Base Ball Pioneers,
1850–1870

Base Ball Pioneers, 1850–1870

The Clubs and Players Who Spread the Sport Nationwide

Edited by Peter Morris, William J. Ryczek,
Jan Finkel, Leonard Levin *and*
Richard Malatzky

McFarland & Company, Inc., Publishers
Jefferson, North Carolina, and London

LIBRARY OF CONGRESS CATALOGUING-IN-PUBLICATION DATA

Base ball pioneers, 1850–1870 : the clubs and players who spread
the sport nationwide / edited by Peter Morris ... [et al.].
p.   cm.
Includes bibliographical references and index.

ISBN 978-0-7864-6843-0
softcover : acid free paper ∞

1. Baseball — United States — History —19th century.
2. Baseball teams — United States — History —19th century.
3. Baseball players — United States —19th century.
I. Morris, Peter, 1962–   II. Title: Baseball pioneers, 1850–1870.
GV863.A1B3748   2012   796.357097309034 — dc23   2012006527

BRITISH LIBRARY CATALOGUING DATA ARE AVAILABLE

© 2012 Peter Morris, William J. Ryczek, Jan Finkel,
Leonard Levin and Richard Malatzky. All rights reserved

*No part of this book may be reproduced or transmitted in any form
or by any means, electronic or mechanical, including photocopying
or recording, or by any information storage and retrieval system,
without permission in writing from the publisher.*

On the cover: The original starting nine of the Niagaras of Buffalo Club, 1857

Manufactured in the United States of America

*McFarland & Company, Inc., Publishers
Box 611, Jefferson, North Carolina 28640
www.mcfarlandpub.com*

To Peter Mancuso

Table of Contents

General Introduction: The Spread of Baseball in the 1860s (Peter Morris) 1
Timeline of the Pioneer Era (Robert Tholkes) 5
Note on Sources and Usage (Peter Morris) 7

❖ CHAPTER ONE: CONNECTICUT AND MAINE ❖

Introduction (Richard Hershberger) 9
Pennesseewassees of Norway, Maine (Peter Morris) 9
Charter Oaks of Hartford, Connecticut (David Arcidiacono) 18
Quinnipiacks of West Meriden (Michael Bielawa) 22
Mansfields of Middletown (David Arcidiacono) 26
Bridgeport's 1866 Clubs (Michael Bielawa) 32

❖ CHAPTER TWO: UPSTATE NEW YORK ❖

Introduction (Richard Hershberger) 42
Hudson Rivers of Newburgh (Peter Morris) 42
Victory Base Ball Club of Troy (Peter Morris) 49
Unions of Lansingburgh (Troy "Haymakers") (Peter Morris) 53
Excelsiors of Albany (Peter Morris) 67
Utica Base Ball Club (Scott Fiesthumel) 69
Syracuse Base Ball Club (Peter Morris) 71
Central City Base Ball Club of Syracuse (Peter Morris) 76
Ontarios of Oswego (Peter Morris) 87
Flour City, Live Oak, Olympic, and Lone Star
 Clubs of Rochester (Priscilla Astifan) 91
Niagaras of Buffalo, Prewar (Peter Morris) 101
Niagaras of Buffalo, Postwar (Peter Morris) 107
Cliftons of Buffalo (Peter Morris) 115

❖ CHAPTER THREE: WESTERN PENNSYLVANIA AND EASTERN OHIO ❖

Introduction (Peter Morris) 118
Mountain Base Ball Club of Altoona (Peter Morris) 119
Allegheny Base Ball Club (Peter Morris) 121
Forest City Base Ball Club of Cleveland (Peter Morris) 125
Independents of Mansfield (Peter Morris) 133

❖ Chapter Four: Cincinnati and Northern Kentucky ❖

Introduction (Peter Morris)   137
Live Oaks of Cincinnati (Greg Perkins)   138
Buckeyes of Cincinnati (David Ball)   141
Cincinnati Base Ball Club ("Red Stockings") (David Ball)   146
Western Unions of Cincinnati (Greg Perkins)   160
Eagles of Brooklyn, Kentucky (Greg Perkins)   162
Covington and Copec Clubs of Covington (Greg Perkins)   163
Holt Base Ball Club of Newport (Greg Perkins)   166

❖ Chapter Five: Michigan ❖

Introduction (Peter Morris)   169
Franklins of Detroit (Peter Morris)   169
Detroit Base Ball Club (Peter Morris)   176
Early Risers of Detroit (Peter Morris)   185
Daybreaks of Jackson (Peter Morris)   189
Kent Base Ball Club of Grand Rapids (Peter Morris)   193
First Nationals of Hancock (Peter Morris)   198

❖ Chapter Six: Indiana, Illinois, Wisconsin, Iowa and Minnesota ❖

Introduction (Peter Morris)   202
Summit City Base Ball Club of Fort Wayne (Robert E. Gregory)   204
Excelsiors of Chicago, Prewar (Peter Morris)   206
Excelsiors of Chicago, Postwar (Peter Morris)   210
Byron (Illinois) Base Ball Club (Peter Morris)   221
Forest City Club of Rockford (Peter Morris)   224
Pecatonica Base Ball Club (Peter Morris)   235
Olympians of Beloit College (Fred Burwell)   239
Mutuals of Janesville (Peter Morris)   247

❖ Chapter Seven: Maryland and the District of Columbia ❖

Introduction (Peter Morris)   252
Excelsior/Pastime Base Ball Club of Baltimore (Peter Morris)   253
Marylands of Baltimore (Peter Morris)   261
Olympics of Washington (Peter Morris)   265
Nationals of Washington (Peter Morris)   271

❖ Chapter Eight: St. Louis ❖

Introduction (Jeffrey Kittel)   281
Cyclones (Jeffrey Kittel)   282
Morning Stars (Jeffrey Kittel)   288
Unions (Jeffrey Kittel)   291
Empires (Jeffrey Kittel)   296

❖ CHAPTER NINE: LOUISVILLE AND ATLANTA ❖

Introduction (William J. Ryczek)   307
Louisville Base Ball Club (Peter Morris)   309
Gate City Base Ball Club of Atlanta (Peter Morris)   314

❖ CHAPTER TEN: SAN FRANCISCO BAY AREA ❖

Introduction (Angus Macfarlane)   318
Eagles of San Francisco (Angus Macfarlane)   323
Pacifics of San Francisco (Angus Macfarlane)   329
Cosmopolitans of San Francisco (Angus Macfarlane)   332
Wide Awakes of Oakland (Angus Macfarlane)   333

General Bibliography   341
About the Contributors   343
Index   345

General Introduction:
The Spread of Baseball in the 1860s
Peter Morris

"In the game of base ball as now played we undoubtedly have a strictly national pastime. As late as the year 1860, base ball was confined to one or two of the middle states — New York being the centre. Now it is played in every state in the union, from Maine to Oregon."[1]

"It has long frustrated me," wrote John Thorn when we first began tossing about the idea of this project, "that there's a painstakingly researched entry in the encyclopedias for every man who played one game in the major leagues after 1870 but nobody knows or cares about what happened to the greatest players of the 1860s." It can be just as difficult to find even the most basic information about many of the key pioneer baseball clubs. To remedy those omissions, John, Richard Malatzky, and I launched what became known as the "Pioneer Project." Our goal was to create a readable reference source that would stimulate more research on this fascinating era and place names and faces on the game's earliest players.

The three years since that decision have never been dull. Some contributors bowed out, but others kept coming forward with new ideas. Details on certain well-known pioneer-era clubs proved too difficult to track down and plans to include those clubs had to be shelved, yet other, less-remembered clubs proved to have left behind treasure troves of reminiscences. By this process of fits and starts, the project began to take shape and its scope to expand.

Eventually it became clear that the richness of the story we were telling would require two volumes. It became just as obvious that the division into parts should reflect the two great movements of baseball's early years. One volume, still being assembled, would chronicle the remarkable synthesis that took place in and around the major cities of the northeastern seaboard: in short order, the "town ball" players of Philadelphia and the "Massachusetts Game" players from that state joined with ballplayers from New York and New Jersey to create a single version of baseball. The other volume, which you now hold in your hands, would cover the other central theme: the spread of this game, which occurred so rapidly that by 1871, as the pioneer era was coming to an end, one writer observed,

"Base-ball ... has passed from city to town, from town to village, till it has overspread the nation. A thriving town in the West is now said to have one church, one school-house, and eight base-ball clubs. It is as much our national game as cricket is that of the English."[2]

So what exactly is the "Pioneer Project"?

Contributors were asked to submit a club history accompanied by profiles of as many club members as possible. They were requested to keep to a minimum player statistics, long lists of the dates and scores of games, and accounts of those games. They were also asked not to summarize the history of baseball in regions other than the one they were covering, and to avoid lengthy explanations of the basic rules, customs, and terminology of early baseball. Beyond that, since the amount and the nature of primary source material varied greatly, the contributors were given a great deal of latitude and were encouraged to present the club's history in the way that seemed most appropriate to them.

In particular, they were asked to give attention in their histories to such key questions as When did the club start playing baseball? Was it one of the first clubs in the region to play by the New York rules and if so why? What made this club tick? Did it exist as a social club as well as a baseball club? What did its members have in common and what made belonging to it special to them? What customs and rituals did they share? Was the club successful on the diamond? Did winning or losing seem to matter? When and where did the club practice? Were practice times designed to allow working men to participate? Where were match games played? Who attended those match games? What role did the club play in its community? How was this club affected by the coming of professionalism and competitiveness? After it ended, how did members reflect on this club?

Thanks to the hard work of the respective contributors

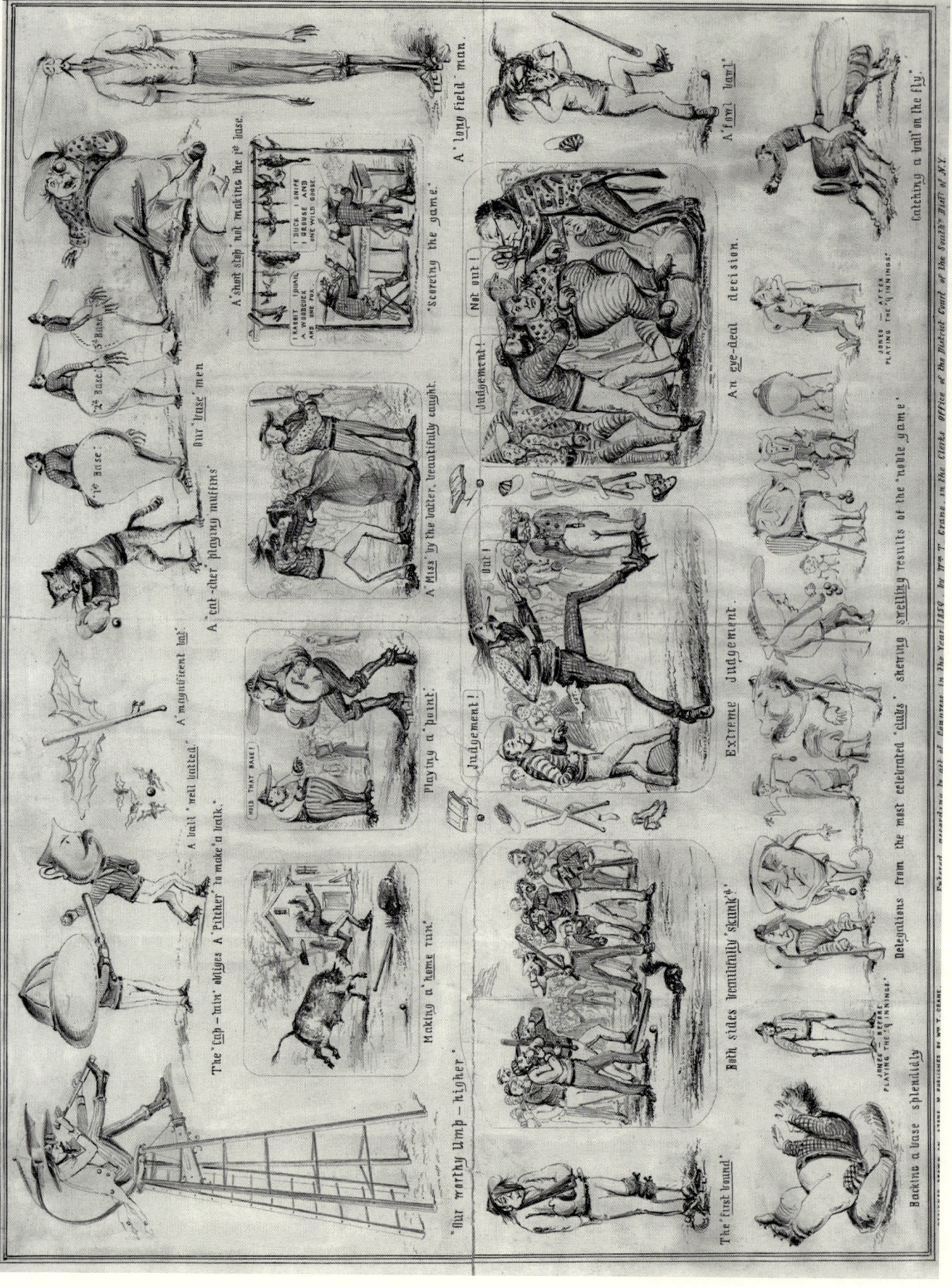

and the expert editing of Jan Finkel and Len Levin, the club histories that resulted are remarkable documents. Each incorporates a great deal of research and each, I have no doubt, will come to be regarded as a standard reference source for baseball historians. Just as important, these engaging narratives bring those long ago clubs back to life — no easy task when dealing with events that occurred 150 years or so in the past.

For convenience, the club histories have been divided geographically. The first chapter describes several clubs in Connecticut and one in Maine that helped to establish the "New York Game" in New England. Chapter two chronicles baseball's spread to the towns and cities of upstate New York, including Newburgh, Utica, Troy, Albany, Syracuse, Oswego, Rochester, and Buffalo. In chapter three, we see the game take root in western Pennsylvania and eastern and central Ohio. The fourth chapter follows the game's entry into Cincinnati, which produced the most celebrated club of the pioneer era.

Chapter five takes baseball into Michigan, and chapter six follows it into the rest of the Midwest. In chapter seven, we learn how the game caught on in Maryland and the District of Columbia. Chapters eight and nine chronicle the early years of baseball in the South and in St. Louis. Our whirlwind tour concludes in the San Francisco Bay Area, during the years that Angus Macfarlane aptly terms the "Era of the Bat."

By design, the player profiles that accompany club histories make for less entertaining reading. From the start, we envisioned this project as a way to turn the ciphers of the pioneer era back into real live men by providing the names and dates necessary for additional research. As a result, the profiles often abound in such dates and potentially tedious details. But we believe that's the least we can do for the men whose labors gave us baseball.

And along the way, we do meet a cast of fascinating characters. There is Frederick Benteen, who fought alongside Custer and parted from the doomed general on the morning of the Battle of Little Big Horn; John Clark, who became a world-renowned opera singer and was Gilbert and Sullivan's original Pirate King; James P. Ball, pioneer African-American photographer who was also a member of a pioneer African-American ball club in Cincinnati; successful politicians such as two-term Ohio governor Judson Harmon, President William Howard Taft, and David Hill (who, after becoming governor of New York, recalled that he and his fellow club members "thought we were some punkins on baseball up in Chemung County" until a decisive defeat proved otherwise); and Alfred T. Goshorn, of whom David Ball writes succinctly, "Goshorn was thus the only knight of the realm associated with the Cincinnati Base Ball Club." All of these men and many others were members of the ball clubs of the pioneer era.

One name that does not appear is Abner Doubleday. The resilient Doubleday myth has been debunked in countless books, but no doubt there will still be readers who will be surprised to learn that its namesake played no role in the history of baseball. Take my word for it — it is the men whose stories appear in these pages and in those of the volume to follow who deserve the credit unjustly bestowed upon Doubleday.

This work does not purport to provide a comprehensive history of these eventful years. For a brief summary, readers are directed to Robert Tholkes's overview of the major events of the period, which follows this introduction. For important in-depth studies of the national baseball scene in the 1860s, readers are directed to William J. Ryczek's *Baseball's First Inning: A History of the National Pastime Through the Civil War* and *When Johnny Came Sliding Home: The Post-Civil War Baseball Boom, 1865–1870*; Warren J. Goldstein's *Playing for Keeps: A History of Early Baseball*; George B. Kirsch's *The Creation of American Team Sports: Baseball and Cricket, 1838–72*; and Tom Melville's *Early Baseball and the Rise of the National League*. My own *But Didn't We Have Fun?*, David Block's *Baseball Before We Knew It*, and Melvin Adelman's *A Sporting Time: New York City and the Rise of Modern Athletics, 1820–70* are recommended for the lively years that led up to baseball's explosion in the 1860s. (See this book's bibliography for publishing details.) John Thorn's *Baseball in the Garden of Eden*, published as this work was going to press, will undoubtedly merit inclusion on this list. Nor is this work meant to take the place of Marshall D. Wright's *The National Association of Base Ball Players, 1857–1870*, an ambitious register of the games played by the major clubs during the pioneer era.

Yet much of the rich material in the entries that follow was not available when these works were written, with the result that promising paths of inquiry can now be examined afresh. Who was really responsible for spreading the game to new regions — Civil War veterans, as was once the orthodox response, or a wider variety of Americans? What caused some areas to be more receptive to the new game? How did the presence of rival bat-and-ball games affect its reception? What factors defined the relationship between a baseball club and the community? Why did the best players in some towns and cities congregate on a single club, while other communities produced balanced in-town rivalries? How did the other members of pioneer-era baseball clubs regard the members of the first nine? Who had a say in a club's key decisions, a few leaders, or the entire membership? What unified these clubs — and what tore them apart? How did the coming of competitiveness and professionalism alter their delicate fabric?

All of these questions have been considered before, but

Opposite: **As this 1859 drawing (titled "A Comprehensive View of Base Ball") amusingly illustrates, baseball had already established its own distinctive jargon before the Civil War (courtesy Library of Congress).**

generally on the basis of the experience of a few clubs from selected regions. Now that the story of all of these additional clubs is available, with more to follow, the time is ripe to reexamine them. Woodrow Wilson once wrote, "Local history is the ultimate substance of national history.... The history of a nation is only the history of its villages written large."[3] His observation is equally applicable to the history of the national pastime.

As a result, for all the work that this book represents, it is not the end of the study of baseball's pioneer era, merely a new beginning. Even as hefty a work as this one barely scratches the surface.... For every club that ended up being included in this volume, there are countless others with stories just as deserving of being told. As an example, the Alert Base Ball Club of Elmira, New York, left behind an official scorebook that abounded in revelations:

> In June 1865, the following entry is found in the book: Bryan, twenty cents, swearing. (Paid.)
>
> Greves, five cents, swearing. (Paid.)
>
> Greves, five cents, swearing. (Paid.)
>
> The official umpire appeared to be the late Colonel D. C. Robinson, and he seemed to rule with an iron hand. Along down in the list are found the names of others who are as well-known as those above mentioned, including John Arnot, W. S. Sherman and Harry W. Beadle. One entry says Frank Blossom was fined for making a home run.[4]

Wouldn't you just love to know why Frank Blossom was fined for making a home run? Alas, every project must end somewhere and so must this one.

Let's give the last word to G. Smith Stanton, a New Yorker who wrote in 1897 of the ballplayers of the pioneer era: "The great national game is indebted to these old veterans in more ways than one. In the first place there was no salary; on the contrary, there was an initiation fee and all had to pay their dues and furnish their own uniforms, and pay their own traveling expenses. The consequence was the different businesses they followed were neglected, and, with few exceptions, they accumulated little of this world's goods."[5]

All baseball fans owe these pioneer clubs and players a tremendous debt, and we all hope that this volume will help to repay that obligation by at last giving credit where it is due. Toward that end, 100 percent of the royalties are being donated to two worthy endeavors: the respective projects of the SABR (Society for American Baseball Research) Negro League and Deadball Era committees to provide appropriate memorials for forgotten stars.

Notes

1. *Chicago Times*, April 7, 1867, reprinted from a New York paper, apparently the *New York Tribune*.
2. William R. Hooper, "Our National Game," *Appleton's*, February 25, 1871, 225.
3. Woodrow Wilson, *Mere Literature, and Other Essays* (Boston: Houghton Mifflin and Company, 1896), 213–214.
4. "The Old Alert Baseball Club," *Elmira Telegram*, August 13, 1916.
5. *Brooklyn Eagle*, August 5, 1897, 5; letter from G. Smith Stanton dated July 28.

Timeline of the Pioneer Era
Robert Tholkes

Baseball's pioneer era, roughly the decades of the 1850s and 1860s, spans the beginning of interclub matches under the ancestor of today's rules to the beginning of the professional era (not yet concluded). Viewed with 150 years' hindsight, the events of the period unspool in a logical sequence of inevitable steps.

1850: Five years after the Knickerbocker Club, of New York, drew up the ancestor of today's rules, the "New York Rules," the Washington Club of New York became the second to adopt them for play. Interclub matches began in 1851. Both were social clubs, collecting dues and sponsoring amateur teams in multiple skill grades from among their members for the purposes of healthful exercise and friendly competition. The social club format, at least, would endure throughout the Pioneer Period and into the first years of professional baseball as the pattern for organized adult play, and emulated by an uncounted number of junior clubs.

1853: The *New York Sunday Mercury* begins publication of game accounts. Other publications shortly follow suit and together spread word from Maine to California of the benefits of the game, information about the playing rules, accounts of match play, and a record of the game's spread.

1857: Several other clubs playing various forms of base ball (then still two words) having also agreed to adopt the Knickerbocker rules, a meeting is held in New York in January to standardize play.

1858: Formation in March of the National Association of Base Ball Players (NABBP) to further regulate play and relationships among the clubs and to promote the expansion of the game. The conventions continue on an annual basis, but NABBP remains entirely a volunteer group, with no paid staff. Its effectiveness against the gambling and professionalism that accompany the game's growth is limited.

1858: The NABBP Rules Committee acts to curb the rising number of pitches thrown in a game, which is making game times too long. Pitchers sought to deceive and exhaust the patience of hitters and to curb base-stealing, while hitters in turn ignored good balls to both exhaust pitchers and to give their mates a chance to steal, to the extent that combined pitch counts ran to hundreds per game. Umpires were directed to begin calling strikes when in their judgment such tactics were being employed. Five years later the ability to call balls was added. Frequently ignored by umpires, who were usually players from other clubs, these were only the first of a series of steps, taken at intervals over the next twenty years, toward the eventual calling of balls and strikes on every pitch.

1858: Admission to matches is charged for the first time, for a series of Brooklyn–New York City all-star games at the Fashion Race Course in Queens. The proceeds are donated to New York's and Brooklyn's fire companies, with which clubs and players were frequently associated. Attendance for the three games was estimated to be in the tens of thousands.

1860: *Beadle's Dime Base-Ball Player*, the first guide to rules, regulations, and play, appears, making available authoritative annotations explaining the rules.

1860: The Excelsior Club of South Brooklyn takes the game on the road, traveling to western New York State, Baltimore, and Philadelphia, while dazzling the locals with their caliber of play. The Excelsior roster includes the first reputed professional, pitcher Jim Creighton. With prestige and the attraction of dues-paying members at stake, various forms of surreptitious compensation are devised as the 1860s progress: payment of club dues, "benefit" games, side jobs requiring varying degrees of actual work, and an outright salary as an employee of the club.

1860: The "conquering" (rubber) game of the three-game match between the Excelsiors and the Atlantic Base Ball Club of Brooklyn ends in unprecedented fashion when the Excelsiors leave the field in protest against the rowdy behavior of the crowd.

1860: Teams composed of compositors employed by two New York newspapers, the *World* and the *Times*, play a game. Teams sponsored by companies and corporations would become a major source of opportunity for organized play by adults and juniors alike over the next several decades.

1861–1865: The War Between the States significantly reduces participation in and public attention to the game, but also to an unknowable degree assists its spread, as it is frequently played in army camps. The United States Government assists by distributing equipment. Baseball writers such as William Cauldwell of the *Sunday Mercury* point out as a precedent the games of cricket played in British camps during the recently completed Crimean War.

1862: The for-profit Union Grounds, the first enclosed playing grounds, opens in Brooklyn. Admission is charged on a regular basis. The effect is to further promote professionalism, as funding shifts from reliance on volunteerism to reliance on selling tickets to the public.

1865: Culminating a six-year struggle, the most contentious rules question of the period is settled after the 1864 season when the "bound rule," whereby fair balls caught on the first bounce put out the batter, is dropped in favor of the "fly rule," which calls for putouts on fair balls only when the ball is caught before touching the ground. The fly rule's proponents have for years criticized the bound rule as "boyish," and a detriment to the game's contest with cricket for the allegiance of young sportsmen.

1865: Paid by a gambler, three Mutual BBC (New York) players "heave" a September game against the Eckford Club of Williamsburg (Brooklyn), are caught, and are expelled from the club. It is regarded as a sign of the times in baseball rather than an isolated incident; the players were later reinstated.

1866: The 10th annual NABBP convention, exceeding pre-war levels, attracts 202 clubs from 17 states and the District of Columbia.

1867: Post-war "base ball fever" peaks, with clubs in virtually every state in the Union. The Nationals of Washington make the first trans-Allegheny tour, traveling as far west as St. Louis.

1868: Several top clubs are demonstrably of "semi-pro" status, with several gradations along the continuum from avowedly amateur social sporting clubs on the Knickerbocker model to clubs pursuing (and paying) top players for the pursuit of prestige, members, and profit.

1869: The NABBP openly recognizes the existence of professional clubs and players, as a response to the sham amateurism and gambling influences by then felt to be damaging the status of the game. At the time, it was estimated that of the thousand or more clubs playing nationwide, fewer than twenty were fully professional, and about fifty paid one or more players.

1869: The Cincinnati Base Ball Club fields the most immediately successful, openly full-time, all-professional team, the Red Stockings, seeking and employing the best players available regardless of location, for a group of civic-minded investor "members." They are essentially, though not in name, stockholders. The Reds firmly establish professional dominance of the sport by touring nationally and going undefeated.

1870: Cincinnati's bitter rival for Western supremacy, Chicago, ups the ante, dropping the social-club format and selling enough stock in the Chicago Base Ball Club to reportedly pay $10,000 in salaries to the all-professional White Stockings.

1870–1871: The professionals break away from the NABBP, forming the National Association of Professional Base Ball Players, and plan the first inter-city "pennant race" for the 1871 season. A separate amateur association is formed and struggles to mid-decade before fading out of sight.

Note on Sources and Usage
Peter Morris

A general bibliography at the end of this work lists key sources on the pioneer era of baseball. Contributors were invited to include their own note on sources used or a selected bibliography at the end of their entry, but were encouraged not to be exhaustive and not to duplicate the books that appear in the general bibliography unless the works were of direct use. In particular, the research done to identify and trace club members was liable to involve the use of dozens of city directory listings, census records, and other genealogical sources. Exhaustive lists of these sources would be more likely to exhaust readers than enlighten them, so every effort has been made to keep these to a minimum.

Contemporaneous newspaper accounts are the primary source for most of these entries, so a few words about their use are in order for those who have not experienced the joys and sorrows of perusing them. Chief among the joys is that reporters of the era were lively and engaging writers, as will be clear from the many excerpts that are reprinted in these pages. Less pleasantly, the concepts of journalistic ethics and plagiarism had only begun to emerge, which meant that some nineteenth-century American newspapers abounded in blatant libel and stolen material.

The latter issue makes accurate acknowledgment of sources difficult, since all newspapers of the era borrowed liberally from one another, but only some of them were meticulous about acknowledging such debts (and many of the ones that did were not very accurate in their attributions).[1] In 1885 *Sporting Life*'s Cleveland correspondent grumbled: "The gentleman who is in charge of [the sporting] department of the [Cleveland] *Leader* evidently has a pair of long scissors, with which he completely cuts up the *Sporting Life* and Cincinnati papers, but fails to credit the source for the news stolen. Nothing original in the sporting line emanates from the *Leader*."[2] It is a state of affairs that makes it impossible to be confident that a note originated in the source cited. So while every effort has been made to cite sources in as precise and helpful a form as possible, there is no way to be certain of the original source. Bylines were very rarely attached to articles, so are included when given in the original, but it is often necessary to refer vaguely to their author as a reporter or writer.

An issue that is more likely to catch readers' attention is that quoted material often contains differences from current standards of spelling, punctuation, and capitalization. Until the 1880s the word "base ball" was almost exclusively written as two words and only in the twentieth century did it become common to spell it as a single word. Other terms, such as "short stop," "team mate," "some one," "every one," and "to-day," also took time to become recognized as compound words. "Innings" with an *s* was used where we would now expect "inning," while British/Canadian spellings of words such as center ("centre"), practice ("practise"), and criticize ("criticise") remained common in the United States. The spelling of city names that ended in "burgh" (e.g., Pittsburgh, Newburgh, Lansingburgh) is too involved an issue to get into here, but suffice it to say that it was not until the twentieth century that the *h* became permanent.

Similarly, placement of commas also varied greatly from today's usage, while capitalization was based on very different principles; "Main Street" was then "Main street" and "Allegheny County" usually "Allegheny county," to cite only a couple of examples. Great care has been taken to ensure that all quoted material has been reproduced verbatim, especially passages that look odd to the modern eye. Rather than regularly interrupting these quotations with the indicator of [*sic*], use of this label has been kept to a minimum, generally only when there was an obvious mistake of fact or grammar or a deviation from the spelling conventions of the day.

The format of club names is also likely to puzzle baseball fans who are accustomed to having the city name come first ("Philadelphia Phillies"). Throughout the pioneer era, formal club names almost always took the following form: the Ontario Base Ball Club of Oswego, or when the city name stood alone, the Utica Base Ball Club. For simplicity's sake, these names were often abbreviated: the Ontario Club of Oswego, the Ontarios of Oswego, the Ontarios; the Utica Club, the Uticas. (Singular construction — the Ontario of Oswego — was sometimes used as well, but was less common, so for consistency's sake the plural form has been given preference.) The modern formulation of "the Oswego Ontarios" did not become common until the 1870s, so the original version has been used. Making things more difficult to follow, two of the best clubs of the pioneer era became known by unofficial nicknames — the Cincinnati Base Ball Club (the "Red Stockings") and the Union Base Ball Club of Lansingburgh (the "Haymakers" of Troy).

Finally, the term "National Association" is likely to prove a source of confusion because it was used to refer to two very different entities. From 1857 to 1870, the game's governing body was known as the National Association of Base Ball Players or NABBP. This entity disbanded prior to the 1871 season and was replaced by separate bodies for the professional and amateur clubs: the National Association of Professional Base Ball Players and the National Association of Amateur Base Ball Players. The latter body was not very active, but the former became the first major league, lasting from 1871 until the formation of the National League in 1876, and it soon came to be known simply as the National Association. Unfortunately, articles from the 1860s often referred to the NABBP as the National Association. To try to keep things as simple as possible, references to the NABBP generally use either the full name or the acronym, and clarification is provided when it seems likely to be helpful.

Notes

1. The profile of Henry Mason Scovell in the Franklin Club of Detroit entry explains some of the reasons why attribution was erratic.
2. *Sporting Life*, May 13, 1885.

Chapter One

Connecticut and Maine

❖ *Introduction* (Richard Hershberger) ❖

New England was the heartland of early ball play in America. It was richly endowed with a wide variety of choices.

The Connecticut River valley was the center of the game of wicket. Almost entirely forgotten today, wicket was a peculiarly American survival of pre-modern cricket, surviving long after cricket was completely standardized in England and modern cricket introduced into America. Wicket was widely played in North America, but it was in the Connecticut River Valley that it reached its height of competitive play. Towns and villages were competing against one another in wicket decades before baseball was routinely seen as a similarly competitive sport.

Baseball came into its own in the 1850s. Players in New England had more choices than in most of the country. Local forms of baseball were played throughout the country. A handful of these rose to become standards of regional competition. Two of them — centered on New York City and on Boston — spread beyond their immediate regions. The "New York Game" is the direct ancestor of modern baseball. The Boston version, traditionally known as the "Massachusetts Game," came to dominate eastern New England, with occasional forays as far away as Pennsylvania.

New England baseball clubs in the late 1850s had three choices to select from: the New York Game, the Massachusetts Game, or the local version. All three choices were popular. In 1859 the club at Colebrook, Connecticut, played a match against the club from Sandisfield, Massachusetts, about ten miles north. They played the local version, stopping because of darkness after only two innings with the score 52 runs in favor of the Sandisfield club. But the year before, the clubs in Alton and Fisherville, New Hampshire, north of Manchester, adopted the Massachusetts Game for their competitions. In the meantime, the first inter-city baseball match ever played occurred when the Portland, Maine, club traveled to Boston to play the New York Game against the local Tri-Mountain club.

By 1862, new clubs forming in Hartford, Connecticut, were specifying that they played under the New York rules. By the end of the Civil War the New York rules were the standard throughout New England, with nearly every town and village having its club competing ferociously against its neighbors, with city clubs competing for the civic championship, and the top clubs playing other cities, and even the New York clubs.

❖ *Pennesseewassees of Norway, Maine* (Peter Morris) ❖

Club History

It was not until 1864 or 1865 that the New York version of baseball appeared in Oxford County, Maine. Before then, recalled Percival J. Parris, the local boys played "Three-year-old-cat, Barnball and the more elaborate Roundball, a name probably corrupted from the English name of Townball." The first two games were designed to be played when only a few boys were on hand, but roundball, which was popular throughout New England, had deeper affinities with baseball along with some conspicuous differences: "The infield was not a diamond, but a parallelogram of varying proportions with the 'gools,' or bases, at the four corners as in Baseball, but the striker or batter stood midway between the first and fourth base, running three-and-a-half bases in place of four bases as in Baseball. In Roundball a runner was put out between bases by being 'plunked' or 'spotted' by a ball thrown by a rival player. The ball was such as could be made from yarn raveled from a cast-off stocking, sometimes with a large bullet at the center to give it weight for long throws, and was covered with calf-skin begged from the family shoemaker."[1]

The arrival of the new version received a great boost from the principal of the Paris Hill Academy, where Percival J. Parris was a student. The principal gave the students a baseball and a copy of the rules of the New York game, on the condition that they practice on Wednesday and Saturday afternoons. The students were left to their own devices for bats, so each player made his own.

In 1865 the academy's Resolute Club squared off against the South Paris Club in what Parris believed to have been the first match game ever played in Oxford County. Played at the County Fair Grounds, which were about a mile from the respective centers of Norway and South Paris, the contest revealed that the players were still learning the rudiments of the game. Although Resolute captain Edward T. Brown did his best to issue orders, "almost every player had his own opinion as to what should be done and was under great excitement. Several would call out different orders and the confusion and clamor was often great."[2]

As was the case in so many states, Maine experienced a baseball boom in the years immediately following the Civil War. Clubs formed all over the state, competition became regular and occasionally heated, and a store in Augusta began boasting in its advertisements that "base ball clubs can procure balls and bats of us as cheap as in New York."[3]

Even regions of the state that were completely unfamiliar with the New York version of the game joined the enthusiasm. After becoming president of the University of California, Benjamin Ide Wheeler recalled that in 1867,

> We decided to play ball at a little town called Saco, where I lived.... One day we sent a man to Portland, Me., twenty miles away, to purchase supplies for a baseball team. He got a bat for twenty-five cents, a ball for $1 and a book of rules for ten cents. The bat was about the size and shape of an indoor baseball bat of today. The ball was fully as hard as those of today but would not travel so far. The rules were contained in a yellow-backed book, which looked like some dime novels. We went out on the prairie, measured off the distances for a field given in the book. There was only one man in the crowd that had ever seen a baseball game and he had only witnessed one contest. When we had finished marking off the diamond we found that we had no bases. We, therefore, took dried cow flaps and used them for bases.

Once they began playing, it proved a struggle "to keep the players from 'plugging' the runner. Hitting the runner with the ball is known as plugging. This practice is followed in rounders and a large number of our young men had played the game. We were so ignorant about the rules of the game that it was necessary for one player to read the rules and for the rest of us to play the game according to the book. It was not long before we learned considerable about baseball and became proficient in the art."[4]

With baseball clubs springing up in many Maine cities at about the same time, competition began to proliferate. Maine's baseball history was not unusual in that regard, but it did differ from other states in one important particular — the emergence of a most improbable collection of underdogs as state champions. Today, such a tale of underdogs overcoming long odds would captivate Americans and end up as a movie. The mindset of the 1860s, however, was a very different one and the Pennesseewassees of Norway, Maine, were ignored by the national press and even by such regional publications as the *New England Base Ballist*. As a result, it was left to club members to tell the amazing story of the Pennesseewassees.

By the fall of 1866, the enthusiasm was intense enough for the Kennebec Union Agricultural and Horticultural Society to offer "a purse of $75 for the best game of base ball" played at its annual fair.[5] There were four entrants — the Cushnocs of Augusta, the Eons and Athletics of Portland, and the Androscoggins of Lewiston — and the Eons captured the purse in front of a "very large" crowd.[6]

The following spring saw the formation of the Maine State Association of Base Ball Players and the announcement that the state's best baseball club was to receive a fourteen-and-a-half-ounce solid silver ball valued at $110 and described by one early player as "a solid affair — made in Boston — encased in a magnificent silk-lined jewel box."[7] The silver ball would initially be awarded to the club that won a tournament in Portland in the first week of August. To keep interest alive, however, the winners of that tournament would then be obliged to defend the silver ball against challengers on a regular basis. The challenge system did indeed prove to be a very effective way of generating excitement, but it also led to considerable controversy.

The August 1867 tournament saw the Eons of Portland crowned as state champions, but it also brought signs that the new trophy would erode the spirit of sportsmanship. Only a few weeks earlier, the Eons had beaten the Cushnocs of Augusta by a single run. Nevertheless, when a spectator had questioned one of the umpire's calls, "the interruption was very properly rebuked by the captains of the two clubs and was not repeated."[8] Yet when those two clubs met again in the tournament championship game, the same Augusta newspaper had a very different take, writing of the rulings of umpire Henry Dennison of the Lowell Club of Boston:

> In the judgment also of impartial and disinterested observers, as we are told, the decisions of the Umpire were grossly unfair, every thing being made to tell against the Cushnocs and in favor of the Portland club. The favoritism and injustice displayed by him were so palpably manifested as to call forth repeated and almost unanimous demonstrations of disapprobation in storms of indignant hisses from the crowd of spectators in attendance, whose sympathies were naturally with their own townsmen, but whose love of fair play prompted this uncomplimentary expression of their feelings. It was very evident throughout the contest that the Augusta club, no matter how well they played, were not to be allowed to carry off the silver ball. The design was effectually carried out, and in a manner which reflects little credit upon the winning club or the umpire who so unscrupulously played into their hands and served their selfish and partisan purposes.[9]

The times, they were a-changing.

The Eons soon had to defend the title and on October 7 they were defeated 39–36 by the Bowdoin College nine. The new holders of the silver ball were in turn deluged with challenges from the likes of the Androscoggins of Lewiston, the Cushnocs of Augusta, and two Portland clubs, the Athletics and the Eons. In addition to these challenges from the state's best-known baseball powers, one was also received from a club so obscure that the *Maine Farmer* described it only as "a Norway club."[10]

Under the rules set down by the state association, the lateness of the season meant that the Bowdoin College club would only have to defend the silver ball one more time that year and could choose which challenge to accept. The result was predictable. As one of the club members later described it, the captain of the college nine listed the challengers and the school president responded, "Why, there is no question which one to accept. Who ever heard of the Pennesseewassees or the Pennie Sawhorses or the Pennie Warhorses, or whatever they are called? I never did." There was unanimous support for this course of action and the only regret anyone expressed was "rather a sorry feeling for the farmers from Oxford County."[11] The Pennesseewassees had their chance to win the silver ball.

The challenging baseball nine was an extension of a social club formed in 1864 by the young men of Oxford County, a largely rural county bordering New Hampshire and Quebec. In order to confer more dignity on their activities, the members borrowed many of the rituals of the Knights of the Round Table. Despite such efforts, it was unmistakably a club of young men who cared most passionately about the various sporting and outdoor activities in which they engaged.

According to club member Clarence Smith, both the club's real essence and the superficiality of effort to disguise that essence were revealed by the club's name — the Cobblers. Smith, who became the left fielder of the ball-club, maintained: "Dr. Young, a famous druggist here, gave us the name. We refused him permission to see our athletic rooms and told him the noise we made was from cobbling shoes. He called us Cobblers, and under that name our club was incorporated."[12] But fellow club member Silas Burnham gave a more prosaic explanation, stating that the club's headquarters were "over Bense Hawkins' cobbler shop on the third floor."[13]

The baseball club was formed on May 4, 1867, by some of the members of the Cobblers Club. The ball-club was centered in Norway, a village of 2,000, but it represented the entire surrounding community, being "made up of five farmer boys and four village boys." Symbolizing this broad constituency, the club was named in honor of Lake Pennesseewassee, "a beautiful lake at the head of the village, seven miles long and one and a half miles wide."[14] As Dr. Charles A. Stephens put it, "We have in our home burg a beautiful lake bearing the long Indian name of Pennesseewassee, which is not wholly unmusical when you learn how to pronounce it, but to do so you must hear a native speak it. As was natural we named our baseball club, The Pennesseewassees."[15]

The new club elected a slate of officers that included James B. Chaffin as president, Cyrus S. Tucker as vice president, Clarence M. Smith as secretary, and E. Stephens as treasurer, and began to line up matches.[16] Its initial contest occurred on May 17 and yielded a win over the Fleetfoots of Mechanic Falls. This victory was followed by wins over the West Paris Club, the Athletics of Portland, and three triumphs against the Ticonics of Paris. But all of these opponents except the Athletics were little-known small-town clubs, and the five wins of the Pennesseewassees were further diminished by two losses to the Androscoggins of Lewiston.[17] Thus as the end of that inaugural season approached, it was generally assumed that, as club member Silas Burnham later wrote of the Pennesseewassees, "of course they could not be expected to compete with the large city teams."[18]

But Burnham added that while the members of the Pennesseewassee Base Ball Club came from a rural area and were inexperienced ballplayers, they were not naïve and indeed took great pleasure in outsmarting the city clubs. So when the players decided to issue a challenge for a silver ball, they carefully studied the association's rules and concluded that their best chance was to continue practicing but avoid playing matches against the state's top clubs. By pursuing this course, they cunningly set a trap for the champions — "naturally we, the Pennies, would have a cinch for the last game, for they would pick the weakest team which naturally would be the farmers from Oxford County, who never had played a game, and being obliged to play away from home, would be frightened and would be easy prey."[19]

Thus when the Bowdoin-Eon game took place on the 7th of October, the Pennesseewassees traveled to Portland with the necessary "challenge in their pockets all ready for the evening paper, with a blank space for the name of the winners to be inserted." The college students did indeed choose the challenge of the unknown Norway club and the championship match was scheduled for the 19th, prompting the Pennesseewassees to begin nonstop practice.[20] Meanwhile, the overconfident collegians were boasting about facing a club of rural hayseeds from "up in Oxford county, the Pennesewassees [*sic*] of Norway or Paris Hill or some other old hill."[21]

Making the forty-mile trip from Norway to Brunswick was no easy matter in those days. Sumner Burnham, the club's captain, left by train two days before the game so that he could pay a visit to an "old sweetheart" in Minot. Two other club members, Sumner's brother Silas and pitcher Gene Fuller, departed at sunrise the next morning "by catching Fuller's old black mare out of the pasture and hitching her to a two-wheeled chaise which Silas had borrowed from Isaac Denison, the leading merchant in Norway." They were joined by two of the outfielders, Cyrus Tucker and Clarence Smith, who were traveling in a horse-and-buggy. After a stop at noon to eat, feed the horses and practice fielding, the four ballplayers arrived at Bowdoin around five in the afternoon and were relieved to discover that the rest of their teammates had "drifted in by various ways and means."²²

Once assembled on the college campus, the members of the Pennesseewassee Base Ball Club were anxious to take a look at the by-now famous silver ball. According to Clarence Smith, "It was in a silk-lined jeweler's box, and as we were looking and admiring it, one of the Bowdoin boys told us that they were going to get a glass case to keep it in, and had picked out the place where it was to be put for the admiration of future generations. That kind of talk riled us up, and Sum Burnham, our captain, told us to come out and practice."²³

The Pennesseewassees then made their way over to the college baseball field, which they found to be very unlike the ones they were familiar with — as Smith recalled, "Our grounds at Norway were soft, and a ball would stick where it struck, but these were as smooth and hard as a wood floor." They were followed to the diamond by several of the college players, who were looking to pick up pointers on the play of their small-town opponents. But once again, it was the Pennesseewassees who ended up gaining the upper hand. According to Smith,

> We were willing to let them see our batting and fielding, for we were good at both, having the name of being the heaviest strikers in the state, but we didn't want to give away our pitching, so I went in and did the twirling. Anyone could hit my pitching with both eyes shut, as I lobbed them us as big as a house. Finally Sum [Sumner Burnham] came to the bat. He was good for three or four home runs in a game, as he used a 42-inch white oak bat, which he swung just as a man does in chopping wood, ending his swing with a grunt. There was a fence round the field, then a road, another fence and some houses. Sum hit the first ball away over both fences, breaking a blind and a window in one of the houses, and the next one he drove into a beet bed about two rods farther on. That made those college boys set up and take notice, and we felt pretty good over the result of the practice.²⁴

Silas Burnham, whose recollection was that his brother's blast landed in a cabbage patch, added, "We were told no one had knocked a ball that far in the memory of the earliest settlers. He hit one more out nearly as far and called up the next batter, who did nearly as well. We stopped right there.... It was not long before a particular friend called and told us that the [college] boys were scared out of their boots. He said, 'They are licked before starting.'"²⁵

But Percival J. Parris, who was now a student at Bowdoin College and the shortstop on the champion nine, had a different recollection. Having grown up in Oxford County, he was aware of the ability of the challengers and tried to warn his teammates of the danger of overconfidence. His efforts proved in vain, however, with another member of the college nine declaring: "Oh — those farmers! They can bat, but they field like oxen."²⁶

The Bowdoin nine offered to have a banquet for the Pennesseewassees, but the visitors "thought they might put something over on us" and so they instead were in bed by nine. When they returned to the ball grounds the next day, they found it beginning to fill up with what Burnham called the "biggest crowd we farm boys had ever seen."²⁷

Special trains had brought curious spectators from such towns as Portland, Lewiston, and Bangor, and it seemed as though the "whole college turned out to watch." Frank Warren Hawthorne, who followed his cousin Nathaniel Hawthorne in graduating from Bowdoin, later penned this description:

> What a scene! A regular Donnybrook Fair in miniature! And what a crowd, too! They had come from all over. The whole town and a good part of Topsham had turned out, of course, and it seemed as if every livery team in Bath, Lewiston and Freeport had been called into commission for the occasion, with nearly all the farm-wagons in the intervening country thrown in for good measure. On both sides of the Delta the Bath road and the Harpswell road were jammed full of teams [of horses] — many of them gay turnouts, with gay young men and women occupying them — and the cavalcade stretched away down into the pines and opposite the Dunlap monument; the grand-stand was filled to overflowing with students and the "college girls" of Brunswick; every window in the Medical Hall had been pre-empted, and "yaggers" swung from the branches of every near-by tree.²⁸

According to one later account, the spectators also included "several of the faculty ... among them old Professor Jonathan Snell, who, on espying the newcomers, pushed up his glasses, glanced across at the row of waiting Pennesseewassees and asked in his soft voice, 'Are those the Penny-sawhorses?'"²⁹

Smith estimated that more than 3,000 people were on hand to watch the champions take on the "'phenomenal farmers,' as they called us."³⁰ It was intimidating enough to play in front of a crowd larger than the entire population of Norway, but to make things worse the spectators were overwhelmingly rooting for the home side. "All the support that we had," recollected Smith, "was from three or four Norway boys in college and three of the Androscoggins who had come up to see the sport."³¹ Burnham added that "while there was great interest and enthusiasm in Norway they did not think it possible for us to win and not a single person except Knight had the courage to go to Brunswick." Although Knight's first name is not provided, he is in all likelihood Enoch Knight, about whom more later.³²

But the Pennesseewassees were not intimidated and surged to an early lead. With the unexpected prospect of a close game, the excitement mounted. According to Frank Warren Hawthorne's account, "In all the buggies and barouches the occupants were standing up cheering lustily for Bowdoin or the 'Wassees' and waving handkerchiefs, hats, canes and improvised flags. The college girls kept up an almost continuous hand-clapping, and as often as it subsided somebody would call for 'three cheers for Hooker!' which would be given with a 'tiger' on the end that awoke the echoes. Bowdoin, like most of the American colleges, had not yet, in the autumn of 1868, arisen to the dignity of a college yell."³³

The contest remained close until a dramatic fielding play in the fifth inning. With two men on base for Bowdoin College and no outs, a brilliant catch by one of the Pennesseewassee fielders led to a triple play. His inspired teammates followed with a seven-run inning and the visitors surged to a lead that they never relinquished.[34]

As the Pennesseewassees continued to pull away, the game lost its suspense and many of the huge throng turned their attention to flirting or to betting on the outcome of specific plays. But even as the result became a foregone conclusion, the play on the diamond continued to produce moments that became part of Maine baseball lore. The spectacular triple play was followed by two dazzling double plays turned by the club that had been expected to "field like oxen." There was also a still more extraordinary sequence of events that yielded only one out. "One of the Bowdoin boys," recollected Smith, "hit a ball into center field that Cy Tucker started for but lost in the sun. I was about two rods back of Cyrus, as he stood looking up, shading his eyes with his hands and trying to get a glimpse of the ball, but before he spotted it, it struck him on the head and caromed off toward me so that I just managed to catch it with one hand, getting the credit of the put-out. That was a sample of the luck that we had in the game."[35]

Another memorable play occurred in the final inning, when Silas Burnham hit a ground ball and arrived at first base at about the same time as the throw. The umpire was slow to make a call, and was surrounded by Bowdoin fielders calling for an out ruling. Burnham started to run toward the umpire to join in the argument, but his brother loudly called out, "Hold your gool, 'Sile'! Hold that gool, Silas!" The quaint expression from the bygone roundball days caused considerable amusement and, according to Hawthorne, "'Hold your gool!' from that moment became a college byword and went down securely in Bowdoin baseball traditions."[36]

Clarence Smith corroborated that particular anecdote, but other elements of Hawthorne's vivid descriptions of the match are less reliable. Most notably, he invoked almost every imaginable stereotype about rustic hayseeds in this description of the Pennesseewassees: "A Norway lad, 'Jud' Parrott ... was spitting on his hands at the home plate and trying the bat in all sorts of positions ... 'Jud's' uniform was not a uniform at all — it was sui generis on that diamond: a coarse-ribbed grey undershirt, with the sleeves rolled well up above the elbows; a visorless red cap; a pair of 'pants' cut off square at the knees; red stockings that didn't come quite up to the 'pants,' thus disclosing a good bit of intervening white cotton flannel; and for shoes a pair of old rubber boots cut off at the ankles. No two of the Pennesewassee [sic] 'uniforms' were alike except in the one feature of abbreviated leg gear, and one of the nine invariably went to the bat barefooted, while others ran their bases in long-legged boots."[37]

This description was a pure fabrication, and it prompted Smith to bluntly retort, "This is not so, for in the first place we had no man on the team by the name of 'Jud Parrott,' and everyone wore a uniform alike, consisting of blue shirts, pants, stockings, cap and belt."[38] So too a claim in the *Portland Eastern Argus* that the players from Norway were "heavy men" was rebutted by the *Oxford Democrat*, which remarked: "The average weight is 145 lbs., but they are used to hard work, and have proved that when 'Old Oxford' goes into the field in good earnest, something is sure to be accomplished."[39]

The championship game ended with the Pennesseewassees on the long end of a 29–8 score. According to Hawthorne's hyperbolic account, at the match's conclusion,

> the riotous element broke loose again. They yelled, hissed, hurrahed, "groaned" for the umpire and did all sorts of things to stir up the excited crowd and add to the general confusion. Skittish horses reared and backed, wheels got interlocked, there were one or two upsets and half a dozen incipient fights stopped promptly by the long-bearded "Pot." On top of it all a chorus of horns swelled up from over on the campus, the big Phi Chi drum boomed a thunderous bass, the "ponderous hewgag that had made Gomorrah hum" for five years back added its notes to the din, and then twenty odd Sophomores, in battered "beavers" and skull-and-cross-bones togas, and led by Charlie "Shep" came trooping into the field. Eye-glassed Seniors and smartly dressed Juniors were carrying members of the defeated nine about on their shoulders just as if they were victors; the president of the baseball association had made a little speech formally surrendering the silver ball to the Norway boys; their captain had replied in an acknowledgment that comprehended little more than "Thank you. By gawd, Silas, we've got that ball!"; the early evening shadows were already gathering, and the crowd was beginning to scatter.[40]

No doubt there was some exaggeration in the description, but Smith at least confirmed Hawthorne's version of Sumner Burnham's speech. Smith also verified another picturesque element of Hawthorne's account — that at the end of the match, recent Bowdoin alumnus "Mose" Owen stood atop the "box" of one of the hacks and regaled the onlookers with this poem that he had composed during the match:

> Majestic Live Oaks! Your names shall stand,
> When broken noses adorn the land,
> And forth, next spring, at your Ricker's call,
> May you strike a blow for that silver ball,
> Which now reposes 'mid cows and hosses,
> Up with the gentle Pennesseewassees;
> For though Bowdoins swore they never would yield,
> They were "choked" to death on their chosen field —
> They got dismayed, and could not rally
> At the cry of "Out" instead of "Tally!"[41]

It seems unlikely that the members of the Pennesseewassees gave much notice to the recital of the poem. Indeed, in their excitement to get home, the old black mare and the two-wheel chaise were forgotten and as soon as they had been presented with the silver ball the happy players hurried to the train station.[42] Once aboard the night train, Sumner Burnham and Gene Fuller spent much of the ride home sitting on the floor of the car and rolling the silver ball back and forth along the aisle.[43]

When the champions disembarked, they found that Mr. Knight — the lone spectator from Norway who attended the game — had telegraphed ahead with the exciting news. As a result, the second nine was waiting at the train depot to greet them and escort them back to Norway.[44] Upon arrival home, the conquering heroes, according to Silas Burnham's recollection, were met by "the whole village" and carried about "on their shoulders."[45] That week's *Oxford Democrat* reported: "A salute of thirteen guns was fired, a torch light procession and an illumination extemporized, after which the club sat down to an Oyster Supper at the Elm House."[46] Later versions, presumably less reliable, added a brass band and fireworks to the celebratory parade.[47]

Despite the great local pride in the accomplishment of the Pennesseewassees, there were many who doubted that they would be able to retain the silver ball. Burnham recalled that an "old codger, looking at it where it was on display in Hod Coles' jewelry window in the old Noyes block on Main Street, remarked, 'Well, I snummy, boys, that's the darndest prettiest thing I ever see. I wish you could keep it but of course next spring those city dudes will take it.'"[48]

But the Pennesseewassees had no intention of surrendering the hard-won trophy so easily. They conducted practices throughout the winter and strengthened their lineup by adding left-handed pitcher Ellis Hersey and catcher Gus Crocker from Paris, giving them an extra battery.[49]

Under the rules of the Maine State Association of Base Ball Players, the champion had to schedule and play a match within two weeks of receiving a challenge. Since the playing season stretched from the start of May to the end of October and the silver ball had changed hands on October 19, 1867, the new champions had not been obliged to defend the title that fall. That didn't stop the issuing of immediate challenges, however, and to the dismay of the Pennesseewassees, the association ruled that the two-week period had started on the date of the challenge, meaning that the first championship match of 1868 would have to take place no later than May 2.[50]

Alas, as Burnham recalled, "The spring season was late and snow drifts covered a portion of our diamond up to very near the first of May, so much so that we had to shovel and throw the snow about in order for it to melt from in front of the catcher's line."[51] Nevertheless, the Pennesseewassees endured their first title defense, beating their old rivals the Androscoggins of Lewiston, 23–21, and followed with a 26–6 win over the Crescents of Saccarappa on May 19.[52]

The next challengers were the Athletics of Portland, and the members of that club were brimming with confidence when they arrived in Norway on May 27. "They came in from Portland in a special train with a big brass band and an immense crowd," recalled Burnham. "As soon as they reached the grounds, one of their enthusiasts holding his arm high with a roll of bills, cried out, 'Any part of a hundred dollars that the Athletics carry home the silver ball.' That was something unheard of with the Pennesseewassees. It is doubtful if the whole team could have raised that much money, with the result that there was a death-like silence for a few minutes." But then Norway butcher Sam Briggs offered to take $50 of the wager and other proud citizens followed his lead.[53]

The match itself proved anticlimactic, as the champions thrashed the Athletics, 38–13. At the conclusion of the catastrophic defeat, the members of the visiting club "returned to their special train so mad that they threw their bats over the fence as they passed the cemetery."[54]

After three championship matches in May, a long gap followed. The primary reason appears to have been that the association's rules permitted aspirants to issue only one challenge per year as long as the same club retained the championship. That bylaw eliminated the Androscoggins, the Crescents, and the Athletics, while the summer recess of Bowdoin College meant that any challenge from the collegians would have to wait until the fall. This left one formidable potential challenger, the Eons of Portland, and, to the surprise of the Pennesseewassees, their rival seemed to be in no hurry to try to regain the silver ball.

Suddenly, it looked as though the upstart club from Norway was going to have an extended reign as state champion. The town of Norway was now rabidly behind the ball club, with a group of local girls who became known as the "corn-fed Beauties" attending all the games and encouraging the players with their cheers.[55] "The silver ball of Maine," quipped a Boston reporter, "has gone up into the county and they are going to keep it indefinitely for no one can challenge them legally — no one knows how to spell their confounded name!" Indeed Clarence Smith, who acted as club secretary, confirmed that few club secretaries even tried to spell the unwieldy moniker ("frequently I received letters addressed to the 'P's, etc.'").[56]

The growing fame of the small-town champions with the odd name also had some unforeseen consequences. Smith recalled, "A funny incident happened when we were topnotchers and drawing cards. One day I received by express a sealed package, all charges prepaid, and was asked to sign a receipt for it. I did so and upon opening the bundle found a bottle of Dr. H—s bitters. I laughed at what I considered a joke. A day or two following, the papers came out with the statement that the great success of the Pennesseewassees, the famous baseball team, was due to the fact that they all used Dr. H—s bitters."[57]

But just when it seemed that the silver ball would remain in Norway all summer, the Eons of Portland finally issued the long-anticipated challenge. And, to the outrage of the Pennesseewassees, it now became clear why the Eons had been so patient. The Athletic Club had disbanded after the catastrophic loss in May and "four or five" of their best players had joined the Eons. Under the rules, these players would not be eligible to play for the Eons for thirty days, which was one reason for the delay.[58]

While the Pennesseewassees resented having to play an all-star squad from the much bigger city, what really infuriated them was that the timing of the challenge meant that the match would have to take place at the height of haying time. More than sixty years after the fact, Burnham was still indignant over this "shrewd trick" and his comments help us understand why so few of the era's top clubs hailed from rural areas: "You might say, 'But surely your folks would not keep you in the haying field and prevent your practicing for such a game.' That might be permitted in these times, but not so with the old New England farmers of that day. Haying in Maine was the most important thing in farming and while we might get off at four o'clock on Saturdays, that would be all we could expect."[59]

Fortunately, the Pennesseewassees were tipped off to the scheme by their old townsman Enoch Knight, who was now editing the *Portland Star*, and with his assistance they crafted a cunning response. Some of the "honorary members of the Norway club" called themselves the Ursa Majors and occasionally engaged in "muffin" games against another club of middle-aged men, the Ulyssians of neighboring Paris. Sizable crowds turned out for these games but nobody took them seriously — as an account of one of their games put it, "The novelty of the thing drew together a large number of spectators, who sent up shouts of applause at the mistakes made and the heavy tread of some of the runners ... good cheer and sore limbs were abundant."[60]

Yet the existence of these clubs gave Knight and the Pennesseewassees an idea. At their urging, both clubs paid the entry fee and joined the Maine Association of Base Ball Players, then sent challenges to Knight. He in turn held on to both challenges until that of the Eons arrived and then published all three in the same issue of the *Star*. This left the champions free to schedule the three matches in any order they pleased and of course they chose to play the Ursa Majors first, the Ulyssians second and the Eons third. The first two "challengers" then obligingly forfeited, buying the Pennesseewassees forty-five days and meaning that they would not have to play during the haying season. In addition, the "farmer boys from Oxford County" had the considerable satisfaction of knowing that they had outfoxed the "smart boys from the city."[61]

The big match was finally scheduled for August 21, a date that would allow the Pennesseewassees a full week of practice beforehand. But on what was to be the first day of practice, an older brother of Sumner and Silas Burnham fell gravely ill with diphtheria. The family rushed to his sickbed but Otho Burnham, who was only 30, died just two days before the date of the match. The Pennesseewassees requested a one-week postponement "as neither Sumner nor Silas would think of playing under the circumstances," but the Eons refused.[62]

During pre-game warm-ups, Percival Parris and Charles Cole of the Bowdoin College nine were spotted in the grandstand and were enlisted to replace the Burnham brothers. But both had to play unfamiliar positions and the Eons won the match, 14–10, to recapture the silver ball.[63] It was the end of the Pennesseewassees' hold on the championship — and of the club itself. The members of the champion nine had been planning to make a tour of Massachusetts and take on famed clubs like the Tri-Mountains after the defense against the Eons. But the loss of the silver ball and the circumstances surrounding the match proved too much to overcome and instead the Pennesseewassee Base Ball Club of Norway disbanded.[64]

Since the challenge system had caused "so much trouble last season," the Maine State Association of Base Ball Players met in the spring of 1869 to devise a more "satisfactory disposition of the 'silver ball.'" It was eventually decided to hold a tournament that July and let the winner keep the emblem forever.[65] In each subsequent season, there would be a new championship bat and ball for the winners of that year's tournament.[66] But that incentives could not tempt the Pennesseewassees to reorganize, since, as described in the profiled that follow, more than a few of the players had already started college or left the state. As for the original ball, Clarence Smith believed that it was "either burned in the famous Portland fire or melted into souvenirs."[67]

While the members of Norway's greatest baseball club had given up the sport for good, the club that spawned it — the Cobblers — lived on. Eventually it became known as the Bass Island Club and helped arrange a variety of outdoor activities on Pennesseewassee Lake that made it "one of the best-known summer resorts in the state."[68] At least two of the starters for the championship nine, Clarence M. Smith and Jimmie Danforth, were prominent members of the Bass Island Club.

Club Members

Marion Louville Bartlett: Second baseman Marion L. Bartlett was born in Maine on October 13, 1846, and grew up on the outskirts of Norway. In an interesting indication of just how rural the area was, he was described as one of the village boys even though his father was a farmer. Bartlett moved to Massachusetts very soon after the Pennesseewassees disbanded and was living in Pepperell in 1910.

Silas H. Burnham: Shortstop Silas H. Burnham was one of the last surviving members of the Pennesseewassees in 1930 when he became "rather nettled" by the erroneous accounts of the club's history. So he decided to write down his recollections of the club, first in an article for the *Norway Advertiser*, and then in a brief self-published book. Burnham was born in Harrison, Maine on April 12, 1848, but at the age of ten moved to a farm in Norway, where his father served as president of the Norway State Bank and in the state legislature. After his heroics on the Pennesseewassee Base Ball Club, Silas enrolled at Dartmouth College and then practiced law in Norway. In 1880, he followed his brother Sumner to Nebraska and helped organize the first banks in two of the state's isolated ranching communities. In 1888, he moved to Lincoln and became involved with the First National Bank of Lincoln, eventually becoming its president. He also became one of Lincoln's best known citizens, yet he never forgot his days on the baseball diamond as is shown by his 1930 book. The last of the Pennesseewassees died in Lincoln on September 2, 1933, and his death warranted a front-page article that declared, "No Western banker has had so interesting and colorful career as Silas H. Burnham."[69]

Sumner W. "Sum" Burnham: Sumner W. Burnham, the club's captain and catcher, and the older brother of Silas Burnham, was born on October 15, 1845, in Harrison, Maine. He left school at the age of seventeen to enlist in the Seventeenth Maine, Company C, and during his three years of service in the Civil War he participated in the main battles of the Army of the Potomac, while earning promotion to first lieutenant and a gold medal for acts of bravery. He spent the next five years farming near Norway, and it was during these years that he led the Pennesseewassees to the state championship. Around 1870 he moved to New York state, then to Kentucky, and in 1876 he settled permanently in Nebraska. He became a successful stock dealer, also serving in the state legislature. Sumner Burnham died on January 12, 1912.

Augustus L. "Gus" Crocker: Gus Crocker from Paris joined the club in 1868 as its "change catcher." Three months old when the 1850 census was taken, Crocker later moved to Minneapolis and worked in real estate. He died in Rochester, Minnesota, on October 14, 1925.

James "Jimmie" Danforth: Third baseman Jimmie Danforth was born on October 10, 1839, in Norway, where his father was the town doctor. He served in the Civil War and contracted rheumatism, which plagued him for the rest of his life. He worked for a while as a traveling salesman, but eventually inherited the family farm. He died in Norway on October 3, 1916.

Eugene F. Fuller: Pitcher Gene Fuller was born on December 16, 1847, in Norway, where his father was a farmer. According to Smith, in the game in which the Pennesseewassees captured the silver ball, Fuller used "an underhand throw, just like pitching horseshoes, which, with his speed, and a slight twist that he got into the ball, fooled the Bowdoin batters completely."[70] In 1875 Fuller married Alice Burnham, the sister of his teammates Silas and Sumner, and he followed them in moving to Nebraska, where he died on October 16, 1879.

Ellis Tristram Hersey: Ellis T. Hersey was born in South Paris on October 18, 1850. A left-handed pitcher, he was one of the two players the Pennesseewassees added in 1868, and he played center field when not pitching. He then attended Amherst College and moved to Colorado to pursue a career in mining. He died in Leadville on December 8, 1878, as the result of an accident.

Enoch Knight: Enoch Knight was probably not a member of the Pennesseewassee Base Ball Club, but as noted in the club history, he played a pivotal role in their championship run. He also led a fascinating and eventful life. He was born near Norway around 1834 and one of his closest friends while growing up was the humorist Artemus Ward. Knight served in the Civil War, attaining the rank of captain, and then became a well-known newspaperman, operating the *Portland Star*. He eventually moved to Los Angeles and became a well-known judge, also writing several pieces about Artemus Ward. He died in Los Angeles on May 16, 1908.

Isaac P. Morrill: First baseman Isaac Morrill was a farmer's son who was born in November of 1848. He grew up in Carthage and taught school there as a young man, but headed west soon after his ball-playing days ended, settling first in Iowa, then in Minnesota, and finally in Hollywood, California. In the late 1920s he visited Maine for the first time in nearly sixty years. He was still living in Los Angeles in 1930, but appears to have died soon afterward.

Percival Josiah Parris: Percival J. Parris was born in Portland, Maine, on January 5, 1849, and grew up in South Paris, Maine. After studying at Bowdoin College and at Union College in Schenectady, New York, he became a teacher and a high-school principal. In the late 1870s, he enrolled at the Hamilton College Law School in New York City and became a lawyer (or, according to his entry on the 1900 census, a "loyer"), practicing in New York City, Whatcom (Washington), and Philadelphia. He married late in life to a much younger woman, but still outlived her—Parris was 96 when he died on October 4, 1945. Baseball obviously remained a passion until the end, as in the last year of his life he wrote a fascinating reminiscence about the early years of baseball in Oxford County.

Clarence M. "Clare" Smith: Left fielder Clarence M. Smith, one of the village boys, was born on April 4, 1846, and was a Civil War veteran. He appears to have served as club secretary and he still had the club's scorebook in 1907, when he gave the second of two interviews that were primary sources for this piece. He worked as a master mechanic and was credited in Charles Foster Whitman's history of Norway with designing a snowshoe that helped the town earn recognition as "the snowshoe capital of the world." A lifelong resident of Norway, Smith died there on February 16, 1923.

Dr. Charles Asbury Stephens (real name Stevens): Charles A. Stephens does not seem to have played for the Pennesseewassees in any match games, but his 1930 reminiscence about the club, though sometimes hyperbolic, suggests firsthand knowledge. So there is a good chance that he was the "E. Stephens" who was listed as club treasurer in an 1867 article that included at least one other typographical error. He was born in Norway on October 21, 1844, and studied at Bowdoin

College before having to drop out to earn a living. He did so as a writer, using the name of C. A. Stephens and becoming a prolific contributor to *Youth's Companion*, the popular American magazine for children and teenagers. He specialized in travel stories and tales about his Maine childhood and was also the author of numerous books. In the 1880s, *Youth's Companion* paid for his tuition to medical school at Boston University so that he could contribute articles on medical subjects. He died on September 22, 1931.

Cyrus Shaw Tucker: Center fielder and club vice president Cyrus S. Tucker was born in Norway on October 11, 1841, and followed his father and grandfather into saddle and harness making. After learning the trade, however, Cyrus enlisted in Maine's Seventeenth Regiment and served for three years. According to a later sketch, the wartime conditions "seriously undermined his health, which he has never fully regained; but by close application to business, while observing hygienic laws, he has been able to accomplish more than many who are physically sound, yet lacking in mental and moral stamina." Cyrus Tucker's fortitude enabled him to start for the state baseball champions and to take over his father's business. He ran it for more than thirty years and rebuilt it after a disastrous fire in 1894. Tucker died on October 31, 1899.

Clinton Young: Right fielder Clinton Young was described as being one of the club's five farm boys and as living in Portland, Maine, in 1907. But efforts to locate him on the census have been unsuccessful.

Other Members: Horace Burnham (a younger brother of Silas and Sumner who was born in October 1852 and died in Westerville, Nebraska, in March of 1903), James B. Chaffin (a Buckfield resident, and the club's first president), Charles Cole, Wallace Cushman, Arthur F. Denison, Julius Fuller, A. E. Herrick (of Bethel, later a lawyer and probate court judge), Charles W. Howe (a Norway storekeeper who was one of the club's scorers), Alton O'Brien, M. S. Partridge (club director), Chandler Swift, Elisha Taylor, Harry Virgin (a Portland lawyer who was another scorekeeper and the captain of the "Ursa Majors," one of the clubs of "elderly men" who helped the scheme of the Pennesseewassees), Judge George A. Wilson (who umpired most of the club's home games).

Notes

1. Percival J. Parris, "Oxford County Baseball in 1865," *Norway Advertiser Democrat*, April 13, 1945.
2. Ibid.
3. Pierce Brothers ad, *Maine Farmer*, November 28, 1867, 4.
4. *Oregonian*, March 21, 1915.
5. *Maine Farmer*, October 4, 1866.
6. *Maine Farmer*, October 11, 1866.
7. "The Champion Game: The Pennesseewassees of Norway the Winning Club!" *Oxford Democrat*, October 25, 1867; "Captured the Silver Ball," *Boston Globe*, June 10, 1906, SM5.
8. *Maine Farmer*, August 5, 1867.
9. *Maine Farmer*, August 8, 1867, 35.
10. *Maine Farmer*, October 17, 1867.
11. Silas H. Burnham, *The History of the Old Pennesseewassee Base Ball Club of Norway, Maine* (Lincoln, NE, 1930), 7.
12. "Captured the Silver Ball," *Boston Globe*, June 10, 1906, SM5.
13. Silas H. Burnham, "Story of the Silver Ball by One Who Played Short-Stop for Every Game," *Norway Advertiser*, July 11, 1930, 10.
14. Burnham, *The History of the Old Pennesseewassee Base Ball Club of Norway, Maine*, 5.
15. Dr. Charles A. Stephens, "The Silver Ball: The Early Days of Baseball in the Old Home Town," *Norway Advertiser*, March 21, 1930, 5.
16. *Oxford Democrat*, June 7, 1867, 2. The club also elected three directors: James Danforth, M. S. Partridge, and "S. M. Burnham." It's not clear which of the Burnhams this was. "E. Stephens" may also be a typo for Charles Stephens, who wrote a 1930 reminiscence about the club that reflected first-hand knowledge.
17. "Pennesseewassees, a Famous Ball Team," *Boston Globe*, June 23, 1907, SM4. It is not entirely clear whether these contests were match games. Clarence Smith reported that they were all included in the club's official score book, but Silas Burnham implied that they were informal or friendly games. One of the games against the Ticonics, played on May 30, was described as "a friendly game ... more for the practice than ascendancy to be gained thereby, as both clubs were young in experience" (*Oxford Democrat*, June 7, 1867, 2).
18. Burnham, *The History of the Old Pennesseewassee Base Ball Club of Norway, Maine*, 5.
19. Ibid., 6.
20. Ibid., 6–8.
21. Frank Warren Hawthorne, "A College Girl's Belated Ideal," in John Clair Minot and Donald Francis Snow, *Tales of Bowdoin: Some Gathered Fragments and Fancies of Undergraduate Life in the Past and Present Told by Bowdoin Men* (Kennebec: Press of Kennebec Journal, 1901), 351.
22. Burnham, *The History of the Old Pennesseewassee Base Ball Club of Norway, Maine*, 8–9.
23. "Pennesseewassees, a Famous Ball Team," *Boston Globe*, June 23, 1907, SM4.
24. Ibid.
25. Burnham, *The History of the Old Pennesseewassee Base Ball Club of Norway, Maine*, 9.
26. Parris, "Oxford County Baseball in 1865," *Norway Advertiser Democrat*, April 13, 1945.
27. Burnham, *The History of the Old Pennesseewassee Base Ball Club of Norway, Maine*, 9–10.
28. Ibid.; Hawthorne, "A College Girl's Belated Ideal," 351.
29. Stephens, "The Silver Ball: The Early Days of Baseball in the Old Home Town," *Norway Advertiser*, March 21, 1930, 5.
30. "Captured the Silver Ball," *Boston Globe*, June 10, 1906, SM5.
31. "Pennesseewassees, a Famous Ball Team," *Boston Globe*, June 23, 1907, SM4.
32. Burnham, *The History of the Old Pennesseewassee Base Ball Club of Norway, Maine*, 11–12. Burnham identified Knight as "the expressman between Norway and Portland" and Enoch Knight had recently left Norway to help run the *Portland Star*.
33. Hawthorne, "A College Girl's Belated Ideal," 355.
34. Silas H. Burnham, in *The History of the Old Pennesseewassee Base Ball Club of Norway, Maine*, 10–11, reported that he had made a running catch to start the triple play. The game account in the *Oxford Democrat* credited pitcher Gene Fuller with making the crucial catch, but it provided no details and it seems odd that both base runners would have strayed so far on a ball hit to the pitcher.
35. "Pennesseewassees, a Famous Ball Team," *Boston Globe*, June 23, 1907, SM4.
36. Hawthorne, "A College Girl's Belated Ideal," 357–358.
37. Ibid., 353–354.
38. "Pennesseewassees, a Famous Ball Team," *Boston Globe*, June 23, 1907, SM4.

39. "The Champion Game: The Pennesseewassees of Norway the Winning Club!" *Oxford Democrat*, October 25, 1867.
40. Hawthorne, "A College Girl's Belated Ideal," 358–359.
41. "Captured the Silver Ball," *Boston Globe*, June 10, 1906, SM5; "Pennesseewassees, a Famous Ball Team," *Boston Globe*, June 23, 1907, SM4; Hawthorne, "A College Girl's Belated Ideal."
42. Burnham, *The History of the Old Pennesseewassee Base Ball Club of Norway, Maine*, 11–12.
43. "Pennesseewassees, a Famous Ball Team," *Boston Globe*, June 23, 1907, SM4.
44. "The Champion Game: The Pennesseewassees of Norway the Winning Club!" *Oxford Democrat*, October 25, 1867.
45. Burnham, *The History of the Old Pennesseewassee Base Ball Club of Norway, Maine*, 11–12.
46. "The Champion Game: The Pennesseewassees of Norway the Winning Club!" *Oxford Democrat*, October 25, 1867.
47. "Pennesseewassees, a Famous Ball Team," *Boston Globe*, June 23, 1907, SM4; "Captured the Silver Ball," *Boston Globe*, June 10, 1906, SM5.
48. Burnham, *The History of the Old Pennesseewassee Base Ball Club of Norway, Maine*, 12.
49. "Pennesseewassees, a Famous Ball Team," *Boston Globe*, June 23, 1907, SM4; Burnham, *The History of the Old Pennesseewassee Base Ball Club of Norway, Maine*, 13.
50. Burnham, *The History of the Old Pennesseewassee Base Ball Club of Norway, Maine*, 12–13.
51. Ibid., 13.
52. "Pennesseewassees, a Famous Ball Team," *Boston Globe*, June 23, 1907, SM4; Burnham gives a slightly different score for the game against the Crescents and has the score of the last game as 28–13. Smith and Burnham also report a 102–4 win over the Ursa Majors on May 23, but this was obviously a friendly game.
53. Burnham, *The History of the Old Pennesseewassee Base Ball Club of Norway, Maine*, 14.
54. Ibid., 15.
55. Carrie Tucker, "Norway's Champion Ball Team of 1867, The Pennesseewassees, and Historic Games Recalled," unidentified clipping, apparently from the *Lewiston Journal*, circa 1928.
56. "Captured the Silver Ball," *Boston Globe*, June 10, 1906, SM5.
57. "Pennesseewassees, a Famous Ball Team," *Boston Globe*, June 23, 1907, SM4.
58. Burnham, *The History of the Old Pennesseewassee Base Ball Club of Norway, Maine*, 16.
59. Ibid., 15–16.
60. *Maine Farmer*, October 24, 1867; Burnham, *The History of the Old Pennesseewassee Base Ball Club of Norway, Maine*, 16–17.
61. Burnham, *The History of the Old Pennesseewassee Base Ball Club of Norway, Maine*, 16–18; "Captured the Silver Ball," *Boston Globe*, June 10, 1906, SM5; "Pennesseewassees, a Famous Ball Team," *Boston Globe*, June 23, 1907, SM4.
62. Burnham, *The History of the Old Pennesseewassee Base Ball Club of Norway, Maine*, 17–18.
63. Parris, "Oxford County Baseball in 1865," *Norway Advertiser Democrat*, April 13, 1945.
64. "Pennesseewassees, a Famous Ball Team," *Boston Globe*, June 23, 1907, SM4.
65. *Maine Farmer*, May 22, 1869.
66. *Eastern Argus*, May 11, 1871.
67. "Captured the Silver Ball," *Boston Globe*, June 10, 1906, SM5.
68. Ibid.
69. *Lincoln Journal and Star*, September 3, 1933.
70. "Pennesseewassees, a Famous Ball Team," *Boston Globe*, June 23, 1907, SM4.

Bibliography

Burnham, Silas H. *The History of the Old Pennesseewassee Base Ball Club of Norway, Maine*. Lincoln, NE, 1930.
_____. "Story of the Silver Ball by One Who Played Short-Stop for Every Game." *Norway Advertiser*, July 11, 1930, 10.
"Captured the Silver Ball." *Boston Globe*, June 10, 1906, SM5.
"The Champion Game: The Pennesseewassees of Norway the Winning Club!" *Oxford Democrat*, October 25, 1867.
Hawthorne, Frank Warren. "A College Girl's Belated Ideal." In John Clair Minot and Donald Francis Snow, *Tales of Bowdoin: Some Gathered Fragments and Fancies of Undergraduate Life in the Past and Present Told by Bowdoin Men*. Kennebec: Press of Kennebec Journal, 1901.
Lapham, William Berry. *Centennial History of Norway, Oxford County, Maine, 1786–1886 : Including an Account of the Early Grants and Purchases, Sketches of the Grantees, Early Settlers, and Prominent Residents, Etc.* Portland, ME: B. Thurston & Co., 1886.
"Pennesseewassees, a Famous Ball Team." *Boston Globe*, June 23, 1907, SM4.
Parris, Percival J. "Oxford County Baseball in 1865." *Norway Advertiser Democrat*, April 13, 1945.
Stephens, Dr. Charles A. "The Silver Ball: The Early Days of Baseball in the Old Home Town." *Norway Advertiser*, March 21, 1930, 5.
Tucker, Carrie. "Norway's Champion Ball Team of 1867, The Pennesseewassees, and Historic Games Recalled." Unidentified clipping, apparently from the *Lewiston Journal*, circa 1928.
Whitman, Charles Foster. *A History of Norway, Maine: From the Earliest Settlement to the Close of the Year 1922* [Ancestry.com]. Lewiston, ME: Lewiston Journal Printshop and Bindery, 1924.

Sources

Special thanks to Charles S. Longley of the Norway Historical Society for his invaluable help in locating sources for this entry.

❖ Charter Oaks of Hartford, Connecticut (David Arcidiacono) ❖

Club History

During the years immediately following the Civil War, the most prominent baseball club in Connecticut was the Charter Oak Base Ball Club. Clarence Deming, former player with Yale, fondly remembered the first Hartford team. "On its list were carried names hardly second, in state fame at least, to those of the baseball *colossi* of the Atlantics and Eckfords.... Seen now through the baseball mist, the old Charter Oaks earned their renown fairly by good discipline, steady work and the germs of team play when that baseball trait was almost unknown."[1]

Although baseball history books typically report the formation of the Charter Oak Club occurring in 1862, that was actually a re-organization of the already existing Independent Club of Hartford. The Independent Club was initially formed on May 18, 1860, at the City Hotel in Hartford. The Independent Club was one of the first baseball clubs organized in the central portion of Connecticut. A handful of clubs, mostly in the southwest corner of the state, near New York City, already existed. Twenty-three-year-old Gershom Hubbell brought the New York game with him to Hartford when he moved there from Bridgeport in 1860. Hubbell found employment in Hartford as a telegrapher at the American Telegraph office on Main Street. He loved multiple sports and was well-known throughout the state for being a champion billiard player.[2]

Members of the Independent club typically gathered two or three times a week to play ball among themselves. At the end of summer 1860, the Independents played an inter-club match with another Hartford team, the Mechanics Club, composed, naturally, of mechanics. The two teams met in Hartford's Bushnell Park, but the game ended abruptly when the Independents, trailing 39–9, left the field, accusing the Mechanics of some unspecified unfair play.[3]

Over the next few summers the Independent Club become very popular with Hartford residents. Hundreds of spectators would watch the club's 4 P.M. practices in the west end of Bushnell Park, near where the Corning Fountain is currently located. The *Hartford Courant* encouraged the Independents, saying, "We hope they will follow the example of some of our sister cities and arrange for matches during the summer."[4]

In the summer of 1862, the Independent Club was re-organized as the Charter Oak Base Ball Club. The objective of the new club was "to establish on a scientific basis the health-giving and scientific game of ball, and promote good fellowship among its members."[5] The name of the club honored one of Hartford's most enduring symbols. The legend of the famous Charter Oak Tree began in 1662 when King Charles II granted the Connecticut Colony the unique right "to have and to hold [the territory] for ever." Obtaining such a charter was an extraordinary diplomatic coup. Twenty-five years later, King James II thought better of the idea and sent an armed delegation to retrieve the document. During the ensuing debate, the charter lay on the table between the King's envoys and the colonists. Suddenly the room went dark. When light was restored, the charter was gone, supposedly hidden by one of the colonial leaders inside a huge oak tree where it remained until the King's men departed.

As the Charter Oak Club quickly learned, the middle of the Civil War was not the ideal time to form a ballclub. The Charter Oaks had trouble filling their ranks as their primary members—young, healthy men—had, as the *Hartford Courant* stated, "answered the call of their country promptly." In 1863, the club issued a plea for new members since so many of their ranks had left to "fight their country's battles."[6]

After the Civil War, the club's games, as well as its victories, became more numerous. Membership grew so popular that it was reported that 40 active members were allowed in the club, and "as soon as there is a vacancy, it is taken up."[7] The Charter Oaks, which had played just two games in 1864, played ten in 1865. Their most noteworthy match of that season took place on July 31, as part of the "College Day" celebration in Worcester, Massachusetts. The opponent on this day was the mighty Harvard nine, which defeated the Charter Oaks 35–13. The next day John Belden, a Hartford resident and avid baseball enthusiast, presented the Charter Oaks with a miniature bat made from the wood of the original Charter Oak. On one end was a silver plate with an engraved picture of the famous tree and the words "Emblem of the Championship of Connecticut." The bat came in a rosewood case and was accompanied by the following letter from Belden.

> As a lover of the manly game of base ball, I take great pleasure in presenting a miniature bat, made of the wood of that famous old oak so rich in historical associations, name of which you have adopted as your own. The bat, which is intended as the emblem of the championship of the State of Connecticut, you are to retain until challenged for and won according to the rules of base ball play by any club in the state. Any challenge must be responded by actual play, within [blank] weeks of the date of the challenge, under the penalty of the forfeiture of the bat to the challenging party.
>
> "May the best play win," is my motto; but I trust it will be pardonable if I express the hope that the Charter Oak boys *will* make the best play.[8]

This was a meaningful gift as the fabled Charter Oak Tree, although felled by a storm in 1856, was still revered in Hartford. Countless stores and businesses were called the Charter Oak such and such, and it seemed that every home in Hartford had a chip from the old tree, or at least claimed to. The ubiquitous adoration of the late tree became tiresome to Mark Twain, who, on one early visit to Hartford, was ushered about by a friend to view all manner of articles fabricated from the cherished tree's wood. "He took me around and showed me Charter Oak enough to build a plank road from here to Great Salt Lake City. It is a shame to confess it, but I did begin to get a little weary of Charter Oak...."[9]

In 1866 and 1867, the Charter Oaks played several of the most famous baseball nines in the country. When a well-known team such as the Atlantics of Brooklyn or the Unions of Morrisania (Bronx) arrived in Hartford, the Charter Oaks greeted them at the rail station and gave the visitors a grand tour of the city. Following the game, entertainment was provided at the Allyn House or the United States Hotel. Occasionally the hosts would even bestow on the visiting club an insurance policy from the Travelers Insurance Company, literally insuring their safe return home.[10]

The most famous game of 1866 took place in Hartford, on Independence Day, against a very strong Harvard nine. Julius Rathbun, a member of the Charter Oaks' second nine, recalled, "There was a great celebration on that day, a parade, balloon ascension by E.U. Bassett, the ball game, and fireworks in the evening. The largest crowd ever seen on the park up to that time gathered to see the great baseball game between the Charter Oak and Harvard University clubs. It was estimated that not less than 10,000 people were present, making it quite difficult to play the game, especially back of third base. The game was closely contested, and at the last half of the ninth inning, with the score 16 to 14 in favor of Harvard, and the Charter Oaks at the bat, with a player on second and third and two men out, H.L. Bunce rapped a two-bagger into the right field, which seemed good for two runs, but by a brilliant play by the Harvard fielder the ball was caught and the game ended with a victory for Harvard."[11]

The 1867 season proved to be the pinnacle of the club's success. That summer the state champion Charter Oaks met the Pequots of New London in a best-of-three series. After splitting the first two games, the clubs played the deciding match on July 4 at New Haven's Hamilton Park. With the very real possibility of the Connecticut championship changing hands, baseball fever swept the state. Extra trains from Hartford and New London accommodated the flood of spectators. Supporters of the Charter Oaks offered special prizes to inspire their best efforts—$30 to the man who made the most total bases, $20 to the fielder who put out the most opponents, and a gold Charter Oak pin to the best overall player. Prospects looked grim when Hubbell severely injured his knee in the first inning and was forced to leave the game, being replaced by Robert Kellogg, an inexperienced player who had never played with the first nine before. Despite this handicap, the Charter Oaks had the game tied at 18 after five innings. From then on the Pequots took charge, and despite Hartford's ten-run ninth inning, New London prevailed, 44–34.[12]

With the loss of the state championship and Gersh Hubbell, who never played again after his injury against New London, the status of the Charter Oaks diminished rapidly. The loss of pitcher Josiah Blackwell, who graduated from Trinity College in 1866, was also significant. By 1868, the club was practically non-existent. Although they still received challenges from top nines such as the Nationals of Washington and the Atlantics of Brooklyn, the Charter Oaks fell into decline. In one of the few games they played that season, Hubbell was reduced to umpiring as a club from Lowell, Massachusetts, embarrassed the Charter Oaks 61–12. The club remained in existence into the early 1870s but was a mere shadow of its former greatness, playing few if any inter-club games.[13]

As explained in the profiles that follow, a number of club members went on to very successful business careers, including three members who became bank presidents.

Club Members

Josiah "Si" Blackwell: Blackwell was a student at Trinity College, graduating in 1866. Clarence Deming, a Yale ball player, remembered that Blackwell "won fame in pick-up catches — then called 'trapping' the ball — a trick used by him as a mere ornament and baseball 'frill,' and with a crudity which would make the modern first baseman or catcher smile, yet not so easy then, long before the era of portly glove and pad." Blackwell handled much of the pitching duties, and it was reported that "he had a peculiar delivery and seemed to be able to curve the ball without trying to do so." Upon his graduation from Trinity and subsequent departure from the team, the Charter Oak muffins gave him a 20 dollar gold piece, smoothed and engraved with the Charter Oak symbol.[14]

Frederic L. Bunce: Frederic Bunce and his twin brother and Charter Oak teammate were born May 4, 1847. Both were still in high school when they played for the Charter Oaks. Deming recalled that they were both "lithe and trusty young players." At age 18, Frederic started work at the Phoenix National Bank in Hartford, where his father was the president. He remained with the bank until his death, becoming president himself. He never married and was devoted to the bank, although he still found time to attend many baseball games in the city. Frederic died of an embolism on November 2, 1915.[15]

Henry L. Bunce: Henry Bunce, Frederic's twin, was also a student at Hartford High School when he played with the Charter Oaks. Like his brother, Henry was also a bank president, becoming head of the United States Bank in Hartford. He died in Hartford on June 28, 1918, of heart disease.[16]

James Daniel Fitzgibbons: Fitzgibbons moved to Hartford in 1862 at the age of 19 and was employed at the Phoenix Iron Works as a machinist. He pitched in 1866, after Blackwell left. While with the Charter Oaks he traveled to Brooklyn in 1867 to play the Excelsiors and found himself unable to hit Candy Cummings' pitching. He left Hartford and went to St. Louis in April 1868. In 1873, he opened his own building and general contracting business and constructed many important buildings in St. Louis. While in St. Louis, Fitzgibbons pitched for the Empire Club and served as one of the club's field captains in 1870. He lived out an active life in St. Louis into his 80s. Alfred H. Spink wrote of Fitzgibbons in 1910: "Two years ago he visited Hartford and while there asked about his former teammates, the Bunce brothers. He found they had become bank presidents. Calling on one of the brothers, the president of the Phoenix Bank at Hartford, Mr. Fitzgibbons was recognized instantly, called by name and given a hearty reception by a fellow player who had seen him but twice in forty years."[17] (For more details on Fitzgibbons, see the entry on the Empires of St. Louis.)

Gershom Hubbell: Hubbell was born in Bridgeport, Connecticut, in 1837. He held the office of the President for the Charter Oaks for their entire existence. In 1874, Hubbell was elected president of the Hartford Dark Blues, Hartford's entry in the National Association of Professional Base Ball Players, the nation's first professional baseball league. Hubbell turned down re-election the following year, paving the way for Morgan Bulkeley, later the first president of the National League, to become the club's president. He was employed with several telegraph companies and was one of the first to appreciate the practical aspects of the telephone. Hubbell died of Bright's disease in Boston on September 5, 1883. He is buried in Bridgeport.[18]

Edward Jewell: Jewell was born in Poughkeepsie, New York, on January 16, 1847. While playing for the Charter Oaks, Jewell was a clerk in his father's hide and leather business, Pliny Jewell and Sons. He typically manned first base and was known for his showboating. Clarence Deming, Jewell's teammate at Yale, from which they both graduated in 1869, recalled that "Jewell, a dashing but too spectacular first baseman, playing more to the gallery than to the score card." He lived in the Boston area for much of his later life and died in Medfield, Massachusetts, on July 6, 1925.[19]

Enos Lane: Lane was a clerk at the George S. Lincoln Co., iron founders, while playing for the Charter Oaks. He also served his country during the Civil War. In his later years he worked as a bookkeeper for the Pratt and Cady Company. He died in Hartford on March 1, 1911, at the age of 71.[20]

Fergus Latta: Latta was known for his big feet and his long strides in running around the bases. He was affiliated with the Alert Hose Company in Hartford in 1872. He died November 2, 1872, in Bridgeport, at age 24.[21]

Carlton L. Perry: Carl Perry, the shortstop, was a nephew of V. D. Perry, who played right field. He worked for many years at D.K. Owen's furniture rooms. He died at his home on Village Street of typhoid fever on November 22, 1884. Perry left a wife, Anna, and an 11-year-old son.[22]

Valette D. Perry: Perry was the uncle of Carl Perry. He was a master mechanic of the Hartford, Providence and Fishkill railroad, famous for his beautifully built passenger cars. In later years he operated a music store. Perry died in Hartford on August 11, 1884.[23]

Jack Reynolds: Reynolds became the Charter Oaks' shortstop after Yergason left in 1866. He was employed as a mechanical engineer at the Sigourney Tool company. Later in life he became vice-president of the Smyth Manufacturing Company. He died in Hartford in May 1927.[24]

Henry Yergason: Yergason was born in 1839. He became a clerk at the Farmers and Mechanics Bank in Hartford in 1857. He was a Yale student while playing for Charter Oaks. In 1864, he joined the Army and became paymaster, headquartered in Vicksburg. In 1866 he accepted a job as a cashier in the Merchants National Bank in Cincinnati and left Hartford and the Charter Oaks. He remained with this bank for the rest of his life, becoming president in 1891. This made him the third Charter Oak player to become a bank president. Yergason was a substitute for the 1867 Red Stockings of Cincinnati, for whom the famed Harry Wright was pitcher. Yergason died June 27, 1916, in Cincinnati.[25]

Notes

1. Clarence Deming, *Yale Yesterdays* (New Haven: Yale University Press, 1915), p. 206.
2. *Hartford Courant*, May 19, 1860, September 17, 1860, and October 27, 1860.
3. *Hartford Courant*, May 19, 1860, September 17, 1860, and October 27, 1860.
4. *Hartford Courant*, June 23, June 30, 1862, May 19, 1862, and February 3, 1916.
5. Phyllis Kihn, "The Charter Oak Nine," *Connecticut Historical Society Bulletin*, April 1961, p. 56; *Hartford Courant*, July 2, 1862.
6. *Hartford Courant*, September 11, 1862, and May 13, 1863.
7. *Hartford Courant*, May 3, 1866.
8. Kihn, "The Charter Oak Nine," pp. 56, 60.
9. *Scribner's Monthly*, November 1876, p. 11; Twain as special correspondent to *San Francisco Alta* (California) newspaper, March 3, 1868.
10. Kihn, "The Charter Oak Nine," p. 63.
11. Major Julius G. Rathbun, "Baseball Here Forty Years Ago," Chadwick Scrapbooks, unidentified clipping, circa 1907.
12. Kihn, "The Charter Oak Nine," p. 64, *Hartford Courant*, July 4, 1867.
13. Kihn, "The Charter Oak Nine," p. 64; *Hartford Courant*, May 15, 1868, June 16, 1868, June 13, 1868, and October 12, 1904.
14. Deming, *Yale Yesterdays*, p. 206; *Hartford Courant*, July 6, 1866, May 10, 1899, and October 12, 1904.
15. Rathbun, "Baseball Here Forty Years Ago"; Deming, *Yale Yesterdays*, p. 206; *Hartford Courant*, November 2, 1915.
16. Rathbun, "Baseball Here Forty Years Ago"; Kihn "The Charter Oak Nine," *Hartford Courant*, June 29, 1918.
17. *Hartford Courant*, October 1, 1866; Alfred H. Spink, *The National Game* (N.p.: National Game, 1910), p. 41.
18. *Hartford Courant*, September 6, 1883; Kihn, "The Charter Oak Nine," p. 55.
19. Deming, *Yale Yesterdays*, p. 206; Kihn, "The Charter Oak Nine," p. 55; *Hartford Courant*, July 8, 1925.
20. *Hartford Courant*, October 12, 1904, and March 2, 1911; Kihn, "The Charter Oak Nine," p. 56; Rathbun, "Baseball Here Forty Years Ago."
21. Rathbun, "Baseball Here Forty Years Ago"; *Hartford Courant*, August 13, 1884, August 13, 1886, January 2, 1872, and November 4, 1872.
22. *Hartford Courant*, November 24, 1884, and October 12, 1904.
23. Rathbun, "Baseball Here Forty Years Ago"; *Hartford Courant*, August 13, 1884, and July 27, 1901.
24. *Hartford Courant*, October 1, 1866, and May 4, 1927; Rathbun, "Baseball Here Forty Years Ago."
25. *Hartford Courant*, March 9, 1866, and June 30, 1916; Rathbun, "Baseball Here Forty Years Ago"; Harry Ellard, *Base Ball in Cincinnati: A History* (Jefferson, NC: McFarland, 2004), p. 34.

Bibliography

Arcidiacono, David. *Grace, Grit and Growling—The Hartford Dark Blues Base Ball Club, 1874–1877*. East Hampton, CT: Self-published, 2003.
Cox, James. *Old and New St. Louis*. St. Louis: Central Biographical Publishing Company, 1894.
Deming, Clarence. *Yale Yesterdays*. New Haven: Yale University Press, 1915.
Ellard, Harry. *Base Ball in Cincinnati: A History*. Jefferson, NC: McFarland, 2004.
Hartford Courant, various dates.
Kihn, Phyllis. "The Charter Oak Nine." *Connecticut Historical Society Bulletin*, April 1961, pp. 56–64.
Rathbun, Major Julius G. "Baseball Here Forty Years Ago." Chadwick Scrapbooks, unidentified clipping, circa 1907.
Spink, Alfred H. *The National Game*. N.p.: National Game, 1910.

Quinnipiacks of West Meriden, Connecticut
(Michael J. Bielawa)

Connecticut's early amateur baseball players must have been a proud and patriotic lot. Neighborhood jingoism during this era is nowhere more evident than in the names clubs chose. Baseball nines adopted cabalistic monikers fondly associated with local character and history. Such is the origin of the Quinnipiack Base Ball Club of Meriden, Connecticut.

The indigenous peoples who once resided in and around the surrounding area of present day New Haven were known as the Quinnipiac. These peoples spoke an Algonquin dialect known as Quinipi.[1] In fact, the English settlers initially recognized the city of New Haven as "Quinnipiac." Roughly translated the word means "long water land." The name is also applied to the 38-mile river flowing through south-central Connecticut and emptying into New Haven Harbor. A portion of the Quinnipiac River meanders through the southwest corner of Meriden in the area initially named by settlers as Falls Plain. In 1832 this south Meriden vicinity formally took the ethno-embracing name "Hanover" in recognition of the German workmen laboring in the local copper mine.[2] It is known that a Hanover Cricket Club existed prior to baseball's advent.[3] Since the game's formative years this neighborhood has remained a baseball stronghold for the city of Meriden. The banks of Hanover Pond still hosts a baseball park, Habershon Field.

The Quinnipiack Base Ball Club of Hanover was organized at some point toward the conclusion of July 1866. The *Meriden Literary Recorder* dated August 15, 1866, corrects an oversight in a previous edition of the newspaper when the editors mistakenly stated there was a lack of local baseball clubs. The *Literary Recorder* then goes on to express that the Quinnipiack club was formed "some three weeks [ago]" in the town's "Hanover" section and that they "number thirty-four members." The initial organization was composed entirely of individuals residing within the Hanover community.[4] Sectionalism, even good-natured, was evident in the members' call to play against "Meridenites."

During 1866 the *Meriden Literary Recorder* usually employed "Quinnipiac," without the letter "k." The following season newspaper writers vacillated between the two usages, but "Quinnipiack" became the generally accepted spelling. "Quinnies" also became a popular nickname. In any event this was by no means the first instance of the Algonquin word being employed by a baseball club — around 1858 a ball club in New Haven played under this Quinipi language banner.[5]

The officers of the Hanover club named the Quinnipiacks were president, Frederick J. Perkins; vice president, Dwight Welton; secretary, Frank Woodstock; and treasurer, Delancy Sawyer. The captain of the first nine was John Thompson. The inaugural match pitted the club's married men against the group's bachelors and took place on Thursday, August 16, 1866. The married men prevailed.

During summer's waning weeks the 1866 Quinnipiacks faced rivals from neighboring towns. The Hanover ballists defeated the Winooski Club of Plantsville, 25 to 24, and in action against two Cheshire, Connecticut, clubs they beat the Athletic Club, 42 to 13, and the Active Club, 32 to 2. Thus, besides the first intrasquad game, the Quinnipiacks participated in a total of three recorded contests during 1866 and went undefeated.

In January 1867 the National BBC of Meriden consolidated with the Quinnipiacks and the newly empowered combine assumed the latter's name. Now numbering 160 members, with sixty involved in baseball, the expanded ball club became identified as the Quinnipiacks of Meriden.[6]

Delegates from the various state baseball clubs, most of which belonged to the National Association, met in Hartford during March 1867 to form the Connecticut Association of Base Ball Players. Gathering in Clinton Hall, the Connecticut ball players committee on credentials reported favorably on allowing admittance to the Quinnipiack Club of West Meriden, represented by John B. Thompson and J. Langdon.[7]

The year 1867 marked a continued legitimization of the Quinnies during an epoch of local "base ball mania."[8] The club fielded three separate nines. Ballists entering the playing field wore a uniform of blue pants, white shirt trimmed in blue, with a black belt and a red and white cap.[9] The club was rated the best in Meriden by the *Literary Recorder,* which ranked them next to the champion Charter Oak BBC of Hartford. The Quinnies also became connected to a bit of Meriden's journalistic history. In a preview of what would one day become a fixture of sports pages across the nation, the June 13, 1867, *Meriden Weekly Visitor* offered the Silver City's first in-depth, inning-by-inning coverage of a baseball game: the Quinnipiacks' victory over the Forest City Club of Middletown.

The significance with which the Quinnipiacks viewed baseball prompted the club to travel north that summer for a weeklong, five-game tournament in Greenfield, Massachusetts. Facing clubs from the western portion of the Bay State, the Quinnies' visit lasted from July 1 to July 8, 1867. The prominence of this series was not lost on participants. Twenty-seven years after the Greenfield gathering, an anonymous member of the highly ranked Florence, Massachusetts, Eagle Base Ball Club reminisced about the tournament: "The first game of any importance [that year] being the defeat at Greenfield of the Quinnipiac Club of West Meriden, Conn. on July second."[10]

Cheers filled the Quinnies' ears when they departed Meriden for Massachusetts that July, but the club ran head-on into reality during the tournament's first game. Quinnipiack was taken down a few notches from their homespun loftiness when the Eagles handily beat them, 55 to 23. Overall, the Meriden men had nothing to be embarrassed about, taking three of the tournament's four remaining games. Greenfield citizens celebrated the Fourth of July 1867 with a cacophony of "bells, cannon, pistols and fire-crackers"[11] before the afternoon ball game between the Quinnipiack and Notunck Clubs (Meriden newspapers mistakenly identified the Massachusetts club, minus the letter "c," as the Notunks). Meriden was victorious 77 to 24. The following evening Captain Thompson, on behalf of the Meriden club, provided the Notuncks a silver goblet manufactured expressly for the tournament by the Meriden Britannia Company. A similar token was presented to the Green River Club. During the course of the week the Quinnies, in turn, were gifted by an elegant china cigar holder from the Notuncks, a solid silver cup by the Green River Club, and a framed engraving by David Simons, the proprietor of the American House in Greenfield where the Meriden club stayed.[12]

Quinnipiack Base Ball Club 1867 Roster

Player	Position	Birth Date	Occupation
Clark	1B		
James Degnan	*C		
John Fletcher	SS		
George W. Francis	CF/SS		harness/saddle maker
Griswold	P/RF		
William A. Harwood	Scorer	abt 1843	burnisher
Charles L. Hyatt**	3B	abt 1844	mechanic
John Jopson*	LF/CF/2B	April 1845	carriage trimming
John M. Kinder*	1B/RF	Sept 1847	Britannia worker
Frank Mason	1B/LF		machinist
C. Parker*	RF		
S. Olin Parker*	LF	April 1847	box maker
Fred J. Perkins**	President & 2B/C	abt 1844	mechanic
Delancy Sawyer	Treasurer	abt 1834	cutler
Edward Haines Shumway**	CF/RF	Feb 28, 1840	Reform School teacher
Planter Sweet	RF/SS	abt 1840	mechanic
John B. Thompson	Captain first nines & P/C		cutter
Dwight Welton	Vice President	abt 1849	
Frank Woodstock	Secretary	abt 1846	mechanic

*Denotes prior membership with the National BBC of Meriden.
**Union soldier serving during the American Civil War.

Several Quinnipiack ballists offer particularly interesting stories. Left fielder S. Olin Parker had been a member of the Nationals of Meriden prior to joining the Quinnies in January 1867. Stephen Olin Parker, who went by his middle name, was born in Meriden in April 1847. His parents were Stephen L. and Martha M. (Andrews) Parker. At about the age of 16, Olin went to work making coffee mill boxes with his father for the

Medals and emblems were popular tokens among 19th century base ball clubs. S. Olin Parker, the 19-year-old former member of the Meriden Nationals BBC, joined the Quinnipiacks in January 1867 and was honored with this emblem. The popular outfielder would work six decades at the Charles Parker Company and serve as an elected official in Meriden's city government (courtesy of the Michael J. Bielawa Baseball Collection).

Charles Parker Company, an expansive factory in the Silver City.[13] Four years later Olin was batting clean-up and patrolling the outfield for the Quinnipiacks. The *Northampton Free Press* complimented Parker on his handling of left field during the Quinnies' 1867 visit to Greenfield, Massachusetts.[14] In 1871 he married Algierose Wylie of Coventry, New York. Later during the decade he became a constable for Meriden, and then one of the city's first special policeman. He also served as a police commissioner. For over sixty years S. Olin Parker continued working with the Charles Parker Company, advancing to patternmaker and eventually foreman in the highly skilled piano stools department. He had served as an alderman in the city's third ward, and at the turn of the twentieth century was nominated second selectman, a civic role he retained into the early 1920s. His love of baseball apparently never waned, Olin helped officially represent the city of his birth during the June 1903 Meriden and Hartford ball game. During S. Olin Parker's lifetime the coffee mill box maker personally took part in the national pastime's inception, and served the city he loved during the Babe Ruth Era. Parker died in 1929 at the age of 82 two months shy of the start of the Great Depression. He is buried in Meriden's West Cemetery.

E[dward] H[aines] Shumway, the articulate outfielder for the Quinnipiacks, may have viewed baseball as more than just a game. The newly crowned national pastime very likely helped

Edward Haines Shumway, former Quinnipiack center fielder, departed New England about 1869 and became a foreman in the Indiana Reform School's chair-caning shop. Shumway was familiar with such institutions. He had been incarcerated in Connecticut's Reform School during the late 1850s before going off to fight in the Civil War. Following his enlistment he took a vocational teaching job in the same Meriden, Connecticut, facility where he had been incarcerated. Baseball was played at both state institutions during Shumway's employment.

transform the ballist's life. It is quite possible that Shumway's first experience on a base path took place at the state's reform school.

Edward was born on February 28, 1840, in Birmingham (what is now Derby), Connecticut. Within ten years he, his father Charles Partridge Shumway, mother Mary, and his four siblings were residing in New Haven. Not long afterwards his father died in New Orleans during the Crescent City's terrifying 1853 Yellow Fever outbreak.[15] Tragedy would not leave Edward's side. A little over six months later, on Edward Shumway's fourteenth birthday, his mother Mary died. Parentless, Edward's life spiraled downward. A single line in the 1860 United States Census illustrates the depths of Edward's difficulties. E. H. Shumway was incarcerated at the State Reform School located in Meriden. Column 14 of the Census inquires if the individual is a convict. The space next to Edward's name lists the word "Forgery."

Opened in March of 1854, the institution was built with the noble intensions of rehabilitation rather than punishment. Theft, assault, and burglary are some of the crimes boys were sentenced for, but inmates were also incarcerated, in Dickensian terminology, for "vagrancy" and even "stubbornness." Parents could also, if so inclined, send incorrigible youths to the "school"; the fee was $2.00 a week to cover their child's room and board. Neither inmates nor boarders were allowed to remain beyond the age of 21.[16] Frank Mason was such a boarder at the reform school in 1860, the same time as Shumway's imprisonment. Certainly Mason's given name is common, but it should be noted that the 1867 Quinnies employed a first baseman by the same name.

Baseball was played at the reform school following the Civil War, on school grounds situated northwest of the institution. We can only speculate if baseball occurred during Edward's incarceration. However, the distinct possibility remains. As early as 1855 it was noted that following the day's work boys "were permitted to play in a spacious piece of ground."[17] In fact, reformers became concerned over this same "common play-ground" becoming a hindrance to rehabilitation. An 1857 *Hartford Daily Courant* article noted that the playing field brought all the boys together in a style reminiscent of a penitentiary. It was feared that the recreational gathering resulted in young children becoming "contaminated and depraved and viciously taught" by the "really bad boys."[18]

A fascinating coincidence took place at the state institution during the time of Shumway and Frank Mason's stays — the appearance of businessman Benjamin Douglas, whose son would one day become an outstanding baseball entrepreneur and manager. In 1858 Ben Douglas Sr. embarked on his nine-year term as a trustee on the State Reform School board. The Douglas family resided in neighboring Middletown, where Ben Jr. as a teenager organized the state champion Mansfields. The trustee's son was about 10 years old in 1860, close in age to Frank Mason. Research does not yet indicate that young Douglas ever toured the reform school's common playing field, but it is interesting to speculate that the trustee's precocious son influenced athletics at the facility and may have introduced two future Quinnipiacks to pick up bat and ball.

Young Edward Shumway worked in the institution's chair manufactory, "slating chairs," until he turned 21, whereupon he volunteered to fight for the Union at the onset of the Civil War. E. H. Shumway was among the first to heed Lincoln's call for troops, enlisting in the 1st Connecticut Infantry during

April 1861. Private Shumway was mustered out following his three-month hitch on July 31, 1861.

Apparently the reform school held a distinct therapeutic pull for the young veteran. Edward returned to the institution about 1864, this time as a state employee appointed by superintendent Dr. E. W. Hatch to be the school's watchman. After two years in this capacity Shumway returned to working in the manufacturing division, now overseeing the Chair Department. Shumway and other "SRS" workers were known to leave the grounds and serenade the townsfolk of Meriden on warm summer nights.

Around 1869 Edward departed New England with his newfound skills as chair maker-cum-social worker. Shumway took a job as a "house father" in the Indiana House of Refuge for Juvenile Offenders, a political euphemism meaning reform school. Shumway continued his trade as foreman of the chair-caning department in the Plainfield, Indiana, facility. Perhaps the sadness he confronted early in life moved him to pursue a more humane approach of educating wayward children. In his December 31, 1870, report to the superintendent of the Indiana House of Refuge, the house father observed that whenever a boy committed an infraction he would, in Shumway's own words, handle the situation by "chiding mildly and appealing to the heart ... knowing that love can conquer the hardest [heart], and reach further than the rod...."[19] An 1870 report on the House of Refuge prepared for the Indiana state government provides an illustration of boys playing baseball on the institution's back lot. The engraver's attempt to convey a tranquil and health-conscious environment was far from successful. Upon closer inspection the tableau strangely lacks a batter, or for that matter, members of an opposing club. The image portrays nine lonely fielders frozen in a sort of baseball purgatory.

In January 1871, a bit shy of his thirty-first birthday, Edward married Arabella Pollard Tomlinson. In 1880 he and Bella were living in Indianapolis, his occupation "chair carver." In the mid-1880s Edward, Bella, and their daughter Clara had relocated to Topeka, Kansas. E. H. Shumway died there at age 67 on August 1, 1907,[20] exactly a week short of his father Charles' passing forty-four years earlier. The young chairmaker who returned from war to play baseball in the town where he'd been incarcerated had reached out to help others. E. H. Shumway ignored the "vicious" lessons of the "penitentiary" ball grounds and followed a noble base path.

Notes

1. Albert E. Van Dusen, *Puritans Against the Wilderness: Connecticut History to 1763* (Chester, CT: Pequot Press, 1975), p. 17.
2. Charles Bancroft Gillespie, *A Century of Meriden* (Meriden, CT: Journal Publishing Co., 1906), pp. Part I, 65–66, and 233.
3. *Meriden Literary Recorder*, August 16, 1865.
4. *Meriden Weekly Visitor*, May 9, 1867.
5. *New Haven Daily Palladium*, May 26, 1863.
6. *Meriden Weekly Visitor*, May 9, 1867. Information concerning the merger of the National and Quinnipiac Clubs appears in a letter to the editor signed "E.H.S." Presumably the letter's author is Quinnie outfielder Edward H. Shumway.
7. Connecticut Association of Base Ball Players, *Constitution and By-Laws of the Connecticut Association of Base Ball Players, with the Laws and Regulations of the Game of Base Ball* (Hartford, CT: Press of Wiley, Waterman & Eaton, 1867), pp. 27, 32. The December 19, 1867, edition of the *Ball Players' Chronicle*, notes the inclusion of "Quinnipiack of New Haven" and "Quinnipiack of West Meriden" in the Connecticut Association organized March 13, 1867.
8. *Hartford Daily Courant*, September 11, 1867.
9. *Meriden Literary Recorder*, May 8, 1867.
10. "The Eagle Ball Club," written by "One of the Players" appears in *The History of Florence, Massachusetts* edited by Charles Arthur Sheffield (Florence, MA: Charles Arthur Sheffield, 1895), p. 183.
11. *Meriden Literary Recorder*, July 10, 1867. The *Meriden Weekly Visitor*, July 4, 1867 and the *Greenfield Gazette and Courier*, July 8, 1867, also provide excellent coverage. The *Greenfield Gazette and Courier* of July 15, 1867, also provides coverage of a Monday, July 8, 1867, game that the Meriden press and Quinnipiack players fail to mention. Nine of the best players from the Notunck and Green River Clubs defeated the Quinnipiacks, 64 to 44.
12. *Meriden Weekly Visitor*, July 11, 1867.
13. *Meriden Record*, August 27, 1929.
14. *Northampton Free Press*, July 12, 1867.
15. Asahel Adams Shumway, *Genealogy of the Shumway Family in the United States* (New York: Tobias A. Wright, 1909), p. 364.
16. *Ninth Annual Report of the Board of Trustees of the State Reform School of Connecticut for the Year 1861, to the General Assembly, May Session, 1861* (New Haven: Carrington & Hotchkiss, 1861), pp. 390–391.
17. *Hartford Daily Courant*, June 14, 1855.
18. *Hartford Daily Courant*, June 23, 1857.
19. *Report of the Commissioners and Superintendent of the Indiana House of Refuge to the Legislature* (Indianapolis: Alexander H. Conner, 1870), p. 50. E. H. Shumway also reprised his Meriden Reform School job in the chair manufacturing shop. The 1875 annual report shows Shumway employed as a House Father and also as foreman of the House of Refuge chair caning department. Shumway's name was associated with institution reports through the 1879 edition.
20. For all that E. H. Shumway accomplished during life, his passing was barely noticed. The date of his death was found on January 12, 2010, using the website: "Irene's KS Genealogy: Kansas Obits," www.carrollsweb.com/ireneksg/s.html. The *Topeka* [Kansas] *Daily Capital*, August 2, 1907, offers merely two sentences announcing E. H. Shumway's death and funeral.

Bibliography

Chadwick, Henry, ed. *The Ball Players' Chronicle.*
Connecticut Association of Base Ball Players. *Constitution and By-Laws of the Connecticut Association of Base Ball Players, with the Laws and Regulations of the Game of Base Ball.* Hartford: Press of Wiley, Waterman & Eaton, 1867.
The [Middletown, Connecticut] *Constitution*, 1867.
"The Eagle Ball Club," written by "One of the Players." In *The History of Florence, Massachusetts*, edited by Charles Arthur Sheffield. Florence, MA: Charles Arthur Sheffield, 1895.
Gillespie, Charles Bancroft. *A Century of Meriden.* Meriden: Journal Publishing Co., 1906.
Greenfield [Massachusetts] *Gazette and Courier*, 1867.
Hartford Daily Courant, 1855–1857, 1867.
"Irene's KS Genealogy: Kansas Obits." www.carrollsweb.com/ireneksg/s.html. Kansas State Census 1885, 1905.
Meriden City Directory for 1873–74. Hartford: Nathan Fenn and Company, 1873.

Meriden City Directory for 1874–75. Hartford: Fitzgerald & Dillon, 1874.
Meriden Literary Recorder, 1865–1867.
Meriden Record, 1929.
Meriden Weekly Visitor, 1867.
Middletown and Meriden Directory 1868–69. New York: Webb & Fitzgerald, 1868.
New Britain [Connecticut] *Record*, 1867.
New Haven Daily Palladium, 1863.
Ninth Annual Report of the Board of Trustees of the State Reform School, of Connecticut for the Year 1861 ... to the General Assembly, May Session, 1861. New Haven: Carrington & Hotchkiss, 1861.
Northampton [Massachusetts] *Free Press*, 1867.
Price, Lee & Co.'s Meriden Directory for 1879. New Haven: Price, Lee & Co., 1879.
Report of the Commissioners and Superintendent of the Indiana House of Refuge to the Legislature. Indianapolis: Alexander H. Conner, 1870.
Shumway, Asahel Adams. *Genealogy of the Shumway Family in the United States*. New York: Tobias A. Wright, 1909.
Topeka [Kansas] *Daily Capital*, 1907.
United States Federal Census 1860–1880, 1900.
Van Dusen, Albert E. *Puritans Against the Wilderness: Connecticut History to 1763*. Chester, CT: Pequot Press, 1975.
Waterbury [Connecticut] *Daily American*, 1867.

❖ *Mansfields of Middletown* (David Arcidiacono) ❖

Club History

The Mansfield Base Ball Club, originally composed of workers from a hydraulic pump factory in Middletown, Connecticut, was no different from any of the hundreds of teams that were formed in the state after the Civil War. It would have been hard to guess from the club's inauspicious debut in 1866, an embarrassing 50–1 loss, that the Mansfields would someday become a major league club. But just six seasons after their start, the club was a member of the nation's first professional league, the National Association of Professional Base Ball Players.

In late summer 1866, 16-year-old Ben Douglas, Jr., was working at the Douglas Pump Company, which had been founded forty years earlier by his father and uncle. Ben was a real lover of the rapidly growing game of baseball, so much so that he once proclaimed, "My whole soul is in base ball." A Chicago newspaper once declared that Douglas "would go ten miles on foot, over any obstacles, rather than miss seeing a good game."[1] As a result, Ben organized some of the factory workers into a team.

Douglas originally designated the baseball nine the "Douglas Club," but quickly changed the name to "Mansfields" in honor of General Joseph Mansfield, a Middletown native and Civil War veteran who was killed at the battle of Antietam. Although General Mansfield certainly deserved the honor, probably the most important factor in naming the team was that he was young Ben's great-uncle.

After limited practice, the naive Mansfields challenged the Lincoln Club of nearby New Britain. Unfortunately, the Lincolns accepted. Upon arriving in New Britain, the Mansfields proceeded to exhibit a keen lack of skill as they were defeated by the humiliating score of 50-1. Despite the magnitude of the loss, the Mansfields agreed to a return match in Middletown. With three additional weeks of practice, the Mansfields somehow managed an incredible reversal of fortune, defeating New Britain 44-31 in front of 200 spectators. This pair of games represented the extent of the Mansfields' 1866 matches.[2]

Over the next three seasons, the Mansfields increased the number of games on their schedule and began traveling longer distances for matches. They also began to draw players from the entire city of Middletown, not just the factory. These seasons were characterized by increasingly intense local rivalries that often featured insulting accusations of ducking games or using ringers. Despite the rivalries, ties to the gentlemanly roots of baseball were still strong during this period. The Mansfields usually entertained visiting clubs at the McDonough House, a famous hotel in town. After games, the Mansfields and their opponents would retire to the hotel where, no matter the score of the game, hard feelings between the two teams were put aside. After a hearty meal, members of each club would stand and toast the opposition. The evening concluded with lively conversation, music, and singing.

During these years, the Mansfields played at several sites throughout Middletown. In 1867, Julius Hotchkiss, a prominent resident and local politician, donated land next to his south-end home for their use as a ballfield. The Mansfields played most of their home games at "Hotchkiss Field"; however, they played some games at other sites throughout Middletown, including Douglas Park.[3]

On the national baseball scene, the 1869 season saw the rise of the famous "Red Stocking" Club of Cincinnati, the first openly professional, all-salaried team. The overwhelming success of the Red Stockings led other clubs to organize themselves in the same fashion, and by the end of 1870 at least five teams in the country paid regular salaries to their players.

Accordingly, Connecticut baseball clubs faced a choice. Should they follow the path blazed by the professionals or cling to their amateur ways? Surprisingly, it was the small city of Middletown, only Connecticut's seventh-largest city, and the Mansfields that led Connecticut's march toward professional baseball.

After steady improvement in the preceding seasons, the Mansfields took three distinct steps toward professionalism in 1870. The first was obtaining an enclosed ball field in which to play their home games. O.V. Coffin, well-known Middletown businessman and later governor of Connecticut, graciously offered some of his land for use as a ballground. The donated lot was located at the corner of Washington and Berlin Streets.[4]

Although locals considered the new ballyard to be one of the best in the state, others disagreed. After a visit to Middletown, the Stars of Brooklyn complained about the field's poor condition, saying, "Now this thriving place, lacking the spirit of emulation which incites other towns to improve their abiding places by adding a first rate ball ground to their local attractions, obliges the baseball fraternity to content themselves with a common rough field, half plowed over, the result is that any display of skillful fielding, except in the way of catching high balls, is out of the question and the local clubs are the sufferers."[5]

Despite the complaints, the Mansfields' enclosed field allowed them to charge for admission to their games. Single game tickets could be purchased for 25 cents apiece and season tickets were also available. The idea of paying to see a ballgame was new in Middletown. The *Wesleyan Argus* wasn't keen on the idea and asserted emphatically that the Wesleyan University ballclub would not follow suit, saying, "We think it comes under the heading of extortion, almost, to charge twenty-five cents to see a game of Base Ball where the score runs as high as it did in the late contest with the Trinity club. Though the Mansfield may have set us the example, we are, by no means, obliged to follow it. A game is rendered much more interesting by having a large number of spectators present, and it seems a little rough to keep people away by the admittance fee, when thanks are due them for climbing the hill [from Main Street] to witness such playing as is usually done there."[6]

Now that they could charge admission, the Mansfields were able to entice better quality opponents to Middletown. The Mansfields offered a 50-50 split of the gate money, a generous proposal, as home teams customarily offered only one-third of the net receipts to visiting clubs.[7]

The Mansfields' second move toward professionalism occurred in August when they took their first out-of-state trip. On August 1, the club boarded the train to Boston, where they spent a week playing local clubs. Although the Mansfields went winless in five games, the road trip was still considered a success as the club gained valuable experience both on the field and in the business of baseball. Upon returning from the Bay State, the confident Mansfields declared themselves champions of Connecticut and challenged all other state clubs, offering a silver ball worth $25 to any club that could beat them two out of three games.[8]

The third advance surfaced in the form of a telegram from Philadelphia saying the Athletic Club would be coming to Middletown in September to play the Mansfields. This was a significant development since it would mark the first time a professional club had ever played in Middletown. News of the Athletics' impending arrival spread quickly, setting Middletown abuzz with excitement.

The day of the game, 2000 people crowded the field for a look at the professionals. The Mansfields arrived at the field smartly attired in their new uniforms, which had been "selected for beauty as well as for service." The uniform consisted of blue checked woolen shirts and caps, white corduroy pants and the Mansfields' signature dark blue stockings. Red piping trimmed the entire outfit.[9]

The Mansfields, who admitted they didn't anticipate winning or even scoring many runs, fulfilled their expectations beautifully. Philadelphia dominated the game from the start and very nearly backed up their pre-game boasting, holding Middletown scoreless over the first six innings on the way to a 32–5 victory.[10]

At the close of the 1870 season, the Mansfields' record stood at 21 wins and 13 losses. The club officially closed its season by sending William Rackliff and Ben Douglas, Jr., to the season-ending convention of the Connecticut Association of Base Ball Players in Hartford. At the meeting, the Mansfields were voted the amateur champions of Connecticut.[11]

The season of 1870 was a coming-of-age year for the Mansfields. They played well enough on the diamond to be recognized as the best team in the state, but their progress off

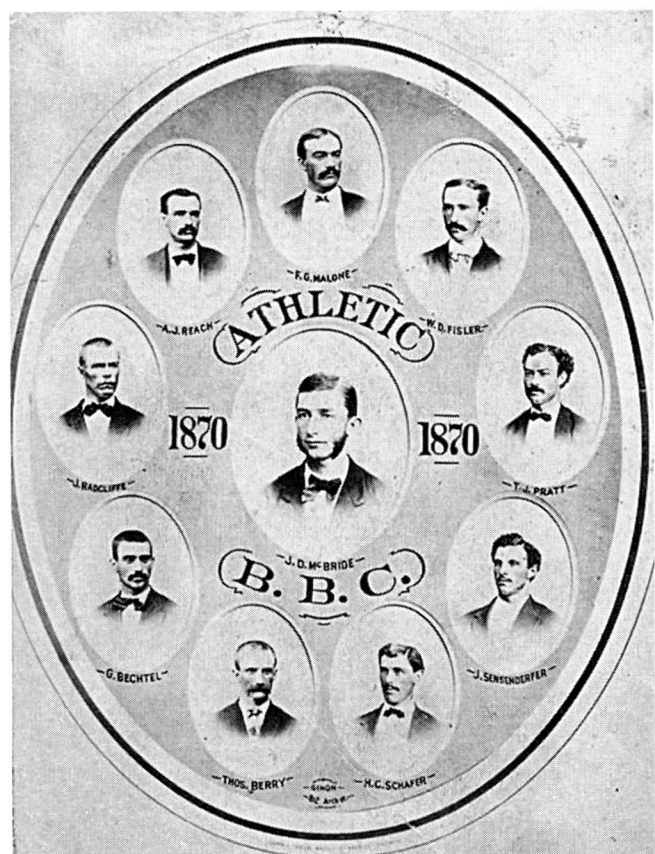

The famous Athletics of Philadelphia created tremendous excitement in September of 1870 as the first professional club to visit Middletown.

the field was even more impressive. Securing an enclosed field was undoubtedly the most important move, but, as would be proven over the next two years, the extended road trip was also extremely valuable. The tour of Massachusetts spread the Mansfield name throughout that baseball-rich state, and as a result, the Mansfields could upgrade their roster by luring players from that area.

Seeing the overwhelming success of the Red Stockings, other clubs organized themselves in the same fashion, and by the end of 1870 at least five teams paid regular salaries to their players. This led to the first professional league in 1871, the National Association of Professional Base Ball Players, in which nine teams battled for the championship.

Despite the establishment of the National Association, the Mansfields continued as amateurs for 1871. With the Mansfields' steady progression toward a more professional organization, however, the administrative duties required to run the ballclub brought about increasing demands on Ben Douglas' attention. In the days before pre-determined schedules and telephones, coordinating playing dates with other teams was an extremely time-consuming chore. This, plus making travel arrangements, signing players, and overseeing ticket sales and the club's treasury all fell to Douglas. As a result, Ben, who had been an active playing member of the Mansfields in their early years, was listed as a substitute for 1871 and never again saw meaningful action on the ball field.

The Mansfields began the 1871 season practicing on the Coffin grounds but had to look for new grounds for the second consecutive year when Mr. Coffin decided to sub-divide the ballfield into building lots. Dewitt Clinton Sage, owner of a Middletown brick factory, offered the Mansfields a portion of his property south of downtown. This was an especially convenient location as the Valley Railroad, which ran from the Connecticut shore northward through Middletown, had a depot close to the field. The land was graded and fenced with a 450 by 350 foot enclosure made of eight-foot boards.[12]

The Mansfields completed the 1871 campaign with 19 wins and 19 losses. Although mediocre compared to their 21–13 record in 1870, they had significantly upgraded their schedule, playing seven professional clubs in 1871, after only having played two the previous year.

Late in February 1872, Ben Douglas, Jr., called together several prominent Mansfield supporters to begin preparations for the upcoming season. After electing officers, it was voted to operate the club according to temperance rules, meaning that no liquor could be sold at the ballgrounds and each Middletown player would be required to sign a pledge swearing off liquor. In addition, the officers announced that the team would remain an amateur one, temporarily laying to rest the persistent rumors of impending professionalism. The club's amateur intentions were further solidified in mid-March when Ben Douglas, Jr., and William Rackliff represented the Mansfields at the national convention of amateur baseball clubs in New York City. While there, Rackliff accepted election as an officer of the amateur association.[13]

Influential sportswriter Henry Chadwick was enthusiastic about the Mansfields' prospects for the season, praising their board of officers and predicting a strong bid for the amateur championship. Chadwick added, "They are well situated in one of the best ball towns in Connecticut, having a fine enclosed park, and guarantee professionals one-half net gate," instead of the more customary one-third.[14]

As the season approached, everything appeared to be in place for the Mansfields' continued operation as amateurs. As part of his annual chore of arranging playing dates, Douglas contacted famed Harry Wright in Boston in hopes of enticing the popular Red Stockings back to Middletown. Wright was reluctant to return to Middletown, where the previous year gate receipts had been lacking. He concluded his message with the fateful suggestion that would eventually put Middletown on the baseball map. He advised Douglas that if the Mansfields were truly interested in playing professional clubs, they should pay the $10 entry fee and join the National Association of Professional Base Ball Players. If the Mansfields were admitted to the league, the professional clubs would have no choice but to play them.[15] Inspired by Wright's novel idea, Douglas wasted no time gathering the Mansfields together for a vote on the matter.

Douglas was undoubtedly aware that this was a risky step, as the Mansfields had failed to defeat a single professional club over the last two seasons. Moreover, Middletown's small population didn't guarantee the club sufficient attendance to remain solvent. With only 11,135 residents, Middletown's population paled in comparison to other National Association cities such as Boston, Philadelphia, Baltimore, and New York. Despite these rather daunting obstacles, the Mansfields authorized Douglas to send the $10 entry fee to Alex Davidson at the League Championship Committee.[16]

Henry Chadwick, who just a few weeks earlier praised the Mansfields, was furious when he heard of their professional intentions. Dead set against allowing Middletown into the league, Chadwick wrote, "The Mansfields state that they have sent on $10 entry fee to Mr. Davidson. Inasmuch as the Mansfields have hitherto claimed to be an amateur club, and not in any way professional, it is not thought that the Professional Championship Committee can allow them to enter, as they were not members of the Association in 1871, nor were they represented in Cleveland [at the convention of professional clubs]. We state this for the information of the Connecticut club, in order that they may understand how the case stands."[17]

Bound by its own rules, though, the Championship Committee was powerless to exclude the Mansfields. As improbable as it seemed, Middletown was now a major league city!

Once the immediate excitement of being allowed to play with the big boys subsided, Douglas had to face the harsh reality that his club desperately needed to upgrade its roster.

By the end of the 1871 season the Mansfields had built a reasonably talented nucleus. The outfield of Frank McCarton, Willis Arnold, and Jim Tipper was solid, while the infield sported Ham Allen, George Fields, and Tim Murnane, with Cy Bentley in the box. This was fine when Middletown was playing local amateur clubs, but much more talent was required to have any hope of beating the pros.

They added catcher John Clapp from Ithaca, New York. With 194 pounds packed on his 5'7" frame, the twenty-year-old Clapp was a natural backstop who could hit. Middletown also lured pitcher Frank Buttery and catcher Jim O'Rourke away from the Osceolas of Stratford. These two men had formed an impressive battery for the amateur Stratford club that over the years had given the Mansfields trouble.

With these additions, the Mansfields had certainly improved themselves, but it proved to be far short of what was required to compete in the professional league. With their young, inexperienced roster, the Mansfields struggled to play well consistently. By early August, with a record of 5 wins and 19 losses, the club disbanded, simply unable to draw enough paying customers. A Middletown newspaper noted the passing of the team saying, "Mr. Benjamin Douglas Junior ... has shown considerable pluck and ingenuity in bringing the club up to rank among the best in the country. He now retires with the best wishes of all concerned."[18]

Two 1872 Mansfield players have been honored by the National Baseball Hall of Fame in Cooperstown. Jim O'Rourke was elected in 1945 based on his prolific 22-year major league career, during which he batted .310 and amassed over 2,300 hits. At the 1978 Hall of Fame induction ceremony, Tim Murnane was honored with the J.G. Taylor Spink award, given by the Baseball Writers Association "for meritorious contributions to baseball writing."

1866: Willis Arnold, N. Birdsey, H. Brown, D. Chase, W. Day, Ben Douglas, Jr., J. Kinyon, Frank Mooney, M. Murphy
1867: Willis Arnold, Birdsey, Brady, D.W. Chase, DeMott, Ben Douglas, Jr., Edwards, Farnam, Herring, Knapp, Plumb, Charles Resedorf, Rollins, Jim Tipper, Ward, Weeks
1868: Willis Arnold, Birdsey, Brady, Chase, Ben Douglas, Jr., Farnam, Harry Furniss, Tom Furniss (son of Harry?), Johnson, Mooney, Plumb, F.A. Ransom, Resedorf, Simonds, A.J. Spencer, Jim Tipper, Wood, Youngs
1869: Willis Arnold, Beekley, Cy Bentley, Brady, Ben Douglas, Jr., Edwars, Johnson, H. Selden Plumb (brother of Seth), Seth Plumb (brother of Selden), Shay, Smith, Jim Tipper
1870: F. Alsop, Willis Arnold, Cy Bentley, Carrigan, Deney, Mike Dorgan, Ben Douglas, Jr., C. Edwards, George Fields, Tom S. Furniss, Charles Goodrich, Kelly, Benson Marks, Tom Noble, H. Selden Plumb (brother of Seth), Seth Plumb (brother of Selden), F. A. Ransom, J. Shay, H.A. Smith, Gustavus (Gus) Smith, Jim Tipper, Vaughan, Webster, E. Young
1871: Ham Allen, Willis Arnold, Cy Bentley, Eddie Booth, Cassiday, George Conway, Dailey, George Fields, William Kelly, David Lenz, Madden, Benson Marks, Frank McCarton, J. Morrison, Tom Noble, Ready, Smith, Jim Tipper

CLUB MEMBERS

Frank Allen: Frank Erwin "Ham" Allen was the Mansfield back-up shortstop. Before joining the Mansfields in 1871, Allen had played with the Marlboro, Massachusetts, club in 1869 and the Fairmounts in 1870. He played for two seasons with Middletown and then played for several clubs in the International Association, including the Lynn (Massachusetts) and Taunton (Massachusetts) clubs.[23] Allen died February 6, 1881, in Natick, Massachusetts. Allen served in Company F, 36th Massachusetts Infantry, during the Civil War.

Willis Arnold: Arnold played with the Mansfield club from its inception. In 1875 he organized the New Haven entry in the National Association, but resigned his post as manager prior to the start of the season. Arnold continued managing on the field for several clubs and found his most success with the Albany club of the International Association in 1878 when he guided his club to an impressive eighteen-game winning streak. The unbeaten string included a victory over the National League Boston Red Stockings and Arnold's old teammate Jim O'Rourke. He resigned after the 1879 season, returning to Middletown where he and his wife, Mary Dorrigan of New Haven, had their first child in September 1880. Arnold died in Albany, New York, in 1899.[24]

Clytus "Cy" Bentley: Cy Bentley, a carpenter by trade, was the 1872 club's number one pitcher, starting 17 of the club's 24 games. After starring for the amateur Mansfields since 1869, Bentley found the professional competition a little too tough. He finished the season with 2 wins and 14 losses and an ERA of 6.10. Besides his struggles on the diamond, Bentley's personal life was filled with tragedy. He missed the Mansfields' first victory of the season due to the death of his mother. Then there was the mid-season death of his infant son. Finally, just six months after the Mansfields' season abruptly ended, Bentley himself died of tuberculosis. He was only 22. His former Mansfield teammates attended the funeral en masse.[25]

Edward Booth: Edward H. Booth played second base and the outfield for the Mansfields. Eddie was the only Mansfield player to continue playing professionally for the remainder of the 1872 season, signing with the Brooklyn Atlantics, who undoubtedly recalled his five hits against them a week before the Mansfields collapsed. A true journeyman, Booth played for six different teams in his five-year career, including the New York Mutuals in the National League in 1876.

In 1877, he played right field with the Buckeye club of Columbus, Ohio, of the International Association.[26] His date and place of death are unknown.

Asa Brainard: Brainard gained fame as the pitcher of the 1869 Red Stockings of Cincinnati. He joined the Mansfields in July of 1872 after playing first half of that season with the Olympics of Washington. This led to some optimism, but he never won a game for the Mansfields. After his stint with the Mansfields, Brainard played only a few more years, showing none of his previous skill. After retiring from baseball he lived with his mother in Staten Island. He later moved to Denver where he operated the Markham Hotel billiards room. He died there of pneumonia in 1888, the first of the famous 1869 Red Stockings to pass away.[27] See the Cincinnati Base Ball Club ("Red Stockings") for more on Brainard's life.

Frank Buttery: Frank Buttery played third base and outfield during the 1872 season, but did his best work as the change pitcher for the Mansfields. After his baseball career, Buttery ran a general store in the Silver Mine section of New Canaan, Connecticut. He wed Mary Guthrie at the age of 38. He died in 1902 of complications of an injury he suffered while on a hunting trip a few years earlier. On that trip, he accidentally shot himself, resulting in the amputation of the toes on one foot.[28]

John Clapp: After his season with the Mansfields in 1872, Clapp had a solid 11-year career, batting a respectable .283 for his career. During that stretch he established the then ironman record for consecutive games played with 212 straight games. This was an amazing feat considering Clapp was a catcher at a time when men of that position wore little or no protection. Starting in 1883 Clapp ran a saloon in partnership with Mets pitcher Jack Lynch. The beer house didn't make much money, though, and Clapp returned to Ithaca as a policeman in 1890. He served on the force for fourteen years until he died of a heart attack while on duty. He was helping carry a drunken man back to the police station when his heart gave out. John was survived by his widow and four children.[29] See the entry on the Independents of Mansfield, Ohio, for more on Clapp.

Ben Douglas, Jr.: Once the Mansfields ceased operations in 1872, most people felt there would never be another professional ballclub in Connecticut. Ben Douglas, Jr., was not one of these people and became the driving force in returning professional baseball to Connecticut. Feeling that the larger market of Hartford would work, he brought baseball back to Connecticut. Upon his resignation from the Hartford club before the 1876 season it was said, "Mr. Douglas has worked hard for the interest of the Hartford club, and had it not been for him the Hartfords would not have attained the celebrity they have. It might be said that he laid the foundation stone of the club...."[19]

After three seasons in Hartford, that team moved to Brooklyn. Douglas attempted to get yet another Hartford team into the NL for the 1878 season After being rebuffed by the league, he went to Providence and assembled backing for a new National League franchise. He served as the club's business manager and secretary. Before the season, Douglas was shocked to learn that the directors had voted to relieve him of his duties as manager.[20]

Incredulous with the club's actions, Douglas refused to sign his release. The directors threatened to withhold the $1,000 he had invested in the club unless he resigned. After all his accomplishments in baseball, Douglas couldn't understand why he was being dismissed. Despite pleas to Harry Wright for help, Douglas' $1,400 annual salary and $500 worth of club stock were bought out.[21]

Later that year Douglas made one final try at baseball, organizing an International Association team in 1878. This team lasted only a few months, spelling the end of his business career in baseball. Douglas returned to Middletown and the family pump factory. In 1893, the 44-year-old Douglas married 20-year-old Nellie Sault. Twelve years later, Douglas died at Connecticut Valley Hospital, an institution for the mentally disturbed in which he spent the last five years of his life.[22]

Ben Douglas, Jr., was a true pioneer of early baseball. Not only did he bring major league baseball to Middletown, but did the same for Hartford and then for Providence. Of the six New England cities that have had major league baseball teams, Ben Douglas, Jr., was responsible for starting three of them!

George Fields: George Fields was the Mansfields' utility player in 1872, playing mostly third base but also some outfield and shortstop. He was born in Waterbury, Connecticut, and returned there to live after his stint with the Mansfields. He worked as a brass turner at the Waterbury Clock Company for many years. In his spare time he helped run the Monitor Baseball club of Waterbury, which was the first team of future Hall of Famer Roger Connor. Fields was the longest-surviving Mansfield, dying in 1933 at the age of 82.[30]

Frank McCarton: Frank McCarton remained in Middletown for several years after the Mansfields disbanded. He became captain of the O.V. Coffin Hook and Ladder Company and married Ann Powers, a local girl who provided Frank with four children while in Middletown. During the years after his lone professional season, McCarton played many games with Middletown amateur teams. In his lone professional season in 1872 McCarton finished second in both batting average and slugging percentage on the Mansfields. He hit .329 for the year, outhitting future stars such as O'Rourke and Clapp. He later moved to the Bronx, where he became a policeman. McCarton died in 1907 at the age of 53, suffering from gangrene of the stomach.[31]

Tim Murnane: Murnane's ball-playing career continued for another six seasons. In 1876 Tim recorded the first stolen base in the new National League. After his career he held several journalism jobs. In 1887 Murnane was employed by the *Boston Globe* and quickly became the baseball editor. In a few short years he was nationally known as a powerful, opinionated editor, highly respected by all. On February 7, 1917, as Murnane and his wife entered Boston's Schubert Theater, Murnane suddenly dropped to the floor, dead of a heart attack. Murnane's death was front-page news in Boston. Many retired and active ballplayers, including Babe Ruth, attended Murnane's funeral. For many years, the Boston Base Ball writers handed out the Tim Murnane Award.[32]

Jim O'Rourke: The most successful Mansfield alumnus was James Henry O'Rourke. During his prolific 45-year career, O'Rourke participated in the game as a player, manager, umpire, and league president. Be it a big game in the pennant race or the latest controversy involving players' rights, O'Rourke was always in the middle of things. In 1876, he recorded the first hit in National League history.

O'Rourke was extraordinarily well educated at a time when most ballplayers weren't. He attended Yale law school in the off-season and graduated with a law degree in 1887. O'Rourke's nickname, "Orator," reflected his law school background and flowery language. With his Ivy League background, O'Rourke was a verbose advocate of player's rights, especially during the Players' League movement in 1890.

O'Rourke retired from the major leagues in 1893. After one season as a National League umpire, Jim returned to Bridgeport and organized the Connecticut Baseball League. In addition to being the founder and president of the league, O'Rourke also found time to manage and play for the Bridgeport club. Although the club was originally dubbed the "Victors," O'Rourke's gift for gab, and his willingness to argue with umpires caused the team's name to be changed to the "Orators."

In 1904, at the age of 52, O'Rourke convinced John McGraw, the manager of his old New York Giant club, to allow him to play in a game at the tail end of the season. The Giants were in the process of wrapping up the pennant and McGraw gave his consent. During the September 22 game, O'Rourke recorded the final base hit and final run of his major league career. He caught the full nine innings in the Giants' pennant-clinching game, making him the oldest player in major league history to play a full game.[33]

At the age of 58, O'Rourke was featured in a *New York Herald* article entitled "Keeping One Foot Out of the Grave." When asked for the secret to his longevity O'Rourke replied, "Secret? Well, if you call it a secret, the secret's just this: Baseball — it is the real elixir of life. It keeps the mind young by association with young minds; it keeps the body young by the best exercise man ever invented. It uses every faculty — every good faculty — a man's got, and amuses him when he's using it. That's what keeps a man young, that's what's kept me young; that's what's kept me feeling twenty." O'Rourke added, "Baseball has kept me so happy and healthy that there is not a minute of my past life I would not willingly live over."[34]

Besides playing ball, O'Rourke spent his later years practicing law, tending to his real estate investments, and dabbling in politics. He was a devoted family man with a wife, six daughters, and a son. His son James also went to Yale and played briefly with the Yankees. O'Rourke died of pneumonia on January 8, 1919. Baseball dignitaries, politicians and fans packed the church for Jim's funeral.

Jim Tipper: Jim Tipper played the outfield for the Mansfields from 1867 through 1872, missing only the Mansfields' first year of existence. In 1873 he played on various amateur teams in Middletown. The next year he returned to the National Association, joining the new Hartford entry. The following year he moved to the New Haven entry in the National Association, making him the only player to play for all three of Connecticut's major league teams. After his stint in the National Association, Tipper bounced around with several International Association clubs including Providence, Lynn, and Rochester. In 1895, while staying at a New Haven lodging house, Tipper died of tuberculosis.[35]

Notes

1. Ben Douglas, Jr., to Harry Wright, April 11, 1878; *Chicago Inter Ocean*, May 24, 1874.
2. *Hartford Courant*, September 25, 1866; *Middletown Constitution*, September 26, 1866.
3. *Middletown Constitution*, April 17, 1867.
4. *Middletown Sentinel and Witness*, May 6, 1870; *Hartford Post*, April 28, 1870.
5. *New York Clipper*, July 16, 1870.
6. *Middletown Sentinel and Witness*, June 24, 1870; *Wesleyan Argus*, June 15, 1870.
7. *New York Clipper*, June 11, 1870.
8. *Hartford Post*, August 11, 1870.
9. *Hartford Post*, September 3, 1870; *Middletown Sentinel and Witness*, February 11, 1870, and May 27, 1870.
10. *Meriden Daily Republican*, September 5, 1870; *Hartford Post*, September 3, 1870.
11. *Hartford Post*, November 3, 1870.
12. *Middletown Sentinel and Witness*, June 2, 1871.
13. *1872 Dewitt Baseball Guide*, p. 99.
14. *New York Clipper*, March 2, 1872.
15. Harry Wright to Ben Douglas Junior, April 8, 1872.
16. *Hartford Post*, April 9, 1872.
17. *New York Clipper*, April 20, 1872.
18. *Middletown Constitution*, August 21, 1872.
19. *Bristol Press*, quoted in *Hartford Times*, April 4, 1876.
20. Ben Douglas, Jr., to Harry Wright, April 9, 1878.
21. Ben Douglas, Jr., to Harry Wright, April 11, 1878, and April 13, 1878.
22. *Middletown Tribune*, October 18, 1893; *Middletown Penny Press*, March 4, 1905.
23. *Hartford Post*, November 9, 1872.
24. *Hartford Post*, April 24, 1876; *Albany Evening Journal*, September 25, 1878, October 11, 1878, and April 12, 1880; Connecticut Vital Records.
25. *Hartford Post*, February 27, 1873.
26. Preston D. Orem, *Baseball (1845–1881) from the Newspaper Accounts* (Altadena, CA, 1961), p. 281; unnamed newspaper clipping in Hall of Fame Library player folder.
27. Asa Brainard to Harry Wright, October 12, 1882, and December 10, 1882; Frederick Ivor-Campbell, Robert L. Tiemann and Mark Rucker, eds., *Baseball's First Stars* (Cleveland: Society for American Baseball Research, 1996), p. 17.
28. Connecticut Vital Records; *Norwalk Hour*, December 16, 1902.

29. William J. Ryczek, *Blackguards and Red Stockings: A History of Baseball's National Association, 1871–1875* (Jefferson, NC: McFarland, 1992), p. 71; Robert L. Tiemann and Mark Rucker, eds., *Nineteenth Century Stars* (Cleveland: SABR, 1989), p. 29; *Ithaca Daily Journal*, December 19, 1904.

30. *Waterbury Republican*, September 23, 1933.

31. *Hartford Post*, September 7, 1875; Connecticut Vital Records; *Hartford Post*, May 1, 1876; *New York Times*, June 18, 1907. McCarton's age is somewhat questionable. The encyclopedias list him as 17 years old in 1872, but four references in the Middletown Vital Records show different ages. All indicate he was born no later than 1851, and one shows him being born as early as 1848, which would have made him 24 years old in 1872. His New York death certificate, however, indicates McCarton was 17 during the 1872 season.

32. *Hartford Post*, November 9, 1872; *Middletown Penny Press*, February 8, 1917; *Boston Globe*, January 15, 1915.

33. Frederick Ivor-Campbell, *Baseball's First Stars* (Cleveland: SABR, 1996), p. 12 and 125; Jordan Deutsch, Richard Cohen, et al., *The Scrapbook History of Baseball* (New York: Bobbs-Merrill, 1975), p. 57.

34. *New York Herald Magazine*, January 16, 1910.

35. *Hartford Post,* March 11, 1876, and April 19, 1876; *New Haven Journal & Courier,* April 22, 1895.

Bibliography

Arcidiacono, David. *Middletown's Season in the Sun: The Story of Connecticut's First Professional Baseball Team*. East Hampton, CT: Self-published, 1999.
Deutsch, Jordan, and Richard Cohen, et al. *The Scrapbook History of Baseball*. New York: Bobbs-Merril, 1975.
Harry Wright Correspondence.
Hartford Post.
Middletown Constitution.
Middletown Sentinel and Witness.
New York Clipper.
Ryczek, William J. *Blackguards and Red Stockings: A History of Baseball's National Association, 1871–1875*. Jefferson, NC: McFarland, 1992.
Tiemann, Robert, and Mark Rucker, eds. *Nineteenth Century Stars*. Kansas City: Society for American Baseball Research, 1989.

❖ *Bridgeport's 1866 Clubs* (Michael J. Bielawa) ❖

Club History

Most folks passing through Bridgeport, Connecticut, never touch the ground. Alas, it's not due to some paranormal reality. The majority of citizens merely find themselves traveling over the coastal city on elevated portions of I-95. Too bad. The acres of land which support the towering highway really *are* spiritual. Sacred ground mired deep within the mythos of baseball's earliest years. For instance, just beyond the large green sign announcing Exit 28, drivers unknowingly witness the abandoned Victorian abode of James "Orator Jim" O'Rourke. The home's famously gregarious proprietor would one day find his visage enshrined in the National Baseball Hall of Fame. This now brooding, dilapidated structure is the last vestige of the city's East Side baseball empire.[1]

Bridgeport has always been a proud conglomerate of distinct neighborhoods, a tradition that continues to this day. After emigrating from Ireland Jim's parents moved into the eastern portion of town.[2] During the mid-nineteenth century the east district was taken under the wing of showman P. T. Barnum. It became the fabulous entrepreneur's goal to develop East Bridgeport into a thriving, temperance-populated community. It was over on this working class side of town that Jim O'Rourke, and his older brother John, learned to play baseball. The ground below this city is fertile with forgotten playing fields. East District meadows, vacant lots on the opposite bank of the Pequonnock River in bustling downtown, and grounds adjacent to the newly established Seaside Park all witnessed the evolution of New England baseball while marching in step with New York Rules.

Bridgeport clubs provide a concise microcosm of baseball's early evolution, tracking the game's semi-hibernation during the Civil War, to its immense popularity within a matter of months following Grant and Lee's meeting at Appomattox. Newspapers of the day related the closing battle scenes of the great rebellion, General Lee's surrender, and soon afterward readers followed the war crimes trial of Andersonville commandant Captain Wirz. Locally, as proof of its popularity, the game of baseball was gathering regular column space, too. Within just two years of war's end the game would distance itself from a rather loose social gathering and begin to mature into a highly competitive sport.[3] Gentlemanly conduct would give way to very public squabbling on both playing fields and in the local press.

To understand baseball's impact across Bridgeport one must start with 1865, a twelve-month lynchpin that altered America. That year marked two important symbiotic events in Bridgeport's social history which illustrate a rising interest in outdoor physical exercise.[4] The Common Council moved to dedicate and improve lands for two public parks. Seaside Park, south of downtown, occupies expansive shorefront property abutting Long Island Sound, and Washington Park, a lovely tree-lined square, on the city's east side.[5]

The second significant fact concerns the birth of serious-minded ball clubs. There was actually a *lack* of nines calling Bridgeport home during most of 1865. On the same page in which the *Bridgeport Evening Farmer* announced the shocking news of Abraham Lincoln's Good Friday assassination, a sports article appeared recounting a "lively" game of cricket. Par for the era, papers listed billiards results, horse racing, and usually the only ball game in town—cricket.[6] Bridgeporters, of course, could turn out to watch baseball played by the Excelsiors and the Stars, but the fielding by these teenage boys was not so crisp. The East End did boast the American Base Ball Club, but members found themselves relegated to playing merely intra-squad games on their grounds just north of Washington Park.[7]

One club's birth immediately altered the city's nineteenth century sportscape. At the end of August 1865, ninety-eight students and administrators from the local college, Bryant, Stratton & Corbin's Bridgeport Business College and Telegraphic Institute, gathered to write a constitution and by-laws creating a thirty-member baseball club.[8] The school's principal, Professor A. Corbin, Jr., was elected president of the "Business College Base Ball Club of Bridgeport." Practice days were selected — Mondays and Wednesdays from five to six o'clock in the afternoon and Saturday mornings at eight. Daniel W. Jones, E. H. Lyon, and L. Vankeuren were named captains of the club's various nines. College vice president W. Stanley Camp served as club umpire during 1865 (the following year he would be elected secretary and treasurer). Grounds were secured downtown, on the upper part of Beaver Street, and the school nine voted to follow the rules of the New York game.[9] Professor Corbin graciously distributed copies of 1865 regulations.

Captains of the college club had an increasingly large student population with which to work. By mid–August the *Bridgeport Evening Farmer* reported that school enrollment was filling now that "the labor of haying and harvesting" was nearly finished.[10] Advertisements offered classes for "Young Men, Boys, Men of middle age, and ladies desiring to act as Bookkeepers, Accountants, Salesmen, Agents, or wishing to perfect themselves as Teachers of Penmanship, or to engage in active business of any kind." The institution, situated above the post office, was a member of a national chain of mercantile colleges. Just as it did with their Ivy League brethren in New Haven, baseball would become a beacon of academic and civic pride.

The summer and autumn of 1865 commenced with scrimmages pitting first and second nines of the Americans against one another. For the most part these men worked at the Wheeler and Wilson Sewing Machine factory.[11] More pointedly, this East Bridgeport club also started to take the field against the new college nine. The eastern portion of the city, populated by factory craftsmen and skilled laborers, would now cross bats with downtown's middle-class clerks, storeowners and college-educated players. Lines of demarcation were now etched in Bridgeport.

In the two games that the Americans faced the College Club, the former found themselves triumphant and celebrating in the east district. The playing season ended with letters appearing in the local press expressing a "quarrelsome and pugnacious spirit" between the two clubs, illustrating just how much the "friendly" competitive spirit had changed.[12]

With baseball season waning, the October 16, 1865, *Evening Farmer* provided a succinct observation:

> Bridgeport is a little behind the age in adopting this excellent game. We have two good junior clubs, The American of the Eastern District, and the Business College Club, but the young, active and muscular men of our city, have so far taken little interest in the subject, and done nothing towards contesting with other cities and towns of the State for supremacy in this athletic sport.

At the end of January 1866, five months after the founding of the Bridgeport college club Corbin was succeeded by his assistant Seth Benjamin Jones, Jr.[13] The new principal aggressively moved the school's sports program forward. The home grounds would also be moved to the foot of Warren Street near the New York and New Haven Railroad tracks.[14]

In addition to public parks and the birth of the college nine a third important development assisted in alleviating the *Farmer's* lament: Bridgeport's volunteer firefighters and the coastal city's expanding industrial base. *Scientific American* of July 8, 1865, boasted, "Bridgeport, Conn., is rapidly becoming an important center of manufacturing operations. Having railroad and water communication with New York and other important seacoast and inland towns, it offers peculiar facilities for the establishment of almost every branch of manufacturing enterprise."

The article trumpeted a number of successful ventures, "Here are located the extensive works of the Wheeler & Wilson Sewing Machine Company, whose famous sewing machine is justly appreciated the world over. Elias Howe, Jr., the original inventor of the sewing mechanism, has recently erected one of the finest establishments in New England for the manufacture of his sewing machine, which has already gained a wide reputation, being adapted to perform all the heavier kinds of work required in harness, shoe and tailoring operations." The local *Evening Farmer* beamed, "Bridgeport is growing very rapidly. When manufactories, new firms, new stock companies have located in this beautiful city during the past year ... people are beginning to prophesy that in a few years Bridgeport will be the largest city in Connecticut."[15] The prediction eventually came to pass. For over a century the Park City vied with Hartford and New Haven for the most populated municipality. Since 1980 this top spot has been awarded to Bridgeport.

Fire companies began safeguarding local citizens as early as 1797.[16] The east district's sprawling Wheeler and Wilson sewing machine manufacturer now sported the Seamstress Fire Company and another firehouse was being constructed by the Protector firefighters. These men and the city's other fire companies would have a vital role in the burgeoning baseball scene. Bridgeport baseball was about to take a large step forward.

Of all the summers across all the decades in which baseball has been played and witnessed in Bridgeport, one special season can be held apart from others. The year 1866 provides a map to that twilight region when events shaped and sharpened the American pastime in New England. During the first full year of peace there was rapid growth in baseball clubs across the nation, a reality that mirrored the local sports scene. Near the conclusion of the playing season the October 16, 1866, *Bridgeport Evening Standard* reported that *Bat & Ball* (a contemporary baseball journal published in Hartford) ran a brief article noting the existence of 14 ball clubs in Bridgeport that year.[17] However, even a casual glance at local newspapers reveals box scores, announcements, and results for at least 26 different

Bridgeport organizations. No longer would the American Club find itself compelled to participate in only inter-squad games or contests exclusively against the Bridgeport College nine:

Bridgeport, Connecticut (Downtown) BBCs of 1866

Alerts
Algonquin (organized May/June 1866; pupils of the Golden Hill Institute)
Americus
Arctic (organized June 4, 1866; members resided along upper Main Street)
Baltic
Bridgeports (originally organized August 28, 1865, as the Bridgeport College club, reorganized May 30, 1866)
Excelsior (organized 1865)
Liberty
Mutuals (organized September 13, 1866)
Pequonnock (organized 1865)
Phoenix
Star (organized 1865)
Swift Foot
Umpire
Veni Vidi Vici (organized June/July 1866)

East Bridgeport, Connecticut BBCs of 1866

Actives
Americans (organized Summer 1865)
Eagle (originally called the Pacifics, organized May 1866)
Eureka (organized June 4, 1866)
Fear Not (organized June 1866)
Ironsides (organized June 1866)
Pembroke (organized 1865, played games on the Old Cricket Grounds east of the Howe Factory)
Pioneer (organized end of May/first week of June 1866)
Protector (organized May 24, 1866)
Wheeler and Wilson (organized May 28, 1866)
Young Americans (organized end of May 1866)

Stratford, Connecticut BBCs of 1866

Osceola (organized June 18, 1866)
Tigers (organized August 10, 1866)

In measurable stages the sport shed its helter-skelter approach and quite quickly expanded into a well-ordered entity. During 1866 these steps could be seen in the abundance of public challenges regularly appearing in the local press; umpires being imported from other cities; and Connecticut towns, as well as Yale University, desiring to play against Bridgeport clubs. Baseball also generated greater interest among spectators. Papers reported sizable crowds of men and women, as well as playing fields surrounded by carriages. As a result, the city became a neutral ground for a match pitting Waterbury against the Unions of Morrisania.

The 1866 season's inaugural game, a well-attended interclub practice among the Americans, took place on Fast Day, Friday, March 30. New England's founding local and state governments had set aside certain days during the year for the purpose of prayer and abstinence called Fast Days. However, by the nineteenth century Puritanical scowls regarding public gaming on Fast Day had largely been ignored, though it was still unacceptable to play baseball on Sundays.[18] Even the journals of philosopher-naturalist Henry David Thoreau connect baseball with this New England spiritual day.[19]

At the beginning of May 1866 the Americans of East Bridgeport announced their newly elected officers. The *Evening Farmer* recognized the roughly year-old club as now being formally organized into "a permanent institution." The members promptly challenged the downtown Pequonnock Club of the Golden Hill district to a game. On May 15, 1866, the Pequonnock and American Base Ball Clubs assembled on the grounds of the latter, located just north of the Wheeler and Wilson Sewing Machine Manufactory.

This game offers an example of how the city's baseball seeds took root across the state. The start time of the May 15 contest was moved an hour forward to allow the timely arrival of umpire Gershom B. Hubbell, Esq., president of the Charter Oak Base Ball Club. The official was received in Bridgeport with "unusual interest."[20]

The game was advertised enthusiastically. The recently christened horse railroad conveniently deposited citizens on the south side of the Wheeler and Wilson factory, allowing for an easy one- block walk north to the Americans playing grounds. In case folks had missed the papers, a red pennant fluttered from carriages of the horse railroad announcing that a ball game was scheduled that day. Chairs for the spectators were thoughtfully provided by the two clubs. The home side donned new uniforms: white shirts with red neck scarves and black leather belts, the word "Americans" embossed in gold lettering on the back of each belt.[21] Despite their sartorial ensemble, the practice-conscientious Americans were shocked to find themselves on the wrong side of a 47–21 score.

During 1866 games took on a bit more formalized schedule for the first time in Bridgeport. As July rolled forward, a rumor began to circulate around town that a special bat was being created for a championship award. Very soon it became evident that the popular East Bridgeport druggist Charles Gay Pendleton had commission the ornate stick to be bestowed upon the city's most worthy club. The handsome 39-inch bat (subsequent coverage placed it at 38 inches) was shaved from rosewood, its handle constructed of satin wood with an ebony knob. A silver plate adorned with the winning club's name would be attached to the barrel. The trophy generated keen excitement while displayed in the window of Pendleton's drugstore.

Pendleton's shop was situated on Noble Street near Washington Park, where he sold medicine, perfume, toilet fixings, wine and liquors "for Medicinal purposes," and a printing press to run off personalized stationery. He made his real money preparing and selling "Pendleton's Compound Camphor Ice and Glycerine" for chapped lips and hands. Ingredients for this compound included wax, tallow, spermaceti, and olive oil. Pendleton was also advertised as "the great Calisaya Bitters man." This form of bitters was derived from quinine, herbs and spices. Its alcohol content could range anywhere up to 30 percent.

On Monday, August 6, delegates from various Bridgeport baseball clubs gathered at the Americans' headquarters located above Isaac W. Smith's grocery store on Noble Street.[22] The nineteen clubs in attendance hammered out arrangements for the Pendleton Bat Championship. Henry Leach of the American Club presided over the meeting while teammate Stephen M. Conger acted as secretary. A number of clubs were gravely disappointed when they discovered their ineligibility because players were deemed too young. Hoping to remove ill feelings, the men's clubs moved to provide a separate Junior Championship Bat. The teenage boys' ball clubs would meet at the end of the month to coordinate their own series schedule.[23]

Eight clubs would participate in the Pendleton Bat contest: Pequonnock, Bridgeport, Protector, Pembroke, Wheeler & Wilson, Eureka, American and the V.V.V. The moniker of this final club, also referred to as the "Three Vs," was derived from Julius Caesar's famous victory report after the Battle of Zela, "Veni Vidi Vici," which translates to "I came, I saw, I conquered."

Representatives voted to play all Pendleton games on the grounds shared by the American and Eureka Clubs, adhere to the rules of the National Association of Base Ball Players, and, for the sake of impartiality, employ out-of-town umpires.[24] Before the evening's meeting adjourned delegates drew lots to decide which club would defend the Bat against the remaining seven other clubs. Bridgeport "drew the lucky number." The first game was scheduled for Wednesday, August 15, pitting the V.V.V. Club against Seth Jones and the former college nine.

The prime force behind the Bridgeport Club were its upper-middle-class members, the Jones brothers: Daniel, club director, left fielder, second baseman and third baseman; Nathaniel, center fielder; Seth Jr., first and third base; and William, club president and catcher.[25] Seth Jones Sr., an early Bridgeport business entrepreneur, and his family resided on Union Street in the heart of downtown. Left fielder George Richards, Jr., had just arrived in Bridgeport with his family a few months earlier. Hugh Sterling was a pitcher and shortstop for the Bridgeport Club.

The appointed day for Game One arrived—but rather than living up to their motto, the Three Vs, for reasons unknown, decided not to take the field. Forfeit in favor of Bridgeport. Perhaps the Three Vs could not gather players. Two weeks earlier the V.V.V.s took a match from the Osceola Club of Stratford but were accused in the press of fielding a number of non-members. Game Two for the Pendleton Bat featured the Wheeler and Wilson Club[26] crossing bats with the Bridgeports. A strong bond was already taking shape within the city's manufacturing fraternity. The Wheeler and Wilson, American, Eureka and Pioneer Clubs each had ties to the local sewing machine industry known the world over.[27] The city's 20th century Industrial League can date its ancestry to the summer of 1866. These early factory baseball clubs established a respected standard that would later captivate t he city's sports pages for over half a century.

The Bridgeport Club drubbed the Wheeler and Wilson Club, 46 to 9. The August 23 *Standard* noted that the winners' "material is of the best and by another season will rank among the first in the National Game." Adhering to the Bridgeport Base Ball Convention's decision to employ impartial out-of-town umpires, Charles Commerford of Waterbury was invited to officiate the Wheeler and Wilson game. Commerford is one of the heroes of 19th century baseball, and his life provides a fascinating portrait of the game and times.[28] A decade earlier he was the shortstop with the Gothams of New York City. Later, during the Civil War, Commerford moved to Waterbury, where he solidified the game in the Brass City. Commerford's exploits were celebrated in *Frank Leslie's Illustrated Newspaper*. Local papers even credit Commerford, a lifelong friend of Henry Chadwick, with inventing the art of scoring.

Controversy was the order of the day for Game Three. The Bridgeport Base Ball Convention had set all contests for Wednesday afternoons at 1:30. However, at a subsequent meeting on August 27 it was brought to the fraternity's attention that the Pembrokes, who were to play in the upcoming match, would not be able to field a club. The game was moved to Friday, August 31.

Trouble began even before a ball was tossed. The Bridgeport Club arrived late, barely squeaking in by the fifteen-minute grace period. Three players short, this time it was the Bridgeport Club who petitioned the Pembrokes to delay the game yet another day. Their request was refused. In fact, the Bridgeporters were so desperate that one of their fielders was required to leave his sickbed. He was allowed a courtesy runner, one of the fastest on the Bridgeport nine. Even with these detriments the former college club held onto a 27–23 lead after seven innings. In the eighth the Pembrokes went ahead by three. But with one out and a runner on third the umpire, once again the esteemed Charles Commerford, called time and announced "no game" because he had to catch the 5:20 pm train back home.

The Pembroke players offered to pay the umpire's overnight accommodations but were rebuffed. Their hard-earned lead was nullified. Several of the Pembrokes angrily cursed the baseball statesman with the "vilest language and went so far as to threaten" Commerford.

Supporters of both sides then unleashed a rivulet of letters to local papers expressing distinct slants of view. After a few days of ink slinging, the *Bridgeport Farmer* on September 5 editorialized that ball players were "working themselves into an unfriendly state of feeling towards members of rival clubs. This they should not allow."

As umpire Commerford had ruled "no game," the match was eventually replayed from the start on September 10 (minus the insulted arbiter). This time there was no questioning the outcome. Bridgeport soundly defeated the Pembroke Club, 44–27. Of special note, this game featured the first box score appearance of East Bridgeport resident John O'Rourke, future member of the original New York Metropolitans and older brother of Hall of Famer Orator Jim O'Rourke.[29]

The largest crowd to ever witness a baseball game in Bridgeport to that date turned out Wednesday, September 19, for the fourth Pendleton match. The Americans, considered a strong nine, would be facing their old rivals formerly known as the College Club. The Americans had easily swept the Bridgeports in the two games they faced each other in 1865. Through the first seven innings of the '66 rematch the Americans did not tarnish any of the public's expectations, as they led 24 to 18. But Bridgeport put the game away in the next frame by plating 18 runners. Powered by the play of shortstop Hugh S. Sterling and Bridgeport's best all-around player, George Richards, Jr., the downtown academicians won handily 39 to 29.

The good natured, "jolly"[30] members of the Protectors fire company confronted Bridgeport in Game Five. The Protectors had just recently become an established volunteer fire organization. The men had been employing a steam hand-pulled apparatus since May 1865, but would soon be celebrating a new firehouse erected that autumn.[31] (This building is still standing. Persistent though unsubstantiated local folklore claims that the brick structure is haunted.[32]) Members held their first annual ball the following February. Their gilded "Protectors No. 2" sign was proudly hoisted above the station's main doors the first week of May 1866, and the ball club was organized three weeks later on May 24. Their gritty motto: "If conquered, we try again."[33] Civil War veteran Sergeant Theron J. Hills served as club secretary.

Any hope the volunteer firemen might have harbored about defeating Bridgeport went up in smoke early. Rain brought the match to a close at the start of the seventh, so the score reverted to the last "even innings," procuring an outcome of 64 for Bridgeport and 11 for the Protectors.

In 1872 the volunteer fire department was superseded by a paid system. Hugh Lawton, original Protector's ball club vice president, pitcher and second baseman, became an assistant chief under the new system. His younger brother Frank, the Protector center fielder, stayed on after the transition and became foreman. Right fielder Asbel Hunt stayed on as a horseman with the company.[34]

Bridgeport pounded the Eureka Club, 43 to 28, in Game Six played on September 27, a contest called because of darkness following just six innings. Another factory nine, the Eureka Club was also composed of Wheeler and Wilson employees. Club officials included Bennett F. Morris, president, and Hylan P. Warren, vice president. Both gentlemen were contractors at the Wheeler and Wilson factory. Dr. William H. Hine served as Eureka Club secretary and treasurer. One player who probably gathered the most attention that afternoon was shortstop Sterling, who belted two home runs in the winning cause.

Recognized by the *Evening Farmer* as "the strongest Club in the city," the Pequonnocks confronted the Bridgeporters for the final game of the Pendleton Championship on Wednesday, October 3. The *Farmer* described the match as "the most interesting game of base ball that was ever witnessed in Bridgeport." Baseball devotees across town knew that if anybody could wrest a victory from the downtown club it was the Pequonnock bunch. Anticipating an exciting match, throngs of spectators made their way to the ball grounds. The audience was so large that police were constantly required to push the crowd back behind the flags marking the field. Cheering and applause reached a pitch that made it difficult to hear the umpire's shouted decisions. Those viewing the game inadvertently lathered pressure on their favorites. Players began pressing due to the stress, as noted by the *Farmer*, and in a few instances fielders acted more akin to muffins than experienced ballists.[35]

The quick-paced 2-hour-and-40-minute contest, officiated by J. Harwood of the Mutuals of New Haven, resulted in yet another Bridgeport conquest. It was close, though, with the old College club beating the Pequonnocks, 50 to 43. The Bridgeport Club was now heralded across the state as city champions.

Bridgeport baseball was gathering attention beyond the solidification of a championship series and growing number of participants. Over the course of 1866 Bridgeport's on-field acumen gained the respect of neighboring communities. A day after pulling duty behind the dish for the Bridgeporters in their clinching Pendleton championship game, W. H. Jones was invited by the Monitors of Westport to umpire their game with the Liberty Club of Norwalk.

The pleasant autumn weather enabled a rematch between the city champion Bridgeports and the American Club. Eager to avenge their loss in the Pendleton series, the Americans faced Bridgeport on October 17. The game was eventually called because of darkness and the score, reverting to the last even innings, resulted in a 35-to-35 tie. Upon closer examination, induced by five days of letters to the editors of the *Farmer* and *Standard*, it was revealed that the Bridgeport Club, and not the umpire, had called time and thereby ended the game. It seems the "unreasonable school boys"[36] were in imminent danger of losing, so they stalled the contest, and then declared it too dark to continue play, even though workers in the Wheeler and Wilson Factory could "distinctly" see the ball up to the point when the game was terminated. Adding further injury to the Americans' plight, players continued to practice batting and catching another twenty minutes after the game was halted. Bridgeport members attempted to reason away the rules through their newspaper letter-writing campaign and as a solution offered another public challenge to the Americans. The dare went unheeded.

The variety of clubs visiting from out of town during 1866 provides another example of how Bridgeport was gaining respectability in state baseball circles. Aware that their neighbors down the road were now playing a "plucky game," the Yale nine decided to challenge the city champions' mettle. The student ballists were cordially received at the train depot by the Bridgeport Club on Saturday, October 20, 1866, and escorted to a ball field at the old State Fair Grounds. Located on a farm owned by Deacon David Sherwood, just beyond the city line within Fairfield, the area had been selected back in 1857 by the Connecticut State Agricultural Society to showcase the state's farming industry.[37]

The well-attended game at the new ball grounds marked the Bridgeporters' first confrontation with Yale — an event that would be repeated several times over the next year and a half.[38] The three-hour contest illustrated the capable fielding of the home side, but they were no match for Yale, which the *Evening Standard* glowed, "was the best ever shown in this city." Yale handily took care of business by a score of 58 to 10 and then caught the five o'clock train back to New Haven.

The Fair Grounds were used again on November 17 when the Waterbury Club played the Union Base Ball Club of Morrisania. These two opponents were already familiar with one another. The Morrisania nine, hailing from the part of New York we recognize today as the Bronx, toured Connecticut during July and faced clubs in Norwich, Hartford, and Waterbury. The Waterbury club in turn also ventured on a brief road excursion to New York, playing among others the Unions in Morrisania.

The appearance of the nationally known New York nine meant that the game was eagerly anticipated. Extra cars were added to the horse railroad, and chairs were promised for the ladies. The clubs arrived at the train depot from their respective cities, crossed the street to the Atlantic Hotel where they donned their uniforms, and enjoyed a cold lunch before boarding horse railroad carriages. Stephen M. Cate, Jr., of the Bridgeport club umpired the three-and a-quarter-hour affair and was roundly complimented for his prompt and loud calls. Nearly 600 spectators gathered to witness the Union Club's defeat of Waterbury 53 to 27. To be fair it should be mentioned that Waterbury was missing two of their regulars and had to rely on members from their second and third nines. After the game the Bridgeport Club generously provided supper for the visitors at the Atlantic Hotel.

Other contests featuring out-of-town clubs included the American Hose Company No. 19, from New York City,[39] which played the American Club of Bridgeport at the grounds near the Wheeler and Wilson Factory; a controversial-rained out match in Waterbury initiated by the Waterbury Club with the Bridgeport Club; and a July contest featuring the Pequonnocks traveling to Waterbury, where they defeated the Monitor Club in a close game, 15 to 14. The Comet Club of New Haven came to the east district and thrashed the Bridgeport Liberty club, 50 to 30. At September's close, the second and first nines of the Monitor Club traveled to Bridgeport from Waterbury on separate trains for a rematch with their Pequonnock counterparts. Between games of the morning-afternoon split doubleheader everybody enjoyed refreshments at Frank Stevens Saloon, where the bar's Water Street address must surely have made for sarcastic chuckles among regular clientele. By the way, the saloon's epicurean specialty was calf's head soup.

As coastal New England advanced into the melancholy days of November, Bridgeport's baseball fraternity was saddened by the passing of one of their brethren, Dr. William H. Hine. Not long after his burial the November 22 *Bridgeport Evening Standard* painted a Currier and Ives picture. That morning's snowfall left the city streets resplendent with "many sleigh rides, jingling bells, slides down hill and other amusements of old winter." On that same page the American Base Ball Club announced their solemn resolution and prayers lamenting the passing of their dear friend, Dr. Hine. The declaration, signed by club president Henry Leach and secretary Stephen M. Conger, Jr., also requested that the American ballists wear "the usual badge of mourning for thirty days."[40]

Despite the time of year ball grounds in and around Bridgeport remained active. In a lighter moment the Bridgeport Club faced a ball field filled with eighteen muffins. The November 28 game took place at the foot of Main Street, making it one of the earliest games to take place within the proximity of the new Seaside Park. Fifty-degree weather proved incentive enough to bring clubs out.[41] East Bridgeport nines, the Fear Nots and Ironsides, faced each other on December 1, 1866, as did the Young Americans of Bridgeport and the Fairfield Club. Just over a century later, Baseball Hall of Fame historian Lee Allen interviewed Jim O'Rourke's daughter, Edith, at her Florida home in 1968. She would recall her father playing with the Ironsides of East Bridgeport, the neighborhood in which the O'Rourke family resided.[42]

Also during December, jewelers in G. W. Fairchild & Company on Main Street began displaying the Pendleton Bat trophy in their storefront windows. The rosewood bat was secured atop a black walnut framed case. A silver engraving proclaimed, "Presented to Bridgeport Base Ball Club, Champions of Bridgeport, 1866. By C. G. Pendleton." The ornate box was constructed on three sides with glass; a mirror in back enhanced viewing of the baseballs taken in victory by the Bridgeport Club. Each ball was inscribed with the name of the defeated club, the date, and the final score. Along with the spheroids from the seven championship contests, the cabinet also included balls won in a game featuring Bridgeport's second nine against the Osceolas of Stratford on October 18, as well as a November 7 follow-up match with the Pequonnocks.[43]

Even as stormy blasts shooed folks away from downtown streets, Bridgeport was still enamored with baseball. Flags on passing horse railroad carriages might announce ice skating on Pembroke Lake, but ballists' thoughts focused on spring. Stephen M. Cate, Jr., and William H. Jones of the Bridgeport Club were duly selected to represent their club at the tenth annual meeting of the National Association of Base Ball Players, held in New York City on December 12, 1866. As a result, the Bridgeport Base Ball Club was added to the association's roll of officially recognized organizations.[44]

Merely a year earlier the local press had wrung ink-stained hands worrying that Bridgeport would fail to maintain pace with healthy postwar American culture. But by the close of 1866 events reshaped the city's sportscape forever. Its burgeoning industrial base readily provided eager ballists, there was a marked growth of serious-minded clubs, and of course neighboring towns began respecting the sports acumen of Bridgeport's amateur athletes. It took merely a handful of months for this coastal factory town to begin marching in step with other communities across the United States. Bridgeport baseball was maturing, and the game's bright future lay down the base path.

Club Members

J. D. Alvord (1824–1877), Williston Isaac Alvord (1847–1894), and Charles Earle Alvord (b. 1849): Master New England machinist Joseph Dana Alvord was president of the Wheeler and Wilson ball club. He was purposely brought to Bridgeport by Wheeler and Wilson superintendent William Perry in the late 1850s to perfect the assembly of sewing machines.[45] When Alvord was not revolutionizing American industry he could be found at his "Shady Dell" estate in East Bridgeport or fishing and fowling from his yacht, *Comet*. Williston Alvord, catcher for Wheeler and Wilson, worked with his father in the sewing machine factory and went on to become an independent machinery inventor. Charles Alvord, son of the master machinist and Wheeler and Wilson's first baseman and club secretary, was also employed by the sewing machine giant. Recognized as a stellar citizen (at 21 years of age he was second lieutenant at the city's Commercial & Military Institute) Charles later in life chose to follow his wanderlust. When his widowed mother died in 1896, Charles declined the $50,000 left to him in her will. Instead he headed back out on the road. The *New York Times* pointed a finger at Charles labeling him "shiftless."[46] A 1908 Alvord genealogy placed Charles' whereabouts someplace vaguely "in the West."[47]

Charles C. Commerford (1833–1920): Charles C. Commerford was born in New York City and as a teen became shortstop with the early Gothams. He moved to Waterbury about 1864 to work for the Great Brook Woolen Mill Company and soon thereafter became the Brass City's baseball mentor. He helped organize, and played infield, for the respected Waterbury Club. Later President Grover Cleveland appointed him postmaster of Waterbury, and he also served as deputy chief of the first state labor bureau. Familiar in political circles Commerford married Elizabeth Hamilton, a descendent of Revolutionary War patriot and first Secretary of the United States Treasury, Alexander Hamilton. Commerford's name would be associated with Connecticut baseball for decades; with his slight figure and long white goatee, he was a fixture at Waterbury's ball yards. He died in the first week of February 1920.

Theron J. Hills (1838–1913): At the Civil War's beginning Hills resided in Bristol, Connecticut, and enlisted as a sergeant during June of 1861. He received a disability discharge in 1863, found himself reduced in rank to private, and located to Bridgeport. Hills served drinks in his establishment, the Hills & Johnson Saloon, on Crescent Place next door to the Protectors' firehouse. Hills died in Addison, Michigan, on January 5, 1913.

Dr. William H. Hine (1840–1866): The Yale graduate was a director of Bridgeport's Eureka Base Ball Club and honorary member of the American Base Ball Club. In addition, he was an honorary member of the Protector Engine Company No. 2 and Americus Hose Company. Hine had located his practice in East Bridgeport in 1864, but sadly fell victim to typhoid fever just two years later on November 12, 1866. Firefighters, benevolent associations and members of the American and Eureka Base Ball Clubs were among the good doctor's long funeral cortege. His body was escorted from East Bridgeport to the train depot for the final trip to his birthplace in Waterbury. The 26-year-old practitioner of allopathic medicine, the scientific treatment of disease using drugs that create the same symptoms in healthy people as the disease, was well respected and a friend to the entire community.

Gershom B. Hubbell (1837–1883): Hubbell, an East Bridgeport resident, left his birthplace to relocate in Hartford about 1860. Roughly a year after his move Hubbell, a telegraph operator, organized Hartford's amateur Charter Oak Base Ball nine, which became reigning state champs from 1865 to 1867. Hubbell was also the club's catcher. In addition to his love of baseball and rowing, Hubbell became a recognized billiards champion and winner of the state's "championship cue." In 1867 he represented the Charter Oaks at the organizational meeting of the Connecticut Association of Base Ball Players and would serve as the association's president. Later the versatile electrician became the first president of the National League Hartford Dark Blues. A three-term member of the Hartford common council, Hubbell is credited with being one of the state's earliest proponents of the telephone and in fact introduced Hartford to the device. Hubbell died of Bright's disease while preparing for a fishing trip in Boston. The remains of one of America's unsung baseball devotees were returned to the city of his birth and interred in Bridgeport's Mountain Grove Cemetery.[48]

The Jones Brothers: Seth Benjamin Jones, Jr., was born in Bridgeport on July 3, 1841. He attended Williams College where he was prominent in athletics and played with the school's Greylock Baseball Club. Following graduation in 1863 he taught in Bennington, Vermont, for roughly two years before returning to Bridgeport and a position at the business college.[49] Seth went on to found the Park Avenue Institute in 1871, a well-known private school for boys. For decades Jones remained the principal of this New England educational landmark. William H. Jones, born about 1845, was a partner in the Lyman & Jones agricultural warehouse, located next to his brother Seth's business college. Nathaniel H. Jones was born in 1839; the real estate agent would later become a teammate of James O'Rourke on the 1871 state champion Osceola Club.

James Henry O'Rourke (1850–1919): O'Rourke's storied nineteen-year major league career, and his .311 lifetime batting average, are anchored by two unique bookends. On one side, Jim is credited with the very first hit in National League history (while a member of the Boston Red Caps he laced a two-out single into left on a Philadelphia afternoon, April 22, 1876) and then twenty-eight years later, at the age of 54, he became the oldest catcher to squat behind home plate for a nine-inning game. In fact, he went one for four that day, September 22, helping his beloved New York Giants clinch the 1904 pennant. Still, his pro career wasn't through. Eight years after that, at the age of 62, he donned a catcher's mask one last time, playing in a game for the Connecticut League New Haven White Wings.

Charles Gay Pendleton (1838–1905): Born in New Haven, the 28-year-old druggist, was an active member of the Bridgeport Masons. A well-to-do citizen, Pendleton served as the city's assistant engineer and ran for Justice of the Peace on the Democratic ticket. He was often found with the rest of Connecticut's elite aboard the steamship Ella heading out for a romp at the summer resort on nearby Charles Island. Still, Pendleton's Bridgeport years were filled with sadness. Two of his four children born here died before reaching the age of three. During 1866 the druggist himself fell prone to recurring fevers of some unknown nature.[50] Later he moved on to Chelsea, Massachusetts, where he continued to ply his trade as a druggist. He died a highly regarded citizen of Holbrook, Massachusetts, in 1905. It's likely few, if any, remembered his contribution to baseball forty years earlier.

George Richards, Jr. (1849–1930): His father, Rev. George Richards, was installed as Shepard of the city's First Congregational Church on January 3, 1866.[51] The younger Richards graduated from Yale and from Columbia Law School. He became a successful New York lawyer and died in New York City on May 24, 1930.

Hugh Sterling (1848–1931): Hugh Sterling was born in London, England. His family migrated to the United States in 1860, and Hugh became a highly skilled ornamenter for cabinets at the Howe Sewing Machine Factory.[52] Apparently he adapted swiftly to American culture, becoming a pitcher and shortstop for the Bridgeport Club. Sterling would later serve as city mayor during the turn of the century, another example of the high social level in which Bridgeport Club members circulated. Sterling died in Bridgeport on May 12, 1931.

NOTES

1. The nine-year plight of this abandoned home brought the author and fellow baseball historians Paul Conan and Bernie Crowley together in an effort to save New England history. Paul Conan is the great-great grandson of James O'Rourke. These gentlemen founded The First Hit, Inc., a not-for-profit social organization dedicated to preserving the memory of National Baseball Hall of Fame member, James H. O'Rourke. The group has helped renew the popularity of this 19th century star and successfully increased appreciation for his accomplishments. See Bill McDonald, "Can This Landmark Be Saved?" *Connecticut Post*, June 25, 2003; C. J. Hughes, "Famous and Forgotten: A Baseball Legend from Bridgeport," *New York Times*, August 8, 2004; Les Carpenter "A House Caught in the Rundown," *Washington Post*, April 21, 2006; Bob Tedeschi, "Touching All the Bases for a Legend," *New York Times*, February 22, 2009. A radio piece concerning the O'Rourke Home won the National Associated Press award for best radio feature of 2007 in Connecticut by a Public Radio personality, Erik Campano. In addition The First Hit, Inc. takes part in Bridgeport's annual St. Patrick's Day Parade, works with the Fairfield County Sports Commission and helped establish their James O'Rourke wing of the Fairfield County Sports Hall of Fame. Sadly, on June 15, 2009, during the preparation of this chapter, the O'Rourke Home was razed to ready the area for development. However, the author, members of The First Hit Inc., sculptor Susan Clinard, Bridgeport's Mayor Bill Finch and the Steelpointe Harbor development company are dedicated to creating a life-size bronze statue of James O'Rourke which will be placed in the plaza outside the Ballpark at Harbor Yard, home of the Atlantic League Bridgeport Bluefish.

2. Paul Conan, O'Rourke Family Genealogy, Personal Papers.

3. So many wonderful sources focus on the antebellum game and baseball immediately following the Civil War. See Warren Goldstein, *Playing for Keeps: A History of Early Baseball, 1857–1876* (Ithaca: Cornell University Press, 1989); Peter Morris, *But Didn't We Have Fun? An Informal History of Baseball's Pioneer Era, 1843–1870* (Chicago: Ivan R. Dee, 2008); and William J. Ryczek, *When Johnny Came Sliding Home: The Post-Civil War Baseball Boom, 1865–1870* (Jefferson, NC: McFarland, 1998).

4. Physical fitness and outdoor recreation were rightfully celebrated. *Bridgeport Evening Farmer*, March 29, 1866, notes, "Now that the season for all outdoor sports and amusements is approaching, everything is being got in readiness by the various clubs and individuals, lovers of field, turf, and aquatics, to make this year one of unusual interest. Amongst the various outdoor sports, that of Base Ball is becoming by far the most popular, and very properly so, being entirely of American origins." *Bridgeport Evening Farmer*, May 26, 1866, states, "Every city, deserving the name, has its public grounds, its breathing places, where the hard-worked and over-worked sons of toil can find pure air, healthy exercise, cheerful scenery, sun and shade, green trees, the fresh earth, blue skies, and sparkling waters.... Boston has her Common, Hartford her Park, New Haven her public Greens and Elms, New York her Central Park. These are all the *peoples' grounds*, the *public parks*, open and free to every man women and child ... so it will yet be with Washington and the Seaside Parks by the people of Bridgeport."

5. Numerous articles in the *Bridgeport Evening Farmer* and *Bridgeport Evening Standard* during 1865 and 1866 provide excellent coverage of the embryonic stages of these parks.

6. Bridgeport's newspapers and the *New York Times* report on Bridgeport's 1857–1866 cricket matches.

7. *Bridgeport Evening Farmer*, August 8, 1865.

8. *Bridgeport Evening Standard*, August 29, 1865.

9. *Bridgeport Evening Farmer* and *Bridgeport Evening Standard*, September 1, 1865.

10. *Bridgeport Evening Farmer*, August 29, 1865.

11. Occupations cited throughout this work have been derived from the U.S. Census of 1860 and 1870 as well as from *1867 Bridgeport City Directories*.

12. *Bridgeport Evening Farmer*, October 27, 1865.

13. *Bridgeport Evening Farmer*, January 30, 1866.

14. The Warren Street grounds were also the home field of the Excelsior Club during 1865, *Bridgeport Evening Standard*, October 14, 1865. The following year they became recognized as the home of the Bridgeport Base Ball Club, *Bridgeport Evening Standard*, September 22, 1866.

15. *Bridgeport Evening Farmer*, March 28, 1866.

16. Samuel Orcutt, *A History of the Old Town of Stratford and the City of Bridgeport, Connecticut Part II* (New Haven: Press of Tuttle, Morehouse and Taylor, 1886), p. 791.

17. By no means the best method in which to conduct research, we'll just have to take the word of the *Bridgeport Evening Standard*. The particular issue of *Bat & Ball* to which the local *Evening Standard* alludes no longer exists. What might be the only extant copy in the world is housed in the Connecticut State Library. The single issue they own is dated 2nd Season, No. 1, May 1, 1867.

18. Even if Sunday was taboo for baseball, another example of public gaming (and probably wagering) occurring on a Fast Day appears in "The Fast Day Trot," *Bridgeport Evening Farmer*, June 2, 1865.

19. Henry David Thoreau, *The Writings of Henry David Thoreau: Journal Vol. VIII, November 1, 1855–August 15, 1856*, edited by Bradford Torrey (Boston: Houghton Mifflin and Company, 1906), p. 270.

20. *Bridgeport Evening Standard*, May 16, 1866.

21. *Bridgeport Evening Farmer*, March 31, 1866.

22. *Bridgeport Evening Standard*, August 4, 1866, mentions a meeting held "at the Room of the American Base Ball Club, over I. W. Smith's store, Noble street [*sic*], East Bridgeport...." The 1867 Bridgeport City Directory paints the complete picture of the business. Note also that the American club used rooms in the Staples House, a hotel at the corner of Noble and Railroad Avenue in the east district, *Bridgeport Evening Standard*, September 6, 1866.

23. *Bridgeport Evening Standard*, September 1, 1866. The Junior Bat was eventually won by the Star Base Ball Club.

24. *Bridgeport Evening Standard*, August 7, 1866.

25. While two of the Jones Brothers (Daniel and William) acted as administrators, the club's focus seemed to sharpen when Seth Jones, Jr., returned to Bridgeport with his own college baseball skills. William Jones was the club's catcher in every 1866 game (except for the match against Yale) which may have marked him as captain. Although the club changed their official name, they still retained a strong tie to the Bridgeport College. The club's secretary and treasurer was W. S. Camp, college vice president. And, of course, Seth B. Jones, Jr., was the college's chief administrator, a role he retained when he founded the Park Avenue Institute in 1871 and held through the beginning of the 20th century.

26. The Wheeler and Wilson Base Ball Club organized on May 28, 1866; J. D. Alvord was selected president, *Bridgeport Evening Farmer*, May 29, 1866.

27. Using the U.S. Census records for 1860 and 1870, it can be seen that many of the ballists were employed within the sewing machine industry. The *Bridgeport Evening Standard*, June 8, 1866 also notes that the Pioneer Base Ball Club "is composed of young men from the Wheeler & Wilson's factory."

28. The information concerning Charles C. Commerford was gathered from "Our Base Ball Illustrations," *Frank Leslie's Illustrated Newspaper*, August 25, 1866, pp. 356–357; John Augustus Spalding, *Illustrated Popular Biography of Connecticut* (Hartford: Case, Lockwood & Brainard Company, 1891) p. 193; *Chadwick Diaries Vol. 37*, 1905, p. 10; and "Commerford Ex-Postmaster Dies, Aged 86," *Waterbury Republican*, February 7, 1920.

29. John O'Rourke played left field and scored four runs, *Bridgeport Evening Farmer*, September 11, 1866, and *Bridgeport Evening Standard*, September 11, 1866.

30. "The Protectors were promptly on hand, all jolly, good-natured, which they retained throughout the game and played with considerable pluck although so badly beaten," *Bridgeport Evening Standard*, September 20, 1866.

31. Orcutt, *History of the Old Town of Stratford*; *Bridgeport Evening Farmer*, August 14, 1865.

32. The unidentified newspaper source for the haunting dates back to 1931 which is covered in Mary Witkowski, "Reporter Told Tale of Haunted Fire Station," *Bridgeport News*, October 30, 1997.

33. *Bridgeport Evening Farmer*, May 25, 1866.

34. The personnel and job titles for the 1872 Fire Department are found in George C. Waldo, Jr., *History of Bridgeport and Vicinity, Vol. I* (New York: S. J. Clarke Publishing Company, 1917), p. 110.

35. *Bridgeport Evening Farmer*, October 4, 1866.

36. A not-so-veiled dig at the ballists' college affiliation. A series of letters and editorial opinion roared back and forth between the Bridgeport and American Clubs. These pieces appear in the *Bridgeport Evening Farmer*, October 18, 1866; *Bridgeport Evening Standard*, October 18, 1866; *Bridgeport Evening Farmer*, October 19, 1866; *Bridgeport Evening Farmer*, October 20, 1866; *Bridgeport Evening Farmer*, October 22, 1866; and *Bridgeport Evening Farmer*, October 23, 1866.

37. The first Connecticut State Agricultural Fair was held in 1854. Sites across the state varied year to year and were selected by an executive committee based upon the dollar amounts offered by each bidding city. Bridgeport was chosen to host the fourth annual fair in 1857 (*Bridgeport Daily Advertiser and Farmer*, April 23, 1857). The grounds were located on "thirty or forty acres" of farmland owned by David Sherwood, a neighbor of P. T. Barnum's. Once a part of Fairfield, Connecticut this area is now within the boundaries of Bridgeport. Researching 19th century maps and land owners it appears that the approximate locale of the 1857 State Fair was on Fairfield Avenue (running south toward Long Island Sound) near the intersection with Lincoln Avenue (today's Clinton Avenue). These ball grounds, near the western terminus of the horse railroad, were capable of accommodating a large crowd, perfect for important games. Not to mention the money proprietors of the horse railroad collected in fares, consider how the games drawing the most spectators are situated on extremes of the railroad.

38. There seems to be a discrepancy in the total number of games played from 1866 to 1867. "Base Ball at Yale," *The Yale Literary Magazine*, December 1868, pp. 131–132, provides a total of four games played between Bridgeport and Yale, while *The Ball Players' Chronicle*, October 10, 1867, mentions additional contests.

39. The *Bridgeport Evening Standard*, July 24, 1866, initially announces the visiting club as "The first nine of the Americus Hose Company No. 19 of New York." However, D. T. Valentine, *Historical Index to the Manuals of the Corporation of the City of New York* (New York: Edmund Jones & Co., 1865) inventories a certain "American" Hose Co. No. 19 being located on Greene Street in New York City. A subsequent box score in the *Bridgeport Evening Farmer* of July 27, 1866, lists the New York club as the Americans.

40. Dr. Hine had a serious relapse as reported in the *Bridgeport Evening Standard*, November 9, 1866. But the article offered that he was improving. When Hine passed away there was a public outpouring of sympathy (*Bridgeport Evening Standard*, November 22, 1866).

41. As a public service basic weather information was maintained at C. G. Pendleton's Drugstore and reprinted in the *Bridgeport Evening Standard* under the heading of "Thermometrical and Barometrical Record Kept at C. G. Pendleton's Store, E. D." At noon on Friday, November 30, 1866, the temperature was 52°F and Wednesday, December 5, 1866, the temperature hit a noontime high of 53°F.

42. Lee Allen, Personal Papers included in the "James H. O'Rourke File," National Baseball Hall of Fame Library, Cooperstown, New York.

43. "A Thing of Beauty," *Bridgeport Evening Standard*, December 1, 1866. The article mentions too that the case contains "the badges" of the rival clubs.

44. Charles A. Peverelly, *The Book of American Pastimes: Containing a History of the Principal Base Ball, Cricket, Rowing, and Yachting Clubs of the United States* (New York, 1866), p. 506.

45. David A. Hounshell, *From the American System to Mass Production, 1800–1932* (Baltimore: Johns Hopkins University Press, 1984), pp. 70–71.

46. "He Declined A $50,000 Legacy," *New York Times*, March 22, 1896.

47. Samuel Morgan Alvord, *A Genealogy of the Descendants of Alexander Alvord: An Early Settler of Windsor, Connecticut and Northampton, Massachusetts* (Webster, NY: A. D. Andrews, 1908), p. 461.

48. Hubbell's biographical information is culled from the *Hartford Daily Courant* July 2, 1862; *New York Times*, August 19, 1865; *Bridgeport Evening Farmer*, May 5, 1866; Hubbell's obituary in the *Bridgeport Evening Farmer*, September 6, 1883, *The Hartford Daily Courant*, September 6, 1883, and September 7, 1883; and David Arcidiacono, "The Hartford Dark Blues," *Hog River Journal*, Summer 2003.

49. Williams College Class of 1863, *Class of Sixty-Three Williams College Fortieth Year Report, 1863–1903* (Boston: Thomas Todd Printer, 1903); accessed January 10, 2009, on www.geneabios.com.

50. *Bridgeport Evening Standard*, October 17, 1866.

51. Charles Ray Palmer, *The Bi-Centennial Celebration of the First Congregational Church and Society of Bridgeport, Connecticut* (New Haven: Tuttle, Morehouse and Taylor Press, 1895), p. 153.

52. Freemasons Michigan, *Sixty-Sixth Annual Conclave: Grand Commandery Knights Templar of Michigan, 1932*, p. 82.

Bibliography

Allen, Lee. Personal Papers included in the "James H. O'Rourke File." National Baseball Hall of Fame Library, Cooperstown, New York.

Alvord, Samuel Morgan. *A Genealogy of the Descendants of Alexander Alvord: An Early Settler of Windsor, Connecticut and Northampton, Massachusetts*. Webster, NY: A. D. Andrews, 1908.

Arcidiacono, David. "The Hartford Dark Blues." *Hog River Journal*, Summer 2003.

"Base Ball at Yale." *The Yale Literary Magazine*, December 1868.

Bielawa, Michael J. *Bridgeport Baseball*. Mount Pleasant, SC: Arcadia, 2003.

_____. *From FarField to Newfield: The Baseball Dream of Orator Jim O'Rourke*. Fairfield, CT: Audubon, 1999.

Bridgeport Daily Advertiser and Farmer, 1857–1858.

Bridgeport Directory and Annual Advertiser for 1867–8. Bridgeport: The Standard Association, 1867.

Bridgeport Evening Farmer, 1865–1866.

Bridgeport Evening Standard, 1865–1866.

Chadwick, Henry. *Henry Chadwick Scrapbooks, 1860–1905*.

_____, ed. *The Ball Players' Chronicle*, 1867.

Conan, Paul. O'Rourke Family Genealogy. Personal Papers.

Connecticut Association of Base Ball Players. *Constitution and By-Laws of the Connecticut Association of Base Ball Players, with Laws and Regulations of the Game of Base Ball*. Hartford: Press of Wiley, Waterman & Eaton, 1867.

Frank Leslie's Illustrated Newspaper, August 25, 1866.

Freemasons Michigan. *Sixty-Sixth Annual Conclave: Grand Commandery Knights Templar of Michigan, 1932*.

Hartford Daily Courant, 1857–1866.

Hounshell, David A. *From the American System to Mass Production, 1800–1932*. Baltimore: Johns Hopkins University Press, 1984.

"Manufacturing Items." *Scientific American*, July 8, 1865.

New York Times, 1857–1859, 1866.

Orcutt, Samuel. *A History of the Old Town of Stratford and the City of Bridgeport*. New Haven: Tuttle, Morehouse and Taylor, 1886.

Palmer, Charles Ray. *The Bi-Centennial Celebration of the First Congregational Church and Society of Bridgeport, Connecticut*. New Haven: Tuttle, Morehouse and Taylor Press, 1895.

Pendleton, Everett Hall. *Brian Pendleton and His Descendants, 1599–1910*. Privately printed, 1911.

Peverelly, Charles A. *The Book of American Pastimes: Containing a History of the Principal Base Ball, Cricket, Rowing, and Yachting Clubs of the United States*. New York, 1866.

Spalding, J. A. *Illustrated Popular Biography of Connecticut: 1891*. Hartford: J. A. Spalding, 1891.

Waldo, George C., Jr. *History of Bridgeport and Vicinity, Vol. I*. New York: S. J. Clarke Publishing Company, 1917.

Waterbury Daily American, 1866.

Webb, Fitzgerald. *Bridgeport and East Bridgeport General and Business Directory: 1867*. New York: Wm. E. Chaplin & Co, Steam Printers, 1867.

Williams College Class of 1863. *Class of Sixty-Three Williams College Fortieth Year Report, 1863–1903*. Boston: Thomas Todd Printer, 1903.

Chapter Two

Upstate New York

❖ Introduction (Richard Hershberger) ❖

Upstate New York was the first hotbed of modern baseball, the "New York Game," as it emerged from the incubation ground of Manhattan and its immediate environs. Orange and Rockland Counties, on the lower Hudson River, had clubs playing the New York Game as early as the spring of 1856. The game spread quickly up the Hudson River to Albany, and from there westward along the Erie Canal corridor.

The New York Game did not move into a vacuum, as the region already had a thriving ball-playing culture. To begin with, the golden age of American cricket had begun with a club in Albany. In addition, the game of wicket, although most closely associated with New England, was popular through much of New York. The area also had a strong pre-modern baseball culture. The earliest recorded baseball challenge was issued in 1825 in the *Delhi Gazette*, some fourteen years before and fifty miles south of where baseball would later be supposed to have been invented, in Cooperstown. Local versions of baseball were played throughout New York state, with some of the early clubs preferring their local versions, but by the end of the Civil War the standardized regulation version was universal among organized baseball clubs.

The region was gripped by baseball fever in the years immediately before the Civil War. One of the first inter-city games occurred in 1859 when the Pittsfield, Massachusetts, club traveled to play the Champion Club of Albany. The first international match was held in 1860, between the Niagara Club of Buffalo and the Young Canadian Club of Hamilton. The first extended tour by any club also occurred in 1860, when the Excelsior Club of Brooklyn journeyed upstate to play the local clubs. The Excelsiors had no problem finding opponents already playing under the new rules, though they taught the local boys a thing or two about how the game could be played better.

Through the early decades of the professional era, upstate teams played at the highest level. There were major league teams at various times in Buffalo, Rochester, Troy, and Syracuse. At the next level down, the Syracuse Stars of 1877 were a famous team, touring through most of the country, and the Buffalo Bisons of 1878 have been judged the best minor league team of all time. To this day the state has more teams in organized baseball than any state except California.

With these essays we see early baseball as it organized and began its spread throughout the nation.

❖ Hudson Rivers of Newburgh (Peter Morris) ❖

Club History

Newburgh lies some sixty miles north of New York City, so it is not surprising that the New York Game had arrived there by 1856. Newburgh was then still a village that was part of the town of Newburgh, a confusing arrangement that resulted from the state's custom of designating as towns all locales that are not either cities or Indian reservations. It was not until 1865 that the village of Newburgh was incorporated as a city and became officially distinct from the surrounding town.

The village's first club was known simply as the Newburghs and played on a field at the corner of South and Johnston streets, with home plate located at the south corner under the shade of a willow tree. The Newburghs faced many clubs from Brooklyn and New York City, but their main rivalry was with the Highlands of New Windsor, a nearby town. The two clubs faced each other on numerous occasions, either on the grounds of the Newburgh Club or on "the plateau west of the brickyards."[1]

According to John Nutt, the Newburgh Club originally had seventeen members: William C. Miller, John Miller, L. S. Straw, S. B. Reeve, Stephen King, Robert Rogers, James W. Miller, Eli Hasbrouck, Isaac M. Martin, George W. Powell, William H. Kelly, H. S. Brewster, John C. Adams, Thomas

Harris, Thomas C. Ring, John McDowell, and George H. Chandler. At least two dozen more members had joined by 1858, enabling the club to stage intrasquad contests when the Highlands were not available. At one such practice session, played on September 18, 1858, "T. C. Ring was fined 50 cents for disputing the umpire, and Wm. C. Miller paid a similar amount to the treasurer, Eli H. Evans, for the use of 'improper language.'"[2]

The rapid-growing club welcomed more than forty additional members in 1859, which must have created issues about playing time. That is probably why a second Newburgh club, the Hudson Rivers, was formed in 1859. The original officers of the Hudson Rivers were William C. Miller as president, Henry Robinson as vice president, and Abram Cassedy as secretary. Several facts point to the close relationship between the new baseball club and the original one. The Hudson Rivers used the same playing field as the Newburghs, although a second small clubhouse was built to differentiate between the two (the clubhouse of the Newburghs was square, while that of the Hudson Rivers was octagonal). More notably, five of the nine men who represented the Hudson Rivers in their first match had been original members of the Newburghs.[3]

The Hudson Rivers played their historic first match on June 23 against the Highlands of New Windsor, winning 29–23. Those same two clubs faced each other four more times that year, with each winning twice. On September 15 the Hudson Rivers played the Newburghs and were beaten by the narrow margin of 29–26. The 1859 season in Newburgh closed on Thanksgiving when the mighty Eckford Club of Brooklyn came to town for a match with the Newburgh Club. Predictably, the visitors won by a score of 58–19, but that wasn't what mattered. Newburgh had had the opportunity to see one of the nation's best ball clubs, and the town's ballplayers had received a valuable lesson in the finer points of the game.

The closely contested series between the two Newburgh clubs resumed in the spring of 1860, with a 27–27 tie taking place on May 30 followed by a rematch a week later in which the Hudson Rivers won by a 29–22 score. On July 5 the club hosted and eked out a win over the Independents of South Brooklyn. Six days later, the Hudson Rivers had a much tougher opponent when the Excelsiors of Brooklyn stopped in Newburgh on a tour of the state. To nobody's surprise, the Excelsiors beat the Hudson Rivers, 65–14.

The Newburgh Base Ball Club traveled to Brooklyn at the end of August for a rematch with the mighty Eckfords. After Newburgh lost by a respectable 36–22 score, the players and many other club members headed to the Odeon for the usual post-match festivities. Alas, this party of about seventy-five arrived to find "a supper prepared for about twenty hungry men," and much of the scant supply of meat caused the men to conclude that "the ox who supplied the tongue, especially, must have been possessed of very bad smelling breath." The indignant diners left for another establishment, and the Eckford Club expressed regret that it had not been able to reciprocate the hospitality received in Newburgh nine months earlier.[4]

That was the last recorded game played by the Newburgh Base Ball Club, and the outbreak of the Civil War seems to have brought that club's activities to an end. But in the summer of 1861, the Hudson River Club reorganized and played two games against the Ulsters of Saugerties, losing both. Then, in September, the Hudson Rivers paid a visit to Poughkeepsie, and a win there was followed by an October trip that included a loss to the champion Eckfords and a win over the Eclipse Club of Kingston.

The activity of the club continued in 1862, beginning with a return visit from the Eclipse Club of Kingston. The contest resulted in another win for the Hudson Rivers and also yielded a treasured souvenir. According to a 1915 article, "The oldest baseball in existence is owned by the president of the East End Church Baseball league of Pittsburgh. The ball is nearly fifty-three years old. It was used first in a championship game between the Eclipse team of Kingston, N.Y., and the Hudson team of Newburgh, N.Y. The game was played on June 20, 1862.... The ball is made of one piece of horsehide, sewed in the center. When it was used underhand pitching alone was permissible. Curves were unknown. The ball carries $500 burglary insurance and $500 fire insurance. It was given to its present owner by John Miller."[5]

The next challenge for the Hudson Rivers came on Independence Day, July 4, 1862, when the Eckfords came to Newburgh for another match. To nobody's surprise, the champions won by the lopsided margin of 74–29. Over the balance of the 1862 season the club didn't lose again, beating the Poughkeepsies twice and closing the campaign with a Thanksgiving Day win over the Resolutes of Brooklyn.

In August of 1863, the Hudson Rivers paid another visit to Brooklyn to test themselves against the country's best clubs. The trip yielded a win over the Resolutes, another drubbing at the hands of the Eckfords, and narrow losses to the Excelsiors and Stars. This latter defeat came on the final day of the trip, and it seems to have left a bad taste in the mouths of some of the forty Newburghers who had accompanied the players. According to an account written fifty years later, at the conclusion of the game the umpire, Colonel Thomas Fitzgerald of Philadelphia, "said he had made a mistake in his decision, for which he felt sorry and that the game should rightly be Hudson Rivers 6, Stars 5. He said the game was the finest he had ever seen and he felt that it would be recorded as 'the' game. He cordially invited the [Hudson River] club to visit Philadelphia, but they came home instead."[6]

The 1863 season closed in October at the Orange County Fair in Goshen, where a silver belt had been offered as first prize. The Hudson Rivers lost an 8–7 thriller to the Resolutes and, once again, there was controversy at the conclusion. The contest had begun at 1:30 in the afternoon, which should have left plenty of time to complete nine innings. Instead, play was interrupted so that the spectators could watch a horse race, with the result that darkness had started to fall by the seventh inning. In the view of many from Newburgh, the Resolutes then began to stall, forcing the umpire to end the game and award the victory to the Brooklyn club.[7]

The two clubs reprised the showdown at the same site in the fall of 1864, and this time the Hudson Rivers came out ahead, earning a silver ball for their efforts. The season also saw Newburgh's representatives manage wins over the Empire State Club of New York and the Enterprise Club of Brooklyn, while losing close games to the Mutuals of New York and the Stars of Brooklyn. A contest against the Eastman College nine of Poughkeepsie was also scheduled, and the club extended "a cordial invitation to all those who take pleasure in out door sports, who prize the health of the young men of our village, who love to witness a good game of ball, and who desire an afternoon of recreation and pleasure, to favor us with their presence.... We would especially invite the *ladies, particularly* those who so often of old were wont to enlighten our grounds with their fair presence, and cause our boys to exert themselves to the utmost for victory. We think that if they attend in force, the chances of our success will be much better, and we may perchance, have another *ball* to add to our case of 'trophies.'"[8] Unfortunately, it is not known whether the Hudson Rivers were able to add to their trophy case.

Clubs that had thrived before the Civil War had to resolve a difficult dilemma in order to continue their success after the war. Baseball was a young man's game in the 1860s, and clubs that stuck with their pre-war players struggled to compete with newly formed rivals. Yet those that opted for radically revamped lineups faced the hurt feelings of older members and often succumbed to internal dissension.

The Hudson Rivers achieved a rare happy medium, injecting new blood into their first nine on a gradual enough basis to keep everyone content while still remaining competitive. A perfect example was the pitching department, which had been in the hands of pre-war stalwart William H. Kelley since he came over from the Newburghs in 1862. But after the war, he agreed to share the pitching duties: "When Frank Brown (Judge Charles F. Brown) came home from Yale on his vacations, and after his graduation, he went in as change pitcher. His delivery was very swift, while Mr. Kelly pitched a slow ball. Judge Brown was one of the first of the speed men to appear in the box."[9]

This arrangement gave the Hudson Rivers the ability to keep opposing hitters off balance. Even more important, such changes were introduced in a way that didn't upset the displaced players. Several pre-war standouts became part of the Hudson River second nine, while others made a different transition: "When the old players retired, they joined the ranks of the rooters."[10] Either way, the essence of the Hudson River Base Ball Club remained intact, even as the first nine changed.

As a result, attendance at home games became all the rage in the years immediately following the war. Match games typically started at three P.M. "or as soon thereafter as W. H. Kelly [*sic*], the school teacher, could arrive from Washington street" and were "attended by the elite of the town." Many prominent Newburgh ladies "were to be seen in the throng," while the regular attendance of the Reverend John Forsyth also helped to confer dignity to the still-young game of baseball. And these bastions of respectability had plenty of company at the match games of the Hudson Rivers. When strong clubs like the Unions of Lansingburgh and the Eckfords came to town, "business was suspended on Water street" so that everyone could watch.[11]

Despite the efforts to appeal to distinguished spectators, wagering was commonplace at the ballpark. "The amount of betting in those days was wonderful," recalled one old-timer in 1896. "Everyone seemed to have money, and in fact such was the case. The war period of inflation was still on, and the stories of men lighting their cigars with greenbacks was not entirely fiction, by any means. The greatest sports in those days were the machinists and moulders, who made from $4 to $6 a day. They had 'money to burn,' and took in all the great ball games and rowing matches. The rolls they would display on the old ball grounds at the South and Johnston street corner struck dismay into the ranks of many a visiting ball club."[12]

The Hudson Rivers began their post-war history with a trip to Poughkeepsie, where they beat the up-and-coming Unions of Lansingburgh.[13] This was followed by a swing through New York that included a loss to the Enterprise Club at Brooklyn's famed Capitoline Grounds, a victory over the Mystics in New York City, and defeats in Hoboken at the hands of the Mutuals and Gothams. After returning home, the Hudson Rivers hosted several more matches against clubs, defeating the Olympics of Paterson, New Jersey, and the Poughkeepsies, and losing to the Mutuals. The eventful season concluded with the Hudson River club defeating the Lorillards of Rhinebeck to capture a silver ball that became the emblem of the "championship of the Hudson River," then beating the Knickerbockers of Albany in November to retain the championship.[14]

The first nine of the Hudson River Club showed more signs of ambition in 1866. In the spring, club secretary Lewis B. Halsey reported,

> We have played in Albany, Saugerties, Kingston, Poughkeepsie, New York, and Brooklyn. We have not been defeated in a return game by any club outside of New York and Brooklyn. In those cities we have lost games with the Excelsior, Star, Eckford, Mutual, and Gotham; which clubs we have never defeated in any game. The Unions, of Morrisania, have won a home-and-home match. We have won from the Empire, Eagle, Enterprise, Resolute, and Mystic Clubs.... Our grounds are situated at the corner of South and Johnson [*sic*] streets, in Newburgh, Orange

county, New York. We practice every Tuesday and Friday of each week. Uniform — white shirt and cap; blue pants. We frequently receive clubs from the cities of New York and Brooklyn, and we cordially extend a general invitation to all clubs in good standing to visit our beautiful city in the future. In 1865, we were the guests of the Enterprise, Mystic, Gotham, and Mutual Clubs, respectively. We have forty active members, ten honorary. The organization has always commanded the respect and esteem of our citizens, and now stands, very high in this community.[15]

Befitting that optimism, the first nine embarked that year on a five-game, six-day tour of upstate New York. According to John Nutt's later account, "Their tour across the State in 1866 was a continued ovation, and the days of their visit were holidays in the towns where they were received. Banquets were given in their honor at hotels, and receptions at private residences."

But while the tour was a success on most counts, the club that had prided itself on being competitive with the best clubs in New York City and better than any other club in the state suffered a significant setback when it reached Buffalo. Bettors offered three-to-one odds on a win by the Hudson Rivers before the match, but instead the hometown Niagaras won by the lopsided score of 40–17.[16]

An 1896 article about the "triumphal tour" said of this lone loss that "the Newburghers succumbed from sheer exhaustion rather than more skillful players."[17] Another club history went to even greater lengths to justify the defeat: "The Newburghers were completely fagged out when they came on the field in the metropolis of Western New York. Banquets, brass band parades through the streets and other forms of hero worship in Elmira, Owego, Binghamton and elsewhere with attendant loss of sleep and change of water from town to town, had made some of the players positively ill, and the entire aggregation was totally unfit to put up any kind of a game against even inferior opposition, whereas the Niagaras had changed and strengthened their nine from day to day as the telegraphic reports came to Buffalo, then as now a great sporting centre, of the triumphal progress of the Hudson River players through the State." The author of the account concluded by despairing of being able to describe "the gloom that prevailed everywhere in Newburgh when the announcement came of the result in Buffalo. The defeat was a local calamity."[18]

As if to demonstrate the extent of that calamity, an 1886 reminiscence described almost every match the Hudson Rivers played on the 1866 tour except the one in Buffalo. The piece recounted wins over the Binghamton Club, the Alerts of Elmira, and the Monitors of Corning before concluding that "the most crushing defeat suffered by any club was that of the Unions of Elmira. The game was played on the return trip of the Hudson Rivers, and was witnessed by nearly 7,000 persons, who fairly went wild over the game. It lasted nearly all the afternoon, and at the close of the ninth inning it was found that the Hudson Rivers had scored 120 runs to the Unions 17. A banquet followed at which David B. Hill, our present governor, delivered a speech. On the return of the victors they were received with as much enthusiasm as was ever accorded a base ball club."[19]

On an 1887 visit to the Orange County Fair, Governor Hill joked that he still held a grudge against the city of Newburgh. He then recounted his own version of the day that the Hudson Rivers "came to Elmira to play our team. We thought we were some punkins on baseball up in Chemung County. But it was simply our vanity for 'we weren't in it' when the Newburghers got in the game. At the close of the game the score stood 126 to 18, or something like that, and we held the small end of the stick."[20]

Despite the warm reception that they received upon arriving home from their tour, the members of the Hudson River Club seemed to lose some of their enthusiasm for baseball. Perhaps the devastating loss in Buffalo had cast a pall over the local baseball scene, but it may also have been that the players were becoming caught up in more pressing concerns. In any event, the first nine played only one more recorded game in 1866 and never again embarked on a tour.

Yet while the first nine of the Hudson River Club began to scale back its ambitions, baseball in Orange County benefited from the club's underlying fabric. Although first nines received most of the newspaper attention in the increasingly competitive post-war environment, the second nines also played an important role. This was demonstrated in 1865 when a new baseball club was organized in the nearby village of Washingtonville (which a century later was the boyhood home of Yankee general manager Brian Cashman). The members of the Washingtonville Base Ball Club "did not have the moral courage or skill to tackle the old boys of the first nine of Newburgh's famous Hudson River Club," so instead they challenged the second nine of the Hudson Rivers. A best-of-three series was played in September and the games "attracted great attention. People all through the county came to witness them."[21]

The Hudson River second nine swept the series, 25–24 and 23–21, but the nail-biting contests had an invigorating effect on baseball in Orange County — something that would have been much less likely if the new club from Washingtonville had faced the Hudson River first nine and been trounced. Many new clubs sprung up, and by 1867 "base ball was at its height in Newburgh.... Hundreds of the youth of the city imitated the achievements of the popular favorites, and the Hudson River Juniors attained almost as wide a reputation as their elders."[22]

The growth of the game also began to include men of different social backgrounds, most notably in the case of a new club known as the Uniteds. The members of the Uniteds were mill workers from a neighboring village by the name of New Mills, which was later annexed by Newburgh and became known as West Newburgh. New Mills was, to say the least, a rough-and-tumble place: "There was a hand engine (Highland) to put out fires, two taverns, several slaughter houses and the United Baseball Club. The police service did not seriously interfere with the fighting habit that flourished at New Mills between the gangs of the rival hotels, the charcoal peddlers, farmers, teamsters, drovers and butcher boys. 'The Turnpike roughs' were still in existence, and fought with anybody who had a local fistic reputation. The fighting began on Saturday nights and continued on Sundays."[23]

The Uniteds reflected their surroundings. According to a 1910 article, "The United team was distinctly a New Mills (West Newburgh) institution, and had more real pleasure out of the game than you can shake a stick at. Villagers themselves, they played many matches out in the country, and Saturday was the day for these jaunts. Starting early in the morning in wagons they made a full day of it, arriving at West street late at night. Their friends would wait in the hotels and the engine house to hear the news, and all New Mills shared in the joy of their victories and the sorrow of their defeats."[24]

The same writer claimed that the Uniteds were one of four men's baseball clubs in or around Newburgh during the 1860s, joining the Hudson Rivers, the Hudson River second nine, and the Alerts. Curiously, however, the Uniteds never faced the Hudson Rivers, and their very existence was never acknowledged in the many articles, both contemporaneous and retrospective, that chronicled the doings of the Hudson River Club. We must at least consider the possibility that the members of the Hudson River Club, whose high social status was frequently mentioned in these articles, wanted nothing to do with the upstarts from New Mills. It could also be that the writer of the 1910 article was mistaken about the time frame and that the Uniteds came into being too late to be a rival to the Hudson Rivers or that the Uniteds themselves didn't want to face the mighty champions and the potential of an embarrassing loss.

In any case, the Uniteds never faced the Hudson Rivers, and none of the other new clubs was able to dethrone them as local champions. The Alerts were thought to have the best chance, but when they got their opportunity in June of 1867 they were routed 65–8 in a game that became the subject of considerable controversy. The supporters of the Hudson Rivers maintained that the Alerts "came on the field with two substitutes half scared to death" and "never recovered from their terrible play."[25] But the Alerts had a very different perspective, with one of them later offering this explanation for the lopsided score: "when the hour arrived to decide the much-talked of contest for local supremacy it was found that the Hudson Rivers had gobbled up three of the Alerts [sic] best men."[26] The Lone Stars of Matteawan also challenged the Hudson Rivers in 1867 and took the series to a third and deciding game, but failed to wrest away local bragging rights.[27]

The Hudson Rivers played a few more games against national powers in 1867, with mixed results. The Mutuals came to town on June 22 and won 27–6 in a game long remembered for a drive by fabled slugger Lip Pike that traveled "into the South side of the yard of the Third Ward school."[28] On Independence Day, the Hudson Rivers paid a visit to the soon-to-be-famous Unions of Lansingburgh and lost a heartbreaker: "The Newburghers had a strong lead until near the finish, when they became rattled by the uproar of the crowd."[29] But in the fall, the Hudson Rivers avenged the loss with a 29–23 win in Newburgh that showed that they were still a formidable adversary.

That victory proved to be the last hurrah for Newburgh's famous baseball nine, as little was heard from the Hudson River Club in 1868. A 44–8 drubbing on July 3 at the hands of the Unions of Lansingburgh seems to have sealed the club's fate, and by 1869 it had quietly disbanded. A short-lived effort at revival was made in 1873, but most of the original members had retired and the new team was the Hudson Rivers in name only. (One retrospective, indeed, referred to this club as the "new Hudson Rivers.")[30]

On September 23, 1886, however, the surviving members were reunited for an old-timers game in Newburgh. In the days leading up to the contest, a photo of the old Hudson River first nine was put on display in the window of a Water Street hardware store owned by Charles J. Lawson and became the talk of the town: "a large crowd has been around the window all day admiring it and making comments. On the top of the frame the gold balls won by the old club are also exhibited."[31]

Rain threatened to ruin the event, but the skies cleared in time for the likes of John C. Adams, Al Lindley, Evert Wilson, William H. Kelley, Jimmie Boyd, Frank Brown, and Nealie Gibb to once more scamper around the baseball diamond. When the game ended, a banquet was held at the Merchants' Hotel and former club president David A. Scott "spoke of the old days of the Hudson Rivers, of the many pleasant times they had, the pleasure of this reunion, and said that it would probably be the last time that the members of the old Hudson River Base Ball Club would ever be together to rehearse the days of the past, in which they had won such glorious victories on the ball ground."[32]

By then the accomplishments of these men and the other members of the Hudson River Base Ball Club of Newburgh had become the stuff of local legend. As one reporter fondly recalled in 1889, "Their deeds have been immortalized in song and story, and can be narrated by thousands of our citizens."[33]

Club Members

John C. Adams: "Jack" Adams was born in Tivoli, New York, on May 16, 1836, and opened a grocery store after settling in Newburgh in 1860. He played for the first nine of the Hudson Rivers from 1861 to 1866 and was one of its heavy hitters; according to a 1909 reminiscence, "On the South street grounds the batting was to the north, and once upon a time John C. Adams put the ball over the building now occupied by the priests of St. Mary's Church."[34] He later served as an alderman, supervisor and postmaster of Newburgh, as a harbormaster of the port, and as president of the Consumers Gas Company. He was president of the Hudson River Club during the brief attempt to revive it in 1873, though by then his playing days were over. A couple of years later he was described as "one of the best umpires and one of the best posted men on base ball in the country." His death in Newburgh on January 12, 1900, warranted a brief notice in *Sporting Life* that recalled his days with the Hudson Rivers.[35]

James T. Boyd: Born in Fishkill, New York, in 1845, Jimmy Boyd was the club's catcher from 1862 to 1867. He soon moved to Boston to work as an engineer, though he returned to play in the 1886 reunion game. Boyd died in Boston on November 3, 1904, but continued to be remembered in Newburgh — a 1911 reminiscence recalled how Boyd "would stand behind the bat on the old grounds and catch all through the long games without complaining. If he split a finger, however, the game was lost, for there was no one to take his place."[36]

Charles Francis "Frank" Brown: Born in Newburgh on September 12, 1844, Frank Brown attended Yale University and then followed his father, Judge John W. Brown, into the legal profession. He began to pitch for the Hudson Rivers while home from Yale on vacations, and had more time to do so after graduating and setting up a law practice with Abram Cassedy (see next profile). According to a 1913 reminiscence, Brown, "who had learned his game at Yale was the speediest pitcher hereabouts. The small boys thought he was the greatest man that lived possibly with the exception of Dan Rice and John Robinson, of circus fame."[37] In 1878, Brown became a judge and spent nearly two decades on the bench. He decided to return to private practice in 1897 and started a new partnership with Cassedy's son. He soon opened an office in New York City and built a thriving practice on Wall Street. After Brown died in Newburgh on June 19, 1929, a tribute by Judge A. H. Seeger enumerated his colleague's many accomplishments. According to Seeger, Brown's "luminous decisions are still quoted and followed in every State in the Union." The judge also alluded to "Judge Brown's interest in sports, among them baseball, rowing, yachting, and riding.... It was a continuance on the farm, said Judge Seeger, which enabled Judge Brown to preserve a sound mind in a sound body to the very last."[38]

Abram S. Cassedy: He was born on November 29, 1833, in Ramapo, New York. He graduated from the State Normal School (in Albany), then studied law in Clarkstown and Goshen before being admitted to the bar in 1857. He settled in Newburgh in 1859 and served as club secretary for the next four years, though he never played on the first nine. He became one of the city's most distinguished lawyers, serving as district attorney, judge, and mayor. He took his own life in Newburgh on April 29, 1896. He had been unwell and was believed to be insane at the time.

James Watson Fisher: He played for both the Hudson Rivers of Newburgh and the Eclectic Club of New York. His death in Elizabeth, New Jersey, on March 12, 1881, warranted a death notice in the *New York Clipper*.[39]

Cornelius Smith Gibb: Born in Newburgh on November 19, 1846, "Nealie" Gibb played shortstop for the first nine in 1867. The son of an undertaker, he continued the family business and served as an alderman from 1887 until his death on April 19, 1891.

Lewis B. Halsey: He was born in Newburgh on January 31, 1841, and graduated from Princeton. He was the club's shortstop from 1864 to 1866 and took over as secretary after the death of A.S. Mapes. He became a lawyer and was very active in Newburgh civic affairs. In 1874, Halsey ran for the Assembly in a contentious campaign marred by his feud with *Newburgh Journal* editor Cyrus Martin. Though both men were Republicans, Martin "denounced Halsey without stint." After losing the election, "Halsey sued the *Journal* for libel, but the case was never tried. He resigned his position as alderman of the Fourth Ward, removed to New York, engaged in the dairying business and became wealthy."[40] Lewis Halsey died in New York City on June 30, 1911.

William H. Kelley (often spelled Kelly): Born in Glens Falls, New York, on June 13, 1839, William H. Kelley graduated from Syracuse University and settled in Newburgh, where he became a schoolteacher and was deeply involved in civic affairs. Kelley was one of the original members of the Newburgh Club and stayed with that club until at least 1860. He joined the Hudson Rivers in 1862 and remained a starter for the rest of the club's existence, also serving as vice president and secretary. He was again a regular during the 1873 revival and also took part in the 1886 reunion game. In later years, he served as an assessor, an alderman, and president of the common council. He taught for more than sixty years before finally retired in 1921. Even then, he continued to serve as president of the Newburgh Board of Education until his death on June 20, 1931, one week after celebrating his ninety-second birthday. An obituary recalled that he had been pitcher of the famous Hudson River nine and reported that he retained his love of baseball to the end of his life.[41]

Stephen King: Stephen King, who played for the Hudson Rivers from 1859 to 1863, was a coal dealer who was born in New York State around 1831. He is not to be confused with the better-known ballplayer of the same name who played for the rival Unions of Lansingburgh.

Colonel Alfred F. Lindley: A.F. Lindley was born in Yorkshire, England, around 1836, and came to New York when he was 14. He learned the tailoring trade and moved to Wappingers Falls, then moved to Poughkeepsie around 1861 to play for that city's cricket eleven. He served as a lieutenant in Ellsworth's Greys during the war, and later became a colonel in the 21st Regiment. Lindley played for the Hudson River Club from 1864 to 1867, years that he fondly recalled. He returned to Newburgh for the 1886 reunion game and, when he died in Brooklyn on January 22, 1894, an obituary mentioned his involvement with the club and described him as "one of its most zealous supporters."[42]

Albert Sidney Mapes: A. S. Mapes was the pitcher of the Hudson Rivers from 1861 to 1864. He became the club's secretary and starting left fielder in 1865 but died that winter. The club's new secretary wrote to Charles A. Peverelly, "Mapes was a great loss, both to efficiency of the nine, and to the welfare of the club. He was widely known as a ball-player, and was not to be excelled in his position by any one."

Charles Mapes: Charles H. Mapes was a partner in a Newburgh dry-goods firm until his partner bought him out. He later worked as a bookkeeper and in the auction and commission business, while also serving on the county board of health. Mapes was born on September 19, 1837, and died on November 6, 1920.

John Miller: John Miller was one of the Hudson River Club's mainstays from its first game until 1864 and remained a member of the second nine in 1865. Born in Newburgh on March 26, 1834, John Miller was descended from one of Newburgh's original settlers. After graduating from Yale University and being admitted to the bar, he became active in the volunteer fire department and was part of the first baseball club. He served as Superintendent of the Newburgh Free Schools and in many other civic capacities before moving to Cornwall-on-Hudson and returning to the private practice of law. When the club celebrated its fiftieth anniversary in 1909, he was the only surviving member of the original first nine. He died at his Cornwall-on-Hudson home on April 30, 1918. Three years earlier, an article in *Baseball Magazine* had reported that Miller was 100 years old, but in fact he was only 84 when he died.[43]

Samuel W. Miller: Samuel Miller was a younger brother of John Miller and was the only original Hudson River Club member to remain on the first nine after the Civil War. He and another brother, James, ran a Newburgh carpet store for many years, and it was there that the ball club held its meetings.[44] Around 1880 Samuel Miller headed west with his family and he was in Nebraska at the time of the 1886 reunion. As of 1910 he was living on a farm in Coffey County, Kansas.

William C. Miller: William C. Miller was club president from 1859 to 1863. He was born in 1817 in Jamaica, Long Island, and moved to Newburgh in 1835. There he taught school and became involved in civic affairs, serving for example as supervisor of the Newburgh Water Works and Superintendent of the Newburgh Almshouse. Even so, when he died in Newburgh on April 14, 1896, his involvement with the Hudson River Club was mentioned prominently in his obituary.[45]

Henry C. Millspaugh: H.C. Millspaugh joined the club in 1862 and remained a regular until at least 1867. He was born around 1845 in New York State and became an attorney and a justice of the peace. He was still in Newburgh in 1880 but had died by the time of the 1886 reunion. Despite his early death, "Hank" Millspaugh was still remembered half a century later for his tendency "to make so many foul hits into the potato patch on Miller Street."[46]

George W. Powell: He was the original catcher of the club, but didn't play for it after 1860. He has not been identified further.

S.B. Reeve: Reeve played for the Hudson River Club from its inception until 1863. There is an S. Belknap Reeve buried in Newburgh's Old Town Cemetery who died at the age of 25 on May 9, 1863, and this may be the man in question.

Captain Henry Robinson: Robinson was born around 1782 and was a sea captain who became a large Newburgh landowner after his retirement. He was credited with introducing the carp to America around 1831— he brought them over from France, bred them in his pond, and released them into the Hudson River. Robinson was also prominent in Newburgh's boating scene. In addition, he served as vice president of the Hudson River Base Ball Club in 1859 and 1860, though of course he did not play the game. He died on March 9, 1866, and part of his estate became the site of the county fair and of a later Newburgh baseball club.

David A. Scott: Born around 1827 in New York, David A. Scott served as club president from 1864 to 1866 but did not play in any match games. A lawyer, he was also surrogate of Orange County. He died in Newburgh on August 24, 1890.

E. Gerry Stevens: E. Gerry Stevens (the E seems to have stood for Elbridge, though it was sometimes spelled Eldrige or Eldridge) was born in New Hampshire around 1836 and played for the first nine in 1859 and 1860. He followed his father into the lumber business and became a well-known Newburgh merchant. He died in June of 1893.

Dr. Lendon S. Straw: L.S. Straw was born on January 22, 1825, in Hopkinton, New Hampshire. His father was a dentist and surgeon, but Lendon initially tried to make his fortune by going to California for the Gold Rush. After five years he returned to the East and followed his father into dentistry. He settled in Newburgh in 1857 and played for the first nine of the Hudson Rivers from 1859 to 1861. As late as 1865, he continued to play for the second nine. Straw died in Newburgh on October 9, 1899.[47]

Charles G. Waring: Early club member Charles Waring was born in New York around 1833 and worked as a painter.

James Evert Wilson: Evert Wilson was a heavy-hitting member of the first nine of the Hudson Rivers; a 1913 article recalled that he "always called for a very low ball, and when he got a fair swipe at it there was something doing, you can believe."[48] Wilson worked as a clerk in the commissary department at West Point and died in Newburgh on July 18, 1904, at the age of 58.

Other Members: Fred Banks, Conklin, W. Garrison, B.

Hanmore, Lansing, C. J. Lawson, Dr. George W. Leonard (this player has been incorrectly identified as Andy Leonard in some sources, but was in fact a local doctor),[49] George Little, John McDowell, James W. Miller (John Miller's brother, who was a member of the Newburghs and treasurer of the Hudson Rivers), Robert Moore, Willard M. Phillips, William L. Smith (played for the club in 1860 and was vice president in 1863 and 1864), George Sneed, John Vernol, B. Verplanck (also with the Highlands of New Windsor), Arthur Wilson, I. Wood, James Young.

SOURCES

This article is primarily based on a detailed history on pp. 328–329 of John J. Nutt's *Newburgh, Her Institutions, Industries and Leading Citizens: Historical, Descriptive and Biographical* (Newburgh, NY: Ritchie & Hull, 1891). Nutt's account is clearly based on the club's scorebooks, since a very similar recount of the club's history appeared in the *Newburgh Telegram* on March 13, 1909. In addition, many details from the club's "Game Keepers' Book" were reprinted in an article published in the *Sunday Telegram* on December 6, 1896. Also helpful were "When Newburgh Had Champion Ball Team," *Newburgh Journal*, October 12, 1912, 10; an entry in Charles A. Peverelly's *Book of American Pastimes* (which in turn was based upon a letter dated April 23, 1866, from club secretary Lewis B. Halsey); and a history by Patrick Mondout at the baseballchronology.com website. Other sources are cited in the notes.

NOTES

1. John J. Nutt's *Newburgh, Her Institutions, Industries and Leading Citizens: Historical, Descriptive and Biographical* (Newburgh, N.Y.: Ritchie & Hull, 1891), 328–329.
2. *Newburgh Sunday Telegram*, December 6, 1896.
3. Those men, according to Nutt's box score, were Straw, John Miller, King, Powell, and Reeve. At least two others, William Kelly and William Miller, would later represent the Hudson Rivers.
4. *Brooklyn Times*, August 30, 1860.
5. "The Oldest Baseball Insured," *Baseball Magazine*, October 1915, 65. This article was marred by numerous inaccuracies, stating that the match was won by the Eclipse Club and that Miller played for the Eclipse Club. It even reported that Miller, who was then 81, was 100 years old!
6. "When Newburgh Had Champion Ball Team," *Newburgh Journal*, October 12, 1912, 10. Fitzgerald was a major figure in early Philadelphia baseball whose contributions will be discussed in the second volume. His title of Colonel was a nickname, rather than a conferred rank.
7. "When Newburgh Had Champion Ball Team," *Newburgh Journal*, October 12, 1912, 10.
8. *Newburgh Daily Telegraph*, June 9, 1864.
9. *Newburgh Telegram*, November 13, 1909.
10. Ibid.
11. Ibid.
12. *Newburgh Sunday Telegram*, May 31, 1896.
13. As noted in the entry on the Unions of Lansingburgh, this game is not well documented and it is possible that Nutt misreported the year. It is also possible that the defeated club was a different Troy or Lansingburgh club, perhaps one of the predecessors of the Unions. But since Nutt had access to the club's scorebooks and the claim was repeated in the *Newburgh Telegram* on November 25, 1911, I am inclined to believe that it occurred in 1865.
14. *Poughkeepsie Eagle*, October 16, 1865.
15. Charles A. Peverelly, *The Book of American Pastimes* (New York, 1866), 448.
16. *Buffalo Courier and Republic*, undated clipping, c. August 19, 1866, Old Fulton Post Card website.
17. *Newburgh Sunday Telegram*, April 19, 1896.
18. *Newburgh Telegram*, November 13, 1909.
19. *Newburgh Journal*, reprinted in the *Oswego Times-Express*, May 21, 1886.
20. "Governors Day at the Orange County Fair: Some Notable Visits to Orange County," *Newburgh Journal*, August 31, 1912, 10–11.
21. *Newburgh Daily News*, September 30, 1886.
22. *Newburgh Sunday Telegram*, July 7, 1889.
23. *Newburgh Telegram*, November 13, 1909.
24. *Newburgh Telegram*, February 12, 1910.
25. *Newburgh Telegram*, February 1, 1913; *Newburgh Sunday Telegram*, July 7, 1889.
26. *Newburgh Sunday Telegram*, July 14, 1889.
27. *Newburgh Sunday Telegram*, July 7, 1889.
28. *Newburgh Telegram*, March 13, 1909.
29. *Newburgh Telegram*, February 1, 1913; clipping from an unidentified Troy paper, reprinted in the *Troy Northern Budget* and in turn in *Sporting News* on December 12, 1896, 6.
30. *Newburgh Telegram*, March 13, 1909.
31. *Newburgh Daily News*, September 20, 1886.
32. *Newburgh Daily News*, September 24, 1886.
33. *Newburgh Sunday Telegram*, July 7, 1889.
34. *Newburgh Telegram*, November 13, 1909.
35. *Sporting Life*, January 27, 1900.
36. *Newburgh Telegram*, November 25, 1911.
37. *Newburgh Telegram*, February 1, 1913.
38. *Newburgh News*, July 8, 1929.
39. *New York Clipper*, March 19, 1881.
40. *Newburgh Telegram*, November 5, 1910.
41. *Newburgh News*, June 22, 1931.
42. *Poughkeepsie Eagle*, January 23, 1894.
43. *Newburgh Telegram*, March 13, 1909; *Newburgh Daily News*, May 1, 1918; "The Oldest Baseball Insured," *Baseball Magazine*, October 1915, 65.
44. *Newburgh Journal*, October 12, 1912.
45. *Newburgh Sunday Telegram*, April 19, 1896.
46. *Newburgh News*, August 24, 1932.
47. *Newburgh Daily News*, October 10, 1899.
48. *Newburgh Telegram*, February 1, 1913.
49. *Newburgh Sunday Telegram*, April 24, 1898.

❖ *Victory Base Ball Club of Troy* (Peter Morris) ❖

CLUB HISTORY

The Victory Base Ball Club of Troy was organized on August 2, 1859, and at first it did not look like its members would be able to live up to their optimistic name. The club's first match game, played on September 9, resulted in a 39–29 loss to the Vanguard Club of Cohoes. It was followed eighteen days later by a 19–14 defeat at the hands of the Excelsior Club of West Troy.

But in October, the players showed a dramatic improvement. On the 1st, the Victory Club posted a convincing win over the Priam Club of Troy at a locale known as Weir's Course or Wier's Course. This site remained the home field of the Victory Club throughout its existence. Also used for cricket and for dog races, it appears to have been located on Lansingburgh Road in Troy's Tenth Ward and been affiliated with a hotel run by John A. Weir, but otherwise little is known about it. The Victory Club built upon its first win with a 30–15 triumph in a rematch against the Vanguards of Cohoes in front of a "large crowd of spectators" from Troy, Lansingburgh, and Cohoes, followed by a second lopsided win over the Priam Club.[1]

This set up a season-ending showdown in Greenbush against the undefeated Champion Club of Albany on October 26. As the big day approached, it stirred "unusual interest. Great preparations have been made by the Albany Club for the match; benches have been provided, and large numbers of the fair sex are expected to honor the occasion with their presence."[2] The game was played the fly rule, perhaps as a concession to the grounds, which were uneven and so inaccessible that a Troy reporter quipped that by the time the Victory Club finally reached the grounds, they were "humming, 'ain't I glad to get out of the wilderness.'"[3]

The game lived up to the anticipation, with the Victory Club pulling out a 29–26 triumph in six hard-fought innings. The papers of both cities cited numerous instances of the "gentlemanly conduct" of the two clubs, and the contest was followed by a shared meal at the Hudson River Depot's saloon and the customary cheers and speeches.[4]

No doubt these sentiments were genuine, but they were accompanied by signs that competitive fervor was starting to emerge. The contest was ended after six innings, and the decision seems to be mutual. Nonetheless, the newspapers of the respective cities had very different opinions of what would have happened had play continued. According to the *Troy Daily Whig*, "It was generally conceded that had the game been continued the Champions would have suffered more than they did."[5] Not so, maintained the *Albany Express*, which pointed out that the Victory Club seized a big lead in the first two innings, when the Champion Club was playing without two regulars, and that when the latecomers arrived the club from Albany steadily began to narrow the margin.[6]

The question of a rematch also produced contrasting viewpoints. An 1861 history of the Victory Club claimed that the nine had found "no other clubs in this vicinity with which to contend," and had therefore wrapped up the season at that point.[7] In fact, a rematch was agreed to immediately after the game.[8] But then it became clear that the Victory Club would be without three players — William Hegeman had had "one of his finger nails torn almost entirely off while practicing," Ben De La Vergne had "chopped off the end of his thumb" (presumably an injury sustained in his butcher's shop), and pitcher Edward Curtis had provided the "climax by unhinging his knee and knocking one of his finger joints out of kilter." The remaining healthy members concluded that they would be "unable to do themselves or the Club justice" and backed out.[9]

In 1859 the Victory Club had sported a fairly simple uniform consisting of "a blue cap, white shirt and red belt.[10] At some point, probably at the outset of the 1860 season, the club adopted a uniform consisting of "white flannel pants, with a blue cord up the seam; white flannel shirt, bound with blue, with a blue wreath in front, enclosing the letters 'Victory,' worked in blue; and a white cap, trimmed with blue."[11] The Victory Club kicked off the 1860 campaign by traveling some seventy miles to take on the Union Club of Whitehall on June 1. That contest produced an easy win, as did a follow-up against the Albany Club that was played in front of a crowd "numbering between four or five hundred" that included "delegations from the Champion, Beaverwycks, Tivoli and other clubs from Albany, Excelsior and Alert from West Troy, Union of Waterford, Van Guard of Cohoes, National of Lansingburgh, and several other clubs of this city."[12]

Then it was time for a July 3 showdown against the mighty Excelsior Club of Brooklyn, which was making a historic tour of the state. The big match, played in front of "quite one thousand spectators — many of them ladies," produced a loss for the Victory Club but earned them additional respect.[13] After falling behind 9–1 after two innings and failing to display "that confidence necessary to successful playing," pitcher Edward Curtis and catcher Ben Follett switched places with Hegeman and De La Vergne.[14] The change paid off, as the Excelsiors scored only four runs the rest of the game to six by the Victory, yielding a very creditable 13–7 final score.

At the conclusion of the match, both clubs adjourned to the Troy House for food and entertainment — "Speeches were made, songs were sung, and the best of feeling prevailed. Dr. Hegeman, on behalf of the Victory, presented the Excelsior Club with a ball and also a regulation bat, suitably inscribed."[15] While the visitors took home the trophy, the narrow margin of defeat was a significant moral victory for the Troy nine. Legendary Excelsior catcher Joe Leggett told De La Vergne "that he wondered that Troy had such a good club."[16] As a Utica paper put it, "The Victory Club gained high honors by giving the Excelsior Club of New York city the closest game they played during their trip through the State."[17] De La Vergne later maintained that the result was also a financial windfall for many Troy residents who accepted bets that the visitors would double the home team's score.[18]

Thereafter Hegeman and De La Vergne comprised the Victory Club's regular battery, and the remainder of the 1860 season saw the club continue its strong play. Over the next month, the club beat two different Champion Clubs — one from Yorkville and one from Albany — and also chalked up wins against the Beaverwyck Club of Albany, the Union Club of Whitehall, the Albany Club, and the Excelsior Club of West Troy. Late that summer, the club looked farther afield and traveled to Chatham, New York, and North Adams, Massachusetts, posting wins in both towns. Hegeman recalled the contest in Chatham with particular satisfaction: "When we went on the field they gave us a great laugh and thought evidently that the game was practically over. They were big fellows and prided themselves on their pitcher and catcher." Instead the Victory Club won 79–11 and the margin would have been worse except that Hegeman's men got so tired from circling the bases that he "directed them to allow themselves to be put out in order to bring the farce to a close."[19]

The Victory Club capped off the splendid season in the fall with four more wins, defeating the Excelsior Club of West Troy, the Champion Club of Albany, the Mohawk Club of Schenectady, and the Utica Base Ball Club. The final contest was considered an especially fine display of ball-playing. Despite the sun being "unfavorable for good fielding," the contest was tightly fought and ended with the Victory Club on the long end of an 18–14 score.[20] The exciting win was the fourteenth of the season, against only the one loss at the hands of the Excelsiors of Brooklyn. With understandable pride the *Troy Whig* boasted, "The Victorys are rather of the invincible order. They are without doubt the strongest club out of the Metropolis."[21]

Buoyed by their success in 1860, the members of the Victory Club proclaimed themselves "ready to accept all challenges" in the spring of 1861.[22] Alas, the outbreak of the Civil War meant that few if any challenges were forthcoming. According to Ben De La Vergne, however, the club did play in an Independence Day match that proved to be his final appearance for the Victory Club: "The last game I played was in July, 1861, at Saratoga. It was on the Fourth and was for a gold cup. I lived then in Greenwich, and at 'Doc' Hegeman's behest I went over. We won the cup. We got eighty odd runs and I don't remember how many the Saratoga fellows got. Oh, in those days, I'd walk twenty miles to play base ball."[23] But there are no contemporaneous accounts of the game, nor any indication that the Victory Club played any other match games in 1861.

The start of the Civil War created several gaps in the lineup of the Victory Club; according to Hegeman, "When that broke out it crippled us some, for the boys enlisted, some of them, and we became scattered."[24] But even in their "crippled" condition, the club forged on. Once warm weather came in 1862, the Victory Club re-formed and won a game against the Knickerbocker Club of Albany. The members also began talking about a tour that would take them to Utica, Syracuse, Oswego, Rochester, and Buffalo. But in the end the tour was cancelled for "various reasons," though there were hopes to do one next year.[25] When the club did play, it was not able to sustain its pre-war reputation for excellence. At a game in Albany on July 14, the Victory Club was defeated by the Knickerbockers of that city 74–35.[26] In September, the Utica Club visited Troy and beat the Victory Club 68–27, prompting a jubilant Utica reporter to suggest that "the members of the Troy Club concede the propriety of changing the name of their organization."[27]

In 1863, plans were made for a June 22 match in Saratoga against the Knickerbocker Club of Albany for a "massive silver cup." This could be the match mentioned in the 1897 article, but no contemporaneous account has yet been found. The Victory Club also apparently played a best-of-three series with the Utica Club, losing two to one. Over the balance of the Civil War there were stray references that suggested the club was still in existence, but no documentation of any match games.[28]

The Victory Base Ball Club of Troy came back to life after the war, though there were many changes in the lineup. In 1866 a slate of officers was elected that included pre-war president William H. Hegeman as vice president and Albert L. Hotchkin, who would go on to be associated with the "Haymakers" (see next entry) and with Troy's National League club, as president. The club played a match on August 1, 1866, against the Endeavor Club of Cohoes, but there is no record of additional activity.[29]

The club organized again in 1867, re-electing Hotchkin as president, along with Robert Green as vice president, George D. Smith as secretary and treasurer, and Hegeman, John MacDonald, L. G. Graves, R. B. Church and George Evans as directors.[30] By this time, the Haymakers were established as the premier local club, and the Victory Club again played sparingly. But the club did beat the Eurekas of Granville, the Griswolds of Lansingburgh, and the Unions of Cohoes to win the second division of a tournament held at the Rensselaer Park in October. All indications are that this tournament was the club's swan song, creating the irony that Troy's first amateur club closed its career by capturing a $200 prize.[31]

The Victory Base Ball Club of Troy thus was one of many clubs that survived the Civil War but could not match its pre-war success. As a result the club was soon forgotten by many, yet there were a few signs that the Victory Club had left a legacy.

The trophy balls won by the club served as one reminder of its glory days. Hegeman later recalled, "The Victory won a great many games and the balls were carefully kept for a long time. We had a case made for them and when we got so many that it wouldn't hold them we got a big basket. The trophies were given into the custody of Al. Hotchkin and he jealously guarded them until a fire destroyed them."[32]

Two of its most prominent members maintained that the Victory Club played a direct role in the rise of the Unions of Lansingburgh (aka Haymakers) to national prominence. According to De La Vergne, "The Victory Club furnished the best material the afterwards famous Haymakers had."[33] Hegeman similarly declared, "All or many of the Haymaker players were broken in in the games of the Victory club."[34] The claims cannot be confirmed by an examination of the rosters of the two clubs, which have almost no overlap. But perhaps the future Haymakers got tips and encouragement from the older club while learning the game, and at the very least the Victory Club helped to create the climate in which the post-war club thrived.

A final distinction was the Victory Club's association with a notable first: Catcher Ben De La Vergne was later credited by a couple of accounts with having been the first ballplayer to wear gloves.[35] While such a claim can never be definitively proven, there are no earlier claimants, and thus it seems likely that De La Vergne did indeed pioneer the use of this basic piece of fielding equipment.

Club Members

Edward Gansevoort Curtis: Edward Curtis, the Victory Club's initial pitcher, was a Brooklyn native who had been born on October 31, 1837, and had come to Troy to study engineering at Rensselaer Polytechnic Institute. He was a member of the Gansevoort family and a relative of author Herman Melville. After graduating, he moved to Washington and became an inspector of customs, where he died on January 29, 1918.

George J. Day: George J. Day, a local lawyer, served as secretary and treasurer of the Victory Club. Although about the same age as his fellow club members (born around 1838), he does not seem to have played on the first nine.

Benjamin De La Vergne: Ben De La Vergne was the catcher of the Victory Club and, while few observers could remember how to spell his name, his play left an impression. One reporter raved, "DELAVAGE of the Troy Club, showed himself a very superior catcher, and the most powerful batter of the game. He also did well at running the bases — in fact as good a player, altogether as we ever saw."[36] Several decades later, he was credited in a couple of accounts with introducing gloves to baseball. De La Vergne's accomplishments are all the more impressive considering that he was already 40 when the Victory Club was formed. A butcher by trade, De La Vergne moved to Greenwich in 1860, thus ending his connection with the Victory Club. But he eventually returned to Troy, and in 1896 he provided his reminiscences about his ballplaying days. He died in Troy on April 23, 1901, at the age of eighty-two.[37]

Benjamin Franklin Follett: Ben Follett was born on December 22, 1840, in Batavia, New York, where his father was a newspaper editor who had fought in Texas alongside Sam Houston. He moved to Troy to work as a telegraph operator, and in 1859 his play caused him to be recognized as "one of the best players" on the Priam Club.[38] He joined the Victory Club in 1860, playing third base and serving as club vice president. But like his father, the Southwest soon beckoned, and he moved to Colorado to go into mining. He died there on March 25, 1914.

Robert Green: Robert Green was an active member of the club. The only man in Troy who seems likely is a sugar maker who was born in 1840 in England.

Dr. William Henry Hegeman: William H. "Doc" Hegeman, the president and pitcher of the Victory Club, was born on February 20, 1828, on a farm in nearby Sand Lake. After graduating from New York University Medical College in 1850, he moved to Troy and became the physician at the local jail. He then became sheriff and then a lawyer, but after the Civil War he returned to farming in North Greenbush. Even then he remembered his baseball days fondly, as in 1896 he reminisced about his role in the formation of Troy's first baseball club. He died on February 12, 1906.

Albert Leet Hotchkin: See Union of Lansingburgh (Troy Haymakers).

John A. MacDonald: John MacDonald, the club's second baseman and treasurer, was born in January of 1842. He became successful in the insurance and real estate businesses. He and his wife Helen were still living in Troy in 1910, but he seems to have died soon afterward. His connection with the Haymakers is discussed in that club's entry.

William Martin: William "Billy" Martin was born in New York state around 1838. He became the janitor of the Troy City Hall, and he and his wife raised fourteen children, at least nine of whom lived to adulthood.

J. D. Parker: J. D. Parker was described as club captain in one 1859 game account (though another listed Hegeman as the captain). It is not clear that he played for the first nine again.

George Henry Sagendorf: Shortstop George H. Sagendorf was born around 1838 and worked for the Mutual National Bank of Troy for many years. He died at the Chalfonte Hotel in Atlantic City on May 14, 1894.

Irvin M. Wickwire: First baseman Irvin Wickwire was born in Troy on July 5, 1838. During one of the Victory Club's games, he was counseled by a reporter to "remember that the umpire's decision is final and that swearing is contrary to the rules of order."[39] He worked as a theatrical agent and died in Troy on March 31, 1898.

Other Members: J. Adams, A. Anthony, Crombie, G. Evans, Daniel W. Ford, McKerrie, I. T. McKoun, Jr., A. Robinson, O. Stewart Warren, E. B. Wood.

Sources

A detailed history of the club in *Wilkes' Spirit of the Times*, May 4, 1861; "Pre-Civil-War Base Ball Games Played in the Capitol Area of New York State," Craig B. Waff's compilation of games on the Retrosheet website; a series of articles about Troy's baseball history that were published in the *Troy Northern Budget* in 1896 and were reprinted in *Sporting News* that winter (see sources section of Union of Lansingburgh entry for details); contemporaneous coverage, as noted.

Notes

1. *Troy Daily Whig*, October 12, 1859, 3.
2. *Troy Daily Whig*, October 26, 1859, 3.

3. *Troy Daily Whig*, October 27, 1859, 3.
4. *Ibid.*, and October 28, 1859, 3.
5. *Troy Daily Whig*, October 27, 1859, 3.
6. Reprinted in the *Troy Daily Whig*, October 28, 1859, 3.
7. *Wilkes' Spirit of the Times*, May 4, 1861.
8. *Albany Express*, reprinted in the *Troy Daily Whig*, October 28, 1859, 3.
9. *Troy Daily Whig*, November 1, 3, and October 27, 1859, 3.
10. *Troy Daily Whig*, September 28, 1859, 3.
11. *Wilkes' Spirit of the Times*, May 4, 1861.
12. *Troy Daily Whig*, July 2, 1860, 3.
13. "Local Matters: Exciting Base Ball Match," *Troy Daily Whig*, July 4, 1860, 3.
14. "A Base Ball Pioneer," *Troy Northern Budget*, May 24, 1896, 8; "Victorious Victorys," *Troy Northern Budget*, June 7, 1896, 9.
15. "Local Matters: Exciting Base Ball Match," *Troy Daily Whig*, July 4, 1860, 3.
16. "Victorious Victorys," *Troy Northern Budget*, June 7, 1896, 9.
17. *Utica Morning Herald and Daily Gazette*, October 30, 1860.
18. "Victorious Victorys," *Troy Northern Budget*, June 7, 1896, 9.
19. "A Base Ball Pioneer," *Troy Northern Budget*, May 24, 1896, 8.
20. *Utica Morning Herald and Daily Gazette*, October 31, 1860.
21. *Troy Daily Whig*, July 25, 1860, 3.
22. *Wilkes' Spirit of the Times*, May 4, 1861.
23. "Victorious Victorys," *Troy Northern Budget*, June 7, 1896, 9.
24. "A Base Ball Pioneer," *Troy Northern Budget*, May 24, 1896, 8.
25. *Utica Daily Observer*, July 2, 1862.
26. *New York Tribune*, July 16, 1862.
27. *Utica Daily Observer*, September 26, 1862.
28. *Utica Morning Herald and Daily Gazette*, August 30, 1864.
29. *Troy Press*, August 10, 1866.
30. *Troy Northern Budget*, reprinted in *Sporting News* on December 12, 1896, 6.
31. *Troy Northern Budget*, October 20, 1867; reprinted in "A Base Ball Pioneer," *Troy Northern Budget*, May 24, 1896, 8. The first "division" was reserved for the "Haymakers" and the Atlantics of Brooklyn, which played a single match.
32. "A Base Ball Pioneer," *Troy Northern Budget*, May 24, 1896, 8.
33. "Victorious Victorys," *Troy Northern Budget*, June 7, 1896, 9.
34. "A Base Ball Pioneer," *Troy Northern Budget*, May 24, 1896, 8.
35. *Sporting News*, June 28, 1886; *Detroit Free Press*, May 17, 1887.
36. *Utica Morning Herald and Daily Gazette*, October 31, 1860.
37. For additional details, see my profile of De La Vergne for the SABR BioProject (*http://bioproj.sabr.org/bioproj.cfm?a=v&v=1&bid=3180&pid=19718*).
38. *Troy Daily Whig*, October 15, 1859, 3.
39. *Utica Morning Herald and Daily Gazette*, October 31, 1860.

❖ *Unions of Lansingburgh (Troy "Haymakers")* (Peter Morris) ❖

CLUB HISTORY

The Union Base Ball Club of Lansingburgh, New York, was one of the most extraordinary clubs of the post-war era and should have brought fame to its hometown, which was then an independent village five miles north of Troy. Instead it became better known by the nickname of the "Haymakers of Troy"—just as Lansingburgh itself would eventually be swallowed up and renamed North Troy. Similarly, the legends that still surround this club have obscured and distorted a far more compelling story of triumph and tragedy.

There are different accounts of when this club got started. Several sources state that it was formed in April of 1861 when the National Club of Lansingburgh and the Priam Club of Troy combined to create the Union Base Ball Club of Rensselaer County. Yet since few if any of the players on this club were the ones who became famous after the war, it is debatable whether this was the same club. The members themselves appear not to have thought so, as the by-laws of the postwar club dated the origin to August 15, 1866.[1] Yet this date is also problematic, since it comes after the club's first major victory. Meanwhile, William Ryczek states that the club began play in July of 1866, while another source reports that the club played a match game on July 4, 1865.[2]

In any event, it was in 1866 that the Union Club of Lansingburgh began play in earnest. The club's first nine that season was a mix of players from Lansingburgh and Troy—Thomas Abrams, Andrew McQuide, Peter McKeon, James Ward, Bub McAtee, and Stephen King from Lansingburgh and Cal Penfield, William H. Craver, and "Sonny" Leavenworth from Troy. Penfield later revealed that he had been playing for such Troy clubs as the Putnam and the Enterprise since 1864, but his love for the game was such that he tried to "wriggle into a place" on another local club whenever those clubs had a day off.

On an afternoon "when the Putnam and Enterprise were both resting Cal. took a stroll up to Lansingburg to see the Unions of that town at practice. Their field was on 'The Green,' north of Twelfth street and near Third avenue, and when the young Troy third baseman got there the Union boys were hard at work. Lansingburgers were base ball mad in those days and a big crowd watched the practice and criticized the plays. Among the observers was [club director] James McQuide, who understood the game thoroughly and took a great interest in the Unions. He recognized Cal, and said to him: 'We're going to have a pretty smart set of New Yorkers up here to-morrow and we'd like to make a good showing, will you come up and play?' 'Why, yes,' said Cal., 'and I'll bring Craver and Sonny Leavenworth too, if you want us.' 'Why, yes,' Mr. McQuide answered, 'bring them along.'"[3]

Even before the additions of Penfield, Craver and Leavenworth, the Union Club had started to make a name for itself. According to an 1896 retrospective, one of the club's first recorded contests was a 146–9 slaughter of the misnamed Champions of West Troy. It took the vanquished Champions "months to recover from the shock.... That score was the talk of both sides of the river for days, and even now it is referred to occasionally by old-time lovers of the game." The Unions showed no more mercy on other local opposition, demolishing the Ancient Citys of Schenectady 107–2 and trouncing a club from Cohoes by a 127–8 margin.[4]

The addition of the three Troy players further strengthened the lineup of the Unions, and the club posted two impressive wins over out-of-state rivals. In the first contest, the Unions beat the visiting Bergen (New Jersey) Club, with the result that, "Everybody in and around Troy began to talk about the Unions." The club next traveled to Williamstown, Massachusetts, to face the Williams College nine, and it was this game in which the Union Club's longstanding image as rural hayseeds first appeared. Before the contest, the college players "believed that they would have a 'soft time' defeating the countrymen, as they were called." Instead the visitors won handily, and then telegraphed the results back home, where "everybody in the village and surrounding country was base ball mad. When the Unions returned in the evening they were met at the depot by a drum corps and escorted to Campbell's Hotel, where a banquet was served and a reception held. The Unions were the hero of the hour."[5]

Plans now began to arrange a contest between the upstarts from Lansingburgh and the national powerhouses in Brooklyn and New York City. A subscription fund was started, and there was soon enough money to send the club down river to face the best clubs the big city had to offer. It was probably around this time that the club elected officers, with local dentist S. P. Welch serving as president of a board of directors that included James McQuide, Thomas H. Morgan, Charles S. Holmes, and William W. Lee.[6]

On the evening of August 7, 1866, many local baseball enthusiasts made their way to the dock to wish the members of the Union Club well as they boarded the steamer Francis Skiddy and headed for New York. On the next afternoon they faced the mighty Atlantics on the famed Capitoline grounds. The contest was close during the early innings, but then Union pitcher Andrew McQuide was hit by a line drive and injured. The Atlantics hit his offerings with ease after that, winning 46–11.[7]

Despite the disappointing outcome, the match with the Atlantics was credited with originating two of the enduring legends that came to be associated with the Lansingburgh club. The visiting players found that they "could not run the bases and slide on the clay ground well in their common shoes, and they had never seen base ball shoes with spikes at that time, and before the game had progressed far the Union players took off their shoes and stockings and rolled up their pants and played in their bare feet. 'Just see the Haymakers,' were the exclamations from all sides, and from this remark according to one version the team derived its name of 'Haymakers.'"[8]

Cal Penfield offered a different version of the origin of the famous nickname. As he told it, when the visiting players got ready to take the field against the Atlantics that day, catcher William Craver hollered, "Now you hay rakers, get out there and see what you can do." A reporter misheard "hay rakers" as "haymakers," repeated the mistake in his account of the game, and the new name stuck.[9]

The play of the Union Club had made quite an impression on the members of the Atlantics, especially the work of the outfielders, of catcher Craver, and of pitcher McQuide. So they let the players from Lansingburgh borrow their spiked shoes for their next match, played in Hoboken two days later against the Mutual Club of New York City. The unfamiliarity of the new shoes made them a hindrance at times, but the players soon adjusted.

With two out in the ninth inning, the upstarts from Lansingburgh were clinging to a 15–13 lead. According to Penfield, the final Mutuals batter hit a towering pop fly that descended toward pitcher Andrew McQuide, as "we all circled around him. He fumbled and it bounded into McAtee's hands. Mac fumbled and I grabbed it and clutched it tight." Three decades later, the ball from that game, now gilded and bearing a suitable inscription, was still hanging in Penfield's hotel.[10]

The defeat of the celebrated Mutuals by an unknown "country club" shocked the baseball world.[11] Meanwhile the victorious players were hailed as heroes, being met by a band and a large crowd when they arrived home. A second banquet soon followed.[12]

After a few weeks of being "subjected to pretty severe criticism" over the stunning upset, the Mutuals traveled to Troy to exact revenge. Their hosts met their boat in Albany and escorted them to the ball grounds on a meadow between Troy and Lansingburgh. The Mutuals ran up nine runs in their first at bat and then shut out the Union Club. But the home side rallied, and by the end of the game the new club had again beaten the Mutuals by a 32–18 score. One local journalist recorded that "the 'country boys' and their best of friends were in high glee at the result, while the New Yorkers were decidedly chop-fallen."[13]

It appears that the club also defeated the National Club of Albany to capture the silver ball that was emblematic of regional supremacy.[14] But that win and a few more trouncings of overmatched local rivals seem to have been all that the Union Club of Lansingburgh played in 1866 after the two upsets of the Mutuals.[15]

While the next three years would bring many changes and a nickname by which the club became universally known, in many ways the defining characteristics of the club would remain constant. The "Haymakers" would become known for their ability to pull stunning upsets (especially of the Mutuals), for the unpredictability of their results, and for the legends and rumors that would always swirl around them, often overshadowing their performances on the field.

A perfect example is the variety of accounts that sprung up about how the club acquired its famous nickname. An unidentified former resident of Troy, quoted in the *Chicago Daily News* around 1924, gave this explanation: "Shortly after the visit to New York the Mutual club came to Troy for a game, riding from New York to Troy on a night boat. A friend of the Troy team asked the captain of the Mutuals whom they were to play, and he replied: 'Oh, a lot of haymakers.' This was told the Troy players and when the Mutuals came to the field that afternoon for the game they saw displayed on a flag pole a white flag, in the center of which was a large yellow sheaf with a sickle stuck through it and underneath the word 'Haymakers.' The Mutuals were given a trimming that day and thereafter the name of Haymakers stuck to the Troy team."[16]

As this account implies, the club members seem to have made a conscious decision to embrace this nickname and the images associated with it. At some point the club adopted a logo that showed two rakes and a bale of hay, along with the words "Hay Makers" and "Lansingburgh, N. Y."[17] In one picture of the players, two hayforks are prominently displayed beside their sides. As a result, new tales continued to emerge, some of which seem to be based in fact while others appear exaggerated or fictitious.

Jack Chapman of the Atlantics of Brooklyn, for instance, later told of how the players stayed at the Grand Central Hotel in Manhattan on one of their visits to New York and "started out early in the morning, dressed in their new baseball uniforms, causing a good deal of amusement among the people on Broadway. Despite their verdancy, the Haymakers had a strong team and they made the older clubs hustle to defeat them."[18] The association of the club with such rural imagery became commonplace, and in 1868 a national magazine explained to readers, "The nickname 'Haymakers' belongs to the Union Club of Lansingburg, N.Y. The fact that many of the nine are well-posted in this branch of farm-work is the probable cause of this name being applied to them."[19]

Accounts like these turned into legends, and in 1887 an especially picturesque description of one of the club's upsets of the Mutuals appeared. The game in question was played in New York, and according to this version, "an old-fashioned hayrick was driven up to the players' gate, and ten men got out and came through that gate. When they got on the ground the crowd laughed till it cried. The team was composed of nine six-footers, who wore blue jean pants and shirts. The pants were rolled up to the knees and the bare legs and feet looked tough as leather. On their hands they wore big straw hats, and in their hands they carried hay rakes. Oh! How that crowd did laugh. Ladies had hysterics and strong men cried, laughing at the ludicrous sight. The visitors took it all in good part, and paid attention to business. The game was called and the Haymakers piled up their rakes and picked out a bundle of small hickory saplings they had brought from home, each man had a stout bat."[20]

There is of course no way to definitively disentangle truth from fiction in such accounts. The members of the club were most definitely not rural hayseeds, and if they indeed brought rakes to New York with them, it was part of an image they deliberately cultivated. At least one contemporaneous account seems to imply that the farm implements were a publicity device. This account was given of a visit to Cleveland: "Shortly after two o'clock the makers of hay, in a metaphorical sense, left the Weddell House in a large wagon, and, shortly before three reached the grounds, singing the 'song of the haymakers' as they entered the gate. They were greeted with enthusiastic applause. Their trim, gentlemanly appearance, as they leaped nimbly from the vehicle, elicited the warmest expressions of admiration. Their uniform, with the exception of their caps, which are of a bright red color, is similar to that of the Forest City. The pants and shirt are white, with the monogram 'H' upon the breast, and the stockings blue."[21]

In fact, the players were raised in Lansingburgh or Troy. Yet while these men had not grown up on remote country farms, it is important to remember that many residents of midsize towns and cities were still involved in agriculture. For example, Joseph King, the father of two of the club's outfielders, Mart and Steve, owned a large estate in Lansingburgh and usually described himself as a gardener, but seems to have essentially been a farmer.

The image of the club playing barefooted also recurred. Journalist W. W. Aulick later maintained that when Mart King joined the club he surveyed his new teammates and scornfully pronounced them "Dudes." The other players were deeply insulted by this "fighting word," but Mart was insistent. "Why the cap?" he demanded. "It'll make you bald if you keep on wearing it — it will, sure's you're a foot high. Whaffor the shoes? Don't you know they'll send you to the chirop's? Sure they will. Can all that soft stuff." He threw his cap and shoes aside and, according to Aulick, his new teammates followed his lead by playing barefooted and bareheaded in their next game.[22]

Even assuming this to be true, it appears that the other players soon went back to wearing caps and shoes. By 1869, the club had donned "very becoming" knickerbocker-style uniforms that included a white flannel shirt emblazoned with the letter "U" in old English text, white corduroy knee-breeches, blue stockings, red belts, and scull-caps.[23] Even Mart King, according to Aulick, began wearing shoes and a cap after joining Chicago — though only because club management insisted.

Another intriguing and difficult-to-resolve question about the club's name is why Lansingburgh was replaced by Troy. One explanation is that the change took place against the will of the membership and was the result of the national press failing to distinguish between the two adjoining towns. This was the view of Warren Broderick, a twentieth-century Lansingburgh historian who maintained that "there was a rivalry over the ball club between Troy and Lansingburgh.... Actually most of the players were from Lansingburgh and the games were played in the 'Burgh' but Troy claimed the team because of its success."[24] And Broderick's contention is supported by the club's logo, which contained the words "Hay Makers" and

"Lansingburgh, N.Y.," and by the 1868 printed constitution, which includes the nickname "Haymakers" alongside the proper name of "Union Base Ball Club of Lansingburgh, N.Y." on the title page but does not have the word "Troy" anywhere.

Yet this is not the whole story. Troy featured several clubs of its own in the immediate aftermath of the Civil War, most notably the Victory Club. But the emergence of the Union Club caused the Troy clubs to disband or scale back and men who had supported these clubs became associated with the Lansingburgh club instead. According to the former Troy resident quoted by the *Chicago Daily News*, "The business men of Troy became interested and furnished the expense money" for the tours of the Union Club and for their first uniform (which was blue "with an American shield on the breast").[25] While it is always difficult to tell who was making the club's decisions at any point, men from Troy did become more prominent in the club's officers over time.

Thus it seems that some sort of tacit agreement was reached by which the players accepted being billed as representatives of Troy in exchange for financial support from the businessmen of the larger city. But if so, not everyone in Lansingburgh was happy with the arrangement. "The Haymakers of Lansingburgh are looked upon by Trojans as a home institution," complained the *Lansingburgh Budget*. "We were aware that some people always looked upon many good things as their own. A slight difference of opinion between such lookers on and actual owners has necessitated courts, police officers, and penitentiaries."[26]

It is especially difficult to tell who was making decisions for the club in the spring of 1867. Thomas Abrams was described as the club's original captain in his obituary, but other sources credited William Craver with playing this role, while by the spring of 1868 Michael "Bub" McAtee was listed as the captain.[27] Whoever was in charge faced a number of crucial choices to make, most notably in picking a first nine.

Shortly after the close of the 1866 season, the first of many tragedies had occurred when pitcher Andrew McQuide was killed in a railroad accident. Replacing McQuide was a dilemma because, while Lansingburgh produced an abundant supply of talent, none of those players had pitching experience. In addition, there were rumors that Craver and other stars would leave town to join one of New York's covertly professional clubs. Eventually, Abrams was chosen as pitcher (even though he had never pitched before) and the other players agreed to remain, while Mart King joined the first nine and "Clipper" Flynn of Lansingburgh became the tenth man.

Other crucial decisions were also made in the spring of 1867. Intriguingly, although the club was still entirely made up of local players, the choices seem clearly designed to position it as a national power. In particular, the club showed little interest in competing against rivals from nearby towns and apparently forfeited the silver ball by declining to accept challenges. "It will be remembered," sniffed a note in a local paper, "that the Unions played for the 'silver ball' with [the Nationals of Albany] last year and won it by one run, but that ball is almost too expensive to keep for the reason that every club that holds it is obliged to go to Poughkeepsie to play for it when challenged."[28]

Thus the club played little in the unseasonably cold spring of 1867 and instead husbanded its resources. Games in 1866 had been played on either the Village Green (between 112th and 113th Streets) or on a plot known as Vail's lot (on Second Avenue between what became 104th and 105th Streets).[29] The latter site was superior, so it was a windfall when the owner agreed to allow it to be used for baseball games again. According to an account in a local paper, "The members of the Union Club are highly elated in view of their good fortune in securing the field used for the playing of games last year, containing about eight acres. The two lots directly south had been rented for the season, but the premises latterly secured are far more desirable for ball playing purposes. The organization feels extremely grateful to Hon. George Vail, the owner, who has kindly tendered his ground without the least charge."[30]

Other efforts were also being made to raise funds to support the club. In July, readers of the *Lansingburgh Gazette* were urged, "Don't forget the base ball picnic at Lansing's Grove this afternoon and evening.... Sullivan's Band had been engaged, and all who love to trip the 'light fantastic toe' will have a chance of doing so to their heart's content. For the accommodation of their Troy friends, two cars will leave for that city after the close of the picnic. The Proceeds of this entertainment will be to the Champion Nine. Go one! Go all!"[31] Residents of Troy and Lansingburgh were also urged to regard baseball as a highly respectable activity, with one game account noting that "representatives were present on this occasion from the bench, the bar and the pulpit, as well as the counting house, the manufactory and the exchange."[32]

With the "spirit of base ball ... rampant in the town and its vicinity," the month of July brought two exciting contests to Vail's Lot. On Independence Day the Hudson Rivers of Newburgh were the visitors, and for much of the afternoon it looked as if a huge crowd estimated at 4,000 would go home disappointed. The Unions trailed 23–11 after six innings, but then staged an impressive rally, scoring eighteen runs in the final three innings and blanking their opponents each time amid a frenzy of shouting, applause, and waving of hats and handkerchiefs.[33]

Five days later, another "immense concourse of citizens ... probably 5,000 of both sexes, young and old" showed up at Vail's Lot: "The field presented a fine sight. Surrounding the players at right angles were three or four lines of spectators, the variegated colors of the dresses of the ladies imparting a holiday appearance to the scene, and back of these, numerous carriages, filled with visitors, took their position. Every eye was turned upon the game, and throughout the entire play, although at times rain fell quite smartly, and threatened each moment to come down with tremendous force, each and every visitor kept his or her standpoint of observation until the game closed."

The visitors also carried the nickname of Union Club, but they hailed from Morrisania, a town that would become part of the Bronx seven years later. Much was made of the contrast between the sizes of the metropolitan regions represented, with the visitors "facetiously" referring to their opponents as the "Haymakers." But if they expected an easy win, they were swiftly set right, as the home team opened with a batting streak that prompted members of the visiting party to moan, "that batting will beat us; it is the most tremendous we ever saw." When the match ended with the Lansingburgh nine on the long end of a 51–23 score, visiting club president Thomas Sutton presented the trophy ball with a "neat speech, in which he said this was the worst defeat his club had ever sustained."[34]

The end of the month, however, brought the first defection when "Sonny" Leavenworth, "accepted a position as a member of the Mutual Club of New York, at a salary of $100 per month." Worse, a local journalist suggested that Leavenworth's departure was the result of a power struggle that threatened to tear the club apart. "Other members of the Union organization," he wrote ominously, "express themselves as being dissatisfied with the way matters are managed, and one or two more will probably retire from the conquerors. We earnestly hope that the present organization will be maintained, and that the disaffected will become reconciled, and in the future as in the past will work harmoniously. The Union Club is now in a way to attain great celebrity; and if successful in the contest with the Athletic Club, it will stand at the head of all baseball organizations in the country. We hope each member will be willing to waive some points of difference for the sake of the 'general good.'"[35]

But Leavenworth felt immediately uncomfortable with the Mutuals, and within days he "returned to the 'burgh and was soon again in full communion with his old club and 'the champion nine was again a unit.'"[36] He was just in time to help the Unions to another impressive win over the Eurekas of Newark in front of an enormous crowd that began arriving two and a half hours before the game and kept growing, as "Every car in the Lansingburgh road was crowded to its utmost capacity, and a large number of carriages were on the ground, filled with eager and interested spectators."[37]

The first nine remained together for the rest of the year and posted some impressive victories, including another win over the Unions of Morrisania, the club that would end the year as the official national champions.[38] Far and away the most dramatic win came against the Nationals of Washington, the celebrated club that had just completed a historic tour of the South and Midwest. The Nationals held a commanding 15–7 lead after eight innings, but the Unions staged an extraordinary nine-run ninth-inning rally and shut out the Nationals in their half of the ninth for a 16–15 win.[39]

But the 1867 season also witnessed several lopsided defeats, showing that the "Haymakers" still lagged a bit behind the Atlantics of Brooklyn and the Athletics of Philadelphia—the two clubs that, despite the official recognition of the Unions of Morrisania, were generally regarded as the country's best nines. There were also signs of the perplexing inconsistency that would become a trademark of the Haymakers—for example, a 39–7 loss to the Irvingtons was followed two weeks later by a 28–9 win over the same club. Similarly, a contest against the Hampden Club of Springfield saw the Haymakers fritter away a large lead by playing in a "don't-care-whether-I-work-or not" fashion, only to rally and pull out the win.[40]

Several tweaks to the lineup were made in 1868, a season that also saw the club move its home games to Rensselaer Park, a forty-two acre horse park now bounded by 108th and 110th Streets and by 5th and 9th Avenues.[41] The club again changed pitchers, with Abrams becoming tenth man. It was initially reported that a mysterious man named Slattery would handle the pitching duties, but instead they went to Rafael Julián de la Rúa, a Cuban studying at Rensselaer Polytechnic Institute. Also joining the club was first baseman "Allie" Davis of Utica, who replaced Leavenworth.

In September, Davis returned to Utica and word also came that "Rua will retire." McAtee moved from shortstop to first base to replace Davis, with Eugene Bonker filling McAtee's old place. Meanwhile, Rúa was replaced by Charles Bierman, previously of the Mutuals of New York. According to the intriguingly worded note that announced the departures of Davis and Rúa, "An effort is now being made to secure Baerman [sic], of the New York Mutuals, as pitcher. He is already a member of the club, having been elected three or four weeks ago."[42] It thus seems likely that Bierman was the club's first imported professional.

With this modified lineup, the club that was now becoming universally known as the "Haymakers" again posted many impressive victories during the 1868 season, highlighted by two more wins in three contests with the Mutuals. Under the deeply flawed method of determining a champion the Mutuals were recognized as the national champion at the end of the 1868 season, making it the second straight year that the club that had originated in Lansingburgh had posted two wins over the nine eventually crowned as champion. One of those triumphs was a 48–11 shellacking at Rensselaer Park that led a local paper the next day to write: "The Haymakers never appeared to better advantage in any game which they have played." Three decades later Mart King also singled out that game as a highlight.[43]

But once again the Haymakers came up short in 1868 when matched against the Athletics, the Atlantics, and a new contender for national supremacy—the "Red Stockings" of Cincinnati. Despite these setbacks, it was an extremely impressive performance for a club composed almost entirely of homegrown talent at a time when the other national contenders were becoming increasingly reliant on imports.

The 1869 season saw the beginning of open professional play, and the "Haymakers" were one of the clubs that opted to be billed as professionals. Yet another new pitcher was brought in—hard-throwing and hard-drinking "Cherokee" Fisher of Philadelphia, who was the club's first imported professional if that distinction had not already been claimed by Bierman or another earlier player. Bierman was also retained, playing second base most of the time and sometimes spelling Fisher. Another new arrival was third baseman Estevan "Steve" Bellán, another Cuban college student who had played for the Unions of Morrisania in 1868. The club also changed grounds yet again in 1869, moving to an area south of Lansingburgh known as Batestown or North Troy. The new ball field was extensively renovated and renamed the Union Grounds in what may have been a last effort to remind outsiders of the club's real origins.[44]

Despite these additions, the club's new incarnation retained far more hometown flavor than many rivals. While the famed "Red Stockings" featured only one Cincinnati native, the first nine of the 1869 "Haymakers" still featured William Craver of Troy and four Lansingburgh natives, McAtee, Flynn, and the King brothers, with Abrams again serving as tenth man. Even the club's other new player, shortstop Mike Powers, hailed from Utica.

On the field, 1869 proved another successful one for the club. Its extraordinary record of triumphs over the Mutuals continued with two more victories, and the second one in early July would have made the Haymakers the official national champions had not the Mutuals had been dethroned a few days earlier. The club also managed two wins and a tie in four contests against the mighty Atlantics of Brooklyn.

But there were also eight defeats, and one of these, at the hands of the amateur Pastime Club of Baltimore, raised eyebrows. The surprise turned to suspicion when the Haymakers rebounded the next day and beat the more highly regarded Maryland Club. A national publication for children informed its readers,

> The Haymaker Club, of Troy, N.Y., are again in disgrace. During their late western and southern tour they arranged to play the Pastime and Maryland Clubs, of Baltimore. The former is but an ordinary skilful nine, while the latter are the recognized champions in their district. The Haymakers played the Pastimes first, and, to the suprise [sic] of every one, were defeated. If the Pastimes could beat them easily, what would not the Marylands do? Yet, in their game with the latter, the Haymakers won by a score of nearly two to one. This set folks to thinking, and it was discovered that the Haymakers had purposely let the Pastimes defeat them, in order that their crowd might profit by the confidence of the friends of the Maryland Club, who were backed to win, and thus enable them to win large sums of money in bets. This base action of the Haymakers is denounced on every hand, and has lowered that club still farther in the estimation of all true lovers of the game. It is by such actions of the professional clubs that our national game is rapidly acquiring a bad name; and if such a course is persisted in, it will soon be placed on a par with horse-racing, and sports of that description. We trust our young friends, when they play base ball, play it fairly and honorably, satisfied to let all dishonorable conduct rest with professional clubs.[45]

There is of course no way to prove that a game was *not* fixed, and the associations between the Haymakers and gamblers created an atmosphere in which such rumors would flourish. Yet in context, there is nothing about the loss to the Pastime Club that looks suspicious. The Pastimes had gotten off to a slow start that season, including a lopsided loss to the Marylands that created the appearance of being weak. But the Pastimes improved dramatically as the season went on and had several impressive results in September, such as a win over the Marylands and a close loss to Philadelphia's mighty Athletics. It was simply the misfortune of the Haymakers to play the Pastime Club before its true strength was recognized.

Similarly, the greatest accomplishment of the Haymakers in 1869 was obscured by rumors and controversy. The Red Stockings of Cincinnati were the dominant club of 1869, and the fact that they were not the official national champion was just a reflection that the Brooklyn and New York City clubs scheduled matches in such a way as to make it all but impossible for the title to leave the area. The irrelevance of the official national championship became clear when the Red Stockings took on all comers that season, including all of the top New York clubs, without losing a single game.

But while the Red Stockings were undefeated in 1869, their record was not unblemished. They faced the Haymakers in Troy early in the season and squeaked out a narrow victory. The two sides met again in Cincinnati on August 26, and the rematch came to an abrupt end when the Haymakers marched off the field with the score tied at 17–17. Efforts to get them to return were unsuccessful, so the umpire declared the game forfeited to the home side. The NABBP, however, later ruled the game a tie, and that was also how Red Stockings manager Harry Wright regarded the contest.

The impetus for the Haymakers' withdrawal from the field was a ruling by umpire John Brockway that catcher William Craver had not caught a foul tip.[46] But this issue soon became lost amid a flurry of charges and countercharges, many of them very far-fetched indeed. Eventually a consensus emerged that the Haymakers had left the field to protect the betting interests of John Morrissey and other supporters, while the Red Stockings were innocent victims.[47]

There is no way to definitively sort out such a controversy, but it is important to point out that this version of events is very one-sided. It overlooks, for example, that even Brockway's defenders conceded that the play was a close one, while many observers were convinced that the call made by the umpire, a Cincinnati native, was wrong. The portrayal of the Haymakers as the bad guys also conveniently leaves out the fact that the players were the victims of vicious assaults after the game.

Since the home club's side of the story has been told so often, it is worth reviewing accounts that told a very different tale. Notably, many of these were written by neutral observers, such as a visitor from Macon, Georgia, who reported that after the unsatisfactory conclusion, "The Haymakers started for their hotel in an omnibus, and were stoned by the mob. The Gibson House, where they stopped, was thronged throughout the evening, and the excitement prevailed everywhere. The receipts at the gate, which in this instance amounted to $2,500, are usually divided between the two clubs, but in this case the Red Stockings held a meeting to decide if any of the gate money should go to the Haymakers. To make a long story short, the Haymakers were shamefully treated."[48]

When the players arrived in Louisville for their next game, a local journalist added these accounts: "The impression seemed to prevail pretty generally yesterday, among those who had read the full particulars of the Cincinnati game, that the Haymakers were shamefully treated at that place, and that, though the Red Stockings are not blamed, the Haymakers have the sympathy and commendation of all unprejudiced persons. This impression too was heightened by the manner and appearance of the latter club at the grounds yesterday. They are a lively, rollicking, full-of-fun, good-natured set of young gentlemen, off on a summer's jaunt and making the best of it.... They are for a wonder, excellent vocalists, and sing together prettily." He added that the players were entitled to their share of the gate receipts from the controversial game but had instead requested that the money be donated to charity.[49]

Meanwhile, a journalist in Albany, New York, read over all the various versions before offering this summary:

> We have refrained from expressing any opinion concerning the recent unfortunate base ball imbroglio at Cincinnati, until we could see the statements upon both sides. Cincinnati papers have come to hand, with full reports of the game and its unfortunate conclusion. They put the best possible face upon the proceedings of their Red Stocking club. But, even from their statements, we cannot avoid the conclusion that the visiting Haymakers were most unfairly treated, and that they were justified in refusing to continue a match in which it was evident that, they must play against a picked nine and an umpire. The treatment of this club by the Cincinnatians, contrasts most unfavorably with that bestowed by Englishmen upon the Harvard rowing crew. It seems to have been settled as a foregone conclusion, that the Red Stockings should not be beaten; and as they manifestly were unable to win the game, the umpire stepped in to help them out of their unexpected difficulty.
>
> It was slightly discourteous, to say the least, for the Red Stockings to propose as umpire a gentleman residing in Cincinnati, who might naturally be expected to show some prejudice in favor of his friends and neighbors — even if he were not personally interested in bets on the result, as is said to have been the case. But in accepting this choice, the Haymakers, who could not know him, did not surrender their claim to fair treatment, or bind themselves to be governed throughout by his decisions, if they were manifestly unjust. A ruling of Mr. Brockway on the second inning, in which he refused to recognize a fair catch by the Haymakers, gave his friends the Red Stockings ten runs, when they would otherwise have gone out with only four. This was a manifest advantage — sufficient in itself to decide any ordinarily contested game. At this early stage, the Haymakers protested against the umpire as prejudiced and unfair, and demanded that he should be changed! They had an unquestionable right to do so, under the laws of the National Association. The refusal of the Red Stockings to make a change showed that they were in the conspiracy, and intended to put their opponent at a disadvantage. From that, moment, the game really ceased. A dishonest umpire has it in his power to win any game, no matter how played, for the club he is engaged to serve. Mr. Brockway was evidently pledged to give victory to the Rod Stockings.
>
> Still, the Haymakers toiled on, and prevented their opponents from taking the lead, until, on the fifth innings, they were brought to a stop by a decision so monstrous as to be unendurable. All who have seen this club play, know that Craver is a magnificent catch, and that it is his specialty to take foul balls, close up to the bat. In this respect, he is probably not equaled by any other player in the country. Having received such a ball, he held it up to show that the striker was caught out; when, to the astonishment of all fair-minded men, the umpire cried: 'Not out.' This was the straw that broke the camel's back. The Haymakers got together and insisted that, in accordance with the well-established laws of the game, the catch should be allowed. But the umpire declined to change his decision. They then asked for a new umpire. This, the Cincinnati club refused to allow. Satisfied that they could not expect justice at the hands of such adversaries, the Haymakers packed up their clubs and withdrew. In this, they were perhaps mistaken. It might have been well to finish the game, entering a protest against every wrong decision, and leaving the public, and the Judiciary committee of the National Association, to decide whether they had been fairly treated. This would have been severe punishment to the Cincinnatians who had bet the Red Stockings would make two runs to one for the Haymakers — as the umpire, by no amount of cheating, could have given his friends such odds. But no one outside of Cincinnati will deny that the Haymakers were justified in refusing to prolong the contest under such circumstances.
>
> The course of the Cincinnati mob, in following the Haymakers to their hotel, hooting, swearing, using obscene language, and threatening violence which was only prevented by the police, was consistent with the whole disgraceful performance. It is of a piece with the rowdyism, on a lower scale, of the roughs collected by the recent prize-fights near St. Louis. A sporting paper recently said: "It is useless for a prize-fighter, a walkist or a runner, to go West expecting to defeat a local celebrity; the crowd won't let him." It seems as though base ball clubs must be added to the list.
>
> We regret this result, because it will ruin the reputation of a celebrated club, and inflict injury upon an athletic and sensible amusement, which is coming to be regarded as "the American game." Previous to this unfortunate rencontre, the Red Stockings enjoyed, as the result of their remarkably successful Eastern trip, a fame such as had been won by no other nine. They might

far better have taken the consequences of the defeat they would undoubtedly have suffered had their game with the Haymakers been fairly played, than sought to avert it by such disreputable means as were resorted to. The case must go before the Judiciary Committee of the Association; and no one can doubt what its judgment will be.[50]

Then there is this account from James H. Spotten, the treasurer of the Haymakers:

No experience of my life made such a lasting impression on my mind as that tie game at Cincinnati. I don't think there ever was such a scene on a ball field, nor do I think the feat performed that day by Steve King ever was surpassed by a ball player with a bat, considering that all of his performances came just at the psychological moments. There were at least 12,000 persons on the ground, and of these about 10,000 had paid 60 cents each to see the game. We were to receive $2,000 as our share of the gate receipts.

After standing for a number of bad decisions President McKeon warned the umpire that if he made another he would take his men from the field. I warned McKeon not to do that in any circumstances, as we needed the money. We had been advertised far and wide as a great club out to beat the Red Stockings, and many in the crowd had come hundreds of miles to witness the struggle. It was the largest gathering seen on a Cincinnati ball field up to that time, and at the start the crowd was with us, as the Red Stockings were chesty because of their success, and rather unpopular in consequence. In one of the early innings when Steve King came to bat there were three men on bases. Harry Wright, the captain and center fielder of our rivals, waved the men back but Steve gave the ball a terrific wallop and it went far over the head of Andy Leonard in left field, for a homer sending in the trio of players ahead of him. When he came up again Steve drove the ball out for three bases, sending two players home, and the third time up he hit another three bagger, sending in a man from third. A total of 10 bases in three times at bat surely was a sensational performance.

Then came the awful fifth inning, with the game a tie at 17 and 17. A foul tip was captured by Craver close to the ground, but the umpire decided that it was caught on the bound and that therefore the man at bat was not out. Even the crowd hooted at the decision, but President McKeon was the one who made the trouble. Indignant at the decision and carried away by the excitement he put his threat into execution and called his men from the field. Thousands among the onlookers had come a long distance and paid their money to see a ball game, and as soon as they realized what had happened there was a riot. The crowd closed in on us from all sides shouting "Kill 'em, kill 'em!" There were threatening gestures everywhere, and in those days, just after the war a Cincinnati crowd was considered about the toughest in the country. Levi Smith of Troy, was one of our party, and just as things were looking mighty black and there was every indication of a lynching, some one in the crowd pointed him out and shouted, "There's John Morrissey, the prize fighter." At that a typical gambler, one of the biggest men I ever saw, pushed his way to Mr. Smith's side and yelled, "no man is going to hurt Morrissey." Then he whipped out a revolver and began to sweep the crowd with the weapon. He kept that gun moving slowly in a semi-circle in the faces of the excited rioters, and while he held them back ordered us to get into the coach which stood waiting. We were driven from the field, followed by a volley of sticks, stones and assorted epithets.

Soon after we reached the hotel the crowd from the grounds arrived, and there was another wild scene. It appeared as if every one in the mob wanted to hang us. We changed to our street clothing as quickly as possible, and some of us went outside, and mingled with the crowd. By midnight the situation became so threatening that a conference of prominent men and the newspaper reporters was held, with the result that we left the city almost immediately. We were scheduled to play three games in Cincinnati, but realized that it would be useless to make the attempt. We actually sneaked across the river to the Kentucky side and made our way to Louisville, where we remained for the next two days.[51]

Finally, the *Troy Press* offered a very novel interpretation, maintaining that the Haymakers should have expected "that all the close decisions would be against them." The *Press* noted, "Mr. Brockway resides in Cincinnati, and would be likely to sympathize with the Red Stockings. The great crowd of spectators were, of course, enthusiastic for their favorite club. But when we add to this that hundreds in the crowd, the boon companions of the umpire, had laid enormous odds upon the Cincinnati Club, it will be seen that the chances that the umpire would not be influenced in his decisions, were small indeed."

Accordingly, the writer called "the action of President McKeon in breaking up the game rash and unfortunate. Very probably he was in the right, but he is absolutely certain to be proved in the wrong. It is never safe to resist the decision of an umpire, unless he is so glaringly partial that even the crowd of spectators, prejudiced as they may be, will see his unfitness for the position. With the umpire, the opposing club, the population and press of a great city against them, what chance have the few Trojans present at the game for making the country believe that the Haymakers did not causelessly break up the game for fear of getting beaten? None whatever, and it will hurt their reputation far more than if they had played the game squarely out and been unfairly beaten by any number of runs. In base-ball 'the absent (from home) are always wrong.'"

He concluded on a wry note,

We can not say that the spectacle of the Haymakers passing along the streets of Cincinnati, followed by fifty groaning bootblacks, and Mr. James McKeon at their head "swearing vehemently," was particularly cheering to gods or men. We have had the pleasure of hearing the President of the Haymakers swear — in moderation — and we can bear cheerful witness to the vigor and fluency with which he discharges this portion of his delicate and responsible duties. But we have never heard him "swear vehemently," at least not enough so as to make it the subject of a telegram to the Associated Press. There are some very able "swearists" in Cincinnati, and when the performance of President McKeon was deemed worthy of such special mention, we leave our readers to imagine the sulphurous halo that must have illumined the features of our friend Jim, as he led his club back to the Gibson House, "few and faint, but fearless still." We wish the game could have been played out. We believe our boys would have been successful in spite of the umpire, and we trust that for the remainder of their tour the telegraph will bring us glad tidings of more victories — and less profanity.[52]

Obviously, these accounts need to be taken with a grain of salt, and they too only tell part of the story. But they certainly bring into question the traditional version of events. In particular, the oft-repeated claim that the Haymakers withdrew to protect the interests of Morrissey and other bettors makes no sense. As noted by the Albany reporter, the Haymakers were heavy underdogs in the match, and many of the wagers were as to whether the Red Stockings would outscore them by two to one. With the score tied, there would be no reason for bettors to want the club to leave the field — instead there would be every reason to want to continue.

In any event, the Haymakers were treated as heroes on their return to Troy. The players "were received at the depot with music and a large crowd of citizens, headed by F. Eddie Hale. In the afternoon they were escorted to their grounds by a crowd of citizens and a band, accompanied by the Niagara Club of Buffalo. Several thousand citizens assembled to witness a game between the Haymakers and the Niagaras, which resulted in a score of 34 to 9 in favor of the former, seven innings being played. In the evening a reception dinner was given by the citizens to the Haymakers, at the Mansion House, the Niagaras being present as invited guests. Speeches were made by C. L. McArthur, William H. Merriam, and others, sustaining the Haymakers in their action with the Cincinnati Red Stockings. George Evans, of the [Troy] *Whig*, who accompanied the Haymakers, gave a detailed account of the unjust decision of the umpire in the Red Stocking game."[53]

That banquet would also prove to be the swan song of the club, at least for the nucleus of local men who had given Lansingburgh and Troy one of the best ball clubs in the country. The fall of 1869 saw Craver and several of the other Haymakers receive a flurry of telegraphs from Tom Foley, the front man for the White Stockings of Chicago, a newly formed professional club that offered exorbitant salaries.[54] In the end, Craver was joined by McAtee, Flynn, and Mart King in leaving town in 1870 for the big salaries of Chicago. Craver would be dropped from the club at midseason under suspicion of game-fixing, but King took his place behind the plate and helped get revenge on the Red Stockings — the White Stockings handed the Cincinnati clubs two defeats down the stretch and at season's end were generally regarded as the national champion.

The Troy Haymakers also continued to play in 1870, but it was the same club in name only. Even after Craver returned home, he and Steve King were the only holdovers who started for a club that consisted almost entirely of imported Philadelphia professionals.

When the National Association was formed in 1871, the Haymakers entered the league and played for two seasons, acquitting themselves respectably. While this club's connection to the Unions of Lansingburgh was now very tangential, native sons such as Flynn, McAtee, Craver, and the King brothers all played for this club at some point. So too did Bellán, thereby making him the first Cuban-born major leaguer.

At the end of the 1872 season, Troy dropped out of the National Association. The city would have an International Association club in 1878 and a National League franchise from 1879 to 1882 as well as many other notable clubs, but never again would it figure as prominently in the national baseball scene as it had when both Lansingburgh and Troy claimed the Haymakers.

The legacy of this remarkable club is a multi-faceted one. The club's shady reputation has become what it is best remembered for and not without some justification. While it is never entirely clear who was making decisions for the club, there were enough suspicious figures around to raise concern. Craver's actions also hurt the club's reputation, as he was frequently accused of involvement with gamblers and finally permanently banned from the National League.

The club's toughness also became the stuff of legend. According to a 1901 account based on the reminiscences of George H. Geer of Syracuse, the "Haymakers were a strong team, but the fighting ability of the players was responsible for most of their victories. They were known as a team which traveled 'on its muscle,' and when they were beaten they generally got satisfaction by whipping the members of the opposing team." Before one game in Syracuse, "the Syracuse team prepared to take the Haymakers in hand in case they 'started anything,' and had Andy Kelley with his Seventh ward gang, known as the 'Swamp Angels,' on hand. Jimmie Johnson, the crack second baseman of the Central Cities, who was a brother to Frank Johnson, now living in this city, hit the ball over the fence, winning the game. The Haymakers sized up the 'Swamp Angels' and decided to take the defeat without a kick."[55]

Yet as with so much of what has been written about this club, the veracity of Geer's comments is debatable. For one thing the Central City Club was nowhere near as strong as the Haymakers, and there is no record of the Syracuse club ever recording such a victory. The depiction of the club's propensity for fighting also seems to be, at the least, grossly exaggerated, as there are no documented instances of actual fights.

In a way, this image of the Haymakers as tough guys with shady pasts is appropriate since, just as the players made a conscious effort to be seen as country rustics, so too they tried to cultivate this perception. Nevertheless, it is regrettable that the portrayal of the club has come to be dominated by these characteristics because there was so much more to the Unions/Haymakers.

Most notably, by whatever name, the club was the embodiment of what so many post–Civil War clubs aspired to be but hardly any achieved: a group of local young men who proved they could compete with the nation's best clubs without hiring outside professionals. The club also represented a bastion of opportunity, featuring two Cuban players and a host of Irish-Americans at a time when the top baseball clubs were overwhelmingly WASPs. There can be little doubt that some of the vicious things written about the players were the result of prejudice. We can be even more sure that their example inspired other youngsters to pursue baseball — one of these was New York Giants owner John T. Brush, who rooted for the Haymakers as a young man and may even have been involved in their management.[56]

Finally, there is the tragedy that stalked the club's original players. Of the eleven men who played in 1866 and 1867, no fewer than seven were dead by 1881— Andrew McQuide died right after the 1866 season, followed by Peter McKeon in 1870, Ward in 1871, Leavenworth in 1874, McAtee in 1876, Abrams in 1880, and Flynn in 1881. In addition, none of the four remaining players reached the age of 65, and many of the men involved in the club's management also died young.

Even club members who didn't die young, such as Craver and the King brothers, seem to have been men of few words. As a result, reminiscences about the club by participants are few and far between. This absence leaves a gaping hole in our understanding of this pioneer club that can never be overcome. And what is known about the Union Club of Lansingburgh/Haymakers of Troy makes that lack of firsthand accounts all the more tantalizing.

Club Members

The 1866 first nine of the Haymakers/Unions consisted of Andrew McQuide, William H. Craver, Carrol F. Penfield, James Ward, Stephen King, Thomas Abrams, Bub McAtee, "Sonny" Leavenworth, and Peter McKeon. Mart King joined the first nine in 1867 after the death of McQuide, but was often referred to as an original member. Clipper Flynn also joined the club that year, but was its tenth man and was never described as an original member. The 1868 additions — Bonker, Davis, Rúa, and Bierman — were looked on as latecomers, as were all of the subsequent additions, whether they were professionals like Fisher and Mike McGeary, or men who appear to have been local amateurs such as Hollister and Woolverton.

Thomas E. Abrams: Thomas E. Abrams, whose obituary described him as the club's original captain, was born in Lansingburgh in 1845. He was the club's top reserve in 1866, then took over as its starting pitcher in 1867 after the death of McQuide although he had not previously pitched. Abrams did a capable job as the club emerged as a national power, but he returned to reserve duty in 1868 when the club brought in Rúa and Bierman to pitch. He became a policeman but died in Lansingburgh on May 7, 1880, after a long battle with tuberculosis. An obituary in the *New York Sunday Mercury* noted that Abrams "was captain of the original Haymakers base ball club, and acquired fame as a heavy batter and sure fielder. Before his illness he was a fine specimen of physical manhood, and prided himself on feats of muscular skill and endurance, and it was little thought he would become a victim of consumption. This leaves only three of the original Haymakers above the sod, Steve King, William H. Craver and Cal. Penfield."[57]

Estevan B. Bellán: Born in Havana on October 1, 1849, to a Cuban father and an Irish mother, Estevan Bellán became known as Steve while a prep student at St. John's College in the Bronx. He also played baseball there and then played in 1868 for the Unions of Morrisania. In 1869, the young third baseman joined the Haymakers and became its second Cuban-born player. He stayed with the club after it joined the National Association, making him the first Hispanic major leaguer. He played his last major league game for the New York Mutuals on June 9, 1873, and then returned to Cuba, and some sources credit him with having "introduced the American game to Cuba."[58] According to a 1911 article in *Sporting Life*, there was even a statue of Bellán in Havana in honor of his role in introducing baseball.[59] Yet little else is known about his life, and even the extent of his contributions to Cuban baseball remains in doubt. He died in Havana on August 8, 1932.

Charley Bierman: Charley Bierman, a well-known New York/New Jersey player who had previously played for the Mutuals, joined the Haymakers in 1868 and pitched seven games for them. He was probably the first outside professional hired by the Haymakers. See the Marylands of Baltimore for more details.

Eugene H. Bonker: Eugene H. Bonker of Lansingburgh was one of the 1868 additions to the club, seeing action at shortstop in at least ten games. He was born around 1848 in New York and grew up in Lansingburgh, where his father worked as an expressman. He did not play for any major club after 1868, yet his occupation on the 1870 census is listed as "base ball player" and in 1871 he signed to play for the Kekiongas of Fort Wayne in the newly formed National Association. Alas, he was released before the season started and thus does not appear in the baseball encyclopedias. By 1880, Bonker and his entire family had moved to Manhattan where Eugene, still single, worked as an engineer. Bonker died in Manhattan on January 2, 1914.

John H. Campbell: John H. Campbell, the club's vice president in 1867, was a Civil War veteran who was born in Ireland around 1835. He worked in the cigar and restaurant business and died on January 31, 1902.

William H. Craver: Bill Craver was born in Troy in June of 1844 and became one of the best-known and most controversial players of the era. After serving in the New York 13th Heavy Artillery during the Civil War, Craver became the catcher of the Haymakers and earned renown for his toughness. He joined the White Stockings of Chicago in 1870 but was soon expelled by the club amid rumors of shady doings. Controversy continued to dog him throughout his career, but clubs were always willing to take a chance on him until he was finally banned from the National League for his involvement in the Louisville game-fixing scandal of 1877. Craver returned to Troy and in 1883 became a policeman; in the summer of 1896, he was badly beaten by a gang of local toughs.[60] He was still on the police force when he died in Troy on June 17, 1901.

Henry Alfred "Allie" Davis: Allie Davis was born in Sauquoit, New York, on December 7, 1847. The family moved to Utica in the late 1850s, where his father ran the Central Hotel and Allie and his brother John became skilled ballplayers. Allie was mostly a pitcher while in Utica, but when he joined the Haymakers in 1868 he mostly played first base. After fifteen games for Troy he returned home to Utica in September. Davis remained in Utica for the rest of his life, working as a hotel clerk, running a café, and becoming known as one of the town's best billiard players. He died in Utica on December 10, 1914.

William Charles "Cherokee" Fisher: Born in 1844 in Philadelphia, Cherokee Fisher was a Civil War veteran who spent more than seven months as a prisoner in the notorious Andersonville prison camp. He was 23 when he became the pitcher of the Haymakers in 1869. After two years in Troy, Fisher played in the major leagues for eight years, winning 57 games and leading the National Association in earned run average twice. When his playing days ended, he became a Chicago fireman and died in New York City on September 26, 1912.

William "Clipper" Flynn: William Flynn was born on April 29, 1849, in Lansingburgh, the son of a successful businessman. He became the club's main substitute in 1867, then was a regular for the next two years before joining the White Stockings in 1870. He returned to play for Troy's entry in the National Association in 1871, and ended his career with the Washington Olympics in 1872. He died in Lansingburgh on November 5, 1881, making him the seventh of the eleven men who played for the club in 1866 and 1867 to die.

John Augustus Griswold: Congressman John A. Griswold was a diehard supporter of the club and reportedly financed an 1867 tour that took the club to Washington and Philadelphia.[61] E. H. Tobias also must have been thinking of Griswold when he wrote, "The Haymakers of Troy, were under the patronage of a large manufacturing establishment, whose head was prominent in politics, both State and National."[62] He was born in Nassau, Rensselaer County, and while sources differ on his year of birth, it appears most likely that the date was November 11, 1818. After moving to Troy, Griswold found work as a drug store clerk and, according to a flowery 1851 profile, "such was his character in that position that he won the confidence of his principal and the respect of all, and in a few years succeeded to the business of the establishment as partner."[63] He was elected mayor in 1855 and also worked in banking and as president of several railroads, including the Troy & Lansingburgh Railroad Company. While president of the Rensselaer Iron Works, he became one of the first American manufacturers to recognize the importance of the Bessemer steel process and he received a number of patents. This enabled him to play a key role in building the Union Navy's famous ironclad, the Monitor. Griswold served in Congress from 1862 to 1869, switching parties from the Democrats to the Republicans after one year. He then was the Republican candidate for governor in 1868 and, according to his *New York Times* obituary, "was undoubtedly elected, but was counted out by frauds." He was a trustee of Rensselaer Polytechnic Institute from 1860 until 1872 so may have had some role in Rúa's joining the club. He died in Troy on October 31, 1872.

Albert Leet Hotchkin, Sr.: Albert L. Hotchkin was born in Chatham, New York, on March 8, 1833, and moved to Troy in 1845. His father died soon afterward, and Albert pursued several occupations before opening a store in Troy and then getting married in 1861. His business was destroyed by the Great Troy Fire of 1862, so he went into business with his new father-in-law, a furniture merchant. He became a partner after his father-in-law's death in 1868 and sole owner in 1878. Hotchkin also became one of Troy's most prominent civic leaders, serving in Troy's Common Council from 1863 to 1866, as fire commissioner for six years, as county treasurer from 1873 to 1876, as treasurer of the Troy Fire Department for nearly two decades, and as sheriff of Rensselaer County. Despite all these accomplishments, one newspaper article about Hotchkin stated, "Although he was Sheriff and County Treasurer for many years, he was best known as the organizer and Manager of the famous Haymaker Baseball Club." While Hotchkin was involved in the activities of the Haymakers, it is unclear whether that description of his role is justified. An article in the *Troy Press* on August 10, 1866, listed him as president of the Victory Club of Troy. He subsequently became treasurer of Haymakers, but the length of his tenure and nature of his role are not well documented. Around 1890, he moved to Washington State and became postmaster of the town of Seabeck. He died in Seabeck on October 16, 1899.[64]

Marshall Ney "Mart" or "Marty" King: Mart King was born in December of 1849, in Lansingburgh, which is now part of Troy. He was one of many children of Captain Joseph King, who was said to be 106 by the time of his death in 1897. According to an obituary, Joseph King "claimed to be of Indian descent and his appearance was a corroboration of his assertion. His title of captain was obtained by his connection with Hudson river sailing vessels many years ago." But the same article quotes Captain King as saying that his father was in the French dragoons and his mother Dutch, which seems to contradict the contention of Native American blood. Joseph King also claimed to have been born on Peeble Island in 1791 and as commander of the sloop LaFayette to have brought the first bunch of radishes to Troy. He soon gave up boating and bought a house in Lansingburgh, where he raised a family and gardened, then remarried and raised a second family after the death of his first wife.[65] According to an obituary, "'Marty' King spent all his spare time as a boy, playing ball on the green in Lansingburgh, the best ball park that that village then afforded. It was on this green, now one of the beautiful parks of Troy, that 'Marty' received that instruction in the art of ball playing that was destined to make him and the team to which he later belonged, famous throughout the country."[66] Mart was only sixteen in 1866 when the Union Club of Lansingburgh began making a name for itself and was not a regular that year. But he joined his brother Steve in the club's outfield in 1867 and became so closely associated with the club that many articles after the turn of the century inaccurately referred to him as the last of the original Haymakers. In particular, a 1911 article by W. W. Aulick credited King with refusing to wear a cap or shoes and in shaming the other players into following his lead by calling them "dudes." It doesn't appear that the club played without shoes and caps for very long, but that became one of the components of the club's legend. What is beyond doubt is that King, who was described by Aulick as being "built on the massive lines of a battleship," was one of the toughest men in an era of tough ballplayers. According to sportswriter T. Z. Cowles, King "served as change catcher when Craver's hand had lost so many finger nails that he could no longer hang on to the ball. 'Mart' was a hero in purpose if not a star in performance. No hurt could drive him out of the game. He, too, spurned all protection contrivances. Once a foul tip landed squarely between his eyes. It didn't even knock him down. He winced a little, shook his head, and went on with the game. A finger nail torn from its roots meant nothing to him. He would wrap a rag around it and go on with the game."[67] King and Craver both joined the high-paying professional White Stockings of Chicago in 1870, and when Craver was expelled, King caught many games for the club that beat the Red Stockings twice and was widely regarded as national champions. The side whiskers of Red Stockings pitcher Asa Brainard also offended King's sensibilities. In one of the victories, King "who was a rough-hewn oak and possessed a rough voice that was inspiring to men of his temperament," loudly urged his teammates to make Brainard "stroke his whiskers."[68] King broke a finger early in that game, but in typical fashion he remained behind the plate "without uttering a single complaint."[69] Mart King played for Chicago in 1871 and got in a few games for Troy in 1872 before, in Aulick's words, he "retired from the game inveighing against an effete civilization which demanded protection where none was asked for." He worked in Troy as a boatman and gardener. In the last year of his life, he engaged in a "fanning bee" (chat session) with Cap Anson and Johnny Evers in which King "maintained that in his day there were players as great, if not greater, than in the days of Anson and Evers."[70] Mart King died at his home on October 19, 1911, which by then had become part of Troy.

Stephen F. King: Steve King was Mart's older brother and was born in 1844 in Lansingburgh. He manned left field for the club from 1866 onward, remaining there after many of the players departed. When Troy left the National Association after the 1872 season, he retired. Steve King died in Lansingburgh on July 8, 1895, and his pallbearers included the two surviving members of the 1867 team: William H. Craver and Cal Penfield.[71]

Seaman or Seamon J. "Sonny" Leavenworth: Sonny Leavenworth, the first baseman of the Haymakers, was born around 1845 and grew up in Troy, where his father worked as a boatman. He was the first club member to accept an offer from an outside club, joining the Mutual Club of New York in the summer of 1867 at a salary of $100 per month. He changed his mind almost immediately and rejoined the Haymakers for the remainder of the season. He did not play for the club after that season, and by 1869 was playing for the Putnams of Troy. He retired after that season and worked as a grocer until his death on June 19, 1874.

John A. MacDonald (often spelled McDonald): John A. MacDonald was a member of the Victory Club of Troy, and a brief summary of his life appears in the entry for that club. After the war, he lived in Buffalo for a few years and was drawn into one of the many controversies involving the Haymakers. An article in the *Syracuse Daily Standard* on April 28, 1868, said that MacDonald would be the third baseman of the Haymakers in 1868. He never played a game for the club, but on August 10, 1868, this article appeared in the *Buffalo Courier and Republic*:

> Mr. John McDonald, of the Niagara club, of Buffalo, umpired the important game at Lansingburgh last week, between the "Haymakers" and the New York Mutuals. The *World* says the New Yorkers claimed that the umpire was against them, and that there was a determination to defeat them at all hazards. The *Troy Whig* defends Mr. McDonald in the following style: "The World reporter is oversensitive. He has the Mutual club on the brain, as he sometimes has it in his pocket. In his version of the matter, he must know that he falsifies and that he willfully misrepresents Mr. McDonald, whose decisions early in the match won the hearty applause of President Wildey, of the Mutuals. The truth is, the New Yorkers were out played at every point, as they will be every time they enter the field with the Haymakers. The decisions of the umpire were governed by the strict rules of the game, and if the Mutuals or their friends think different, the matter can be easily decided by an impartial committee who understand the game. The Mutuals can find in Troy, at any time, plenty of gentlemen who will wager money and give odds on the decision of such a committee relative to Mr. McD.'s umpiring. It is an old dodge with defeated clubs to find fault with the umpire."

Michael James "Bub" McAtee: Bub McAtee is listed in the encyclopedias as being born in March of 1845 in Troy, but this may be a mistake as he grew up in Lansingburgh. While with the Haymakers, he showed unusually versatility by playing both first base and shortstop. He was one of four Troy players who joined the White Stockings of Chicago in 1870, and he remained with that club until the Great Chicago Fire. He returned to play in Troy in 1872 but by then was showing signs of tuberculosis. After a long battle, he died in Troy on October 18, 1876. According to an obituary in the *Clipper*, the surviving members of the original nine "attended in a body," but by then only four of them were still alive.

McCormick: According to the article in the *Chicago Daily News* from around 1924, a man by this name was a utility player around 1865 or 1866.

James McKeon: Club president James McKeon was born around 1835 and was the brother of Peter. According to Spotten, McKeon was the one who made the decision to pull the club off the field in the famous game in Cincinnati. He was a local alderman during the 1860s and the sheriff of Rensselaer County from 1870 to 1873 but seems to have left town or died soon afterward.

Peter McKeon: Peter McKeon (often spelled McCune) was born in Lansingburgh around 1846. He worked as a saloonkeeper and merchant before dying in Lansingburgh on December 9, 1870, leaving a wife and young son.

Andrew McQuide (often spelled McQuade): Andrew McQuide was born in Ireland around 1848 and was the club's pitcher in 1866. He was fatally injured in Albany on November 22, 1866, when his horse-drawn wagon was struck by a railroad engine. McQuide died in the City Hospital the following day, and his funeral "was attended by the members of the Union Base Ball Club of Lansingburgh in a body."[72] Sadly, that scene would be repeated often in the coming years as the club's original members one by one passed away.

James McQuide: While it's difficult to be sure who was running the club at any time, James McQuide was one of the prime movers, and Cal Penfield credited him with putting the original first nine together. An obituary added: "When the old Haymaker baseball club was famous throughout the country he was its president and it seldom made a trip away from home without its chief officer. He took great interest in the national game and did much to make the old Haymakers what they were." Born in Ireland in 1832, James McQuide arrived in Lansingburgh in 1849 and went to work at one of the town's many brush factories. He mastered the business quickly and opened his own factory on Thirteenth Street, where a patent for a new type of sash brush made him wealthy. He became a prominent civic leader and served two terms as village president. McQuide died at his home on Thirteenth Street on June 7, 1902.[73] His relationship to club pitcher Andrew McQuide has proved difficult to determine — they may have been brothers, cousins, or even uncle/nephew.

John Morrissey: The name of John Morrissey is closely associated with the Haymakers, although the extent of his involvement with the club is far from clear. Morrissey, who was born in Templemore, County Tipperary, Ireland, on February 12, 1831, moved to Troy at age two and became a celebrated boxing champion, gambler, gang member and eventually, with a lot of help from Tammany Hall, a U.S. Congressman and State Senator. Morrissey was not a member of the Haymakers (although his son was).[74] He did attend many games, however, and one that was played at Saratoga Springs between Haymakers and Atlantics was reported to have been arranged under his "patronage."[75] His appearance at games always led to rumors of huge sums being bet on the outcome, and sometimes to suspicions of game-fixing. This was most notably the case in the famous tie game against the Red Stockings, though there is no proof that he influenced the outcome. Morrissey died in Saratoga on May 1, 1878.

Carrol F. Penfield: Cal Penfield was born in June of 1845 and grew up in Troy. As described in the club history, he played third base for the Putnams (or "Puts"), the Enterprise, and several other Troy clubs before joining the Unions/Haymakers in 1866. He was one of the few original club members who didn't die young, but his life was also touched by tragedy. His father Nelson enlisted in the 125th New York in the Civil War and rose to the rank of major. But ill health forced Nelson Penfield to accept a disability discharge near the end of the war and he remained bedridden until his death in February of 1866. Cal Penfield began playing for the Haymakers that year and remained the club's third baseman until being replaced by Bellán in 1869. He rejoined the club in a reserve role in 1870. Interestingly, Cal's brother Burr Penfield, who ran a cigar store in Troy, issued "Base Ball Photograph Cards of the Haymakers" that year. Cal Penfield then retired from baseball and remained in town, working as a collar cutter, a clothing store clerk, and as proprietor of a billiard hall and a hotel known as the Troy House. In 1896, he reminisced about those long-ago days, and his eyes were said to "sparkle with delight as he rehearses the scenes and incidents connected with that memorable contest. Years have rested lightly on Cal., and he does not look like a man who was one of the foremost professional base ball players in the land when the game was in its infancy thirty years ago."[76] But then Penfield's wife died at the age of 42, followed in 1900 by the deaths of his mother and seventeen-year-old daughter. Cal Penfield left Troy soon afterward and moved to New York City and was soon forgotten in Troy, as several notes after the 1901 death of Craver referred to Mart King as the last surviving member. In fact, Carrol Penfield was still alive, dying in Manhattan on January 28, 1910.

Mike Powers: Mike Powers was a Utica native who became the shortstop of the Haymakers in 1869 after having previously played the same position for clubs in Albany.

Rafael Julián de la Rúa: Rafael de la Rúa was one of the new additions to the club in 1868, doing much of the pitching that season. He was born on January 28, 1848, in Matanzas, Cuba. By 1860, the twelve-year-old was a student at a small school in Newton, Massachusetts. Also enrolled at the school was a Finomen Rúa, age 18, who was likely Rafael's brother.

In June of 1864, according to a note in the *New York Times*, he arrived in New York on the steamship *Havana* to begin preparatory studies at St. John's College. He studied there from September 1864 through July 1867, where his fellow students included Estevan Bellán and his brother Domingo. The official student catalogues give his name as Julián R. Rúa. In 1868, he enrolled at Rensselaer Polytechnic Institute in Troy and began pitching for the Haymakers. His work in a win over the Mutuals on August 4 led the *Troy Times* to write, "Rúa's pitching was the acme of perfection — not too swift to be unreliable, and with just enough of the 'twist' to prevent the Mutuals from making their heaviest batting." The *New York Clipper* also mentioned that Rúa used a "screw" pitch.[77] He left the school without graduating after a single year and that seems to have ended his baseball career. Rafael de la Rúa was next heard from on September 23, 1874, when he applied for U.S. citizenship, giving his occupation as merchant and his address as 15th and 32nd Streets in New York. His trail ends there.

John W. Scofield or Schofield: This man was a local bookkeeper who served as secretary and club scorer in 1866 and later served as secretary of the National Association. He appears to have been a Civil War veteran. Schofield eventually moved to Chicago, where he died on July 17, 1909.

J. Slattery: An article in the *Syracuse Daily Standard* on April 28, 1868, said that a player by this name would pitch for the Union Club in 1868. But he does not appear to have ever played a game.

James H. Spotten: James H. Spotten was born around 1841 in New York state and became the club treasurer. Spotten worked in the coal business and later served as a town supervisor. He was also an officer of the club known as the Haymakers that represented Troy in the International Association, making him apparently the only man to be an officer of both clubs.[78] He died in Troy on December 11, 1925. Several of Spotten's reminiscences are quoted in Richard Puff's history of the club.

James Ward: Second baseman Jim Ward, like so many club members, had a short life that was touched by tragedy. He was born around 1848 in Lansingburgh. His father Philetus worked as an engineer at the John G. McMurray brush factory and was killed in a boiler explosion in December of 1865. After leaving the baseball diamond, Jim Ward got married and found work as a brushmaker, but he died on March 6, 1871.

Dr. Seth P. Welch: S. P. Welch, a Lansingburgh dentist, was the initial president of the Union Club and remained in that role in 1867. Welch was born in New York State around 1825 and served as village president of Lansingburgh from 1869 to 1872. He died there on October 23, 1890.

Other Members: In addition to Welch, the club's initial officers included these directors: James McQuide, Thomas H. Morgan, Charles S. Holmes, and William W. Lee. Beginning in 1870, many professional players from Philadelphia joined the Haymakers and those men (who included Mike McGeary, John McMullin, Dicky Flowers, Jim Foran, and Tom York) have not been included here. Also joining the club that year were two reserve players named Hollister and Woolverton. These were probably local amateurs, but have not been identified.

Sources

There is no end of sources of information on this club, but deciding which ones are trustworthy is no easy task. My aim has been to rely as much as possible on primary sources and on authors who relied upon primary sources. The best source of information was an 1896 series of articles in the *Troy Northern Budget*. (There were apparently nine parts to the series but only seven of them could be located in the pages of that paper: "Famed Old Haymakers," *Troy Northern Budget*, April 19, 1896, 5; "Famous Old Haymaker Base Ball Club," *Troy Northern Budget*, April 26, 1896, 8; "Haymakers' Palmy Era," *Troy Northern Budget*, May 10, 1896, 2; "It Was A Great Game," *Troy Northern Budget*, May 17, 1896, 8; "A Base Ball Pioneer," *Troy Northern Budget*, May 24, 1896, 8; "Victorious Victorys," *Troy Northern Budget*, June 7, 1896, 9; "Mutuals Outplayed," *Troy Northern Budget*, June 21, 1896, 8. The series was reprinted in *Sporting News* on December 5, 12, and 19, 1896, and January 2 and 9, 1897 [all on page 6], with most if not all of the missing material included.) A great deal of research on this club was conducted by a man named Warren F. Broderick, who detailed his findings in two articles in the *Troy Record*—one on August 23, 1969, entitled "Haymakers' Bats Brought Fame" and a follow-up one week later, entitled "Haymakers Tie Red Stockings in Exciting Game." In addition, many of Broderick's notes were donated to the National Baseball Hall of Fame and are now housed in the Hall's file on Troy baseball. Also valuable is Richard Puff's "Haymakers and Daisycutters: Troy and the National Pastime," in *Troy's Baseball Heritage*, ed. Richard A. Puff (Troy, 1992). William Ryczek's *When Johnny Came Sliding Home* is another very helpful source, as was the "Constitution and By-Laws of the Union 'Haymakers' Base Ball Club of Lansingburgh" (published in the office of the *Lansingburgh Gazette* in 1868), a photocopy of which can be found in the Hall of Fame's Troy file. An article about the club appeared in the *Springfield* (MA) *Republican* on May 12, 1907, and was said to be based on an interview with Mart King (the "last surviving member"), which had recently appeared in a Troy paper. It is likely, but not certain, that the article in question was an undated and incomplete clipping in the Troy file of the Hall of Fame. The article in the *Republican* also repeats some statements from one that appeared in the *Duluth News-Tribune* on December 30, 1906, and that may also be a source. Other sources are cited in the notes.

Notes

1. "Constitution and By-Laws of the Union 'Haymakers' Base Ball Club of Lansingburgh."
2. William J. Ryczek, *When Johnny Came Sliding Home* (Jefferson, NC: McFarland, 1998), 92; John J. Nutt, *Newburgh, Her Institutions, Industries and Leading Citizens: Historical, Descriptive and Biographical* (Newburgh, NY: Ritchie & Hull, 1891), 329.
3. "Famous Old Haymaker Base Ball Club," *Troy Northern Budget*, April 26, 1896, 8.
4. "Famed Old Haymakers," *Troy Northern Budget*, April 19, 1896, 5.
5. *Ibid*.
6. *Ibid*.
7. *Brooklyn Eagle*, August 9, 1866, 2; "Famed Old Haymakers," *Troy Northern Budget*, April 19, 1896, 5. The latter article reports that McQuide had to leave the game after the injury. Game accounts do not mention the injury, but do indicate that he lost his effectiveness.

8. "Famed Old Haymakers," *Troy Northern Budget*, April 19, 1896, 5.
9. "Famous Old Haymaker Base Ball Club," *Troy Northern Budget*, April 26, 1896, 8.
10. *Ibid.*
11. *New York Tribune*, August 11, 1866.
12. "Famed Old Haymakers," *Troy Northern Budget*, April 19, 1896, 5; "Famous Old Haymaker Base Ball Club," *Troy Northern Budget*, April 26, 1896, 8.
13. *Troy Press*, August 29, 1866.
14. *Troy Northern Budget*, reprinted in *Sporting News* on December 12, 1896, 6.
15. "Famed Old Haymakers," *Troy Northern Budget*, April 19, 1896, 5.
16. *Chicago Daily News*, undated clipping, c. 1924.
17. Warren F. Broderick, "Haymakers' Bats Brought Fame," *Troy Record*, August 23, 1969.
18. *Brooklyn Eagle*, March 26, 1905, 13.
19. *Oliver Optic's Magazine*, August 1, 1868.
20. *Chicago Inter-Ocean*, April 24, 1887.
21. *Cleveland Herald*, August 24, 1869.
22. W. W. Aulick, "One Hundred Notable Figures in Baseball: Mart King, Who Scorned All Precautionary Measures," *Auburn Citizen*, March 10, 1911.
23. *Chadwick Scrapbooks*, account of September 1869 game from unidentified source.
24. Warren Broderick, contributions to the Troy file at the National Baseball Hall of Fame.
25. *Chicago Daily News*, undated clipping, c. 1924.
26. Quoted in Richard A. Puff, ed., *Troy's Baseball Heritage* (Troy, 1992), 8–9; no date provided.
27. *Syracuse Daily Standard*, April 28, 1868.
28. Quoted in the *Troy Northern Budget*, reprinted in *Sporting News* on December 12, 1896, 6.
29. Warren Broderick, contributions to the Troy file at the National Baseball Hall of Fame.
30. Clipping from an unidentified local paper on June 19, 1867, quoted in the *Troy Northern Budget*, reprinted in *Sporting News* on December 12, 1896, 6.
31. *Lansingburgh Gazette*, July 25, 1867; quoted in Broderick, "Haymakers' Bats Brought Fame," *Troy Record*, August 23, 1969.
32. *Troy Whig*, September 2, 1867; reprinted in the *Troy Northern Budget* and in turn in *Sporting News* on January 2, 1897, 6.
33. Clipping from an unidentified local paper, reprinted in the *Troy Northern Budget* and in turn in *Sporting News* on December 12, 1896, 6.
34. Quoted in the *Troy Northern Budget* and in turn in *Sporting News* on December 12, 1896, 6.
35. Unidentified clippings from July of 1867, quoted in "Haymakers' Palmy Era," *Troy Northern Budget*, May 10, 1896, 2.
36. "Haymakers' Palmy Era," *Troy Northern Budget*, May 10, 1896, 2.
37. Quoted in "Haymakers' Palmy Era," *Troy Northern Budget*, May 10, 1896, 2.
38. According to Broderick, the club also managed another win over the Mutuals, but Marshall Wright does not list the game and no account has been found.
39. "It Was A Great Game," *Troy Northern Budget*, May 17, 1896, 8.
40. *Troy Whig*, September 2, 1867; reprinted in the *Troy Northern Budget* and in turn in *Sporting News* on January 2, 1897, 6.
41. Puff, ed., *Troy's Baseball Heritage*, 7.
42. *Troy Whig*, undated clipping from September of 1868.
43. "Mutuals Outplayed," *Troy Northern Budget*, June 21, 1896, 8.
44. Warren Broderick, contributions to the Troy file at the National Baseball Hall of Fame.
45. *Our Boys and Girls*, October 23, 1869.
46. Foul balls that were caught on the first bounce were outs until the mid–1880s, while foul tips were outs if caught in the air. The latter is what Craver claimed to have done.
47. See, for example, Ryczek, *When Johnny Came Sliding Home*, 188–189.
48. *Macon Weekly Telegraph*, September 17, 1869.
49. *Louisville Courier-Journal*, August 29–30, 1869, 5.
50. *Albany Evening Journal*, August 30, 1869.
51. Edwin A. Goewen, *Leslie's*, reprinted in *Auburn Citizen*, July 24, 1919.
52. *Troy Press*, reprinted in *Cleveland Herald*, September 1, 1869, 3.
53. *New York Herald*, September 10, 1869.
54. "Haymakers' Palmy Era," *Troy Northern Budget*, May 10, 1896, 2.
55. *Syracuse Evening Telegram*, June 17, 1901.
56. *Sporting News*, November 28, 1912.
57. *New York Sunday Mercury*, May 22, 1880.
58. *Boston Globe*, January 17, 1915.
59. *Sporting Life*, March 4, 1911, 13.
60. "Famed Old Haymakers," *Troy Northern Budget*, April 19, 1896, 5.
61. *New York Clipper*, September 7, 1867; quoted in Ryczek, *When Johnny Came Sliding Home*, 187.
62. "Paid Players: Amateur Ball Began to Wane in 1869," E. H. Tobias, seventh of sixteen-part history of baseball in St. Louis up to 1876, *Sporting News*, December 14, 1895, 5.
63. *The Unique*, November 1, 1851, reprinted in the *Troy Northern Budget*, June 17, 1900, 10.
64. *Seattle Post Intelligencer*, October 20, 1899; *Descendants of John Hotchkin of Guilford, CT*, by Edgar Hotchkin (see http://hotchkingenealogy.com/).
65. *Albany Evening Journal*, May 10, 1897.
66. *Troy Northern Budget*, October 22, 1911, 19.
67. *Chicago Tribune*, May 26, 1918.
68. *Duluth News-Tribune*, December 30, 1906.
69. *Cincinnati Daily Gazette*, October 18, 1870.
70. *Troy Northern Budget*, October 22, 1911, 19.
71. *Troy Northern Budget*, July 14, 1895, 5.
72. *Lansingburgh Weekly Chronicle*, December 5, 1866.
73. *Troy Northern Budget*, June 8, 1902, 6.
74. Ryczek, *When Johnny Came Sliding Home*, 186–187.
75. *New York Clipper*, August 21, 1869.
76. "Famous Old Haymaker Base Ball Club," *Troy Northern Budget*, April 26, 1896, 8.
77. *New York Clipper*, June 27, 1868.
78. *Troy Record*, October 16, 1946.

❖ *Excelsiors of Albany* (Peter Morris) ❖

Club History

The Excelsior Base Ball Club of Albany had a brief existence that ended in mystery. Nevertheless they deserve to be remembered as a reminder that the most imposing challenge faced by many early clubs was that of finding anyone willing to play them.

The Excelsior club was organized on May 12, 1856, during

what proved quite an active year for baseball in Albany. The Excelsiors faced the Empire Club of Albany in their first match and won. That seems to have ended the ambitions of the Empire Club, but another new club was soon formed to challenge the Excelsiors for local supremacy. In an intriguing and rather saucy move, the new club called itself "The Rivals" but announced that it intended to take the name of Excelsior if they won the match.

The original Excelsior Club emerged triumphant from the match, thereby retaining local honors and its name. The Rivals immediately issued a challenge for a rematch but when the appointed day rolled around the challengers did not show up. That ended the 1856 baseball season in Albany.

On April 1, 1857, the Excelsiors organized for the year, electing Walter C. Osborn as president, Thomas L. Goodwin and George S. Dawson as vice presidents, A. DeGraff as secretary, and W.A. Van Rensselaer as treasurer. In addition to the officers, the club chose a five-man board of managers that consisted of Dr. J. L. Babcock, R. M. Sherman, J. G. Waldron, John M. Rankin, and Charles W. Gibbs. The club also completed arrangements to use the grounds of the Albany Cricket Club for its matches and announced itself ready to accept challenges.

All of this activity suggests that the Excelsiors expected 1857 to be a banner year for baseball in Albany. Instead, no challenges seem to have been forthcoming and that is the end of the known activities of the Excelsior Base Ball Club of Albany. The members may soon have tired of intrasquad games and turned to other forms of recreation. It is also entirely possible that they continued to play for several more years, but attracted no attention.

At any rate, when a different Excelsior Club — the mighty Excelsiors of Brooklyn — paid a visit to Albany four years later, there was no indication that anyone remembered that a club by that name had once been the local champions. In the ensuing years, Albany was represented by several prominent clubs, most notably the Nationals and Knickerbockers of Albany, who flourished in the late 1860s. But the Excelsior Club seems to have passed entirely from local memory.

Club Members

Dr. James L. Babcock: A member of the Excelsior Club's board of managers, Babcock was born in 1824 in New York state, and was living in the town on Bethlehem, near Albany, in 1850. He later moved to Albany and practiced medicine there for many years. According to an online genealogy, he moved to Colorado and then to Humboldt, Nebraska, where he died on April 23, 1912.

George Seward Dawson: George S. Dawson, the club's second vice president, was born on November 7, 1838, in Rochester, New York. His Scottish-born father, also named George, grew up in Rochester and worked for Thurlow Weed, a newspaper editor and the organizer of a baseball club in the 1830s. Weed later moved to Albany to become the proprietor of the *Albany Evening Journal*, and George Dawson followed him, initially as assistant editor and later as editor and proprietor. The younger George worked as a printer for Thurlow Weed's publishing company. When the Civil War broke out, he volunteered but was rejected due to poor eyesight. But he was eventually able to obtain a lieutenantcy in the 2nd New York Artillery and earned a promotion to captain. At the siege of Petersburg on June 16, 1864, Dawson was shot in the leg. At first the wound appeared minor, but his condition deteriorated and the leg had to be amputated. Finally, on December 6, 1864, Dawson died in Albany of his wounds.[1]

A. DeGraff: DeGraff was the club's secretary, but has not been positively identified.

Charles W. Gibbs: Charles Gibbs, a member of the club's board of managers, was born around 1838 in New York and grew up in Albany. He enlisted in the Union Army as a lieutenant and served in the 44th New York Infantry for more than two years, earning promotion to captain. He died in Albany on February 11, 1914.

Thomas Laing Goodwin: Goodwin, the club's first vice president, was born on January 24, 1835, near Albany, and moved to Albany to work as a lithographer. He and his family eventually moved to the small nearby town of Watervliet. He died on November 7, 1888.

Walter C. Osborn: Osborn was the club president. The only man by that name was born around 1834 in New York state, served in the Civil War, and later worked as a clerk in Binghamton, dying on August 30, 1900.

John M. Rankin: Another member of the board of managers, John Rankin was born around 1834 in New York and worked as a clerk and later ran an advertising bureau. He died in Albany on February 29, 1888.

R. M. Sherman: This member of the board of managers has not been positively identified but may be a man named Rufus M. Sherman.

Dr. Walter A. Van Rensselaer: Walter A. Van Rensselaer, the club's treasurer, was born on November 24, 1836, and like Babcock became a doctor. In the late 1850s he moved to Kingston, New York, to begin a practice. When the Civil War broke out he enlisted and earned promotion to major. He was wounded at Gettysburg and mustered out as a result. He returned to Kingston to practice medicine and raise five children. He died on November 17, 1879, and his death was attributed to his war wounds.

James G. Waldron: James G. Waldron of the board of managers was born around 1831. Like Babcock, he was living in the nearby town of Bethlehem in 1850 but later moved to Albany and worked as a coal dealer. He died in Albany on February 18, 1899.

SOURCE

Porter's Spirit of the Times, May 23, 1857, from *Albany Transcript*.

NOTE

1. *Albany Journal*, August 10, 1896, reprint of an article by Fred Mather in *Forest and Stream* containing his memories of both George Dawsons; Rufus Wheelwright Clark, *The Heroes of Albany* (1866), 318–335.

❖ *Utica Base Ball Club* (Scott Fiesthumel) ❖

CLUB HISTORY

In December 1860, the Utica Base Ball Club from upstate New York was one of 58 clubs represented at the New York City convention of baseball clubs. The club had played eight games during the summer of 1860, posting a 5-2-1 record against rivals from the Utica area, and the single and married members of the club had also faced each other in a game. The members were looking forward to the next season, not knowing that the onset of the Civil War would curtail the number of games played in 1861. Some of the club members and officers were not players, or played in only one or two games a year. A majority of club members were businessmen or white-collar workers and several were connected to volunteer fire companies. Every spring the club met to elect officers for the new season. At the 1861 meeting, the club decided on a uniform of blue coat with gray flannel shirt and cap, and in 1864 the members decided the dues would be $2 for existing members and $3 for new ones.

The Utica Base Ball Club's scorebook for 1860 through 1865 gives a good portrait of the club. The scorebook was in the possession of LaMott Thomson when he died in 1909 and now is in the collection of the Oneida County Historical Society. During that six-year period, the club played 39 games against other clubs, posting a 25-13-1 record, as well as some intrasquad exhibitions between the married and single members. The star was Thomson, who played in 38 of those 39 games. He led all players with 128 runs scored and was the main pitcher, posting a 20-7 record. LaMott's brother Mortimer was second to him with 33 games played and 83 runs scored. Several other pairs of brothers played for the club.

Most of Utica's early games were against opponents from the Utica area, such as Whitestown and Hamilton College, but Utica soon began playing nines from Syracuse, Rochester, and the Albany area, such as the Victory Club of Troy and the Knickerbockers of Albany. The home side often hosted a reception or dinner after the matches, which were as much a social event as a sporting event. In 1864 Utica played two of the best-known clubs of the time, the Mutuals of New York City (a Utica loss) and the Atlantics of Brooklyn (the Atlantics led 4-2 when rain came in the fourth inning).

The Mutuals played several games against upstate clubs and after they returned home had special thanks for their Utica hosts:

To the Utica Base Ball Club, of Utica, whose guests we were while there, we cannot find words fitting to express our gratitude. Their liberal and warm reception, their marked attention to our slightest wishes, their gentlemanly courtesy on each and every occasion, where they could, by any possibility, tender us a favor, and their handsome entertainment after the game has left in our hearts an obligation which we must at some period, no matter how distant, have an opportunity to cancel in a small degree as we cannot exist with the knowledge that even to these gentlemen we shall be forced to remain forever indebted to so great an extent. To Messrs. Griffin, Thompson [*sic*], Taylor, and each and every member of that excellent club, we trust that the personal friendships formed on the occasion of our brief stay in the City of Utica may be as lasting as they are strong at the present time.

Obviously the game, a 26–8 Mutuals victory, was secondary to the social bonds between the clubs.

Some of Utica's games were played for a silver cup or ball, or for cash, and there was often betting on the games. A game against the Oneida Castle club in 1867 was played for a $30 stake. Utica won, 48–32, even though the club began the game with only eight players and finished it with seven after one suffered an injury. Some of the game accounts in the Utica scorebook contain notes written by the scorer regarding the weather, umpiring, and spectators. In September 1863 Utica traveled to play the Knickerbockers of Albany. According to the scorebook, "On account of the interference of the spectators & other excitement on the fair grounds it was impossible to catch any fly balls tho the Knicks done all that could be done to keep the field clear. Game closed on account of darkness. On the part of Ford [of Albany] as pitcher ⅔ of his balls were to [*sic*] high to be struck at & generally his pitching was very irregular."

Two years later, Utica was hosted by the Nationals of Albany. The 75–17 Utica win produced this notation: "A beautiful day & many spectators on the grounds, including quite a delegation of ladies. There was a strong west wind that against Utica did some of the finest batting ever witnessed on the grounds." Two weeks after that, Utica played a game in Albany against the Knickerbockers that they were much less happy with: "The umpire in this match made 8 or 9 errors against Utica. 4 of which were errors against the plain rules of the game. His errors lost the game for Utica." The umpire happened to be Y.E. Lane of the Nationals club, so perhaps he wasn't happy with the way Utica had defeated his club two weeks before.

An 1864 game in Albany against the Knickerbockers gave Utica a chance to exhibit good sportsmanship when it started to get dark during Utica's last at-bat. Trailing 32–17, Utica scored 11 runs to get within four runs of the Knicks with only one out. Not wanting to win the game because the Knickerbocker players couldn't see in the dark and with the umpire refusing to call the match, two Utica players purposely struck out to end the game. The Knicks then hosted the Utica club at a local dining establishment and the members of the two clubs spent an agreeable couple of hours together.

Amateur baseball remained popular in Utica for many years even as the professional game evolved. Utica's entry in the 1878 International Association featured longtime major league stars Hardy Richardson and Doc Bushong and in 1885 the city received its first of several New York State league franchises.

Club Members

Lewis H. Babcock was a lawyer.

Moses M. Bailey was a clerk at the Butterfield House hotel and ran the Apollo Billiard Saloon.

Thomas Bailey was a spinner.

Samuel Barnum was the first president of the Utica Base Ball Club. He later moved to Chicago, where he was a successful businessman until he lost nearly everything in the Great Fire of 1871. He recovered from those losses. Born July 19, 1828; died May 28, 1900, in Chicago.

M. P. Callender was a player and officer. He was a printer for the *Utica Herald* newspaper.

Thomas Carton was a bookkeeper.

George B. Chase was a conductor on the city railroad.

Albert DeForrest Crocker was the club's original first baseman. He was a clerk at the American Express Company and was in the lumber business. He was also a volunteer fireman with the Tiger Hose Company and ran the first skating rink in Utica. Born August 21, 1841, in Utica; died September 13, 1896, in Utica.

George Langford Curran was an officer and player. He was a successful businessman who was well respected for his charitable work in Utica and was known as the "father of night schools" for his efforts in promoting education. Born March 10, 1840, in Utica; died November 18, 1925, in Utica.

Charles M. Dagwell was born on October 7, 1843, in Utica, and died on July 22, 1912, in Utica. When he was 17, Dagwell enlisted in the Union Army and served during the first two years of the Civil War. After his enlistment expired, he worked at the Remington Armory for a year before enlisting in the Navy for the rest of the war. In 1870, he became a Utica police officer and became police chief in 1889. He resigned in 1898 after being found guilty of neglecting his duty to enforce laws regarding taverns and saloons. He was an officer of the volunteer Washington Engine Company No. 7 and the Exempt Fireman's Association.

John J. Davis, died May 6, 1878, in Utica, owned the Central Hotel and was a volunteer fireman.

Dr. Horace Day was a medical doctor and insurance agent. Died August 24, 1870, in Utica.

William J. Doolittle was a player and officer. He was a bookkeeper at the Bank of Utica. See the Mutuals of Janesville for more details. Born June 13, 1833, in Utica; died August 9, 1912, in Cleveland, Ohio.

F. Louis Faass was born on January 18, 1847, in Meintzheim, Baden (Germany), and died on January 25, 1926, in Utica. His family had a grocery business and he later became a contractor and city employee involved in many public-works projects. He served as an alderman and was an officer of the volunteer Washington Engine Company No. 7 and the Exempt Fireman's Association. He was a pitcher during his playing days. He financed early Utica amateur and professional baseball clubs, often acting as umpire.

James G. French was a lawyer. Born November 9, 1823, in Utica; died October 27, 1915.

Henry Griffin ran the Apollo & Metro billiard halls.

Frederick J. Harding was one of three players to appear in more than half of the Utica club's games from 1860 through 1865. He was born in Ireland in 1842 and was employed as a bookkeeper for local breweries. Died December 8, 1907, in Utica.

John S. Hill was a player and officer who was a clerk at several businesses. He was a volunteer fireman with the Tiger Hose Company. Born on June 25, 1828, in Martinsburg, New York; died August 1, 1905, in Utica.

John C. Kelley was the proprietor of the Sherwood House.

John D. Kernan and **Nicholas Kernan** were brothers and players. The Kernans were lawyers, and their family is well known in Utica's history. Their father served as a U.S. congressman and senator.

Charles E. Kirtland was a telegrapher at the Butterfield House hotel.

Samuel Y. Lane served as a club officer and umpired many games. He was a volunteer fireman with Rescue Hook & Ladder Company No 1, and was involved in several businesses, including an express company. After illness affected his hearing in 1897, he complained of unbearable ringing noises in his head that drove him to suicide in 1899 at the age of 68.

Ichabod Collins McIntosh was a player and officer. He was a lawyer who served as a city attorney and a Utica alderman. Born September 17, 1831, in Steuben, New York; died February 1, 1904, in Utica.

John W. McQuade was a lawyer involved in real estate and his family's business, McQuade & Sons. The company is still in business.

Marcus M. Miles was a student.

Edward Eames Millard (born 1843; died 1919 in New London, Connecticut) was a physician. In 1908 he was injured in a train crash that killed three. The same year his daughter married Wilford Bacon Hoggatt, the governor of Alaska.

John D. Mosher was a railroad engineer.

James Murdock was a jeweler and a volunteer fireman with the Tiger Hose Company.

George S. Porter played first base, third base, and catcher. He was a post office clerk and an insurance agent. He moved to New York City in 1897 and later to New Jersey. (Born in Utica. Died October 1, 1901, in Glen Ridge, New Jersey).

A. Stuart Potter was the barkeeper at the Baggs Hotel.

James B. Richardson was a clerk at the provost marshal's office.

George J. Sicard and **Stephen G. Sicard** (George born February 24, 1838; died August 26, 1904, in Buffalo, New York; Stephen born June 1, 1835; died November 5, 1890, in Utica) were born in New York City. Both were players and George also served as a club officer. George was a lawyer who moved to Buffalo, where he became a partner in a law firm after Grover Cleveland left the firm. Stephen was a bookkeeper at a bank and at a grain wholesaler. Their brother was Rear Admiral Montgomery Sicard, who served with the Union Navy during the Civil War.

William Taylor. Born April 1826 in Utica; died November 30, 1908, in Utica.

LaMott Thomson was born on September 27, 1825, in Paris Hill, New York, served as a Utica club officer and was the main pitcher for the club during the 1860s. After his death, the *Utica Daily Press* said he was "the originator, it is said, of the underhand curve.... The principle which Mr. Thomson employs was afterward adopted by others." Thomson was also called the "father of chess" in the Utica area. He was involved in numerous successful businesses in Utica, including insurance, real estate, and express companies. He left a large estate upon his death in Utica on August 7, 1909.

Mortimer G. Thomson, Lamott's younger brother, served as a club officer and as a player, mostly as a second baseman. He was involved in many of the same businesses as LaMott. Mortimer was also a well-known horseman in the Utica area. Born December 24, 1826, Paris Hill; died January 12, 1900, in Utica.

David P. White was a school commissioner.

Nathan Curtis White was a player and officer. He was a lawyer. Born September 24, 1822, in Torrington, Connecticut; died February 14, 1900, in Osprey, Florida.

Calvin H. Williamson was a druggist. Died August 16, 1903, in South Pines, South Carolina.

Other Members: Carpenter, Calvin Hall, Henry Hall, G. Pier.

Sources

This entry is based primarily on the Scrapbook of the Utica Base Ball Club, now at the Oneida County Historical Society. City directories and census records were also used to identify club members and newspaper obituaries provided additional details.

❖ Syracuse Base Ball Club (Peter Morris) ❖

Club History

There were some signs before 1858 that Syracuse would be a fertile ground for baseball clubs. Townball was played near Clinton Square as early as the 1830s, prompting the Syracuse Common Council to ban ballplaying in both Clinton and Hanover Square in 1845.[1] An 1856 article reported, "Ball playing is all the fashion now. It's excellent exercise, and the men as well as youngsters enjoy it."[2]

A list of rules based upon the Knickerbocker Rules was even printed in the *Syracuse Standard*, apparently in 1855.[3] Nonetheless, it took several more years before baseball activity in Syracuse began to take shape. Some subsequent accounts suggested that the Syracuse Base Ball Club began play in 1857, which is entirely possible, but contemporary documentation of this claim is lacking. Instead, an article in the *Standard* on October 6, 1858, reported that the "Syracuse Base Ball Club has been organized but a few weeks" and listed the officers of the new club, including president George Gratton, vice president William H.H. Geer, secretary M.H. Avery, and treasurer Frank Carroll.[4]

Once established, the club showed considerable enthusiasm, playing at least seven intrasquad contests that were reported in the *Standard* during October and November of 1858. The first two games seem to have been rather informal — six players facing seven in the first one and ten playing against nine in the second, with "short fielders" and "long fielders" scattered about as needed. In addition, the two sides in these matches were chosen by the captains.[5]

But the remaining contests became more structured, with clubs of nine per side representing the married and single members. The club established grounds for these matches near West Fayette and Geddes Streets and spectators began turning out to watch. According to Syracuse historian Ron Gersbacher, the club even added reversible belts (black on one side, white on the other) to their uniforms in order to choose and distinguish the two sides.[6] The play also showed signs of improvement, with increased emphasis on "scientific playing" and on showing "an eye to the strong points, and a will and muscle to go in for them, that would do honor to much older clubs."[7]

Competition between the married and single members

of the Syracuse Base Ball Club continued well after the weather began to turn cold. After one November game, the *Standard*'s reporter noted that a large crowd of spectators had turned out despite the inclement conditions. The writer added optimistically that "the interest they manifested during the progress of the game, showed that Base Ball is bound to be an institution in Syracuse as well as elsewhere."[8] A few days later, he added, "Base ball playing has become an institution in our goodly town, sure enough. The Club formed here during the season has increased to a goodly number, and with numbers comes good players and good spunk."[9]

When the spring of 1859 rolled around, it became clear that baseball had indeed taken root. The Syracuse Base Ball Club organized in early May and set up grounds on Lodi Street as well as regular practice days.[10] After beginning the season with another married-versus-single contest, it began facing outside competition.

The first such match was scheduled to be played against a club called the Salt Point Club, but there is no record of the result.[11] By contrast, the first contest between the Syracuse Base Ball Club and an outside opponent attracted very thorough coverage. The match was played in Canastota on August 18, 1859, and the emphasis was on ceremony.

"The Canastota Club," began a game account, "desirous of a pleasant day's sport in competition with one of older date than their own, sent a friendly challenge to the Syracuse Club, which was accepted, and the game came off yesterday afternoon at Canastota." The Syracuse players brought several other club members along with them and the party was "cordially received" by their hosts.

The playing field itself proved most unsatisfactory, as "too much grass formed a very slippery and insecure footing, and the very many little depressions and elevations of an ordinary meadow field rendered entirely uncertain the course of a bounding ball." Nevertheless, "good fellowship" prevailed throughout the match, as there was "not a harsh or unkind word between the contestants…. All and each quietly but vigorously plied himself to the game."

When play concluded with the Syracuse Base Ball Club victorious by a 44–38 count, the winners "gave three lusty cheers and a tiger for the Canastota Club, which was promptly and as heartily responded to by Capt. Plank's men; and then all adjourned to—(did you think I was going to say drink?—you are mistaken—I did not see a drop of *the ardent* taken during the afternoon)—supper." After the two clubs did "ample justice" to the feast prepared by the host nine the Syracuse Club returned home and passed a resolution thanking the Canastota Club for the generous hospitality.[12]

It was a model of how a baseball match was supposed to be conducted, and the same spirit prevailed when a rematch was staged in Syracuse in September. After the contest concluded with another narrow win for the Syracuse Base Ball Club, the two clubs enjoyed a hearty supper at the Timby & Sherman saloon and "the best of feeling prevailed." The Canastota Club presented the host club with the baseball that symbolized victory, toasts and brief speeches were made, and a good time was had by all.[13]

Good fellowship again prevailed at a match played in Oswego on September 23. After the Syracuse Club beat the host Frontier Club, an Oswego newspaper wrote that the visitors "are a fine looking company of men, and are very handsomely uniformed. Each member is a gentleman in every respect."[14]

In the next recorded match of the Syracuse Club, however, a new spirit of competitiveness emerged for the first time. The opponents were the Olympics, a local club that had already lost to the Syracuse Base Ball Club at least once, although the date and score are unknown. As a result, it was announced that the rematch on September 28 would feature the Olympics and the second nine of the Syracuse Club.

Unfortunately, there was confusion on this point and on almost every other aspect of the ill-fated contest. A game account reported that "many of the players" who showed up to represent the Syracuse Club were in fact members of the first nine, although this was denied by both clubs. Worse, only seven Syracuse players were on hand at the scheduled hour and the umpire had already announced a forfeit when two more men arrived. The Olympics sportingly agreed to go ahead with the match, but the late start made it impossible to play nine innings. Some sort of agreement was reached, but when darkness began to fall with the score close, it turned out that the two sides had very different understandings of what had been decided. Play was finally ended in the seventh inning with the Olympics one run ahead.

An account of the game in the *Standard* dwelled mostly on positive aspects, describing the fine fielding plays that were made and the home runs that "were unequalled, and elicited hearty applause." But the author of the account was apparently a member of the Olympic Club and his comments about the disputed points provoked more controversy. A member of the Syracuse Club angrily denounced misstatements in the account and accused the Olympics of doing "all in their power to protract the game" while they were winning so that the umpire would have to stop play. Meanwhile a member of the Olympics conceded that the Syracuse Club had not used members of its first nine and tried to be conciliatory, remarking that "the Syracuse Club … has always taken the deepest interest in our welfare." Yet he couldn't resist the urge to add that his club did "not wish to make our victory appear greater than it really is," thereby further antagonizing the members of the Syracuse Club who disputed the outcome.

For his part, the editor of the *Standard* was disgusted by the squabbling. He apologized to his readers for publishing the letters at all, explaining, "We were not aware that the report published yesterday, contained anything of an objectionable character, and having admitted that we can do no less than publish an answer. But we desire to give notice that we do not consider a discussion of Base Ball disputes, of sufficient interest to the public to fill our columns hereafter."[15]

Not surprisingly, the Onondaga Historical Association's collection of clippings from the *Standard* includes no more articles about baseball. It's possible that the *Standard* did continue covering baseball and that those issues were unavailable or were not examined. But the timing suggests that the editor of the *Standard* had decided that baseball no longer merited attention.

This means that we don't know much about the activities of the Syracuse Base Ball Club in October and November of 1859. It's possible that weather or scheduling problems prevented additional play. But an article the next year stated that the Frontier Club of Oswego had been beaten twice by the Syracuse Base Ball Club in 1859, and the lack of known coverage of the second match suggests that the squabbles had prompted the *Standard* to boycott baseball.[16]

In any event, the Syracuse Base Ball Club began preparation for another season of play in the spring of 1860. Officers were elected, details attended to, and the campaign launched with another game between the club's single and married members. Significantly, however, it was a new paper — the *Journal*— that carried accounts of the club's doings.[17]

Matches against rival clubs soon followed, but they proved far more contentious than in 1859 (or at least the *Journal* was far more willing to report on disputes than the *Standard* had been). In particular, a series against a club from Cazenovia caused no end of controversy. The first match was played on neutral grounds in the village of Chittenango and attracted a sizable crowd that included "hundreds of ladies" along with ballplayers from the towns of Oneida, Canastota, Chittenango, Syracuse, Manlius, and Cazenovia. "Considerable sums of money" were bet on the contest, which saw the Cazenovia club come out on top by the score of 32–20.[18]

The second game was played in Cazenovia and this time it was the Syracuse nine that emerged victorious. But the loss prompted the Cazenovia Club to allege that there had been "collusion between the umpire and the Syracuse players." In response, the Syracuse Club maintained that the umpire was a "man of honor" from Utica who had been selected by the Cazenovia Club and was "a stranger to the Syracuse Club."[19]

The Syracuse Club won the third and deciding game and was declared "champions of the field in Central New York."[20] The bold proclamation led to more challenges. Matches against the Frontier Club of Oswego and the Union Springs Club ensued in September, both of which were won by the Syracuse Club without any reported incidents.[21] The Cazenovia Club also issued a challenge, but there is no record of its being accepted.[22]

Perhaps that is just as well because the two recorded matches that were played by the Syracuse Base Ball Club in October of 1860 both ended in acrimony. On the 10th, the opponent was the Utica Club, and game accounts suggested that all had gone smoothly. The Syracuse players cut an impressive figure in "a picturesque, Zouave-like uniform, consisting of blue cap, white flannel jacket, red breeches, and cricketer's shoes." After a closely fought 20–19 win by Syracuse, the host Utica Club treated their guests to an elegant supper. The presentation of the ceremonial ball was accompanied by speeches, singing, and "the utmost good feeling."[23]

Yet as soon as the Syracuse Club left town, the bickering began. Both the *Utica Observer* and the *Utica Telegraph* complained that umpire John Wilkinson, Jr., of the Olympic Club of Syracuse had favored the victors. Another Utica paper, the *Herald*, offered a tepid defense of Wilkinson, noting that the "rules of the New York game" require acceptance of the umpire's decisions. But the piece went on to criticize those decisions and to state that it was a mistake to let Wilkinson umpire, since "the Olympics are only an offshoot of the Syracuse City Club, and feel as much interest in the latter's success as in their own."[24] The article concluded by declaring that "the Utica Club can beat Syracuse any day in the week."[25] The *Syracuse Journal* responded in kind, gloating: "We admit that it is decidedly 'tough' that both the Cricket and Base Ball Clubs of boasting Utica should be beaten in the same week by the Syracuseans, but it seems to us that it would be much better for the beaten parties to keep their temper."[26]

The next match for the Syracuse Club, a rematch with the Union Springs Club on the 12th, followed a similar pattern. The match was played at Auburn for a purse of $20 and was ended by darkness after seven innings with the Syracuse Club clinging to a narrow lead. At the finish, "cheers were given by the Syracuse boys for the Union Springs Club, which were heartily responded to by the latter Club." Both clubs were also thanked by the Logan Club of Auburn, which had offered the purse in order to watch the "scientific playing" of "such masters of the game."[27]

Once again, however, the good will was destroyed by subsequent grumbling in the newspapers. Syracuse scorer Alfred Wilkinson was forced to defend himself against unspecified allegations.[28] This was followed by a claim that the pitcher and catcher of the Syracuse nine had been "imported" for the occasion, a charge that brought an equally sharp retort.[29]

On that sour note, the 1860 season came to an end and to all intents and purposes, so too did the career of Syracuse's pioneer baseball club. Over the winter a match on ice was proposed against the Union Springs Base Ball Club, but there is no record that the ice became strong enough to allow it to take place.[30] By the spring of 1861 the Civil War was under way and baseball activity in Syracuse pretty much came to a halt. One meeting was held to try to organize a new Syracuse Union Base Ball Club, and a couple of attempts were made to arrange contests with clubs from Utica and Union Springs.[31] But the reality that "most of our best ball players are playing 'ball' with the rebels" proved too much to overcome.[32]

By the time the war ended, the first baseman of the Syracuse Base Ball Club had lost his life at the Battle of Peach Tree Creek and many other club members had decided to retire from active play. As a result, the new Central City Club was formed to represent Syracuse and was mostly made up of younger players. Yet the members of Syracuse's pioneer club did not lose their interest in baseball. An 1886 article reported that men like Harrison Geer, Frank Carroll, Charles Tamkin, and Alfred Wilkinson of the Syracuse Base Ball Club were still in town and "may be seen at Star Park at almost every game. They still retain their old-time interest in the game."[33]

Club Members

Matthew Henry Avery: Matthew Avery was born in Middletown Springs, Vermont, on March 27, 1836, the son of a Congregational minister. He operated a book and stationery store in Syracuse before the Civil War, but at the outbreak of the war he raised a company of cavalry at Syracuse and was soon appointed as captain. He commanded the 10th New York Cavalry for most of the next four years and became a colonel. He was brevetted brigadier general on March 13, 1865, for "gallantry in action at Sailor's Creek, Va., and for faithful and meritorious services." He went into the oil business after the war and died on September 1, 1881, in Geneva, New York.

Charles Barnes: See Central City Base Ball Club of Syracuse.

George Barnes: George Barnes was born in Tenterden, England, on October 1, 1827. He began working in the office of a local solicitor at the age of 13, then four years later was persuaded by his uncle to emigrate to the United States. Upon arriving in Syracuse, he worked as a mason and then as a clerk in the office of pioneer lawyer John Wilkinson. Wilkinson helped him obtain a good position with the Syracuse and Utica Railroad. In 1856 Barnes moved to Ohio to work for the Marietta and Cincinnati Railroad, but that railway soon experienced financial setbacks and he returned to Syracuse. It was over the next few years that he was an active member of the Syracuse Base Ball Club. In 1860 he and a partner opened a business that manufactured mower and reaper knives and cast steel. Eventually the two parts of the business were divided, and Barnes created a knife-making firm that became highly successful, employing some 1,500 workers and doing business all over the world. George Barnes also helped found the State Bank of Syracuse and the Trust and Deposit Company of Onondaga County. Barnes was a large, powerfully built man who retained an interest in baseball and cricket throughout his life. During the 1880s, however, he became afflicted by locomotor ataxia, a disease that left him in constant pain. He died on October 17, 1892, in New York City, while returning home from a trip to Europe that he had taken in hope of reviving his flagging health.

James Barnes: James Barnes was a brother of Charles and George. He was born around 1833 in Tenterden, England, and moved to London to study music. He followed his brothers to Syracuse, where he was the organist for several churches and ran a music store. He later went to work for the Onondaga Savings Bank. In 1879 he became secretary of the Trust and Deposit Company of Onondaga County and remained in that position for many years. He was still living in Syracuse in 1906 and is believed to have died in 1916.

Peter John "P.J." Brumelkamp: P.J. Brumelkamp was born in Holland in August of 1838, immigrating to the U.S. at the age of 9. He became a successful Syracuse businessman, running a men's furnishing store and working as a contractor. He also became prominent in Democratic politics and was eventually named superintendent of the Onondaga Salt Springs. He died on February 17, 1902.

Jacobus C. Bruyn: J.C. Bruyn died in Syracuse on October 30, 1868, age 48.

John Germond Butler: John G. Butler was born on March 16, 1834, in Utica. His family settled in Syracuse when he was 4. He worked as a bank teller before the Civil War, then enlisted in a regiment that became known as Butler's Zouaves (Company D, 3rd New York). He rose to the rank of colonel but had to be mustered out when he contracted typhoid fever, a development that he later described as one of the "great sorrows" of his life. After the war he worked in Annapolis and Mexico before returning to Syracuse in 1885 to become secretary and treasurer of the Syracuse Water Works. When the Spanish-American War broke out, Butler again enlisted. He lived long enough to see the outbreak of World War I and to express regrets that he was too old to serve his country again, although his son did enlist. Butler died in Syracuse on October 4, 1917.

Francis Edward Carroll: See Central City Base Ball Club of Syracuse.

Augustus Byron Cheney: A.B. Cheney was born on August 7, 1829, and his was a life marked by tragedy. When he was 11, two of his uncles were killed in a powder explosion at the Syracuse factory where they worked. His younger brother George was a gifted chess player who was killed in the Civil War. A.B. Cheney was married by then, but his wife died around 1869, leaving him a widower with five young children. He moved to a farm on the outskirts of Syracuse, eventually remarrying and living there until his death in late May 1905.

Charles D. Davis: Charles D. Davis was born around 1833 in Massachusetts and was simply listed as a "gentleman" on the 1860 Census.

William Henry Harrison "Harry" Geer: Harry or Harrison Geer was born on July 25, 1814, in Utica. He moved to Syracuse and became a professional photographer. His son George played professional baseball in the 1880s and then became a minor-league manager. William H.H. Geer died in Syracuse on June 12, 1894, just shy of his 80th birthday.

Sidney Brooks Gifford: Sidney Gifford was born in Syracuse around 1834 and lived there his entire life. He went to work for the New York, Albany & Buffalo Telegraph Company as a messenger boy while still a teenager. The company was bought by Western Union and Gifford went along, eventually rising to become the local telegraph superintendent. After a 52-year career in the telegraph business, he retired and devoted his last years to studying in his large personal library. He also retained his love of baseball to the end. He died in Syracuse on July 13, 1920, at the age of 85.

George W. Gratton: George Gratton was born in England around 1838 and became the first plumber in Syracuse, at one point being a partner of Frank Carroll. He and his family moved to Baltimore in 1862 and set up what was described as a "base-ball emporium." As described in the entry on the Excelsior/Pastime Club of Baltimore, he was credited with making major contributions to the growth of baseball in Maryland. Around 1869 he moved to Omaha, Nebraska, where he worked as a gas inspector.

John H. Ireland: John H. Ireland was born in Herefordshire, England, on February 3, 1833, and arrived in Syracuse in 1848. His name appeared in the first Syracuse directory of 1853 and when he died on May 2, 1921, at the age of 88, his obituary stated that he was the last man who could make that claim, as well as the last survivor of the city's first baseball club. For most of the intervening years, Ireland had worked as a dry-goods clerk.

John F. Kidder: John Kidder was born around 1831 in New York State and was listed on the 1860 Census as a city engineer.

Francis A. Marsh: Francis A. Marsh was a printer who was born around 1819. He appears to have been strictly a non-playing member.

Levi Snow Mayo: Levi Mayo was born around 1839 and worked as a local agent for the United States Express while living in Syracuse. He eventually moved to New Haven, Connecticut, and went into the insurance business. He died in New Haven on February 25, 1915.

David McClelland: David McClelland was born in New York City on April 29, 1825. He worked as a clerk before the war and later became a hatter. He died in Syracuse on September 18, 1882.

John McNamara: John McNamara was born in Ireland around 1830 and was listed as a tailor on the 1860 Census.

Alfred Moore: Alfred Moore was born in England around 1823 and was listed as a railroad baggageman on the 1860 Census.

William W. Ostrander: William Ostrander was born around 1837 and served in the 149th New York for nearly three years during the Civil War. He later worked as an undertaker, a clerk, and a hardware salesman. His war service remained a vivid memory and in 1913 he traveled to Chattanooga to attend a reunion of Confederate veterans. While there, he enjoyed swapping tales with his onetime enemies, and especially enjoyed listening to descriptions of the Battle of Gettysburg from the opposite perspective. He died in Oran, New York, on August 24, 1922.

Richard Paine, Jr.: Richard Paine was born in New Rumney, England, in 1824. He worked as a wig maker and died in Syracuse on December 2, 1892. Some later accounts referred to him as Richard Page but contemporary records make it clear that this was a mistake.

Richard Husted Parker: R. H. Parker was born on January 22, 1831, in Onondaga Hill, New York. He became a successful cigar manufacturer. He died in Syracuse on January 4, 1911.

Thomas Garret Putnam: Thomas G. Putnam was born in Fultonville, New York, on January 24, 1840, and studied law in the office of Syracuse lawyer George Comstock. Putnam served as a captain in the Fifteenth New York Cavalry during the Civil War and then settled in West Virginia, where he practiced law and was a member of the House of Delegates. He relocated to Denver in 1870 and was a prominent member of that city's bar until his death on September 6, 1903.

Charles B. Randall: Charles B. Randall was born around 1837 and he too became a lawyer. When the Civil War broke out, the first baseman of the Syracuse Base Ball Club enlisted in the 12th New York. He earned promotion to lieutenant colonel and was assigned to the 149th New York. He was severely wounded at Gettysburg but soon returned to active duty. While leading his troops to victory at Peach Tree Creek on July 20, 1864, Randall was killed. After the war a 30-page commemorative book was issued that paid tribute to his bravery.

George Davis Redfield: George Redfield was born around 1833. He died at St. Anthony, Minnesota, on March 27, 1871, at the age of 37, leaving a wife and three children.

Stiles Mortimer Rust: Stiles Rust was a lifelong resident of Syracuse, being born there on October 16, 1825, and passing away on August 10, 1896.

Harvey C. Sherwood: Harvey Sherwood was born around 1835 and grew up in DeWitt, a town near Syracuse. He moved to Syracuse and worked as a liveryman, then headed west to Michigan. He died in Watervliet, Michigan, on August 10, 1888.

William D. Stafford: William Stafford was born around 1839 in New York state and is listed as a railroad conductor on the 1860 Census.

Charles Tamkin: Charles Tamkin was born in March of 1835 in Tenterden, England. He was apprenticed to the father of the Barnes brothers and during one of George Barnes's visits home he heard him speak favorably of life in the United States. He followed the Barnes brothers to Syracuse, then to Ohio and back to Syracuse. After settling permanently in Syracuse in 1861, he opened a billiard parlor that became a popular hangout for the city's fashionable young men. Over the next 40 years he ventured into making pianos and bicycles but billiards remained his primary business and he operated the parlor for four decades. Like the Barnes brothers, he continued to play cricket after giving up baseball.

Horace H. Walpole: Horace Walpole was born in March of 1837 in New York state and served in the 122nd New York Infantry for nearly three years, attaining the rank of lieutenant colonel. After the war he ran a Syracuse insurance agency for many years. During the 1890s his health began to fail and the widowed Walpole spent his last years at a home for disabled veterans in Dayton, Ohio. He died on June 3, 1903.

Alfred Wilkinson: The Wilkinson brothers were the sons of pioneer Syracuse resident John Wilkinson, the city's first lawyer and first postmaster. The elder Wilkinson also selected the name of the city because of the resemblance between its salt-water springs and those of the ancient Sicilian city of Siracusa. Alfred Wilkinson was born around 1832 and he and his brother both became prominent Syracuse bankers. He died in Syracuse on July 7, 1886.

Joshua Forman Wilkinson: J. Forman Wilkinson was Alfred's older brother. He was born on June 12, 1829, and graduated from the Rensselaer Polytechnic Institute. He was a railroad man before the war, but then like many club members, served in the 149th New York during the Civil War. After the war he became a banker. He died in Syracuse on May 4, 1889.

J.W. Yale: See Central City Base Ball Club of Syracuse.

Other Members: Baker, William Beebe, H. D. Brewster, Brockway, Byron, J. R. Clark, A. G. Cook, James R. Mann, Franklin D. Mosher, M. Myers, Palmer, T. R. Radcliff, Roberts, John Ryan, John W. Sherman, Tracy, Van Houten, A. J. Young, A. C. Younglove.

Sources

My principal source is the clipping collection of the Onondaga Historical Association. The articles are hand-dated, which is why some dates are unknown and others questionable. Thanks to Larry McCray for providing me with copies of the articles. Also valuable were Charles E. Colton, "Saltine Town Early Power in Diamond," *Syracuse Post-Standard*, January 3, 1910; Ron Gersbacher, "Play Ball! A History of Early Organized Baseball in Syracuse," in *Portraits of the Past* (a publication of the Onondaga Historical Association) 7 (1994), n.p., and an untitled piece in *Sporting Life* on January 13, 1886.

Notes

1. Ron Gersbacher, "Play Ball! A History of Early Organized Baseball in Syracuse," *Portraits of the Past* (a publication of the Onondaga Historical Association) 7 (1994), n.p.
2. *Syracuse Standard*, April 30, 1856. In an unusual move, the writer of the article expressed regret that "fashion deprives" womanhood of "the benefits that might be derived from indulgence in such sports."
3. A copy of the clipping in the files of the Onondaga Historical Association is hand-dated May 16, 1855. The list includes 17 rules and is based upon the Knickerbocker Rules, but the numbering is different and there are a number of other differences.
4. *Syracuse Standard*, October 6, 1858.
5. *Syracuse Standard*, October 6 and 15, 1858.
6. Ron Gersbacher, "Play Ball! A History of Early Organized Baseball in Syracuse," *Portraits of the Past* (a publication of the Onondaga Historical Association) 7 (1994), n.p.
7. *Syracuse Standard*, October 15 and November 8, 1858.
8. *Syracuse Standard*, November 11, 1858.
9. *Syracuse Standard*, November 15, 1858.
10. *Syracuse Standard*, May 9, 1859.
11. *Syracuse Standard*, July 6, 1859.
12. *Syracuse Standard*, August 19, 1859.
13. *Syracuse Standard*, September 16, 1859.
14. *Oswego Times*, reprinted in *Syracuse Standard*, September 24, 1859.
15. *Syracuse Standard*, September 29 and 30, 1859.
16. *Syracuse Journal*, September 22, 1860.
17. *Syracuse Journal*, May 3, 19, and 23, 1860.
18. *Syracuse Journal*, August 1, 1860.
19. *Syracuse Journal*, August 25, 27, and 28, 1860.
20. *Syracuse Journal*, September 9, 1860.
21. *Syracuse Journal*, September 22 and October 30, 1860.
22. *Syracuse Journal*, September 19, 1860.
23. *Syracuse Journal*, October 12, 1860, based on accounts in the *Utica Herald* and *Utica Telegraph*.
24. Wilkinson, indeed, was the younger brother of two members of the Syracuse Club, one of whom was the club's scorer in the match.
25. Quoted in the *Syracuse Journal*, October 13, 1860.
26. *Syracuse Journal*, October 13, 1860.
27. *Auburn Advertiser*, reprinted in the *Syracuse Journal*, October 15, 1860.
28. *Syracuse Journal*, October 20, 1860.
29. *Syracuse Courier*, October 30, 1860.
30. *Syracuse Journal*, December 21, 1860.
31. *Syracuse Journal*, July 10 and October 15, 1861; *Syracuse Courier*, September 18, 1861.
32. *Syracuse Courier*, September 18, 1861.
33. *Sporting Life*, January 13, 1886.

❖ Central City Base Ball Club of Syracuse (Peter Morris) ❖

Club History

Like so many of the clubs formed during the post–Civil War baseball boom, the Central City Base Ball Club of Syracuse experienced many ups and downs between its formation in 1865 and its demise at the close of the 1869 season.

A meeting to organize the new club was held in April of 1865, within days of Lee's surrender at Appomattox Court House. A few days later, potential members were invited to stop by the Central City Bank and affix their name to the new club's constitution and bylaws. Although in many ways a continuation of the prewar Syracuse Base Ball Club, it was decided to select a new name and the choice was Central City — a name that served as their city's informal nickname and also paid tribute to the bank that initially served as the club's headquarters.[1]

The announcement of the new club's existence appeared on the same day as the terrible news of President Lincoln's assassination. A country longing to return to normalcy after the

Civil War was plunged back into mourning, and it was not until late May that Syracuse's new ballclub was heard from again. When the Central City Club did begin in earnest, it did so with a series of intrasquad games at Armory Park between the married and single members of the club. Somewhat surprisingly, these games attracted large crowds and "considerable interest ... as to the result," which spurred the new club to begin arranging matches against clubs from other towns.[2]

The first such match was played in Syracuse on June 2, 1865, and the opponent was the Utica Base Ball Club. Not surprisingly, the more experienced visiting side won by the decisive score of 38–17. But the result was not discouraging because, as the *Utica Telegraph* explained, "The Central City is a newly organized Club, and, as yet, have had but little practice. They have the material for a good club, and it only needs practice to secure for themselves a first class organization."[3]

A more noteworthy element of the day's events was the post-match feast. Such meals had been a prominent feature of antebellum matches, but the visitors from Utica "made it a condition of their trip not to accept or expect any of the usual club entertainments after the game, believing it to be for the best interest and support of the national game, which should be generally adopted." But the Central City Club "insisted that Utica money was not good in Syracuse, and handsomely entertained their visitors at the Sherman House" after the match.[4] The intriguing exchange was a portent of things to come, as many of the cherished rituals associated with prewar baseball would prove impractical and had to be abandoned.

The Central Citys faced several other outside clubs in 1865, including the Nationals of Oswego, the Monitors of Homer, and the Mutuals of Rochester. Yet the most notable aspect of the season's competition was the difficulty that the club had in arranging matches. On several occasions the club was forced to decline challenges because players were out of town or unavailable, while another match was delayed when one of the nine failed to show up.[5]

Efforts to arrange a rematch against the Utica Base Ball Club proved especially messy. The shared feast after the June 2 match had inspired expectations of "a lasting and endearing friendship between the respective clubs."[6] Instead, the men from Utica became increasingly frustrated as the Central City Club captain, J. W. Yale, made excuses that "the greater portion of the men are absent from town."

The underlying problem was not an unwillingness to contest matches. Rather the first nine of the Central City Club included many holdovers from the prewar Syracuse Base Ball Club and these men had now reached an age where there were many other claims on their time. Finally, the Central City Club offered to send its nine to play Utica's second nine. But what point was there to having a first nine at all if only the second nine was available for matches?[7]

It had become clear by the end of the 1865 season that some of the Central City Club's veterans had to be replaced with young blood. As a result, the most important match that the club played that year was probably one against a nine from Hamilton College of Clinton, New York. While eking out a 12–10 win, the Central City players became very impressed by the performances of two of the collegians, pitcher Byron Baker and left fielder George Porter. Over the winter the club bowed to the inevitable and began bringing in younger players, with Baker and Porter being two of the new men who were recruited. In addition, a junior club called the Olympics acted as a feeder club for the Central Citys, providing fresh young talent whenever needed.[8]

Thus the 1866 campaign began with several new players who brought renewed enthusiasm and energy. The season got off to an early start with the election of new officers and selection of practice days taking place in the first week of April, followed soon afterward by the first practice.[9]

When the club began to face outside competition, it appeared that there was good basis for optimism. After warming up against the Arctics, a local junior club, the Central Citys faced their first major challenge of 1866 on June 23 when they hosted the Pacifics of Rochester. The Pacifics were billed as the champions on Monroe County, so a large crowd turned out for the match and they were rewarded with an impressive 18–7 win for the home nine.

The match afforded more evidence that the prewar emphasis on baseball matches as ceremonies was being threatened by the emergence of a new outlook. The Central City Club did its best to uphold the gentlemanly traditions, meeting their guests at the station the night before and escorting them to their hotels, then joining them in post-match cheers ("three rousers and a tiger") and a hearty match. Yet a game account also noted that "considerable money changed hands on the result."[10]

Beating a strong club like the Pacifics was impressive enough, but still more striking was the fact that the Central Citys had held their opponents to only seven runs and had blanked them in five of the nine innings. These were remarkable accomplishments under the rules of the day and much of the credit went to the battery of catcher David Sanford, who was charged with only two passed balls, and new pitcher Byron Baker.

Despite the restrictions of the day, which forced pitchers to deliver the ball with a strict underhand motion and without bending their arms, an account in a Rochester paper claimed that Baker gave "a great bias [spin] to the ball, and at the same time it is slowly delivered, so as to drop on the bat, and the consequence is, that, unless the ball is struck fairly, its twist throws it in the air, giving, of course, a greater chance to the out fielders." In later articles, Baker would be described as having used "the modern twists and curves now so common in the pitchers of to-day" and even as "the first man to pitch a curve ball in Syracuse."[11] These two assertions must be taken with skepticism in light of the delivery restrictions that he worked under, but it seems clear that Baker's offerings featured an amount of twist or spin that was very unusual for the time.

Sadly, however, the match against the Pacifics would be Baker's last. He contracted typhoid fever and died on August 26, only a few months after having graduated with honors from Hamilton College.

The Central Citys were forced to regroup again and when they returned to the field the results were disappointing. In a lopsided September loss to the Excelsiors of Rochester, several players were absent and the play of those on hand was "decidedly 'muffy,' it being the poorest game we ever remember to have seen played by that Club."[12] The club concluded the season by entering a tournament in Auburn in which the prize for first place was a gold ball that was to become the symbol of regional supremacy over the next three years. George Porter of the Central Citys won a prize at the tournament for being the best fielder, but his club did not distinguish itself, being eliminated after a 44–29 loss to the Pacifics of Rochester. The lopsided loss to the same club that Baker had held to seven runs just a few months earlier provided another reminder of what a devastating loss his death had been to the Central Citys.

This disheartening ending to so promising a season meant that the winter of 1866-1867 was a second straight offseason of reflection. One local journalist offered this very pointed advice for the Central City Club:

> There are some very instructive lessons to be drawn from the contests which have just closed.... [A] first class club must, if we may so express ourselves, possess a certain amount of homogeneousness. Its members must be somewhere nearly of an age, somewhere nearly of equal size and strength, somewhere nearly of equal temperaments. Above all, they must be young. At a certain age it is impossible, except in extraordinary cases, for a person to possess the requisite quickness and the requisite muscularity to play well. He may indulge in games for mere pleasure, he may even play in matches of little importance, but when he comes to be pitted against youthful agility and youthful strength he fails. The crack clubs of the sea-board cities are all composed of comparatively young men. The two best clubs on the grounds at Auburn were made up of players whose similarity of age and stature were evident to every beholder. One of the Syracuse clubs — and singularly enough the one which enjoyed the highest reputation — was notoriously unsuccessful. This fact is mainly owing to the circumstances that the members of its first nine differ so greatly from each other. The ages of the oldest and youngest are many years apart; the statures of the tallest and shortest vary by many inches; the weight of some must exceed the weight of other by as much as three score of pounds. Under such circumstances it is surely not expected that the nine will pull together with sufficient strength and uniformity to successfully combat an association where there are no such differences as these.

The writer was just as adamant that the club's first nine needed to be chosen from men who were not so busy with work as to be unable to practice or attend matches.

> Our clubs ought already to be making their arrangements for next summer. Let each association select with great care its first nine. In making this selection, let it look with the utmost circumspection at the physical features and physical capacities of the nine men upon whom the reputation of the organization must rest. Let it insist that these men shall devote as much time to practice as possible. Let it insist that if there be a member who can do better in any position on the grounds than the one who holds the place, then the possessor shall gracefully give way. Let no man be allowed to retain a post on the bases or in the field, merely because he is a good fellow, or because he is warmly interested in the game. If he be not the right man in the right place, he should make room for his successor.[13]

The Central City Club's decision-makers seem to have reached a similar conclusion, so when the spring of 1867 rolled around, several of the older members of the first nine had been replaced by younger men. The result of the decision was that the club had its most stable lineup that season, rarely having to replace one of its first nine. Not surprisingly, the young players had some early struggles, including two losses to the Auburn Base Ball Club and one to the Utica Base Ball Club. But then the squad began to gel and produced the best season in the club's history.

On September 30, the Central Citys embarked on a five-day, five-city tour that turned out to be one of the highlights of the club's existence. After wins in Binghamton and Owego, New York, and Erie, Pennsylvania, the club arrived in Buffalo to contest for the gold ball — and left town as possessors of the coveted trophy after a thrilling 39–27 victory over the Niagaras. The Central Citys completed their tour with an impressive victory over the Excelsiors of Rochester, then returned home and successfully defended the gold ball against the Knickerbockers of Albany.

The great winning streak and the capture of the gold ball "raised 'base ball excitement' to fever heat" in Syracuse and the nine men who became known as the "champion nine"— David Sanford, Ed Yale, Will Cruttenden, George Porter, new pitcher Fred Dodge, Jimmy Johnson, Eugene Boswell, Teddy Adams and Will Telford — were the toast of the town. The new champions were treated to a sumptuous banquet at the "Plymouth Rock" and feted with speeches.[14] Local poet John Albro even commemorated the victors with a lengthy poem that began, "Honor to the 'Central Citys!'/ Shout it long and loud;/ They're the champion players/ Of which we may be proud."[15]

Yet even in their moment of greatest triumph, there were ominous signs of trouble ahead. At the banquet in their honor, club captain George Porter was asked to say a few words and he had a blunt message to deliver. Porter compared the gold ball to "a 'white elephant,'" and added that "the question of holding it remained with our citizens. He stated that the financial condition of the club was such that a proper fixing up of the grounds of the club was out of the question, and unless something was done the 'white elephant' might take its departure."[16]

In response to Captain Porter's challenge, the banquet attendees donated $125 to replenish the club's purse and a committee was formed to raise additional funds. Nevertheless, Porter's words ensured that the winter would not merely be spent exulting in the triumph of the Central Citys, but would also witness concern about whether the club could adapt to the changes that were accompanying the sport's shift to professionalism.

One consolation was that, for the only time in the club's existence, the Central City Club didn't have to worry about its playing lineup for 1868 that offseason — it had the luxury of knowing that its young and talented "champion nine" would return intact. So instead the club was able to focus on the off-field challenges it was about to face.

The 1868 annual meeting of the Central Citys was held on April 1 and for the first time a board of directors was elected along with the other officers. This was no doubt a sign that the club was serious about addressing its financial challenges and its need for a new home site, but the meeting also produced some worrisome signs. Alfred Wilkinson, a Syracuse businessman who had been involved in the local baseball scene since before the war, was re-elected as president but declined to serve. Porter was chosen in his stead, but he too would step down after a month.[17]

Despite the unsettled leadership, the club pressed ahead with efforts to address its key needs. The first priority was finding a suitable place to play. While the Central Citys had had no trouble getting youngsters to come watch them play at Armory Park, attracting older citizens had been a problem. As George Geer recalled, "The crowds that attended the games [at Armory Park] never knew or heard of the luxury of a grand stand — no, not even a bleacher, — and all stood up through the entire nine innings of play. Occasionally some gallant would appear on the ground with a camp stool, which he would place in the shade of some tree for his lady, but this was a rare sight, as the crowd would interfere with persons so situated, and it was the regular rule that if you desired to see the game you had to stand up."[18]

An effort had been made to address the problem after the 1866 season. At that time, Armory Park had been pronounced too small and a committee had been appointed to find grounds that would suit the needs of both the Central City Club and the Syracuse Cricket Club. The Pavilion Race Course was identified as a possibility and negotiations were started with its proprietor.[19] But they appear to have fallen through, as few notable matches were played in Syracuse in 1867.

It was thus essential to find a more commodious place to play in 1868, and the club settled upon a ten-acre site on West Onondaga Street on the outskirts of town. (The precise locale, according to a 1900 article by Geer, was "the lowlands on the south side of Onondaga street just below its present junction with Delaware street."[20]) Choosing such a remote site raised the obvious question of whether spectators would find it convenient to attend. In response, the initial article that announced the club's move stressed that the field was only a short distance from the terminus of the Fifth Ward streetcar, while a follow-up piece noted that passengers were dropped off within "forty rods" of the field.[21]

The new site did have the great advantage of a level tract of ground measuring 450 feet by 700 feet, but even so, there were many preparations that needed to be completed in the three weeks between the lease-signing and the home opener. Work began immediately on rolling the ground to remove imperfections and on enclosing the field with an 11-foot fence. Seating was hastily constructed, and as opening day neared it was confidently announced that there was seating for 3,000 and that the arrangements for carriages and standing-room spectators would accommodate a crowd of 10,000.[22]

All of this industry forced the club's hands on two other fronts. The first decision was to begin charging a hefty admission to home matches — the club announced that all spectators would have to pay 25 cents to attend, with "the season tickets of last year" not being accepted. The wording suggests that some sort of admission fee had been charged the previous year, but it seems likely that this was only for special seating arrangements. Now spectators had to pay 25 cents just to get in, even though most of them would have to stand around the field and hope to be able to see the action. An additional quarter was to be charged to anyone who chose to watch the match from a carriage.[23]

These were considerable sums to expect spectators to fork over, which in turn meant that the Central Citys would have to schedule matches against national powerhouses. As a result, the opponent for the home opener on June 13 was the mighty Atlantics of Brooklyn. Scheduling opponents of this caliber became inevitable with the move to a new home park, but it remained a course that was full of risk. There were countless logistical issues to surmount in making the new site comfortable and convenient to spectators, and there was always the threat that bad weather could ruin the best of preparations. Perhaps of greatest concern, the Central City Club had never before faced one of the country's best clubs and there was no way to be sure that the players were up to the challenge.

Anticipation was high in Syracuse as the visit of the Atlantics approached. The Ontario Club of Oswego chartered a special train to Syracuse to witness the match and brought 800 Oswego residents to the new field. "Large delegations" from many other nearby surrounding towns poured into Syracuse and of course locals turned out in droves for the big event. "The capacity of the grounds of the C.C. Club," predicted the *Syracuse Journal*, "will probably be tested to its fullest extent this afternoon."[24]

Overall, the opening of the new field was a success. According to a later article, the new field was not as ideal as expected because "there were no ground limits and the ball was just as apt to roll a few hundred yards down hill when hit into left field as not."[25] But there were no major problems with the arrangements, while the weather — which had forced cancellation of the Atlantics' game in Albany on the previous day — proved accommodating. The Central Citys didn't win the match, but they proved very competitive in a 20–14 loss to the Atlantics.

Yet after this promising beginning, the 1868 season soon began to go downhill. The club's ambitious plans had been fueled by the faith that "the 'Champion Nine' of the Central City in full" would again represent the club.[26] Instead, one of the club's vital cogs, catcher David Sanford, who had earned national acclaim for his work behind the plate, was missing from the club's lineup in all of the club's early matches. The specific reason for his absence was never stated, but one article predicted that Sanford would rejoin the Central Citys "at the urgent request of his many friends," an assertion that suggests that his decision was voluntary and that he was expecting more money.[27]

Whatever the reason, Sanford's absence continued and it was not until an Independence Day game against the Nationals of Albany that the star catcher made his first appearance and finally enabled the Central Citys to present their celebrated "champion nine."[28] When the Central Citys next faced a top club, Sanford was once again conspicuously missing, "contrary to the expectation of every one present."[29] He was back in the lineup by the end of the month, but then suffered a string of injuries. He had to be removed from one game on the orders of a doctor, and was unable to play at all in most other contests.[30]

Having to play without Sanford was a devastating blow to the Central Citys. The catcher's position had become far and away the game's most crucial one, because without a capable man behind the plate a pitcher was unable to use his best offerings (since they would end up at the backstop, allowing the batter to reach first base even on a strikeout). Worse, his absence forced the club to move another fielder behind the plate and thereby weakened another defensive spot. Making matters worse, Telford and Boswell also disappeared from the club's lineup. No reason for their absence was given, but there were several references to the club being crippled with injuries so that is a likely explanation.

The play of the shorthanded Central Citys deteriorated quickly after the match against the Atlantics and the season proved a major disappointment. While Sanford's absence was the most glaring reason for this turn of events, it was far from the only one. Judging from game accounts, the performance of other players was subpar. It also seems likely that the expectations of the club had been unrealistic from the outset. This was, after all, a club that had never previously faced top competition, and indeed the Central City Club won most of its 1868 matches against its traditional rivals from towns like Oswego, Fulton, and Albany.

But that was no longer good enough, as the expectation had been created that Syracuse was ready to emerge on the national baseball stage. Instead, every match against a top-flight opponent produced not just defeat but embarrassment for the Central Citys: a 41–12 thrashing by the Athletics of Philadelphia, a 34–7 manhandling by the Unions of Morrisania, and lopsided losses by 48–6 and 35–14 margins at the hands of the Unions of Lansingburgh (the club that became known as the Haymakers of Troy). As the losses mounted, dissatisfaction in Syracuse grew and things began to unravel.

This was most noticeable in newspaper coverage of the club. The *Syracuse Journal*, which had previously been supportive and even a cheerleader for the Central Citys, changed its tone entirely. In the club's first match of the season, its performance was described as "not up its usual standard, except in one or two cases."[31] Once the losses began, the coverage became increasingly harsh. Game accounts began to be dotted with statements such as "several bad plays ... made by the C.C.'s ... which should not have been, and in closely contested games are hardly justified" and "We do not remember of having seen a game in which so much poor infielding was done by the Central Citys as that of yesterday."[32] Occasionally the comments took on a personal tone. One report noted, "The loose playing of the Central City and also their muffing continued during the game, with occasionally an exception.... Several of the members of the C.C.'s seemed to take delight in muffing everything that came to their hands."[33]

In addition to such grumbles in game accounts, the *Journal* published one lengthy essay that expressed concern that baseball had "become the means of a system of gambling only rivaled by the monte table and dice boxes of professional sports." The writer maintained that "base ball as base ball alone, is noble; but when base ball is sold to the highest bidder, it becomes degrading." He then turned to the Central Citys, and while he made no specific accusations, his comments left no doubt of his disapproval:

> During the present summer our city has been honored — we believe that is the term — by the presence of foreign clubs. The first were met and hotly contested; the second achieved an easy victory; while they have also been unable, from reasons unknown, to hold their own against obscure clubs from the east. We had hoped, for the honor of Central New York, that our city would have been able to retain its reputation. We have no comments to make upon the playing of the home club, further than that we consider it unfortunate that it is so crippled in its selection of men. As it now stands, the olive crown has departed, prestige gone, and the relaxation of energy taken the place of earnest action.[34]

As the mood in Syracuse soured, a similar dissatisfaction became evident among the players. During the trouncing at the hands of the Athletics, "they became more 'demoralized' than was the Union army at the battle of Bull Run."[35] After another match, the Central City players were chastised for indulging in "chin music," a term that could refer to either arguing with the umpire or internal disputes.[36] Captain George Porter, who had already resigned the club presidency, now stepped down as captain and was replaced by Ed Yale.[37]

The conduct of spectators at the matches also became a concern. A group of "young roughs" began climbing the trees near the field to watch the game for free and then directing "insulting epithets, hisses, groans, et cetera" toward the visiting players.[38] The Central City Club was forced to saw off the lower branches of these trees near the field and tar the trunks.[39]

Some of the paying spectators also joined in the catcalls, but a much more serious problem was convincing these people that they should continue attending games. The match against the Athletics attracted a sizable crowd, but a "large portion of the spectators left the ground about the middle of the game, having become disgusted with the loose work on the part of the C.C.'s."[40] Naturally, those who made early exits were not inclined to return to future matches.

The decrease in attendance at the expensive new park had a predictable effect on the club's finances. The club president was forced to place a statement in the local paper to the effect that only members of a three-man committee were authorized to make contracts for the Central Citys and that no other bills would be honored.[41]

The club did not stand idly by as the season unraveled, and considered several different approaches for reviving local baseball enthusiasm. The most obvious course was to bring in imported professionals, but the club's directors appear to have concluded that the mood in Syracuse to such new arrivals would be too hostile. Indeed, throughout the club's five-year existence, it frequently enlisted players from surrounding towns — pitcher Fred Dodge from Skaneateles, Baker from Lafayette by way of Hamilton College, Will Cruttenden from Cazenovia, and Leonard Fancher from Baldwinsville — but never once brought in a player from any greater distance.

The wisdom of this decision was revealed when the club began using Patrick Grace to fill the huge hole left behind the plate as a result of Sanford's absence. Grace had been living in Albany and was the catcher for the Knickerbockers of Albany in 1867. He joined the Central Citys in June of 1868 and although at the time there was no allusion to his being a professional, his obituary acknowledged that a business position in Syracuse had been found for him. Intriguingly, Grace was still living with his parents and younger siblings at the time and they joined him in moving from Albany to Syracuse. His departure prompted a complaint from his old club, although the *Syracuse Journal* insisted that Grace had resigned from the Knickerbockers in October of 1867 and become a member of the Central Citys on June 26, 1868.[42] The controversy soon died down, but the fact that even bringing in Grace could raise ire made it very clear that Syracuse would be hostile to outside professionals.

So the Central City Club focused on other alternatives. One of the first proposals was to schedule a tour, an idea that had worked so successfully the previous season. Arrangements got far enough to make tentative plans for a fourteen-game, three-week tour that would take the club to Buffalo, Cleveland, Detroit, Chicago, Milwaukee, Madison, Rockford, St. Louis, Cincinnati, and Pittsburgh.[43] But for unknown reasons, the tour was canceled.

A variety of other ideas were considered, including even discussion of changing to a new uniform. (No contemporaneous description of the uniform of the Central Citys has been found, but a later account described it as "a deep plaid black and white check flannel with a red 'C.C.' monogram on the breast."[44]) Eventually, however, the club ceased playing national powers and refocused its attention on the gold ball that symbolized supremacy of Central and Western New York. By doing so, they were able to revive some of the lost enthusiasm for baseball in Syracuse, though their success was mixed.

The Central Citys successfully defended the gold ball on July 30 with a 33–21 win over the trophy's previous holders, the Niagaras of Buffalo. Just as important, more than 1,200 spectators flocked to the club's new grounds to watch the match, and the next day's *Syracuse Journal* published a long and laudatory account.[45] Things were looking up again.

In their next title defense, however, the Central Citys fell victim to "overconfidence." Against the visiting Ontarios of Oswego, the Central City Club grabbed a big early lead but then commenced to play in a way that "would not have reflected credit upon even a 'juvenile' club." Going to the eighth inning the home side was still ahead, 25–15. Then the bats of the Ontarios got hot and those of the Central Citys became cold, with the result that the visitors scored eleven unanswered runs and captured the gold ball by the margin of a single run.[46]

The Central Citys immediately issued a challenge for a rematch, and when the game came off on September 15 it provided a vivid demonstration of just how much the competition for the gold ball had done to renew baseball enthusiasm. A special train was run from Syracuse to Oswego to accommodate the hundreds of spectators anxious to see if the Central Citys could recapture the prized trophy. Before the game began, there was a dispute over the intention of the Ontarios to use pitcher Gerrit Miller, a Harvard student who had grown up in the area and had recently returned home. (See the entry on the Ontarios of Oswego for more details.)

Finally, the match was commenced under protest and it proved a tense and disputatious contest. The Central Citys staved off a couple of runs by means of a tactic described only as "sharp practice," while their use of Charles Colton in relief of a tiring Fred Dodge led to a ruling that he was illegally "jerking" the ball, which forced Dodge to return to the pitcher's box. The Central Citys surged to the early lead, only to see the Ontarios rally and narrow the margin to one run. But they could get no closer and when the match ended the Central Citys had pulled out a hard-fought 30–27 victory to reclaim the gold ball.[47]

In October, the Central Citys made one final defense of the gold ball against the Excelsiors of Rochester. The Excelsiors held a commanding 30–16 lead after completing their at-bats in the top half of the fifth inning, but it proved too dark at that point to record the three additional outs needed to make the game official. The result was that the game ended in rancor; the Central Citys retained the gold ball, while the Rochester papers accused the Syracuse players of having deliberately "jockeyed the game until darkness came on and it had to be called."[48] It was an unfortunate way to end the 1868 campaign, but in some ways an appropriate finale to a season that had fallen far short of the lofty expectations of the Central Citys, but which had at least seen a significant revival in interest during the final two months as a result of the increased emphasis on the gold ball.

The up-and-down 1868 season ensured that the winter would be another one in which the club's direction would be subjected to re-examination. Quite a bit of thought appears to have gone into the matter, with one meeting of the board of directors even taking place in mid–February.[49] By the time the spring rolled around, a decision had been made.

The Central Citys reorganized for the 1869 season in the middle of April and announced a new board of directors, a new captain (Jim Johnson), a new practice schedule and a new direction—the club adopted a resolution to henceforth be "strictly an amateur organization."[50] Precisely what was meant by this resolution cannot be determined because we cannot be sure of the extent to which professionalism had infiltrated the club in 1868. It is known that Grace was offered a position in Syracuse, and it seems likely that Sanford's mysterious absences had a financial component. But beyond that lie only unanswerable questions: Were the players dividing the gate receipts? Were those proceeds divided evenly or based on ability? Were any or all of the players receiving supplementary income or preferential treatment at work? Were such payments, if they occurred, looked upon as reimbursements for expenses and lost wages or as a salary?

Since there is no definitive way to settle these issues, it is impossible to be certain of the extent to which the new policy represented a change. But even without knowing the specifics, this very public retreat leaves no doubt that many members of the Central City Club believed that the club had gone too far down the road toward professionalism in 1868. To emphasize the new course, a three-man committee of Alfred Wilkinson, F.A. Marsh, and Park Wheeler—all of whom previously had served as club president—was appointed to "carry out the sense of the resolution."[51]

Yet even while the club was redefining itself as a purely amateur organization, it was reaffirming its intention to remain active. Plans were announced to host a "grand tournament" in June, with the celebrated gold ball as a reward to the victors.[52]

The plan to revert to strict amateurism was met with initial optimism and brave talk of "a return to the old feeling of interest which characterized the club in the palmy days of yore."[53] One early-season game account reported that the club's play was again beginning to resemble "that done two years since."[54] Instead, as the 1869 season unfolded it more closely resembled the disastrous first two months of the preceding campaign.

The first scheduled match of the year was to be a marquee showdown in which the Central Citys were to host the "Red Stockings" of Cincinnati, at the outset of the first road trip of the Red Stockings' historic undefeated season. But in a portent of things to come, that match was rained out, while the planned tournament was also canceled for reasons unknown. When the Central Citys finally did play their first match of the season the opponents were the Pastimes of Little Falls, New York. It was quite a comedown from playing the Red Stockings—especially when the club from Little Falls won.

Baseball matters in Syracuse remained sluggish until mid–June, when the Central City Club held a meeting and elected an official first nine for the season. Gone were stalwarts like Dodge, Cruttenden, Yale, Telford, and Sanford (although all but the final two did play for the club that season). In their places were a slew of new faces, including teenagers liked Horatio White and Herbert Stark. It was the latest youth movement for the Central Citys, and it would prove to be their last.

The new lineup made its debut on July 2, 1869, and the game ended in disappointment when the Alerts of Rochester staged a ninth-inning rally to send the Central Citys to another defeat. The opponents in the club's next outing were the Shermans of Utica, and this match ended in a tie, leaving the Central Citys still winless for 1869. Undeterred, the club set out on a tour—only to lose in Buffalo, lose in Cleveland, lose in Detroit, and lose twice in Cincinnati before finally beating the Niagaras of Buffalo 18–15 on August 7 to at last record the elusive first win of the season.

The club returned home and soon discovered that Syracuse had lost all interest in their doings. They played two more matches against top-flight nines, but neither produced satisfactory results. A match against the Eckfords of Brooklyn resulted in a 41–13 loss that prompted the *Journal* to write, "The Central City Club won no laurels by their playing of yesterday, and with several exceptions, we seldom saw more 'muffs' and 'logy' actions than were exhibited yesterday."[55] One final attempt was made, but the 39–11 loss at the hands of the Forest Citys of Cleveland was wearily described as "one of the poorest we ever saw them play."[56]

In 1868, the Central City Club's lackluster performances against top-notch clubs had been partly offset by renewed enthusiasm over the gold ball. By contrast, nothing the club tried during the 1869 season generated local interest. In August, for example, the club again announced its intention to host a tournament, only to see the plans fall through once more.[57] Even a benefit game played for the victims of a catastrophic fire at a Pennsylvania mine yielded a turnout that "was disgraceful to the people of Syracuse, considering the charitable uses for which the receipts are intended."[58] Meanwhile the few fans who did show up were berated for "getting inside the barriers" and for "the hoots and yells of mischievous boys and loaferish men."[59]

Toward the end of the season, the Central Citys finally managed to string together a few wins before closing their season with a contest against the Ontarios of Oswego on October 9. The game proved tightly fought and exciting, with the Ontarios pulling out a 29–27 victory. It was the last match ever played by the Central City Base Ball Club of Syracuse.

That winter the Central Citys passed quietly out of existence. But Syracuse was not without a marquee baseball club for long. The city was full of "young Syracusans who stood about Armory park and watched the Central Citys play ball" and then formed their own junior clubs.[60] One of these clubs, the Stars, soon stepped into the void left by the demise of the Central Citys and by the mid–1870s had acquired a national reputation.

The final two campaigns of the Central City Club had been difficult ones and some signs of bitterness over the way things ended would surface during the next few years. Eventually, however, any ill will faded and locals began to look back on the Central Citys with nostalgia.

In particular, reminiscences that discussed the whereabouts of the gold ball began to abound. An 1878 article boasted that "the ball is still the property of the C.C.'s and remains 'on deposit' in one of our banks. At the time of its coming into possession of the Central Citys, we learn that one of our jewelers pronounced it worth nearly $500."[61] Around 1889 the gold ball resurfaced when it was used to pay a bill at a Syracuse hotel, though expectations that the ball was of solid gold were disappointed when it was "examined and found to be only gold-plated."[62] The ball passed into the possession of a cigar dealer named Homer A. Ostrander and he was still displaying it at his store as late as 1900. By then, the ball looked "badly dilapidated," but Ostrander did his best to compensate by housing it in an attractive new case.[63] At some point between 1900 and 1920, the ball passed into the possession of Will Cruttenden.

Time's healing powers gradually cause the struggles of the Central Citys to be forgotten, while the better memories continued to be treasured. In 1910, Charles Colton, by then a renowned architect, reminisced about the club and provided a version of events that often differs from the historical record. Nonetheless, he surely captured an essential truth when he wrote, "Those were halcyon days for local pride over baseball victories. Great crowds surrounded the telegraph office to hear the results by innings and good news was the signal for gladsome shouting."[64]

Club Members

George E. "Teddy" Adams: Teddy Adams was the most baffling mystery among the players of the Central Citys. He became the club's shortstop in 1865 and was a fixture there for most of the club's existence, with the exception of the 1866 season. George Geer later called him "the famous Ted Adams" and maintained that "the press of the country had it that Adams played the [shortstop] position second to none," even comparing him to George Wright. No doubt this was an exaggeration, but Adams was deemed good enough to spark rumors he would sign with the professional Troy Haymakers after the Central Citys gave up baseball in 1870. Articles in 1878 and 1886 reported that he was still living in the area, yet there was no Theodore Adams who could possibly be the ballplayer. The mystery was solved by the discovery of the reminiscences of a Rochester newspaper editor named Rossiter Johnson who described growing up with a George Adams who was always known as Teddy and went on to become a noted ballplayer. This led to a George E. Adams who was born in 1841, grew up in Rochester, moved to Syracuse to work as a railroad machinist, and died in New Durham, New Jersey, on October 26, 1894. His tombstone at Rochester's Mount Hope Cemetery lists him as a veteran who had served in the 1st New York Light Artillery.[65]

Byron W. Baker: Baker was born on December 15, 1842, in Lafayette, New York, and in 1862 he entered Hamilton College in Clinton. During his four years there, he became known for his skill in oratory and for his work as the pitcher for the baseball nine. He pitched so well in an 1865 contest against the Central City Club that that club soon enlisted his services and that of teammate George Porter. Baker earned his degree from Hamilton College with honors in the spring of 1866 and became the pitcher of the Central City Club. He did brilliantly in his first match and, as described in the club history, was credited with using some sort of predecessor of the curveball. But shortly thereafter he contracted typhoid fever and returned to his home in Lafayette, where he died on August 26, 1866. His death prompted the Sigma Phi Society of Hamilton College and the Central City Base Ball Club to meet and pass resolutions in honor of his memory. The members of the ball club also resolved to wear badges of mourning for the next 30 days.

Charles Barnes: Charles Barnes was born in Tenterden, England, on May 22, 1837, and followed his brother to Syracuse while still young. In March of 1865, he graduated from the Philadelphia Dental College and returned to Syracuse to practice dentistry. He became a regular for the Central City Club in 1865 and 1866. But by then he was nearly 30 and no doubt he was one of the players that a local sportswriter was thinking of when he counseled the club that it was time to begin using younger players. Barnes was used only as a replacement in 1867 and not at all thereafter. He switched to playing cricket and was still playing in the late 1880s. He also helped organize the Dental Society of the State of New York and served as its secretary for many years. His health began to fail in 1894 and he died on June 3, 1894, in Middletown, New York.

George Barnes: See Syracuse Base Ball Club.

Frank Manley Bonta: Bonta was the club's longtime scorer and also played for the second nine. He was born on April 14, 1845, in Amber, New York, and eventually moved to the nearby city of Syracuse, where he became a teller for the Salt Springs National Bank. He was still alive as late as 1930, living in Manhattan at the time, and is believed to have died in 1939.

Eugene S. Boswell: Eugene "Buzzy" Boswell was born around 1851 and became a prominent part of the Central City Club's 1867 youth movement. While playing for the club, he worked as a postal clerk and route agent. In 1870 he went into business in Syracuse, but before long he decided to move west. He ran a hotel in Denver for many years, and as of 1920, he was living in Long Beach, California.

Oscar L. Brownell: Oscar Brownell was born in Solon, Cortland County, New York, on June 9, 1841. He moved to Syracuse and opened a grocery store at the corner of James and Warren streets, while also serving as recording secretary and one of the principal decision-makers for the Central Citys. He retained an interest in baseball and played a major role in the transition of the Syracuse Stars to fully professional status in the mid–1870s. Brownell later ran a Syracuse hotel. He died on April 21, 1900.

George G. Campbell: George Campbell was born around 1845 in New York state. He became a saloon keeper in Syracuse and was prominently involved in the management of the Syracuse Stars of the 1870s and of several of the minor-league clubs that represented the city in the mid–1880s. He later moved to Manhattan, where he was living as of 1910. He appears to have died around 1920.

Francis Edward Carroll: Frank Carroll, the first president of the Central City Club, was born in Philadelphia on November 16, 1830, the son of Irish immigrants. He moved to Syracuse in 1849 and opened a store that sold gas fixtures and plumbing supplies. He served as an alderman during the 1860s and was elected mayor in 1871. After serving two one-year terms, he returned to private life but his business had suffered while he was mayor and he was forced to close the store. He became a plumber and remained in Syracuse until his death on April 16, 1912.

Charles Erastus Colton: Charles Colton was born in Syracuse on November 12, 1847. He saw some action for the Central Citys in 1865, then played for another local club, the Arctics, in 1866 and 1867 before rejoining the Central City Club for its final two seasons. In the mid–1870s he began to study in the office of a local architect. He became one of Syracuse's best-known architects, designing City Hall and many other public buildings, schools and firehouses. He was eventually offered the position of state architect by New York Governor David Hill but declined. In 1910 Colton wrote a reminiscent article about the "halcyon days" when he played baseball for the Arctic and Central City clubs. Around then his health began to fail and he died in Syracuse on July 18, 1914.

William Henry Cruttenden: Will Cruttenden was born in May of 1843 and grew up in Cazenovia, New York. He briefly attended seminary, then moved to Syracuse to learn the jewelry trade in the store of Syracuse jeweler and watchmaker Dennis Valentine. While there, he became a regular for the Central Citys during their youth movement of 1867 and remained on the first nine for the next two years. He worked as a jeweler in several cities over the next few years; in 1870 he returned to Cazenovia and opened a jewelry store. He became one of the city's best-known merchants, and in 1920 celebrated his golden anniversary of doing business in Cazenovia. He was a prominent civic leader, serving as president, clerk, trustee, and treasurer of the village offices and as chief of the volunteer fire department, while also leading and being drum major in a twenty-four-man town band. In addition, Cruttenden retained his interest in baseball, managing the Cazenovia town team and frequently returning to Syracuse to cheer on the minor-league Stars. A 1920 article stated that Cruttenden had become the possessor of the famous gold ball from the 1866 Auburn Tournament. He lived a long life and had the misfortune of outliving his wife and both of his children before dying in Cazenovia on March 28, 1928.

Fredric Dodge: Fred Dodge was born around 1845 and was a native of Skaneateles, New York, not far from Syracuse. After pitching for a club called the Lake Shores, he became the Central City Club's pitcher in 1867 after the death of Byron Baker. He was the club's primary pitcher for two years, but returned to Skaneateles for good in 1869. There he worked as a printer and as the manager and editor of the *Skaneateles Democrat*. He died unexpectedly on September 5, 1886, of an apparent heart attack.

Patrick Ambrose Grace: Patrick Grace was born in Ireland around 1847 and moved to the States while young. He was living in Albany and playing for the Knickerbockers of Albany in 1867 when his fine work behind the plate caught the eye of members of the Central City Club. He soon joined the Central Citys, in a move that created considerable controversy. At the time there was no overt admission that he was a professional, but his obituary was a bit more forthright, stating that "a business position was found for him in Syracuse." Interestingly, his parents and siblings moved to Syracuse at the same time. In 1874 Grace moved to California where he worked for the next 12 years. Shortly after returning to Syracuse, his health failed and he died there on December 18, 1886, leaving a wife and five young children.

John E. Harwood: John Harwood was born around 1846

and served in the 8th Regiment of the New York Heavy Artillery during the Civil War. He became the pitcher of the Central Citys in 1869, then later owned an engraving store in Syracuse. He died there on September 21, 1929.

James T. Johnson: Born in 1845 and raised in Syracuse, Jim Johnson became one of the mainstays of the Central City Club. A later article described Johnson as "the famous batsman of the team, and it was the regular thing for the favorite Jimmy to hit that ball clean over the old armory building and into the old creek in the rear." He was one of the few members of the first nine to be involved in the club's business affairs, serving as the club's treasurer in 1868. Johnson was the son of the local grocer and he was being groomed to take over the business. But he died on September 13, 1875, at the age of 30.

James G. Noakes: James Noakes was born on February 4, 1840, in Sussex, England. After emigrating to the U.S., he married a Syracuse woman in 1862. He served in the Civil War as a musician with the 149th New York and was taken prisoner at Chancellorsville. After the war he became a regular in the outfield of the Central Citys in 1868, and later played for a local cricket club. He worked as the foreman of a picture frame shop and died in Syracuse in July of 1919.

George A. Porter: George Porter was born in Syracuse around 1846 and attended Hamilton College. When the Hamilton College nine played the Central Citys in 1865, the play of two collegians — pitcher Byron Baker and Porter in left field — attracted attention and both were asked to join the Central City Club. Upon graduation, he joined his father in the salt business. He and his father also established a successful foundry, with George Porter becoming its treasurer and general manager. He was also the longtime organist of Syracuse's First Presbyterian Church and a member of the National Guard. He moved to Chicago in 1889 and died there two years later, on October 5, 1891, of Bright's disease, leaving a wife and five children.

David Sanford: David Sanford was born on December 20, 1845, in Glens Falls, New York. His father was a well-to-do lumber dealer and the family moved to Syracuse in 1857. David Sanford became the Central City Club's regular catcher in 1865 and his work behind the plate made him the club's most celebrated player. In 1900 George Geer maintained,

> Sanford is said to have been the first player in the country who stood up close behind the batsman to catch the ball. On the occasion of Sanford's first attempt at this new mode of catching there was great amazement expressed by the players of both clubs and the onlookers, and there were those present who were certain that Dave Sanford had gone clean crazy. Fred Dodge, the Central City's pitcher, refused to pitch the ball unless Sanford went back to his old position near the backstop. The police came onto the ground and notified Dave that he would be placed under arrest if he persisted in catching up close to the batsman. The police insisted that Sanford was attempting suicide. After much persuasion Sanford was prevailed upon to forego the attempt for the time being, but after the game was over Dave induced Jimmy Johnson to pitch to him, and one of the other players took a bat, and it was only a few moments before Sanford convinced those present that the trick could be done.

Geer's account is marred by numerous misstatements and exaggeration and there is no reason to believe that Sanford was the first catcher to stand directly behind the plate, but it does make for entertaining reading. Geer also claimed that Sanford's picture appeared on the front page of the *New York Clipper* with the inscription, "David Sanford, Champion Catcher" while another article reported that Sanford was featured in Frank Leslie's magazine. But his success did not last. As discussed in the club history, Sanford played only a few games after the triumphant 1867 season and his absence was one of the reasons for the club's decline. After his playing days ended, Sanford worked for a local picture framer. On the evening of Saturday, December 3, 1893, he went to a local tavern for an evening of heavy drinking. In the wee hours, he fell down a flight of stairs and by morning he had died from his injuries.

Herbert Stark: Herbert Stark was born in 1853 and was a member of the Stars before joining the Central Citys for the 1869 season. He later moved to Trinidad, Colorado, and reported in 1882 that he was a confectionery manufacturer, the holder of the city seal, foreman of a volunteer fire company, "end man" in a church choir, and captain of the Trinidad Base Ball Club. As of 1887, he was postmaster of Trinidad but may have died soon afterward.

William L. Telford: Will Telford was born in Iowa around 1847 and moved to Syracuse at a young age with his widowed mother. He became known as a great all-around athlete and was one of the Central City Club's mainstays in 1867. In the late 1870s he moved with his wife and daughter to Emmetsburg, Iowa, where he worked as a law clerk. He died there on December 31, 1897.

Horatio Stevens White: Horatio White was born in Syracuse in 1852 and became the catcher of the Central Citys in 1869. He then enrolled at Harvard, where he captained the baseball nine for three straight years (1871–73). A few years later, another Harvard catcher would introduce the catcher's mask, but White used no form of protection except, as he later recalled, that he "was accustomed to bite upon a large rubber eraser, to prevent dental demolition, with a surreptitious supplementary duplicate to lend to envious and suppliant professional backstops. But this was the principle [*sic*] concession made for defensive armor."[66] Horatio White's catching at Harvard was so skillful that it was later claimed that Harry Wright offered him a generous contract to play professional ball for the Boston Red Stockings. But White was more interested in continuing his education, which he did at the University of Glasgow, earning a law degree. He joined the faculty at Cornell University in 1876, teaching German and Latin and becoming the dean in 1888. After a quarter-century on the Cornell faculty, he returned to his alma mater in 1902. White had continued to take a great interest in athletics during his years at Cornell and he also did so upon his return to Harvard, serving as chairman of the Athletic Committee — thus effectively being the school's athletic director. He also taught German and was the author of a number of books, including *Elementary German, Deutsche Volkslieder: A Selection from German Folk-Songs, Selections from Heine's Poems* and *Memorials of Willard Fiske*. White retired in 1919 but remained in Cambridge as a professor emeritus until his death on December 12, 1934. He never lost his fondness for baseball and mentioned in 1932 that he often got together with George Wright to reminisce about the early days of the game.[67]

A.E. Yale: Ed Yale was a prominent member of the Central Citys, and George Geer would later rave, "Yale was known as 'Old Bushel Basket' on account of the size of his hands. It seemed almost an impossibility for Yale to miss a thrown ball." Information on him is nonetheless scarce. He was a younger brother of John W. Yale. He was born around 1835 and his full name appears to have been Andrews Edward Yale. He was living in Harrison, New Jersey, as of 1910.

John Wesley Yale: John W. Yale was born on December 17, 1832, in Scipio, New York. During the Civil War, he moved to Syracuse and became a very successful wallpaper merchant. He was prominent in Democratic politics and served as a colonel in the National Guard. Yale remained involved in the activities of Syracuse's professional clubs during the 1880s and one of his daughters married George Frazier, manager of Syracuse's National League club. The marriage, however, ended in divorce and with Frazier suing his father-in-law for alienation of affection. Yale died in Syracuse on June 26, 1900.

Other Members: Jerome Clark (player in 1866; Lyman Clark, proprietor of the St. Charles Hotel, was also involved but was not a player), Leonard Fancher (from Baldwinsville), Henry Farrer, T.W. Fitch, T.H. Gilbert, W.H. Graves, H. Loomis, F.A. Marsh (club president in 1866), Levi Mayo (see Syracuse Base Ball Club), Franklin D. Mosher (possibly the former catcher of the Lone Stars of Rochester), Matthew J. Myers, Will Page (manager), John Ryan, Schoeffel (possibly Frank Schoeffel of the Lone Stars of Rochester), Sedgwick, Stone, W.P. Stewart, Frank Waggoner, E.E. Weiskotter, Major Park Wheeler (club president), Alfred Wilkinson (see Syracuse Base Ball Club), D.P. Wilkinson.

Sources

The Onondaga Historical Association has an excellent collection of clippings from the *Syracuse Journal* during the five-year existence of the Central Citys that are the primary source of this piece. The articles are hand-dated, which is why some dates are unknown and others questionable. Several very helpful retrospective accounts of the club's doings appeared in later years: an article in the *Syracuse Sunday Times*, August 18, 1878, a reminiscence by Charles Colton in the *Syracuse Post-Standard* of January 3, 1910, pieces in the *Syracuse Herald* on March 1, 1908, and in *Sporting Life*, January 13, 1886, and a reminiscence by an unidentified member of a Syracuse amateur club that appeared in the *Syracuse Journal* on November 2, 1906. Tony Kissel's "The Pumpkin and Cabbage Tournament of 1866," in the *Baseball Research Journal* 24 (1995), 30–33, offers a fine summary of the tournament at which the gold ball was first offered. Joseph M. Overfield's "Baseball in Buffalo—1865 to 1870, Heyday of the Niagaras," *Niagara Frontier*, Spring 1965, 1–14, is a splendid history of one of the chief rivals of the Central City Club and proved very valuable. Also of use was a long club history by George Geer in the *Syracuse Telegram* of March 22, 1900. Unfortunately, Geer's account includes many details that appear to be simply fiction—most notably a tie game that the Central Citys supposedly played against the Red Stockings of Cincinnati—so I have used it with great caution. Charles E. Colton's "Saltine Town Early Power in Diamond," from the *Syracuse Post-Standard*, January 3, 1910, is also marred by questionable statements, but useful at capturing the spirit of the club. Obituaries of several club members were helpful in filling in additional details as was Ron Gersbacher, "Play Ball! A History of Early Organized Baseball in Syracuse," in *Portraits of the Past* (a publication of the Onondaga Historical Association) 7 (1994), n.p. Special thanks to Larry McCray and Craig Potkay for their help.

Notes

1. *Syracuse Journal*, April 15, 1865.
2. *Syracuse Journal*, May 27 and June 20, 1865.
3. *Utica Telegraph*, reprinted in the *Syracuse Journal*, June 7, 1865.
4. *Ibid*.
5. *Syracuse Journal*, September 14 and October 12, 1865.
6. *Utica Telegraph*, reprinted in the *Syracuse Journal*, June 7, 1865.
7. *Syracuse Journal*, undated clipping.
8. Charles E. Colton, "Saltine Town Early Power in Diamond," *Syracuse Post-Standard*, January 3, 1910.
9. *Syracuse Journal*, April 7 and 18, 1866.
10. *Syracuse Journal*, June 25, 1866 (copied from the *Standard*).
11. *Syracuse Sunday Times*, August 18, 1878; *Syracuse Journal*, November 2, 1906.
12. *Syracuse Journal*, September 14, 1866.
13. *Syracuse Journal*, October 5, 1866.
14. *Syracuse Journal*, October 7, 1867.
15. *Syracuse Journal*, October 22, 1867.
16. *Syracuse Journal*, October 7, 1867.
17. *Syracuse Journal*, April 2 and May 8, 1868.
18. George H. Geer, "Old Central City Nine," *Syracuse Evening Telegram*, March 22, 1900.
19. *Syracuse Journal*, October 15, 1866.
20. George H. Geer, "Old Central City Nine," *Syracuse Evening Telegram*, March 22, 1900.
21. *Syracuse Journal*, May 23 and June 12, 1868.
22. *Syracuse Journal*, May 23, June 10, and June 12, 1868.
23. *Syracuse Journal*, June 10, 1868.
24. *Syracuse Journal*, June 10, 12 and 13, 1868.
25. *Syracuse Herald*, March 1, 1908.
26. *Syracuse Journal*, June 13, 1868.
27. *Syracuse Journal*, July 3, 1868.
28. *Syracuse Journal*, July 6, 1868.
29. *Syracuse Journal*, July 10, 1868.
30. *Syracuse Journal*, July 31 and September 29, 1868.
31. *Syracuse Journal*, May 16, 1868.
32. *Syracuse Journal*, July 6 and August 14, 1868.
33. *Syracuse Journal*, July 10, 1868.
34. *Syracuse Journal*, July 13, 1868.
35. *Syracuse Journal*, July 2, 1868.
36. *Syracuse Journal*, July 10, 1868.
37. *Syracuse Journal*, July 25, 1868.
38. *Syracuse Journal*, July 10, 1868.
39. *Syracuse Journal*, July 28, 1868.
40. *Syracuse Journal*, July 2, 1868.

41. *Syracuse Journal*, June 26, 1868.
42. *Syracuse Journal*, August 12 and 14, 1868.
43. *Syracuse Journal*, August 5 and 13, 1868.
44. *Syracuse Sunday Times*, August 18, 1878.
45. *Syracuse Journal*, July 31, 1868.
46. *Syracuse Journal*, undated clipping.
47. *Syracuse Journal*, September 14, 1868; *Oswego Advertiser*, reprinted in the *Syracuse Journal*, September 17, 1868; *Syracuse Journal*, September 16 (?), 1868.
48. *Rochester Democrat*, reprinted in the *Syracuse Journal*, October 9, 1868.
49. *Syracuse Journal*, February 19, 1869.
50. *Syracuse Journal*, April 24, 1869.
51. *Ibid.*
52. *Ibid.*
53. *Syracuse Journal*, June 20, 1869.
54. *Syracuse Journal*, undated clipping.
55. *Syracuse Journal*, August 11, 1869.
56. *Syracuse Journal*, September 15, 1869.
57. *Syracuse Journal*, August 23, 1869.
58. *Syracuse Journal*, October 2, 1869.
59. *Syracuse Journal*, August 11, September 1, and September 13, 1869.
60. George H. Geer, "Old Central City Nine," *Syracuse Evening Telegram*, March 22, 1900.
61. *Syracuse Sunday Times*, August 18, 1878.
62. Joseph M. Overfield, "Baseball in Buffalo—1865 to 1870, Heyday of the Niagaras," *Niagara Frontier*, Spring 1965, 10; Tony Kissel, "The Pumpkin and Cabbage Tournament of 1866," *Baseball Research Journal* 24 (1995), 33.
63. Geer, "Old Central City Nine," *Syracuse Evening Telegram*, March 22, 1900.
64. Colton, "Saltine Town Early Power in Diamond," *Syracuse Post-Standard*, January 3, 1910.
65. Rossiter Johnson, *The Grandest Playground in the World* (Rochester: Rochester Historical Society, 1918), 21; *Rochester Democrat Chronicle*, October 28, 1894; George E. Adams Find a Grave Memorial.
66. Robert Sidorsky, "How Harvard Invented the Tools of Ignorance," *Harvard Crimson*, April 24, 1979, is the source of this quotation; Sidorsky attributes it to a 1927 article in the *Crimson*.
67. [Alphonse] Martin, More about First Curve: Scrapbook, 1869–1932, National Baseball Hall of Fame.

Ontarios of Oswego (Peter Morris)

CLUB HISTORY

The population of the village of Oswego, on Lake Ontario in upstate New York, hovered around 3,000 throughout the 1860s, making it an unlikely locale for a nationally prominent baseball club. Predictably, the Ontario Club never beat any of the powerhouse clubs that stopped in Oswego on their way to or from New York City. Yet Oswego's representative club did gain a reputation for pluck and perseverance and did manage one signal victory that allowed the club to briefly claim to be the champion of Central and Western New York.

There are gaps in the contemporary record of the Ontario Base Ball Club, but retrospective accounts make an overview possible. The club was first organized in 1859, according to initial president Edwin D. Stacy. Bylaws and a set of rules were adopted then, along with the election of a slate that consisted of Stacy as president, Horatio Morse as vice president, Oliver J. Root as secretary, and Thomas Kehoe as treasurer.[1] But little is known about the club's activities and it seems to have died out when the Civil War began, if not before.

The "Old Ontario Base Ball Club" was next heard from in 1864, when a new set of officers was chosen and a new committee on bylaws appointed. Plans were announced for an organizational meeting and a practice in the West Public Square, but whether these efforts bore fruit is not known.[2] There were signs of life again in 1865, with a Utica newspaper announcing the formation of a "new" Oswego club called the Ontarios.[3]

Once again, however, the club's activity was unimpressive. One reason was that many of the young men of Oswego seem to have preferred cricket to baseball.[4] Worse, the members of the Ontarios were unable or unwilling to find enough time for baseball. According to a summary of the 1865 season, "The Ontario Club, on account of the migratory character of its members, never had a regularly organized nine. They have, therefore, played but few matches and those under very discouraging circumstances. The Club was small, and the absence during the summer of five or six of their best players, rendered it difficult to get out enough for practice."[5]

Adding to the woes of the Ontarios, a rival Oswego club known as the Nationals had emerged during the 1865 season. The members of the first nine of the Nationals had the key advantages of being in general younger and having more time for baseball, so it looked to be just a matter of time before theirs became the city's dominant club.

Instead, the Ontario Club began to exhibit a new sense of purpose in the fall of 1865 season. Thirty to forty new members joined the club, including three members of the first nine of the Nationals: Dundas Havill, J. Irving Weed, and the pitcher, an unidentified man named Farwell. The renewed enthusiasm carried over to the spring, when the club leased an impressive club room in the Hungerford block and prepared for the season with a spirited practice game.

The new dedication paid off during the 1866 season as the Ontario Base Ball Club played ten match games, winning seven of them. Fully half of those games were against the crosstown National Club, with the Ontarios winning four of those five contests. The Ontario Club also recorded victories against the Arctic Club of Syracuse and a Fulton club, while splitting a pair of matches with the X.L. Club of Sandy Creek. The only loss that wasn't avenged came at the hands of the Falley Seminary of Fulton—a club that boasted a young pitcher named Arthur "Candy" Cummings, who would earn induction to the Baseball Hall of Fame for his role in the development of the curveball.[6]

In 1867 the Ontario Club assembled the first nine that became the basis of its legacy. The new lineup was made possible when the rival National Club decided to disband as a result of its series of losses to the Ontarios in 1866. Four of the stalwarts of the Nationals, "Brick" Parker, J.H. Mattoon, David Torrey, and Charley Lewis, became members of the Ontarios. With these additions to a club that already included such holdovers as Dundas Havill, Simeon Golden, George Dodge, George Cooper, and Martin Wadleigh, the Ontarios became a very formidable adversary.[7]

Even in their glory years, contemporary accounts of the Ontario Base Ball Club are scarce, but later reminiscences allow us to fill in many details. We know, for example, that the club was named in honor of the nearby Great Lake and that its uniforms also reflected that theme, being blue with white trim and topped with white caps.[8] Like many clubs of the era, the Ontario Club enjoyed a close relationship with a local newspaper, as the publisher and business manager of the *Palladium* handled the club's arrangements and acted as spokesmen. We also know that club headquarters moved to the Richardson block on East First Street and that the Ontarios played most of their home matches in East Park.[9] (Their former rivals, the Nationals of Oswego, had been literally cross-town rivals as they were based in West Park.)

It appears that the club used a different field when charging admission. Many years later a former resident of Oswego recalled attending a match against the famed Red Stockings of Cincinnati. "The game," he recollected, "was played up on Orphan Asylum Hill, as an admission fee was charged to see the game, and up on this far away hill was the only lot in the city with a fence around it, and I a boy of ten, tramped from East Seventh to see the game."[10]

After being strengthened by the reinforcements from the Nationals, the Ontario Base Ball Club of Oswego defeated rivals from such nearby towns as Fulton, Sandy Creek, Mexico, Phoenix, and Pulaski.[11] But little is known about these contests, and none of these clubs appear to have given the Ontarios much of a challenge.

A much better-known aspect of the club's history was the many occasions on which a national powerhouse stopped in Oswego to take on the Ontarios. In 1869 the visitors included the Eckfords of Brooklyn, the Niagaras of Buffalo, and the Alerts of Rochester, while in 1870 the Olympics of Washington, the White Stockings of Chicago, and the Red Stockings of Cincinnati all came to town. The Ontarios did not win any of these matches and many of the losses were by lopsided margins. Nonetheless, there was no quit in the Ontarios, and the club continued to schedule professional clubs like the Red Stockings and White Stockings in 1870 when many other strictly amateur clubs had stopped doing so.

The Ontarios did have better success against clubs from Canada. When baseball began to catch on in Canada, a number of clubs traveled south to Oswego to gain experience. One of the vanquished clubs was the Maple Leafs of Hamilton, a club that later earned recognition as champions of Canada.[12]

But of all the triumphs of the Ontario Club of Oswego, none compared to the one that earned the club the gold ball that was emblematic of the championship of Central and Western New York. Although the Ontarios retained the gold ball for only a few weeks, that win remained a fond memory more than 43 years later when a retrospective article appeared in the *Palladium*. Fortunately, while many details about this club are lost in the mists of time, a great deal is known about this particular victory.

The Central City Club of Syracuse had captured the gold ball in the fall of 1867 and the club retained possession of it for most of the 1868 campaign. During the early months of 1868 the Central Cities had twice beaten the Ontarios, once by the close score of 22–15 and then on the second occasion by the decisive count of 65–10. As a result, when the Ontarios issued a challenge to play for the gold ball, there was no reason to expect that the championship was likely to change hands.

The match took place in Syracuse and saw the Central City Club grab a big early lead. After seven innings, the home side held a commanding 25–15 lead but then the Ontarios staged an extraordinary rally, scoring ten unanswered runs in the eighth inning and then counting the only run in the ninth inning to pull out a 26–25 win. A Syracuse newspaper account attributed the result to the "overconfidence" of the Central Cities, adding that the late rally was the result of a "streak of luck" by the visitors, coupled with "terribly loose playing" by the home side. He added uncharitably, "it is rather humiliating to allow by no means a first class club to wrest the insignia from them, after successfully defending it against the attacks of far superior clubs."

But such slights didn't matter to the jubilant new champions. According to the same Syracuse reporter, "The Ontarios had not the remotest idea of winning the ball, and the surprise attendant upon the favorable result, for a few seconds, fairly dumbfounded the club, but remembering their victory, they made the air resound with demonstrations of joy at their unexpected good luck."[13]

The Central Cities immediately issued a challenge for a rematch, and arrangements were made to play it in Oswego on September 15, 1868. When the big day arrived, it was clear that the Syracuse club would not underestimate the Ontarios again. A special train had to be run from Syracuse to Oswego to accommodate the hundreds of spectators anxious to watch the two clubs compete for the gold ball. Then the match was almost canceled because the Central Cities protested the Ontarios' use of pitcher Gerrit Miller, who had recently returned to the area after studying at Harvard.

To prevent disappointment, the match was finally played under protest and it lived up to the advance billing. The

Central Citys jumped out to an early lead but the Ontarios clawed their way back to within a run. With the lead slipping away, the Central Citys stanched the bleeding by employing tactics that were not specifically described but were referred to as "sharp practice."[14] They also tried switching pitchers, but the deliveries of the replacement were ruled illegal and the original man was forced to return. When the dust finally settled, the Central Citys had hung on to win 30–27 and reclaim the gold ball.[15]

Although the gold ball returned to Syracuse to stay, the Ontarios of Oswego had left no doubts that they were worthy rivals. "Now that the thing is over," wrote one Oswego reporter proudly, "the Ontarios can see various points in which they might have made a stronger game, but they did all and even more than could have been expected. They certainly demonstrated their ability to play with any of the crack clubs of this section of the state."[16]

Baseball's amateur era soon ended and the members of the Ontario Club moved on to new phases of their lives, but in the years to come, they were able to look fondly back on those days — and in particular on their short but sweet tenure as champions of Central and Western New York. As of 1912, six of the club's regulars were reported to be living, and they kept alive memories of their long-ago glory on the baseball diamond. As a *Palladium* reporter put it, "Oswego has had many baseball teams since and will undoubtedly have many more, but the Ontarios' victories and records will long be remembered."[17]

By 1921 all of the members of the champion nine were said to be dead (although that statement overlooked Torrey and Cooper, both of whom had left town and died the following year, and excluded Miller, who lived for another 16 years).[18] As a result, memories of the Ontarios gradually faded. They deserve, however, to be remembered as an important pioneer club.

Club Members

Coman Cheney Ames: C. C. Ames was born in Oswego in 1843 and was the son of Cheney Ames, one of the city's best-known businessmen. He graduated from Oswego High School and Hamilton College, also finding time to play on the first nine of the Ontario Club in 1866. He then went into the grain commission business, eventually moving west to Chicago and then Minnesota. He died in Deerwood, Minnesota, on February 20, 1928.[19]

George W. Cooper: George Cooper, who was described as being "a catcher of State reputation," was raised in Oswego by his widowed mother. He became a tinsmith and married in the late 1870s. He and his wife moved to Rochester, where he died on December 30, 1922.

George Henry Dodge: Second baseman George Dodge was born on January 10, 1845, in Saratoga Springs, New York. Upon turning 18 he enlisted in the Union Army and over the next two years he served in the 76th, 91st, and 147th New York Infantry regiments. After the war he settled in Oswego and married, working first as a machinist and later as the proprietor of a hat and cap store. He died on July 1, 1907.

Simeon Golden: The 1912 article stated that Golden was living in Jersey City, while a 1923 article described him as being dead, but he has proved very difficult to trace.

Dundas Havill: Dundas Havill was born around 1845 and worked as a bookkeeper for the Lake Ontario National Bank of Oswego. He played for the Nationals of Oswego in 1865 and then joined the Ontarios in 1866. He moved to Syracuse in the 1870s and became the manager of a meat company. He lived there until his death on March 1, 1920.

Myron Holly: Myron Holly played for the Ontarios in 1866, before moving on to the Niagaras of Buffalo. See that club's entry for details on his life.

Simeon Holyrod: Simeon Holyrod was born around 1845 and grew up in Waterford, New York. He settled in Oswego after the war and became business manager of the *Palladium*. He also served as secretary of the Ontario Club and, as one later account put it, became "a prominent factor in everything that pertained to baseball during those days." After many years with the *Palladium*, he moved to Albany and became a successful manufacturer of knit goods. In 1896 Holyrod was the Democratic candidate for the House of Representative in New York's 20th District. He remained in Albany for the rest of his life, dying on June 29, 1917.

Gale B. Kingsley: Born in the nearby town of Mexico on March 24, 1837, Gale Kingsley served in the 24th New York Infantry for more than two years during the Civil War. He was a regular on the Ontario Club in 1866 but lost his spot after the influx of new talent. He became a mason contractor and a well-known singer, dying in Oswego on June 16, 1900.[20]

Charles Lewis: Charles Lewis may have been dead by 1912, and little is known about him. Lewis had played for the Nationals in 1866 and an article that year stated that he had recently returned to Oswego. The only plausible candidate to be him was a traveling agent named Charles F. Lewis who was living in St. Louis in 1910.

John Henry Mattoon: Center fielder John Henry Mattoon was born in Brooklyn on August 17, 1845, moving to Oswego as an infant. His father, Abner, rose from humble beginnings and served as a state senator in 1868–69. John became a lumber merchant and real estate agent. He never married and died in Oswego on September 7, 1916.

Gerrit Smith Miller: Gerrit Smith Miller was born on January 30, 1845, and was named in honor of his maternal grandfather, a wealthy social reformer and abolitionist who ran for president three times. Susan B. Anthony was also a relative. Gerrit Miller grew up on the family's large estate near Peterboro, New York. In 1860 he was sent away to Boston to attend Epes Sargent Dixwell's School. While there, Miller organized the Oneida Foot Ball Club, which played its games on the Boston Common. According to a monument erected on the Common in 1925, this pioneer club took on all comers between 1862 and 1865, never losing a game and never having its goal line crossed. The ball used by the club is now displayed at the National Soccer Hall of Fame in Oneonta, and Miller has occasionally been referred to as the father of American soccer. The problem with this, however, is that descriptions by Oneida Foot Ball Club member James D'Wolf Lovett make it clear that the game they played borrowed generously from rugby, with the result that Miller is sometimes claimed as a football pioneer as well. Lovett and Miller were also members of the Lowell Base Ball Club. Miller entered Harvard in 1865 and during the next few years played for the Harvard nine and the Lowells. On October 4, 1867, he pitched the Lowells to victory over the famed Excelsiors, which James D'Wolf Lovett described as the first-ever win by a New England club against a prominent New York club. One month later, he married Susan Dixwell, the daughter of his former schoolmaster. His grandmother died shortly thereafter, and Miller decided to leave Harvard and attend to the estate. His return also allowed him to pitch for the Ontarios of Oswego, although the Central Citys of Syracuse protested his involvement in the gold-ball match on September 15, 1868. One later account maintained that "for three years [Miller] pitched for the Ontarios and did not lose a game. The only trouble was it was very difficult to find a catcher who could hold his terrific speed." While the statement that he was never beaten seems very unlikely, the claim that his pitches were hard to corral seems more plausible. Miller continued to attend to the estate for the rest of his life, but his farming practices were far from routine. He established the first registered American herd of Holstein cattle, later describing his

> interest in "making two blades of grass grow where one grew before" and in producing two quarts of milk where one was produced before. In October, 1869, I established a herd of Holstein cattle imported from Holland on my farm, with the intention of improving the dairy cattle of the country. At that time a cow that would give six thousand pounds of milk per year and twelve pounds of butter per week was considered a good cow. We now have Holstein cows which under official tests have given over thirty thousand pounds of milk per year, one thousand pounds in seven days, one hundred and fifty pounds in one day, over fifty pounds of butter in seven days, and fifteen hundred pounds in three hundred and sixty-five days. Most of the cows making the above-named records trace back to my herd.

Miller's son and namesake inherited this fascination with the Holstein cattle. Gerrit Smith Miller, Jr., was educated at Harvard and became one of the country's best-known zoologists and mammalians. He was perhaps best known for his involvement in the Piltdown Man controversy. Gerrit Smith Miller, Sr., died on his beloved Peterboro estate on March 10, 1937, at the age of 91.

Clark Morrison: Clark Morrison, the publisher of the *Oswego Palladium*, served as president of the Ontario club and also officiated as umpire in many of the contests. He arrived in Oswego on March 17, 1864, to work for the *Palladium* and soon purchased a controlling interest and remained involved with the newspaper for more than 65 years. He also served two terms as mayor of Oswego. He celebrated his 90th birthday on December 12, 1929, and died less than a month later, on January 3, 1930.

Raymond S. Myrick: R. S. Myrick, the club secretary in 1864, was born around 1843 and was a lifelong resident of Oswego. He established a steamship and railroad ticket agency in Oswego for many years and was viewed as being very successful. But eventually he suffered financial reverses and exhausted his savings. Too proud to accept charity, he and several other men in similar straits were allowed to sleep on a chair in the courtroom by the sympathetic police chief. By the time of his death in 1913, Myrick had been a guest of "Chief Richardson's Hotel" for around a dozen years.[21]

Charles Adelbert "Brick" Parker: C. A. "Brick" Parker was born in July of 1846 and became a railroad man. Around 1878 he moved to New York City to work for the Manhattan Railway Company. He was transferred to Boston a few years later and settled in Somerville, Massachusetts. He died on January 31, 1912.

Edwin D. Stacy: Edwin D. Stacy, Sr., the original president of the club in 1859, was born around 1831 and became a successful Oswego grocer. Around the turn of the century, he retired to the town of Texas, New York, where he died on March 30, 1905.

David Torrey: David Torrey eventually moved to Manhattan, where he died on January 25, 1922, at the age of 74.

Martin V. "Mart" Wadleigh: Mart Wadleigh was born around 1843 and the hard-hitting first baseman was said to be such a fine ballplayer that he received many offers to play professionally. Instead he remained in Oswego and became a marble dealer. He never married and retained his love of baseball throughout his life. An article in the *Palladium* on October 17, 1916, noted that Wadleigh and several other old-time ballplayers were among those following the World Series on the newspaper's bulletin board. (Others included Tom Cunningham, Tom Dalton, and Billy Finley, who was said to have pitched for the Ontarios.) Wadleigh died in 1919.

Jonathan Irving Weed: J. Irving Weed was the club treasurer in 1864. He apparently played for the rival Nationals in 1865, but rejoined the Ontarios in 1866 and occasionally played for the first nine that year. Weed was born on February 26, 1846, and became a successful Oswego grain commission merchant. He ran for mayor in 1880s, but was defeated by Morrison and soon left town, spending the rest of his life in New York City and Colorado. He died on November 4, 1932.

Other Members: W. Ames, Bates, Alfred Crolius (president in 1864), Craft, Farwell, George Garland (secretary in

1865), Thomas Kehoe (1859 treasurer), Philo Knox (mentioned in a couple of retrospective accounts but apparently not a member of the first nine), Joseph Lathrop, Merriman, J. F. Miller, Horatio Morse (1859 vice president), William Mott, Oliver J. Root (1859 secretary), Scott, Watson (played shortstop when the Ontarios captured the gold ball but was not mentioned in later accounts).

Sources

The primary source was a long article that appeared in the *Oswego Palladium* on January 19, 1912 (and was later reprinted with some changes in the *Syracuse Herald* on May 19, 1912). Other valuable sources included a letter from George Oliver printed in the *Oswego Palladium* on October 18, 1919, and a brief article that appeared in the *Oswego Palladium* on March 5, 1921. These were supplemented by contemporary coverage in a variety of newspapers, as cited in the notes.

Notes

1. *Oswego Times-Express*, June 8, 1886.
2. *Oswego Palladium*, August 24, 1864; *Oswego Commercial Times*, August 24, 1864.
3. *Utica Herald*, July 18, 1865.
4. *Oswego Times*, November 19, 1910, in an article about the history of the Oswego Cricket Club.
5. "Base Ball in Oswego," *Oswego Daily Palladium*, May 8, 1866.
6. *Oswego Palladium*, January 8, 1867.
7. *Oswego Palladium*, January 19, 1912. These nine men appeared in a photo that accompanied the article and they were generally regarded as the club's first nine in retrospective articles.
8. *Oswego Palladium*, October 18, 1919, letter from George Oliver.
9. *Oswego Palladium*, January 19, 1912; "Base Ball in Oswego," *Oswego Daily Palladium*, May 8, 1866.
10. *Oswego Palladium*, October 18, 1919, letter from George Oliver.
11. *Oswego Palladium*, January 19, 1912; *Syracuse Herald*, May 19, 1912
12. *Oswego Palladium*, January 19, 1912.
13. *Syracuse Journal*, undated clipping.
14. An 1886 article made the unconfirmed claim that the game ended with the Central Citys playing the hidden ball trick (*Syracuse Standard*, December 19, 1886).
15. *Syracuse Journal*, September 14, 1868; *Oswego Advertiser*, reprinted in the *Syracuse Journal*, September 17, 1868; *Syracuse Journal*, September 16 (?), 1868.
16. *Oswego Advertiser*, reprinted in the *Syracuse Journal*, September 17, 1868.
17. *Oswego Palladium*, January 19, 1912.
18. *Oswego Palladium*, March 5, 1921.
19. *Oswego Palladium-Times*, February 21, 1928.
20. *Oswego Times*, June 16, 1900.
21. *Oswego Times*, February 3, 1913; *Oswego Palladium*, February 4, 1913.

❖ *Flour City, Live Oak, Olympic, and Lone Star Clubs of Rochester* ❖ (Priscilla Astifan)

A number of senior and junior Rochester, New York, baseball clubs made contributions to the early development of organized baseball in the three years that preceded the Civil War. However, four senior clubs became especially significant: the Flour City, the Live Oak, the Olympic, and the Lone Star. The Live Oaks and the Lone Stars won the first two city championships, and the Olympics were close contenders as they made their own enduring contributions to the rich history of local baseball. All three of these clubs cultivated noteworthy players. The Flour City Club never came close to a championship, winning only three first-nine matches against other senior clubs from 1858 to 1860.[1] Yet, the Flour City Club made its own indelible contributions.

Early Rochester newspaper accounts, pioneer players' reflections, and Rochester city directories indicate that these clubs had between 25 and 40 active members who worked at a variety of occupations and played primarily for the purpose of combining social recreation with healthful outdoor exercise. Pioneer player Sidney Avery, represented in his 1903 memoir as "Third Base," reveals that it was common for clubs to rely on the financial support of inactive members who contributed financial support.[2] As in New York City, Rochester clubs played under the regulations of the recently organized National Association of Base Ball Players (NABBP). They held monthly business meetings and elected officers, including a president, vice president, treasurer, secretary, and a board of directors. Members paid initiation fees, monthly or weekly dues, and fines for such offenses as missing a monthly meeting or practice session, using profane language, or disputing an umpire's decision.[3]

"These fines ranged all the way from ten cents to one dollar," Live Oak pioneer James Backus recalled in 1902, and "they were religiously collected."[4] The game was strictly amateur then, but according to Backus, membership was eagerly sought, and failure to pay a fine meant dismissal from the club.

Each club held regular weekly or bi-weekly practice sessions, and in spite of long (but perhaps flexible) hours at a variety of professional and non-professional occupations, players gathered at the ball fields on weekday or Saturday afternoons or evenings, or early in the morning. "We used to get out of bed at 3 o'clock and wait for the sun to come up so we could practice until it was time for us to go to work," Backus recollected.[5] Sunday baseball of any kind was illegal and subject to a fine, jail sentence or both.

Practice sessions or field meetings served a variety of purposes. Club members worked on ground maintenance or practiced their batting, pitching, and fielding skills during intra-club scrimmages. These sessions also aided in the selection of first and second nine players. Such casual contests might include more than nine players per side. More serious contests, sometimes played in uniform before the public, might pit married club members against single members. Occasionally a club's second nine competed against the second nines of another prominent club, or the first nine of a prominent junior club.

THE FLOUR CITY CLUB

The Flour City was the first club formed in Rochester, an occasion that was announced in the *Rochester Democrat and American* on May 3, 1858.[6] "When the organization was perfected, by order of the treasurer I ordered the first white horsehide ball that came to town (just one) and what a host of the boys called just to see it and have a kindly handling," Avery recalled in 1903.[7]

The Flour City Club played Rochester's first reported match game on the hot afternoon of June 18, the day after the city celebrated the anniversary of the Battle of Bunker Hill. "The day was fine and carriages lined up on the street and the youth and beauty of the town were there to see the first game of ball played here," claimed Avery. A former grazing meadow recently designated for the new campus of the University of Rochester served as the site of the city's first formal contest, with the opposition being formed by members of a recently organized social club from the University of Rochester.[8]

The Flour City players took the field in their new uniforms, which included white flannel shirts trimmed with blue braid and pearl buttons, blue pantaloons with white stripes down the outside seams and fancy trimmings of pearl buttons from ankle to knee. The Flour City Club won the game 25–8, and a basic box score noting last names, positions, runs, and "hands lost" (outs) for each player appeared in the *Rochester Union and Advertiser* on the following day.[9]

The Flour City Club did not play another outside match until August. However, the club did send a representative to the historically significant match between picked men from all the best Brooklyn and New York clubs at the Fashion Race Course, Long Island on July 20. The New York/Brooklyn match attracted at least 10,000 onlookers, each of whom paid a ten-cent fee to enter the enclosed stone grandstand and thereby helped to initiate baseball as a paying spectator sport. The unnamed Flour City delegate telegraphed the score — New York 22, Brooklyn 18 — back to Rochester where it was printed in the next day's *Democrat*.[10]

The Flour City Club played its second outside match on August 5, losing 24–13 to the Live Oak Club. Later that month the Rochester City Council took notice of baseball's new popularity by granting Rochester clubs permission to play on Brown Square. This proved a significant aid to the game's development as the new location became a favorite playing field for the remainder of the season. Matches also continued at the University Ground.

Although the Flour Citys played only two other first-nine matches that season, these were significant as they comprised a home-and-home series with the Niagara Club of Buffalo, thus initiating Rochester's first inter-city competition. After the Flour Citys sent an official challenge to the Niagaras, the first game was played on Brown Square in Rochester on Friday, September 3. The Niagara, organized in 1857, was also an older and more experienced club and the Flour Citys lost the well-attended game, 25–16.[11] The return match was played in Buffalo three weeks later. An account of the game in the *Democrat*, copied from the Buffalo papers, indicated that Rochester played a good game in the early innings but eventually lost 35–20 to a nine who were "cooler than the Flour Citys and their fielders did better execution."[12]

No doubt the Flour City players, other club members, and guests were encouraged by the festive post-game supper, hosted by the Niagaras, after which they were presented with the nation's first published piece of baseball music. *The Base Ball Polka*, composed by J. Randolph Blodgett, a Buffalo ballplayer and musician, was dedicated to the Flour City Club.[13] Another Niagara Club member, Everett L. Baker, immortalized the Flour City nine in the words of *Impromptu*, a poem sung by the composer.[14]

Competition for Brown Square had often been intense in 1858, so in March of 1859 members of Rochester clubs leased a ten-acre plot in the city's Third Ward on the corner of High and Troup Streets that became known as the Babbitt Tract or Babbitt Ground. Players immediately began conditioning the field, and the majority of match games played that season took place at the new site.

Rochester's baseball clubs grew more competitive in their outlook in 1859, motivated by the public display of the city's first pennant, won by the Live Oak Club the previous September at the Monroe County Agricultural Fair.[15] Even so, Flour City members seem to have remained content to make healthful recreation their primary goal. They played only one first-nine match, losing to the Live Oaks 21–11 on July 14. A second match, scheduled with the Lone Star Club for October 14, was deferred, probably due to unfavorable weather conditions.

On January 14, 1860, the Flour Citys joined with the Live Oak, Olympic, and Lone Star clubs for an experimental game on ice skates. This was held on the frozen waters of Irondequoit Bay, an inlet of Lake Ontario adjacent to the city, near the float bridge crossing. "Sides were chosen up and the playing went on in the presence of about a hundred spectators, who were attracted to the spot by the novelty of the scene. Eight innings were had on each side and when the game closed the score stood 27 to 25. The play was very lively and exciting — less difficulty being experienced than had been apprehended."[16]

The first reported Flour City match of the 1860 season was the pending match with the Lone Star on June 21. The Flour Citys lost, 22–18, and apparently played no other first-nine matches until August 16 when they opposed the Union Club of Brighton, a nearby town club. Again the Flour Citys lost, 31–24. But they won the return game on September 7, 23–10.

The 1860 season brought the Flour Citys national recognition and immortality when they became the first of two Rochester clubs to oppose the touring Excelsiors of Brooklyn on Saturday, July 7, 1860. The game "could hardly be considered a match game," the *Democrat* lamented following a 21–1 loss. "The fact that the Rochester boys made only one run, was owing less to their own want of skill, than to the remarkable amount of it possessed by the Excelsiors."[17] The members of the Flour City Club considered themselves fortunate to score at all and were pleased to have kept the Excelsiors' score comparatively low. Although the nationally renowned visitors had beaten them with ease, only one other opponent on their tour — the Victory Club of Troy, which was defeated 13–7 — had held the Excelsiors to fewer runs. This was hailed as a significant achievement.[18] The Flour Citys played only two other reported major games that season, achieving one win and one loss against the Union Club of Brighton.

In December the Flour City Club sent a delegate to the annual National Association of Base Ball Players convention in New York City, making them the only pre–Civil War Rochester club to become a member of the NABBP.[19] Whether this would have spurred the members to greater activity in 1861 season remains unknown because on April 13 news of the attack on Fort Sumter arrived through the telegraph wires at the Reynolds Arcade. During the Civil War years that followed, local baseball managed to stay alive due to the efforts of students, junior clubs and other younger players, town teams, and game accounts from the camp grounds. But it would be five years before it regained its pre-war momentum.

Twenty-two men served as first-nine players for the Flour Citys from 1858 to 1860. The club was "vivified by the bluest of blue blood," according to an untitled 1883 reflective essay by a writer identified as "Historicus."[20] His statement has merit, as most of the surnames of Flour City members correspond to those of early Rochester settlers, and a contemporary reference in the 1859 *Rochester Daily Express* labeled the Flour City "a fancy club, most of its members being bankers, brokers, clerks, and such like, whom a little smart work speedily 'knocks up.'"[21]

Flour City players who can be readily identified include Sidney S. Avery, Darius Cole, George Dana, George S. Harris, Charles Powers, Richard Tarrant, and Charles Upton. Sidney S. Avery, a book seller, played third base in 1858 and first base in 1860. Darius Cole, an accountant at Rochester Savings Bank, caught and played center and right field. George Dana, a bookkeeper at the Eagle Bank, caught and played right field in 1858 and center field from 1859 through 1860. He also caught in 1860. George S. Harris, a treasurer at Rochester Savings Bank, fielded in 1858 and played shortstop from 1858 through 1860. Charles Powers, an attorney, pitched and fielded in 1858, pitched and caught in 1859, and caught in 1860. Richard Tarrant, a shoemaker, played third base and pitched from 1859 through 1860. Charles Upton, a teller at the Commercial Bank, played third base and center field in 1858; third base in 1860.[22] Unfortunately, very little biographical information or commentary concerning Flour City members survives and includes only Charles Powers and Charles Upton.

Charles Powers gained notoriety as a general during the Civil War but was otherwise remembered as a modest attorney whose value was known only to those immediately acquainted with him.[23]

In his 1883 article, "Historicus" attempted to apply a dab of polish to the newly tarnished image of Charles Upton, then the recently demoted president of City Bank in Rochester. Upton was at the time of the article on trial for embezzlement after a disastrous oil speculation tempted him to overdraw funds and ruin his reputation. Perhaps it was sympathy that led "Historicus" to credit Upton with making the single run for the Flour Citys in the July 7, 1860, game against the Excelsiors of Brooklyn.[24] However, the game box score clearly awards this enduring honor to first baseman Sidney S. Avery; Charles Upton did not play that day.[25] Upton died tragically in a Rochester hotel on March 20, 1886, from an overdose of laudanum after he had nearly completed restoring the embezzled funds.[26]

The Live Oak Club

The Live Oaks, who held their first regular meeting on May 3, 1858, were reportedly the second Rochester club organized that year. On July 1 they wore their new uniforms comprised of a Marie Louise blue flannel shirt[27] trimmed with white silk and "neatly embroidered springs of oak" encircling the letters L.O. on the left breast. Their pants were white flannel with a blue stripe on each side, and they wore jockey-style caps of white flannel corded with blue, and front trimming of the same color.[28]

The Live Oaks played their first outside match with the Flour Citys on the University Grounds on August 5, winning 24–13, and they remained undefeated when they vanquished the newly formed Olympic Club on August 11 by the whopping margin of 65–10. On September 16, when they beat the Genesee Valley Club 39–7 in a contest played at the Monroe County Agricultural Fair, they became Rochester's first city champions. Their only immediate award, other than the prestigious title, was an invitation to take tea with the managers of the fair and to aid the tasting committee in judging "domestic manufactures" such as bread, biscuits, cakes, and native wines.[29]

The following spring the Monroe County Agricultural Society presented the Live Oaks with Rochester's first championship banner. The *Rochester Democrat and American* gave the following description: "The prize is the American colors, 12 feet long and 6 wide, attached to a blue and white staff, which is mounted at the top with a gilt ball. On either side of the flag is a green silk wreath of Oak leaves. Inside the wreath is the inscription 'Live Oak B. B. C.,' and underneath is the following: 'Presented by Monroe County Agricultural Society, 1858.'"[30]

Soon afterward, Live Oak member Henry ("Harry") Hartman took a photograph of the club in front of their prize. Forty-four years later, the photo and a club score book were presented to President Higgins of the Flower City Baseball Association[31] by Live Oak pioneer James Backus shortly before the opening day of the 1902 Rochester Bronchos of the Eastern (International) League. A reduced version of the image appeared in the *Rochester Post Express* along with Backus's 1902 reminiscences, beneath the headline "They Won a Pennant."[32]

Back in 1859, as the city's first pennant hung in the Reynolds Arcade, it immediately encouraged a more fiercely competitive spirit in Rochester baseball. The Live Oaks fought to defend their championship while other clubs tried to wrest it away from them. The members of the Live Oak Club, later described by the *Rochester Evening Express* as "tough and muscular young mechanics inured to toil and equal to any amount of exertion," would have no problem defending themselves against the genteel Flour City Club.[33] But the Olympic and Lone Star clubs would each be another matter.

Although the details are unknown, the first Live Oaks vs. Olympics match game of the season, played on May 26, ended in a heated dispute. The following day the *Union and Advertiser* proclaimed the game a failure and suggested an apology be made to the public.[34] Four days later, a sternly worded follow-up article in the same newspaper declared that petty rivalry between ball clubs was causing the publication of false and misleading information. Accordingly, the *Advertiser* announced that it would grant no more promotional free advertising, and that local clubs would have to pay the regular rates for their announcements.[35]

The two clubs eventually settled their differences, and on June 16 the Live Oaks won the replayed game, 26–13. A challenge from the rising Lone Star Club, briefly mentioned in the *Advertiser* on July 30, remained pending while the Live Oaks won a game with the Lockport Club at Lockport, New York, 43–18 on August 4. They challenged the Niagaras of Buffalo to a best-of-three series, but this also remained pending. On August 30 the Live Oak Club played the Canandaigua Club in Canandaigua, New York. No score was reported, only that "the Rochester club was victorious by large odds."[36]

On September 22 the Live Oaks and the Lone Stars finally met to play the long-deferred and much-anticipated match in front of a large crowd, including a sizable delegation from Buffalo as well as other towns and cities. The contest would achieve legendary status as the earliest local forerunner of what we now call a pitching duel. The combatants were Ed Loder, who stood on the line for the Live Oaks, and Richard Willis of the Lone Stars, both of whom would later be associated with what was referred to as "irregular" or "curve" pitching—pitching techniques that deviated from the NABBP rule then in effect, which called for the ball to be thrown for the advantage of the striker, not to deceive him. The closely contested afternoon game progressed so slowly that by the eighth inning, darkness was falling. The Lone Stars, ahead by one run, 8–7, declared the game should be called. The Live Oaks, who hoped to benefit by additional innings, claimed it should continue on another date. Before umpire John Stebbins, a Rochester attorney, could an-

Dedicated to the Live Oak Base Ball Club by composer J.H. Kalbfleisch in 1860, this has the distinction of being the second published piece of baseball music. If you look closely, you can see James Backus at bat. (Information taken from the *Rochester Democrat and American*, May 29, 1860, p. 3, col. 4.)

nounce his decision, an angry crowd stormed the field. In his animated (and perhaps fanciful) 1918 description of the game, noted Rochester author Rossiter Johnson claimed that Stebbins, who seemingly had to flee for his life, ran off the field and into a waiting carriage to be hastily driven away by a friend. Johnson blamed the dispute and game break-up — and even the long deferral of the game — on a growing objection to Willis's deceptive style of delivery.[37] These details were not mentioned in contemporary newspaper accounts, but the *Advertiser* did accuse the Live Oaks of prolonging the game in order to take advantage of the dark innings.[38]

An editorial in the *Advertiser* the following morning condemned the loss of the spirit of honorable rivalry in the community, which seemingly had been replaced by "wrangling, contention, betting, bluffing, and all those concomitants of horse races and prize fights." Women especially will cease to attend such exhibitions, they cautioned. In addition, the editorial defended the supreme authority of the umpire, maintaining that he alone should decide the outcome of a game — not contending club members.[39] One day later, Stebbins' explanation appeared in a letter: the unruly crowd had taken the game out of his hands and left him no choice but to advise captains to seek a settlement, he claimed.[40]

The disputed game was much discussed but never replayed that season. When the Monroe County Agricultural Society did not sponsor a championship contest, the 1859 city championship went undecided. The proposed match between the Live Oaks and Niagaras also remained pending. Meanwhile, the Live Oaks won the second of two games played with the Erie Club of Buffalo, 29–23, in Rochester, on October 10. (They had lost the first by a convincing 22–7 score in Buffalo on September 27.)[41] A third match to decide the superiority of the two clubs was never played after a misunderstanding over a suitable location, as well as the lateness of the season and poor weather. The Live Oaks also hosted the Lockport Club on October 6, defeating the visitors 49–21.

The first Live Oak baseball activity of 1860 was the January 14 game on ice that featured members of the Live Oak, Flour City, and Olympic clubs. The official Live Oak season began on May 23 with the Olympic match that had been pending since the previous fall. Olympic Club pitcher John Stebbins opposed Ed Loder for the second time, and the narrow 25–24 Olympic victory surprised the members of the Live Oaks, who considered their club superior.[42]

The month of May also brought the publication of *The Live Oak Polka*, which was composed by J. H. Kalbfleisch, self-published in Rochester by Joseph P. Shaw, and dedicated to the Live Oak Base Ball Club. Unlike the black-and-white cover of the 1858 *Base Ball Polka*, the *Live Oak Polka* featured a colored lithograph of the uniformed club in action, with player James Backus prominently awaiting his turn at bat.[43] The piece has the distinction of being the second published piece of baseball music.

Unfortunately, the second game of the Live Oak match with the Olympics, played on June 6, ended in another dispute and walk out in the sixth inning after Live Oak players protested a call made by umpire Henry Daniels. With the score 15–14 in favor of the Live Oaks and the Olympics at bat with no hands out in their sixth inning, Daniels ruled a runner safe at first. Live Oak players heatedly objected, claiming he was fairly put out. When Daniels refused to change his ruling, they stormed off the field.[44] The dispute was finally settled when Olympic secretary Daniel Wood queried the *New York Clipper*, baseball's voice of authority. The *Clipper*'s response, published

This 1859 image of the Live Oaks in front of their championship flag appeared in the *Rochester Post Express* on May 1, 1902, shortly before the opening of the new baseball season.

in the *Express* on June 21, agreed with the previously published Olympic stand: the decision of the umpire should have been accepted. Therefore, the Live Oak players were wrong to quit the game and leave the ground, and the victory should be awarded to the Olympics.[45]

On July 4 at the Independence Day Agricultural Fair, the Live Oaks and Lone Stars met on the fair grounds to compete for the 1860 city championship, the second such contest sponsored by the Monroe County Agricultural Society. The day did not go well for the Live Oaks, particularly when a lame wrist caused a one-inning replacement of pitcher Ed Loder in the sixth and enabled the Lone Stars to mount a seven-run rally. Hopelessly behind at the end of the eighth, the Live Oaks humbly acknowledged defeat and relinquished the 1860 championship to the Lone Stars.[46]

Four days later, on July 9, the Live Oaks had the distinction of being the second Rochester club to compete against the Excelsiors of Brooklyn, the fabled club that was making the first organized tour in baseball history. With Ed Loder pitching and his brother George catching, the Live Oak Club was defeated 27–9. However, the score was far from embarrassing, as the Live Oaks had earned the distinction of achieving a tie with the Champions of Albany for the second-lowest loss margin of the six upstate New York clubs the national experts had faced. The Victory Club of Troy, defeated 13–7, had earned the lowest.[47]

The Live Oaks played three more first-nine matches that season, winning all three. On September 6 they beat the Olympics 21–18. Later they won both games of a home-and-home series with the Pioneers of Canandaigua, New York; the first 26–13 on September 19, in Canandaigua, and the second 34–16 on October 11, in Rochester.

On November 5, a Live Oak intrasquad game unsuccessfully attempted to forecast the result of the 1860 presidential election. Each of the eighteen members competed on the side of his chosen candidate and Abraham Lincoln was defeated 28–14. The eventful 1860 season ended on December 25, when the Live Oaks issued a challenge to "any base ball club in the state" to a match on skates, ten men to a side, to be played on Irondequoit Bay near the city.[48] The Lone Stars accepted the challenge and defeated the Live Oaks 21–8 in a game played at 1 P.M. on New Year's Day.

Early in the spring of 1861, the Live Oak and Olympic clubs joined forces for greater strength and established the Union Club. Unfortunately, the promising new organization never had a chance to test its might. By April the city was enveloped by news of the outbreak of the Civil War, and regularly scheduled Rochester baseball was limited for the next five seasons.

The Live Oaks left behind greater evidence of their club than any other Rochester pioneer baseball organization. Theirs is the only club of which a team image survives or was ever preserved — Harry Hartman's 1859 photograph, which was published in the *Rochester Post Express* in 1902.[49] The ten men who were featured in that photograph did not include two 1860 additions to the first nine: George Ellerbeck, who briefly played third base and right field, and George Loder, who caught for his brother Ed throughout that season.

Here is what is known about the men who do appear in that historic image. Cyrus Beardsley, a civil engineer, played left field from 1858 to 1860. R. Heintz (spelled Hines in the newspaper accounts), whom Backus referred to as "an old cricketer," played third base throughout the 1859 and 1860 seasons. George Putnam, whose occupation is unknown, played first and third base in 1858 and right field throughout 1859. Harry Hartman, the ambrotype artist who took the picture, played third and second base in 1858, second base in 1859, and second base, center field and left field in 1860. Henry Whittlesey, a clerk, pitched one game in 1858, then played shortstop throughout 1859 and 1860. Henry Putnam played first base in 1859 and 1860 and became a well-known miller. Daly (first initial unknown), spelled Dailey in newspaper accounts, played first base in 1859 and center field, right field and second base in 1860. Richard Barker, a clerk at the Masonic Hall Building, caught throughout 1858 and 1859. He apparently did not play in 1860. According to Backus, he died in Mississippi after the end of the war.[50]

The most notable Live Oak player was pitcher Ed Loder. Loder, a tinsmith, pitched and played third base in 1858. He then pitched throughout 1859 and, with the exception of one game, throughout 1860. Fellow club member James Backus recalled in 1902 that Loder was one of three early Rochester pitchers associated with irregular or curve pitching. "I think Loder was the first man to pitch a curved ball in Rochester," Backus claimed. "The batters against whom we were playing, did not know what was happening to them and when they found the ball was approaching them and then curving away, they declared it to be unfair."[51] Ed Loder, who served for a time in the Monroe County Legislature, died on June 5, 1890, in the midst of Rochester's single season of major league baseball.[52]

Finally there was James Backus, a city grocer, who served as a scorer in 1858, and then played center and right field during the 1860 seasons. The 1902 article that included Backus's reminiscences also described him as the club's manager, but that title didn't exist before the Civil War and it would be more accurate to say that he helped to oversee the club's affairs.[53] James Backus, a well-known grocer for many years, remained a sponsor and friend to Rochester baseball until he died on December 24, 1902, at 68 years of age, seven months after the publication of his recollections.

In addition, two young men from Rochester — Theodore Frost and Matthew M. Yorston — have been credited with helping to introduce the New York version of baseball to Cincinnati. As Greg Perkins discusses in his entry on his club elsewhere in this book, the extent of their role in early Cincinnati baseball is not entirely clear. Neither Frost nor Yorston had been members of the first nine of the Live Oak Club of Rochester and we don't even know for sure that they were club members. Yet Frost, Yorston and a third member of the Live Oaks of Cincinnati, Sylvester Hicks, had grown up in Rochester, so it seems likely that the Live Oak Club of Rochester helped to contribute to its Cincinnati namesake.

THE OLYMPIC CLUB

The first newspaper notice concerning the Olympic Club appeared in the *Rochester Democrat and American* on July 14, 1858, to announce a match between the married and single men on the University Grounds. It also described the newly adopted club uniform: cashmere checked pants with a stripe, and checked caps.[54] The first outside club the Olympics opposed that year was the Live Oaks, which walloped them 65–10 on August 11. The Olympics did not confront the Live Oaks again until October 23. They lost again, but by a lesser margin of 36–26. The Olympics had, however, defeated the Genesee Valley Club in a "great slaughter" on October 9. (The microfilm account of the game is unclear, but the final score appears to be 74 to 25 or 20.)[55]

The Olympics opened the 1859 season with a formal intra-club game, in uniform, on Brown Square on March 12. By May the club had improved enough to pose a serious threat to the champion Live Oaks. The first game of a Live Oaks vs. Olympics home-and-home series on May 26 ended in a dispute. The rescheduled game was played on June 16, resulting in a 26–12 loss to the Live Oaks, and on June 29 the Olympics played their first match with the rising Lone Star Club. John Stebbins, who had previously played right, center field, or shortstop, stood on the pitcher's line and opposed Richard Willis. The Olympics lost 28–12.

The Olympic Club's 1860 season unofficially began on January 14 when they joined members of the Live Oak, Flour City, and Lone Star for a game on ice. Their official season began on May 23 when they opposed the Live Oaks for their first outside match. John Stebbins pitched, John Morey caught, and the Olympics rejoiced in a narrow 25–24 victory. The outcome surprised the members of the Live Oaks, who continued to consider their club superior.[56] The second game of the series, on June 6, ended with another dispute and walkout in the sixth inning with no hands out and the score 15–14 in favor of the Live Oaks. When the dispute was eventually settled, the Olympic Club was awarded the win.

The Olympics did not play another first-nine match until August 25. Again, they opposed the Live Oak Club, which had since relinquished the championship to the Lone Stars (on July 4). Unfortunately, rain ended the game in the top of the first inning; a great disappointment, as the level of skill demonstrated by the two clubs highly impressed both the *Democrat* and the *Express*. "Thus far the game had been played in regular Excelsior style — not a miss-play [*sic*] being made on either side," the *Express* proclaimed.[57] On September 6 the game was replayed, and John Stebbins opposed Ed Loder in a well-contested 21–18 victory for the Live Oaks. This was apparently the Olympic Club's last first-nine match of the 1860 season.

Early in the 1861 season, the Live Oak and Olympic clubs decided to join forces for greater strength. They never had ample opportunity to test their might, however. On April 13, Fort Sumter was fired upon, the Civil War began, and regularly scheduled baseball games in Rochester would be rare until 1866.

The most memorable Olympic player was pitcher John Stebbins, a Rochester attorney. "Stebbins was a natural pitcher," Olympic player John Van Voorhis recalled in a 1903 article that included the reminiscences of both men. "Tall, powerfully built, with broad shoulders and long arms, he could twist those balls into the batsman like cannon shots." In order to comply with the NABBP rules of the day, which necessitated a straight-armed delivery, "Stebbins hit upon the scheme of tightly bandaging his elbow with cloths and then in someway [*sic*] discovered by himself hurl [*sic*] those balls in like lightning." Van Voorhis added that Stebbins "practiced hour after hour at his home, and he never 'ran up,' as most of the pitchers did in those days."[58]

After Stebbins' questionable style of pitching was protested, Van Voorhis recalled, "The matter was referred to [Jim] Creighton, the great pitcher of the New York Excelsiors, and he was to have come up, and after watching Stebbins's methods, give final decision." This didn't happen, however, as club members couldn't afford to pay for Creighton's travel expenses.[59]

At the beginning of the first season of the Rochesters, the city's first fully professional base ball club in 1877, a *Rochester Union and Advertiser* article wistfully recalled that the present system of delivering the ball in Rochester was first practiced by the Honorable John W. Stebbins: "It is our belief that this style of pitching originated with Mr. Stebbins, and if so, he is responsible for important modifications in the national game. Long ago there was a general opinion in this city that Mr. Stebbins' style of pitching was not regular, but although clubs against which he played murmured deeply they took no effective action to suppress that style of delivery, and now we see the dreadful effect … it has spread over the country and no one can tell what the last effect will be."[60] More likely, Stebbins was among a number of innovative early pitchers who influenced the evolution of pitching — and therefore the game.

Also significant was John Morey, who stood behind Stebbins to catch his powerful pitching. "Morey was a powerfully built man," Stebbins recalled. "His hands were long and flexible, and I have seen him twist his wrist about and snatch a wide ball from apparently hopeless distances and put the batsman out almost without stirring from his tracks." He also claimed that Morey's shins, ankles and knees, which also aided him in catching, were black and blue from foot to knee. Both Stebbins and Morey, it was claimed, gained the valuable experience that would aid them in baseball from wicket, a modification of cricket that preceded baseball in Rochester; Stebbins as a bowler and Morey as a dreaded batsman.[61]

John Stebbins was a Rochester attorney, and John Morey was listed in the 1859 city directory as the proprietor of the *Rochester Union and Advertiser*.[62] Stebbins died in Rochester on July 30, 1905, while Morey died in Rochester on September 11, 1890 (toward the end of Rochester's single year of major league baseball). Several other Olympic players were identified only by matching mentions in newspaper coverage to directory listings. Ezra R. Andrews, a printer, played third base and shortstop in 1858, caught in 1859, and played third base and left field in 1860. He also served as a director in 1859. Later a city councilman, Andrews died in Rochester on August 13, 1900. William D. Andrews, also a printer who apparently worked with or for Ezra, may have been a brother or cousin. Andrews caught in 1858, played shortstop in 1859, and third base in 1860. Philip H. Curtis pitched one game each in 1858 and 1859 and then played right field in 1860. Curtis and his wife founded the Livingston Park Seminary and Curtis was past ninety when he died in 1914. Sylvanus A. Ellis, a merchant, pitched one game in 1858, played second base for one game, and served as captain that year. He played second base in 1859. He later became a school superintendent and died in Rochester on March 24, 1896. Edwin T. Huntington, listed in the directory as a proprietor of the *Rochester Democrat and American*, played right field in 1859 and center field in 1860. Thomas Stanton, a jeweler, served as a fielder and catcher in 1858. He caught and served as a director in 1859 and played shortstop in 1860. James Tone, a bank teller, played third and second base in 1860. John Vickery, a bookkeeper at a cotton factory, fielded briefly in 1858.

THE LONE STAR CLUB

The organization of the Lone Star Club was announced in the *Rochester Union and Advertiser* on August 16, 1858.[63] The new club played only one reported game that season, defeating the Genesee Valley Club by an overwhelming score of 76–22 on October 2. The Lone Stars impressively opened their 1859 season on June 29 by beating the Olympics 28–12 in an eight-inning game. One month later, on July 28, they appeared in their new uniform: a white flannel shirt and pants trimmed with blue, topped by a blue and white jockey-style cap.[64]

The Lone Stars did not play another game until they played the long-deferred match with the Live Oaks on September 22. The closely contested game ended in a protest and walk-out after seven innings. The disputed game was never replayed that season, and a game scheduled with the Flour Citys on October 11 was postponed.

On January 14, 1860, the Lone Stars joined the Live Oak, Olympic, and Flour City clubs for an experimental game on ice skates. The regular 1860 Lone Star playing season opened on June 21 with a 22–18 victory from the Flour City Club in the match rescheduled from the previous October. Less than two weeks later, the Lone Stars won the city championship from the Live Oaks on July 4, defeating them 24–14 during a contest sponsored by the Monroe County Agricultural Society at their Independence Day fair on the county fairgrounds near Rochester.

On September 5, the Lone Star Club's newly awarded championship banner was hung in the Reynolds Arcade. No contemporary newspaper description of the banner was found. However, forty-one years later the faded "bit of dingy bunting" was brought out by pioneer player John Barnes for the inauguration of the 1901 Eastern (International) League Rochester championship season. Barnes apparently thought the old pennant might encourage the modern-day Bronchos to earn the city a pennant. The 1860 prize pennant measured 8x14 feet, and was white with a blue outer border. In the center of a red inner border stood a large red star, and a dark blue inscription which read: "Presented to the Lone Star B. B. C., July 4th, 1860, by the Monroe Co. Agricultural Society."[65] The antique banner obviously did work some magic as the Bronchos claimed the championship for Rochester that season after miraculously winning 14 consecutive games, including twelve on the road, near the end of the season.[66]

The Lone Star Club played only one other match that season, when they opposed the Niagaras of Buffalo for the first game of a home-and-home series for the championship of Western New York State on September 20. The game was scheduled to be played at 2:00 on Jones Square, a public park on the west side of the city, which became a popular and significant ball ground in the post–Civil War years. Both clubs were undefeated, with the exception of the Niagara Club's loss to the visiting Excelsiors of Brooklyn. But according to the *Democrat*, the odds were not in favor of the Lone Stars: "The [Niagara] players are said to be 'extraordinary on the bat' and having had an unusual amount of practice this season, the Lone Stars will have to 'dust themselves' to keep up their laurels. Should they be beaten in this first game, it is to be hoped that they will court the practice they need so badly, in order to win the other two (and the match), for the sake of the 'village' which they represent."[67]

With Richard Willis standing on the pitcher's line for the Lone Stars, the highly unexpected happened. When darkness ended the game after the seventh inning, the score stood at Lone Star 32, Niagara 10. "The victory is one to be proud of, as the Niagaras have always claimed the position of the Champions of Western New York," the *Democrat* boasted.[68] "Willis ... never 'let up' on his 'cannon ball' delivery," the *Express* remarked, "not forgetting to mention his trying to dig a hole in the ground with his head." The later comment suggests that Willis, like Creighton, may have had a low, sweeping delivery that caused his head to dip below knee level. Willis may have learned this by studying Creighton, the nation's best pitcher, when the Flour City and Live Oak clubs opposed the Excelsiors in July.[69]

"The pitching of Willis bothered the Niagaras some…. They were not quick enough for him, although his balls were fair," the *Democrat* observed. However, a strong wind did much to challenge both pitchers and fielders as well.[70] The members of the Niagara Club, who were hospitably entertained at the Osborn House, graciously accepted their defeat. The following day, however, the *Buffalo Daily Courier* claimed, "Our boys attribute their defeat, in a great measure, to the wild pitching, if it can be called pitching, of Ellis [sic] of the Lone Stars."[71]

A second and deciding match with the Niagaras was intended but never played, probably due to the lateness of the season. Most likely, it was postponed until the following season. However, the official Western New York championship of 1860 remained forever undecided as the Civil War broke out before the 1861 season could get underway.

At their final meeting on November 20, the members of the Lone Star Club presented Richard Willis with "a beautiful seal ring and a massive gold pen and case" to show their appreciation. The popular pitcher, known for his modesty, graciously accepted. A similar present awaited Willis's star catcher, Mosher, who was absent.[72]

An unidentified eyewitness claimed in 1903 that Willis "was the greatest pitcher, in the estimation of many people, that this city ever saw." He explained: "The rules prescribed the underhand pitch, with a stiff elbow. Many of the pitchers, to get up speed, would 'run up.' Neither Willis nor Stebbins would do this. They stood still in their tracks and fired the ball in almost as fast as the high-priced overhand thrower of the present day can do it."[73]

John Stebbins maintained in the same article that Willis "had an arm as hard as marble, and many a time, after a difficult inning, I have seen them lead him almost fainting to a tent and rub him down and put cold cloths on his arms, as they do to prize fighters to-day in their corners." "Willis," he said, "gave up his life to his love for the game. It did not kill him outright, but I mean his devotion shortened his days."[74] Richard Willis also served as club treasurer for the Lone Star Club in 1860.

Richard Willis was born in England and came to the United States with his parents when he was eight years old and remained in Rochester until his death on September 21, 1869. He worked as a machinist, was active in public affairs, and continued to play baseball until his health failed. After being ill and bed ridden for nearly a year, Willis succumbed to an early death from consumption (later known as tuberculosis) at 33 years of age.[75]

Unfortunately, nothing is known for sure about Willis's faithful catcher other than that his surname was Mosher and that the club valued him as much as they did Willis. Mosher stood behind Willis and caught during every Lone Star game from 1859 through 1860. A likely possibility is that he was Franklin D. Mosher, who later caught for the Central Citys of Syracuse. George "Teddy" Adams played right field in one game and shortstop in one game in 1860. For details on his life, see the Central City of Syracuse entry. George R. Angell, a machinist, served as club president and caught in 1858, and played third base and right field in 1859. Angell moved to Detroit and became very successful, being the president of the City Savings Bank by the time of his death on April 18, 1900. Henry C. Daniels, a clerk, served as club secretary and played second base in 1858, throughout 1859, and in 1860, when he also served as a director. Daniels later became a Rochester police commissioner.[76] Frank Schoeffel played first base from 1858, when he also served as club vice president, through 1860 when he also became president. Intriguingly, an April 1859 article reported that Schoeffel recently had organized a ball club in Galveston, Texas, yet by the start of the ball season he was back in Rochester and playing his usual position.[77] Schoeffel died in Rochester on March 15, 1908. Patrick Sullivan, a gas works employee, played first base in 1859, and right field and third base in 1860. Sullivan became a prominent Rochester player in the post-war years and was a police captain when he died in 1882.[78]

Once the Civil War began, many Rochester ball players traded their baseball clubs for war weapons. "I do not think it is an exaggeration to say that nine-tenths of the old ball players went to war," Olympic player John Van Voorhis claimed later. "They were the flower of the city, all athletic, sturdy young fellows, hard as oak boards, trained down to the pink of condition, and possessors of keen eyes, good heads and rapid judgment." After the war the old clubs were "thinned by death, business responsibilities or other interests," Van Voorhis added. "But in its heyday I do not believe there was a city in this country which could have shown as clever and enthusiastic ball players as Rochester."[79] Although Van Voorhis's reflections included some fanciful statements, they also hold a fair amount of truth.

When baseball activity resumed after the war and gathered momentum, Rochester baseball would continue to rise to a new level of significance. Many of the senior pre-war players stepped aside and were replaced by former junior players and new players. The years immediately after the war produced such notable Rochester clubs as the Excelsiors, Pacifics, Mutuals, Athletics, Washingtons, and Alerts and such star players as Ezra Sutton, Samuel Jackson, John McKelvey, and Eugene Kimball, all of whom went on to enjoy successful professional careers. In 1890, the Rochesters enjoyed a single season as a major league team in the American Association. After that Rochester would continue as a significant minor league city and becoming the longest-running franchise in the International League.[80] The city would also gain a prominence that endures to this day with the community-owned International League (AAA) Rochester Red Wings, currently an affiliate of the Minnesota Twins and one of the most successful franchises in minor league baseball. In 1998, Rochester was declared "Baseball City USA" by *Baseball America*.[81]

Notes

1. Only first-nine matches will be discussed in this piece, although the members of second, third and muffin nines made important contributions to clubs of the era.

2. "Record of the Flour Cities," *Rochester Post Express*, March 28, 1903, p. 5, col. 4.

3. Three club record books still exist: a Live Oak Club field book kept from July 20, 1858 – October 4, 1859; a Washington (Jr.) Club secretary's book kept for the year 1859, and a Charter Oak (Jr.) Club treasurer's book kept from 1859 to 1860. An entry in the Charter Oak Club secretary's book indicates that existing members made moves to nominate new ones. The Live Oak and Charter Oak club books are housed with the Rochester Historical Society in the Rundel Memorial building of the central Rochester Public Library. The Washington Club book, however, is owned by the Rochester Public Library and housed in the Manuscript File in the Local History Division in the Rundel Memorial building.

4. "They Won a Pennant," *Rochester Post Express*, May 1, 1902, p. 9, col. 5–7.

5. Ibid.

6. *Rochester Democrat and American*, May 3, 1858, p. 3, col. 3.; also *Rochester Union and Advertiser*, May 4, 1858, p. 3, col. 2.

7. "Record of the Flour Cities," *Rochester Post Express*, March 28, 1903, p. 5, col. 4.

8. *Ibid.*; *Rochester Union and Advertiser*, June 19, 1858, p. 3, col. 4; Arthur J. May, *History of the University of Rochester, 1850–1962* (Rochester: University of Rochester Press, 1977), p. 142; *Interpres Universitatis* (student newspaper), University of Rochester, June 1858, Vol. I, p. 3, housed at the University of Rochester Rare Books library.

9. *Rochester Democrat and American*, May 29, 1858, p. 3, col. 3; *Rochester Union and Advertiser*, June 19, 1858, p. 3, col. 4.

10. *Rochester Democrat and American*, July 21, 1858, p. 3, col. 3.

11. Joseph Overfield, *The 100 Seasons of Buffalo Baseball* (Kenmore, NY: Partners' Press, 1985), p. 17. See the two entries on the Niagaras elsewhere in this chapter for additional details on the club.

12. *Rochester Democrat and American*, September 27, 1858, p. 3, col. 2–3.

13. *Ibid.* An original copy of *The Base Ball Polka* can be found in the Sibley Music Library of the Eastman School of Music of the University of Rochester. See the Niagara Club pre-war entry for a profile of Blodgett.

14. *Buffalo Daily Courier*, September 25, 1858, p. 3, col. 2.

15. *Rochester Democrat and American*, March 7, 1859, p. 3, col. 2.

16. *Rochester Democrat and American*, January 16, 1860, p. 3, col. 2. The game was also mentioned in *The New York Times*, January 23, 1860, p. 8, col. 3.

17. *Rochester Democrat and American*, July 9, 1860, p. 3, col. 3.

18. Preston D. Orem, *Baseball (1845–1881) from the Newspaper Accounts* (Altadena, CA: Preston D. Orem, 1961), p. 30.

19. Marshall D. Wright, *The National Association of Base Ball Players, 1857–1870* (Jefferson, NC: McFarland, 2000), p. 63.

20. *Rochester Union and Advertiser*, March 12, 1883, p. 4, col. 1.

21. *Rochester Daily Express*, August 10, 1859, p. 3, col. 4.

22. Occupational information taken from the *Rochester Daily Union City Directory of 1859* (Rochester: Curtis, Butts, & Co, Union and Advertiser Office, 1859). (Directories were published every other year at this time; therefore, there was no directory in 1858.) Unfortunately, with the exception of prominent persons (and even these can be disappointing), obituary information is disappointingly brief. Also, pioneer player information for this early period is inhibited by little mention of names; even first initials were not usually provided in newspaper accounts unless two players shared the same surname.

23. *Rochester Democrat and Chronicle*, August 29, 1882, p. 3, col. 3. Rochester pioneer baseball players' achievements in the Civil War will not be included in this chronicle.

24. "An Historical Reminiscence – Score Him One," *Rochester Union and Advertiser*, March 12, 1883, p. 4, col. 1.

25. *Rochester Democrat and American*, July 9, 1860, p. 3, col. 3.

26. *Rochester Union and Advertiser*, March 22, 1886, p. 2, col. 6.

27. In a November 21, 2010, message, nineteenth-century historian John Thorn explained that "Marie-Louise" apparently referred to the shade of blue, rather than the type of flannel the shirt was made of. Thorn also mentioned that a Google search confirmed "Marie-Louise blue" as "a new shade of bright light blue named after the Empress," most likely the Empress Marie-Louise of France (1791–1845), the second wife of Napoleon I of France, and later Duchess of Parma.

28. *Rochester Democrat and American,* July 2, 1858 p. 3, col. 2.

29. *Rochester Democrat and American*, September 17, 1858, p. 3, col. 1.

30. *Rochester Democrat and American*, March 7, 1859, p. 3, col. 2.

31. By the start of the twentieth century, flour milling had declined, and the nursery business that replaced it caused the city's longtime nickname to change from the "Flour City" to "Flower City."

32. "They Won a Pennant," *Rochester Post Express*, May 1, 1902, p. 5, col. 7.

33. *Rochester Daily Express*, August 10, 1859, p. 3, col. 4.

34. *Rochester Union and Advertiser*, May 27, 1859, p. 2, col. 4.

35. *Rochester Union and Advertiser*, May 31, 1859, p. 2, col. 1.

36. *Rochester Union and Advertiser*, September 1, 1859, p. 2, col. 2

37. Rossiter Johnson, "The Grandest Playground in the World," *The Rochester Historical Society Publication Fund Series*, Historic Monographs Collection, Central Library of Monroe County, New York.

38. *Rochester Daily Express,* September 23, 1859, p. 3, col. 1; *Rochester Democrat and American*, September 23, 1859, p. 3, col. 1; *Rochester Union and Advertiser*, September 23, 1859, p. 2, col. 2.

39. *Rochester Union and Advertiser*, September 23, 1859, p. 2, col. 2.

40. *Rochester Union and Advertiser*, September 24, 1859, p. 2, col. 2.

41. *Rochester Union and Advertiser*, September 29, 1859, p. 3, col. 4.

42. *Rochester Democrat and American*, May 24, 1860, p. 2, col. 5.

43. *Rochester Democrat and American*, May 29, 1860, p. 3, col. 4.

44. *Rochester Democrat and American*, June 7, 1860, p. 3, col. 2.

45. *Rochester Evening Express*, June 21, 1860, p. 3, col. 3.

46. *Rochester Union and Advertiser*, July 5, 1860, p. 2, col. 7.

47. *Rochester Evening Express*, July 10, 1860, p. 3, col. 3.

48. *Rochester Union and Advertiser*, December 29, 1860, p. 2, col. 5.

49. "They Won a Pennant," *Rochester Post Express*, May 1, 1902, p. 9, col. 5–7.

50. Occupational information compiled from the *Rochester Daily Union City Directory of 1859*, or the *Rochester Daily Union City Directory for 1861–62* (Rochester: Curtis, Butts & Co., Daily Union and Advertiser Office, 1861).

51. "They Won a Pennant," *Rochester Post Express*, May 1, 1902, p. 9, col. 5–7.

52. This and other death dates found in the Deaths Index card file in the Local History division of the Rochester Central Library; *Rochester Democrat and Chronicle*, June 6, 1890, p. 4, col. 1.

53. "They Won a Pennant," *Rochester Post Express*, May 1, 1902, p. 9, col. 5–7.

54. *Rochester Union and Advertiser*, July 14, 1858, p. 4, col. 2.

55. *Rochester Union and Advertiser*, October 11, 1858, p. 3, col. 1.

56. *Rochester Democrat and American*, May 24, 1860, p. 2, col. 5.

57. *Rochester Evening Express*, August 27, 1860, p. 3, col. 3.

58. "Baseball Half a Century Ago," *Rochester Post Express*, March 24, 1903, pp. 4–5.

59. *Ibid.*
60. *Rochester Union and Advertiser*, May 10, 1877, p. 2, col. 2.
61. "Baseball Half a Century Ago," *Rochester Post Express*, March 24, 1903, p. 4, col. 5.
62. *Rochester Daily Union Annual Directory of 1859*.
63. *Rochester Democrat and American*, August 16, 1858, p. 3, col. 3.
64. *Rochester Union and Advertiser*, July 28, 1859, p. 2, col. 2.
65. "There Will Be a Pennant," *Rochester Union and Advertiser*, April 23, 1901, p. 5, col. 1.
66. Bill McCarthy, *Rochester Diamond Echoes from the Hop Bitters of 1880 to the Red Wings of '49* (place, publisher, and date of publication unlisted), p. 30; Jim Mandelaro and Scott Pitoniak, *Silver Seasons, The Story of the Rochester Red Wings* (Syracuse: Syracuse University Press, 1996), p. 13.
67. *Rochester Democrat and American*, September 18, 1860, p. 3, col. 3.
68. *Rochester Democrat and American*, September 21, 1860, p. 3, col. 4.
69. *Rochester Evening Express*, September 22, 1860, p. 3, col. 2.
70. *Rochester Democrat and American*, September 21, 1860, p. 3, col. 4.
71. *Buffalo Daily Courier*, September 22, 1860, p. 2, col. 3.
72. *Rochester Union and Advertiser*, November 22, 1860, p. 2, col. 2.
73. "Baseball Half a Century Ago," *Rochester Post Express*, March 24, 1903, p. 4, col. 6.
74. *Ibid.*
75. *Rochester Democrat and Chronicle*, September 22, 1869; *Rochester Evening Express*, September 22, 1869, p. 3, col. 3.
76. "'Twas a Famous Team: The Forgotten Alerts," *Rochester Democrat and Chronicle*, June 3, 1895.
77. *Galveston News*, reprinted in the *Rochester Democrat and American*, April 6, 1859.
78. Edmund Redmond, "Subject of Famous Verse, 'Casey at the Bat,' Played Ball on Early Team Here," *Rochester Democrat and Chronicle*, July 24, 1927, p. 6, col. 1–6. Occupational information for Lone Star members compiled from the *Rochester Daily Union City Directory for 1859* and the *Rochester Daily Union City Directory for 1861–62*.
79. "Baseball Half a Century Ago," *Rochester Post Express,* March 24, 1903, p. 4, col. 6. It is interesting to note that John Van Voorhis, a Rochester attorney and second-nine player for the Olympics, defended local resident Susan B. Anthony after she voted in rebellion during a national and state election on November 5, 1872. For details, see *The Concise History of Woman Suffrage*, edited by Mari Jo Buhle and Paul Buhle (Urbana: University of Illinois Press, 1978, 2005), 293.
80. Bill O'Neal, *The International League* (Austin: Eakin Press, 1991).
81. A list of significant distinctions earned by the community-owned Rochester Red Wings organization includes the following:

"Baseball City USA"—1998: presented by *Baseball America* in recognition of the Red Wings year-after-year excellent operation for approximately a century of minor league baseball

John H. Johnson Presidents Trophy — 2001: presented by Minor League Baseball to recognize the best minor league operation in the country. This is the second time that the Red Wings were honored with this award.

Prism Award — 2006: Presented by the University of Massachusetts to the minor league sports franchise which exhibits the best operational performance (includes all sports).

On-going Excellence — 2008: Presented by *Ballpark Digest* to the minor league team which displays operational excellence year-after-year

Also, on July 24, 2007, the International League held a press conference at Frontier Field in Rochester to announce plans for the League to celebrate its Quasicentennial Season (125th Anniversary) in 2008. Rochester was chosen because it had been represented in the League longer than any other team — 120 of the 124 years since the league's earliest beginnings (as New York State League) in 1884.

❖ *Niagaras of Buffalo, Prewar* (Peter Morris) ❖

CLUB HISTORY

Like most cities, Buffalo had been the scene of ballgames for as long as anyone could remember. As Joseph M. Overfield discovered, when Buffalo was incorporated in 1832, its city council was specifically authorized to regulate "the rolling of hoops, flying of kites, playing at ball or any other amusement or practice having a tendency to annoy persons passing in the streets and sidewalks of said city or to frighten teams or horses within the same."[1]

It was not, however, until 1857 that the Knickerbocker rules were introduced in Buffalo and the game began to take on formal structure.[2] Indeed, as late as that summer, the earliest known reference to baseball in a Buffalo newspaper indicated that "sundry" players from the seventh ward would be playing an "equal" number from the city proper by "old-fashioned" rules.[3]

The impetus for change was the arrival in Buffalo in the fall of 1857 of two members of the Excelsior Club of Brooklyn, James B. Bach and Richard Oliver. Bach and Oliver found a receptive group of Buffalonians and familiarized them with the rules that had been adopted by the newly founded National Association of Base Ball Players earlier that year. The two Brooklynites then demonstrated how to lay out a diamond according to those rules, an event that took place on a vacant lot on the corner of Pennsylvania and 7th streets. In deference to the city council's authority to prevent ballplaying when it had a "tendency to annoy persons passing in the streets," the location chosen was not just a vacant lot but one that was described as being in a part of town that "was all vacant lot ... in those days."[4]

Bach and Oliver also showed the locals the bylaws of the Excelsior Club and persuaded them of the need to organize a club. The existence of the new club and its intention to follow the national rules were announced in the *Buffalo Express* on September 12, 1857, along with an impressive list of club officers. Neither of the Brooklynites served as an officer, but Bach's brother Robert became the club's secretary and was joined by president George C. Webster, vice president Edwin Richards, and directors William T. Wardwell, Thomas Shiels, and Orlando Allen, Jr. The Niagara Base Ball Club had been born.[5]

The list of officers also tells us much about the ties that bound the members. Wardwell, Allen, Shiels, and Robert Bach were all members of the volunteer Taylor Hose Company, and throughout the history of the Niagara Base Ball Club it retained a close alliance with that company of volunteer firefighters.[6]

The Niagaras restricted themselves to intrasquad competition that fall and when the spring of 1858 rolled around, it was far from clear that the new version would catch on in Buffalo. The first recorded game that year was played on August 20 with fifteen players a side and old-fashioned rules. The two combatants were the Star and Buffalo clubs, which a local paper described as the "two crack clubs of the city," and the Stars won 82–71 in three innings.[7]

But the Niagaras had not abandoned the new way of playing and six days later they met another local club called the Eries in the first match game of baseball played in Buffalo by the Knickerbocker rules. The Niagara Club had moved their grounds from the vacant lot at 7th and Pennsylvania to a much more accessible location at the northwest corner of Main and Virginia streets, which they shared with a younger club, the Frontier Club. The August 26 match, however, was played at the old site, which was now the home field of the Erie Club.[8]

The match was arranged so as to be not just a game but an event. The *Express* announced the match beforehand and suggested that it would be appropriate if a large number of female Buffalonians turned out to "inspire the players and urge them on to derring do before their ladies fair." The contest was indeed witnessed by a crowd of several hundred that included a significant number of women, some of them in seats around the field and others in the carriages that flanked the field. The match was played with "good feeling throughout" and the sense of ceremony was underscored after it ended with the Niagaras winning by the score of 25–16. The Niagaras joined in offering three cheers for the Eries, who responded with three times three.[9]

One week later, the Niagaras played their first match against an outside club when they took the Genesee Valley train to Rochester and faced that city's Flour City Club.[10] Once again the match was as much ceremony as competition, with the home nine meeting the Niagara Club at the depot and escorting their guests to the Osburn House. At the conclusion of the match, the players from both clubs joined in an "elegant supper" and listened to speeches.[11]

While the result of the game may not have been of primary concern, the Niagara Club members had the pleasure of coming away with another victory, this time by the score of 30–20. Any doubt that the result mattered was erased by a report in the *Express* that "there was considerable money bet on the result, with some of our citizens wagering on the Rochester boys."[12]

One week later, the Niagaras played their first match at their new home grounds at Main and Virginia, once again beating the Eries, by the score of 22–18. Then the 1858 season was brought to a fitting conclusion when the Flour City Club paid a visit to the new grounds.

The Niagaras won the match, 35–20, but once again the on-field competition was only part of a much larger event. The visiting players were accommodated at the American and Clarendon Hotels, and the contest was played in front of a crowd estimated at 2,000 that included many ladies. When it ended, both sides regaled the other with three cheers and a "tiger" (an odd noise popularized by Princeton students) and then they adjourned to Bloomers for a banquet and to the American Hotel for more festivities.

The eating, drinking, and merriment continued into the wee hours, accompanied by music from Poppenberg's Orchestra. The players also listened to a song by a man named Everett L. Baker, who chronicled the exploits of the Niagaras in twenty-three verses such as this one:

> Sidway's bat sends a rolling ball,
> And he makes his first base,
> As Demarest strikes an airy one,
> Sidway has gained a base.

They also listened to a song entitled *The Base Ball Polka*, which was written by Niagara Club member J. Randolph Blodgett and became the first published piece of sheet music devoted to baseball.[13]

The post-match festivities also included many toasts and speeches, beginning with one from M.E. Gelston, a member of the Eagle Club of New York City, who had come to Buffalo to serve as umpire. One of the more notable toasts was given by *Buffalo Courier* publisher Joseph Warren, who responded to one entitled "The Music of the Ball Clubs, their Thorough Base is full of Harmony" as follows: "May your innings at this fireside hearth be the best of all, and when the short-stop is put out by the great umpire, may he find his home base where celestial music is struck by angel bands on golden lyres."[14]

It was a fitting close to a season that had seen baseball rapidly gain popularity in Buffalo. The game did receive a setback when the city's aldermen voted to enforce an ordinance prohibiting ballplaying in the centrally located Franklin Square, but there were still plenty of vacant lots available. The Knickerbockers' version of the rules had also made significant inroads in the city during 1858. Despite the continued existence of nines like the Buffalo Club that still played by less structured rules, the new version now had more prestige and more prominence.

The 1859 season was another strong one for the Niagaras, as the club retained the informal city championship by again besting the Eries. One unpleasant exchange did take place, however, when the Niagaras declined to accept a challenge from the Live Oaks of Rochester. The Niagaras maintained that they did not have to accept the challenge because the Live Oaks hadn't established themselves as Rochester's best club, but the *Rochester Democrat* dismissed this reasoning as a "miserable subterfuge."[15]

The Niagaras also had a photograph made of themselves that year. Since photography was still in its infancy, each player had to be photographed separately and then all nine were pasted on to an appropriate background. Despite the contrived nature of the image, it was kept by John Van Velsor and eventually donated to the Buffalo Historical Society.[16]

The 1860 season saw several more milestone events for baseball in Buffalo. Things began with an early July game in which the Niagaras hosted the mighty Excelsiors of Brooklyn.[17] The Excelsiors were in the midst of an unprecedented 12-day, 1,000-mile railway tour of New York state that began on June 30, 1860, and included matches in Albany, Troy, Buffalo, Rochester, and Newburgh.

The point of the excursion was not so much competition as providing a showcase for the game. As one reporter noted in previewing the game, "The Niagaras look upon the Excelsiors as their parent club, for it was through the enthusiasm of one of their members, that they were organized, and being anxious to make their acquaintance, and also of giving the citizens an opportunity of seeing a first class club play, they extended the invitation to them for the match. The Niagaras expect to be beaten, and as one of its members remarked, 'its [sic] only proper, that the parent should be the first to whip the offspring.'"[18] Indeed, none of the games on the tour of the Excelsiors were close, including the one in Buffalo. The Excelsiors won in convincing fashion, 50–19, handing the Niagaras the first loss in the club's history.

The outcome was a disappointment to some overly optimistic Buffalonians who had wagered on the home nine, but in all other respects the match was a rousing success. A crowd of more than 3,000 turned out to witness the spectacle, filling all of the seats that had been set up in tiers and even overflowing into the windows and roofs of the surrounding buildings. And it was indeed a spectacle that they saw, as the Excelsiors played the game with a skill and finesse that inspired awe. One account noted: "No such ball playing was ever before witnessed in Buffalo. The manner in which the Excelsiors handled the ball, the ease with which they caught it, under all circumstances, the precision with which they threw it to the bases, and the tremendous hits they gave into the long field made the optics of the Buffalo players glisten with admiration and protrude with amazement."[19]

As usual, the Niagaras went to great lengths in hosting their guests. The Excelsiors were met at the train depot and escorted to Bloomfield's Hotel for dinner, given a tour of Niagara Falls, and then lodged in comfort.[20]

In August it was the Niagara Club's turn to play the role of ambassadors, as the players and their supporters traveled to Hamilton, Ontario, to face the newly formed Young Canadian Club. The game proved such a mismatch that one of the Niagara players, John B. Sage, later claimed that "the visitors finally struck out purposely in order to catch a train for home."[21] But the Hamilton players weren't discouraged and they paid a return visit to Buffalo, where the Niagaras beat them by the less lopsided score of 45–13.

The Niagaras continued to reign as Buffalo's top club in 1860, twice beating a new local rival called the Queen City Club. But their status as the champions of Western New York was brought into doubt in September when they traveled to Rochester and were handed their second-ever defeat. Their vanquishers were the Lone Stars of Rochester, who won by the surprisingly easy score of 32–10 in a match that reportedly dragged on from 2:10 until 6:45.[22]

That was the last important match played by the original incarnation of the Niagara Base Ball Club of Buffalo and may have been their last game of any sort. The club apparently made preparations to play again in 1861, but the onset of the Civil War led several of the club's best players to enlist in the Union Army. In June of 1861, the club that had introduced the Knickerbocker version of baseball to Buffalo went on a hiatus that lasted until the war ended in 1865.[23]

After the war the Niagara Base Ball Club reorganized and again established itself as the standard-bearer for Buffalo baseball. Of the antebellum players, only David Burt remained active and even he soon gave up playing, meaning that the postwar roster was almost entirely made up of new faces.

Yet while in many ways the postwar version of the Niagaras was a distinct club, in other ways it was a continuation of Buffalo's pioneer club. As before, the club was closely associated with the volunteer Taylor Hose Company. In addition, as a retrospective article explained, "Towards the close of the brief history of the original Niagara Baseball Club, the pioneers of the National game in Buffalo, full teams for practice were filled on occasion from the young lads who attended every practice and every game — the original rooters — and unconsciously schooled the material for a team to carry on the reorganized club and make a name for it quite as honorable as that bequeathed by the original organizers."[24]

Club Members

The antebellum Niagara Club was a who's who of Buffalo's influential young men. As one later account of the club's membership put it, "It was in the days of the old volunteer fire companies when membership therein was the test of a young man's good citizenship, and the leading baseball clubs were largely composed of young men drawn from one company or another. Later on, these same individuals shouldered the responsibilities of making this good city a leader among the cities of the United States."[25]

Another later summary noted, "The players were all young gentlemen of irreproachable family connections and plenty of money to swing the thing. The Niagara, from its organization, was really a men's social club with sixty or seventy members. The nine were merely the athletic features."[26]

This description is undoubtedly true and it shows why

it is tricky to paint an accurate portrait of the membership of the Niagara Base Ball Club. While we know the names of the men who played on the first nine, those men are just the tip of the iceberg. Yet there is no reliable way to determine which of the other club members looked at it as a social club and which were genuinely participants in the club's baseball activities. Another trouble is that retrospective accounts of the club tended to mention the members who became socially prominent or successful, rather than those who were active in the club's activities. As a result, this listing may not be entirely representative and probably tends to overstate the social prominence of the club's members. Nonetheless, there can be no question that the club membership was a distinguished one.

Orlando Allen, Jr.: Allen was an original Niagara Club director in 1857 and his highly recognizable name was a boon to the club. His father and namesake arrived in Buffalo in 1818, learned the language of the native Indian tribes, became a translator between the natives and the new settler and later served as mayor of Buffalo in 1848–49. The younger Allen was born in Buffalo in July of 1830 and, like many of the members of the ball club, was a volunteer in the Taylor Hose Company.[27] He enlisted in the Civil War and died on February 14, 1862, in Cairo, Illinois.

James Brown Bach: Bach was one of the two Brooklynites who helped form the Niagara Club. Although he spent only a few years in Buffalo, he was an appropriate figure to bring regulation baseball to the city. Bach's parents were married in New York City in 1831, then moved to Buffalo, where his father became one of the young city's leading businessmen. James was born in 1836 but his father died four years later at the age of 33 and his mother moved her young family back to Brooklyn. James remained in Brooklyn and went into business, also joining the Excelsior Club of that city in 1855. But his mother eventually was remarried to a Buffalonian and returned there. In 1857 James Brown Bach visited his brother in Buffalo and, along with fellow Brooklynite Richard Oliver, help to introduce the Knickerbocker rules. He was soon back in New York City, where he continued to enjoy success in business, eventually moving to New Jersey, where he died in July of 1914.

Robert Bach: Robert Bach was James's older brother and the original secretary of the Niagara Club. Like many other members, he belonged to the Taylor Hose Company, but there is no trace of his whereabouts after 1857.

Albert W. Bishop: Bishop was the center fielder of the Niagaras' original nine and one of the most distinguished members of the club. Born in Alden, New York, in 1832, he graduated from Yale University in 1853. He returned to Buffalo and began studying for the bar exam while working as chief clerk for the local law firm of Rogers & Bowen. When he passed the bar, he started his own practice and was succeeded as chief clerk by a junior clerk — future President Grover Cleveland. When the war broke out, Bishop enlisted, rising to the rank of general and being appointed adjutant general of Arkansas in 1864 by President Lincoln. He remained in Arkansas after the war, serving as president of the University of Arkansas and running unsuccessfully for governor in 1876. He returned to Buffalo in 1879, becoming a prominent member of the local Bar and a writer of some note. He died there on November 30, 1901.

John Randolph Blodgett: Blodgett was born in New York state around 1830 and celebrated his allegiance to the Niagaras by writing a song called *The Base Ball Polka*, which in 1858 became the first baseball-themed composition to be published as sheet music. Blodgett owned a Buffalo music store and became a prominent music dealer, director, and organist. He married in 1886 and sold his store to move to Chicago. The marriage proved an unhappy one, and the couple were

The original first nine of the Niagara Club wearing the natty uniforms that were adopted in 1857. Right fielder James Sidway (fourth from left), a member of one of Buffalo's most prominent families, perished in the disastrous 1865 American Hotel fire.

living apart when Blodgett died at his brother's house in Cortland, New York, on March 21, 1873, leaving an infant son.

David Wales Burt: Burt was born in Buffalo around 1842, the son of a successful businessman and state legislator who also served as a brigadier general and commanded the Erie County regiments during the so-called "Patriot War" of 1830. The older David Burt died in 1848. His namesake became the youngest member of the prewar starting nine of the Niagaras, being the club's shortstop when the photograph of 1859 was taken. Still in his early 20s when the war ended, Burt became the only prewar player to continue to represent the Niagara Club, but before long retired from active play. He also served as foreman of the Taylor Hose Company. Burt became a Buffalo banker, but around 1889 he opted for a quieter life and moved to the small community of Alexander, where he operated a small hotel and a large farm. He gave up the hotel after a decade, but continued to farm until his death in 1914, even after the deaths of all the other members of his immediate family. He died on June 8, 1914, in Corfu, New York.

Edward Payson Chapin: Chapin was the shortstop of the Niagaras in their third 1858 match against the Eries. Chapin was born in Waterloo, New York, in 1831, and moved to Buffalo to become an attorney. At the outset of the Civil War, he enlisted and became captain of Company A in the 44th New York Volunteers, nicknamed Ellsworth's Avengers. Chapin was promoted to lieutenant colonel after being wounded at the Battle of Hanover Court House in Virginia. He was then appointed a colonel in the 116th New York Volunteers in September and selected two of his fellow Niagaras to help command the regiment, George M. Love as lieutenant colonel and John Higgins. Chapin was killed on May 27, 1863, at Port Hudson, Louisiana. President Lincoln posthumously promoted Chapin to brigadier general. Buffalo's Chapin Parkway is named in his honor.

Frank Demarest: This man was listed as the shortstop of the Niagara Club when the club played its first game in 1858. The only plausible candidate is a man named James F. Demarest who was born into one of Buffalo's pioneer families on January 14, 1826, and became a successful broker, dying in Buffalo on July 8, 1891. His father was also named James, so it seems likely that the younger man was known by his middle name.

John Higgins: John Higgins, who was born around 1833, was the second baseman of the Niagaras before the war. The 1860 Census shows him working as a leather dealer, unmarried, and living at the St. James Hotel, where fellow club members J. Randolph Blodgett and Edward Chapin also lived. In 1862 Higgins and another young man, Charles F. Wadsworth, led efforts to recruit a company to represent Buffalo in a new regiment. When the 116th Infantry was formed, Higgins became a captain and was joined in command of the regiment by fellow club members Edward Chapin and George M. Love. Higgins received several promotions and was a lieutenant colonel when he was given a disability discharge on September 19, 1864. After the war he worked as a bookkeeper for the Buffalo firm of A. Rumsey & Co. He was reported as being dead by 1897, but the details of his passing are not known.

George B. Ketchum: The appropriately named Ketchum was the catcher of the Niagaras in 1858. He was injured in the club's game at Rochester, had to leave the game, and did not represent the club after that. His first child was born that year, which may have had more to do with his withdrawal from the first nine. Born around 1830 in New York, Ketchum was a member of the Taylor Hose Company and a prominent businessman. His father had been a cheese merchant and George followed him into the business, then later went into insurance. Ketchum served briefly in the Civil War and eventually filed for a disability pension. The 1910 Census shows a man who appears to be Ketchum living in a home for incurables in New York City. This man died in the Bronx on March 19, 1913, at the age of 81.

William Nelson Loomis: Loomis, born in 1836 in New York, played left field for the Niagaras. He was the son of Horatio N. Loomis, a physician who moved to Buffalo at about the time of his son's birth. On August 28, 1862, the *Buffalo Courier and Republic* reported that W.N. Loomis had enlisted as a lieutenant in the Subsistence Department of the Army of the Mississippi, serving under General William S. Rosecrans. On November 5 the same paper brought the news of Loomis's death. The account reported that Loomis had led a battalion into combat at the Battle of Corinth and "acquitted himself under fire like a hero." But he contracted a severe fever and was sent home, where he died on November 4, 1862.

George Maltby Love: A foreman for the Eagle Hose Company and city fire marshal in 1860, Love was the Niagaras' third baseman in their first match. Born on the first day of 1831, Love was the son of a Buffalo judge who had been a prisoner of war during the War of 1812. George M. Love went on to earn military glory of his own in the Civil War, serving three tours of duty, the last of them with the 116th New York Infantry. Although severely wounded at Port Hudson, where his cousin and fellow Niagara member Edward Chapin was killed, Love rose to the rank of brigadier general and was awarded the Medal of Honor for capturing the battle flag of the 2nd South Carolina at the Battle of Cedar Creek, Virginia, on October 19, 1864. He remained in the Regular Army after the war, but he continued to be affected by wartime injuries and retired in 1883. Love died on March 15, 1887.

Wells B. Miller: This man was later listed as the pitcher of the 1858 club but I have found nobody by that name in Buffalo.

William F. Miller: William F. Miller, who was born in New York around 1822, was the first baseman of the Niagaras. He was a prominent Buffalo attorney, who was in a partnership with Albert P. Laning, later a partner of Grover Cleveland. He died between 1880 and 1882, but passed the photograph of the Niagara players along to his son.

Richard Oliver: Oliver was one of the two Brooklynites who helped introduce the Knickerbockers' version of baseball to Buffalo in 1857. Oliver was then the president of the Wayne Base Ball Club of Brooklyn, and later served as president of Brooklyn's Excelsior Club in 1868 and again from 1871 to 1877.

Edwin Richards: Richards was the vice president of the club in 1857, but his identity is a mystery.

John B. Sage: Sage, who played right field for the Niagaras, was born around 1832. He served as foreman of the Taylor Hose Company and joined the family business in lithography and printing. His playing days ended with the war, but he remained prominent in the Buffalo sporting scene. He served as president of Buffalo's National League club from 1881 to 1885 and was later named official printer of National League. He was still alive in 1900 but was reported seriously ill in May of 1903 and appears to have died soon afterward.

Thomas Shiels: Thomas Shiels was a club director in 1857 and like so many other members was prominently associated with the volunteer fire department, serving as city fire marshal in 1859. Born in Earlstown, Scotland, on February 15, 1831, he moved with his family to Canada as a young child and then to Buffalo around 1840. He moved to Detroit in 1860 and then on to Minnesota and Montana, where he died on September 11, 1912.

Franklin Sidway: Frank Sidway, a starter for the Niagaras in both 1858 and 1859, was born on July 23, 1834, into a Buffalo family so wealthy that he was simply listed as a "gentleman" on the 1860 Census. His father, who had made his fortune in shipping, banking, and real estate, died when Frank was 13. Frank Sidway graduated from Yale University and during the war was commissioned to raise a regiment of volunteers. He was unable to raise an entire regiment because of the decision to stop paying bounties, and his recruits were transferred to another regiment. Sidway later became vice president of the Farmers and Mechanics' National Bank. He married a daughter of Buffalo Mayor Elbridge Spaulding and raised a large family, eventually moving to Grand Island, New York, near Buffalo, and becoming a gentleman farmer. After the turn of the century, he and his wife began to winter in St. Augustine, Florida, where he died on March 7, 1920. Although Sidway had a long and successful life, his name is now best remembered because, as executor of a friend's estate, he became the defendant in *Hamer v. Sidway*, a landmark case in U.S. contract law.

James Henry Sidway: James Sidway, Frank's younger brother, became one of the youngest members of the Niagaras' first nine in 1859. Sidway was a member of the volunteer Taylor Hose Company and he responded when a fire broke out at the American Hotel around midnight on January 25, 1865, and spread to the surrounding buildings. A blizzard prevented the firefighters from using their gas lamps and the fire raged on despite their best efforts. When it was finally put out, the dead bodies of three prominent young Buffalonians — Harrison Tifft, Harry Gillett, and James Sidway — were discovered under fallen walls. The whole city went into mourning. Sidway was only 25.

George S. Wardwell: George Wardwell was part of another pair of brothers who played for the original Niagaras. His father was in the whale, linseed, and tanning oil business. George, who was born in Rhode Island in 1829, graduated from Harvard, passed the bar and then became city attorney and a local judge. He died in Buffalo on October 18, 1895.

William T. Wardwell: William Wardwell was George's brother and he too played on the first nine, as well as serving as a club director and as a volunteer for the Taylor Hose Company. He was born in Bristol, Rhode Island, on February 1, 1827, and at 13 was sent to Buffalo to become clerk for his uncle, who worked in the oil refining business. He went into the business himself and after the 1859 discovery of oil near Buffalo, he built a refinery and became very wealthy. His company was eventually bought out by the Standard Oil Company and Wardwell became treasurer of the company. He moved to New York City, where he was a generous supporter of the Prohibitionist Party. He was the party's candidate for mayor of New York City in 1896 and for governor in 1900. He also became a major donor to the American Red Cross. William T. Wardwell died on January 3, 1911.

Joseph Warren: Warren was the publisher and proprietor of the *Buffalo Courier* and he gave the memorable toast at the banquet that concluded the 1858 season. Warren was born in Vermont around 1829 and graduated from university and taught Greek and Latin before turning to journalism. In 1854 he arrived in Buffalo to become local editor of the *Courier*. He purchased part-ownership of the paper in 1858 and soon gained a controlling interest. He remained the newspaper's president and editor-in-chief until his death in 1876, also serving as a park commissioner and as superintendent of schools and being prominent in Democratic politics.

George C. Webster: Webster was selected as the first president of the Niagara Club. He too was a volunteer firefighter, although unlike many members of the ballclub, he belonged to the Red Jacket company. He was born in Litchfield, Connecticut, around 1822, and his family moved to Buffalo when he was 3 months old. His father became a Buffalo pioneer in the transportation business and George Webster followed him, then became an oil refiner, and finally went into life insurance. He married the daughter of a local judge and they raised four children. George Webster died suddenly on February 1, 1873, at 50.

Sources

This entry relies primarily on Joseph M. Overfield, "Baseball in Buffalo Before the Civil War," *Niagara Frontier*, Summer 1964. Other sources are cited in the notes and in the source note for the entry on the postwar Niagaras.

NOTES

1. Joseph M. Overfield, "Baseball in Buffalo Before the Civil War," *Niagara Frontier*, Summer 1964, 54.
2. "When Baseball Was a Fledgling," *Illustrated Buffalo Express*, October 7, 1897.
3. *Buffalo Express*, August 7, 1857; cited in Overfield, "Baseball in Buffalo Before the Civil War," *Niagara Frontier*, Summer 1964, 54.
4. "When Baseball Was A Fledgling," *Illustrated Buffalo Express*, October 7, 1897.
5. *Buffalo Express*, September 12, 1857; cited in Overfield, "Baseball in Buffalo Before the Civil War," *Niagara Frontier*, Summer 1964, 55; "When Baseball Was a Fledgling," *Illustrated Buffalo Express*, October 7, 1897. Shiels' name is incorrectly given as "Shields" in the Overfield article.
6. Matt Endres, *History of the Volunteer Fire Department of Buffalo, N.Y.* (1906), especially 134–140, is the source of rosters of the Taylor Hose Company and of other Buffalo firefighting companies.
7. Overfield, "Baseball in Buffalo Before the Civil War," *Niagara Frontier*, Summer 1964, 56.
8. "When Baseball Was a Fledgling," *Illustrated Buffalo Express*, October 7, 1897; Overfield, "Baseball in Buffalo Before the Civil War," *Niagara Frontier*, Summer 1964.
9. Overfield, "Baseball in Buffalo Before the Civil War," *Niagara Frontier*, Summer 1964, 57.
10. According to Overfield, "Baseball in Buffalo Before the Civil War," *Niagara Frontier*, Summer 1964, 57, the game took place on September 3, while the article "When Baseball Was a Fledgling," *Illustrated Buffalo Express*, October 7, 1897, stated that the game occurred on the 4th.
11. Overfield, "Baseball in Buffalo Before the Civil War," *Niagara Frontier*, Summer 1964, 57, citing the *Express* and the *Rochester Democrat*.
12. Cited in Overfield, "Baseball in Buffalo Before the Civil War," *Niagara Frontier*, Summer 1964, 57.
13. Overfield, "Baseball in Buffalo Before the Civil War," *Niagara Frontier*, Summer 1964, 58.
14. Kate Burr, "Handsome Captain Hawley Still Live Wire," *Buffalo Times*, July 10, 1927; Overfield, "Baseball in Buffalo Before the Civil War," *Niagara Frontier*, Summer 1964, 58.
15. Overfield, "Baseball in Buffalo Before the Civil War," *Niagara Frontier*, Summer 1964, 59.
16. "When Baseball Was a Fledgling," *Illustrated Buffalo Express*, October 7, 1897.
17. Most sources have this game occurring on the 5th, but Overfield, "Baseball in Buffalo Before the Civil War," *Niagara Frontier*, Summer 1964, 59, places it on the 4th.
18. "The City and Vicinity: Base Ball—Excelsiors and Niagaras," *Buffalo Courier*, July 4, 1860, 2.
19. Unidentified Buffalo paper, reprinted in the *Brooklyn Eagle*, July 9, 1860.
20. Charles A. Peverelly, *The Book of American Pastimes* (New York, 1866), 409; Overfield, "Baseball in Buffalo Before the Civil War," *Niagara Frontier*, Summer 1964, 59.
21. "When Baseball Was a Fledgling," *Illustrated Buffalo Express*, October 7, 1897.
22. *Ibid*. This article states that the game took place on the 11th, while Overfield gives the date as the 21st. There was also a minor discrepancy about the exact score.
23. "When Baseball Was a Fledgling," *Illustrated Buffalo Express*, October 7, 1897.
24. *Ibid*.
25. *Ibid*.
26. Burr, "Handsome Captain Hawley Still Live Wire," *Buffalo Times*, July 10, 1927.
27. Endres, *History of the Volunteer Fire Department of Buffalo, N.Y.*

❖ *Niagaras of Buffalo, Postwar* (Peter Morris) ❖

CLUB HISTORY

As was the case with many clubs, the postwar version of the Niagaras of Buffalo was made up of an entirely new group of players and they faced challenges that the prewar players never could have anticipated. One of the prominent postwar members suggested that he viewed the two incarnations as separate entities when he commented, "I began playing ball in 1859 with the Olympics, a Buffalo high school team, and after serving through the Civil war became a member of the Niagaras, a team organized to take the place of the Niagaras of former days."[1]

Yet the Niagaras differed from most similarly placed clubs in a very important way—they were able to manage a signal victory against one of the country's top clubs without sacrificing the traditions of the era when players were strict amateurs for whom the pride of wearing the dapper uniform of their club meant everything. Symbolizing that fidelity, a member of a rival club in Rochester later recalled: "The suits of the Niagaras of Buffalo were the objects of envy on the part of the Alerts of this city. The whole thing was a check suit, trousers, shirt and cap. The trousers were long and buttoned about the bottom, so as not to interfere with locomotion."[2] As another later summary put it, "The famed Niagaras of the sixties were for the most part young men in the social strata, and in their natty uniforms looked like dudes. But they played ball like fiends."[3]

The Niagaras played only two matches in 1865, both of which took place in October when the Niagaras took a brief tour to face two small-town opponents, the Ellicott Club of Jamestown and the Excelsiors of Dunkirk. To no one's surprise, the Niagaras won both matches handily.

Although the year in which the war ended saw the Niagaras face no serious rivals or play any matches in Buffalo, the club made important steps toward laying the foundation for the success of the ensuing seasons. The club established a new practice field at the Arsenal grounds, located on Broadway between Milnor and Potter streets. There is no way to be certain how often the Niagaras practiced, and the game in Jamestown prompted a local reporter to remark that the players had had "little practice."[4]

Nevertheless, the club members did play at least one intrasquad game (with the squads divided into light and heavy members) and may well have staged others that were not recorded. They also established a new first nine that consisted of catcher Al Wheeler, pitcher J. Sprague Sawin, first baseman John Van Velsor, second baseman John Dobbins, shortstop Ed Hawley, third baseman Charles Pickering, left fielder Stanley Cowing, right fielder John Bartow, and center fielder Townsend Davis.[5] Some of these players were soon replaced on the first nine, but Cowing, Van Velsor, and Hawley remained fixtures, and several of the others had lengthy tenures.

Just as importantly, the Niagaras maintained the traditions of the prewar amateur club. The club's headquarters were at the Taylor Hose Company and as before the war, several of the players were volunteer firefighters. While even some amateur clubs charged admission to cover their expenses, it was not until 1867 that the Niagaras did so.[6] For now, members continued to bear the burden — Stanley Cowing later recalled, "We had 350 members who each paid five dollars annually toward the support of the club."[7]

The club also retained the gentlemanly customs of their predecessors. After their trip to Jamestown, that town's newspaper wrote, "The manly appearance and easy manner of the Niagaras won for them the respect of all. The Buffalonians showed themselves to be polite, courteous and polished gentlemen by every action."[8] While the next four years would see many challenges and periodic breaches of decorum, the Niagaras always strove to live up to those words.

One of the most dramatic changes occurred at the start of the 1866 season when the Niagaras received permission from the Buffalo Common Council to create permanent grounds on Market Square, at the corner of Sixth and York Streets. The council turned down a request to contribute to building a ballfield at the site, so the Niagaras went about creating one. By summer, the club had a fine home field that could accommodate the significant crowds that were beginning to flock to the club's games. Eventually the field was enclosed and a grandstand erected for the comfort of spectators.[9]

The Niagara Club continued to try to maintain the prewar customs of hospitality. When the Ellicotts of Jamestown visited Buffalo in August, they were met at the train station and escorted to the Tifft House. After the match, both clubs joined in a ten-course meal that featured mutton, beef, softshelled crabs, and broiled prairie chicken, with the food accompanied by plenty of speeches and socializing.[10]

But some of the club's other matches showed that the delicate fabric of baseball's gentlemanly era was beginning to fray. The Hudson River Club of Newburgh, New York, visited a couple weeks later and their members were treated with similar hospitality. The *Buffalo Courier and Republic* reported afterward, "The spirit of betting, at present so rife on account of the Horse Fair, caused considerable investment in the game, at odds of about three to one on the Hudson River. The result shows either that the Niagara's [sic] are better, or their visitors poorer, players than was thought."[11]

The upset win over the highly regarded Hudson River Club also showed that the Niagaras were becoming a force to be reckoned with (although, as described in the Hudson River Club's entry, that club blamed its defeat on travel-related fatigue and sickness). The first nine of the Niagaras in 1866 included only two new players, Tom Emerson and Ed Atwater, both local young men. But their additions, coupled with the players who had joined the club in 1865, created the strong nucleus that would achieve several significant victories over the next few years.

Atwater in particular was crucial to the club's success. The son of a prominent Buffalo businessman, Atwater became the club's pitcher and his work against the Hudson Rivers prompted the *New York World* to rave, "Atwater of the Niagaras is one of the best pitchers in the country, there being no one on any of the New York or Buffalo clubs who can approach him in throwing a difficult ball."[12]

While the match against the Hudson Rivers demonstrated the promise of the Niagara Club's young players and their commitment to maintaining the prewar gentlemanly customs, other matches were less satisfactory. One such match occurred when the Niagaras made a late July trip to play the Excelsiors of Rochester. The match was tied after nine innings, but then an injury forced Niagara catcher Al Wheeler to leave the game and the Excelsiors won in the tenth inning. Worse, the hotly contested match prompted the *Buffalo Express* to make wild accusations that the Buffalo players "were browbeat by the mob and assailed with boorish and ungentlemanly epithets and howls by their opponents."[13] While other newspapers tried to downplay the controversy, ill will between the ballplayers of Buffalo and Rochester continued to fester.[14]

Particularly disturbing was a season-ending tournament in Auburn that was intended to determine regional supremacy. After winning their first match, the Niagaras again faced the Excelsiors of Rochester and were again tied when darkness fell. It was agreed to decide the outcome with a rematch on the following day and this time the Excelsiors squeaked out a narrow win.

The Excelsiors now had only to beat the Pacifics of Rochester to take home the gold ball that symbolized the championship of the region. Instead, controversy erupted over who was to receive the second-place trophy and after a lengthy dispute, the championship game was canceled. The Niagaras were offered the trophy, but they declined.[15]

The Auburn tournament was a troubling sign of things to come, as was the outcome of an October challenge from the Detroit Base Ball Club. The Niagaras declined the challenge, explaining that the club intended to play no more games that year but would be glad to schedule a match for 1867.[16] The club's position was entirely understandable, considering the likelihood of bad weather at that time of year and that the members of the Niagaras were amateurs with business concerns to keep them busy. Yet there was no way for a challenging club to know whether such a response was genuine or just an excuse, so bad feelings could ensue.

When the season ended, the Niagaras officially joined the National Association of Base Ball Players and the club's certificate of membership, dated December 12, 1866, was carefully preserved and was eventually donated to the Buffalo Historical Society.[17] After getting off to a late start, the 1867 season saw several indications of new ambition on the part of the club.

In July the Niagaras beat the Auburn Base Ball Club and were awarded the gold ball that had caused so much controversy the previous fall. Possession of the trophy created great excitement in Buffalo, and it was put on display at the Main Street music store of club member J. Randolph Blodgett. But in other cities the match renewed the old controversy and many wondered what right the Niagaras and Auburns had to play for the gold ball.

Challenges were quickly made to the Niagaras to defend the trophy, and more ill will was created when the club was slow to defend its title. In an attempt to clarify matters, the Niagaras even went to the extent of placing an advertisement in the *Ball Players' Chronicle* spelling out challenge rules for the gold ball.[18] But this backfired, as others found it presumptuous for the holders to create such rules, and the *Syracuse Herald* published a devastating parody of the rules. Included were such gems as mock provisions that the Niagaras reserved the right "not to play after the acceptance of a challenge if there is any prospect of their being beaten," that the championship would consist of a single game "except it be that the Niagaras should be beaten in that game; in such case best two in three to decide the matter," and that "the season shall commence May 1st and end when the Niagaras will."[19]

The humor masked a serious issue that plagued the challenge system: the club possessing the championship might very well have legitimate reasons for declining a challenge, yet the challenging club understandably felt frustrated when this happened.

Whether or not the reasons were legitimate, it was not until October that the Niagaras defended the gold ball. In the interim, the club went on a brief tour that included matches in Detroit, Toledo, Cleveland, and Erie (in the last city, the Niagaras faced a club from Williamsport). The Niagaras and their guests took a boat across to Detroit, and many members of the party spent the voyage singing along to tunes made by a guitar, flute, and banjo. Unfortunately, rough seas spoiled the idyllic scene and many of the players were seasick upon arrival in Detroit. The Niagaras lost their match to the Detroit Base Ball Club, but recovered quickly and concluded the tour with convincing victories over the Toledo Base Ball Club, the Forest Citys of Cleveland, and the nine from Williamsport.[20]

Upon their return to Buffalo, the Niagaras commenced a series against an up-and-coming Buffalo club called the Cliftons. The Cliftons were still considered a junior club but the matches proved competitive and the Cliftons even won one when the Niagaras played two men short.[21] The emergence of the Cliftons was an important development because it gave the hope of a spirited in-city rivalry, but as we shall see that prospect was nipped in the bud.

The Niagaras also began making arrangements to defend the gold ball. The first such match took place on October 3 at the Sixth Street grounds and the challengers were the Central Citys of Syracuse. For the first time ever, admission was charged for a match in Buffalo, and a huge crowd estimated by the local press at 4,000 turned out to watch.[22] They went home somewhat disappointed, however, when the visitors won by the score of 38–27 and took the coveted championship trophy back to Syracuse.

Next up was a home-and-home series between the Niagaras and their archrivals, the Excelsiors of Rochester. The two matches had none of the acrimony that had plagued earlier contests between the two clubs. The first match was played in Rochester and prompted the *Ball Players' Chronicle* to conclude that "it seems as if the hostility so long existing between the two clubs will be turned into a generous rivalry." After the return match in Buffalo, "the Rochesters were entertained lavishly after the game."[23]

While the restoration of harmony between the two clubs was welcome, the Niagaras were defeated in both matches and this spelled trouble. Twenty-five-cent admission had again been charged for the match in Buffalo, and advertisement beforehand had produced another enormous crowd that was once more estimated at 4,000. The concept of paying to watch baseball did not by itself seem to trouble Buffalonians, with an *Express* reporter even writing after the gold ball match, "The idea of charging admission was an excellent one. It excluded the offensive rabble of urchins who heretofore had monopolized the portion of the ground reserved for spectators."[24]

But what the matches did reveal was that charging admission created heightened expectations. The *Express* was so dismayed by the losses at the hands of the visitors from Syracuse and Rochester that it published an editorial entitled "Base Ball, a Buffalo Invention" that observed sarcastically, "The Niagaras were playing a game of their own invention, a version of one-old-cat, while the Rochesters were actually playing the national game as it is recognized the country over."[25]

Thus the 1867 season ended with the Niagara Club facing a dilemma. Buffalo's excitement about baseball had reached new levels during the exciting campaign, but in order to maintain that interest, the Niagaras were going to have to start winning matches against the strong foes.

The Niagaras did just that in their first major match of 1868. After a warm-up win over the Cliftons, the club hosted the mighty Atlantics of Brooklyn on June 16. The city of Buffalo was in a state of frenzy on the day of the game — newspaper accounts suggested that some 2,500 spectators paid to watch while three times as many did their best to follow the match from outside the fences.[26]

But few of the Buffalonians really believed that the home side had a chance to win, with 5-to-1 odds being offered on the Atlantics. The visitors felt even more certain of victory, and they made no effort to disguise their confidence. According to John Van Velsor of the Niagaras, "The Atlantics had brought along with them a large number of photographs of the team which they purposed selling to the baseball enthusiasts in the various cities included in their tour. Printed across the cards on which the photographs were mounted were the words, 'Champions of the World. Never Beaten and Never Will Be Beaten.'"[27]

Yet that boast was soon proved wrong as, behind the sterling pitching of Ed Atwater, the Niagaras did the unthinkable. As one later article put it,

> These stars in the baseball firmament arrived in Buffalo with much flourish of trumpets. The Niagaras had new suits of black and white material with caps to match, the visor being of white. They wore baseball shoes, but their long trousers buttoned over the top of the shoe. Captain [Ed] Hawley, just at the age when a mustache seemed important, wore a red necktie. The nines met at the Front. All Buffalo was there. Society turned out in tandem, coach, four-in-hands, drags, carriages, barouches, phaetons, dog carts and every conveyance known to the sixties. Buffalo's belles were there in their stiffly starched piques and brilliant sashes. And everybody else was there to see ours take their trimming, hoping against hope that the stars would score low enough to save the face of the Niagaras. When the game was over that bright June day the score stood 19 to 14 in favor of the Niagaras.... You couldn't hold that Buffalo crowd. It yelled itself hoarse. The ladies fluttered their handkerchiefs and smiled on the conquerors. Staid business men threw their hats in the air, dignified bankers uncorked their throats to hurrah for the Niagaras.[28]

Legendary sportswriter Henry Chadwick had come up from New York to report on the match and had the same expectation about the result as everyone else. At the conclusion of the remarkable game, a dumbfounded Chadwick turned to John B. Sage, the former president of the Niagara Club, and asked, "Who are these players?" "Young gentlemen of the town," was Sage's heartfelt reply. Perhaps the most satisfying moment came after the game when the Atlantic players glumly packed up the photographs with the taunting inscriptions and sent them back to Brooklyn.[29]

While these accounts undoubtedly include some measure of exaggeration, it was impossible to overstate the magnitude of the upset. Back in New York City, some assumed that the Niagaras' win must have been the result of a fix, so it was fortunate that Chadwick was on hand to defend the legitimacy of the contest.[30] But even in Syracuse, news of the outcome "created great interest and much astonishment among the ball players of this city. The general impression seemed to be that the Atlantics could not have tried to win the game."[31]

The victory over the legendary Atlantics was one of the highlights of the Niagara Club's existence and one of the biggest upsets of the era. Even so, it was a mixed blessing for the surprise winners and in some ways was a pyrrhic victory.

To begin with, the club's only serious rival in Buffalo, the Cliftons, almost immediately disbanded because the members of the younger club were so anxious to join the more established club. This development provided the Niagaras with a few new players, but in the long run it left Buffalo with no in-city rivalry, while also meaning that there would be less new talent available in the future.[32] The club tried to address the situation by organizing a second nine, but such clubs were more difficult to sustain than ones that flew under their own masthead.[33]

An even more serious problem was that the upset of the Atlantics put the Niagaras in an impossible situation. In big cities, recognition had begun to dawn that a single baseball game sometimes produced an anomalous result. Henry Chadwick referred to the Niagaras as a "country club" in describing the match against the Atlantics, prompting a peeved Buffalonian to ask, "Has a man got to live in New York or Philadelphia to be a first-class ball player?"[34] One New York paper went much further, describing the result as an "accidental victory."[35]

By contrast, in regions where baseball was new, there continued to be an assumption that the winner of a game could endlessly repeat that triumph. The result for the Niagaras was that expectations in Buffalo were raised to such a height that disappointment became inevitable. Enormous throngs started turning out at the Sixth Street diamond and the home club rewarded them with some impressive victories, including wins over strong clubs like the Excelsiors of Rochester and the Detroit Base Ball Club. There was also a triumph at a tournament in Niagara Falls, which earned the club another gold ball that was proudly exhibited at S.N. Lawrence & Son's furnishing goods store.[36]

Yet victories such as these paled by comparison with the one against the great club from Brooklyn, while every defeat created disappointment. The first loss came against another national power, the Athletics of Philadelphia, in front of another huge throng of Buffalonians reported as numbering 10,000. Defeat at the hands of such a club was understandable, especially since Atwater was handicapped by an injury, but the mood changed and the crowds began to thin when the Niagaras began losing to clubs from nearby cities.[37]

The next loss came when the Niagaras challenged the Central Citys for the gold ball, and the Buffalo public found it hard to understand why a club capable of beating the mighty Atlantics couldn't defeat one from Syracuse. The puzzlement grew when the Niagaras dropped a game to the Alerts, a *junior* club from Rochester (though in fact a very strong one). Even when the Niagaras rebounded with two convincing wins to capture the series with the Alerts, this just provided another reason to be perplexed about the earlier loss.

The kneejerk reaction would have been to jump to the conclusion that the game had been fixed. Indeed, the "betting feature" at the second game of the series "was quite prominent, several sporting characters having come down from the Flour City [Rochester], with their greenbacks carefully folded in wrapping paper, which they appeared greedy to invest upon the result of the game. The betting generally ruled at evens, though in some cases odds were laid on the Alerts. As far as our observation extended, offers did not go begging on either side. We should judge that two thousand dollars, or thereabouts, was invested on the game."[38] On the basis of such circumstantial evidence, accusations of game-fixing by imported professionals frequently flew in other cities. But the Niagara Club was still made up of local young men from good Buffalo families, and there was no reason to believe that there was anything fishy about the result, so other explanations had to be sought. One sportswriter wrote,

> Base-ball is very uncertain. Last Saturday the Niagara club went to Rochester, and were beaten by the Alerts by the decisive score of thirty to thirteen. All who witnessed the game united in the opinion that the Rochesterians out-batted and out-fielded the Buffalonians, and such was the fact. Judging from that fact alone, the fair inference would be that the Alerts were much the superior club. Yesterday the return game was played here, and the boot was on the other leg. The Niagaras won, by a score of twenty-three to eleven, nearly equivalent to that by which they were defeated at Rochester, and no one will gainsay that yesterday they out-batted and out-fielded the Alerts. Judging from that game alone, the inference would be equally fair that the Niagaras can "lay out" the Alerts any day in the week. From which premises, "without fear of successful contradiction," as the man says in the play, we can reiterate our original proposition that base-ball is very uncertain, and we may add, speaking from a local stand-point, peculiarly uncertain when the Niagara club is concerned.[39]

Local bewilderment further increased after a lopsided September loss at the hands of the Excelsiors of Chicago. As one sportswriter observed, previous results made the result difficult to understand:

> The Excelsiors, of Chicago, beat the Niagaras, of Buffalo, at Detroit yesterday, by a score of thirty-one to twelve. Last Saturday the Detroit club beat the Excelsiors, on their own grounds, the score standing fifteen to twelve, and yesterday the Niagaras "warmed" the Detroit club to the tune of thirty-eight to seventeen. The ways of base ball are mysterious. A logical mind would have concluded from the above premises that Chicago would have been wax in the paws of Buffalo, but the very peculiar rules which govern base ball ruled otherwise. We understand that some twenty or thirty of the Buffalo nine were afflicted with "Grecian colic" or some other complaint, and that the decisive defeat they experienced is to be attributed to that circumstance. But we have little sympathy with excuses after the game is played. Chicago has a right to crow, it knows how to crow, and let it crow.[40]

By the time the Niagaras concluded their tumultuous 1868 campaign with a match against the Red Stockings of Cincinnati, the Buffalo public was starting to accept the fact that the club was not on a par with the national powers. As a result, the 1,500 spectators who turned out expected that the visitors would beat the "somewhat rusty" Niagaras and indeed the Red Stockings won by the score of 28–11. Although coverage of the game included high praise of the play of the visitors, there were still signs that expectations of the Niagaras remained very high. The local players were criticized for having failed to "play up to their ordinary standard. Bettinger was unusually ineffective behind the bat; Van Velsor muffed one ball squarely and missed another; Myron was not himself at second, and was powerless on the inside; Smith was very strong on the inside, but made several wild throws; Emerson muffed a ball and Holley [sic] misjudged one. This is a record not wont to be written of the Niagaras when they have serious work to do."[41]

Thus the 1868 season ended with the Niagara Club at a turning point. Baseball's governing body elected to allow open professionalism, with the result that the already large gap between the top clubs and the rest of the country became a gaping chasm. The Niagaras opted to remain an amateur club made up entirely of locals, with the result that expectations for 1869 needed to be tamped down. "The intense base ball enthusiasm of last year has not worn off," warned the *Buffalo Express*, "but if base ball continues at the high degree of interest it did last year, we fear its days are numbered, for the public, fickle as it is, will have had too much of it, and seek entertainment elsewhere."[42]

Adding to the troubles of the Niagaras, they were facing the loss of the Sixth Street grounds, which the city was planning to turn into a park. Since it was unclear that baseball would be allowed there, the Niagaras began playing at a harness racing park on East Ferry Street. Unfortunately, the ground at the new field left much to be desired, while spectators understandably "did not fancy the long walk from the street railroad in a hot day."[43]

A far more serious result of the move was that it became "impossible to get the nine together there sufficiently often for practice."[44] In consequence, the Niagaras did not play their first match of 1869 until June, when the mighty Red Stockings again passed through town. The rust of the Buffalo players was obvious in the game, and their "fatal nervousness" resulted in a 42–6 trouncing at the hands of the visitors.[45]

The next match played by the Niagaras was to become their most celebrated victory, coming to overshadow even the historic upset of the Atlantics. The game was played on June 9, 1869, against another Buffalo club, the Columbias, and saw the Niagaras win by the extraordinary score of 209–10, with every member of the nine crossing the plate at least 20 times. Perhaps even more amazing was the fact that the carnage was completed in a mere three hours.

News of the result spread throughout the country and for many years later the game would be cited as a record for runs scored in a match. Yet more than anything else, what the match revealed was that the demise of the Cliftons had left the Niagaras without the strong local competition needed to keep the players sharp.

This reality was underscored in the club's next game, which took place nearly a month later and saw the Niagaras cross the border to take on a club from Dundas, Ontario. But the game proved another mismatch, as the batters of the Niagaras walloped the speediest offerings of the Canadian pitcher with ease. In desperation, he began tossing slow pitches, but this played right into the hands of slugging Buffalo first baseman John Van Velsor. He picked out the heaviest bat he could find, asked for a high pitch and "drove it away into the woods adjoining the ball grounds." Years later, the drive was a fond memory for Van Velsor, who recalled, "I never saw anything like it. I think it's going yet."[46]

While matches against clubs like these created fond memories, they did nothing to enable the players to improve. Over the remainder of the 1869 season, the Niagaras played several matches against professional clubs and they kept them all close, but lost every time. The most impressive win came when the Niagaras finally beat their old nemeses, the Central City Club of Syracuse, but the Central Citys were also slumping. Still more luster was removed from the win when the Syracuse club won a rematch.

By the end of the 1869 season, it was painfully obvious that the Niagaras were never going to become a national power. In addition, the club's nucleus was breaking up. After using a fairly set lineup in previous seasons, the combination of players having to attend to business responsibilities and the inaccessible practice grounds took a toll. No fewer than 18 different players represented the Niagaras in 1869, with three positions becoming revolving doors.[47]

These disheartening trends continued in 1870, with pitcher Ed Atwater turning professional and joining the Red Stockings and Myron Holly doing the same with the Olympics of Washington, while longtime captain and shortstop Ed Hawley retired from competitive play to pursue business. The club did regain the use of the Sixth Street grounds and pluckily scheduled many top clubs that year. But the results were predictable — a string of losses, most of them lopsided, to clubs like the Forest Citys of Rockford, the White Stockings of Chicago, the Harvard University nine, the Athletics of Philadelphia, the Forest Citys of Cleveland, the Olympics of Washington, the Atlantics of Brooklyn and the Pastimes of Baltimore. The only wins the Niagaras could boast in 1870 came against a nine from the Cortland Normal School and one called the Gobblers of Nunda.[48]

Despite the dismal results, there was serious talk of keeping the Niagara Club going in 1871. But by June reality had set in. "There was a time," wrote the *Express* mournfully, "when the mere mention of the name Niagaras would excite a thrill of pride in the heart of every Buffalonian. Yesterday was practice day and only a few men showed up to play, knock up a few, and catch. The national game is not thriving in Buffalo. Good men are impossible to get. Some have left the city; others are in business. The Queen City will have to go without a nine, or form a stock company and hire one. Meanwhile, the lawns are being rolled for croquet."[49]

August brought the welcome news that the Niagaras, who had been "thought dead," were "only sleeping."[50] A first nine consisting of Sawin, Emerson, Van Velsor, Greene, Cowing, Tanner, Bostwick, Hawley, and a player named Walker was selected and a game was played against the Haymakers of Troy, now in the National Association. But after the predictable loss, the club soon lapsed back into inactivity.[51]

The spring of 1873 saw another effort to revive the Niagaras — appropriately, it was at the Liberty firehouse that the meeting was held and a motion to reorganize the Niagara Club was adopted. But while such Niagara stalwarts as Thomas Emerson, John Van Velsor, and Edward S. Hawley were involved in this effort, nothing seems to have come of it.[52]

A few years later, professional baseball finally arrived in Buffalo, and men such as Emerson, Van Velsor, and Hawley would play a prominent role in running those clubs. But by then the days when a club made up of "the young gentlemen of the town" could compete on a national basis were gone forever.

Perhaps the best epitaph for the Niagaras was provided in 1927 by a *Buffalo Times* reporter. After interviewing Ed Hawley, who by then was one of the few surviving members of the club, she wrote, "The Niagara, from its organization, was really a men's social club with sixty or seventy members. The nine were merely the athletic features. But, as on those memorable occasions when the tail wags the dog the nines swallowed the Niagara."[53]

Club Members

Edward Pease Atwater: Ed Atwater was the star pitcher of the Niagaras and the only club member to go on to play professional baseball. His speedy pitching was one of the keys to the historic win over the Atlantics and his deliveries overwhelmed many of the local clubs the Niagaras faced. His pitching in a match against a nine from Lockport prompted a spectator to marvel, "Why don't they shoot the balls from a cannon, certainly they could not go swifter." In another match, the Lockport club tried using light pine bats instead of bats made of ash, but "the first one to come in contact with one of Atwater's redhot liners was splintered in matchwood, and it is stated that everyone of the lot shared the same fate." Atwater, who was born in 1845, was described in one article as being the son of Edward M. Atwater, a successful Buffalo oil refiner. But if so he was not raised by his father. It appears instead that his mother died when he was young and Ed and his two sisters were raised by an aunt, while Edward M. Atwater remarried and started a new family. On the 1860 Census, the Atwater children are even listed with the surname of their aunt, suggesting that they may have been formally adopted, though this could also be a census-taking error. Edward P. Atwater turned professional in 1870 and spent the year playing for the legendary Cincinnati Red Stockings, although he saw limited playing time. In 1871 he signed to play with the White Stockings of Chicago, but was released before the season started. He remained in Chicago, found work as a bookkeeper, and he and his wife raised a daughter. He died in Chicago on November 11, 1903.

James H. Barker: James H. Barker, the club's scorer, was born around 1844 and later worked as a bookkeeper.

John H. Bartow: John Bartow was born on April 9, 1846, in Flint, Michigan. He belonged to the Eagle Hose Company and served in the U.S. Navy during the Civil War. He was on the first nine of the Niagaras in 1865, but soon was replaced. He later moved to Cleveland, where he worked as a broker. He died in Cleveland on July 11, 1912.

Stephen Bettinger: Niagara Club catcher Stephen Bettinger was born in December of 1847 and grew up in Buffalo, where his French-born father was a successful dry-goods merchant. The younger Bettinger earned a degree from St. John's College (now Fordham University) and then became a bookkeeper. He was still living in Buffalo as late as 1930.

Henry Bull: Henry Bull, the corresponding secretary of the Niagara of Buffalo, was born on February 6, 1844. He became a member of the Taylor Hose Company, and nearly died in the 1865 fire that claimed the life of prewar Niagaras member James Sidway and two other prominent Buffalonians. Bull was buried under debris after the collapse of a wall on that freezing cold night and was only rescued after a search of several hours. But he made a full recovery and lived for another 70 years.

Stanley Bagge Cowing: Stanley Cowing was born in Buffalo in 1844, the son of a wholesale grocer. While in high school he played baseball for a junior club called the Olympics. When war broke out, he enlisted as a Private in Company K of the 2nd New York Mounted Rifle Regiment. After the war he joined the Niagaras, usually playing third base or the outfield. He eventually moved to Kalamazoo, Michigan, where he worked for the Puritan Corset Company. He died in Kalamazoo on February 11, 1921.

Townsend Davis: Townsend Davis was a member of the first nine of the Niagaras in 1865, but he soon lost his place to younger players. Davis had a good position as assistant secretary of the Western Insurance Company while playing for the Niagaras, but the company failed as a result of claims from the Great Chicago Fire of 1871. Davis, however, regrouped and formed his own company, which he ran until his death in Buffalo on September 14, 1898.

John R. Dobbins: John Dobbins was born in October of 1843 in Pennsylvania. He served in the 116th New York Infantry during Civil War, earning promotion to first lieutenant by the time he was mustered out. He was a member of the first nine of the Niagaras in 1865, and worked in the insurance business while living in Buffalo. Around 1870, he moved to California and started a fruit ranch. He made a brief return to Buffalo, but then went back to California, where he died on April 21, 1905.

Thomas E. Emerson: Tom Emerson, an outfielder for the Niagaras, was born around 1845. His enthusiasm for baseball never dimmed, as he was part of an attempt to revive the Niagaras in 1873, and then headed the committee on grounds in an unsuccessful 1875 attempt to form Buffalo's first professional club. Emerson was associated with the M. & T. Bank and later worked as a clerk in the office of the city comptroller. Like many club members, he was also a volunteer fireman. He died in Buffalo on May 2, 1890.

John B. Greene: John B. Greene, who sometimes pitched for the Niagaras when Atwater was not available, was born in 1849. He graduated from Princeton, then passed the bar and returned to Buffalo to become a city attorney. He died in Buffalo on October 16, 1893.

Edward Selden Hawley: Edward S. Hawley was born in Buffalo on October 13, 1846. His father was a businessman who also served as a city alderman and state assemblyman. Edward joined the Taylor Hose Company. He became the shortstop and captain of the Niagaras, but retired from baseball in 1870 because of the constraints of his job with Sidney Shepard & Co. Even then he retained his interest in the game, supporting an 1873 attempt to revive the Niagaras and then becoming one of the backers of the professional club that represented Buffalo in 1877. Hawley later became a partner in the Woodworth-Hawley Company. He was still living in Buffalo when he died on December 12, 1937.

Alfred A. Holly: Myron Holly's younger brother Alfred was born in 1851 in New York. He left Buffalo after playing the outfield for the Niagaras and his whereabouts after that have been hard to trace.

Myron Holly: Myron "Mina" or "Mynie" Holly played the infield for the Niagaras and later became the club's catcher. He was born in June of 1842 in Oswego, but his father moved to Buffalo and went into the flour business. Myron made a reputation for himself in a number of sports, including cricket and baseball. In 1870 he was one of the two Niagara players who turned professional, joining the Olympics of Washington. He later became a customs inspector but his marriage ended in divorce and he became a wanderer, living for a while in Canada's Northwest and in Manitoba. He eventually settled in Michigan, where he worked as a musician until he went blind. After being admitted to the Pontiac Valley Asylum, he escaped in 1904 and tried to take his life by slashing himself with a razor. But his "wonderful constitution" allowed him to survive, and when he continued to try to remove his bandages he was handcuffed. "It has been more than eighteen years since I played a game of ball," he told a reporter from his hospital bed. "I used to play professionally. I caught behind the bat before Charlie Bennett was ever heard of, and I caught many games opposed to him. He was the greatest catcher in the business. I have played professional ball in Detroit as a member of other teams. I was catcher for the Buffalo team, for the Rochester team and for Syracuse, and was in Cincinnati at the time the old Cincinnati Reds were organized. But don't bother me now. I am in pain. Oh, how I wish I could end it all." When Holly had recovered from his wounds, he was returned to the Pontiac Valley Asylum, where he died on January 22, 1907.[54]

Charles E. Pickering: Charles Pickering, a member of the Neptune Hose Company, was the club's third baseman in 1865. Born around 1844, Pickering later became a chemist.

Jay Sprague Sawin: Jay Sprague Sawin, the pitcher of the Niagaras in 1865, was born in New York state in July of 1847 and belonged to the Neptune Hose Company. By 1870 he had left Buffalo and moved to Illinois to go into the dry-goods business. He eventually settled in Chicago, where he ran a restaurant. He died there on January 2, 1927.

Edward B. Smith: Edward B. Smith, the club president in 1868, was born in December of 1837 and became a prominent Buffalo builder. He later was president of Buffalo's National League club in 1879 and 1880. Smith then moved to St. Paul, Minnesota, and owned the city's minor-league park.

Henry S. Sprague: Born around 1844, Henry S. Sprague was the secretary of the 1869 team and played in a couple of games. He worked as the receiving teller of the Manufacturers' and Traders' bank. He retained his interest in baseball and served as secretary and treasurer of Buffalo's National League franchise. He also took a great interest in science and helped found the Buffalo Natural History Society. Sprague became a teller at the new Merchants Bank in 1880 but by then his health had begun to fail. He died in Buffalo on April 5, 1889.

William E. Tanner: See the entry for the Cliftons Base Ball Club of Buffalo.

John W. Van Velsor: Slugging Niagaras first baseman John Van Velsor was born in New York state in August of 1839. After baseball he opened a bakery on Main Street in Buffalo that he eventually passed down to his son. He also became the custodian of the trophies of the Niagaras, as well as a backer of the city's first professional club. He was alive when the 1910 census was taken on April 23 but appears to have died later that year.

Algar Monroe Wheeler: Al Wheeler was born in Buffalo on May 23, 1841, the son of a soap and candle maker. He served for four years in the Civil War, reaching the rank of captain. He later became deputy postmaster, before moving to Virginia and then to North Carolina. When he died in North Carolina on the last day of 1932, the death and connection with the Niagaras of the 91-year-old Wheeler were noted in *The Sporting News* even though he had only played on the first nine in 1865.

Other Members: Bostwick, Samuel Holly (umpire, and a brother of Myron and Alfred), George Laverack (see the entry on the Cliftons), Lewis, John MacDonald (umpire; see the entries on the two Troy clubs), Rogers, G. Smith, Walker.

Sources

The primary source for this entry is Joseph M. Overfield, "Baseball in Buffalo—1865 to 1870, Heyday of the Niagaras," *Niagara Frontier*, Spring 1965, 1–14. Two other articles by Overfield were also of great value: Joseph M. Overfield, "Professional Baseball in Buffalo—How It Began," *Niagara Frontier*, Spring 1954 (Vol. 1, #2), 29–35, and Joseph M. Overfield, "Baseball in Buffalo Before the Civil War," *Niagara Frontier*, Summer 1964. Game accounts in various newspapers filled in key details, as did these later reminiscences: Kate Burr, "Handsome Captain Hawley Still Live Wire," *Buffalo Times*, July 10, 1927; "Ah, Those Were the Days When Local Volunteers Ran with the Machine," *Buffalo Express*, 1924 clipping, exact date unavailable; Matt Endres, *History of the Volunteer Fire Department of Buffalo, N.Y.* (1906); "When Baseball Was a Fledgling," *Illustrated Buffalo Express*, October 7, 1897; untitled articles in the *Kalamazoo Evening Telegraph* on March 26, 1906, and the *Buffalo Times* on May 17, 1928.

Notes

1. Stanley B. Cowing, quoted in the *Kalamazoo Evening Telegraph*, March 26, 1906.
2. "Base Ball in Old Times," *Rochester Democrat and Chronicle*, June 10, 1895.
3. *Buffalo Times*, May 17, 1928.
4. *Buffalo Express*; quoted in Joseph M. Overfield, "Baseball in Buffalo—1865 to 1870, Heyday of the Niagaras," *Niagara Frontier*, Spring 1965, 3.
5. *Buffalo Express,* November 21, 1897, letter from Sawin.
6. Kate Burr, "Handsome Captain Hawley Still Live Wire," *Buffalo Times*, July 10, 1927; Overfield, "Baseball in Buffalo—1865 to 1870, Heyday of the Niagaras," *Niagara Frontier*, Spring 1965, 4.
7. *Kalamazoo Evening Telegraph*, March 26, 1906.
8. *Jamestown Journal*; quoted in Overfield, "Baseball in Buffalo—1865 to 1870, Heyday of the Niagaras," *Niagara Frontier*, Spring 1965, 3.
9. Overfield, "Baseball in Buffalo—1865 to 1870, Heyday of the Niagaras," *Niagara Frontier*, Spring 1965, 3–4; "When Baseball Was a Fledgling," *Illustrated Buffalo Express*, October 7, 1897.
10. Overfield, "Baseball in Buffalo—1865 to 1870, Heyday of the Niagaras," *Niagara Frontier*, Spring 1965, 5; *Buffalo Express,* August 9, 1866
11. *Buffalo Courier and Republic*, undated clipping.
12. Quoted in Overfield, "Baseball in Buffalo—1865 to 1870, Heyday of the Niagaras," *Niagara Frontier*, Spring 1965, 5.
13. Quoted in Overfield, "Baseball in Buffalo—1865 to 1870, Heyday of the Niagaras," *Niagara Frontier*, Spring 1965, 4.
14. Overfield notes that the response of the *Rochester Union* to these charges was much more temperate. The *Buffalo Courier and Republic* also implied that the claims of the *Express* were unfounded.
15. Tony Kissel, "The Pumpkin and Cabbage Tournament of 1866," *Baseball Research Journal* 24 (1995), 30–33; Overfield, "Baseball in Buffalo—1865 to 1870, Heyday of the Niagaras," *Niagara Frontier*, Spring 1965, 5–6; *Syracuse Journal*, October 6, 1866.
16. *Detroit Advertiser and Tribune*, October 15, 1866.
17. "When Baseball Was a Fledgling," *Illustrated Buffalo Express*, October 7, 1897.
18. *Ball Players' Chronicle*, August 29, 1867, 2.
19. *Syracuse Herald*, August 27, 1867.

20. Overfield, "Baseball in Buffalo—1865 to 1870, Heyday of the Niagaras," *Niagara Frontier*, Spring 1965, 7
21. *Ibid.*
22. *Ibid.*
23. *Ball Players' Chronicle*, both quoted in Overfield, "Baseball in Buffalo—1865 to 1870, Heyday of the Niagaras," *Niagara Frontier*, Spring 1965, 8.
24. Quoted in Overfield, "Baseball in Buffalo—1865 to 1870, Heyday of the Niagaras," *Niagara Frontier*, Spring 1965, 8.
25. Quoted in Overfield, "Baseball in Buffalo—1865 to 1870, Heyday of the Niagaras," *Niagara Frontier*, Spring 1965, 8.
26. Overfield, "Baseball in Buffalo—1865 to 1870, Heyday of the Niagaras," *Niagara Frontier*, Spring 1965, 8–9.
27. "When Baseball Was a Fledgling," *Illustrated Buffalo Express*, October 7, 1897.
28. Burr, "Handsome Captain Hawley Still Live Wire," *Buffalo Times*, July 10, 1927.
29. "When Baseball Was a Fledgling," *Illustrated Buffalo Express*, October 7, 1897.
30. Overfield, "Baseball in Buffalo—1865 to 1870, Heyday of the Niagaras," *Niagara Frontier*, Spring 1965, 9.
31. *Syracuse Journal*, June 17, 1868.
32. "Baseball in '67," *Illustrated Buffalo Express*, November 7, 1897.
33. *Buffalo Courier and Republic*, September 2, 1868.
34. Quoted in Overfield, "Baseball in Buffalo—1865 to 1870, Heyday of the Niagaras," *Niagara Frontier*, Spring 1965, 9.
35. *New York Sunday Mercury*, reprinted in the *Buffalo Courier and Republic*, August 5, 1868. The Niagaras' win over the Atlantics led to a great deal of talk that the club would go on a tour of New York City and Philadelphia, and matters got to the point that club president Edward B. Smith went to New York to arrange the details (*Buffalo Courier and Republic*, September 2, 1868). But the tour never occurred.
36. *Buffalo Courier and Republic*, July 2, 1868.
37. Overfield, "Baseball in Buffalo—1865 to 1870, Heyday of the Niagaras," *Niagara Frontier*, Spring 1965, 9.
38. *Buffalo Courier and Republic*, August 27, 1868
39. *Ibid.*
40. *Buffalo Courier and Republic*, September 18, 1868.
41. *Buffalo Courier and Republic*, October 10, 1868.
42. Quoted in Overfield, "Baseball in Buffalo—1865 to 1870, Heyday of the Niagaras," *Niagara Frontier*, Spring 1965, 11.
43. Overfield, "Baseball in Buffalo—1865 to 1870, Heyday of the Niagaras," *Niagara Frontier*, Spring 1965, 11; *Buffalo Courier and Republic*, May 2, 1870.
44. *Buffalo Courier and Republic*, May 2, 1870.
45. Overfield, "Baseball in Buffalo—1865 to 1870, Heyday of the Niagaras," *Niagara Frontier*, Spring 1965, 11.
46. "When Baseball Was a Fledgling," *Illustrated Buffalo Express*, October 7, 1897.
47. *Buffalo Courier and Republic*, undated clipping from the spring of 1870, showing these games played in 1869: Bettinger 7, M. Holley 8, Cowing 9, Hawley 14, Emerson 13, A. Holley 14, Tanner 13, Van Velsor 13, Bostwick 5, Dobbins 7, G. Smith 7, Atwater 13, John Green 2, H. Sprague 2, Burt 2, H. Green 2, Laverack 1, Rogers 1.
48. Overfield, "Baseball in Buffalo—1865 to 1870, Heyday of the Niagaras," *Niagara Frontier*, Spring 1965, 13; *Syracuse Daily Standard*, April 20, 1870.
49. *Buffalo Express*, June 2, 1871; reprinted in Joseph M. Overfield, "Baseball in Buffalo—1865 to 1870, Heyday of the Niagaras," *Niagara Frontier*, Spring 1965, 13.
50. *Buffalo Express*, August 19, 1871.
51. *Buffalo Courier*, August 24, 1871.
52. *Buffalo Courier and Republic*, March 8, 1873.
53. Burr, "Handsome Captain Hawley Still Live Wire," *Buffalo Times*, July 10, 1927.
54. "Blind Man Tried to End Life," *Detroit Free Press*, June 8, 1904, 5; "Would-Be Suicide an Old-Time Ball Player," *Detroit Free Press*, June 9, 1904, 3; *Oswego Times*, June 9 and 11, 1904.

❖ *Cliftons of Buffalo* (Peter Morris) ❖

CLUB HISTORY

During the baseball boom that followed the Civil War, the Niagara Club emerged as Buffalo's premier club. Every club of the era needed an in-town rivalry to keep interest high and at first "the Niagaras found foemen worthy of their white-ash weapons in the Cliftons."[1] The Cliftons, however, soon disbanded and an 1897 article provided an intriguing explanation of why they did so.[2]

One of the major gaps in our understanding of early baseball comes from the fact that the vast majority of the clubs formed during the explosion of 1866 and 1867 had disbanded by 1869 without leaving any explanation. We often have a rough idea as to when they gave up baseball because accounts of their games ceased to appear in the local newspapers, but even that can be misleading since some newspapers simply decided to stop covering baseball. More crucially, the specific reasons for giving up the young sport usually remain shrouded in mystery.

The result is that plausible explanations can be offered— lack of success on the baseball diamond, the interference with work and family life, inability to find a suitable home field or convenient practice time, financial constraints, internal friction, injuries, defections of key players, etc., etc.— but there is no way to be sure which factors were really responsible for the decision to disband. The story of the Cliftons is thus an important one because it suggests yet another fate that could befall clubs of the era.

The Cliftons were one of many clubs to emerge when a frenzy of baseball enthusiasm swept Buffalo in 1867. Leslie Lyman was credited with organizing the club and it established playing grounds in a vacant lot on Virginia Street. Like most of the city's clubs, it played on Wednesday and Saturday afternoons. A photo of the club published in 1897 shows that the players wore natty checkered uniforms.

The Cliftons soon established themselves as an up-and-coming club when they beat the Stars of Batavia in an exciting three-game series, with the decisive game being played at a neutral site in the town of Le Roy. Then in August, a nine known as the All-Buffalos defeated the mighty Niagaras. While the All-Buffalos were an all-star squad, all but a couple of the players were members of the Cliftons, suggesting that the Niagaras' reign as Buffalo's top club was in jeopardy.

Subsequent matches showed that the Cliftons were indeed a worthy opponent for the Niagaras, and yet they kept coming up second best. In the next match between the two clubs, the Niagaras pulled out a hard-fought 50–42 victory. In a major tournament in Auburn, New York, in 1868, the Cliftons tied for second place — but it was the Niagaras who took home a gold ball valued at $500.

The Cliftons did manage signal triumphs such as a win over the Alerts of Rochester, but it wasn't enough. The Niagaras handed the Cliftons two decisive defeats in June of 1868 and a few weeks later a pair of members of the Cliftons, William Tanner and H. L. Fairchild, left the club and joined the archrival Niagaras. It was the death knell for the Cliftons and by 1869 the club had "lost its identity" entirely and it passed out of existence.

While it is tempting to look at Tanner and Fairchild as traitors whose defection destroyed the Cliftons, that wasn't how the situation was portrayed in the 1897 article. Instead its author wrote, "It was the ambition of the other local teams to be drafted into the Niagaras." It is a simple but important declaration.

We know that ballplayers of this era took fierce pride when they donned their uniforms and took the field because they were representing their cities and their clubs. Yet it is important to remember that these two sources of pride were often at odds, which forced players to choose between them. Should the members of a club like the Cliftons continue to work toward dethroning the top local nine? Or should they join forces with the Niagaras and perhaps form a club good enough to put Buffalo on the national map?

In the case of the Cliftons, the latter option must have seemed especially appealing since in between their two wins over the Cliftons, the Niagaras had pulled off a historic upset over the mighty Atlantics of Brooklyn. Many Buffalonians undoubtedly figured that enlisting the services of a few members of rival clubs would be the ideal way to establish a local club as a national powerhouse.

As it turned out, the addition of Fairchild and Tanner did little to strengthen the Niagaras. Fairchild does not appear even to have made the first nine, and while Tanner did become a regular in the club's outfield, the Niagaras were unable to build on their historic win over the Atlantics. No other major victories occurred in 1868, and by 1869 the Niagaras were headed toward dissolution themselves.

Meanwhile the city of Buffalo had lost its best rivalry. The importance of this absence was demonstrated at the start of the 1869 campaign when the Niagaras beat a local club called the Columbias by the count of 209–10. The extraordinary score was a record even by the high-scoring standards of the era and it attracted considerable attention. But what it really showed was that the Niagaras no longer could get meaningful competition in Buffalo.

Nevertheless, the 1897 article conveys no sense that the other members of the Cliftons were bitter toward Tanner and Fairchild for their decision to join the Niagaras. Club pride and civic pride, it would seem, were both understood to be powerful bonds and the decision to choose the former over the latter was not considered a betrayal.

Club Members

Almost all of the members of the Cliftons were born in the late 1840s and grew up together in Buffalo. While not exclusively the case, an impressive number of them were the sons of some of the city's most successful businessmen.

Augustus C. Allen: Allen, an outfielder on the original first nine of the Cliftons, was born in 1847 in New York state and was the son of a land agent. By 1880 the whole family had moved to Brooklyn.

Henry Barnum: Barnum, another outfielder, was born in 1847 and was the son of a wealthy Buffalo merchant who owned Barnum's Bazar. He was listed as a clerk on the 1870 Census, but died not long after that.

Charles F. Bingham: Bingham was not listed as a member of the first nine but was described as a former player in the 1897 article. The reason for that may be that Bingham, who was born in August of 1843 and was therefore several years older than the other members of the club, married in 1868 and his first child was born in the first week of 1869. Bingham was born in New York to the Welsh-born owner of a successful Buffalo foundry, and he eventually became the co-proprietor of the foundry. The Binghams lost their only child in an 1879 horseback-riding accident. After the turn of the century, Bingham and his wife spent most of their time in Palm Beach, Florida. She died there in 1912 and he followed two years later, leaving an estate of over $400,000 that became the subject of a court battle.[3]

John Bullymore: Bullymore was born in Buffalo in 1847 to emigrants from Northampton, England. His father operated a successful pork-packing business and John became a prominent Buffalo maltster. He died in Buffalo on February 6, 1914.

Tommy Castle: Castle was born in 1848, the son of a wealthy Buffalo jeweler. He was accepted into Cornell University in the fall of 1868 and was on the verge of graduating when he fell victim to a smallpox epidemic and died on April 18, 1872.

William K. Cowing: Cowing, who was described as "the star catcher of the nine in its palmiest days," was born in Buffalo in 1842 and was a member of one of the city's pioneer families. When the Civil War broke out, he joined the first regiment from Buffalo, the 21st New York Infantry, serving for more than two years and rising to the rank of sergeant. He became a bookkeeper and worked in New York City for several years, but eventually returned to Buffalo. He was the cashier of the Buffalo Mill Supply Company during the last 15 years of his life and died in Buffalo on November 12, 1909. His obituary in the *Buffalo Express* stated that he had once played for the Niagaras, another piece of testimony to how the Cliftons had been forgotten.

H. L. Fairchild: Fairchild was the second baseman for the Cliftons and one of the two players who left the club to join the Niagaras. The 1897 article reported that he had left Buffalo and headed west, but efforts to identify him have been unsuccessful.

Benjamin Allen Holloway: Holloway was born in New York state on November 17, 1847, and worked as a foreman until his untimely death on November 1, 1877.

Le Dran B. Lamphier: Lamphier was born in New York state around 1848 and worked as a painter, fireman, and foreman. He was still in Buffalo in 1908 but had died by 1909.

George Edward Laverack: Laverack was born on October 10, 1846, in Buffalo. His father was one of Buffalo's first grocers and George became a partner in the business in 1865. He took over full control after his father's death in 1888 and also acquired several other businesses. He was very prominent in Buffalo's civic and cultural affairs, being one of the founders of the city's country club. He was a member of the Taylor Hose Company, serving alongside many members of the Niagara Club. Even after the demise of that company, he remained a volunteer firefighter for many years. He died in Buffalo on March 1, 1924.

Henry Leslie Lyman: Leslie Lyman, the founder of the Cliftons, was born in Lynchburg, Virginia, on April 20, 1848. He moved to Buffalo and became a confidential clerk to H. L. Lansing. He married in Buffalo in 1871, but after becoming the father of four children he returned to Virginia in the late 1870s. He died in Charlottesville, Virginia, on July 6, 1933.

Cyrenius Chapin Pickering: C.C. Pickering was born on November 30, 1849, in Buffalo and became a manufacturing chemist and wholesale liquor dealer. The younger brother of Charles Pickering of the Niagara Club, he was still living in Buffalo in 1917 but may have died that year.

Clark Wilder Rice: Rice was born around 1850 and worked as a bookkeeper. He died in Buffalo on February 10, 1907.

George W. Robertson: George Robertson was the older brother of Richard, born around 1846, but little else is known about him. He may have moved to Eau Claire, Wisconsin.

Richard L. Robertson: Richard Robertson was born in New York state around 1848, the son of a well-to-do hat and cap maker, and he eventually succeeded his father in the business. He married in 1883 and had one child. He was still living in Buffalo in 1923 but his wife was listed as a widow in the 1925 city directory.

William Stimpson: Stimpson was the original pitcher of the Cliftons and later the club secretary. There was a William Stimpson in several city directories but he never appeared in the censuses, so his identity remains a mystery.

William E. Tanner: Tanner, one of the two players who left the Cliftons to join the Niagaras, was born in New York City around 1848, the son of a wealthy merchant. As of 1870, he was working as a telegraph operator, and the 1880 Census shows him as a city fireman with his wife, Cora, and their baby. Soon after that he headed west for parts unknown.

Edward Bennet Townsend: Townsend, the club secretary, was born on April 10, 1846, in Lafayette, Indiana. His parents had previously lived in Buffalo and they soon returned there. Edward Townsend married in 1868 and worked as a bookkeeper, passing away on October 15, 1898.

Albert Barnes Young: Young was the official scorer of the Cliftons and preserved the photo of the club that was published in 1897. He was born in New York state in October of 1848 and eventually became president of the Cling Surface Company. Young lived in Buffalo until his death in 1930.

SOURCE

"Baseball in '67," *Illustrated Buffalo Express*, November 7, 1897.

NOTES

1. "When Baseball Was a Fledgling," *Illustrated Buffalo Express*, October 7, 1897.
2. "Baseball in '67," *Illustrated Buffalo Express*, November 7, 1897.
3. *Buffalo Express*, February 19, 1915.

Chapter Three

Western Pennsylvania and Eastern Ohio

❖ *Introduction* (Peter Morris) ❖

"As late as the year 1860," a New York sportswriter observed in 1867, "base ball was confined to one or two of the middle states — New York being the centre. Now it is played in every state in the union, from Maine to Oregon. New York has in a measure lost its ascendancy in the game, Philadelphia now being the base ball centre of the country. There are ten clubs in the Quaker city to one in the metropolis, and last year the best record made by any club in the United States was made by the champion club of Pennsylvania — the gallant Athletics of Philadelphia — whose average score of 51 to a match, against the strongest clubs in the country, and of over six runs to a match at the hands of their best individual players presents the best record known in the annals of the game."[1] Philadelphia's "base ball fever" spilled over into the rest of Pennsylvania and eastern Ohio, but the new clubs formed in that region were typically short-lived and none of them rivaled the Athletics as a national force. Geographical and economic factors had much to do with baseball's sluggish development.

As late as 1776, a mapmaker had ended his efforts at the Mississippi River and dismissed much of central Pennsylvania as "Endless Mountains."[2] Rampant land speculation and the opening of the Erie Canal had led to a massive population shift — in 1820 the geographical center of the U.S. population was only 40 miles from Washington, D.C., but by 1860 it lay in Pike County, in southeastern Ohio.[3] Baseball inevitably followed this trend and such clubs as the Kickenepawlings of Johnstown, Arcadias of Doylestown, Susquehannas of Wilkes-Barre, Tyroleans of Harrisburg, Alerts of Danville, Starks of Canton, Resolutes of Oberlin, and Stars of Painesville sprang up.

Yet at the same time the larger forces that would doom many of these clubs were becoming evident. The Erie Canal had opened up shipping, but land travel remained cumbersome, especially in the vicinity of the Allegheny Mountains and the other mountains now known collectively as the Appalachians. The coming of the railroad solved some of those problems but created new ones, such as the tendency of towns to overflow with railroad workers and then face an inevitable rapid downsizing. Moreover, both new modes of transportation tempted settlers to skip over western Pennsylvania and eastern Ohio in favor of the emerging West.

Tours by the first great baseball clubs provided stimulation, but even these proved a mixed blessing. The Athletics made several ventures into central Pennsylvania but no suitable rival emerged and the club chose to concentrate its efforts on foes from large cities such as Brooklyn, Baltimore, and Washington. In 1867 the Nationals of Washington launched a celebrated tour billed as the first trans–Allegheny tour, but even they bypassed the ballclubs in the shadows of the great mountain range, starting in Columbus, Ohio, and proceeding to the South and West. An 1869 tour by the Olympics of Washington helps us to appreciate the wisdom of that choice — as described in memorable terms in that club's entry, the players made a nonstop overnight trip from Cincinnati to Philadelphia in a freight train "over a rough mountain road, for such was the Baltimore & Ohio in those days.... They arrived in Philadelphia one hour ahead of the time set for the game, but every one of the players took a portion of that hour for a bath in the waters of the Schuylkill river. But they presented a sorry sight when they appeared on the field."[4]

The result was that the baseball clubs in central and western Pennsylvania and eastern Ohio reflected a region in flux. The entry on the Mountain Club of Altoona reveals a baseball nine made up primarily of railroad men who soon left town, leaving little trace of the club they had formed. In addition, the unique site of the club's home field provides a vivid reminder of the practical impediments faced by ballplayers in a mountainous terrain. Allegheny and Pittsburgh also faced the challenges of an unsettled population, with the result that the ballclubs of these adjoining cities had a history so discontinuous that even club members had trouble keeping the various incarnations of the Allegheny Base Ball Club straight. The Independents of Mansfield had the good fortune to enlist the services of one of greatest catchers of the nineteenth century, yet soon found that a city the size of Mansfield could not compete against well-financed professional nines from big cities.

Even Cleveland was hard-pressed to keep pace, as is reflected by the fits-and-starts history of the Forest City Club, a club that struggled with the dilemma that its best pitcher and its best catcher were one and the same: the incomparable Jim "Deacon" White. An even better example was provided by the Forest City Club's first great in-city rival, the Railway Union Club of Cleveland, which vanished entirely when members moved on, making that club impossible to include here.

It is thus small wonder that it was not until the 1880s that baseball become firmly established in even the large cities of Pittsburgh and Cleveland. Yet that does not diminish the accomplishment of the men who forged these pioneer clubs.

Rather, it makes their efforts to play baseball in spite of the obstacles all the more impressive.

Notes

1. *Chicago Times,* April 7, 1867, reprinted from a New York paper, apparently the *New York Tribune.*
2. James MacGregor Burns, *The Vineyard of Liberty* (New York: Vintage, 1983), 3.
3. Christopher Clark, *Social Change in America: From the Revolution Through the Civil War* (Chicago: Ivan R. Dee, 2006), 207.
4. Chadwick Scrapbooks, unidentified clipping.

❖ *Mountain Base Ball Club of Altoona* (Peter Morris) ❖

Club History

The Mountain Base Ball Club of Altoona was formed in 1862, and within a few months the new club accepted a challenge to play their first match game against the Keystone Club of Harrisburg. The match was played in Harrisburg on August 20, and saw Altoona's new club jump to a big early lead. But then the Keystone switched to a pitcher who delivered "balls to which Mountain Club was unaccustomed, and which they could not bat." As a result, the home side rallied with thirteen runs in the ninth inning to tie the game at 33–33, then added eight more runs in the tenth inning to win 41–38.

Under the circumstances, some discouragement might have been expected, but there was no sign of that emotion in an account of the game that was published in the *Harrisburg Telegraph* and proudly reprinted in the *Altoona Tribune.* The article noted that the umpire, Colonel DeWitt C. Moore, a member of the Athletic Club of Philadelphia and the vice president of the National Association of Base Ball Players in 1861, had "complimented the players of both clubs for their good playing, considering the short time they have practiced." It added generously, "Considering that Mountain Club was on a new field, they did exceedingly well, and on their own ground would be likely to lead the Keystone more than three runs in ten innings." Indicative of just how new the Knickerbocker rules were to the region, the *Tribune* felt obliged to explain to its readers that "nine innings constitute a single game."[1]

At the match's conclusion, the captain of the Mountain Club presented the customary "prize ball" to the victorious host club, and that seems to have ended the first season of Altoona's first regulation baseball club. As soon as the spring of 1863 had rolled around, however, the club reorganized for another campaign. The meeting took place at the Military Office of the Pennsylvania Railroad on March 26 and saw the Mountain Club elect a new slate of officers and make plans for the upcoming season.

Once again the 1863 season saw the Mountain Club play only one match game (although no doubt many practices were held). And that lone match game was a very special one as the mighty Athletics of Philadelphia had agreed to pay a visit to Altoona. Excitement built as the day of the game approached, with the *Tribune* gushing, "The old victorious Athletic 'nine' have kindly consented to show their country brethren how the game is played, and will bring with them several of the most distinguished ball men of New York, Brooklyn and Philadelphia, to participate in the excursion and crown the occasion. Very brilliant plays will be exhibited on the part of the Athletics, being the picked men of a large city, and the tried men of many well fought contests; while the Mountaineers will endeavor to atone by their hospitality for deficiency in science."[2]

The match was played on September 11, 1863, beginning at 10 A.M., and to nobody's surprise the visitors won by the lopsided score of 73–22. In addition to revealing the ball-playing shortcomings of the Mountain Club, the match also showed that the club's home field on Prospect Hill was far from ideal. The field was quite literally on the side of the hill, which made fielding an ordeal and caused a reporter for the *New York Clipper* to remark that it was difficult to see the outfielders from the diamond, making it necessary to hire "the tallest kind of umpire to watch the movements of the out fielders as fully as should be done."[3]

Yet such matters caused little concern in Altoona, where the mood after the match was again a sunny one. The club had gone to considerable lengths to show hospitality to the visiting Athletics and their party, meeting their guests at the train depot and escorting them to their lodgings at the Mountain House.[4] After the match, these efforts were acknowledged in the *Philadelphia City Item*, which in turn prompted the *Tribune* to express pride that the Mountain Club had succeeded in being gracious hosts, and had thereby "made for themselves a good name among the fraternity."[5]

The 1864 baseball season once again got off to an early

start in Altoona, with the club's annual meeting taking place at the Military Office on March 31.[6] The election of officers and arrangement of other details was followed by an initial practice session on April 23 that left many of the players feeling sore.[7]

The Mountain Club had scheduled a "special meeting" to be held on April 29, 1864, at the office of club member B.F. Rose.[8] That announcement suggests that the club had big plans for the upcoming season, and we do know that the club visited Philadelphia on September 27, where the Mountains were beaten by the Athletics by the very convincing score of 63–2. Otherwise, however, little is known about the Mountain Club of Altoona that season.

The end of the war caused a baseball boom in much of the northeast and Midwest, with Altoona at first being no exception. The Mountain Club played at least four match games in 1865, including one on September 20 in which the club again hosted the Athletics of Philadelphia and lost by the more respectable score of 41–16. The club was even more active in 1866, playing at least six match games. By season's end, the Mountain Club boasted seventy-seven active members, and Benjamin F. Rose of the club was elected president of the Pennsylvania Base Ball Association.[9]

Yet the known history of the Mountain Club ends at that point. The club was at least nominally still in existence in 1867 and may have mustered on in 1868 as well, but no record of match games in either year survives. By 1869, a new club called the Mountain City had been formed, suggesting that Altoona's pioneer club had passed out of existence.

The demise of any pioneer baseball club is the result of a combination of factors, some known but most of them unknowable at this point. That makes it a dangerous topic to speculate about, but in the case of the Mountain Base Ball Club of Altoona two likely reasons stand out. As is clear from the player sketches below, many of the club members were well past thirty by the end of the war. Thus, although club members remained optimistic after losses in 1862 and 1863 against more experienced rivals, this outlook became more difficult to maintain as the losses continued and the players aged. More important, most of the club members who could be identified were railroad employees who had few ties to Altoona. Several of them are known to have left Altoona at about the time that the club's activity began to taper off, while many more had left Altoona by 1870. Their departures no doubt hastened the demise of the city's first ball club.

Club Members

Joseph Wilkinson Askew: J.W. Askew was born on November 8, 1829, in East Nottingham, Maryland, and worked as a railroad office clerk for the Pennsylvania Railroad in Altoona. He was secretary of the Mountain Club from 1864 to 1866 and remained in Altoona until at least 1880. Askew retired from the railroad at age seventy and lived for another seventeen years, dying on March 18, 1917.

David T. Caldwell: David Caldwell played center field for the Mountain Club and served as treasurer in 1865–1866. He was born around 1836 in Pennsylvania and differed from most of his fellow club members in two important regards — he did not work for the railroad and he remained in Blair County for his entire life. After getting married in Altoona in 1859, Caldwell worked as a banker and notary public, also serving as a director of the First National Bank of Altoona. Eventually he moved his large family to nearby Snyder and then to Tyrone, where he sold insurance. He was still living there in 1920.

Robert Brown Gemmell: R. B. Gemmell was born in Greensburg, Pennsylvania, on April 27, 1839. He began working for the Pennsylvania Railway Company in 1854, beginning in the telegraph department, working his way up to division operator, and then becoming chief clerk to the superintendent of the state's middle division in 1861. In 1863, he was appointed trainmaster for the middle division and spent the next three years in Altoona, serving as vice president of the Mountain Club in 1865 and 1866. He resigned his position in 1866 to move to Kansas and become chief clerk and superintendent of telegraphs on the Kansas Pacific Rail Road. He eventually settled in Topeka and came to be in charge of all telegraphs in a region that comprised over 6,000 square miles. A devout Presbyterian, Gemmell was also president of the Y.M.C.A. of Topeka for ten years. He died in Topeka on September 14, 1896.

Henry Wynkoop Gwinner: H. W. Gwinner, the president of the Mountain Club in 1862, was born in Philadelphia on January 11, 1824. After a brief stint at Lafayette College, he became a printer, then entered the railroad business in 1858. He became general passenger agent for Pennsylvania Central Railway and became a very prominent and popular railway man. He resigned from the railway in 1880 and moved to New York to become president of the Hoole Manufacturing Company. Three years later, in October of 1883, Gwinner's many friends were stunned to learn that he had fatally shot himself. Gwinner was a wealthy man by that time and to all appearances was happy as well, and no plausible reason for his suicide other than overwork was advanced.

William C. Keller: Will Keller played shortstop for the Mountain Club, also serving as club secretary in 1862 and 1863. He was born around 1840 in Pennsylvania and was listed as a telegraph operator on the 1860 census. He had left Altoona by 1870, and may have moved to Harrisburg, but his common name makes it difficult to be certain.

Enoch Lewis: Enoch Lewis pitched for the Mountain Club and was its president in both 1863 and 1864. By that time, however, he was already past 40, having been born around 1820 in Wilmington, Delaware. Lewis worked as a superintendent for the Pennsylvania Railroad and, like so many of his fellow club members, he left Altoona shortly after his association with the Mountain Club. He moved to Philadelphia around 1866 and became the Pennsylvania Railroad's purchasing agent, a prestigious position in which he served until retiring in 1893. He died in Philadelphia on November 15, 1902.

Robert Pitcairn: Robert Pitcairn was treasurer of the Mountain Club in 1862 and 1863; this appears to have been his only involvement with baseball during a long and successful life. Pitcairn was born on May 6, 1836, in Johnston, Scotland, and immigrated to Pittsburgh in 1846. His boyhood friend Andrew Carnegie helped him get a job with the Pennsylvania Railroad, and he was soon transferred to Altoona. While in Altoona, he got married and became involved with the local ball club. But then Carnegie decided to leave the railroad business to start the steel business that made him extraordinarily wealthy, so Pitcairn returned to Pittsburgh to take Carnegie's position as the Pennsylvania Railroad's local supervisor. He remained in that position for more than three decades, becoming immensely popular with the railroad workers, who referred to him as "R.P." or as "Uncle Robert." Then in 1906 he was reminded that he had reached the company's mandatory retirement age of seventy. In vain, Pitcairn, who had created the policy, protested that he had not intended it to apply to him. After over half a century with the Pennsylvania Railroad, he "was utterly miserable at not being at his accustomed place" and his health declined rapidly. He died three years later, on July 25, 1909. Pitcairn was also very active in civic affairs and the Allegheny County borough of Pitcairn is named in his honor.[10]

Benjamin Franklin Rose: Born in Pennsylvania around 1821, B.F. Rose served as club president in 1865, and the special meeting of the club on April 29, 1864, was held at his office. He was then elected president of the Pennsylvania Base Ball Association after the 1866 season. Like many civic leaders of the era, he was chief of the volunteer fire department. Rose became a judge in 1865 and later served as a city alderman. He died in Altoona on March 8, 1896.

Other Members: C.L. Kitchel (club treasurer in 1864), Darlington (second baseman), Downer (right fielder), Pettit (first baseman), Miller (left fielder), John Reilly (third baseman and club vice president in 1863 and 1864), L. M. Stewart (club vice president in 1862), Watt (catcher) and E. H. Williams (club president in 1866). None of these men could be identified in Altoona on the censuses of either 1860 or 1870. Of course in a few cases, most notably Miller, the problem was the man's common surname and absence of a given name. But in most cases, there was nobody by that name in Altoona on either census, suggesting that many of these members were also railroad men who lived in Altoona for only a brief time.

Notes

1. *Harrisburg Telegraph*, reprinted in the *Altoona Tribune*, August 28, 1862.
2. *Altoona Tribune*, September 9, 1863.
3. *New York Clipper*, September 26, 1863.
4. Charles A. Peverelly, *The Book of American Pastimes* (New York, 1866), 480.
5. *Altoona Tribune*, September 23, 1863.
6. *Altoona Tribune*, March 23, 1864.
7. *Altoona Tribune*, April 27, 1864.
8. *Ibid.*
9. Peverelly, *The Book of American Pastimes*, 514; *Pennsylvania Patriot*, October 18, 1866.
10. "'R.P.' and 'Uncle Robert'; How He Earned the Titles," *Pittsburgh Gazette-Times*, July 26, 1909, 6; "Robert Pitcairn Dies in Pittsburg," *New York Times*, July 26, 1909, 7.

❖ *Allegheny Base Ball Club* (Peter Morris) ❖

Club History

In some cities, the history of regulation baseball was a continuous one from the day the Knickerbocker rules were introduced. In other cities, a hiatus occurred during the Civil War, with the result that the postwar players were mostly different from the men who played before the war. In still others, the establishment of the new way of playing was discontinuous, with a series of unsuccessful attempts being made before a permanent club was formed.

A prime example of the third pattern is the adjoining cities of Pittsburgh and Allegheny City (which became a single metropolis when the latter was annexed in 1907). There remain huge gaps in what is known about early baseball in this vicinity, so any conclusions remain provisional and subject to revision as new sources emerge.

A notable exception to the general dearth of information was a match played in the spring of 1857 on the West Common in Allegheny City. This "long talked of game" attracted "a large concourse of citizens" to watch the two sides, which represented Pittsburgh and Allegheny. A detailed account of the contest appeared the following day in the *Pittsburgh Post*. While the account does not provide specifics about the rules being used, it is clear that the Knickerbocker rules were not being followed closely if at all. Most notably, fifteen players a side were used, and all players had to be retired before an inning was completed.[1]

Those are the only details about how the match was played that appeared in the original 1857 report, but additional information was provided in a 1904 reprint. According to that article, which was based upon the recollections of one of the players, Allegheny police sergeant Michael F. Lynch, the 1857 match was "first baseball game played in Allegheny county, under the regulation rules and upon a regulation diamond." That description suggests that an effort was made to incorporate some of the Knickerbockers' innovations, such as the reconfiguration of the bases.

But even if that was the case, many elements of the match reflected the looser approach of earlier versions. The participants used a "soft, rubber ball" that was delivered by the pitcher so that its flight "described a semi-circle." Instead of a stick, the batter "employed a paddle resembling in a great degree that used in playing cricket. It was next to impossible to miss the ball and so light was the ball that it often went far afield and home runs were the rule rather than the exception." One of the results was that Lynch, who played shortstop, had little to do, since there were no "hot grounders to encounter, and the flies were usually of that high order, which made their capture by a man at his position well nigh impossible."

That is all we know about the rules by which the historic match was played, but the account in the next day's *Post* does provide many additional details about the contest itself, as well as giving some hints as to why it took some time for baseball to become established in Allegheny County. Three innings were scheduled to be played, but the difficulty of retiring so many batters meant that darkness was approaching by the end of the second inning.

The Pittsburgh side then had 68 runs to only 49 for the Alleghenys, so were naturally willing to end the match at that point. But the Allegheny squad insisted on playing the third inning and umpire T. M. Smith agreed with them, so play continued. The Alleghenys took advantage to double their score with a 49-run outburst. Pittsburgh finally got its chance to bat and had scored nine runs with ten batters "still in" (i.e., not retired) when the Alleghenys decided that it was too dark to continue.

As a result, the game account reported that "there was some little dissatisfaction manifested at the conclusion of the game, the Pittsburghers holding that the match should have been played out, and that were it not for this understanding they would not have commenced the third inning at the hour they did; the umpire, however, gave in his adhesion to the course pursued, and has ordered the game to be resumed this afternoon. We do not know whether the Pittsburghers will abide by his decision or not, but, as he was the mutual choice of both parties, we presume they will." Adding to the controversy, the *Post*'s account included this cryptic statement: "Below we give the result of the game as far as played, and in doing so, we are requested to state by the umpire, Mr. T. M. Smith, that figures calculated to mislead the public as to the part the Alleghanians took in the game have been given out."

The 1904 account gave no indication as to whether the interrupted match was ever completed or of whether the ruffled feathers were ever smoothed. Perhaps they were not, as it does not appear to have been until 1860 that a serious attempt was made to form a club in the Pittsburgh-Allegheny region that played by the Knickerbocker rules.

The Allegheny Base Ball Club was organized on June 8, 1860, and played at least four match games that year, winning all of them. The club played one more match game in 1861; then, like so many, it lapsed into inactivity. Other than a list of 1860 officers, which consisted of President J. J. Moore, Vice President James M. Carr, Secretary W. H. Lockhart and Treasurer Robert Elton, nothing is known about the makeup of this club.[2]

The only known game played by the Allegheny Club during the war occurred in 1863 against the Duquesne Base Ball Club. Typifying the fragmentary history of the region's early baseball history, the lone surviving account of the game is a clipping of a reprint of an 1863 article that was published in the *Pittsburgh Leader* during the 1920s. Also typical was that the game ended in a 27–27 tie, with confusion about the outcome forcing the umpire, one Dr. Dilworth, to explain a crucial ruling.[3]

The Allegheny Base Ball Club sprang back to life after the war and described itself as a continuation of the pre-war club, but it is difficult to be sure how true this was. James M. Carr, the vice president of the prewar club, was a director in 1866 and did represent the club at that year's convention of the National Association of Base Ball Players, but none of the prewar officers were included on the listing of officers.[4]

Details about other activities of the postwar Allegheny Base Ball Club also include many gaps. In 1865, the club played its first match in mid–July and completed only five contests. The most notable one occurred in September when the mighty Athletics of Philadelphia traveled to Pittsburgh for four days of competition with the best ball clubs in the area. To nobody's surprise, the Alleghenys were walloped 65–15, and similar fates befell the Lincoln Club of Pittsburgh, the Enterprise Club of Allegheny, and a picked nine of the best local players. Nonetheless, the trip was a milestone event for baseball in Pittsburgh-Allegheny, with the Athletics being met on their arrival by a delegation from the three host clubs and accommodated at the Allegheny House.

The only road trip that the Alleghenys made in 1865 was a visit to East Liberty, Pennsylvania, that resulted in a win over the Collins Club. Otherwise, all of the Allegheny Club's matches in 1865 were against the newly organized Enterprise Base Ball Club of Allegheny City. The Enterprise Club won two of the three contests, with a fourth match that was attempted on November 29, 1865, having to be abandoned because of "a snow-storm coming up and driving off the contestants." In addition to winning the head-to-head series, the Enterprise Club lived up to their name by playing nearly twice as many matches as the Allegheny Club. Thus at the end of the 1865 season, it looked as though the younger club was on its way to becoming the local standard-bearer.

The 1866 incarnation of the Allegheny Club boasted sixty active members and thirty-one honorary members, along with a uniform of blue pants and a white shirt with blue facings, topped with a white cap with "blue hand."[5] Once again, however, it was the Enterprise Club that earned local bragging rights in 1866 by winning both of the contests between the two clubs. In addition to being able to bill itself as "champions of Allegheny County," the Enterprise Club again showed far more initiative, playing at least ten matches that year and making a tour that took it to Johnstown, Altoona, Harrisburg, and Philadelphia. In stark contrast, the Allegheny Club played only five known matches in 1866, all of them against clubs from Allegheny City. The club did not even try its luck against any rivals from Pittsburgh, although that city was now home to the Anchor, Atlantic, Eureka, Good Will, Laurence, Lincoln, Mutual, Olympic, and Osceola Clubs.[6]

As a result, by the spring of 1867 it looked as though the Enterprise Club would continue to be regarded as the premier club in Allegheny City. The younger club even announced plans to make a Western tour in the summer of 1867.

Instead, the activities of the Enterprise Club fell off in 1867, and the Allegheny Club again became the most prominent club in the city. The reasons for this are not entirely clear, but one interesting explanation stands out. In 1866, an eighteen-year-old Civil War veteran named Al Pratt had been the catcher of the Enterprise Club, handling the offerings of another teenager named Woodruff McKnight. But in 1867, Pratt joined the Allegheny Club as a pitcher, and his acquisition proved vital.

When the summer of 1867 arrived, it was Allegheny Club rather than the rival Enterprise Club that made a couple of westward excursions. The club celebrated Independence Day by taking a train to Canton, Ohio, to play that city's Stark Club. The contest resulted in the expected easy win for the Alleghenies, but the real highlight was the supper afterward, at which Canton's "young ladies were out in full force." When everyone had eaten their fill, "the tables were cleared away, the musicians came, and the dance commenced, which was kept up till the 'wee sma' hours, when after exchanging goodbyes and mutual well-wishes, the happy party separated."[7]

Then in August the Allegheny first nine was accompanied by a party of thirty in traveling to Detroit to compete in an event that was billed as a world championship tournament. Although efforts were made to attract powerhouse Eastern clubs, the Alleghenys turned out to be the only entrant that didn't hail from either Michigan or Ontario. As such they were the favorites to win, but instead were upset in the championship game when the Unknowns of Jackson, Michigan, staged a ninth-inning rally.

Despite the disappointing outcome, the Allegheny Club did not go home empty-handed. The club's battery of Pratt and Ambrose Lynch was selected as the tournament's best pitcher and catcher, respectively — Pratt was presented with a gold-mounted opera glass while Lynch received a belt mounted with solid silver. For finishing second, the club was awarded an eight-piece tea set with a baseball design, created by Detroit jeweler M. S. Smith and valued at $250. The Alleghenys were also recipients of a set of blue silk flags for being the entrants that had come from the greatest distance.[8]

Just as importantly, the Allegheny Club earned considerable acclaim at the tournament for both their fine play and their gentlemanly conduct. While the tournament was marked by rancor between the champion Unknown Club and their Detroit hosts, both sides agreed that the conduct of the Allegheny Club was exemplary. In particular, the club's first baseman, a man named H. Nichol, was singled out for praise as a result of his sportsmanlike acknowledgment that he had not in fact retired a Jackson batter who had been ruled out by the umpire.[9]

That, however, was pretty much the club's swan song. In 1868, Al Pratt accepted an offer to pitch for a club in Portsmouth, Ohio, receiving in return $60 per month plus college tuition.[10] The Allegheny Club did continue to compete in 1868, including a couple of matches with the Detroit Base Ball Club, but that seems to have marked the end of the club.

Pratt went on to a long professional career, but it was not until the mid-1870s that the Pittsburgh-Allegheny area boasted its first prominent professional club. Even that club made few ripples, and Al Spink would later maintain that it was not until the 1880s that Denny McKnight and Horace Phillips first gave Pittsburgh "a real place on the professional baseball map."[11] McKnight, incidentally, was the brother of Woodruff McKnight, the onetime pitcher of the Enterprise Club.

Thus the years between the 1857 match that supposedly brought regulation baseball to Pittsburgh-Allegheny and the establishment of professional baseball some two decades later, the history of baseball in the region was characterized by a series of fits and starts. The sense that the city's history was discontinuous is accentuated by several intriguing stray ends.

The most notable is that Al Pratt, who was born and raised in Pittsburgh, claimed to have been unfamiliar with the game until after he enlisted in the Union Army in 1864.[12] Adding to the confusion, an obituary for a man named Thomas McNally reported that he had organized the area's first professional club, the Allegheny Base Ball Club. But McNally was born in 1847 and did not come to the United States until 1869, so if the claim was true it referred to a later incarnation.[13] Then in 1935, an obituary of a man named "Ike" Ross credited him with introducing baseball to Pittsburgh sixty-nine years earlier.[14] While claims such as these must be taken with a grain of salt, they increase the impression that Pittsburgh-Allegheny was one place where the baseball seed had to be planted numerous times before finally flourishing.

Club Members

Algernon Sidney Bell: A. S. Bell was an attorney and the club president in 1866. He was born on August 8, 1825, and died in 1879.

William John Blackstock: William J. Blackstock, who was the catcher and lead-off batter for the Allegheny Club in the 1863, was born in Prince Edward Island on May 21, 1826. He moved to Allegheny City as a young man and lived in the area for the rest of his life, dying on August 2, 1906.[15]

Alf. Bryan: Bryan was the shortstop of the first nine in 1866. The only man in Pennsylvania by that name was a Civil War veteran who was born in 1834 and died in Crafton, Pennsylvania, on January 3, 1930.

Addison M. Cameron: A. M. Cameron was a club director and the catcher for the first nine in 1866. (There was also an Alex Cameron on the first nine that year.) He was a Civil War veteran, having served in the 123rd Pennsylvania Infantry. He worked as a cashier and died on June 22, 1904.

James M. Carr: James Carr was the club's vice president in 1860, the scorer in the 1863 game, and the club's representative at the NABBP convention in 1866. He was listed on the 1870 census as having been born around 1831 in Pennsylvania but was last listed in the Allegheny city directory in 1871.

Robert Elton: Robert Elton was the club treasurer in 1860. The only man by that name on that year's census in Allegheny County had been born in 1818 in Pennsylvania. But that man's age suggests a non-playing member, while Elton was the shortstop in the 1863 game.

John Ewer: John Ewer was the club's third baseman in the 1863 game.

Albert R. Girty: A. R. Girty, a Civil War veteran and bank teller who was born around 1842, was the first nine's pitcher in 1866. He was last listed in the city directory in 1875.

W. K. Hamilton: Hamilton was the club's vice president in 1866.

William H. Lockhart: W. H. Lockhart, who was born in Scotland in May of 1838, served as club secretary in 1860 and was the center fielder in the 1863 game. He later served in the Civil War and died on November 22, 1900.

Ambrose Lynch: Ambrose Lynch, the star catcher of the Alleghenys, was born in Ireland in 1839. At the time of the 1860 census, he was living with the Lane family, which included Samuel, who would later pitch for the Lincolns of Pittsburgh and the Detroit Base Ball Club, and George, who would have a brief major league career. He enlisted in the Union Army and served for three years in Pennsylvania's 38th Infantry. After his ballplaying days ended, Lynch was convicted of murdering a deputy sheriff. He was pardoned in 1885, but had contracted tuberculosis while in prison and died of the disease in late June of 1888.

Michael F. Lynch: Michael F. Lynch was the police officer who played in the 1857 game and later reminisced about it. He was born around 1837 and became a cabin boy as a young man. When the Civil War broke out, he enlisted and was wounded in battle. He returned to Allegheny City and worked for the police force until his retirement. When he died on September 7, 1921, at the age of 84, his obituary mentioned that he had once been a ballplayer.[16]

J. C. McLaughlin: McLaughlin was the left fielder of the first nine in 1866.

J. J. Moore: Moore was the club's president in 1860.

H. Nichol: Nichol was the club's first baseman at the Detroit tournament who was commended for his honesty. The only man with a similar name in that year's city directory was Henry Nicholls. In 1866, there was a Henry C. Nickolls who ran a billiard parlor.

Albert G. Pratt: Al Pratt was born in Pittsburgh on November 19, 1847. Though only 16, he enlisted in the Union Army in 1864 and had a distinguished service record. After a three-month stint in the 193rd Pennsylvania Infantry, Pratt reenlisted in the 61st Infantry Regiment, which became one of Pennsylvania's most famous fighting regiments. After his regiment played a key role at Petersburg, Pratt joined in the pursuit of Robert E. Lee. Along the way, Pratt was also exposed to baseball for the first time and upon his return home he joined the Enterprise Club as a catcher. He then became the pitcher of the Allegheny Club in a move that likely tipped the local balance of power back to that club. After the 1867 season, he accepted an offer of $60 per month plus college tuition to play for a club in Portsmouth, Ohio. He joined the Forest Citys of Cleveland in 1869 and would play professional baseball for several more seasons, earning a reputation as one of the hardest-throwing pitchers in the game. When Pittsburgh finally got a professional club, Pratt became its first manager. He was involved in the Pittsburg Fire Arms Company until 1886, when he received the local franchise of A. G. Spalding's sporting goods business. Pratt died in Pittsburgh on November 21, 1937, two days after his ninetieth birthday.

William Ralston, Jr.: William Ralston, Jr., was born around 1844 in Pennsylvania. He served as club secretary in 1866 and was the club's second baseman. He was also captain of the club when they attend the tournament in Detroit and had the honor of giving a speech at the tournament's conclusion that was warmly received.

Frank Rhinehart: Frank Rhinehart played right field for the first nine in 1866.

Thomas A. Sproul: Thomas Sproul, who was born in Pennsylvania around 1843, was the Allegheny Club's third baseman in 1866.

Other Members: T. M. Blair (first baseman in 1863 game); J. M. Bryant (right fielder in 1863 game); C. Cutler (pitcher in 1863 game); A. S. Milligan (left fielder in 1863 game). Men who played in the 1857 match included Beckler and Frefogle for Pittsburgh and Stevenson for Allegheny.

Sources

Samuel Fleming and Samuel Kilgore, *The Iron City: a compendium of facts concerning Pittsburgh and vicinity, for strangers and the public generally* (Pittsburgh: G.W. Pittock and K. McFall, 1867); *Pittsburgh Post*, April

4, 1904 (reprint of account of 1857 game); "TOWN BALL; Game Played in 1863 in This City Is First On Record," *Pittsburgh Leader* clipping from the 1920s (exact date not given; thanks to the Blackstock family for donating this article); *Detroit Post*, numerous issues in August of 1867, especially August 21, 1867, and *Detroit Advertiser and Tribune*, numerous issues in August of 1867, especially August 22, 1867, for Detroit tournament; *Sporting News*, March 23, 1895, for Al Pratt's reminiscences.

Notes

1. *Pittsburgh Post*, April 4, 1904 (which reprints the account of the 1857 game and adds Lynch's reminiscences).
2. Charles A. Peverelly, *The Book of American Pastimes* (New York, 1866), 489.
3. "TOWN BALL; Game Played in 1863 in This City Is First on Record," *Pittsburgh Leader* clipping from the 1920s (exact date not given; special thanks to the Blackstock family for donating this article).
4. Peverelly, *The Book of American Pastimes*, 489.
5. *Ibid.*
6. Samuel Fleming and Samuel Kilgore, *The Iron City: a compendium of facts concerning Pittsburgh and vicinity, for strangers and the public generally* (Pittsburgh: G.W. Pittock and K. McFall, 1867).
7. *Canton Repository*, July 10, 1867; reprinted in James M. Egan, Jr., *Base Ball on the Western Reserve* (Jefferson, NC: McFarland, 2008), 13.
8. *Detroit Post*, August 21, 1867.
9. *Detroit Advertiser and Tribune*, August 19, 1867.
10. *Sporting News*, March 23, 1895.
11. A. H. Spink, *The National Game* (N.p.: National Game, 1910), 86.
12. *Sporting News*, March 23, 1895.
13. *Pittsburgh Press*, October 25, 1902.
14. *Sporting News*, July 18, 1935.
15. *Pittsburgh Press*, August 3, 1906.
16. *Pittsburgh Press*, September 10, 1921, 7.

❖ *Forest City Base Ball Club of Cleveland* (Peter Morris) ❖

Club History

There are contemporaneous references to baseball being played in Cleveland's public square as early as 1857. When local police tried to intervene, the ballplayers appealed to "one of the city authorities" and "he quietly informed the players that there was no law against ball-playing there, for had there been he should have put a stop to it at the commencement. The crowd sent up a shout and renewed the game, which was continued until dark, while the Police went for further orders from head quarters."[1]

By the following year, the interest in baseball was so great in Cleveland that the *Herald* reported,

> Never within the memory of that venerable old fogy, "the oldest inhabitant," has the "base ball" epidemic raged so fiercely as at present. Fields, open lots, streets, alleys, and yards, everywhere can be found a troop of boys and men with a ball and a couple of bats, working at play as earnestly as if it were the great business of the day. All ages and classes have caught the infection. The toddling, unbreeched youngster crows as he hits the tiny ball with the little wand; the school boys make the streets echo with their uproar as they dispute about a "tip" or a "first bound"; out in the fields the portly men grunt as they run past the bound, and grey-bearded Nestors plant themselves firmly to await the swift coming ball. The ragged and shoeless urchin enters with heart and soul into the game he is playing on the street; the staid merchant, the cautious banker, and the millionaire are just as excited and eager over the same game a little out of town.

In addition, the new sport had the enthusiastic support of this reporter, who added:

> Hurrah for base ball! There is no game superior to it in strengthening the muscles, expanding the chest, invigorating the frame, and enlivening the spirits. It is a thoroughly republican game. The possession of wealth or social station does not make a man hit the ball better nor run his rounds faster, nor will the mechanic who bowls shrink from hurling a swift shot after the running millionaire. Cricket is a very good game, but there is too much looking on in it. The good "bat" has all the time to himself, and the green hand loses his first chance, and has to sit on the grass for the remainder of the day. "Keep the pot boiling" is the only way for health and fun, and this "base ball" does.[2]

Nevertheless, local interest in the sport soon faded and it was not until after the Civil War that "the regular game of base ball [took the] place of what was known as 'long ball,' 'square ball' and 'sock ball,' in which a soft ball was used [and in which] one of the ways of getting a batter or base runner out was to hit or 'sock' him with the ball before reaching or while off his base."[3]

Even in 1865, efforts to give the city a representative baseball club proved less than successful. On April 14 the *Cleveland Herald* contained an announcement that a meeting of the Forest City Base Ball Club would be held on the following day.[4] But fatefully it was that same evening that President Lincoln was assassinated and the national mourning put all ideas of fun out of the minds of Americans.

Two months later, a newcomer from the East who identified himself only as "A.R.S." wrote to the *Herald* to express his regret at Cleveland's lack of a baseball club.[5] His complaint initially fell on deaf ears and the only local players that summer appear to have been a group of clerks and high-school students who gathered together and formed sides on an ad hoc basis. But finally in late August of 1865 the Forest City Base Ball Club was permanently established, with a slate of officers elected and a first nine chosen.[6] One of the members of that first nine was catcher Austin R. Smith, a recent arrival from New York state and almost certainly the man who had written to the *Herald* to complain of the lack of ballclubs. Although already in his 30s, "Pikey" Smith was to become the mainstay of Cleveland baseball and of the Forest City Club in the years to come.

The club's historic first match game occurred at the old State Fair Grounds on October 20, 1865, and was far from auspicious. Playing in a "fierce gale," the Forest City Club was "roundly beaten" by a score of 67–28 by the Penfield Club of Oberlin College. Although the match lasted nearly 4½ hours, only seven innings were played — as the *Herald* explained, "The rules of the game, fix nine innings as the full game; but contain a proviso, that, if foul weather, or any other unforeseen impediment should occur, seven innings may constitute a game." To make things worse, L. D. Leffingwell of the Forest City Club suffered a severely sprained arm, while Smith lost three teeth after colliding with a teammate while both were pursuing a popup.[7]

Yet the Cleveland players were "not discouraged," taking consolation in their lack of practice and determining to do better in 1866.[8] In the spring, the Forest City Club held a series of organizational meetings at the law offices of club member Samuel Williamson and, once the weather permitted, began practicing at the corner of Case Avenue and Kinsman Street.[9] Matches followed and they showed that the club had indeed improved. On June 16 the club's first nine took the morning train down to Hudson and defeated the Western Reserve college nine, then joined the students for supper in the school library before returning home on the evening train.[10]

Baseball fever was now sweeping Cleveland and the summer of 1866 saw the formation of at least 11 new clubs in the city, the most prominent being the Young America, the Occidental, the Eagle, the Star, the Alert, and the Railway Union.[11] In recognition, local businessmen offered a silver ball and a silver-inlaid rosewood bat made at Tiffany's of New York to the champions of the Western Reserve, with the stipulation that any club that held on to the bat and ball for an entire year would get to keep it. The first championship match occurred at the grounds of the Forest City Cricket Club on July 4, 1866, and the hometown Forest Citys, dressed in natty white and blue uniforms, handily defeated the Penfield Club of Oberlin, 48–14, to claim the cherished trophies. They then successfully defended the championship in a rematch on August 25, and the bat and ball were proudly put on display in the local storefront of John Sargent.[12]

Their success against the two college nines prompted the Forest City Club to look farther afield and in October the club hosted the Detroit Base Ball Club. The visitors won, 36–18, but as had been the case the preceding fall, the relative inexperience of the Forest Citys meant that the setback was taken in stride. "Under the circumstances," commented a reporter for the *Cleveland Leader*, "we believe that [the Forest City Club] should feel highly encouraged at the result of the match. It has played with confessedly the finest club in the West, a club its senior by four years, and one whose members by long practice under a most excellent drill master have become almost perfect." The writer went on to express pleasure that the home nine had "demonstrated the possession of material" that, with more practice, would make them competitive with the Detroiters.[13] The spectators had a harder time keeping a philosophical outlook because of instances when "the ball would ricochet into the party of ladies and gentlemen, producing as much consternation as a bomb shell in a militia camp." But no injuries resulted, and the female spectators reportedly "enjoyed the sport immensely."[14]

The contests against the Detroit Base Ball Club became regular events and created new fans in Cleveland, including one who was destined for fame. Many years later, John Hinchman of the Detroit Club met John D. Rockefeller at a business meeting and "the oil king associated the Detroit name immediately with the times when as an unknown young bookkeeper he had attended all the ball games between Detroit and Cleveland."[15]

The Cleveland baseball scene continued to heat up in 1867. The Forest City Club organized for the season in April and it soon became apparent that it now had a formidable local adversary. That rival was the Railway Unions, a club made up of local railroad workers that, according to early Cleveland sporting editor Robert S. Pierce, was "backed by a number of railroad officials, among whom were Robert Bice, then superintendent of the Big Four, afterward mayor of Cleveland; William Thornburg, Charles A. Davidson and C. H. Gale. These gentlemen furnished the players with uniforms and generally stood good for their expenses." The rivalry between the two clubs was made all the more intense by the fact that "Pikey" Smith, though "himself a railroad man, preferred to cast his lot with the Forest Citys instead of with the Unions. He was a crack player and both teams coveted his services. It was said that the offer of the captaincy was the weight in the balance that finally settled the question in favor of the Forest Citys."[16]

The Railway Union Club and the Forest City Club played a series of closely contested matches in the next two years. A typical example of the excitement generated by these matches was one played that August in which the hard-hitting Railway Unions jumped to an early lead. But then the Forest City Club fought back by means of a very different weapon — the use of "what may be defined as a characteristic of the club, stealing bases. Among base ball men this is called the science of the game. It is something beyond the usual playing of ordinary clubs, where no risk is taken, but only the most promising chances accepted, and which fails to awaken an interest in the members of the club or the spectators. In the stealing of bases while the ball is in the air, there is a decided risk, and when successful always elicits from the audience a hearty applause. Besides this, it awakens a spirit of emulation among the members of the club, and if done with proper decision results well and adds materially to the score." Among the excited crowds was a group of young Cleveland ladies who regaled the players with calls like "Why don't you catch it, you silly thing!" "Why, what a spooney to run so much!" "run, run, you great dunce!" "you dear fellow, that was fine!" and "don't miss it, you scamp!" Eventually their aggressive base-running helped the Forest Citys pull out a 48–40 victory.[17]

But while the Railway Unions were regarded as the main rivals of the Forest City Club, it was another adversary that briefly wrested away the silver ball and bat. In late June, less than a week before the trophies would have become the permanent possession of the Clevelanders, they were beaten 37–36 by the Western Reserve college nine.[18] A month later, the Forest City Club reclaimed the championship bat and ball by eking out a 40–36 win over the collegians. The match was played in front of 5,000 excited Cleveland spectators, with the most memorable moment coming when the unlucky Smith was again "injured, while recovering a ball which fell under a horse, by the animal jumping while he was beneath it."[19]

The Forest City Club also continued to represent Cleveland in matches against distant opponents in 1867, but the results showed little progress. A surprising road win over the Detroit Base Ball Club on Independence Day created high hopes that were deflated by a convincing defeat when the rematch was played in Cleveland in September. Similarly, a victory over the Quickstep Club of Toledo was followed by a loss to a club that was alleged to be an all-star aggregation of Toledo's best players. Worse, a match against the Niagaras of Buffalo ended with a demoralizing 66–11 loss.[20]

Such defeats had been brushed aside in the two preceding seasons as the product of inexperience, but the Forest City Club had passed the stage for such justifications. As a result, the 1868 campaign was a transitional one for Cleveland baseball.

Hoping to take advantage of the large crowds that baseball had begun to attract, the Forest City and Railway Union clubs joined forces to build a new enclosed baseball field at the Case Commons. Covered stands were erected at the park, which became known as the Association Grounds, providing an appropriate site for hosting visiting clubs and a way to collect admission to baseball games for the first time.[21]

Not everyone saw the new field as an improvement. "The new grounds are very snug and pleasant," observed a journalist, "but to our mind, the high fence and the comparatively limited space, convey an idea of confinement that is not particularly agreeable. One misses the pretty rural scene that was an accessory of the old Kinsman street grounds, where there was a boundless wealth of green turf, with distant glimpses of grove and shrub. Then a vigorous strike that sent the ball away from the fielders was sure to result in a 'home run,' with its accompanying shouting and excitement."

But the loss of such idyllic images was the price that had to be paid for progress. The reporter went on to point out the advantages of the covered seats and other new amenities. He concluded, "The new arrangement, too, insures an income to the proprietors, which is as it should be. Under the old plan the public were constantly being treated to delightful entertainments, free, while the entertainers had the expenses to bear."[22]

The two Cleveland clubs began lining up visits from some of the country's most prominent clubs, including the Athletics of Philadelphia, the Atlantics of Brooklyn, and the Unions of Morrisania. But first, however, the new grounds hosted the renewal of the rivalry between the Forest Citys and the Railway Unions. The latter club gained the upper hand in the first match that spring, beating their rivals 21–14 to earn the coveted bat and ball. But the Forest Citys quickly regrouped, improving their first nine by the addition of several young players from local rivals such as the Peconic Club of the Humiston Academy. After a hard-fought tie on Independence Day, the Forest City Club beat the Railway Unions three straight times to re-establish local supremacy.

The Forest Citys also squared off against many national powerhouses in 1868, but they experienced only mixed success. The club did split with the Detroit Base Ball Club and managed wins over visiting clubs from several other cities, some of which created excitement that the club's nucleus of young Cleveland players was poised for greatness. After a 38–18 win over the Mutual Club of Pittsburgh, for example, a local reporter raved that Forest City second baseman William P. Johnson "is 'lightning on a catch.' He and [outfielder Arthur] Burt belong to the rising generation of players who are bound to excel their predecessors. Like the small boys that inhabit the tops of neighboring trees during the progress of a game, they feel full of enthusiasm, take pride in being successful all the time, and seldom ever make a mistake or muff a ball. They, and others like them, will soon out-play those who introduced the game, and, when able to do so, should be admitted to all the honors of this truly National, exciting, and popular sport."[23]

Yet matches against powerhouse clubs from Philadelphia and the New York resulted in lopsided defeats and made it clear that the young Cleveland players were not ready for the national stage. The 1868 lineup of the Forest Citys consisted almost entirely of local amateurs with one notable exception — Jim "Deacon" White from Corning, New York.[24] White was destined to a 20-year major-league career as one of the greatest ballplayers of the 19th century and his play showed just how far the young members of the Forest City Club still had to go. When White pitched, his twisting deliveries were able to perplex the best hitters in the country — even the mighty Red Stockings of Cincinnati "couldn't knock them crooked balls all to pieces no how."[25] Unfortunately, the club tried all of its best players behind the plate with White pitching and found that none of them were consistently able "to stop the balls." Inevitably, "the deal had to be changed ... and White went behind the plate."[26] Once there, he displayed the form that was to earn him recognition as one of the game's best catchers, yet all too often he didn't get the chance to show his skill because the offerings of less skilled pitchers like Charles Brown and Theo Branch were being driven to the farthest reaches of the Association Grounds.[27]

By the end of the 1868 season, there were signs that the Cleveland public was running out of patience with the Forest City Club. After three years of defeats being taken philosophically, an October loss to the Excelsiors of Chicago prompted a sportswriter to write that the string of losses, "without explanation, would lead the general reader to suppose that the nine had been rusticating in some spot where base ball was unknown."[28]

These developments meant that the Forest City Club had to make a crucial decision after the 1868 campaign. The National Association of Base Ball Players finally sanctioned professional play that offseason and it was now clear that bringing in outside professionals was the only way to be competitive with the country's top clubs. Yet it was not clear whether Cleveland was ready to support a fully professional nine.

The same dilemma confronted every top amateur club, but the case of the Forest Cities of Cleveland was an especially interesting one. In a real sense there was no turning back for the club because local competition, which had been so vibrant when the silver ball and bat were initially offered, now created little enthusiasm. By adding promising players from the best Cleveland junior clubs, the Forest City Club had prevented any of those clubs from becoming serious rivals, thereby enriching the city's top club at the expense of local competitive balance. As a preview of one match between the Railway Unions and the Forest Citys put it, between those two clubs "virtually lies the championship of the Western Reserve, there being no others which can have any hope of securing the prize bat and ball."[29] Then the Railway Unions disbanded after their three straight 1868 losses to their crosstown rivals, leaving Cleveland with only one notable baseball club.

A reversion to focusing on local competition thus was no longer an option for the Forest City Club, but they still had a choice to make about the direction they would take in 1869. The demise of their strongest rival meant many strong local players were available and the Forest Citys could become an all-star lineup of Cleveland's best players while still remaining nominally or strictly amateur. But would such a lineup prove competitive against top professional clubs? If it didn't, it was safe to assume that attendance would soon fall off.

Alternatively, the Forest Citys could follow the example of the cross-state Red Stockings of Cincinnati and sign a nine that consisted almost entirely of Eastern professionals. But this course would create hard feelings by thrusting longtime regulars out of their positions, and would ensure a backlash unless wins ensued.

At first it appeared that the Forest City Club would embrace full-fledged professionalism. To raise the necessary capital, the club signed up 275 members and opened new club rooms in the Lyman block, concurrently announcing plans "to furnish such entertainments there during the winter as will keep up the interest in the club, especially among members, and make it pleasant for them to spend their evenings in their own society, instead of seeking amusements elsewhere."[30] The club immediately began the hunt for "renowned players" and at a meeting in January of 1869, "it was resolved to make the nine a strong one, and for that purpose instructed the Secretary to open a negotiation with [pitcher Al] Pratt, of the Riverside Club [of Portsmouth], and Joe Doyle and Eb. Smith, of the Nationals, of Washington."[31]

Pratt and Smith were indeed signed, as were two more Eastern professionals, Art Allison and John Ward. But Doyle slipped away, and a far more serious mistake was made when Jim White was allowed to leave town. As a result, the Forest City Club began the 1869 season with an almost equal mix of imported professional players and local stalwarts.[32]

As a symbol of just how difficult it was to tightrope between the two polar opposites, this amalgam roster was implausibly billed as an amateur club, with a club representative writing, "We are charged with having secured professional players in our nine, which assertion is positively untrue. We have strengthened our nine somewhat by the acquisition of Pratt, Ward and Allison, but neither [sic] of these players is a professional, all being in business in this city, and making base ball a secondary matter to business requirements. Our club is strictly an amateur organization."[33] Not surprisingly, few observers believed this claim and the Forest Citys were generally listed as a professional club.

The season opened with an optimistic declaration that the club's finances were in "good shape," and even a 25–6 loss to the cross-state Red Stockings was met by brave talk about the improvement of the Forest Citys and predictions that "with a little more practice they will place themselves on a footing second to none in the State."[34] In hopes of matching the success of the Red Stockings, the club adopted uniforms that looked strikingly similar except that the stockings were blue.[35]

But as the season wore on, the results of the decision to use the half amateur-half professional lineup were predictable: an undefeated record against amateur clubs, with most of the victories coming by lopsided margins, but only one win in seven contests against professional rivals.[36] After a "galling defeat" in July, Jim White was brought back, but the "Blue Stockings" continued to come up short in their matches with all-professional nines.[37]

The 1869 season also saw the Cleveland Base Ball Association have to fend off efforts to take their new park away. A group of citizens, with the backing of the City Council, contended that the club had illegally blocked a street by enclosing their field. The matter loomed over the club until May, when the city attorney ruled in favor of the ballclub.[38]

At the close of the campaign, the *New York Clipper* maintained that the season had been a successful one for Cleveland's most prominent baseball nine. "The Forest City club," wrote its baseball reporter, "was not gotten up with the idea of their obtaining the championship; such an idea never entered the Clevelanders' heads; they simply wished to keep pace with the times. Extensive tours being the order of the day, and Cleveland being a favorite stopping place on account of the hospitable manner of its denizens and their liberality in patronizing the games, at once a source of gratification and reward, they (the Forest Citys) wished to have a club which would give all the visitors a good struggle, and they have done it finely."[39] But it may be doubted whether that was in fact the outlook in Cleveland.

At any rate, the developments of 1869, especially the phenomenal success of the Red Stockings of Cincinnati forced the hand of Cleveland's top club. In March of 1870 a meeting was held at the Amereon House

> for the purpose of selecting the nine for the coming season, and to devise ways and means for their support. A committee consisting of Messrs. Mason, Andrews and Olmsted, was appointed for the purpose of selecting ten men to canvass the city for subscriptions. The Club for some time has been struggling with debt, and have got along, so that now, with a little assistance from the admirers of Base Ball, it will be able to make "buckle and strap" come together and enable this city to have an efficient organization. Several first class players have signified a desire to play here, and the officers of the club are now corresponding with them. To have a first class club, men must be paid for their services, and the success that this committee which is to be appointed to solicit subscription, shall meet with, will instruct the officers how good a club is wanted here. The town of Rockford, Illinois, contributed $7,000 in one evening, and Chicago, always to the extreme, contributed $20,000 in one day, and it remains to be seen whether the many friends of base ball in this city will not give the boys a handsome send off. The season of 1870 promises to be one of unusual activity. Everywhere reorganization and preparations are being made, and if our citizens desire the club to make a record, even as good as they did last year, they must be ready and liberal with their assistance.[40]

The first nine that the Forest City Club ended up fielding in 1870 consisted entirely of professionals from New York and Pennsylvania, including both Jim White and his cousin Elmer White. The club got off to a slow start and a series of losses in June prompted talk that the hired players were a "humiliation" and a "disgrace" to Cleveland and that "'reorganization,' 'practice,' and 'discipline'" were urgently needed.[41]

The club did indeed regroup and in late July posted a signature triumph over the visiting Mutuals of New York. The 7–5 victory was hailed as the "Finest Game Ever Seen in Cleveland" and at its conclusion, "the crowd went wild with joy. They sprang over the ropes, old men and young flung their hats into the air and shouted till compelled to desist from sheer exhaustion."[42]

The big win was followed in August by a tour of New York, Maryland, the District of Columbia, and Pennsylvania that was billed as the Forest City Club's "first trip to meet on their own grounds the famous clubs of the east."[43] With their work already cut out for them, Pratt became ill at the start of the trip, which meant that the club was back in the awkward position of 1868 when Jim White was both the club's best catcher and its best pitcher. To make matters still more difficult, a Brooklyn umpire ruled White's delivery illegal in a one-run loss to the Mutuals.[44]

The three-week, 15-game trek included four other hard-fought losses. But overall, it was a rousing success, with the Clevelanders posting victories over such legendary clubs as the Eckfords of Brooklyn, the Nationals of Washington, and the Unions of Morrisania and proving that they had become a force to be reckoned with on the national baseball scene.

Just as important, the tour of August 1870 changed the Cleveland public's view of the imported ballplayers. The *Herald* published lengthy accounts of the doings of the Forest City Club while in the East, and the descriptions stressed the club's role as ambassadors. Attention was drawn, for example, to the club's "new traveling uniform, which is very neat and tasty. It is a suit of light gray, dark shirt, white hat and blue-edged neck tie."[45] Upon arrival in New York, a trip was paid to Central Park, where, as a result of the "natty" attire of the visitors, "a great deal of speculation was indulged in as to who they were. Some said they are the 'Harvards,' but the largest number seemed to think that they belonged to the yacht Cambria."[46]

When the weary travelers finally returned home, they were treated to a dinner at the Kennard House at which the players received toasts and compliments for their "gentlemanly deportment and fair, honest play."[47] Although the 1870 season continued for another month, that evening proved to be the pinnacle of Cleveland's first entry into professional baseball.

With most of the same players, the Forest Citys entered the National Association in 1871 and posted a 10–19 mark in the first season of major-league baseball. The club made a concerted effort to upgrade its talent in 1872, but the fates were against them. The Great Chicago Fire had led both Chicago and Rockford to drop out, leaving Cleveland as the only "Western" city in a league of East Coast clubs. The Eastern clubs were reluctant to travel to Cleveland, and the Forest Citys struggled on the field as well.[48] The club disbanded at mid-season and, according to Robert Pierce, "attorney W. M. Reynolds was made receiver, and Arnold Green, an attorney for the stockholders, paid all debts in full."[49] In the five years "following the inglorious break-up ... base ball interest in and about Cleveland was confined to games played by high school and other amateur nines."[50]

During its nearly seven years of existence, the makeup of the Forest City Club changed dramatically and by the end all of the original players had been replaced by Eastern professionals. Nonetheless, memories of the original members did not fade as quickly. Robert Pierce recalled that the early players "were nearly all scions of the best families in Cleveland, and the games always attracted a good turnout of fathers, mothers, sisters, sweethearts and the usual following of ardent and admiring supporters. All contests took place in the open field with no seating accommodations except the green grass. The game was played for pure love of it, and some of the players become quite expert. So far as history records, no umpires were mobbed in those days, but feeling often ran high and long disputes over questionable decisions frequently occurred, to be settled only by the substitution of a new arbitrator."[51]

Club Members

The Amateur Years: 1865–1868

Theodore Francis Branch: Theo Branch was the pitcher for the Peconics of Humiston Academy, then became one of the outfielders of the Forest City Club in 1868, occasionally pitching as well. But his pitching aspirations came to an inglorious end when he surrendered 15 runs to the famous Red Stockings of Cincinnati in the first inning of a game that October. Branch was born in Prussia on May 28, 1849, and became a civil engineer. He moved his family to North Dakota in 1880, working there as a surveyor and as the clerk of the district court for Stutsman County. He returned to Ohio shortly before the turn of the century and died in Cleveland on October 16, 1916.

Thomas Hope Brooks: Thomas H. Brooks does not appear to have ever been a member of the first nine of the Forest Citys, but his prominent place in Cleveland society meant that he was often mentioned in later articles about the club. He was born in Patriot, Indiana, on October 10, 1846. His father, a doctor, moved the family to Cleveland the following year. Thomas graduated from Williams College in 1870, and established the Brooks Foundry in 1875. He remained a successful Cleveland businessman until his death on May 29, 1919.

Charles Brown: Charles Brown was the regular pitcher of the Forest Citys in 1868, but was not mentioned in later accounts of the club and his common name makes it impossible to identify him.

Harvey Huntington Brown: Harvey H. Brown was the third baseman of the Forest City first nine in 1868 and a backup in 1869 and 1870. An 1886 article about the Forest City Club singled him out as "a great natural ball player" who "astonished the natives by a great triple play against the famous Cincinnati Reds."[52] Brown was born in Allegheny City, Pennsylvania, on June 30, 1848, and became a noted Cleveland iron and steel manufacturer. He joined other old-time players like Sheffield and Hanna in helping to fund Cleveland's 1879 National League entry. He died in Cleveland on August 2, 1923.

Arthur Edwin Burt: Arthur Burt was born in Liverpool, Ohio, on April 30, 1851. He attended Humiston Academy and played for the school team, the Peconics, before joining the Forest Citys and becoming one of their regular outfielders in 1868. He lost his spot to new recruits and became a successful seed dealer. But when he died in Cleveland Heights on April 16, 1939, his status as the last living member of the Forest Citys was prominently mentioned in his obituary. In addition, an editorial in the *Plain Dealer* noted that his death coincided with the start of the baseball season, describing Burt as "a baseball pioneer of more than local fame" who "kept his interest in baseball for many years, in spite of the burdens of managing a successful business and the demands of civic obligations."[53]

James Waite Clarke: J.W. Clarke was the club's regular first baseman from 1865 to 1868 and its president in 1867. His play in his club's first match against the Detroit Base Ball Club prompted the *Leader* to rave, "His play was accurate and scientific from beginning to end. One catch of his, in particular, received enthusiastic cheers, and was pronounced by *connoisseurs* the finest they had ever seen." But like most of the original Forest Citys, he eventually lost his spot in the first nine. He was born in Sardinia, New York, on June 8, 1843, the son of a Baptist pastor, and earned an undergraduate degree after studying at both Yale University and Oberlin College. After moving to Cleveland, Clarke became a partner in a firm of book sellers. Like fellow club member Theo Branch, he moved to North Dakota during the 1880s and finally settled in Ashland, Wisconsin. Clarke died in Chicago on June 19, 1905.

Charles Long Cutter: C.L. Cutter was born on February 20, 1842, and served as club secretary in 1865, then as both secretary and treasurer in 1866. He also played for the second nine. He worked as a clerk and died in Cleveland on January 13, 1915.

John Melancthon "Lank" Gorham: "Lank" Gorham was born in or near Cleveland on January 2, 1841, and worked as an accountant. He died in Cleveland on November 30, 1916.

Leonard Colton "Doc" Hanna: One of the unfortunate anomalies of the Forest City Club was that its early members died when there was more pressing world news and were deprived of detailed obituaries. Several died during World War I, while Brooks died on the day that many Cleveland troops returned home from the war and Burt died as the Second World War loomed. In addition, the passings of others coincided with major tragedies — Stockley died on the day after the San Francisco Earthquake, Vilas died in Chicago on the day before the Iroquois Theatre Fire, and Harvey Brown on the same day as President Harding. As a result, Leonard C. Hanna's death was singular in receiving extensive coverage of his long-ago days on the ball field. Hanna was born in Lisbon, Ohio, on November 30, 1850, the younger brother of Mark Hanna, the U.S. senator who masterminded William McKinley's rise to the presidency. Mark Hanna also founded the M.A. Hanna Co., which became a very successful coal and iron shipper. Leonard Hanna attended Doctor Holbrook's Military School and then joined his brother in operating the M.A. Hanna firm. He too became wealthy and influential, but when he died in Cleveland on March 23, 1919, it was his baseball career as "Doc Hanna" that was the focus of an article in the *Cleveland Plain Dealer* by W. R. Rose. Rose recalled that "everybody called him 'Doc'" and that he was a "hard hitter and quick on his feet and always tractable." He usually played left field, "that section of the garden being considered in the early days the most important." The era "when the game was a pastime pure and simple, staged on commons or cow pastures, with neither enclosed grounds or grand stands, where the ball was lively, the batting vigorous and the scores ran high, the contests often lasting from noon till dark," soon passed and amateurs like Hanna were replaced with professionals. But Hanna never lost his affection for the game, being a backer and board member of many later clubs, holding a private box at League Park until his death, and even umpiring one major-league game. "Some day," concluded W. R. Rose, "when a list is made of all the prominent Clevelanders who have helped along the game of baseball during the past half century, it will be found that the roll of names includes a large proportion of the men who have built up the city — and L. C. Hanna's name will be near the top."

William L. Hulbert: William Hulbert, whose name was often misspelled as Hurlbut or Hurlburt was born in Binghamton, New York, on January 28, 1844. (He is not to be confused with William Ambrose Hulbert, the founder of the National League.) He worked in the coal business and died in Cleveland on August 4, 1918.

William P. Johnson: William P. Johnson first played for the Occidentals and then joined the Forest Citys in 1868. He was born in Ohio around 1848 and worked as a bookkeeper for the Commercial National Bank. After the turn of the century, he became president of the American Lumber Company of Albuquerque, New Mexico. He died in Albuquerque on September 25, 1909.

John Henry Kirkwood: John Kirkwood was born in Baltimore on September 8, 1850. He played for the Occidentals of Cleveland before joining the Forest Citys in 1868 and seeing spot duty in the outfield. He became a bookkeeper and died in East Cleveland on October 5, 1929.

Everton Judson Latimer: Everton Latimer was described by Robert S. Pierce as the pitcher for the first nine in one of the club's first games, but his involvement with Cleveland baseball ended then and was no doubt the casualty of his budding academic career. Latimer was born in Norwalk, Ohio, on October 14, 1849. He graduated from the Cleveland High School and spent a year at the Western Reserve College before enrolling at Yale in 1869. After graduation, he attended Columbia Law School and became an attorney in Cleveland, dying there on February 11, 1915.

Lucius Dexter Leffingwell: L. D. Leffingwell was born on September 20, 1846, and was a member of the board of the directors and the first nine of the Forest Citys in 1865. But his playing career seems to have pretty much ended when he suffered a severe arm sprain in the club's game against the Penfields of Oberlin that fall. Leffingwell died in Cleveland on June 16, 1884.

Lemuel O. Rawson: Lem Rawson was born in Connecticut in March of 1838 and served separate terms in the Union Army in the 84th and 150th Ohio regiments. He became an officer of the Forest City Base Ball Association in 1869 and a wealthy and successful businessman as president of the Cleveland Brass & Iron Bedstead Co. But his health began to fail and led to a nervous breakdown. On June 11, 1902, he took his own life.

Charles J. Sheffield: Charles Sheffield was born on September 6, 1845, in New Haven, Connecticut, where his father was the founder of Yale's Sheffield Scientific School. He graduated from Yale himself, then moved to Cleveland and went into the mining and shipping of coal while playing for the Forest City Club in 1868 and 1869. In the early 1890s, his health began to fail and a trip to Europe did not provide relief. He became bedridden and died in Cleveland on July 26, 1895.

Austin R. "Pikey" Smith: Austin "Pikey" Smith was the captain of the original Forest City nine and was much older than most of his teammates, having been born in New York state around 1833. He is very likely the "A.R.S." who described himself as a new arrival from the East in 1865 and who complained about Cleveland's lack of baseball clubs. If so, he worked hard to address that deficiency, by playing a major role in the Forest City Club while working as a ticket agent at the Union Station. After his playing days ended, he remained involved with the local baseball scene and a note in the *Cleveland Herald* on June 26, 1872, stated that he had been elected secretary of the Forest City Club and would travel with club management. He died in Cleveland on January 8, 1881.

George W. Stockley: George Stockley was born in Cleveland in December of 1843. He studied for the law but instead went into business. After a stint as a banker, he became president of the Telegraph Supply Co. Later his close friendship with inventor Charles F. Brush led to his selection as president of the Brush Electric Company. After many years as one of Cleveland's most prominent businessmen he moved to New Jersey, and died in Atlantic City on April 19, 1906.

Taylor: A man named Taylor played six games for the Forest Citys in 1868. He can't be positively identified, but given how many of the club's new players that year had previously been with other Cleveland clubs, he was probably a man named William Taylor of the Peconics of the Humiston Academy.

Royal Cooper Vilas: R.C. Vilas was born in Ogdensburg, New York, on November 19, 1842. He was still living in Ogdensburg in 1860 but had moved to Cleveland by the end of the Civil War and became the club's initial president in 1865. He played shortstop for the club that year and was its regular third baseman in 1866, but that seems to have ended his involvement with baseball. Vilas moved to New York City in

1869 and became a successful railway executive, later becoming the president of the Pyle National Electric Headlight Company. He died at his home in Chicago on December 29, 1903.

James Laurie White: Jim "Deacon" White was born on December 7, 1847, in Caton, New York. In 1868, he moved to Cleveland to take a job at the McNairy and Claflin car shops and play ball for the Forest Citys. He joined the Central Citys of Syracuse in 1869, but it is not clear whether he played any games before rejoining the Forest Citys in August. He agreed to play for the White Stockings of Chicago in 1870, but had another change of heart and remained in Cleveland. He remained with the Forest Citys until the club disbanded in 1872 and then announced his retirement. But he again change his mind and played in the major leagues for two full decades, winning six pennants and establishing himself as one of the greatest players of the 19th century. He died on July 7, 1939, in Aurora, Illinois.

Willard Elmer White: Elmer White played for the Forest Citys along with his first cousin, Jim White, for a few games in 1868. He rejoined the club in 1868 and played with it until his death from tuberculosis on March 17, 1872, in Caton, New York, at the age of 22.

Judge Samuel E. Williamson: Samuel Williamson is not known to have ever been a member of the first nine of the Forest Citys, but he was mentioned in several accounts as one of the early crowd of ballplayers. More important, the club's meetings at the start of the 1866 season were held at his law offices.[54] He was born in 1844 and died at his home in Glenville, Ohio, on February 21, 1903.

Darwin E. Wright: Like Williamson, Darwin E. Wright does not appear to have ever belonged to the first nine. He was born in February of 1844, became the city's public service director under Mayor Robert E. McKisson, and died in Cleveland on November 15, 1907.

Other Members: Bradbeer, Castor, Coit, Frank Collins, Crumbie, Dodge, Samuel E. Eddy, D. M. Graham, W. B. Hall, Herse or Herss, W. N. Hudson, William P. Johnson, William C. McEwen, George W. Melton, T. H. Miles, Parker, Patterson, N. E. Pearse, Fred Partridge, J. Quay, Skaits or Skates, A. I. Truesdale, John Wheeler, H.P. Wolcott, B. H. or R. H. Wright.

The Professional Years: 1869–1870

Arthur Algernon Allison: Art Allison was one of the professionals who joined the Forest Citys in 1869 and he remained a starter until the Forest Citys disbanded in 1872. He played professional baseball for four more seasons. The brother of Doug Allison, star catcher of the Red Stockings, Art was born on January 29, 1849, in Philadelphia, and died on February 25, 1916, in Washington, D.C.

James Leslie Carleton: James Carleton was an Easterner who became the starting first baseman of the Forest City Club in 1870. Carleton, who was born on August 20, 1848, in Clinton, Connecticut, remained with the Forest City Club until it disbanded in 1872. He stayed in Cleveland for several years after that, working as a real-estate agent, before giving professional baseball another try with a club in Natick, Massachusetts. He was back in Cleveland by the early 1880s, and one article stated that he was "interested in the Bell telephone and has made a pile." He eventually settled in Detroit, where he worked as a stockbroker until his death on April 25, 1910.

Charles John "Chick" Fulmer: Philadelphian Chick Fulmer played eight games for the Forest Citys in 1870 and went on to a long major-league career.

Georg (George) A. Heubel: German-born Georg Heubel was another Philadelphian who joined the Forest Citys in 1870 and went on to play in the majors. He later worked as groundskeeper of the Philadelphia park, but was blamed for a disastrous fire after the 1894 season and was dismissed. He died two years later.

Eugene Boynton Kimball: Gene Kimball was born on August 31, 1850, in Rochester, New York, and played ball there before becoming the second baseman of the Forest Citys in 1870. He became more famous as a professional billiards player than as a ballplayer. Kimball died in his native Rochester on August 2, 1882.

Albert G. Pratt: The career of pitcher Al Pratt is described in the entry on the Allegheny Club.

John Riley: John Riley (or Reilly) was a regular for the Railway Unions in 1868, but became a starter for the Forest Citys in 1869. By 1872 he was playing for the Mutual Club of Kansas City, but little else is known about him.

Eben Griffin Smith: Eb Smith was a Brooklyn native and the brother of another well-known ballplayer, Sydney Smith. He had played for various New York clubs and the Nationals of Washington before joining the Forest Citys and becoming captain in 1869.[55] He was born in Brooklyn on August 11, 1846, and died there on July 22, 1875.

Ezra Ballou Sutton: Ezra Sutton was born on September 17, 1850, in Palmyra, New York, joined the Forest Citys in 1870, and became one of the game's best third basemen, remaining in the major leagues until 1888. He died on June 20, 1907, in Braintree, Massachusetts.

John Ward: Jack Ward had played for the Eckfords of Brooklyn, the Haymakers of Troy, and the Nationals of Washington before joining the Forest Citys in 1869. In 1921, Cleveland journalist W.R. Rose wrote, "It is believed that Jack Ward was the first player on the Cleveland team to receive pay for his services. He was a little fellow, quick and agile, a hard hitter and a fearless catcher."[56]

In addition to the imported players, the club elected new officers who included president Charles B. Pettingill (1838–1888); recording secretary Philip L. Kessler; corresponding secretary John J. Reed; and directors H. L. Melton, Frank H. Mason, George W. Rouse and T. A. Andrews.

Sources

Two primary sources were relied upon in this entry. The first was James M. Egan, Jr., *Base Ball on the Western Reserve* (Jefferson, NC: McFarland, 2008), a documentary history of 19th-century baseball in Cleveland and its surrounding area. Egan's work is impressively detailed and anyone wishing to learn more about the Forest City Club and of other clubs in the region will find a wealth of information. The second was a ten-part history of local baseball written by early Cleveland baseball editor Robert S. Pierce, which was published in the *Cleveland Press* from February 11 to 21, 1908. Pierce's memory about details is sometimes imprecise, but he brings the perspective of an eyewitness. Several retrospective articles by Cleveland journalist W.R. Rose were also helpful. Additional information has been culled from contemporaneous press coverage, mostly the *Cleveland Herald*, as cited in the notes. Details of the contests between the Forest Citys and the Detroit Base Ball Club come from my *Baseball Fever: Early Baseball in Michigan*.

Notes

1. *Porter's Spirit of the Times*, April 18, 1857. There was another mention of ball-playing three weeks later in the May 9 issue.
2. *Cleveland Herald*, May 4, 1858. Another article in the same paper on March 30 had reported, "A grand tournament in the grand old American game of base-ball is in progress on 'The Hights.' The participants are the players of former days, and perhaps are entitled to no inferior grade now. The game will continue until six o'clock."
3. Robert S. Pierce, "Score of the First Professional Base Ball Game Ever Played in Cleveland of Which an Official Record Has Been Kept," *Cleveland Press*, February 11, 1908, 6.
4. *Cleveland Herald*, April 14, 1865. The meeting was to be held at W.H. Rugg's Painting Rooms and a man named "C. Burt" was identified as club secretary.
5. *Cleveland Herald*, June 21, 1865.
6. *Cleveland Herald*, October 10, 1865, and October 21, 1865. The August date is based upon the statement in the latter article that the Forest City Club was "only organized six weeks."
7. *Cleveland Herald*, October 21, 1865.
8. *Ibid.*
9. *Cleveland Herald*, April 2, 16, 17, 24, and 28 and May 8, 1866.
10. *Cleveland Herald*, June 19, 1866.
11. *Cleveland Herald*, August 27, 1866.
12. *Cleveland Herald*, July 10 and August 27, 1866; James M. Egan, Jr., *Base Ball on the Western Reserve* (Jefferson, NC: McFarland, 2008), 5–8.
13. *Cleveland Leader*, reprinted in the *Detroit Advertiser and Tribune*, October 19, 1866.
14. *Cleveland Herald*, October 17, 1866. The Forest City Club closed the 1866 season a week later with a win over a club representing Columbus (*Cleveland Herald*, October 26, 1866).
15. "Detroit's Old Time Baseball Clubs," *Detroit Free Press*, November 13, 1904, D3.
16. Robert S. Pierce, "Old Railway Unions Played a Fine Game," *Cleveland Press*, February 13, 1908, 10.
17. *Cleveland Herald*, August 23, 1867.
18. *Cleveland Herald*, June 29, 1867.
19. *Cleveland Herald*, July 27, 1867.
20. Egan Jr., *Base Ball on the Western Reserve*, 20–22; Peter Morris, *Baseball Fever* (Ann Arbor: University of Michigan Press, 2003), 155–156, 172.
21. Egan Jr., *Base Ball on the Western Reserve*, 23–24.
22. *Cleveland Plain Dealer*, June 5, 1868.
23. *Cleveland Herald*, August 26, 1868.
24. White's cousin, Elmer, also from Corning, played in a few games. Marshall Wright lists Eb. Smith playing for the club in 1868 but notes from the time identify him as Pikey Smith.
25. *Cleveland Herald*, October 13, 1868.
26. *Cleveland Herald*, October 5, 1868.
27. *Cleveland Herald*, September 21 and October 13, 1868.
28. *Cleveland Herald*, September 21, 1868.
29. *Cleveland Herald*, August 31, 1868.
30. *Cleveland Herald*, November 21, 1868.
31. *Cleveland Herald*, January 15, 1869.
32. John Riley of the Railway Unions had been added to the first nine and he was described as a professional by several sources. The remaining four were locals, and were at least billed as amateurs.
33. *New York Clipper*, June 19, 1869.
34. *Cleveland Herald*, April 8, 1869; *Cleveland Herald*, June 3, 1869.
35. *Cleveland Herald*, June 30, 1869.
36. *Cleveland Herald*, March 16, 1870, record of the Forest City Base Ball Club for 1869 along with statistics for all players.
37. *Cleveland Herald*, July 31, 1869. The "galling defeat" was officially not a loss at all, because rain ended play after three innings. But by then the Forest Citys were behind their Rockford namesakes 23–0 and the Cleveland press treated the outcome as a defeat and an embarrassing one at that.
38. Egan Jr., *Base Ball on the Western Reserve*, 32–33.
39. Quoted in the *Cleveland Herald*, January 17, 1870.
40. *Cleveland Herald*, March 21, 1870.
41. *Cleveland Herald*, June 23, 1870.
42. *Cleveland Herald*, July 30, 1870.
43. *Cleveland Herald*, August 11, 1870.
44. *Cleveland Herald*, August 25, 1870. This decision, along with another questionable ruling by umpire Jack Chapman, on a fly ball, prompted much second-guessing, even in the New York papers.
45. *Cleveland Herald*, August 11, 1870.
46. *Cleveland Herald*, August 17, 1870.
47. *Cleveland Herald*, September 2, 1870.
48. Egan Jr., *Base Ball on the Western Reserve*, 66–72.
49. Robert S. Pierce, "Bubble Bursts As Era of Big Salaries Begins," *Cleveland Press*, February 17, 1908, 6.
50. Robert S. Pierce, "Hollinger Comes and the Fans Are Happy," *Cleveland Press*, February 18, 1908, 8; see also Egan Jr., *Base Ball on the Western Reserve*, 72–76.
51. Robert S. Pierce, "Famous Players in Early Games Here," *Cleveland Press*, February 12, 1908, 6.
52. *Cleveland Plain Dealer*, December 1, 1886, 4.
53. *Cleveland Plain Dealer*, April 18, 1939, 4.
54. *Cleveland Herald*, April 2 and 16, 1866.
55. Marshall Wright lists him playing with the Forest Citys in 1868, but contemporaneous notes identified this player as Pikey Smith.
56. *Cleveland Plain Dealer*, July 1, 1921.

❖ Independents of Mansfield (Peter Morris) ❖

Club History

John C. Carrothers became known as "the acknowledged head of the base ball fraternity in Mansfield," and it is largely thanks to him that we know as much as we do about the history of early baseball in Mansfield.[1]

According to Carrothers, the city's first game took place on September 12, 1866, near the depot on East Fourth Street and featured the Mansfield and the Exercise clubs.² The players for the Exercise club were Roberts, Emminger, Decamp, Snyder, Cobean, Sturges, Rowland, McIlvain, and Dougherty, while Mansfield countered with Rowland, Guernsey, Thomas, Lacy, McMann, Ritter, Hade, Leiter, and Strong. Playing with a lively ball and straight-arm pitching, the Mansfields won 45–31, with Hade leading all scorers with seven runs. The umpire was John M. Jolley, a wealthy banker.

The following May 1, the two clubs consolidated as the Mansfield Club, with the lineup consisting of L. A. Strong, c; R. H. Rowland, p; G. W. Blymyer, 1b; J. D. Bell, 2b; J. Cobean, 3b; Gail Thomas, ss; Jacob Hade, rf; George Snyder, cf; George A. Clugston, lf. The substitutes were A. Sturges, A. Emminger, and E. Snyder. The club selected grounds on a vacant lot on East Market Street and faced Ohio clubs from Ashland, Delaware, and Galion, winning all three matches by lopsided margins.³ After the game against the Delaware club, John C. Burns of that club joined the Mansfields and became a regular.⁴

In July, however, the club faced a much tougher rival from Akron. The game saw R.H. Rowland make what Carrothers called "the great hit of the day," with the ball ending up 195 feet from home, the distance speaking volumes about the liveliness of the ball they were using.⁵ Despite the mighty blow, the Mansfield Club suffered its first-ever defeat by the score of 46–31.

Soon afterward, disharmony split the club, and the first nine broke off to form a new club called the Independents. The new club showed signs of new ambition in October when it entered the top division of a tournament in Norwalk. Unfortunately, the Independents had to play without three injured players and their regular catcher and were defeated by the Forest City Club of Cleveland.⁶

In 1868 two New Yorkers, John Clapp and Henry Dietz, were added to the Independents' regular nine. The club now played on grounds on the south side of Newville Road near a cemetery and faced opponents from as far away as Pittsburgh and Washington. The reinforcements enabled the Independents to beat strong rivals like the Railway Unions of Cleveland and the Akrons. But they were still not on a par with the Forest Citys, which beat them twice.⁷

The first defeat prompted a Cleveland journalist to write, "The Mansfield Club has some good material. The catcher [Clapp] received great praise in every quarter. A good pitcher would make it a more formidable opponent. The present incumbent [Rowland] is, probably, the best the club can afford, but all base ball men agree that he is not as efficient in that position as the merits of that club deserves."⁸ It was a portent of things to come.

In 1869 the Independent Club played the most celebrated match in its history when it squared off against the mighty "Red Stockings" of Cincinnati, the first openly professional club in the Midwest. The Red Stockings' fame made them a tremendous draw, and a huge crowd turned out at the fair grounds to watch the Independents lose 48–11. This was followed by an almost equally lopsided loss at the hands of the Independents' old nemesis, the Forest City Club of Cleveland, in which the Mansfield batters were not "able to do anything with those dreadful balls that [Forest City professional pitcher Al] Pratt sent in red hot."⁹

In August, the Forest Citys paid a visit to Mansfield, but a dispute prevented the match from being completed. The visiting club alleged that the Independents had insisted on having the game umpired by James D. Bell, a member of their club. The Forest Citys agreed to start the game that way under the stipulation that a change would be made if he proved unsatisfactory. In the fourth inning, with the home club leading 16–12, the visitors complained that Bell was giving the home batters "bases on three balls with astonishing regularity." But the Independents refused to allow a replacement to be made, and the game ended at that point. To make matters worse, "attendance was not very large, and the gate money was not sufficient to buy a box of matches."¹⁰

As so often happens, the dispute was continued in the newspapers. George Clugston, the secretary of the Independents, wrote to the *Cincinnati Commercial* and alleged that Forest City pitcher Al Pratt had been ordered by teammate Jack Ward to throw at the Mansfield batters and that the visitors stopped play in the fourth inning because Pratt was too tired to continue. An indignant Pratt responded that the first charge was "a falsehood, as I neither received any instructions from Mr. Ward or any other person how I should deliver the balls, as I am presumed to know my own business." He concluded, "As for my being 'tired to death' or 'fagged out' by pitching four innings, I will let those judge who know me, and have frequently seen me pitch nine innings without being 'fagged out.'"¹¹

The matches against the Red Stockings and the Forest Citys showed that clubs like these created a dilemma for less proficient rivals in the region. Clearly, the Independents could not compete with such juggernauts unless the decision was made to plunge wholeheartedly into professionalism. As a result, as the season went on, the Independents dropped more locals in favor of imported players from Philadelphia.

By the end of the season, there was widespread dissatisfaction with this course of action, and the Independents disbanded. It was five years before Mansfield again had a notable club, and when it did, appropriately enough it was Carrothers who managed the new club.¹² This club, known as the Athletics, played its games on a lot located on the north side of East Fourth Street.¹³

As the profiles suggest, the club's players were drawn from the most prominent families of Mansfield, and most of them went on to successful careers in the law, business, or civic matters. By the late 1860s many of them were married and starting families, which undoubtedly also contributed to the demise of Mansfield's first prominent club.

Club Members

James Dorland Bell: Infielder James D. Bell was born on April 19, 1843, in Homer, Ohio. He worked as a leather dealer and died in Mansfield on December 23, 1912.

George Washington Blymyer: George W. Blymyer was born in Shellsburg, Pennsylvania, on October 31, 1839. Three years later, his father moved the family to Mansfield in a covered wagon and set up a hardware store that made him one of that city's pioneer merchants. George and his brother eventually took over the store. By the time he died on April 17, 1930, the street on which he lived was known as Blymyer Avenue in honor of his family's contributions to the city.

George H. Bowman: George H. Bowman served as vice president of the Independents when the club split off in 1867. According to the 1860 census, he was born around 1839 in Ohio. He had left the city by 1869.

John Caldwell Burns: John C. Burns was born on January 26, 1847, in Mansfield, the son of lawyer Barnabas Burns. He served in the Civil War, then attended Hamilton College in New York and graduated from Ohio Wesleyan. Following in his father's footsteps, he also earned a degree from the University of Cincinnati Law School and practiced law in Mansfield as well as serving as city clerk. Eventually he moved to Chicago, where he died on February 11, 1931.[14]

John Clapp: John Clapp was born on July 17, 1851, in Ithaca, New York. He came to Mansfield as a teenager and was the only member of the Independents to play in the major leagues, having an eleven-year career as one of the game's best catchers. At one point, Clapp's services were in such great demand that he actually staged a closed-bid auction and provided his services to the highest bidder. In 1903, Carrothers reported that he was corresponding with Clapp, who was again living in Ithaca and had experienced a run of bad luck in recent years. He had started a business, but lost it as a result of a lengthy illness and had also lost his wife to death. Clapp was starting over as a policeman. The following year, on December 18, 1904, Clapp died in Ithaca. See the Mansfields of Middletown for more on Clapp's life.

George A. Clugston: George Clugston was born around 1843 in Pennsylvania. He co-owned a prominent Mansfield insurance firm and was later mayor and the president of the city's Tri-State league club. He died on September 3, 1911, at the Elks National Home in Bedford City, Virginia.

James Cobean: Infielder James Cobean was born around 1848 in Ohio, and was living in Portsmouth, Virginia, in 1920.

Henry C. Dietz: Henry Dietz was born around 1844 in New York State. He and Clapp were listed as painters in the 1869 city directory. Dietz stayed in Mansfield for several years and worked as a painter, but was gone by the mid–1870s. He may have moved to Denver.

Jacob Hade: Jacob Hade was born on May 17, 1846, and worked as a bookkeeper at the Farmers' National Bank while living in Mansfield. He mostly played the outfield for the Independents but later became the pitcher of the Athletics. He moved to Toledo around 1880 to work as a railroad clerk, and that is where he died on June 17, 1910.

John N. Mowry: John N. Mowry, a doctor, became president of the Independents after the split of August of 1867. He was born in Pennsylvania around 1824 and served as a surgeon for the 86th Ohio Infantry during the Civil War. He lived in Mansfield for twenty-five years before moving to Cleveland, where he died on October 27, 1893.

Robert H. Rowland: Pitcher R. H. Rowland was born in Mansfield on September 8, 1842, the son of a clergyman. He worked as a teller of the Richland National Bank and became county treasurer in 1873. He then moved to Chicago and became a lawyer. He died in Milwaukee on July 1, 1892.

George Snyder: Second baseman George Snyder was born around 1847 and worked as a railroad clerk.

Lyman Arlington Strong: Catcher Lyman A. Strong was born in Bellville, Ohio, on March 2, 1839. He worked as a commission merchant, selling grain, seeds and wool. He died in Mansfield on July 9, 1916.

Arthur Dimon Sturges: Arthur Dimon Sturges was born in Mansfield on August 17, 1847, and became a lumber dealer. He died in Oberlin on May 30, 1923.

Gaylord "Gail" Thomas: Shortstop Gail Thomas was born in Mt. Vernon, Ohio, on July 15, 1841, and moved to Mansfield when very young. During the war, he served in Company D, 102nd Infantry Regiment, but he had to be discharged after seven months due to lung trouble. Thomas's father operated a restaurant until his death in 1860, at which time Gail and one of his brothers took over the business. In the 1870s, he added a billiard room that became popular among the young men of Mansfield. But the 1890s brought a series of tragedies. Gail Thomas sold the restaurant after the death of his only son in 1891. His wife died the next year, and he passed away one year later, on November 10, 1893, at his sister's home in Mt. Vernon.

Other Members: W. Dougherty, Hunt, Manchester, Smith, Webber.

Sources

Cleveland Leader, April 7, 1881; *Mansfield News*, June 3, 1895; *Mansfield News*, December 17, 1902; *Mansfield News*, May 2, 1903; James M. Egan, Jr., *Base Ball on the Western Reserve* (Jefferson, NC: McFarland, 2008); contemporaneous accounts, as noted.

Notes

1. *Cleveland Leader*, April 7, 1881.
2. *Mansfield News*, June 3, 1895.
3. James M. Egan, Jr., *Base Ball on the Western Reserve* (Jefferson, NC: McFarland, 2008), 15.
4. *Mansfield News*, June 3, 1895.
5. *Ibid.*

6. Egan Jr., *Base Ball on the Western Reserve*, 15, 22.
7. *Ibid.*, 26.
8. *Cleveland Herald*, August 22, 1868.
9. *Cleveland Herald*, June 30, 1869.
10. "Tour of the Forest City," *Cleveland Herald*, August 4, 1869, 1.
11. Quoted in the *Cleveland Herald*, August 13, 1869, 3.
12. *Cleveland Leader*, April 7, 1881.
13. *Mansfield News*, December 17, 1902.
14. *Chicago Tribune*, February 12, 1931, 25.

Chapter Four

Cincinnati and Northern Kentucky

❖ *Introduction* (Peter Morris) ❖

The Cincinnati Base Ball Club, which became familiarly known as the Red Stockings, remains the most famous club of the pioneer era of baseball. As masterfully told here by David Ball, that remarkable story emerges in all its fascinating detail: we read in amazement as a legendary baseball nine emerges from a club of Cincinnati lawyers so unambitious that the members complained that the purchase of a $20 chest for bats and balls was "the height of extravagance." Yet it would be a mistake to think that the Cincinnati Base Ball Club was synonymous with the city's baseball scene during the pioneer era.

Instead, as we learn from the other entries in this rich chapter, the 1869 Red Stockings were just one part of an explosion of "base ball fever" that took place in Cincinnati during these years. There was also the Buckeye Club, which came to be remembered as the foils of the Red Stockings, but which, as Ball shows, deserved a better fate. Then there was the Live Oak Club, often credited with bringing the New York Game to Cincinnati although the claim, as Greg Perkins explains, is dubious. Finally, we have the Western Union Base Ball Club, a pioneer African American club that has been rescued from undeserved obscurity by Perkins (with a big hand from early Cincinnati sportswriter Harry Millar).

The fervor also spilled over into the towns of northern Kentucky, especially after the 1867 opening of the John A. Roebling Suspension Bridge connected them to Cincinnati. The Eagles of Brooklyn, Kentucky, indeed, may have predated all of Cincinnati's baseball clubs, as the *Cincinnati Commercial* described them as the "the oldest organization of the kind in this vicinity." The Covington and Copec clubs of Covington began that city's proud baseball heritage and established Willow Run Bottom as the home of Covington baseball. The Holt Club of Newport experienced only fleeting success but does have the distinction of being referred to on a Hall of Fame plaque at Cooperstown.

In the process we also become aware that the early baseball clubs of Cincinnati and Northern Kentucky were closely tied to the townball-playing clubs that preceded or were contemporaries of them. This has long been a source of confusion, with sportswriter William Phelon examining the score sheet from an 1866 townball game between the Buckeye and Magnolia clubs in 1917 and commenting: "The ancient score books also reveal the strange fact that teams of fifty years ago, contrary to the universal modern belief, were NOT limited to nine men per game, and nine only. On the contrary, these ancient clubs threw fifteen or sixteen players into action every afternoon. Puzzling almost beyond explanation, though, is the fact that the last six or seven men on the score cards do not appear merely in late innings, but as taking part in every inning, first as well as last, while the nine men in the upper spaces are shown as scoring right along, without leaving the game."[1] We are at last in position to give the pioneer townball clubs of Cincinnati the recognition they deserve.

Even the abundance of clubs that appear in this chapter is only part of the story of what went on in Cincinnati and surrounding areas during the 1860s. As described by Harry Ellard in *Base Ball in Cincinnati*, the baseball-mad city also included clubs that bore such names as the Woodburns, the Pickwicks, the Great Westerns, the Hun-ki-do-ris, the Crescents, and the Pastimes. "By the middle of 1867," Ellard recalled, "the influence of baseball was being felt in every direction, and new clubs were forming all around the vicinity of the city."[2] One such suburban club was the Mount Auburn Base Ball Club, which featured a young man named William Howard Taft, who would retain his love of the national pastime even after becoming the 27th president of the United States.

Not all of those clubs could be included in this chapter but, thanks to the expert sleuthing and keen eye for detail possessed by Greg Perkins and David Ball, the stories of eight of those clubs have been brought to life. Without further ado, here are the stories of the pioneer clubs of Cincinnati and vicinity and the men who made them possible.

Notes

1. William A. Phelon, "The Team That Never Was Licked," *Baseball Magazine* (January 1917), 74.
2. Harry Ellard, *Base Ball in Cincinnati* (1907; reprint Jefferson, NC: McFarland, 2004), 42.

❖ *Live Oaks of Cincinnati* (Greg Perkins) ❖

Club History

In announcing the birth of the Live Oak National Base Ball Club in July 1866, the *Cincinnati Daily Enquirer* expressed hope that the new team "may be but the beginning of a great number of these clubs, for it [baseball] is decidedly *the* American game." Actually, the new Live Oak Club signaled not a beginning, but a surge in popularity for a game that Cincinnatians had known for almost a decade. Cincinnatians had played New York rules baseball since at least 1858, when a group who called themselves the Base Ball Club held weekly games. Nevertheless, historians of Cincinnati baseball have long followed the *Enquirer's* lead by crediting the Live Oaks, especially Rochester, New York, transplants Theodore Frost and Matthew M. Yorston, with introducing baseball to Cincinnati.[1]

Yorston took his first steps as the reputed "father of Cincinnati baseball" in the spring of 1861 when he and several other young men who lived in Cincinnati's West End founded the Buckeye Base Ball Club. He reportedly had to make baseballs for the team to use because they were not available for sale in Cincinnati. The Buckeyes arose to answer a challenge from nearby Brooklyn, Kentucky, for a game of baseball. Officers of the Buckeye Club included Samuel A. Butts, Jr., President; Matthew M. Yorston, Vice-President; John S. Conner, Secretary; and John Draper, Treasurer. The club's Directors were William Hollenbeck, Octavius Tudor, and Marcellis Dyer. Other club members included Wash Blair, John C. Davis, and James Fogarty, Jr. An 1870 newspaper account suggested that recently migrated Easterners comprised the Buckeyes; however, nearly all the known Buckeyes, except for Yorston, were Ohio natives. The Buckeyes played three times a week at the Orphan Asylum lot in the West End. The coming Civil War doomed the young Buckeye Club. In a 1919 interview, James Fogarty, Jr., blamed the war for breaking up the club. Several Buckeyes, including Draper, Butts, Hollenbeck, and Yorston joined the Union armed forces.[2]

Joined by new players, the erstwhile Buckeyes emerged after the war as the Live Oak National Base Ball Club. During the war, another group had usurped the name "Buckeye" for their townball club. Fogarty recalled that he and his friends selected the name "Live Oak" as the Buckeye Base Ball Club's new name to honor a tree that his teammates had seen during their military service in the South. The new name also may have served as a tribute to the Live Oak Club of Rochester, New York. Rochester had been home to Yorston, Frost, and Sylvester Hicks during the late 1850s. The Live Oaks of Cincinnati kept their home grounds in their West End neighborhood at the foot of Richmond Street. According to an 1866 article, the Live Oak uniform consisted of "skyblue caps, white shirts with an oak leaf design, and dark blue pants." A photo of Matthew Yorston in his Live Oak uniform later appeared in Albert G. Spalding's *America's National Game* (1911).[3]

As a pioneer baseball team, the Live Oaks became linked with many early Cincinnati baseball milestones. Cincinnati's first match game of baseball pitted the Live Oaks against the Eagle Base Ball Club of Brooklyn, Kentucky, on September 8, 1866. Later that season, the Live Oaks also joined the region's first baseball tournaments held at the Florence, Kentucky, fair grounds and the Union Cricket Club grounds in Cincinnati. The Union Cricket Club tournament may have attracted baseball's first paid audience in Cincinnati. Although the Live Oaks failed to win a game in the Florence tournament, the club finished as the runner-up to the Cincinnati Base Ball Club in the Cincinnati event. Moreover, the Live Oak Club won three games and captured a second place prize in the 1867 Ohio State Base Ball Tournament. Besides tournament play, the Live Oaks also supported baseball in Cincinnati by sponsoring a junior club and joining the Cincinnati and Buckeye clubs as local members of the National Association of Base Ball Players.[4]

Unlike the Cincinnati and Buckeye Clubs, the Live Oaks remained an amateur team. As it became apparent that the Live Oaks would, observed the *Cincinnati Daily Gazette*, "depend solely on home talent," the club transformed itself from a neighborhood team to a metropolitan organization. The Live Oak Club made several changes to its first nine as its membership spread from the West End to the rest of the city. Expanding streetcar services and the 1867 opening of the Roebling Suspension Bridge that connected Cincinnati to Covington, Kentucky, made it easier for players to go across town for practices and games. For the 1868 season, the Live Oaks recruits included Michael Beckler, a noted catcher of the Excelsior Town Ball Club, and Will Skiff of the Buckeyes. The Live Oaks also lost players, including founders John Draper to the Cincinnati Club in 1867 and John Brockway to the Great Westerns in 1869. Although the Live Oaks could not compete with professional teams, the club remained a good enough draw locally to stay on the schedules of the professional Buckeyes and Red Stockings. A rained-out 1869 game with the Live Oaks and the ensuing lost gate receipts left the Cincinnati Club in dire financial straits as it commenced an Eastern tour.[5]

During the 1870 and 1871 seasons, the Live Oaks probably fielded their strongest nines. The Live Oaks lured local players from the Cincinnati and Buckeye clubs who had been replaced by professionals. Former Buckeyes Ben Brookshaw, William Boake, John Boake, and George W. Smith switched to the Live Oak Club. Several ex–Red Stockings including J. William Johnson, John Condit How, and Oak Taylor also joined the Live Oaks.[6]

When the Cincinnati Red Stockings stopped hiring players after 1870 season, the Live Oaks at last became Cincinnati's leading baseball team. The Live Oaks played several games that season with National Association clubs as they took their Western tours. Amateur clubs from as far as Chicago and Brooklyn, New York, came to Cincinnati to play the Live Oaks in 1871.[7]

The Live Oaks faded from existence sometime after 1871, a likely victim of the malaise that beset baseball in Cincinnati and the West during the early 1870s. In 1871, the National Association of Professional Base Ball Players had teams in Chicago; Rockford, Illinois; Fort Wayne Indiana; and Cleveland, Ohio. Only the Cleveland team remained in the National Association for the 1872 season. By 1873, the National Association had no teams west of the Alleghenies. The Great Chicago Fire of 1871 kept Chicago from fielding a National Association club until 1874. Cincinnati's Union Grounds, home of the Red Stockings, was dismantled in April 1872 — an event that led the *Cincinnati Daily Gazette* to declare an end to baseball in Cincinnati for the foreseeable future. The lack of western travel obligations and no enclosed grounds in Cincinnati left Eastern teams in the National Association with little incentive to come to Cincinnati and play top amateur clubs like the Live Oaks. By July 1872, the *Cincinnati Daily Gazette* could lament a "dull" baseball market in Cincinnati with meager "offering of first class, second class, or third class matches."[8]

Members, Buckeye Base Ball Club (1861) and Live Oak Base Ball Club

Robert Allison: President Live Oak Base Ball Club (1868). Born March 4, 1831, in Philadelphia, Robert Allison moved to Cincinnati as a young man. He became superintendent of the Franklin Type Foundry and a city council member from the Second Ward. He died in Cincinnati on March 23, 1904.[9]

Michael Beckler: Catcher and Captain (1868). Beckler was a catcher for the Excelsior Town Ball Club in Cincinnati before the Civil War. He later leased one of Cincinnati's most historic houses — the Jacob Strader mansion on Third Street — and converted it to a resort.[10]

James R. Blair: Director, Live Oak Base Ball Club (1867). Blair was born in Cincinnati around 1844 to Samuel and Mary A. Blair. Blair worked in his family's ice dealership. He died in Cincinnati on November 17, 1887.[11]

David M. Bleaks: Director, Live Oak Base Ball Club (1868). Bleaks was born around 1823 in Wallsburg, Virginia, to John and Dorcas Bleaks. Bleaks worked as a bank detective and later became police chief in Cincinnati during the 1870s. David Bleaks died in Cincinnati of Bright's disease on December 17, 1887.[12]

John R. Brockway: Director, Live Oak Base Ball Club (1867). Brockway served in the 30th New York Volunteer Infantry. He was a photographer with a studio at 161 West 4th Street in Cincinnati. While a member of the Live Oaks, Brockway won honors as best team captain at the 1867 Ohio State Base Ball Tournament. Brockway was a well-known umpire for several years — he worked three games for the National League during the late 1870s. Brockway lived in Cincinnati's West End on Laurel Street until moving to Newport, Kentucky, where he died in 1899.[13]

Samuel A. Butts, Jr.: President of the Buckeye Base Ball Club (1861). Butts was born in Kentucky around 1839 to Samuel and Lucinda Butts. His father was a cooper. Samuel became a teacher in the Cincinnati school system. During the Civil War, Butts served as a 2nd Lieutenant in Company E of the 138th Ohio Volunteer Infantry. This company included several members of the Buckeye Town Ball Club. Butts does not appear to have been involved with the Live Oak Club after the name change.[14]

John Sanborn Conner: Secretary of the Buckeye Base Ball Club (1861). A Cincinnati native, Conner was born June 30, 1844, to Dr. Phineas and Eliza A. Conner. Dr. Conner passed away when John was ten years old. John S. Conner attended his father's alma mater, Dartmouth College, class of 1865, and later became a prominent Cincinnati attorney and judge. He died in Cincinnati on July 11, 1911.[15]

John Corwin Davis: President, Live Oak Base Ball Club (1866–67); Vice-President, Live Oak Base Ball Club (1868). Davis was born May 15, 1841, in Cincinnati. His father was a native of Wales. Davis graduated from Cincinnati's Woodward High School and became a clerk in the firm of R. O'Leary Company, a cigar manufacturer. He died in Cincinnati on August 14, 1924.[16]

Dr. John Draper: Treasurer, Buckeye Base Ball Club (1861); Director, Live Oak National Base Ball Club (1866). Draper was born January 20, 1844, in Cincinnati to Joseph and Martha Draper. He served in Company D, 137th Ohio Volunteer Infantry during the Civil War. Draper was the catcher and captain of the Live Oaks in 1866. In 1867, Draper organized a junior team for the Cincinnati Base Ball Club. Like John R. Brockway, Draper later became a well-known umpire in the Ohio Valley. He umpired games for both the National Association and the National League. Draper studied to become a physician, but apparently never practiced medicine. For thirty years Draper served as secretary to the chief of police in Cincinnati. He died of tuberculosis on December 3, 1911, in Cincinnati.[17]

Robert A. Dunlap: Director, Live Oak Base Ball Club (1868). Born in Ireland in 1830, Dunlap had moved to Cincinnati by the early 1850s. He later became the secretary of the Cincinnati Street Railway Company. Dunlap died in Cincinnati in 1904.[18]

Marcellis Dyer: Director of the Buckeye Base Ball Club (1861). Dyer was born around 1845 in Ohio to Charles and Emeline Dyer. The 1861 Cincinnati Directory lists Charles

Dyer as a notions dealer and residing at 37 Everett Street in the Eighth Ward.[19]

James Fogarty, Jr.: Member, Buckeye Base Ball Club (1861); Secretary, Live Oak Base Ball Club (1867–68). Fogarty was born May 11, 1845, in Cincinnati. He was a buyer of tea and coffee for what later became the Cincinnati-based Kroger supermarket chain. Fogarty died on October 28, 1936, in Cincinnati.[20]

Theodore Carr Frost: Director, Live Oak Base Ball Club (1866). Frost was born December 20, 1844, in Rochester, New York. He first came to Cincinnati when his family moved to the area in 1858. His father, George Frost, was a printer for a Cincinnati newspaper. Theodore Frost returned to Rochester by the summer of 1860. In 1862, he enlisted in the 140th New York Volunteer Infantry. Frost spent about six months in a Confederate prison camp. He returned to Cincinnati to stay after the war and worked as a machinist. Frost was a pitcher for the Live Oaks in 1866. He moved to Toledo, Ohio, after 1920, where he died on November 16, 1928.[21]

Sylvester Hicks: Second Base, Live Oak Base Ball Club (1866). Hicks was born in New York around 1846. He moved to Cincinnati from Rochester before 1866. Hicks returned to Rochester before 1870, where he worked as a salesman. He later moved to Seattle, where he died on December 18, 1920.[22]

William Hollenbeck: Director of the Buckeye Base Ball Club (1861). Hollenbeck was born around 1845 in Ohio. His parents, Martin and Annie, were immigrants from Hanover, Germany. William fought for the Union during the Civil War, serving in the 21st and 128th Ohio Volunteer Infantry. In 1870, Hollenbeck still lived in Cincinnati and worked as a clerk in a grocery store. He died before April 1895, when his widow Matilda applied for his military pension.[23]

Benjamin E. Hopkins: Treasurer, Live Oak Base Ball Club (1868). Hopkins was born in Cincinnati on March 27, 1834, to Benjamin and Rachel Hopkins. Benjamin graduated from Cincinnati's Woodward High School and later became a banker. During the Civil War, Hopkins served as a lieutenant in Company C of the 137th Ohio Volunteer Infantry. Hopkins, who was a Quaker, was the superintendent of the Friends' School in Cincinnati. He died in Cincinnati on January 7, 1889.[24]

William Irwin Torrence: President, Live Oak Base Ball Club (1868). Torrence was born in Cincinnati on September 9, 1835, to George P. and Mary Torrence. The Torrence family was one of Cincinnati's pioneer families. William graduated from Cincinnati's Woodward High School. During the Civil War, Torrence served as a captain in Company A of the 138th Ohio Volunteer Infantry. He worked as a clerk in the Torrence family's mercantile stores. William I. Torrence died of consumption (tuberculosis) in Cincinnati on July 4, 1881.[25]

Octavius Tudor: Director, Buckeye Base Ball Club (1861). Octavius Tudor was born July 29, 1844, in Cincinnati to John and Anne Tudor. He later became a banker and joined the Cincinnati Base Ball Club. He died on July 15, 1904, of consumption (tuberculosis) in Cincinnati.[26]

Matthew McKay Yorston: Vice-President, Buckeye Base Ball Club (1861); Director, Live Oak National Base Ball Club (1866–67). Born September 5, 1842, in Glasgow, Scotland, Matthew Yorston immigrated to the United States in 1851. Yorston's family lived in Rochester, New York, where young Matthew probably first encountered the New York game. By 1858, Yorston had moved to Cincinnati, where for several years he worked for and boarded with DeRobigne M. Bennett, a Rochester druggist who had moved to Cincinnati in 1859. Bennett later became a well-known publisher of free-thought literature. His trial and subsequent conviction for sending obscene literature through the mail made Bennett a standard-bearer of free-speech reformers. During the Civil War, Yorston served in the Union Navy as a mate on the gunboat *Kenwood*. After the war, Yorston opened his own drugstore and became one of Cincinnati's leading pharmacists. He played shortstop for the Live Oaks in 1866 and 1867. Yorston suffered a debilitating stroke in 1898 and died December 18, 1914, in Cincinnati.[27]

Notes

1. *Cincinnati Daily Enquirer*, July 7, 1866; Greg Perkins, "The Cincinnati Game: Townball in Cincinnati, 1858–1866," *Base Ball, A Journal of the Early Game* 2 (Fall 2008), 35–46; For early histories of Cincinnati baseball see *Cincinnati Daily Times*, April 15, 1868; *Cincinnati Commercial*, August 21, 1870; *Cincinnati Commercial*, March 2, 1879; Harry Ellard, *Base Ball in Cincinnati: A History* (Cincinnati: Johnson & Hardin, 1907; reprint, Cincinnati: Ohio Book Store, 1987), 34.

2. *New York Clipper*, April 21, 1861; *Cincinnati Commercial*, August 21, 1870; *Cincinnati Commercial*, March 16, 1879; *Cincinnati Post*, August 14, 1919; 1860 census; *Williams' Cincinnati Directory 1861*; *Cincinnati Daily Enquirer*, March 14, 1861; *Cincinnati Post*, August 14, 1919.

3. *Cincinnati Post*, August 14, 1919; *Rochester* (NY) *Evening Express*, July 26, 1866, cited in Priscilla Astifan, "Baseball in the 19th Century, Part 2," *Rochester History* 62 (Spring 2000), 4; *Cincinnati Daily Times*, September 10, 1866; Albert G. Spalding, *America's National Game* (New York: American Sports Publishing Company, 1911), 72.

4. *Cincinnati Daily Times*, October 18, 1866; *Cincinnati Daily Gazette*, October 18, 1866; *Cincinnati Commercial*, October 19, 1866; *Cincinnati Daily Times*, November 3, 1866; *Cincinnati Commercial*, November 4, 1866; *Cincinnati Daily Gazette*, September 19, 1867; Ellard, *Base Ball in Cincinnati*, 67.

5. *Cincinnati Daily Gazette*, May 4, 1869; *Cincinnati Daily Gazette*, May 6, 1868; *Cincinnati Commercial-Tribune*, August 15, 1912.

6. *Cincinnati Daily Gazette*, June 21, 1871; *Cincinnati Commercial*, August 13, 1871.

7. *Cincinnati Daily Gazette*, June 1, 1871; *Cincinnati Commercial*, June 8, 1871; *Cincinnati Commercial*, July 6, 1871.

8. Information about National Association teams came from http://www.baseball-reference.com/; *Cincinnati Daily Gazette*, April 11, 1872; *Cincinnati Daily Gazette*, July 12, 1872.

9. *Cincinnati Daily Gazette*, May 6, 1868; Robert Allison burial record — Spring Grove Cemetery, Cincinnati, Ohio; *Cincinnati Commercial Tribune*, March 26, 1904.

10. *Cincinnati Daily Times*, April 15, 1868; *Cincinnati Commercial-Tribune*, August 10, 1912.

11. *Cincinnati Daily Gazette*, March 11, 1867; 1870 census; James R. Blair burial record — Spring Grove Cemetery, Cincinnati, Ohio.

12. *Cincinnati Daily Gazette*, March 16, 1868; Charles Theodore Grieve, *Centennial History of Cincinnati and Representative Citizens* (Chicago: Biographical Publishing Company, 1904), Vol. 1, 970; David M. Bleaks burial record—Spring Grove Cemetery, Cincinnati, Ohio.

13. *Cincinnati Daily Gazette*, March 11, 1867; Ellard, *Base Ball in Cincinnati*, 66; *Kentucky Post*, October 28, 1899. For information about Brockway's umpiring career see http://www.retrosheet.org/.

14. 1860 census; Greg Perkins, "The Cincinnati Game: Townball in Cincinnati, 1858–1866," *Base Ball, A Journal of the Early Game* 2 (Fall 2008), 35–46.

15. John Sanborn Conner burial record—Spring Grove Cemetery, Cincinnati, Ohio; Dr. Phineas Conner burial record—Spring Grove Cemetery, Cincinnati, Ohio; the Rev. George T. Chapman, *Sketches of the Alumni at Dartmouth College* (Cambridge: Riverside Press, 1867), 470, available at http://books.google.com/books.

16. *Cincinnati Daily Gazette*, March 11, 1867; *Cincinnati Daily Gazette*, March 16, 1868; *Cincinnati Commercial-Tribune*, August 10, 1912; *Memoirs of the Ohio Valley* (Chicago: Robert O. Law Co., 1920), Volume III, 269–270; John C. Davis, burial record—Spring Grove Cemetery, Cincinnati, Ohio.

17. *Sporting Life*, December 16, 1911, 12; Dr. John Draper burial record—Spring Grove Cemetery, Cincinnati, Ohio. For information about Draper's umpiring career see http://www.retrosheet.org/.

18. *Cincinnati Daily Gazette*, March 16, 1868; *Cincinnati Commercial-Tribune*, August 10, 1912; *Williams' Cincinnati Directory for 1852–53*; *Cincinnati Enquirer*, January 11, 1904.

19. 1860 census; *Williams' Cincinnati Directory 1861*.

20. James Fogarty burial record—Spring Grove Cemetery, Cincinnati, Ohio; *Cincinnati Post*, 14 August 1919.

21. *History of Cincinnati and Hamilton County, Ohio: Their Past and Present* (Cincinnati: S. B. Nelson & Co., 1894), 991; 1860 census; Theodore C. Frost burial record—Spring Grove Cemetery, Cincinnati, Ohio.

22. Ellard, *Base Ball in Cincinnati*, 34; *Rochester* (NY) *Evening Express*, July 26, 1866, cited in Astifan, "Baseball in the 19th Century, Part 2," 4; 1870 census.

23. 1860 census; *Williams' Cincinnati Directory 1861*; 1870 census; William Hollenbeck Civil War pension index card.

24. *Cincinnati Daily Gazette*, March 16, 1868; "Old Woodward" Club, *"Old Woodward," A Memorial* (Cincinnati: Robert Clarke & Company, 1884), 200; Benjamin E. Hopkins burial record—Spring Grove Cemetery, Cincinnati, Ohio.

25. *Cincinnati Daily Gazette*, March 16, 1868; "Old Woodward" Club, *"Old Woodward," A Memorial*, 293; William I. Torrence burial record—Spring Grove Cemetery, Cincinnati, Ohio.

26. 1850, 1870, and 1900 censuses, *Williams' Cincinnati Directory 1861*; Octavius Tudor burial record—Spring Grove Cemetery, Cincinnati, Ohio; Ellard, *Base Ball in Cincinnati*, 123.

27. *Cincinnati Enquirer*, December 19, 1914; *Cincinnati Times-Star*, December 19, 1914; *Rochester* (NY) *Evening Express*, July 26, 1866, cited in Astifan, "Baseball in the 19th Century, Part 2," 4; Matthew Yorston burial record—Spring Grove Cemetery, Cincinnati, Ohio; 1860 census. For information about DeRobigne M. Bennett, see Roderick Bradford, *D.M. Bennett, The Truth Seeker* (Amherst: Prometheus Books, 2006).

❖ Buckeyes of Cincinnati (David Ball) ❖

CLUB HISTORY

Remembered today as the foil and unsuccessful local rival of the famous "Red Stockings" of Cincinnati, the Buckeye Club originated as a group of school teachers and probably some students who started playing ball, probably a little before 1860, in a vacant lot at the Commercial Hospital, later called the Cincinnati Hospital. By 1861 they had moved to the Orphan Asylum Lot on Elm Street, where Music Hall sits today. Both playing fields were located in the East End and the bottoms of the Mill Creek Valley, an area that was the heartland of Cincinnati baseball up until the construction of Riverfront Stadium downtown in the 1970s.

Although the group played ball, they were not yet actually playing baseball. When they met on October 1, 1863, in the office of a local jeweler to organize formally, they did so as the Cincinnati Buckeye Townball Club. Townball was the name given in Cincinnati to a locally popular variation of the family of games from which modern baseball developed. Much of the information traditionally used to tell the story of Cincinnati townball comes from baseball-centered reminiscences published in later years, and they tend to depict townball as a minor pastime enjoyed in a desultory way by small numbers of adult Cincinnatians. More recently, we have begun to examine newspaper sources from the late 1850s and early 1860s that make it possible to see that the townball scene in the area of Cincinnati was actually fairly active, starting earlier, continuing longer and participated in by more people on a more organized basis than has hitherto been apparent.

Various townball clubs were active across the Ohio River in Northern Kentucky, but in Cincinnati the most prominent names were the Excelsiors and the Buckeyes. Later accounts suggest that the Excelsiors and the Buckeyes were related in some way, but disagree on exactly what that relationship was. They may actually have been a single group operating under two different names, first as the Excelsiors and then in more organized form as the Buckeyes. The Buckeyes may have broken off from the Excelsiors in an amoeba-like schism of the sort that typifies such groups. We do know that another club played baseball under the name of Buckeyes before the Civil War, and when they re-formed after the conflict they called themselves the Live Oaks because the Buckeyes name was now taken, and this does suggest that it was only some years after they started playing at the Commercial Hospital that the club remembered as the Buckeyes took that name. What is clear, at any rate, is that the core membership of the Buckeye club that formed in 1863 was made up of the school teachers who had been playing for several years, although by this time, if not earlier, some members followed other professions.

After their formal organization the Buckeyes played a few games but disbanded in the spring of 1864 when several members were mustered into military service. Their enlistments were only for one hundred days, however, and by the following year the Buckeyes were playing match games of townball again.

In 1866 Cincinnati was swept by a wave of enthusiasm for the more sophisticated New York game, the game we simply call baseball. The Buckeyes are known to have piled up a 146–21 victory at townball over an aggregation called the Magnolias as late as May 1866, but they were also beginning to play the new game. In the fall they reorganized as the Buckeye Base Ball Club, adding new members including Mayor Charles Wilstach, who was probably just an honorary member but seems to have been generally willing to lend a helping hand to baseball clubs, for he also donated money to the Red Stockings.

The change to baseball may have been good for the growth of the organization in numbers and finances; at any rate, the Buckeyes were soon thriving, and perhaps the most striking testimony to that fact is the election in December 1867 of club president George Sands to the presidency of the National Association of Base Ball Players. Sands became the first man not from the eastern seaboard to hold that office. In April 1868 it was announced that the Buckeyes were to play at the Buckeye Trotting Park in the suburb of Carthage, farther up the Mill Creek Valley and north of their Elm Street location. The Orphan Lot had probably been unenclosed, and so it would not have been possible for the club to charge spectators an attendance fee, as they could at the trotting park. Before long, the Buckeyes moved back toward town, to a location about a mile west of the Orphanage, where they leased a new field with the odd name of the Iron Slag Grounds. Their new grounds were just north of Lincoln Park, where their Cincinnati Club rivals played. The Buckeyes intended to pay the rent there by having ice skating in the winter as well as charging admission to their ball games.

By 1868 the Buckeye Club was traveling out of Ohio, touring Midwestern cities including Chicago and St. Louis. On the tour, they won all eleven games they played, meeting second-tier opposition but defeating strong clubs such as the Excelsiors and Atlantics of Chicago and the Forest City clubs of Cleveland and Rockford, Illinois. Against several of the strongest professional clubs of the day — the Athletics and Atlantics of Philadelphia and Brooklyn, for example — they lost by respectable margins, and against most Cincinnati rivals they won by such impressive scores as 40–13, 53–4, and 83–11.

The Buckeyes did not achieve these results with a lineup featuring the mix of school teachers and other ordinary Cincinnatians who made up their core membership. Their 1868 roster featured four professional players imported from the heartland of the game in the east. Besides Charlie Sweasy and Andy Leonard from the Irvington club in New Jersey, they brought in a battery from Philadelphia, Cherokee Fisher, a hard-throwing pitcher, and tough catcher Patsy Dockney, who captained the nine, filling most of the duties of a modern player-manager. The rest of the Buckeyes were local players. The best of them, shortstop Ben Brookshaw, is said by Harry Ellard, chronicler of early Cincinnati baseball, to have been among the founding members of the Buckeyes in 1863, but this is probably a mistake, for Brookshaw lived in northern Kentucky across the Ohio River from Cincinnati and had played for a strong club named for his native Covington, Kentucky, until the Covingtons disbanded, and this does not appear to have occurred until after 1863. Brookshaw did not appear in the Buckeyes' first nine until 1868, which is unlikely if he had been a club member, for he was one of the very finest local players and retained his place in the 1868 lineup although he never practiced with the club, probably because he could not get the time off from his job as a tobacco worker. Like the paid Eastern players, it seems likely that he had been recruited into the club for his playing abilities on the field rather than for personal qualities that made him fit in well socially with the other Buckeye Club members.

As rapidly as the Buckeyes had advanced in the brief time since they had converted to the new game, they did not by any means have things all their own way. Another organization, known simply as the Cincinnati Base Ball Club but soon to be famous under their Red Stockings nickname, had organized in July 1866. The Cincinnati's membership included Ivy League–educated attorneys, with an admixture of local businessmen. Among them were movers and shakers in the city, and although their members had less experience as ball players than the Buckeyes, they would not be content to take second place to anyone. In the waning days of their first season the Cincinnatis played four games, all but one against the Buckeyes. The Buckeyes won the first by a close 20–18 score, although some of their players were so inexperienced at baseball that they threw the ball at base runners, a feature of townball. After the Cincinnatis easily won the second game, the Buckeyes came back for a 41–31 win on October 27, giving them a win in the series and bragging rights as the best club in the city. This was also the last time a Buckeye nine would ever defeat the Red Stockings.

In 1867 the Cincinnatis had recruited a much stronger lineup that beat the Buckeyes convincingly on four separate occasions in a season during which their only loss was to the professional Nationals of Washington. After the season, the Red Stockings raided the Buckeyes to acquire the services of Charlie Gould, who would go on to play first base for the Red Stockings and become the only Cincinnati player of his generation to go on to a professional career. The Red Stockings brought in a contingent of professionals, as well, to compete with those of the Buckeyes, and enjoyed another successful season.

For the Buckeyes, on the other hand, the year was a frustrating one, in spite of their unbeaten string on the Midwestern tour and their domination of most local opposition. They lost to the Red Stockings 28–10 in their first game on May 23. During the last half of the season their professional players were constantly rumored to be planning to leave the club. Patsy Dockney, a talented catcher but a very rough character, missed time early in the season after being stabbed in a bar fight, then jumped the club in August after quarreling with club officials. The Buckeyes recruited three Washington professionals for their return match with the Red Stockings, leading to a protest by the Cincinnati Club that turned out to be moot when the Cincinnatis won again. By the end of the season, Sweasy and Fisher had jumped ship as well, and the Buckeyes were using more of their amateur players to fill out their lineup.

The experience with hired mercenaries had been unpleasant, but it may be that the defections were due at least in part to a failure on the Buckeyes' part to pay the men as promised, for it is clear the club was having difficulty meeting the financial responsibilities it had taken on by renting a new facility and fielding a partially professional nine. During the off-season, Sweasy, Leonard and Dick Hurley, a late recruit, all went over to the Cincinnati Club, which set out to field a complete team of professionals. The Buckeyes announced in January that their lineup would also be fully professional, only to reverse course in March, reporting that, if any of their players were paid at all, they would limit themselves to a professional battery backed by amateur fielders. A correspondent to an Eastern newspaper wrote sourly, "One year's experience with an imported nine was sufficient; home players were debarred from playing, or even practicing, while their pockets were taxed for those whose only interest in the club was their weekly salaries." Given that the Buckeyes had been planning to hire players only a few months before, these words are easily dismissed as sour grapes, but the sentiments seem plausible as an expression of how many club members may have perceived the experience of the previous season.

The Buckeyes were in a difficult position, though. They could decide not to pay salaries to professional players, but they could not as easily renounce the lease they had signed, and they needed strong gate receipts to do that. Although no one could know that the Cincinnati Club's Red Stockings were about to start on one of the most famous seasons in baseball history, it must have seemed obvious to the Buckeye leadership that income would dwindle if they could present only an amateur club playing almost literally in the shadow of the Red Stockings' Union Grounds to the immediate south. By April, the club was in court, requesting a receiver. The lease on their park was given to S. K. Stephens, a club member, who made the field available to the Buckeyes as well as to bicyclists. The Buckeyes, amateurs once again, played a lackluster series of games. On July 22 they met the Cincinnati Club and fell, 71–15 in five innings. By the end of August, the club's financial condition was bad enough that the Red Stockings played them another game as a benefit for the Buckeyes, who received all the receipts, and this time the Red Stockings rolled over them by a score of 103–8. Such as it was, it was the last hurrah for the Buckeyes, who disbanded after the 1868 season and never played again.

In histories of early baseball, the Buckeyes are forever cast as unsuccessful rivals of the famous Red Stockings. A Cincinnati newspaper suggested that, had the Red Stockings' manager Harry Wright been a Buckeye, the latter club might have emerged as Cincinnati's strongest. The Cincinnatis were indeed fortunate to have secured the services of the first great baseball manager, but strong as the Buckeyes' organization probably was in comparison with the ordinary baseball club, it is questionable whether they could have prevailed under any circumstances in a contest against the array of money and civic leadership the Cincinnati Club enjoyed. The Buckeyes' experience, at any rate, was not unusual among baseball clubs of their day. For the greater part of a decade they had been a stable organization, playing ball among themselves in apparent contentment. Ambition and a year's trial of running a partially professional team had virtually broken them, as professional baseball would break so many other clubs, and it seems that interest was lacking to reconstitute the club on its old basis. The Buckeyes' disappearance seemed to seal the Red Stockings' triumph over them, but the Cincinnati Club, for all its spectacular success, would follow essentially the same path to extinction within about a few years.

Club Members

John Leonard Boake: Born September 24, 1841, Pennsylvania. Boake was the eldest son of John Boake, who came to Cincinnati around the late 1840s and operated a wagon-making business until his retirement about 1880. Harry Ellard's history of Cincinnati baseball listed the younger John Boake as the Buckeyes' left fielder in 1866 and 1867. He had served two brief enlistments in the Union Army and worked with his father as a wheelwright. Around 1880 he separated from the family firm and started businesses of his own, primarily as a stationer, printer and bookbinder. By 1910 he was working as a salesman for someone else's printing firm and living in Covington, Kentucky, across the Ohio River from Cincinnati. He died in Covington on July 22, 1912.

William H. K. Boake: Born on October 1, 1846, in Philadelphia. Boake played center field for the Buckeyes alongside his older brother John. Like his brother, William served two brief enlistments during the Civil War and subsequently worked in his father's wagon business, which does not appear to have thrived after the elder Boake's retirement in 1880, for his three sons subsequently worked in relatively menial jobs, William as a cigar packer and then as a rodman in the county engineer's office. He died in Cincinnati on December 11, 1910.

Ben Brookshaw: See the Covington and Copec Clubs of Kentucky.

B.O.M. (Bodo Otto Morgan) DeBeck: Born March 1830, New Jersey. Relatively old for a member of an amateur club, DeBeck was apparently not related to Jesse DeBeck, a fellow founding member of the Buckeye club. He was not a teacher as were a large number of the Buckeyes, but for many years he was secretary of the Cincinnati school board. His wife Martha died in March 1912, and he passed away the following September 9.

Jesse P. J. DeBeck: Born around 1844, Ohio. DeBeck was the son of William DeBeck, a New York–born painter, and his wife Martha. Like many of the Buckeyes, he served in the Union Army, but DeBeck enlisted in a Kentucky regiment in November 1861. A *Daily Illinois State Journal* account of the Battle of Chickamauga claims he was originally discharged as underage, and later reenlisted. He suffered serious wounds at Chickamauga but recovered to become one of the Buckeyes' founding members after the war. After teaching for some years, around 1884 he became the Covington reporter for the *Cincinnati Times Star*. He died in December 1898.

Patsy Dockney: Born around 1844, Ireland, and a Civil War veteran. When the Buckeyes decided to import hired professional players from the East in 1868, Dockney was chosen to fill the crucial roles of captain and catcher. A preseason newspaper article described Dockney and Harry Wright, the Cincinnati Club's captain, as old and mutually respectful friends as well as rivals (*Cincinnati Times*, April 15, 1868). In truth, the pairing of the upright and abstemious Wright with Dockney fell little short of the bizarre, for Dockney was a roisterer and wastrel whose lifestyle was summarized as "to play ball every afternoon and fight and drink every night." Less than two weeks after the *Times*' pleasant notice of him, Dockney was severely knifed in a Cincinnati dive. He recovered to play in June but jumped the club in August and went to New York. Moving rapidly from club to club, or "revolving," was a habit with Dockney, but, confirmed reprobate that he was, it is not impossible that on this occasion Dockney may have been as much sinned against as sinning. Most of the Buckeyes' professional players were dissatisfied with their treatment, and it would not be surprising if the club had difficulty keeping up with their salaries. Dockney's hard lifestyle drove him from the game early, and he died some time in the 1880s after another barroom stabbing.

Stephen Faulkner: Harry Ellard, historian of early Cincinnati baseball, lists "Steven Faulkner" as a member of the club from about 1867. He is one of the few individuals we know of who was not either a founding member of the club or a later addition to the first nine. Ellard's "Steven Faulkner" should probably be identified as Stephen Faulkner, who was born in Boston on May 29, 1825. About 1855 Faulkner established a Cincinnati company running a planing mill, in partnership with two brothers named Taylor. He died at his home in nearby Madisonville on April 13, 1877, and by the early 1880s the Taylors appear to have sold the business.

Cherokee Fisher: One of the hardest-throwing pitchers of his generation, Fisher was imported along with catcher Patsy Dockney to be the Buckeyes' battery in 1868. Fisher returned east in 1869 and continued his baseball career until age and the introduction of new pitching techniques such as the curveball eroded his value in the late 1870s. See the Unions of Lansingburgh (Troy "Haymakers") for more details on Fisher's remarkable life.

Charles Gould: See Cincinnati Base Ball Club ("Red Stockings").

Judson Harmon: Born Newton, Ohio, February 3, 1846. A law student who was not a particularly prominent member of the Buckeyes, Harmon later became better known than any of his fellow club members as attorney general and two-term governor of Ohio. His membership in the club is mentioned in a letter to the editor of the *New York Times* (April 24, 1908, p. 8).

Frank Harvey: Born England, around 1849. A clerk by occupation, Harvey was elected the Buckeyes' secretary at their first meeting. He was one of two club delegates to the convention of the National Association of Base Ball Players in December 1866 and was elected the Ohio state association's secretary at its initial organizational meeting the following September. In the early 1880s he disappears from the Cincinnati city directories.

William F. "Dick" Hurley: See Olympics of Washington.

Andrew J. Leonard: See Cincinnati Base Ball Club ("Red Stockings").

Philip N. Lishawa: Born in Philadelphia around 1842. As a one-armed pitcher and a delegate to the National Association of Base Ball Players convention in New York in December 1866, Lishawa was a conspicuous figure, yet information on him is difficult to find, in part because the family name is sometimes spelled Lishewa or Lishauer. He was employed as an assessor before his untimely death in February 12, 1869. His widow, Mary (Mollie) Price Lishawa, was a teacher. He was also survived by a daughter, Luella.

George Fox Sands: Born on March 9, 1836, in Cincinnati, Sands was the Buckeyes' second baseman. More importantly, he served as the club's first president — the only one, so far as we know — and in December 1867 he was elected the president of the National Association of Base Ball Players, the first chosen for the office from west of the Alleghenys. During and for many years after his involvement with the Buckeyes, he served as a principal in the Cincinnati school system. He died in Cincinnati on June 18, 1922.

John B. Scheidemantle: Born on October 8, 1842, Cincinnati. Scheidemantle played shortstop for the Buckeyes until they imported professional players, and he was also the organization's treasurer. Like other members, he worked as a school teacher and served a 100-day enlistment in the Union Army in 1864. Around 1880 he became a school principal and subsequently acted in that capacity for a succession of public schools, serving as president of the city's Principal's Association in 1894–95. He died of a stroke, passing away in his sleep at his home on Cincinnati's east side, on December 7, 1912.

James Edmund Sherwood: Born in Cincinnati on February 9, 1840. The son and son-in-law of physicians, Sherwood was the club's vice-president when they organized in 1863 and played catcher for the 1866 team, a crucial defensive role that indicates he must have been one of the club's better players before they started upgrading with hired professionals and local all-stars recruited from other clubs. Cincinnati baseball historian Harry Ellard says he was "afterwards a teacher in the public schools," but the 1860 census shows him already acting in that capacity at the relatively tender age of 20. He became principal of Cincinnati's 1st District School, where he served for many years. He died on August 6, 1910.

George W. Smith: Smith was the pitcher of the club in 1866 and 1867, and at this period a battery member is always likely to have been one of the more talented players in his club. Otherwise, he is a hard man to follow because of his common name. He can, however, confidently be identified with "Friend George" W. Smith of Woodward High School in Cincinnati, to whom Harry Wright, formerly the manager and captain of Cincinnati's famous Red Stockings, addressed letters on March 24 and May 8, 1875 (Harry Wright collection, SABR). Wright, now managing Boston's National Association (NA) club, was making arrangements to play exhibition games during a planned western swing. In his second letter, Wright confirms that on June 1 Boston would play a club on whose behalf Smith was negotiating; he does not name that team, but Boston did visit the Cincinnati area and played the Ludlows on June 1. The Ludlows were an ambitious new team taking their name from the small northern Kentucky town in which they were based, and in the words of a club announcement, they had engaged "picked players of the Stars of Covington, Ky. and of various Cincinnati Clubs," had secured enclosed grounds that would enable them to charge spectators an admission fee, and they were eager to schedule professional teams (*New York Clipper*, April 16, 1875 p. 18, col. 6).

On the basis of these letters we can assume that, among several men with that name in Cincinnati city directories of the period, the ball-playing George Smith was the same one listed as a school teacher, the profession of many of his fellow Buckeyes. We can also identify him as one of only a few men active during baseball's first flowering in Cincinnati in the late 1860s, and the only one of the original Buckeyes, who remained active in the game in some capacity during later decades, in an administrative capacity if not as a player.

Charley Sweasy: See Cincinnati Base Ball Club ("Red Stockings").

Henry Hammond (Harry) Tatem: Tatem was born in 1841, the child of Henry Lea Tatem, who came to Cincinnati as a child in 1812, and of Sarah Ann Hall Tatem, a Cincinnati native born in 1809. Tatem was therefore an old settler by the standards of a new town, able to trace his family's roots in his home town back to a time before it had been chartered as a city. Tatem served four years as city auditor and subsequently as Secretary of the Board of Trade, and from the late 1860s he was an official and member of the board of trustees of several local railroads He was also a trustee of Longview Mental Hospital and an active member of the Masons. In a title-happy age, his military service during the Civil War earned him the life-long courtesy title of Captain Tatem.

In his late twenties when the Buckeyes flourished, Tatem was a little older than the typical active ball player of the day, and he does not appear to have been very active in the club. His membership may in fact have merely honorary, yet he is of some interest as an example of the ties that bound the club to Cincinnati's educational system, for beginning in 1867, Tatem spent 24 years as a member of Cincinnati's school board, serving two terms as president. A graduate of the city's Hughes High School, he also acted as trustee for the estate of Thomas Hughes, out of which that school was endowed. A 1912 local history praised Tatem for having given "his time and thought ungrudgingly to the interests of [Hughes] with no expectation of reward beyond the consciousness of having performed a public duty and having served his Alma Mater faithfully." After retiring from business he removed to the town of Hartwell, north of Cincinnati, where he was again elected to the Board of Education, serving for periods as its president and clerk. Tatem died in Hartwell on December 1, 1895. (*Supreme Council: Sovereign Grand Inspectors-General of the Thirty-Third and Last Degree Ancient Accepted Scottish Rite for the Northern Masonic Jurisdiction of the United States of America* [S.n: s.l., 1895]).

Other Members: Joe Doyle (see Forest City Club of Rockford), Febiger, C. S. Foote, W. D. Gibson, Eugene Hammett, F. J. Hannon, Samuel Hughes, Charles Jones, Lowe, J. P. Mack, John Meagher, George P. Miller, W. J. Ogden, William H. Skiff, Thomas Tallow, George Wehmer, William P. Wright.

Sources

Details of the Buckeyes' organizational history and amateur players are largely taken from Harry Ellard's *Base Ball in Cincinnati* (1907, reprint, Jefferson, NC: McFarland, 2004); the club's brief career as a professional organization, from William J. Ryczek's *When Johnny Came Sliding Home: The Post–Civil War Base Ball Boom, 1865–1870* (Jefferson, NC: McFarland, 1998) and two articles that appeared in the *Cincinnati Times* on April 15, 1868, and May 8, 1868. Information on the club members comes largely from local newspapers, especially the *Cincinnati Enquirer*, city directories and census reports. Much of the profile of Patsy Dockney comes from Peter Morris, *Catcher: How the Man Behind the Plate Became an American Hero* (Chicago: Ivan R. Dee, 2009), 175–177 and William J. Ryczek, *When Johnny Came Sliding Home* (Jefferson, NC: McFarland, 1998), 143–144. Also useful were Charles Frederic Goss's *Cincinnati, the Queen City, 1788–1912* (Chicago, Cincinnati: S.J. Clarke, 1912) and William A. Phelon, "The Team That Never Was Licked," *Baseball Magazine* (January 1917), 69–75.

Cincinnati Base Ball Club ("Red Stockings") (David Ball)

Club History

On the evening of July 11, 1866, a group of Cincinnati businessmen and lawyers met in the offices of the law firm of Tilden, Moulton and Tilden on a matter of no very profound importance.[1] A wave of enthusiasm for the new game of baseball was sweeping the country, and although some of the participants had never seen a baseball game — even the meeting's chairman, a certain Dr. May, confessed himself "ignorant of the rudiments" — they intended to form a baseball club.[2]

Not all the members were unacquainted with the game. J. William Johnson, a young lawyer, had played on the Harvard nine. He and insurance executive Henry Glassford had been involved with another group of ball players who had been playing baseball and the predecessor game called townball under the name of the Resolute club. In their honor the new organization took the Resolutes' name, elected officers and chose management committees, with Glassford accepting the presidency. About a dozen years later an anonymous club member published a wry account in the *Cincinnati Commercial* in which he recalled "the quiet feeling of indignation" that arose among the membership at a meeting a little later when attorney Drausin Wulsin, their one-man supply committee, announced he had spent twenty dollars on a chest to hold the club's balls, bats and other accoutrements. "The transaction was considered the height of extravagance," recalled the anonymous memoirist. "Subsequently, when the management was at an annual outlay of $30,000 for professional players, traveling expenses and grounds, the incident was considered very amusing."[3] By the time that happened, however, the club was no longer the Resolute, having changed its name to the Cincinnati Base Ball Club, famous today under the nickname Red Stockings.

Sporting goods dealer George Ellard, whose son later wrote an early account of early Cincinnati baseball, was the first club member to wear the socks that became a trademark. The club's first nine adopted the red stockings in 1867 and by 1868 had taken up the white uniforms with red stockings and trim that eventually became traditional for Cincinnati teams. How the name of the club itself was changed to Cincinnati is more difficult to determine. Records directly reflecting the change do not survive, and reminiscences from even a few years afterwards are contradictory. Given the aggressive effort the club made to field a powerful professional nine and the prominence that was ultimately attained, one might naturally suspect that the name was intended to bring attention to Cincinnati. The cities of what we now call the Midwest were then young and jostling for prominence, with Cincinnati in what would prove to be a losing struggle to retain its early primacy ahead of Chicago and St. Louis as the Queen City of the west. Anything that brought one of these towns before the national public was welcome to its business community — as an enthusiastic follower could cry when the professional nine was at its peak of success, "Glory, they've advertised the city — advertised us, sir, and helped our business, sir."[4] Obviously, a nine representing the Cincinnati Club advertised its city more effectively than if it were called the Resolutes.

None of the surviving accounts point to this consideration as a reason for the name change, however. Two versions later published imply that the change was made fairly soon after the organization in the summer of 1866, at the suggestion of J. William Johnson, as one version has it, or by a formal motion of Aaron Champion, the vice president and future president of the club, according to the other. Another account published many years later by *Cincinnati Commercial Tribune* reporter Harry Millar gave still a different version, and the fullest one we have. Millar referred the change to the period after the group had formed an alliance with Cincinnati's Union Cricket Club. The original intention, wrote Millar, was to change the name to the Cincinnati Union club, but when time came to incorporate the organization, Champion, S. S. Davis, Thomas G. Smith, and John Joyce simply decided that name was too long, so they had the papers made out in the name of the Cincinnati Base Ball Club.

Whatever it was calling itself at the time, the club at first practiced and played games on a field they shared with the earlier established Live Oak club at the foot of Eighth Street in the valley of Cincinnati's Mill Creek Bottoms. Little Mill Creek flowed down to the Ohio River through Cincinnati's relatively highly populated West End, passing through terrain that was flat enough for use for baseball fields and too frequently flooded to be very attractive for more economically productive uses. The Mill Creek Valley was therefore the cradle of baseball in Cincinnati and the site of almost all the city's major ball parks up to the 1970s. The club practiced for a while and in the fall played four match games, three against the club that soon became their archrivals, the Buckeyes, which beat them two times out of three. Their opposition was probably not very good, while the Cincinnati Club's players themselves were a mixed lot but mostly of indifferent skill at best. A few, notably J. William Johnson, were talented and experienced amateurs, but others, such as president Glassford, forty years old and bespectacled, showed little capacity for the game.

The field on Eighth Street was soon abandoned, but later accounts again differ as to the reason. One version has it that the grounds were too small, another that drainage was a problem, still another that the landlord, the city's mayor, had allowed the use of the field free of charge until he sold the land, at which point the Cincinnati Club as well as the Live Oaks had to move. The Cincinnati Club made an arrangement with the Union Cricket Club to share their Union Grounds on the west side of Lincoln Park, not far from where they had been playing. The baseball club agreed to raise $2,000 in capital and take joint ownership of the grounds.

The coalition with the cricketers brought in a number of new members who took up baseball after playing the British game. An incomparably more valuable addition, however, was Harry Wright, the cricket club's property man and club professional, a job roughly equivalent to a golf pro at a modern country club. Wright took up the same duties with the Red Stockings and became its captain and manager. The son of a professional cricketer who had emigrated from England to the United States, Wright had played cricket in New York and had also been a prominent baseball player before coming to Cincinnati to work for the Union Club. Wright had proven himself as a player in New York, the home of modern baseball, and his work at the Union Club had given him administrative and managerial experience that would be invaluable in running a baseball nine.

Considerable expense was put into refurbishing the Union Grounds, and the improved facility was opened on July 1, 1867, with a game against a Louisville club. The Cincinnati Club played a much more ambitious schedule in 1867 than it had the previous season. A large crowd was the first in Cincinnati history to pay an admission price to play a game. On July 13, the Red Stockings hosted the National Club of Washington, which was making a highly publicized tour of the Midwest. Although the Nationals were not among the very top clubs of the day, they brought state-of-the-art baseball from the heartland of the game to an area in which it was just developing. On their tour the Nationals demonstrated the finest standard of play for their hosts, and the highly publicized games they played with their various Midwestern hosts focused attention on the newly popular game of baseball, besides filling the home clubs' coffers with large receipts from their games.

In retrospect, we can see that already in 1867 the Cincinnati Club had perhaps taken a first step away from its origin as a social club designed to give all its members an opportunity for enjoyable and healthy exercise. On the disbandment of the Covington Club, a particularly strong nine based across the Ohio River in Covington, Kentucky, Cincinnati's leading clubs gobbled up the Covingtons' best players. The Live Oaks and Buckeyes each grabbed two men while the Cincinnatis added Mose Grant. So far as we can tell from the historical record, no one ever had a negative word to say about Grant, yet it appears likely he was recruited less for any social qualities that made him a suitable member of the Cincinnati Club than for his playing abilities, and now he took the left field position that otherwise would have gone to an old club member.

The 1868 season saw a much more significant move in the direction of an organization intended more to win games than to allow its members to play ball. Over the preceding winter the Union Cricket Club's financial problems had threatened their control over the Union Grounds, and to protect their own playing field the baseball club agreed to become its sole proprietor, assuming the outstanding debts and taking over the lease. Meanwhile, the club's leadership decided to recruit a nucleus of professional players. According to later reports, the Buckeyes were the first to go professional and the Red Stockings followed, recruiting New York professionals John Hatfield, Asa Brainard, and Fred Waterman to go with Harry Wright, besides luring Charlie Gould away from the Buckeyes. Gould, a local ball player, was the only Cincinnatian of his generation to go on to a substantial professional career. Later Doug Allison, a relatively inexperienced catcher, was discovered in Philadelphia. Because of regulations against professionalism, the new players were given sinecures in companies run by members of the Cincinnati Club, but if anyone imagined that the crack third baseman Fred Waterman, for example, had come out from New York to Cincinnati in order to take a position as a shipping clerk, he could walk by Waterman's place of business any day and see him lounging around, talking baseball with passers-by, and letting the shipping business take care of itself, with help from the company's legitimate employees.

With a mixed nine of professionals and some of the best amateur players in the area, the season was a successful one for the Red Stockings. They defeated all local opposition and late in the season made the first tour of the East by a Midwestern club, winning 10 of 14 games and beating the Mutuals of New York, one of the strongest clubs in the country. At home the Cincinnatis defeated the Buckeyes twice, although for the second game the Buckeyes brought in several paid players from Washington, and there were even claims that attempts had been made to drug or bribe Red Stockings players. John Hatfield was withheld from the game, but the Cincinnatis still won, cementing their position as the best club in the city and probably the Midwest.

Over the ensuing winter, the Cincinnati Club reorganized as a stock organization, with the current members receiving half of the $15,000 in stock, leaving the other $7,500 to be sold to the public. The primary purpose of the stock offering was to raise capital, of course, but Henry Glassford reportedly advanced the idea as a way of bringing in a large number of small subscribers in order to spread interest in the club. Another result, of course, was that a fraternal club composed of men with at least a passing interest in baseball now changed its fundamental character. Originally, membership had been set at a maximum of forty, a number considered large enough to allow a sufficient number of players to get up two full sides for practice days, but sufficiently restricted, in the language of the *Commercial* memoirist, "to insure exclusiveness, as it was feared at the time that some one might join who was a loafer and would swear." When membership grew to six hundred, there were more than enough players to get up a practice game — more in fact than could possibly be accommodated if all wished to participate — but "the latter [consideration] was winked at." The organization became a company selling stock to anyone who wanted to buy it, rather than a club. Probably few if any of the stock subscribers saw their purchase as a profit-driven business decision, but it is likely that many or most had no participatory interest in the game at all and had purchased stock for reasons of civic pride or a fan's interest in the success of the club's increasingly well-known first nine.

Professionalism was the next logical step, and a raid on the Buckeyes' roster brought over New York area professionals Andy Leonard, Charley Sweasy, and Dick Hurley, and essentially pushed the beleaguered Buckeyes over the edge. Their club had suffered a money-losing season and endured difficulties with their hired professionals who, to be fair, may have been legitimately angry at not receiving their promised pay. After some hesitation the Buckeyes made a disillusioned retreat from professionalism and fielded a weak amateur lineup before giving up the ghost entirely before the season was over.

The legendary unbeaten 1869 "Red Stocking" Club of Cincinnati made professional baseball respectable, but that achievement also brought an end to the pioneer era of baseball.

As for the Cincinnatis, they lost John Hatfield, who jumped the club and was formally expelled from membership, a fate that did not prevent him from joining the Mutuals in New York. More than making up for the loss of Hatfield was the addition of Harry Wright's brother George, probably the best player in the game, and Cal McVey, a young player from Indianapolis who would prove in the long run to be one of the most talented players on a great team. Under the capable leadership of Harry Wright the Cincinnati Club now fielded a lineup that could reckon with any opponent — quite literally, for they went undefeated during the season of 1869. The story is too well known to need retelling in detail — how, having manhandled all local opposition, they proceeded to make their way unbeaten through the best baseball nines in existence, in Philadelphia, New York, and Brooklyn; finished the season with a trip to the West Coast, so that by the time winter came they had traveled literally from coast to coast without finding a rival that could beat them even once.

In 1870 they took the field with an unchanged starting nine and again had excellent luck on the field, but their own example had moved other cities to put together aggregations of strong players, and this fact, together with the inexorable law of averages, made an end to the Red Stockings' unbeaten string inevitable. On July 14, they lost to the Atlantics in Brooklyn, 8–7 in eleven innings. Aaron Champion, now club president, sent his famous telegram home, "Though beaten, not disgraced." Yet although Champion's sentiment seemed valid, the season began gradually to go downhill for the Red Stockings. They lost several other games as the season advanced, cracks appeared in player discipline, and attendance fell off at the Union Grounds. In early August, Champion appeared before a club meeting to deliver a report that showed the club's finances in good condition. Champion, club secretary John Joyce, and director Thomas G. Smith then all offered their resignations, pleading the press of their own business affairs.

After a face-saving minuet in which the club membership refused to accept the resignations while the officials demanded them, everybody compromised and agreed that they would keep their positions until the club's regular annual elections in the fall. With that, Champion was succeeded by vice-president A.P.C. Bonte, who presided over the decision not to field a professional team in 1870. After some unseemly squabbling by club officials and newspaper writers over whether unreasonable demands by the players, especially the two Wrights, had helped push the club to drop its professional team, Harry Wright went off to organize a new club in Boston, taking the Red Stockings nickname and several of his Cincinnati players while the remainder signed up with the Olympic club in Washington. The Cincinnati Club would go back to playing amateur baseball, but interest now seems to have flagged and by the spring of 1872 the club's effects were sold at auction.

The story is simple to summarize. What is not so easy is to see how and why the Cincinnati Club experienced such a dizzying rise and decline. In the summer of 1866 the club had formed with a handful of experienced and talented players and a probably far larger number who had little experience or understanding of the game, and all their hopes and ambitions for worldly success concentrated on other fields than baseball. When the Buckeyes and the Live Oaks, the other leading club in town, had sent representatives that December to the convention of the National Association of Base Ball Players in New York, the Cincinnatis had gone unrepresented while John Draper of the Live Oaks took a seat on the playing rules committee, thereby becoming the first member of a club west of the Allegheny Mountains to hold a seat on any NABBP committee. Another year passed, and in December 1867 the Buckeyes were prominent enough on the national scene to garner the honor of having their president, George Sands, elected the first president of the NABBP from beyond the Alleghenies.

Of the Queen City's three leading clubs, two had now been recognized with signal honors on the national stage, but the Cincinnatis were not one of them. By the following winter, however, the Cincinnati Club was strong enough to launch a devastating raid on the Buckeyes' roster that effectively destroyed that now shaky club, while the Live Oaks declined to follow their rivals into professionalism. Less than three years after their own club had formed, the Cincinnatis set out upon their famous unbeaten season, and within another two years the Cincinnati Club got out of the professional baseball business altogether, and less than eighteen months later the club ended its existence, less than half a dozen years after its first organization.

The Red Stockings' remarkable though brief success no doubt owed much to the club's good luck in securing the services of Harry Wright, the first great manager in baseball history. Contemporaries also gave much credit to the capable president Aaron Champion and club secretary John Joyce. However, the spectacular rise of the Cincinnati Club probably also reflects the composition of its membership. Following Harry Ellard, later writers have described the club as an organization of Yale- and Harvard-educated attorneys. In fact, of those members we can identify, many were not Ivy-educated, and a large number were businessmen rather than attorneys — for example, Harry Ellard's father George was a sporting-goods dealer who probably had no higher education at all. Nevertheless, it is clear the new club included few if any members below the middle class and a disproportionate number of Harvard graduates, and that among them were a substantial number of men either already prominent in Cincinnati's affairs or looking forward to promising futures in the city. While the Buckeyes' core membership was composed of school teachers and principals and the Live Oaks seem to have been essentially a neighborhood ball club, at the heart of the Cincinnati Club were men from the city's leadership, men with the confidence and the means to accomplish what they set their sights upon.

Nevertheless, surviving accounts suggest that the club's rise to prominence in the baseball world most probably was not really the work of determined and able men acting on a plan, but rather something the membership drifted into without really intending to. To us, the key moment in the club's history — in fact, a crucial moment in the history of baseball — seems to be the decision to field a nine made up of the best professional players of the day. We now have little in the way of first-hand accounts of how the crucial policy decisions were reached. Most of what we do have consists of articles written years after the fact, and our one contemporary document, the financial report by president Champion at the meeting at which he handed in his resignation, probably was crafted to meet criticism of Champion's leadership and so cannot be taken completely at face value. That said, the most striking fact that emerges from a perusal of the accounts we do have is that they say surprisingly little about the decision to professionalize and focus instead on the financial consequences of the club's decision to take over its playing field from the Union Cricket Club. Moving in with the cricketers had already required the raising of $2,000 in capital — enough for one hundred of Drausin Wulsin's extravagant chests — and the takeover of the Union Grounds raised the stakes drastically. This was the step that committed the baseball club to paying an annual rent and investing large sums in improvements. This was the decision that, in the good-humored but rueful formulation of the *Commercial* memoirist, had first nudged a club whose members originally had blanched at the expenditure of twenty dollars toward annual expenditures in five figures. In order to produce revenues that matched this new level of expenditures, the club had to field an attractive team that could draw spectators at the gate and appeal to subscribers for their stock issue. Competition from the Buckeyes, now fielding a professional team playing at a field virtually adjoining the Union Grounds, spurred the race toward an entirely paid team, but the heavy investment in the Union Grounds seems to have been the decision that ultimately led almost naturally to the decision to hire professionals. As best we can tell from our somewhat sketchy evidence, it appears that, rather than recruiting a high-priced team and then putting it in an attractive playing facility, the club had been led into acquiring their expensive roster of players to support the field they were committed to.

With professionalization, of course, came a hefty payroll that only added to the budget. Local games could not bring in the revenue needed, and so the team had to be sent on the road for much of the season, thereby incurring still more expenses for travel. Over the seasons of 1869 and 1870 the team seems to have done well financially. The frequently repeated statement that the club turned a profit of exactly $1.39 in 1869 seems to ignore that fact that much of the club's receipts went to liquidate the debt, an important accomplishment. By the time he addressed a meeting of the club in August 1870, president Champion was able to tell the membership that the club had entered the season of 1869 in debt to the tune of more than $15,000—equivalent to well over a quarter million dollars today—after the stock offering the previous fall brought in only $3,000 of the intended $7,500, and the team had started its famous 1869 Eastern tour with only $500 to cover travel expenses. In the East, however, the Red Stockings' income had finally started to exceed expenses, and by the time Champion spoke, the debt had been entirely liquidated, with money in the treasury.

A successful enterprise, it would seem, but Champion would not have been making such an elaborate statement if there had not been discontent among the club members. He and Joyce had been the primary advocates of the aggressive policy that had made the club leaseholders on an improved Union Grounds and brought in a team of professional players, and their joint resignation probably represents an easy way out after it had become apparent that they had lost the confidence of much of the club membership and might not or would not be reelected in the fall. Many of the original members must have wondered how they had come so far and whether the comparatively small profit earned could justify the hazarding of large amounts of capital on what had begun as a modest recreation.

Moreover, although Harry Wright's careful management had made the experience relatively trouble-free, the club members had experienced enough of the difficulties that came with employing relatively highly paid ball players. John Hatfield was the worst case, but some of the other Red Stockings had proved disciplinary problems or squabbled over money. Baseball salaries around the country were increasing, and the club would need to go back into debt in order to organize another professional team for the next season. Nor were some of the members happy to see a club organized for recreation turn into a business venture that relegated them to spectators. A statement by the new board of directors promised "a development of the amateur talent of our club ... and ... the pleasure of witnessing many exciting contests on our grounds." Champion's replacement A.P.C. Bonte told an interviewer, "You can wave the Star Spangled Banner, and talk about the glory of the Red Stockings, and the nine that meets with no defeat, but you must put your hands in your pocket and pay the bills. You can't run the club on glory."[5] Thus the decision to end professionalism after the 1870 season.

But the Cincinnati Club, like the Buckeyes before them, seem to have found that, having had their adventure running a professional team, they could not go back to a placid existence as a club providing harried young businessmen and lawyers an opportunity for exercise and amusement. The club put an amateur nine on the field in 1871, but it does not seem to have spawned much interest. William Johnson and Con Howe, two of the best of the old Cincinnati Club amateurs, were playing for the Live Oaks, who had never professionalized and were by now considered the city's leading club. That same summer Aaron Champion attempted to reignite interest in professional baseball by bringing Boston and the Olympics, the two teams that had divided the Red Stocking stars, to play in Cincinnati. Attendance at the Boston-Olympic matches was disappointing, and by the following spring the *New York Clipper* reported that "the Cincinnati Club has given up the ghost," selling its assets at auction.[6] The club had experienced an eventful round trip from obscure and casual amateurism to management of a professional team and finally extinction. The citizens of many cities during this period would have similar experiences during this era, but few would have as eventful a journey as the people of Cincinnati.

CLUB MEMBERS

At its peak the Cincinnati Club was very large, and the names of individuals known to have been members stretches literally into the hundreds, including players both amateur and professionals, some who played little if at all but were active in administrative capacities and others who became financially interested after stock was offered for sale but may not have taken a very active part in any way. We can give here only a large sample of the most important members. For an exhaustive list, see Harry Ellard's *Base Ball in Cincinnati*, pp. 77–83.

Doug Allison: Allison was a Philadelphia bricklayer and catcher for the Geary Club of that city. He was reportedly discovered by Cincinnati Club secretary John Joyce, who acquired him to catch for the Red Stockings in 1868. Allison went on to play professionally for nearly a dozen different professional clubs. He spent most of his later life working for the Post Office in Washington, where he died in 1916.

A.P.C. Bonte: The owner of a picture-frame factory, Albert Pearley Cross Bonte was born on March 4, 1833, in Lockport, New York, and came to Cincinnati in the 1850s. By the late 1860s he was a trustee of the Board of Trade and member of the city council and also served as president of the Young Men's Gymnastic Association. His listing in the 1870 census credits him with $86,000 in real and $60,000 in personal property, a considerable fortune for the day. Although he is not known to have been active as a player in the Cincinnati Club, Bonte was elected its vice president in March 1870. At the end of the season he succeeded Aaron Champion in the presidency and subsequently presided over the decision to deprofessionalize the Cincinnati team. Bonte died in Cincinnati in March 1879.

Asa Brainard: Brainard, a former member of the famous Excelsiors and other well-known clubs in New York and elsewhere, was one of the professionals imported to play in Cincinnati. With the Excelsiors, Brainard had watched Jimmy Creighton, the first great pitcher, from his position at second base, becoming the Excelsiors' pitcher after Creighton's untimely death. Aaron Champion later told *Sporting Life* that when he had gone to New York to sign third baseman Fred Waterman, he had found that Waterman's friend and teammate Brainard was considered the best young second baseman in the New York area and therefore had taken Brainard back to Cincinnati along with Waterman. Brainard played some second base for the Red Stockings, but he was the regular pitcher during the unbeaten 1869 season and the highest paid player except for Harry and George Wright. Always something of a prima donna and a drinker, Brainard's work declined sharply after he left Cincinnati. Probably he could not compete with the new generation of curve ball pitchers who broke into baseball in the early 1870s, and by 1875 he was out of the game. He abandoned the wife he had met in Cincinnati, managed a succession of retail businesses such as pool halls and archery ranges, and died in Denver in 1888.

Cecil Calvert: According to the anonymous memoirist of the *Cincinnati Commercial,* Calvert joined the club late in 1866 and was subsequently "known as 'old posish,' from his Mercury-like manner of skipping around the bases and striking attitudes, to the intense admiration of the ladies." His attitudes were apparently less conducive to winning baseball than feminine admiration, for he was replaced in the lineup of the first nine. Calvert's background is a contrast to that of some of the more eminent club members. He was born in Ohio around 1846, the son of comb-maker George Calvert and his wife Deborah. The 1866 city directory shows him employed as a clerk, not one of the more eminent club members. He subsequently married and relocated to Cleveland, where he worked as a bookkeeper and traveling salesman and later ran a newspaper depot. Eventually he moved to Brown County in rural Indiana, where he and his family ran a hotel. He seems to have died in the 1920s.

Aaron Champion: A center fielder of moderate skill at best, Aaron B. Champion nevertheless bore as much responsibility as anyone for the Red Stockings' success. Champion was a native of Columbus, Ohio, who was compelled to go to work early after the death of his father but later attended Antioch College. After reading law in Columbus, he was admitted to the Ohio bar in 1863 and shortly afterward moved to Cincinnati, where he became a leading authority on the laws applying to the new electric utilities.

In 1866 Champion became a charter member and director of the Cincinnati Club. He succeeded to the presidency in 1867 and pushed the aggressive policies that led the club to take over the Union Grounds and hire a team of professional players. At a club meeting in August 1870 Champion presented a statement showing that the club's affairs were in favorable condition and then submitted his resignation, but he was persuaded to remain in office until a successor was found. At season's end, vice president A.P.C. Bonte was elected president, and the club opted to return to amateurism. Champion attempted to revive professional ball in the city by bringing in pro clubs containing former Red Stocking players to play several games in the summer of 1871, but attendance was disappointing, and when a new professional team was organized several years later Champion was not involved. He remained a leading citizen of Cincinnati until his death September 1, 1895, while visiting London.

William Chapman: The first treasurer of the Cincinnati Club and briefly its shortstop, Chapman was an Ohio-born druggist. The 1875 city directory lists his wife as a widow.

Quinton Corwine: Corwine was a charter member and the club's first vice president. His father Richard was a Cincinnati attorney in partnership with future president Rutherford B. Hayes and cast one of the deciding votes for Abraham Lincoln at the Republican convention of 1860. Born in 1843, Quinton Corwine was educated at Miami University of Ohio and Harvard. After serving in the Union Army during the Civil War, he practiced law in Cincinnati, served as assistant U.S. Attorney, and later practiced in Washington and New York. He died on August 28, 1906, in New York.

S.S. Davis: Simon Stevens Davis was one of a number of club members, including presidents Alfred Goshorn and A.P.C. Bonte, who were officials of the Board of Trade. Sources mention Davis only as an organizer, and since he was nearly fifty when the club was formed, it is likely he did not play. Davis was born December 19, 1817, on a farm in Rockingham, Vermont. After working on his family's farm and as a teacher, Davis had lived in various cities, including Cincinnati, before returning there to set up in business as a banker in 1853. By the time the firm of S.S. Davis and Company dissolved in 1885, it was one of the last private banking firms in the city. Davis was elected mayor in 1871 and was narrowly defeated for reelection two years later. He died May 11, 1896, in Newton Highlands, Massachusetts.

John Draper: Draper, a particularly prominent figure in early Cincinnati baseball, is sometimes mistakenly described as a founder of the Cincinnati Club, but in fact he transferred from the Live Oaks only in 1867. Known as a player but more so as one of the most sought-after umpires in the region, Draper had represented the Live Oaks at the 1866 convention of the National Association of Base Ball Players in New York, where he was appointed to the Rules Committee, becoming the first member of a club west of the Alleghenies to be named to any NABBP committee. After switching to the Cincinnati Club, he organized a Cincinnati Junior Club composed of players between the ages of fifteen and twenty. His founding of the Cincinnati Juniors caused him to be misidentified in his obituary as a charter member of the parent club. See the Live Oaks of Cincinnati for details on Draper's life outside of baseball.

George Brabazon Ellard: A sporting goods dealer and

president of the Union Cricket Club who joined the Cincinnati Club after the baseballers rented the cricket club's grounds. Ellard played left field for a while and is credited with having introduced the club's famous red stockings. He may have played a far more important if indirect role in the Cincinnati Club's success, for Ellard is said to have hired Harry Wright to come out from New York in 1865 to take a position as the Union Club's professional, the position Wright subsequently left to become the captain and manager of the Red Stockings. Ellard later served as secretary of the Longworth estate. His son Harry published a history of the city's early baseball teams, written in large measure from memorabilia kept by the elder Ellard. Born in Swinford, County Mayo, Ireland, on April 18, 1829, George Ellard died in Cincinnati on September 28, 1916.

James Fowler: The original Cincinnati Club amateurs had boasted a heavy representation of young Harvard graduates, but James Fowler, an extra player on the 1869 professional team, was a Yale man. With Dick Hurley as chief substitute Fowler had little to do on the field, but he played a few times, sometimes kept the official score, occasionally acted as an umpire for local teams, and may have reported on the team for a Cincinnati newspaper during road trips. At a banquet celebrating a successful road trip at the beginning of July, Fowler said, "[Club president] Champion says that I slept through all those matches; if I didn't play, I talked and helped in that way. I am happy to be a member of the Cincinnati Nine or rather Eleven." The obscure eleventh man Fowler would have been utterly forgotten had he not enjoyed a fictional second life as the inspiration for Samuel Clemens Fowler, the first-person protagonist of Darryl Brock's historical novel of the Red Stockings, *If I Never Get Back*.

Identifying Fowler has been difficult. Writing many years later about the Resolutes, the organization from which the Cincinnati Club sprang in the mid–1860s, Cincinnati *Commercial* reporter Harry Millar wrote, "Among their players was a red-headed knock-kneed young fellow named Jimmie Fowler who when it came to general all-around good ball playing, was a regular terror." Identifying this redheaded Fowler with the player of the same name who later appeared for the unbeaten Red Stockings is an attractive possibility, but that player was clearly identified as a Yale man by a contemporary item in the *New York Clipper*, and the only Yale graduate named James Fowler during this period does not seem to have had any connection with Cincinnati earlier (or later) than 1869.

This Fowler, an 1869 graduate of Yale, was born on May 8, 1849, in Westfield, Massachusetts. An obituary makes no mention of any baseball playing but says he lived in Syracuse and Philadelphia after graduation and then worked as a civil engineer in various Western cities. He died in Caldwell, Idaho, of pneumonia on November 26, 1892. What would have brought this Fowler to Cincinnati is unclear. However talented he may have been, there seems little reason to import a player all the way from Connecticut to fill such a minor role on the team, especially a Yale graduate who was not likely to remain in professional baseball long enough to develop any potential he showed. When the Red Stockings played in Rochester, the *Daily Chronicle* of that city referred to Fowler as a correspondent for the *Cincinnati Gazette*. We may speculate that he conceivably may have come to Cincinnati in the first place as a writer for the *Gazette*, perhaps with the understanding that he would also play for the team and write game reports and perhaps handle general correspondence from the road. Whether that is true or not, it has not been possible to find mention of Fowler in Cincinnati newspapers after mid–August 1869, while Oak Taylor, another substitute, accompanied the Red Stockings on the season-ending trip to the Pacific Coast that Brock uses poetic license to make the climax of Fowler's adventures with the Red Stockings. Meanwhile, a Fowler shows up playing for Syracuse ball clubs in the fall of 1869, a fact that fits what we know of the Connecticut native Fowler's biography.

Henry Glassford: Canadian-born insurance man Henry A. Glassford was the club's first president, serving until he resigned and was replaced by A. T. Goshorn immediately after the celebrated game between the Red Stockings and the touring Nationals of Washington in July 1867. At the club's start, he had at least a little more experience with baseball than many, perhaps most, of his fellow members, having reportedly been involved as president of an earlier ball club called the Resolutes, with which J. William Johnson also played. Unlike Johnson, Glassford, bespectacled and forty when the club was formed, was a player of no particular distinction. Playing with the Cincinnati muffins (a term used for inept amateurs), Glassford is reported to have stopped a hard line drive but lost his glasses throwing the ball back to the pitcher.

Alfred Goshorn: Alfred Traber Goshorn was the club's second president. Goshorn was born July 15, 1833, and so was of somewhat advanced years in comparison with the young men who made up a large portion of the club's membership. The son of a Cincinnati manufacturer of paints and varnishes, Goshorn was educated at Marietta College and the Cincinnati Law School, from which he graduated in 1857 before serving as a major in the Union Army during the Civil War. He later made a specialty of organizing expositions, beginning with a series of successful industrial expositions in Cincinnati, moving on to be Ohio's delegate to Philadelphia's great Centennial Exposition in 1876 and finally serving as director-general of the International Centennial Exposition in London, for services to which he was decorated by Queen Victoria. Goshorn was thus the only knight of the realm associated with the Cincinnati Base Ball Club. Sir Alfred died in Cincinnati on February 19, 1902.

Charlie Gould: Charles H. Gould was the only Cincinnatian on the 1869 team. The son of a businessman, Gould worked for his father and played for the strong Buckeyes in 1867, then joined the Red Stockings, for whom he played first base, a position his considerable height suited him for. Never a real star, Gould went on to a respectable professional career with several Eastern teams before returning to Cincinnati after his New Haven club disbanded in 1875. He finished his career with the newly formed Reds team, retiring in 1877. Subsequently, Gould did not keep a very high profile in Cincinnati, although he played in several old-timers games. He lived in Cincinnati's West End, filling a variety of blue collar and clerical positions, and at one point is said to have driven a streetcar on a line that regularly passed the ballpark. He died in 1917 in Flushing, New York, where he appears to have moved in order to live with a son.

Moses Grant: Called both Mose and Moses, Grant was playing second base in 1866 for the Covingtons, one of the strongest clubs in the area. The Covingtons disbanded at a time when the strongest Cincinnati clubs were consolidating the better talent in the area onto their rosters, and while other stars went to the Buckeyes and Live Oaks, the Cincinnati Club added Grant. He was good enough to keep playing frequently in 1868, by which time a majority of the starting positions had been filled by professionals imported from the East. When suspicions were raised that gamblers had gotten to outfielder John Hatfield before a key game against the Buckeyes, Cincinnati's archrivals, Grant was the player chosen to replace Hatfield in the lineup. See the Covington and Copec Clubs of Covington for the details of his life.

Holmes Hoge: Hoge was a charter member and director of the club, and must have been one of its best amateur players as well, for he was the club's first pitcher and its captain until professional Harry Wright came in to fill that role. Yet his name never appeared in the Cincinnati city directory, so he is almost certainly a Chicagoan by that name who had served as captain of the Atlantics of Chicago. This man was born into a prominent family in Allegheny, Pennsylvania, in 1842, moving to Chicago in 1848. He enlisted as a private in the Chicago Mercantile Battery Illinois Light Artillery in 1862 and then, following a lengthy correspondence between his mother and President Lincoln, received an appointment to the Quartermaster's Department and was assigned to William T. Sherman's 15th Corps. He served in the Army of the Tennessee and the Department of the Gulf until being mustered out in October 1865.[7] His doings in the immediate aftermath of the war are difficult to trace, but his absence from the Chicago city directory in 1866 and 1867 suggests that he was in Cincinnati on some sort of business and found time to play for the Cincinnati Base Ball Club. He returned to Chicago for good in 1868 and had a long career as a banker with the First National Bank of Chicago. He died in Pasadena in 1924.

Con Howe: The family name of John Condit "Con" Howe was often spelled "How," although rarely if ever in a baseball context. A *Cincinnati Times* article of May 8, 1868, discussing the leading clubs of the city, remarks that, while the area's best players and most polished talents were professionals hired from the Eastern states where organized baseball had first developed, "many among our own are not naturally inferior to any of the East. Howe, Gould and Brookshaw could, with practice, play in any nine." While the enthusiasm of a home-town reporter may be discounted, it is a fact that Ben Brookshaw did go on to a brief professional career and Charlie Gould became a regular on the unbeaten Red Stockings and several National Association and National League teams, so it is quite possible that Howe may likewise have had the potential to develop into a professional player if he had given the game enough attention. A cricketer who joined the Cincinnati Club after it rented the Union Cricket Club's grounds, Howe played first base and then shortstop. He still retained the latter position in 1868 after most of the lineup had been professionalized but was replaced in 1869 by the great George Wright.

Howe was born in 1846 in Kentucky, but by 1860 his family had moved to Cincinnati, where his father Joseph worked as an inspector and then a dealer of tobacco. By 1871, with the Cincinnati Club disbanded, Con Howe was pitching for the Live Oak Club, which was regarded as the best amateur club in Cincinnati. Later he served as club secretary for the National League Reds under the administration of another former member of the original Cincinnati Club, Wayne Neff. Howe and Neff thus stand on a very short list of club members who are known to have taken an active part in baseball after the club disbanded.

Howe's brother Fulton married a relative of the Kemper family, one of whose members (the ill-fated Sammy Kemper) also played for the Cincinnati Club. Fulton became a director of the Cincinnati and Queens Railroad, but Con Howe himself never married and appears to have spent his life in relatively modest employment as a clerk and bookkeeper. He died in Cincinnati on March 23, 1918, reportedly of pneumonia, but in view of the fact that his sister-in-law, who lived with him, died within two days and with the same cause given, it seems possible that rather than dying of pneumonia, a noncommunicable disease, the two may have been unrecognized victims of the great worldwide influenza epidemic, then in its very early stages.

William F. "Dick" Hurley: See Olympics of Washington.

J. William Johnson: One of the more experienced baseballists among the Cincinnati Club's charter members, Johnson was an important figure on and off the field. As a newly minted college graduate, he was the club's first recording secretary while older men held more prominent positions, but according to a later newspaper historian, "it was J. William Johnson to whom is greatly due the credit of being the prime leader in the organization," as he enthusiastically pushed the idea of a baseball club and recruited members.

Johnson had played ball at Harvard and therefore had experience of baseball on the eastern seaboard, where the organized form of baseball was longer established and better developed, and to this advantage of experience he added physical skills that allowed him to play on the club's first nine as an outfielder late as 1868, when most of the players were eastern professionals. He is said to have been a good all-around player, but especially noted for speed.

Born in Wales on November 15, 1842, Johnson came to Cincinnati in childhood and served in the quartermaster corps during the Civil War under Colonel C.W. Moulton. After graduating from Harvard in 1866, he attended the Cincinnati Law School, meanwhile serving as an assistant in Moulton's law firm, and it was in the offices of Tilden, Moulton and Tilden that the first meeting of the Cincinnati Club was held in July 1866.

One Cincinnati amateur turned professional, Charlie Gould, remained in the lineup after the club had turned entirely pro in 1869, and it is not impossible that Johnson likewise had the ability to hold down a regular position even on the famous unbeaten Red Stockings, but having graduated from law school in April 1868 and married Sarah Belle Morse the following December, he probably would have found it impossible to spare time for the team's intensive schedule and frequent traveling. A career in the fledgling profession of baseball couldn't have held much appeal for a promising young lawyer. However, Johnson continued to play amateur ball, appearing with his former Red Stocking teammate Con Howe in the lineup of the strong Live Oaks by 1871 if not earlier. In later decades he turned up occasionally in newspaper features as a figure from the city's baseball past and a still interested fan.

Johnson settled down to a successful career as an attorney in Cincinnati and rose to a partnership in the Moulton firm, which after various changes in membership ultimately became Johnson and Meyer. He acted as vice president for the Western and Southern Life Insurance Company and the Victor Safe and Lock and as a trustee of the Eclectic Medical College, besides serving two terms in the same office for the Cincinnati Bar Association. He died in Cincinnati on June 5, 1917.

John Joyce: Modern accounts usually cast manager Harry Wright as the star of the Red Stockings' rise, with club president Aaron Champion in the primary supporting role, but contemporaries gave nearly equal billing to capable club secretary John P. Joyce, whose service to the club earned him a reputation in baseball circles around the country as well as in Cincinnati for excellence in the new art of running a baseball team. John Joyce is a common name, and he seems to have led at least a somewhat peripatetic early life; moreover, important details of his story come from a series of articles by Harry Millar, a *Cincinnati Commercial Tribune* reporter who had known Joyce but was writing from memory three decades after Joyce's death, so his testimony must be treated with some caution. As a result, it has been somewhat difficult to come by reliable information about a figure of interest and considerable importance in the early development of baseball.

Joyce was born in County Galway, Ireland, in 1839. Millar calls him a Canadian, probably a simple error that may indicate that Joyce had arrived in Canada before coming to the United States. According to Millar, Joyce lived for a while somewhere in the eastern United States, where he learned "rounders," a term Millar uses as a catchall to describe folk variants of the game from which modern baseball developed. Millar says that Joyce came to Cincinnati to work in the lottery business under William "Policy Bill" Smith. Joyce first appears in Cincinnati city directories in 1865, employed as a clerk, his job description until 1869. In later years newspapers referred to him from time to time as Colonel Joyce. Ambitious and capable as he undoubtedly was, so young a man occupied in relatively modest employment during the late 1860s is not likely to have been a Civil War colonel. The years after the Civil War were a time when military titles were ubiquitous, and not all of them were obtained through active service in the Army; how Joyce came by his is unknown.

A small, slight man, Joyce is not mentioned as having played baseball with the Cincinnati Club. Millar implies that Joyce was a club member from the first, saying that he interested Smith and others in the club but surviving lists of club officials do not mention him until 1868. Until that year, the secretary's position would in fact have been a relatively undemanding one to fill. As the team professionalized and began to arrange longer schedules with more time spent on road trips, everything had to be negotiated and planned game by game by the Red Stockings. Since there were no leagues to provide centralized scheduling, the job became a considerable challenge. Joyce appears to have managed the ordinary business of the club efficiently while apparently also taking a hand in questions of policy and long-term strategy. When Aaron Champion rose to the presidency, Joyce worked closely with him to push an aggressive policy that led to the acquisition of the Union Grounds and eventually an entirely professionalized team. The idea of making major improvements to the Union Grounds is credited to Joyce, as is the discovery of catcher Doug Allison in Philadelphia after Joyce and Alfred Goshorn had gone there in a futile attempt to sign John Radcliffe. He is also credited with recruiting Cal McVey for the team. The Red Stockings' spring trip to New Orleans in 1870, one of the first such Southern trips by a Northern team, was another of Joyce's ideas.

By 1870, the Cincinnati city directory listed Joyce as "secretary, Cincinnati Base Ball Club," a change that must reflect the amount of time and energy he was devoting to the ball club, whether or not he still remained in Smith's employ. About the time the city directory was in the hands of the public, however, Joyce was on his way out as a club official. In company with Champion and Thomas G. Smith, a director and former vice president, Joyce resigned his position at a club meeting in early August 1870, citing the pressure of other business. The three eventually agreed to remain in their positions until the regular election of new club officials in the fall, at which time a new slate of officers changed the course of the club's policy drastically, dropping the professional team altogether.

During subsequent years Joyce remained an interested observer of the baseball scene and sometimes an active participant. When a new professional team was established in Cincinnati in July 1875, Joyce was a natural choice for manager. He recruited a team to finish out the year and then during the subsequent offseason represented the club during at least one meeting preparing for the establishment of the new National League. It is not clear whether Joyce continued to work for the club during the following season; at any rate, primary owner Josiah Keck and his brother George stepped forward as the dominant figures in its management. Joyce certainly retained his interest in the game. In 1878, according to Albert Spalding, it was Joyce's skepticism that a baseball could be made to curve that led to a famous demonstration of the curve's reality by Cincinnati pitcher Will White.

More or less immediately upon resigning as club secretary Joyce was set up in business as a stockbroker. Evidently he remained close to Aaron Champion, for he boarded from the early 1870s at Champion's home on Baymiller Street in Cincinnati's West End. Little past forty, he died on November 22, 1882, at a private home in New Carlisle, Ohio, northeast of Cincinnati, where he had presumably gone for a visit. His remains were returned to Aaron Champion's home for the funeral and Champion paid for Joyce's plot at Spring Grove Cemetery.

Samuel L. Kemper: Sammy Kemper was a "fragile little lad" who had earned a name for himself as an accomplished cricketer before earning a spot on the first nine of the Cincinnatis in 1866. He retained his spot after Harry Wright's arrival but then a terrible accident befell him during an 1867 game at the Union Grounds: "Sammy, in making a sharp turn at third, caught his foot in some way and fell to the ground. The snap of his thigh-bone was heard distinctly by the spectators. He was laid up for months."[8] It ended Kemper's playing career and two years later, on the eve of his club's legendary undefeated season, he died of smallpox. Sammy Kemper was only 20 years old and his death prompted the club to pass resolutions on April 6, 1869, acknowledging that "for the first time since the organization of the Cincinnati Base Ball Club, death has deprived us of a member" and that "in the decease of Samuel L. Kemper the club has lost one of its most active and efficient members; one of the first to become associated with the club, and identified with its objects and attainments, and who has in no small degree contributed to its success."

Rufus King: Although he played some second base in 1868, Rufe King was most commonly found in center field for the Red Stockings. He appeared in only twenty-six out of more than forty match games, which may indicate that he was a player of some talent but found it difficult to retain a regular position against tough competition that included many of the best players in Cincinnati along with five Eastern professionals.

But an upper-middle-class amateur might also have found it difficult to spare time from other engagements to participate in the Red Stockings' increasingly busy and travel-heavy schedule.

King's family was in fact not only prosperous, but eminent. One great grandfather had served as one of Ohio's first pair of governors and later as governor and a second, the ballplayer's namesake, was a signer of the Constitution as well as the Federalist candidate for president and vice-president. Rufus King the future ball player was born in 1846 in Cincinnati, the eldest of three sons of Thomas Wentworth King and his wife Elizabeth. After Thomas King died in 1851, young Rufus spent at least some of the ensuing years in Columbus, Ohio, where his mother probably had family. Her husband's early death does not seem to have crippled the family financially, for the 1860 census shows her living with all three of her sons and a servant, and she is credited with $20,000 in real and personal property, a very considerable amount for the time.

Young Rufus went east to Harvard in 1863. After graduating in 1867, a year after his future Red Stocking teammate William Johnson, he returned to his original home town of Cincinnati and entered the law firm of the eldest brother of his father, also named Rufus. Although the addition was not strictly appropriate, in Cincinnati the younger Rufus was regularly called Rufus King, Jr., presumably to differentiate him from the very prominent attorney and civic leader with whom he shared his name. Perhaps while he was still playing for the Cincinnati Club, King returned to school and received a master's degree in 1870. Like most of his fellow members of the Cincinnati Club, he seems never again to have participated seriously in baseball after his brief membership in the club's first nine.

In short order King was admitted to the bar in 1870, married Louise Estes Miller early the next year and fathered a son, yet another Rufus, the year after that. However, King never actually practiced law, instead entering the firm of Phillips and Jordan, a dealer in pig iron. A few years later, a report by his Harvard class secretary noted that King had been in the rolling mill business until the fall of 1875 but "since then he has been out of business." It is reasonable to suppose that the laconic tone was intended to avoid a plain statement that the firm had foundered during the business depression that began in 1873.

We have some indication that during subsequent years, King had a difficult time getting back on his feet, probably as a result of the collapse of his business and perhaps because of ill health as well. He may have left Cincinnati for a while, for he disappears from the city directory entirely in 1877, but by August of that year he was in town and working as paymaster and purchasing agent for the Cincinnati Southern Railroad. The directory for 1879 lists him as living at his uncle's residence, perhaps in order that he might receive better care during his final illness, for by the time that directory was in the hands of the public Rufus King, Jr., was already dead, having passed away May 3, 1878, of tuberculosis.

Andy Leonard: Born in Ireland and raised in Newark, New Jersey, Leonard played alongside his friend Charlie Sweasy on the Irvingtons of Irvington, New Jersey, and then with the Buckeyes of Cincinnati in 1868. The two then jumped to the Cincinnati Club for its final two triumphant seasons. Leonard played left field for the Red Stockings and after leaving Cincinnati became a solid second-rank star, primarily for Harry Wright's Boston team. A good hitter and excellent outfielder, Leonard was a more than competent infielder as well. He finished his career with a return to Cincinnati in 1880, but by this time the last-place Reds were a far cry from the unbeaten team of eleven years earlier, and Leonard himself was over the hill, reportedly in large measure due to failing eyesight. Leonard later worked for Wright and Ditson, the sporting goods firm co-owned by his former Cincinnati and Boston teammate George Wright. He died in Boston in 1903.

John McLean: John Roll McLean was born September 17, 1848, the son of *Cincinnati Enquirer* publisher Washington McLean. Like many members of the Cincinnati Club, McLean was a Harvard student. He filled the critical position of catcher for the Cincinnati team in 1867 and is said to have been a talented player. Cincinnati baseball historian Harry Ellard says that, in a day when catchers wore no protective equipment of any type, McLean was the first man to stand directly behind the bat, but that is a distinction claimed by many players in many cities.

As a result of his fearless technique, however, McLean failed to last a full season with the team. He was struck on the left eye by a foul tip, an injury so severe that it appeared for a time he might lose the eye. He never played again, a loss that weakened the Red Stockings coming as it did just before their highly anticipated match with the touring Nationals of Washington.

McLean subsequently went to work with the *Enquirer*, learning the business from the ground up and eventually succeeding his father as publisher. Particularly strong baseball coverage was an important element in helping the *Enquirer* thrive on the basis of its appeal to a large and broad constituency of readers. He played a role behind the scenes in the organization of later Cincinnati professional teams, not to mention the vicious feuding among the backers of Cincinnati's professional clubs in the early 1880s. McLean was active in Democratic politics in Ohio, but after acquiring the *Washington Post*, he relocated to the national capital in 1886. When he died in June 9, 1916, at his home near Washington, he left an estate estimated at nearly one hundred million dollars.

Cal McVey: The talented McVey is comparatively little known today, but he might be recalled as a peer of great contemporaries such as Cap Anson, Jim O'Rourke, and Deacon Jim White had he not interrupted his major league career soon after his thirtieth birthday to move west and settle in California. After the dissolution of the Cincinnati Club, McVey batted .346 through nine seasons of play with various clubs in the National Association and National League. The right fielder for the famous Red Stockings was always most at home in the outfield and the infield corners, but he could play virtually any position, even catching on a regular basis several seasons and filling in as a backup pitcher for Chicago.

McVey was born August 30, 1849, in Montrose, Iowa, but grew up in Indianapolis, where he learned the game. He played for the Actives of Indianapolis until John Joyce made several trips to that city to sign the nineteen-year-old for Cincinnati in 1869. After the breakup of the Red Stockings, McVey spent most of the next five seasons playing for Wright's perennial champion Boston teams, then joined three other stars in moving to Chicago, where his team won another championship. In 1878 he returned to Cincinnati with a three-year contract but found himself at liberty when the club disbanded at the end of the 1879 season, to be replaced by a new organization taking the Cincinnati franchise. In order to avoid a money-losing post-season exhibition season, the players were released early and lost a month's salary and, in McVey's case, the last year of his contract. The disgusted McVey traveled to California with a barnstorming team that fall, and liked the West so much he never moved back. He was involved intermittently in the active West Coast baseball scene but made his living in various pursuits and became a dim memory to fans and reporters. He lost everything in the great San Francisco earthquake and suffered other setbacks but survived to be brought back to Cincinnati in 1919 as one of the few survivors of the unbeaten team during festivities honoring the Reds' championship team. McVey died in San Francisco on August 20, 1926.

J. Wayne Neff: James Moore Wayne Neff was always known in baseball circles as J. Wayne Neff, but city directories and formal documents in Cincinnati generally referred to him as J.M.W. Neff. On his father's side, Neff was a member of a family that had come west to Cincinnati around the 1830s to establish a dealership in hardware, although the firm had dissolved by the time Wayne, born April 8, 1847, had come of age.

Neff evidently was an amateur player of some skill, as he held down the first base position for the Cincinnati Club's first nine in 1866 and 1867. Neff's real moment in the sun, as far as Cincinnati baseball was concerned, would come in 1877, when the city's National League team fell apart in midseason. By this time, Neff was a considerable success in business. According to the 1870 census, he was involved in Cincinnati's leading industry, the pork business, and was worth almost $50,000, a very comfortable fortune for the time; he served as secretary of the Cincinnati Board of Trade at the same time. When the Reds ran into trouble in 1877, Neff had the money and reputation to lead a consortium of local businessmen who picked up the pieces and reorganized the club, with Neff taking the club presidency. The new management scored a success the following season when the Reds, last-place finishers in their first two seasons in the National League, finished a strong second. The following season, however, a high-priced roster failed to produce results, and Neff was faulted for spending too much money on a few star players and meddling in the team's management when it did not win. By season's end, Neff had wearied of heavy losses. To the disgust of local fans and the press he engineered the premature release of the team's players to save money. He then took the organization out of business, leaving another group of new investors to take over a franchise handicapped by a late start in organizing and signing players. As a result, Neff exited the National League with few friends in Cincinnati's baseball community, but he remained a prosperous Cincinnati businessman. He died in New York on May 31, 1903, apparently while on a visit.

David Schwartz: Schwartz played twelve games for the Cincinnatis in 1867 and posted one of the best runs-per-game averages of any player on an NABBP club. He moved on to Detroit in 1868 but did not stay there long either and a man by that name played for the Lone Star Club of New Orleans in 1870.

Thomas Smith: Our sources do not mention Thomas G. Smith as a player, but he was vice president of the club in 1869 and a director in 1870. In company with president Aaron Champion and secretary John Joyce, he handed in his resignation at a club meeting on August 3, 1870, a fact that suggests Smith was associated with Champion and Joyce in their advocacy of an aggressive policy of expenditure and professionalization. Smith later was president of the City Board of Affairs.

William B. Smith: "Policy Bill" Smith plays little or no role in most accounts of the club's history, but in a long series of articles published in the *Cincinnati Commercial Tribune* in 1912, Harry Millar, who had been active as a reporter and follower of the game as far back as the days of the Red Stockings, describes Smith as an important backer of the club through moral as well as financial support. A great admirer of Smith, Millar claimed the club's organization had first been put on the tracks in a meeting at Smith's home, before the formal inauguration of the club at the meeting of July 11, 1866. Millar implies that Smith played a crucial role in finding money to send the Red Stockings on their early summer road trip in 1869 and goes so far as to describe him as "the man to whom world is indebted for most famous of all clubs." Born in Cincinnati on October 3, 1829, Smith was of comparatively advanced years to have taken up a new athletic sport in the middle and late 1860s, so it is not surprising to see him missing from accounts of the club's early players; what is more unexpected is that according to Millar he never joined the club at all. This may account for his absence from other accounts of the club's history, if Millar is not grossly exaggerating his role. Millar notes Smith's failure to become a member as a remarkable fact, without making any attempt to account for it.

Possibly the explanation may be that Smith seems to have been the sort of man who operated most comfortably in the shadows. Historian Mark Wahlgren Summers describes him as a Cincinnati gambler and an operator of lotteries — the "policy" games that account for his nickname — who was accused in 1873 by *Cincinnati Commercial* editor-publisher Murat Halstead of having managed the bribery of state legislatures to prevent the illegalization of his lotteries.[9] Summers regards the accusations as baseless, but it is clear that Smith was a behind-the-scenes political operator and fixer. Even an admiring obituary in the *Commercial Tribune*, possibly written by Millar, says he had played "a large part in directing the affairs of the city through his close relationship with the politicians and officials in power," a characterization that could be taken in a sinister sense, although the author clearly did not intend it so. According to the *Commercial* obituary, at some point he suffered financial reverses as well as an onset of bad health and moved to Denver to recuperate, but he had returned with health and fortunes recovered and died at his home in Cincinnati on August 18, 1914.

Bellamy Storer: In 1867 Storer played second base, and he still appeared in center field a few times in 1868, but his greatest distinctions were achieved off the baseball field. Born in Cincinnati on August 28, 1847, Storer was another member of the Cincinnati Club who was a Cincinnati Law School student and an alumnus of Harvard, from which he had graduated in 1867. Storer's father was a Cincinnati attorney and judge who had served in Congress. Storer followed in his father's footsteps by obtaining a judgeship and spending two terms in Congress. Later, he became ambassador to Belgium, Spain, and Austria-Hungary. Storer's wife Maria founded the famous Rockwood Pottery, and Nicholas Longworth, speaker of the house in the 1920s, was his nephew. He died November 11, 1922, in France.

Charley Sweasy: Born on November 2, 1848, in Newark, New Jersey, Charles Sweasy came west to Cincinnati in 1868 with Andy Leonard, his friend and teammate on the Irvington Club of Irvington, New Jersey. The two played for the Buckeyes and then jumped to the Cincinnati Club in 1869. Sweasy was never a great hitter and was something of a discipline problem, but his play at second base attracted admiring attention during his two years with the Red Stockings. When the club disbanded at the end of the 1870 season, Sweasy was signed by the ambitious Olympics of Washington and given the captaincy, a position roughly equivalent to that of a modern field manager. However, he came down with a debilitating illness in the summer of 1871. He recovered to play again but seems to have been permanently weakened by his ailment and soon dropped out of top-flight competition. Along with Charlie Gould, another old Red Stocking hero, Sweasy was back in Cincinnati in 1876, but he batted only .211 for a last-place team. His last National League team was Providence, and he seems to have taken up taken up employment in that city as a hatter. In the mid–1880s he returned to New Jersey, living in Irvington and Newark, where he died on March 30, 1908. (Sweasy has often been confused with Charles Swasey, a different player associated with the Forest Citys of Rockford, and for a long time encyclopedias listed "Swasey" as Sweasy's real name. His listed middle name of James may also be a mistake.)

Oak Taylor: Born in Cincinnati on March 27, 1852, Oakley Robinson Taylor had barely turned seventeen when the 1869 season began, but he had already played for the Great Westerns and Walnut Hills clubs and the Cincinnati Junior nine formed by John Draper as a kind of junior varsity for the Cincinnati Club. Evidently, he showed enough promise that Harry Wright tapped him to be one of the substitutes on the Red Stockings. He saw little action but filled the role of scorer, which regularly went to a substitute, and stayed with the team for the entire year, joining the rest of the Red Stockings for a trip to the Pacific Coast at the end of the season. After that, he seems to have disappeared from the professional baseball world. The son of a well-to-do businessman, Taylor married a local girl in 1873 and became a traveling salesman living in Ohio until he moved south in the mid 1890s. The obscure substitute joined 1869 stars George Wright and Cal McVey in attending the festivities celebrating the Cincinnati Reds' 1919 championship and the fiftieth anniversary of the championship team. He eventually moved to the Atlanta area and died in Hapeville (near the Atlanta airport) on April 27, 1931.

Fred Waterman: Frederick A. Waterman was born in 1845 in New York, where he learned to play ball. He was playing for the famous Excelsiors when Cincinnati president Aaron Champion brought him west to play third base in 1868. Waterman was given a sinecure as a shipping clerk in the office of one of the club's members in order to stay on the right side of the anti-professionalism rules. Waterman was one of the more highly paid Red Stocking professionals, but drinking and a tendency to gain weight took a toll on his career, and he accomplished little after the Cincinnati Club broke up. Like many of the veterans of the undefeated team, especially the less successful ones, Waterman eventually wound up back in Cincinnati, returning during the 1875 season to take a position as the team captain and probably the only player paid more than semipro wages of the Cumminsville Blues in a suburb just north of downtown Cincinnati. Alec Voss, a Blues player who went on to a long professional career, later remembered that "old Fred" had played very well; old Fred was in fact not yet thirty. Late in the season Waterman was picked up by Chicago and played five games, but that seems to have been his last hurrah in baseball, and he subsequently hit the skids. "Drunk and friendless," according to *The Sporting News*, in 1899 Waterman returned to his old stomping grounds in Cincinnati, where he died of pneumonia.

William Worthington: Worthington was the team's scorer until 1868, after which substitute players took over the job. He was born in Cincinnati on August 3, 1847, and was yet another Ivy-League-educated attorney, taking his Harvard degree in 1867. That he was scorer suggests that he may not have been much of a player, but had a knowledge of the game superior to that of many of his peers. This background he may have acquired, as seems to have been true of some of the other club members, while he was in school in the East. In 1877 Worthington formed a legal partnership with Drausin Wulsin, another old member of the Cincinnati Club. Worthington resigned from the firm in the early 1880s to take what turned out to be a short-lived judgeship and then participated in the formation of the firm of Worthington, Strong and Stettinius, the predecessor of today's large law firm Taft Stettinius & Hollister. In 1886 he served on a commission to replace the Cincinnati courthouse, which had been destroyed in rioting two years before. He died in 1923, but his name lives on today in the form of the William Worthington Prize for Best Case Note annually awarded to a student at the University of Cincinnati Law School.

George Wright: The brother of manager-captain Harry Wright, George was the son of English-born professional cricketer Sam Wright, who had immigrated to New York to serve as a club professional for cricket clubs there. Harry and George were both excellent cricket players but drifted into baseball because it provided better employment opportunities in the United States. George in particular was something of a boy wonder, catching at a very young age for clubs in the New York area before switching to shortstop. He played for the National Club of Washington in 1867 when it toured the Midwest and handily beat the Cincinnati Club with brother Harry as well as their local rivals the Buckeyes. By this time he was considered the best player in the country. In 1869 George Wright was added to the Cincinnati roster, and he contributed mightily toward the unbeaten season. He later accompanied his brother to Boston, where he remained until he moved to Providence in 1879 and won a pennant in his only season as manager. Injuries, age, and perhaps difficulties adjusting to batting the newly developed curve ball had diminished his value somewhat, but he remained a viable player well into his thirties. In 1880 he wanted to return to Boston to watch over his interests in the sporting goods firm Wright and Ditson, but Providence held his right under the new reserve rule. Wright became the first player to hold out for almost an entire season, and although he made brief comebacks later, his career was virtually ended. His sporting goods business thrived, and Wright became interested in the new game of tennis, paying rather little attention to baseball except to complain occasionally that fielders' gloves had made the game too easy, a strange point of view for a man who sold sporting goods. He died on August 21, 1937, in Boston, the last survivor of the famous Red Stockings.

Harry Wright: The son of a cricket professional who had emigrated from Great Britain to the United States, Wright played both his father's game and baseball, originally coming to Cincinnati to serve as property man and club professional for the Union Cricket Club. A center fielder and sometimes pitcher, Wright was a fine player, but by 1869 he was 34 and already past his prime; his real fame lies in having been the first great baseball manager. His background in cricket, at the time a far more developed and sophisticated game than baseball, probably played a part in helping him develop the tactics and training methods that contributed to his standing. His success in Cincinnati made his name in the baseball world, and he augmented his reputation by building a new team in Boston that won six championships in eight years before going on to manage Providence and Philadelphia. After 1878 the championships stopped coming, and Wright spent the last fifteen years of his career without ever bringing home a first-place team, although his clubs were usually winners. Nevertheless, he remained a man immensely respected for character as well as ability. After his retirement in 1893 he served briefly as chief of the National League's umpires and died October 3, 1895, in Atlantic City.

Drausin Wulsin: Wulsin, besides playing second base during its first season, was a charter member and director of the club. He was also the one-man supply committee who scandalized the membership by his extravagant purchase of a twenty-dollar chest. Wulsin was born June 10, 1842, near New Orleans, and moved in childhood to Cincinnati. Wulsin's brother Lucien became the owner of the well-known Baldwin Piano Company, while Drausin went into the law, one of a number of Cincinnati Club members who were alumni of the Cincinnati Law School.

After playing shortstop for the club early in its history, Wulsin was pushed out of the lineup. An article published some years later and written with tongue perhaps partly in cheek says his chief weakness was unsteadiness catching pop flies. A weakness on popups is not necessarily a fatal weakness for an infielder, as the career of Rogers Hornsby demonstrates. Wulsin was most certainly not a Hornsby, but he does seem to have been a serious player and not an entirely inept one. When the Cincinnati and Holt clubs put on a game featuring teams of muffins — the term then used to describe inept amateurs who could be relied on to muff any ball hit to them — Wulsin, being the best of this bad lot of Cincinnati players, was captain of his team, and is said to have "played an earnest game throughout and was much perturbed over the comic stunts of his team."

After the Cincinnati Club passed out of existence, Wulsin became a leading corporate attorney in the city. At different times he was the law partner of two other former Cincinnati Club members, Alfred Goshorn and William Worthington. On his death on November 3, 1910, Wulsin left behind a diverse record of professional, civic, and scholarly activities, including a term on the city council, several stints as president of the Cincinnati Bar Association, a variety of club memberships, life membership of the Ohio State Archaeological and Historical Society, and service for many years as a trustee of Cincinnati's public library. Nevertheless, his involvement in the brief-lived Cincinnati Base Ball Club almost half a century earlier found a space in his obituaries. "He was a charter member of the Cincinnati Base Ball Club, which was which was organized ... as a purely amateur club, its members playing purely for the physical benefits to be derived from the game," reads a typical example.

Henry Yergason: See Charter Oaks of Hartford, Connecticut.

SOURCES

The sources on the Red Stockings are incomparably fuller than those available for the vast majority of contemporary clubs, and in fact dwarf those for even the most famous of the Cincinnati Club's rivals. The following are a sample of items that have proven useful for this article.

NOTES

1. This law firm went through various changes of name as partners came and went, with a former Red Stocking outfielder eventually taking pride of place as senior partner; see the biographical sketch of J. William Johnson. Accounts of the Red Stockings' formation usually refer to the firm as Sherman, Moulton and Tilden, but judging by the listing in the 1866 city directory, the form given here seems to have been the one in use during the summer of 1866.
2. *Cincinnati Commercial*, March 2, 1879, p. 2, col. 5.
3. *Cincinnati Commercial*, March 9, 1879, p. 2, col. 1.
4. Stephen Guschov, *Red Stockings of Cincinnati* (Jefferson, NC: McFarland, 1998), 68.
5. Christopher Devine, *Harry Wright* (Jefferson, NC: McFarland, 2003), 82–83.
6. *New York Clipper*, April 20, 1872, p. 19, col. 1.
7. "President Lincoln and Mrs. Hoge," *Lincoln Editor* 2:4 (October–December 2002), 2–3; Mrs. A.H. Hoge, *The Boys in Blue: or Heroes of the "Rank and File"* (New York: E.B. Trent and Co., 1867).
8. *Cincinnati Commercial*, reprinted in the *New York Sunday Mercury*, May 22, 1880.
9. Mark Wahlgren Summers, *The Era of Good Stealings* (New York: Oxford University Press, 1993), 83–84.

BIBLIOGRAPHY

Cincinnati Commercial, especially a series of articles in March 1879.
Cincinnati Commercial Tribune, especially a lengthy series of articles by Harry Millar published during the summer of 1912.
Cincinnati Enquirer.
Cincinnati Times, especially articles on April 15, 1868 and May 8, 1868.
Devine, Christopher. *Harry Wright: The Father of Professional Base Ball.* Jefferson, NC: McFarland, 2003.
Ellard, Harry. *Base Ball in Cincinnati: A History.* Cincinnati: Ohio Book Store, 1987 (reprint of original self-published in 1907).
Guschov, Stephen D. *The Red Stockings of Cincinnati: Base Ball's First All-Professional Team.* Jefferson, NC: McFarland, 1998.
McKenna, Brian. "Asa Brainard," SABR BioProject. http://bioproj.sabr.org/bioproj.cfm?a=v&v=1&bid=3041&pid=1466.
Morris, Peter. *But Didn't We Have Fun? An Informal History of Baseball's Pioneer Era, 1843–1870.* Chicago: Ivan R. Dee, 2008.
New York Clipper, July 1, 1871; Aug. 12, 1871; April 20, 1872.

Rhodes, Greg, and John Erardi. *First Boys of Summer: The 1869–1870 Cincinnati Red Stockings*. Cincinnati: Road West Publishing, 1994.

Ryczek, William J. *When Johnny Came Sliding Home: The Post–Civil War Baseball Boom, 1865–1870*. Jefferson, NC: McFarland, 1998.

❖ *Western Unions of Cincinnati* (Greg Perkins) ❖

Club History

The following was written by Harry M. Millar and published in the *Cincinnati Commercial Tribune*, August 28, 1912.[1]

The baseball fever had become not only national but general in its character and on Walnut Hills, in that delectable locality then known as the "stone jug," the cry "play ball" among the colored baseball organizations became one of the daily customs—I say daily, but I mean upon week days only, because these colored people did not break the Sabbath in baseball just then.

There was as much favoritism, discussion, contention and enthusiasm among the colored clubs as at that time existed among their white opponents and brethren of the diamond field.

There was one club in particular, known as the Western Unions, that played ball with a vengeance and its nine was made up of the sons of the best-known colored people in Cincinnati.

The Western Unions had as their president that prominent and nationally known educator, Peter H. Clark, of the Gaines Colored High school, and there never was in this part of the country a more zealous or earnest tutor of colored youth than he.

I did not know much about this colored club of ballplayers except by hearsay, and upon the merits of which Prof. Ball, Cincinnati's famous photographer and one of the best in that profession in the United States, would grow exceedingly eloquent.

There was another club up in Newtown called the Independents that gave the Western Unions many an exciting tussle.

Colonel Robert M. Harlan, a very prominent colored citizen of this city, was another who took a fatherly interest in the Western Unions, as did "Major" Travis, a Vine street barber who studied law and became quite a distinguished character in police court and magistrate practice.

Those admirers of the game determined that the Western Unions should present as striking and favorable appearance at play as the white ballplayers and took up a subscription list to get the players of that organization a suitable uniform.

On Thursday afternoon, Aug. 12, 1869, on the Iron Slag Grounds of the Buckeye club the Western Unions and the Independents of Newtown crossed bats in one of the most remarkable games of baseball of the period for the colored championship of Hamilton County.

In the crowd of more than 2,000 persons who attended the game probably more than half were white people drawn there out of curiosity, while the grand stand was about one-third filled with colored women and children.

The Western Unions appeared for the first time in their new uniforms.

It was the most gorgeous combination that had ever lent color to the diamond field.

The grand stand had in one end a band composed about equally of colored people and Italians, the latter playing guitars, mandolins and harps, and the colored aggregation keeping the dust of the diamond lively with the tintinnabulations of base drums, cornets and other discordant brass instruments.

When the Western Unions marched upon the ground the parade of the Red Hussars was matchless to it.

Their pitcher, Watson, by name, wore a yellow fez like that of a drum major, with a long red feather at the top.

They marched around the bases in single file, all wearing flaring red shirts, short green pants, black sashes and black and white checkered stockings and yellow caps.

When the pitcher reached his position and the others had posed themselves a photograph of the scene was taken by the colored Fourth street, photographing firm of Ball & Thomas, after which Pitcher Watson removed his fez, laid it on the grass beside him, put on his yellow cap to one side of his head, imitated the lawdyda characteristic pose of Brainard [Cincinnati Red Stockings pitcher Asa Brainard] and let go with a yell that was enough to frighten the life out of the batter of the opposition club had he not been "on" to the game.

And talk about baseball mannerisms!

It kept one's head in a whirl to watch the antics of the men at bases and when they swat the ball and the player broke away to first, the Cherokee, Chicopee, Comanche Indian yells would be weak whispering compared to the present-day style of coaching of the fellow players of the batsman.

While it was a game chock full of intense excitement the players of the Red Stocking nine in all their practical experience never had, in the closest of contests, witnessed anything that was of more grave earnestness than this game of baseball between two crack colored organizations.

The game was won by the Independents of Newtown, the score standing 38 to 26.[2]

Without Harry Millar's vivid article, the Western Unions would be another pioneer Ohio Valley African American baseball club known only by brief mentions in local newspapers. Ohio Valley community histories and newspapers from the nineteenth century tended to ignore African American accomplishments and institutions. Even Harry Ellard's *Base Ball in Cincinnati* (1907)—long considered a definitive source for early Cincinnati baseball history—did not identify any African American baseball clubs. The stigma attached to any public contact with African Americans prompted the Alerts, an all-white Plainville, Ohio, baseball club, to publish a vehement denial when the *Cincinnati Commercial* reported in 1869 that the club had played the Independents of Newtown. The Alerts' denial reflected a hostile racial environment that allowed a Cincinnati newspaper to matter-of-factly announce a baseball game involving the Ku-Klux Club of nearby Covington, Kentucky, without offering any comment about the club's name.[3]

People Associated with the Western Union Club of Cincinnati

James Pressley Ball: Born a free African American in Virginia in 1825, James P. Ball learned photography from another African American photographer, John B. Bailey. By 1849, Ball had settled in Cincinnati and opened his own photography studio. He attained a national reputation as a photographer. Ball's photographic subjects included Charles Dickens, Queen Victoria, Frederick Douglass, and Jenny Lind. Ball used his art to advance the abolitionist cause; his 1857 panoramic exhibition on the African slave-trade was shown in Cincinnati and Boston. After encountering financial difficulties due to bad investments, Ball left Cincinnati in 1871 and continued his photography in several Western cities. Having moved around frequently, he died in Honolulu on May 4, 1904. The Cincinnati Museum Center has the largest collection of Ball's images held by a single repository.[4]

Peter Humphries Clark: President of the Western Union Club. Clark was born a free man in Cincinnati in 1829 to a mixed-race family. His father was the manumitted son of a slave and her white master. Before the Civil War, Peter Clark was an outspoken abolitionist and an associate of Levi Coffin and Frederick Douglass in their anti-slavery activities. Educated at Oberlin College, Peter Clark became a teacher and later the principal of the all-black Gaines High School. Clark favored school segregation because he feared that integrated schools would compromise the quality of education provided for African American students. He also believed that integrated schools would take away jobs from African American teachers in addition to diminishing African American self-determination. Clark was a visible civil rights political activist who would forge alliances with Republicans and Democrats to advance his goals. In regards to Clark's talent and intellect, Ohio Governor George Hoadly observed, "His color has kept him in the shadows: had he been a white man, there is no position in the State to which he might not have aspired." Clark later moved to St. Louis, where he died on June 21, 1925, three months after celebrating his ninety-sixth birthday.[5]

Colonel Robert James Harlan: Born a slave in Virginia on December 12, 1816, to the elite Harlan family, Robert Harlan was rumored to be the half-brother of United States Supreme Court Justice John Marshall Harlan. Robert was raised in the Harlan home near Harrodsburg, Kentucky, and educated by the Harlan family. The Harlans permitted Robert to hire himself out. He eventually owned a barber shop in Harrodsburg and a grocery store in Lexington, Kentucky. Freed by the Harlans in 1848, Robert James Harlan went to California for the 1849 gold rush and made a fortune. Shortly thereafter, he settled in Cincinnati and invested in real estate and a photography studio. In 1851, Harlan attended the Great Exhibition in London. In 1858, Harlan moved his family to England to escape the pervasive racism in America. He returned to Cincinnati in 1868, where he helped start an African American militia company and became a leader in the Republican Party. As an Ohio state legislator, Harlan helped secure the repeal of Ohio's discriminatory "Black Laws" in 1886. He died in Cincinnati on September 21, 1897.[6]

Major William H. Travis: According to the 1870 census, William H. Travis was born in Tennessee around 1835. Travis was African American, but it is not known whether he had been a slave. By 1867, Travis was working as a barber in Cincinnati. During the early 1870s, he led a Cincinnati militia company comprised of African Americans. Like Peter H. Clark and Robert Harlan, Travis was politically active. As leaders of rival Republican Party factions, Travis and Harlan often clashed. Like Peter H. Clark, Travis would switch his party affiliation to punish the party that had neglected the interests of African American voters. In addition to owning a barber shop, Travis studied law and was the first African American to be admitted to the Cincinnati bar. He also fought for civil rights. Travis once sued a druggist who had refused to serve him on account of his race. William H. Travis died of consumption (tuberculosis) in Cincinnati on October 4, 1880.[7]

Notes

1. Harry M. Millar (1849–1920) worked for sixty years in the newspaper business. His father, Constantine D. Millar, was an editor for the *Commercial*. Harry traveled with the 1869 Cincinnati Red Stockings on their historic cross-country tour and, along the way, sent correspondences to the *Commercial*. Millar's article about the Western Unions was part of a series he wrote on early baseball and the Cincinnati Red Stockings. For biographical information about Harry M. Millar, see the *Cincinnati Commercial Tribune*, January 18, 1920. Also see George Mortimer Roe, ed., *Cincinnati: The Queen City of the West* (Cincinnati: The Cincinnati Times-Star Co., 1895), 403–404.

2. The Independents also won the return game with the Western Unions played at Newtown by a score of 68 to 20. See the *Cincinnati Commercial*, September 8, 1869.

3. A partial list of these clubs included the Modocs of Cincinnati, Ohio; the Chocolate Stockings of Ripley, Ohio; and the Black Stockings of Newtown, Ohio — see *Cincinnati Commercial*, July 10, 1870 and *Cincinnati Commercial*, November 6, 1869. Also *Cincinnati Commercial*, August 12, 1869; *Cincinnati Commercial*, August 14, 1869; Darrel E. Bigham, *On Jordan's Banks: Emancipation and Its Aftermath in the Ohio River Valley* (Lexington: University Press of Kentucky, 2001), 141–150; *Cincinnati Daily Gazette*, July 29, 1871.

4. The Cincinnati Museum Center is making its collection of Ball images available online. For biographical information about James P. Ball and a searchable collection of his photographic images, see http://library.cincymuseum.org/ball/jpball.htm.

5. Bigham, *On Jordan's Banks*, 39–40, 287–288; Lawrence Grossman, "In His Veins Coursed No Bootlicking Blood: The Career of Peter H. Clark," *Ohio History* (Spring 1977), 76–96.

6. William J. Simmons, *Mark of Men: Eminent, Progressive, and Rising* (Cleveland: George M. Rewell & Co., 1887), 613–616; *Cincinnati Commercial Gazette*, June 8, 1884; *Cincinnati Enquirer*, September 22, 1897.

7. 1870 census; *Williams' Cincinnati City Directory for 1867*; *Cincinnati Daily Gazette*, September 6, 1870; *Cincinnati Daily Gazette*, August 7, 1877; *Cincinnati Commercial*, March 26, 1872; *Cincinnati Daily Gazette*,

March 30, 1872; John Clay Smith, *Emancipation: The Making of the Black Lawyer, 1844–1944* (Philadelphia: University of Pennsylvania Press, 1993), 411; *Cincinnati Commercial*, May 23, 1873; *Cincinnati Commercial*, August 10, 1873; *Cincinnati Commercial*, October 5, 1880.

❖ *Eagles of Brooklyn, Kentucky* (Greg Perkins) ❖

CLUB HISTORY

In 1874, a Northern Kentucky newspaper cited former Eagle Base Ball Club of Brooklyn, Kentucky, member Henry Pudder as claiming credit for "first introducing baseball to this part of the West." Indeed, Brooklyn, Kentucky, cast a long shadow over the game's origins and early growth in the region. Located on the Ohio River across from Cincinnati, Brooklyn had a townball club before the Civil War and, apparently, some baseball players. In 1859, a group of Brooklyn's young men reportedly challenged anyone within a one-hundred mile radius to a game of baseball. This declaration spurred the creation of Cincinnati's Buckeye Base Ball Club in 1861.[1]

The Civil War disrupted sports and everything else in Brooklyn. A reported 40 of Brooklyn's 58 families had a family member in the Union Army. Probably sometime after the war ended in 1865, the Eagle Base Ball Club of Brooklyn commenced activities. In an 1866 article, the *Cincinnati Commercial* described the Eagles as the "the oldest organization of the kind in this vicinity."[2]

Metropolitan Cincinnati's first match game of New York rules baseball took place in Brooklyn on September 8, 1866, when the Live Oak Club of Cincinnati crossed the Ohio River to play the Eagles. The Eagle Club's grounds were located next to a school that bordered Brooklyn and neighboring Jamestown, Kentucky. In a 1919 interview, James Fogarty, Jr., of the Live Oaks recalled the impression made that day by the "rolling mill toughs" that comprised the Eagles. He remembered the long fly balls James Mahaffey hit over the schoolhouse in his first two times at bat. The Live Oaks placed an outfielder behind the schoolhouse to counter the Eagle slugger. Cincinnati baseball historian Harry Ellard described Mahaffey as a strong hitter who "used only one hand and a short bat eighteen inches long." In its account of the game, the *Cincinnati Daily Times* also noted the Eagles' imposing size. The *Times* described the team as "a stout, hardy set of men" who wore "Scotch caps ... very becoming to them." Despite Mahaffey's power hitting, the Eagles lost to the Live Oaks 52 to 41.[3]

The Eagle Club's working-class reputation reflected Brooklyn's ties to the Ohio River. Besides having wharves and other river-related businesses, Brooklyn was also connected by ferry to boat-building facilities in Cincinnati. A review of census records and extant city directories show that several Eagle Base Ball Club members had river-related jobs. Henry Pudder was a river boat pilot. David Bricker, Michael Kennedy, William Lusk, and John Swift were caulkers — a job that involved making boats watertight by caulking their seams. James Mahaffey was a ship's carpenter.[4]

With their strong neighborhood and working ties, the Eagles may have measured baseball success by the game's social benefits rather than wins and losses. At least for the 1866 season, the Eagles lost all of their known games. Nonetheless, the Eagles actively participated in early Cincinnati baseball. The club played in two local tournaments in 1866 — one at the fair grounds in Florence, Kentucky, and another at the Union Cricket Club grounds in Cincinnati. The Eagles were Northern Kentucky's sole representative at the Cincinnati tournament. In 1867, the Eagles entered the Ohio State Base Ball Tournament held at the Cincinnati Club's Union Grounds; the Eagles lost the only game they played. The Eagle Club apparently kept their baseball activities local. Like other Northern Kentucky teams, it did not join the National Association of Base Ball Players.[5]

Judging by their absence from Cincinnati-area newspapers after the 1867 season, the Eagle Club probably ceased baseball activities soon thereafter. Yet at least one member stayed involved with the game in Brooklyn, which was renamed Dayton after an 1867 merger with Jamestown. During the mid-1870s, Henry Pudder led the McArthur Base Ball Club of Dayton. The name Eagle Club survived in Dayton through at least the 1930s as a fraternal organization whose activities included sponsoring a baseball team.[6]

CLUB MEMBERS

Bricker: second base. This was probably David Bricker. He lived in Brooklyn and had both military and occupational ties to other Eagle players. The Pennsylvania-born Bricker served in Company H, 15th Kentucky Infantry of the Union Army during the Civil War. He worked as a caulker. Bricker died in November 1887 in Dayton, Kentucky.[7]

Kennedy: right field. This is likely Michael Kennedy. Like David Bricker, he also had military and occupational ties to other Eagle players. Born in Canada, Kennedy also served in Company H, 15th Kentucky Infantry. He, too, was a caulker.[8]

James Mahaffey: catcher and captain. Born in Pennsylvania around 1842, Mahaffey moved to Dayton, Kentucky, where he worked as a ship's carpenter. He died in Newport after 1931.[9]

Henry Pudder: pitcher. A Pennsylvania native and a river boat pilot, Pudder moved to Brooklyn sometime around 1865 while in his early thirties. He probably learned about baseball while living in Allegheny, Pennsylvania, during the late 1850s and early 1860s. Pudder also led the McArthur Base Ball Club of Dayton during the 1870s before moving back to Pittsburgh sometime before 1880. Pudder died there on February 22, 1907.[10]

John W. Swift: shortstop. Born in Boston in February 1846, Swift became a Brooklyn resident at the close of the Civil War. During the war, Swift served in Company H, 15th Kentucky Infantry of the Union Army. He was active in the Grand Army of the Republic for several years. During his years with the Eagle Base Ball Club, Swift worked as a caulker. Later, Swift served as Dayton's police chief for twenty years. He died in Dayton, Kentucky, on February 15, 1925.[11]

NOTES

1. *Ludlow (KY) Reporter*, August 15, 1874; *Cincinnati Commercial*, July 12, 1859; *Cincinnati Commercial*, August 21, 1870.
2. *Cincinnati Daily Enquirer*, December 16, 1863; *Cincinnati Commercial*, September 9, 1866.
3. *Cincinnati Commercial*, September 9, 1866; *Cincinnati Post*, August 14, 1919; Harry Ellard, *Base Ball in Cincinnati: A History* (Cincinnati: Johnson & Hardin, 1907; reprint, Cincinnati: Ohio Book Store, 1987), 37–38; *Cincinnati Daily Times*, September 10, 1866.
4. See "Dayton," *The Kentucky Encyclopedia*, John E. Kleber, ed. in chief (Lexington: University Press of Kentucky, 1992), p. 259; 1860 and 1870 censuses; 1872–73 Dayton City Directory. Only last names were given for the Dayton starting nine. This makes identifying players difficult but not impossible. The men referenced in this entry had other things in common besides baseball — namely age, residency, occupation, and military experience.
5. In addition to losing to the Live Oaks, the Eagles also lost to the Holt Club of Newport, Kentucky — see *Cincinnati Daily Enquirer*, October 1, 1866; *Cincinnati Daily Times*, October 18, 1866; *Cincinnati Commercial*, November 4, 1866; Ellard, *Base Ball in Cincinnati*, 55–59.
6. *Ludlow (KY) Reporter*, August 15, 1874; *Kentucky Post*, September 16, 1932.
7. Ellard, *Base Ball in Cincinnati*, 37–38; *Williams' Dayton, Kentucky Directory for 1872–73*.
8. Ellard, *Base Ball in Cincinnati*, 37–38; *Cincinnati Commercial-Tribune*, August 1, 1912.
9. Ellard, *Base Ball in Cincinnati*, 37–38; Census records —1870, 1919, 1920, 1930; *Williams' Dayton, Kentucky Directory for 1872–73*.
10. Ellard, *Base Ball in Cincinnati*, 37–38; *Cincinnati Commercial*, September 9, 1866; Census records —1860, 1870, 1880, and 1900; *1864–65 Directory for Pittsburgh and Allegheny Cities*; *Williams' Dayton, Kentucky Directory for 1872–73*.
11. Ellard, *Base Ball in Cincinnati*, 37–38; Census records —1870, 1880, 1900, 1910, 1920; *Kentucky Post*, February 16, 1925; *Williams' Dayton, Kentucky Directory for 1872–73*.

❖ *Covington and Copec Clubs of Covington* (Greg Perkins) ❖

CLUB HISTORY

Covington, Kentucky, located on the Ohio River across from Cincinnati, made several contributions to the rise of baseball in Cincinnati and its environs. Although Covington's early baseball clubs lacked the stability and longevity of their Cincinnati counterparts, Covington supplied competition and players for Cincinnati in its struggle to achieve baseball supremacy, first on a regional level and then nationally. Two of Covington's more prominent clubs, the Covingtons and the Copecs, are representative of the city's early contributions to baseball. Through shared players, the clubs became intertwined throughout their sporadic existence. One of their descendant clubs, the Star of Covington, helped lead a professional baseball revival in Cincinnati during the mid–1870s.

Of the early Covington baseball teams, the Covington Club probably emerged first. Before the founding of the Covington Base Ball Club, many of its constituents had played townball for the Olympic Club before switching to baseball. Many townball clubs in the Ohio Valley underwent similar conversions. The Covington Base Ball Club's formal birth occurred on July 28, 1866, at the home of Covington attorney William L. Grant. The Covington Club and the Live Oak Club of Cincinnati played in the Cincinnati area's second match game of baseball on September 15, 1866, at Covington's Willow Run Bottom, where a crowd estimated in excess of two thousand watched the Covington Club defeat the Live Oaks, 28–21. Covington's long history of baseball played at Willow Run Bottom has been memorialized by a mural on the city's floodwall.[1]

In October 1866, the Covington Club entered the Cincinnati region's first baseball tournament, held at the fairgrounds in nearby Florence, Kentucky. Other participating Northern Kentucky clubs included the Eagles of Brooklyn and the Holts of Newport. The Live Oaks and Buckeyes represented Cincinnati in the Florence tournament. The contestants played for an engraved silver ball for the tournament winner and a mounted silver bat for the runner-up.[2]

Adding a baseball tournament to the Florence Fair brought an urban bustle to an otherwise rural venue. Anticipating a large crowd, the tournament's organizers arranged for horse-drawn omnibuses to take baseball fans from Covington to Florence, an eight-mile journey. The *Cincinnati Daily Times* described the chaotic scene the morning of the tournament: "The day was very pleasant, and at an early hour the Lexington pike — the only approach to the grounds — was besieged with vehicles of all kinds, making their way to the tournament. It was about 10 o'clock when we arrived, and even then a very large crowd had assembled. A continuous in pouring [*sic*] of men, women, children, horses, and vehicles was kept up during the entire morning, so that by noon there must have been present nearly 6,000 or 7,000 persons."[3]

Those who endured the traffic saw a full day of baseball. The one-day tournament consisted of five-inning games to save time. In the first game, the Live Oaks defeated the Eagles 45 to 24. The second game matched the Buckeyes of Cincinnati with the Holts of Newport. Despite a home run and six runs scored by Charlie Gould, the Buckeyes surrendered a five-run lead and lost, 33–32. In the third game, the Covington Club routed the Live Oaks, 29–9, making for an all–Northern Kentucky championship match with the Holts. The Covington Club won 19–4 in a three-inning game shortened by darkness.[4]

Despite its strong start, the Covington Club soon faltered. Covington Club president Bushrod W. Foley, Jr., moved to Europe in April 1867 to pursue a doctoral degree in music. Without its leader, the Covington Club reportedly succumbed to dissension. Several former Covington Club players joined Cincinnati teams. Moses Grant of the Covington Club played for the Cincinnati Base Ball Club's first nine during the 1867 and 1868 seasons. Another Covington Club member, Ben Brookshaw, joined the Buckeyes. Two other Covington Club players joined the Live Oaks. The January 1, 1867, opening of the John A. Roebling Suspension Bridge that connected Cincinnati to Covington eased travel between the two cities and probably aided the dispersion of Covington Club players. The Roebling Suspension Bridge helped make residency a less important factor in the composition of metropolitan Cincinnati baseball clubs than it had been just one season earlier. Despite the loss of its best players, the Covington Club continued its baseball activities, but received only sporadic mention in Cincinnati newspapers during the 1867 and 1868 seasons.[5]

With the Covington Club in decline, the Copec Club emerged as Covington's leading team. Organized on October 4, 1866, the Copec Club took its name from a race horse. Though considered a junior club, the Copecs had talent, most notably John Shoup, James C. Ernst, and Pearce Barnes. Shoup had a long professional baseball career; Ernst later played first base for the Princeton University baseball team; Barnes played baseball at Yale University. The Copecs defeated the Holt Club of Newport and finished in third place in the 1867 Ohio State Base Ball Tournament played at Cincinnati's Union Grounds. Pearce Barnes won a Tournament prize as best left fielder. In 1868, the Copecs lost to the "Red Stockings" of Cincinnati twice, but in one game held the score to a respectable 30–14.[6]

Based on their absence from local newspapers after the 1868 season, the Copecs may have disbanded. Several Copecs joined the still extant Covington Club. In 1869, the Covington Base Ball Club secured two former Cincinnati Red Stockings, ex–Covington Club member Moses Grant and Cincinnati attorney Rufus King. Grant and King withdrew from the Cincinnati Base Ball Club after being displaced in the Red Stocking first nine by professional players. Ben Brookshaw also returned to the Covington Club. The *Cincinnati Commercial* praised the rebuilt Covington Club as having "many of our best amateur players." Despite the infusion of players, the Covington Club apparently became defunct again after the 1869 season.[7]

For the 1870 season, several of the former Covington and Copec Club players started a new baseball team — the Star Base Ball Club of Covington. The new Star Club included former Copec John Shoup along with what the *Cincinnati Daily Gazette* called "the best amateur talent in the Western country." The Stars defeated the Live Oaks of Cincinnati and undertook a tour of Kentucky, playing clubs in Lexington, Louisville, and Maysville. For the 1874 season, the Star Club included several former Copecs and Covington Club members such as Shoup, Ben Brookshaw, James C. Ernst, and Charles H. Thomas. The Stars, along with the Ludlow Base Ball Club of Ludlow, Kentucky, returned professional baseball to Cincinnati in 1875 when they began fielding paid nines. Their success on the field and at the gate inspired the creation of a new Cincinnati Red Stockings professional club later that season.[8]

Club Members

Pearce Barnes: Catcher and left field, Copec Club. Born in Mount Sterling, Kentucky, on September 14, 1851, to banker Thomas C. and Emily Barnes, Pearce Barnes moved to Covington, Kentucky, as a teen where he lived with his sister and prepared for college. Barnes attended Yale University — class of 1874 — and played on its baseball team. After graduation from Yale, Barnes earned a law degree from Columbia University in 1876. Barnes practiced law in New York City. He died on November 22, 1925, in Kent, Connecticut.[9]

Ben Brookshaw: Shortstop, Covington Club. Born 1845 in Covington to English immigrants Joseph and Dorothy Brookshaw, Ben Brookshaw was one of the Ohio Valley's most prominent early baseball players. As a young man, Brookshaw played townball for the Buckeye Town Ball Club. In September 1862, Brookshaw was mobilized into the Union Army to defend Northern Kentucky and Cincinnati from an approaching Confederate Army. He served in the 41st Kentucky Volunteer Infantry Regiment. Brookshaw later played professional baseball in Louisville, Memphis, and Rochester, New York. Ben Brookshaw died in Covington, Kentucky, on May 6, 1904.[10]

James Clarence Ernst: Copec Club (1867–68). Born July 10, 1853, in Covington, Kentucky, James C. Ernst had a privileged childhood. His father, William Ernst, made a modest fortune in banking and railroading. James Ernst attended Princeton University, where he played baseball. He also played baseball professionally for the Covington Stars in 1875. Afterwards, Ernst became one of the region's most visible business leaders in the utilities, banking, and transportation industries. He died in Asheville, North Carolina, on September 20, 1917.[11]

John Preston Ernst: Vice-President, Covington Base Ball Club (1868); President, Covington Base Ball Club (1869). Born November 16, 1845, in Covington, John P. Ernst was the older brother of James C. Ernst. He attended Miami University and became a prominent banker like his father. He died in Covington on January 13, 1925.[12]

Bushrod Walton Foley, Jr.: Catcher and President, Covington Club (1866). Bushrod W. Foley, Jr., was born January 31, 1845, in Covington. His father served as mayor of Covington. The successful escape of several Foley family slaves in 1853 provided abolitionists with hope for slavery's decline in urban Northern Kentucky. As a young man, Foley played townball for the Olympic Club of Covington. Leaving Covington in May 1867, Foley went first to Leipzig, Germany, and then to Paris, France, to study music. Upon his return to Covington in 1870, Foley started his career as a professor with what would become the Cincinnati Conservatory of Music. He was also a well-known church organist and choir director. Professor Foley died in 1924 in Cincinnati.[13]

Moses V. Grant: Second Baseman, Covington Club (1866); Director and Captain of the First Nine, Covington Club (1869); also a member of the Cincinnati Base Ball Club (see that club's entry for details). Grant came from one of Covington's most politically influential families. His grandfather, Moses V. Grant, was the mayor of Covington during the 1840s. Grant's father, William Letcher Grant, was a longtime Covington city councilman, who, with the support of African American voters, served in the Kentucky legislature, where he became an advocate of African American education. Moses V. Grant worked as an insurance agent. He died on December 10, 1883, in Newport, Kentucky, at age 35.[14]

Richard Grant: First Base, Copec Club. The younger brother of Moses Grant, Richard Grant was born in Covington around 1852. Grant moved to Chicago, where he died on February 19, 1890.[15]

William S. Grant: Center Field, Covington Club (1866). The brother of Moses and Richard Grant, William S. Grant was born around 1847 in Covington. During the Civil War, he played townball for the Kentucky Club. Grant worked as a railroad clerk. He stayed connected to baseball by serving as the Corresponding Secretary of the Covington Stars in 1875; his father was the team's President. William S. Grant died in Covington on August 29, 1885.[16]

Orrin B. Hallam: Secretary, Covington Club (1868). Born in Owenton, Kentucky, on April 22, 1849, Orrin B. Hallam was the son of prominent Kentucky attorney James R. Hallam. Like his father and brothers, Orrin B. Hallam became an attorney and an influential Democrat. Hallam moved from Covington to Washington, D.C., in 1885 when President Grover Cleveland appointed him a deputy auditor in the Treasury Department. Hallam remained in Washington and continued his legal practice until his death on July 13, 1913.[17]

Thomas Reed, Jr.: Center Field, Copec Club. Born in England, Thomas Reed, Jr., came to Covington as a toddler. As an adult, Reed took over the family's undertaking business. He died on December 22, 1927, in Covington at age 86.[18]

John H. Shoup: Copec Club. Often referred to as "Jack Shoup" or "John Shoupe," John H. Shoup was born on September 30, 1851, probably in western Virginia to Henry Shoup and the former Mary Elizabeth Haymaker. Shoup moved to Covington before 1860. As a young man, Shoup worked in a rolling mill to help support his family. In 1875, Shoup started his long professional baseball career as an infielder with the Covington Stars. He played for several teams, most notably the National League's Troy Haymakers. While playing in the Tri-State League in 1890, a hotshot prospect told Shoup that he looked too old to be a beginner like himself. Shoup retorted, "Why you young whipper-snapper, I was getting paid for playing ball before you were out of long dresses." Shoup died in Cincinnati on February 13, 1920.[19]

Dr. Charles Henry Thomas: Pitcher, Copec Club; Treasurer, Covington Club (1869). Born January 6, 1851, in Pomeroy, Ohio, to surgeon Dr. Charles F. Thomas and Hannah Thomas, Charles Henry Thomas moved to Covington as a boy. He graduated from Yale University in 1873. Thomas studied medicine at Miami Medical College in Cincinnati and Bellevue Hospital Medical College in New York City. He received his medical degree in 1875. As a medical student, Thomas had to miss baseball games with the Star Club of Covington to attend class lectures. He practiced medicine in Covington for several years. Dr. Charles H. Thomas died in Baltimore on October 29, 1904.[20]

NOTES

1. *Cincinnati Daily Enquirer*, July 28, 1868; *Cincinnati Daily Times*, May 5, 1865; *Cincinnati Daily Times*, April 15, 1868; *Cincinnati Commercial*, April 5, 1869; *Cincinnati Commercial*, August 21, 1870; *Cincinnati Daily Enquirer*, September 13, 1866; *Cincinnati Commercial*, September 15, 1866; *Cincinnati Commercial*, September 16, 1866.

2. *Cincinnati Daily Enquirer*, October 10, 1866; *Cincinnati Commercial*, October 19, 1866.

3. *Cincinnati Daily Enquirer*, October 10, 1866; *Cincinnati Daily Times*, October 18, 1866.

4. *Cincinnati Daily Times*, October 18, 1866; *Cincinnati Daily Gazette*, October 18, 1866; *Cincinnati Commercial*, October 19, 1866.

5. *Cincinnati Daily Times*, April 15, 1868; *Cincinnati Daily Enquirer*, April 17, 1867; *Cincinnati Daily Gazette*, July 27, 1867; *Cincinnati Daily Gazette*, November 25, 1867; *Cincinnati Daily Gazette*, July 29, 1868; *Cincinnati Daily Gazette*, September 12, 1868. The opening of the Suspension Bridge and the concurrent expansion of the streetcar system started an unprecedented population and real estate booms in Covington. Many Cincinnatians made homes in less densely populated Covington and crossed the Suspension Bridge daily to work in Cincinnati. On the John A. Roebling Suspension Bridge's effect on Covington, see Paul Tenkotte, "Rival Cities to Suburbs: Covington and Newport, Kentucky, 1790–1890," (Ph.D. diss., University of Cincinnati, 1989), 345–382.

6. *Cincinnati Daily Gazette*, September 19, 1867; *Cincinnati Enquirer*, September 21, 1917; Clarence Deming, *Yale Yesterdays* (New Haven: Yale University Press, 1915), 203; Henry Ellard, *Base Ball in Cincinnati* (Cincinnati: Johnson & Hardin, 1907; reprint, Cincinnati: Ohio Book Store, 1987), 56–59; *Cincinnati Daily Gazette*, May 22, 1868.

7. *Cincinnati Daily Gazette*, July 29, 1868; *Cincinnati Daily Gazette*, March 15, 1869; *Cincinnati Daily Gazette*, April 6, 1869; *Cincinnati Daily*

Gazette, May 12, 1869; *Cincinnati Daily Gazette*, May 27, 1869; *Cincinnati Commercial*, May 14, 1869.

8. *Cincinnati Daily Gazette*, July 22, 1870; *Cincinnati Daily Gazette*, August 2, 1870; *Cincinnati Daily Gazette*, August 19, 1870; *Cincinnati Commercial*, May 18, 1874; *Cincinnati Daily Gazette*, July 20, 1874; *Cincinnati Daily Gazette*, August 5, 1874; *New York Clipper*, October 3, 1874; *Cincinnati Daily Times*, July 12, 1875; *Cincinnati Daily Commercial*, July 12, 1875; *Cincinnati Daily Gazette*, July 13, 1875.

9. Ellard, *Base Ball in Cincinnati*, 127–128; 1870 census; Henry W. Farnam, Secretary, Yale University Class of 1874, *Biographical Record of the Class of 1874 in Yale College, Part Fourth, 1874–1909* (New Haven: The Tuttle, Morehouse & Taylor Company, 1912), 6–7; Deming, *Yale Yesterdays*, 203; *New York Times*, November 25, 1925.

10. Ellard, *Base Ball in Cincinnati*, 33; 1900 census; Benjamin Brookshaw death certificate, Kentucky; *Louisville Courier-Journal*, July 8, 1875; *Chicago Tribune*, December 24, 1876; *The Ticket* (Covington), October 12, 1877; *Kentucky Post*, May 7, 1904.

11. Ellard, *Base Ball in Cincinnati*, 127–128; *Cincinnati Enquirer*, September 21, 1917; *Cincinnati Daily Enquirer*, May 12, 1875.

12. *Cincinnati Daily Gazette*, July 29, 1868; *Cincinnati Daily Gazette*, April 6, 1869; *Kentucky Post*, January 14, 1925.

13. Ellard, *Base Ball in Cincinnati*, 38; *Covington* (KY) *Journal*, December 10, 1853; *Cincinnati Daily Times*, May 5, 1865; W. S. B. Matthews, Ed., *A Hundred Years of Music in America* (Chicago: G. L. Howe, Publisher, 1900), 603; *Cincinnati Commercial Tribune*, January 2, 1924.

14. Ellard, *Base Ball in Cincinnati*, 38; *Cincinnati Daily Gazette*, April 6, 1869; *Daily Commonwealth* (Covington), December 10, 1883.

15. Ellard, *Base Ball in Cincinnati*, 127–128; census records — 1870 and 1880; *Cincinnati Commercial Gazette*, February 21, 1890.

16. Ellard, *Base Ball in Cincinnati*, 38; 1870 census; *Cincinnati Commercial*, April 19, 1864; *Cincinnati Daily Gazette*, July 1, 1875; William S. Grant burial record — Linden Grove Cemetery, Covington, Kentucky.

17. *Cincinnati Daily Gazette*, July 29, 1868; *Washington Post*, July 14, 1913.

18. Ellard, *Base Ball in Cincinnati*, 127–128; *Kentucky Post*, December 23, 1927.

19. John Shoup Death Certificate, John F. Shoupe Player File, A. Bartlett Giamatti Research Center, National Baseball Hall of Fame Library, Cooperstown, New York. Shoup's birthplace was listed as Virginia or West Virginia in the 1860, 1870, 1900, 1910, and 1920 censuses; *Wheeling Register*, September 9, 1890.

20. Ellard, *Base Ball in Cincinnati*, 127–218; *Cincinnati Daily Gazette*, April 6, 1869; *Cincinnati Commercial*, September 26, 1874; *Kentucky Post*, October 31, 1904; *Obituary Records of Graduates of Yale University* (New Haven: Yale University Press, 1905), 460.

❖ *Holt Base Ball Club of Newport* (Greg Perkins) ❖

Club History

Though not mentioned by name, the Holt Base Ball Club of Newport, Kentucky, occupies a prominent spot in the National Baseball Hall of Fame and Museum — Harry Wright's Hall of Fame plaque. The last sentence on the plaque reads, "Hit 7 home runs in game at Newport, Ky. in 1867." That day, the Holts surrendered 23 total home runs to Wright's Cincinnati Base Ball Club in a 93–22 defeat. The *Cincinnati Daily Gazette* attributed the Cincinnati club's heavy hitting to the rough outfield at the Holt Club's home grounds that led to "bases, which otherwise would not have been made."[1]

Long before padding Harry Wright's Hall of Fame credentials, Newport nurtured Ohio Valley sporting culture. Since at least the late 1820s, Newport's tracks contributed to horseracing's popularity in American and spurred the construction of courses just across the Ohio River in Cincinnati and upriver in Maysville, Kentucky. Founded in 1845, Newport's Kentucky Cricket Club promoted the early progress of team sports in the West. A decade later, the Kentucky Town Ball Club of Newport entertained crowds on both sides of the Ohio River.[2]

The Holt Base Ball Club started in September 1866 as the "Newport Base Ball Club." The team soon became known as the Holts in tribute to William Holt, one of the Newport Club's founders. Years later, Cincinnati newspaper reporter Harry M. Millar remembered the Holts as comprised of the "cultured and refined people of Newport." Holt Club President William C. Davis, Treasurer William Holt, and Secretary James R. Morin were all Newport grocers. Moreover, Holt served on Newport's City Council, and Morin was a county commissioner.[3]

The early Holt Club appeared to attract Republican Party supporters, a rarity at the time in heavily Democratic Northern Kentucky. William Holt was a staunch Republican. James Root came from a prominent Republican family. James R. Morin and Root's father, Ira Root, were arrested the previous autumn when they and others seized control of Newport's Taylor Street Methodist Church. The Methodist Episcopal Church Conference South had sent pro–Confederate Reverend Lorenzo D. Huston to lead the Taylor Street Church. Union Army veteran Morin would not tolerate a Confederate pastor, so he, along with Root and other church members, seized the building to prevent Huston from assuming the pulpit. Showing support for Reverend Huston, the Democratic *Cincinnati Daily Enquirer* wondered how Union stalwarts Morin and Root "relish being called secessionists." The crisis resolved when Root, Morin, and the other rebels left the Taylor Street Church and started a new congregation.[4]

At least initially, the Holts fared well against other amateur teams in the region. Several Holts had played townball for the Kentucky Club, so they were already familiar with hitting and basic fielding when they took up baseball. During the 1866 season, the Holts defeated the Buckeyes of Cincinnati in the tournament played at Florence in October 1866. A controversial umpiring call contributed to the Holt's one-run victory, much to the Buckeyes' chagrin. Ill feelings between the two clubs lingered the next season. In August 1867, the Buckeyes refused to play the Holts until the Holts apologized for the insults they heaped on Buckeye Club member John L. Boake during a Holt game that he umpired.[5]

By 1867, the Holts could no longer match Cincinnati's

elite clubs. Though trounced twice by the Cincinnati Club, the Holts fared better against other opponents. The Holts won a game during the 1867 Ohio State Base Ball Tournament. In addition, two Holt players won prizes as the best players at their position during the Tournament. In 1868, the Holt Juniors went to Memphis, Tennessee, where it defeated two local clubs. During the 1870 season, the Holts played the Red Stockings again. Although the Holts lost again, they held the now famous Cincinnati club to only 32 runs.[6]

After a dormant period during the early 1870s, the Holt Base Ball Club reappeared during the summer of 1874. Former Cincinnati Red Stocking Charlie Gould joined the Holts that season. For the 1874 season, the Holts played their home games at the enclosed Newport Driving Park. Earlier, the Holts had often played on Taylor's Bottoms, near the Ohio River in Newport. By the late 1870s, the Holt Club apparently disbanded. Holt Club founder William Holt died in 1877. Several of the old Holts reportedly were still playing in 1878 under the name Navy Blues. Blue had been a prominent color in the Holts' uniform — blue pants with white stripes, bright red shirts, and blue caps with a red tip.[7]

Club Members

William Air: Born around 1833 in Ohio, William Air owned and operated the Newport ferry. Before the Civil War, Air played townball with the Kentucky Club of Newport. During the war, Air sided with the Union and served in the 23rd Kentucky Volunteer Infantry, Company S. In 1867, he played in a muffin game for the Holts against the Cincinnati Club. Air died in Newport in 1907.[8]

Frank Buchanan: captain of the Holt Juniors. Buchanan was born July 28, 1850, in Newport to Henry and Mary Buchanan. In 1875, he played professional baseball as an outfielder and first baseman for the Star Base Ball Club of Covington, Kentucky. A broken finger from a hard grounder disabled Buchanan for much of the season. The Stars released Buchanan late in the 1875 season. Afterward, Buchanan worked for his family's insurance agency. He died on February 12, 1912, in Newport.[9]

George Creighton: third baseman. Born in Canada in 1846 to Scottish immigrants, Creighton moved to Newport sometime before the Civil War. During the war he fought for the Union in the 53rd Kentucky Volunteer Regiment. He later served several years as a Newport policeman. In 1914, Creighton still had the Holt Club's scorebooks and other records. He died in 1919 in Newport.[10]

William C. Davis: President of the Holt Base Ball Club (1866). Davis was born around 1817 in Ohio. Davis owned a stove foundry in Newport, where he was still living in 1880.[11]

William Holt: Treasurer (1866). Born in Quinceton, Massachusetts, in 1812, Holt came to Cincinnati in 1858, where he operated a grocery store. Holt was a member of Cincinnati's Excelsior Town Ball Club. By 1860, Holt moved across the river to Newport, where he served on the city council for eight years. William Holt died on August 10, 1877, at his Newport home.[12]

Ed Mariani: Born in Ohio to Italian immigrants, Mariani played townball for the Kentucky Club of Newport before the Civil War. After the war, he operated a confectionery shop. Mariani died in Newport in 1892 at the age of 54.[13]

James Riley Morin: Secretary (1866). Morin was born April 1, 1831, in Campbell County, Kentucky. During the Civil War, Morin supported the Union as a First Lieutenant in the 8th Kentucky Volunteer Cavalry, Company E. After the war, he owned a butter and egg store in Newport. By 1870, Morin moved to Chicago and then to Cedar Rapids, Iowa, where his butter and egg company, J. R. Morin & Company, thrived until the firm went bankrupt in 1894. Thereafter, Morin resumed his butter and egg dealings in Chicago, where he died on February 25, 1915. Morin and his wife Sarah were the parents of nine children, including Charles R. Morin, a national champion billiards player.[14]

George Nealeans: center field. During the Civil War, Nealeans fought for the Union in Company C, 53rd Kentucky Volunteer Infantry. A printer by trade, he died in 1910 in Newport at age 67.[15]

George Prather: catcher. Aside from his baseball exploits, little is known about Prather. In addition to playing for the Holts, Prather also played for the Cincinnati Juniors. In 1875, Prather played baseball professionally for the Covington Stars, with whom he won praise as an excellent defensive catcher. Prather left the Stars in protest after the club released his friend Frank Buchanan.[16]

James Clinton Root: left field. Root was born July 11, 1846, the son of prominent Newport attorney Ira Root. James also became an attorney. He died December 19, 1871, in Newport.[17]

Albert C. Seddens: first baseman. Per the 1870 Kentucky census, Seddens was born in Kentucky and worked as a clerk. He died in Covington in 1903 at age 58.[18]

Frank Stein: Born in Germany around 1830, Stein played for the Kentucky Town Ball Club before the Civil War. Stein and thousands of others were mobilized in September 1862 to defend Cincinnati and Northern Kentucky from the approaching Confederate Army. He served in Company D of the 42nd Kentucky Volunteer Infantry. Stein died in Newport in 1894.[19]

Notes

1. An image of Harry Wright's plaque at the National Baseball Hall of Fame and Museum can be found at http://baseballhall.org/hof/wright-harry; *Cincinnati Daily Gazette*, June 27, 1867.

2. *American Turf Register and Sport Magazine* 1 (October, 1829): 107; *Spirit of the Times* 8 (July 14, 1838): 172; Greg Perkins, "The Cincinnati Game: Townball in Cincinnati, 1858–1866," *Base Ball, A Journal of the Early Game* 2 (Fall 2008), 35–46.

3. *Cincinnati Commercial-Tribune*, July 30, 1912; 1870 census; 1868 Newport City Directory; *Cincinnati Daily Gazette*, August 30, 1878.

4. *Cincinnati Daily Enquirer*, September 21, 1865; for biographical information about Ira Root, see E. Polk Johnson, *History of Kentucky and Kentuckians*, vol. 3 (New York: The Lewis Publishing Company, 1912), 1,223–1,224.

5. *Cincinnati Daily Times* October 18, 1866; *Cincinnati Daily Gazette*, October 18, 1866; *Cincinnati Commercial*, October 19, 1866; *Cincinnati Daily Gazette*, August 9, 1867; *Kentucky Times-Star*, April 11, 1914.

6. Harry Ellard, *Base Ball in Cincinnati: A History* (Cincinnati: Johnson & Hardin, 1907; reprint, Cincinnati: Ohio Book Store, 1987), 55–56; *Cincinnati Daily Gazette*, October 7, 1868; *Cincinnati Daily Gazette*, October 13, 1868; *Cincinnati Daily Gazette*, September 26, 1870.

7. *Cincinnati Daily Gazette*, June 15, 1874; *Ludlow (KY) Reporter*, September 26, 1874; *Cincinnati Daily Gazette*, September 5, 1874; *Newport Local*, August 11, 1877; *Cincinnati Daily Gazette*, August 30, 1878; *Cincinnati Daily Gazette*, August 19, 1867.

8. *Cincinnati Daily Commercial*, July 26, 1860; *Cincinnati Commercial-Tribune*, August 1, 1912; *Kentucky Post*, February 2, 1907.

9. *Cincinnati Daily Gazette*, July 15, 1870; *The Ticket* (Covington), July 20, 1875; *Cincinnati Daily Enquirer*, September 3, 1875; Frank Buchanan burial record—Evergreen Cemetery, Southgate, Campbell County, Kentucky.

10. Ellard, *Base Ball in Cincinnati*, 48; *Kentucky Times-Star*, April 11, 1914; *Kentucky Times-Star*, March 28, 1919.

11. *Cincinnati Daily Enquirer*, September 14, 1866; *Cincinnati Commercial-Tribune*, August 1, 1912; 1880 census.

12. *Cincinnati Daily Enquirer*, September 14, 1866; *Newport Local*, August 11, 1877; *Cincinnati Daily Gazette*, August 11, 1877.

13. *Cincinnati Daily Commercial*, July 2, 1860; *Cincinnati Commercial-Tribune*, August 1, 1912; 1880 census; *Kentucky State Journal* (Newport), November 25, 1892.

14. *Cincinnati Daily Enquirer*, September 14, 1866; *Daily Commonwealth* (Covington), October 8, 1879; 1870 and 1880 censuses; *Chicago Daily Tribune*, March 11, 1894; *Chicago Daily Tribune*, July 6, 1947.

15. Ellard, *Base Ball in Cincinnati*, 48; *Kentucky Post*, March 22, 1910.

16. *Cincinnati Daily Gazette*, September 26, 1870; Harry Ellard, *Base Ball in Cincinnati*, 68; *Cincinnati Daily Enquirer*, September 3, 1875.

17. Ellard, *Base Ball in Cincinnati*, 48; E. Polk Johnson, *History of Kentucky and Kentuckians*, vol. 3, 1,223–1,224.

18. Ellard, *Base Ball in Cincinnati*, 48; *Kentucky Post*, March 21, 1903.

19. *Cincinnati Daily Commercial*, July 2, 1860; *Kentucky State Journal* (Newport), January 4, 1895.

CHAPTER FIVE

MICHIGAN

❖ *Introduction* (Peter Morris) ❖

On the eve of the 1860 season, the Detroit Base Ball Club was the only club west of New York represented at the convention of the National Association of Base Ball Players in New York City. But in the ensuing years no Michigan nine emerged as a national power and at the 1866 NABBP convention there was not a single Michigan club to be found among the 202 clubs from seventeen states. As a result, it would be easy to conclude that the state was not a baseball hotbed during the pioneer era.

In fact, as I showed in *Baseball Fever: Early Baseball in Michigan* (2003, University of Michigan Press), nothing could be further from the truth. While the focus was on in-state competition rather than national honors, Michigan was a baseball-mad state during these years, especially once the Civil War had ended. At the forefront of this flurry of activity were the six clubs profiled in this chapter: the Franklins of Detroit, the state's first organized club; the Early Risers of Detroit, whose members rose at the break of dawn to play on the Campus Martius; the Detroit Base Ball Club, the state champions for most of the period; the Daybreaks of Jackson, a pioneer club that broke up so its members could serve in the Civil War; the Kent Club of Grand Rapids, which took part in western Michigan's first great baseball rivalry; and the First Nationals of Hancock, one of the first clubs to bring the new passion for baseball to the state's Upper Peninsula.

While these six clubs played crucial roles in the growth of baseball in the Great Lakes State, their histories are only part of a larger story. It takes two clubs to play a game, a reality that doomed the Franklin Club and that made survival difficult for other prewar clubs. But there was no such shortage after the war: By 1867 the state boasted 240 documented clubs, representing 117 cities and 36 counties, and it is safe to assume that even those impressive totals are incomplete. It was this abundance that made up for the lack of a nationally recognized club and allowed baseball to thrive in Michigan.

As a result, the story of the pioneer era of Michigan baseball is about much, much more. It's also about clubs like the Custers of Ionia, which handed out honorary memberships to five local clergymen and to its namesake, George Custer. And about a club from the University of Michigan, which, many years before the development of varsity athletics, trounced the reigning state champions in one of the biggest upsets in Michigan baseball history. It's about the Wolverines of Benton Harbor, which starred an African American named Luck Hackley during the heady years of Reconstruction. It's about the North Stars of East Tawas, which traveled to Au Sable on a tug and started Iosco County's first baseball rivalry. It's about the Mutuals of Jackson, which produced Fred Andrus, the first Michigan-born major leaguer, and many other talented players.

The story of the pioneer era of Michigan baseball is also the tale of thrilling contests, of budding rivalries, and of trial-and-error experiments to find an appropriate method of competition. Most of all, however, it is the story of young men whose love of baseball led them to carve out baseball diamonds on the most implausible terrains and trek great distances to find suitable rivalries. What follows are the stories of some of those pioneers and how the six clubs they formed brought baseball to Michigan.

❖ *Franklins of Detroit* (Peter Morris) ❖

CLUB HISTORY

The Franklin Club of Detroit was founded in 1857 and its adoption of the Knickerbocker Rules made it one of the first clubs west of the Alleghenies, if not the first, to do so. The existence of the new club was announced in a letter to the New York–based *Porter's Spirit of the Times* that fall. In the letter, club president Walter H. Foster wrote,

Dear Spirit— Having organized a Base Ball Club in this city, we would be pleased to have you place the fact on record in the SPIRIT as we claim to be the pioneer Club of the West. We have twenty-seven good members, and think we could give a good account of ourselves even in a match with some of the other old clubs of the East. The following are the officers. Franklin Base Ball Club, organized August 18, 1857. President Walter H. Foster; Vice-President, Theodore Robinson; Secretary, Marsh Robinson. By publishing the above, you will much oblige numerous admirers of the SPIRIT. Truly yours, W.H. Foster.[1]

While Foster's letter suggests that the new baseball club recognized its status as pioneers, other accounts reveal a less serious side. In particular, Henry Starkey, a leading member of the Franklins, described in 1884 how he "organized the first base ball club in Detroit, or assisted to do so." Starkey explained that the only game previously played in Detroit was "the old-fashioned game of round ball. There were no 'balls' or 'strikes' to that. The batter waited until a ball came along that suited him, banged it and ran. If it was a fly and somebody caught it, he was out and couldn't play any more in the game. If the ball was not caught on the fly, the only way to put a batter out was to hit him with the ball as he ran. There were no basemen then; everybody stood around to catch flies and throw the ball at base runners."

According to Starkey, that changed when an "old fiddler here in the city named Page" showed him a copy of the *New York Clipper* that included "quite a lengthy description of the new game of base ball." Soon several Detroiters reached "the conclusion that the new way must be an improvement over the old … so I wrote to the *Clipper* for a copy of the new rules, and paid $1 for it. After we got the rules we organized a club — the first in Detroit."

But the rest of Starkey's comments show the lightheartedness of the endeavor. In the course of explaining that most of the club members were local printers and that games were played on a pasture on the Beaubien Farm, he threw in one silly joke and several asides. And when asked what became of the Franklins, Starkey replied, "Oh, Bob Anderson and others soon formed the Detroit Club, got fine grounds out on Woodward avenue and so far eclipsed us that we died a natural death. Bob once knocked the ball four miles out into the country; took them three weeks to find it. I heard him telling about it the other day. It's a fact!"[2]

The activities of the Franklin Club received considerable attention in the *Detroit Free Press* and the *Detroit Advertiser* in the summer of 1857, no doubt at least in part because so many of the club's members worked for the two papers. Local historian George Catlin later gave the date of the club's formation as August 1, 1857, but contemporaneous accounts suggest this to be an error.[3] On August 15 the *Detroit Free Press* reported that "a Base Ball Club is about being organized in this city, by the admirers of the 'good old Yankee sport.'" This was followed by accounts of the club's formation and its election of officers in the *Detroit Advertiser* on August 25, 1857, and in the *Detroit Free Press* of the following day. So it appears that Foster was correct in giving August 18, 1857, as the date of the club's birth.

The historic meeting took place at the Congress Hall Saloon at 3 Congress Street, a saloon frequented by printers and other employees of the two newspapers and run by Jere Calnon. It appears that the meeting was not a long or very formal one, as the surviving accounts provide almost no details other than the names of the three officers who were elected. Twenty-seven men joined the club, no fewer than sixteen of whom were closely associated with either the *Free Press* or the *Advertiser*.[4]

The club's members had already played together several times, and they celebrated their formal organization with two intrasquad games on Saturday, August 22, followed by a meal at the home of vice president Theodore Robinson. Another practice session was announced for the following Saturday, to be played at the grounds of the Detroit Cricket Club on August 29, but there is no record of whether it took place and that ends the recorded history of the Franklin Club in 1857. Indeed, it is not even clear that the club had yet chosen that name for themselves, as that name was not used in any accounts that year and the *Free Press* referred to the new organization as the Detroit Base Ball Club.

The spring of 1858 brought more structure. Detroit's first baseball club held its annual meeting at the Congress Hall Saloon on April 9 and became formally known as the Franklin Base Ball Club of Detroit. President Foster and vice president Theodore Robinson were re-elected, while Henry Starkey became secretary and treasurer and Eugene Robinson and George Atkins were elected captains. The club was described as being in a "very prosperous condition," with twenty-four active members and a "large number" of additional applicants "in the hands of the committee."[5]

The new season also brought the first inklings that baseball might come to play a major role in the life of the city. The start of the new season was accompanied by an article in the *Advertiser* that offered this endorsement: "The game of base ball is an American game, and that it is one of healthy and manly exercise as well as one of many excitements, no one who ever played it will deny. Last year, for the first time, we believe was there a regular organized club formed and conducted upon regular rules, and by-laws, in this city, and as far as we know in the State. It has had one preliminary meeting this season, and we understand will have regular meetings throughout the season. When governed by strict rules, it is a beautiful game. It has become very popular about New York City, and the highest classes of professional gentlemen — Doctors, lawyers, and clergymen — engage in it. There was recently a large convention held, composed of delegates from the various clubs on Manhattan Island, to revise and adopt rules governing the game. The rules and constitution, &c., may be found in

Porter's Spirit of the Times of April 3, (for sale by Ross,) which will be useful to those contemplating the formation of clubs."[6]

Those comments were followed a few days later by a hint that it was time to establish appropriate grounds for baseball in Detroit ("so that this club, and others which are soon to be formed, may have a suitable place for their field exercise").[7] Later that month, the *Advertiser* again suggested that "There should be a rival base ball club here."[8] But nothing came of these hints and newspaper coverage of the Franklins stopped at that point.

It is of course possible that the Franklins continued their practice and intrasquad games in 1858 and 1859. On June 14, 1859, after the formation of the Detroit Base Ball Club, the *Free Press* reported that there were two baseball clubs in Detroit, which could mean that the Franklin Club was still in existence. But there was no mention of the club between April 1858 and 1860, suggesting that, as the *Free Press* later put it, the pioneer Franklin Club had arrived "unheralded and departed unwept."[9]

By 1860 Detroit boasted several baseball clubs and this development inspired the Franklins to reorganize on June 26.[10] The club played two games against the Detroit Base Ball Club in September, winning the first one but losing the second one. It was probably this year that John Drew was thinking of when he described the Franklins challenging the Early Risers ("a club mostly of young clerks, etc., who had rather a high opinion of themselves") and beating them handily. But there is no contemporaneous record of the game and Drew's claims should be taken with a grain of salt — he was not a member of the Franklins and his reminiscences, written four decades after the fact, included some obvious errors, such as calling the Early Risers the "Rising Suns."[11]

The club also re-formed in 1861, holding an annual meeting on May 21 and electing a slate of officers.[12] But by then the first shots of the Civil War had been fired, and that spelled the end of the Franklin Club. Quite a few club members enlisted in the Union Army, while the ones who remained in Detroit formed a "Ben Franklin Guard" to support the war effort by keeping watch around the city.[13]

One later account concluded that the Franklin Club "succumbed to the war, a large portion of its members going into the service."[14] There is no question that the outbreak of war was a major factor in the demise of the Franklin Base Ball Club, but it is a mistake to think of it as the only one. For one thing, the members of the club were assuming new business and family responsibilities that left them with little time for sport. That was a problem common to all baseball clubs of the era, but the Franklins faced additional challenges that were unique to them.

As of 1855, Detroit boasted five daily newspapers, an extraordinary number for a town its size and one that could not possibly be sustained. The *Democrat* and the *Inquirer* soon merged, and the new paper was in turn swallowed up by the *Advertiser*. Then the *Advertiser* merged with the *Tribune*, and finally, when the war came, the *Advertiser and Tribune* temporarily joined forces with the *Free Press*, leaving the city with a single newspaper during the war years.

This naturally caused a sharp drop in the number of printing jobs in Detroit. Making matters worse, according to John Drew, "Occasionally a very rapid compositor would come along, but as a rule, would soon leave for Chicago, which seemed to be the Mecca for all fast men. The Chicago scale of prices being always considerably higher than that of Detroit."[15] The "Chicago scale of prices" refers to the then-prevailing wage.

The trend accelerated in 1861 when mercurial *Detroit Free Press* publisher Wilbur F. Storey bought the *Chicago Times* and took many of his employees with him to Chicago, including several prominent members of the Franklin Club. Several other club members left Detroit for Chicago in the next few years, making it inevitable that the Franklins would not reorganize at the end of the war. There was thus the sad irony that the club that put Detroit on the baseball map ended in part because a significant percent of its members left for brighter prospects in Chicago.

The discontinuous history of the Franklin Club also makes it difficult to determine exactly where the club played its matches. Starkey reported that the club played in a pasture on the Beaubien Farm, while a 1908 article stated that the club "played on the sand lot bounded by First and Second, Lewis and Jones streets."[16] One practice was also scheduled for the grounds of the Detroit Cricket Club, and it is likely that other locations were used for the club's practices. Reflecting its membership, the Franklin Base Ball Club was an itinerant organization that had yet to feel the need to set down permanent roots.

Note: In 1874 another baseball club calling itself the Franklins was organized in Detroit. None of its members were holdovers from the pioneer club by that name, but it did have several parallels with its namesake. To begin with, the club's organization came after a prolonged dry spell for baseball in Detroit and it proved a harbinger of renewed interest.[17] In addition, the club was made up entirely of printers from the city's newspapers — the city directory listed Patrick O'Grady as a *Tribune* printer, James Murtagh as a *News* printer, and six others, Bernard and Henry McAndrews, Albert Stewart, Converse Cook, Marcus Heaslip, and John Walker, as printers for the *Post*. The ninth player, J. Dougherty, could not be located in the city directories under that occupation, but the *Jackson Daily Citizen* said he was also a printer for the *Post*. Finally, like the original Franklins, the 1874 incarnation had little pretension to expertise at baseball. The players were described as small and clumsy, and they were outfitted in assorted garb — the only thing uniform about their attire was a white cap with a blue star.[18] Yet another Franklin Club was formed in Detroit in 1884, but was unrelated to the previous ones.

Club Members

Edward Atkins: Edward Atkins was the youngest of three brothers who were members of the Franklin Club. He was born in Vermont around 1839 and the family was still living in Burlington, Vermont, in 1850. Soon after, they moved to Detroit, where Edward worked as a printer. But he left Detroit along with his brother George in 1861 and moved to Chicago.

George E. Atkins: George Atkins was the oldest of the three Atkins brothers, being born around 1832. He too became a printer and worked as foreman of the newsroom of the *Free Press*. But he became one of many *Free Press* employees to follow publisher Wilbur Storey to the *Chicago Times* in 1861. George Atkins fought in the Civil War and then returned to work at the *Times*. Franc Wilkie recalled that Atkins was on duty as foreman of the printing department on the night that the Great Chicago Fire destroyed the *Times* building. John Drew had less than fond memories, recalling that

> when the *Times* and Chicago union failed to harmonize, Atkins and his brothers remained with the [*Times*] office, which remained as a non-union office during Story's [*sic*] management. Atkins became such a bitter opponent of unions that he used to send men from the *Times* office to the various cities where trouble existed between the employers and compositors. In one of their expeditions of this nature his brothers and others, who accompanied them, were so roughly received and got such a general shaking up that future attempts were abandoned. It is said that George became so costly and useless to his employer that his services finally had to be dispensed with.

He died in Chicago on January 24, 1894.

John H. Atkins: John Atkins was a third brother who was born in Vermont around 1837. Unlike his brothers, he became a brick mason and was still living in Detroit in 1890.

William Henry Baxter: W.H. Baxter was the vice president of the Franklin Club when it reorganized in 1860. He was born in Hull, England, on February 9, 1836. The family crossed the Atlantic when he was an infant and eventually settled in Chatham, Ontario. According to a profile in *Landmarks of Detroit* by Robert Budd Ross, George Byron Catlin, and Clarence Monroe Burton, Baxter was "of a roving disposition" and at the age of nine he went to sea with his uncle. Upon returning to Chatham, he was apprenticed as a printer and in the late 1850s he moved to Michigan to work as a compositor and the foreman of the newsroom of the *Detroit Tribune*. Despite his recent arrival and a young family, Baxter served in the Union Navy as a seaman from 1862 to 1864. After the war he joined the editorial staff of the newspaper, now known as the *Detroit Advertiser and Tribune*, first as its court and municipal reporter and later as city editor. He was also the paper's main baseball reporter and the secretary of the Detroit Base Ball Club.[19] He served two terms as a Detroit alderman in the 1870s, and also helped organize the city's first health board, serving as health officer from 1876 to 1880. In 1880 he became the city's fire marshal and remained in that position for 26 years. His main assistant was B.F. Wright, who had been the *Post*'s baseball reporter while Baxter was covering baseball for the *Advertiser and Tribune*. He died in Detroit on June 25, 1913.

Jeremiah Calnon: Jere Calnon was the proprietor of the Congress Hall Saloon, where the Franklin Club was organized. He was born in Ireland around 1832 and was still single at the time the club was organized. He married in 1860 and by the time of the 1870 Census he was listed with considerable wealth and he and his wife were the parents of four children. But by the end of the decade he was a widower with only one surviving daughter, and Calnon himself died on September 13, 1882.

Ad Cowan: Ad Cowan was a *Free Press* printer but little else is known about him.

Thomas Crane: Thomas Crane was the club's vice president in 1861. He was born in Canada in April of 1833 and immigrated to the United States when he was five. After apprenticing in Mount Clemens, he moved to Detroit and became a newspaper printer, while also serving on the board of directors of the Detroit Typographical Union. He played second base for the Franklins and in 1897 John Drew described an incident when Crane covered second base on an attempted stolen base. According to Drew,

> Up to this period the game was played with a "soft ball" but on this occasion a hard ball was used.... [The throw to second base] came with great force (being very hard) and Tom missed it with his hands but caught it with his eye, causing him to drop immediately. After the optic was bathed and rubbed for a while, Tom tried to resume the game, but was still so confused that he thought he was playing with the other side.... Tom says he can feel the force of that blow yet whenever he thinks of it.

Crane later gave up the printing business due to health problems and went to sea. But in 1874 he returned to the newspaper business as a circulating agent for the *Detroit News* and remained in that position until his death in Detroit on November 29, 1912.[20]

Michael Dempsey: Michael Dempsey was born in New York state around 1833 and became a printer. Along with fellow club member Malachi O'Donnell and many other Detroit printers, he enlisted in the 24th Michigan Infantry in 1862. He earned promotion from sergeant to lieutenant and, according to an official report, "Lieut. Dempsey was conspicuous for his gallantry in the charge across Willoughby's Run." Dempsey was wounded at Gettysburg, where the 24th suffered devastating casualties, and again at Spotsylvania. While recovering at Annapolis Hospital in July of 1864 he "left without leave" and was eventually dismissed. According to John Drew, Dempsey was never the same — before the war he had been known as "one of the dudes of that period," but afterward he "became dissipated and a 'wanderer.'" He reportedly died in Detroit in March of 1890 but confirmation has not been found.

Benjamin French Duncklee: Ben Duncklee was born in Newport, New Hampshire, on October 12, 1835. The family moved to Buffalo three years later and then to Detroit around

1850. Ben became a printer and died in Detroit on February 9, 1894.

Henry R. Durney: Henry Durney was born in Albion, New York, on January 25, 1830. He began working as a printer for the *Rochester Democrat* in 1847, after signing a contract of apprenticeship in which he promised "to learn the art of newspaper and job printing and that he will give his undivided and constant attention to the interests of his employers, from July 13th, 1847, to January 24th, 1851." He moved to Detroit and started work at the *Free Press* on March 9, 1856. He spent close to half a century in the *Free Press* composing room, becoming known to his fellow printers as "Dad" Durney as he adapted to a slew of changes over the years. Through them all, he "peacefully pursued his calling, with judicious intermingling of fishing expeditions." He retired around the turn of the century and died in Detroit on June 16, 1905.[21]

John Jacob Duryea: John Duryea was born on Long Island, New York, in November of 1840 and his family moved to Michigan when he was young. He became a printer for the *Tribune* and served as a director of the Franklin Club when it was reorganized in 1860. In 1862, he enlisted in the 24th Michigan Infantry. On June 18, 1864, Duryea suffered a severe head wound at the Battle of Petersburg. After many months in the hospital, he was discharged. He subsequently moved to Ann Arbor and Chicago. After the death of his wife he resided in the National Home for Disabled Volunteer Soldiers near Milwaukee, where he died on March 1, 1912.

Clarence E. Eddie: Clarence Eddie was an attorney. He left Detroit around 1862 and moved to Houghton in the Upper Peninsula to practice law. In 1865 he was elected a circuit judge but he died in early 1869 without completing his term.

Frank Folsom: See Detroit Base Ball Club.

Walter H. Foster: Walter H. Foster, the club's first president and the man who wrote to *Porter's Spirit of the Times* to announce the club's existence, was born in New York state around 1826. He worked as a printer for the *Free Press* while in Detroit, but like so many club members left for Chicago around the start of the Civil War. He died there on January 23, 1881.

Robert Gibbons: Robert Gibbons was another newspaperman who was described as one of the few surviving members of the Franklin Club in an article that appeared in the *Free Press* on June 1, 1908. His name did not appear in any contemporaneous accounts, but given the sketchy coverage that appeared at the time, there is no reason to doubt the claim. Gibbons was born in New York on April 20, 1839, and died in Detroit on November 16, 1917.

Thomas S. Gillett: Thomas Gillett was the son of Shadrach Gillett, a pioneer settler of Detroit who arrived in the city in 1815 and ran a general store. Thomas was born around 1824 and became a partner in his father's business, which became known as Gillett and Son. But he left Detroit around 1865 and moved to St. Joseph, Missouri.

Julius Porter Gilmore: J.P. Gilmore was secretary of the Franklin Club in 1860 and 1861 after it reorganized. He was born in Massachusetts on August 26, 1838, and moved to Detroit at the age of 16. He worked as a bookkeeper for the Preston National Bank and after the death of his first wife he married a daughter of the proprietor, David Pearson. From 1886 to 1891 Gilmore served as a Detroit alderman. He died in Detroit on September 16, 1903.

Grieve: Though not identified by first name, this member was almost certainly Robert Grieve, who was foreman of the *Free Press*. Born around 1830, he moved to Honolulu, Hawai'i, in 1863, and lived there until his death on July 1, 1899.

Milo Dwight Hamilton: Milo D. Hamilton was born in Blandford, Massachusetts, on October 5, 1828. When he was seven, his family moved to Michigan and Milo grew up on a farm near Homer. He began an apprenticeship at the *Marshall Statesman* in 1846 and began a long career in newspapers. He worked as foreman of the *Liberty Press*, a Battle Creek newspaper, until its plant was destroyed in a fire. He went to work for the *Detroit Free Press* in 1850, and became the commercial editor of the *Detroit Advertiser* the next year. He remained in that position for seven years and helped organize the Detroit Board of Trade in 1856. Hamilton moved to Cincinnati in 1858 and spent two years working for the *Enquirer*. In 1860 he returned to Michigan to become editor of the *Monroe Commercial*. He soon became the owner of that newspaper as well and continued to publish it until 1888, also serving as city postmaster from 1870 to 1874. He sold the newspaper in 1888 and moved to Washington, D.C., where he died on February 7, 1899.

John H. Hudson: The only man in Detroit by this name was a ship carpenter who was born in England around 1822 and died in Detroit on April 9, 1867.

J. J. Maledon: J. J. Maledon was the circulating agent for the *Daily Advertiser*. It appears that his full name was Joannes Jacobus Maledon and that he was born in Germany on April 24, 1830.

Jordan P. McMillan: J.P. McMillan, who was born in Canada around 1835 and moved to Detroit in 1852, was the club president in 1861. He was a printer for the *Free Press* and continued to work as a printer in Detroit for many years. He was living in Detroit in 1897 and apparently was still there in 1910, but the census listing is confusing enough to raise some doubts.

William F. Moore: William F. Moore, who was a director when the club was reorganized in 1860, was yet another printer. He was born in 1835 in Dublin, Ireland, and was very active in the Typographical Union. In 1865, after a strike of Detroit printers broke out, he was one of six men who started a new paper called the *Detroit Daily Union*, which survived until 1874. He was still a Detroit job and book printer when he died in Detroit on December 5, 1897.

Malachi J. O'Donnell: Malachi J. O'Donnell was born

in Ireland around 1839 and became foreman of the composing rooms of the *Free Press*. When the Civil War broke out, O'Donnell enthusiastically volunteered for the 24th Michigan Infantry, giving a patriotic speech that was recorded in the *Free Press* on August 23, 1862. His co-workers presented him with a sword, sash and belt with the inscription, "Presented to Lieut. M.J. O'Donnell by the proprietors and employes [sic] of the Free Press.'"[22] O'Donnell began his service as a second lieutenant and earned promotion to captain. After being wounded, he left the army hospital over the protests of nurses and was killed at Gettysburg on July 1, 1863.

John Philips: John Philips appears to have been a lumber dealer who lived in Detroit until at least 1871.

Earl F. Plantz: Earl F. Plantz was born in New York State around 1831 and worked as a collector and grocer. He married in 1859 but died three years later, on December 13, 1862, at the age of 32.

Charles C. Robinson: Charles C. Robinson was a coppersmith who was born in the state of New York on July 19, 1834, and died in Detroit on April 1, 1914.

Eugene Robinson: See Detroit Base Ball Club.

Marshall D. Robinson: Marsh Robinson was born on April 14, 1832, in Union, New York. He worked for the *Free Press* for more than four decades, beginning as a printer and later working for the newspaper in a variety of functions. As of 1881 he was running the *Free Press*'s stock room, which was described as

> one of the most important places in the building. Here the entire stock used in show, card, book, railway, label or law printing is kept. Two men are constantly employed in cutting with immense machines cardboard and paper into the required sizes. A business man has only to leave his order and "copy" and within a few hours he has a tastefully printed letter head with envelope to match for almost what the white paper would cost him.[23]

Robinson died in Detroit on December 17, 1903.

Theodore Pearson Robinson: Theodore P. Robinson was the vice president of the Franklin Club in 1857 and the man who hosted a meal after their intrasquad games on August 23, 1857. He was born on July 27, 1830, in Nanticoke, New York, and worked as an accountant until his premature death in Detroit on September 22, 1865.

Franklin D. Ross: Franklin D. Ross was born in Canada around 1833. He moved to Detroit in the mid–1850s and worked for the *Free Press* as a printer and circulating agent. Around 1865 he moved to Chicago and continued to work as a printer. He died in Chicago on November 23, 1914.

Charles M. Rousseau: This club member was listed as "E. Rousseau" in one newspaper account, but it appears very likely that that was a mistake and he was in fact Charles M. Rousseau, a longtime Detroit printer. Rousseau was born in 1842 in Canada, and immigrated to the United States as a baby. He died in Detroit on April 26, 1910.

Henry Mason Scovell: Harry Scovell was born around 1830 in New York state, the son of a doctor who had moved the family to Detroit by the mid–1840s. At the age of 14 Harry went to work at the *Detroit Advertiser* as a printer's devil, or apprentice. After becoming an expert compositor, he joined the *Free Press* in 1852 and soon became its exchange editor. As a colleague explained in Scovell's obituary, the role of the exchange editor was a crucial one in those days. Telegraphs were still "new, expensive, and uncertain," so the exchange editor went through out-of-town newspapers manually to determine what items to reprint.[24] As another reminiscence of those early days put it, Storey was "the heavyweight and penned all the editorials," Starkey was "local," Scovell was "scissors," and everyone else set type.[25] Scovell acquired such "a reputation for speed, judgment, and accuracy in getting the news out of other papers into his own" that publisher Wilbur F. Storey took him along when he took over the *Chicago Times* in 1861.[26] With the *Times*, Scovell continued to prove invaluable. Fellow newsman Franc B. Wilkie recalled that the New York papers did not arrive until 11 P.M. each evening, giving the exchange editor only an hour before the paper went to press. Wilkie explained,

> It was not enough to cut them out and prepare their headings. Each article must be treated according to its value; one must be cut down one-half or more; others must be condensed by rewriting; and only here and there were there instances in which an article could be used in its entirety. It may readily be seen that the news editor who could well perform this task must be one capable of the exercise of infinite swiftness in action and judgment. The man who performed this work for the *Times* was Harry Scovel [sic], who justly merited the reputation of being the very best of his kind on the continent. He would go through a hundred newspaper "exchanges," apparently only glancing at them, and yet would never miss an item of the smallest consequence.

Then in 1865, Charles A. Dana started a new paper called the *Chicago Republican* (which later became the *Inter-Ocean*). Dana's first step was to offer better salaries to the best talent of the *Times* and, as Wilkie put it, "Several of the old employes were thus seduced, among others the famous news editor, Harry Scovel." Scovell eventually moved on to become news editor of the *Tribune* before his failing eyesight forced him to retire. When the Detroit Typographical Union celebrated its golden anniversary in 1902, he was one of the few surviving charter member.[27] He died in Chicago on April 9, 1912.

Beecher Skinner: Beecher Skinner, the treasurer of the Franklin Club in 1861, was a printer who was born in Ireland in 1839. In 1865 he joined fellow Franklin Club member William F. Moore and four other men in responding to a strike by starting a new paper called the *Detroit Union*. Skinner was only 35 and unmarried when he died in Detroit of tuberculosis on December 21, 1874.

Henry Mitchell Starkey: Henry Starkey was born in Binghamton, New York, on May 11, 1828. His father moved the family to Michigan in 1833, eventually settling in Kalamazoo and serving in the Senate of the second state legislature. After being trained in the printer's trade, Henry volunteered and fought in Mexican War. Upon his return he followed his brother to Detroit to work for the *Free Press*. He helped organize the Detroit Typographical Union and represented it at the National Convention of Typographers in Buffalo in 1854. Later in the decade he succeeded his brother as city editor of the *Free Press*. Starkey named his first son Henry Scovell Starkey in honor of *Free Press* co-worker and fellow Franklin Club member Harry Scovell. By the end of the decade, Starkey had drifted into civic affairs and in the next few years he served as county clerk, clerk of the first Recorder's Court, and a member of the volunteer fire department. When the Civil War began, Starkey enlisted and was appointed a lieutenant in the 5th Michigan Cavalry, Company H, until an injury at the Battle of Gettysburg led to his discharge. In 1865 Starkey was elected to a two-year term as city clerk, and was twice re-elected. Then in 1872 he was named secretary of the Water Commission, a position he fulfilled until his death, coming to be known as "the encyclopedia for all information relating to the proper methods by which the city and its inhabitants are supplied with water; the appliances, cost and dispensing were as familiar to him as the letters of the alphabet." He also found time for a wide variety of other civic activities, including being credited with having "devised the present system of house numbering in Detroit, giving each twenty feet a number, whether occupied or not." Baseball too remained a part of his life, as he served as treasurer of the Aetna Club, umpired games from time to time, and in 1884 provided the *Free Press* with an enchanting account of the origins of the Franklin Club. Starkey died in Detroit on October 28, 1888.

George Thurston: George Thurston was another printer but his name soon disappeared from the Detroit city directories.

Jonas H. Titus, Jr.: Jonas H. Titus, Jr., was born in New York state around 1832. He worked as a printer before enlisting in the war and serving in Brady's Sharpshooters. He later moved to Saginaw and then to Chicago, where he died on April 2, 1895.

Charles H. Vernor: See Detroit Base Ball Club.

James Henry Walker: James H. Walker, who was born on May 16, 1836, in Plattsburgh, New York, was the president when the Franklin Club reorganized in 1860. He was a charter member of the Detroit Typographical Union and a *Free Press* printer, but unlike most of the club members he remained in Detroit after Storey's departure. Walker later worked for both the *Tribune* and the *Evening News* and eventually became the financial secretary of the Detroit Typographical Union. When he died in Detroit on April 11, 1915, he was one of two surviving charter members of the union and was described as "probably the most widely known man in the printing business in the state."[28]

Other Members: L. Boismuir (director in 1861), Knapp, McLogan, A. McMillan (director in 1861), Patten, George Staring, Taylor.

In addition, an article about the club that appeared in the *Free Press* on June 1, 1908, listed these three additional men, "all now dead," as having been members. The first was Albert Henry Raynor, a printer, who was born on February 1, 1836, in Vermilion, Ohio, married the sister of Franklin Club member Ben Duncklee, and died on January 28, 1898, in Detroit. The other two names were Chauncey Crofut and Rudolph Duryea, neither of whom could be identified. None of these three men's names appeared in contemporaneous pieces. While that doesn't rule out their membership, it is possible that someone confused John Duryea's name with that of Rudolph Duryea.

Sources

The main source for this piece is my book *Baseball Fever*, which relied heavily on contemporaneous newspapers and on Henry Starkey's reminiscences in the *Detroit Free Press* on April 4, 1884. John Drew's five-part series "Old-Time Printers of Detroit" (*Detroit Sunday News-Tribune*, every Sunday from October 17 through November 14, 1897) was extremely helpful, though Drew's memory was far from reliable. Franc B. Wilkie's *Personal Reminiscences of Thirty-five Years of Journalism* (Chicago: F.J. Schulte & Company, 1891) was also most valuable, as was Justin Walsh's fascinating biography of *Free Press* editor Wilbur F. Storey (*To Print the News and Raise Hell! A Biography of Wilbur F. Storey*, Chapel Hill: University of North Carolina Press, 1968). Orson Blair Curtis's *History of the Twenty-fourth Michigan of the Iron Brigade, Known as the Detroit and Wayne County Regiment* provided details on the military service of Dempsey and O'Donnell. Other helpful sources included the article about the club that appeared in the *Free Press* on June 1, 1908, and the obituaries of numerous players, as cited in the notes.

Notes

1. *Porter's Spirit of the Times*, October 3, 1857, letter from Walter H. Foster dated September 21, quoted in its entirety.
2. *Detroit Free Press*, April 4, 1884. John Drew stated that the club played "between First and Second, Lewis and Jones streets, a block which at that time was mostly a common." But Drew was not a club member and his account was written four decades after the fact.
3. Letter to Clarence Burton dated October 17, 1927, in the Burton Collection of the Detroit Public Library.
4. *Ibid.*
5. *Detroit Advertiser*, April 12, 1858.
6. *Detroit Daily Advertiser*, April 7, 1858.
7. *Detroit Daily Advertiser*, April 12, 1858.
8. *Detroit Daily Advertiser*, April 27, 1858.
9. *Detroit Free Press*, December 26, 1884.
10. *Detroit Daily Advertiser*, June 27, 1860; *Detroit Tribune*, June 27, 1860; *Detroit Advertiser*, June 27, 1860.
11. John Drew, "Old-Time Printers of Detroit" (five-part series), *Detroit Sunday News-Tribune*, October 17–November 14, 1897.
12. *Detroit Daily Advertiser*, May 24, 1861.
13. *Detroit Advertiser*, September 23, 1861; John Drew, "Old-Time Printers of Detroit" (five-part series), *Detroit Sunday News-Tribune*, October 17–November 14, 1897, although Drew calls this the "Lion Guard."
14. *Detroit Daily Advertiser and Tribune*, May 2, 1867. A nearly identical claim was made in the article that appeared in the *Free Press* on June 1, 1908.

15. John Drew, "Old-Time Printers of Detroit" (five-part series), *Detroit Sunday News-Tribune*, October 17–November 14, 1897.
16. "Challenge Early Risers," *Detroit Free Press*, June 1, 1908, 8.
17. *Detroit Daily Post*, May 5, 1874.
18. *Jackson Daily Citizen*, June 27, 1874.
19. "Pioneer Ball Players," *Detroit Free Press*, December 2, 1888, 6.
20. "Death Ends Long Newspaper Career," *Detroit News*, December 1, 1912, 10.
21. "Dad Durney's Apprenticeship," *Detroit Free Press*, September 1, 1901, C6; "Saw Many Changes; H. R. Durney, Veteran Printer, Dead at Ripe Old Age," *Detroit Free Press*, June 17, 1905, 2.
22. "Old Printers Fought in the Civil War," *Detroit Free Press*, March 10, 1902, 5.
23. "Poor Job!," *Detroit Free Press*, January 30, 1881, 8.
24. "Dana's Old Partner Dead," *Chicago Tribune*, April 10, 1912, 10.
25. "Saw Many Changes; H. R. Durney, Veteran Printer, Dead at Ripe Old Age," *Detroit Free Press*, June 17, 1905, 2.
26. "Dana's Old Partner Dead," *Chicago Tribune*, April 10, 1912, 10.
27. *Detroit Free Press*, March 2, 1902, 12.
28. *Detroit Free Press*, April 12, 1915.

❖ *Detroit Base Ball Club* (Peter Morris) ❖

Club History

The Detroit Base Ball Club was the most prominent ballclub in Michigan throughout the 1860s, and the club's history is at the center of my book *Baseball Fever*. As a result, this entry will provide an overview of the club's history along with profiles of key club members.

The Detroit Base Ball Club was formed in the fall of 1858, after the city's first club, the Franklins, had either disbanded or become inactive enough to amount to the same thing. The newly formed club did not take the field that fall, but members did begin practices when the spring of 1859 arrived. Those practices were scheduled for 4 P.M., a choice that proved fateful because it conflicted with the work schedules of many prospective members. This led to the organization of another new club, which called itself the Early Riser Club of Detroit in honor of its break-of-dawn practices.[1]

The rivalry between the two clubs was a friendly one but it was a rivalry nonetheless. Not surprisingly, the members of the Detroit Base Ball Club tended to be older, wealthier, and better established than the Early Risers, although several men belonged to both clubs. Two contests were played in 1859, with the Detroit Club winning both by convincing margins. But the competition proved much closer in 1860, with the two rivals splitting their first two matches before the Detroit Base Ball Club pulled out the rubber game to retain its distinction as local champion.[2]

The 1860 season also saw the start of intercity competition in Michigan, with the Detroit Base Ball Club defeating the Daybreak Club of Jackson. Baseball clubs were formed in several other Michigan cities that year and the new game seemed poised to sweep the state. But then the outbreak of the Civil War in the spring of 1861 put that possibility on hold.

While relatively few members of the Detroit Base Ball Club enlisted, many became involved in the war effort in some way or other and the club's activities came to a virtual halt. The club played only one match per season in 1861 and 1862, losing both times. In 1863 the club elected officers but never took the field, and in 1864 all baseball activity in Detroit seems to have ceased.[3]

The war finally ended in the spring of 1865 and the revival of the Detroit Base Ball Club soon followed. But while this club carried on the name and many of the traditions of its prewar counterpart, in many crucial ways it represented a break with the past. To begin with, most of the antebellum first nine members lost their places to younger men. In addition, two of those younger men — pitcher/captain Henry Burroughs and first baseman John Clark — were recent arrivals from the East (Newark and Brooklyn respectively). The extent to which these men were professionals is debatable, but there was no question that a new era of baseball in Michigan had begun. Symbolic of that new era was the club's decision to establish permanent enclosed grounds — a move that created the possibility of charging admission to games.[4]

No contemporaneous descriptions of the club's uniform have been found, but according to one of the men who covered the team: "The Detroit Club's uniform consisted of blue flannel pantaloons, full length, which the players tied at the ankles with strings. They also wore a blue blouse and caps to match, but later on changed their uniform to white."[5]

Although the Detroit Base Ball Club was now prepared for a new era of baseball, it was less clear whether the rest of the state would follow suit. The Early Riser Club did not reform after the war, leaving the Detroit Club without a local rival. Ball clubs sprang up in a few other Michigan towns that year, but the players were mostly novices who were still learning the basics of the game. As a result, the Detroit Base Ball Club played few outside clubs in the first five months after its postwar reorganization.

Matters changed dramatically when the news broke that the 1865 Michigan State Fair, which was to be staged in Adrian on September 20–21, would feature a baseball tournament. There was excitement about the event as far away as New York, where the *New York Clipper* noted, "We have had almost every other kind of tournament but base ball, but this exception, it appears, is not to be for long."[6] The anticipation increased when word came that the winner was not only going to be recognized as state champions but would also be awarded a goblet consisting of "a silver cup, mounted on three miniature bats. The lid of the cup is of oval shape, and in a depression carries a silver ball, the emblem of success. Between the bats, constituting the standard, are also placed fac similes of the square and circular bases. The prize is thus very appropriate, in addition to being of a novel model."[7]

When the State Fair opened, it showed the predicament that the Detroit Base Ball Club faced. Despite the interest generated by the tournament, several small-town clubs realized that they stood no chance of winning and elected not to play. In the end, there were only three other entrants — from Adrian, Jackson, and Lansing — and the Detroit Base Ball Club won both its matches handily to take home the championship trophy.[8]

A challenge system for defending the trophy had been adopted at the State Fair and two championship matches were staged at the enclosed grounds of the Detroit Base Ball Club that fall. The first one was billed as featuring an admission charge, but if one was charged the spectators must have been disappointed as the day was very cold and the visiting club from the small town of Salem was badly overmatched. The second one proved more competitive, with the hosts staving off a late rally by the Anchora Club of Adrian to retain the title.[9]

The eventful season of 1865 thus finished with an unresolved question. Would Michigan produce strong enough rivals for the Detroit Base Ball Club to sustain the enthusiasm over the state championship and, in the process, pay for the club's enclosed ballpark? Or would Detroit's status as far and away the state's biggest city prevent any meaningful rivalry from developing?

Unfortunately, the 1866 season showed that the latter situation still prevailed. Few challenges from in-state rivals were forthcoming, and even a match against an all-star club of players from around the state proved one-sided. Forced to look beyond the state boundaries for competition, in late June the Detroit Base Ball Club traveled to Rockford, Illinois, to compete in a tournament billed as being for the championship of the region. But this trip too proved disappointing when the club lost a tightly contested match to the Excelsiors of Chicago.[10]

The defeat was a bitter pill to swallow. More than two decades later, *Detroit Post* reporter B. F. Wright recalled, "It took the boys many weeks to satisfactorily explain how it all happened. In this connection I may say that that was the first instance of an umpire stealing a game that ever came under my notice. The barbarous decisions of the umpire in that game were dwelt on at great length and with painful particularity."[11] Nearly forty years after the contest, Detroit Club third baseman David Barry was still bitter that umpire H. G. Teed had "robbed us of that game…. That old grudge rankles deeply in our hearts yet. He was supposed to be from Laporte, Ind., but in reality was a member of the Chicago club."[12] The animosity between the Excelsiors and the Detroit Base Ball Club grew when efforts to stage a rematch at the enclosed field in Detroit were unsuccessful.[13]

After the disappointments of 1866, captain Henry Burroughs left town and the other Easterner, John Clark, temporarily stopped playing. The efforts of the club in 1867 were instead focused on hosting an August tournament in Detroit that was billed as being for the "World's Championship." In many respects, the tournament proved a success, but it was marred by ill will between the host club and the eventual winner, a club representing Jackson.[14]

The Detroit Base Ball Club did not compete in its own tournament and when it did return to action the results suggested that the leadership of Burroughs was sorely missed. The tournament was supposed to conclude with a match between the hosts and the champions, but the Jackson club refused, so the Detroit Club instead faced the runners-up and lost, prompting one reporter to comment that the "Detroit club is composed of good material when properly worked down, but it has been so much overrated as to become too lazy to practice."[15] More shocking was a match in which a club from the University of Michigan routed the state champions, 70–18.[16] And at times the Detroit Base Ball Club seemed just to be going through the motions, as when only five of the first nine were on hand for a loss to the Quickstep Club of Toledo.[17]

In spite of these setbacks, the 1867 season had many highlights. The Detroit Base Ball Club showed flashes of brilliance in wins against such clubs as the Niagaras of Buffalo and the Forest Citys of Cleveland. The friendly rivalry with the Forest Citys prompted great interest in Cleveland and helped spur the growth of baseball in the city. In 1903 John Hinchman of the Detroit Club met John D. Rockefeller at a business meeting in Chicago and "the oil king associated the Detroit name immediately with the times when as an unknown young bookkeeper he had attended all the ball games between Detroit and Cleveland."[18] The tournament hosted by the Detroit Base Ball Club similarly contributed to the explosive growth of baseball all across southern Michigan — the number of cities with clubs doubled and the number of clubs in the state enjoyed a corresponding surge.[19]

With the Detroit Base Ball Club no longer invincible and the game's appeal on the upswing, it would seem that the competitive imbalance that had plagued the state's baseball scene in 1866 and 1867 would end. Yet that didn't prove to be the case. Since most University of Michigan students went home for the summer, that club could not compete for the championship trophy or provide an ongoing rivalry. Meanwhile, the hard feelings between the ballplayers of Detroit and Jackson prevented that rivalry from being contested on the field, while the newly formed clubs in other towns were not ready to challenge the Detroit Base Ball Club.

The result was that the club once again faced few challenges for the trophy that was emblematic of the state championship. By the rules established in 1865, the Detroit Club's retention of the goblet against all challengers for two years meant that it became the club's permanent possession in September. This was a significant accomplishment, but it was less satisfactory than would have been the case if the trophy had inspired the number of championship matches that had been intended.

Also unsatisfying was the series that concluded the Detroit Base Ball Club's 1867 campaign. Two matches against the Excelsior Club of Chicago had finally been arranged for that October, giving Detroit its long-awaited chance for revenge. But the first contest, played in Chicago on October 5, resulted in a one-sided victory for the Excelsiors. The rematch was played in Detroit two weeks later and was much closer, with the Michigan club clinging to a narrow lead as darkness approached. Then the Excelsiors rallied and surged back in front. In desperation, the Detroit players resorted to allowing the visitors to score at will in hopes that the inning would not be completed and the score would revert to that of the previous inning. But eventually the inning came to an end and so too did another tumultuous season for the Detroit Base Ball Club.[20]

In the spring of 1868, Detroit's marquee ballclub announced plans to take a new direction. "We lost sight of the best interests and legitimate objects of base ball when we began to have an itching for foreign aid," declared club president Jonathan Van Norman at the outset of the new season. "What we haven't the brain and muscle to accomplish ourselves, by education and practice, we had better leave unaccomplished. So soon as our club becomes possessed with a hankering after professionals, that moment there is danger of its becoming prostituted from its beneficial and noble aims, and thus can no longer either claim or expect countenance from the public."[21]

Yet instead of staying true to this resolution to revert to amateurism, the club vacillated. The *Detroit Advertiser and Tribune* rejected allegations that the Detroit Base Ball Club was employing professionals and maintained that the nine was "composed of only home talent; notwithstanding the ungenerous assertion of our wise neighbors to the contrary."[22] But in fact the club employed several imported players in 1868 and most if not all of these men were paid for their services.

B.F. Wright, who covered the club for the *Detroit Post*, later recalled a meeting at the Russell House at which club members discussed whether to hire professional players. By this time it had become "quite the fashion to belong to the club" and more than 200 Detroiters were paying $5 a year for honorary memberships. This created a sizable war chest and, after a lengthy debate, a committee was appointed to hire professional players. Even so, it was "deemed necessary that the men be nominally amateurs, and it was determined to establish them in business."[23]

George Dawson of the University of Michigan club was hired for the summer and his obituary revealed that he was paid $75 per month to do so.[24] The club's pitcher was another new arrival, S. C. Lane from Pittsburgh. Henry Burroughs returned to town, now playing shortstop, and it seems likely that he was compensated in some way. In addition, a catcher named John Brown and an infielder named Snedaker arrived from New York, while a Jackson newspaper claimed that yet another new player, a Detroiter named T. Collins, received $15 a week for his services.[25]

With these reinforcements, the Detroit Base Ball Club pluckily agreed to play matches against the top Eastern clubs that had chosen to make their first Western tours in 1868. These matches finally provided the club with an opportunity to take advantage of their enclosed home field by collecting admission. Unfortunately, while matches against clubs like the Atlantics of Brooklyn and the Athletics of Philadelphia drew large crowds and swelled the coffers of the Detroit Base Ball Club, they resulted in lopsided defeats that showed that the club was still not able to compete on a national scene.[26]

Worse, because the members of the Detroit Base Ball Club were not amateurs who played for civic pride, they could no longer count on the support of the press. While the *Advertiser and Tribune* remained sympathetic, B.F. Wright of the *Detroit Post* lambasted the club for its use of imported players at every opportunity. "They have good material within the Club, but fail to develop it," he complained after one loss. He predicted that "just so long as they blindly overlook this fact and strain for players from a distance, even so long will the public not sympathise with them when they are defeated. A few years ago, when home talent alone was called into play, victory almost unceasingly perched on the banner of the Detroit club."[27] As the losses mounted, the rhetoric escalated and before long Wright had characterized professional ballplayers as "drones on the community. They have no noble aim in life, and ought not to be tolerated in a thrifty community."[28]

The Detroit Base Ball Club had one last hurrah on September 12 when it finally defeated its bitter rivals, the Excelsiors of Chicago, for the first time. But by this time the Excelsiors were also on the decline and the win was not as meaningful as it would once have been. As a result, the 1868 season ended with the Detroit Club facing the same dilemma that confronted clubs all over the country. Would it take advantage of the National Association of Base Ball Players' decision to permit open professionalism and hire a professional nine or would it revert to amateurism?

In light of the disappointing results of 1868 and the harsh criticism that had ensued, it came as no great surprise when the Detroit Base Ball Club decided to use only amateurs in 1869. A first nine of locals was assembled, almost all of whom were new players 20 years of age or under. Symbolizing the new direction, David Peirce of the prewar days was elected club president.

The club pinned its hopes for a return to glory on a young pitcher named Charley Ward, the son of Michigan's wealthiest industrialist. Ward's talent was such that the members of the Forest City Club of Rockford pronounced him the equal of any pitcher they faced during a tour of Illinois, Michigan, and

Ohio.[29] But Ward was as unreliable as he was gifted and his inconsistency was reflected in the club's performances, prompting speculation that the "Detroit Club may retire."[30] In August, the Detroit Base Ball Club made one last effort to revive its fortunes by announcing that it would again accept challenges for the championship trophy.[31] The anticipated flurry of activity did indeed result and in October the goblet was captured by a club from Ann Arbor.[32]

That match proved to be the last one ever played by the Detroit Base Ball Club. An effort was made to reorganize the club in April of 1870 but it came to nothing.[33] In May came word that the club owed $115.71 in taxes on its enclosed ballpark.[34] It was a final sad reminder that the Detroit Base Ball Club, for all its triumphs, had never quite succeeded in establishing baseball as a spectator sport in Michigan.

Club Members

Robert Henry Anderson: Robert H. Anderson was born in Patchogue, New York, on February 22, 1827. He followed the gold rush to California in 1848 but headed back east in 1855 and settled in Detroit. He went back to New York for a couple of years, but soon returned to Detroit to stay. He became a successful commission merchant and a member of the Board of Trade and the Light Guard. He was also one of the mainstays of the Detroit Base Ball Club, being involved in its founding in 1859 and, unlike many early members, remaining involved after the war. Even after losing his spot on the first nine, he continued to play for the second nine and serve as a director. He died in Detroit on January 26, 1898.

Lyman Hayden Baldwin: Lyman H. Baldwin was secretary of the Detroit Base Ball Club and one of the 16 club members who attended the 1866 Rockford tournament. He was born into a prominent Detroit family on April 18, 1844, and according to an obituary, "He early fell in with a group of youngsters who took kindly to athletics and he became an expert boxer; but rowing was his especial ambition. He was stroke oar of the famous Excelsior Victory of the early 70s and later commodore of the local navy."[35] Baldwin became the secretary and treasurer of the Hargreaves Manufacturing Company, one of the biggest frame manufacturers in the world. He died in Detroit on November 2, 1918.

David E. Barry: David Barry was born in Detroit on October 12, 1845, and played for the first nine in 1865 and 1866. As a young man, he worked in the railroad business but he later became associated with the Hoffman Coal Company. He died in Detroit on June 29, 1917.

William H. Baxter: See Franklins of Detroit.

Bergen: Like so many of the Eastern imports, mentions of this player were brief. On August 4, 1868, the *Advertiser and Tribune* described him as a new arrival from the East and then on April 22, 1869, the *Detroit Post* stated that he had left town. It's possible that he was Lem Bergen, a well-known Brooklyn player, but there's no way to be certain.

William Shepard Biddle: William S. Biddle, a Harvard-educated lawyer, became the Detroit club vice president when it was founded in 1859. When the Civil War broke out, he became involved in drilling troops and his connection with the ballclub ended. After the war he moved to Grosse Ile. Biddle was born in Detroit on April 24, 1830, and died in Grosse Ile on November 14, 1901.

John A. Brown: John Brown was an import from New York who started playing for the Detroit Base Ball Club in late 1867 and remained a mainstay until the club disbanded. B. F. Wright, who covered the club for the *Detroit Post*, had less than fond memories of Brown. Wright recalled that Brown was set up in a barber shop, "but if capable of shaving[,] it was never found out, as no one was venturesome enough to attempt to discover his tonsorial ability. It is certain he couldn't play ball. He failed miserably as a catcher and was then put on second base, where he developed great ability for dropping fly balls."[36] Brown was born in Florida around 1843 and brought along his young family when he arrived in Detroit from New York. He left Detroit and moved to Chicago during the 1870s and, despite Wright's reservations, he ran a barber shop there. Brown appears to have died in Chicago on February 8, 1893.

Henry S. Burroughs: Henry S. Burroughs was born on February 3, 1845, in Newark, New Jersey, and first played baseball for the Eureka Club of that city. After the war he moved to Detroit and became a "professor" of gymnastics at the Detroit Gymnasium and the captain and pitcher of the Detroit Base Ball Club. While he did offer courses in gymnastics, rival cities viewed him as the state's first professional import. An Ann Arbor paper explicitly described Burroughs as a "professional player," while the University of Michigan student newspaper wrote of Burroughs: "We don't blame Detroit for thus holding out inducements to good players: she must do it to keep pace with her sister cities. But it is somewhat difficult for us to distinguish between these men and 'professional players,' or those who play for 'place or emolument.'"[37] His play and captaining skills earned praise over the next two years, but professionalism gradually fell into disfavor and he resigned from club in the spring of 1867. He did return to play for the Detroit Club in 1868 and, according to Wright, he brought back from the East "a new wrinkle in fielding" and "proceeded to astonish the natives. His wrinkle was to rush at a ground ball and try to scoop it. He was successful about once in ten times."[38] After the demise of the Detroit Base Ball Club, Burroughs played professional ball for several seasons, including stints in the National Association in 1871 and 1872. He then returned to his native Newark, where he died of tuberculosis on March 31, 1878. An obituary noted that Burroughs had "gained celebrity as a base ball player, travelling over the United States" and was mourned by "hosts of friends, throughout the West and South as well as Newark being known as a genial and whole souled gentleman."

John Clark: John Clark was a second Easterner who joined the Detroit Base Ball Club after the war and went on to a remarkable career as an opera singer. Clark was born in County Cork, Ireland, on September 26, 1841, but came to Brooklyn as a child. After the Civil War he moved to Detroit to work as a proofreader for the *Advertiser and Tribune*, also becoming the first baseman of the Detroit Base Ball Club. He held down both positions for the next three years, and was likely also responsible for many of the unsigned articles about baseball that appeared in the paper during these years. After returning to Brooklyn, he continued his career as a journalist for several years and also began singing. He proved to have such an exceptional bass voice that a subscription was raised in Brooklyn to send him to Europe for voice training. As a tribute to his hometown, Clark adopted the stage name of Signor Brocolini. After four years as an opera singer in Europe, he returned to New York in 1879 to create the role of the Pirate King in the original New York City production of Gilbert and Sullivan's *The Pirates of Penzance*. The evidence suggests that Clark also played a key role in the creation of the Pirate King's signature song. Clark continued to tour in comic operas for the next decade, mostly in the United States, but he also made a tour of Australia. Rheumatism forced him to give up the stage at last and he became the music critic of the *Brooklyn Eagle*. He died in Brooklyn on June 7, 1906.[39]

James Craig: James Craig served as club vice president in 1863 and played for the first nine before the war. He was born on December 2, 1823, in Ticonderoga, New York, and moved in 1847 to Detroit, where he and his brother were in the fish and grocery business. In 1875 he served in the state legislature. He died on November 11, 1895.

George Ellis Dawson: George Dawson was a University of Michigan student who caught for the Detroit Base Ball Club in the summer of 1868. According to his obituary, he was paid $75 a month to do so, and while his professional status was not explicitly mentioned in the press, it seems to have been well enough known to cause resentment. That is ironic because Dawson embodied the gentlemanly era of baseball. He was born on June 23, 1847, in Loami, Illinois, and sang in Lincoln's funeral choir while a student at Springfield High School. Only weeks before joining the Detroit Base Ball Club, Dawson gave a speech at his sophomore class commencement on "The Desire for Knowledge." His career after graduation would exemplify that theme, as he became principal of Flint High School in 1870, then taught in Buffalo before passing the Bar in 1881 and becoming a successful attorney. Dawson died in Ludington, Michigan, on August 19, 1935.[40]

William DeGraff: William DeGraff, who was born around 1846 in Michigan, was a club member from 1866 to 1868. He mostly played with the second nine, but was one of the 16 members who attended the 1866 Rockford tournament. DeGraff was a cashier at the Detroit National Bank.

Dr. Justin J. Dumon: J.J. Dumon was a dentist who was born in New York state around 1832. He was the club's regular catcher before the war and played a couple of games in 1865, also serving as a club director. In 1868 he was accused of larceny and acquitted, then disappeared.

Charles Dupont: Charles Dupont was born in Detroit on February 12, 1842. His mother was a Simoneau, so he was presumably related to fellow club members Henry and Leander Simoneau, in whose drugstore he worked as a teenager. He also worked as a printer's apprentice at the *Free Press* alongside many members of the Franklin Club. Dupont enlisted in the 4th Michigan Infantry at the start of the Civil War and was shot in the face at the battle of Gaines' Mill and reported dead. In fact, he had been captured by the Confederates and was held in Libby Prison in Richmond for four months before being exchanged and being able to notify his family that he was still alive. Although the shooting cost him his right eye, he re-enlisted and was eventually placed in command of more than 1,400 men. Among his regiment's many accomplishments was helping to capture accused Lincoln assassination conspirators Samuel Mudd and George Atzerodt. After the war Dupont served as a director of the Detroit Base Ball Club and, despite his war injuries, even played in a few games for the club's second nine. He went into the laundry business and was also elected Detroit's Register of Deeds. He never married and died in Detroit on December 16, 1901.

Morgan S. Fellers: Morgan Fellers was born around 1836 and played for the first nine of the Detroit Base Ball Club in 1859. He enlisted in the 1st Michigan Infantry on April 18, 1861, and served until that August. He then ran a grocery in Detroit until he moved to Kansas City around 1877. By 1910 he was living in a home for disabled veterans in Leavenworth, Kansas. He died on October 13, 1922, and is buried in Leavenworth National Cemetery.

Dexter Mason Ferry: Dexter M. Ferry, Sr., was born in Lonville, New York, on August 8, 1833, and moved to Detroit in 1852. He became a partner in a seed company in 1856, and then in 1867 founded D. M. Ferry Seeds, which became one of the world's largest seed companies and is still in existence. Ferry's involvement with the Detroit Base Ball Club was limited, as he played one game for the club's second nine in 1866 and then served as a club vice president in 1867. That was the year that Ferry started his seed company and was married, and his involvement with the Detroit Base Ball Club appears to have ended there. Nonetheless, he was often mentioned in later reminiscences about the club. In 1903, David Peirce recalled, "D. M. Ferry played with us and he was a great hitter. He had an ankle sprained in one game and it laid him up for a long time. We had some new bases, fastened to stakes in the ground. Mr. Ferry made a long hit that proved to be a home run, but on the way around the bases he stepped on one of the posts, and turned his ankle severely. He kept on, and made the run, but it was his last for a long time."[41] After becoming a very successful businessman, Ferry continued to take an interest in baseball. In 1876 he made a $50 loan to the Aetna Club of Detroit. During the 1880s he sponsored a company baseball team known as the Seeds and one of his employees, pitcher Frank McIntyre, briefly reached the major leagues. Ferry died in Detroit on November 10, 1907.

Frank Folsom: Frank Folsom was born in Southbridge, Massachusetts, on June 25, 1839, and moved to Detroit with his father, a wool dealer. He helped his father in the business. Like several others, he belonged to both the Detroit Base Ball Club and the Early Riser Club and was a director of the latter club. He also belonged to the Franklin Club, making him the only man who is known to have belonged to the city's first three prominent clubs. But he seems to have restricted his appearances in match games to the Detroit Base Ball Club, earning a reputation as "one of the fastest runners of bases in the country." His interest in baseball continued after his playing days ended, as he served as vice president of Aetnas in 1876. He married an opera singer who performed with John Clark under the name of Debbie Clemelli.[42] She died in 1887 and Folsom eventually moved back to Southbridge, where he died on April 27, 1895.

Charles Harvey Force: Charles Force was born in Manchester, Michigan, on October 10, 1838. After the Civil War he moved to Detroit, where he married in 1866 and joined the Detroit Base Ball Club. He won the best baserunner competition at that year's Rockford tournament. He died in Manchester on September 15, 1870.

Ford De Camp Hinchman: Ford Hinchman was born at the house of his grandfather, former Detroit Mayor Marshall Chapin, on September 3, 1847. The Chapin House was directly across from Lewis Cass's home, symbolizing the prominence of his family. He played for the first nine of the Detroit Base Ball Club after the war and won the prize for the best throw at the 1866 Rockford tournament — indeed all three of his throws were better than the best one of the runner-up. In 1869, he gave up baseball and became a partner in his father's business, which became known as T.H. Hinchman and Sons. He did, however, continue to play cricket as the wicket-keeper for the Peninsular Cricket Club. He also served as the city's park commissioner under Mayor William Thompson. He died in Detroit on March 26, 1929.

John Marshall Hinchman: John M. Hinchman, Ford's older brother, was born in Detroit on August 14, 1845. He attended the University of Michigan from 1862 to 1865 and helped found the school's first baseball club. After the Civil War, he became the shortstop of the Detroit Base Ball Club. He gave up baseball in 1868 and became a partner in his father's business, which became known as T.H. Hinchman and Sons. He died on May 3, 1912, in Detroit.

John Horn, Jr.: John Horn, Jr., was born in Sidmouth, Devonshire, England, on September 7, 1843. In 1852 the family moved to Detroit, where the elder John Horn operated a saloon known as Gorman's or The Shakespeare, which became a popular hangout of printers. John Horn, Sr., played cricket but his son took up baseball and was a regular in the outfield of the Detroit Base Ball Club from 1865 to 1868. John Horn, Jr., became renowned for saving well over a hundred people from drowning in the Detroit River. An 1875 book described how Horn "saved the life of a poor little newsboy, who fell into the water in the presence of two boat-loads of people, not one of whom was willing to jump into the river." But Horn "ran immediately to the place, and without an instant's hesitation, sprang into the water and rescued the child just as he was sinking, which made the number of one hundred and twenty people, whom he has saved from drowning. He is a good swimmer and his method is to hold the person at arm's length, aiming to keep only the head of the drowning person out of the water; this requires very little strength, only of a few pounds."[43] For his heroism, Horn received the Congressional Gold Medal in 1874. Horn served as a Detroit alderman during the 1870s and was spoken of as a potential candidate for governor.[44] He later served as president of the board of health and as a deputy sheriff. He also continued to rescue people from the river, including an incident in which he saved nine people after the explosion of an oil tank on a ferry, and was so seriously injured that he spent several weeks in bed.[45] Following in his father's footsteps, he later became a member of the Peninsular Cricket Club. In 1901 his Congressional Gold Medal was stolen and the U.S. Congress voted to create a replacement medal. Horn died in Detroit on April 12, 1920. An obituary credited "Captain Jack" with having saved 135 lives, adding,

> For many years he was a picturesque and familiar figure about the docks. His rescues included every sort of person, ragged newsboys that fell from the docks at play, giant Negro laborers, women who sought death, once a baby that slipped from its mother's arms, sailors who came to the docks seeking their ship with a cargo of hard liquor aboard that treacherously led them to the water's edge, boys who had ventured out in the stream in leaky boats, victims of accidents to every sort of craft. He was one of the best swimmers in the country, of great strength and daring, and in time came to hold a feeling of responsibility for every endangered man or woman along the river. He failed in but two efforts.[46]

Butler Ives: Butler Ives had one of the longest tenures with the Detroit Base Ball Club, being a regular before the war and resuming that role in 1865 and 1866. He was noted for sliding into bases during an era when that was a very unusual tactic. Ives was born in Detroit on June 17, 1843, and joined his father in the banking business. The Ives Bank was successful for many years but it fell victim to the difficult economic climate of the 1890s and folded on May 24, 1896. Butler Ives died on April 11, 1916.

S. C. Lane: S. C. Lane, who was described by the *Detroit Post* as a mechanic who had recently moved to town, became the club's pitcher in 1868. The circumstances and other references to him in the local papers suggest that he was a professional player, while other notes had him being from Allegheny, Pennsylvania (now part of Pittsburgh), and having formerly played for the Lincolns of Pittsburgh. Based on these facts, he was almost certainly a man named Samuel C. Lane, who was born in Allegheny around 1847. On the 1860 Census the Lane household included Ambrose Lynch, who was the catcher of the Allegheny Base Ball Club and was voted best catcher at the 1867 Detroit tournament. Also of note is that Samuel Lane's younger brother, George, played in the major leagues in the 1880s. Samuel Lane later worked as a painter and was living in Pittsburgh in 1910.

Heber LeFavour: See Early Risers of Detroit.

George Howard Lothrop: George Lothrop was another University of Michigan student who joined George Dawson in playing for the Detroit Base Ball Club in the summer of 1868. The indication, however, is that Lothrop was not paid for his services, as he was not even a regular. Lothrop was born in Detroit on April 18, 1850. He left the University of Michigan after his sophomore year and completed his degree at Cornell University. He passed the Bar and became such a respected patent lawyer that President Grover Cleveland offered him the position of commissioner of patents in 1885. But he declined the appointment, although he did later serve on Detroit's first Public Lighting Commission. He died in Detroit on November 21, 1896.

John F. McMillan: John McMillan, the club's secretary in 1863, was a civil engineer.

E. F. Myrick: E. F. Myrick was the club president in 1863.

John Stoughton Newberry, Sr.: John S. Newberry was born on November 18, 1926, in Waterville, New York. The family moved to Michigan when he was young and he graduated from the University of Michigan in 1845 with honors, then was admitted to the Bar in 1853, and specialized in maritime law. He was married in 1855 but soon widowed, and after his wife's death he moved to a downtown hotel and began to play with both the Detroit Base Ball Club and the Early Risers. When the Civil War broke out, Newberry was appointed provost marshal of Michigan in 1862, as well as serving as the associate secretary of the U.S. Sanitary Commission. During the war he also established a firm called the Michigan Car Company and received many wartime contracts to make railway cars. The business remained very successful after the war, making Newberry and his partner, James McMillan, very wealthy men. Newberry later started several other businesses, including the Baugh Stearn Forge, Griffin Car Wheel Works, Fulton Engine Works, and several foundries and grain elevators. He was elected to Congress in 1879 but did not run for re-election. He died in Detroit on January 2, 1887.

Samuel S. Newberry: Samuel Newberry does not appear to have been related to John Newberry. He was born in Indiana and graduated from Union College before moving to Detroit and playing for the Detroit Base Ball Club in 1860. He enlisted in the Civil War and rose to the rank of captain before being shot and killed near Petersburg on August 18, 1864.

George Niles: George Niles was born in Painted Post, New York, on May 27, 1820. His father, Johnson Niles, soon moved the family to a farm in Oakland County, Michigan. The site later became the city of Troy, but at the time it was so isolated that Niles's childhood playmates were Native Americans and he did not own a hat or a pair of shoes until he was 12. According to an 1877 book, Johnson Niles was one of the men who played in a "game of base-ball" that was part of the Independence Day celebrations in 1826.[47] George Niles was widowed twice before the age of 30. Around 1850 he moved to Detroit with his third wife and the children from all three marriages. For the next two decades he worked as a traveling salesman for a Detroit dry-goods merchant. He also served as a 2nd Ward alderman from 1856 to 1858. During these years, although quite a bit older than most of the players, he became involved in the Detroit Base Ball Club. As a result, he was later remembered as "a well-known character, somewhat older than the rest." Around 1870 George Niles returned to Oakland County to help his father run the farm and he remained there after his father's death two years later. By 1891 he was farming 90 acres of the original homestead plus an additional 55 acres. He died there on January 31, 1899.

O'Brien: Several men named O'Brien were involved with the club in the postwar years and it's difficult to keep them straight. The one who was mentioned most often was Noel C. O'Brien. In 1866 W. C. O'Brien was listed as a club director, although it's possible that this was a typographical error and the man in question was actually Noel. Other O'Briens in these years were H. L. and T. J. When these men played, it was almost always with the second nine.

Edward S. Orr: Edward S. Orr was born in Bedford, New Hampshire, on February 26, 1826, and ran a dry-goods store after moving to Detroit. He was active in the Detroit Cricket Club, but also became interested in the newer sport of baseball, serving as an officer of the Detroit Base Ball Club and hosting its first organizational meeting in the fall of 1858. After many years as a Detroit merchant, he moved to a farm in Macomb County during the 1870s. He died on March 8, 1884.

William K. Parcher: William K. Parcher, who was born in Maine around 1835, was a starter for the club in 1860 and during the lone games the club played in 1861 and 1862. He later became the vice president of the Globe Tobacco Company.

David Russell Peirce: David R. Peirce was born in Ogdensburg, New York, on October 25, 1827, and grew up in Montreal. In 1849 he started for California to join the Gold Rush, but when he passed through Detroit he "decided it was good enough for him" and he remained there for the rest of his life. He initially worked as a bookkeeper at Senator Zach Chandler's dry-goods store on Woodward Avenue and as a daguerreotypist (daguerreotypes were a predecessor of the photograph). Peirce became very active in civic life, joining one of the early fire companies, helping to found the Detroit Light Guard and the city's Audubon Club, and showing a special fondness for athletics. According to a 1903 article about his early years in the city,

> The young men of the city were enthusiastic over athletics, and every noon and every night they met at Merritt's gymnasium, on Jefferson avenue, between Bates and Randolph streets. Mr. [David] Peirce says the boys used to do all the tricks that the athletes do in circuses today. Mr. Peirce did not have time during the days to take boxing lessons, so he got up early in the mornings and walked four miles to Canniff's farm on the Pontiac road, to take his lessons. He was very quick on his feet, and in those days he would rather box than eat. At night when the boys assembled at the gymnasium, the first event on the program usually was a foot race from Jefferson avenue to the foot of Woodward avenue and back. Then the boys adjourned to the gymnasium and boxed, wrestled and took part in other sports.[48]

He was also involved in the formation of the Detroit Base Ball Club and was a starter in 1859 and 1860. His election as club president in 1869 was a sign of the club's intention to return to its amateur roots. By then Peirce was secretary and treasurer of the Detroit Locomotive Works, a position that he held for more than 40 years. It was the first Detroit business to pay all of its workers in cash — the others "paid a small amount in cash, and the remainder in store orders of all kinds." Peirce made all of the monthly payments himself and knew every employee by name, even after the ranks grew to include more than 500 workers. He remained an enthusiastic baseball fan right up to his death in Detroit on January 21, 1905.[49]

Frank J. Phelps: Frank J. Phelps first played for the Detroit Base Ball Club in 1862 and he became a mainstay after the war, mostly playing the demanding position of catcher. Phelps was born around 1838 in Michigan and ran a store at 256 Jefferson in downtown Detroit. He served as club vice president in 1866, and meetings were sometimes held at his store. In addition, by 1867 his store was advertising baseballs made by three different manufacturers, bats, caps, belts, spikes, and other baseball implements. He left the city directory around 1887 and a 1903 article stated that Phelps had died around 1889, but no death certificate has been found in Michigan, suggesting that he died out of state.

Eugene Robinson: Eugene Robinson was born in Binghamton, New York, on May 15, 1837. His father died in 1840, one year after the family moved to Detroit. He joined the Detroit Light Guard in 1857 and then enlisted in the 1st Michigan Infantry at the start of the Civil War. He fought at the Battle of Bull Run and was promoted to sergeant-major. Upon his return to Detroit, he alternated between serving in the Michigan Guard and working as a civil engineer. In the former capacity, he was elected lieutenant colonel of the Michigan Guard, then promoted to colonel on July 23, 1885, and to brigadier general on October 1, 1890. He also became the city surveyor and received the contract to pave Jefferson Avenue. The latter job, however, caused him great trouble and he repaved it several times at his own expense. Robinson also found time for baseball, playing for the first nine before the war and serving as treasurer in 1863. After the war, he was relegated to the second nine but remained one of the club's directors. He also served as a director of the Cass Base Ball Club in 1876. Robinson died in Detroit on October 28, 1897.

W. Rogerson: W. Rogerson played only one game for the Detroit Base Ball Club in 1867, but he is noteworthy because the *Detroit Post* described him as having previously played for the Union Cricket Club, apparently of Cincinnati. He soon left for Buffalo.

Henry Simoneau: Henry Simoneau was born around 1833 in Canada and he and his brother Leander ran a Detroit drugstore in the 1850s. Henry moved to Peoria and continued to work there as a pharmacist until after the turn of the century.

Leander Simoneau: Leandre or Leander Simoneau was born in St. Nicolas, Quebec, on February 5, 1834, but moved to Detroit while young. He and his brother Henry were partners in a Detroit drug business before Leander moved to East Saginaw in 1864 to run his own business. Leander Simoneau served two terms as mayor of East Saginaw, in 1871–72 and again in 1882–83. He sold his business in 1883, subsequently serving as register of deeds and as a justice of the peace. On the morning of January 21, 1894, he fell into the frozen Saginaw River and drowned. It was nearly two months before his body was recovered.

W. C. B. Teller: W. C. B. Teller was born around 1843 and served as treasurer of club in 1866 and 1867. He worked as the paying teller of the American National Bank but in 1878 he absconded with $5,300. He was captured in Montreal the following year and sentenced to five years in the House of Correction. But he received a presidential pardon because of failing health and he died on April 15, 1883.

J. W. Toms: The Detroit Base Ball Club was represented in New York at the 1860 convention of the National Association of Base Ball Players by two men whose involvement with the club was otherwise minimal. One of these men was listed as either J. W. Tomes or G. W. Toms and the other as J. S. Davies or J. E. Jarvis. Neither has been positively identified, but the former may be Justus W. Toms, who was born in New York state on March 12, 1827, and grew up in Oakland County. He later moved to Wisconsin and Chicago but returned to Michigan and died in Pontiac on November 17, 1913.

Arthur Van Norman: Arthur Van Norman was Jonathan's younger brother and he played a variety of positions for the club between 1865 and 1867. Like his brother, he was born in Canada. He worked as a bookkeeper while living in Detroit, but by 1873 had moved to Jackson to work as superintendent of the Michigan Central Railroad shops. He was subsequently promoted to secretary and manager and also served as a city alderman. In 1878, he returned to Detroit as proprietor of Biddle House but was dogged by financial troubles. Notes in 1879 placed him in both Colorado and Ohio, but his whereabouts after that are difficult to trace. A 1903 article stated that he had been dead for several years and, according to an online genealogy, he died on June 17, 1895.

Dr. Jonathan Mack Van Norman: Jonathan Van Norman was born in 1824 in Canada and attended McGill Medical School in Montreal. He graduated in 1850 and established a medical school in Bronte, Ontario, with Dr. Anson Buck. He later moved to Detroit and served as one of the Detroit Base Ball Club's directors and as club president in 1867 and 1868. In the latter year he gave a speech announcing the club's intention to revert to amateurism. He occasionally played when the club was short-handed, and usually handled the umpiring duties, which he did while "sitting well to one side, out of danger of foul balls, an umbrella over his head, and his silk hat on the ground beside him."[50] He also served as unofficial team doctor, and John Clark became notorious for the frequency with which he requested Dr. Van Norman's attentions. Major league player and manager Dan O'Leary later recalled, "When Clark made an error he invariably shook his fingers, as though hurt, and the small boys always yelled, 'Get the doctor.'"[51] On April 18, 1873, the *Detroit Advertiser and Tribune* reported that Van Norman had been convicted of smuggling. He subsequently moved to Cleveland and apparently died there in 1894.

Charles H. Vernor: Charles H. Vernor was born in Albany, New York, in 1839 and moved with his family to Detroit in 1849. During the Civil War he served in the Detroit district quartermaster's office. He played for the first nine of the Detroit in its first two games in 1865. Thereafter, he played only occasionally and usually did so for the second nine, but remained involved in the club's activities as secretary in 1866 and as treasurer in 1869. When the Detroit Base Ball Club hosted the major 1867 tournament, Vernor's brother James was one of the vendors. At the time, James Vernor was in the process of perfecting a new soft drink, so it seems likely that tournament attendees were among the first to try the beverage that became famous as Vernor's Ginger Ale. Charles Vernor worked as a bookkeeper for the Second National Bank. After a long life, he died in Detroit on March 4, 1928.

Charles Harrison Ward: Charley Ward was born on September 19, 1850, and he and fellow club member Milt Ward were the sons of Eber Ward, a ship magnate and Michigan's richest man. Charley attended the state agricultural college (now Michigan State University) from 1864 to 1866, then took courses at Bryant & Stratton and worked in a bank from 1867 to 1869. As described in *Baseball Fever*, he became the pitcher of the Detroit Base Ball Club in 1869 but he was better known for being a spendthrift who wasted every cent his father let him have. In 1893 a relative described him as "a kind of roving renegade" and a 1900 Michigan State alumni directory listed him as a banker in Cape Town, South Africa.

Milton Duane Ward: Charley Ward's older brother, Milt, was born in May of 1848. Like his brother, he attended the state agricultural college but never settled down. He died of tuberculosis in Bermuda on May 26, 1877.

Other Members: Altman (1860), Andrews (1869 club), S.C. Andrews (1859), George F. Bagley (1859), Gov. John J. Bagley (1859), B. Franklin Baker (1859), George A. Baker (nonplaying officer), W. S. Biddle (1859), John H. Bissell (1867), W. Bissell (1867), T. S. Blackmer (1859), Bowler (1869), M. R. Campin (1859), John M. L. Campbell (1869 secretary), Carrier (1866 and 1868), Charles F. Clark (1859), T. Collins (1868), William J. Crittenden (1860), Charles P. Crosby (1859), Dr. L. L. Davenport (1859), Davis (1869), A. D. Dickinson (1859), Joseph A. Eagle (1859), Elliott (1867), John G. Erwin (1859), G. J. Fellers (1859), George L. Finney (1859), Henry W. Fisher (1859), Henry R. Hallock (1859), John Heffron (1859), J. W. Hooker (director in 1867), Hull (1869), William Hull (prewar scorer), Irving (1868), Albert Ives, Jr. (prewar), DeGarmo Jones (1859), M. M. Kelly (1867), George C. Langdon (1859), Joseph Law, Jr. (1859), A. R. Linn (1866), Mahon (1869), E. R. Mathews (1863 director), E. R. McDonald (1859), McLaughlin (1867), Robert McMillan (1859), Andrew McPherson (1869 director), Pasco (1869), Pickering (1866), S. Pittman (1859–60), Fred B. Porter (1859), Pressley (1869), John J. Regan (1869 vice president), W. W. Robbins (1859), J. Seaman (1860), Sheehan or Sheeran (1869), James Sines (1860–62), James Slocum (1866–67), Snedaker (1867), Snow (1860), Sprague (1869), George Staring (1867–68), J. B. Staring (1859), D. Swarts (one game in 1868 — apparently an import from the Buckeye Club of Cincinnati), Thompson (1859), Albert Tonn (1859), Trempe (1869), Webster (1860 and 1869, presumably different people), Daniel T. Wells (1859), N. N. West (1859), Charles H. Wetmore (1859), DeGarmo J. Whiting (1859), Ned G. Williams (1859), C. S. Witbeck (1859), Wood (1869), Smith R. Woolley (1859), H. B. Wormer (1866–67), Peter Young (1859).

Sources

The main source for this entry was the research in contemporaneous newspapers done for my book *Baseball Fever: Early Baseball in Michigan*, which has far more details about the context in which the club emerged and competed. Especially useful in compiling the list of club members was an "An Old-Time Ball Club," *Detroit Free Press*, April 23, 1893, 18, which listed the 50 active club members in 1859 and discussed their current whereabouts.

Notes

1. Peter Morris, *Baseball Fever* (Ann Arbor: University of Michigan Press, 2003), 33–34.
2. *Ibid.*, 36–43, 54–61.
3. *Michigan Gazetteer 1863*; Morris, *Baseball Fever*, 80.

4. Morris, *Baseball Fever*, 90–93.
5. "Old-Time Base Ball," *Detroit Free Press*, December 16, 1888, 10.
6. *New York Clipper*, August 8, 1865.
7. *Detroit Advertiser and Tribune*, September 13, 1865.
8. Morris, *Baseball Fever*, 96–99.
9. *Ibid.*, 99–101.
10. *Ibid.*, 110–115.
11. "Old-Time Base Ball," *Detroit Free Press*, December 16, 1888, 10.
12. *Detroit News-Tribune*, March 15, 1903.
13. Morris, *Baseball Fever*, 116–117.
14. *Ibid.*, 161–170.
15. *Chicago Times*, August 21, 1867.
16. Morris, *Baseball Fever*, 146–148.
17. *Ibid.*, 171.
18. "Detroit's Old Time Baseball Clubs," *Detroit Free Press*, November 13, 1904, D3.
19. Morris, *Baseball Fever*, Appendix B.
20. *Ibid.*, 175–176.
21. *Detroit Post*, April 7, 1868.
22. *Detroit Advertiser and Tribune*, June 13, 1868.
23. "Old-Time Base Ball," *Detroit Free Press*, December 16, 1888, 10.
24. *Chicago Tribune*, August 20, 1935.
25. *Jackson Daily Citizen*, June 5, 1868.
26. Morris, *Baseball Fever*, 218–219.
27. *Detroit Post*, June 5, 1868.
28. *Detroit Post*, June 22, 1868.
29. *Rockford Republic*, June 24, 1922, 6.
30. *Detroit Free Press*, July 24, 1869.
31. *Detroit Advertiser and Tribune*, August 23, 1869.
32. Morris, *Baseball Fever*, 232–233.
33. *Ibid.*, 244.
34. *Detroit Free Press*, May 21, 1870.
35. *Detroit Free Press*, November 5, 1918.
36. "Old-Time Base Ball," *Detroit Free Press*, December 16, 1888, 10.
37. *Ann Arbor Peninsular Courier and Family Visitant*, June 20, 1866; *University Chronicle*, June 22, 1867.
38. "Old-Time Base Ball," *Detroit Free Press*, December 16, 1888, 10.
39. For a much more detailed account of Clark's life, see Peter Morris, "From First Baseman to Primo Basso: The Odd Saga of the Original Pirate King (Tra La!)," *Nine: A Journal of Baseball History and Culture* 15:2 (Spring 2007), pp. 46–65, 169.
40. *Chicago Tribune*, August 20, 1935.
41. "When D.M. Ferry Played Ball," *Detroit Free Press*, June 14, 1903, D3.
42. *Detroit Free Press*, May 12, 1883.
43. William Whitty Hall, *How to Live Long* (London: Hurd and Houghton, 1875), 269.
44. *Detroit Evening News*, August 22, 1874.
45. "Captain Jack Loses Lifeline," *Detroit News*, April 14, 1920, 1.
46. *Ibid.*
47. Samuel W. Durant, *History of Oakland County, Michigan* (Philadelphia: L. H. Everts & Co., 1877), 295.
48. "When D.M. Ferry Played Ball," *Detroit Free Press*, June 14, 1903, D3.
49. *Ibid.*; "Old Citizen Passed Beyond," *Detroit Free Press*, January 22, 1905, 9; "Tried to Break Peirce Will," *Detroit Free Press*, December 14, 1908, 1.
50. "Old-Time Base Ball," *Detroit Free Press*, December 16, 1888, 10.
51. "Pioneer Ball Players," *Detroit Free Press*, December 2, 1888, 6.

❖ *Early Risers of Detroit* (Peter Morris) ❖

CLUB HISTORY

The Early Riser Base Ball Club of Detroit was in existence for less than two years and disbanded for good when the Civil War broke out. Yet the club created Michigan's first major rivalry and offered a striking testament to the sacrifices the earliest ballplayers were willing to make to play baseball.

The Early Riser Club commenced play in 1859, when the city already boasted at least one other club, the Detroit Base Ball Club. (There is contradictory evidence about whether Detroit's first club, the Franklins, was still in existence, but that club had no recorded activity in 1859.) Practical considerations were behind the formation of the new club, as the Detroit Base Ball Club held afternoon practices that conflicted with the work schedules of many Detroit men who were interested in playing baseball. As a result, the Early Riser Club was made up of "young men employed in stores and offices, whose occupations prevent their taking any recreation during the day."[1]

While this description might seem to suggest that the Early Risers came from a lower social class than the Detroit Base Ball Club, that generalization does not appear to hold. The Early Risers represented a broad swath of the social spectrum but by and large the club's membership was not that different from that of the Detroit Base Ball Club. Both were made up of young men who were still striving to define their status in a young, rapidly growing city. The common bonds between the two clubs were underscored by the fact that several men belonged to both.

The most important difference was the extraordinary time at which the Early Risers got out of bed for their practices. One of the first articles about the club stated that its practices began at 4 A.M.[2] That piece was written shortly after summer solstice, but even so it is surprising that enough daylight was available for practice at such an early hour. Yet they were not alone — a member of another pre-war club, the Live Oaks of Rochester, New York, later recalled, "All of the young fellows who played on the 'Live Oaks' were employed in the city. We used to get out of bed at 3 o'clock and wait for the sun to come up so we could practice until it was time for us to go to work."[3]

Subsequent articles about the Early Risers gave somewhat later start times for their sessions, which could mean that the club rethought the question. But it is also possible that they made adjustments as the seasons changed. Adding to the confusion, this was before standard time was instituted. In any case, the decision to name the club in honor of Ben Franklin's maxim about the benefits of early rising was very apt.

There is also conflicting information about the exact date of origin of the Early Riser Club. An article in the *Free Press* on July 12, 1859, announced that the club had been formally organized at a meeting on the previous Friday — which was the 8th — and boasted 22 members. But on Thursday the 7th, a piece in the *Daily Advertiser* had reported: "A Base Ball Club has been organized by some of our enterprising young men, which meets every morning at four o'clock in front of the Russell House for practice. It is very fine exercise, and most emphatically causes those who enter into the arrangement to comply with one of the conditions given as requisite by Dr. Franklin to become healthy, wealthy and wise, viz. 'early to rise.'" In addition, the *Free Press* of June 14, 1859, noted that the city had two baseball clubs, which could mean that the Early Riser Club was already in existence by then.

What we do know is that by July of 1859 the club was up and running and that it soon began to attract attention. The Early Risers held their crack-of-dawn practices beside the Campus Martius, the large open space set aside for public assemblies in the original design of Detroit. The location was convenient, but also had a major disadvantage — batted balls broke so many windows in the nearby Russell House hotel that the club began paying a flat rate.[4]

Nevertheless, the club's practices attracted good turnouts. To help the players shake off their slumbers, a local marketwoman, Mrs. Martin, "established her quarters on our playing grounds every morning and furnished us coffee and light refreshments which very often was our only breakfast." The Early Risers also began storing their bats and balls in a large box located behind a nearby grocery store.[5]

Before long, the success of the early-morning practices prompted the Early Risers to challenge the Detroit Base Ball Club to the first match game ever played in Michigan. The historic event took place on August 8, 1859, and to nobody's surprise the older club won by the convincing score of 59–21. Yet the Early Risers earned plaudits because they "were offered odds in the match by the other club on account of their inexperience and acknowledged inferiority, but with the true Young America spirit they declined accepting the offer, and went in on equal terms. They were of course beaten, but, as they expected this they took it in good part, consoling themselves with the recollection that they had had an even share of the sport, as well as the opportunity of practicing with superior players."[6]

A rematch was held eleven days later, on August 19, with the Detroit Base Ball Club winning again, by a count of 51–30. By this time, a couple of other baseball clubs had been formed in Detroit and a new club of employees of the Michigan Central Rail Road soon arranged a match against the Early Risers. The match took place on September 30 and ended in a tie, bringing the Early Risers' first season to a conclusion.

The club reorganized for the 1860 season in April and began practicing as early as it became light enough. They played their first match on June 30, beating the younger Brother Jonathans, and then prepared for another series with the Detroit Base Ball Club. The Detroit Club won the first game, on July 17, but by only a slim 25–22 score, prompting the *Free Press* to describe the contest as "decidedly the best played game that has ever taken place in this city."[7] Then on August 6, the Early Risers finally beat their nemesis, downing the Detroit Base Ball Club 39–32 in front of a large crowd. "This is the first defeat of the Detroit Club," noted the *Free Press*, "and is, in consequence, the more creditable to their more juvenile competitors."[8]

The stage was set for a third and deciding game to determine local supremacy, but first the Early Risers played a home-and-home series against the Daybreak Club of Jackson. The clubs split two very close games, but despite the narrow margins of victory, good will prevailed. After the first contest, there was praise for the "gentlemanly manner in which the game was conducted."[9]

The 1860 season concluded with the deciding game between the Early Risers and the Detroit Base Ball Club. The big showdown was scheduled for September 27 and was played at a larger venue than usual because of the expected crowd. Unfortunately for the Early Risers, one of their players failed to appear on time and the play was "not very spirited." When darkness ended play after seven innings, the Detroit Club had won 34–19.[10]

Befitting a match between clubs with such close ties, the contest was played in the gentlemanly fashion that usually characterized prewar baseball. Nonetheless, there was one sign of increased competitiveness. After the match, the *Detroit Tribune* reported that the Detroit Base Ball Club had never lost a match game. The error prompted one of the Early Risers to write in with a correction and to grouse that the concluding game "reflects doubtful credit upon the 'Detroiter,' as they played the early part of the game against eight men, and through the whole game against three of the 'Early Risers' second nine. The 'Detroit' club had two practiced pitchers, while the 'Risers' had to fill that post by their first base man, thus disarranging the whole field, their regular pitcher being unavoidably absent."[11]

During the first few months of 1861, it looked as though baseball enthusiasm in Detroit might continue to increase. On February 21 the Early Risers and Detroit Base Ball Club met for a match on ice skates. By early April, both clubs had held their annual organizational meetings to prepare to renew their rivalry during the coming season. But then came the onset of the Civil War, and the history of the Early Riser Base Ball Club was brought to a dramatic end.

One later account claimed that half of the club's members enlisted in the Union Army.[12] While the exact proportion cannot be verified, the accompanying player profiles confirm that many of the Early Risers served their country with distinction.

Memories of the Early Riser Club faded in the ensuing years, but the prominence of club members like Trowbridge and Fyfe ensured that they were not entirely forgotten. In particular, that legacy was recalled in 1908 when the Detroit Tigers used the unveiling of the club's first American League pennant to honor earlier Detroit baseball clubs.

Sporting Life correspondent Paul Bruske explained,

> The proceedings will take the form of a gigantic testimonial to base ball, as exemplified from the earliest days of the National pastime in this city, right down to the present. Every amateur club in the city, averaging 18 years or more of age, that has been in existence prior to 1903, will be the guest of the management on the eventful occasion. Gray-haired men will parade with their old comrades of twenty, thirty, forty, yes fifty, years ago on the base ball diamond. Along side them will be the present generation of players, uniformed and marshalled by their various officers. All will be on hand to do honor to the victorious Tigers and the management will reserve ample space for them all in the grand stand, freely inviting them to share in the celebration and in the details of the flag raising. The actual hoisting of the pennant will be entrusted to Gen. Luther S. Trowbridge, U.S. Appraiser of Customs, as the oldest exponent of amateur base ball in Detroit. At least one of Gen. Trowbridge's old team mates on the "Early Risers" who played ball on the present site of Cadillac Square away back in 1859, will be at the side of the whitehaired old veteran when he gives the halyards the pull and sends the pennant up the tall shaft of Michigan pine that has been erected out in centre field to bear it. This is R.H. Fyfe, who played shortstop on the team for which Gen. Trowbridge pitched. Ranged with them from side to side will be the players of other nines, famous in the early days of base ball in Detroit and flanking these the amateur teams with which the present generation is identified and acquainted.

Bruske added,

> The Early Risers of which Gen. Trowbridge and Mr. Fyfe are believed to be the sole surviving members, but whose roll also includes such names as John S. Newberry, Edwin S. Barbour, Frank Phelps and others since dead, took their name from the fact that all the members worked hard during the day and were forced to play their base ball before the opening of their working day. Every pleasant, clear, morning of the year found them hard at it at 4 A.M. and a lively practice was the rule up to breakfast time. Gen. Trowbridge believes that the early morning work was what fitted the team for its many victories over the various mushroom nines which it played. He plainly thinks that such a policy would be a fine thing if the Tigers strike another slump or want to win their pennant without waiting for the final sprint this year. Just imagine the Tigers routed out in the still watches of 4 A.M. There is no use arguing; the old-time players had "pep" that would have made Hughey Jennings happy had he been born at that time, only he wasn't. The old Cadillac Square diamond wasn't much but it had to do and the citizens of the little town which Detroit was then, were rightly proud of its denizens.[13]

The image of Luther Trowbridge and Richard Fyfe standing on the same baseball field as Ty Cobb and Sam Crawford is an appealing one indeed.

CLUB MEMBERS

Edwin S. Barbour: Edwin Barbour, the 1861 club president, was born on November 19, 1832, in Canton, Connecticut. He moved to Detroit in 1856 and worked for Edward Orr's dry-goods store until leaving Orr's employ in 1861 to open his own dry-goods store. In 1870 he became secretary of the Detroit Stove Works. He later became president of the firm and helped it become one of the world's largest stove manufacturers. Barbour was in poor health after being injured in an 1892 train wreck and he died in Detroit on April 3, 1897.

Dr. George Lindsey Field: George L. Field was born on April 19, 1835, in London, England, but his father, a Swedenborgian minister, brought the family to Detroit when George was three. The family moved on to St. Louis in 1850 and while there George was apprenticed to a dentist. He returned to Detroit in 1857 to open a practice at a time when dentistry still lacked professional prestige. As he later recalled,

> I had not one dollar in my pocket. Detroit then had about 40,000 inhabitants and I determined to get a footing here if possible. A friend lent me $60 and with that modest capital I set up my tent. That is to say, for $8 a month I rented desk room in a building on Jefferson avenue.... I papered the walls, whitewashed the ceiling and bought some second-hand furniture at an auction store. Among these movables were a lounge, for which I paid $1, and an old easy chair, which had to serve as an operating chair. For my carpet I paid seventy-five cents a yard. Of course, I had to hew sharp to the line, so I sewed my carpet and laid it myself.... A common deal table, two or three wood-bottom chairs and a severely plain box stove completed my outfit. Then I hung out my sign and waited for business.

His first year in business consisted "mainly of waiting" and at year's end he had only $150 in income, which barely sufficed to pay the annual rent of $96 and meet his living expenses. But he endured and became a local fixture after moving into the city's business district. He served as a club director for the Early Risers and played in at least one match game for the club, then married the sister of fellow club member Frank Folsom in 1861. Field remained a Detroit dentist until his retirement in 1907, fifty years after opening his dental practice, and treated the grandchildren of many of his original patients. He died on October 30, 1916, in Detroit.[14]

Dr. Henry G. Field: George Field's younger brother, Henry, was born in New York in 1838 while the family was en route to Michigan. He played several positions for the Early Risers and also served as a director. During these years, he was training to become a doctor and around 1861 he moved to the Paw Paw area on the western side of the state to set up a practice. While there, he helped organize and served as president of the Lafayette Base Ball Club of Paw Paw, the area's first such club. On September 20, 1870, Field made a long horse ride to Lawrence to attend to a patient. Upon arrival, he collapsed of a heart attack and died. He was only 32 and left a wife and two young children.

Frank Folsom: Folsom was a playing member of the Detroit Base Ball Club and his life is described in more detail in that club's entry. But in a sign of the close links between the two clubs, it was Folsom, then working at a local bookstore, who took initial applications for membership in the Early Risers. Fyfe also recalled Folsom practicing with the Early Risers. In addition, Folsom was a member of the Franklins, making him the only man to belong to all three of Detroit's most important prewar clubs.

Richard Henry Fyfe: More than any other man, Richard Fyfe exemplified the spirit of the Early Riser Club. He was born on January 5, 1839, in Old Orchard Creek, New York. When his father lost all his money through bad business speculation, Fyfe was forced to begin working at the age of 11. When he was 17 he moved to Detroit and found work for a boot and shoe dealer, while sleeping in a room over the store to save money. It was during these years that he served as catcher and the original president of the Early Risers. By 1865 he had saved enough money to buy the shop, but he continued to sleep over the store until he was sure of its success. Before long, the store was prospering, and Fyfe continued to expand the business until he was the owner of the largest retail shoe store in the country. But even after becoming a millionaire, Richard Fyfe hewed to the work ethic that had made him a success, always preaching the value of hard work and giving the customer what he paid for. He enjoyed his business so much that he continued to work until the age of 90, while also remaining a big fan of baseball. He died in Detroit on October 27, 1931.

Rufus William Jacklin: Rufus Jacklin was born in England on April 18, 1842, and came to the United States as a child. He was a club director but there is no record of his playing in match games for the Early Risers. In 1862 he enlisted in Brady's Sharpshooters, a company that was attached to the 16th Michigan for the balance of the war. He was promoted to captain in June 1864 and subsequently served as "chief of sharpshooters" for the 5th Corps. After being mustered out in July of 1865, he returned to Detroit, married, and worked at city hall as a tax collector. In 1898 he published his war memoirs, which included a memorable account of the Battle of Gettysburg. He stood unsuccessfully for Congress in 1900. He died in Detroit on September 14, 1906.

Heber LeFavour: Early Riser vice president Heber LeFavour was born in Pawtucket, Rhode Island, on May 3, 1837. He moved in the 1850s to Michigan, where his uncle, Henry P. Baldwin, would later serve as governor. Like several others, he belonged to both the Detroit Base Ball Club and the Early Risers, but he played match games only for the latter club. He was appointed the state's assistant adjutant general on April 1, 1861, but after the Civil War broke out on April 12, he enlisted as a captain in the 5th Michigan Infantry. After being wounded at Williamsburg, he was commissioned a lieutenant colonel in the 22nd Michigan Infantry, which was commanded by former Governor Moses Wisner. Wisner died at Lexington in January of 1863 and LeFavour was promoted to colonel. LeFavour was captured at the Battle of Chickamauga in September 1863, and was held prisoner for the next nine months. After being exchanged, he joined Sherman's March on Atlanta. He was finally mustered out in June 1865, but was reportedly "wounded for life." He returned to Pawtucket, and became adjutant general of Rhode Island. He died on February 25, 1878, after being thrown from a carriage.

John Stoughton Newberry, Sr.: Newberry's life is described under the Detroit Base Ball Club entry but according to Fyfe, he practiced with the Early Risers "every morning." Since the widowed Newberry was then living at the Russell House, the hotel outside of which the Early Risers practiced, he may not have had much choice!

John C. Pierce: John C. Pierce played for the Early Risers in both 1859 and 1860 and also served as a club director, but his identity remains unclear. The only John Pierce in Detroit on the 1860 Census was a bookkeeper who had been born around 1830 in New York state. But no middle initial was provided and this man has proved difficult to trace. The 1861 city directory did list a John C. Pierce as a corporal in the Detroit Light Guard.

Simeon B. Smith: Simeon B. Smith served as treasurer and then as club secretary. He died in Detroit on March 18, 1865, murdered during a failed burglary. The case became one of the most notorious homicides in Detroit's early history and William H. Baxter, a member of both the Franklins and the Detroit Base Ball Club, published a pamphlet describing it. A man named Billy Holt was eventually convicted on circumstantial evidence and he spent 18 years in the State Prison in Jackson. But many Detroiters were convinced of Holt's innocence and pleas for a pardon were regularly made to the governor. In 1883 Holt was at last pardoned by Governor Josiah W. Begole, leaving the true identity of Smith's murderer an abiding mystery.[15]

General Luther Stephen Trowbridge: Luther S. Trowbridge, the club president in 1860, was born on July 28, 1836, on a farm near Troy, Michigan, his father and uncle having been among the earliest settlers of Oakland County. He graduated from Yale in 1857 and soon passed the Bar, but as fate would have it he rarely practiced law. Like Folsom and Newberry, he was a member of both the Early Risers and Detroit Base Ball Club. In 1862 he enlisted in the Union Army and marched more than 2,000 miles during Civil War, becoming a comrade of George Armstrong Custer and fighting alongside him. After the war Trowbridge was named inspector general of the state militia by Governor John J. Bagley, and then in 1875 President Grant appointed Trowbridge to the prestigious position of collector of customs for Michigan's Eastern District. He later served as Detroit's city comptroller and as vice president of the Wayne County Savings Bank. He then received another much-coveted appointment when President Theodore Roosevelt appointed him appraiser of the port of Detroit. Through all these successes, General Trowbridge remained attached to baseball and raised the pennant after the Tigers won their first American League flag. When he died in Detroit on February 2, 1912, one obituary described him as the "last member of the 'Early Risers,'" although in fact Richard Fyfe outlived Trowbridge by nearly two decades.

Joseph Winter: Joseph Winter was born in Germany around 1838 and appears to have grown up in Michigan's Upper Peninsula. By 1859 he had moved to Detroit, where he worked as a saddler. By 1870 he had married and returned to the Upper Peninsula. He first lived in Portage, then in Negaunee, working as a butcher in both places. He died in Negaunee on October 30, 1895.

Charles S. Wright: Along with Henry Field, Charles Wright was one of only two players to represent the Early Risers in all of their known contests. The only Charles Wright in Detroit in the 1860 Census was a 22-year-old blacksmith who had been born in England.

Benjamin Rush Young, Jr.: B.R. Young was born in New York state on June 9, 1839. He worked as a clerk and salesman while living in Detroit, and was also one of the club's regular outfielders. After his wife's death he moved to Alpena, where he remarried and opened a hardware store. By 1900, he had moved his family to Montana, where he operated a mine. But he returned to Alpena before his death on May 12, 1915.

Other Members: H. Biglow, Edwin B. Chope (a director who was born around 1815 so probably a nonplaying member), Elisha B. Gorton, Morton H. Hawley, J.M. Moberly, Frank J. Phelps (of the Detroit Base Ball Club), Tyler, William W. Wright.

SOURCES

This piece is based upon my book *Baseball Fever: Early Baseball in Michigan*. Primary sources used included contemporary newspapers and a letter written by Richard Fyfe, now housed at the Burton Collection, Detroit Public Library.

NOTES

1. *Detroit Free Press*, May 20, 1860.
2. *Detroit Daily Advertiser*, July 7, 1859.
3. James Backus, quoted in "They Won a Pennant," *Rochester Post Express*, May 1, 1902, 5.
4. Richard Fyfe, letter to Clarence Burton, Burton Collection, Detroit Public Library. According to a 1908 article, the exact location was "that part of Fort street on which stands the public drinking fountain between city hall grounds and the McMillan store" ("Challenge Early Risers," *Detroit Free Press*, June 1, 1908, 8).
5. Richard Fyfe, letter to Clarence Burton, Burton Collection, Detroit Public Library.
6. *Detroit Free Press*, August 9, 1859.
7. *Detroit Free Press*, July 18, 1860.
8. *Detroit Free Press*, August 7, 1860.
9. *Detroit Free Press*, August 31, 1860.
10. *Detroit Free Press*, September 29, 1860.
11. *Detroit Daily Advertiser*, October 1, 1860.
12. *Detroit Advertiser and Tribune*, May 2, 1867.
13. Paul H. Bruske, *Sporting Life*, June 6, 1908, 7.
14. "A Prominent Detroit Physician," *Detroit Free Press*, August 8, 1893, 8; "Dr. George Field, Aged Dentist, Dead," *Detroit Free Press*, October 30, 1916, 3.
15. "Billy Holt," *Detroit Free Press*, January 4, 1883, 6.

❖ *Daybreaks of Jackson* (Peter Morris) ❖

CLUB HISTORY

The Daybreak Club of Jackson, Michigan, was one of many pioneer clubs whose history was inextricably tied to the Civil War. Like so many of those clubs, at the war's end the Daybreak Club was succeeded by ones that included new players and earned greater glory. Yet in many ways, those later clubs merely built on the tradition established by the Daybreak Club.

The exact date of the formation of the Daybreak Club is unknown. In 1858 a local reporter wrote dismissively, "We notice that the lawyers, doctors and gentlemen of Detroit, Pontiac and other towns are forming 'cricket clubs' for amusement, recreation, etc. It may do for the people of those 'dull towns' to engage in such things, but the people here are always *too busy* to engage in play of any kind."[1] But by 1860 the mood in Jackson had changed and the city had its first baseball club.

With Michigan still having very few organized clubs, the Daybreak Club played only three matches in its first season of competition, all of them against clubs from Detroit. The historic first match was a "very spirited" 62–38 defeat at the hands of the Detroit Base Ball Club on July 20, 1860.[2]

The opponent in the other two matches was the Early Riser Club. The Early Risers traveled to Jackson on August 28 and the Daybreaks eked out their first victory by a 21–20 count. The Jackson club members went all out to prove themselves excellent hosts and the *Detroit Free Press* wrote that their "gentlemanly courtesy and generous hospitality will long be remembered."[3] A rematch in Detroit in September was just as closely contested, with the Early Risers pulling out an 18–16 win. There were hopes of playing a third and deciding game, but it couldn't be arranged and that ended the inaugural season for the Daybreaks.[4]

The outbreak of the Civil War in the spring of 1861 put an abrupt halt to the activities of many baseball clubs, including the Early Risers and the Detroit Base Ball Club. The Daybreaks still had enough members in town to field a club, but it was a challenge to find competition. As a result, their opponents were mostly ones like the newly formed Red, White and Blue Club of Marshall. The Daybreaks traveled to Marshall on June 17, 1861, and barely eked out a 24–23 win.

Accounts of this game made it very clear that it was the

spirit that mattered and not the result. One Marshall journalist observed,

> It was gratifying to observe so many spectators gather to witness the sport and doubly gratifying to see so many ladies. The nine men selected by the Daybreak Club, of Jackson, showed themselves superior players, both at the bat and in the field, and for their kind and courteous treatment to our club, as beginners, they have the sincere thanks of our club. The first nine of the Red, White and Blue Club, although beaten by one run, did nobly for beginners, every man both in batting and fielding, acting his part well. With a little more practice they will not fear to cope with any nine players in the state.... Previous to the commencement of the game, the Jackson Club were welcomed to our city in appropriate remarks by William Powell, Esquire, President of the Marshall Club, which were handsomely responded to, by Mr. Proudfit of the former. After the game the Jackson players presented ours with a splendid bat, with appropriate ceremonies. The sport was highly entertaining, and we hope our Jackson friends were well pleased with their visit to our city.[5]

An account in another Marshall newspaper noted, "Nothing occurred to mar the pleasure of the meeting." It also reported that after the match had ended and the ball had been presented to the winners, the two clubs divided their members up and played a "promiscuous" game.[6]

Later that summer a Grand Rapids newspaper reported that the Daybreak Club was the best in the state and had been challenged by one from Kalamazoo.[7] It appears that the Daybreaks did face this new rival and several others, as they were later said to have compiled a 6–0 record in 1861.[8] The details of these matches, however, are lost to history. We do at least know that the Daybreaks concluded the season in October with a game between their first and second nines for an oyster supper.[9]

By 1862 Jackson had sent several more regiments to fight in the war, including many local ballplayers. In June it was reported that 17 of the 34 members of the Daybreaks were away at war, including one captain, two lieutenants, three orderly sergeants, one hospital steward, two corporals, and six privates.[10] Yet this still left enough members to field a nine and the Daybreaks decided to elect a board of officers and organize for another season.[11]

Finding opponents to play proved a bigger challenge than ever in 1862, but the club did play two matches against the Hickory Club of Howell, winning both.[12] The Daybreaks also suffered their first defeat since the start of the war, losing 28–14 to the Monitor Club of Ann Arbor in Jackson on June 23. In a revealing detail that tells us much about the spirit of baseball at the time, the match was umpired by John H. Weller of the Daybreak Club, yet nobody seems to have been concerned by the apparent conflict of interest.[13]

By 1863 a significant number of Jackson's enlisted men had completed their war services and baseball activity picked up. In April the club held a series of meetings to reorganize for the season, elect officers, and make other arrangements.[14]

When the club hit the field for the 1863 season, it soon became evident that there would be more competitiveness than ever before. By June the Brother Jonathan Club of Detroit, the University nine of Ann Arbor, and the Daybreak Club were all claiming to be champions and challenges were flying. In particular, a claim by a member of the Brother Jonathans that his club was the state champion ruffled the feathers of the Daybreak Club and prompted an indignant response.[15]

The exam schedule of the University nine made it impossible to schedule a match with that club, but a series between the Daybreaks and the Brother Jonathans was arranged. The first contest took place in Detroit on August 5 and was close until the late innings, when the defense of the Brother Jonathans collapsed and allowed the Daybreaks to win, 43–16. The result led one Jackson resident to boast, "We trust that Detroit will fling out no more championship banners until he has earned the right to do so."[16] The second game was played in Jackson on September 3, and saw the home side squeak out a 23–22 win that earned the Daybreaks recognition as the state champion.

Despite the bickering that had preceded these showdowns, they were contested in a spirit of harmony. The Daybreaks brought nearly a hundred friends with them to Detroit for the first game, and the Jackson players were hosted and accommodated in style by their Detroit counterparts. The rematch witnessed similar hospitality, and concluded with "three rousing cheers" from "the Detroit boys for their conquerors."[17]

Signs of a new competitiveness also appeared after a July match in which the Daybreaks beat the Monitor Club of Niles. A dispute arose over the calls of the umpire, which led a member of the Monitors to complain: "We do not claim it [a victory], nor do we care for it, but we have made these statements for the purpose of showing that if we *were* beaten, we were not beaten by the Day Breaks as a club *but by a single member of the club and that member the Umpire*." A representative of the Daybreaks responded that his club "cared very little ... to win the game" and "regret exceedingly that anything occurred to mar the pleasure of the game."[18]

It is a revealing exchange, for despite the lip service, there can be no question that both clubs did care about the result of the game and that that new outlook jeopardized the harmony of the matches. It also made it apparent that having a member of one of the clubs serve as umpire — a practice that had gone unquestioned a year earlier — was no longer viable.

Nevertheless, courtesy and good will prevailed in most of the series played by the Daybreaks in 1863. A match against a new club from Concord that was "looking to learn" from the more experienced Jackson club was characterized by harmony and followed by a hearty meal.[19] Two victories against the Dowagiac Club were played in a similar spirit. The second contest, played in Dowagiac, prompted a member of the Daybreaks to write that the members of his club would "long remember the hospitality extended to them by the Club and

Citizens of Dowagiac, and with them will be associated the humorous sayings and caprices of T.H. Campbell."[20] Although a new spirit of competitiveness had begun to manifest itself, the members of clubs like the Daybreaks clearly still looked at themselves first and foremost as ambassadors for their native cities and for the game of baseball.

In 1864 references to baseball almost entirely disappeared from Michigan newspapers and the Daybreak Club played no recorded matches. What remains unknown is whether that means that the Daybreaks stopped their practices, or whether they couldn't find rivals to play, or whether match play continued and the results were just not reported by newspapers with more serious war news to report. When the war finally did end in the spring of 1865, the decision was made to represent Jackson with a newly formed club called "The Central."[21]

The history of the Daybreak Club of Jackson was thus a brief one and both the club and its members were buffeted by the war. Moreover, with the Civil War foremost in everyone's mind, there is much about the club that we don't know. Not a single description of the club's uniform, for example, is extant. Doubt also remains about where the club played — one article mentioned that the club was to practice at the old race track and it seems likely that was where the Daybreaks usually played, but even that cannot be said with confidence.[22]

Even so, the accomplishment of the Daybreak Club was impressive. The club compiled a 14–1 record in known matches played during the war and it was hailed as "the Champions of the state."[23] The club also paved the way for Jackson to become one of Michigan's foremost cities for baseball. When the Central Club was formed after the war, several of the Daybreaks were selected for the first nine. The Unknowns of Jackson, an amalgam nine that won the Detroit "world's championship" tournament of 1867, included no fewer than four former members of the Daybreaks — Hooker DeLand, Thomas Conely, Melville McGee, and Stephen Welling. Even the Mutuals of Jackson, a powerhouse of the 1870s, enlisted Welling's services as club secretary.

Perhaps most important, the Daybreak Club of Jackson served as ambassadors for the game of baseball in Michigan. Clubs in such towns as Marshall, Niles, Kalamazoo, Howell, Concord, and Dowagiac received instructions in the New York rules from their matches with the Daybreak Club, and the familiarity that they gained was important in the postwar baseball boom.

Club Members

Billie J. Billings, Jr.: B.J. Billings, Jr., was born in Batavia, New York, in 1838. The son of the owner of one of Jackson's biggest stores, Billings later moved to Toledo and died there on May 24, 1905.

Thomas Jefferson Conely: Thomas J. Conely was born in New York City on July 12, 1836, and was educated at the New York Free Academy. He was the catcher for the Daybreaks in 1860, then enlisted in the Union Army in 1861. He served for three years, including five months as a prisoner of war at the Confederacy's Libby Prison, in Richmond, Virginia, and was promoted from lieutenant to captain. His letters from the Civil War are archived at the Bentley Library of the University of Michigan. After the war, he married and became the chief of the fire department. Yet he still found time for baseball, serving as treasurer of the Central Club and playing for the Unknowns of Jackson when they captured the 1867 Detroit "world's championship" tournament. After growing too old for baseball, he turned to cricket. In 1872 Conely accepted a position as a railroad superintendent and spent a few years in Ionia. But he soon returned to Jackson, where he became the recorder of the city's common council and served in the Jackson Guard. Conely died in Jackson on July 2, 1899.[24]

Hooker Ashton DeLand: Hooker DeLand was born in Speedsville, New York, around 1843, and played the outfield for the Daybreak Club in 1860. The following year, he enlisted in the 1st Michigan Sharpshooters, under the command of his cousin, Charles V. DeLand. The regiment was decimated by casualties and desertions, and in 1864 Hooker DeLand was court-martialed and convicted of cowardice. In addition to being dishonorably discharged and losing his shoulder insignia, DeLand had the humiliation of having his name and a list of the charges printed in the Jackson newspaper. In 1867 he was selected to the first nine of the Central Club but declined due to illness. Later that year, however, he was a member of the Unknowns of Jackson when they captured the 1867 Detroit "world's championship" tournament. He married in 1868 and soon moved to Grand Rapids to work in the pressroom of the *Grand Rapids Democrat*. He even resumed playing baseball in 1875. But new sorrows awaited him four years later when DeLand alleged that his wife, while in Berlin to study music, had been seduced by her pastor. Eventually DeLand moved back to New York and, as described in Raymond J. Herek's book *These Men Have Seen Hard Service: The First Michigan Sharpshooters in the Civil War* (Detroit: Wayne State University Press, 1998), he spent many years unsuccessfully trying to clear his name of the court-martial conviction. He died on April 5, 1931, in Seneca Falls, New York.

Howard Hampton Gridley: H. H. Gridley was one of the oldest members of the Daybreaks, having been born in New York state on November 15, 1824. But he played in several matches for the club, and continued to umpire after the war. Gridley owned a livery stable and omnibus line. In 1870 he became involved in an argument and struck and killed a farmer, Abel Williams. But his conviction for manslaughter brought him only a fine of $200. Gridley died in Jackson on March 20, 1882.

Harrington: This man, who played for the Daybreaks in 1860, has not been positively identified because his first name was never given. But he never again played for the club and was specifically described as being away fighting the Civil War. As a result, it seems highly likely that he was George L. Harrington, who enlisted as a private on August 22, 1861, at the age of 18 and was assigned to the 8th Michigan Infantry, serving until September 22, 1864. After the war he became a farmer and remained in the Jackson area for most of his life, dying in Jackson on August 1, 1912.

William F. Hewitt: William F. Hewitt was president of the Daybreak Club and a member of the first nine. He and fellow club member Stephen Welling purchased the Jackson grocery owned by C. L. Mitchell in 1863, but Hewitt left town soon afterward and settled in nearby Marshall. Born in Byron, New York, on February 4, 1835, Hewitt died in Marshall on October 3, 1889.

Melville McGee: Melville McGee was born in Bolton, New York, on January 24, 1828, and his family moved to the Jackson area when he was 4. The area was then very sparsely populated, and he later reminisced about playing ball at barn raisings. As he put it, "It seems to me now as I look back and recall those early days that the young people enjoyed their sports and games and entered into them with far more zest then young people do at the present day. There was no feeling of envy or superiority, or the feeling that you don't belong to my set. All were on a level, and everyone was just as good as any other." McGee became a distinguished judge but continued to play baseball and scored the tying run for the Unknowns of Jackson in the championship game of the 1867 Detroit "world's championship" tournament. He also earned recognition as a hard hitter who reportedly once batted a ball clear over a sturdy oak at the corner of Fourth and Franklin. McGee died in Jackson on February 20, 1909.

Hiram Bacon Pierson: Born in Vermont on February 29, 1836, Hiram Pierson's odd middle name was his mother's maiden name. When the war broke out, he enlisted in the 10th Michigan Infantry and served for more than a year. When he returned home, Thomas J. Conely enlisted and Pierson took his place as the club's regular catcher. Pierson retained his interest in baseball after the war, playing for the Central Club while holding the office of president in 1865 and later that of vice president. He moved to Grand Rapids during the 1870s and worked as a messenger. He died in Grand Rapids on March 9, 1918.

George Proudfit: George Proudfit was born in Hopewell, New York, on January 28, 1838. He became a lawyer and was practicing in Jackson when the Civil War erupted. Proudfit enlisted in the 8th Michigan Infantry and served for 15 months. After the war he returned to the practice of law and in 1878 was elected Circuit Court Commissioner. He was enumerated for the 1880 Census on June 9, 1880, and was listed as being sick with consumption (tuberculosis). Nine days later the disease claimed his life.

Francis A. Sharpsteen: Francis Sharpsteen was one of the mainstays of the 1863 Daybreaks, but two years later, on December 2, 1865, he died in Jackson of tuberculosis. He was still several weeks shy of his 23rd birthday.

Henry W. Shipman: Henry W. Shipman enlisted in the Civil War in 1861 at the age of 30. He died on September 11, 1864, at Nashville of wounds suffered at the Battle of Peachtree Creek in Georgia on July 21.

Stephen Alling Welling: Stephen Welling, the pitcher of the Daybreaks, was born in New York state on October 24, 1830. He owned a saddle and harness business on Main Street in Jackson until 1863, when he and fellow club member William F. Hewitt bought a Jackson grocery store. Welling later owned a men's furnishings store. Despite the demands of business and his age, Welling remained very involved in Jackson baseball after the war. At the 1865 state fair he was elected secretary of the state baseball association. He also served as secretary of the Central Club and played for the Unknowns of Jackson when they captured the 1867 Detroit "world's championship" tournament. After his playing days ended, he served as secretary of the Mutual Club of Jackson in the early 1870s. Welling later moved to Detroit, where he died on July 29, 1908.

Charles Beers Wood: Charles B. Wood was the vice president of the Daybreak Club in 1862 and its left fielder in 1863. He was born on October 13, 1839, in Waterloo, New York. His family moved to Jackson in 1844. His father, James B. Wood, was a lawyer and became the first mayor of Jackson under the city charter. Charles B. Wood graduated from the University of Michigan, then enlisted in the Union Army in 1862, serving for more than three years in the 17th and 4th Michigan infantry regiments. After the war he became editor of the *Hastings Home Journal* and then passed the bar examination. He practiced law in several Michigan cities, then divorced his wife and moved to Chicago, where he died on November 14, 1910.

Other Members: Charles E. Barker (scorer), H.W. Camp (scorer), Case (likely N. Case, later a member of the first nine of the Centrals, the successors of the Daybreaks), Crittenden, (likely George Crittenden, also a member of the Centrals' first nine), L.J. Curtiss (scorer, on the board in 1862), Hall, D. Holder, Hulbert or Hilbert, Kassick, McConnell, Saulpaugh, G. Shiverton, Van Horn, John H. Weller (board member in 1862), Woodworth.

SOURCES

This entry is based on my book *Baseball Fever: Early Baseball in Michigan*, which relied primarily on contemporary accounts in the newspapers of the era. Also helpful were later reminiscences, such as one that appeared in the *Jackson News* on September 22, 1918.

NOTES

1. *Jackson American Citizen*, May 6, 1858.
2. *Detroit Free Press*, July 21, 1860.

3. *Detroit Free Press*, August 31, 1860.
4. *Detroit Free Press*, September 19, 1860.
5. *Marshall Democratic Expounder*, June 20, 1861.
6. *Marshall Statesman*, June 19, 1861.
7. *Grand Rapids Eagle*, July 31, 1861.
8. *Jackson Eagle*, June 28, 1862.
9. *Jackson American Citizen*, October 17, 1861.
10. *Jackson Eagle*, June 7, 1862.
11. *Jackson American Citizen*, July 2, 1862.
12. *Jackson Eagle*, June 21, 1862.
13. *Jackson American Citizen*, June 25, 1862.
14. *Jackson Eagle*, April 4 and 18, 1863.
15. *Jackson Eagle*, June 13, 1863; *Detroit Advertiser and Tribune*, April 8 and 14, June 12, 15, 18, 19 and 20, 1863; *Jackson American Citizen*, June 17, 1863; *Michigan State News*, June 23, 1863. See Chapter 7 of my *Baseball Fever* for a detailed discussion.
16. *Jackson Eagle*, August 8, 1863.
17. *Detroit Advertiser and Tribune*, September 5, 1863.
18. *Niles Republican*, July 25, 1863.
19. *Jackson Eagle*, June 6, 1863.
20. *Jackson American Citizen*, August 19, 1863; *Jackson Eagle*, August 29, 1863
21. *Jackson Daily Citizen Patriot*, May 25, 1865, 1.
22. That sole reference to playing at the race track appeared in the *Jackson American Citizen* on July 2, 1862.
23. *Niles Republican*, July 4, 1863.
24. "Death of Capt. T.J. Conely," *Jackson Citizen Patriot*, July 3, 1899, 6.

❖ *Kent Base Ball Club of Grand Rapids* (Peter Morris) ❖

CLUB HISTORY

Regulation baseball arrived in Grand Rapids, Michigan, in 1859 and the city's first organized club was made up of many prominent citizens — the president of the club was destined to become attorney general of the state. But the activities of the Pioneer Base Ball and Wicket Club were cut short by the Civil War and it was not until 1867 that Grand Rapids featured sustained baseball competition.[1]

The two clubs were the Kents and the Peninsulars and for two years they forged a friendly yet intense rivalry. In 1883, an unknown writer penned this idyllic description of those two seasons:

> Grand Rapids's first glory in the base ball profession was radiated from the Peninsulars and the Kents, which were formed about 1867. The ball grounds were all of the "green" or open field between Lyon and Bronson streets which had been the camping ground of the old Tenth cavalry under Col. Foote. The present residence of Mr. James A. Rogers on Lyon street was then the last house on the east of the city settlement, the grove which surrounded his house ceasing just beyond. The ground was admirably adapted for any sort of field sport and there was room for a dozen ball diamonds. This place was the scene of many hard fought contests on emerald aceldama. [Aceldama is a biblical term meaning, literally, field of blood.] Often during the period following the organization of these clubs a number of games would be going on especially during practice hours. A silver ball suitably engraved was "hung up" as gift of the citizens to the champion club and this ball was many times transferred to a different nine which had been compelled to work hard for its possession.

Another interesting aspect of the rivalry was that prior to each contest, "the contestants considered it absolutely essential to health to suck lemons."[2]

Of course the realities of fielding and administering a baseball club were much more mundane and we know more about this facet of the Kent Base Ball Club than is the case with most of the club's contemporaries. A variety of rich sources have much to say on the subject — the club's log book has been preserved and is now housed at the Grand Rapids Public Library; contemporaneous newspaper accounts filled in many additional details; and even the 1883 article cited above provided insight.

An initial abortive effort to organize the Kent Base Ball Club was actually made in the spring of 1866. The club held at least one meeting and elected a slate of officers who included Lewis H. Withey as president, C.W. Wright as secretary pro tem, and T. Stewart White as secretary. They also chose Wednesday and Friday evenings as their practice days and staged a few practice sessions at the old campground on Lyon Street. But within a few weeks the members appear to have lost interest and no more mention of local baseball clubs appeared in the Grand Rapids papers that year.[3]

Another effort was made in 1867 and it prompting one sportswriter to remark, "An attempt was made, last spring and summer to organize and keep alive a Base Ball Club in our city. A club was formed, officers elected, and one or two meetings held, and from some unaccountable cause, no more after, and nothing more was heard of it, except when some of our young men would get together and talk over the things that were."[4]

This time the Kent Base Ball Club proved more successful. The initial organizational meeting was held on the evening of April 4 at "Perkins' boot and shoe store in the old Abel block on Monroe street." Some 20 young men were in attendance, and they adopted a club constitution. Eventually signed by 43 members, it included such provisions as one stating that a "fine of twenty-five cents be imposed for disputing the decisions of the umpire, for refusing obedience to the captain and for non attendance." A slate of officers was also elected, consisting of president Silas K. Pierce, vice president D.K. Hulburt, secretary Lawrence C. Earle, treasurer A.P. Sinclair, and directors W.S. Earle, L.H. Withey, and John M. Avery.[5]

Balls, bats, and bases were ordered and the members of the Kent Base Ball Club were so anxious to get started that they could hardly wait. They even staked out the grounds so that everything would be "in readiness" when the equipment arrived.[6] As soon as the eagerly awaited implements made their appearance, the club staged a practice game at the campground. In an account of the session, a reporter for the *Daily Democrat* noted that he hadn't noticed the winner, "nor do we care muchly, and that, in our opinion, is about as deep an interest as our readers or the boys themselves have in the result. They want exercise and fun and that they get in this athletic game."[7] But a reporter for the *Daily Eagle* filled in the missing details, supplying the names of both sides and the final score for a series of scrimmages that were held over the next few weeks.[8]

Before long the club was approaching its constitutional limit of 50 members and the members were keen to face outside competition.[9] When a challenge was received from the Custer Club of Ionia, a special meeting was held to accept the challenge and arrange the details.[10]

The match took place on May 24, 1867, and proved a big event in Grand Rapids. Readers of the *Daily Eagle* were instructed the day before that they could reach the grounds of the Kent Club by traveling east on Lyon Street past Division Street until they reached the "brow of the hill."[11] Some 2,000 spectators did indeed turn out and were treated to seeing the hometown ballplayers dressed in black pants, white shirts "tastefully embroidered in blue," leather belts, white caps trimmed in blue, and canvas shoes.[12]

The Custer Club won the match handily, but that didn't spoil the festive mood at all and both clubs shared in supper at the Rathbun House afterward.[13] Even more important, the "base ball fever" soon spread all over Grand Rapids and at least five new clubs were organized during the next week.[14]

The most important of these clubs was one formed by "the middle aged and youthful sporting men of the 4th and 5th Wards" that called itself the Peninsular Club. The first nine of the new club consisted of John J. Belknap, captain and catcher; Walter S. Gee, pitcher; Henry Covell, first base; Frank Ward, second base; Dick Blumrich, third base; Dwight Marvin, short stop; Henry Bolen, center field; Charles Gee, right field; A. S. Stevens, left field. Over the next year and a half this club's rivalry with the Kent Base Ball Club would become the focus of local baseball interest.

The object of both clubs was a silver ball that originally was donated by local jeweler P. J. G. Hodenpyl for a tournament held in Grand Rapids on July 4, 1867.[15] The Kent Club captured the silver ball that day with an 88–39 win over another local club called the Centrals, but instead of its becoming their permanent possession, the silver ball was transformed into the symbol of local supremacy.

The Peninsulars were the first challengers and competition between the two clubs began on July 26, 1867, with the more experienced Kents winning by a 58–30 score. Undeterred, the Peninsulars issued another challenge and won the rematch, although the silver ball was not at stake this time.[16] The third and final contest between the two clubs occurred in September during the Kent County Fair and saw the Peninsulars squeak out a 68–67 victory to win a $25 purse.[17]

By the close of the 1867 season, the Peninsular and Kent clubs were recognized as the two best clubs in Grand Rapids, and the Kent Club had managed wins over several other Grand Rapids clubs as well as ones from Grand Haven and Muskegon. Nonetheless, neither club had any success against Ionia's two top clubs. As a result, when a baseball tournament was held at the Ionia County Fair in October, the Peninsular and Kent pooled their forces to create an all-star squad known as the Valley Citys. Even so, the representatives of Grand Rapids were handily defeated. The loss was a portent of things to come.

Despite the preparations that had been made and the lack of emphasis on competitiveness, the summer of 1867 had demonstrated that the Kent Club was looking for more than "exercise and fun." This was reflected in the minutes of the club's meetings. After only three months, the three-man board of directors, "for non-performance of duty were dishonorably discharged July 15, and Fred Joslin, Will Hubbard and Charlie Mills chosen in their place. A resolution was also adopted punishing neglect of duty by any officer with expulsion. On July 8 the secretary, L. C. Earle, was discharged and G. W. Perkins chosen to his place, and Charlie Eaton was discharged for non-payment of dues."[18]

Other signs of unrest also emerged from the meetings. The original plan to stage 5 A.M. practices on Mondays and Thursdays and 4 P.M. practices on Tuesdays and Fridays "continued but a little while, as the days and hours were constantly changed." Even the meetings themselves were changed from weekly to biweekly, and "were occasionally noisy, but good order was general, for stringent rules were adopted."[19]

In the spring of 1868, the Kent Club organized in late March and chose new officers who included president John White; vice president Fred C. Joslin; secretary A. B. Porter; and directors Henry Baars, N. B. Scribner, and C. W. Mills.[20] While quite a few of the players from the previous year had "retired on their laurels," there were still plenty of players available and no shortage of enthusiasm.[21] The rivalry for the silver ball was soon renewed and a lengthy set of rules were adopted to ensure fairness.[22]

The first championship match was played on May 28 and it saw the Peninsulars pull out a thrilling 21–20 victory that earned them possession of the silver ball. The Kents soon issued a challenge for a rematch, which was played on June 23. This contest was also close until the seventh inning, when the Peninsulars put together a 26-run inning. It was the end of the rivalry and it pretty much ended the Kent Base Ball Club, with the silver ball "falling as a legacy to the Peninsulars."

The Kent club played at least one more game that summer, but it was called after five innings because of excess heat.[23] Thereafter, the activities of the Kent Club faded out. According to the 1883 history, "The meetings through the summer were semi-occasional, and on Sept. 29, 1868, the last recorded meeting was held. The season was closed and the wonderful organization never revived."[24]

An effort was made to reorganize the club in the spring of 1869 but it proved unsuccessful.[25] While we cannot be certain of the reasons for the club's demise, it seems logical to blame it on three factors that led many clubs of the era to disband. The first was that the players were growing old and, as a later account put it, becoming "too busy in business to toss the sphere."[26] The second was the club's lack of success against its rivals from Ionia and, ultimately, against the Peninsulars. Finally, there was the coming of open professionalism in 1869 — a development that left clubs like the Kent Base Ball Club with no reason to believe they would become more competitive.

The experience of their crosstown rivals suggests that it was wise for the Kent Club to disband when it did. The Peninsular Club continued to play until 1870, when it lost to a local club called the Dexters that consisted of "mere boys." Nor did the club receive any sympathy after the stinging defeat, with one reporter advising them never "to appear in the base ball arena again, unless they are challenged by some old woman's club. With one or two exceptions, the players are worse than bad, and the several defeats they have suffered already this season should convince them that they cannot play base ball."[27] When the Peninsulars did indeed elect to give up baseball, the same reporter sniffed, "After their terrible defeat by the Dexters, a lot of small boys, they concluded wisely that they could not play the national game and disbanded."[28]

With both the Kents and the Peninsulars defunct, the 1870s were dreary ones for baseball in Grand Rapids. An 1874 article noted that it had been quite a few years since baseball had "been a rage in the Valley City."[29] The next year saw several efforts to re-establish baseball in the city, including the formation of one club called the Kent Base Ball Club.[30] But none of them really took, and by 1879 a reporter observed, "It has been pretty thoroughly demonstrated that no amateur club can keep up the interest in the 'National Game' in our city, from the fact that they cannot compete successfully with the professional clubs with which they may cross bats, and it is not at all encouraging to have a club that can be beaten all of the time."[31] That same year, members of the Kent and Peninsular clubs played a series of old-fashioned games that attracted as much notice in the local press as did the activities of any of the city's younger clubs.[32]

Professional baseball finally arrived in Grand Rapids to stay in the early 1880s and caused many locals to forget the earlier days. Yet there were still a few who retained vivid memories of those earlier clubs. As the 1883 article put it, "Among those who today display but little outward interest in base ball are some who were the fiercest of players fifteen years ago. And the games played when every inning would tally from a dozen to forty runs were as exciting then as those when it often takes nine full innings to get a single run."[33]

Club Members

George Roderick Allen: George R. Allen was born on November 1, 1844, in Painesville, Ohio. After the family moved to Grand Rapids, George and his brother Stanley operated a furnishing establishment on Monroe Street. He subsequently became associated with the Grand Rapids Savings Bank and served as a school board officer. Allen was still living in Grand Rapids in 1920.

John M. Avery: John M. Avery was born in Ovid, New York, on July 20, 1847, and came to Grand Rapids in 1851. He was the third baseman for the first nine of the Kent Club. In 1868, he and T. Stewart White became partners in a lumber firm. White became one of the city's most successful lumber men, but Avery didn't live to share in that as he died of lung disease on May 17, 1873, in Grand Rapids.

John Frederick Baars, Jr.: J. Fred Baars, Jr., was born in Rhode Island in 1849. The family moved to Michigan around 1858 and the elder John Frederick Baars became city treasurer of Grand Rapids. The younger J. Fred worked as treasurer of a Grand Rapids furniture company, but his marriage ended in divorce and he left town in 1895. He conducted a lumber commission business in Duluth, Minnesota, and eventually moved to New York City, where he died on April 7, 1915.[34]

William Henry Baars: J. Fred Baars' brother William was born in Rhode Island in 1851 and died in Grand Rapids on November 13, 1880.

Otis Hunt Babcock: Otis H. Babcock was born around 1851 in New York state and came to Grand Rapids at the age of 6. He began his career as a messenger for the City National Bank, later being promoted to teller and then vice president of what became known as the Grand Rapids National City Bank. He worked for the bank for 52 years, and when he died in Grand Rapids on August 1, 1919, one obituary stated that Babcock "had no other interests but the bank, and his home."[35]

Andries Bevier: Andries Bevier was born in Warwick, New York, on August 12, 1846, and moved to Grand Rapids to work for the Grand Rapids and Indiana Railroad Company. He later became general manager of the city's streetcar company. He returned to New York around the turn of the century to pursue new business ventures, but these proved unsuccessful and he took his own life in Manhattan on January 30, 1912.[36]

Charles Herman Deane: Charles H. Deane was born in Portland, Michigan, on November 16, 1839, and came to Grand Rapids as an infant. At the time, the city's population was said to be 175, two-thirds of whom were Native Americans. Deane became a master machinist and, like many other club members, the end of his days on the diamond coincided with his starting a family — he married in 1866 and his first son was born in 1869. He lived into his 80s and even survived a serious automobile accident in 1922.[37] Charles Deane died on May 10, 1923.

Lawrence Carmichael Earle: L.C. Earle was born in New York City on November 11, 1845. His family moved to Grand Rapids in 1857 and he became the secretary of the Kent Club in 1867, as well as the right fielder for the first nine. Although he was soon replaced, his enthusiasm for the game was so great that his art studio contained "several sketches of base ball players in different attitudes." His water color paintings soon made him famous, and he moved to Chicago in 1869 and then to Munich. Of all his paintings, the best known was one of a Dutch boy that became the trademark of the National Lead Company and later of Dutch Boy Paints. In 1910 he returned to Grand Rapids, where he died on November 20, 1921.

William Sylvester Earle: William S. Earle was born in New York City on September 10, 1845, and was Lawrence Earle's first cousin. By 1884, he was superintendent of Grand Rapids Postal Carriers. Earle then moved with his family to San Diego, where he lived until at least 1910.

Charles W. Eaton: Charlie Eaton was born in Grand Rapids in 1840, apprenticed as a printer and then was elected city clerk. He served in the 21st Michigan Infantry in the Civil War and, according to his obituary, was "promoted for gallantry on the field through the various ranks from private to captain. He was captured at the battle of Kingston, N.C., while serving on the staff of General [Thomas Francis] Meagher, but escaped three days later." After the war he became a successful Grand Rapids merchant, building and owning the Eaton block on South Division Street and being the president of the Eaton Printing Company. Although he was drummed out of the Kent Club for not paying his dues, he was welcomed back to play in the 1879 old-fashioned games. He died in Daytona, Florida, on March 20, 1902.[38]

Clayton Eugene Gill: Clayton E. Gill was born on March 14, 1850, in Wethersfield, New York. He moved to Grand Rapids after the Civil War and became a banker, but eventually returned to New York and was living in Warsaw, New York, in June of 1915. In 1919 he was a candidate for the New York State Assembly. Gill died in 1925 and is buried in Warsaw.

Henry B. Grady: Henry B. Grady was born in Pensacola, Florida, on March 17, 1848, and was reared in New York, where he attended the school now known as Fordham University. He then moved to Grand Rapids and became a traveling salesman for a grocery house. Grady later became a partner in Kortlander and Grady, a Grand Rapids liquor distributor, and died in Grand Rapids on September 9, 1914.

Deloney Gunnison: Deloney Gunnison was born around 1848 in Michigan. His father, Captain John Williams Gunnison, was a West Point graduate who led surveying expeditions of the areas around the Great Lakes for Corps of Topographical Engineers. In 1853, Captain Gunnison and seven of his men were murdered in Utah while on another government surveying expedition. Deloney Gunnison became a real estate agent and Deloney Street in Grand Rapids was named in his honor. Little else is known about him.

George D. Herrick: George D. Herrick was born in Mt. Morris, New York, on June 28, 1840, and came to Michigan as a boy. After attending Kalamazoo College and Ypsilanti Normal School (now Eastern Michigan University), he enlisted in the 17th Michigan Infantry. He was recommended for promotion to captain for his service in the Army of the Potomac but the Civil War ended before the promotion came through. He settled in Grand Rapids after the war and showed such ability as a singer that he gave concerts all over the state. He became the superintendent of music in the public schools of Grand Rapids and then in Muskegon. Later he founded the Herrick Piano Company and became a successful music dealer. He died in Grand Rapids on February 18, 1919.[39]

William O. Hubbard: William O. Hubbard, the left fielder of the first nine, was born in Oswego, New York, and worked as a clerk.

Dwight K. Hulburt: Dwight Hulburt, the original vice president of the club and the catcher of the first nine, was a successful wool and grain dealer who was born in Michigan around 1845. He later moved to Chicago and seems to have fallen on hard times.

Edward H. Hunt: Edward H. Hunt was born July 10, 1838, in either Ithaca or Utica, New York (sources differ). He moved to Grand Rapids in 1854 to work for a private banking house operated by his uncle. He enlisted in the 8th New York Cavalry in 1861 and was taken prisoner the following year at the Battle of Harper's Ferry. He was immediately released and spent the balance of the war in Washington as a clerk in the office of the Quartermaster-General. He returned to Grand Rapids after the war and became assistant cashier of the Old City National Bank, where he worked with Otis Babcock and J. Fred Baars. He joined the City Trust and Savings Bank when it was organized, eventually becoming vice president. He died in Grand Rapids on September 19, 1914.[40]

Fred C. Joslin: Fred Joslin was a Civil War veteran who was born in 1843 and moved to Oakland, California, and worked as a stationery engineer. According to Civil War pension records, he died on February 17, 1913.

Benjamin Franklin McReynolds: Benjamin F. McReynolds was born in Detroit on October 31, 1842, and came to Grand Rapids in 1850. He was a student at Hobart College when the Civil War broke out, at which point he enlisted in the Union Army. He spent a year in Washington after being discharged and was in Ford's Theatre when Abraham Lincoln was assassinated. He then returned to Grand Rapids and opened a store. Initially, he tried to convince customers that his business was thriving by filling the back of the store with empty boxes and chests that purportedly held merchandise, but eventually he had plenty of real business. He gave up the store in the 1870s when his health began to fail. After three years of trying everything, he resorted to what he called the "heroic treatment" of unstinting hard work — he cleared 26 acres of shrubs and trees on his own. His health restored, he served as secretary of the Grand Rapids Police and Fire Commission from 1882 until his death on January 12, 1907.[41]

Charles Warren Mills: Charles Warren Mills was born in Grand Rapids on August 31, 1850. He was one of the first graduates of the College of Pharmacy of the University of Michigan, in 1870. He died in May of 1892 in Tela, Honduras.

Arthur R. Morgan: Arthur R. Morgan was born in Michigan around 1851 and worked as a boot salesman and in insurance and real estate.

George H. Morgan: George H. Morgan was born around 1845 in Massachusetts and became a shingle dealer.

Frederick Barker Perkins: Fred B. Perkins was born in Michigan on June 13, 1843. He enlisted in the Grand Rapids Greys when the Civil War broke out but does not appear to have ended up serving. In the 1870s he moved to Albany, New York, and operated a retail grocery store. He died in Grand Rapids on April 2, 1890.

Gaius William Perkins: Fred's younger brother G.W. Perkins was born in Grand Rapids on July 16, 1847. He served as president of the board of education from 1882 to 1884. He later became president of the American School Furniture Company as well as a wool merchant. He moved to Los Angeles for a while, but returned to Grand Rapids before his death on April 23, 1934.[42]

Silas Kellogg Pierce: Silas K. Pierce was the club's left fielder and its initial president, and he brought experience to the position, having captained the Custer Club of Ionia in 1866. He was born on June 28, 1842, in Livingston County, New York, and moved to Grand Rapids as a teenager. When the war broke out, he and his two brothers all enlisted, with Silas becoming a sergeant in the 4th Michigan Cavalry. During his three years of service, his photograph was taken by Mathew Brady. After the war, he had a short stint in Ionia and then returned to Grand Rapids to work in the clothing business. Late in life, Pierce moved to Lansing and then to Detroit. While visiting in Grand Rapids on September 14, 1904, he died unexpectedly. Vintage Base Ball players in West Michigan today compete for the Silas K. Pierce Trophy.

Alonzo Burton Porter: Lon Porter was born on December 15, 1849, in Utica, New York, and came to Grand Rapids as an infant. He became the shortstop for the first nine and was the club secretary in 1868. Unlike most club members, he was still playing baseball in the mid–1870s and was also a director of an 1874 organization that sought to bring a "first-class base ball club" to Grand Rapids. He became a bookkeeper for the National Bank and was later manager of the Grand Rapids Clearing House and secretary-treasurer of the Wales Barrel Works. He died in Detroit on January 20, 1928.[43]

Leonard C. Remington: Leon C. Remington was born on May 28, 1840, in New York state and came to Michigan as a boy. He served along with Silas K. Pierce in the 4th Michigan Cavalry Regiment, enlisting in 1862 and rising to the rank of lieutenant before being mustered out in 1865. He married the daughter of a Grand Rapids judge in 1867 and worked in the shirt business. He died in Grand Rapids on May 27, 1921.[44]

Nestell "Ness" Bonee Scribner: Ness Scribner was born in Grand Rapids on March 15, 1849, and was the captain of the second nine. He and his brother ran a copper, tin, and sheet iron manufacturing firm. They became involved in a long-running lawsuit with the city of Grand Rapids that became known as the "Scribner sidewalk case." Having never married, he headed to Alaska in the 1890s but eventually returned to Grand Rapids, where he died on December 29, 1906.

Alexander Porter Sinclair: A. Porter Sinclair was born in Dixboro, Michigan, on February 16, 1845, and served in the 14th Michigan Infantry Regiment. After the war he became an insurance agent and also served as a Grand Rapids alderman during the 1880s. Business took him to San Francisco in 1885 and on to Salt Lake City in 1894, where he died suddenly on July 22, 1897.[45]

Sam B. Sinclair: Sam B. Sinclair was born around 1846 in Michigan and became a grocer.

Charles Robert Sligh, Sr.: Charles R. Sligh was born in Grand Rapids on January 5, 1850. When he was 11, his father enlisted in the Michigan Engineers and Mechanics' Regiment and was fatally wounded. Sligh worked as a tinsmith and a traveling salesman, then founded the Sligh Furniture Company in 1880. The firm became one of the city's most successful businesses and Sligh sat on the boards of several other Grand Rapids companies. He also got into politics, running for governor of Michigan in 1896 for the Silver Party and serving two terms as mayor of Grand Rapids from 1906 to 1910. He died at sea en route to New York on September 15, 1927. His furniture company went under two years later, which was a major setback for Grand Rapids, but his son ultimately revived the firm.

Benjamin F. Stevens: Benjamin F. Stevens was born in Massachusetts on May 3, 1837, and served in the 6th Michigan Cavalry, then became a bookkeeper. He died on April 8, 1919, at the Old Soldiers' Home in Grand Rapids.[46]

Lewis F. Waldron: Lewis F. Waldron was born around 1850 in Illinois and worked as a store clerk. Along with Porter, he took part in the 1874 effort to bring a "first-class base ball club" to Grand Rapids. He moved to California after the death of his wife in 1916 and he died in Berkeley on April 6, 1918.[47]

John Baldwin White: John B. White, the second baseman of the Kent Club's first nine, was the brother of T. Stewart White. He was born on June 14, 1836, and joined his brother in the lumber business. He died in Grand Rapids on April 27, 1905. Despite his brother's prominence, his passing was only briefly noted in the Grand Rapids papers.

Thomas Stewart White: T. Stewart White was born in

Grand Haven, Michigan, on June 28, 1840. He served in the Quartermaster's Department during the war, then moved to Grand Rapids. He was the Kent Club's secretary in 1866 and became a prominent lumberman, eventually having charge of all of the logs that ran through Grand Rapids. He helped organize the Michigan Trust Company and was also the director of the National City Bank of Grand Rapids. His son Stewart Edward White became a well-known novelist; one of his books, *The Blazed Trail*, was based on his father's tales of early lumbering days. T. Stewart White died at a private hospital in Flint on October 14, 1915. An editorial in the *Grand Rapids Herald* described him as "a self-made man — one of that generation, now fast passing, which made history and made Michigan in the 'lumber days.' His rugged personality found reflection in rugged ideals. In loyalty to these ideals he never flinched. The result is written in a life-record of rare accomplishment — yet a record which is as clean as driven snow."[48]

Walter L. Wilkins: Walter L. Wilkins was born in August of 1842 in Vermont and worked as a salesman while he lived in Grand Rapids. In 1876 he and his brother James opened a factory in Hastings, Michigan, to make croquet equipment and baseball bats. Walter Wilkins let his brother buy his interest in 1878, and James then brought in A.G. Spalding as a partner. The Spalding and Wilkins Manufacturing Company soon became the country's leading manufacturer of baseball bats. Although no longer a partner, Walter Wilkins remained involved in the factory until it was destroyed by fire. He later moved to Chicago.

Lewis H. Withey: Lewis H. Withey was born in Grand Rapids on January 21, 1847, the son of a judge. He was the club's first baseman, but like many members his time for baseball was limited. After attending Williston Seminary in Massachusetts, in 1867 he founded a lumber firm called Lewis Withey and Company. In 1889, he also became president of the Michigan Trust Company, which was the first to organize under the Michigan legislature's new Trust Company Act and took advantage to pursue many new courses, such as handling receiverships. He died in Grand Rapids on July 1, 1925.[49]

Other Members: Blevins, R. A. Blumrich, A. E. Dick, Edward H. Donnelly, C. T. Henderson, C. F. (or J. F.) Nelson, Henry W. Pierce, and A. W. Stevens. The Kent Club log book lists at least 29 additional club members, though most of these men probably did nothing more than pay the membership fees and occasionally attend practices.

Notes

1. Peter Morris, *Baseball Fever* (Ann Arbor: University of Michigan Press, 2003), 49–51.
2. *Grand Rapids Daily Democrat*, May 18, 1883.
3. Ibid., May 15, 16, 18 and June 7, 1866; *Grand Rapids Daily Eagle*, May 16, 17 and 18, 1866.
4. *Grand Rapids Daily Eagle*, April 6, 1867.
5. *Grand Rapids Daily Democrat*, May 18, 1883; *Grand Rapids Daily Eagle*, April 6, 1867.
6. *Grand Rapids Daily Eagle*, April 9, 1867.
7. *Grand Rapids Daily Democrat*, April 13, 1867.
8. Ibid., April 13, 19, 20, 24 and 25, 1867.
9. *Grand Rapids Daily Eagle*, April 25, 1867.
10. Ibid., May 9 and 10, 1867.
11. Ibid., May 23, 1867.
12. Ibid., May 24, 1867.
13. Ibid.
14. Ibid., May 29 and 31 and June 1, 1867.
15. Ibid., June 10, 1867.
16. Ibid., August 30, 1867.
17. Ibid., September 27, 1867.
18. *Grand Rapids Daily Democrat*, May 18, 1883.
19. Ibid.
20. Ibid.
21. *Grand Rapids Daily Eagle*, May 29, 1868.
22. Ibid., May 26, 1868.
23. Ibid., July 18, 1868.
24. *Grand Rapids Daily Democrat*, May 18, 1883.
25. *Grand Rapids Daily Eagle*, April 5, 1869.
26. *Grand Rapids Eagle*, April 16, 1879.
27. *Grand Rapids Daily Democrat*, August 9, 1870.
28. Ibid., August 12, 1870.
29. Ibid., May 10, 1874.
30. Ibid., June 29, 1877.
31. Ibid., September 18, 1879.
32. *Grand Rapids Eagle*, April 16, May 23, June 4 and June 11, 1879.
33. *Grand Rapids Daily Democrat*, May 18, 1883.
34. *Grand Rapids Herald*, April 9, 1915.
35. Ibid., August 2 and 3, 1919.
36. *Grand Rapids Press*, January 31, 1912.
37. Ibid., January 6, 1922, 1.
38. Ibid., March 21, 1902.
39. *Grand Rapids Herald*, February 19, 1919.
40. Ibid., September 20, 1914, 3.
41. "Man of Character and Experience," *Grand Rapids Herald*, January 29, 1899, 16.
42. *Grand Rapids Herald*, April 23, 1934.
43. Ibid., January 22, 1928, 18.
44. Ibid., May 28, 1921, 6.
45. *Salt Lake Herald*, July 23, 1897, 11.
46. *Grand Rapids Herald*, April 10, 1919, 6.
47. Ibid., April 9, 1918, 3.
48. Ibid., October 15, 1915, 6.
49. Ibid., July 2, 1925, 3.

❖ *First Nationals of Hancock* (Peter Morris) ❖

Club History

There are challenges in recreating the history and makeup of the Hancock Base Ball Club of Michigan that reflect the highly mobile nature of the U.S. population at the time. But what we do know provides a vivid example of how the mobility of Americans helped baseball spread so quickly during the 1860s and 1870s and establish itself as the national pastime.

The village of Hancock, situated on the north shore of Portage Lake in Michigan's Upper Peninsula, was not even settled until 1858. But the Quincy Mining Company set up a base there the following year and the prospect of steady work in the copper mines caused Hancock to swell to a town of 1,600 by the time of the 1860 census. The population remained fairly steady in the ensuing years, as women and children gradually joined the miners and turned Hancock from a mining camp to a true community. Although the 1863 Michigan directory conceded that Hancock was surrounded by "an uninhabited wilderness ... covered with swamps," it boasted that the village did have "seven mails per week" along with "several stores, groceries, and mechanic shops, three hotels, etc."

Population stability was more difficult to achieve than an initial surge of population and many settlers in Hancock soon moved on because they could not adjust to the harsh climate and the isolation. This was especially the case among the many European immigrants who spent their first few years in the town and then decided to cast their lot elsewhere. Hancock was particularly hard hit by such departures after a calamitous fire destroyed much of the village on April 11, 1869.

As a result, many efforts were made to foster a sense of community. The 1863 Michigan directory reported that Hancock had "three churches ... a masonic society, known as 'Quincy Lodge,' and an association called 'St. Patrick's Society.'" More social organizations were added after the Civil War, including a baseball club.

Several baseball clubs sprang up in the Upper Peninsula in 1868, representing such towns as Negaunee, Marquette, Houghton, and Ontonagon.[1] It's possible that Hancock also had a club that year, but if so, all trace of it was obliterated by the fire of 1869. As a result, the town got its first known club in 1870 when a club was organized that took its name from the First National Bank.

Of course 1870 was very late for a town to get its first baseball club, but the spread of baseball to remote regions like Hancock was an important development nonetheless. By this time, many of the areas in which baseball was well established were beginning to lose interest because of the advent of professionalism. As a result, baseball's introduction to remote regions like the Upper Peninsula was an important way to keep the true spirit of the game alive.

The First Nationals of Hancock played series in 1870 with the German Socks of Calumet and the Houghton Base Ball Club. The latter series was especially hard fought, with the Houghton Club winning the first game by a single run and the First Nationals rebounding to capture the second contest. Hancock eked out the third and deciding game, 52–50, and a game account in the Houghton newspaper implied that the outcome had much to do with the support that the First Nationals received from the community. "The Hancock people," the report observed, "are proud of their nine, and showed it by the way they backed them up. If the residents on this side of the Lake would have a good nine, they should be willing to aid them in clearing up a place where they could both practice and play match games."[2]

The excitement built in 1871 and in August the First National Club went on a tour that saw it play five clubs from Marquette County — the First City Club of Marquette, the Negaunee and Ishpeming nines, the Independent Club of the New York Mine, and a picked nine from Marquette County. All five matches resulted in victories for the First Nationals, so the players returned home as conquering heroes.

Alas for Hancock's champion ballclub, the tour prompted the members of the Ishpeming Club to go into practice and then embark on a tour of their own. Traveling in the Upper Peninsula in late September was not ideal, and the club spent two days stranded in Marquette by rough seas. But after many adventures, they made it to Hancock and defeated the First Nationals, a win that enabled the men from Ishpeming to proclaim themselves "the champion base ball players of the Upper Peninsula."[3]

The rivalries between the baseball clubs representing these towns continued in the ensuing years, despite the abbreviated ballplaying season permitted by the climate. The preparations of the First Nationals for the 1872 season led to this bold proclamation appearing in a Houghton newspaper: "This club, having won the championship of Houghton county and Lake Superior for the season 1871, is now prepared to hear from all other clubs on Lake Superior." Whether the boast originated with the club is unclear, but the Calumet Club assumed that it did and its secretary issued a curt rejoinder. "Will the Secretary of the First National Club," he inquired, "please inform the readers of the *Gazette* how they obtained the championship of Houghton county, and at the same time how they lost it?"[4]

In any event, the First National Base Ball Club of Hancock ended the 1872 season by capturing that very honor. In the summer, a convention was held and a method was arrived at to determine a champion from among Houghton County's four clubs. Although not all games were completed by the time the weather became too cold, it was generally acknowledged that the First Nationals had won and the club members received a badge signifying that distinction.

More important than any badge was the boost that baseball received from so many becoming passionate about the sport. A Houghton reporter expressed this eloquently when he wrote:

> To one who has been inclined to belittle the importance of base ball as a game of sport, the scene at the Hancock grounds last Saturday, when the Independents, of Ripley, and the First Nationals played, was surprising. The crowd present was large. It was composed of all classes, and included many strangers sojourning in the neighborhood. The ladies, too, were well represented, and apparently enjoyed the game. That many people are not only interested in base ball, but that they grow as enthusiastic over it as do the members of political parties during

a hard-fought campaign over the respective issues in contest, was last week fully illustrated. Though the game was between two local clubs, the lines were well drawn, and each side was continually urged on and encouraged by the cheers and bravos of its friends. It can no longer be denied that base ball is in reality the national game in the United States. When, day after day, it can call together crowds of people throughout the land, it is useless to deny it the position it claims. That it does furnish innocent amusement and excitement to thousands is patent, and, so doing, much of its alleged abuse can be forgiven.[5]

Inevitably, however, the same troubles that had started to plague other communities in the 1860s made their way to Michigan's Upper Peninsula. Baseball, for example, had a strong tendency to interfere with work. A newspaper in Sault Saint Marie provided this description of a practice session of a baseball club composed of tugmen: "With three tugs at the bay, tied up to the dock, with one man left to blow the whistle if a wild tug comes in sight, the rest go out and practice. At the first signal from the lookout, all hands ran, helter-skelter, get up steam and run up as far as the mission, discover a steam barge coming with three vessels in tow, they hold a hurried consultation and agree to d — n the barge and then return to practice."[6] The account is humorous, but the underlying problem real.

By 1874 matches in the Upper Peninsula were being played for large stakes and tournaments were starting to be marred by accusations of imported players and questionable tactics. The disputes continued in 1875, making it clear that the spirit of the amateur era was coming to an end even in areas that had been late to catch "base ball fever."[7]

A beautifully preserved photograph at the Michigan Technical University Archives and Copper Country Historical Collections captures the nine men who played for the First National Base Ball Club of Hancock in the decisive game of the 1870 series against Houghton. They are regaled in spiffy uniforms consisting of white shirts (many of them offset by ties of various descriptions), dark pants, and belts that bear the name of their club. There is no mistaking the pride the men felt in representing the town of Hancock.

But while the photograph vividly demonstrates the role that a baseball club could play in building a sense of community, it also carries suggestions of how fleeting that civic pride could be. Only three of the men in the photo went on the tour of Marquette County the following season. And as is shown by the profiles that follow, while several of the club members remained in Hancock and became pillars of the community, more than a few of them soon left to pursue opportunities elsewhere.

Club Members

John Bittenbender: Left fielder John Bittenbender was born in Pennsylvania around 1850 and worked in a sawmill while living in Hancock. He left town within a few years of playing for the First Nationals, and there are enough men with similar names and ages to make him very difficult to trace.

Albert A. Brockway: Center fielder Albert Brockway was born in Copper Harbor, Michigan, around 1848. His father, Daniel, was a mine agent who was one of the pioneer settlers of Lake Superior County, while his mother's diaries of those early years can be found in the Michigan Technical University Archives and Copper Country Historical Collections. Albert became county treasurer of Keewenaw County in 1883 and held that position for many years. He never married, and as of 1930 was living in Livonia, outside of Detroit.

William Harry: William Harry, the third baseman of the First Nationals, was born in Rudruth, England, on August 14, 1843. He arrived in the United States as a teenager and settled in Hancock around 1862. After beginning his career as a tinsmith, he branched off into banking, becoming an officer in the First National Bank of Hancock and numerous other Upper Peninsula financial institutions. He represented Houghton County in the state legislature in 1891–1892. He eventually moved to Detroit, where he died on April 20, 1914.[8]

Joseph Johnson: Joseph Johnson was the club's right fielder in 1870. The only man by that name in the 1870 census was a 23-year-old Canadian-born miner who was living in Franklin. But even assuming that is the right man, he had vanished by the time the 1880 census was taken.

David S. Kendall: Club vice president David Kendall was born in New York state on October 15, 1828. He worked as a retail merchant and bookkeeper and never married, dying in Hancock on June 18, 1906.

Otto Charles Kunath: Otto Kunath, the club's first baseman, was born in Wisconsin on September 26, 1850. The family moved to Michigan's Upper Peninsula while he was young, and Otto worked as a tinsmith while living in Hancock. By 1880 he had moved to Austin, Minnesota, where he worked as a butcher. Eventually, he settled in the delightfully named town of What Cheer, Iowa, where he ran a jewelry shop. He died on November 7, 1929, and is buried in Keokuk, Iowa.

Max H. Mandelbaum: Max H. Mandelbaum, the club president in 1872, was born in Dennenlohe, Bavaria, on September 28, 1828. After immigrating to the United States, his family lived briefly in New York City before settling permanently in Cleveland. In 1855 Mandelbaum moved to northern Michigan, settling first in LaPoint and then moving to Hancock five years later. After initially working as a clerk, he started his own business in 1864 and became one of the city's most respected merchants. By the early 1870s, Mandelbaum was serving as president of the baseball club and as village president (forerunner of the office of mayor). But he died in Hancock on October 18, 1873, leaving behind a wife and five children, the youngest of whom had been born only ten days earlier.

Thomas D. Meads: Thomas Meads, the club's shortstop, was born in Brighton, England, on April 12, 1839, and immigrated to Cleveland in 1856. He moved to Michigan's Upper

Peninsula three years later and in 1868 settled in Hancock, where he worked at first as a watch maker and jeweler. In 1876 he was elected county clerk and register of deeds, serving for at least three terms. He got into real estate in the mid–1880s and moved to Marquette. In the mid–1890s he moved to Calumet and became the township's assistant township clerk and supervisor pro tem. By then he was "considered an authority on upper peninsula historical subjects and a frequent contributor to the press." Meads died in Calumet, Michigan, on May 1, 1912.[9]

Archibald J. Scott: A.J. Scott, the club's catcher, was born near London, Ontario, on January 24, 1849. Orphaned at a young age, he was raised by his uncle Donald and at the age of 15 during the Civil War enlisted in the 52nd Wisconsin Regiment, Company D, which was led by his uncle. He moved to Houghton in 1867 and found work as a clerk in a drugstore. After the great fire of 1869, he opened his own store and became a successful druggist. He also led the organization of a town fire department in 1870 and was fire chief for 26 years, as well as starting the *Hancock Times*. He served seven terms as village president and then became Hancock's first mayor after incorporation as a city in 1903. Scott was also director of the Superior Trust, president of the Eva Mining Company, builder and proprietor of the Hotel Scott, and vice president of First National Bank. He even employed Charles L. Fichtel, the captain and manager of the 1887 Hancock Base Ball Association. Despite these obvious signs of leadership skills, when he served as captain of the First Nationals in 1871 the choice was questioned by a reporter who wrote that Scott "did not appear to be the best man for the position; he was too easily excited, and dropped too many balls." Scott was elected to another term as mayor in 1907 but by election day he was in Hot Springs, Arkansas, for his health. A paralytic stroke followed a few years later, and he was admitted to a sanitarium in Milwaukee, where he died on March 8, 1915.[10] One obituary said that Scott possessed "almost as many sides as Ben Franklin, whom he much resembled in face and figure as well as in mental characteristics."[11]

James Walls Trembath: Second baseman James Trembath was born on February 21, 1852, in Cornwall, England. His family crossed the Atlantic and settled in northern Michigan in 1866, where James became a miner. He eventually moved on to Colorado, where he died on November 22, 1924.

John T.V. "Victor" Trembath: The club's pitcher Victor Trembath was not a brother of James Trembath but presumably was a relative. Born in Cornwall around 1848, he remained in the area and worked as a miner for the Atlantic Mine. Trembath died of tuberculosis in Houghton on November 10, 1890, leaving a wife and eight children.

Other Members: Frank Atwood, Jacob Baer (one of four vice presidents in 1872), Bryant, Corey, McLaughlin, Edward Ryan (another of the vice presidents in 1872), W.J. Robinson, Sackle.

Sources

This entry is based upon the research I did for my book *Baseball Fever* (Ann Arbor: University of Michigan Press, 2003). Specific newspaper sources are either listed in the footnotes or can be found in that book. Special thanks to Cathy Greer of the Michigan Technical University Archives and Copper Country Historical Collections for providing a great deal of information about the club members.

Notes

1. Peter Morris, *Baseball Fever* (Ann Arbor: University of Michigan Press, 2003), 222–223.
2. *Portage Lake* (Houghton) *Mining Gazette*, August 11, 1870.
3. *Marquette Mining Journal*, October 21, 1871.
4. *Portage Lake* (Houghton) *Mining Gazette*, April 18 and 25, 1872.
5. *Portage Lake* (Houghton) *Mining Gazette*, June 18, 1874.
6. *Sault Saint Marie Enterprise*; reprinted in the *Ishpeming Iron Home*, September 19, 1874.
7. Morris, *Baseball Fever*, 325–326, 350–351.
8. "William Harry, Banker, Former Legislator, Dies," *Detroit Free Press*, April 21, 1914, 6.
9. *Hancock Evening Copper Journal*, May 1, 1912; *Calumet News*, May 1, 1912.
10. *Portage Lake* (Houghton) *Mining Gazette*, March 10, 1915.
11. *Hancock Evening Copper Journal*, March 9, 1915.

Chapter Six

Indiana, Illinois, Wisconsin, Iowa and Minnesota

❖ *Introduction* (Peter Morris) ❖

Eastern settlers flocked to the Midwestern states of Indiana, Illinois, Wisconsin, Iowa, and Minnesota during the 1840s and 1850s, reshaping a mud-infested "upstart village" named Chicago into a booming metropolis and transforming other sleepy farming towns into bustling cities.[1] Baseball clubs soon burst into existence in these new communities and often reflected the breathtaking ambition of the people who had abandoned civilization as they knew it to make the westward trek. An 1857 club in Nininger City, Minnesota, for example, declared its bold intention to "extend a challenge to the 'whole West.'"[2]

Easterners were often bemused by this earnestness and by the very notion of organizing baseball clubs in remote outlets, with the *New York Clipper* drily referring in 1863 to the formation of two clubs in Dubuque as proof that "civilization is gradually proceeding westward."[3] Even Midwesterners were sometimes taken aback — an 1884 history of Milwaukee offered this description of a pioneer club formed in the city: "April 5th, 1860, and a club organized.... Play grounds on Spring street hill. The rules and regulations of this Club occupied one entire column in the *Sentinel* of April 7th, the Constitution alone containing thirty-eight sections. No wonder it died of plethora or something."[4]

Yet new baseball clubs continued to spring up and when the Civil War ended, the flow became a torrent as town after town became caught up in "base ball fever." Typical was the experience of Nevada, Iowa, from which word came that "A club for the practice of this game (base ball) has been organized in our village with a membership of some thirty persons. The club has sent for the necessary 'traps,' elected officers and soon will be in trim to lug off honors and carry in health and muscle. It will be refreshing to see something better than pitching old horse-shoes, resorted to for amusement on our streets."[5]

As was the case elsewhere, few of these new Midwestern clubs had the success envisioned by their members. On December 6, 1865, fourteen ambitious clubs representing the states of Indiana, Michigan, Illinois, Missouri, Iowa, Ohio, Wisconsin, and Minnesota met in Chicago to form the Northwestern Association of Base-Ball Players.[6] By the time of its second annual convention, in December of 1866, the number of member clubs had more than doubled, to thirty-two, but there were obvious indications that the new association lacked direction. Much of the meeting was spent expressing resentment of the Eastern bias of the National Association of Base Ball Players and the most heatedly debated issue was whether the Northwestern Association should disband in favor of state associations.[7]

Nor was everyone impressed by the new game. A newspaper editor in Racine, Wisconsin, observed in 1867 that "it is base ball, base ball everywhere; our local and foreman are members of base ball clubs with high sounding titles. We have heard so much about base ball, and once having been an expert at a game we used to call base ball, we took it into our head to go up to their grounds and see the incipient specimens of humanity of the present age play base ball." What he found was a source of great aggravation: "[O]f all the sickly games we have ever seen played the new fangled base ball takes them all down. It was the old fashioned game of base ball, but shorn of all its life and animation, to suit the sluggish youth of this deteriorated age." He instead expressed his longing for the days when "fifty or a hundred men would get together, after log raising perhaps," and play by the rules that allowed fielders to retire base-runners by hitting them with the baseball.[8]

Even the seven clubs featured in this chapter learned that success could prove fleeting. The Pecatonica Club became synonymous for overwhelming defeat, while the Excelsiors of Chicago were crushed beneath the lofty expectations of the city they represented. The Byron Base Ball Club and the Summit Citys of Fort Wayne soon gave way to more ambitious clubs, while the Beloit College nine died the natural death that befalls all college nines when their stars graduate. The Mutuals of Janesville did endure, but even they experienced so many ups and downs that their eloquent chronicler, Frank L. Smith, was often plunged into despondency as he penned his reminiscences.

There was, however, one notable exception. The Forest Citys of Rockford (Illinois) exploded onto the national scene in July of 1867 when they pulled their historic upset of the touring Nationals of Washington. In retrospect, it can be argued that the outcome shouldn't really have come as such a surprise. Yet the reality is that the upset was entirely unexpected, with the result that a single game changed the baseball landscape — it enabled Midwestern ballplayers to believe that they could topple the best East Coast clubs. Moreover, the Forest City Club was no one-trick pony. The club built upon that legendary game by remaining a national power while continuing to rely (primarily) on local talent. It was apt that, when the first celebration of early baseball was held on Harry Wright Day in 1896, the primary event was held in Rockford.

Nor was the glorious career of the Forest Citys a solitary case. While no other pioneer-era club from the states of Indiana, Illinois, Iowa, Wisconsin, and Minnesota rivaled the long-term success of the Forest Citys, there was no shortage of memorable contests and legendary players. Indianapolis's first-known club, formed in 1865 by W.S. Pratt, the brother of Eastern star Tom Pratt, included the great Cal McVey and another budding professional named Harry Deane. A town club from Marshalltown, Iowa, featured the town's founder and his two sons, one of whom amused onlookers by impertinently urging his father on balls hot over his head to "Hurry, Pop, darn ye, hurry, or he'll make a home run."[9] That cheeky youngster was none other than Adrian Anson, who himself became known as Pop or Cap Anson during his illustrious career as player-manager of the Chicago White Stockings. Then there were clubs like the Kekiongas of Fort Wayne, a little-known nine that brashly embarked on a tour of the east. As Bob Fisher, one of the club's organizers, later recalled: "We left Fort Wayne, full of enthusiasm for a series of contests with the teams of the east. It was a memorable trip. Everywhere they joshed us as small-town Hoosiers, and made fun of the name 'Kekionga,' but we stood the jokes all right and carried off enough honors to make us feel good."[10]

Even more importantly, for every player and club that proved itself on the national stage, there were dozens that became local legends. In Pana, Illinois, for example, "the first baseball club was named the Excelsiors. J.C. McQuigg, still a leading attorney of Pana, was the star catcher and batter of the club. He was known as the Babe Ruth of Central Illinois, and won the state championship by knocking the ball out of the state fair grounds at Decatur, Illinois, for a home run and brought in three men with him, winning the game and the silver cup."[11] Meanwhile, in nearby Decatur, a law student named W. Corwin Johns laid out the first baseball diamond and earned a local reputation comparable to a Decatur Hall of Famer of a later generation — according to a 1905 article, Johns "was the star pitcher for the McPhersons, the great prehistoric ball team in Decatur. In that day Corwin Johns was as famous as a baseball pitcher as was Joe McGinnity in modern times. Corwin could throw a ball further than any other man in Decatur."[12]

Was J.C. McQuigg in fact deserving of comparison to Babe Ruth? Did W. Corwin Johns actually possess a pitching arm that rivaled that of Iron Man McGinnity? It seems very unlikely, but that scarcely matters. What is important is that their exploits inspired Midwestern boys with the desire to emulate them and thereby permanently planted the seed of baseball in the American heartland.

In 1870 businessmen from the now-thriving metropolis of Chicago became fed up having their local clubs embarrassed by rivals from Cincinnati and Rockford. So they tried to buy supremacy by offering such unheard-of salaries that the resulting team was dubbed the "$10,000 nine." It was the end of the pioneer era and its "take-on-all-comers" spirit — soon nines from towns like Rockford would no longer be able to compete with Chicago clubs, while clubs from villages like Pecatonica would be relegated to their own divisions.

But by then the game of baseball had been firmly established in the heartland by clubs like the Saxon Base Ball Club of St. Paul, which traveled to Lake City on the steamer Mollie McPike in August of 1869 to compete for the championship of Minnesota.[13] And by players like the hardy members of the Fort Dodge (Iowa) Club, who made the thirty-mile trip to Boone to play for the championship of northwestern Iowa on a "wet and disagreeable" day in 1866 and "managed to drive dull care away with songs, stories, anecdotes, sells [tall tales], and yarns.... [We arrived] in Boonsboro about dark; singing as we passed through to Boone, every thing known to vocalists, from 'One Hundred' to 'Babble, babble, little brook.' The inhabitants stared at us; children looked amazed; dogs barked."[14] And by countless similar clubs, including the seven whose stories follow.

NOTES

1. Quoted in Donald L. Miller, *City of the Century: The Epic of Chicago and the Making of America* (New York: Simon & Schuster, 1997), 61.
2. *Porter's Spirit of the Times,* August 29, 1857.
3. *New York Clipper,* September 19, 1863.
4. James Smith Buck, *Pioneer History of Milwaukee* (Milwaukee: Milwaukee News Co., 1876), 381.
5. *Nevada Yegis,* undated 1867 article; quoted in William Orson Payne, *History of Story County, Iowa* (Chicago: S. J. Clarke, 1911), 391.
6. *Chicago Tribune,* December 7, 1865.
7. *Detroit Advertiser and Tribune,* December 21, 1866.
8. "The Great National Game—A Sickly Thing," *Racine Journal*, August 14, 1867. This intriguing article, written by *Journal* editor Colonel William L. Utley, was first unearthed by Tom Melville, who quotes briefly from it in *Early Baseball and the Rise of the National League* (Jefferson, NC: McFarland, 2001), 11. Michael Epstein offers an extended commentary and quotes more extensively from the original piece in "A 'Yaller

Kivered' Game: New York–Style Baseball Comes to Racine," *Nine* 16:1 (Fall 2007), 10–20.

9. *Rockford Register-Gazette*, April 26, 1912.

10. "'Bob' Fisher Talks of Old Kekiongas," *Fort Wayne News*, April 1, 1908, 7.

11. Dorothy Jordan, "The Old Home Town," *Decatur Daily Review*, July 17, 1921.

12. *Decatur Daily Review*, August 11, 1905.

13. *St. Paul Daily Pioneer*, August 7, 1869.

14. *Iowa North West* (Fort Dodge, Iowa), exact date not given, approximately September 26, 1866; quoted in John Liepa, "Baseball Mania Strikes Iowa," *Iowa Heritage* 87:1 (Spring 2006), 6.

❖ Summit City Base Ball Club of Fort Wayne (Robert Gregory) ❖

Club History

In 1862 several men in Fort Wayne, Indiana, organized their city's first baseball club. Choosing the name the Summit City Base Ball Club because Fort Wayne was the highest elevation point on the Erie-Wabash Canal, which linked Lake Erie to the Ohio River, the organization was typical of most clubs of that time. Although bat-and-ball games had probably been played in Fort Wayne by children before 1862, the Summit City Base Ball Club was the first adult group in Fort Wayne to see the possibilities for healthy exercise and career-advancement opportunities. More social club than athletic team, the members of the club were young professional gentlemen, many of whom would rise to national renown and esteem.

On Tuesday, April 22, the morning paper, Dawson's *Daily Times and Union*, informed the city that a meeting to organize and elect officers would be held the next evening. At the meeting, thirty-three men joined the club, electing Charles S. Brackenridge president, William B. Fisher secretary, and Thomas B. Shoaff treasurer. It is likely that Brackenridge, a student "back East" in 1862, brought the game home with him when the school year was over. At the next weekly meeting (April 30), banker Allen Hamilton donated land directly behind his residence for use as the ball grounds. (Today it is the Fort Wayne Community Schools Administrative Center, south of Lewis Street, between Calhoun and Clinton Streets.) It was also decided that games would be played each week on Monday afternoons at 2 o'clock.

The first game was played on May 5. Before the game it was announced that a beautiful silver cup worth $10 would be presented to the member making the greatest number of runs in nine innings. Unfortunately, no box score exists from the game. It was reported that the game was "pleasant and exciting," and that a number of ladies were in attendance to witness the game. When the nine innings were over, the side captained by John E. Hill defeated the side captained by Samuel Lewis, 57–37. After the game, the silver cup was awarded to Thomas Shoaff, who scored the most runs, seven.

If there was a game the following week, no evidence of it has survived. Only once more that year would the Summit City Base Ball Club be mentioned in the local paper. On Saturday, May 17, members were reminded that Monday was the regular match game day. All members who wished to play were asked to arrive promptly by 2 o'clock. John McArthur was to present a handsome cane to the man making the greatest number of runs. As before, no details of the game were published.

As expanding needs of the Civil War became critical that summer, nearly half of the club members joined the military. After only a few weeks of ballplaying, the Summit Citys disbanded and quietly faded away, leaving behind no photographs, no box scores, and no memorabilia.

After the war numerous clubs organized (one even took the name Summit Citys), perhaps in memory of the original. Though long forgotten even by its city, the Summit City Base Ball Club of Fort Wayne is due its legacy as the founding baseball club in northeast Indiana.

Club Members

The thirty-three men who joined the Summit Citys were middle- and upper-middle-class men, or at least, aspiring to attain that level. A list of members, their ages and professions in 1862, as well as any additional achievements worth noting, follows:

Stephen Cooper Ayres, 21, physician: Ayres was born in Troy, Ohio, on June 5, 1840, and grew up in Fort Wayne. After serving in the Civil War as a surgeon, he studied in the ear and eye clinics of London and Vienna, returning to the Cincinnati area to become a world-renowned oculist. He also taught ophthalmology at what is now the University of Cincinnati. He wrote several reminiscences about the Civil War, including *The Battle of Nashville: With personal recollections of a field hospital*. He died in Cincinnati on September 2, 1921.

Jared D. Bond, 23, bank teller: Born in Lockport, New York, on May 31, 1838, Bond served in the Civil War as an adjutant. After the war, he spent many years as cashier (in the 19th century, the cashier was a management position, similar to an accountant) at the First National Bank. He died in California on June 9, 1912.

Lafayette M. Bowser, 25, attorney: Born in 1837 in Ohio, Bowser was a leading local Democrat until his death on September 26, 1877.

Charles Starr Brackenridge, 20, student: From a prominent Fort Wayne family, Brackenridge, after graduating from college, became a civil engineer for the city, working specifically with water-treatment plants. Born in 1842, he helped design and construct the water works in Fort Wayne and other nearby smaller Hoosier towns, as well as Saginaw, Michigan. He died in Fort Wayne on January 10, 1902.

William Hartman Brady, 27, dry goods salesman: Born in Montoursville, Pennsylvania, in 1834, Brady came to Fort Wayne to work for the dry-goods firm of fellow club member Ernst Rurode. He was still working for the firm when he died in Fort Wayne on July 1, 1900.

John G. Bright, 25, merchant: Born in Ireland, Bright served as an orderly sergeant in the Civil War and then moved to Pittsburgh, where he died on September 23, 1915.

Erastus L. Chittenden, 28, attorney: Born in New York City in 1833, Chittenden served as Fort Wayne's city clerk for many years after the Civil War. Active in local politics, he served on the city council and was elected to the state legislature. He died in Fort Wayne on June 19, 1886.

Ward B. Chittenden, 25, auditor for the county clerk: Erastus Chittenden's younger brother Ward was born in New York City in 1836. After the war he moved to St. Louis, dying while on vacation in Florida in 1913.

Frederick J. Drake, 27, dry-goods dealer: Fred Drake was born in Yonkers, New York, on February 22, 1835, and moved to Fort Wayne in 1849 to work at the dry-goods store of his brother Moses. When his brother was appointed postmaster of Fort Wayne by President Lincoln, Fred became his assistant and remained as chief delivery clerk until his death on June 24, 1898.

William Augustus Dripps, 22, railroad draftsman: Born in New Jersey in 1840, Dripps enlisted in the Navy during the Civil War and spent time on the famous ironclad USS *Monitor*. He returned east after the war and eventually re-enlisted in the Navy and became a career military man. He died in Pennsylvania on November 10, 1927.

Alexander J. Erwin, 23, physician: A.J. Erwin, born in 1837 in Pennsylvania, was an oculist like fellow Summit City Club member Stephen Ayres. He served for many years on Fort Wayne's Board of Health, then moved to Mansfield, Ohio. He was critically wounded in an 1881 assassination attempt but recovered and lived in Mansfield until his death on October 9, 1913.

William B. Fisher, 23, bank cashier: Born in Little Falls, New York, in 1838, Fisher moved to Indiana while young. He was involved in private banking until the First National Bank, the first national bank in Indiana, was organized in 1863. He was elected cashier, making him the first cashier in the state, a position he held until 1871 (Jared Bond succeeded him), when he left for New York City to be an import/export merchant. He died in New York City on January 22, 1891.

Joseph B. Fry, 21, leather manufacturer (shoes and boots): Fry, born in Fort Wayne in 1840, served as the chief of the volunteer fire department for many years. He died in Green Bay, Wisconsin, in 1908.

Andrew Holman Hamilton, 27, attorney: Hamilton, whose father donated the land for the baseball club, ran the First National Bank for many years after his father's death in 1864. Active in national politics, he served in the U.S. House of Representatives for two terms. Born in Fort Wayne in 1834, he passed away there in May 9, 1895.

Washington H. Haskell, 21, produce merchant: Haskell died in New York City in 1883.

John Evans Hill, 21, milling merchant: Hill, born in 1840 in Ohio, took over his father's mill and warehouses when his father decided to retire, and ran them until his own retirement many years later. After the war, Hill reorganized the Summit Citys and played with them in 1866. He was the only 1862 member to play in 1866. He passed away in California in 1915.

Thomas Lewis Jefferds, 20, railroad agent: Born in 1842, in Indiana, Jefferds served in the Union Navy during the Civil War. He died in Fort Wayne on September 5, 1870.

George S. Kauffman, 26, jeweler (with Byron Thompson): Born in Ohio in 1835, Kauffman died in German, Indiana, near South Bend, in 1881.

Carl C. Kingsbury, 31, physician: After the Civil War, in which he served as a regimental captain, Kingsbury left for Wisconsin. He never married and died in Grand Rapids, Michigan, on June 21, 1895.

Samuel L. Lewis, 19, gentleman: Nothing further is known at this time.

John W. McArthur, 25, surveyor: Born in Scotland in 1836, McArthur was a civil engineer and surveyor in Fort Wayne until his death in 1913.

Charles McCulloch, 21, bank teller: McCulloch's father, Hugh, had significant influence on Reconstruction as he was the Secretary of the Treasury under Lincoln and Andrew Johnson. (See the National Club of Washington entry for a description of Hugh McCullough's association with that club, many of whose stars were lured to Washington by the promise of Treasury Department clerkships.) Following in his father's footsteps, Charles went into the banking industry. With his father away in Washington, McCulloch, along with Hamilton (and other board members) ran the First National Bank for many years. He lived his entire life in Fort Wayne, being born in 1840 and passing away on March 18, 1921.

William Rockhill Nelson, 21, clerk of the Circuit Court: Nelson, born in Fort Wayne in 1841, founded or bought many newspapers, starting in and around northeast Indiana. By the time he died in Kansas City on April 13, 1915, he had owned and operated many newspapers that exist still today. He founded and ran the *Kansas City Star* for many years.

Henry G. Olds, 21, machinist in family lumber business: Born in Auburn, New York, in 1839, Olds was a leading manufacturer of spokes and hubs for the local railroad business until his death on May 14, 1902.

Henry H. Robinson, 21, hotelier: After serving in the

Civil War, Robinson continued his education, becoming an attorney and serving in the Indiana legislature as a recording clerk in the 1880s.

Marvin S. Robinson, 23, bookkeeper: Born in New York in 1837, Robinson was one of the original tellers at the First National Bank. Shortly thereafter, he moved to Peru, Indiana, to run the local bank. He died there in 1912.

Ernst Christian Heinrich Rurode, 23, dry-goods merchant: Born in Hanover, Germany, in 1838, Rurode came to Fort Wayne in 1860 and started the Rurode Dry Goods Company, which he ran until his death at age 87 on July 20, 1925. Although some club members' death dates are unknown, it appears that Rurode was the last surviving Summit City ballplayer.

Thomas B. Shoaff, 20, saddler: Shoaff, born in Fort Wayne in 1842, epitomizes the type of entrepreneur who utilized his baseball connections to advance his career. After starting out in his father's saddle shop, Shoaff sold the business upon his father's death and went to college. He then invested money in a retail carpet partnership. After learning the business, he sold out and took his nest egg to New York City, where he continued to invest in businesses just as they were taking off. By the time of his death in New York on January 4, 1900, he was a multimillionaire, with holdings in a variety of interests.

Francis A. Stapleford, 21, merchant: Born in Indiana in 1841, Stapleford moved to Ohio and died there in 1902.

Byron S. Thompson, 21, jeweler (with Kauffman): Thompson was born in 1840 in Fort Wayne and lived his entire life there, dying in 1923. After the Civil War, he was engaged in the real-estate business for many years and assisted in laying out many subdivisions on the south side of the city.

William J. G. Thompson, 19, merchant: The brother of Byron Thompson, William J. G. Thompson was born in Fort Wayne in 1843. He enlisted in the Army in 1862, was given the rank of second lieutenant, and began his 90-day enlistment on June 1. On August 29, 1862, Thompson was shot and killed at the Battle of Richmond, Kentucky. His enlistment had been scheduled to end on the 31st.

Joseph H. Wilder, age unknown, shoe merchant: No further information known at this time.

Charles B. Woodward, 27, merchant: In articles about the Summit Citys, this name is usually listed as C.B. Woodworth, most likely because there was a well-known Fort Wayne pharmacist by the name of Charles B. Woodworth in the 1890s and 1900s, and the noted Fort Wayne historian, B.J. Griswold, assumed that the original newspaper misprinted the name. The correct name is Woodward. He left Fort Wayne just after the Civil War. Nothing else is known at this time.

Sources

This entry is based upon B.J. Griswold, "A Pictorial History of Fort Wayne," and contemporary newspapers.

❖ *Excelsiors of Chicago, Prewar* (Peter Morris) ❖

Club History

Chicago may be known as the second city, but its sports fans are quick to grow impatient with second-rate performances. As true as that is today, it was much more so when the city's first notable baseball clubs emerged. It was the misfortune of the Excelsior Club to be Chicago's best club during those years and to be saddled with the weight of expectations that they could not meet.

Chicago's earliest known ballclub, the Union Club, was organized on August 12, 1856, while the city was in the midst of its extraordinary transformation from tiny outpost to major metropolis.[1] According to sportswriter John Kelley, baseball and like games had been "played long before this by schoolboys, but there was no regularly organized club until the Unions, a West Side aggregation of prairie players, challenged 'any and all comers for money, chalk or marbles.'"[2]

As far as we can tell, that gauntlet was not picked up until 1858. On July 7 of that year, the Union Club hosted a club from Downers Grove, Illinois, and were beaten by the "country boys" in the first known match game played in Chicago.[3] The loss did nothing to diminish interest in the new game, and two days later the rules of the New York version were published in the *Chicago Press and Tribune* along with the announcement that a convention of Chicago baseball clubs would be held on the 21st.[4]

The Union Club no doubt expected a challenge from one of the new clubs, but none was forthcoming. So Chicago's oldest club took the initiative and sent a challenge to the Excelsior Club. The members of the Excelsior Club met on August 14 and authorized secretary John R. Floyd to commit the club to playing a match game on the 26th. Chicago's very first intracity rivalry was ready to start!

While the Excelsiors had only recently adopted the New York rules, they had more experience at playing bat-and-ball games. According to one early resident, the club initially played with five bases on grounds located "in the middle of a bleak prairie, and except when used by the Indians for an occasional sun dance they practically belonged to the Excelsiors and were rent free." Then in 1857, the club adopted the New York rules.[5]

How and why they made that decision is not known. Many of the early members would later call G. Charles Smith the father of the club, but Smith maintained that the club was already organized when he joined. In any event, the club never regretted adopting the New York rules: "After the alteration was made in the style of play and the boys got some new bats the game picked up fresh interest."[6]

Excitement mounted as the date for the historic showdown between the Union and Excelsior clubs approached. A newspaper account on the day of the match gushed, "The Nines comprise the flower of each Club, and have been in rigorous training for some time past." Despite the fact that the match was being played at 2 P.M. on a Thursday, a big crowd was anticipated. The setting was the Prairie Cricket Club grounds, located at Chicago's western city limits on Madison Street between Loomis Street and Ogden Avenue. To ensure that spectators could get to the site, special arrangements were made for the Madison Street omnibus to run to and from the ground every 30 minutes. In addition, a committee was organized to make sure that all attendees were accommodated and to prepare special tents for female spectators.[7]

Unfortunately, as would happen 130 years later at the first night game at Wrigley Field, rain spoiled all of the planning. The match was eventually played on the following Monday and the Excelsiors' victory by a 17–11 score received only brief mention in the local press. It was a portent of things to come for a club that would repeatedly find its triumphs overshadowed by its misfortunes.

Chicago's first cross-town rivals played a rematch a couple of weeks later, and the Excelsior Club again emerged victorious, this time by a count of 30–17. After the match all of the players from both clubs "returned to the Union Park House to partake of a collation, and adjourned at a late hour, the time being spent in speech making, pleasant repartee, merry jokes, and singing."[8] It was a fitting way to end the season that had witnessed the birth of formal baseball competition in Chicago.

The following spring, the Excelsiors kicked off the new season by holding their annual meeting on April 12, 1859, and electing Dr. W.C. Hunt as club president, James Malcomb as vice president, W.W. Kennedy as secretary, and G. Charles Smith as treasurer. By then, their first rivals, the Union Club, had passed quietly out of existence. Several new Chicago clubs, however, had sprung up and the presence of the Olympic, Columbia, and Atlantic clubs ensured that the 1859 season would witness heightened local interest in the game that was already being hailed as the "national pastime."

A few weeks later, the secretary of the Excelsiors wrote to the New York–based publication *Spirit of the Times* and predicted that all of the new clubs would make the 1859 baseball season a "lively one." The letter added the boast that the Excelsior Club was Chicago's "most prominent" club and reported that its players would "make a nice appearance on the ball field in their new uniforms, which consist of long white pants and white shirts made of English flannel."[9]

Despite this initial enthusiasm, coverage in the *Press and Tribune* suggests that the Excelsiors' activity in 1859 was mostly restricted to the practices that were held on Tuesdays and Fridays at their new grounds at West Lake and Ann streets.[10] On at least one occasion, a practice session was enlivened by a match between married and single members.[11]

The Excelsiors also defended their local supremacy against a couple of new challengers in 1859. They beat the Columbia Club handily enough that the customary rematch appears to have been called off, but the Atlantic club proved another matter. In early June the Excelsiors beat the Atlantics by a 31–17 score in front of "some five hundred spectators, not a few of whom were ladies."[12] But the Atlantics evened the best-of-three series in July to force a deciding game. That match took place in August at the Prairie Cricket Grounds, and the Atlantics squeaked out an 18–16 win, thereby wresting away the honor of being considered Chicago's top baseball club.[13]

The Excelsiors reorganized for the 1860 season in late April. G. Charles Smith remained the club's treasurer, but Dr. Hunt stepped down as president, so James Malcomb assumed that role and Kennedy became vice president, while a new officer, Abraham Voorhies, became the club's secretary. The club's first nine was reportedly strengthened by the addition of several players who had formerly belonged to the Columbia Club.[14] Yet it was hard to tell that from the club's level of activity, as the *Press and Tribune* contained more accounts in 1860 of the doings of the club's second and junior nines than of its first nine.

The first nine did again face the Atlantics for local supremacy, but the results were the same. After splitting two games, they played the rubber game at the Prairie Cricket Club on August 26, 1860, and the Atlantics won by a convincing 23–12 score in front of "a much larger crowd than has heretofore attended during a match."[15]

A likely explanation for the lack of match play by the Excelsiors' first nine in 1860 is that the city's attention that summer was consumed by the presidential election, which featured Illinois favored sons Stephen A. Douglas and Abraham Lincoln and was further enlivened by the threat of Southern cessation. Emblematic of that, the most notable game played by the Excelsior Club in 1860 was an intrasquad contest between nine club members who supported Lincoln and an equal number of Douglas loyalists. The Douglas partisans won, prompting the fiercely pro–Lincoln *Press and Tribune* to predict: "Never mind, Lincoln boys, there's a victory in store where Douglas will make no 'runs.' He is a lame 'short stop,' and has been 'caught out.'"[16]

Lincoln did indeed win that fall's election, and over the winter the country headed inexorably toward disunion and war. One later account claimed that most of the Excelsior Club's members enlisted in the Union armed forces and, as the accompanying profiles show, many of them did indeed either become soldiers or helped out on the home front. As a result, by the time the Excelsiors played their next match game, both Lincoln and Douglas were dead and the United States had been changed forever by a long, devastating civil war.

Club Members

Francis H. Bostock: Frank Bostock, a druggist who was born in England on April 7, 1820, played for the first nine in 1859. Despite his age, he served in the 65th Regiment, Illinois Infantry (Scotch Regiment) during the Civil War. He later became a doctor and moved to Palisade, Nebraska, to practice medicine. He retained his love of baseball until his death in Palisade on March 17, 1923, at the age of 102.

Simeon Farwell: Simeon Farwell played for the first nine in 1858 and 1859. Born on March 22, 1831, in Campbelltown, New York, he was the younger brother of Charles B. Farwell, a U.S. senator from 1887 to 1891, and John V. Farwell, one of Chicago's best known dry-goods merchants. The family moved in 1838 to Ogle County, Illinois, which was still so rural that the county seat was described as "the great city of Oregon City, three houses and a smoke house." Eventually, the family moved to Chicago and John V. Farwell became a partner of Marshall Field until he formed his own dry-goods business in 1865. Farwell would eventually take three of his brothers on as partners and the firm became extremely successful. It would later sponsor one of Chicago's best-known company baseball teams. Simeon Farwell joined his three older brothers as a partner in the dry-goods firm in 1870, and by 1880 he and his wife and two children had moved to Evanston. Widowed in 1905, he died in Evanston on February 12, 1911.

John R. Floyd: Floyd was the club secretary in 1858. Born in Butler County, Pennsylvania, around 1837 to Scottish-born parents, he was working for the penny post at the time of the 1860 census. He and his wife, Sarah, were living with the family of a Joe Malcomb, so he may have been related by marriage to fellow club member James Malcomb. In 1862 he enlisted in the 65th Regiment, Illinois Infantry (Scotch Regiment), serving with fellow club member Frank Bostock. He became a captain in Company E and served until September of 1864. After the war he became a cashier for the American Express Company. Floyd died in Chicago on January 8, 1900.

John J. Gillespie: Gillespie first belonged to the Union Club and then switched to the Columbias, but had joined the Excelsiors by 1860 and played with the Lincoln men in that July's intrasquad game. Once joining the Excelsiors, he became one of the club's most prominent members and served as its president after the war. Another early ballplayer recalled in 1888 that the early members of the Excelsiors were "all natural ball players, as a matter of fact, and chief among the ancient veterans was John J. Gillispi [sic], who at one time was president of the club. Mr. Gillispi was a veteran ball player when Al Spalding was in the care of a nurse."[17] Gillespie was born in Scotland in 1833 and was assistant chief of Chicago's fire department by 1860. After the demise of the Excelsiors, like other members, he moved on to other pursuits. In 1875 the *Tribune* reported that the Excelsiors' former president and first baseman was now the vice president of the Chicago Gun Club. The new interest also provided him with a livelihood, as Gillespie, who had worked for a time as a lime burner, became a clerk at a gun store. Around 1889, Gillespie suffered a paralytic stroke. He died on the last day of 1901 without ever having left his room during the last 12 years of his life.

W. Hartshorne: Hartshorne played in 1858 and 1859 but no man by that name has been found in Chicago.

William Haughton or Houghton: Haughton/Haughton played in 1858. He is probably William B. Haughton, a merchant, who was born in 1834, arrived in Chicago in the early 1850s and lived there until his death on April 22, 1901.

J.A. Hays/Hayes: Hayes has not been identified.

Dr. William Carlton Hunt: Dr. Hunt, who was born in Litchfield, Connecticut, on November 8, 1826, was a physician who served as club president in 1858 and played in 1859. Although married and in his mid–30s, Hunt enlisted as a surgeon in Company S, 51st Infantry Regiment on October 21, 1861, serving for six months. He died in Chicago on February 28, 1891.

William Wallace Kennedy: Kennedy served as club secretary in 1859 and as vice president in 1860. He does not appear to have played for the first nine, but he was probably a member of the second nine as he did play in the Lincoln-Douglas game. Alec Kennedy, later a member of the first nine, was a relative, probably a cousin once removed. W. W. Kennedy was born in Greene County, Alabama, in 1830, at the crossroads country store on the Tombigbee River operated by his Scottish-born father. Around 1847, his father, William, sold the store, bought a wagon and headed north with his wife and eight children — by the time they arrived in Chicago in June, a ninth child had been born. W. W. Kennedy opened a hardware store at the corner of Lake and Wells streets along with his brother George, but eventually sold it and joined the city police force in 1860. By 1868 he had risen to the command of the West Side station and the following year he was appointed Chicago's chief of police by Mayor Roswell Mason. During the fall of 1869, he served as acting mayor and controller while those men were away on vacation. His three-year tenure as chief of police was an eventful one that included the Great Fire, but it came to an abrupt end in 1872 when he was fired by Mayor Joseph Medill. After his firing, Kennedy remained in Chicago but faded out of the limelight entirely. He never married and in 1880 accepted an appointment in the mailing division of the Chicago post office. He still held that position when he died in his room at McEwen's Hotel on September 20, 1900. The then police chief, Joseph Kipley, commented, "During the last few years I have heard little of Kennedy. His time on the police force was just before I joined the department, but I knew of him by reputation. I knew that he resided on the West Side, but he appeared to be of a reticent disposition and we seldom heard of him. There are few men connected with the Police department now who will remember Kennedy."[18]

James Malcom/Malcomb/Malcolm: Malcolm played for the Excelsiors from 1858 through 1860, serving as vice president in 1859 and president in 1860. In 1888 G. Charles Smith informed an inquirer that

> James Malcolm was president of the club in his day, and that all the old Excelsiors recall what a wonderful player Mr. Malcolm was. He continued to play with the club long after Mr. Smith and "Sim" Farwell retired, and was famous as a pitcher. There is not much in Mr. Malcolm's picture, which was taken long ago when Baby Anson was in short clothes, to indicate that he was at one time the star twirler of Chicago. That's what he was, though. On days when a big match was to be played Jim Malcolm himself alone would attract two-thirds of the crowd's admiration, for he was a born ball player, and in those days the game was played for fun — no sordid motives such as at present govern the game and make it a mere financial speculation.[19]

Despite being so well remembered, Malcolm remains a mystery. Various spellings of his surname have been cited, and the only census listing for him is in 1850 when he is listed as James Malcom, age 25, engineer, born in Illinois to Scottish-born parents. A James Malcomb died in Chicago during the 1893 World's Fair as the result of an accident. He was a visitor from California and his reported age was quite a bit off from that of the ballplayer. Since he was traveling alone, however, that age was likely an estimate and it's conceivable that the one-time ballplayer had returned to his former home for the great event.

W. C. Nichols: Nichols played in 1858 and 1859 but no strong candidate appears on the censuses.

N. F. Ousterhout: Ousterhout played in 1859 but nobody by that name has been found.

M. F. Prouty: Prouty played in 1858 and 1859. The name is so unusual that it's very likely he was Merrick Franklin Prouty, who was born in Spencer, Massachusetts, on March 27, 1829, and lived almost his entire life in the Boston area. If he was indeed the ballplayer, his stay in Chicago was a brief one, as he was back in Chicago by the time the 1860 census was taken and subsequently served for three years in Company C of the 25th Massachusetts Infantry.

G. Charles Smith: Smith played in 1858 and '59 and was treasurer in both 1859 and 1860, a position he again held in 1866. He was still in Chicago in 1888, when a newspaper account reported, "Many of the old members say G. Charles Smith was the father of the Excelsior base ball club. Mr. Smith shakes his head at this and modestly declares that the nine was already organized when he became a member. He gives a reflective tug to his gray mustache, runs his hand through the thick, silvery locks on his forehead, and becomes pleasantly reminiscent."[20] Stephen Freedman, in "The Baseball Fad in Chicago, 1865–1870," identifies Smith as being George C. Smith, a prominent banker. The basis of this identification, however, is not clear, and it seems unlikely; this banker was frequently mentioned in the newspapers, but was always referred to as George C. Smith, while the member of the Excelsiors was also referred to as G. Charles Smith. For that reason, I suspect that he was instead a man who died a few months after the above article was published and whose obituary described him as G. Charles Smith, age 61, and one of the oldest cutters in Chicago.[21]

George Throop: George Throop was born in Michigan on January 24, 1840. His father, Amos Throop, moved the family to Chicago and became a very successful businessman. Amos Throop twice ran for mayor and as city treasurer at the time of the Chicago Fire played a major role in the rebuilding of the city. He eventually moved to California and founded the university now known as Cal Tech (which was originally called Throop University). George Throop enlisted in the famous Chicago Mercantile Battery on August 6, 1862. After being promoted to sergeant and then lieutenant, he was mortally wounded and died on April 8, 1864, at the battle of Mansfield, Louisiana (where the battery was nearly wiped out). His wartime diary and letters are now at the Library of Congress.

A. Voorhies: Voorhies was the secretary of the club in 1860. The only candidate in that year's census was a lawyer named Abraham Voorhees who had been born in 1832 in New Jersey. This man died in Chicago on July 23, 1898.

Other Members: Charles Burgess, Byron (first name not given), G. C. Carpenter, Davids (first name not given), R. D. Hughes, A. Kennedy (presumably Alec, then a teenager, who became a regular after the war), G. H. Kennedy, W. Lowe (probably William Lowe, secretary after the war), Prime or Prince (first name not given), L. Quick, Ed Simonds, George Simons or Simonds (also a member of the Union Club).

Note: According to the *Atlanta Constitution* of March 14, 1909, the Pullmans were charter members of the Excelsiors. An article in *Sporting Life* on June 20, 1908, stated that George Pullman's brother Frank was a financial backer of the Excelsiors and also cited Henry Blair, William Blair, and William B. Whitehead as club members who went on to attain local prominence. The Pullman brothers were involved in the founding of Chicago's professional White Stockings in 1870 and one of them was the pitcher for a Chicago club called the Mutuals in 1867. But the Pullmans were never mentioned in contemporary accounts about the Excelsiors (and neither were the Blairs or Whitehead), so this appears to be a mistake.

See Excelsiors of Chicago Postwar for a list of sources.

Notes

1. *Chicago Tribune*, October 19, 1919.
2. *Ibid.*
3. *Chicago Press and Tribune*, July 8, 1858.
4. *Ibid.*, July 9, 1858; cited in Federal Writers Project, *Baseball in Old Chicago* (Chicago: A.C. McClurg, 1939).

5. "Baseball in Days Gone By," *Davenport Tribune*, August 24, 1888.
6. *Ibid.*
7. *Chicago Press and Tribune*, August 26, 1858.
8. *Chicago Press and Tribune*, September 14, 1858.
9. *Spirit of the Times*, exact date not provided but letter dated May 1, 1859, reprinted in Alfred H. Spink, *The National Game* (N.p.: National Game, 1910), 63.
10. *Spirit of the Times*, exact date not provided but letter dated May 1, 1859, reprinted in Spink, *The National Game*, 63. This letter did not mention the site of the grounds, but three accounts gave this location, while a fourth had them playing at the corner of West Lake and May.
11. *Chicago Press and Tribune*, June 3 and August 8, 1859.
12. *Ibid.*, June 13, 1859.
13. *Ibid.*, August 12, 1859.
14. *Ibid.*, August 24, 1860.
15. *Ibid.*, August 27, 1860.
16. *Ibid.*, July 25, 1860.
17. "Baseball in Days Gone By," *Davenport Tribune*, August 24, 1888.
18. *Chicago Tribune*, September 21, 1900.
19. "Baseball in Days Gone By," *Davenport Tribune*, August 24, 1888.
20. *Ibid.*
21. *Chicago Inter-Ocean*, September 22, 1888.

❖ *Excelsiors of Chicago, Postwar* (Peter Morris) ❖

Club History

As discussed in the first part, the Excelsior Base Ball Club of Chicago played several notable matches in the years before the Civil War. When the war began, however, baseball in Chicago shut down to a greater extent than was the case in any of the other cities where it had become established. "The early 60's were not a season for base ball," recalled one observer who had been involved in Chicago baseball before the war. "More serious business was to be attended to and the young man capable of making a good two-base hit was relieved of his bat and given a musket and sent south to face the rapid delivery of the Confederates."[1]

Accordingly, it appears that not a single match game of baseball was played in Chicago in either 1861 or 1862. Two new clubs did compete for the city championship in 1863, with the Garden City capturing the best-of-three series by beating the Osceolas on August 23, but these contests attracted little attention. No match games were played in 1864, but the year did see the only noteworthy baseball development that took place in wartime Chicago.

Soldiers in the 19th Illinois Infantry had formed a club known as the Turchin Base Ball Club, which was named in honor of its commander, Russian-born Brigadier General John B. Turchin. On March 18, 1864, the members met at their camp in Graysville, Georgia, and passed an intriguing resolution. One of the soldiers had picked up a piece of chestnut wood on the battlefield of Chickamauga that was ideally suited for a baseball bat. So the members of the Turchin Club sent it to the *Tribune* office with instructions to finish it and then award the bat to the city's best baseball club. In return for this generous gift, the members of the 19th Illinois asked only that they be allowed to challenge the winners upon their return from the war.[2]

Yet even this donation failed to revive baseball in Chicago. Indeed, the only recorded game played in the city in 1864 was an intrasquad game played in late June by members of the Turchin club, as the 19th Illinois had returned to Chicago in June in preparation for being mustered out.[3]

The Civil War ended in April 1865, but the assassination of Abraham Lincoln on April 14 again cast a pall over Chicago. The Excelsiors did reorganize that year, and were joined by their old rivals the Atlantics and by at least three new clubs, the Pacifics, the Pioneers, and the Ogdens. But most of the men who had been active ballplayers before the war had ended their playing days, and formal competition between the Excelsiors and the other local clubs was limited at best.

According to a Rockford baseball historian, the Excelsiors did compete in a September tournament held at the Winnebago County Fair Grounds. After a 37–8 victory over the Shaffers of Freeport, the Excelsiors faced the Empires of Freeport in the championship game. But in the third inning, with the Excelsiors clinging to a 16–15 lead, the Empires disputed a close call at third base. When the umpire yielded to their arguments and reversed his original decision, the Excelsiors walked off the field in disgust and refused to continue. As a result, the Empire Club was awarded the tournament trophy, "a sterling silver baseball of regulation size, and a miniature bat of rare wood, mounted with a heavy ferule of silver, appropriately inscribed."[4]

The local baseball scene began to perk up in December 1865, when a meeting was held in Chicago to form the Northwestern Association of Base-Ball Players. The Excelsiors were represented at that meeting by G. Charles Smith and A.J. Smith.

By the following spring, the Excelsiors were raring to go. As had been the case before the war, the players sported stylish uniforms, "consisting of white trousers extending to the ankle and a white shirt of English flannel."[5] The club members also spent a great deal of time considering the possibility of adopting a badge to complement their uniforms. A special committee was appointed to come up with a design, and the committee's report provoked a lengthy discussion among the membership, with the result that the matter was eventually returned to the committee.[6]

The Excelsiors now boasted a spanking new playing nine. A few of the prewar players continued to participate in intrasquad games, but the remainder retired from active play.

Their places were taken by promising young local players, with the apparent exception of pitcher C. J. McNally, who was described by one source as an arrival from the East.[7] With this young squad, the Excelsiors did not challenge any of the top Eastern clubs, nor did they pursue the Eastern course of charging admission to home matches.

As a knowledgeable observer explained, "No gate money was charged except to tournament games. Public liking for the game wasn't educated up to the standard where it was willing to let go of its money unless something particularly great in the way of base ball was promised. This could be had only when a half-dozen or more clubs got together and played a series of games, lasting five or six days. Such an occasion was called a tournament. These tournaments came off in country towns, almost invariably during fair time, and it was a great day for every one at the fair when in addition to the regular program, including horse-races and the like, a game of base ball was to be seen."[8]

One of the reasons for this policy was that the Excelsiors faced a dilemma that would plague Chicago ball clubs for most of the nineteenth century. Chicago was still a small city in area, but it was surrounded all on sides by prairies that were inviting for ballplaying. This made it easy for baseball clubs to find a location on the outskirts on which to play, but prohibitively expensive to set up grounds within the city limits. As a result, the Excelsiors never found a permanent base of operations. When they first reorganized after the war, they held their practices at their old grounds at West Lake and Ann streets. But the site was unsuitable for spectators, which meant that the Excelsiors had to make special arrangements for any important match played in Chicago.

Because of that daunting reality, the biggest events on the Excelsiors' schedule in 1866 were a tournament in Rockford at the end of June and another one in Bloomington in September.[9] The Excelsiors took home first place in both tournaments and ended the season with a perfect 6–0 record, marking them as a club that might soon threaten the dominance of baseball by the Eastern squads.

Despite the successes, the 1866 season also brought signs that trouble lay ahead. The Excelsiors had won a tightly fought game against the Detroit Base Ball Club at the Rockford tournament, and the Michigan club soon issued a challenge for a match to determine regional supremacy. But instead of a series that could have created a new level of excitement for baseball in both Chicago and Detroit, the challenge led to a nasty spat.

The Detroit Base Ball Club angrily accused the Excelsiors of being poor sports when the Chicago club would not agree to play a home-and-home series, even after the Michigan club offered to pay the Excelsiors' train fare and hotel bills.[10] They were not the only club to express irritation with the Excelsiors, as the up-and-coming Forest City Club of Rockford passed an angry resolution declaring that "we regard the reply of the Excelsior Base Ball Club, of Chicago, deferring the acceptance of our challenge till next spring, as a virtual refusal to play with us."[11]

For their part, the Excelsiors maintained that they were being asked "to exhibit themselves in the inclosed grounds of the Detroit club, to provide a fund from which the Detroit players can so generously 'pay their expenses,' leaving a handsome surplus."[12] They noted that they were amateurs who worked for a living and could not afford to accept every challenge issued to them. They added, "Such a course would involve them in an endless series of games with clubs of questionable ability."[13]

The wording of the last remark seems deliberately provocative and may help to explain why the Excelsiors were involved in so many disputes. But if the Excelsiors sometimes showed a lack of diplomacy, both they and the Detroit Base Ball Club were responding in reasonable fashion to the difficulties created by the game's awkward transition to professionalism. This dilemma applied with special force to ambitious clubs in cities like Detroit and Chicago, which is why each club was so adamant about its position.

In East Coast cities like New York City and Philadelphia, there were plenty of strong clubs that could create spirited local rivalries that spectators were willing to pay to watch. Trips to other cities were also viable and could lead to even more intense competition and still larger crowds. But states like Michigan and Illinois that boasted only one large city had no such options and this created a difficult dilemma for the best clubs in those cities.

The modest scale on which the Excelsiors operated was revealed by the club's financial statement, which showed that the club spent only $1,399 during the 1866 season. But with no opportunity to collect admission fees, the club's receipts were an equally modest $1,453. While the sources of this income were not spelled out, it is likely that membership fees made up most, if not all, of it.[14] Accordingly, it is understandable that club members were reluctant to take on additional expenses, since these would necessitate increased dues. Most likely, this also explains the controversy over the proposed badge.

So both the Excelsiors of Chicago and the Detroit Base Ball Club were trapped in a dilemma that neither would manage to solve. Detroit's representative club rented a nice enclosed ballpark to host matches, but — as was symbolized by the exchange with the Excelsiors — the club proved singularly unsuccessful in its efforts to attract strong rivals to pay visits. The Excelsiors took a very different course, initially choosing a home ground that was not suitable for charging admission and subsequently struggling to find a better site.

These challenges made both clubs slow to switch from amateur play to professionalism, and it caused them further difficulty when they finally hosted the top Eastern clubs. The hiring of professionals made Detroit's top club subject of many attacks and it had disbanded by 1869. But the Detroit Base

Ball Club was lucky by comparison with the Excelsiors of Chicago, which would be the recipient of far more abuse than any other baseball club of the era.

Such an outcome could not possibly have been foreseen by the Excelsiors after their two tournament triumphs in 1866. All was optimism in Chicago, and the mood was best symbolized in December when the Excelsiors used the occasion of the second meeting of the Northwestern Association of Base-Ball Players to unveil a new clubroom in the Phoenix Block of LaSalle Street. "The rooms are fitted up in a very tasteful manner," remarked a *Tribune* reporter, "and are 'set off' considerably by the trophies which the Excelsior boys have won within the last two years from clubs in various parts of the West. Among the silver-ware is a handsome set which was given to the Excelsiors by citizens of Rockford, last summer, for gracefulness in attitude while playing."

The centerpiece of the display, appropriately enough, was the bat "presented to the Club by the Nineteenth Illinois Infantry. It was taken from a tree in Chickamauga swamp, and sent to Chicago in the rough. Soon after its arrival it was put into proper shape, and a piece of silver, with engraving, showing from whom received and for whom intended, inserted in its side. We venture the assertion that the Excelsiors will never willingly part with that bat."[15]

As the start of the 1867 season approached, the Excelsiors were described as "in arms and eager for the fray.... Practising is still diligently pursued, and a marked improvement in batting and fielding is discernible.... Instead of resting supinely upon the laurels of last year, they manifest a thorough appreciation of the severity of future contests, and are preparing vigorously. They recognize the fact that they are the champions, as well as the duties and labors which the preeminence entails."[16]

They also busied themselves in making preparations. Some of the decisions were straightforward, such as the selection of a uniform consisting of a blue shirt, cricket flannel pants, a web belt, and a white hat with a blue star. Other choices, however, reflected the pressures resulting from the game's relentless shift toward professionalism. To show that they appreciated the honorary members who financed the first nine's activities, the club made plans to reward these members with engraved certificates.[17]

The Excelsiors also accepted a challenge from the Atlantic Club of Chicago, which remained a very strong rival and had narrowly lost to the Excelsiors in the championship game of the Bloomington tournament. The stellar match-up had the potential to attract a large crowd, but the lack of a suitable home field was beginning to haunt the Excelsiors. For the showdown with the Atlantics, they initially asked the Amateur Club for permission to play the match on their grounds, at Michigan Avenue and 30th Street.[18]

The need for a permanent solution led the city's clubs to put their heads together. On May 10 a meeting was held "to discuss the advisability of establishing common base ball grounds for general practice."[19] A committee was formed to investigate and it reported back that "the most available place was a piece of ground in the vicinity of State and Twenty-second streets, which could be secured."[20] But at a follow-up meeting, no consensus was reached on how to proceed.[21]

Meanwhile the selection of the 1867 "match nine" of the Excelsiors was left to a three-man committee of Alex Kennedy, Tom Foley, and a player named Oliver.[22] Their picks included several new men, including David Alston, who had played for the crosstown Atlantics in 1866. None of the new players, however, seem to have been imports from the East, which meant that, with the probable exception of McNally, the club was still made up of amateurs.[23]

The optimism surrounding the Excelsiors grew when they defeated the Atlantics and followed up with a victory over the next strongest in-state rival, the Forest Citys of Rockford. But even in victory, the Excelsiors were subject to press criticism, with a reporter from the *Times* attributing the win over the Forest Citys to "unaccountable circumstances." He maintained that the Excelsiors had never played worse, accusing them of "reprehensible slouchiness," "over-confidence," and being "lazy," and then enumerated many specific shortcomings—the outfielders were "lax in ... vigilance," the three bases "were not guarded with care," and the batters "showed a marked deterioration."[24] Meanwhile one Rockford paper accused the Excelsior players of using a "a system of jockeying" by "standing at the base, bat in hand, 'till three balls were called and then stalking up to the next base," with the result that darkness ended the game after seven innings. The accusation was denied by the Forest City players, but it was a sign of things to come.[25]

On July 4, 1867, the Excelsiors beat the Forest Citys for a second time, setting the stage for the biggest baseball event yet undertaken in the city. The powerful Nationals of Washington were scheduled to come to town in late July for a showdown that would finally give the Excelsiors the chance to flex their muscles against one of the top Eastern clubs.

Yet the matter of finding a suitable site remained unresolved. The match against the Atlantics and the home game against the Forest Citys had been played at the corner of Laflin and Jackson and spectators were counseled that the "Madison street cars run within two blocks of the ground."[26] The Forest City match was played in front of a crowd described as the "largest ever" in Chicago, with "accessions from Rockford, Belvidere, and other towns" helping to create a throng estimated at 5,000 people.[27] But newspaper coverage pointedly said little about the site and the fact that a new locale was chosen for the tournament implies that it was not ideal. In another telltale sign, the scores of both games were unusually high, suggesting that the field itself was ill suited to baseball.

Perhaps mindful that Chicago residents were willing to pay to watch baseball only in the tournament format, a "tournament" was announced for the visit of the Nationals. In fact, it was a tournament in name only: over a five-day period, the visitors would first play the Forest City Club, then the Excelsiors, and finally the Atlantics. Other matches were scheduled for the off days, including one for the junior championship of the state. In addition, a meeting was to be held to form an association of the state's baseball clubs.

But where to play the tournament? The initial plan was to use Brighton Driving Park but then the organizers caught a break. Work had begun in the spring on Dexter Park, a new racetrack close to the stockyards that was designed to give Chicago "the model park of the west, equaled by few, and unexcelled."[28] Construction of the new park was completed just in time to switch sites and so Chicagoans were advised that "the means of reaching the grounds whereon the tournament is to take place, Dexter park, are numerous."[29]

Even before the arrival of the Nationals there were signs of overconfidence in Chicago. The Excelsiors' second win over the Forest Citys of Rockford led the *Chicago Times* to editorialize that the triumphs of the Excelsiors "refute the popular idea that city life weakens men in place of strengthening them." The ability of Chicago's best club to "so persistently vanquish Rockford, Detroit and Milwaukee," concluded the editorial, demonstrated that Chicago was "at once a great city, and yet a town of the most remarkable healthfulness."[30]

The overconfidence grew when the opening match of the tournament produced a stunning upset. On a rainy day, the young Rockford club and teenage pitcher Albert Goodwill Spalding pulled out a 29–23 victory that amazed the baseball world. To many, the outcome of the next day's game was now a foregone conclusion — with the Excelsiors having recently beaten the Forest Citys and the Forest Citys having knocked off the Nationals, it seemed only logical to assume that the Excelsiors would easily handle the visitors from the East and establish themselves as one of the best clubs in the country. As one reporter put it, "With such wonderful ease have [the Nationals] vanquished all competitors that their invincibility was beginning to be regarded as a fixed fact. The result of the game yesterday, however, disproves the latter theory, and the belief now obtains that the Nationals have 'no license' to beat any of our first-class western clubs."[31]

Those expectations could not have been more wrong. According to an account written in 1874,

> The crowd of the first day was small compared to that which assembled to witness the second discomfiture of the "Nationals." Fully 15,000 people were on the grounds. They came to see the victory. They sat around and poked fun at those materials, and offered large odds against them, and cheered their own boys on to triumph, and swore with emphasis that Chicago could not be beaten, even in the little matter of base-ball. The game commenced, and the crowd soon stopped singing and commenced to whistle; their open countenances grew cadaverous, and they looked bewildered as they contemplated the progress of events. They had seen enough before the game was over, and moved for the gates. Chicago had been betrayed; her confidence had been misplaced; her proud escutcheon had been trailed in the mire by the men she thought invincible. In fact, the Excelsiors were beaten by a score of 49 to 4, and the sport-loving community pocketed their losses and reserved their crows for some future occasion. The Excelsiors were a by-word and a reproach, and they proceeded to disintegrate as rapidly as possible. They couldn't be hired for money to play the veriest "muffers" in the city after that Waterloo.[32]

Needless to say, this account includes some exaggeration and by no means did the Excelsiors cease to play baseball after this match. Yet it is difficult to overstate the extent to which this single game served to transform Chicago's top club from a source of pride into the object of scorn and ridicule.

The initial response to the trouncing of the Excelsiors was to assume that a fix had occurred. Baseball was still a novelty to Americans, and most of them saw no reason why a superior club should not always be able to beat a slightly lesser rival (just as one might expect a faster runner to always beat a slower one every time they raced). This viewpoint was most prominently voiced by the many Chicagoans who had bet on the Excelsiors, but it also found official expression in the *Chicago Tribune*. In an editorial entitled "Base Ball As A Confidence Game," the *Tribune* accused the Nationals of deliberately losing the game to Rockford "to induce the sporting men of Chicago to venture their money. They did so and the Nationals have pocketed it. It is estimated that $20,000 changed hands, that that amount of money has been withdrawn from circulation here, and will go East, and we shall not draw against it immediately."[33]

The editorial prompted Frank Jones, the president of the Nationals, to pay a visit to the *Tribune,* and a retraction was published the following day.[34] But the magnitude of the Excelsiors' defeat remained the talk of the town.

A number of theories emerged. The Excelsiors themselves advanced the most likely explanation, pointing out that the Nationals were tired from a schedule of nonstop travel and matches when they lost to the Rockford club. In addition, they noted that the rain and the treacherous playing conditions during that game negated the superior skill of the Nationals.[35]

Others, however, were intent on pointing the finger at the Excelsiors. One popular theory was that the players became overconfident: "The modest people of Chicago lauded them to the skies, and with petting spoiled them.... The boys began to think they were invincible, and they daily grew in pride and self-complacency."[36] One writer even claimed the Excelsior players had "felt it incumbent on them to do a little entertaining" of their guests on the evening before the game, with the result that "some of the boys weren't as steady as they ought to have been the day of the game."[37]

The 49–4 score reminded many of a similar score recorded the year before. At the Rockford tournament, an overmatched country club from Pecatonica, Illinois, had been trounced 49–1 by the Detroit Base Ball Club and had received a horn inscribed with the word "practice." When the Pecatonica nine learned of the Excelsiors' defeat, they held a meeting and concluded that "the Excelsiors have fairly taken from us our hard-earned laurels; therefore, be it *Resolved*, That the Secretary be instructed to send the horn to the Excelsior Club."[38]

The Pecatonica club was not the only one that took advantage of the opportunity to remind the Excelsiors that they were no longer invincible. A nine made of up newspapermen issued a sarcastic challenge to the club, "to play a game of base ball during the present month, with a view of showing to the world that the Excelsiors are not the worst players in the State."[39] A brand-new club in Newton, Iowa, also joked about issuing a challenge.[40] Before long, it was reported that many "muffin" clubs had been formed with the aim "of resting from the Excelsiors their victorious laurels.... But it was all in vain.... The silver-mounted horn still remains with the Excelsiors."[41]

In public the Excelsiors seem to have taken the gibes in good humor, but their true feelings can readily be imagined. The game against the Nationals had itself been humiliating, with one later account maintaining, "It was great fun for the visitors and spectators. The latter howled and roard [sic] and screamed and jeered and addressed the Excelsiors in inimical terms till they felt like committing hari-kari. When the game was over the Chicago players stole home through the back streets, and they didn't talk base ball again for many a day."[42] The ongoing barbs only made the sting worse.

The Excelsiors now began to move toward professionalism, though they started off by providing players with job offers rather than salaries. John Zeller, a longtime starter for the Mutuals of New York, was lured to Chicago in the aftermath of the game against the Nationals and "set up in the saloon business by the club, on Randolph street, near La Salle."[43] A player named Keenan from Bloomington was added to the first nine and he too reportedly received some form of remuneration.[44]

The eight weeks after the Waterloo defeat saw a "general dullness prevailing" in the Chicago baseball scene.[45] The Excelsiors played only twice, trouncing the overmatched Rustics of Danby by the score of 124–2 and beating a scrub nine 120–4. But the club was not entirely inactive, as it did finally adopt the controversial badge, which featured "a blue ground ... divided into four divisions by two intersecting lines, with emblems of base ball, viz: balls, a cap and shoes, one in each quarter; while in each corner of the square there will be a base."[46]

By mid–September the club's revamped lineup was "in excellent practice" and anxious to test its strength at a tournament in Decatur.[47] Unfortunately, as so often happened, the Excelsior Club "did not exert itself at all" in winning the tournament. With Zeller and Keenan now in the lineup, the Excelsiors routed the Egyptians of Centralia, 79–9 in five innings, and then beat a picked nine of the best players, 44–6 in six innings.[48]

The Excelsiors finally got a stiff test on September 27 when the Bloomington (Illinois) Club came to town for a match at Dexter Park. The Bloomingtons had knocked off the Forest Cities of Rockford and, according to the *Chicago Times*, they brought with them "a splendid reputation" and "a belief in their own superiority." For once, the contest lived up to the advanced billing as the Excelsiors rallied from behind in the sixth inning to pull out an exciting victory.[49]

The stage was now set for the long-awaited showdown against the Detroit Base Ball Club, but before that series could begin the Excelsiors made yet another addition to the roster. As one reporter put it, Rockford's young star pitcher, A.G. Spalding, was "seduced" into joining the Excelsiors.[50] As Spalding himself told it, he was given a $40-a-week position as a bill clerk at a Chicago wholesale grocery "with the understanding that I was to pitch for the Excelsiors during the Base Ball season." He was also specifically warned not to mention his salary to his fellow employees, since, as he soon discovered, more experienced clerks were making only $10 per week.[51]

The first game of the series with Detroit took place in Chicago on October 5 and did not live up to the advance billing. Spalding did not play, and Keenan instead pitched the Excelsiors to a surprisingly easy 49–20 victory. A reporter from the *Detroit Post* blamed umpire Ambrose Lynch for allowing Keenan to deliver endless wild pitches, while warning Detroit's pitcher not to lift his forward foot after delivering the ball. The reporter also grumbled that there were hardly any women and only one policeman in attendance, with the result that the spectators engaged in "betting, hissing the umpire, getting in the way of Detroit players, and oaths and loud talk." The Detroit players, however, maintained that they had been fairly beaten.[52]

The second game of the series took place in Detroit on October 19 and was a different story. With Spalding and Keenan sharing the pitching duties for the Excelsiors, the game was tightly fought throughout and the hometown side was clinging to a three-run lead when the visitors began their final at-bats. Then, with the fans who had made the trip from Chicago enthusiastically blowing on the famed Pecatonica horn, the Excelsiors mounted a furious comeback. Clutch hitting, along with "wild throws and foolish plays" by the Detroit fielders, enabled the visitors to bat around a couple of times and cruise to a 36–24 win.[53]

Upon their return to Chicago, the Excelsiors held a meeting and passed a resolution thanking those who had made the trip an enjoyable one, including the members of the Detroit Base Ball Club and the proprietors of the Russell House, where they had lodged. They expressed especial gratitude to H. C. Wentworth of the Michigan Central Railroad for "his kindness in placing at their disposal, for the trip, the magnificent sleeping car 'Kalamazoo,' and in other ways enhancing the pleasure of the otherwise tedious journey."[54] The resolution is an important reminder that, while the Excelsiors became embroiled in more than their share of disputes, the club also had many pleasant interchanges that received less publicity.

In a summary of the season, a reporter called the Excelsiors' 1867 campaign one "of almost unvarying success. Excepting the defeat by the National club of Washington, they have 'scooped' every club with which they have competed." He also commended the club for making "invaluable accessions to their nine. By judicious management, their in-field and out-field has been strengthened.... Next season the Excelsior nine and subs will compare in ability to any in the country."[55]

Although it was true that the Excelsiors had lost only one game since the end of the war, that defeat had been decisive and embarrassing. In addition, baseball was moving rapidly toward professionalism and it was becoming all but impossible for truly amateur clubs to compete. The result was that that winter was another pivotal and tumultuous one for the Excelsiors.

With little alternative, the Excelsiors continued to bring in new players. The grocery that had employed Spalding failed and he and Keenan both moved on, being replaced by a new pitcher from Philadelphia named Harry Lex. Another new player named James Hoyt was also added. Hoyt ended up playing little and his identity remains mysterious, but there was a Philadelphia player by that name so he likely accompanied Lex to Chicago. Zeller and McNally were also retained, giving the Excelsiors a distinctly East Coast look.

What is notable is that Chicago's marquee club does not appear to have had any more professional players than it did at the end of the 1867 season. But the distinctively East Coast flavor of the club changed how it was perceived. As a later article put it, "The Excelsior Ball Club of Chicago, by hiring Lex and one or two other outside players, made themselves virtually a professional organization — or, as we should say now-a-days, a 'semi-professional club.'"[56]

Mention of this new reality was tactfully avoided by the local press in the lead-up to the 1868 season, but there can be no doubt that the residents of Chicago were well aware of the changing composition of the Excelsiors. By bringing in these imports and creating a lineup that was a mix of Eastern professionals and Chicago amateurs, the ingredients for public disfavor and internal dissension were in place. If the new nine could emerge as a national power, then all was likely to be forgiven, but losing would now be unacceptable.

Another new element in the mix for 1868 was that the Excelsiors finally had the use of a home field that was well suited to hosting visiting clubs and large crowds. The site in question was the commons at State and Twenty-Second that had nearly been acquired the preceding spring. As had been contemplated at that time, several Chicago baseball clubs had joined together to lease the site. The Atlantics were not party to the deal, having chosen instead to use Ogden Park on the North Side, but the Enterprise Club had agreed to use the grounds on Tuesdays and Fridays and it was expected that the Eurekas would also rent the park on specified days.[57]

The work of turning the "ample grounds" into a suitable facility commenced on May 11, and a crew set to work building "a spacious amphitheatre" for spectators, along with such amenities as "suitable cloak-rooms, refreshment rooms, and stables." Surrounding the entire field was an eight-foot fence that would ensure that every spectator paid to enter.[58] When construction was completed, the new park was pronounced "probably the finest ball grounds in the country, possessing every facility for observation and comfort."[59]

To capitalize on their new site, the Excelsiors had finally put together an ambitious schedule. Unfortunately, it soon became evident that the players were not up to the challenge, with the result that the early part of the 1868 season was a disaster. After opening with a win over the lightly regarded Eurekas of Chicago, the Excelsiors lost on June 12 to the Forest Citys of Rockford, who now again included Spalding. It was an ominous sign that, despite the Eastern imports, the Excelsiors were no longer even the top club in Illinois. The second-guessing began immediately, with the *Times* declaring that the Excelsiors made a "great mistake when they allowed Spalding to return to Rockford."[60]

The following week saw the Excelsiors get trounced by the Athletics of Philadelphia and the Atlantics of Brooklyn. The press's comments about the losses were tactful, but at least one fan was blunt. In a letter to the *Times*, he suggested that it would have made more sense for the Athletics to have played the Atlantics, explaining, "I can't see that it is much credit to these clubs to come out here to defeat some of our green country clubs." He concluded by suggesting that the Excelsiors should rename themselves the "Inferiors."[61]

Matters got worse when the Excelsiors hosted their rivals from Rockford on Independence Day. The game was played in front of a crowd estimated at 2,500 and "considerable money quietly changed hands" on the result. Those who had wagered on the Excelsiors went home unhappy when the home side jumped out to a 12–2 lead after four innings and then collapsed, losing 36–27. "The effect of the defeat upon the Excelsiors is undeterminable," wrote the baseball reporter of the *Times*, "but it probably will inspire them to more thorough practice."[62]

The Excelsiors had two weeks to prepare for the next visitors, the Buckeyes of Cincinnati, and they took advantage. By game day, the *Times* reported that the Excelsiors "have been practicing with commendable assiduity, rising before sunrise, and playing in the cool of the morning. The club feels keenly its recent defeats; members attribute their want of success to want of practice; and manfully resolved that, if defeat results in future contests, it will not be occasioned by lack of practice."[63] The Buckeyes had just squeaked out a one-run win over the Detroit Base Ball Club, so the Excelsiors were confident of finally posting a victory. Instead things hit rock bottom for the Excelsiors as the Buckeyes won by the lopsided score of 43–22.

A club that had lost only one match in the first three seasons after the war had taken on an Eastern face and promptly lost five games in rapid succession. Outrage predictably followed, with a *Tribune* reporter writing,

> The Excelsiors must do one of two things. They must give up playing entirely, and disorganize, carrying with them the prospects of base ball in this section, or they must practice. They cannot hope to make players at a moments [sic] notice. Base ball requires practice, if any game does, and enough of it. If they hope to retrieve their fortunes and again hold the first place among Western clubs, they must root out from among themselves the men who have rested upon them like so many incubi, who have clogged their progress and made them weak at the bat and in the field, and replace them by others who are willing to practice, and who are devoid of the conceit that good fortune must attend them. It is better to have poor players who have the will to practice, than to rely upon those who rest upon laurels gained in the past. There are men among the Excelsior nine who have no right to be there, and until this truth is recognized, it will be idle for the club to expect to win.[64]

The *Times* chipped in, referring to the club as "the celebrated muffin nine, known as the Excelsior club of this city."[65]

The extent of the Excelsiors' woes was revealed at a meeting held at the club's LaSalle Street rooms the following week to discuss "ways and means to redeem the reputation of the club."[66] Club president W.F. Wentworth chaired the meeting and listened to one discouraging report after another. Two longtime members of the first nine, C.J. McNally and Alec Kennedy, had resigned, as had the mysterious James Hoyt. With several gaping holes in the lineup, the Committee on Nines was instructed to hold a practice game and fill with members of the second nine. There was even serious discussion of consolidating with the Eurekas.

The club's financial picture mirrored the gloomy mood. A Mr. Treadway, who was a member of the Committee on Subscriptions, "said he had made several attempts to collect funds, but met with no success. He was sure some small sums could be obtained from the members of the Board of Trade, but they felt somewhat diffident at present about contributing."

Only B.R. Chambers expressed a glimmer of optimism, maintaining, "The Excelsior club had as good material in it as any other, and because the club had sustained two or three defeats was no reason that the members should become disheartened. The Rockford Club had one player who received a salary of $250 a year. That club had no better record than the Excelsiors. They had lost more balls than the Excelsiors had won. The Detroit Club was in about the same situation." He believed that the problem was that the club was forced to play Foley at catcher instead of his natural position, and that if a good catcher were secured and Foley could again play third base, the club would improve dramatically.

Chambers also thought the club's finances were not in all that bad shape. While he admitted that he had been too busy with business to try to collect any money, he believed that a subscription drive could raise the needed funds. At last, it was agreed to replenish the club's treasury by means of an "assessment" of $5 for honorary members and $3 for active members.[67]

The fund-raising initiative did collect enough money to keep the club going, and a rout of the Rough and Readys of South Bend followed. But the Excelsiors' losing ways resumed on August 12 when they met that year's eventual champions, the Unions of Morrisania. The defeat was by a respectable 31–21 score, but the Excelsiors received more bad news when John Zeller fractured his knee so severely while rounding the bases that there were concerns that he would be crippled for life.[68]

With the losses mounting and their contingent of Eastern imports now reduced to just Lex, the Excelsiors brought in a new platoon of New York professionals — Fred Treacy, Joe Simmons, and the much-needed catcher, Bill Lennon from Brooklyn. The club also began making optimistic plans for its first-ever real tour, which would see the club play games in Detroit, Buffalo, Cleveland, and Cincinnati.[69]

The club warmed up for the tour with easy wins over two local rivals, the Enterprise and the Garden City. Next up was a home game against the Detroit Base Ball Club that saw the Excelsiors end up on the short end of a 15–12 score in front of a "very meagre" crowd. It marked the first loss to the rivals from Michigan and several explanations were offered. Some attributed the low score to the baseball — "an imitation 'Ross,' [which] was soft and flabby." Others pointed to the twist that Detroit pitcher S. C. Lane gave to his offerings, which caused the Excelsiors to hit the ball foul.[70] But all such analysis seemed unimportant when it was learned that James Alston, the brother of Excelsior outfielder David Alston, had fallen off a streetcar on his way home from the contest and been fatally injured.

The Excelsiors' tour proved a mixed bag. Impressive wins over the Niagaras of Buffalo and the Forest Citys of Cleveland prompted a rare note of commendation in the press. "The national game is in great favor in Chicago at present," crowed a *Tribune* reporter. "The present season the play has been nearly up to its old mark, and within a few days it has been exceeded."[71] Lennon's play behind the plate was especially good and he was declared "the best catcher in the West."[72]

But other stops were less successful. In Detroit the Excelsiors jumped to a 17–3 lead after two innings, only to see the home team come back and tie the score at 31 apiece. When the game was called due to darkness in the ninth inning and declared a draw, the Excelsiors angrily protested. According to the Detroit papers, the Chicago players neglected the "customary courtesies" of cheering for their opponents and the umpires, declaring "It ain't our style."[73] A Chicago reporter responded with allegations that the Detroit spectators greeted the Excelsiors "with groans, hisses, catcalls, and every indignity that could be offered."[74]

The next stop was Cincinnati, where the Excelsiors were beaten by the embarrassing score of 22–4. Four runs was an extraordinarily low score for 1868, but of the Excelsior batters only "Woody" Stearns was able to hit the tantalizingly slow deliveries of Harry Wright with any effect.[75] The Excelsiors received the chilliest of welcomes on their return to Chicago — the *Times* wrote that "the feeling against this club, for allowing themselves to suffer such a 'Waterloo defeat' at the hands of the Cincinnati club, was expressed very strongly on their return from their 'starring' tour."[76]

The Excelsiors next made a trip to St. Louis, lured by a $500 purse offered by the St. Louis Agricultural Society.[77] They posted lopsided wins against three of that city's best clubs, but none of these clubs were national powers and the results received little attention in Chicago. On their way back to Chicago, the Excelsiors stopped in Bloomington for a return match with that city's strong club, but in the fourth inning captain Tom Foley pulled the Excelsiors off the field to protest a call by the umpire and the game ended at that point.[78]

Adding to the indignity, upon their return home, the Excelsiors found that the "high board-fence" around their new grounds had been "spirited away by some person or persons unknown."[79] The Excelsiors soon bowed to the inevitable and disbanded.

With all eyes on the presidential election, little attention was paid to the demise of the club that had received so much coverage. The *Tribune* did, however, offer this obituary:

> The Excelsior Base Ball Club is no more, it having dissolved its organization. Several reasons for the event are assigned, among them the insolvency of the club, which fell badly in arrears for its current expenses; and also the fact that several of the star players have left the city. It is probable, however, that the remaining members of the first nine will constitute the nucleus for a stronger organization to be formed next spring, although, perhaps, under a different club name. This will undoubtedly be done, since it is imperative that Chicago should boast of a base ball club which can not only beat anything in the West, but which shall be able to vindicate Chicago's importance as the first city on the continent, by bidding defiance to any and all clubs in America. We look to see such an organization perfected next year.[80]

That offseason the National Association of Base Ball Players bowed to the inevitable by acknowledging professionalism. Many cities took advantage of the new opportunity by rushing to sign up players, but no such activity occurred in Chicago. As the season began, a New York reporter commented, "The Excelsiors may be doing something to bring up the club to first-class playing merit; but, if so, they are doing their work very quietly."[81]

But the Excelsiors were in fact dead, and the Chicago baseball scene in 1869 was restricted to amateur play that received little attention. The Atlantic Club also disbanded and was unsympathetically eulogized as "a gentlemanly but awkward and somewhat indolent group of ball tossers."[82] The Garden City Club came to be regarded as the city's best ballclub, but was considered so weak that after it had been thrashed by the Forest Citys of Rockford, a Rockford reporter complained about the subpar performance of the Forest Citys.[83]

In 1870 Chicago got its first professional club and at least one Excelsior player, Fred Erby, became prominently involved in the city's professional clubs. Several of the outside imports also became major figures in professional baseball, while a few Excelsior officers became involved in operating the White Stockings. But almost all of the young Chicago men who had built the Excelsior Club turned their back on baseball and appear to have remained bitter about the treatment they had received from the public and press.

Even reunion games, which became common in other cities, were rarely staged in Chicago. Reminiscences about the Excelsiors were occasionally published. "There was more fun in the games then than there is now," wrote one old-timer in 1888. "The old Excelsiors say so."[84]

But nostalgic references to the Excelsiors were rare, and subsequent mentions of the club usually dwelt upon the humiliating loss to the Nationals or other failures. An 1869 summary maintained that the "lamented Excelsior" club "grew as suddenly into notoriety as a mushroom into existence. They beat everything around Chicago — the candymakers' clubs, the dry goods clerks' clubs, the newsboys' clubs, and the bootblacks' clubs. And then they grew ambitious. Chicago grew ambitious with them. The Excelsiors became venturous; Chicago became venturous also. And then the celebrated Nationals, of Washington, were played with...."[85]

The 1874 article cited earlier was just as blunt. After stating that the Excelsiors became "a by-word and a reproach" after the loss to the Nationals, it added that the club members "abandoned the sports of the diamond and contracted matrimonial alliances, and went into mercantile pursuits. Most of them are still doing business in the city, but they take no interest in base ball; in fact they say they never did admire the game."[86]

Club Members

The unusual history of the Excelsiors, which saw the club receive relentless coverage in the press but most of the members eventually distance themselves from the game, makes it a challenge to re-create their identities. An additional problem is the number of different club members whose surname was Stearns. The following is my best effort.

David Gordon Alston: David Alston was born on September 24, 1846, in Chicago. Like many of the prewar club members, his ancestry was Scottish and both of his parents had been born in the old country. His father became a wealthy

Chicago businessman who owned an oil and paint store, in which David worked as a clerk. After playing for the crosstown Atlantics in 1866, David Alston became one of the Excelsiors' regular outfielders in 1867. But he appears to have been one of the locals who lost playing time to imports in 1868, as he did not play regularly for the Excelsiors. Tragedy struck his family that year when his brother James was fatally injured on the way home from the club's September 12 game. Alston did serve as umpire in a few National Association games in the 1870s, but he is not known to have otherwise remained involved in baseball. He later worked as a salesman and was a widower when he died in Chicago on April 20, 1893.

Benson Beriah Banker: Ben Banker was born in Peasleeville, New York, on March 19, 1843, and the family moved to Boston during the 1850s. In 1864 he served a three-month stint in the Union Army. After the war, the whole family relocated to Chicago and Banker became one of the Excelsiors' regulars in 1867, only to lose his spot on the first nine in 1868. He stayed in Chicago for a few years, working as a schoolteacher, but by 1873 he had returned to Boston, where he married and lived for the rest of his life, raising five children and working as a clerk and as an accountant. He died on February 28, 1913.

Blakeslee: This man played for the Excelsiors for most of the 1867 season, but he made so little an impression that the 1888 article that provided details on almost all of the other regulars said of him only, "Blakesly, whose first name is forgotten, was pitcher."[87]

Stephen B. Budd: Stephen Budd was one of the few players to see regular action for the Excelsiors in both 1866 and 1867, also serving as a club director in 1866. When the Excelsiors played in the 1866 Rockford tournament, the *Chicago Times* listed a "J. W. Budd" as being one of their starters, but this was almost certainly a mistake. Stephen Budd was born in Chatham, New Jersey, in 1835 and moved to Chicago around 1859. By 1870 he had a wife and son and was working as a commercial merchant. His death in Chicago on August 21, 1886, came while his days with the Excelsiors were still well enough remembered for his passing to warrant a mention in *Sporting Life*.

Frederick C. Calloway: The Excelsiors had more than their share of umpires, including Calloway, who was described as "the first umpire that was ever brought from the East. Mr. Calloway, the name of the gentleman, came from Newark, N.J., and from long practice dodging the mosquitoes of his native swamp land was able to see all over the diamond at once, and thus made a most excellent umpire. There is something blithe-like and debonair about Mr. Calloway. Those lissome whiskers, that jaunty straw hat, bespeak the New Jersey sport, and Mr. Calloway, there is every reason to believe, was on easy terms with himself. He liked Chicago after a fashion and as a mark of his good favor had his picture taken here."[88] Calloway was born in New Jersey around 1842 and he returned to Newark after the Excelsiors disbanded.

Beverly R. Chambers: B. R. Chambers was the only club member to express optimism at the club's meeting in late July of 1867. Chambers was born in Ithaca, New York, and came to Chicago in 1858. He worked as a clerk and a bookkeeper, then joined his father's jewelry business. Chambers, who was described as a "popular society and club man," never married. In 1879, he contracted Bright's disease and he never recovered his health, dying on April 9, 1886, ten days after his 40th birthday.

Frederick Wise Erby: Fred Erby was not a member of the first nine but he was very active in the club's doings and was one of the few Excelsior members who took an active role in the professional clubs that succeeded them. Born on April 9, 1845, in Pennsylvania to German-born parents, he worked in a hat store, at city hall and as a restaurant proprietor while living in Chicago. He also did some umpiring in the National Association. After his wife died, he moved to Seattle and again worked as a restaurant manager. Erby died in Seattle on September 5, 1918.

Thomas J. Foley: Tom Foley, who was born in Chicago around 1847, was the only homegrown member of the Excelsiors to play professional baseball after the club's demise, being a regular for the White Stockings in both 1870 and 1871. (He is not to be confused with the Tom Foley who acted as the effective manager of the White Stockings.) His playing days ended after the Chicago Fire, though he did umpire a few National Association games. He became a mail carrier on May 6, 1874, and died in La Grange, Illinois, on January 4, 1896.

John J. Gillespie: Gillespie was a prominent prewar member who served as club president in 1866 and was still on the second nine as of 1867. His life is described in the prewar section.

Alphonso Goodrich: Goodrich was a member of the Excelsiors' first nine in 1866 and won the base-running prize, a silver-mounted belt, at the Bloomington tournament.[89] He was also a club director that year and served as vice president in 1868, but he was identified only as "A. Goodrich," leaving some doubt about his identity. He had good reason to be reticent, as an 1872 article reported:

> For umpire, the two nines agreed upon Mr. Goodrich, the fearful and wonderful catcher of the Amateurs of 1870. Goodrich was always distinguished as the worst ball-player in Chicago, but it was not until yesterday afternoon that he acquired the distinction of being positively the poorest umpire on record. He evidently entertained a lofty scorn for all rules relating to the calling of balls and strikes, while his ideas as to fair and foul balls, and the proper time of expressing his views with reference thereto, are entirely original, to say the least. Most umpires would, on the spur of the moment and under the excitement of the occasion, sing out "foul" as soon as the hit was made. So would Goodrich, unless there was a man on first base, in which case he retains his presence of mind to a remarkable degree. His eminently judicial mind deplores a hasty utterance, and the result is that the man on first is down to second by the time that

Goodrich has concluded the hit to be foul, and then the rash runner receives his punishment by being easily put out. Goodrich's umpiring is of a kind calculated to make the game more interesting on account of the delightful uncertainty as to his rulings, which also tend to develop forcible and explosive expressions on the part of players and spectators.[90]

The 1888 article, however, identified Goodrich as a lawyer, leaving no doubt that he was Alphonso Goodrich, a Chicago divorce lawyer who acquired considerable notoriety during the 1870s. The scandal-mongering *Chicago Times* dubbed Goodrich the "divorce shyster" and ran a long, successful crusade to have him disbarred.[91] Even after being disbarred, Goodrich continued to find himself in hot water, being accused among other things of involvement in several fraudulent schemes and of continuing to practice law after his disbarment.[92] Goodrich was born in Logansport, Indiana, on January 28, 1843, and died in Chicago on January 9, 1915.

James Henry Haynie: Haynie was yet another club umpire and, according to the *Detroit Post* of August 27, 1867, he was also the baseball reporter for the *Chicago Republican*. Haynie was born in Winchester, Illinois, on July 19, 1841, and became a very well-known reporter. He served in Company D of the 19th Illinois Infantry during the Civil War and was taken prisoner. After the war he became a journalist, while also playing for the second nine of the Excelsiors. After the 1870 season, he was elected recording secretary of the National Association of Base Ball Players just as it broke into separate professional and amateur organizations. By 1871 he was working as a sports reporter for the *Chicago Tribune*. After a domestic scandal, he chose to go abroad to Paris, spending many years as a foreign correspondent for the *New York Times* and other newspapers. He returned to the United States in 1895 and settled in Newton Centre, Massachusetts, where he wrote a couple of notable books—*The Captains and the Kings* (1904), about his experiences as a foreign correspondent, and *The Nineteenth Illinois: A Memoir of a Regiment of Volunteer Infantry Famous in the Civil War of Fifty Years Ago for Its Drill, Bravery, and Distinguished Services* (1912). He died on May 14, 1912, in Newton Centre.

James Hoyt: The mysterious Hoyt appears to have been from Philadelphia, as there was a player from that city by that name and he arrived with Lex. He remained in Chicago after quitting the Excelsiors and joined another local club. An 1877 article described him only as being out of baseball.

Keenan: Keenan was reportedly from Bloomington but nothing more is known about him.

Alexander D. Kennedy: Kennedy was secretary and captain of the Excelsiors in 1866. He was born in Illinois in 1842 to Scottish-born parents, and appears to have been a cousin of early club member W.W. Kennedy. He became a fire insurance agent and was still alive in 1895.

Billy Lennon: Lennon was the catcher the Excelsiors desperately needed when he arrived in late 1868. Born in Brooklyn around 1848, he had previously played for the Excelsiors of Brooklyn. He and Treacy were members of the Mohawks of New York when both joined the Excelsiors. Lennon later played in Philadelphia, where he and teammate Ed Mincher married sisters. He played a few more years of professional baseball, including stints with two major-league clubs, then returned to Baltimore, where he worked as a saloon keeper and for his father-in-law. He died on August 19, 1910, in Philadelphia.

Harry Lex: Harry Lex, the professional pitcher imported for the 1868 season, is believed to have been from Philadelphia. The most likely candidate is a Harry J. Lex who was born in Philadelphia on March 9, 1848, worked as a stockbroker, and died at his Philadelphia home on September 6, 1907.

William Lowe: Lowe was the club secretary.

C. J. McNally: McNally is another mysterious player who was described as an Eastern import by one source. He was listed as both C. J. McNally and C. McNally, but in 1888 an old-timer referred to him as John McNally. He pitched the decisive game of the 1866 Rockford tournament, prompting a Detroit reporter to complain: "McNally, the Chicago pitcher, did not pitch his balls but bowled instead. That the Detroit boys did not ask judgment and obtain the ruling out of this pitching, can only be explained on the supposition mentioned that they thought themselves able to beat their opponents against all odds."[93]

John Oberlander: Oberlander was born in New York City on May 17, 1846. By 1860 the family was living in Chicago, where his father worked as a shoemaker. John enlisted in the 134th Illinois Infantry in 1864, serving six months. He moved to New Orleans to play ball in 1870 and remained there for many years, operating a turf club and a billiards parlor at the St. Charles Hotel. He and his wife returned to Chicago in the 1890s and eventually retired to Norwalk, Ohio, where he died on October 11, 1923.

Guss R. Owen: Owen was the club secretary in 1866.

Joe Simmons: Simmons was one of the New Yorkers who joined the Excelsiors toward the end of the 1868 season. He was born Joseph Chabriel on June 13, 1845, in New York City, but used the name Simmons for baseball. He had previously played for the Gotham and Empire clubs, and went on to a long professional career as a player and manager. He died in Jersey City on July 24, 1901.

G. Charles Smith: The club's treasurer in 1866, he is described in the section on the prewar Excelsiors.

Albert Goodwill Spalding: Spalding played only one game for the Excelsiors but went on to a Hall of Fame career as a player, manager, executive, and sporting-goods magnate. See the Forest City Club of Rockford for a summary of his life.

George Stearns: There were at least four men with the surname of Stearns who were actively involved in the Excelsior Club, plus one on the Forest Citys of Rockford, and the habit of the newspapers of the day to refer to men only by their surnames makes it very difficult to keep them straight. Several notes in 1868 stated that a new player named George Stearns had joined the Excelsiors, and he does not appear to have been related to the three Stearns brothers. Other notes suggest that the new player had formerly been with the Forest Citys of Rockford, but that player's name was Warren Stearns.

James Stearns: James Stearns was a brother of John and Woody Stearns who died unexpectedly in 1873 at the age of 33. An obituary said that the Excelsior club was "largely indebted to Mr. Stearns for its high character," but it appears that he was mostly an organizer rather than a player.

John Walker Stearns, Jr.: Stearns was the captain of the Excelsiors and appears to have played catcher and first base, though it is very difficult to keep all the men named Stearns straight. John Stearns also won a wreath for scoring the most runs at the Rockford tournament. He followed his father into the wholesale grocery business. He was born on June 19, 1846, never married, and died in Chicago on October 20, 1918.

Woodbury Eaton "Woody" Stearns: Woody Stearns was born on March 2, 1851, in Peru, New York, and followed his brother into the grocery business. He too never married and lived for most of his life with his brother and two unmarried sisters. He died only five days before his brother, on October 15, 1918.

H.G. Teed: Teed umpired the pivotal game at the Rockford tournament between the Excelsiors and the Detroit Base Ball Club. In the *Detroit News-Tribune* of March 15, 1903, David Barry maintained that Teed, who was supposed to be from La Porte, Indiana, was in fact a member of the Excelsiors. Whether that was true or just sour grapes has not been determined.

Fred Treacey: Treacey was one of the three New Yorkers who joined the Excelsiors late in the 1868 season. He went on to a fine major-league career, but remained a shadowy figure. He may have died in Brooklyn on January 26, 1891, but that has not been proven.

Willard Francis Wentworth: Wentworth was the president of the Excelsior Club and also a leading figure in the 1870 professional White Stockings. Born on January 31, 1838, in Alstead, New Hampshire, he was proprietor of the Tremont House and the Briggs House, as well as city treasurer of Chicago from 1865 to 1867. Yet when he died on December 28, 1910, his *New York Times* obituary began by describing him as "Willard F. Wentworth, formerly Treasurer of the old Chicago White Stockings baseball team."[94]

Gardner Goodrich Willard: Willard was a Harvard student who played for the Excelsiors when not in school. He was born on April 8, 1845, in Metamora, Illinois, but the family moved to St. Louis in 1857 and then to Chicago in 1861. Gardner served as a private in the Chicago Mercantile Battery during the war. He entered Harvard in 1865, graduating with a degree in history and political economy, while also serving as the president and captain of the baseball nine. He then passed the bar and joined the Chicago law firm of Willard & Evans. He never married, and died in Chicago on March 20, 1915.

John H. Zeller: Zeller played for the Excelsiors in 1867 and 1868. The knee injury he suffered in the club's game against the Unions of Morrisania was compounded when he fell again three months later and suffered another fracture.[95] The injury proved so severe that it not only cost him his career but also his leg. He returned to New York and became a saloon and lunch counter owner, dying there on February 13, 1900.

Other Members: Ackley (1867 second nine); C. J. Blair (the club's vice president in 1867); George S. Cleveland (another of the club's umpires); Crum (1867 second nine); Eggleston (1867); J. S. Gibbs (a club officer); Grant (1867–1868); Herbert (member of the second nine in 1867); E. Hill; Mackey (first nine in 1865); E. Morris; Oliver (1867); J. Owens; Quick (first nine member in 1865, probably the L. Quick who played for the Excelsiors before the war); Shumway (member of the second nine in 1867); C. Sweet; Taylor; D. B. Thompson (a member of the first nine in 1866); Treadway; Whitney.

Sources

Research on early Chicago baseball remains sparse, with material on the Excelsiors especially meager. As a result, the two pieces on the Excelsiors rely primarily upon contemporaneous newspaper coverage, as cited in the notes. Two retrospective pieces were of great value: "Baseball in Days Gone By," *Davenport Tribune*, August 24, 1888; Letter to the *Chicago Evening Post* from "Byron, An Original Excelsior," reprinted in the *Milwaukee Sentinel*, July 30, 1868. Also of help were Stephen Freedman, "The Baseball Fad in Chicago, 1865–1870: An Exploration of the Role of Sport in the Nineteenth-Century City," *Journal of Sport History* 5 (Summer 1978), 42–64; Alfred H. Spink, *The National Game* (1911) (reprint: Carbondale: Southern Illinois University Press, 2000); Larry Names, *Bury My Heart at Wrigley Field* (Neshkoro, WI: Sportsbook, 1990); Federal Writers Project, *Baseball in Old Chicago* (Chicago: A.C. McClurg, 1939); and Robert Pruter, "Youth Baseball in Chicago, 1868–1890: Not Always Sandlot Ball," *Journal of Sport History* 26:1 (Spring 1999), 1–28. Special thanks to Richard Smiley for his assistance.

Notes

1. "Baseball in Days Gone By," *Davenport Tribune*, August 24, 1888.
2. *Chicago Tribune*, April 18, 1864.
3. *Chicago Tribune*, June 28, 1864.
4. *Rockford Republic*, March 25, 1922, 10.
5. "Baseball in Days Gone By," *Davenport Tribune*, August 24, 1888. The *Chicago Inter-Ocean* of April 12, 1874, also observed that the Excelsiors were noted for their stylish uniforms.
6. *Chicago Tribune*, August 9, 1867.
7. Letter to the *Chicago Evening Post* from "Byron, An Original Excelsior," reprinted in the *Milwaukee Sentinel*, July 30, 1868..
8. "Baseball in Days Gone By," *Davenport Tribune*, August 24, 1888.
9. The championship match of the Bloomington tournament, against the Atlantics of Chicago's North Side, had to be postponed due to rain and was eventually played in Chicago in early October.
10. *Chicago Tribune*, October 11, 1866; *Detroit Advertiser and Tribune*, September 29, 1866.
11. *Chicago Tribune*, November 21, 1866.

12. *Chicago Times*, October 14, 1866.
13. *Detroit Advertiser and Tribune*, September 29, 1866.
14. *Chicago Tribune*, April 12, 1867.
15. *Chicago Tribune*, December 19, 1866. The *Chicago Inter-Ocean* of April 12, 1874, also mentioned these "handsome club rooms."
16. *Chicago Times*, April 28, 1867.
17. *Chicago Tribune*, January 18, 1867. Intriguingly, the club also decided to apply to the state legislature for a charter. The reasons for this decision are unknown, as is whether the charter was granted.
18. *Chicago Tribune*, May 22, 1867.
19. *Chicago Times*, May 12, 1867.
20. *Chicago Times*, May 18, 1867.
21. *Chicago Times*, May 26, 1867.
22. *Chicago Times*, May 22, 1867.
23. An article in the *Chicago Tribune* on December 30, 1877, listed all of the professionals who had played in Chicago. Of the men on the Excelsiors at the start of the 1867 season, only McNally and third baseman Tom Foley were listed, and the article specifically noted that Foley did not become a professional until 1869.
24. *Chicago Times*, June 23, 1867.
25. *Rockford Republic*, April 22, 1922, 1, 8.
26. *Chicago Times*, June 8, 1867.
27. *Chicago Times*, June 21, 1867.
28. *Chicago Times*, February 19, 1867.
29. *Chicago Times*, July 25, 1867.
30. *Chicago Times*, July 7, 1867.
31. *Chicago Times*, July 26, 1867.
32. *Chicago Inter-Ocean*, April 12, 1874.
33. *Chicago Tribune*, July 28, 1867.
34. *Chicago Tribune*, July 29, 1867.
35. Letter from the Excelsior club signed by vice president C.J. Blair and secretary Will Lowe, published in the *Chicago Tribune*, July 31, 1867. Similar explanations were given in the *Chicago Tribune*, July 29, 1867, and in "Baseball in Days Gone By," *Davenport Tribune*, August 24, 1888.
36. *Chicago Inter-Ocean*, April 12, 1874.
37. "Baseball in Days Gone By," *Davenport Tribune*, August 24, 1888.
38. *Chicago Tribune*, July 31, 1867.
39. *Chicago Tribune*, August 9, 1867.
40. *Chicago Tribune*, August 5, 1867.
41. *Chicago Tribune*, August 17, 1867.
42. "Baseball in Days Gone By," *Davenport Tribune*, August 24, 1888.
43. Letter to the *Chicago Evening Post* from "Byron, An Original Excelsior," reprinted in the *Milwaukee Sentinel*, July 30, 1868.
44. *Chicago Tribune*, December 30, 1877.
45. *Chicago Times*, September 1, 1867.
46. *Chicago Times*, September 13, 1867.
47. *Chicago Times*, September 15, 1867.
48. *Chicago Times*, September 20 and 21, 1867.
49. *Chicago Times*, September 27 and 28, 1867.
50. *Detroit Post*, October 21, 1867.
51. A. G. Spalding, *America's National Game* (New York: American Sports Pub. Co., 1911), 512.
52. *Detroit Post*, October 8, 1867.
53. *Detroit Post*, October 21, 1867.
54. *Detroit Advertiser and Tribune*, October 24, 1867.
55. *Chicago Times*, October 13, 1867.
56. *Chicago Tribune*, September 27, 1876. The article erroneously stated that these events occurred in 1869.
57. *Chicago Times*, May 12 and 24, 1868.
58. *Chicago Times*, May 12, 1868.
59. *Chicago Times*, June 17, 1868.
60. *Ibid.*
61. *Chicago Times*, June 24, 1868.
62. *Chicago Times*, July 5, 1868.
63. *Chicago Times*, July 19, 1868.
64. *Chicago Tribune*, July 22, 1868.
65. *Chicago Times*, August 4, 1868.
66. *Chicago Times*, July 24, 1868.
67. *Chicago Tribune*, July 28, 1868.
68. *Chicago Tribune*, August 20, 1868.
69. *Chicago Tribune*, September 10, 1868.
70. *Chicago Times*, September 13, 1868.
71. *Chicago Tribune*, September 20, 1868.
72. *Ibid.*
73. *Detroit Free Press*, September 19, 1868; *Detroit Post*, September 19, 1868.
74. *Chicago Times*, September 20, 1868.
75. *Chicago Tribune*, September 22, 1868.
76. *Chicago Times*, September 27, 1868.
77. *Ibid.*
78. *Chicago Times*, October 14, 1868.
79. *Chicago Times*, October 25, 1868.
80. *Chicago Tribune*, November 7, 1868.
81. *New York Tribune*, April 3, 1869, reprinted in the *Chicago Tribune*, April 7, 1869.
82. *Chicago Times*, June 13, 1869; quoted in Stephen Freedman, "The Baseball Fad in Chicago, 1865–1870: An Exploration of the Role of Sport in the Nineteenth-Century City," *Journal of Sport History* 5 (Summer 1978), 60.
83. *Winnebago County Chief*, July 22, 1869.
84. "Baseball in Days Gone By," *Davenport Tribune*, August 24, 1888.
85. "The Failure of Base Ball Here," *Chicago Tribune*, September 1, 1869.
86. *Chicago Inter-Ocean*, April 12, 1874.
87. "Baseball in Days Gone By," *Davenport Tribune*, August 24, 1888.
88. *Ibid.*
89. *Chicago Times*, September 15, 1866.
90. *Chicago Tribune*, July 27, 1872, 6.
91. *Chicago Times*, reprinted in the *Indianapolis Sentinel*, February 11, 1876.
92. *Chicago Tribune*, November 14, 1893; *Chicago Inter-Ocean*, May 10, 1889.
93. *Detroit Advertiser and Tribune*, July 3, 1866.
94. *New York Times*, December 30, 1910.
95. *New York Herald*, November 15, 1868.

❖ *Byron (Illinois) Base Ball Club* (Peter Morris) ❖

CLUB HISTORY

In 1862, four years after the death of her husband, Harriet Spalding of Byron, Ogle County, Illinois, sent her twelve-year-old son, Albert, to board with his aunt and uncle in the nearby town of Rockford. A year later she traded her Byron farm for a house in Rockford and moved there along with her two younger children.

Harriet Spalding attributed the decision to bad influences in Byron — specifically that other youngsters called her children "stuck-up" for wearing nice clothes and that the men of Byron spent far too much of their time at local stores, "with their trousers tucked into their boots, sitting on kegs, cracking jokes and talking." Fearing that her children would come to see such slackers as role models and lose their ambition to rise in the world, the widow opted for the "simple life at Rockford."[1]

As it turned out, Albert Spalding's relocation from Byron to Rockford had a defining effect on baseball in the region. Most obviously, it propelled the Forest City Club of Rockford to the forefront of the national baseball scene — Albert's interest in the game was whetted by his cousin Henry Warner and at sixteen he led the Rockford club to its historic 1867 upset of the Nationals of Washington. In addition, Spalding's move from Byron to Rockford initiated a recurring pattern by which the Forest City Club strengthened itself by adding the best players from nearby towns.

It was this pattern that enabled the Forest City Club to compete with great success against the representatives of much larger cities. But it also meant that there was little competition from other clubs in the region. The Byron Base Ball Club, in particular, could well have become a strong rival to the Forest City Club. Instead, it supplied two additional starters to the Forest Citys and thereby became simply a feeder to the Rockford powerhouse.

The members of the Byron Base Ball Club included James Barry, Ezra Evans, Joseph H. Hunt, Edwin A. Irvine, William H. Mix, brothers Morris P. and W. Ballard Osborn, Nahum F. Parsons, Gat Stires, and David W. Spalding (who was another of Albert's cousins). Stires and Ballard Osborn would become stalwarts of the Forest City Club, but the rest of the men typified the small-town ball club: pretty much every willing and able adult male was a starter. Indeed, we may well wonder how able-bodied the club members were, since Parsons and Evans were both over 30, while at least five of their younger teammates were Civil War veterans. To make matters worse, most of the club members were involved in farming, which left little time for play and practice.

Under the circumstances, it is not surprising that few details about the Byron Base Ball Club's history survive. We know that the club was founded in 1866.[2] In addition, the results of two contests against the Forest City Club are known: a 59–4 loss in 1867 and a more commendable 43–25 defeat in 1868.

After the 1868 game, the two stars of the Byron Base Ball Club made the predictable decision to cast their lots with their conquerors. As Stires later told it, his tryout was no mere formality: "It was a hurrying, pushing time on the farm and I had to plow three acres of land that day for Jap Hewitt, my brother-in-law. I got up before the crows did in the morning and chased that team right to a finish; got the fastest horse on the farm and burned the road to Rockford. Then I surprised both myself and Mr. Waldo by playing the best baseball in my life, and winning the place."[3] Osborn soon followed and, now deprived of their two best players, no more was heard of the Byron Base Ball Club.

History is always told from the perspective of the victors rather than the vanquished, so it is no surprise that the Forest Citys have gone down in baseball history, while the Byron Base Ball Club is forgotten. Given the many obstacles facing such clubs, it might not have been much different even if Albert G. Spalding had still been living in Byron in 1866. Nevertheless, it is an interesting topic for speculation — how would baseball history have been different if Harriet Spalding had decided to stay in Byron?

Club Members

James S. Barry: James Barry was born in Ogle County, Illinois, in January of 1848 and grew up in a log house his father built on a forty-acre farm near Byron. He farmed in the area for most of his life, dying in Byron on November 22, 1928.

Ezra H. Evans: Ezra Evans was born on November 22, 1829, in Taberg, Oneida County, New York. He arrived in Ogle County in 1848 and became a prominent farmer. His skilled oversight of his fifty-five-acre farm led to his being described as "one of the self-made men of Illinois, who, in carving out their own fortunes in the west, have added to the wealth, importance, and stability of the community."[4] Evans died in 1914.

Joseph H. Hunt: Joseph Hunt was born in New Jersey in April of 1845. He had moved to Byron by the time of the Civil War and he enlisted in Company B of the 92nd Illinois Infantry on February 29, 1864, serving alongside four future Byron Base Ball Club teammates. After being mustered out, he re-enlisted in the 65th Illinois Infantry, serving with Morris P. Osborn. After the war he helped his father run the family farm. Eventually he moved into Byron and became the local postmaster. Hunt died in 1906.

Edwin A. Irvine: Ed Irvine was born in Illinois around 1843. Like so many of his future teammates, he served in Company B of the 92nd Illinois Infantry during the Civil War. He became a farmer after the war and the demise of the Byron Base Ball Club came at the same time as the birth of his first child. Irvine later moved to Rockford and became a railroad clerk. He died there on December 1, 1911.

William Harry Mix: William H. Mix was born in 1846 and was the son of a Byron merchant. As was the case with so many of his future teammates, he served in Company B of the 92nd Illinois Infantry during the Civil War. He then married Adelaide Osborn, the sister of two of his teammates, and became a farmer. The young couple welcomed their only child in 1869, just as the Byron Baseball Club ended its short career. Mix died in Byron on May 25, 1917.

Morris P. Osborn: Morris Osborn, the older brother of Ballard Osborn, was born in September of 1845. During the Civil War, he served with Hunt in both the 92nd and 65th Illinois Infantry regiments. He died in Rockford on January 25, 1929.

William Ballard Osborn: Ballard Osborn was born in

February of 1847, shortly before his parents moved from Glenmore, New York, to a farm in Rockvale Township, near Byron, Illinois. In 1868 he became the regular third baseman of the Forest Citys and he remained a backup in 1869. In 1871 Osborn agreed to play for Rockford's entry in the National Association, signing a contract in which he pledged to "play first class baseball in any position for the sum of sixty-six and two thirds dollars per month." But he was released without playing in a regular-season game, thereby missing out on the honor of having his name in the encyclopedias. He returned to farming in Rockvale Township, Illinois, where he lived until his death on April 12, 1924.[5]

Nahum Fisher Parsons: Nahum F. Parsons was born on December 4, 1834, in Bloomfield, Massachusetts, and became a farmer and cattle dealer in Ogle County. He died on April 24, 1906, in the village of Winnebago.

David W. Spalding: David W. Spalding, a cousin of Albert G. Spalding, was born in Illinois in December of 1844. Like so many of his future teammates, he served in the 92nd Illinois Infantry, Company B, during the Civil War. After his ballplaying career, Spalding owned the Quarter Circle-Pan-Bar ranch in the Dakota Territory. He later moved to Wyoming and died on September 21, 1924, in Wilson, Wyoming.

Garret C. Stires: Gat Stires was born on October 13, 1849, in Hunterdon County, New Jersey. In 1856 his father moved the family to a stock farm and ranch near Byron, Illinois. Gat Stires joined the Forest Citys in 1868 and became one of the mainstays of the club. He remained with the club when they joined the National Association in 1871 but then his services were needed on the ranch and he retired from baseball. Long after his retirement, however, stories continued to be told about Stires's phenomenal hitting. Stires was only 5-feet-8 but weighed 180 pounds and descriptions suggest that every ounce of that weight was sheer muscle. One writer recalled that Stires was known "as the 'terrible hayseed,'" and elaborated:

> Stires was the phenomenon of those days. He knew nothing of headwork, but he had the strength of a giant. The places under the arms where the shoulders join the body are usually hollow. In Stires' case they were filled with muscles. The man could run like a deer, and had hands like hams covered with hide. No fly passed him, and his field record was generally errorless save in the matter of throwing. When he returned the ball to the diamond it was always at lightning speed, and no one could tell whether the sphere would reach the catcher or go over the fairground fence. But it was at the bat that Stires won his name as the "terrible hayseed." He was not like Anson or Barnes a sure base hitter, but when his club and the ball did meet the result was nearly always a home run. I once saw Harry Wright, the Philadelphia veteran, who then played center field for the Bostons, wade Kent's creek and toil up a bluff beyond to recover the sphere after it had collided with Stires' six pound bat.

Fred Cone similarly recollected, "Many a time I have heard Al Spalding say Stires could hit the ball harder and send it further than any man on earth." Stires did not possess similar gifts in other aspects of the game, and reportedly "always was lame and had to have somebody run for him."[6] After retiring from baseball, Stires continued to "gravitate toward the frontiers and the open spaces," and spent much of the next two decades mining in Colorado, surveying in Minnesota and South Dakota, and farming and hunting in the "duck paradise" of northwestern Iowa. In the mid–1880s, he and former teammate Dave Spalding were the only white men among 4,000 Sioux at the last Sun Dance ever held on the Pine Ridge reservation. Stires eventually returned to cattle ranching and stock buying near Byron and became quite wealthy, though he enhanced his mythic status by "wearing his hair long after the frontier fashion."[7] He never married, and when his health began to fail in the 1920s he moved into Byron. By then, a new slugger had begun to revolutionize baseball and he reminded some of the exploits of Stires — Horace E. Buker pronounced Stires "the Babe Ruth of pre-league ball."[8] He died in the Ogle County Home in the nearby town of Oregon on June 13, 1933.[9]

Sources

A forty-four-part history of the club that was written by Horace E. Buker and published serially in the *Rockford Republic* in 1922; A.G. Spalding, *America's National Game* (New York: American Sports Publishing Company, 1911), Harriet Spalding, *Reminiscences of Harriet I. Spalding* (East Orange, NJ: 1910); Peter Levine, *A.G. Spalding and the Rise of Baseball*; "Baseball Thirty Years Ago," *Lima News,* July 15, 1899 (reminiscences of Fred Cone); a four-part series by John Molyneaux that appeared in *Nuggets of History*, a publication of the Rockford Historical Society ("The Sinnissippi Base Ball Club," 43:1 (March 2005); "The Forest City Base Ball Club: The Amateur Years," 45:1 (March 2007); "No Longer Amateurs: The Forest City Base Ball Club in 1868," 46:2 (June 2008); "'We Can Beat the Spots Off the Best Club That Ever Lived': The Forest City Base Ball Club in 1869," 46:3 (September 2008).

Notes

1. Peter Levine, *A.G. Spalding and the Rise of Baseball* (New York: Oxford University Press, 1985), 4; Harriet Spalding, *Reminiscences of Harriet I. Spalding* (East Orange, NJ, 1910), 70–72, 80.
2. *Rockford Republic*, September 9, 1922, 1.
3. *Ibid.*, 11.
4. *Ogle County Portrait and Biographical Album* (Chicago: Chapman Bros., 1886).
5. "Wm. Osborn of Anson's Team Dead at Byron," *Rockford Register-Gazette*, April 12, 1924, 11.
6. *Rockford Republic*, September 9, 1922, 11.
7. *Ibid.*
8. *Rockford Republic*, August 12, 1922, 9.
9. For more on Stires, see my SABR BioProject profile: http://bioproj.sabr.org/bioproj.cfm?a=v&v=1&bid=3110&pid=13662.

Forest City Club of Rockford (Peter Morris)

Club History

The Forest City Club of Rockford came to be best remembered for a stunning upset of the mighty Nationals of Washington and for producing legendary pitcher, executive, and sporting-goods magnate Albert Goodwill Spalding. In fact, the Forest City club had a wide range of impressive accomplishments: it regularly defeated the representatives of much larger cities, it yielded several other stars and made the transition from amateurism to professionalism so smoothly that it participated in the first major league, and it produced several star players.

Spalding later gave an intriguing account of his introduction to the game. In 1863, at the age of twelve, he was sent to Rockford to board with a relative and

> became associated with a number of my school companions in the organization of a junior base ball club. The way it came about was this. One of our young townsmen, while in the east, had seen several games of ball played by New York clubs at the Elysian Fields, Hoboken, N.J., then the home of the game; and becoming interested in it, on his return home to the west he brought with him some base ball materials, and a copy of *Beadle Dime Book of Base Ball*, the standard book of the game at that period. It was edited by Mr. Chadwick, who was then, as now, the leading writer of the national game. From the pages of this book, aided by personal instructions by our teacher, we were initiated in the mysteries of base-ball, and of course we became infatuated with the sport.[1]

At other times, Spalding maintained that a disabled Civil War veteran first explained the game to him.[2] In addition, it must be stressed that this is a description of how Spalding was introduced to baseball, and since he was a brand-new arrival to Rockford in 1863, it is very possible that the New York version of baseball had been played there earlier.

The other first-hand source on baseball's origins in Rockford is Spalding's mentor, local bookseller Hiram H. Waldo. "I came West fifty-nine years ago, in 1846," Waldo wrote, "and found 'Town Ball' a popular game at all Town meetings. I do not recall an instance of a money bet on the game; but, at Town meetings, the side losing had to buy the ginger bread and cider." He pointed out the similarities between baseball and town ball and concluded that the national pastime was "an evolution from Town Ball."[3]

One more tantalizing fragment also survives, though its original source remains unknown. According to a much later account, "An old rubber shoe, melted down, became the core of the first ball manufactured [in Rockford]. Around it, yarn was wrapped. An orange peel was quartered and used as a model for the leather cover which was sewn by George Lane, harness maker."[4]

Organized baseball came to Rockford in 1865 when at least five clubs were formed: the Sinnissippis, the Forest Citys, the Pioneers, the Mercantiles, and the Unions. It was the Forest City Club that emerged as local champions by posting two victories over the rival Sinnissippis in 1865. The first was a five-inning contest, but the second was a decisive season-ending 55–17 win at the County Fair Grounds on September 23. Having establishing themselves as the city's standard bearer, the Forest Citys began a rapid growth that would see them eventually enlist 150 members.

Despite having earned recognition as Rockford's top club, the Forest Citys showed no signs of future glory in 1865. The decision to form the club received this matter-of-fact acknowledgement in the local paper on June 3: "Some of our young men are organizing the Forest City Base-ball Club. It will be an excellent institution to develop muscle."[5] Four days later the Forest City Club was formally organized and it played six match games that year. Yet the club won only one match against out-of-town competition that year, losing matches at a September tournament at the Winnebago County Fair Grounds to the Empires of Freeport and Atlantics of Chicago before beating the Shaffers of Freeport. Just as important, the club's lineup in 1865 included only a few players who would be part of the glory years, and none of its stars.

As a result, the most significant contest played by the Forest Citys in 1865 was an informal game on November 7 against a "picked nine" selected by Waldo. The champions won, 31–19, but what made the game important was that the pitcher for the picked nine was the fifteen-year-old A. G. Spalding. His pitching on that day was enough of a revelation to earn him a spot on the 1866 Forest Citys, thereby beginning the club's long tradition of recruiting the best players from its rivals. It was the club's success in this regard that enabled the representatives of a sleepy Illinois town of 8,000 to compete with and often beat the national powers.[6]

As Spalding later told it, when the club began practicing for the 1866 season, his pitching was so impressive that his cousin, club captain Henry Warner, named him starting pitcher of the Forest Citys. Some of the older club members objected that the fifteen-year-old would "go to pieces" against strong competition, but the youngster won his first game against the Mystics of Belvidere by the score of 123 to 8 and the doubters were silenced.[7]

Spalding pitched for the Forest City Club in most of its 1866 contests, and the club enjoyed a stellar season. The Forest Citys twice defeated their crosstown rivals, the Sinnissippis, although for unknown reasons Spalding did not pitch in either match. The club also began to look further afield for competition, with the highlight being the announcement that the club would host a major tournament at the end of June that was billed as being for the championship of the Northwest.

Hiram Waldo was elected president of the Forest City Club in April of 1866 and he served as the club's de facto manager for the remainder of its existence. Under his leadership, the club continued to enlist new recruits. Many of these newcomers hailed from the surrounding region, making the club less of a true town club.

The most notable addition of 1866 occurred after the Forest City Club visited Rochelle, Illinois, and, as Spalding later recalled, "unearthed Bob Addy, who afterward became a celebrated character. He was originally a Canadian cricketer. He showed wonderful ability as a ball player in this game, by practically playing the whole game, captain of the team, pitcher, catcher, and, in fact, took every position where the player had developed weakness by making an error. We won the game without difficulty, but were so impressed with his playing abilities that Addy was afterward invited to join the Forest Citys and was a member of that club all the time I was connected with it."[8]

Addy was followed in August by Mart Wheeler of the Sinnissippis and in September by a young infielder named Roscoe Barnes. Like Spalding, Barnes had been a member of the Pioneer Club of Rockford and he too was destined for major-league superstardom. The foundation for greatness was now in place.

The new additions raise the difficult question of whether the Forest City Club offered any financial inducements to persuade these men to switch clubs. Spalding was adamant that this was not the case, and that money was not involved in the club's doings until several years later. He maintained that he was docked pay when he had to miss work at a Rockford grocery to play for the club, and that he left the club briefly in the fall of 1867 and joined the Excelsiors of Chicago because he had been offered what amounted to a salary to play baseball for the first time.[9]

In 1884 Rockford native and minor-league manager James F. McKee provided a brief history of the Forest Citys in which he stressed that the club's early years were the "days when salaries to play ball was unheard of." He then quoted an unnamed "eminent writer" who had written, "The members of the first nine are neither sporting men, gamblers or hired experts, but they are boys who have grown to manhood in this city, have received liberal educations and every one of them is engaged in business, filling stations of profit and honor."[10] One year later, McKee wrote a very confusing article that reiterated that the original Forest City Club was strictly amateur but then characterized the 1870 version as baseball's "first regular salaried professional team."[11] But this is sheer nonsense, since the Red Stockings of Cincinnati had openly paid salaries in 1869.

Perhaps it was McKee who led Alfred H. Spink to refer to the Forest City Club as the "first to pay regular salaries to their players."[12] On another occasion, Spink repeated this assertion and added that the people of Rockford objected to the claim that the Red Stockings were the first to receive salaries and believed that the distinction belonged to the Forest Citys.[13] Yet immediately after making the above-quoted declaration, Spink proceeded to describe the playing members of the Forest City Club in the exact same words that had been quoted by McKee in 1884, even adding that the players had "only the hours of evening after their day's work was done to practice."[14] So had Spink been the "eminent writer" cited by McKee or was he just copying the same source without attribution? Or was it McKee who led Spink astray? In any case, while it seems clear that the Forest Citys began paying salaries to their players in 1870, there is no reason to believe that they were the first club to do so.

But there are other sources that suggest that the Forest Citys were not lily-pure amateurs during the 1860s. An undated article stated that after the 1867 upset of the Nationals, residents of Rockford began "freely forking down their greenbacks to pay their players for the time spent in practicing."[15] Gat Stires, who joined the club in 1868, confirmed that "the division of gate receipts and the liberality of local fans amply covered the personal expenses of each member of the nine."[16] Even Spalding's mother recalled that her son's employer, the editor of the *Rockford Register*, "was so much interested in baseball that he was always ready to let Albert off to play ball."[17]

Given the contradictory evidence and the wide differences in definitions of what constituted an amateur club, there is no way to be certain of the status of the Forest Citys. It seems most likely, however, that no salaries were paid in 1866 or 1867, and that the 1868 and 1869 seasons saw the club beginning to make the transition to professionalism. Horace E. Buker suggested that the club pursued such a gradual course: "Rockford was a small prairie town. Where wealthy clubs were attracting players by imaginary 'jobs' at high pay, the nearest the Forest Citys came to this brand of lure was to offer promising players real jobs at fair pay, with the understanding that the employer would not be opposed to a limited number of lost afternoons."[18] Buker also disclosed that after one 1867 match in Rockford, "Receipts of $400 were divided between the two teams — which is one idea of amateurism."[19]

The loyal support of Rockford residents also played a key role. The members of the Forest Citys were regarded as "social lions," and "Carriages were provided for them whenever they went to other cities to play and all sorts of invitations were extended to them. The fans were as enthusiastic as they are today and the spectators used to become familiar and take the players into their confidences. Batting and fielding averages formed the small talk at sociables and dinner parties. An astonishing amount of loyalty to the home team was displayed by business men, lawyers, judges and the profound thinking economists."[20] Before long, the club's renown was such in the region that "every time a game was advertised stores shut up, banks closed and the town turned out, as well as the country for thirty-five miles around."[21]

The players also began sporting a snazzy "uniform consisting of white shirts, white flannel pants, with blue cord, white caps, and black patent leather boots."[22] Presumably this expense too was funded by donations from the club's rabid supporters.

The aforementioned June 1866 tournament was another opportunity for Rockford residents to open their wallets and show their support. A local dentist, Dr. Joseph Norman, was the primary sponsor, offering the winning club a ball "of full regulation size, two and three-quarters inches in diameter, of eighteen carat gold, and put up in a satin-lined Morocco case," and a bat "of solid rosewood, elaborately mounted with the same quality of gold, and cased the same as the ball." Many Rockford businesses and groups chipped in by donating additional prizes to lure clubs and players.[23] A local monument cutter even offered to donate a free tombstone to the first player killed during the tournament.[24]

Fortunately, this last prize was not claimed, but the Rockford tournament did feature its share of bizarre moments. The generous prize fund attracted clubs from cities like Chicago, Detroit, and Milwaukee, but the questionable decision was made to place all the entrants in one division. This discouraged most small-town clubs from entering, with the notable exception of the Pecatonica Club, which went down to a notorious 49–1 loss (that is described more fully in that club's entry).

Another problem was the field at the county fairgrounds, which prompted widespread complaints about its being "badly disfigured in a base ball point of view, by trees."[25] One attendee later recalled that

> a poorer field, to my mind, has never been known. Trees in every direction. There was a cluster of five around third base. The catcher was hemmed in by trees with the exception of a space about 30 by 50 feet. The umpire could not see a foul unless it hit back of the plate or a few feet on either side of the base lines. Between the plate and second base the terrain was fairly level, but approaching third base there was a noticeable rise and from third to the plate there was a depression and the baserunner had to dig in for life. At the edge of the outfield was a deep gutter to take care of water from the quarter-mile race track and why more fielders did not break legs in this trap was because Providence protected them.[26]

Yet another tree impeded the right fielder, although one of the men stationed in that field took advantage by making "an excellent rebound catch" of a ball that ricocheted off a branch.[27]

Things also went badly for the Forest Citys, which lost a 14–13 nail-biter to the Cream City Club of Milwaukee and were knocked out of the single-elimination tournament. But a one-run loss to a club from a much bigger city was nothing to be ashamed of and that was the general outlook. According to Horace E. Buker, "Among the Forest City players there was more joy at their good showing than sorrow at the game lost. They didn't consider themselves anything more than county champions — and they were about right."[28]

As a result, the Forest City Club was quick to rebound. The club did not lose another match in 1866, and the players were particularly exhilarated when they gained revenge on the Cream Citys by the decisive margin of 24–10. A challenge was even issued to the Excelsiors of Chicago, the club that had won the Rockford tournament and had earned recognition as the best club in the Midwest. But the response was unsatisfactory, prompting the Forest City Club to pass a resolution stating, "[W]e regard the reply of the Excelsior Base Ball Club, of Chicago, deferring the acceptance of our challenge till next spring, as a virtual refusal to play with us."[29]

As Horace E. Buker observed, the Forest Citys ended the 1866 season as "champions of Winnebago county, nothing more," and remained unknowns on the national scene.[30] Yet the pieces of the dynasty had been assembled, with the last one being added on September 26 when Ross Barnes played his first game in a Forest City uniform.

When the spring of 1867 rolled around, the Forest City and Excelsior Clubs did indeed play two matches. The first contest, played on June 20, saw the Forest Citys clinging to a narrow lead after five innings, only to be on the short end of a 45–41 score when darkness ended play after seven innings. The hard-fought setback prompted one Rockford paper to claim that the Excelsior batters had unsportingly engaged in "a system of jockeying" by "standing at the base, bat in hand, 'till three balls were called and then stalking up to the next base." The Forest City players, however, responded to these allegations with "hearty condemnation." When the second game of the series was played in Rockford on Independence Day, it was much the same story — the Forest Citys led 17–12 after five innings, but their Chicago rivals rallied to pull out a 28–25 win.[31]

While the close losses were frustrating for the Forest City Club, they also earned new respect for the small-town club and earned it an invitation to participate in a historic event. The Nationals of Washington had embarked on baseball's first-ever trans–Allegheny tour and were due to arrive in Chicago at the end of July. To welcome them, three days' worth of matches were scheduled at Dexter Park, with the opponents being the Forest Citys, the Excelsiors, and the Atlantics of Chicago.

The match against the Forest Citys was widely viewed as a warm-up contest for the Nationals, and few expected it to be competitive. A correspondent for the *Chicago Times* believed that even the Forest City players felt that way, and "commenced the play with not the slightest hope of success."[32] Spalding, who was still only 16, later said, "A great lump arose in my throat, and my heart beat so like a trip-hammer that I imagined it could be heard by everyone on the grounds." He added that his teammates shared his apprehension, and although they tried to reassure him, "I recognized the fact that everyone of them was so scared that none could speak above a whisper. The fact is, we were all frightened nearly to death, with possibly the exception of Bob Addy, who kept up his nerve and courage by 'joshing' the National players as they came to bat with his witticisms."³³ The contrast was also apparent in the uniforms of the two adversaries: the Nationals sported "dark blue pants, white shirt with blue cord trimming, 'Shakspeare' [sic] collars, ornamented on either side with the letter N, and a white jockey cap, ribbed with blue cord. The Forest Citys wore white pants and shirt, and blue and white cap."³⁴

But to everyone's surprise, the Forest City Club surged ahead and clung gamely to the lead. The Nationals redoubled their efforts, but their bats continued to be subdued by Spalding's pitching and by a steady drizzle that forced two interruptions and left the players and spectators "thoroughly drenched."³⁵ By the seventh inning, time was running out and in desperation the club's president loudly reminded star player George Wright that "to lose this game would be to make our whole trip a failure." His words spurred on the Forest Citys, and they completed the historic upset, ending up on the long end of a 29–23 score.³⁶ The win put the city of Rockford on the baseball map — as one reporter put it, the Forest City club had been "unknown to fame outside of Illinois, and it will undoubtedly puzzle many of the Eastern players to assign Rockford a location without the assistance of a gazetteer."³⁷

The embarrassed Nationals bounced back in their next game and thrashed the Excelsiors, 49–4. This prompted allegations that the loss to the Forest Citys had been fixed, but the charges were angrily denied by the Nationals and were withdrawn. Upon their return to Rockford, the Forest Citys were hailed as conquering heroes. A banquet was held at the Holland House, followed by a public reception at Brown's Hall at which the triumphant ballplayers were feted with speeches, toasts, and a song that concluded: "While we with festive mirth and songs/ Our tribute now are bringing/ The champion ball to them belongs/ Thro' all the land was ringing." Spalding was singled out and presented with a "fine American silver watch and chain" that bore a suitable inscription.³⁸

It was another indication that the Forest Citys were not lily-pure amateurs, yet the generous gift was not enough to keep Spalding in Rockford. He soon accepted a $40-a-week clerkship for a Chicago grocery with few duties, as long as he agreed to pitch for the Excelsiors.³⁹ His departure left the Forest Citys without an experienced pitcher, and the club went more than two months without playing, then lost badly to the Bloomingtons of Bloomington, Illinois.

By the spring of 1868, the Chicago grocery that employed Spalding had gone bankrupt, and the young pitcher returned to Rockford. He found work for an insurance agency and the *Rockford Register*, both of which — by coincidence or perhaps not — were managed by officers of the Forest City Club. Not surprisingly, he also resumed his old role as the club's pitcher. Joining him on the first nine were several players who had previously played for the Forest City juniors, including Dent Sawyer and Fred Cone. Players from other junior clubs were also being grabbed up; as Chandler Starr later put it, "As rapidly as the players in the smaller clubs became proficient, they were drafted into the Forest Citys."⁴⁰

The 1868 season proved an up-and-down one for the Forest Citys. The highlights came when they finally beat the rival Excelsiors of Chicago on June 12 and then repeated the feat on July 4. These wins, along with eleven other decisive triumphs over clubs from Illinois, Wisconsin, and Iowa, firmly established the Forest Citys as the top club in the state and the surrounding area.

But when Eastern clubs came for visits, the Rockford club proved incapable of repeating the signal triumph it had achieved in 1867. The first such opponent, the Athletics of Philadelphia, overwhelmed the Forest Citys by a 94–13 margin as the visiting batters found Spalding's offerings "just to their liking ... frequently sending the ball far beyond the reach of the outfielders. This strong work soon demoralized the Rockford players, and they became fearfully 'rattled,' playing wildly and without a particle of confidence."⁴¹ When the Atlantics of Brooklyn came to Rockford, the Forest Citys grabbed a big lead on the strength of a grand slam home run by Gat Stires, only to have the Atlantics rally to pull out a two-run win. Visits from the Buckeyes of Cincinnati and the Unions of Morrisania also ended in hard-fought defeats.

The match against the Unions of Morrisania was especially frustrating. The visitors were the defending national champions and, according to first baseman Fred Cone, anticipation was so high in Rockford that "the banks closed, business men shut up their stores and the judge of the county court gravely informed his lawyer friends that the court had to sit en banc with a number of other estimable judges — of baseball — in a well-known stand out in the remote part of the city given over to baseball players."

But as Cone related wistfully, "That game with the Unions was one of the best we ever played, although we lost. We had a new man that showed up so well in practice that we let him play first base in my place — I had broken my wrist in a game. He was unable to hold the ball and in desperation Stires was called in to supplant him by our captain. Stires was little better. There were fourteen bad plays at that bag that game, and with that for a handicap we were only beaten by a narrow margin."⁴²

After the 1868 season, clubs like the Forest City faced a crucial dilemma. The National Association of Base Ball Players finally recognized professionalism that offseason, giving clubs the choice of amateurism or professionalism, and the related decision of whether to use local players or import outsiders.

Like many clubs, the Forest Citys opted for a compromise. They remained nominally amateurs and brought in no Eastern professionals. But as Horace E. Buker put it, the club's "interpretation" of amateurism "was beginning to follow the lead set by the east, in that there was nothing to prevent life being made as comfortable and work as easy as possible for men who contributed to local fame." As a result, several new players "were attracted here from neighboring towns by the prospect of playing on a winning club and being well paid for not too much real work in shop or store."[43] The first two "new accessions," Scott Hastings and Lee Cheney of the Bloomington Club, enlisted in February, while Tom Foley of the now-defunct Excelsiors of Chicago followed in July when he moved to Rockford and opened a bindery.[44]

Unlike most of the clubs that sought a middle ground between pure amateurism and open professionalism, the course of the Forest Citys proved a success in 1869. The club managed twenty wins and only four defeats during the season, with all four losses coming at the hands of the Red Stockings of Cincinnati, including one in Cincinnati on July 24 by the narrow margin of 15–14. The Forest Citys led 14–12 after eight innings and were on the verge of a historic upset until a couple of misplays allowed the home side to rally and preserve their undefeated season. (Even so, the string of losses to the rival from Cincinnati prompted the *Winnebago County Chief* to write on July 15 that the Forest City batters, "as usual, went to the bat nervous and fearful" when they played the Red Stockings.)

The gaudy record of the Forest Citys is made less impressive by the reality that the demise of the Excelsiors meant none of the top Eastern clubs paid visits to Illinois. Nevertheless, a season that includes losses only to a legendary undefeated club remains quite an accomplishment. As one Rockford reporter put it, "When the boys of the F.C.B.B.C. meet any other than the nine red legged giants gathered from the four quarters of the Union, and rendezvoused at Cincinnati they can 'scoop them,' 'gobble them up,' 'clean them out,' 'get away with them,' and crow like victorious game cocks, but when they run against these nine 'scarlet runners' they come in contact with nine gentlemen whom they cannot handle.... One fact is pretty well settled, and that is, that the Red Stockings is the finest club in the world, and that Rockford stands next to them."[45]

As good as the Forest City Club was in 1869, the nine could have been even stronger if it had not had to play without two of its stars—George King retired from baseball to concentrate on business, while Gat Stires missed the entire season due to a dangerous bout of typhomalarial fever.[46] With good reason, Horace E. Buker speculated that the Forest City Club might have beaten the Red Stockings out for the championship if those two men had been available.[47]

The strong performance in 1869 inspired Rockford residents to raise $7,000 to fund the club's first tour of the East Coast.[48] Later accounts leave little doubt that the influx of money led the Forest Citys to begin paying salaries in 1870 (if they weren't already doing so). Yet at the time the club continued to describe itself as an amateur nine, maintaining that all profits were donated to charity. These claims are difficult to believe in light of references to the players having "business connections, which are prosecuted in their absence and to which they return at the close of the baseball season."[49]

Even with the ability to pay salaries, the club's roster was already such a strong one that only two new players were brought in—first baseman Joe Doyle, a Washington native who had been playing for the Buckeyes of Cincinnati, and New Yorker Joe Simmons, an outfielder who was another former Excelsior of Chicago. Simmons had been driving a horsecar in Chicago when a Rockford director tracked him down and offered a job in Rockford that allowed him to be absent for ballgames.[50] Simmons lived that year at a hotel operated by club member Harry Starr and was joined there by numerous other club members, including Bob Addy, James Manny, Fred Cone, Gale Barstow, Rufus Bailey, and Scott Hastings (who, oddly, was listed as a hotel clerk!).

The 1870 campaign proved another successful one for the Forest City Club, as it compiled 42 wins and a tie in 56 outings. Most impressively, in a year that produced no clear-cut national champion, most considered the Red Stockings and the White Stockings of Chicago to be the best clubs and the Forest Citys managed wins over both of them.

The strong season led the Forest City Club to join the first major league, the National Association, in 1871. Alas, the move had to be made without Spalding, Barnes, and Cone, all of whom had signed to play for Boston. But club manager Hiram Waldo enlisted some capable replacements, including Chick Fulmer, George Bird, Denny Mack, Cherokee Fisher, and a young player named Adrian Anson. The Forest Citys finished the year with an 8–17 record, only to have four of the wins turned to losses when Scott Hastings was ruled ineligible. The club was still using the ill-suited fairgrounds for its home games, with the result that the field has been described as the "strangest major league ballpark in history."[51]

The Great Chicago Fire forced the White Stockings to drop out of the National Association at the end of the 1871 season, making it inevitable that the Forest Citys of Rockford would do the same. Many of the club's players joined other major-league clubs and fashioned impressive careers. But the club that had produced them and had managed one of the greatest upsets of baseball's era had come to the end of the road. (It appears that other clubs called the Forest Citys represented Rockford in subsequent years, but without stars like Spalding and Barnes, these were to all intents and purposes new clubs.)

In later years, Spalding and other members of the Forest City Club of Rockford looked back on the club's heyday with great fondness. Spalding, for example, later told of a memorable trip from Rockford to Rochelle that was made

> in an old-style picnic side-seat wagon. On our return from Rochelle in the evening after the game, it rained very hard. The harness broke, and it took us about half an hour to fix it with the assistance of a neighboring farmer. The wheels of the wagon had struck a log, imbedded in the mud, lying across the road.

It was suggested that we all get out and help it over the obstruction, and I remember Major Sine, a fleshy man, weighing about 250 pounds, then chief of police of Rockford, objected to getting out because he had on low shoes and white stockings. It took us about a half hour to fix the harness. In the meantime Major Sine had fallen asleep and when the wagon started up the lurch in crossing the log tipped Sine out in the deep mud, soiling not only his white stockings, but considerably more of his person as he went out of sight. Before we had missed him we heard a voice asking us to hold up, and then Sine climbed in, covered with mud, uttering expletives which do not look well in print.[52]

No doubt the smooth manner in which the club navigated the transition from amateurism to professionalism was one of the main reasons that the memories were so fond. Appropriately, in 1896, when Harry Wright Day was celebrated with reunion matches all across the country, it was in Rockford that the most celebrated game was played. There was a great turnout of the club's former members, and while rain washed out the game after only an inning, it didn't put a damper on the good spirits and the affectionate reminiscences about bygone days.

Club Members

Note: This includes only men who belonged to the club before its 1871 entry into the National Association.

Bob Addy: Bob Addy, the player whose memorable discovery was chronicled by Spalding, remained a regular for the Forest Citys for several years and became known as quite a character. One writer aptly described him as "big hearted, bow legged, profane Bob Addy." Even during his time in Rockford, Addy was talking seriously about heading west to "seek his fortune."[53] He played professionally for several years after leaving Rockford, but according to Cap Anson he was "an odd sort of a genius and quit the game because he thought he could do better at something else."[54] That "something else" lay to the west and Addy lived first in Wyoming and then settled permanently in Pocatello, Idaho. There he ran a hardware and sporting-goods store and raised cattle as a sideline. He died in Pocatello in 1910. The circumstances of his birth have been a source of confusion, and he is often listed as being born in Rochester, New York, but in fact he was born and raised in Port Hope, Ontario, making him the first Canadian major leaguer.[55]

Rufus C. Bailey: Rufus Bailey, the secretary of the Forest Citys from 1865 to 1872, was born in Auburn, Maine, on July 28, 1833. After graduating from Amherst College in 1853, he headed west and settled in Rockford. He worked as a railroad engineer for several years, but then desired to study law. After passing the bar, he worked as a city attorney. As of 1870, the unmarried Bailey was living with many of his fellow club members at Henry Starr's hotel. In 1873 Bailey was elected a county judge and he served in that position for more than 30 years. As of 1910, he was still living in Rockford but appears to have died shortly afterward.

William Blakney Barbour: William Barbour was born around 1848 in Ireland and immigrated two years later. He became a prominent Rockford businessman, owning a dry-goods store, being in business with fellow club member Henry Price and eventually becoming president of the Rockford Insurance Company. He was also involved in the management of the Forest City Club and after he died in Rockford on January 26, 1921, an account book was found in his possession that included entries from 1871 like "Mending Fisher's shoes — 25 cents; bat for Anson — 50 cents; shirt for Ham — $1.75." Spalding jocularly recalled in 1896 that Barbour "used to manage the team. I used to think he was about the meanest man on earth about giving up money when we were away on a trip. But somehow or other he had a faculty of never letting us walk home."[56]

Alfred L. Barker: Al Barker was born on January 18, 1839, in Lost Creek, Indiana. The family moved to Illinois in 1848 and settled in Rockford five years later. He enlisted in the Civil War and served tours of duty in the 11th and 74th Regiments. One of his brothers died at the Battle of Kennesaw Mountain. Barker became the catcher for the Forest City nine in 1865 and was the only member of that year's first nine to represent the club during the professional era. He remained a member of the first nine for several more years, though work obligations prevented him from traveling with the club. He even played one game for the Forest Citys in 1871, good enough to earn him a place in the baseball encyclopedias. Along with his wife, Barker then opened a dance school and "abandoned chasing the horsehide for the gentler occupation of guiding faltering footsteps across the slippery floor of the dance hall." But even after turning his attention to being a band leader, orchestra manager, dance instructor, and choir leader, he continued to share "more reminiscences about old times than any member of the team" and to "tell them in a peculiarly happy manner." Spalding recalled that Barker had been the club member who "always used to remind us of practice days, and ... always saw that the necessary paraphernalia was at hand."[57] Barker died in Rockford on September 15, 1912.[58]

Charles Roscoe Barnes: Ross Barnes was born in Mount Morris, New York, on May 8, 1850, but grew up in Rockford. Like Spalding, he graduated from the junior Pioneers to the senior Forest Citys and then went on to become a major-league superstar. He averaged an extraordinary .397 between 1871 and 1876, leading the National Association in batting twice and the National League once. He became known for his adeptness at hitting fair-fouls, leading one sportswriter to observe that Barnes "studies up the position, and makes his hits according to circumstances.... In fact, as 'a scientific batsman' — one who goes in to place a ball advantageously — we never saw his superior."[59] In 1877 Barnes fell seriously ill and was never the same player. (His decline has often been attributed to a new rule that eliminated fair-foul hits, but contemporaries blamed the illness.) He eventually moved to Chicago and pursued business. He died in Chicago on February 5, 1915.

Galen W. Barstow: Gale Barstow was the main backup for the Forest Citys in 1868. On the 1870 census he is listed both in Morris, Illinois (as a "base ball player") and in Rockford. He soon moved to Chicago, where he remained until his death on May 14, 1900, at the age of 49.

Royal Miller Buckman: R. M. Buckman was born on September 4, 1846, in Morristown, New York. He moved with his family to Illinois and became a starter for the Empire Club of Freeport after the war. He joined the Forest Citys in 1867, but remained a regular for only one year before losing his spot to new players. He returned to Freeport for a few years, then moved to Chicago and became an insurance adjuster. He died in Wilmette, Illinois, on February 27, 1918.

Owen Lee Cheney: Lee Cheney was born in Cheney's Grove, Illinois, a community founded by family members, on January 19, 1847. He grew up in Bloomington and served in two infantry regiments during the Civil War before being wounded. He then saw sporadic duty for the Forest Citys in 1869. An 1896 article described Cheney as "probably the most intellectual young man that ever stood in a base ball uniform," but he bounced around from job to job.[60] He mostly worked as a promoter of such events as balloon ascensions, boxing matches, and horse races. One of his most ambitious schemes saw him buy the former county fairgrounds and try to convert the site into an amusement park. He was also a noted billiards player and remained involved with baseball as manager of the Bloomington Reds. In that capacity he became a close friend of an up-and-coming player named Charley Radbourn who went on to a Hall of Fame career. Cheney was also an inventor and held 27 patents at the time of his death in Bloomington on November 2, 1911.[61]

Joseph Frederick Cone: Fred Cone was born in May of 1848 and grew up on his parents' farm four miles south of Rockford. As a boy he played for a junior club called the Unions and then joined the Sinnissippis. He was the regular first baseman for the Forest City juniors in 1867 and then for the Forest Citys in 1868 and 1869, but moved to the outfield in 1870 when Joe Doyle was signed. During these years he worked for Harry Starr as a clerk at the Holland House. He joined Spalding and Barnes in signing with Boston in 1871, but spent only one year in the major leagues. He then became the night manager of the Grand Pacific Hotel in Chicago and later worked for other Chicago hotels. His reminiscences about the Forest Citys appeared in the July 15, 1899, issue of the *Lima News*. Cone died in Chicago on April 13, 1909.[62]

Joseph E. Doyle: Joe Doyle was born around 1849 and was a native of the District of Columbia. He grew up in a sporting family, having one brother who was a major leaguer and another who became a noted Washington sportswriter. He joined the Buckeyes of Cincinnati and then became the first baseman of the Forest Citys in 1870. His signing moved Fred Cone to the outfield, but Cone would graciously acknowledge that to be a good move, saying of Doyle: "He wore no big glove to protect his hands, yet he was lightning on thrown balls, no matter how badly they broke. Up in the air, down on the ground, in fact any old way, he would get them and save many an error. In getting into fast double plays, he was a wonder."[63] After baseball, Doyle lived for a while in Cincinnati and New York but eventually returned to Washington. By 1920, the widowed Doyle was living at a home for the aged and infirm. He died in Washington on April 12, 1928.

Elisha Charles Dunn: Dr. E.C. Dunn was a Rockford physician who was born in Bethel, New York, on July 27, 1840. He grew up in Sandusky, Ohio, and Battle Creek, Michigan, and studied at the University of Pennsylvania before moving to Rockford in 1863. He was the second baseman of the Forest Citys in 1865 and was still representing the club at the time of the 1866 Rockford tournament, as he came second in a base-running contest staged at the tournament. Dunn was also a club director in 1866, but soon lost his place on the first nine. In 1871 he was appointed secretary to the U.S. ambassador to Turkey. He traveled the world during the next three years and was shipwrecked twice. On one of these occasions he was stranded on a desert island and his wife believed him dead for six months until word came of his rescue. Soon after returning home to Rockford, Dunn gave up medicine and became a lecturer on medical topics and on the many countries he had visited. He later got into local politics, serving as a member of the Rockford city council and running unsuccessfully for mayor in 1897 and 1899. Dunn died in Rockford on March 23, 1914.[64]

Thomas J. Foley: Tom Foley was a future major leaguer whose life is described more fully in the entry on the Excelsiors. His arrival in Rockford to play third base for the Forest Citys and operate a book bindery was reported in an article that referred to Foley as the "Old Reliable."[65] According to Cone, the book bindery "did well" during Foley's two years in Rockford.

Edward H. Griggs: Edward H. Griggs, who was born on March 19, 1835, in Dedham, Massachusetts, moved to Rockford in 1865 and became the associate editor and publisher of the *Rockford Register*. He married Hannah Fowler, the daughter of Rockford Mayor Albert Fowler. He also served as secretary of the Forest City Club, so perhaps it was no coincidence that he employed Spalding. Griggs also played a prominent role in the National Association of Base Ball Players. He moved in 1876 to Chicago, where he worked as a bookkeeper and as an actuary for an insurance company, and served as a state senator. He died in Chicago on October 25, 1909.

Winfield Scott Hastings: Scott Hastings was born on August 10, 1847, in Hillsboro, Ohio. His family moved to Illinois and Hastings served in the Illinois 145th Infantry, Company B, during the Civil War. He spent the 1869 and 1870 seasons with the Forest Citys, playing second base initially but eventually showing an aptitude for catching. He again played for Rockford after the club joined the National Association in 1871, but he was ruled ineligible and the Forest Citys forfeited four of their eight wins as a result. Hastings played in the majors for several more years, and his catching skill prompted one observer to maintain that he was "the only man who could catch" hard-throwing pitcher Jim Devlin. When his major-league career ended, Hastings moved to California. He died at a Veterans Home in Sawtelle, California, on August 14, 1907.

George Jerome Hitchcock: Jerome Hitchcock, who was born in New York state around 1836, worked for a dry-goods firm while in Rockford. He served in the Civil War, as a private in the 11th Illinois Infantry and as a hospital steward in the 52nd Illinois Infantry. He later moved to Janesville, Wisconsin, where he died in January of 1905.

Isaiah Smith Hyatt: Isaiah S. Hyatt was born in Chemung County, New York, in 1829. At the tender age of 19 he was put in charge of the *Cortland Democrat*. He then moved to Illinois and became the publisher and editor of the *Rockford Register*. He was vice president of the Forest Citys in 1866 and, according to Harriet Spalding, "was so much interested in baseball that he was always ready to let Albert off to play ball." In 1868, Hyatt's brother John read that a $10,000 reward was being offered to anyone who could find a substance that would replace ivory in billiard balls. The two brothers began to work on the problem, and on June 15, 1869, they received a patent for an "Improved Method of Making Solid Collodion." Isaiah Hyatt eventually gave the product the name of celluloid, and it came to be recognized as the first industrial plastic. They formed the Celluloid Manufacturing Company to produce their invention and Isaiah Hyatt moved to Albany, New York, and then to Newark, New Jersey, to help with its development. In 1884, the two brothers designed and patented a system of water filtration that was the first to make use of a coagulant. This invention is now recognized as a milestone in water filtration, and began to be used in municipal water supplies in 1885. But I. S. Hyatt didn't live to reap the rewards, as he died on March 18, 1885, in Eden, Florida.

George E. King: George King was born in Wappingers Falls, New York, on April 30, 1844. He was secretary of the Forest City Club in 1865 and its regular catcher in 1867 and 1868, including the celebrated upset of the Nationals. Spalding later recollected "how kind and considerate [King] used to be to me when I was a colt of 16 ... saying ... 'Steady, Albert, take your time, you're doing all right. They can't hit you.'"[66] Unlike most of the starters from the club's early years, he left the first nine voluntarily. Horace E. Buker deemed King to be one of the club's unsung heroes:

> George King passes from the line-up as catcher with the end of 1868 but played a few games in the field. This was a serious loss to the Forest Citys, removing one of the greatest players of early base ball and taking Bob Addy from the infield to catch. While George King elected to separate his future from that of his old associates who followed the game into the days of professionalism, it is only fair to express here the opinion that he was as great a ball player as those who became nationally famous at the game. An examination of his record will prove this. Sometimes I wonder if the absence of George King, peer of catchers, and Gat Stires, king of the bat ... was not all that kept Rockford from the world's championship of 1869.[67]

As a young man, King helped his father run a grocery store on South Main Street. He became a cashier for the Second National Bank in 1864 and was a bank president by the time of the 1896 Harry Wright Day celebrations, having also served as a Rockford alderman. But his later years were marred by tragedy and scandal. His only child, a daughter, died of diphtheria while a student at Rockford College. Then his bank collapsed, amid revelations of financial impropriety. King denied involvement in these transactions, but the dual blows left him a broken man in health and spirit. In 1897 he and his wife, Alice, moved to Circle City, Alaska, where he became an Alaska agent for the North American Transportation and Trading Company. After several years in Alaska, he moved to Seattle, where he died on April 28, 1905.[68]

Wallace "Fred" Lighthart: Wallace Lighthart was born around 1851 and played for the Empire Club of Freeport before joining the Forest Citys in 1867. By 1870 he was back in Freeport working as a grain buyer, but he later moved to St. Louis and became a railway man. Wallace Lighthart died in Minneapolis, Minnesota, on November 16, 1917.

James H. Manny: J. H. Manny, one of the club's two scorers, was born in New York state on April 17, 1836. During the Civil War, he served in the 11th Illinois Infantry for three months. In 1870 Manny and his wife were living at Henry Starr's hotel along with many other club members. He umpired one major-league game in 1871 but his shaky work led the *Chicago Tribune* to advise him to familiarize himself with that year's new rules. Manny worked for his cousin, John Manny, whose reaper manufacturing company was Rockford's largest firm. He was still living in Rockford in 1880 but eventually moved to Chicago, where he managed a furnace company. Manny died in Chicago on April 21, 1909.

Alfonzo Noble Nichols: Major A. N. Nichols was another key figure in the management of the Forest Citys. Born in Wilkes-Barre, Pennsylvania, on April 19, 1841, Nichols was working as a bank cashier in Milwaukee when the Civil War broke out. He was named a paymaster and a major, serving in those capacities until 1865. After the war he moved to Rockford and went into the insurance business. In addition to serving as secretary of the Forest City Club, he employed Spalding in his insurance office. He died in Rockford on June 26, 1912.[69]

William Ballard Osborn: See Byron (Illinois) Base Ball Club.

Charles T. Page: Charles Page was born in Hillsdale, Michigan, on April 18, 1849. He played first base for the Forest

Citys in 1865, but lost his spot when new players like Spalding joined the club. Page and Spalding remained close friends, and Spalding eventually married Page's niece. Page became a successful banker and the president of the Englewood Lumber Company. He lost both his wife and son in Chicago's Iroquois Theatre Fire tragedy of 1903, and then moved to Atlanta. He died in Atlanta on May 20, 1921.

Henry W. Price: Henry W. Price, the other scorer of the Forest Citys, was born in New York state in May of 1837. He became a very successful Rockford businessman, serving as president of the Manufacturers' and Merchants' Mutual Fire Insurance Company and also owning the Henry W. Price Company, which at one time was the largest glove manufacturer in the United States. The glove firm made the "Price" line of gloves and Price even patented a catcher's glove on October 27, 1891. But he suffered financial reverses when his investments in a watch company and a railway were busts and by 1896 he was struggling to avoid bankruptcy. He died on May 20, 1903.

Denton F. "Dent" or "Danny" Sawyer: Dent Sawyer was born around 1850 in either Illinois or Wisconsin. He played with Barnes and Spalding on the Pioneers in 1865, then joined the Forest City juniors in 1867 and played a backup role for the first nine in 1868. When the 1870 census was taken, he was living at the American House in Springfield. His occupation was listed as "base ball pitcher" and was rooming with a young man named Amos B. McKay, who was listed as a "base ball catcher." Sawyer was married around 1878 and moved to Iowa City, where he worked for the Iowa City Power Company and as a clothier. By 1910 he had retired and was still living in Iowa City.

Dr. Sylvester J. Sawyer: S. J. Sawyer was born in Hooksett, New Hampshire, in 1828, and studied at Columbia College (later University), earning his medical degree from the New York College of Physicians and Surgeons in 1854. While practicing in St. Paul, Minnesota, in 1859, he met and married Helen Sibley, the 18-year-old daughter of Minnesota Governor Henry H. Sibley. Sawyer began a practice in Raymond, Wisconsin, only to see Helen and their newborn daughter die of scarlet fever a mere ten months after their wedding. He then enlisted in Union Army's medical corps as a surgeon. After the war he moved to Rockford, where he pitched for the first nine of the Forest Citys in 1865 and then played third base in 1866. But he had moved to New York by 1867 when Spalding's absence created the need for a pitcher. Sawyer started a new family, but died in New York City on November 25, 1870.

Joe Simmons: Joe Simmons was another transplanted New Yorker who came to the Forest Citys by way of the Excelsiors of Chicago. Simmons had been driving a horsecar in Chicago when a Rockford director tracked him down and offered a job in Rockford that allowed him to be absent for ballgames. He had a long involvement with baseball that is described more fully in the entry on the Excelsiors.

Albert Goodwill Spalding: A. G. Spalding moved from the junior Pioneers to the senior Forest Citys in 1866 and went on to a Hall of Fame career. He was born on September 2, 1850, in Byron, Illinois, and was sent to Rockford in 1862 after the death of his father. In the first half of the 1870s, he was the best pitcher in baseball, relying on a devastating change of pace to lead Boston to four straight National Association pennants. In 1875 he was the key figure in Chicago's signing of Boston's "Big Four," a move that was crucial in the formation of the National League and in Chicago's winning that league's first pennant. But by then the curveball was changing baseball, and Spalding chose to play first base in 1877 and then retire. He had meanwhile started a sporting-goods firm that would make him a millionaire. He remained involved in baseball as president of the Chicago team, and his reminiscences about baseball — often not very accurate — are one of the best-known sources of anecdotes about the early years of baseball. He eventually moved to San Diego, California, where he died on September 9, 1915. His life story is told in much greater detail in his own book, *America's National Game*, and in Peter Levine's *A. G. Spalding and the Rise of Baseball* and Mark Lamster's *Spalding's World Tour*.

Chandler Starr: Chandler Starr was born on April 29, 1851, and was Spalding's first catcher on the Pioneers. He primarily belonged to the second nine of the Forest Citys, but was occasionally used on the first nine. He was the younger brother of Harry Starr; their father, Melancthon, was an early Rockford settler and a prominent banker. Chandler Starr graduated from East Hampton College in Massachusetts and then returned to Rockford, where he worked as cashier of his father's bank, the Winnebago National Bank. He later became vice president and director of the Rockford Trust Company. He died on October 9, 1930.

Henry Nevins Starr: Harry N. Starr was Chandler's older brother and was prominent in the club's doings. His time on the first nine of the Forest Citys was brief and he mostly played right field, but it was reported in 1896 that he had once been a "very good pitcher." He was born in New York state around 1840 and when he was 10 his father moved to Rockford to run the Winnebago National Bank. Harry Starr went into the dry-goods business and then became the proprietor of the Holland House, the hotel where many players and club members lived. In 1891, the former Forest City Base Ball Club vice president was elected to a two-year term as mayor. At the time of the 1896 reunion, it was reported that "time has left no impression on his love for the national game, and he was one of the most enthusiastic when the idea of a base ball reunion was broached."[70] He died in Rockford on the last day of 1920.

Warren S. Stearns: W. S. Stearns was born on September 18, 1846, and grew up in Bloomingdale, Illinois. I believe he was the man who played for the Forest Citys from 1865 to 1867, but there were numerous men named Stearns who played for the top two clubs in Illinois and with newspapers generally referring to ballplayers only by their surnames it is very difficult to be sure of who was who. Several notes referred to the 1867 player as George, but the preponderance of evidence suggests that he was in fact Warren. He joined the Excelsiors in 1868, but eventually returned to Rockford, where he manufactured bags and hosiery. Warren Stearns died in South Beloit, Illinois, on July 30, 1931.

Garret Stires: See Byron (Illinois) Base Ball Club.

Charles James Swasey: Charles J. Swasey was born in Haverhill, New Hampshire, on September 3, 1847. He moved to Chicago when young and in 1864 served a six-month stint in the 134th Illinois Infantry. He became a member of the Excelsiors in 1865 but could not crack the first nine. In 1866 he moved to Rockford and was a member of the Forest Citys for the next three years. Once again, he did not become a regular, but he filled in at third base in quite a few games. In 1873 Swasey moved to Fort Worth, Texas, where he became a cigar and liquor wholesaler. Swasey, who never married, lived in Fort Worth for the rest of his long life and remained an avid follower of baseball until the end. He enjoyed reminiscing about his long-ago days on the baseball diamond and he was interviewed by several reporters. Some of the resulting accounts confused Swasey with Charles Sweasy, who was a starter for the undefeated 1869 Red Stockings of Cincinnati. This appears, however, to have been the fault of the reporters and not an attempt by Swasey to take credit for the other player's achievements. In 1922 Swasey was described as being "in feeble health" and in "his last days." Nevertheless, he lived until March 24, 1939.

Frank Edward Trumbull: Frank Trumbull was born in Hamden, New York, on February 21, 1850, and grew up in Rockford. He was captain of the Union Club of Rockford, then joined the Forest City juniors and saw sporadic duty for the Forest Citys in 1868 and 1869. He briefly moved to Memphis and played for the Reds, but an arm injury ended his playing days. He returned to Rockford and initially worked as a carpenter, then spent more than two decades as a clerk at David Turkenkoph's clothing store. It was reported that he "would not part with his collection of photographs and score cards of the early days for any sum of money."[71] He died in Rockford on July 8, 1912.[72]

Hiram Hungerford Waldo: Hiram H. Waldo was born in Elba, New York, on November 23, 1827, and moved to Rockford in 1846. After working as a schoolteacher and post-office clerk, he decided to open a bookstore in 1855. His first store was a shanty on West State Street that was suspended on stilts to keep it safe from the river. He moved down the street to a new location four years later and ran the store until his death in 1912, taking only one vacation during those years.[73] He became the president of the Forest Citys and acted as unofficial club manager thereafter. Once the Forest Citys began charging admission, tickets were sold at Waldo's bookstore. Spalding described Waldo as "Rockford's Grand Old Man" and recalled how he advised him to accept a better-paying job and join the Excelsiors even though Waldo was then president of the Forest Citys. When Rockford joined the National Association in 1871, he remained very active in the club's doings and was credited with discovering Cap Anson. In addition, Hiram Waldo was an active civic leader who served as the county's school commissioner. According to Spalding, Waldo sometimes "interceded with my teacher to let me off early whenever the Forest Citys had a ball game on for that afternoon."[74] He also helped organize Rockford's Church of Christian Union. He remained devoted to baseball until the end of his life, although he had to stop going to games in his later years because he became too excited. Waldo died in Rockford on April 26, 1912.[75]

Henry Spalding Warner: Henry Warner was born in Pennsylvania around 1845 but lived in Rockford from infancy. His father, U. M. Warner, was the third mayor of Rockford. Henry was the shortstop of the Forest Citys in 1865 and club vice president, as well as captain in 1866. He probably played a role in enlisting the services of A. G. Spalding, who was his cousin. Yet like many early regulars, he lost his starting status when such new players joined the lineup. Warner graduated from the University of Michigan Law School in 1864 but never practiced law, working instead in a variety of Rockford business enterprises. He died in Rockford on May 23, 1921, just a week after Charles Page.[76]

Ernest L. Waxham: Ernest Waxham was born in La Porte, Indiana, on February 5, 1848. He had moved to Rockford by 1867 and played for the Forest City juniors that year, then became a semi-regular for the Forest Citys in 1868. The 1870 census found Waxham and Charles Page living in the home of Hiram Waldo, with Waxham working as a clerk in Waldo's bookstore. As noted in the entry on the Mutuals of Janesville, players identified only as Waxham, Bird, and Barker joined that club late in the 1870 season and it seems a safe bet that these were Ernest Waxham, George Bird, and Al Barker of the Forest Citys. Waxham later became a commercial traveler for the Henry W. Price Company, the glove firm owned by his fellow club member. He and his wife later traveled extensively in Europe and North Africa before settling in Los Angeles. That is where Waxham died on June 9, 1928.

Martin L. Wheeler: Mart Wheeler was born in Rockford on December 19, 1847, and was the first student to graduate from the city's East Side High School. He played a single game for the Forest Citys in 1865, but then switched to the rival Sinnissippi club of Rockford. He rejoined the Forest Citys in 1867 and remained a starter until he suffered a serious injury in a game against the Excelsiors on June 11, 1868. After attending Northwestern University, he worked as a music teacher and as a clerk in a boot and shoe store. He lived in Lincoln, Nebraska, in the early 1870s, then passed the Bar exam and moved to Chicago to practice law. He was also known for his tenor voice and toured with the Chicago Pinafore Company. He was found dead at a Chicago railway depot on September 27, 1908. Foul play was initially suspected, but the police concluded that he had slipped and fallen to his death.

Other Members: J. Brown (1865 player), Horace and John T. Buker, J. H. Burns, Thomas Butterworth (club president in 1869), L. F. Farwell, Thomas B. Gault (club vice president), Goss, J. W. Hall (treasurer), Hurd, Keeler, S. Lakin (1865 player), George W. LaRue, John Lewis (director), C. G. Manlove (director), Dr. Joseph Norman (main patron of 1866 tournament; probably Joseph Prentice Norman, who died on May 14, 1883), George P. Ross (treasurer), W. B. Thomas (Freeport), Webb, T. T. Webster (second baseman and club director in 1865), Hon. Charles A. Works (Rockford).

Note: The April 29, 1899, issue of *The Sporting News* reported that Robert J. Martin of the Forest Citys of Rockford had died recently at the age of 52. But no record for such a player could be found and the mystery at last was solved by a lengthier piece in *Sporting Life*. It recorded that Martin had died in Austin, Illinois, on the 17th and added:

> Old members of the Forest Citys say that he was never a member of that organization, although he played with the Pioneers and may have been in several games with the Forest Citys. Martin played right field for the Pioneers and was one of the good "youngsters" of the early days. He was much younger than the Forest Citys and was at one time the star of what was called the "second nine." [Frank] Trumbull, one of the first fans in the old days, does not remember Martin, but said to-day that it was possible that Martin came into prominence as a player after he left the city. Mike Golden remembers Martin, and said that he did some very nice work in the outfield in the early games. Uncle Hi Waldo told a reporter that he had an indistinct recollection of Martin, but that he thought he played in the old Pioneers. He thought Martin was not conspicuous or he should have remembered him.[77]

Sources

The Forest City Club of Rockford is mentioned in countless books and articles, but most of them offer brief descriptions of the club's celebrated win over the Nationals. As a result, this entry relies primarily on two sources. The first was an extraordinary forty-four-part history of the club that was written by Horace E. Buker and published serially in the *Rockford Republic* in 1922. The other was a five-part series by John Molyneaux that appeared in *Nuggets of History*, a publication of the Rockford Historical Society ("The Sinnissippi Base Ball Club," 43:1 [March 2005]; "The Forest City Base Ball Club: The Amateur Years," 45:1 [March 2007]; "No Longer Amateurs: The Forest City Base Ball Club in 1868," 46:2 [June 2008]; "'We Can Beat the Spots Off the Best Club That Ever Lived': The Forest City Base Ball Club in 1869," 46:3 [September 2008]; "The Eastern Tour — The 1870 Season of the Forest City Baseball Club," 47:3 [September 2009]). Because Dr. Molyneaux is at work on a book about the Forest City Club, I have used these articles sparingly. Numerous other articles contributed to my understanding of the club. Rockford was central to the 1896 Harry Wright Day celebrations and the activities were described in great detail in the *Rockford Register-Gazette* on April 13 and 14, 1896. Coverage also appeared in the *Chicago Tribune*, the *Chicago Inter-Ocean* and the *New York Times* between April 8 and 14, 1896. The reminiscences of Fred Cone ("Baseball Thirty Years Ago," *Lima News*, July 15, 1899) and Charles Page (E.C. Bruffey, "Bruffey Tells of Charles T. Page," *Atlanta Constitution*, August 10, 1919, A4; *Atlanta Constitution*, March 14, 1909) were also helpful. A.G. Spalding's *America's National Game* (1910; reprint: Lincoln: University of Nebraska Press, 1992) is a gold mine of information, but not entirely reliable. Other useful pieces about Spalding include "Spalding's Start," *Sporting Life*, June 20, 1908, 16; Harriet Spalding, *Reminiscences of Harriet I. Spalding* (East Orange, NJ: 1910); Peter Levine, *A.G. Spalding and the Rise of Baseball: The Promise of American Sport* (New York: Oxford University Press, 1985), and Mark Lamster, *Spalding's World Tour: The Epic Adventure that Took Baseball Around the Globe — And Made It America's Game* (New York: PublicAffairs, 2006). Other sources that were of help included: a brief history of baseball in Rockford written by James McKee that appeared in *Sporting Life* on April 9, 1884, 4; Harvey T. Woodruff, "Forest Citys a Noted Team," *Chicago Tribune*, March 31, 1912, C2; "Sport's Progress," *Sporting Life*, February 4, 1905, 10; Alfred H. Spink, *The National Game* (1911) (reprint: Carbondale: Southern Illinois University Press, 2000); William J. Ryczek, *When Johnny Came Sliding Home: The Post–Civil War Baseball Boom, 1865–1870* (Jefferson, NC: McFarland, 1998); David L. Fleitz, *Cap Anson: The Grand Old Man of Baseball* (Jefferson, NC: McFarland, 2005); and untitled pieces in the *Chicago Tribune* on February 4, 1877, in the *Bismarck Daily Tribune*, July 7, 1891, and the *Brooklyn Eagle* of December 6, 1885.

Notes

1. Chadwick Scrapbooks, vol. 4, handwritten by Spalding.
2. "Sport's Progress," *Sporting Life*, February 4, 1905, 10; A.G. Spalding, *America's National Game*, 509–511.
3. Letters from H.H. Waldo, Rockford, Illinois, to the Mills Commission, April 8 and July 7, 1905; Protoball website.
4. Edward Prell, "Cities That Pioneered Sports in Chicagoland: Albert G. Spalding, Horatio Alger Character, Sports Giant of Rockford," *Chicago Tribune*, January 31, 1954, A3. Prell's article is largely based on Spalding's *America's National Game*, but this statement appears to come from some other source.
5. Quoted in *Rockford Republic*, March 29, 1922, 1.
6. *Rockford Republic*, March 18, 1922, 1 and 10.
7. "Spalding's Start," *Sporting Life*, June 20, 1908, 16.
8. *Chicago Inter-Ocean*, April 12, 1896.
9. A. G. Spalding, *America's National Game* (New York: American Sports Publishing Company, 1911), 119–122.
10. *Sporting Life*, April 9, 1884, 4.
11. *Sporting Life*, August 12, 1885, 2.
12. A. H. Spink, *The National Game* (N.p.: National Game, 1910), 5.
13. Syndicated column, *Reno Evening Gazette*, March 31, 1922.
14. Spink, *The National Game*, 5.
15. Chadwick Scrapbooks, quoted in William J. Ryczek, *When Johnny Came Sliding Home* (Jefferson, NC: McFarland, 1998), 163.
16. *Rockford Republic*, September 9, 1922, 11.
17. Harriet Spalding, *Reminiscences of Harriet I. Spalding* (East Orange, NJ, 1910), 83.
18. *Rockford Republic*, April 19, 1922, 10.
19. *Rockford Republic*, April 22, 1922, 8.
20. "Baseball Thirty Years Ago," *Lima News*, July 15, 1899.
21. *Sporting Life*, August 12, 1885, 2; see also *New York Clipper*, August 22, 1868.
22. *Chicago Tribune*, June 21, 1867.
23. *Detroit Advertiser and Tribune*, June 21, 1866.
24. *Rockford Republic*, April 1, 1922, 1.
25. *Chicago Times*, June 27, 1866.
26. *Rockford Register*, August 16, 1939.
27. *Chicago Times*, June 28, 1866.
28. *Rockford Republic*, April 1, 1922, 11.

29. *Chicago Tribune*, November 21, 1866.
30. *Rockford Republic*, April 19, 1922, 10.
31. *Rockford Republic*, April 22, 1922, 1, 8.
32. *Chicago Times*, July 26, 1867.
33. Spalding, *America's National Game*, 109–111.
34. *Louisville Journal*, July 29, 1867, 3.
35. *Chicago Times*, July 26, 1867.
36. Spalding, *America's National Game*, 112.
37. *Chicago Times*, July 26, 1867.
38. *Rockford Republic*, May 6, 1922, 1, 8.
39. Spalding, *America's National Game*, 119.
40. Quoted in John Molyneaux, "The Sinnissippi Base Ball Club," *Nuggets of History*, 43:1 (March 2005).
41. *Chicago Times*, June 19, 1868.
42. "Baseball Thirty Years Ago," *Lima News*, July 15, 1899.
43. *Rockford Republic*, June 10, 1922, 1.
44. *Winnebago County Chief*, February 25, 1869; "A New Book Bindery," *Winnebago County Chief*, June 10, 1869.
45. *Winnebago County Chief*, August 5, 1869.
46. *Rockford Republic*, June 24, 1922, 6.
47. *Rockford Republic*, June 17, 1922, 3.
48. A. G. Spalding, *America's National Game*, 125. The Forest City Club had toured Ohio and Michigan in 1868.
49. William J. Ryczek, *When Johnny Came Sliding Home* (Jefferson, NC: McFarland, 1998), 163; citing *New York Clipper*, November 5, 1870.
50. *New York Clipper*, June 4, 1870; quoted in William J. Ryczek, *When Johnny Came Sliding Home*, 163.
51. Philip J. Lowry, *Green Cathedrals* (Reading, MA: Addison-Wesley, 1992), 196.
52. *Chicago Inter-Ocean*, April 12, 1896.
53. *Winnebago County Chief*, April 15, 1869.
54. Adrian C. Anson, *A Ball Player's Career* (1900: reprint, Mattituck, NY: Amereon, n.d.), 51.
55. For more on Addy's life, see my SABR BioProject profile: http://bioproj.sabr.org/bioproj.cfm?a=v&v=1 &bid=3182&pid=78.
56. *Rockford Register-Gazette*, April 14, 1896.
57. *Ibid*.
58. "Al Barker in Death's Sleep," *Rockford Register-Gazette*, September 16, 1912, 3; "'Al' Barker," *Rockford Register-Gazette*, September 16, 1912, 4; "Al Barker Passed Away Sunday," *Rockford Republic*, September 16, 1912, 9. For more on Barker, see my SABR BioProject profile: http://bioproj.sabr.org/bioproj.cfm?a=v&v=1 &bid=3111&pid=605.
59. *New York Clipper*, May 3, 1879.
60. *Rockford Register-Gazette*, April 13, 1896.
61. "Lee Cheney Found Dead in Chair," *Bloomington Pantagraph*, November 3, 1911, 11.
62. *Rockford Register-Gazette*, April 15, 1909.
63. "Baseball Thirty Years Ago," *Lima News*, July 15, 1899.
64. "Dr. Dunn Died at His Home," *Rockford Register-Gazette*, March 23, 1914, 1, 9; "Dr. Dunn Died This Morning," *Rockford Republic*, March 23, 1914, 1.
65. *Winnebago County Chief*, June 10, 1869.
66. *Rockford Register-Gazette*, April 14, 1896.
67. *Rockford Republic*, June 17, 1922, 3.
68. "George E. King Dies in West," *Rockford Register-Gazette*, April 29, 1905, 1.
69. "Major Nicholds Dies Suddenly," *Rockford Register-Gazette*, June 26, 1912, 7.
70. *Rockford Register-Gazette*, April 13, 1896.
71. *Rockford Register-Gazette*, April 13, 1896.
72. "F.E. Trumbull Passed Away at 3 A.M.," *Rockford Republic*, July 8, 1912, 7; "Death Claims F. Trumbull," *Rockford Register-Gazette*, July 8, 1912, 3.
73. *Rockford Register-Gazette*, April 26, 1912.
74. *Rockford Register-Gazette*, April 14, 1896.
75. *Rockford Register-Gazette*, April 26, 1912. For additional details on Waldo's life, see my SABR BioProject profile: http://bioproj.sabr.org/bioproj.cfm?a=v&v=1 &bid=3112&pid=19715.
76. "Henry Warner Expires After Brief Illness," *Rockford Register-Gazette*, May 23, 1921, 1, 2; "Pioneer Baseball Captain Dies Today," *Rockford Republic*, May 23, 1921, 2.
77. "A Veteran Gone," *Sporting Life*, April 29, 1899, 6.

❖ *Pecatonica Base Ball Club* (Peter Morris) ❖

CLUB HISTORY

The Pecatonica (Illinois) Base Ball Club had a very brief existence and lost by a lopsided margin in the only one of its games that has been recorded for posterity. Nevertheless the club remained alive in the popular imagination long after playing its last game. As is so often the case, the myths and legends that surrounded this club have only a limited basis in reality.

In 1866 the city of Rockford, Illinois, hosted a major tournament that was billed as being for the championship of the Northwest. The event attracted the likes of the Cream City Club of Milwaukee, the Julien Club of Dubuque, Iowa, the Detroit Base Ball Club, the Excelsior Club of Chicago, the Forest Citys of Rockford, and a number of other strong Illinois nines. Also among the entrants was a club from Pecatonica, a village about twenty miles from Rockford.[1]

The participation of this club, which had been formed only four months earlier, created a problem. Tournaments of the era were usually broken into several divisions, so as to allow junior and small-town clubs to compete among their peers. But when the captains met at the outset of the tournament, a proposal to create different classes was voted down, forcing the Pecatonica Base Ball Club to either play against the big-city teams or not compete.[2] The Pecatonica Club elected to play and became the tenth entry in the field.

The small-town upstarts were pitted against one of the tournament's favorites in the opening game of the single-elimination tournament and the result was predictable. The Detroit Base Ball Club beat the Pecatonica Club by the jaw-dropping score of 49–1.

While the lopsided result was no surprise, a couple of factors made the game memorable. The first was that the Pecatonicas had managed only a single run at a time when the rules and conditions so favored hitters that scores almost always reached double digits. Indeed, while box scores did not yet include hits, and the game accounts were a bit vague, it appears that the club did not even get a base hit until at least the sixth inning and managed only a couple of safe hits in the entire game.[3]

An eyewitness blamed the club's lack of success at the bat on "the wind being directly in the face of the batting, making it [a] comparatively rare occurrence to knock the ball very far from the bases."[4] In light of the 49 runs scored by the opponents, this excuse sounds unconvincing. In their defense, however, the box score shows that 14 of the Pecatonica hitters were retired on fly balls, plus quite a few more on foul outs, which suggests that they were accustomed to hitting the ball in the air and thus were handicapped unduly by the wind.[5] Whatever the reason, the 49–1 score attracted widespread attention, with the *Chicago Times* describing it as "a victory ... only to be equaled by the Athletics of Philadelphia."[6]

The second factor was that the tournament's organizers had arranged to have numerous prizes presented to the clubs and to individual players. One of those prizes, the "Chandlers and Humphrey Prize," was a silver-mounted tin horn bearing the inscription "Practice" that was to be awarded to the club that was beaten by the greatest margin.[7] Naturally the Pecatonica Base Ball Club was the recipient of the horn, which was described as "an ornate specimen of German silver workmanship."[8]

After the conclusion of the tournament, which was won by the Excelsiors of Chicago, the Pecatonica Club returned home. There is no contemporary documentation that its members ever played another game, but Forest City of Rockford historian Horace E. Buker reported that the Pecatonica Club hosted one subsequent tournament. According to Buker, the other entrants were the Plow Boys of Seward, the Prairie Boys of Seward, the Farmers of Winnebago, the Clippers of Lysander, the Eurekas of Lysander, and the Bummers of Winnebago. As Buker noted, "The names selected indicate that the farmer boys were not taking themselves very seriously," yet even against this lesser competition, the Pecatonica Club failed to finish in the top three.[9]

In any event, the Pecatonica Club's legacy long outlived the nine's existence. The next year the mighty Nationals of Washington came to Chicago to play a series against the top clubs in Illinois. To everyone's surprise, the Nationals were beaten in the first game by the Forest Citys of Rockford. In the next match, the Eastern visitors faced the Excelsiors of Chicago, and since the Excelsiors were the state's number one club, it was now assumed in Chicago that the Excelsiors would win.

Instead the Nationals beat Chicago's pride and joy by the shocking score of 49–4. The loss ended any hope that the Excelsiors would become a national powerhouse. It also reminded many people of the game at the Rockford tournament that had ended with a very similar score. The resemblance was also noticed in Pecatonica, and shortly thereafter the Excelsior Club received a package from that village. In it was the horn the Pecatonica Club had received at the Rockford tournament along with a good-natured note that commended the Chicago club for having "fairly taken from us our hard-earned laurels."[10]

The Excelsiors seem to have taken the tin horn in equally good humor, allowing some of their supporters to bring it to Detroit and blow on it throughout a match against the vanquishers of the Pecatonica Base Ball Club. As a result, the horn — now universally known as the "Pecatonica horn"— passed into baseball lore.

The lopsided score of the Pecatonica Club's only documented game was one aspect of the appeal, and many of these references invoked the idea of a hopelessly overmatched club. This was especially noticeable in Chicago, where the ensuing years brought periodic reminders of the club. For example, in 1878, after Chicago's National League team coughed up a 7–2 advantage, a *Tribune* sportswriter referred to the lead as one "that ought to have enabled even the Pecatonica Horn-blowers to win if they played even fairly steadily."[11]

But memories of the Pecatonica Club also remained alive in other quarters, and in these instances it was the club's rural origins that were emphasized. For example, in 1869 a club from a Michigan farming community named itself the Pecatonica Club of Shepardsville and played a series with a rival known as the Forlorn Hope Club of Ovid.[12]

Several reminiscences offered exaggerated or fictitious anecdotes based upon the club's rural origins. The most notable was a widely reprinted 1878 description of the Rockford tournament game that was presumably made up. This account described a Pecatonica farmer who made the trip to Rockford for the game and wagered three loads of hay and a yearling calf on its outcome. At the outset of the game, he keeps track of the score by making notches in a stick with his knife. But with all the scoring on one side, he gradually becomes disheartened. Finally, an explanation occurs to him and he exclaims, "Why the goldarned fools are after the horn!"[13]

The enduring appeal of this image of a plucky rural nine that suffers an overwhelming defeat was shown in 1914 when Finley Peter Dunne, the popular creator of Mr. Dooley, included a mention. In Dunne's column, an old-timer reminisced in an exaggeratedly rural dialect about having watched Harry Wright, Cap Anson, Jim White, and "th' Forest Citys bate th' Pecatonica Blues be a scoor iv two hundhred an' eight to nawthin.'"[14]

Legends such as these were kept alive and expanded upon in the oral story-telling tradition of 19th-century America. The resulting tales could be very tall. For example, an 1887 article maintained that the Pecatonica Club themselves donated the horn, expecting to finish last and win it, only to have the Excelsiors finish last.[15] Then there was this version that appeared in 1882: "The Rockford citizens gave a great base ball tournament for clubs from all over the country in 1866, at Rockford, and the Pecatonica Club, which had the lowest average of games won, was presented with a fish horn handsomely decorated, and carried it home amid the good natured chaff of all the players. In 1867 the old Excelsior Club of this city played so poorly and got beat so often that the horn was sent here by special messenger from the village of Pecatonica with the compliments of that club. It then traveled back and forth among a number of national clubs and finally stayed in the East somewhere. It is still owned by some club there, but no one knows what club."[16]

And in 1896, as part of an article about the stories being told about early baseball, the *New York Times* reported as follows:

> The most famous of these annals is that of the "Pecatonica Horn," or rather, of the great tournament of 1869, devised and carried out by "Uncle Hi" Waldo, and which gave rise to the horn and the story. At this tournament there were gathered as guests of the Forest Citys the Mutuals of New York, the Atlantics of Brooklyn, the Cincinnati Red Stockings, and such local clubs as the Maple Leafs of Guilford, the Ducklegs of Belvidere, the Rustlers of Cherry Valley, the Plowboys of Stillman Valley, and the Pecatonicas of Pecatonica. It fell to the lot of "Uncle Hi" Waldo to provide the prizes and trophies to be played for, and when he thought he had done the thing up handsomely and was all through, the Hon. "Bob" Tinker, a famous joker and afterward Mayor of the town, remarked:
> "Why, Uncle Hi, you have forgotten a prize for the club having the lowest score."
> "That's so," said "Uncle Hi." "Well, what is suitable for the club coming out at the small end of the horn? I have it. We'll give 'em a horn." And forthwith he ordered constructed the largest tin horn ever made. The last day of the tournament was the one on which the Pecatonicas of Pecatonica were to play the Red Stockings, and as it was generally conceded that they would win the horn, it was taken to the Fair Grounds on a float, with great ceremony, and during the game, rousing blasts were blown upon it by enthusiasts to encourage the Pecatonicas to sustained effort.
> When the Pecatonicas came on the field a young farmer was conspicuously in evidence close to the umpire and scorers. He had a lath, whittled down to a fine edge on both sides, ready to notch in keeping tally. The game started, and developed into one long inning, which lasted all through the afternoon, and the Pecatonicas of Pecatonica were sweating, shouting, and running breathlessly all over the field during the long and phenomenal inning of the Red Stockings. The Pecatonica enthusiast had started out by betting a yearling calf on his home favorites, and later on added a load of hay and another of wood to his wager. Just as dusk was falling that stalwart batter George Wright swiped the ball a fair stroke, and sent it over the centrefield fence into Kent's Creek, and it floated away on the current, while four runs in succession came in, the score then standing something like 121 to 0.
> The young farmer carefully notched up the four runs on his lath, which was already full of the nicks on one side, and, as he was obliged to turn over the end to the other side, he rubbed his hand carefully over the notches, and then, looking up in surprise and astonishment, he gazed upon the laughing bystanders with a dawning expression upon his face of the calamitous fate that had overtaken the Pecatonicas and burst out with the exclamation, "Why, the goll darned fools are after the horn!"
> Thus started the story of the famous Pecatonica horn, which in various forms has found place in baseball annals ever since.

> The Red Stockings begged the horn from the Pecatonicas and carried it in triumph throughout the country, exhibiting it with pride as a trophy of their famous victory and of the greatest baseball tournament ever held in the West.[17]

While accounts such as this one bore little relation to the actual events of the 1866 Rockford tournament, they did serve to keep memories of the Pecatonica Base Ball Club alive long after the club's very short career had ended.

CLUB MEMBERS

Although later accounts implied that the members of the Pecatonica Base Ball Club were rural hayseeds, the reality was very different. Pecatonica remains to this day a small village of about 2,000 and it was slightly smaller at the time — the 1860 census shows a little over 800 residents, a figure that had grown to about 1,800 by 1870. The town's population in 1860 included only about 80 males who would have been in their twenties as of 1866 when the Pecatonica Base Ball Club was formed, and that number had risen only to 120 as of 1870.

There was thus an extremely small population from which to select a baseball nine, and the pool of available players was reduced by several other factors. To begin with, the Civil War had taken the lives of many young men who would have been of ideal age to play baseball in 1866, while leaving many others unfit for baseball activity. Other young men couldn't join a baseball club because of business or family obligations or just lacked interest. Of course the club could have drawn on the surrounding farm population, but it was a daunting task to get farmers' sons into town on a regular basis for practice.

As a result, it can safely be assumed that the Pecatonica Club had few members beyond its first nine and that those nine represented every able-bodied local man who was willing to practice, whether or not they possessed much athletic ability. A closer look at those nine men follows, and it produces some surprising results. In particular, none of the nine were farmers, while many of them would eventually move to large cities and engage in the law, business, or medicine. Several of the men were well into their 30s, which again suggests how difficult it was for a village as small as Pecatonica to field a baseball nine.

Another striking feature is that two of the club members had attended the University of Michigan, with one playing on that school's highly successful baseball nine, a squad that would beat the Detroit Base Ball Club in 1867. It seems likely that these two young men were responsible for organizing the Pecatonica Base Ball Club. Yet this intriguing element of the club was never mentioned, with reports instead exaggerating the club's rural ties.

John Comly Bigger: J. C. Bigger was born in Massillon, Ohio, on April 11, 1844, and his family eventually moved to Freeport, Illinois, a town some 17 miles from Pecatonica. He enrolled at the University of Michigan in 1862, but put his studies on hold that summer to enlist in the Union Army. He served in Illinois's 92nd Infantry Regiment for 16 months, earning his discharge on December 29, 1863. He then returned to school, earning a law degree and playing the outfield for the school baseball nine in the fall of 1866. Bigger was also a member of the same fraternity as Henry B. Farwell, so it is probably no coincidence that both had ended up in Pecatonica in 1866 when the club's first baseball nine was formed. He was the left fielder for the nine, and scored their lone run in their 49–1 loss at the Rockford tournament. Bigger earned his degree in 1868 and by 1870 he had moved to St. Louis to begin a law practice. During the 1870s, he relocated to Dallas, where he became a United States Attorney and was active in the Republican Party. He died in Dallas on September 24, 1900.

Dr. Thomas Mifflin Butler: Born in Lycoming County, Pennsylvania, on June 21, 1833, Dr. Thomas M. Butler graduated from Lewisburg University and then earned a medical degree from Cincinnati Medical College. He arrived in Pecatonica in 1861 to begin a medical practice and married a local woman three years later. In 1876 he took a break from medicine after being elected circuit clerk. He eventually returned to medicine, practicing in Milwaukee, Detroit, and Rockford before retiring around 1903. The onetime first baseman and cleanup hitter for the Pecatonica Base Ball Club died in Rockford on November 28, 1912.

Henry Byron Farwell: Henry Byron Farwell was born on October 1, 1845, on a farm near Freeport. He graduated from Freeport High School and then in 1862 enrolled at the University of Michigan, where he belonged to the same fraternity as J. C. Bigger. Around this time, his family moved to Pecatonica. Bigger and Farwell both became members of the Pecatonica Base Ball Club in 1867, with Farwell serving as the club's pitcher. Farwell never graduated from the University of Michigan, but was admitted to the bar and began a law practice in Rockford. He later moved to St. Paul, where he served as a police-court judge for a few years before returning to private practice. He died in St. Paul on April 20, 1903.

Charles C. Stevens: C. C. Stevens was the first baseman of the Pecatonica Base Ball Club. He also served as club secretary, and in 1867 he had the responsibility of sending the famed horn to the Excelsior Club and of writing the accompanying letter. Charles C. Stevens was born in Cuba, New York, on November 6, 1832. Since his father was born in the same New York town as fellow club members Erastus and Thomas Stevens, it seems very likely that he was their first cousin. Stevens married in 1854 and moved to Pecatonica the following year to work as a master saddler. After training his son Frank in the same profession, he sold his business to his son in 1883, and then worked in real estate and loans and collections. He also served as a notary public and was village president when he died in Pecatonica on December 30, 1902. Many of Pecatonica's stores closed for his funeral.

Erastus Corning Stevens: Erastus Stevens was born in Illinois on March 27, 1837. His father, Josiah, had brought the family to Illinois from New York by covered wagon three years earlier, and Josiah found work for the railroad. As a result, the family moved several times, and there are conflicting accounts of the exact location of Erastus's birth. Eventually the family settled in Pecatonica, where Erastus became a carpenter. He was married and had a young daughter when the Civil War broke out, but nonetheless enlisted in the 1st Illinois Cavalry and served for 15 months. While at war, his first son was born and he learned the news when a letter arrived from home that included a little blond curl off the infant's head and a request that he suggest a name. He chose Josiah Halleck in honor of, respectively, his father and the general under whom he was serving. Stevens suffered hearing loss during the war and became very deaf as a result. After his brief tenure as third baseman for the Pecatonica Base Ball Club, Erastus Stevens did not remain in the town for long. Around 1868 he relocated to Chicago and worked as a carpenter and builder. After about a decade in Chicago, he, his wife, and their four children moved to the Dakota Territories during the Great Dakota Boom. Their first winter was a discouraging one that featured a notorious blizzard, but the family persevered and eventually settled in Chamberlain, South Dakota, where Erastus Stevens's building skills proved invaluable. Along with his oldest son, Josiah, and his brother Thomas, he built most of the town's houses as well as the Indian school and numerous other important buildings. Stevens then opened a meat market in Chamberlain, which he ran until 1895, when he moved to Vermillion. He died there on May 22, 1903.

Thomas Asaph Stevens: Thomas Asaph Stevens was the younger brother of Erastus Stevens and the catcher of the Pecatonica Base Ball Club. He was born in Elgin, Illinois, on January 26, 1840. On the day after President Lincoln's first call for volunteers, he enlisted in the Union Army as a member of the Rockford Zouaves. When his three-month enlistment ended, he helped recruit a company in the 1st Illinois Cavalry, then served as a first lieutenant in that company for more than a year, alongside his brother. He eventually enlisted for a third tour of duty in the 146th Illinois Infantry, finally being mustered out on August 1, 1865. He returned to Pecatonica and was married later that month. Thomas Stevens opened a meat market in town, but was soon itching for new surroundings. He caught "gold fever" and spent time staking claims and prospecting in several Western states but always returned to Pecatonica. In 1872 he finally left for good, moving to Chicago and working there as a bookkeeper for a decade. After his brother Erastus relocated to Chamberlain, Thomas followed him in 1882 and helped him build many of the town's homes and buildings. He then served as register of deeds and held several other prominent positions in Chamberlain, culminating in 1898 with his appointment as local postmaster. He died in Chamberlain on March 15, 1917.

Daniel A. Stitsel: D. A. Stitsel was born around 1828 in Pennsylvania, making him nearly 40 and the oldest club member when he played right field for the Pecatonica Base Ball Club. He arrived in Pecatonica in 1854 and married his landlady's daughter six years later. He became a hardware and iron merchant and, aside from briefly relocating to Chicago, lived in Pecatonica for the rest of his life. The 1900 census shows him as retired and he died a few years later (the cemetery lists his year of death as 1905, while a death index gives the date as January 8, 1906).

Andrew M. Thompson: A. M. Thompson was the center fielder of the Pecatonica Base Ball Club and the only club member known to have been involved with baseball after the Rockford tournament. Thompson was born on November 9, 1845, in Seward Township, near Pecatonica. By 1860 the family had moved into Pecatonica and, according to his obituary, Andrew served as a drummer boy in the Civil War. After the war he worked as a saloon keeper, then married in 1875 and moved to St. Paul, Minnesota, where he worked in real estate. In 1884 he became involved in the affairs of the local minor-league club, eventually becoming its manager. Late in the year St. Paul joined the Union Association, making Thompson briefly a major-league manager. He remained involved in the local baseball scene for several more years, managing a club in 1886 and subsequently purchasing an interest in it. In 1889 Thompson even mortgaged his house to keep professional baseball in St. Paul alive, only to see the club have to disband the following year. But apparently he came out of the experience solvent and undiscouraged, as two years later he purchased a stake in another local minor-league club. Andrew M. Thompson returned to Pecatonica in 1893 and his health began to decline. In February of 1895, he was hauling wood when his sleigh overturned and flung him to the ground. He suffered a spine injury that led to his death in Pecatonica on the 17th.

E. J. Thompson: E. J. Thompson is almost certainly Edward J. Thompson, who was born in 1836 in Ohio, served in the Civil War, and died on May 20, 1873. Edward had a twin brother named Edwin who died in 1875 and it is possible that Edwin was the man who played center field for the Pecatonica Base Ball Club. But the Pecatonica Cemetery lists Edwin's middle initial as D, which points to Edward.

Other Members: Scorer G. W. Keys.

NOTES

1. *Chicago Tribune*, June 29, 1866.
2. *Detroit Advertiser and Tribune*, July 3, 1866.
3. *Chicago Times*, June 27, 1866.
4. *Chicago Tribune*, June 29, 1866.
5. The *Tribune*'s box score states that 14 fly outs were recorded by the Detroits and only 9 by the Pecatonicas, a huge discrepancy considering that the Michigan club had about three times as many at bats. That suggests a difference in hitting approach, though no doubt fielding skill played a role as well. The foul outs were 6 to 4, but the wording is ambiguous, so it's not clear which figure belonged to which club. Either way, at least two-thirds of the Pecatonica hitters were retired on balls hit in the air. In addition, Detroit managed only one home run, which lends more credence to the theory that the wind and a difference in batting approach were major factors.
6. *Chicago Times*, June 27, 1866.
7. *Chicago Tribune*, June 25, 1866.
8. *Chicago Times*, July 31, 1867; *Ball Players' Chronicle*, August 15, 1867.
9. *Rockford Republic*, April 8, 1922, 1, 12.
10. *Chicago Tribune*, July 31, 1867.
11. *Chicago Tribune*, May 27, 1878.
12. *Clinton* (MI) *Independent*, September 1, 1869.
13. The piece appeared in the *New York Sunday Mercury* on October 12, 1878. It also appeared in the *New York World* and other newspapers.
14. Syndicated column; *Boston Globe*, March 8, 1914.
15. *Chicago Inter-Ocean*, August 10, 1887.
16. *Chicago Herald*, June 11, 1882.
17. *New York Times*, April 12, 1896.

❖ *Olympians of Beloit College* (Fred Burwell) ❖

CLUB HISTORY

A contemporary photograph shows nine ballplayers nattily dressed in new uniforms, wielding massive bats that look hewn from tree trunks. Two or three fresh-faced kids are surrounded by a group of grizzled Civil War veterans. In 1866, the Olympian Base Ball Club of tiny Beloit College tested the mettle of clubs hailing from much larger cities, winning several games and apparently losing only one. The following year they were the champion baseball club of Wisconsin. Then, as fast as they rose, they faded away.

At that time, the city of Beloit, Wisconsin, had just over 4,000 citizens and had been in existence for only thirty years. Founded in 1836 by New England emigrants, the city nestled along two sides of the Rock River, the southernmost city in Rock County, only a few steps from Illinois. The new city drew entrepreneurs who built a paper manufactory and a steam planing mill among other enterprises. Downtown Beloit became a hub for commerce and a market for the many farmers tilling the nearby fertile prairie.

Almost from its inception, the city planned to have a college. After four founding conventions a group known as the Friends of Education adopted the Beloit College charter in 1846, with classes beginning in 1847, based on the Yale model of a classical curriculum. By 1866, fledgling Beloit College had 82 students in the college proper, with another 159 in its Preparatory Department. Fully one half of its alumni had served in the Union armed forces during the Civil War. Many veterans returned to the college to resume their studies.

Although since the 1840s Beloit College students had enjoyed a variety of sports among themselves, they had never played a contest with a club from outside the college. With the introduction in 1866 of a new sport, that was about to change, as a reporter for the college newspaper explained: "The term for out-door sport and exercise has returned. The rough and exciting game of foot-ball has been in a great measure superseded by a more agreeable one called 'New York Base.' The corporeal calamities attending our 'exercise for health' are no longer bruised shins and broken collar-bones, but simply blistered hands and occasionally a black eye."[1]

The same issue announced the formation of two "complete organizations" for the new game, the "Olympian Base Ball Club" of Beloit College, and the "Union Base Ball Club" of the Preparatory Department, along with a roster of officers.[2] According to alumnus Joel B. Dow, class of 1869, "Base-ball was born and christened in '66. Aaron Skinner, of '69, proposed the name of 'Olympians' for the College Nine, and it was a go. Aaron was commended for his classic thought."[3] A founder of the Olympian Club, Henry T. Wright, Beloit College class of 1866, wrote in 1920, "W. A. Cochran is the man I selected and coached for the Olympian Baseball club, the first college baseball club west of the Allegheny Mountains so far as I can learn."[4]

Although they probably played several undocumented games during 1866 and 1867, the first known match of the Olympian Base Ball Club took place on Saturday afternoon, June 2, 1866, against the Union Base Ball Club, resulting in a resounding 57–12 victory, featuring a 13-run second inning and a 15-run eighth inning. The line score did not list the players, but mentioned that there were four Olympian home runs.[5]

In one of its editorials, *The Beloit College Monthly* reflected on changing times, describing a country and people ready at last for fun and leisure after the turmoil of the war years:

> Did we say, a moment ago, the summer is a time of activity? Yes, and of recreation too. And this summer is specially so. In the last war were many scenes of fierce excitement. The people at times have boiled over with rage, patriotism, bitterness or grief. Now peace has come and the popular heart demands some food for excitement. So a host of festivities, celebrations and tournaments have risen all through the land.... We rejoice in the rising popularity of manly sports....[6]

Such was that popularity that both Olympian and Union clubs even featured a "second nine" which played each other on June 9, this time with the Union Club on top, 87–59.[7] By year's end, the Olympian Club boasted fifty-four members and a full directorship, led by its president, William A. Cochran.[8]

The Olympian Base Ball Club played its first game against a club from another city on June 17, losing to the Capital Club of Madison, 49–26, in a contest lasting two hours and forty-five minutes. "Though beaten, our boys won great honor by their fine playing toward the close," reported *The Beloit College Monthly*. "A few more months of practice and we may well be proud of them. The other Club, the Capital, from Madison, played quite scientifically and has good prospects before it in the future."[9]

A few weeks later, the college graduated seventeen students. Apparently, baseball did not resume again until the fall. The *Janesville Gazette*, from Beloit's neighboring city, remarked on the growing popularity of baseball in an article headlined "Base Ball the National Game," in which it affirmed that "the game of base ball is attracting more attention from the American people than any other game (played purely for recreation) ever did in this or any other country in ancient or modern times. There were 25,000 persons present to witness a game played last week in Philadelphia, 10,000 at Hartford, Conn. And in our sister city of Beloit, 4,000 people were on the grounds to witness a game between the Freeport and Beloit boys. The Badger club of this city have re-

Beloit Olympian Base Ball Club. Top row: Edward S. Chadwick, William A. Cochran, Robert M. Town, George W. Marston. Bottom row: Milo C. Jones, Arthur Burrall, Charles H. Bicknell, Willard T. Hyde, Harmon B. Tuttle (courtesy Beloit College Archives).

ceived and accepted a challenge from the Olympian club of Beloit. Game to be played on the grounds of the Badger boys in this city on Saturday next October 13th."[10] The writer, perhaps not as knowledgeable about the game as his editor might have hoped, apparently confused the Badger team of Beloit with Janesville's own, because the following issue mentions the upcoming game as being between the "Olympian Club of Beloit and the Bower City Club of Janesville."[11] The contest, apparently the first "match game" ever played in Janesville, began promptly at 1:30 P.M. under a gloomy sky, according to the Janesville paper: "The dark heavy clouds which veiled the sun during almost the entire day, threatened to somewhat allay the excitement...." The reporter noted the Bower City uniform of "black pantaloons, white jacket and tarpaulin hat" and the players' apparent nervousness. "It could easily be seen that the Janesville boys were afraid of their adversaries, as they did not go in with a will, but seemed to draw back." More than thirty years later, Beloit's pitcher, William A. Cochran, recalled how the Beloit team intimidated their neighbors:

> The Olympians won the toss and took the field, and then for a few moments before the game was called the Janesvillians were given an exhibition of ball throwing, fancy catches, hand springs and various other gymnastic exercises, which made their eyes open with astonishment, and they were practically beaten before the first ball was pitched.[12]

The Olympian Club also played in "full regulation dress — white zouave pants, red stripes down the outside, red jackets, white regulation caps, and shoes. They took hold as though they came up to win, all playing together."[13] The Olympian Club trounced the Bower City Club, 61–8, after which "the boys formed the usual circle and gave three cheers each for the umpire (Capt. Taggart) and the respective clubs, when the Bower City escorted the Olympians to the Myers House, where they all partook of the hospitalities...." The newspaper chalked up the Bower City Club's poor showing to a lack of experience playing together. The reporter noted one player's performance: "Mr. Cochrane [sic] appears to be the champion of the Olympians...." William Avery Cochran, class of 1867, pitched the entire game, hit three home runs, and scored ten times.[14]

The Olympian Base Ball Club played at least one more match that fall. On October 26, in Beloit, they defeated the local Badger Club, 60–22.[15]

On April 10, 1867, the Badger Club of Beloit sponsored a convention for all of the baseball clubs in the state "for the purpose of forming a State Association of Base Ball Clubs."[16] Meeting at the Bushnell House in downtown Beloit, seven participating clubs chose two delegates each, and a committee nominated officers of the Association. The Olympian Club chose pitcher William Avery Cochran and center fielder Edward Sanborn Chadwick, who also served on the nominating committee, although none from the club became an officer of the Association. The newly formed association declared as its main purpose the desire that Wisconsin's baseball clubs gain representation in the National Association of Base Ball Players.[17]

Spring 1867 found the Olympian Base Ball Club reconvening for another season on the diamond. "Base Ball especially, [sic] bids fair to 'become the rage' again, this summer," reported the student newspaper. "The boys may be seen at almost any time of day, practicing in throwing and catching.... The 'New York game' is a truly noble one, and has become the national sport."[18]

Practice was "very rigorous," according to an article published many years later:

> They made a practice game as severe and as much like a match game as possible. They used to play a team consisting of the regular second nine with three or four extra men, making a team of twelve in all, the extra men being put into the field, with an extra shortstop and men to back up the basemen. They used to give their battery to the second team and thus, pitted against their equals, they kept themselves in the pink of condition. From one of the players, I have learned that they had as doubtful contests with the Unions under these conditions as they did with the strongest teams and occasionally lost games.[19]

The Whitewater Club challenged the Olympians and set a match for May 25, on neutral territory in Janesville at the grounds of the Bower City Club. "Base Ball is at present receiving a good deal of attention from the students, as it does from all other classes of the community," a writer noted in the college paper.[20] *The Janesville Gazette* commented, "They are said to be two of the best clubs in the State and it will be an occasion of no small interest to the lovers of good playing ... we may predict a large attendance of spectators."[21]

James L. Foley, a student in the Preparatory Department of Beloit College, kept an extensive diary, and described the Olympian and Whitewater contest held on May 25. He was a member of the committee that hired "Wood's omnibus" to carry twelve students at seventy-five cents each. That morning, Foley and his comrades set off on the journey to Janesville, despite not receiving permission from Preparatory Department Principal Fisk, who at morning chapel warned the students that those who went "would have to take their marks." Foley and his fellow students rushed through morning recitations in time to make the trip. "We were a jolly set of school-boys just let loose from school, or rather just broke loose from school," he wrote.[22] They stopped for dinner at the American House, where for 40 cents, Foley's meal "was the very best that I have eaten since leaving home." The proprietor expressed amazement when the prep boys refused cigars. "Not one of us took the filthy weed. I told him that we were from Beloit, and that at once satisfied him." After dinner, the students hurried on to the game: "The game was hotly contested and for the first few innings it was very doubtful which party would be victorious, but at the close of the [4th] inning the Olympians stood 26 to Whitewater's 12. Our boys now played with high hopes of success. And as a natural consequence they were successful beyond the expectation of every one."[23]

The Olympian Base Ball Club of Beloit defeated Whitewater 59–19 in a contest which lasted three hours and fifty-five minutes. A *Janesville Gazette* reporter commented that "the constant practice and training of the Beloit boys manifested itself in every move of the game. In fact they are hard to beat, and would make it warm for any organization of the kind in the State to handle."[24]

On the way home just before sundown, Foley and his schoolmates celebrated, telling stories, shouting "hurrah" and striving "with each other to see who could make the most hideous noise. Indeed we made perfect fools of ourselves after coming to town, as we went through the principal streets, shouting like madmen and proclaiming the victory of the Olympians."[25]

James D. Eaton was another Beloit College student passionate about baseball and, in fact, had served as one of the scorers of the Bower City match in 1866. Although Eaton missed the Whitewater game, in a May 29 letter to his younger brother Edward Dwight Eaton, later to become Beloit College's second president, he took up the story where Foley left off: "We heard a loud cheer, and running down found several loads of students riding into town with noisy demonstrations, and we trotted down to the city to see them. They formed a regular triumphal procession and marched up one street and down another by the gaslights, stopping frequently at the corners to cheer, and we who went on foot helped to swell the sound. If anybody went to bed in Beloit before ten o'clock it is pretty certain that he couldn't sleep for a while." Eaton crowed over the Olympian Club's dominating play, which included five home runs and "three 'whitewashes' against none on the other side. The 'Cream City' of Milwaukee, the first in this state, beat the latter by but one tally. Wherefore it follows that we are probably the *first* club in the state!" According to Eaton, a new faculty edict forbade the Olympian Club from playing outside town and so the students hoped that the Cream City Club would challenge them. "The challenged party, you know, chooses the field for playing."[26]

Frank L. Smith, writing nearly forty years later, recalled a spectacular play during the Beloit-Whitewater game "which I think has never been duplicated on any field":

> Cochrane [sic], the pitcher of the Olympians, was coming home from third base at full speed when the ball was fielded in to the Whitewater catcher so low that he caught it while resting on one knee, and, in that position, awaited the coming of Cochrane, [sic] who jumped clear over the catcher, touched the plate and scored his run, justly meriting the loud applause from quite a crowd of spectators.[27]

William Cochran remembered the reaction of the opposing side, though he believed that the contest was against the Capital Club of Madison, rather than Whitewater. "The shortstop was completely dumbfounded. He looked up and down and all around and would not have been more surprised if the earth had opened and swallowed up the Olympian."[28]

Such a sound defeat caused speculation about the Beloit nine's ranking in the state. The *Madison Union* claimed that the hometown Capital Club had achieved second ranking in Wisconsin because both the Olympians and Capitals had defeated the Whitewaters, although the Whitewater-Madison contest had taken place a year before. The *Beloit College Monthly* would have none of it, describing the *Union's* "would-be logician" as drawing his conclusions from "false premises":

> How the Capital Club makes such an enormous leap as to pass entirely over the Whitewaters, who not long ago worsted them in a well contested game, our friend, the logician, does not explain. He has evidently forgotten that the world moves, and with it our College Olympians. However, the truth or falsity of his conclusions will soon appear if the Capital Club accept the challenge, to play the Olympians on the 15th of June in this city, which has been sent them. We earnestly hope that then and there it will be proved that poor logic is one thing and good ball playing quite another.[29]

As noted in James Eaton's letter, the Beloit College faculty, fearing disruption of academic life, decided to clamp down on the students' incipient baseball mania with new rules. In those days, faculty took on a paternal role regarding student life outside the classroom and strictly enforced a variety of rules and regulations. In the minutes of their meeting on May 27, the faculty noted that "match games ... which involve more or less absence from the exercises of the College tends to material interference with the proper college duties and the order of the institution." As an aside, the faculty also fined two baseball crazy students "50cts each for throwing ball in front of the Chapel."[30]

The edict certainly put a damper on ball-playing field trips, but it did not initially lessen the enthusiasm of the students or prevent the Olympian Club from competing on its home turf. William Cochran recalled that, despite their decision not to allow the team to travel, the faculty was supportive of the team:

> The faculty of the College in those days was in hearty sympathy with the boys, and cheered them by their presence as well as by their voices. The grave, sedate, dignified President was a habitué of the ball ground, and it is reported that he would become so enthused at times that he would rise in his carriage and wave his silk hat, in a very dignified manner, of course, to cheer the boys.[31]

The Whitewater Club wasn't ready to admit defeat or give up. Smarting from their loss, they issued another challenge to the Beloit club and traveled to Beloit for a rematch on June 8, although the game had been planned for a few days earlier and canceled due to the death of a relative of one of the Whitewater players. James D. Eaton explained in a June 4 letter to his brother that the Whitewater Club had what he considered a new and possibly devious strategy: "Two or three of our men are rather unwell, and we have heard that the Whitewaters have sent to Milwaukee for two, who belonged to the club awhile ago, + [sic] [and] intend to give us a tight game, but we are quite confident of beating them, though we shall be on the watch for any unfairness in getting members."[32]

Eaton's next letter, dated June 12, reported that "a *large* crowd of people from the city and country on foot and in carriages witnessed the game."[33] Although Whitewater battled hard and the game lasted four and a half hours, and despite some careless play by the Olympian Club, the verdict was the same. Beloit won 49–33, thumping nine home runs to Whitewater's five. Eaton commented that "there is no need of the Whitewater's [sic] playing us again, for we have taken their place, and it only remains for us to play the Milwaukee's [sic] who are going to challenge us. They will probably beat us by a few tallies, but who knows?[34]

One week later, the Capital Club of Madison journeyed down to Beloit for a contest which the student newspaper described as "the best game we have ever seen."[35] Eaton concurred in a June 19 letter: "The Madison B.B. Club played us last Saturday — score 23–12 as follows;

	1	2	3	4	5	6	7	8	9	
"Olympian"	3	2	0	3	1	0	1	9	4	— 23
"Capital"	2	2	0	0	0(!)	3	0	5	0	— 12

You will perceive that the game was a closely contested one — the best any of us ever saw: but we came out gloriously ahead."[36] And as the *Beloit College Monthly* succinctly summed up, the "Capitals went home 'mum.'"[37]

The Cream City Club of Milwaukee telegraphed a challenge to the Olympian Club and at 4 A.M. on June 19, they arrived in Beloit. Like his fellow students, and in fact, city and country folk in the region, James Eaton was thrilled about the prospect of the Olympian Club possibly meeting the "champion club of Wisconsin."[38] In a letter to his brother, Eaton was realistic about the college's chances against such a powerhouse: "We expect to get beaten, but it will be no disgrace. Their pitcher is hired for a salary! He throws behind him to any base he wishes without turning his head and *very* swiftly! Our pitcher is very good; but he can't come up to Milwaukee.... The latter say that the Olympians have been thrown in their face for a month past and they want to wipe us out. It is very unusual for the best club to challenge an inferior."[39]

The day before, the *Janesville Gazette* claimed that at least two hundred people would attend from Janesville. "If [the Cream City Club] get away from Beloit with the belt tomorrow, it will be the best day's work they ever performed."[40]

With boosterish fanfare, the paper bragged about Olympian chances for winning what they described as "probably the most spirited game of Ball ever played in this State":

The Capt of the Olympians first nine has dangling at his belt the scalps of the Bower City and White Water Clubs, besides numerous others of less pretensions and if the setting sun does not find the scalps of the Cream City added thereto, put us down for the Lager, or some other equally salubrious Milwaukee drink. We bet our pile on the Olympians.[41]

William Cochran recalled the Cream City Club's overconfidence:

The Cream City boys came to Beloit with a great flourish of trumpets and a large following of friends. They were boastful and confident of an easy victory. They came with their pocketbooks well lined with greenbacks, and offered the Olympians almost any odds — ten to one on general result; two to one that we would not make a home run during the day, and various other offers.[42]

Cochran concluded that there was no suspicion of any betting by Olympian players; however, James D. Eaton commented in a diary excerpt published in 1922 that "every carriage in Janesville was engaged to bring the people to see the game between the two crack clubs; and Madison, Rockford and other towns sent their quotas. Large sums of money were staked on the game, one man from Rockford risking $1,000."[43]

The teams met on the grounds of the Badger Club in Beloit in front of "a large crowd of spectators consisting of both ladies and gentlemen, estimated at 2,000."[44] Such a sizeable crowd perhaps became magnified in memory, as Frank Smith of Janesville recalled in 1905 that "there was said to be 5,000 in attendance."[45] James D. Eaton set the number at "4,000 to 5,000," according to his diary.[46] "There were 600 vehicles on the ground by actual count, and but a small minority occupied seats in them. The spectators formed a complete ellipse, encircling the players."[47]

To keep things fair, the teams used neutral umpires drawn from other baseball clubs, with two official scorers, one from each team playing. The Cream City Club won the toss and took the field. Despite the Milwaukee club's use of a "professional" pitcher, the Olympian Club once again showed superior firepower, swatting five home runs to the opposing team's two, and squashing the Cream City Club, 44–25. The Olympian Club scored 14 runs in the third inning and 11 in the fourth to take a commanding lead, also shutting out the Cream Citys in three of nine innings.[48] The *Janesville Gazette* reported that, though "both clubs played splendidly ... the Olympians ... showed superior playing in all the details and minutiae of the game, and all their throwing, catching, knocking and running exhibited their excellent discipline and contrasted strongly with the maneuvering of their opponents."[49] Despite the partisan crowd, the paper explained that the "decisions of the umpire were fair and just, and the betting was largely in favor of the Milwaukeeans on the start. As far as we could learn, nobody who wished to put up his money on the Creamers, went off without having the opportunity, and a large amount of money changed hands."[50]

The Olympian Club hosted the Cream City club to a banquet at the Salisbury House, where, according to William

A. Cochran, they "tried to jolly them up, but it was of no use. With drooping plumes they left the city in the night time."⁵¹

The *Beloit College Monthly* described the Olympian Club as "the Banner Club of Wisconsin," commenting magnanimously, "we all would acknowledge the generous and manly conduct of the Milwaukee boys."⁵²

However, William A. Cochran remembered two further games with the Cream City Club played away from Beloit, despite faculty rules. The Olympian Club fell to the Cream City Club in the first game, played at Milwaukee. According to Cochran, a playoff game took place in Janesville: "In order to strengthen its team and make victory certain, the Cream City club imported a pitcher from the old National league club at Washington. But it went down in a disastrous defeat, with the score 61–12."⁵³

Later that year, a student summed up the season:

> The Base Ball mania has prevailed quite extensively during the year, but has proved fatal to none except visitors. The Olympians have met all of the principal clubs in the State the past year, and not suffered a single defeat. This would not seem to indicate that the students of Beloit are a puny race. No, we develop muscle as well as brains.⁵⁴

Edward S. Chadwick was among the Olympian players graduating at the college's Commencement, held at Beloit's First Congregational Church on July 11. Like his fellow seniors, Chadwick had to read an oration, and he chose "Commemorative Architecture" as his topic. According to the Beloit newspaper, along with "the usual quota of bouquets, 'Chad.' the 'center-fielder,' was honored with a regulation ball, gaily trimmed in the national colors, thrown from the gallery, but which he failed to take 'on the fly.'"⁵⁵

Also in July, Beloit College held a dedication ceremony for the laying of the cornerstone of Memorial Hall, a gothic limestone edifice completed in 1869 in honor of those from the college and city that died in the Civil War. Still residing among the treasured items placed in its cornerstone: "The ball won by the College Olympian Base-Ball Club from the Cream City Club."⁵⁶

Despite their phenomenal success, the Olympian Base Ball Club of Beloit College soon faded away, replaced briefly in 1868 by the Beloit College Base Ball Club.⁵⁷ The college did not field a regular team for many years until it finally had an official athletic department. Frank Smith, in one of his articles on local baseball history for the *Janesville Daily Gazette* in 1905, lamented their passing: "The Olympians were certainly a great ball nine and probably the best, all things considered, that ever represented the college.... It was a pity they could not have kept together for several seasons, as they were of the improving kind...."⁵⁸

Club Members

Charles H. Bicknell, Jr.: Charles H. Bicknell, Jr., was born on November 3, 1849, in Beloit, Wisconsin. He attended Beloit College as a member of the class of 1871, but did not graduate. He played shortstop on the 1866 and 1867 teams and also pitched. Reminiscing in 1898, William Cochran described Bicknell's play: "It was a great delight to Charley Bicknell, shortstop, to open the eyes of the uninitiated. His arm seemed to have more than the regulation number of joints. He would take the ball, give his arm a peculiar twirl, bring it behind his back and send the ball far up in the air. He would then turn a number of hand-springs, stand on his feet and catch the ball behind his back as it descended." Bicknell lived in Boise, Idaho, and Chicago, and eventually moved to Minneapolis, where he became president of the Landers-Morrison-Christenson Company, dealers in lime and cement. He died there on December 19, 1921.

Arthur Burrall: Arthur Burrall was born on May 9, 1848, in Jingles Corners, Illinois. He played first base for the Olympian Club in 1866 and 1867. He was a member of the class of 1871, but he did not graduate. Burrall spent several years in Texas overseeing his grandfather's land and cattle business, once participating as a cowboy in a cattle drive from Texas to Newton, Kansas. He settled in Rock Island, Illinois, where he farmed four hundred acres, served for many years as county supervisor and for five years as a government gauger. A busy man, he was also a real estate agent, a maltster, and a general agent for the Rock River sandstone quarry. He died in Rock Island on February 14, 1927.

Edwin F. Carpenter: Edwin F. Carpenter was born on May 12, 1845, in Moretown, Vermont. His family moved to Wisconsin in 1863, and he graduated from Beloit College in 1870, after having served two years as a sergeant of Company K, 17th Illinois Cavalry, during the Civil War. He served as treasurer of the Olympian Club in 1866 and in 1867 played right field and center field. Carpenter later became a lawyer, for two terms serving as city attorney of Janesville, Wisconsin. He was for many years circuit court commissioner of Rock County. Carpenter died in 1917.

Edward Sanborn Chadwick: Edward Sanborn Chadwick was born on July 28, 1847. In 1864 at age 17, he enlisted as a private in Company B, 40th Wisconsin Infantry as a "100 day" man and served with his regiment at Memphis. Chadwick graduated from Beloit College in 1867. He taught and studied law for a time, eventually moving to Beatrice, Nebraska, where he practiced law and served one term as Police Judge. He practiced law in Bloomington, Nebraska, where he also served as County Judge of Franklin County, beginning in 1876. He died on July 27, 1926, at the Rock County Insane Asylum, where he had resided since 1889. Edward Chadwick roamed center field for the Olympian Club and served as one of its directors. William Cochran well remembered "the brilliant catches of the long gaunt Chadwick.... Time and again he would make a long run for a ball, which to the spectators seemed far beyond his reach, but somehow he would get near enough to stretch out one of his long arms and slip his hand under the ball just before it touched the ground." Charles B. Salmon described Chadwick, Town and Tuttle as each "standing over six feet two in their stockings" and being "fleet of foot and very muscular."[59]

William Avery Cochran: William Avery Cochran was born on January 8, 1842, at Ripley, Chautauqua County, New York, moving with his family to a farm four and a half miles outside of Beloit in 1854. Like his fellow Olympian, Edward Chadwick, he served four months in 1864 as a private in Company B, 40th Wisconsin Infantry during the Civil War. While stationed at Memphis, he worked as assistant in the Commissary department and also served on picket duty and as a train guard. After pitching for the Olympian Club for two seasons, and graduating from Beloit College in 1867, Cochran became a teacher at the State School for the Deaf in Delavan, Wisconsin, for three years. He filled a similar position at a school in Flint, Michigan, for five years, before returning to Delavan in 1875, where he taught for the next fifty years, also coaching the school's baseball team. He also served in city and county government, including terms as an assemblyman for Walworth County and as an alderman and member of the school board in Delavan. He died on August 8, 1929. According to Charles B. Salmon, Beloit College class of 1870, Cochran "was the leading underhand pitcher of the Northwest until Al Spaulding [sic] of the Forest Cities, of Rockford, appeared."[60]

Henry Chester Hammond: Henry Chester Hammond was from Chicago, and in 1866 played left field for the Olympian Club. He graduated from Beloit College in 1868. Hammond became a teacher in deaf schools in Illinois, Indiana, Iowa, and Arkansas, and eventually served as superintendent of the Kansas School for the Deaf. Hammond died on September 9, 1922, in Olathe, Kansas.

Willard Tenney Hyde: Willard Tenney Hyde was from Polo, Illinois, and graduated from Beloit College in 1868. He became a lawyer and died in 1874. William Cochran recalled one example of Hyde's sharp play at third base for the 1867 team: "Hyde, the third baseman, among his many good catches, made one, at least, that was an astonishment to all. It was during the game with the Cream City Club. A hot ball from the bat went sailing, as everyone supposed, far over his head, but he made a leap into the air and stretched up his left arm to its fullest extent and captured the ball and then threw it to second base, cutting off the man who, supposing the hit a safe one, had started for the home plate."

Milo C. Jones: Milo C. Jones was born in 1849 in Fort Atkinson, Wisconsin. He attended the Beloit College Preparatory and Beloit College with the class of 1872, but did not graduate. Jones worked on the family dairy farm and eventually became well known as a sausage maker. He died in 1919. His company, the Jones Dairy Farm, still exists. Jones is in the Wisconsin Meat Industry Hall of Fame. He played third base in 1866 and left field on the 1867 Olympian Club, also serving as Vice President that year.

George White Marston: George White Marston was born on October 22, 1850, in Fort Atkinson, Wisconsin and attended the Preparatory Department of Beloit College, beginning in 1866. He played in only a few Olympian contests during 1867, alternating between right and left field, and also serving as one of the club's directors. He also pitched for the Beloit Preparatory team against a local high school in 1868, losing 79–40. He recalled the Olympian Club losing to the Forest City Club of Rockford, Illinois, 70–7 yet at another time remembered the score as "twenty odd runs to seven." In 1869, Marston played third base for a Janesville club, the Mutuals, which became state champions after defeating Whitewater, 50–24. After leaving his studies in Beloit, Marston worked in a grist mill and clerked in a bank, before attending the University of Michigan as a pre-med student. Marston moved to California in 1870 where he clerked and then went into business as a store owner, also joining a volunteer fire company and eventually serving as the San Diego Fire Commissioner. He continued to play baseball on an informal basis and in 1878 organized a team in San Diego known as the "Olympians," which evolved into the Bay City Base Ball Club. Marston served as their president. In the 1880s he became the business manager of the San Diego Base Ball Club.[61] Marston ran the Marston Company, San Diego's leading department store, and became increasingly involved in civic affairs, serving on the city council and founding the San Diego Historical Society, of which he became the first president, also donating land and a building. Among other accomplishments, Marston donated the Serra Museum to San Diego and funded the designs of Balboa Park and the first formal plan for San Diego's development. Marston ran for mayor of San Diego in 1913 and 1917 and lost both times — ironically, his opponents tagged the highly successful businessman "Geranium George" and convinced voters that he would be unfriendly to business and would be more interested in city beautification than development. He was a trustee of Pomona College. He died in San Diego in 1946.

Charles B. Salmon: Charles B. Salmon was born on August 16, 1850, in Peru, Ohio. He was a member of Beloit College class of 1870, but did not graduate. In 1873 he helped found the Eclipse Windmill Company, which eventually became Fairbanks, Morse & Company. In 1885, Salmon founded the Beloit Water Works and for many years he was engaged in the milling business as well as building several commercial blocks in Beloit. He served as a Beloit College trustee from 1901 until his death on October 15, 1929. Salmon played shortstop on the 1867 Olympian Base Ball Club.

Lester Samuel Swezey: Lester Samuel Swezey was born on July 25, 1840, in Rockford, Illinois. Before graduating from Beloit College in 1868, he spent two tours of duty for the Union Army during the Civil War. He enlisted in 1862 as a private in Company K, 74th Illinois Infantry, serving in Kentucky, Tennessee, and Alabama. He was promoted to fifth corporal before being discharged because of an unidentified disability. He enlisted again as a private, later attaining the rank of orderly sergeant for Company B, 40th Wisconsin Infantry, serving in Memphis from May to September of 1864. Swezey went on to study law in Rockford and Chicago, later practicing in Chicago and Sioux Falls. He died in 1890. Swezey played right field for the 1866 team and served as one of its directors.

Robert Miller Town: Robert Miller Town (sometimes spelled Towne) was born on November 12, 1844, in Batavia, Illinois. He enlisted for 100 days in 1864 as a private in Company B, 141st Illinois Infantry, eventually promoted to fifth sergeant. He served with his company in Kentucky and Tennessee. Town played second base for the 1866 and 1867 Olympian teams and served as its vice president in 1866 and president in 1867. He graduated from Beloit College in 1868. He moved to Los Angeles in 1869, where he was a charter member of the Historical Society of Southern California. The society's 1901 obituary states that "for some years he was engaged in sheep-raising. Afterwards he went to New Mexico, where he did a freighting business between Las Vegas and the mines.... Mr. Towne was a man of much decision of character; he was ever a good citizen, and was highly respected by all who knew him." Town developed tuberculosis and died on April 24, 1900, in Los Angeles.

Harmon Bascom Tuttle: Harmon Bascom Tuttle was born on June 10, 1845, in Roscoe, Illinois. He enlisted in 1862 as a private in Company C, 67th Illinois Infantry, as a "100 day man." He served with his regiment guarding prisoners at Camp Douglas, Chicago. Tuttle graduated from Beloit College in 1870 and from Chicago Theological Seminary in 1873. He became a clergyman and teacher, living for a time in St. Charles, Minnesota, and eventually settling in Fairmont, Minnesota, where he served as city clerk and Minnesota state head of the G.A.R. Tuttle was the Olympian captain and catcher in 1866 and 1867. His battery mate Cochran mentions that

> it was often a mystery to the members of contesting clubs to understand how the Olympian pitcher knew when an opponent was off from a base, as he very seldom turned around and seemed to pay but very little attention to base runners. He was accused of having eyes in the back of his head. The fact is, he depended upon the eyes of the catcher to give him information in that particular. They had between them a number of signs, and whenever the catcher saw a man stealing away from the second base the signal would be given and the ball would be in the hands of Bob Town, second basemen, and placed on the man before ever realized that such a move was about to be made.

Charles B. Salmon recalled that "stealing bases from Tuttle and Cochran was sure death, as Tuttle's right arm itself would reach a long ways towards the second base."[62] Tuttle died on October 13, 1922, in Fairmont, Minnesota.

Sources

Most sources relating to the Olympian Base Ball Club of Beloit College are available at the Beloit College Archives, including original college documents and publications. *The Beloit College Monthly* provided much commentary on individual games and on the national pastime in general. Its later incarnation, *The Round Table,* as well as the Beloit College annual, *The Codex,* included several useful retrospective articles and reminiscences. Letters by student James D. Eaton and a diary by student James L. Foley vividly brought the college scene of the 1860s to life. Unfortunately, only scattered issues of Beloit city newspapers of the era exist on microfilm and none so far online. However, newspapers from neighboring Janesville reported on college activities, including baseball, and are available online at www.newspaperarchive.com.

Notes

1. *Beloit College Monthly*, May 1866, p.168.
2. *Ibid.*
3. *The Codex '92*, Beloit College, p. 235.
4. *The Round Table*, December 11, 1920, p. 2.
5. *Beloit College Monthly*, June 1866, p. 192.
6. *Beloit College Monthly*, July 1866, p. 212.
7. *Ibid.*, p. 214.
8. *Beloit College Register*, December 1866, p. 35.
9. *Beloit College Monthly*, July 1866, p. 214.
10. *Janesville Gazette*, October 11, 1866, p. 1.
11. *Janesville Gazette*, October 12, 1866, p. 1.
12. "The Olympians," *The Round Table*, April 22, 1898, p. 253.
13. *Ibid.*
14. *Janesville Gazette*, October 15, 1866, p. 1.
15. James L. Foley diary, typescript copy at the Beloit College Archives, original on microfilm at the Wisconsin Historical Society.
16. *Janesville Gazette*, March 26, 1867, p. 1.
17. *Janesville Gazette*, April 17, 1867, p. 1.
18. *Beloit College Monthly*, May 1867, p. 166.
19. "The Beloit Olympics," *The Round Table*, March 20, 1891, p. 159.
20. *Beloit College Monthly*, June 1867, p. 189.
21. *Janesville Gazette*, May 20, 1867, p. 1.
22. James L. Foley diary, typescript copy at the Beloit College Archives, original on microfilm at the Wisconsin Historical Society.
23. *Ibid.*
24. *Janesville Daily Gazette*, May 27, 1867.
25. James L. Foley diary, typescript copy at the Beloit College Archives, original on microfilm at the Wisconsin Historical Society.
26. James Demarest Eaton letters, Beloit College Archives.
27. *Janesville Daily Gazette*, February 9, 1905, p. 5.
28. "The Olympians," *The Round Table*, April 22, 1898, p. 254.
29. *Beloit College Monthly*, June 1867, p. 190.
30. Beloit College Faculty Minutes, May 27 1867, Beloit College Archives.
31. "The Olympians," *The Round Table*, April 22, 1898, p. 255.
32. James Demarest Eaton letters, Beloit College Archives.
33. *Ibid.*
34. *Ibid.*
35. *Beloit College Monthly*, July 1867, p. 211.
36. James Demarest Eaton letters, Beloit College Archives.
37. *Beloit College Monthly*, July 1867, p. 211.
38. James Demarest Eaton letters, Beloit College Archives.
39. *Ibid.*
40. *Janesville Gazette*, June 18, 1867, p. 1.
41. *Janesville Gazette*, June 19, 1867, p. 1.
42. "The Olympians," *The Round Table*, April 22, 1898, p. 255.
43. *The Beloit Alumnus*, May 1922, p. 10.
44. *Ibid.*
45. *Janesville Daily Gazette*, February 9, 1905, p. 5.
46. *The Beloit Alumnus*, May 1922, p. 10.
47. *Ibid.*
48. *The Beloit College Monthly*, July 1867, p. 212.

49. *Janesville Gazette*, June 20, 1867, p. 1.
50. *Ibid.*
51. "The Olympians," *The Round Table*, April 22, 1898, p. 254.
52. *Beloit College Monthly*, July 1867, p. 211.
53. *Milwaukee Journal*, October 17, 1926.
54. *The Beloit College Register* 1867, p. 5.
55. *Beloit Free Press and Journal*, July 11, 1867, p. 2.
56. *Janesville Gazette*, July 11, 1867, p.1
57. *The Beloit College Register* 1868, pp. 5 and 38.

58. *Janesville Daily Gazette*, February 9, 1905, p. 5.
59. "The Old Famous Olympians," *The Codex*, Beloit College, 1899, p. 160.
60. *Ibid.*
61. Michael J. Epstein, "George White Marston: Baseball Player," *The Journal of San Diego History* Summer/Fall 2004, vol. 50, nos. 3 & 4, pp. 90–101.
62. "The Old Famous Olympians," *The Codex*, Beloit College, 1899, p. 160.

❖ *Mutuals of Janesville* (Peter Morris) ❖

CLUB HISTORY

The Mutual Base Ball Club of Janesville, Wisconsin, rose from the ashes of two earlier clubs in 1868 and went through numerous ups and downs before re-emerging at the end of the 1870s as a formidable professional club that featured such stars as John Montgomery Ward and Albert "Doc" Bushong. As such, the story of the Mutuals' early years gives us a fascinating window into the struggles that occurred in many towns to determine which baseball club would become the local standard-bearer.

At least three ballplaying clubs were active in Janesville in 1860: the Janesville Club, the Bower City Club, and the Badger Base Ball Club. The competition was intense enough for several matches to take place and for a tournament of sorts to be staged on Independence Day to determine the local championship of the "old fashioned American game of base ball." But this was very much an old-fashioned game — one of the versions that would collectively come to be known as "town ball" — as matches featured twelve players to a side and were played to fifty runs.[1]

Ball-playing disappeared from Janesville entirely during the Civil War, and it was not until 1866 that the Knickerbockers' version was introduced. Frank L. Smith, whose reminiscence is the primary source of this piece, recalled that he attended school in Connecticut that spring and was first exposed to the more regimented way of playing baseball. He returned home to Janesville in July eager to pass along his knowledge, only to find that a New York hardware businessman named W. J. Doolittle had relocated to Janesville and had already begun to introduce the new version.

Over the remainder of the summer, a small group of players began to practice the new version. Periodical announcements would appear in the *Gazette*, such as one that read: "Ball players will meet on the old ground at 6:30 this evening by order of Smith, Grand 'Bawler,'" and the result would be a gathering at the ground established on Court Street. Many of the players who turned out did not think highly of the new way of playing, and continued to throw the ball at the baserunner. As Smith puts it, their adherence to the old way of playing was "amusing to the spectators ... [but] rather annoying to the party who was hit."[2]

Gradually, however, the "indifferent practices" gave way to more satisfactory ones and by the fall a club had been formed to represent Janesville. Known as the Bower Citys to reflect the city's nickname (which in turn was a tribute to Janesville's many shade trees), the club relocated to better grounds in the block bounded by Milton Avenue, Prospect Avenue, Fifth Avenue, and Glen Street. The club also arranged its first-ever game against an outside club, to be played in Janesville on October 13 against the Olympians of Beloit College.

For the historic match, members of the Bower City Club arrayed themselves in spiffy uniforms consisting of "black trousers, white dress shirts, cuffs and collars, black necktie, glossy black tarpaulin hats and boots shined to order." Other aspects of the match were attended by similar ceremony, with postgame cheers for both clubs and the umpire being followed by a feast at the Myers House. Unfortunately, a couple of problems also manifested themselves. The first was that the visiting collegians won by the lopsided score of 61–8. The second was that Smith, who was only 15 years old, was told that he was "too small to take part in match games" and had to settle for being official scorer of the historic match.

As a result, when the spring of 1867 rolled around and the Bower City Club reorganized, Smith had decided to form a new club consisting of lads of his own age. This was a solution that had many advantages, since it created two homogeneous clubs while also giving Janesville the potential for a spirited in-town rivalry. Initial signs suggested that the division into two clubs had indeed infused energy into the local baseball scene. A State Association of Base Ball Players was formed at Janesville on July 22, 1867, and plans were announced for a state baseball tournament in Beloit. Both the Bower Citys and Smith's club, the Excelsior Juniors, arranged several matches against clubs from other towns.

But it soon became apparent that the new arrangement was far from perfect. When Smith entered his club in the junior bracket of the state tournament, he received a response that read, "I think you will stand a good chance, as no other junior clubs have entered." Two other junior clubs eventually signed up, but both of the matches the Excelsior Juniors were supposed to play were canceled due to misunderstandings. The club was given the second-place trophy, a silver ball said to be valued at $75, but Smith and his fellow club members were nonetheless disgusted at having made the trip to Beloit for nothing.

The matches played by Janesville clubs in 1867 proved no more satisfactory. The Bower Citys showed a tendency to poke fun at Smith's junior nine, so the younger club challenged them to a match and won a tightly fought contest. The result was very exciting to the Excelsior Juniors, but demoralizing to the Bower Citys, who were forced to recognize that they were not destined for much success on the baseball diamond. That message was reinforced by convincing defeats at the hands of two Wisconsin college squads, which pretty much sounded the death knell for the Bower City Club.

By the end of the 1867 season, as Smith put it, it had become apparent that Janesville did not "cut a very wide swath in the baseball world. The Seniors did not seem possessed of the right material — or were too old when they commenced to play — and the Juniors were too young to successfully go out of their class. Probably with a full realization of these facts, both clubs silently passed away in the mellow autumn."[3]

In the spring of 1868, with both the Excelsiors and the Bower City Club having passed out of existence, the Mutual Club of Janesville was formed and it enlisted many of the strongest players from its two predecessors. This arrangement had the great advantage of giving Janesville the most competitive baseball club the town had ever possessed. But at the same time it meant that the club members did not share much in common — the Mutuals were a baseball club, as opposed to a social club that happened to play baseball. This was an important development because it meant that the club's existence was entirely tied up in its ability to win baseball matches.

During their inaugural season, the Mutuals devoted themselves primarily to competition against clubs in the immediate vicinity. They won a hotly contested series against the Titans, a club from the west side of Janesville that was mostly made up of railroad employees. The club also won several other matches against nearby rivals, culminating in September when they earned the title of county champions at the Rock County Fair. For doing so, the Mutuals received a familiar trophy: the same silver ball that the Excelsior Juniors had won at the previous year's state tournament. According to Smith, when that club had passed out of existence, the silver ball that was supposedly worth $75 had been taken to a jeweler for appraisal. His response had been, "If it was silver it would be worth about twelve dollars but as it is only thinly plated it would be of no value to us." So it had been donated to the county fair and now, like a bad gift, was being recycled.

While the Mutuals beat all of the clubs in the vicinity in 1868, their only game against a well-known club produced a very different result. The Forest Citys of Rockford paid a visit to Janesville in mid–July and, in Smith's dry account, "the Rockford boys ceased to run the bases when they had accumulated 88 runs, during which time, it being a very warm day, the Mutuals were seemingly contented with six."[4]

The same pattern repeated itself in 1869. The Mutuals again proved themselves the top club in the region, winning matches or series against the crosstown Titans, the Athletes of Whitewater and the Capital Citys of Madison and retaining the county championship. They even managed a very significant victory against the Cream Citys of Milwaukee. The match was especially gratifying to Frank L. Smith, who had spent the summers of 1868 and 1869 working for a railroad and playing in few of the club's matches, but who was so anxious about the match against the Milwaukee club that he quit his job so that he could play. The game was tied at 46–46 after seven innings, the point at which it had been previously been agreed the game would end so that the Mutuals could catch their train home. But the Cream Citys persuaded the Janesville players to stay and complete the game, and the visitors scored nine runs in the next two innings without surrendering any.[5]

The triumph in Milwaukee led the Mutuals to bill themselves, not without justification, as the champion club of Wisconsin. Nevertheless, when pitted against a club from Chicago in a late-season showdown, the Mutuals were once again badly outclassed. This left the Mutuals with a dilemma to mull over in the winter of 1869-1870. With baseball's national body having now legitimized professionalism, many amateur clubs were forced to decide whether to take this route. From the start, the Mutuals had been more baseball club than social club, so it seemed likely that they would begin to gravitate toward professionalism.

The 1870 season started with the Mutuals mostly using the same local players who had represented the club over the preceding few years. But the club opened the season by being trounced 74–5 by a strong club from Chicago, an embarrassing loss that prompted the *Milwaukee Sentinel* to chortle, "We don't know how Janesville will regard this record made by the Chicago club. With their usual presumption they will no doubt still claim the championship of the state, and will sling ink fast and furious to establish their pretensions. The other portions of the state will at once see the utter nonsense of calling that club champion that has been hard at practice for the last two months and after all could only make five runs against the White Stockings."[6]

While the Mutuals improved in their next few games, in July the club was reorganized and, in Smith's words, the "executive talent was becoming slightly top-heavy." His description of the remainder of the season leaves little doubt that the new directors were calling the shots and that longtime players like Smith felt left out. His comments about professionalism remain vague, leaving it impossible to be certain how many of these players were receiving money and how much. Newspaper coverage that year was also vague, though there was a suggestive mention of a "misunderstanding" between the members that caused several players to miss a key match.[7]

What is known is that the ensuing months saw several new players suddenly appear, while other mainstays of the club left town and joined rival clubs. One of the young men who departed was Orion Sutherland, who had been born and raised in Janesville and spent almost all of his long life in the town. But in 1870 he played a match for the Mutuals in Oshkosh and was approached afterward by a man named Charley Brown, a former Janesville resident who now owned a boot and shoe store in Oshkosh. When asked what he was doing, Sutherland's reply was "Playing ball and hunting." Brown offered him $30 a month plus board to join the Oshkosh ballclub, along with use of a team of horses for hunting whenever he wanted. Needless to say, Sutherland moved to Oshkosh and spent the next two years there playing ball.[8]

Meanwhile, the new lineup of the Mutuals was first tested in a three-game tour that took them north to Beaver Dam, Fond du Lac, and Oshkosh. All three games ended in triumphs, but none of the opponents were highly regarded, and the *Sentinel* again raised Smith's ire by writing dismissively,

> There have been several games of baseball lately at different points along the line of the Northwestern railroad — all of which have been won by the Champion Muffers of Janesville. They are able to play ball just well enough to be beaten by respectably strong clubs and on their own grounds, at the rate of five to one. Their game of blowing can discount their game of base ball. Cheek, too, is one of their best points. Give them pen and paper and they will demonstrate without danger of contradiction that if they have not won the championship of the state at base ball by playing a game they are partly entitled to it by reason of the remarkable dexterity with which they sling ink in their endeavor to prove themselves such. They can also incontestably show that as blowers they are a decided success. How fortunate for the world that the telegraph and the press are sufficiently capable of heralding the vast achievements of the Muffers.[9]

By this point, the rivalry between the Mutuals and their Milwaukee counterparts had reached fever pitch and it was time to decide matters on the diamond. Unfortunately for the Mutuals, however, the first game was scheduled to be played in Milwaukee and when the day rolled around the Mutuals were unable to assemble a creditable nine. So several last-minute substitutes were enlisted, including a third baseman who, to the disgust of Smith, threw a ball to first base that soared over the fence and clear out of the enclosure. Not surprisingly, the Mutuals were trounced, 64–20.

That set the stage for a return match between the Cream Citys and the Mutuals in Janesville on the last day of August. This time the Janesville directors made certain to have enough players on hand but they overcompensated and ended up with a surplus. As a result, as Smith poignantly describes it, he "was asked by some of the directors to abdicate in favor of players to whom we had to offer liberal inducements when short handed, as they might be offended if dropped from the list — and of course 'I didn't care.'" Even 35 years after the fact, Smith admitted that it was a difficult subject for him to write about and that he had become "worked up over a recollection of the affair."[10] It is a heart-wrenching portrayal of the conflicting emotions of a proud amateur member of a club that had begun bringing in professionals.

Thus the man who had helped introduce regulation baseball to Janesville, who had been a mainstay of the local baseball scene ever since, and who had even arranged this match, was forced to watch from a buggy as the opposing clubs warmed up before the start of the critical match. Suddenly, however, the Mutuals' new pitcher reached for a ball and came up clutching his finger, which turned out to be broken. The directors asked Smith to replace him and, "after a few minutes of conflicting emotions I took to the field, 'Sans' uniform, not to please them, but because I, above all others on the grounds, was anxious for victory." After beginning the game in the outfield, Smith then had the great satisfaction of being called upon to pitch the final two innings and preserving a 19–17 win over his club's archrivals.

The Mutuals followed the big win over the Cream Citys with several more wins, but just when it seemed that the 1870 season would end on a high note, the unthinkable happened. The club received a challenge from a rival in Elkhorn, which as Smith puts it, was "a town that had been scarcely heard of at that time, being known only as a place where Whitewater did its 'courting,' and where cases were sometimes taken from other courts on a change of venue." But instead of the easy victory that was anticipated, "after locating the place on the map we drove across the country and were effectually done up to the tune of 36 to 21."[11]

Naturally, the upset was viewed in Janesville as a "fluke" and a "good joke," and a rematch was scheduled at which it was assumed that the Mutuals would exact revenge. Once again, however, the club from Elkhorn emerged triumphant, and the two shocking results changed the local outlook on baseball.

In Smith's words,

> So we went into winters quarters with our conceit somewhat shattered and the enthusiasm of the capitalists almost flooded. This sad ending of an otherwise successful season was not the only discouraging feature as the arrangement of all our games was fraught with more or less difficulty. Most of the home players were engaged in business, making it uncertain as to when they could indulge in practice or take part in games and the gate receipts were insufficient [for] the outlay necessary to the securing of outside players — who seldom made good. The final straw was a judgment secured against the club by a liveryman, for the loss of a horse in a trip to Rockford to secure players. It seems that the young man selected to make the trip had never before driven horses, but he had some personal errand to do in that city so two birds (and one horse) were killed with one stone at a cost of about $200 to the club. With all these drawbacks it is not surprising that there was no reorganization of the club in the spring of 1871.[12]

Only a few games were played in Janesville in 1871 and none at all in 1872. In 1873 arrangements were made for a game on

Independence Day. But after Smith and Orion Sutherland spent all morning preparing the grounds, a big rainstorm came and, as Smith dryly put it, "[T]hat is the nearest Janesville came to having a ball game in 1873."[13]

As it turned out, however, the Mutuals were not dead but merely hibernating. A rebirth of baseball enthusiasm came in 1874 and over the next few years a familiar pattern repeated itself. At first Janesville was represented by enthusiastic local amateurs, including holdovers such as Smith and Sutherland from the clubs of the 1860s. But eventually, these men were replaced by younger men such as brothers Tom and John Morrissey — both of whom were destined to play in the major leagues — and by imported professionals.

By 1877 the lineup of the Mutuals of Janesville included such stars as John Montgomery Ward and Albert "Doc" Bushong and defeated many strong professional nines. But in a close parallel to 1870, the season ended with two disappointing losses and, in Smith's words, "[I]f we had won the last two games and the attendance during the week had come anywhere near up to expectations, there is no doubt but what we should have continued for another year."[14] Instead, the Mutuals' best players soon signed with other professional clubs for the 1878 season and the Mutuals of Janesville passed out of existence for good.

Club Members (1868–1870)

"Del" Bump: The identity of the player Smith referred to as "Del" Bump remains in some doubt. There was only one man with a plausible name: Delos S. Bump, who was born around 1837 in New York State and spent much of his life on a farm in Buffalo County, Wisconsin. In 1864, he enlisted in the 36th Wisconsin Infantry, serving for 16 months. Eventually he returned to Buffalo County, where he farmed and later worked as a carpenter. He died there on July 31, 1902. But I've found no indication that this man ever lived in Janesville, which is in an entirely different part of the state than Buffalo County. Also, Del Bump was still playing for the Mutuals in 1874, which seems unlikely for a man born in 1837. Did Delos Bump move to Janesville after the Civil War and continue to play until quite a bit older than might have been expected, or was Del a nickname of one of the men named Bump who did live in Janesville?

Theodore Pearson Conant: Theo Conant was born in Irasburg, Vermont, on August 8, 1850, and his family settled in the Janesville area while he was a child. In the early 1870s he moved to St. Louis and found work as a salesman for an iron merchant. He worked his way up to becoming secretary and treasurer of the Sligo Iron Store Company, a leading manufacturer of carriage lamps, and eventually became the president of the company. His success allowed him to become prominent in St. Louis society and to send his son to Yale. Conant lived to a very old age, dying in St. Louis on August 9, 1938.

William J. Doolittle: W. J. Doolittle was not a playing member of the Mutuals, but Frank L. Smith credits him with introducing regulation baseball to Janesville in 1866. Doolittle was born in Utica, New York, on June 13, 1833 and attended Hamilton College. He was an active member of the Utica Base Ball Club, serving as the club's first secretary in 1859, and appeared in at least 17 games as a player between 1860 and 1865. In the mid–1860s, he moved to Janesville with his wife and young family to become a hardware merchant. He eventually moved on to Milwaukee to accept a job with the Northwestern Mutual Life Insurance as an actuary. He worked for the firm until 1911, then retired to Cleveland, where he died on August 9, 1912.

William G. Heller: William Heller was born in Wisconsin in 1852 and grew up in Janesville. Intriguingly, he was listed on the 1870 census as a "ball player," but later censuses had less glamorous occupations such as "bookkeeper." He never married, and remained in Janesville until his death in 1934.

Pete Lenehan: Pete Lenehan was born around 1851 in Ontario, Canada, to Irish immigrants who eventually moved to Janesville. Lenehan was still living in Janesville in 1880, but he becomes hard to trace after that.

George White Marston: See Olympians of Beloit College.

Frederic Brown Pullan: Fred Pullan was born on February 4, 1849, in New York City and grew up in Janesville. The son of a clergyman, Fred followed in his father's footsteps. After earning a degree from Beloit College and then graduating from Yale's Divinity School, he led Congregational churches in East Orange (New Jersey), San Francisco, and Providence (Rhode Island), among other places. He died in Newport, Rhode Island, on January 6, 1927.

Dr. James W. St. John: Dr. St. John was a local doctor who was quite a bit older than the other members of the Mutuals, having been born in Janesville on October 30, 1839. Smith recalled that Dr. St. John used his great strength to hit "haymakers" that "went so high and far that they had to be relayed back through the entire nine." According to another account, "[T]he doctor had a willow club of his own that he used to swing when he came up to bat which weighed in the neighborhood of seven pounds and that every time he took his position at the bat the crowd were [sic] much disappointed if the doctor did not make a home run." Dr. St. John helped out on his family farm until he was 18, at which point he spent a year studying at a seminary in Vermont and then began the study of medicine. He served as a medical cadet during the Civil War, then graduated from the Chicago Medical College and returned to Janesville to practice medicine. He served as the city's mayor in 1875 and 1876, and later as president of the Board of Education. He died in January of 1912.

Edgar M. Smith: Ed Smith was Frank L. Smith's older brother, born around 1849. He appears to have died young, as no trace of him has been found after 1870.

Frank L. Smith: Frank L. Smith was one of the leading figures in Janesville baseball for many years and he wrote the 1905 series of articles on the history of baseball in the city upon which this piece is based. Smith was born in Janesville on April 7, 1851, the son of dry-goods merchant Morris C. Smith. In addition to his baseball exploits, Frank Smith captured the state skating championship as a young man. He was educated in Connecticut, then followed his father into business, although, as he revealed in his history of local baseball, on several occasions he was forced to choose between business and baseball. After working as a railroad clerk and businessman, he went to work for the city of Janesville in 1908 and became the city's first full-time assessor four years later. Although past 60 when he accepted the position, he remained city assessor for three decades, retaining his "remarkable memory" and still continuing to report to his office on a daily basis until his health began to fail in the winter of 1942. Widowed three times, Smith died on June 14, 1943 at the age of 92.[15]

James A. Sutherland: Born on November 7, 1847, James A. Sutherland was the older brother of club member Orion Sutherland. Like his brother, James was an underage Civil War enlistee, serving in the 40th Wisconsin Infantry in 1864. He joined his father and brother in the bookstore business and remained in Janesville for the rest of his life. His health began to fail around 1912, and he applied for a Civil War disability pension in that year. His final years were also saddened by the death of his only child. He died in Janesville on October 16, 1918. Note: J. A. Sutherland was described by Smith as a member of the Excelsior Juniors. Smith later refers to "Duck" Sutherland as a member of the Mutuals (primarily during the mid– to late '70s). Orion was on the club at the same time, so "Duck" cannot be Orion. I'm therefore inclined to believe that Duck is a nickname for James, but it's possible that "Duck" was a different brother.

Orion Sutherland: Orion Sutherland was born in Janesville on September 15, 1849, the son of a bookstore owner. Like his older brother, James Sutherland, Orion was an underage Civil War enlistee, serving as a private in the 46th Wisconsin Infantry under the alias of Samuel Statelin or Satelin. After the war Orion began working as a clerk at his father's bookstore, but by his own account spent most of his time "playing ball and hunting." As described in the club history, he was recruited to join the Oshkosh club in 1870 with an offer of $30 per month plus board and the use of a team of horses for hunting. He spent the next two years there playing ball and "hunting up the Wolf river through Butte des Morts, Winneconne, Lake Poygan, going through the cutoff and up the Wolf river, passing Big and Little Partridge lakes up as far as Stanley's Landing." His time in Oshkosh also reunited him with James Rea, who had been one of the lieutenants in the 46th Infantry. In 1871 Orion Sutherland returned to Janesville, married, and joined his father's business, which became known as J. Sutherland & Sons, Booksellers and Stationers. Both the marriage and his association with the store lasted for more than 60 years, as it was not until the 1930s that he finally retired. Sutherland remained very active throughout his life, receiving several medals as a long-distance bicycle rider. In 1933, at the age of 83, he reported that he still played 18 holes of golf a day and had marched in that year's Armistice Day parade, carrying the colors. He died in Janesville on April 11, 1937.

Other Members: Harry Adler (of the firm of Adler and Irwin, president of club); Eager (who was described as a newcomer to the city in 1868 when he joined the club); Hart (a member of the Bower Citys before joining the Mutuals); Hitchcock (a newcomer to the city in 1868, later with Fond du Lac — quite possibly Jerome Hitchcock of the Forest Citys of Rockford); Nash; B. and/or T. Smith; Stoddard; and White. Men who played for the club during the latter part of the 1870 season included Barker, Bird, Waxham, and Hulse. Their first names were not given, but the first three were almost certainly Al Barker, George Bird, and Ernest Waxham of the Forest Citys of Rockford. After reorganizing, the Mutuals included many strong professional players, such as John Montgomery Ward and Albert "Doc" Bushong from Pennsylvania, along with locals such as Tom and John Morrissey, Thomas and W. D. Cantillon, Cornelius J. McGinley, and Joseph Doe.

Sources

Frank L. Smith, twenty-part history of baseball in Janesville, *Janesville Daily Gazette*, February 8–May 4, 1905; *Oshkosh Northwestern*, November 21, 1932, 7 (article summarizing a letter from Orion Sutherland); contemporary coverage in various Wisconsin newspapers.

Notes

1. *Janesville Daily Gazette*, July 3, August 11, August 24, and September 1, 1860.
2. *Janesville Daily Gazette*, February 8, 1905, 5.
3. *Janesville Daily Gazette*, February 13, 1905, 5.
4. *Janesville Daily Gazette*, February 14, 1905, 2.
5. *Janesville Daily Gazette*, February 16, 1905, 2.
6. Quoted in *Janesville Daily Gazette*, February 18, 1905, 2.
7. *Janesville Gazette*, September 1, 1870.
8. *Oshkosh Northwestern*, November 21, 1932, 7; summary of a letter from Orion Sutherland
9. Quoted in *Janesville Daily Gazette*, February 18, 1905, 2.
10. *Janesville Daily Gazette*, February 18, 1905, 2.
11. *Janesville Daily Gazette*, February 22, 1905, 2.
12. *Ibid.*
13. *Ibid.*, February 23, 1905, 2.
14. *Janesville Daily Gazette*, April 17, 1905, 2.
15. *Janesville Gazette*, June 14, 1943.

Chapter Seven

Maryland and District of Columbia

❖ *Introduction* (Peter Morris) ❖

In October of 1860, the Potomac Club of Washington, D.C., climaxed a successful season by defeating their biggest local rival, the Nationals, 33–16. The triumph prompted one local paper to observe: "The game was a good one, and it settles the local championship. The victors are quite anxious to get a game or two in Baltimore, but the clubs there have decided not to give them a 'final hearing' till the spring. We would be glad to see the intercourse between the 'B.B's' of the two cities established on a more equitable footing."[1]

By the end of the decade, competition between the top clubs from Washington and Baltimore was firmly established and much of the baseball interest in the two cities had come to revolve around the intra-city rivalries between the four clubs profiled in this chapter. In Baltimore, it was the Excelsior/Pastime and Maryland clubs that vied for supremacy, while in Washington the National and Olympic clubs competed for local bragging rights. But while those four clubs received much of the attention, it would be a mistake to imagine that they were the only pioneer nines in the region that mattered.

In 1861, as James Bready observed, "the Association of Base Ball Clubs of Baltimore was formed: from Alpha to Zephyr, by way of Deluge, Freethinking, and Quicksteps, thirty-eight teams in all."[2] By 1867 the state of Maryland boasted enough clubs for a statewide association to be organized, with the wealth of Baltimore clubs augmented by such new entries as the Alert of Cumberland, Antietam of Hagerstown, Excelsior of Sudlersville, Avalanche of Cecil, Mountain City of Frederick, Patapsco of Westminster, and South River of Anne Arundel.[3] The purchase of a silver ball to symbolize the state championship offered additional stimulus and, according to William Ridgely Griffith, the president of the association and later the first historian of Maryland baseball, "clubs sprang into existence in nearly every section of the State."[4]

Meanwhile in Washington, the nation's capital was the scene of an equally impressive flurry of activity. The Potomacs were the city's pre-eminent antebellum club, holding the local championship when the Civil War broke out and billing themselves as the "first base ball organization instituted in the city of Washington" and as having "introduced the National Association, or New York Game, into the District of Columbia."[5] After the war's end, the city became the site of a wealth of ballclubs, with much of the action taking place on three diamonds laid out on the White Lot, behind the White House.

As an eyewitness later recalled, "The rivalry between the clubs playing on the White Lots in 1867 and 1868 was keen and fierce, but between no two teams was this feeling so developed and so bitter as between the Jefferson and the Union. Just why this special hostility existed no one knew, but these two never met without a great display of feeling on the part of spectators and players. It was hinted that the real cause of the enmity lay in the fact that many of the members of the Jefferson outfit clung to the feelings of the south, while the Unions were all former Union soldiers with well-gained knowledge of the war just over. But no matter what the cause was the hostility existed. And the games attracted even more attention than their more finished neighbors, the Nationals and the Olympics. There was, too, more of a display of the gambling interest, as 'Rum Row' always turned out in force when these two were scheduled to meet."[6]

Another memorable aspect of play on the White Lot was the participation of Ulysses S. Grant's youngest son, Jesse, who was ten years old in 1869 when his father was inaugurated as president. According to a 1904 account, Jesse Grant became "captain and manager of a boys' team which played in the White Lot. ... Gen. Grant was a lover of the national game. With members of his Cabinet and personal friends he frequently strolled down to the White Lot and witnessed the ball games. It was not an unusual occurrence to see President Grant with the late Senator Stockton, of New Jersey, beside him, the two men discussing the relative merits of their respective sons as baseball players. 'Dick' Stockton played first base and Jesse Grant played in the outfield. Vice President Wilson, Gen. O.E. Babcock, Senator Simon Cameron, and Judge-advocate General Townsend could always be depended upon to join President Grant when there was a baseball game going on in the White Lot. Like regular up to date baseball rooters, these distinguished men smoked innumerable cigars and worked themselves up to a high pitch of excitement as the game progressed for or against the team in which they were directly interested."[7]

Many other Washington and Baltimore ballclubs stirred up similar excitement during these years, but it was the Excelsior/Pastime and Maryland clubs of Baltimore and the National and Olympic clubs of Washington that dominated their respective landscapes. Here are their stories.

NOTES

1. Quoted in *Wilkes' Spirit of the Times,* November 17, 1860.
2. James Bready, *Baseball in Baltimore* (Baltimore: Johns Hopkins University Press, 1998), 7; William Ridgely Griffith, *The Early History of Amateur Base Ball in the State of Maryland* (Baltimore: n.p., 1997), 26–27.
3. Griffith, *The Early History of Amateur Base Ball in the State of Maryland,* 49–51.
4. *Ibid.,* 49.
5. Charles Peverelly, *Book of American Pastimes* (New York: n.p., 1866), 113.
6. Chadwick Scrapbooks, unidentified clipping, c. 1907.
7. R.M. Larner, "President Roosevelt Is a Baseball Crank," *Washington Post,* June 19, 1904, S4.

❖ *Excelsior/Pastime Base Ball Club of Baltimore* (Peter Morris) ❖

CLUB HISTORY

Exactly when Baltimore residents first began to play bat-and-ball games remains unknown, but all indications are that they are nearly as old as the city itself. For example, John W. Oliver, later the editor of the *Yonkers Statesman*, claimed to have played "baseball pure and simple" in Baltimore in 1825 and to have done so with childhood friends who included Edwin Booth, the famous Shakespearean actor, and Edwin's younger brother, the notorious assassin John Wilkes Booth. Oliver recollected:

> A dozen or more of us would get together in an old field for a game. A couple of the leaders were selected to handle the bat. It was thrown from one boy to the other. Hand over hand they went up the handle of the bat, and the boy whose hand reached the extreme top of the handle first got first choice to bat. Then the leaders selected their favorite players out of the crowd and the game began. There were four bases, the same as in the game of the present day, but there was no pitcher. The man at the bat tossed the ball into the air and hit it, and the man running from base to base was put out of the game if hit with the ball between bases. In those days the boys always used a paddle instead of the round heavy modern bats. The ball was the old-fashioned ball of our fathers, a light yarn ball made by winding yarn raveled from old stockings and covered with buckskin. It was a very light affair and it was impossible for any player to be injured by it.[1]

By contrast, the arrival of the Knickerbockers' version of baseball can be dated much more precisely. In 1858, Baltimore grocer George F. Beam made a business trip to New York and was invited by colleague Joe Leggett — the catcher of the Excelsiors of Brooklyn — to witness a game. He returned home "so much enthused" that he convinced his fellow "Merchants of the Wharf" to form a club and to name it in honor of Leggett's club.[2]

An initial meeting was held at the office of Woods, Bridge & Co. on Commerce Street to elect officers and arrange other details. Then the club established a meeting room on the second floor of the Mount Vernon Hook and Ladder Company on Biddle Street and began to hold practices near a row of five gum trees at Flat Rocks, a picturesque locale down by the lakeside. Their gatherings soon began to attract attention: "An omnibus twice a week, Wednesday and Saturday afternoons, would wait at or near the corner of Exchange Place and Commerce Street, take up the members engaged in business in that section, and pick up members in business or residing up town, on its way to 'Flat Rocks,' and as it passed out Madison Avenue, large numbers of young men living in that section of the city, would follow to see THE NEW GAME."[3]

A second diamond was laid out nearby, but before long the game had outgrown Flat Rocks altogether. The Excelsiors moved to a vacant lot at the corner of Madison and Boundary Avenues and left behind Baltimore's first regulation baseball diamond (which was soon underwater as part of what became known as Druid Hill).[4]

In the first few years of their existence, the Excelsiors played sparingly. According to William Ridgely Griffith, an early club member and the author of an 1897 history that is the source of most of what we know about this pioneering club, the Excelsiors' score book was lost and, "the old members having no recollections of any games played in 1859, except with the Potomac Club, of Washington, D.C., it is quite probable that the time was devoted to practice."[5]

That changed in 1860 as the Excelsiors took several important steps toward putting Baltimore on the national baseball map. In March, club president Hervey Shriver was elected second vice president of the National Association of Base Ball Players. He became the body's first officer from outside New York and an important symbol that the game already being billed as the "national pastime" was in fact becoming national in scope.[6]

The next important development came when the Excelsiors accepted a challenge to visit Washington and play the Potomacs.[7] Appropriately enough, this historic match was played on a field near the White House and was won by the Excelsiors, 40–24.[8] In an amusing indication of how unfamiliar baseball still was to many, the *Baltimore Sun* reported that the Excelsiors had won "by sixteen rounds."[9]

Even more exciting was the news that the club's Brooklyn namesake had accepted an invitation to travel to Baltimore and "instruct them on the game."[10] The big game was scheduled for July 22, 1860, and it proved a landmark for Baltimore baseball in many ways. Since the grounds of the Excelsiors were far too small to host such an event, the match was scheduled for the Madison Avenue grounds of another local club, the Waverlys. This diamond proved so well suited that the location remained the center of Baltimore baseball for the next decade.

The arrival of the famous Brooklyn club and of stars like Leggett and Jim Creighton was eagerly anticipated, although not even the most optimistic local "thought that the Baltimore Club had the least show to win." Rather, "it was to be a game of instructions" by which the Baltimore club and the many spectators would "learn a few new points before the game closed." As such, nobody was disappointed when the visitors won by the lopsided score of 51–6. Instead, they took careful note of the unique pitching style of Creighton — "The Baltimore boys picked up their bats very cautiously.... The first ball thrown to the bat went like a bullet, the stroke of the bat being made simultaneously with the ball entering the catcher's hands. The batter had never struck at such a ball, and three misses followed, and he stepped aside." The home players took equally close note of Leggett's "daring, almost reckless" decision to "take fly-tips close behind the bat," as well as of the expert support of the other fielders and the expert work of all nine visiting batters.[11]

After the match came the customary banquet, at which the hosts outdid themselves in showing "true Southern hospitality." At a cost of more than $700, the two clubs shared in a sumptuous dinner at Guy's Monument House on North Calvert Street, "at which flowers in profusion decorated the tables' toasts and songs abounded." From the arrival of the celebrated visitors until their departure, they "were occupied in one entire round of pleasure."[12]

Yet while there was no expectation that the Baltimore club would win this historic match, there was a presumption that improvement would result. Griffith boasted that one of the visitors from Brooklyn had pronounced the host club "the greatest amateur Base-Ball Club the United States *ever saw*."[13] Even if we take that claim with a grain of salt, no doubt many of the members of Baltimore's first club dreamed of achieving that goal.

But it was not to be, as instead of improving, the Excelsiors regressed. Shortly after the visit of the Brooklyn club, the club received a challenge from a newly formed Baltimore club called the Waverlys. No doubt intending to be gentle on their younger rivals, the Excelsiors sent "nine of the second-rate players of the club," only to have this lineup beaten handily. Embarrassed, the senior club now arranged for their first nine to meet the Waverlys, yet when this match occurred on October 17, 1860, it produced an even more convincing victory for the younger club. According to Griffith, the second setback was the main factor in the merger of the Excelsiors and the Waverlys under a new name: the Pastime Base Ball Club of Baltimore.[14]

In fact Griffith was confused about the sequence of events, which is understandable in light of the passage of time, the loss of the scorebooks of both clubs, and the fact that parts of the surviving clippings had been damaged by mice.[15] The merger actually occurred ten months after this disastrous loss, and during the interval the Excelsiors suffered a third defeat to the Waverly club in May of 1861. Only then did the sting of repeated defeats, coupled with the outbreak of the Civil War and the reality that the members of the Excelsiors were past the ideal age for baseball, lead to the merger with the younger club. On August 15, 1861, the Pastime Club was formed with the hope that this step would enable the city's first club to maintain both its baseball reputation and its reputation as "A Club of Gentlemen." The unified club scheduled practices for Wednesday and Saturdays and adopted a uniform consisting of a "cap of blue cloth with white leather visor, a white flannel shirt with a large capital 'P.' of blue in the front, and blue cloth pants."[16]

The Pastime Club had around fifty members in 1861, though for obvious reasons, "quite a number seldom played."[17] Competitive play remained sporadic throughout the war, yet steadier than in many other cities, and Baltimore's first regulation club managed to survive the war years and remain a power in Baltimore baseball circles until the end of the decade. As a result, it seems reasonable to regard the merger of the Excelsiors and the Waverlys as a successful move.

As Griffith notes, what is really remarkable is that the Pastime Club survived the war despite a membership that was deeply divided in its political sympathies.[18] Griffith supported the Confederates, as did the majority of the club's members. Especially staunch was the Waverly Club — one of the reasons given for the merger was that many of the clubs' first nine had already joined the Southern cause, including William Murray, who had been one of the stars of the 1860 upset of the Excelsiors, and who was killed at Gettysburg.[19] Two more Waverly members, Philip Minis and Neilson Poe, Jr., became officers in the Pastime Club but eventually also enlisted in the Confederate Army. Yet the club also had many Union loyalists, such as Thomas J. Mitchell and Eugene Van Ness. Nevertheless, Griffith reported that never during the war was there "trouble among members, due to feelings born of those unhappy days."[20]

Eighteen sixty-one in particular saw an extraordinary amount of baseball activity considering how close Baltimore was to the battle lines. Throughout the summers, new clubs kept forming, and by the end of the year at least thirty-eight clubs had seen action.[21] This surprising flurry of activity prompted Griffith to proclaim with pride that "in the three years since Mr. George Beam brought the game to Baltimore it had become the *game of games* in the hearts of the young men of the city."[22] No doubt he was just as elated that in September the Pastimes convincingly beat the young club that was to become their greatest rival — the Maryland Club — and earned general recognition as the city's top baseball club.[23]

Baltimore also boasted a vibrant baseball association in 1861, and in order to keep the excitement going this body created a new incentive for the 1862 season: a silver ball emblematic of the local championship. Even so, the Pastimes played rarely in 1862. Griffith, who was elected to the first nine that spring in a vote of all club members, reported that the club played only three matches all year. Yet the club did remain active enough to establish a new club room in a one-story house behind Geiglein's Restaurant and to win each of those matches, highlighted by a 30–21 victory over the Maryland Club that made the Pastimes the possessors of the silver ball.[24]

The war continued to limit the doings of the Pastime Club over the next two years. Yet all things considered, Baltimore's most prominent baseball club maintained an impressive level of activity. There is even evidence that the city's proximity to the battlefront proved a stimulant to local baseball. Griffith recalled that in 1864 a Philadelphia hundred-day regiment "camped on the wooded hill, opposite of the Pastime base-ball grounds. On one of the practice afternoons of the Pastime Club, the writer, who at that time was President, noticed several soldiers in uniform, who seemed to take great interest in the game.... These soldiers, during the practice, did not show any very remarkable skill, but after the game, approached the writer and stated, that in their regiment were a number of base-ball players, and they wished a match game could be made up with the Pastime Club.... Somehow, when the game came off, this taller soldier, turned out to be Dick McBride, the famous pitcher, and the shorter one, Al. Reach, the second baseman, and in fact the nine were the players of the great Athletic Club, of Philadelphia.... From this grew a strong friendship between the two clubs that continued during the existence of amateur base-ball."[25] It is likely that Griffith was confused about Reach, who did not join the Athletics until 1865 and for whom no service record is extant, but McBride and many other members of the Athletics did serve in the Pennsylvania 196th, a hundred-day regiment, so there is no reason to doubt the basic fidelity of his recollection.

The final years of the war also saw a memorable series of matches between the Pastimes and the Nationals of Washington. In August of 1863, the Nationals traveled to Baltimore on the early morning train and were met by a committee of the host club. After treating them to "a refreshing lunch," the visitors were escorted to the ball field. When the match concluded with the Pastimes victorious, the members of both clubs went for a ride in the country, before returning to Charles Haffcke's saloon for a supper that "embraced many delicacies of the season." According to the *Baltimore American*, "The company did not rise until the evening had far advanced, having devoted much time to sentiments, cheering table talk and brief speeches. These base-ball clubs are composed of our best young men in the city, and conducted with strict regard to morality and decorum."[26]

In September, it was the Pastimes' turn to travel to Washington for a rematch that proved close and exciting. The Baltimore club staged a late rally to pull out a narrow victory, prompting one newspaper to declare that, since each club was the champion of its respective city, the Pastimes were now "Champions of the South." It was a most peculiar claim to be making in the midst of the Civil War and suggests that competitiveness was beginning to emerge. Yet the emphasis was still very much on decorum. When the match ended, National Club president (and future U.S. Senator) Arthur Pue Gorman presented William C. Pennington of the Pastimes with the game ball and made "a few neat and appropriate remarks, which were responded to by Capt. Pennington." Then the members of the visiting club members "were sumptuously entertained" until it was time to return home.[27] The site of the post-game festivities was not mentioned in contemporary accounts, but on what apparently was a different wartime trip to Washington to play the Nationals, Griffith recalled the match being followed by "a grand entertainment in the U.S. Senate Restaurant."[28]

The final years of the Civil War saw some other moments in which baseball provided a welcome respite from the horrors of warfare. Griffith, for example, recalled taking a business trip to New York City in 1864 and returning to Baltimore with "the first willow bats" ever seen in the city. Naturally, the novel implements were greatly "appreciated by the club."[29] Another cherished memory was assembling the 1863 first nine and taking a photograph that remained in existence more than three decades later.[30]

While events like these carried symbolic importance, it was a relief when the war ended and regular practice became possible. In the immediate aftermath of the war, it looked as though the Pastime Club was poised to emerge as a national power. Plans were made to continue the rivalry with the Nationals of Washington and to take advantage of the wartime coincidence by beginning one with the Athletics of Philadelphia. The club's longtime grounds on Madison Street were extensively renovated in 1865, the additions including a new grandstand, a high fence around the field, and a third clubhouse.[31]

Even so, the grounds were far from ideal. Because of the adjoining streets, the field was "in the shape of a parallelogram" with little room behind first and third base, which meant that the ball was occasionally sent "whizzing over the west fence into an adjoining garden, from whence it could not be recovered, and a new ball had to be obtained." With baseballs a large part of a club's expenses, this was no minor matter. Yet the location also had some important advantages, such as proximity to the terminus of the Madison Avenue City Railway and a "fine grove of lofty trees" in the southwest corner of the grounds that provided welcome shade to sun-drenched spectators. The site remained the home of Baltimore baseball through the end of the decade.[32]

Unfortunately, the postwar performance on the field failed to live up to expectations. By all indications, the Pastimes did not lose a match between the 1862 merger and the end of the war.[33] While the total number of matches played by the club was not great, its string of victories did include the sweep of the Nationals. That streak, however, ended in 1865 with a pair of losses.

The first came at the hands of the Athletics and the growing reputation of that club meant that that defeat could be taken philosophically in Baltimore. The arrival of the Athletics on August 29, 1865, was a hailed as a great event and a learning experience — much like the visit of the Excelsiors of Brooklyn five years earlier. The visiting nine was met at the train depot, escorted around town, treated to an "elegant lunch" at the Eutaw House, and then "conducted in carriages" to the ball grounds.

The Pastimes expected to be beaten, and that was indeed what transpired, but the 39–27 margin of defeat was deemed very commendable. The *Baltimore Sun* noted proudly that the game "was one of the most closely contested ... that has ever been played by the Athletic Club with any antagonist." That newspaper's account also drew attention to the fact that the Athletics had just beaten the rival National Club of Washington by the lopsided score of 87 to 12.

As a result, the match and the surrounding events were characterized by sportsmanship and ceremony. According to the *Sun*,

> The greatest good feeling prevailed during the entire game, and all decisions of the umpire were received with loud applause. Committees of the various clubs of the city were on the ground and extended many courtesies to the Athletics. A committee of the Empire Club presented [Athletic Club president] Col. Fitzgerald with a badge, and miniature picture of *two bats*, ball and base. After the game was concluded, the visitors, with the Pastimes, and a number of invited guests, returned to the Eutaw House, where an elegant dinner was partaken of. The beaten club, as customary, presented to the victorious club the ball that was played.... Subsequently the Athletic Club was escorted to the Philadelphia depot by the Pastime, and at 9.25 P.M. left for home, all expressing themselves highly pleased with their visit. They exacted a promise from the Pastime that the visit would be returned during the month of September. There were about 5,000 persons upon the ground, a large proportion being ladies, and much interest appeared to be felt on the occasion.[34]

The other loss, however, came at the hands of the Nationals, and this was an entirely different matter because it suggested that the Pastime Club was losing ground to its longtime rival. Significantly, Griffith, who often included pages of descriptions of the triumphs of his club, provides no details of this game at all, acknowledging the loss only by including a clipping that mentions that the Pastimes were hoping for a rematch after an earlier loss to the Nationals.[35]

A likely explanation for Griffith's conspicuous silence about this match became evident in the ensuing years. The starting nine of the Nationals already featured imported New Yorkers and over the next few years this trend accelerated. More alarmingly, the new players had invariably been lured to Washington by offers of well-paying jobs in the Treasury Department, in which Gorman was a high-ranking official. The unfairness of the resulting competitive imbalance would create a steadily rising tide of resentment in Baltimore.

First, however, many efforts were made to encourage Baltimore's ballplayers. In response to the steadily growing incursion of money, the Pastime Club took advantage of its newly enclosed field to begin charging fifteen-cent admission to 1866 games. The erection of the third clubhouse was another bow to this new economic climate — the Pastimes began using their grounds only on Wednesdays and Saturdays, renting them to the Maryland and Enterprise clubs on other days.[36]

Another infusion of fresh life in the local baseball scene occurred when George Gratton, a founding member of the first club in Syracuse, New York, arrived in Baltimore and opened a store. Although Gratton's shop sold a variety of goods, Griffith described it as "a regular Base-Ball Emporium ... [that] became a kind of headquarters for base-ball in the city. He sent out travelling salesmen over the State of Maryland, who so enthused the young men that clubs sprang into existence in nearly every section of the State." In addition, Gratton served as corresponding secretary of a state association that included thirty-three clubs, and in the spring of 1886 he donated a new silver ball to stimulate local competition.[37]

These developments led to the formation of many new clubs in Baltimore and also provided a temporary boost to the Pastimes. Over the next two years, the club enjoyed many pleasurable moments. In September of 1866, the Excelsiors of Brooklyn paid another visit to Baltimore, and the Pastimes showed that they had made considerable progress, losing by the respectable margin of 28–19.[38] Perhaps inspired by the ambassadorial example of the Excelsiors, the Pastimes embarked on a tour of Virginia in August of 1867, making stops in Richmond and Petersburg and easily beating the local representatives. But of course the score wasn't the point and, according to Griffith, "this trip of the Pastime was one of the most enjoyable they ever took, and the members of the club left, still speak in the WARMEST, HEARTFELT terms of the great pleasure of their trip to the dear old South. The writer at this time remembers so well his having been urged by Major Beckham to sing for Ex-Governor Wise, the Pastime's club song of 'Go down, Moses, way down into Egypt's land, and tell old Pharaoh to let my people go.' Dear Old Major B. chose to think it referred to the South."[39]

Another memorable accomplishment came when the Mutuals of New York paid a visit at the end of that month. According to an account in the *Sunday Telegram*, the Mutuals "came to our city elated by their triumphs and achievements, doubtless expecting to demolish a club which conceded defeat in advance." Instead, the Pastimes won by the convincing score of 47–31 and did so in spite of what the *Sunday Telegram*'s correspondent described as "a partial and biased umpire" whose "decisions were frequently so reprehensible, so flagrantly partial and unjust, as not only to provoke the murmurs of the Pastimes, but to call forth the criticism of the fair minded members of the Mutuals, in whose favor he constantly awarded."[40]

Unfortunately, such signal victories were few and far between for the Pastimes. Especially frustrating was the mounting awareness that the Pastimes had little hope of competing with the government-subsidized Nationals. By 1867, the string of losses to their old rivals had become so discouraging that a national publication offered these comments: "It is a singular fact that the business men of Baltimore are decidedly opposed to base ball; and when it is remembered that a majority of base ball players are employed in stores where their presence is required till sunset, instead of in the public service, as are a majority of Washington players, who are at liberty at an early afternoon, the difficulties with which a Baltimorean ballist has to contend may be appreciated. A member of one of the prominent clubs of this city recently sought a situation there, and upon giving his name was at once asked whether he was connected with the _____ club. He replied in the affirmative, whereupon the merchant instantly informed him that he would give employment to no base ball player, however capable to transact business."[41]

Adding to the woes of the Pastime Club was that the 1867 season also saw the loss of local supremacy. After narrowly defeating one of their tenants, the Enterprise Club of Baltimore, the Pastimes were challenged by their other tenant, the Maryland Club. The Pastimes won the first game of the best-of-three series, but the Maryland Club rebounded with two decisive victories to capture the silver ball donated by George Gratton.[42]

It was now clear that the Pastime Club was not destined to become a national powerhouse, and over the next few years it switched roles with the Maryland Club. Until the championship changed hands, the Maryland Club had traditionally been made up of up-and-coming young players, while the Pastimes were the local standard-bearers and at least dabbled with professionalism. But beginning in 1868, a reversal of places occurred, which in turn led to numerous changes in the lineups of both rivals. The Maryland Club came to be made up of imports and of local players with ambitions to play professionally, while the Pastimes contented themselves with being a strong aggregation of homegrown amateurs.

The final years of the Pastime Club saw the club remain competitive against the growing number of professional nines and even manage some impressive victories. In 1869, for example, the Pastime Club pulled a 15–14 upset of the Unions of Lansingburgh (better known as the Haymakers of Troy). But by then, the Pastimes were so lightly regarded that the defeat of such a strong club by one that "is but an ordinary skilful nine" prompted unfounded rumors of a fix.[43]

In 1870, the Pastimes played an especially ambitious schedule and faced professional nines in most of their games. Once again, there were a few impressive victories and some narrow losses. Especially noteworthy was a trip to New York in August that saw the club beat the Stars of Brooklyn and post a second win over the Unions of Lansingburgh, prompting the *New York Tribune* to describe the Baltimore players as having "shown themselves to be expert players, but gentlemen both on and off the field."[44]

It was a fitting note on which to end the club's history. As Griffith noted proudly, "With 1870 *ended amateur baseball*; in fact, with the exception of the Pastime Club, of Baltimore city, every one of the leading clubs of the United States had, during 1870, nines who were paid, or members of nine who were paid, and if not paid a salary, situations were procured for them. In fact, the Nationals, of Washington, had for years procured situations in the departments for some of its best players. During the years of 1868, 1869 and 1870, the Pastime Club, which was composed almost entirely of business men and clerks, who could not always get off to *even practice*, had been obliged to place in the field nines that could get off from business, but who did not always represent the very best playing ability of the club. The club was recognized all over the country as *strictly amateur*, and yet, as will be seen in this record for 1870, in its trip North, won three out of six games played against the very leading clubs."[45]

CLUB MEMBERS

Note on the identification of Baltimore players: Positive identification of players of the 1860s is a challenge in any city, but especially so in Baltimore. As elsewhere, contemporaneous references to Baltimore ballplayers usually referred to players by their surnames alone. In most cities, however, later articles make identification of key players possible by providing first names and identifying details. Unfortunately, most of what is known about Baltimore's early clubs comes from William Ridgely Griffith, who rarely provided first names of players except in a list of more than 600 "old players" at the end of his book. In many cases, he listed multiple players with the same surname, making it impossible to be sure which of the men corresponds to a particular player. In the following, players are identified only when there is a specific basis for that identification, while doubt remains in the cases of many players, even prominent ones.

John I. Armistead: J. I. Armistead, an outfielder on the first nine in 1870, was born around 1851 in Virginia and grew up in Baltimore, where his father was a prominent businessman. He went into the clothing business and died in Harrisburg, Pennsylvania, on August 30, 1896.

George F. Beam: George F. Beam was the grocer who helped introduce baseball to Baltimore and the Excelsiors' first pitcher, but he didn't live to see it become popular. He was in his mid-thirties when he died in Baltimore on January 15, 1866, after a brief illness.

Dr. Thomas Brown: Dr. Thomas Brown was the secretary of the Pastimes in 1863. A man named Brown also played for the club in 1866, but this may have been Robert Brown or some other man with this surname.

Nicholas P. Chapman: N. P. Chapman, a clerk and bookkeeper, was a member of the Excelsiors who became the first secretary of the Pastimes after the 1861 merger. He was then in his mid-thirties, and there is no indication he was a playing member. He died on March 20, 1881, at his home on Druid Hill Avenue, near the site of Baltimore's first baseball field. (Griffith lists a "Nat. P. Chapman" in his list of "Old Players" but contemporaneous sources suggest this to be a mistake.)

James A. Courtney: James Courtney of the Excelsiors was the first president of the Pastimes after the 1861 merger and served as club treasurer in 1863. He was born in Virginia around 1830 and was a merchant who was involved in the volunteer fire department. He left Baltimore after the war and is believed to have died in Atlantic City on February 4, 1901.

Addison K. Foard: A. K. Foard was a native of Baltimore County, having been born there in 1824. He was a prominent Baltimore broker and then the secretary of the Maryland Life Insurance Company, before retiring in the mid–1880s. He died on December 22, 1897, in Howard County, Maryland.

John Newton Gregg: Newton Gregg, who played left field for the Pastimes after the war, was born on December 14, 1840, in Clear Spring, Maryland. After moving to Baltimore, he pursued a career in business and eventually became secretary of the Silver Valley Mining and North Carolina Smelting Company. He died in Baltimore on April 22, 1894.

William Ridgely Griffith: Colonel William Ridgely Griffith's 1897 book is the primary source of our knowledge about the early days of Baltimore baseball, but it was not his only claim to fame. He was one of the organizers of the 1860 Democratic Convention in Baltimore that was divided between party nominee Stephen A. Douglas and John Breckenridge, his secessionist rival. Born into one of Baltimore's leading families on January 31, 1837, Griffith served in General William Walker's Army in Nicaragua in the 1850s. He returned to the States after contracting a near-fatal case of cholera, living in Kansas and Illinois before returning to Baltimore for good in 1859 and going into business. Griffith also began a lifelong involvement in Democratic politics and, among his many activities, was president of the Pastime Club from 1864 until 1867. In his later years, he wrote on a wide range of subjects and served as president of the Sons of the Revolution. He died in Baltimore on October 22, 1910.

Dr. John William Fletcher Hank: Dr. J. W. F. Hank, the third baseman of the Excelsiors in 1860, was born on March 11, 1826, in Jefferson County, Ohio. After graduating from Dickinson College, he received his M.D. from the University of Pennsylvania in 1850 and settled in Baltimore, where he became a vaccine physician, also serving as physician to the Maryland Penitentiary and as Assistant Board of Health Commissioner. In addition to being the third baseman of the Excelsiors in 1860, he was also club president and gave a toast to the visiting Excelsiors of Brooklyn after that year's celebrated game. Dr. Hank died in Baltimore on November 3, 1881.

Boston Hazlitt: Boston Hazlitt, the first baseman of the Excelsiors in 1860, was a liquor dealer who died in Baltimore on March 8, 1867, age 35.

Dr. Frederick Porteous Henry: Fred Henry was born on his grandfather's farm in Middlesex County, New Jersey, on July 21, 1844. His father died while he was young, and in 1859 his mother took Fred and his four sisters to Europe, where Fred attending schools in Dresden, Germany, and Tours, France. In 1861, they moved to Baltimore, and Henry became the pitcher of the Pastimes in 1862, making quite an impression. According to Griffith, Henry "was the first to introduce slow-curved balls, which if hit, nearly always resulted in an infield high fly. He was in the estimation of the writer the most graceful player and best pitcher ever seen on a ball ground. This may be prejudice, perhaps not, but it is certain that he was the first to pitch slow curve and drop balls."[46] Henry enrolled at Princeton University, and continued to refine his technique. His work in an 1863 game against the mighty Athletics of Philadelphia prompted one of that city's newspapers to write, "The Nassaus' pitcher helped them greatly. He gave the ball with a heavy twist that was extremely irregular. The Athletics found it difficult to bat him for two or three innings."[47] Henry left Princeton without graduating to pursue a medical career. He received his M.D. in 1868 from Columbia and moved to Philadelphia, where he practiced for more than forty years, specializing in pathology and doing research on the spread of smallpox, Addison's Disease, Reynaud's Disease, among others. He was on the staffs of the Episcopal Hospital, the Philadelphia General Hospital, and the Woman's Medical Hospital, while also serving as Professor of Medicine at the Philadelphia Polyclinic Institute. Fred Henry died in Philadelphia on May 24, 1919. Despite his lengthy list of accomplishments, an obituary in the next day's *Philadelphia Inquirer* prominently highlighted his role in the development of the curveball.

Otis Keilholtz: Otis Keilholtz was born around 1836 and educated at St. Mary's Seminary and Georgetown College. He followed father into business and then in the 1870s began a successful political career that saw him serve as president of the city council, acting mayor, and Speaker of the Maryland House of Delegates. But his health began to decline at the end of the decade, and he was only 47 when he died on September 13, 1883, of Bright's Disease.

Louis Warner Mallinckrodt: Brothers Louis and William Mallinckrodt were both involved in the club, but only Louis played for the first nine, pitching for the Pastimes from 1863 to 1867. Louis was born in July of 1844 and had been the scorer for the Waverly Club before its consolidation with the Excelsiors. Yet when Griffith wrote his 1897 history, Mallinckrodt, by then a successful broker, told him that he had no idea of the meaning of most of the notations he had written in the club's scorebook. In 1902, Henry Chadwick reported that Mallinckrodt was one of several former members of the Pastime Club who were now active in the Baltimore Cricket Club. He died four years later, on April 5, 1906.

William Mallinckrodt: William Mallinckrodt was born around 1842 and served as secretary of the Pastime Club from 1864 until his death on Christmas Day, 1866. The large turnout of club members at his funeral was cited by Griffith as an example of the club's "great good fellowship."[48]

Louis McKim: Louis McKim was born around 1848 and worked as a bank clerk until his premature death in 1876.

Philip Henry Minis: Philip H. Minis was one of the three members of the Waverly Club who became an officer of the Pastime Club after the 1861 merger. Born in Savannah, Georgia, on December 14, 1842, Minis was the grandson of William Livingston, one of the signers of the Declaration of Independence. When the Civil War broke out, he returned to Georgia and served in the Confederate Army, being briefly held as a Prisoner of War during the final weeks of the war. After marrying in Baltimore in 1868, he moved to New York City and became a stock broker. He died in Manhattan on October 22, 1911.

Thomas J. Mitchell: Griffith described Mitchell as a very loyal supporter of the Union cause and referred to him as "dear old Tom Mitchell," suggesting he was dead. As such, he is believed to be a Thomas J. Mitchell who served in the 2nd Maryland Infantry from 1861 to 1865 and who died on September 8, 1895. The ballplaying Mitchell was on the first nine of the Pastimes in 1862 and 1863, which seems on first glance to rule out this soldier, but according to the official history of the 2nd Maryland, the regiment was "on duty along the eastern shore of Maryland and Virginia," until the summer of 1863, spending much of that time in Baltimore.

William Morris Orem: W. Morris Orem was born in 1838 and was a member of a prominent Baltimore family whose estate was near the site of the city's first baseball diamond. After graduating from Princeton, he was on the first nine of the Excelsiors in 1860 and also played for the Pastimes during the war. Orem went into business and died in Baltimore on March 10, 1900.

William C. Pennington: William C. Pennington was on the first nine of the Pastimes in 1862 and 1863 and president of the Pastime Club. There were two Baltimore men named William C. Pennington of the same approximate age and it is a challenge to keep them straight. The ballplayer is believed to be William Clapham Pennington, who was born on March 4, 1829, in Baltimore, where his father was a lawyer. Like his father, he became a lawyer and also became president of the Baltimore Fire Insurance Company. Pennington died in Baltimore on April 12, 1913.

Edward G. Pittman: Edward G. Pittman, who was born in Maryland in May of 1830, was club secretary in 1860 and the shortstop of the first nine. He later worked as a broker and died in Baltimore on August 13, 1908.

Major Neilson Poe, Jr.: Neilson Poe, Jr. — whose given name was pronounced and often misspelled Nelson — was born in Baltimore on September 6, 1834. He and his younger brother William both became members of pioneer Baltimore baseball clubs — Neilson with the Waverly Club and William with the Ivanhoe Club. When the Waverly Club merged with the Excelsiors in 1861, Neilson Poe, Jr., was one of the three members of the Waverly Club to become an officer of the newly formed Pastime Club, serving as its secretary. His father, Neilson Poe, Sr., a lawyer, was the second cousin of Edgar Allan Poe, while his mother, the former Josephine Clemm, was the half-sister of Poe's child bride, Virginia Clemm. The elder Neilson Poe made an unsuccessful attempt to break up this proposed marriage, causing the poet to term his cousin his "bitterest enemy." Yet Neilson Poe, Sr., was one of the handful of attendees at the 1849 funeral of the great writer. The younger Neilson Poe served in the Confederate Army during the Civil War. After the war he married Alice Minis, the sister of Philip Minis, who had been a fellow member of the Waverly Club and a fellow officer in the Pastime Club. He worked as a bank clerk and a police magistrate, retiring in 1906. He died in Baltimore on May 11, 1919.

George J. Popplein: George Popplein was born in Baltimore in August of 1840, and he and many of his brothers were involved in Baltimore's earliest baseball clubs. According to Griffith, George and Andrew Popplein joined him in becoming members of the Maryland Club in 1860, but all three soon resigned to join the Pastime Club.[49] One of the Popplein brothers played a single major league game in 1873, and the game has been credited to George, but it is much more likely to have been one of his brothers since George played sparingly after about 1867. He died in Baltimore on March 31, 1901.

Joseph Popplein: Joe Popplein, George's younger brother was born around 1849 and joined the first nine of the Pastimes in 1867, making him the most likely candidate to have been the one-game major leaguer. He later joined the fire department. He never married and was a very wealthy man when he died on November 12, 1927.

John K. Sears: John K. Sears, the first baseman of the Excelsiors in 1860, was born in September of 1827. He was a tobacco importer and a liquor dealer who served as club president in 1862 and 1863. He remained involved in the baseball during the 1870s as a member of the association that supported Baltimore's National Association entry.[50] By 1900, he had retired to Hundred Bay, Maryland, and he died between the 1910 and 1920 censuses.

J. Hervey Shriver: Hervey Shriver, who was club president and second vice president of the National Association of Base Ball Players in 1860, was born on July 18, 1829, in Frederick, Maryland. He and his brother operated Shriver Brothers, a Baltimore. Hervey Shriver eventually moved to Oswego, New York, where he was still living but in very poor health as of 1904.

William D. Shurtz: William D. Shurtz, the president of the Excelsior Club in 1859, was a merchant. He was born in New Jersey around 1816, so appears to have been a non-playing member. He died in Baltimore on July 19, 1888.

Richard P. Southard: Richard Southard was born in Massachusetts around 1853 and joined the first nine of the Pastimes in 1870 as the club enlisted new blood.

George W. Tinges: George W. Tinges, one of the officers of the Excelsiors, was born in Baltimore around 1815 and there is no record of his ever playing for the first nine. He worked as a bank clerk and in several other businesses before getting into real estate in 1861. By the time he retired and left the business to his son in 1884, he was one of Baltimore's best-known and longest-tenured real estate agents. Tinges was also involved in the local Episcopal church, spearheading its outreach to the poor and infirm. He died in his native city on September 21, 1887.

Nesbitt Turnbull: Nesbitt Turnbull, another of the new recruits of 1870, was born around 1848. He later became a bookkeeper at City Hall and lived in Baltimore until his death on November 8, 1924.

Eugene Van Ness: Eugene Van Ness, who was born around 1841, was one of the three members of the Waverly Club who became an officer of the Pastime Club following the 1861 merger. He worked for the banking house of Alexander Brown and Sons and married Helena Shriver, a descendant of Charles Carroll, a signer of the Declaration of Independence. He was the victim in a sensational poisoning case in the early 1870s but survived and died in Baltimore on March 31, 1900.

Jacob B. Waidner: Jacob Waidner was born around 1840 and worked as a grocer, becoming a partner with John C. Bridges after Bridges split from Alexander P. Woods (see below) in 1864. He later worked as a coffee importer and a tax clerk. He died in Baltimore on November 14, 1892; in an odd coincidence, his elderly father died on the same day and a joint funeral was held.

Alexander P. Woods: Alexander P. Woods was the younger of two brothers who played for the first nine of the Excelsiors in 1860. He was born near Portland, Maine, around 1838 and became a partner in Woods, Bridges & Co., the Commerce Street grocery firm that hosted the initial meeting of the Excelsior Club. Woods split from Bridges in 1864 and became a coffee importer. He died in Baltimore on March 1, 1909.

Daniel C. Woods: Daniel C. Woods was born around 1836 near Portland, Maine. He became a very successful sugar broker when Baltimore was one of the major hubs of the sugar industry. But the rise of the sugar trust and a disastrous fire that destroyed his warehouse put him out of business in 1904. Although then around 70, Daniel Woods began a new career as a real estate broker. He died in Baltimore on November 10, 1910.

Other Excelsior/Pastime Club Members: William H. Annan (see Marylands), Barrett, Robert J. Bayley, Buck, William Chenoweth, Clarence Doyle, M. N. Howe, Fielding Lucas (see Marylands), Morris McDonald, C. McDowell, Nelson Mowton (secretary in 1869), John M. Nelson (secretary in 1868), Andrew Popplein, W. R. Presstman, Reese, Frank Sellman (see Marylands), William M. Shoemaker, William J. Walker, James Williams, Oliver A. Winchester (secretary in 1867).

SOURCES

This piece was primarily based upon William Ridgely Griffith's 1897 book *The Early History of Amateur Base Ball in the State of Maryland* (Baltimore: n.p., 1997). Also valuable were contemporary newspaper accounts, as cited in the notes, and James Bready's *Baseball in Baltimore* (Baltimore: Johns Hopkins University Press, 1998), especially pages 5–7. After this piece was completed, Brian McKenna began a blog on early Baltimore baseball (*http://baseballhistoryblog.com/*) that is far more detailed about many aspects of the Pastime and Maryland clubs.

NOTES

1. "Oldest Baseball Man," *Baltimore Sun*, December 27, 1905, 8.
2. William Ridgely Griffith, *The Early History of Amateur Base Ball in the State of Maryland* (Baltimore: n.p., 1997), 4.
3. Ibid., 5.
4. A helpful map of the sites of early Baltimore baseball diamond appears in James Bready's *Baseball in Baltimore*, p. 4.
5. Griffith, *The Early History of Amateur Baseball in the State of Maryland*, 5.
6. *New York Atlas*, March 18, 1860.
7. *Baltimore Sun*, April 10, 1860.
8. Griffith, *The Early History of Amateur Baseball*, 12–13.
9. *Baltimore Sun*, June 7, 1860.
10. Griffith, *The Early History of Amateur Baseball*, 5.
11. *Wilkes' Spirit of the Times*, October 6, 1860, 69; Griffith, *The Early History of Amateur Baseball*, 6.
12. *Wilkes' Spirit of the Times*, October 6, 1860, 69; Charles Peverelly,

The Book of American Pastimes (New York, 1866), 410; Griffith, *The Early History of Amateur Baseball*, 6.

13. *Ibid.*; italics in original.
14. *Ibid.*, 7, 14–15, 28.
15. *Ibid.*, 30. To make matters worse, when Griffith tracked down early club members in the mid–1890s, he found that many of them "had altogether forgotten that they were officers of their clubs in 1860 and 1861, until informed of the fact, when they would thank him, with a smile or pleasure, as recollections of the past would come before them" (p. 25).
16. *Baltimore Sun*, August 17, 1861; reprinted in Griffith, *The Early History of Amateur Baseball*, 10, and supplemented by Griffith's commentary.
17. Griffith, *The Early History of Amateur Baseball*, 10.
18. *Ibid.*, 36.
19. *Ibid.*, 7.
20. *Ibid.*, 11; see also 36–37.
21. *Baltimore Sun*, August 10, 1861; Griffith, *The Early History of Amateur Baseball*, 26–27.
22. Griffith, *The Early History of Amateur Baseball*, 25.
23. *Baltimore Sun*, September 23, 1861; Griffith, *The Early History of Amateur Baseball*, 22.
24. Griffith, *The Early History of Amateur Baseball*, 31–33.
25. Griffith, *The Early History of Amateur Baseball*, 36–37. Griffith recalled this happening in either "1863 or 1864," but regimental histories clearly record that it was in 1864.
26. *Baltimore American*, August 8, 1863; reprinted in Griffith, *The Early History of Amateur Baseball*, 33–34.
27. Unidentified clipping, September 12, 1863, and *Baltimore American*, September 17, 1863; both reprinted in Griffith, *The Early History of Amateur Baseball*, 34–35.
28. Griffith, *The Early History of Amateur Baseball*, 31.
29. *Ibid.*, 11.
30. *Ibid.*, 33.
31. *Ibid.*, 11.
32. French Scrapbooks; reprinted from *The Ball Player's Chronicle*, apparently in September of 1867.
33. This statement that the club did not lose during these years is made explicitly in an article in the *Baltimore Sunday Telegram* of August 27, 1865 — reprinted on page 37 of Griffith — and my research has found no reason to dispute that claim.
34. *Baltimore Sun*, August 30, 1865; reprinted in Griffith, *The Early History of Amateur Baseball*, 37–39. Italics are from Griffith.
35. *Baltimore Sunday Telegram*, August 27, 1865; reprinted in Griffith, *The Early History of Amateur Baseball*, 37.
36. Griffith, *The Early History of Amateur Baseball*, 11.
37. *Ibid.*, 49 and 43. Griffith described Gratton as a former member of the Putnam Club of Brooklyn and stated that he arrived in Baltimore in 1866. But city directories make clear that he was wrong about the year, while the articles cited in the entry on the Syracuse Base Ball Club establish his membership in (and presidency of) that club. That of course does not preclude him also being a member of the Putnams, a statement that was also made in contemporaneous newspaper accounts, but it has not been corroborated. For more on Gratton, see the entry on the Syracuse Base Ball Club.
38. *Ibid.*, 47–48.
39. *Ibid.*, 54–55.
40. *Baltimore Sunday Telegram*, September 1, 1867; reprinted in Griffith, *The Early History of Amateur Baseball*, 56–60.
41. French Scrapbooks; a clipping from *The Ball Player's Chronicle*, apparently in September of 1867.
42. Griffith, *The Early History of Amateur Baseball*, 54–56.
43. *Our Boys and Girls*, October 23, 1869.
44. *New York Tribune*, August 4, 1870; reprinted in Griffith, *The Early History of Amateur Baseball*, 83.
45. Griffith, *The Early History of Amateur Baseball*, 84–85 (italics in original). The Pastime Club also recaptured the silver ball from the Maryland Club in the fall of 1870, but little credit should be attached to this feat, since, as even Griffith acknowledges, it occurred after the majority of the players of the Marylands had left to play elsewhere (*Baltimore Sun*, September 10, 1870; reprinted in Griffith, 84).
46. *Ibid.*, 32.
47. Quoted in J. C. Kofoed, "Early History of Curve Pitching," *Baseball Magazine*, August 1915, 56.
48. Griffith, *The Early History of Amateur Baseball*, 11.
49. *Ibid.*, 31. Griffith states that this occurred in 1861, but the game account on page 16 and other evidence contradict that assertion.
50. *Baltimore Sun*, December 8, 1874.

❖ *Marylands of Baltimore* (Peter Morris) ❖

Club History

For much of its history, the Maryland Club of Baltimore was overshadowed by the Excelsior/Pastime Club. But then in 1867 the club captured the local championship, and the distinction prompted the Marylands to become Baltimore's first professional baseball club.

The club's first known match game took place on November 27, 1860, and saw the Marylands lose 23–16 to the Waverly Club.[1] Many of the nine players who represented the club on that date cannot be positively identified, and three of the ones who can — William Ridgely Griffith, George Popplein and Andrew Popplein — soon quit to join the more established Excelsior Club.[2] It was not an auspicious start, and when the Civil War began a few months later, there was no reason to think that the Maryland Club would be heard from again.

But the club was made of sterner stuff, as Griffith himself would later acknowledge. "The Maryland Club," he wrote in 1897, "was a club composed of a large number of the most enthusiastic, and best ball players of the State during the years of Amateur ball. It was a great antagonist of the Pastime Club — the Champions. Although beaten in the contest year after year, yet it would not down, but came back as each season opened, stronger than before, until in 1867 it won from the Pastime the Silver Ball, and Championship of the State. The victory was deserved, for each player had been constantly drilled by their Captain, Mike Hooper *first*, and to the President, Robert Green, *next*, if the writer's recollections be correct, and after, to the large number of *earnest members*, who never tired of working for the best interest of their club, is due great praise for the splendid record of the Maryland Club, in and out of the State."[3]

As with so many clubs, the activities of the Maryland Club were limited during the war. They did, however, manage several notable victories, including two wins over the Peabody Club of Baltimore in 1861, triumphs against the National Club of Washington in 1861 and 1862, and a victory over the Jeffersons of Washington in 1864. But the Marylands never could quite manage to beat the older Pastime Club and earn recognition as local champions.

That state of affairs continued in the first few years after the war, and the frustration of the Marylands must have been increased by having to rent grounds from the champion Pastimes. In the spring of 1867, the *Sunday Telegram* reported that the Maryland Club and another local nine, the Enterprise Club, "intend straining every nerve this season to win the title of Champions."[4] The Enterprise Club made the first try but was defeated in two straight games by the champions. Since the Marylands had already lost to the Enterprise Club, nobody gave them much chance against the Pastimes, especially when they dropped the first game of the series. But then the Maryland rebounded with two convincing victories—47 to 26 and 47 to 15.[5] At long last, the Marylands were the champions of Baltimore!

Thereafter the Pastime Club and the Maryland Club essentially exchanged roles, with the Pastimes settling for remaining a strong amateur nine and the Marylands plunging into the new world of professional baseball. In the process, many of the men who had helped the club win the city championship lost their places on the first nine. At the same time, however, the Maryland Club helped make Baltimore a fertile ground for developing new talent, as it sent numerous young Baltimore players on to professional careers. That was quite an accomplishment in a city whose merchants had become so hostile to baseball that one declared "that he would give employment to no base ball player, however capable to transact business."[6]

While the Marylands retained the city championship for the next three years, they had limited success against clubs from the large Northern cities. In 1868, the club vanquished its local rivals and then beat the Nationals of Washington to earn recognition as "Champions of the South."[7] But a few weeks after the big win over the Nationals the Marylands embarked on a tour of Philadelphia and New York with high hopes, only to lose all four games.

The 1869 season saw the Marylands bring in two professionals, pitcher Elias Cope from Philadelphia and catcher Bill Lennon from New York. The result? Once again, the club outdid its local rivals and even managed upset wins over the Mutuals of New York and the Eckfords of Brooklyn. Yet it still lost nearly two-thirds of its games against professional clubs, several of them by embarrassing margins. In addition, the decision to bring in outside players caused several former starters to quit the Marylands and join the Pastimes.

These dispiriting trends continued in 1870. At the annual meeting on January 4, it was decided that the same nine would represent the Maryland Club in 1870, an announcement that led the club to be commended as "a good instance of non-revolving."[8] But by the start of the season there was a new set of directors that pledged major changes, including 2,000 additional seats and a new nickname of "Blue Stockings" in honor of the club's white and blue uniforms. Most important, several more imported professionals were signed, and it was pledged that every member of the nine, along with the substitutes, would practice on a daily basis.[9]

But for all the promise of change, the 1870 season was very much like the two preceding years. The new imports caused several more veteran players to switch to the Pastimes, yet the Marylands did not improve and instead lost 14 of their 16 professional games. To cap things off, the club ran out of money on an August tour of Illinois, Indiana, and Ohio, with the result that several players quit and joined the Kekiongas of Fort Wayne. The remnant who did return to Baltimore then lost the city championship to the Pastimes in September.

Although these years were not successful ones for the Marylands, they weren't unmitigated failures. The club did manage to develop homegrown product Bobby Mathews into one of the game's first pitching superstars, while sending at least seven other young Baltimore players on to brief major league careers. Many of those players got their chance with the Kekiongas of Fort Wayne, but several more did so in 1873 when the Marylands regrouped and entered the National Association. As with the club's previous experiments with professionalism, however, entering the major leagues was not a success—the Marylands lost all six games and were outscored 152 to 26 before disbanding.[10]

Club Members

William Howard Annan: William H. Annan was the son of a physician and was born in Louisville on December 14, 1850. The family was living in St. Louis in 1860, and then settled in Baltimore. William Annan played shortstop for both the Marylands and the Pastimes and garnered quite a reputation. According to Griffith, one 1866 game account contained "not much praise for any one but Annan, S.S. of the Marylands, who it predicts will become one of the famous shortstops of the country."[11] He then enrolled in Harvard, playing on the school's baseball nine in 1873 and even umpiring one National Association game. He then spent three years studying in Europe (possibly at Cambridge), before returning to Harvard Law School and earning a law degree. During his second stint at Harvard, he apparently remained interested in baseball, as the *Harvard Crimson* of February 21, 1879, reported that Annan of the law school was trying out for the baseball nine. Annan practiced law in Baltimore from 1880 to 1885, went to Scotland and studied medicine at the University of Edinburgh, and then moved to London. He returned to New York in 1895, but vanished in 1898, telling his landlord that he would return for his trunk but never doing so. Nothing is known about his whereabouts thereafter; one alumni publication suggested that he was living in Cambridge, Massachusetts, in 1903, but no confirmation has been found, and mystery continues to swirl around Annan.

Robert L. Armstrong: Outfielder Robert L. Armstrong was a giant by the standards of the time at 6'2" and was known as an "extraordinarily heavy batter" who had "made the longest hit on record on the Maryland grounds."[12] After playing with the Marylands from 1866 to 1870, he went on to a brief career in the National Association with the Kekiongas of Fort Wayne. While the baseball encyclopedias list no vital information for him, he was identified as Robert L. Armstrong in newspaper accounts and an 1870 profile in the *Clipper* described him as being 20 years old and a lifelong resident of Baltimore. Based on this, it seems virtually certain that the ballplayer was Robert Livingston Armstrong, the son of a local farmer who was listed as 21 on the 1870 census. This man moved to Fort Worth, Texas, in 1881, and died there on December 3, 1917.

Charles S. Bierman: Charley Bierman was one of the imported professionals who joined the Marylands in 1870. He was born in Hoboken, New Jersey, around 1845, and his development of a "slow drop ball which is very effective" enabled him to play for numerous professional clubs, including a brief major league stint.[13] He died in Hoboken on August 4, 1879.

Thomas Joseph Carey: Tom Carey was born in Brooklyn around 1846 and served in the Civil War before joining the Marylands in 1870. He played in the major leagues for nine seasons before heading west and settling in San Francisco. In 1896, he was admitted to a Veteran's Home in Napa, California, where he remained until being discharged in October of 1905 for "noncompliance with pension rules and deserting with $6.50 of clothing." He returned to San Francisco (arriving just in time for the Great Earthquake) and died there on August 16, 1906.

Elias P. Cope: Elias Cope was born in Philadelphia around 1845. He enlisted in the 104th Pennsylvania Infantry, Company D, in February of 1862 and received a disability discharge seven months later. He played for the Keystones of Philadelphia from 1864 to 1867, being the primary pitcher for most of that time. In 1868, he followed battery mate Fergy Malone to the Olympics of Washington in 1868 and then he joined the Marylands of Baltimore in 1869. Already married and with two young children, Cope retired from baseball in 1870 and returned to Philadelphia where he became a butcher like his father and raised six children. On the 1900 census, Cope's wife is listed as married but Elias was not living with her.

Thomas J. Forker: Tom Forker joined the Marylands in 1870, having previously played for various Brooklyn clubs, including the Mohawks and the Excelsiors, and for the Nationals of Washington. According to an 1870 profile, he was born in Brooklyn around 1846 and grew up there.[14] Based upon this,

it appears that he was a Civil War veteran, but other information about his life has been difficult to pin down.

Warren "Wally" Goldsmith: Wally Goldsmith was born in Baltimore in 1847 to a well-to-do family. He played for the junior Monumental Club in 1863, then spent several years with the Enterprise Club before joining the Marylands. He then played professionally until 1875, seeing action with four different major league clubs. He became a bit of a drifter after baseball, worked in Peoria as a hotel clerk for several years, then moved to Chicago, and finally settled in Washington around 1903, where he worked as the manager of a hotel. He died there on September 16, 1915.

Robert F. Green: Robert Green was the president of the Maryland Club during its early years. Born in Baltimore around 1831, he became secretary of the board that was responsible for opening streets. He died in Baltimore on January 13, 1898.

Walter Gwynn: Walter Gwynn was the name of a Confederate Civil War general who spent many years in Baltimore, but the man by that name who played for the Maryland Club was a different man and does not appear to have been a close relative of the general. The ball-playing Walter Gwynn was born in Virginia around 1847. In the late 1860s, he moved to De Soto County, Mississippi, where he worked as a railroad agent. He died there in June of 1880.

George Payson Heiner: G. Payson Heiner, the club secretary in 1863, was born in Maryland around 1846 and was the son of a prominent Baltimore clergyman. He was also active in the local boat club. He was incapacitated by a painful illness in the late 1860s and died on November 17, 1869.

Michael H. Hooper, Jr.: Mike Hooper, the longtime captain of the Marylands, was a native of Baltimore who earned a reputation as a "very swift runner" and a "sure, heavy batter." Although listed in the encyclopedias as being born on February 7, 1850, censuses and newspaper profiles suggest that he was actually born in 1845 or 1846. One profile even claimed that he had been playing for the Marylands since 1858, although this seems highly unlikely.[15] Hooper played for the Marylands during their brief foray in the National Association. He also umpired several major league games, having the unique experience of being fired by the Union Association "on account of his weak voice."[16] He remained in Baltimore, working as a driver and as a storekeeper and raising a large family. He died there on December 2, 1917.

George Henry Keerl: George Keerl was born in Baltimore on April 10, 1847, and played for the Marylands from 1866 to 1869. He then played for several professional clubs, including the White Stockings of Chicago in 1875. He moved to Marinette, Wisconsin, working there as a plumber until his death on September 9, 1923.

Joseph Kernan: Joe Kernan joined the Marylands as a substitute in 1870 and played two games for the club's National Association entry in 1873. He has not been positively identified, but there is only one plausible candidate: a Joseph S. Kernan who was born in Baltimore in June of 1851, later worked as a railroad conductor, and died in Baltimore on February 16, 1911.

William H. Lennon: Bill Lennon was born in January of 1845 in Brooklyn and played for the Excelsiors, Stars, and Mohawks of that city and the Excelsiors of Chicago before becoming one of the Maryland Club's first imports in 1869. He remained with the club for two years, and in 1872 married a young Baltimore woman whose sister married his teammate, Ed Mincher. After retiring from baseball in 1874, Lennon worked for the City of Baltimore. After the death of his wife, he moved to Philadelphia to be closer to his daughters. He died there on August 19, 1910.

Fielding Henry Lucas: Fielding Lucas was born in Baltimore on October 12, 1851, and played first base for the Marylands in 1868 and 1869. On a trip to New York in 1869, he was praised as "a very superior first base man; his one hand catching, although more showy than prudent, is very fine."[17] After attending Loyola College, he began a long career in the Baltimore fire department in 1879, eventually becoming its fire chief. He died in Baltimore on July 9, 1918.[18]

Robert T. Mathews: Alone among Baltimore players of the 1860s, Bobby Mathews went on to major league stardom, winning 297 major league games from 1871 to 1887 and playing a major role in the development of the curveball. Mathews was born in Baltimore on November 21, 1851, the son of Irish immigrants. Though a diminutive man (he is officially listed as five feet, five-and-a-half inches tall and 140 pounds but was described in many accounts as even smaller), Mathews joined the Marylands as a substitute in 1869 and became their primary pitcher in 1870. Along with several other players, he joined the Kekiongas of Fort Wayne after the Marylands ran out of money while on tour. As a result, when the Kekiongas joined the National Association in 1871, he had the distinction of pitching in the first major league game ever played. Not only that, but Mathews also pitched the first major league shutout on that day — one of only four shutouts pitched that season. His success was due in large part to his development of a lethal curveball at a time when the underhand delivery restriction made the pitch very rare. While "Candy" Cummings is usually credited with "inventing" the curve, many contemporaries believed that Mathews had played just as large a role in its development. Even Cummings acknowledged Mathews's contributions, and at least one very credible source, pitcher Alphonse "Phonney" Martin, believed that Mathews had more to do with the advent of the pitch than Cummings.[19] Martin also believed that Mathews was throwing a spitball long before the pitch became recognized as such, and was joined in that belief by such authorities as William Rankin.[20] Unfortunately, by the time debates about the origin of the curveball and spitball were held, Mathews was not able to contribute to them, as he died in his native Baltimore of paresis on April 17, 1898.

Edward M. Mincher: Ed Mincher was born in Baltimore on June 17, 1851, and played for the Enterprise Club of Baltimore before joining the Marylands in 1868. He played for numerous professional clubs during the 1870s, but his career began to wind down after he was blacklisted in 1877. He and Maryland Club teammate Bill Lennon married sisters, but Mincher became a mysterious figure after baseball. He moved to Philadelphia for a while and was still listed in the city directories as a ballplayer as late as 1890, though by then his playing days were long over. He finally moved to New York and, for reasons unknown, changed his name to Henry McElwee. He died in Brooklyn on December 18, 1918.

Arthur W. Sellman: Arthur W. Sellman was born in Baltimore on February 11, 1847, and was involved with the Marylands from 1864 onward, mostly in off-the-field roles. He worked as a bookkeeper and never married, dying in Baltimore on April 8, 1915.

Charles Francis Sellman: Frank Sellman was Arthur's younger brother and a much more accomplished ballplayer. He played for the Marylands and other Baltimore clubs from 1867 to 1871, then had brief stints with five National Association clubs. Although he played only 37 major league games, he was the ultimate utility player, seeing action at every position except left field. He often used the alias "Williams" because of parental disapproval, but little effort was made to disguise his true identity. When his baseball career ended, he returned to Baltimore, where he died on May 6, 1907.

John Tolly Worthington: Tolly Worthington was born into a wealthy Baltimore family around 1846 and played for the Marylands from 1868 to 1870, earning a reputation as a "strong heavy batter" and a "splendid outfielder" who "covers as much ground as any player." He attended the University of Virginia, then spent time abroad before returning to Baltimore to look after a large property inherited from his father in the section of the Baltimore Valley known as Worthington's Valley. Even after retiring from active play, Worthington still retained an interest in the Lord Baltimores and once became so excited when a player made a fine defensive play that he ran from the grandstand to the player and, removing a diamond pin stick from his own scarf, attached it to the player's uniform. He never married and died on March 22, 1894.

Other Club Members: William Bennett, Fred Benteen (it's conceivable that this was Fred W. Benteen, who is discussed in the St. Louis chapter, but is more likely a Baltimore man named Frederick D. Benteen, Jr., who died on January 2, 1864, at the age of 20), E. P. Bertrand, Blanford, Buck, William Caughey, Doyle, Frush, Hazlehurst, Hess, Henry Kohler, Edward C. Lefebvre, George Lilly, W. P. Montague, Charles A. Richardson, Rorke, Reese, John Shannon, Alex Stewart, E. O. Thomas, William P. Vaughan, Col. Henry Q. Weigel, Edward Williams, James Wilson, Yardley, Charles E. Young.

SOURCES

As with the article about the Excelsior/Pastime club, this piece was primarily based upon William Ridgely Griffith's *The Early History of Amateur Base Ball in the State of Maryland* (Baltimore: n.p., 1897), with help from contemporaneous newspaper accounts, as cited in the notes. After this piece was completed, Brian McKenna began a blog on early Baltimore baseball (*http://baseballhistoryblog.com/*) that is far more detailed about many aspects of the Pastime and Maryland clubs.

NOTES

1. William Ridgely Griffith, *The Early History of Amateur Base Ball in the State of Maryland* (Baltimore: n.p., 1897), 16. Griffith stated that the club was first organized in 1860. Some later articles suggest that the club was formed in 1858, but there is no contemporaneous confirmation of the earlier date.
2. Griffith, *The Early History of Amateur Base Ball in the State of Maryland*, 31. Griffith states that this occurred in 1861, but the game account he provides on page 16 and other evidence seems to contradict him.
3. Ibid.
4. *Baltimore Sunday Telegram*, April 28, 1867; reprinted in Griffith, *The Early History of Amateur Base Ball in the State of Maryland*, 52.
5. Griffith, *The Early History of Amateur Base Ball in the State of Maryland*, 52–56.
6. French Scrapbooks; see the Excelsior/Pastime of Baltimore entry for the entire quotation.
7. "The Championship of the South," *New York Clipper*, October 10, 1868, 211
8. *New York Clipper*, January 15, 1870.
9. *New York Clipper*, April 23, 1870.
10. William J. Ryczek, *Blackguards and Red Stockings* (Jefferson, NC: McFarland, 1992), 97, 115.
11. Griffith, *The Early History of Amateur Base Ball in the State of Maryland*, 47; the original article appeared in the *Baltimore Sunday Telegram* on September 16, 1866.
12. *New York Clipper*, April 23, 1870.
13. *New York Clipper*, April 2, 1870.
14. *New York Clipper*, April 23, 1870.
15. Ibid.
16. *Cleveland Herald*, May 21, 1884.
17. *New York Tribune*, July 30, 1869.
18. "Chief Lucas Dead," *Baltimore American*, July 10, 1918.
19. Phonney Martin Curveball Scrapbook, National Baseball Hall of Fame.
20. Francis C. Richter, *Richter's History and Records of Base Ball* (Jefferson, NC: McFarland, 2005), 270; *Sporting News*, February 13, 1908.

❖ Olympics of Washington (Peter Morris) ❖

CLUB HISTORY

In the years immediately following the Civil War, the National Club of Washington lacked a strong rival in the nation's capital. The Olympic Club had been formed in 1865, but its first two seasons of play were undistinguished, and the ages of some of its early members suggest that it may have been a junior club. Even as late as 1867, a pair of contests between the Nationals and the Olympics ended in easy 46–7 and 33–7 victories for the older club. But the Olympic Club did capture a prize bat at a local fair that fall, and that triumph was a sign of things to come.[1]

In 1868, the Olympics emerged as a legitimate challenger for local supremacy. They displayed their new ambition at an early-season meeting at which a new uniform of dark blue pants, gray shirts with dark blue trimmings and gray caps was adopted and at which plans to challenge clubs from all over the country were announced.[2] Matches against the Nationals proved harder to arrange, and the two clubs spent much of the year embroiled in tedious disputes over the circumstances under which they would compete. Eventually, two late-season contests were held, with the Nationals prevailing both times, 21–15 and 18–13. Even so, the Olympic Club's status as an up-and-comer became clear during a season highlighted by a win over the Cincinnati Base Ball Club (the club that became known as the Red Stockings).

Several factors had contributed to the rapid rise of the Olympic Club, including the maturation of young players such as pitcher Ed Leech and the decision of National Club players like Harry McLean and Val Robinson to cast their lots with the newer club. In addition, the Olympics borrowed from the Nationals a couple of tactics that had enabled that club to become a national power.

The first of these was enlisting wealthy supporters as honorary members. Washington attorney Simon Wolf later described how he became club president and a generous patron. Wolf recalled that he became acquainted with Ezra B. French of the Treasury Department, who "was an intense lover of the game and managed to get as many of the clerks in his bureau as were good baseball players, and in this way, I also became interested. Accepted the honor at a cost of $1,000 a year, bought a big flag for the organization and went with them to several cities, where I became more or less initiated in the curriculum of baseball."[3]

The other ploy was one alluded to in Wolf's comments: using Treasury Department jobs to lure promising players from New York. A. G. Mills later acknowledged that catcher and shortstop Davy Force came to New York because he was offered a government job, though he insisted that Force "earned every dollar that was paid him."[4] Dick Hurley and Waddy Beach were other players recruited by the lure of Treasury Department clerkships.

Despite the improvement of the Olympics, their inability to beat the Nationals remained a source of considerable frustration. As one Washingtonian later recalled, "The great ambition of the Olympics was to beat the National, but game after game went against them. Strong clubs came here from the North and often times they would defeat the National

Club easily, to be as easily defeated by the Olympics. Even the Capitols and the Unions pointed to balls that they had won from the sturdy Nationals, but the Olympics, as strong a club in every respect, was always defeated. They strengthened their nine in every position, but for two years they could not win a ball from the Nationals."[5]

The "ice was broken" in the summer of 1869 when the Olympics at last defeated the Nationals. As the writer of the above recollection recalled, "it was a memorable day, celebrated by a banquet, that the Olympic won a ball from the Nationals."[6] The descent of the Nationals was rapid after that, while the Olympics picked up many players from the Nationals and became the capital city's foremost baseball club.

That new role brought new responsibilities, and the Olympics embraced them. In July of 1869, the club followed in the footsteps of the Nationals by embarking on an ambitious tour. One of the "hardy patriots" who made the trek later described it as "the longest of its kind up to that time" and provided a harrowing account:

> We had trouble everywhere, even in such small jumps as from Cincinnati to Mansfield, Ohio, nothing went properly but our worst time came when turning our faces eastward for the return trip, we ran up against a snag of huge dimensions at Cincinnati.
>
> On that trip the Olympics played the Red Stockings four games. In the last one they defeated us 10 to 7, the game being delayed by a rain storm. Our boys were anxious to play it out, as they imagined they had a chance of defeating the unbeatables. Well, the game was played out, but the train we were expected to take for Philadelphia was at that time many miles to the east, and there was no other train out that night for us to take in order to reach Philadelphia in time for our next game. But right here came the "do or die" spirit of the Olympic management, Secretaries N. E. Young and Fred Schmidt in particular.
>
> A freight was due to leave Cincinnati at 1 A.M. and after many consultations with the agent of the railway company it was decided to add a "box car" for the players. Say, you haven't any idea what a box car of those days was, nor can you imagine what a trip of 700 miles meant over a rough mountain road, for such was the Baltimore & Ohio in those days. It was the days before the use of air brakes, but rough as the ride, and tedious as the trip proved to be, the band never wailed, the only desire being to reach Philadelphia in time to keep their word with the Keystones of that place.
>
> They arrived in Philadelphia one hour ahead of the time set for the game, but every one of the players took a portion of that hour for a bath in the waters of the Schuylkill river. But they presented a sorry sight when they appeared on the field to play the Keystones, then the best team in the city of Philadelphia. Though fatigued, they played a wonderful game against their opponents, that is for that period of ball playing.[7]

The Olympic Club also made a courageous and admirable decision in the fall of 1869 by accepting a challenge from the Alert Base Ball Club, a local African American club. The proposed match was described as "the first game between white and colored clubs in the District."[8] Controversy ensued, with the Maryland Club of Baltimore reportedly passing a resolution to refuse to complete a series with the Olympics if the match was played. The Maryland Club used the flimsy pretense that the Alert Club was not a member of the NABBP, but such contests were played all the time, and there can be little doubt of the real reason for the threat.[9]

The Olympics went ahead with the match against the Alert Club, winning easily, and subsequently played a much closer contest on October 12 against another African American club, the Mutuals of Washington. The Maryland Club later denied having made the threat and resumed playing the Olympics the following season.

The Olympic Club wrapped up the breakthrough season with an exciting 13–11 win over the National Club, followed by a celebration at the Sweetzer House. Suitable toasts were offered by club president Colonel C. M. Alexander, captain Davy Force, and many other players and club officers, each of which was "received and applauded in hilarious fashion. Then followed a spirited

The Olympic Club's rise to national prominence in 1868 included contests against such legendary clubs as the Atlantic and Eckford nines of Brooklyn.

song by one of the worthy gentlemen present, recounting his experience 'Up in a Balloon,' the chorus being generously sustained by all present.... In the midst of the general good feeling and good cheer the Olympics did not forget the courtesy due to a vanquished foe, but duly condoled with the Nationals in their 'unprecedented bad luck' and unprofitable playing on Monday last."[10]

After the successful conclusion to the campaign, the club immediately began laying the foundation for greater success in 1870. By November, the first nine and "nearly all the playing members" of the Olympic Club were engaged in gymnastic practice at the Washington Gymnastics Association. They earned commendation for taking this "wise step," which had been inspired by the example of the Red Stockings' undefeated season.[11]

Another key part of the transition to the professional era was establishing suitable grounds, and in 1870 the Olympic Club opened a new home field. Henry Chadwick reported approvingly: "The Olympic Club ... has not been idle. Heretofore they have had no grounds of their own on which to practice; but they have secured grounds now near those of the Nationals, and have fitted them up in a style superior to any in the country, paying cash down as they go. A fine club house, plenty of seats and a fine pagoda over the back stop, secluded from the crowd, for the scorers and reporters of the press, has been erected. The field is level and dry and can be played upon within two hours after a heavy rain."[12]

The conversion to professionalism was a rocky one for every amateur club, and the Olympics were no exception. On the eve of the 1870 season, Olympic Club secretary Nick Young expressed disgust at how "revolvers" such as Ed Pinkham were taking advantage by signing multiple contracts and then disregarding all but the most lucrative one.[13] In spite of such setbacks, however, the able leadership of Young as secretary and A.G. Mills as club president enabled the Olympics to adapt to professional baseball.

Young in particular played a crucial role in the 1871 launch of the first professional league, the National Association. The historic meeting to organize the league took place on March 17, 1871, at Collier's Rooms, a saloon located at the corner of Broadway and Thirteenth in New York City. While Henry Chadwick is sometimes credited with arranging the meeting, in fact Chadwick specifically noted, "The origin of this convention should be placed on record, viz., Mr. N. E. Young, the efficient Secretary of the Olympic Club of Washington."[14]

The Olympics placed a strong team on the field in 1871 in which the holdovers were supplemented by new recruits from the famous Red Stockings, including Asa Brainard, Doug Allison, Andy Leonard, and Fred Waterman. As in the past, it appears that civil service jobs were used to lure at least some of the new players, since Leonard received an appointment as a War Department messenger that corresponded with the start of the 1871 baseball season and Allison spent most of the rest of his life working for the post office.

The Olympics got off to a solid start in 1871 and were over .500 for most of the National Association's inaugural campaign. The turning point for the club took place on July 4 with Boston in town. According to Nick Young, on the evening before the match, Charley Sweasy of the Olympics told Young and two of his companions that a Boston backer wanted to bet $150 on his team. The wager was accepted, and, to Young's chagrin, "next day [Olympics' third baseman] Fred. Waterman was so full that he couldn't see the grand stand from first base. The Olympics were beaten, and our $50 apiece gone into the stranger's pockets."[15]

Nine days later, with the team's record at 12–8, Mills stepped down as president, citing the demands of his position as chief clerk of Supervising Architect of the Treasury. In his resignation letter, Mills explained, "The time has at length arrived when I can, without detriment to the club, retire from the office I hold.... To those of you who stood by the club with me in its dark hours — and it has seen many — and to those who, more recently, contributed your means and influence to ensure its success, I beg to return my hearty thanks.... Standing among the foremost of the clubs competing for the national championship, with the finest playing and most popular nine in the country, a full treasury [of $3,500], and a fine ground with unrivalled conveniences for spectators, the Olympic Club may well congratulate itself on what it has accomplished, and look forward with confidence."[16]

Despite the optimistic tone, the Olympic Club was never the same. Nick Young cited the pressures of his own civil service job and declined to take over the presidency. A man named W. D. Whipple eventually was elected, and the Olympics won only three of their final ten contests to end the 1871 season with a 15–15 record. Young was then hired to run the Chicago team in 1872 and promptly signed such Olympic stalwarts as Allison, Everett Mills, and Davy Force. The Great Chicago Fire put an end to these plans, but the Olympics lost all three players and several other key performers.[17]

Despite the losses, the Olympic Club entered the National Association again in 1872, but its makeshift lineup won two games and lost seven before disbanding in late May. Fittingly, the team's final game was played on May 24 against the Nationals and resulted in an exciting 11–7 victory.

Club Members

Waddy Beach: Waddy Beach was a former star of the Eckfords of Brooklyn whose actual first name was probably Washington. Little is known about him, and one article about the Eckfords reported that he had disappeared.

Harry Berthrong: See Nationals of Washington.

James Irving Burns: J. Irving Burns was one of the Olympic Club's regulars at the start of the 1867 season but lost his spot to more talented players. Born in Biddeford, Maine, on August 10, 1843, Burns was educated at Colgate and Union College and then earned a law degree at Columbian University (later George Washington University). He served in the New York State Senate in the 1890s and remained prominent in Republican politics until 1901. Burns died in Yonkers on December 17, 1925.

Henry Burroughs: See Detroit Base Ball Club.

Elias Cope: See Marylands of Baltimore.

Philip Culp: See Philip Kulp.

Henry Willard Denison: Henry Denison of the Olympics of Washington is not to be confused with the Henry Dennison who played for the Lowells of Boston at the same time. Henry Willard Denison was born in Guildhall, Vermont, on May 11, 1846, and moved to Lancaster, New Hampshire, in 1860. After apprenticing as a printer, his father's cousin, Charles Dana, obtained a position in the War Department for Denison. He subsequently transferred to the Treasury Department and became a customs clerk. He was the first baseman for the Olympics in 1867 and 1868 and also began studying law at the Columbian University (later George Washington University). When the war of 1868 opened up Japan to Westerners, Denison obtained a consular position in Yokohama and soon became enthralled with the country. He went back to the United States to complete his legal studies and get married, but he returned to Japan in 1880 as legal advisor to the Japanese Department of Foreign Affairs. He lived in Japan for the rest of his life and became a powerful and highly respected figure. In 1905, he returned to New Hampshire to represent Japan in drafting the Treaty of Portsmouth, which ended the Russo-Japanese War. When the peace treaty had been signed, he returned to Lancaster to visit the grave of his sister. Denison died in Tokyo on July 3, 1914, after becoming the first foreigner to receive the Grand Cordon of the Rising Sun.[18]

William S. "Billy" Dick: Infielder Billy Dick played for the Keystones of Philadelphia from 1865 to 1867, then played for the Olympics in 1868 before rejoining the Keystones in 1869 and ending his career in 1870 with the Haymakers of Troy. His identity is not well established, but he may be a man who was born in New York in 1839 and died in Manhattan on July 22, 1903.

George W. "Shorty" Ewell: Catcher George "Shorty" Ewell was born in Philadelphia on October 29, 1850, and, like so many of the Olympics, had previously played for the Keystones of Philadelphia. He was listed as a "base ballist" on the 1870 District of Columbia census but his career pretty much ended at that point and he later worked as a sailor and an oysterman. He died in Philadelphia on October 20, 1910.

David W. Force: Davy Force was born on July 27, 1849, in New York City and, even by the standards of the era, was a very small man. He is listed as 5'4", 130 pounds, but descriptions by contemporaries suggest that that was generous. According to sportswriter Byron Clarke, Force "was not much bigger than Tom Thumb. He was the smallest man playing ball, and there has not been as small a one since. He was a fair player at short, but the crowd was always with him. He looked so funny on the ball field that whatever he did was funny.... It was quite a contrast between Force and Anson when they were walking together on the ball field — they looked like a giant and a midget."[19] Despite his lack of stature, Force played major league baseball for fifteen seasons.

Force began making a name for himself with the Unknowns of Harlem, where he was Charlie Pabor's catcher.[20] A. G. Mills, then the pitcher for the Olympics, lured Force to Washington in 1867 "to handle my pitching. I shall never forget the first time I saw him on the playing field. I looked down on him pityingly, thinking that my swift ones would perforate his anatomy, and what a revelation it was to me to see him stand up behind the bat and not only stop but hold every ball."[21]

Force soon moved to shortstop, and it was there that he made a name for himself. He was a surprisingly good hitter for a man of his size, batting .418 in 1872, and was such a dependable fielder that he remained a National League regular until 1886. He then played two more seasons in the minor leagues before finally retiring from baseball. The most notable incident in his career came after the 1874 season when he signed two different contracts, an event that led to a controversy that played a significant role in the formation of the National League. He settled in New Jersey when his career ended, and Mills helped him obtain a job with the Otis Elevator Company. Force briefly returned to the headlines in 1896 when he was accused of murder, but it was a case of mistaken identity. He died on June 21, 1918, in Englewood, New Jersey.

George Fox: See Nationals of Washington.

Andrew Gibney: See Nationals of Washington.

John Glenn: See Nationals of Washington.

John "Holly" Hollingshead: See Nationals of Washington.

William F. "Dick" Hurley: William F. "Dick" Hurley remains one of the most mysterious players from the early years of professional baseball. Before joining the Olympics during the 1869 season, Hurley had played for the Buckeyes of Cincinnati and been the first substitute of the famous 1869 Red Stockings. Shortly after joining the Olympics he married a young Washington woman named Ophelia Mahagan, and the marriage produced a son. Hurley worked for the Treasury Department for several years, but then the marriage broke up, and he left Washington for parts unknown. His wife finally obtained a divorce in 1884, claiming that she had last seen him in New York years earlier. She soon remarried and their son died in China, but no trace of Dick Hurley's subsequent whereabouts has been found. According to census data, he was born in Pennsylvania in the late 1840s, but careful examination of various possibilities has not produced a likely candidate.

Philip Kulp (aka Culp): Philip Kulp, whose name was

often given as Culp, was born in 1849. His death certificate lists Germany as his place of birth, but that may be wrong as he was already in Trenton, New Jersey, on the 1850 census and the censuses always gave New Jersey as his birthplace. He played third base for the Keystones of Philadelphia in 1868 and 1869 and then played the same position for the Olympics in 1870. He later worked as a brickmaker and served on the Trenton City Council from 1885 to 1892. He was also a member of the National Guard. He died in Philadelphia on January 29, 1902.

Edward Owen Leech: Edward O. Leech was born in Washington on December 9, 1850, and received his education at the Everett Institute and Columbian University (later George Washington University). By age sixteen, he was pitching for the Olympics and remained in that role through the 1870 season, with the exception of 1868 when he shared the pitching duties with Elias Cope. Leech graduated from the Columbian University in 1869, earning second honors in his class. His father died that same year, so he accepted a clerkship in the Treasury Department's Bureau of Statistics and soon gave up baseball for good. When the Bureau of the Mint was created in 1873, its first director recruited Leech to become one of his assistants. He became known for his expertise in monetary systems and even found time to earn a law degree in 1886, though he never practiced. In 1889, he became the youngest director of the U.S. Mint. Leech resigned the directorship in May of 1893 and joined the National Union Bank of New York City, where he lived until his death on May 1, 1900, after an operation for appendicitis. Despite his many accomplishments, an obituary mentioned his days as pitcher of the Olympics and noted that he retained his love of baseball throughout his life.[22]

Fergus G. Malone: Fergy Malone was born in August of 1842 in County Tyrone, Ireland. After serving in a hundred-day regiment during the Civil War, he became the catcher of the Keystones of Philadelphia in 1865. He went on to a long career that saw him catch in the major leagues from 1871 to 1876. In 1902, he gave this summary of his career:

> I started out as a cricketer with the Oxford Club. In 1863 I joined the Athletics as pitcher. After two years' service in the Army I returned and played with the Keystone Club. From there I went to the Diamond State Club of Wilmington, Delaware. This was a gentleman's organization and included such afterwards famous men as Ambassador and Secretary of State Thomas F. Bayard, United States Senator Anthony Higgins, the great Bancroft, W. J. Pussey and the Rev. Mr. Thomas. 1867 found me back in Philadelphia. After playing a time with the noted Olympics, of Washington, I returned to the Athletics and helped defeat the champion Atlantics, of Brooklyn, in what was destined to be a memorable series of games. It was the first club that bore the name 'Philadelphia.' This was in 1873 and we trimmed the Athletics eight times out of nine. I was captain of the team and trained it until 1886. I continued as a player, then I quit the game and sought other means of livelihood.[23]

After retiring, Malone worked in Philadelphia as a baker, a grocer and a policeman before receiving a United States Custom Service appointment and moving to Seattle. That is where he died on January 18, 1905.

Samuel Stewart Marr: Samuel S. Marr was one of the players who lost his spot on the first nine of the Olympics when the club became more ambitious. After working as a law clerk, he studied medicine at Georgetown and became a well-known Washington physician. Marr died in Washington on September 26, 1915, at the age of 71.

Harry Clay McLean: Harry McLean was born in Rahway, New Jersey, around 1845. His father, George Washington McLean, was a colonel in the 2nd New Jersey Infantry during the Civil War, and his brother William was killed in the war. In 1866 Harry moved to Washington to join the Treasury Department. He was initially a member of the National Club and went on the 1867 tour, but then joined the Olympics and played with that club for several seasons. He remained in the Treasury Department for many years, and it couldn't have hurt his career when Ulysses S. Grant wrote a letter to Treasury Secretary Benjamin Bristow in 1876 requesting that the young clerk receive "your most favorable consideration." According to Grant, McLean "comes of an historic family, his grandfather a Revolutionary officer and the first Adj't Gen'l of the State of New York. His father Genl G W McLean and his brother Major William McLean were among the Nations [sic] bravest defenders, in its last struggle."[24] McLean rose steadily through the ranks and by 1893 was chief clerk in the Supervising Architect's Office, a powerful branch of the Treasury Department that oversaw federal building design. He was then fired by newly appointed Supervising Architect Jeremiah O'Rourke. The decision was controversial and was one of several reasons that O'Rourke held the office for only seventeen months.[25] McLean then became deputy health officer for the District of Columbia and remained in that position until his death in Washington on June 2, 1917.[26] McLean frequently reminisced about his ball-playing days, and our knowledge of early Washington baseball is richer as a result.

William Miller: William Miller was a substitute on the 1869 Olympics and is likely the man who played one game for the Nationals in 1872 (a game credited to Joe Miller in the encyclopedias). His common name has made it impossible to identify him.

Abraham Gilbert Mills: A.G. Mills was born on March 12, 1844, in New York City and served in the Union Army during the Civil War, where he reportedly carried a bat and ball along with his military equipment. He settled in Washington after the war, where he studied law at Columbian Law School (now George Washington University), held a key post in the Treasury Department, and continued to play baseball as the pitcher of the Olympic Club. His stay on the first nine was brief, but he remained involved in the club as an officer and helped it enter the National Association. He resigned the club presidency in the middle of the 1871 season, and the Olympic Club was never the same. Mills soon left the civil service and moved first to New York City and then to Chicago. While in Chicago, Mills became a trusted advisor of National League president William Hulbert, and when Hulbert died in 1882, Mills was chosen as his successor. His term lasted only two years, but included such milestone events as the signing of the first National Agreement and the strengthening of the reserve clause. He also helped the National League successfully withstand the challenge posed by the Union Association. Mills left baseball for good after the 1884 season, though he later sat on the committee that became known as the Mills Commission. He became vice president of the Otis Elevator Company and died on August 26, 1929, in Falmouth, Massachusetts.

Frank Prescott Norton: See Nationals of Washington.

Robert Reach: Bob Reach, the younger brother of Al Reach, played for the Olympics in 1869 and 1870, then had a brief major league career. Reach was born on August 28, 1843, shortly after the family had emigrated from England to Brooklyn. A Civil War veteran, he died on May 19, 1922, in Springfield, Massachusetts.

Alfred Valentine Robinson: Val Robinson was a native Washingtonian, being born there on August 31, 1848, the son of a veteran of the War of 1812. He belonged briefly to the National Club, but did not make the first nine, and in 1867 he and Harry McLean joined the Olympics and became regulars. Robinson was a starter in the outfield of the Olympics for four seasons and then played seven games in the major leagues. Like most Washington ballplayers, Robinson worked as a government clerk for several years, but his doings after his father's death in 1876 are a mystery. He died in Washington on August 2, 1896.

M. E. Urell: See Nationals of Washington.

Simon Wolf: Simon Wolf was a prominent Washington attorney, civil servant, and philanthropist. In a 1921 article, Wolf described how he became president of the Olympic Club and a large contributor to its coffers, but the extent of his involvement in the club is not clear.[27] Wolf was born in Bavaria in 1836 and died in Atlantic City in 1923.[28]

Edward P. Woods: Eddie Woods was born in Philadelphia around 1838. According to his obituary, "'Neddy' Woods took part as catcher in the initial game of baseball in the Quaker City, which was played on Thanksgiving-day, Nov. 18, 1858, and from 1859 to 1870, inclusive, with the exception of one season, he was one of the nine of the famous Keystone Club." During the war, he served in the 196th Pennsylvania Infantry, a 100-day regiment. Then "on Aug. 21, 1864, at the formal inauguration of the grounds — a portion of which is now used by the Athletic Club — Woods represented the Keystones, and played second-base for the Pennsylvania nine that contended unsuccessfully with a nine selected from New Jersey clubs." He remained the shortstop of the Keystones until joining the Olympics in 1868. He returned to the Keystones in 1869 and then retired to help raise his young family. He worked as a police officer, then a watchman at the Philadelphia Navy Yard, and finally a painter. His wife died in 1881, leaving him to raise eight children. On November 15, 1886, Woods was painting one of the city's public buildings when he slipped and fell to his death. His funeral drew a large crowd that included several Keystone teammates, with William Deal serving as one of the pallbearers. Many politicians also attended, with Congressman Samuel J. Randall and Councilman William McMullen sending flowers.[29]

Sam Yeatman: As noted in the profile of William Yeatman under the entry on the Nationals, the two ball-playing Yeatmans have been a source of confusion. It is most likely, however, that the man who was a substitute for the Olympics in 1868 and a "cup of coffee" major leaguer was Samuel B. Yeatman, a graduate of Georgetown Law School who died in Washington on December 13, 1905.

Nicholas Ephraim Young: Nick Young was born on September 12, 1840, in Amsterdam, New York, and played cricket as a youth. He enlisted in the Twenty-Seventh New York Regiment during the Civil War and was joined by ten other members of his cricket club. After beating "all comers" at cricket, they were forced to switch to baseball, and that change was the start of a remarkable career.[30] Young settled in Washington when his military service ended and received a clerkship in the Treasury Department. He continued to play baseball and was a regular on the Olympic Club through the end of the 1870 season, mostly at right field or first base. Although a slightly built man who weighed only 115 pounds, Young was one of the club's top hitters and a terrific base-runner. When his playing days ended, he became involved in the club's management and it was he who organized the March 17, 1871, meeting that launched the National Association. Five years later, the National League replaced the National Association, and Nick Young was elected secretary, handling such important matters as the league's schedule and record keeping. In 1885, he succeeded fellow Olympic Club member A. G. Mills as National League president and served in that capacity for seventeen eventful years. Young is frequently characterized as a weak-kneed executive who did not stand up to the league's owners, but this is unfair. The league presidency was not even his full-time job for much of his tenure, and the National League owners did not give him the authority to exert much power. So instead he focused on doing his best to make things run as smoothly as possible and to give the league's beleaguered umpires much-needed support. In 1897, "Uncle Nick" finally resigned from the Treasury Department to devote all his time to the league presidency, but by then the National League was in dire straits and Young found it all but impossible to find anyone willing to take the abuse and threats heaped on umpires. After five more tumultuous years, he retired under pressure in 1902. Nick Young died in Washington on October 31, 1916.

Other Members: Barrett, W. Burchard, Clark, Dr. Marr, Robbins, Seymour, West, Williams.

Notes

1. *Daily National Intelligencer*, December 11, 1867.
2. *Daily National Intelligencer*, May 11, 1868.
3. Simon Wolf, "Noted Men on Baseball Team," *Washington Post*, March 13, 1921, 62.
4. A. G. Mills letter to Francis Richter, March 17, 1914, A. G. Mills Collection, National Baseball Hall of Fame.
5. *Washington Post*, May 8, 1889, 2.
6. *Ibid*.
7. Chadwick Scrapbooks, unidentified clipping. The person reminiscing is not identified, but the fact that he had also been on the 1867 tour of the Nationals means that he is most likely Harry McLean, though Val Robinson is also a candidate.
8. *Daily National Intelligencer*, September 20, 1869.
9. *Daily National Intelligencer*, September 22, 1869.
10. *Daily National Intelligencer*, October 22, 1869.
11. *Daily National Intelligencer*, November 5, 1869.
12. *New York Clipper*, February 19, 1870.
13. *New York Clipper*, April 17, 1870.
14. *New York Clipper*, March 25, 1871; William J. Ryczek, *Blackguards and Red Stockings* (Jefferson, NC: McFarland), 11–14.
15. *Cincinnati Times-Star*, March 28, 1891, quoted in Howard W. Rosenberg, *Cap Anson 2* (Arlington, VA: Tile Books, 2004), 321–322.
16. *New York Clipper*, July 22, 1871.
17. *New York Clipper*, September 23, 1871.
18. *New York Times*, July 4, 1914, 7; http://portsmouthpeacetreaty.org/.
19. Byron Clarke, *Atlanta Constitution*, December 30, 1907.
20. *New York Clipper*, May 10, 1879; *New York Sun*, October 17, 1915, 7.
21. A. G. Mills, letter dated February 28, 1916, A. G. Mills Collection, National Baseball Hall of Fame and Museum.
22. "Edward O. Leech Dead," *Washington Evening Times*, May 2, 1900, 2.
23. *Philadelphia Inquirer*, May 18, 1902.
24. *The Papers of Ulysses S. Grant: January 1–October 31, 1876*, ed. John Y. Simon (Carbondale: Southern Illinois University Press, 2005), 81.
25. Antoinette Josephine Lee, *Architects to the Nation: The Rise and Decline of the Supervising Architect* (New York: Oxford University Press, 2000), 156.
26. *Washington Post*, June 3, 1917, 8.
27. Simon Wolf, "Noted Men on Baseball Team," *Washington Post*, March 13, 1921, 62.
28. *Washington Post*, June 5, 1923, 8.
29. *New York Clipper*, November 20, 1886, 571.
30. Letter from Nick Young to Henry Chadwick, quoted in the *Washington Post*, February 29, 1904, 8.

❖ *Nationals of Washington* (Peter Morris) ❖

Club History

The National Base Ball Club of Washington took on the role of ambassadors for the still-young game of baseball in 1867 by becoming the first club to tour west of the Allegheny Mountains. To many contemporaries, that tour embodied the club's rare ability to play brilliant baseball while staying true to the ideals of amateurism and fair play. The legacy of the Nationals, however, was more complex because the club also exemplified baseball's awkward transition to professionalism.

The origins of the National Club date back to May of 1859, but the play remained informal at first. During those early months, the club did not "desire or expect to succeed in any contests with other clubs, as a majority of its members were far advanced in life, only playing ball for exercise, and to have a pleasant time socially."¹ That changed on November 29, 1859, when the club formally organized and elected a slate of officers that consisted of James Morrow (President), Joseph L. Wright (Vice President), Arthur Pue Gorman (Secretary), and A. Dodge (Treasurer). It soon adopted a "uniform of dark blue pants and jackets and red belts with jockey caps and chamois leather gaiters, 'well clogged at heels and ball.'"² The initial first nine, according to a later account, consisted of Gorman pitching to Morrow, Edmund F. French and players named Wallace and Brown manning the three bases, one of the Hibbs brothers at shortstop, and Wright in the outfield along with two players named Law and Carlisle.³

Gorman, Morrow, and French were driving forces over the next few years, which saw the members of the National Club "became ambitious to have it rank with the finest clubs of the country."⁴ The young club played for awhile between 6th and 7th Streets East, near Maryland Avenue, but then in June of 1861 a new location was found in the square south of the White House.⁵ The "entirely unimproved" field became known as the White Lot, and that was where the Nationals played such local rivals as the Pythian, Jefferson, Washington and Potomac clubs, as well as an 1861 game against a nine chosen from the 71st New York Regiment.⁶

The early years of the Civil War brought many experienced baseball players to Washington and thereby exposed local enthusiasts and players to a higher caliber of play. In 1861, a newspaper advertisement advised: "To the Base Ball Players of Washington. There will be a match played at Camp Wood, above the Park, on Saturday afternoon, June 29th, at 4 o'clock, between the first nine of the Baldwin Base Ball Club (company D) and the first nine of the Steers Base Ball Club (company E). Those interested in the noble game of Base Ball are invited to witness the contest, as the above clubs are composed of some of the best players of Brooklyn and New York. A very interesting game may be expected."⁷

Another large crowd was on hand at the White Lot for

an April 1862 match between the Nationals and the Potomacs, but as the Civil War dragged on, time available for ball-playing became scarce and the "sport languished considerably."[8] The Nationals played only a handful of match games in 1863 and 1864, but their level of activity picked up dramatically after the war's end. The National Club soon adopted a uniform that consisted of "blue pants, white shirt with blue shield, and white cap" and boasted more than one hundred members.[9] Most of these members were of the honorary, non-playing type, but their generous contributions to the club's coffers made its famous tour possible. The sport of baseball also received the support of the Washington press, with one reporter writing: "As a means of physical cultivation, base ball is one of the most commendable in vogue. As a remedy, also, for many of the evils accruing from the immoral associations the youths of our cities and towns are liable to, this game merits the endorsement of the best classes of the community."[10]

Few of the National Club's local rivals maintained their strength after the war, so the next two seasons were highlighted by several trips that laid the foundation for that great tour. Several key members were natives of Brooklyn, so there was great excitement when the Excelsior Club of Brooklyn included Washington on its October 1865 tour. The celebrated tourists arrived in the national capital on October 8, 1865, and were met at the depot by a delegation of the host club, who conducted them to Willard's Hotel. The game was played near the White House on the following day, and the Nationals claimed a 36–30 victory.[11]

The Nationals returned the visit the following July, and upon arrival they were escorted to Brooklyn City Hall and introduced to the mayor. Their next stop was Green-Wood Cemetery, where they were shown the elaborate monument to legendary Excelsior pitcher Jim Creighton. It was a symbolic passing of the torch from the most famous prewar touring club to the one that was to assume this important function.

When the match against the Excelsiors was concluded, the Nationals "were taken to the Mansion House in Hicks street, and here was found a feast prepared such as the gods of the olden time were wont to indulge in, every delicacy of the season contributing to make the entertainment one of the most complete on record. Not content with palatial luxuries, a perfect feast of delightful vocal and instrumental music was provided, the artists present excelling in their vocal offerings. The charming singing of Messrs. Stein, Lingard, Lockwood and Lockhart being a vocal treat of the very first order; the instrumental performance of Mr. Abbott, too, being noteworthy. For some three or four hours there was quite 'a feast of reason and a flow of soul,' speeches from the two presidents and remarks from distinguished military and civil guests present marking the occasion."[12]

The Excelsiors paid a second visit to Washington in the fall of 1866 and were accorded another lavish reception. The fifty club members who made the trip from Brooklyn were again met at the depot and escorted to Willard's Hotel in carriages and stages. In addition to the usual banquets and related festivities, during their stay the visitors were shown such attractions as the Little and Great Falls of the Potomac, Mount Vernon, the Lower Potomac, Indian Head, and Fort Washington, where they were received with military honors. The Brooklynites were also treated to performances by a Marine band, including a special dirge that was played during their visit to George Washington's tomb.[13]

The match itself took place in front of an enormous crowd. According to Harry McLean, who played for the Nationals in that game, the grounds of the White Lot

> had been partially enclosed by the reception of an amphitheater of seats on the east and west sides of the diamond, the remaining portion of the field being inclosed [sic] by a rope fence extending from the seats around the field. For the seats in the amphitheater a charge was made, but the crowd in general were admitted free to the grounds outside the rope line. The lowest estimate placed on the attendance outside of the rope line was 8,000, while the seats accommodated 3,500. The seats on the west side of the diamond were reserved exclusively for ladies, but so great was the pressure of the fair sex (which included the ladies of the diplomatic circle, Cabinet, Senators, and Representatives, etc.) that a large portion of the seats on the east side had to be given up to them.... Such a galaxy of beauty, fashion, and enthusiasm never before or since has graced a Washington ball field, and I question whether any such assemblage will ever be witnessed again.

After the Excelsiors eked out a narrow victory, the players from both sides and their many guests adjourned to Willard's for a "princely feast." There were also the usual speeches and toasts, one of which made clever use of the names of many leading baseball clubs while also suggesting that the role of baseball ambassadors was being passed to the Nationals: "May our National game, the best and prettiest of all Pastimes, never become extinct until it has winged its flight to parts Unknown, and every Active man, whether in or out of the Union, for or against Liberty, become determined to march together hand in hand with the noble Keystone, by the light of the guiding Star, under the banner of Excelsior."[14]

While the Nationals were acquiring a reputation for carrying on baseball's prewar pomp and circumstance, there were also signs of the changing times. Such ball club officials as Charles E. Coon, Colonel Frank Jones, Arthur Pue Gorman, and Edmund F. French held prominent roles in the Treasury Department under new Secretary Hugh McCullough and that department developed a close association with the Nationals. When the club hosted a tournament in late August of 1865, McCullough expressed pleasure in the performance of "his boys from the Treasury Department" and offered assurances that President Andrew Johnson would attend the next match.[15] (See the Summit City Base Ball Club of Fort Wayne entry for a profile of McCullough's ballplaying son Charles.)

In addition to offering moral support, the Treasury Department became a major financial supporter of the National Base Ball Club. As French put it, after the war "every member of the home team was provided with a Government office, and this was in the nature of a salary for their services as ball players for the club did not pay them anything."[16] Gorman confirmed this with an intriguing recollection of a game in which the Nationals played a club from Georgetown College. According to Gorman, the Nationals were very impressed by one of the college players and "upon inquiry we ascertained that the heavy batter was George Fox, and that he had just graduated and was preparing to go to live in New York. He was questioned, and urged to remain in Washington, one of the inducements offered him being a position in a Government department, for in those days there was no such thing as civil-service reform, and the majority of our members were men who held official positions and wielded a great deal of influence. Our arguments proved too potent for Fox, and he consented to remain with us."[17]

There is no way to be sure how much work was expected of the ballplayers who were employed by the Treasury Department. Some of them must have been undoubtedly valuable employees — such National Club starters as Dennis Coughlin, Harry Berthrong, and Billy Hodges had successful careers that extended well beyond their ball-playing days. But others seem to have contributed far less to the department and moved on as soon as they left the first nine. Hall of Famer George Wright, most notably, was a member of the club in 1867, but his clerkship seems to have been nominal and his address in the city directory seems to have corresponded to a public park.[18] As sportswriter Robert M. Larner put it, "Civil service examinations cut but little figure if a promising baseball player was discovered in the locality. It was an easy task to get him a government position with the understanding that he was to play with the National club."[19]

Even assuming that none of these players were being specifically paid for playing baseball, the government-subsidized positions gave the Nationals a huge competitive advantage. The 1867 additions of Wright and several Brooklyn players elevated the club to a level that few local rivals could hope to attain. At the end of that season, a national publication offered these revealing comments: "It is a singular fact that the business men of Baltimore are decidedly opposed to base ball; and when it is remembered that a majority of base ball players are employed in stores where their presence is required till sunset, instead of in the public service, as are a majority of Washington players, who are at liberty at an early afternoon, the difficulties with which a Baltimorean ballist has to contend may be appreciated. A member of one of the prominent clubs of this city recently sought a situation there, and upon giving his name was at once asked whether he was connected with the _____ club. He replied in the affirmative, whereupon the merchant instantly informed him that he would give employment to no base ball player, however capable to transact business."[20]

Shortstop George Wright, one of the brightest stars of the pioneer era, played for the Nationals of Washington and the "Red Stockings" of Cincinnati, among other clubs.

The Nationals and most of the other prominent Washington clubs were continuing to use "the White Lot, where, for several years, through the indulgence of the President, spectators often crowded to see a match game. And this might have gone on for many years longer but for the vociferous demonstrations of the rooters at a famous game between the Actives and Eagles in 1867, when the din of cowbells so exasperated Col. William G. Moore, secretary of President Andrew Johnson, that the privilege was withdrawn at the end of the season."[21]

By then the Nationals had opened new grounds that were bounded by S and T Streets and by 15th and 16th Streets. The new field possessed the important natural advantages of being very level and a spacious 400 square feet. The Nationals further improved the site by enclosing it with an eight-foot fence, and by adding a covered grandstand and refreshment booths.[22] All of these features made it possible to recoup expenses by charging admission and the club added to its revenues by flooding the site during the winter so that it could be used as a skating rink.[23] According to an account written after the grand opening in June, the grounds "are easy of access, the 14th street cars running directly by the entrance. The Nationals, for several months past, have been steadily engaged in improving the grounds, until now they present a very respectable appearance. It is nicely fenced in and seats for the accommodation of a large number of spectators have been erected on the north side. The ground, being situated rather low, was, owing to the rain of Tuesday, in a muddy condition, but with proper draining this objection will be entirely overcome. A large number of spectators were present, the fair sex being largely represented. There must have been as many as 1,500 persons on the ground at once."[24]

Shortly after the opening of the new ball field, the Nationals undertook their historic tour of the region then known as the west. (What we now call the west was then referred to as the "wild west.") The 3,000-mile expedition included stops in Columbus, Cincinnati, Louisville, Indianapolis, St. Louis, and Chicago and stirred up great excitement in those cities. In St. Louis, for instance, there was "joy when it became known that the National Club of Washington would include St. Louis in a tour to the West.... The Nationals' reputation and the fact of it being the first of the great clubs of the East to 'Westward Ho!' created great interest among the steadily increasing admirers of the game and when the gates of the new park were opened to the public on July 22 at fifty cents a head, there was no kick coming from the thousands who flocked there to see the Union boys throw themselves against the famed Nationals."[25]

The players similarly viewed themselves as ambassadors. Four decades later, substitute outfielder Harry C. McLean recalled:

> It was a trip that proved of incalculable value to the youth of the great agricultural districts of the west and south. A dearth of healthy means of recreation had led as a natural sequence to the adoption of sport neither physically nor morally elevating. After the labors of the day it was customary for the young farmers and mechanics to seek recreation and imagined pleasure at the village tavern, where cards and other games of chance were played; then waiting and wasting for the excitement of the race track, and between times seeking relief from the tedium of their daily occupations, which the dissipations of a city life offer ... youths with vicious tendencies were transformed into beings with manly characters.... We entered every contest with kindly feeling, gentlemanly conduct and skilful in every position on the field, no fault-finding for accidental errors, no murdering of umpires, no attributing motives to victorious opponents, no boasting exultation when triumphant; only happy, exultantly happy, giving vent thereto singing this our anthem to the tune of "Benny Havens, Oh."

McLean exaggerated the importance of the trip, but his words do convey the outlook of the touring players.[26]

Not all went smoothly on the trip, with travel arrangements being especially vexing. An unidentified old-timer later recalled: "There were no prearranged schedules, every team had its own private arrangements and went ahead and made dates without taking into consideration any other team, hence 'jolts' sometimes took place that at the last minute had to be changed, trips revised and schemes worked out to reach the points where the next games were dated. The pioneer trip of the Nationals in 1867, which was arranged by Mr. 'Jimmy' Patterson, was carried through admirably, because the advent of the Nationals into the west was a novelty and a day's delay made no great difference. Still the players had trouble on the western roads that if experienced today would send the modern gladiator over to the home on the hill beyond Anacostia."[27]

Troubles continued throughout the trip. Charles Coon of the Nationals acted as umpire for the game in Louisville and he had a "hot time of it"—the crowd could not understand why he ruled "a man out who was forced off by the purposed dropping of a fly ball to catch men on bases."[28] Walter F. Hewett, who became president of Washington's National League entry in the late 1880s, was then a boy of five who accompanied his father on the tour. "Ball players were a pretty tough set in those days," Hewett afterward recalled, "and when we were in Indianapolis some of them stole the flag from the State-house flagstaff. The whole team came near being put in jail. I remember one man we had who could not read. He always used to get next to me at the table, and after I had ordered he invariably took the same."[29]

The biggest problems were encountered in Chicago. After winning all of their previous contests by enormous margins, the Nationals lost their first game in Chicago to the Forest Citys of Rockford. That upset was followed by an equally surprising result when the Nationals rebounded to trounce the Excelsiors of Chicago, 49–4. Since the Excelsiors were the Illinois champions, Chicagoans could not understand the disparate results, and wild allegations began to fly. The *Chicago Tribune* accused the Nationals of being a professional club that had deliberately lost the first game in order to win wagers on the second game. Officials of the National Club paid an immediate visit to the *Tribune*'s editors, and a retraction was published the next day.[30]

Despite the controversy, the trip was a rousing success. Upon their return to Washington, the Nationals were greeted by a crowd of 300 people and a band that played "Home, Sweet, Home." They listened to "the things that are always told on such occasions" until they finally pleaded fatigue and further speech-making was deferred for a banquet at the Kirkwood House, which was "the headquarters for the players in those days." The banquet occurred on the following Friday, and all had "a jolly good time" as they listened to toasts predicting that the tour would "elevate the standard of our national game, and perpetuate our favorite pastime for all future generations."[31]

Four decades after the tour, Harry C. McLean could still recall all the words of the lengthy song, which climaxed with the chorus: "We're going westward ho, we're going westward ho/ Success to all who toss the ball, we're going westward ho." After waxing eloquent about the tour, he concluded:

For the remainder of my allotted days I must, however, be content with singing the praises in my humble way of the game, of which no "fan" tireth, and hum to myself, as time speeds by:
"My base ball battles are all fought,
And all my bases run,
I can but wait my turn at bat
To make my last 'home run.'
And though our flags long ceased to fly
Where I so oft did go,
I ne'er forget those jolly days
When we went westward ho!"[32]

The tour was the highlight of the National Base Ball Club's career and also marked the end of the club's time as a national power. The club lost several matches in the fall of 1867, and Wright returned to New York at season's end. Another costly departure was pitcher Billy Williams, who was never adequately replaced.

New players did continue to arrive from Brooklyn and Rochester, most of whose names ended up on the payroll of the Treasury Department. The Nationals also established a Junior National Club with the aim of developing young players to "replace retired stagers who may become played out."[33] Nonetheless, the club's fortunes continued to decline.

By 1868, the Nationals again had a formidable local rival in the Olympic Club. It was a golden opportunity to create new excitement among Washington baseball lovers, but instead the two clubs spent much of the season exchanging barbs before playing two tightly fought late-season games, both won by the Nationals. In 1869, the Olympics beat the Nationals for the first time, and the "ice was broken." The Olympics assumed the mantle of Washington's top club and "soon the National club was but a small opponent for their old-time victors. It came near being the death of baseball in this city, however, as many of the old friends of the Nationals lost heart and gave up baseball."[34] Before long the men who had earned the club a national reputation were "spread all over the country."[35]

After a miserable 1870 season, the National Base Ball Club kept a very low profile in 1871. A club using that name competed in the National Association in 1872 (losing all twelve of its games), but it is debatable whether it was the same club. Larner, for example, wrote in 1904: "The march of improvement caused the National and Olympic parks to be abandoned, and the professional baseball park of the city was located on the then vacant square bounded by Ninth, Tenth, R, and S streets northwest. The old National club went out of existence when the park at Fifteenth and S streets was closed. The name 'National' was used off and on by the professional organization, but finally was changed to the Washington club."[36]

The last team known as the Nationals had concluded operations in 1899, and by the time of Larner's article, Washington had an entry in the American League known as the Senators. But the team had suffered through four straight seasons, culminating with an abysmal 38–113 record in 1904 and so it

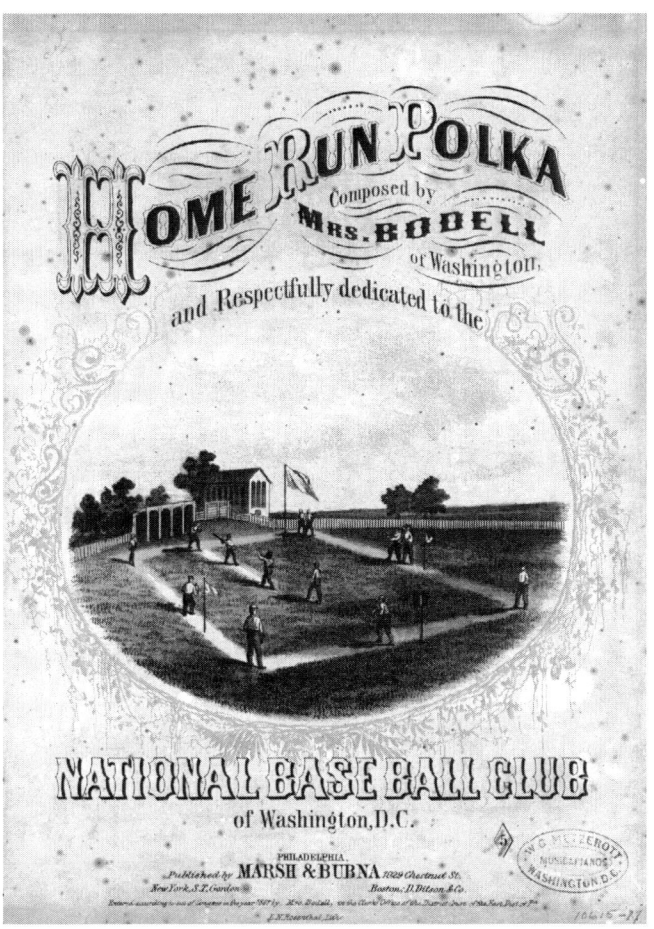

Published in 1867, the "Home Run Polka" was one of several musical compositions of the era that paid tribute to the national pastime.

was decided to scrap the "hoodoo" (unlucky) nickname. A name-the-team contest was held and many innovative suggestions were submitted, but there was an overwhelming consensus for bringing back an old name. "The old Nationals were very popular with the Washington people," wrote one fan, "and the name is still dear to some of the older followers of the game." Another commented, "The name Nationals has greater significance, and will be more appropriate than Senators. It will incite the players to greater efforts. When Washington had a club called the Nationals, it was a winner, and the people were proud of and supported it."[37]

Oddly, the name change never caught on, and the club continued to be predominantly known as the Senators until it left for Minnesota in 1961, as did the expansion club that succeeded it. But the name of Nationals was once again revived in 2005 when the National League returned to Washington for the first time since 1899. None of these latter-day clubs have much in common with the original National Base Ball Club of Washington but they do bear the name of the hardy pioneers who headed "westward ho" in 1867.

Club Members

Henry Washburn Berthrong: Harry Berthrong was born on January 1, 1844, in Mumford, New York, the son of a blacksmith, and grew up in nearby Rochester. Shortly after his eighteenth birthday he enlisted in the New York 140th Infantry, Company E, serving until the war's end in the regiment that became known as the "Rochester Racehorses." He then accepted a clerkship in the War Department and joined the National Base Ball Club, two events that were probably related. He was a regular for the Nationals for four seasons, playing catcher and outfield and earning a reputation as one of the fastest base-runners. In July of 1868, in an exhibition at Baltimore, Berthrong was credited with rounding the bases in a record time of just over 14 seconds. He left the Nationals after that season but played occasionally for the Olympics after that, including seventeen major league games in 1871. By then, however, his civil service career had begun to blossom. After a year in the War Department, Berthrong transferred to the Treasury, where he was assigned to help establish a new mint in Carson City. He later moved to Boston and worked as a custom house officer, while also becoming well known for painting portraits of such luminaries as Ulysses S. Grant. Berthrong also continued to follow baseball, and when another player was reported to have broken his base-running record, he vigorously protested. Harry Berthrong died in Chelsea, Massachusetts, on April 24, 1928.[38]

David Solomon Birdsall: Dave Birdsall was one of the mainstays of the Unions of Morrisania before joining the Nationals and then going on to a professional career. He was born in either Westchester County or New York City on July 16, 1838, and died on December 30, 1896, in Boston.

Asa Brainard: See Cincinnati Base Ball Club ("Red Stockings").

Charles Edward Coon: Born in Friendship, Allegany County, New York, on March 15, 1842, Charles E. Coon was a member of the Eckford Club of Brooklyn before enlisting in the Civil War. After the war, he settled in Washington and became a prominent Treasury Department official, while also becoming heavily involved in the National Club. Coon was sent to London in 1871 to handle the re-funding of the country's Civil War debt and he spent much of his time in London during the next decade. By 1884, he had ascended to the rank of Assistant Secretary of the U.S. Treasury and then briefly became Acting Secretary of the Treasury. He resigned in 1885 and returned to Brooklyn. Then in 1897 Coon settled permanently in Port Townsend, Washington, where he later served as mayor and as a member of the state House of Representatives from Jefferson County. Charles Coon died on January 8, 1920, in Port Townsend.[39]

Dennis H. Coughlin: Like Harry Berthrong, Dennis Coughlin was born in January of 1844, grew up in Rochester, and enlisted in the regiment known as the "Rochester Racehorses" (140th New York Regiment, Company E). Coughlin fought at such legendary battles as Gettysburg, the Battle of the Wilderness, and Petersburg, being wounded at the last battle site. He earned promotion to Full Sergeant before being mustered out on June 3, 1865. Coughlin returned to Rochester and played for a local club called the Excelsiors for three years. In 1868, presumably on Berthrong's recommendation, he joined the Nationals of Washington and accepted a position in the Treasury Department that he held until his death. Coughlin played for the Nationals for three seasons and then played for the Olympics in the National Association in 1872, making him the only known combat-wounded Civil War veteran to have played major league baseball. He died in Washington on May 14, 1913, and is buried at Arlington National Cemetery.

William Darcy Craven: William Darcy Craven does not appear to have ever been a member of the first nine of the Nationals, but his life and role as baseball ambassador make him worthy of being remembered as a member of this famous touring club. Craven was born in Newark, New Jersey, on July 6, 1846, and played baseball for the junior Pioneers and then for the famous Eurekas. His father was a physician who enlisted in the Civil War and became a prominent Surgeon in the Union Army. When Jefferson Davis was arrested, Craven was initially put in charge of his treatment. The family moved to Washington during this period, and William became a member of the Nationals. In 1867, he moved to Savannah, Georgia, and founded a baseball club there. In 1893, he moved to London, England, and again was responsible for forming a baseball club. William Darcy Craven later published a revised edition of his father's book about Jefferson Davis. As of 1939, he was still alive and living in Ridley Park, Pennsylvania.[40]

Richard A. Cronin: R.A. Cronin was born in the late 1830s and became a member of the National Club in 1860. After serving briefly in the Civil War, he became a club officer and also played a unique role. According to an 1866 article: "The base-ball fraternity will be glad to learn that a base-ball headquarters has been established in this city, where they can learn all the latest ball news from all parts of the country. Mr. R.A. Cronin, for a number of years connected with the National Club of this city, and known to all ball players in town, has bought the cigar store No. 238 Pennsylvania avenue, which he intends to make the headquarters for the ball fraternity of this city. Next season he will keep a bulletin of the latest ball news. He will also keep a register of all base-ball clubs of the city, address of secretaries, &c., besides all the implements pertaining to the game. The remarkable success of the national game in this city makes such an establishment necessary."[41] Cronin was later a small shareholder in the local National League team and died in Washington on April 3, 1890.

George Horace Elliot Fletcher: George H.E. Fletcher was born on April 21, 1845, in Brooklyn, New York, and played for the Excelsiors from 1864 to 1866. He joined the National Club in March of 1867 and was part of that year's historic tour. That was Fletcher's only season with the Nationals, but he remained in Washington for several years as a Treasury Department clerk. After returning to Brooklyn he played in two major league games in 1872. Fletcher was only 34 and a newlywed when he died in Brooklyn on June 18, 1879.

Tom Forker: See Marylands of Baltimore.

George H. Fox: As described in the club history, George Fox joined the Nationals in 1866 after graduating from Georgetown College (now Georgetown University). Originally from Brooklyn, Fox played for the Nationals for four seasons and then played briefly for the Olympics. After the 1867 season he was presented with a silver ball that bore the inscription: "Awarded to George Fox by the National Base-Ball Club for the best average during the season of 1867."[42] Nonetheless, his identity has proved difficult to pin down. Several later notes had him in San Francisco, while one placed him in Alaska. While it's possible that both are correct, it seems most likely that he was a Brooklyn-born San Joaquin County horse owner who died in San Francisco on July 28, 1910.

Edmund Flagg French: E.F. French was a founding member of the National Club, and his scrapbooks were invaluable in recreating the club's history. Born in Chester, New Hampshire, on July 17, 1819, he worked as a Treasury Department clerk for more than forty years. Despite his age, he played on the first nine of the Nationals before the war, and one game account noted that he had "played in his usual reliable manner."[43] French died in Washington on September 30, 1901.[44]

Andrew Gibney: Born near Jersey City around 1844, Andrew Gibney began his career with the Gothams of New York, joining the Nationals in 1867 and spending three seasons with them before finishing his career in 1870 with the crosstown Olympics. His first wife died while he was playing for the Nationals, leaving him with a young son. He is difficult to trace after that, but according to an on-line genealogy, he died in Jersey City in 1909.

John W. Glenn: John Glenn was born in Rochester, New York, in 1850 and played for both the Nationals and the Olympics in 1870 before going on to a long major league career. His life after baseball was, to say the least, unsavory. After numerous run-ins with the law, in 1888 he was accused of assaulting a nine-year-old girl. Glenn was accidentally shot by a police officer who was trying to protect him from a lynch mob and died from his wounds a few days later.[45]

Arthur Pue Gorman: Arthur Pue Gorman was one of the founding members of the Nationals and a driving force in the club's rise to prominence. While he had a significant influence on baseball's early development, his involvement with the game was just a small part of a long and distinguished life. Born in Woodstock, Maryland, on March 11, 1839, Gorman became a page in the House of Representatives when he was only thirteen. He showed such promise that Stephen A. Douglas made him his private secretary. After serving in both the Maryland House and Senate, Gorman was elected to the U.S. Senate in 1881 and remained there for most of the remainder of his life. He was a member of the so-called Mills Commission but died in Washington on June 4, 1906, before the report was released.

Nathan Woodhull Hicks: Nat Hicks was born in Hempstead, New York, on April 19, 1845, and went on to a legendary career as one of the greatest catchers of his era. His fearless play was still remembered when he died in Hoboken on April 21, 1907, and numerous papers described his passing as the end of an era in which catchers had demonstrated incomparable skill and courage.[46]

William H. Hodges: Billy Hodges was the Nationals' first baseman in 1866, a substitute for the next couple of years, and again became a regular during the dismal 1870 campaign. Hodges was born in New Jersey around 1839 and worked as a clerk in the quartermaster corps. He had been a government employee for more than half a century by the time of his death in Washington on December 21, 1917.[47]

Patrick Hoey/Hoyle/Hoy: Henry Chadwick observed after an 1867 game, "The pitching of Hoy [Patrick Hoey of the Excelsiors of Rochester] in this game was very effective. His delivery is from the ground, and the ball comes to the batsman 'on the raise,' so that they are hard to control."[48] Hoey followed many Rochester ballplayers to Washington in 1870 but pitched ineffectively as the Nationals suffered through a very disappointing season. Notes in the late 1890s stated that he and wife Ellen were in such bad straits in Rochester that they had nearly starved to death, but Hoey's eventual fate is unknown.

John Samuel Hollingshead, Jr.: "Holly" Hollingshead was born in Washington on January 17, 1853, and was only sixteen when he began playing for the Nationals in 1869. He became a regular in 1870 and then played for Washington representatives in the National Association in three different seasons. Hollingshead obtained a clerkship in the Treasury Department's Internal Revenue office but remained heavily involved in the local baseball scene. Despite the lack of success of earlier Washington professional clubs, Hollingshead gave up his government job to become manager of an 1884 entry in the American Association.[49] Before the season, he told a reporter, "the Washington nine will have one reserve man, who will be in trim and ready to play ball at a moment's notice. His name is 'Holly.'"[50] Instead, the Washington lineup became a revolving door, with a team that won only 12 games using 25 different players — none of them named Holly. The team disbanded in the first week of August, prompting one reporter to observe: "Hollingshead now regrets the chucking up of his government position at Washington in order to manage the bum representative club of that city in the American Association. His governmental position he had held for about fourteen years, and his baseball job lasted him about fourteen weeks."[51]

Hollingshead returned to the civil service and remained in Washington until his death on October 6, 1926.

Colonel Frank Jones: Frank Jones was born in Boston on April 24, 1832, and by the outbreak of the Civil War was living in Brooklyn, where he belonged to the Excelsior Club. Jones enlisted in the Union Army on May 24, 1861, as a lieutenant and had a distinguished military career, attaining the rank of full colonel. After the war, he settled in Washington, becoming prominent in the Treasury Department and in the affairs of the National Club. He played a major role in the acquisition of so many fine Brooklyn ballplayers and in organizing the 1867 tour. Colonel Jones eventually transferred to the War Department and remained in Washington until his death on March 15, 1916. He is buried in Arlington National Cemetery.

John Jones: A man named Jones became the pitcher of the National Club in 1868. But he lasted only one season and, in a telling sign of the club's declining fortunes, little notice was paid to him in the papers. An 1886 note stated that old National pitcher John Jones was now a baggage master at Central Station in Rochester, so this is probably the man in question, but little else is known about him.[52]

George Joyce: George Joyce was born in Washington around 1847 and played the outfield for the Nationals in 1869. He later worked in the cigar business, but remained involved in the local baseball scene. As a result, when Sadie Houck wrenched his back during an 1886 National League game, Joyce took his place in center field and earned a place in the baseball encyclopedias.[53]

Harry C. McLean: See Olympics of Washington.

Frank Prescott Norton: Frank Norton was born on June 9, 1845, in Port Jefferson, New York, and was one of the earlier players to aggressively change clubs. After playing for the Stars of Brooklyn from 1863 to 1865, Norton received an offer to play for the champion Atlantics in 1866. But when he got a better offer from the Excelsiors of Brooklyn, Norton deserted the Atlantics along with Dickey Pearce and Fred Crane. In 1867 he became one of the many members of the Nationals recruited from New York with offers of clerkships, playing catcher, second base, and shortstop over the next two seasons and taking part in the famous tour. He then played for the Olympics in 1870. Like George Joyce, Norton became a major leaguer by accident, entering Washington's opening day game in 1871 when catcher Doug Allison split his thumb. After baseball, he returned to New York and became a successful contractor. He also inherited money, which enabled him to move to Connecticut and live in luxury. By 1920, he was living in a large country house on the Boston Post Road at Greenwich and wintering in South Carolina. Frank Norton died at his home in Greenwich on August 1, 1920.[54]

Osborn: Osborn was the regular pitcher for the Nationals in 1869, but it says much about the club's rapid decline that no clues to his identity have been found.

Edward Parker: Ed Parker joined the Nationals in 1862 and was a regular through the 1867 season, taking part in that season's historic tour. Parker was a government clerk in the internal revenue office and was dead by 1878, but little else is known about him.

Jimmy Patterson: Jimmy Patterson joined the club in 1866 and was credited with a large role in the travel arrangements for the 1867 tour. He then served as the club's recording secretary. He is believed to be a government clerk who was born in New Jersey around 1838 and died in Washington on November 5, 1915.

Ed Shelley: Shelley played third base for the Union Club of Morrisania before joining the Nationals. He worked in law enforcement and was also an Assemblyman but little else is known about him.

Pete Shreves: The rather nomadic career of Pete Shreves included stints with the Gotham, Empire and Mutual clubs of New York and the Nationals of Washington. Shreves was born in New Jersey around 1844 and when his playing days ended he operated a ball park in Jersey City for a while.[55] He was last heard of living in Hoboken in 1900.

E.G. "Eb" Smith: See Forest City Base Ball Club of Cleveland.

Seymour Studley: Seymour "Seem" Studley was born in May of 1841 in Bryan, New York, and grew up in Rochester. As a young man he played for the Charter Oaks and Stars and was a volunteer firefighter with the Live Oak, Engine Number 3. Around 1860, he appears to have moved to the New York City area, possibly to pursue a baseball career. While there, Studley enlisted in the 54th New York Infantry and suffered such severe sunstroke while loading horses onto a car that he was unconscious for 20–30 minutes. He was advised to never go out in the sun again, which would have greatly hampered his ball-playing career, so he ignored the advice. (Most of the games on the Nationals' 1867 tour were played with the sun shining "brightly and the thermometer not far off the nineties."[56]) By 1865, Seymour and his brother Henry had both moved to Washington and joined the National Club, with Seymour accepting a Treasury Department clerkship. He remained a starter for five seasons, making him one of the few players from the club's glory days to hang on until the bitter end. He also played in five major league games in 1872. Studley married while in Washington, but that and two other marriages were tumultuous, as was the rest of Studley's life. He died July 9, 1901, at the Soldier's and Sailor's Home in Grand Island, Nebraska.[57]

Myron Augustus Tappan (original name may have been Tappen): M.A. Tappan joined the Nationals in 1864, and an obituary credited him with being one of the driving forces in the club. Tappan became the Washington representative for A.G. Spalding's sporting goods business and later operated his own store. Born in Kingston, New York, in 1832, Tappan was a Civil War veteran (47th New York Infantry) who died in Washington on May 9, 1911.[58]

General Michael Emmet Urell: M.E. Urell played for the Nationals on occasion during their early years, but soon settled for playing an administrative role. Urell was born in Nenagh, County Tipperary, Ireland, on November 8, 1844, and moved to the United States as a child. He enlisted in the 82nd New York in the Civil War and earned a Congressional Medal of Honor for bravery. Despite being wounded and left for dead at the Battle of Bristoe Station, he reenlisted when the Spanish-American War broke out. Urell died while on a trip to Cork, Ireland, on September 6, 1910.[59] Most obituaries focused on his military career, but one recalled "Mike Urell, with his flowing whiskers, facing Colonel Jones, the pitcher of the Nationals, who also wore a full beard ... a picture that attracted attention." It added that Urell "always argued that the game was just as good and strong in the old days, when 'first bounce was out,' as it is at present."[60]

William F. Williams: Billy Williams was born in Washington in 1844 and began playing baseball for the Pythian Club of that city. He joined the Nationals in 1862 and became the club's pitcher, while also enrolling at Georgetown at around the same time. His pitching for the Nationals prompted one fan to recall: "I can remember when my sole ambition in life was to rise to the glory attained by Billy Williams, who in his day was the boss pitcher. We boys used to sing a song about him with a refrain that ran: 'Billy Williams, he could split a two-inch plank.' Billy was one of the old-fashioned pitchers, they call 'em 'twirlers' now, who believed in express trains, and pitched the ball over the plate. Billy was lightning."[61] Williams's "great velocity" and the "peculiar 'twist'" he imparted to the ball made him very effective and all of the club's success was experienced while he was pitching.[62] By 1867, he was studying the law, but when his father died, he gave up his studies and quit playing baseball to support his mother. He worked as a teller in the U.S. Treasury Department until his death in 1892. At the time of his death, it had been a quarter of a century since the end of his pitching career, yet an obituary said of Williams "although a brainy man, with a classical education, his national fame was the result of his wonderful pitching for the old National Baseball Club."[63]

George Wright: See Cincinnati Base Ball Club ("Red Stockings").

William Suter Yeatman: Two unrelated men named Yeatman played baseball in Washington within a few years of each other, and it is very difficult to keep them straight. But it appears that the man who played for the Nationals in 1865 and 1866 was William Suter Yeatman, who was born in March of 1839 in Alexandria, Virginia, joined the club in 1865 and died on April 20, 1901, in York, Pennsylvania. The one who played for the Nationals in 1872 has been listed as being William, but is probably in fact Samuel.

Other Members: W.H. Andrews, Beale, C.P. Benedict, A.R. Benner, James A. Brow, A.N. Brown, Navy Commander George Brown, J. Buell, Carlisle, L.C. Carpenter, C.H. Cherry, W. Choate, Joseph R. Cowen, W.C. Cutler, J.F. Dobbyn, A. Dodge, James F. Dooley, Hon. John W. Douglass, E. Droop, J.G. Eck, C.Z. Eddy, C.C. Edwins, Finney, R. Goodhart, S.S. Gredy, E.J.B. Gunning, C.L. Hart, Charles Herzberg, Ed Hibbs, George D.C. Hibbs, D.S. Holland, John D. Hyer, C.C. Ivey, Charles James, H. James, General Noah L. Jeffries, E.J. Jennings, H.W. Jennings, Lake, Law, J.T. Leavy, T.J. Leonard, Lusk, H.M. Maguire, F.A. Marden, S.W. Marsh, L. Mason, George B. McCartee, H.A. McCormick, McCutchen, E.M. McLeod, H.H. McPherson, W.G. Metzerott, S.E. Middleton, J. Molan, W.G. Moore, J.R. Moorhouse, W.J. Moran, James Morrow, W.B. Moses, H. Munson, N. Nicholson, S.C. Palmer, General Eli S. Parker, J.D. Patten, F. Philp, W.B. Pope, O.O. Potter, Joseph Y. Potts, J.C. Poynton, F.W. Pratt, M.T. Prouty, George Randall, W. Randall, H. Reeb, H.G. Roach, "Val" Robinson (see Olympics), B.C. Root, B.R. Ross, J.A. Sample, M. Sanstag, S.M.B. Servoss, R.A. Shinn, C.B. Smith, Goodrich Smith, H.H. Smith, T.R. Smith, A.H. Solomon, N. Spencer, L.S. Sprague, E.C. Sterling, H.H. Stewart, C.H. Stocking, Strong, Harry C. Studley, E. Totten, Le Roy Tuttle, E.H. Waddell, C.C. Walden, J.O. Walker, Wallace, Dayton Ward, L. Washington, R.E. Williams, W.V.S. Wilson, J.B. Wimer, Frank Wright, Joseph L. Wright.

Sources

The primary sources for this article were contemporaneous newspaper coverage and the Edmund F. French Baseball Scrapbook and Memorabilia, 1859–1871, which are housed at the Historical Society of Washington, D.C., and have also been microfilmed. Other sources included Peverelly, *Book of American Pastimes*; Stephen Fox, *Big Leagues: Professional Baseball, Football, and Basketball in National Memory* (New York: William Morrow, 1994); Harry C. McLean, "Baseball in Infancy; Famous Game Recalled That Drew Immense Crowd," *Washington Post*, March 23, 1902, 24; Robert M. Larner, "Old-Time Baseball in the White Lot," *Washington Post*, June 26, 1904, S4; R. M. Larner, "Beginning of Professional Baseball in Washington," *Washington Post*, July 3, 1904, S3; Frank Ceresi and Carol McMains, "Early Baseball in Washington, D.C.," *Baseball Research Journal* 34 (2005), 19–25; "Old Time Baseball," *Washington Post*, March 31, 1889, 10; and Jim Roberts, *Hardball on the Hill: Baseball Stories from Our Nation's Capital* (Chicago: Triumph, 2001).

Notes

1. Charles A. Peverelly, *The Book of American Pastimes* (New York, 1866), 492.
2. Wilhelmus Bogart Bryan, *A History of the National Capital from Its Foundation through the Period of the Adoption of the Organic Act, 1790–1878* (New York: Macmillan, 1914), vol. 2, p. 495.
3. "City's Pastimes Vastly Changed in Half Century," *Washington Post*, December 6, 1927, E1. There are few box scores from the club's first two seasons to confirm the accuracy of this first nine and one that did appear in *Wilkes' Spirit of the Times* on November 17, 1860, featured a quite different lineup: George Hibbs, p; Gorman, c; Frank Wright, 1b; French, 2b; Ed Hibbs, 3b; McCutchen, ss; Dooley, lf; Beale, cf; Benner, rf.
4. Bryan, *A History of the National Capital from Its Foundation through the Period of the Adoption of the Organic Act, 1790–1878*, vol. 2, p. 492.

5. Edmund F. French Scrapbook.
6. Bryan, *A History of the National Capital from Its Foundation through the Period of the Adoption of the Organic Act, 1790–1878*, vol. 2, p. 495.
7. *Daily National Intelligencer*, June 29, 1861.
8. *Washington Star*, April 23, 1862, cited in Bryan, *A History of the National Capital from Its Foundation through the Period of the Adoption of the Organic Act, 1790–1878*, vol. 2, p. 495; E.F. French, quoted in "Old Time Baseball," *Washington Post*, March 31, 1889, 10.
9. Peverelly, *The Book of American Pastimes*, 494.
10. *Daily National Intelligencer*, April 16, 1866.
11. Peverelly, *The Book of American Pastimes*, 412.
12. Edmund F. French Scrapbook.
13. Harry C. McLean, "Baseball in Infancy; Famous Game Recalled that Drew Immense Crowd," *Washington Post*, March 23, 1902, 24; Peverelly, *The Book of American Pastimes*, 414.
14. McLean, "Baseball in Infancy; Famous Game Recalled That Drew Immense Crowd," *Washington Post*, March 23, 1902, 24.
15. Edmund F. French Scrapbook.
16. *Washington Post*, March 31, 1889, 10.
17. *Chicago Tribune*, January 26, 1890.
18. William J. Ryczek, *When Johnny Came Sliding Home* (Jefferson, NC: McFarland, 1998), 116–117; Harold Seymour, *Baseball: The Early Years* (New York: Oxford University Press, 1960), 48; Stephen Fox, *Big Leagues* (New York: William Morrow, 1994), 190–191.
19. R.M. Larner, "President Roosevelt Is a Baseball Crank," *Washington Post*, June 19, 1904, S4.
20. Edmund F. French Scrapbook; reprinted from *The Ball Player's Chronicle*, apparently in September of 1867.
21. "When Washington Nine Was 'Champion of the South,'" *Washington Post*, November 20, 1910, S4.
22. Fox, *Big Leagues*, 190.
23. R. M. Larner, "Beginning of Professional Baseball in Washington," *Washington Post*, July 3, 1904, S3.
24. Edmund F. French Scrapbook, 1867, article with handwritten date of June 19.
25. E.H. Tobias, third of sixteen-part history of baseball in St. Louis up to 1876, *Sporting News*, November 16, 1895, 5.
26. Chadwick Scrapbooks, unspecified article, circa 1907.
27. Chadwick Scrapbooks, unidentified clipping quoting unidentified old-timer. The writer's knowledge of the 1867 Nationals and the 1869 Olympics suggests that he may have been Harry McLean, who was the only prominent player to belong to both clubs.
28. Chadwick Scrapbooks, clipping of 1886 article by Chadwick in an unidentified source.
29. "Old Time Baseball," *Washington Post*, March 31, 1889, 10.
30. *Chicago Tribune*, July 28 and 29, 1867. William J. Ryczek reports that the *Chicago Republican* made similar charges and did not withdraw them. See Ryczek's *When Johnny Came Sliding Home*, 116–120, and Fox, *Big Leagues*, 190–196, for full accounts of the incident and the tour, which was also covered in great detail by Henry Chadwick in *The Ball Player's Chronicle*.
31. "When Washington Nine Was 'Champion of the South,'" *Washington Post*, November 20, 1910, S4; *Ball Player's Chronicle*, August 15, 1867.
32. Chadwick Scrapbooks, unspecified article, circa 1907.
33. French Scrapbook, unidentified clipping from May, 1868.
34. *Washington Post*, May 8, 1889, 2.
35. *New York Clipper*, March 23, 1878.
36. Larner, "Beginning of Professional Baseball in Washington," *Washington Post*, July 3, 1904, S3.
37. "Senators' New Name; Washington Team Rechristened the 'Nationals,'" *Washington Post*, March 26, 1905, S1.
38. *Washington Post*, November 27, 1904, S4, reprint of story from a Boston newspaper about Berthrong, who was incorrectly identified in the headline as "Charles J. Berthrong"; *Chicago Tribune*, March 20, 1881; *Boston Globe*, March 4, 1906; *Sporting Life*, March 31, 1906.
39. *New York Clipper*, April 26, 1884; *Seattle Daily Times*, January 11, 1920.
40. *Richmond Times Dispatch*, May 7, 1939.
41. Edmund F. French Scrapbook, article from late 1866.
42. *Daily National Intelligencer*, March 23, 1868.
43. *Wilkes' Spirit of the Times*, November 17, 1860.
44. *Washington Evening Star*, October 2, 1901, 8.
45. *Sporting Life*, November 14, 1888, 1.
46. Peter Morris, *Catcher: How the Man Behind the Plate Became an American Folk Hero* (Chicago: Ivan R. Dee, 2009), passim.
47. *Washington Post*, December 23, 1917.
48. *The Ball Player's Chronicle*, August 29, 1867.
49. *St. Louis Post-Dispatch*, February 2, 1884.
50. *Washington Post*, March 16, 1884.
51. *National Police Gazette*, August 23, 1884.
52. *Sporting Life*, April 14, 1886.
53. *Philadelphia Press*, August 15, 1886.
54. *New York Times*, August 3, 1920.
55. *New York Sunday Mercury*, June 10, 1876.
56. *Ball Player's Chronicle*, August 15, 1867.
57. *Rochester Democrat and Chronicle*, July 13, 1901.
58. *Sporting Life*, May 20, 1911, 7.
59. *Washington Post*, September 8, 1910, 2.
60. "Famous Ball Player Dead," *Aberdeen American*, November 8, 1910. The article reported that word of Urell's death had recently been received, though in fact it was published two months after his death.
61. *Boston Globe*, May 30, 1886.
62. Edmund F. French Scrapbook, clipping dated May 10, 1866.
63. *Washington Post*, August 10, 1892.

Chapter Eight

St. Louis

❖ *Introduction* (Jeffrey Kittel) ❖

Edmund Tobias, in his seventeen-part history of early St. Louis baseball, wrote that it "was in the latter years of the '50's that base ball found a permanent lodging [in St. Louis] and ... it became quite 'the craze'...."[1] St. Louis, during this era, was booming. Between 1840 and 1870, the population of the city grew from 16,469 to 310,869. Physically, the city itself grew from a small town hugging the banks of the Mississippi to one that had quadrupled in size in thirty years and had a series of smaller satellite towns dependent upon it. When the game of baseball came to St. Louis in the late 1850s, it found the first great Western boomtown.

Although it was experiencing extraordinary growth, St. Louis was still a young city, especially when compared to the major metropolises of the East. Founded as a small fur trading village in 1764, St. Louis did not become part of the United States until 1804. The first streets were not paved until 1818, and there were no sidewalks until 1821. It was not until 1822 that St. Louis was incorporated as a city. This combination of a Creole frontier town and a thriving, modern city whose growth was fueled by immigration and Eastern investment created fertile soil in which baseball could take root.

This fertile soil included a tradition of bat-and-ball games and club infrastructure that baseball was able to use to establish itself and grow. Before the introduction of the regulation game of baseball in St. Louis, cricket, as Tobias noted, "had long had a strong hold on lovers of out door sport" in the city.[2] There were attempts in the early 1850s to establish a cricket club in St. Louis,[3] and in 1858 there were at least three cricket clubs playing matches in the city.[4] The Gamble Lawn Grounds, site of some of the earliest baseball games in St. Louis, was first used by cricket clubs in the city[5] and the game would remain popular throughout the 19th century.

There is also substantial evidence of a variant of American baseball being played in St. Louis during the antebellum period. Tobias wrote that town ball "had quite a footing"[6] in the city during this era, and while there are few contemporary references to town ball in the St. Louis newspapers, one such reference in 1860 refers to the game as "old" and speaks of a revival of play, implying that town ball had been played in St. Louis in the past.[7] Richard Perry, a member of the Morning Star Base Ball Club of St. Louis, mentioned that the club was originally established as a town ball club several years before the Civil War.[8] In 1858, two clubs were formed in Alton, Illinois, a satellite town located a few miles upstream from St. Louis, and a match game of "Base Ball" was played between them in June of that year. This variant version involved twelve men a side and five innings per game.[9] The economic, social, cultural and geographical ties between Alton and St. Louis would suggest that a similar game was likely being played in St. Louis. There is also an interesting reference in the *St. Louis Daily Bulletin* in 1860 that mentions the "good old social game of base ball, which we used so much to delight in when a student, and which, semi-occasionally, we have indulged in since arriving at man's estate...."[10] Although the author was speaking specifically about the organization of a baseball club in St. Louis that was playing the New York game, the implication is that there was a variant of American baseball being played in St. Louis during the antebellum era, possibly as early as the 1840s.

As the New York game began to be played in St. Louis in the late 1850s, there already existed a culture of adult bat-and-ball games and clubs, and, as the game grew in popularity, this established club infrastructure was subsumed to the point where town ball clubs became baseball clubs and cricket grounds became baseball grounds. While the older traditions of bat-and-ball games survived the arrival of the regulation game, in general these traditions facilitated the acceptance and growth of the game in St. Louis.

The unique geography and history of the city also helped the establishment of baseball in St. Louis. The original three streets of the town were built parallel to the Mississippi River, below a limestone bluff that slopped gently westward and rose about forty feet above the river. Beyond the bluff was "a broad rolling prairie containing infrequent clumps of timber [reaching] to the horizon."[11] Sections of this prairie, which became known as the Commons, were allocated to residents of the town and cultivated. By the 1840s, as St. Louis began its boom period, parts of the Commons were still uncultivated and the city made a decision to preserve sections of it through the establishment of a series of parks. As a result, large areas of prairie land, within walking distance of the city center, were available in which to play baseball and establish grounds. St. Louis clubs used Lafayette Park, Carr Square Park, and the St. Louis Fairgrounds, all of which just a few years earlier had been a part of the Commons, as sites for intramural games and matches during the antebellum period. Baseball was played in at least eight different locations in St. Louis during the antebellum period and well over twenty before 1875. When clubs went in search of a suitable location in which to play baseball in St. Louis, they discovered a wealth of land available for their use.

With a tradition of bat-and-ball games and clubs as well as a large availability of land upon which to play the game, baseball flourished after its introduction to St. Louis in the late 1850s and by 1860 there were at least ten baseball clubs playing games in the city. There is some difficulty, however, in trying to ascertain the order in which the clubs were founded. Major sources—Tobias, Merritt Griswold, and Richard Perry—all identify a different baseball club as the first established in St. Louis. Griswold makes the case for the Cyclones, Perry for the Morning Stars and Tobias for the Unions. Other sources point to the Empire Club as being St. Louis' first baseball club. While Tobias and Perry make important points about the establishment of the earliest clubs, the best available evidence supports Griswold's claim that his Cyclone Club was the first to organize and play baseball in St. Louis.

There is also a great deal of misinformation in modern historical baseball sources about how specifically the rules of the regulation game were introduced in St. Louis. It is common to see references to Jeremiah Fruin, a Brooklyn native who moved to St. Louis and joined the Empire Club, as the "father of St. Louis baseball" and as the man who brought the game to the city. This, however, is demonstrably false and Fruin himself explicitly stated that the game was being played in St. Louis upon his arrival in 1861. Again, the best available sources point to Merritt Griswold as the first to bring the rules of the regulation game to St. Louis and the first to organize games based on those rules.

Regardless of how specifically the regulation game was introduced in St. Louis and which club was the first to organize, by the summer of 1859 clubs were being organized and games were being played. By the summer of 1860, the first match games were taking place and baseball had established a strong hold on the people of St. Louis. Although the outbreak of the Civil War would have a damaging effect on the growth of the game in the city, in 1859 St. Louis was well on its way to becoming one of the nation's great baseball towns.

❖ *Cyclones* (Jeffrey Kittel) ❖

Although there is a dearth of contemporary sources describing the formation of the earliest baseball clubs in St. Louis, there is substantial evidence, including the later testimony of players, which supports the idea that the Cyclone Base Ball Club of St. Louis was the first formed in St. Louis. The club had a short existence, lasting at most for less than two years, and never captured the imagination of the local sporting public as the Empire and Union Clubs later would but, in its short life, the Cyclone Club had an extraordinary impact. Besides being the first to form and take up the New York game, the club spread the new gospel of baseball by publishing the rules of the game in a local newspaper and by convincing a local town ball club to take up the game. As the first club to play the game in St. Louis, their example inspired others to do the same so that less than a year after their formation there were eight other baseball clubs in the city. Having successfully established and spread the game in St. Louis, the Cyclones led the way in the arrangement of match games and were the first to play another club in the first match game played west of the Mississippi. The collapse of the club was also significant. While the establishment of the Cyclone Club is illustrative of the spread of the New York game in the antebellum era, their break-up at the beginning of the Civil War speaks to the political divisions and tensions that existed in St. Louis at the time. In many ways, the life and death of the Cyclone Club mirrors the history of St. Louis at the outbreak of the war and captures that history in microcosm.

The Cyclone Club, described variously as "[among] the very first of regularly formed clubs in St. Louis,"[12] "the first base ball club"[13] and "the first in St. Louis to set the ball in motion,"[14] was founded in 1859 by Merritt W. Griswold, a recent arrival to St. Louis who had played baseball with several clubs in Brooklyn, and Edward Bredell, Jr., Griswold's co-worker at the Missouri Glass Company. "In the summer of 1859 a meeting was held in the office of the old Missouri Glass Company.... M.W. Griswold, ... aided by the exertions of Ed. Bredell, had gathered together the nucleus of a club, and after one or two preliminary meetings, the Cyclone Base Ball Club was organized, the first in St. Louis.... The uniform adopted was blue flannel cap, blue flannel pants, with a white stripe and white leather belt."[15] Leonard Matthews, who was elected president of the club, wrote in his autobiography that the Cyclones were formed "for exercise, recreation and social intercourse"[16] and the *St. Louis Republic* noted that the object of the club "was exercise and amusement."[17]

According to Matthews, the club "leased what is now

Lafayette Park. At the time it was surrounded by an osage [sic] orange hedge. We spent $600 to put the grounds in shape."[18] Lafayette Park was one of the earliest baseball grounds in St. Louis and was used by several of the antebellum clubs besides the Cyclones. Tobias wrote that the clubs "obtained permission from the city council to use a certain portion of Lafayette Park providing they would arrange and maintain the grounds at their own expense. This was done at an outlay of several hundred dollars by each club...."[19] One of the reasons that the club chose Lafayette Park as their home grounds was that Edward Bredell, Sr., the father of club member Edward Bredell, Jr., was on the board of improvement for the park. For many years after the park was established in 1851, all of the monies used for improving the park came from private sources, raised by the board of improvement, and Bredell Sr. may have seized on an opportunity to raise funds for the park's improvement at the expense of the newly formed baseball clubs in St. Louis.

Having successfully established the game in St. Louis, the Cyclone Club, and specifically Merritt Griswold, began the process of evangelization and of building up the nascent game in the city. To this end, Griswold published the rules of the game "as adopted by the United States Convention of Base Ball Players" in the April 26, 1860, issue of the *Daily Missouri Democrat*. Along with the rules, Griswold published a diagram illustrating how the field was laid out and how the players were positioned. Griswold's act of informing a new audience of the rules of the game is illustrative of one of the ways in which the New York game was spread to new locations. Using the new information technology of a mass-produced, cheaply priced, daily newspaper, Griswold was able to illustrate to a large St. Louis audience the unique nature of the New York game in comparison to the local baseball variant.

At the same time he was spreading the word about the new game, Griswold was taking direct action in educating the public about the merits of the New York game. In a letter to Al Spink, Griswold related the tale of how he taught a local town ball club how to play the New York game. One day Griswold discovered the Morning Star Club playing the local St. Louis baseball variant and "after considerable coaxing and urging" convinced them to try the new game under his coaching. While the Morning Stars were initially disgusted with aspects of the game play, after an hour of play and instruction they invited Griswold to return and give them further instruction, as some of the players stated that they "kindy [sic] like it."[20] According to Griswold, after these coaching sessions, the Morning Star Club were converted to the New York game and never played the St. Louis variant again.

Griswold's evangelical baseball activities in St. Louis found fertile soil and brought forth abundant fruit. When he arrived in St. Louis in 1859, the New York game was unknown in the city but within a year of the establishment of the Cyclone Club, there were at least ten clubs in St. Louis organized around the playing of baseball. Besides the Cyclones and Morning Stars, these clubs included the Unions, the Empires, the Commercials, the Lone Stars, the Resolutes, the Olympics, the Lacledes, and the Tigers. The existence of all of these clubs, the growth of the popularity of the game in St. Louis in 1860, and the attention that the game received in the local press were all an outgrowth of Griswold's baseball missionary work.

With the establishment of so many clubs in St. Louis by the summer of 1860, it was only a matter of time before two of the clubs would meet in a match game. On July 9, 1860, "the first match of base ball ever played in St. Louis"[21] as well as the first "that was ever played West of the Mississippi, under the rules of the National Association,"[22] took place between the Cyclone Club and Griswold's pupils, the Morning Star Club, on grounds located just west of the St. Louis Fairgrounds. Either Griswold taught the club well or the Morning Stars were a quick study because they won the game by a score of 50 to 24. The game was attended by "a large number of spectators, among whom were several ladies. A very great interest was manifested by all present, who expressed their delight at the many instances of fine play displayed by both clubs."[23] The star of the game for the Cyclone Club was third baseman Edward Farish, who scored eight runs without making a single out.

According to Griswold, "the ball in that first match game was for years used as the championship trophy [of the city], it going from one club to the other.... I personally sent to New York for the ball to be used in this first match, and after the game it was gilded in gold and lettered with the score of the game."[24] After the ball had been properly ornamented, the Cyclone Club held a dinner for the Morning Stars at the Planter's Hotel and the game ball was awarded to the victors of St. Louis's first match game. This trophy ball was believed by both Griswold and Tobias to have last been in the hands of the Empire Club. However, in reports of the Empire Club's 1873 anniversary game where the club's most prominent trophies were on display, there is no mention of the ball. Tobias does mention the legend that Jeremiah Fruin, the former field captain of the Empires, borrowed the ball and "forgot" to return it.[25]

The contest against the Morning Stars is to date the only known match game played by the Cyclones, and this disappointing lack of information is likely because, according to Tobias, the club's records were lost in a fire that destroyed club member Maurice Alexander's drug store. While this irreplaceable source is lost forever, one story about a spectacular play made by club shortstop Ferdinand Garesché survives. In a game for which no other details exist, Garesché made a play "which now would be almost impossible, namely, to put out, unassisted, three men on one batted ball. On this occasion, knowing where the batter was in the habit of knocking the ball, he as shortstop was playing down near second base, with a man on first and second. Catching the ball on the fly he ran across second base, which had been vacated for third, and succeeded in catching and touching the runner for first who had attempted to make a second, before he could regain first."[26] It's probably safe to assume that this was the first unassisted triple play in St. Louis baseball history.

The Cyclone Club did not survive the outbreak of the Civil War, and Griswold wrote that the club disbanded as a direct result of its members "taking part [in the war] on one side or the other."[27] Griswold's statement is an extraordinary example of understatement as the historical record reveals that the club members were intense partisans who played important roles with both Union and Confederate forces during the Civil War. The political divisions within the club and the coldness that crept into club relationships as a result was a reflection of dynamics at work in St. Louis society generally in 1860 and 1861. Both the city and the club were divided among staunch Unionists, conditional Unionists who supported the Federal government but not abolition, staunch Secessionists who wished to see Missouri join the Confederacy, conditional Secessionists who supported the right of a state to secede but wished for Missouri to remain in the Union, and those who were ambivalent about the entire matter. These divergent forces were organizing, and violence was breaking out in St. Louis even before the beginning of the war.

The divisions within the club and the city are illustrated by the attitudes of three members of the club. Merritt Griswold, who was originally from Brooklyn, was a staunch Unionist and a member of a pro–Union paramilitary organization that operated in St. Louis prior to the outbreak of war. When the war began, Griswold's group was organized into a Federal militia and he took part in a successful assault on the Missouri state militia in May of 1861 that helped Federal forces gain control of St. Louis. Basil Duke, who was originally from Kentucky, was a staunch Secessionist and one of the leaders of pro–Confederate forces in St. Louis. As the Federal government tightened its control over St. Louis, Duke left the city and joined the Confederate Army, where he rose to the rank of brigadier general. Leonard Matthews, the club president, stated that he found the war inconvenient and purchased a substitute to serve in the Union Army for him. At the same time, he tried to convince his brother and fellow club member, Orville Matthews, to resign his commission in the United States Navy and not to fight in the war. The Cyclone Club, like St. Louis and the nation itself, was torn apart by the Civil War. What is truly amazing is not that the club broke up at the beginning of the war but that a club of such diverse men could hold together throughout 1860 as tensions rose and the drumbeat of war grew louder.

Matthews tells a rather bittersweet story about the club as the nation was on the verge of war. He wrote: "[one] afternoon some of us, Ed Bredell among the rest, were lying in the shade of the hedge, pitching a ball from one to the other, when someone remarked — 'Boys, we will soon have another kind of ball to pitch'— and poor Ed caught one in battle in Virginia, early in the war."[28]

Club Members

The Cyclone Club, according to Tobias, "included in its membership some of the brightest young men of St. Louis, among them a number of whom have left the impress of their handiwork in almost every honorable calling."[29] Matthews describes his fellow club members as high rollers. Matthews' description of the club's membership may be a bit of an exaggeration, but there is no doubt that the former Cyclones rose to prominence in fields as varied as politics, business, and the military. While the membership is diverse and there is no one link that ties the men together, among the club were co-workers, brothers, in-laws, and friends.

Maurice W. Alexander: Alexander, a merchant and pharmacist, was born on February 9, 1835, in Philadelphia. Graduating from the Philadelphia College of Pharmacy in 1854, he moved to St. Louis and, after initially working for wholesale druggists Bacon, Hyde & Co., he opened the first of several drug stores. Alexander operated his business in St. Louis for forty-two years and was recognized as one of the leaders of the industry in Missouri and the West, serving as Commissioner of Pharmacy for the State of Missouri and president of the American Pharmaceutical Association. Alexander died in St. Louis on June 6, 1898.

Frederick Benteen: Frederick William Benteen was born in Petersburg, Virginia, on August 24, 1834. Benteen's father moved the family to St. Louis in the spring of 1849 after the death of his wife and set up a paint and glass supply company, where Frederick Benteen worked as a sign painter until the outbreak of the Civil War. Under the influence of his fiancée, Benteen supported the Union cause much to the dismay of his secessionist father. When Benteen joined the Union Army, his father stated that he hoped his son would be killed by the first bullet fired at him.

In July of 1861, Benteen began a lifelong military career by supervising the training of soldiers at the St. Louis Arsenal. During the war, he was involved in battles at Wilson's Creek, Dutch Hollow, Pea Ridge, and Vicksburg. In 1865, Benteen's Cavalry unit was involved in a baseball game on the Solomon Fork of the Republican River in Kansas against another Cavalry unit. Benteen named his team the Cyclones in honor of his former club.

Benteen is best known for his actions at Little Big Horn in 1876 when he commanded Company H of Custer's Seventh Cavalry. There is a great deal of controversy surrounding what Benteen did during the battle, and there have been accusations that Benteen was derelict in his duties and abandoned Custer's main force to their fate while others claim that after Custer was killed Benteen, assuming command, saved the remnants of the Seventh Cavalry through his calm leadership. One thing that is known for certain is that Custer's last message was to Benteen, commanding him to "Come on.... Be Quick. Bring packs."[30]

Frederick Benteen, who retired from the army in 1888 with the rank of brigadier general, died on June 22, 1898, and is buried at Arlington National Cemetery.

Edward Bernoudy: Edward A. Bernoudy was born in Louisiana in 1835, worked as a merchant and died in St. Louis in January of 1871.

Edward Bredell, Jr.: Ed Bredell was born in St. Louis in 1839, the only child of a wealthy family. His father, Edward Bredell, Sr., was an attorney and one of the founders of the firm of Bredell & Bro., one of the first wholesale dry goods houses in St. Louis. Bredell Sr. also founded and was the president of the Missouri Glass Company where his son and Merritt Griswold worked.

Bredell and his family had strong Southern sympathies, supported the Confederacy, and favored Missouri's secession from the Union. At the outbreak of the Civil War, Bredell joined the Confederate Army as a staff officer but resigned his commission and joined Mosby's Rangers as a private. On November 16, 1864, Bredell was killed in a battle at Whiting's House.

In *Reminiscences of a Mosby Guerilla*, John William Munson wrote that on "the day of the fight the boys laid [Bredell] to rest where he fell, but afterwards we brought his body over to our side of the mountain and buried it near Oak Hill.... Before the war ended young Bredell's father came down to Virginia and took his dead son's body home. When he reached St. Louis, owing to bitter feeling there towards Southerners, he was informed that the body could not be buried in any of the cemeteries. He thereupon had a grave dug in his own handsome grounds, and his son's body found its final rest in the shadow of his old home."[31]

Jonathan Collier: Jonathan Pierre Collier was born on December 12, 1842, in Missouri. The brother of fellow club member William Bell Collier, Jack Collier, as he was commonly referred to, was a successful wholesale grocer in St. Louis. He died in St. Louis on December 31, 1876.

Alexander Crosman: Born in 1838, Alex Crosman, like fellow club member Orville Matthews, was a graduate of the Naval Academy and a life-long naval officer. During the Civil War, he commanded the *Commodore M'Donough* in the South Atlantic Blockading Squadron. While there is a report that Crosman drowned in 1872 while commanding the steamer *Kansas* in the Caribbean,[32] according to *The New York Times*, he was "eaten by sharks in Panama waters in the late sixties while trying to save the lives of two sailors."[33]

Jonathan Davis: Jonathan T. Davis was born in 1845 and was the son and heir of Samuel C. Davis, one of the largest dry goods merchants in St. Louis. Sam'l C. Davis & Co. fielded an amateur baseball team in St. Louis during the 1870s and '80s that was organized and equipped by John Davis, who also played for the club.[34] Davis died in St. Louis in 1898.

Basil Duke: Born in Kentucky in 1838, Basil Wilson Duke attended Georgetown College and Centre College before obtaining a law degree from Transylvania College in 1858. After graduating from law school, he moved to St. Louis where his cousin, also named Basil Duke and also a lawyer, had a thriving practice. In St. Louis, Duke became one of the leaders of pro–Southern St. Louisans and a member of the Minute Men, "their paramilitary organization."[35] Originally a conditional Unionist, after the arrival of Federal troops in St. Louis Duke became an ardent Secessionist.

Upon the outbreak of the war, Duke was sent by Missouri Governor Claiborne Jackson to Montgomery, Alabama, to obtain material support from the Confederacy. Successful in his mission, Duke returned to St. Louis on May 9 aboard a steamboat loaded with siege guns and howitzers which he promptly delivered to the Missouri Militia at Camp Jackson. It's arguable that it was the delivery of these weapons that precipitated the Union attack on the camp.

Returning to Kentucky, Duke joined the Second Kentucky Cavalry under the command of his brother-in-law, John Hunt Morgan. Twice wounded in battle, Duke was captured during a raid on the Indiana-Ohio border in 1864 but was exchanged. After the death of Morgan, he was promoted to brigadier general and was given command of "Morgan's Raiders."

After the war, Duke settled in Louisville where he became head of the law department of the Louisville & Nashville Railroad Company. For twenty years, he served as a member of the Kentucky House of Representatives. Duke also was involved in several Confederate veterans associations and wrote two histories of the Civil War.

Basil Duke died on September 16, 1916, "due to shock resulting from the removal of one of his legs."[36]

Edward Farish: Edward Tilghman Farish was a prominent St. Louis lawyer who was born on August 7, 1836, in Woodville, Mississippi. Farish lost both of his parents by the time he was eleven and in 1847 came to St. Louis to live with relatives. He graduated from St. Louis University in 1854 and was admitted to the bar two years later. Farish formed a partnership with Alexander Garesché and P.B. Garesché, the brother and cousin, respectively, of fellow club member Ferdinand Garesché. In 1857, Farish would marry Ferdinand's sister Lilly.

At the outbreak of the Civil War, Farish "[declined] to take any part in the great civil contest"[37] and focused his energies on building his law practice. He served as City Councilor in the 1870s and was one of St. Louis's most prominent civil law attorneys.

Edward Farish died in St. Louis on July 21, 1904.

Joseph Fullerton: Joseph Scott Fullerton was born in Chillicothe, Ohio, in December of 1835 and graduated from Miami University in 1855 and Cincinnati Law School in 1858. After graduating from law school, Fullerton moved to St. Louis, where he set up a practice and became involved in the Union cause in Missouri. In the fall of 1861, he was appointed by President Lincoln to a committee that oversaw the military affairs of the Department of the West.

After being relieved from the commission in the fall of 1862, Fullerton entered the Union Army as a private although he was quickly appointed a lieutenant in the Second Missouri Infantry. Rising through the ranks as a staff officer, Fullerton was eventually brevetted a brigadier general "for most valuable services and distinguished personal gallantry."[38]

Unhappy with his postwar assignments, Fullerton resigned his commission in September of 1866 and was appointed postmaster of St. Louis. In 1868, he left that post to set up a private law practice. Retiring in 1890, he served as chairman of the Chickamauga and Chattanooga National Military Park Commission.

Joseph Fullerton was killed on March 20, 1897, in a train accident near Oakland, Maryland.

Joseph Gamble: Joseph Gamble was born on September 6, 1842, in St. Louis. He attended a Presbyterian seminary from 1864 to 1867 and was ordained as a minister in April of 1868. For almost thirty years, Gamble was the pastor of the First Presbyterian Church of Plattsburgh, New York, and was described as one of the best-known clergymen in the state.[39] He died on April 8, 1909. His brother Rufus E. Gamble, who was a Methodist minister, was also a club member.

Ferdinand Garesché: Ferdinand Garesché was born on December 7, 1827, in New York City into a wealthy, landed Creole family. Ferdinand's father settled the family on the Garesché holdings near St. Louis in 1839.

Garesché was at Camp Jackson in May of 1861 when the Union forces, including Merritt Griswold's 3rd regiment, attacked. He was captured, imprisoned, and later paroled. Under the terms of his parole, Garesché promised not to take up arms against the United States and he honorably abided by these terms. His brother Alexander, who also was at Camp Jackson, claimed that neither he nor Ferdinand were Secessionists but rather were Democrats who were opposed to the war and the Federal policies that they believed started the conflict.

After the war, Garesché was involved in Democratic machine politics in St. Louis and, through the patronage of the Democratic Party, held several civil service and elected positions, including chief clerk of the St. Louis County Court and St. Louis Commissioner of Supplies. While serving as clerk of the County Court, Garesché was involved in an election-fraud scandal investigated by the United States Congress in 1877 when he was accused of tampering with ballots in a congressional race.

Ferdinand Garesché, who was also a member of the Union Base Ball Club of St. Louis, died in St. Louis on July 16, 1903.

Merritt W. Griswold: Born in 1835 in New York, Griswold played baseball with the Putnam Club of Brooklyn in 1857 and the Hiawatha Club of Brooklyn in 1858 and 1859. He came to St. Louis, where his mother had family, in 1859 and found employment with the Missouri Glass Company.

While living in St. Louis, Griswold served as an officer with the 3rd Regiment of the United States Reserve Corp, the "Home Guards," from May 8, 1861, until August 17, 1861. Griswold's unit was involved in the capture of Camp Jackson in May of 1861, an action that helped secure St. Louis for the Union at the beginning of the Civil War. An engineer by trade, Griswold lived most of his adult life in Englewood, New Jersey, where he died on March 24, 1915.

It's Griswold's claim that his founding of the Cyclone Club and publication of the rules of the game in the *Daily Missouri Democrat* was "the commencement of the game in its first introduction into Missouri...."[40] Almost all of the statements that Griswold made in his letter to Al Spink regarding the origins of the New York game in St. Louis have been verified by other sources, lending great credence to his claim.

Besides being one of the founders and the field captain of the Cyclone Club, Griswold also served as an umpire for several games in antebellum St. Louis.

Charles Kearny: The son of General Stephen W. Kearny, Charles Kearny was born at Jefferson Barracks, just south of St. Louis, on March 7, 1834. Living the life of an itinerant young man, Kearny, between 1855 and 1866, moved six times between Missouri, Texas, and Kansas, never living in one place for more than two years. He worked a variety of jobs including grocery store clerk, ranch hand, grain merchant, and steamboat agent. Kearny finally settled down in 1868, buying a farm near Wathena, Kansas. In the 1880s, he moved to St. Joseph, Missouri, and worked as a clerk at the Pacific Hotel.

Charles Kearny died in 1904.

Leonard Matthews: One of three Matthews brothers who were members of the Cyclones, Leonard Matthews was born on December 17, 1828, in Baltimore. During the California Gold Rush of 1849, Matthews journeyed by wagon to Sutters Creek where he panned $2500 in gold in two weeks time. After losing the money in a failed business venture in San Francisco, he returned to St. Louis. Along with his brother and fellow club member William Matthews, he ran an apothecary business that had originally been started by his father, John Matthews, Jr. Selling the business to the Meyer Brothers' Drug Company after the Civil War, Matthews became an investment banker. Upon his retirement, he devoted most his time to the development of Shaw's Garden in St. Louis.

In his 1927 autobiography, *A Long Life in Review*, Matthews states that he was the first president of the Cyclone Club. He also notes that due to divisions within his family, his business interests, and a young bride, he had no desire to fight in the Civil War.

Leonard Matthews died on May 5, 1931, at his home in St. Louis. He was 102 years old.

Orville Matthews: The third, and youngest, of the Matthews brothers, Edmund Orville Matthews was born in Baltimore in 1836. After graduating from the Naval Academy in 1855, he was stationed in St. Louis and, at the outbreak of the

Civil War, Matthews' family encouraged him to resign his commission. Refusing to do so, he took part in several naval engagements during the war including one that resulted in the capture of forts at Hatteras Inlet in 1861. In December of 1864, Matthews, serving with a detachment of Marines, took part in the assault on Tullafinny Crossroads.

During the course of his naval career, Matthews commanded several ships and served as Chief of the Bureau of Yards and Docks from 1891 to 1894. On June 19, 1897, he was promoted to Rear Admiral.

Matthews retired from the navy on October 24, 1898, and died at his home in Cambridge, Massachusetts, on January 30, 1911.

Gratz Moses: Born on November 11, 1839, in New Jersey, Gratz A. Moses was a St. Louis physician who served as a surgeon with the Confederate Army during the Civil War. He was the son of S. Gratz Moses, a prominent St. Louis physician. Moses died on June 6, 1898, in St. Louis.

Griff Prather: Born on June 16, 1834, in Clermont County, Ohio, John Griffith Prather worked on riverboats from a young age, moving to St. Louis in 1850. In 1852, he moved to California where he worked as a salmon fisherman before returning to St. Louis in 1855 to assist in his uncle's wholesale liquor business. During the Civil War, Prather served as an officer with the 5th Regimental Missouri Militia.

After the war, Colonel Griff Prather, as he was commonly known, took over his uncle's business and specialized in selling wine, liquor and tobacco to the many steamboats that frequented the St. Louis riverfront. He also owned shares in several steamboats throughout the 1860s and '70s that worked the Mississippi, Missouri, Ohio, Red, and Arkansas rivers.

Prather, like Garesché, was involved with the Democratic political machine in St. Louis. He was a member of the Democratic National Committee and was instrumental in securing the 1888 Democratic National Convention for St. Louis.

Griff Prather died on December 27, 1903.

John Riggin: John Riggin, Jr., was born in St. Louis in 1837 and worked for his father as a real estate agent. During the Civil War, he served as a staff officer to General Grant and was promoted to Brigadier General on March 13, 1865. After the war, he returned to St. Louis before moving to Florida in 1874. He died in Bradenton, Florida, on June 13, 1886.

John Waddell: John Waddell was born on September 18, 1836, in New York and was working as a clerk in St. Louis in 1860. He died on April 20, 1922, in Sedalia, Missouri.

Willie Walker: Willis Collins Walker was born in Adair County, Kentucky, in April of 1831 and moved to St. Louis sometime in the 1850s where he was engaged in the dry goods business, eventually becoming a partner in the firm of Ely, Walker & Co. During the Civil War, Walker was a member of the 1st Missouri Light Artillery Battery and took part in the capture of Camp Jackson as well as in the battle of Wilson's Creek. He died on January 7, 1918, in St. Louis.

Robert Whitney: Robert Sanford Whitney was born on June 9, 1825, in Westfield, Massachusetts. While in St. Louis, he worked as a teller for Boatman's Savings and was a member of the First Congregational Church. In the church records it states that "[the] name of Robert S. Whitney will long be dear to all among us who loved modest, unassuming, genuine Christian worth, and gentle but firm Christian principle. His character was one pervaded, lighted up and established by a godly sincerity; one of delicate and shrinking diffidence, but of thorough, genuine, manly truth. His fidelity was like the sun; his honor and integrity among business men would have secured him any trust. His aim was to be useful in any sphere. He was singularly free from ambition of precedence or display."[41]

Whitney, who died on April 25, 1864, was credited by Merritt Griswold with coming up with the club's name.

Other known members of the club include Alfred Bernoudy, Louis Hutchinson, John Lapsley, Paul Prewitt, and John Stetinius.

Notes

1. E.H. Tobias, letter to *The Sporting News*, October 26, 1895.
2. *Ibid.*
3. *Spirit of the Times*, August 7, 1852.
4. *Missouri Republican*, November 22, 1858.
5. *Daily Missouri Republican*, September 10, 1858.
6. Tobias, October 26, 1895.
7. *St. Louis Daily Bulletin*, May 4, 1860.
8. *St. Louis Globe-Democrat*, April 24, 1887.
9. *Alton Weekly Courier*, June 24, 1858.
10. *St. Louis Daily Bulletin*, June 6, 1860.
11. St. Louis City Planning Commission; *Physical Growth of St. Louis*.
12. Tobias, October 26, 1895.
13. Al Spink, *The National Game* (N.p.: National Game, 1910).
14. *St. Louis Republic,* April 21, 1895.
15. *Ibid.*
16. Leonard Matthews, *A Long Life in Review* (1927).
17. *St. Louis Republic*, April 21, 1895.
18. Matthews, *A Long Life in Review*.
19. Tobias, October 26, 1895.
20. Spink, *The National Game*.
21. *St. Louis Daily Bulletin*, July 11, 1860.
22. *Porter's Spirit of the Times*, July 17, 1860.
23. *St. Louis Daily Bulletin*, July 11, 1860.
24. Spink, *The National Game*.
25. E.H. Tobias, first of sixteen-part history of baseball in St. Louis up to 1876, *Sporting News*, November 2, 1895.
26. *St. Louis Republic*, April 21, 1895.
27. Spink, *The National Game*.
28. Matthews, *A Long Life in Review*.
29. Tobias, November 2, 1895.
30. *New York Times*, November 8, 1988.
31. John Williams Munson, *Reminiscences of a Mosby Guerilla* (New York: Moffat, Yard and Co., 1906).
32. *Bangor Daily Whig & Courier*, April 29, 1872.
33. *New York Times*, February 9, 1902.
34. *St. Louis Daily Republic*, February 9, 1896.
35. Louis Gerteis, *Civil War St. Louis* (Lawrence: University of Kansas, 2001).

36. *New York Times*, September 17, 1916.
37. L.U. Reavis, *Saint Louis: The Future Great City of the World* St. Louis: C.R. Barns, 1876).
38. William H. Powell, *Officers of the Volunteer Army and Navy Who Served in the Civil War* (Philadelphia: L.R. Hamersley & Co., 1893).
39. *New York Times*, April 9, 1909.
40. Spink, *The National Game*.
41. Whitney Research Group, biographical sketch of Robert Whitney.

❖ *Morning Stars* (Jeffrey Kittel) ❖

CLUB HISTORY

An antebellum town ball club that began playing baseball before the Civil War, the Morning Star Base Ball Club of St. Louis was largely made up of employees of a St. Louis dry goods store who lived in the neighborhood around Carr Square Park. While the club did not survive the outbreak of the war, it was involved in four of the earliest match games in St. Louis baseball history.

Although there are two different accounts of how the Morning Star Club came to play baseball, the club is a significant example of the popularity of bat-and-ball games in St. Louis prior to the advent of baseball in the city. They are also an example of how baseball was able to use the infrastructure already created by town ball and cricket clubs in St. Louis to quickly establish itself in the years leading up to the Civil War.

It is unknown when exactly the Morning Star Club was established, but Richard Perry, a member of the club, stated that the club was in existence "[about] two years before the war."[1] He also went on to say that the club played town ball every day at Carr Square Park between 5:30 and 7:00 A.M. This is consistent with Merritt Griswold's recollections. Griswold wrote that the "Morning Star Club was a 'town ball' club and played from 5 A.M. to 6 A.M. on Tuesday and Friday mornings in Carr's Park."[2]

In its June 6, 1860, issue, the *St. Louis Daily Bulletin* reported that the club reorganized as a baseball club with twenty-four members. An election of officers was held, and David Naylor was selected as club president; Robert Henry, vice-president; George Franklin, secretary; and C.C. Ferguson, Henry Franklin and Charles Scudder, directors.

For the most part the members of the Morning Star Club were young men, "all strong, well-built athletes, quick of action and all wide awake for business"[3] employed in various capacities by Ubsdell, Pierson, & Co., a St. Louis dry goods store that was the forerunner of Wm. Barr & Co. Seven of the fourteen known members of the club worked for Ubsdell, Pierson, & Co. as clerks, salesmen, or cashiers. Two other members worked for a wholesale grocery store, another worked at the Merchant's Exchange, and one was a produce salesman. It is safe to say that the vast majority of club members were modestly employed in the retail business.

Not only did the club members share a common trade, many of them also lived in the same neighborhood. Half of the known members of the club lived within three blocks of Carr Square Park, either on Carr Street, 15th Street, or 16th Street. The choice of Carr Square Park as the location for the Morning Star Club's games was obviously made for the convenience of its members. Interestingly, Perry stated that "[nearly] all of us moved to the neighborhood of Twenty-second and the Pacific Railroad, and we continued our game there."[4] This area around the Pacific Railroad machine shop would be a popular site for baseball games in St. Louis into the 1890s. The Empire Club played numerous games there in 1866, and both the Veto Grounds and the Compton Avenue Grounds would be established there. Based on Perry's statement, it appears as if the Morning Star Club was the first to play games in the neighborhood.

The Morning Star Club played in four known match games before the outbreak of the Civil War. The first took place on July 9, 1861, when they defeated the Cyclone Club, 50 to 24, in the first match game played in St. Louis. Before that game, the Empire Club had issued a challenge to the winner of the match, and the Morning Stars accepted their challenge. What is most likely the second match game ever played in St. Louis took place on July 17, 1860, at the Laclede Grounds and the Empires emerged victorious, 41–33. According to the *Daily Bulletin*'s account of the game, "Each club displayed a great deal of skill during the three hours they played."[5]

On September 14, 1860, the two clubs played again. The match was held at the Gamble Lawn Grounds, and again the Empires defeated the Morning Stars, this time by a score of 37–18. The following day, the *Daily Bulletin* supplied an interesting account of the game. They reported that the "large crowd in attendance seemed to take great interest in the game, and frequently applauded the players when an extra play was made, but we regret to say that a great many boys and others, of whom we should have expected better conduct, crowded around the scorers so as to make it almost impossible for them to keep an account of the game. It was utterly impossible for them to make a correct report of the fielding, and they soon abandoned the attempt.... Soon after the game began, two of the players attempted to catch a ball on the fly, and one of them, Mr. W.A. Hudson, was struck in the pit of the stomach by the other player's knee, and was so disabled that he had to quit, and his place was filled by Mr. D.H. Naylor."

The last known game played by the club was in the spring of 1861 when they lost to the Empire Club 31 to 17. This match was "was played on grounds adjoining the old cemetery, then located where now is the junction of Franklin Avenues, Wash and Twenty-eighth Streets. It commenced at five o'clock in the morning, was umpired by Captain Griswold, of the Cyclone Club, under the National Association rules."[6] The club arrived for their match with the Empires "seated in two of Ubsdell, Pierson & Co.'s wagons attired in their handsome uniforms of heavy white flannel. As they alighted they made a fine impression."[7]

All of the known matches played by the Morning Star Club are significant. Obviously, their first two matches are the first two match games played in St. Louis and the first two played west of the Mississippi. With the disruption caused by the Civil War, their game against the Empire Club in 1861 is one of only two known match games played in St. Louis during the war years. Also, their two games against the Empires in 1860 represent the first known instance of a series, or at the very least a return match, played between two clubs in St. Louis baseball history.

Although it's been established that the Morning Stars were a town ball club that converted to baseball, there are two different versions of how that conversion came about. Richard Perry stated that the club members became aware of baseball and "our secretary wrote on for the rules of the game. We received a little book that told how it was played, and we changed our name to the Morning Star Base-Ball Club."[8] Merritt Griswold, however, wrote that he discovered the club playing town ball at Carr Square Park and

> after considerable urging and coaxing on my part they passed a resolution at one of their meetings that they would try the national rules for one morning if I would coach them, or more properly, teach them, which I consented to do if they would agree to stick to it for the full hour without "kicking," for as I told them they would not like it until after playing it for a sufficient length of time to become familiar with some of its fine points, all of which they agreed to and kept their word like good fellows as they were, but in ten minutes I could see most of them were disgusted, yet they stuck to it for their hour's play. At the breaking up of the game to go home they asked me if I would coach them one more morning as they began to "kindy [sic] like it." I was on hand their next play day, or rather play morning at 5. Result they never played "town ball" after that second inning....[9]

These two accounts seem at odds, but they do not necessarily contradict each other. It's entirely possible that the Morning Star Club was aware of the rules of baseball before Merritt Griswold met them. It's also just as possible that after some coaching from Griswold, the club sent away for a copy of the rules. Regardless of how the chain of events played out, the Morning Star Club gave up town ball for baseball by the summer of 1860 and was one of St. Louis's first baseball clubs.

At the outbreak of the Civil War, the club was "disorganized ... [with] most of the Stars going into the Union Army under Maj. Zagonyi, in command of Gen. Fremont's Body Guard, and of this brilliantly uniformed battalion eighteen were from the dry goods house of Ubsdell, Pierson & Co."[10] There is no record of any of the known members of the Morning Star Club playing for any of the other major clubs of St. Louis after the war.

CLUB MEMBERS

Martin Burke: Burke, a pitcher for the Morning Stars, was born in Canada in 1836. Living in St. Louis by 1860, he was a partner in a small grocery store and lived on N. 16th Street near Carr Square Park.

While living in St. Louis, Burke joined the St. Louis Greys, the oldest volunteer militia unit in the city and by 1861 he was the Greys' commanding officer. The Greys were mustered at Camp Jackson in May of 1861 and it can be assumed that Burke surrendered to Union forces along with the other Missouri militia units at Camp Jackson. While he was most likely released upon promising not to take up arms against the Union, Burke joined the 1st Missouri Infantry on the Confederate side, serving as a Captain. In "short time [he] was brought home severely wounded. He did not long survive...."[11]

Edwin Fowler: Born in Dover, New Hampshire, in 1829, Fowler played second base for the club and was the long-time St. Louis representative of the Mutual Benefit Life Insurance Company. A successful life insurance agent, Fowler became a rather wealthy man who was active in St. Louis society, joining numerous clubs and contributing to several prominent charities.

Fowler died in St. Louis in 1902.

Henry Franklin: It is unknown when exactly Henry H. Franklin was born, but it's assumed that he was the brother of Joseph Franklin and was born in Ireland in the 1830s. An outfielder with the club, in 1860 he was working as a salesman for Ubsdell, Pierson, & Co. During the Civil War, he served as a private with Searcy's Battalion of Missouri Sharp Shooters.

Franklin died in Missouri in 1866.

Joseph Franklin: Born in Ireland in 1836, Franklin played third base for the Morning Star Club. In 1860, he was working as a bookkeeper for Ubsdell, Pierson, & Co. and living on Carr Street between 16th and 17th Street. During the Civil War, he served in the infantry on the Union side with the 1st Regiment of the Missouri State Militia.

After the war, he returned to Ubsdell, Pierson, & Co. and, by the 1880s, rose to become the managing partner of Wm. Barr & Co., as the firm was by then known. In 1884, Franklin was also a trustee of the Lindell Hotel, which was owned by fellow club member Charles Scudder.

Franklin's wife, Jane, passed away in November of 1887. Her funeral serves as an example of the enduring friendships that were created in Morning Star Club as well as in the St. Louis baseball fraternity during the antebellum era. At the funeral were fellow Morning Star Club members Richard Perry,

Robert Henry, and George Wright, all of whom served as pallbearers. Also at the funeral were Leonard Matthews and Maurice Alexander, formerly of the Cyclone Club, and Robert Duncan, who had played with both the Empire and Union Clubs.

Joseph Franklin died on February 22, 1904, in Kirkwood, Missouri.

John Henry: One of three Henry brothers who were members of the Morning Star Club, John Henry was born in Ireland in 1837. In 1860, he was working as a salesman with Ubsdell, Pierson, & Co. and living with his two brothers on 16th Street, near Carr Square Park.

An outfielder with the club, John E. Henry died in St. Louis in 1896.

Robert Henry: The oldest of the three Henry brothers, Robert Lind Henry was born in Ireland in 1835. A catcher, he was the field captain of the Morning Star Club. By 1860, he was working for Ubsdell, Pierson, & Co. and living on 16th Street in a household that included his wife, children, and two brothers. During the war, Henry served with the 49th Regiment of Missouri Infantry on the Union side.

After the war, it appears that he returned to work for Ubsdell, Pierson, & Co. and remained in the dry goods business as a salesman and merchant for the rest of his life. Robert Henry died in St. Louis in 1892.

William Henry: The youngest of the Henry brothers, William H. Henry was born in Ireland in 1840. Working for Ubsdell, Pierson, & Co., Henry played both first base and the outfield for the Morning Stars before joining the 1st Regiment of the Missouri Cavalry at the outbreak of the Civil War.

Returning to St. Louis after the war, William Henry worked as a traveling commercial agent. He died in Kansas City on November 14, 1882.

William Hudson: William Allen Hudson was born on January 11, 1832, in Wales. By 1857, he was living in St. Louis and working with his brother, Benjamin, selling produce. In 1884, the brothers incorporated their business under the name of the Hudson Brothers Commission Company, with William acting as president. One of the leading produce companies in St. Louis during the 19th century, Hudson Brothers expanded their business to other cities, including Chicago, and continued operations into the 1920s.

William Hudson died in St. Louis on April 20, 1915.

David Naylor: David H. Naylor, born in New York in 1832, was an outfielder with the Morning Star Club who was living in St. Louis by 1852. In 1860, he was a partner with Naylor, Mosley, & Co., a corrugated iron roofing company.

In 1878, Naylor was elected to the Missouri State Senate and was described as one of the hardest working men of that body. "He is so rotund and rosy ... and jolly, that one would expect him to be satisfied with the labor of drawing his per diem and calculating his mileage, but on the contrary, he attends all his committees, and when the giddy throng is playing pool at the Madison, he is engaged in manufacturing bills and resolutions of the most patriotic stamp."[12]

After his term in office expired, Naylor returned to St. Louis and was a partner in the John J. Daly Stationery and Printing Company. He died in Washington, D.C., on August 17, 1904.

Richard Perry: The club's shortstop, Perry was born in England in 1838; by 1860 he was living in St. Louis on Carr Street and working as a reporter for the Merchant's Exchange. After the Civil War, he worked as a flour importer and served for many years as President of the Merchant's Exchange Board of Flour Inspection. In 1887, Perry claimed that he was still playing baseball with an amateur club made up of workers from the Merchant's Exchange.

He died in 1895 in St. Louis.

Charles Scudder: Scudder, who played second base for the Morning Star Club, was born in Kentucky on November 2, 1834, and, after moving to St. Louis, was one of the first graduates of Jones Commercial College in the 1850s. In 1860, he was living on Carr Street and was a partner in Weirick, Scudder & Co., a grocery store. After the Civil War, Scudder served as a member of the St. Louis School Board and as city treasurer. He also was one of the owners of the Lindell Hotel.

In August of 1884, Scudder was vacationing in Minnesota with several friends from St. Louis and played in a "very exciting and closely contested game of ball."[13] Playing the outfield, he helped his team to an 11 to 10 victory. According to reports, the game was umpired by General William T. Sherman.

Scudder died in St. Louis on March 15, 1912.

Other known members of the club: J. Brazil, Archibald G. Duff, Charles C. Ferguson, George Franklin, Thomas Houllhan and George N. Wright.

Notes

1. *St. Louis Globe-Democrat*, April 24, 1887.
2. Spink, *The National Game*.
3. Tobias, November 2, 1895.
4. *St. Louis Globe-Democrat*, April 24, 1887.
5. *St. Louis Daily Bulletin*, July 18, 1860.
6. Tobias, November 2, 1895.
7. *Ibid*.
8. *St. Louis Globe-Democrat*, April 24, 1887.
9. Spink, *The National Game*.
10. Tobias; November 2, 1895.
11. *Ibid*.
12. *St. Louis Globe-Democrat*, February 10, 1879.
13. *St. Louis Globe-Democrat*, August 10, 1884.

Unions (Jeffrey Kittel)

CLUB HISTORY

The Union Base Ball Club of St. Louis was one of the two most prominent and successful clubs in the city during the pioneer era. In many ways the Union, under the leadership of Asa W. Smith, was the vanguard club of the period, leading the development of the game in St. Louis. One of the first organized clubs in St. Louis, the Union helped push St. Louis into the baseball mainstream by advocating such innovations as a state association, enclosed grounds, payment for admission to games, matches against the powerful Eastern clubs, and possibly compensation of players.

With a membership that included the sons of some of the most prominent families in St. Louis, the Union Club was a testament to the fact that the popularity of the game in the city knew no class boundaries. Also, it is arguable that the participation of members of "the silk stocking element"[1] helped to popularize the game in St. Louis and gave it a veneer of respectability that it might not have otherwise had.

The Union's rivalry with the Empire Base Ball Club of St. Louis, which possibly began as early as 1859, defined baseball in St. Louis during the era. After the end of the Civil War, the two clubs engaged in a multi-year battle for supremacy in St. Louis and for the state championship of Missouri. This struggle was marked by fiercely balanced competition on the field and by the class differences between the club members off of it.

Edmund Tobias describes the Union Club as being among "the very first of regularly formed clubs in St. Louis" and states that the club was founded in 1859, going so far as to list several match games that the club played that year against the Lone Star, Excelsior, and Empire clubs.[2] However, the first documented match game in St. Louis did not take place until July of 1860, and the best available evidence suggests that the Cyclones were the first organized baseball club in St. Louis.[3]

While it is certainly possible that the Union Club organized in 1859, other available evidence suggests that the club was founded after April of 1860. In *The National Game*, Al Spink explicitly states that the Empire Club was founded on April 16, 1860, and that the Union Club was only organized after that.[4] Most likely, the statement by Tobias that the Union Club was playing match games in 1859 is a simple error, and the club was founded in the spring of 1860 and began playing matches that year. Regardless of whether the club organized in 1859 or 1860, the Union Club was certainly active before the outbreak of the Civil War, playing games at the Ham Street Grounds and at Lafayette Park, and is one of ten antebellum clubs known to have existed in St. Louis.

The first documented reference to the Union Club and the first record of a match game involving the club appears in the October 9, 1860, issue of the *St. Louis Daily Bulletin*. On October 8, the Union Club played the Lone Star Club in "one of those charming contests for athletic superiority ... upon the grounds of the [Empire Club].... The day was exceedingly fine, and the play drew a large number of spectators, who appeared to enjoy the sport almost as much as those directly engaged in it. The match was contested with much spirit." The Unions won the match 41 to 23.

The antebellum Union Club was founded by a group of teenage students. Tobias notes that the club was "composed of high school pupils"[5] but it's more likely that the young men who formed the club were students at Washington University and St. Louis University. Not only did numerous club members attend both universities, but several members of the club were also related to the founders of Washington University. The members of the antebellum Union Club were all old enough to have been attending a 19th century university, and the idea that they were high school students is probably an anachronism. These members included sixteen-year-old Asa Smith, club president; fifteen-year-old Robert Niggeman, vice-president; sixteen-year-old James Freeman, secretary; seventeen-year-old Edward Finney, treasurer; and seventeen-year-old William Greenleaf.

Like most clubs in St. Louis, the Union did not survive the outbreak of the Civil War. However, one of the things that make the club unique is that immediately after the war ended, Smith, Greenleaf, and Freeman reorganized the Union, and by 1866 the club was challenging the Empires for the baseball supremacy of St. Louis. In both 1867 and 1868, the club won their season series against the Empire Club and thereby the championship of St. Louis and Missouri. The Union was the only club during the pioneer era that was able to wrest the championship from the Empire Club.

The true significance of the Union Club, however, lies not in their success on the playing field but rather in the influence that the club and its president, Asa Smith, had in shaping the game in St. Louis. Smith in many ways was a visionary who recognized the trends that had emerged on the national baseball scene and sought to change the game in St. Louis so that it reflected those trends.

As a result of Smith's vision, in 1867 the Union became the first St. Louis club to join the National Association of Base Ball Players, and that same year, Smith began pushing the idea of a Missouri state baseball association. On April 22, 1868, the Missouri State Association of Base Ball Clubs was formed with Asa Smith as its first president and fellow Union Club member Henry Carr as vice-president.

The Union Club, under Smith, was also in the vanguard in establishing permanent baseball grounds in St. Louis. In the spring of 1867, the club began playing on grounds opposite

Saint Alphonsus Liguori Rock Church on Grand Avenue. The Union Grounds, as it was known, was the first enclosed baseball park in St. Louis and the first that charged admission. On July 22, 1867, the Unions entertained the Nationals of Washington at their new home, and not only did the Nationals defeat the Unions by a score of 113–26, but they also disparaged the new grounds, referring to them as inadequate. As a result of this assessment from the Nationals, the Unions began looking for a new home in 1868 and entered into an agreement with the Empire Club that resulted in the building of the Grand Avenue Base Ball Grounds. The first game at the new ballpark, where baseball would be played for the next century, was an exhibition between the first and second nines of the Union Club.

As the first club in St. Louis to play in an enclosed ballpark and the first to charge admission to its games, it is rather likely that the Union Club was also the first baseball club in St. Louis to compensate its players. While there is no direct evidence to indicate this and there are many sources that speak to the amateur purity of the club, the relationship between the charging of admission to enclosed grounds and the payment of players has been noted by 19th century baseball historians. Some form of compensation for members of the Union Club's nine would fit with the idea of Smith's adapting to national patterns as well as his goal "to advance his club to the foremost and to maintain that position."[6]

All of these activities can be seen as an attempt by Smith to place the Union Club in a position to compete nationally. Before 1867 (with a couple of notable exceptions), baseball in St. Louis was a local affair and a competition between the home clubs. But upon conquering the clubs in St. Louis, Smith set his sights on the elite clubs of the nation and began corresponding with Eastern clubs in an attempt to arrange matches with them. Between 1867 and 1870, the Union Club would play matches against the Nationals of Washington, the Athletics of Philadelphia, the Atlantics of Brooklyn, the Buckeyes of Cincinnati, the Union Club of Morrisania, the Excelsiors of Chicago, the Southerns of New Orleans, the Forest City Club of Rockford, Illinois, the Red Stockings of Cincinnati, and others. However, this attempt to compete nationally was a dismal failure as the Union Club of St. Louis was not only unable to win a game but was generally uncompetitive against elite competition. This failure would have severe consequences for the Union Club specifically and the popularity of baseball in St. Louis generally.

One of the more interesting aspects of the Union Club was the makeup of its membership. Collectively described as "made up of the silk stocking element"[7] or being "of wealthy families,"[8] there were certainly members of the club who came from some of the more prominent families of St. Louis. In the club were several members of the Laclede-Chouteau family who had established the city of St. Louis in 1764 as well as members of the prominent Lucas family. These two families were the largest landowners in St. Louis during the 19th century. Several other members of the club were from families that had political connections in Washington. Alton, Illinois, is named after the father of one of the club members. Clearly, the membership of the Union Club was dominated by what passed for an aristocracy in St. Louis.

At the same time, however, there were also members of the club who did not belong to the St. Louis elite. Several members of the club worked as clerks for the city or as merchants. There also were several newspapermen in the club. So while there is a strong "silk stocking element" to the Union Club, the membership was not homogeneous.

It is noteworthy that many of the sons of the St. Louis elite embraced the game and were members of one of the most prominent baseball clubs in the city. This certainly speaks to the general popularity of the game in the 1860s. It may also be one of the factors in the acceptance and popularity of the game in St. Louis. The acceptance of the game by the elites of a city as socially stratified as St. Louis certainly had an impact on how the game was viewed by the masses. This embrace of the game by the St. Louis elite would also have an impact on the future of the game in the city as several prominent members of the Union Club, as well as the Lucas family, would be involved in the establishment of the Brown Stockings in 1875.

The class distinction that is noted in the membership of the Union Club helped to fuel the rivalry with the Empire Club. Tobias noted a "very jealous feeling"[9] that existed between the clubs and was due in large part to the differences in class between some of the members of the clubs. The Unions, Tobias wrote, "being mostly of wealthy families, had plenty of time and facilities to practice every day if they so desired."[10] The Empire Club, to which Tobias had belonged, was made up of members who had to work for a living. He insinuates that this distinction had a great deal to do with the success of the Union Club in 1867 and 1868.

Despite the best laid plans of Asa Smith, the Union Club was never able to compete on a national level and quickly lost its position as the championship club of St. Louis. In 1869 and 1870, the club lost the season series, and the championship, to the rival Empire Club. Coupled with the severe defeats that the club had suffered at the hands of nationally elite clubs, the Unions' interest in baseball began to ebb, and they did not field a team in 1871.

Several explanations for this exist. The most likely scenario is that, after Asa Smith decided to retire from active play in 1870, the baseball club was unable to survive the loss of their founder and leader. *The New York Times* reported that the club disbanded because "its social status is too high for Sunday playing, which is in vogue in St. Louis."[11] However, this is unlikely because St. Louis's unique cultural heritage had never produced a stigma against Sunday baseball. The *Times* is certainly wrong in stating that the club itself had disbanded, as is evident by the fact that they had annual elections for officers between 1871 and 1874. Tobias, in noting the demise of the Union Club as a baseball entity in 1871, simply states that the "arrangement of its playing nine was deferred until quite late in the season."[12] The Union had lost several of its best players to other clubs, and several others were away at college, making it difficult to put together a team.

Efforts by the club over the next several years to field a nine met with little success. A final attempt by the Union Club to put together a team was made in 1874, but this was essentially ended by the death of Asa Smith in July of that year.

Club Members

One of the two most popular baseball clubs in St. Louis in the postbellum period, the Union Club had a large membership roster. On a list of active members, dated January 1, 1869, there are seventy names and, in total, almost two hundred former members of the club have been identified. However, the vast majority of those identified as Union Club members were non-playing and honorary members. In the following biographical sketches, the emphasis — with one notable exception — will be on those who have been identified as players for or officers of the club.

Shepard Barclay: A lawyer, jurist, and Chief Justice of the Missouri Supreme Court, Barclay was born on November 3, 1847. A member of the St. Louis University baseball club, he graduated in 1867 and received his law degree from the University of Virginia in 1869. After studying law at the University of Berlin, Barclay returned to St. Louis in 1872 and set up his practice.

In 1882, Barclay was elected as a judge to the circuit court in St. Louis and in 1888 he won election to the Missouri Supreme Court. Barclay was named the Chief Justice of the Missouri Supreme Court in 1897 and resigned that position the next year, returning to St. Louis to practice law as a partner in the firm of Barclay, Fauntleroy, & Cullen. In 1901, he returned to the bench after being appointed to the St. Louis Court of Appeals and served until 1903, once again returning to private practice.

Barclay, who played center field for the Union Club, passed away in St. Louis on November 17, 1925.

Henry Berning: Berning, who played first base and right field for the Union, was born in 1849. The son of a bricklayer, he was involved in the banking business, providing bonds to the city of St. Louis for the building of sewers. Described as a prominent businessman, Berning also was involved in the city's Democratic Party machine as an election supervisor.

C. Orrick Bishop: Campbell Orrick Bishop, a prominent lawyer and judge in St. Louis, was an officer of the Union Base Ball Club as well as a member of the board of directors of the 1875 Brown Stockings.

Bishop was born in Union, Missouri, on December 28, 1842, and graduated from St. Louis Central High School in 1858. After attending Westminster College in Fulton, Missouri, he went to law school in Louisville, Kentucky, graduating and being admitted to the bar in 1867.

A partner in the Bishop & Rollins law firm in St. Louis, Bishop also served as assistant circuit attorney from 1883 to 1897 and again from 1901 to 1905. A close associate of Missouri Governor Joseph Folk, he was named to the circuit court bench in March of 1905 and served as a judge until 1907. The highlight of his public career was his involvement with Folk in uncovering the 1902–1904 "Boodle Scandal," helping to ferret out corruption among the political and business class in Missouri. Ironically, one of those caught up in the scandal was fellow Union Club member Charles Hunt Turner.

Bishop, who according to W.E. Kelsoe "used to play [baseball] a little,"[13] served as the secretary of the Union Club in the early 1870s, and Kelsoe also mentions that he was the last president of the club. In 1875, he was a member of the board of directors of the newly formed Brown Stockings (along with, again, Charles Turner) and, spending a month in the East, signed Dickey Pearce, Lip Pike, Herman Dehlman, and Jack Chapman for the club.

Bishop was also involved in the governing of the National Association in 1875 and the organization of the National League in late 1875 and 1876. When William Hulbert was trying to organize the League, according to Harold Seymour, "he traveled to St. Louis ... to confer with Charles Fowle ... and Campbell Orrick Bishop, an attorney who had played with the St. Louis Unions in the 1860s and then became Vice President of the Association and a member of its Judiciary Committee. Bishop drew up a constitution for a new league based upon a draft submitted to him by Hulbert."[14]

A lifelong bachelor, Bishop died on August 26, 1929.

Joseph Cabanne: Joseph Charless Cabanne, the founder of the St. Louis Dairy Company and a member of the prominent Laclede/Chouteau family, was born in St. Louis on October 16, 1846. A graduate of the Christian Brothers Academy, Cabanne studied at colleges in the East, most notably Flushing (New York) Institute, before returning to St. Louis to start his business career.

Upon the advice of an uncle, Cabanne founded the Mont Cabanne Dairy in 1868 on the family farm in what is now Forest Park, and in 1882 he established the St. Louis Dairy Company. An innovative businessman, Cabanne was the first to introduce covered milk wagons, a creamery, the delivery of milk in bottles, and the selling of whole milk at a cheaper price than skim milk in St. Louis.

An active member of the community, Cabanne was the first president of the Civics League. He was also a member of the Citizens' Industrial Association, the Missouri Athletic Club, the Amateur Athletic Club and, of course, the Union Base Ball Club of St. Louis, for whom he played first base, third base, shortstop, and both corner outfield spots.

On March 17, 1922, Cabanne, after being ill with pneumonia for several weeks, cut his throat with a straight razor and died.

Henry Carr: Henry Chills Carr, an infielder for the Union Club, was born in 1849 and was a bookkeeper for the Simmons Hardware Co., which was owned by Union Club member E. C. Simmons. Carr was related by marriage to fellow club member Joseph Cabanne and the Laclede-Chouteau family. He died in 1904.

John Dillon: John A. Dillon was born on October 29, 1843, in St. Louis. A newspaperman, Dillon worked as an editor for the *St. Louis Globe-Democrat* and was the founder of the *St. Louis Evening Post*. On January 25, 1865, he married Blanche Valle, a member of the Laclede-Chouteau family. Dillon died in St. Louis on October 17, 1902.

William Duncan: Duncan, who played center field for the Union Club, was born in Birkenhead, England, on August 20, 1845, and came to St. Louis with his family at a young age. A self-made man, Duncan began his career as a clerk with the Ohio & Mississippi Railroad in 1863 and, by 1893, rose to become the vice-president of the Baltimore & Ohio Railroad. He resigned this position in 1896 to start the Charter Oak Stone and Range Company. Duncan died on April 4, 1921. His brother Robert was an infielder with the Union Club.

Archibald Easton: Archibald G. Eason was born on November 21, 1851, and played both in the infield and outfield for the Union Club. He was the grandson of Rufus Easton, a United States Congressman and the founder of the city of Alton, Illinois, and the son of Alton Easton, a West Point graduate and prominent businessman in St. Louis.

William Edgar: William Boyce Edgar, who served as an officer with the Union Club, was born on November 26, 1843. A businessman involved in metal manufacturing, Edgar died in St. Louis on March 7, 1928.

Edward Finney: Edward Forsyth Finney, born in St. Louis on March 30, 1843, was the first secretary of the Union Club. A clerk at the St. Louis City Hall who played first base for the club, he died January 10, 1925. Finney was also a member of the Olympic Club of St. Louis.

William Greenleaf: William Eugene Greenleaf played every position except catcher and shortstop and also served as an officer with the Union club. Greenleaf, who was born in 1844, was the cousin of William Greenleaf Eliot, the co-founder and chancellor of Washington University, and poet T.S. Eliot.

Rufus Lackland: A catcher and infielder with the Union Club, Rufus James Lackland, Jr., was born in 1845. His father was the president of Boatman's Bank and the president of the board of directors of the St. Louis chamber of commerce and his step-mother was the sister of William Greenleaf Eliot, the co-founder and chancellor of Washington University. Lackland ran a wholesale sugar manufacturing company and died in St. Louis on June 15, 1901.

Robert Lucas: A member of the prominent Lucas family of St. Louis, Robert Lucas caught, pitched, and played the outfield for the Union Club. The grandson of J.B.C. Lucas and son of James H. Lucas, he was an attorney and, like many members of his family, involved in the real estate business. His older brother, J.B.C., would become the president of the Brown Stockings of St. Louis in 1875, and his younger brother, Henry, would launch the St. Louis Maroons and the Union Association in 1884. His cousin Charles Lucas was also a member of the Union Club. Robert Lucas died on May 18, 1922.

Wayman McCreery: A first baseman, Wayman Crow McCreery was born in 1851 and was the grandson of Wayman Crow, a prominent St. Louis businessman and politician who, along with William Greenleaf Eliot, was the co-founder of Washington University. McCreery, who was involved in the real estate business, was related to the Laclede-Chouteau family and several of his fellow club members through his marriage to Mary Louise Carr. His daughter, Marie, was the St. Louis Veiled Prophet Queen in 1896, which speaks to his family's high social standing in the city.

McCreery was a man of many talents. He was the musical director of Christ Church Cathedral in St. Louis for twenty-five years and a leader of an amateur theater club. He wrote an opera, *L'Afrique*, which was performed in New York and was a champion billiards player. McCreery was also remembered as an outstanding athlete. Augustus Thomas wrote that "[few] men are so physically and intellectually equipped as he was. There was nothing that an athlete could do with his body that in a notable degree Wayman McCreery could not do. He was boxer, wrestler, fencer, runner, and swimmer, and all-round athlete. In addition to these he was a graceful dancer."[15]

McCreery died in St. Louis in 1901.

Edward Meacham: Edward C. Meacham played second and third base for the Union Club and served as field captain in 1867. He was born in 1845 and died in St. Louis on March 26, 1895. Meacham was also a member of the Olympic Club of St. Louis.

Robert Niggeman: Niggeman was born in Prussia in 1845 and immigrated to St. Louis with his parents in the 1850s. The first vice-president of the Union Club and a third baseman, Niggeman worked as a shoemaker and merchant. He died in St. Louis on December 16, 1890.

William Sherman: William Tecumseh Sherman, the Commanding General of the United States Army, moved his headquarters to St. Louis in 1874. While he lived in the city, Sherman enjoyed going to baseball games with his friend Colonel Alton Easton, the father of Union Club member Archibald Easton. Taking note of this, club secretary Orrick Bishop had the Union elect General Sherman as an honorary member. Sherman sent the club a letter thanking them for the honor that they had conferred upon him.

Edward Simmons: Edward C. Simmons was born in Frederick, Maryland, on September 21, 1839, and moved to St. Louis with his family as a child. As president of the

Simmons Hardware Company, "he made St. Louis the greatest hardware centre on earth...."[16]

In 1854, Simmons, at the age of 16, was working for Child, Pratt, & Co., the largest wholesale hardware store in St. Louis at the time. By 1860, according to Kennedy's St. Louis city directory, he was working for Wilson, Levering, & Waters, the company that would become the Simmons Hardware Company.

Jeremiah Fruin stated that Simmons, who played center field for the Union Club, was its first captain but "he was so overbearing and arbitrary that his players fell out with him and he went in another direction and started a team of his own."[17] However, there is no evidence that Simmons played with the Unions prior to 1865, and Tobias names him as a member of the antebellum Commercial Base Ball Club of St. Louis.[18]

Simmons died on April 18, 1920.

Asa Smith: The founder, longtime president, and "leading spirit"[19] of the Union Club, Asa W. Smith was born in 1844. A "young man of many bright and endearing traits ... it was his personal magnetism that gathered into the Union Club that galaxy of young athletes whose names adorned its role of membership."[20] Smith was described as "a genial and accomplished gentleman whose pleasant disposition, agreeable manner and kindly heart endeared him to all who were favored with his friendship."[21]

A shortstop, third baseman, and outfielder, Smith was a visionary leader who "devised plans to advance his club to the foremost and to maintain that position being animated mainly by that true spirit of sportsman and athlete love of the game...."[22] Smith's plan was to place the Union Club in a position to compete nationally by adapting St. Louis baseball to the national trends in the game. His plan included improving the baseball grounds in St. Louis, building the first enclosed grounds in the city, charging for admission, arranging games against elite competition, building a state baseball association, joining the National Association of Base Ball Players, and most likely compensating players. Although Smith failed in his goal of turning the Union Club into a national power, he did succeed in bringing St. Louis into the national baseball mainstream. When Smith reorganized the Union Club in 1866, St. Louis was a baseball backwater. A year after his death, the city had two professional teams competing in the National Association and was a baseball hotbed. No one in the history of baseball in St. Louis had a more profound impact on the game than Asa Smith.

Little is known about Smith's life outside of baseball. His father, Sol Smith, was a successful attorney in St. Louis. Smith's brother Thaddeus, who was also a member of the Union Club, worked as a clerk and bookkeeper. Another brother was an actor. Asa Smith, himself, listed his occupation in the 1870 census as bank clerk and later founded a successful banking house. He was described as a "fine violinist and an excellent amateur actor."[23] But his primary activity, before his retirement as a player in 1870, was the management of the Union Base Ball Club.

In the summer of 1874, as the Union Club struggled to put together a nine and revive its baseball fortunes, Smith visited his family's vacation home in Biddeford, Maine. On the morning of July 31, Smith went swimming at Biddeford Pool "and ventured too far or was drawn out by a hidden reflux of the tide ... and after a gallant struggle for life was compelled to succumb before the [lifeboat] could be gotten to him.... The dispatches, which are very meager and unsatisfactory, say that every effort was made to save him, but without avail. Whether he was taken with cramp or drawn out by the undertow, or died from exhaustion, is a matter of conjecture; but most likely the latter, as the lifeboat seems to have been brought into requisition and strong efforts made to rescue him."[24]

The news of Smith's death was received by Sol Smith, Jr., in St. Louis on August 1, 1874. A telegram was sent from Maine that read: "Your brother Asa was drowned this morning, while bathing. Every effort was made with a lifeboat to save him. Your mother desires you to come here at once."[25] Tobias wrote that the "sad and unexpected death of Asa W. Smith created a profound feeling of regret throughout the city and in no circle was it more keenly felt and deplored than amongst the base ball fraternity by whom he was respected and beloved to an unusual degree."[26] A match between the Union Club and the Westerns of Keokuk was cancelled and a memorial "was held ... by representatives of the Base Ball Brotherhood with whom [Smith] had long borne a prominent part. The following clubs were represented: Union, Empire, National, Turner, Rowena, Red Stockings, Benton, Niagara, Rival, Artisan and Western of Keokuk."[27]

Julius Smith: Julius H. Smith, Jr., was a third baseman with the Unions. Born in Dayton, Ohio, on July 20, 1844, Smith worked as a clerk with the St. Louis sewer department. He died on March 24, 1920. There is no known family relationship between Julius Smith and Asa and Thaddeus Smith.

Thaddeus Smith: The older brother of Asa Smith, Thaddeus Smith was born in 1840 and served as an officer with the Union Club. A member of the 13th Regiment, Missouri Cavalry during the Civil War, after the war Smith worked as a clerk and bookkeeper. He died in St. Louis in August of 1913.

Henry Stansbury: Stansbury was born in St. Louis on November 30, 1846, and played shortstop, third base, and left field for the Union. A clerk for the city of St. Louis, he died on February 3, 1917.

William Steigers: William Colbert Steigers was a prominent St. Louis newspaperman and one of the organizers of the 1875 Brown Stockings, serving as vice-president of their board of directors.

Steigers was born in St. Louis on September 15, 1847, and educated at the Wyman School and Christian Brothers College. He enlisted with the 8th Missouri Volunteers on September 15, 1862, his fifteenth birthday, and fought in numerous battles, including the siege of Vicksburg. On July 5, 1863, a day after the fall of Vicksburg, he became seriously ill while traveling from Vicksburg to Jacksonville, Tennessee, and spent three months in a hospital. Steigers was mustered out of the army on October 22, 1863, due to the illness and returned to St. Louis.

In April of 1864, Steigers began his career in the newspaper business with the *St. Louis Evening Dispatch* as a collector before rising to head the advertising department. In 1872, he became the advertising manager of the *St. Louis Times* before returning to the *Dispatch* in 1874. In December of 1878, the *Post* and the *Dispatch* merged to form the *St. Louis Post-Dispatch* with Steigers running the advertising department. A close associate of Joseph Pulitzer, Steigers was named vice-president and business manager of the *Post* in 1897.

Steigers died on May 25, 1923.

Charles Turner: Charles Hunt Turner was a catcher, pitcher, infielder, and officer with the Union Club and was involved in the founding of the Brown Stockings in 1875.

Born in 1850, Charles Turner was one of the more prominent citizens of St. Louis in the late 19th century. Not only was he a member of the wealthy Lucas family, he also married into another prominent family. His wife Margaret was the daughter of Stephen Barlow, the cousin of Stephen Douglas and a wealthy politician and railroad magnate in St. Louis. Turner himself was the president of the Suburban Railway Company, which owned the St. Louis street car system, and the Commonwealth Trust Company. He was described by Lincoln Steffens in "Tweed Days in St. Louis" as a millionaire and served on the St. Louis Board of Police Commissioners in the 1880s. Turner also was a member of the Board of Directors of the Louisiana Purchase Exposition Company, which raised the money to put on the 1904 World's Fair in St. Louis.

In 1902, Steffens exposed the extent of Turner's influence in what became known as the Boodle Scandal. Steffen showed that Turner was a member of a cabal that bribed city aldermen and state legislators in an attempt to get legislation passed that was favorable to their business interests. Witnesses testified before a grand jury that Turner had paid over $144,000 in bribes in an attempt to secure legislation that would double the value of the Suburban Railway Company, which Turner was looking to sell. The case was tied up in court for several years and Turner died in 1906 before facing the legal consequences of his actions.

The USS *Turner Joy*, a destroyer that was involved in the Gulf of Tonkin incident in 1964 and served the nation with distinction until it was decommissioned in 1982, was named after Charles Turner's grandson, Admiral Charles Turner Joy.

Eugene Wolff: Eugene Ulrice Wolff was born on April 14, 1848, and played second base, shortstop, and center field for the Unions. The brother of fellow Union Club member and third baseman Wally Wolff, he worked for the *St. Louis Globe-Democrat* and died on February 3, 1907. The Wolff brothers were members of the antebellum Olympic Base Ball Club of St. Louis before joining the Unions.

Other known playing members of the Union Club include Henry Berning, Robert Duncan, William Duncan, F. W. Kennon, Thomas McCorkell, E.W. Mudge, H.C. Pearce, Robert P. Renick (also an officer), George Arthur Strong and William A. Yore. Other known officers of the club include James P. Freeman, F.C. Dillon, William Keiselhorst, Joseph P. Carr, and Joseph H. Holliday.

Notes

1. Spink, *The National Game*.
2. Tobias, October 26, 1895.
3. *Missouri Democrat*, July 1860.
4. Spink, *The National Game*.
5. *Ibid*.
6. Tobias, November 23, 1895.
7. Spink, *The National Game*.
8. Tobias letter, October 26, 1895.
9. *Ibid*.
10. *Ibid*.
11. *The New York Times*, November 29, 1870.
12. Tobias, December 28, 1895.
13. W.A. Kelsoe, *St. Louis Reference Record: A Newspaper Man's Motion-Picture of the City* (St. Louis, 1927).
14. Harold Seymour, *Baseball: The Early Years* (New York: Oxford University Press, 1960).
15. August Thomas, *A Print of My Remembrance* (New York: C. Scribner's Sons, 1922).
16. Bertie Charles Forbes, *Men Who Are Making America* (New York: B.C. Forbes, 1917).
17. Spink, *The National Game*.
18. Tobias, November 2, 1895.
19. Tobias, November 23, 1895.
20. Tobias, November 16, 1895.
21. Tobias, January 25, 1896.
22. Tobias, November 23, 1895.
23. *The Milwaukee Sentinel*, August 3, 1874.
24. *Ibid*.
25. *Ibid*.
26. Tobias, January 25, 1896.
27. *Ibid*.

❖ *Empires* (Jeffrey Kittel) ❖

Club History

The largest and most successful club in St. Louis during the pioneer era, the Empire Base Ball Club, often styled the "Champions of the West," was founded in the antebellum period and survived the Civil War to dominate baseball in St. Louis, winning the championship of Missouri eight times in the decade following the war. Their success on the diamond and the excitement generated by their championship series with rivals such as the Union Club and the Red Stockings helped to create the conditions that allowed St. Louis to grow and flourish as a baseball city. By the end of their run as St. Louis's first great baseball team, the city had successfully entered professional clubs in the National Association and the National League, and there were almost two hundred amateur clubs playing baseball in St. Louis. The interest and support for baseball that existed in the city was largely due to the efforts and success of the Empire Club.

In contrast to the Union Club, whose members were sons of some of the wealthiest families in St. Louis, the Empire Club was generally made up of members of St. Louis's working class. Within the membership was a large component of men who made their living in the construction business, as laborers, masons, bricklayers, painters, and roofers. The club was large enough that its membership contained men who achieved prominence in business and the law, but most of the club members were largely anonymous men who made their living as cigar makers, railroad workers, brass finishers, and bar keepers. It was, as Al Spink wrote, a club of "mechanics and tradesmen,"[1] and the club's longtime field captain, Jeremiah Fruin, described the members as "a rough and ready set."[2] Edmund Tobias, another member of the club, stated that "all of its members ... were tough, hardy men."[3]

One of the more interesting things about the Empire Club is the ties that its membership had to the St. Louis Fire Department (StLFD). While there is some evidence to suggest that the fire department was represented in the club membership from its founding, it was not until after the Civil War that the leadership of the StLFD took control of the club. This quickly led to a club membership that was heavy with firemen and men who played ancillary roles in the operation of the fire department. Although it does appear that jobs with the StLFD were used as a form of compensation for some playing members, contemporary newspaper accounts describe playing members of the club actually fighting fires in St. Louis. The fact that several club members were injured and at least two were killed while fighting fires supports the idea that, for the most part, these members were firemen who played baseball rather than baseball players who were being compensated with make-work jobs at the fire department.

These firemen and tradesmen found a social outlet in the Empire Club that, while focused on the diamond, certainly extended beyond it. The club was large enough to field at least three nines, "matches between these being of frequent occurence."[4] A "finely furnished hall at the corner of Sixth and Morgan streets"[5] was available to the members for meetings and banquets. For those members who were not particularly good baseball players, muffin games were regularly scheduled. The Empire Club's anniversary game, held every year in April, was one such game, pitting the married members against the bachelors. Another annual social event was a ball, held during the winter, for the members and their wives or lady-friends.

Equally important from an economic standpoint was the opportunity the club offered for members to socialize among members of their own and ancillary professions. One of the largest construction companies in the United States was formed by members of the Empire Club, and with numerous members in the construction business, the opportunities for club members to find work were numerous. Many members also found work with the StLFD, either as firemen, engineers, teamsters, or mechanics, and those already employed by the department found success and promotion. The Empire Club clearly aided the economic success of many of its members.

The renown gained by the club, however, was largely due to their success on the diamond. Winning eight of the ten state championships following the Civil War, the Empire Club was known as the "Champions of the West" and was involved in almost every significant baseball game played by a St. Louis club prior to 1875. They were involved in some of the earliest match games in the city and were the first St. Louis club to travel outside the city for matches. The club, according to numerous sources, played in the first fly ball match west of the Alleghenies in 1865 and dominated Midwestern amateur clubs during the era. By the late 1860s, the club was hosting some of the more prominent Eastern baseball clubs, including the Nationals of Washington and the Red Stockings of Cincinnati among others. The Empire Club's greatest success, of course, was among its peers in St. Louis. From 1865 to 1875, the club lost only two championship series and had a stretch of eight years where it did not lose a series to a St. Louis club.

On April 16, 1860, according to Al Spink, "the Empire Baseball Club was organized under a regular set of rules and by-laws ... at a meeting held in the office of Justice [Charles] Hequemberg."[6] "The origin of the Empire Club," Tobias wrote, "was mainly due to Joseph Hallenbeck, a deputy under Constable Dan Manning, who acted as such for both Justices Ed A. Allen and Peter W. Johnstone. Hallenbeck was a New Yorker, and had played with the old Knickerbocker Club before his arrival in St. Louis, and he was assisted by L.P. Fuller in forming the club."[7] While there is no evidence and it is unlikely that Hallenbeck ever was a member of the Knickerbocker Club, Spink noted that the new club did adopt the constitution and by-laws of their famous predecessors. Among those at the first meeting of the club were Bernard Higgins, John O'Connell, John Walton, Daniel Coyle, Patrick Cooney, Herman Barklage, J.C. Adams, James Utley, Patrick Tobin, Jacob Ruppenthal, James Fitzgerald, and William Henley. Although most of the members had a working-class background, there is little evidence suggesting what may have brought these men together to form a baseball club other than a mention in *The Book of St. Louisans* that O'Connell and Tobin were childhood friends.

In general, the original membership of the Empire Club was relatively diverse when compared to the other antebellum clubs in St. Louis. The Morning Star Club was made up of young men who lived in the Carr Park neighborhood and worked in the dry goods business. The Cyclone Club members had family and business ties. The Union Club members were young students. The original membership of the Empire Club can not be summed up so neatly, and this may speak to the fact that these members did not, for various reasons, fit the profile of the kind of members that the other clubs were looking for. As the baseball fever spread in St. Louis, members of the city's working class felt the need for a club of their own.

Regardless of why it was formed, the club certainly found early success on the diamond. Of the seven match games the Empire Club played prior to the outbreak of the Civil War for which there is a record, the club won five and lost two. The split of four games with the Union Club was a precursor to the evenly matched rivalry between the clubs in the post-war era.

The war years themselves were an interesting period in the history of the club. One of only two antebellum clubs, along with the Commercials, to survive the outbreak of the war, the Empire Club was the only St. Louis baseball club to field a nine every season during the Civil War. How active the club was is not clear, but it is known that they held annual elections for officers and continued to bring in new members, including Jeremiah Fruin and Henry Clay Sexton, two of the most influential members the club ever had. Although we may not know exactly how often the Empires played, it's likely that their activity during the war years, along with the leadership of Fruin, gave the club a competitive advantage over new and reorganized St. Louis clubs in the postbellum era.

Of the seven known baseball games that took place in St. Louis during the Civil War for which contemporary documentation currently exists, five are intramural matches played by the Empire Club. More specifically, these were matches held to celebrate the anniversary of the founding of the club. Normally held around April 16, the matches pitted the married club members against the single members. The Empire Club's annual anniversary game became a St. Louis baseball tradition that would continue into the late 1870s, but the first few games illustrated the difficulties that the club experienced in a city divided by civil war and, at times, living under martial law.

The first anniversary game of the Empire Club, and the first game in St. Louis after the outbreak of the war, was played on April 16, 1861, three days after the fall of Fort Sumter. The game was forcibly broken up by the pro–Union St. Louis Home Guard who believed that the blue and gold flag the club was flying above their refreshment and changing tent was a "Secesh banner."[8] Their fifth anniversary game was scheduled to take place on April 19, 1865, but was postponed a week after the assassination of Abraham Lincoln. The game was finally played on April 26, the same day that Confederate General Joe Johnston surrendered to Union forces. In many ways, the Empire Club's anniversary games marked the beginning and the end of the Civil War in St. Louis.

After the Civil War, the Empires generally remained a club whose members were involved in working class professions. Although the club included such men as William V.N. Bay, a Missouri state legislator, a United States Congressman, and Justice on the Missouri State Supreme Court, speaking broadly, one can say that the membership of the Empire Club was largely composed of two groups: those employed in the construction business and those affiliated with the St. Louis Fire Department.

Several of the founding members of the Empire Club, such as Henley, Fitzgerald, O'Connell, and Tobin, were involved in construction-related businesses and the club included as members men like Jeremiah Fruin, who founded some of the largest construction-related companies in St. Louis. One explanation for the large number of club members involved in the construction business is that construction was a growth industry in St. Louis at the time and employed a great number of young men. The city was the fourth largest in the nation in 1870, and its population had jumped from 77,000 in 1850 to over 300,000 just twenty years later. Business — and construction — was booming. "Tough, hardy men"[9] who were successful in the construction business were also just the type of young men a baseball club would look for to form a successful nine.

The other large group that composed the Empire Club's membership, one even larger and more prominent than those in the construction business, was made up of men affiliated with the St. Louis Fire Department. James Utley, at the first meeting of the club in 1860, was listed in the 1860 St. Louis city directory as a fireman and may have been responsible for bringing other firemen, such as William Thorn and John Reynolds, into the club prior to the end of the Civil War.

But this group really came to the fore near the end of the war after Henry Clay Sexton, the first chief of the StLFD, was elected club president in 1864. The election of Sexton as club president certainly suggests that the fire department had a large and influential presence in the club prior to 1864, but as the war ended and the club expanded, so did the number of members who were affiliated with the StLFD. The club membership would come to include two men who served as chief of the StLFD, three men who were assistant chiefs, at least thirteen men who were firemen or engineers, and several others who served the department in ancillary roles such as telegraph operator or teamster.

The St. Louis Fire Department developed contemporaneously with baseball in the city. An all-paid fire department was founded in St. Louis on September 14, 1857, less than two years before the founding of the Cyclone Club. By 1910, the department had grown to fifty-one steam engine companies and seventeen hook and ladder companies. Like the construction business, the StLFD expanded rapidly in the post–Civil War era and employed a great number of young men who were exactly the kind of people who could help a baseball club.

One question that must be addressed is whether or not the Empire Club was using their ties to the StLFD to compensate their players. There is at least one prominent case in which this does appear to be the situation. In 1869, Tom Oran jumped from the Union Club to the rival Empires and shortly thereafter was employed by the StLFD. While there were other members of the club who would come to find work with the fire department, Oran's situation seems like a *quid pro quo* and a form of compensation.

Although we don't know if other members of the Empire's first nine were given jobs with the fire department specifically because of their playing abilities, the *St. Louis Globe-Democrat* in 1881 mentioned a form of special treatment received by those who were employed by the StLFD. Specifically reporting on a proposed winter trip by the Brown Stockings to New Orleans, the question of whether or not Bill and Jack Gleason would be able to get away from their jobs with the fire department was raised. The *Globe* stated that this should not be a problem because "on other occasions Chief Sexton has let firemen go to New Orleans with ball clubs and stay there for weeks. He did this when the old Empire Club was in existence, and did it season after season."[10]

The Oran case and the report of the New Orleans trip certainly make it appear as if the StLFD was used by the Empire Club to further their baseball prospects. However, there is ample evidence to suggest that the playing members of the Empire Club who also happened to be members of the fire department were honestly employed and did more than earn their pay. Joe Schimper, who pitched for the club in 1874 and 1875, and John Shockey, an outfielder who also served as field captain in 1869, both lost their lives in the line of duty while serving with the StLFD. Adam Wirth, a mainstay of the club's first nine, the field captain in 1868 and 1872, and arguably the best St. Louis player of the era, was seriously injured while fighting a fire in 1881. Although the nature of the relationship between the StLFD and the Empire Club can be questioned, it's obvious that many members of the Empire Club served the city of St. Louis honorably as members of the fire department.

An important aspect of the club for its membership was the social components that it brought to their lives and certainly the playing of baseball was central to this. With a club membership in the early 1870s that exceeded one hundred seventy, the Empire Club was large enough to field multiple nines as well as a junior nine. While most contemporary sources focused on the first nine, the other nines not only provided the club with an avenue for player development but also allowed other members to participate in the baseball activities of the club.

Another social activity for club members was the muffin game that became an annual event on the club's calendar. The anniversary game, played between married and bachelor members, was an important event that celebrated the club's founding. Edmund Tobias was an annual participant in the anniversary game and chronicled the outcome, and his own play, with a tone of amusement that properly captures the spirit of the game. In this same spirit was a game played in 1873 between the first nine and a nine composed of "poor decrepit Vets"[11]—former playing members of the club. Tobias notes that he took the field for the old-timers "in the original uniform of the club having preserved it since his retirement from the nine."[12] Like the anniversary games, this old-timers game was celebratory in nature, and the club took the opportunity to publicly display its banners, trophies, and championship belts. Another muffin game that Tobias mentions was one played between fat and skinny club members. So while the Empire Club's first nine was gaining the glory, the rest of the club was at least having fun on the diamond.

If one looks at the employment history of members of the Empire Club, it becomes apparent that one social function of the club was to serve as a networking facility for its members. One can argue that the club attracted men who worked for the fire department and in the construction business, but it's also true that club members were instrumental in getting work in their fields for other club members. John Barrett, David Duffy, and William Thorn are all examples of this. In 1860, Barrett was working as a tinner and "helped to organize the Empire Club."[13] By 1862, he was working with the fire department and was there for twenty years, receiving several promotions. Duffy, in 1860, was working as a bricklayer and, like Barrett, he moved on to the fire department after joining the Empire Club. William Thorn, interestingly, had the opposite experience of Duffy as he was working for the StLFD in 1860 but after joining the club found better employment as a mason. Club members were not only finding work for other members but they were also going into business together as Fruin and Swift and O'Connell and Tobin did. It also appears that several prominent promotions in the StLFD, under the management of Sexton, went to Empire Club members. So while the members of the club were, generally, not as successful as their rivals in the Union Club, it certainly appears that they were doing their best to take care of each other and using their connections within in the club to further their own careers.

The prominence of the Empire Club in the history of St. Louis baseball is, of course, owing to on-the-field success. In 1865, "having successfully demonstrated that it was cock of the home walk"[14] and after winning matches in Freeport, Illinois, and Davenport, Iowa, the club was declared "Champions of the West." Over the next five years, the Empire Club would engage in an epic struggle with the Union Club to determine the true champion of St. Louis. Playing a championship series of originally three and then later five games, the Empires would lose their title to their rivals in 1866 and 1867 before winning it back in 1868, 1869, and 1870. The contest for supremacy between the Empire and Union Clubs defined baseball in St. Louis during this era as the two evenly matched clubs brought out the best in each other. When the Union Club failed to field a nine in 1871, the rivalry ended with the two clubs having played sixteen championship matches and each club winning eight. Counting the matches played in the antebellum era, the Empire Club split its match games with the Union Club ten victories apiece.

After the demise of the Union Club, the Empire Club handily won the Missouri championship in 1871 and 1872. It was not until 1873 that another club seriously challenged the club. That year and the next, the newly formed Red Stockings seized an early lead in the championship series only to see the old champions come back to defend their title in five games. The excitement generated by the 1873 and 1874 Empire/Red Stockings contests pushed interest in baseball in St. Louis to a new level and set the stage for 1875 season, when two professional St. Louis clubs would compete for the championship in the National Association. That year, the Brown Stockings of St. Louis, by winning their season series against the White Stockings of Chicago, would claim the title of "Champions of the West," supplanting the Empires as the dominant team in St. Louis.

While the Empire Club played many memorable games, including numerous games against visiting Eastern powers, two deserve to be specifically mentioned. The first is a match game against the Morning Star Club on July 17, 1860, which was most likely the second match game ever played in St. Louis. On July 3, 1860, in advance of the match game between the Cyclone Club and the Morning Stars, the Empires passed a resolution challenging the winner of the upcoming game and also stating, if the challenge was not accepted, they were willing to play any baseball club in Missouri.[15] The Morning Star Club, of course, accepted the challenge and lost to the Empires, 41–33.

Probably the most significant game the Empire Club played was their July 4, 1865, match against the Empire Club of Freeport, Illinois. The club's match in Freeport is not only the first recorded road game by a St. Louis baseball club, but, according to both Tobias and Spink, it was also the first fly match played in the West. "No definite arrangements were made as to whether it would be 'a bound or a fly' game until the two club captains faced one another on the diamond when in reply to the question as to what it should be, Fruin promptly responded: 'Just as you please' and the answer came promptly: 'Fly it is.'"[16] It appears that the Freeport players had been practicing for a fly match, and their captain believed that he had gained an advantage over his guests, but their St. Louis namesakes, who "just doted on fly balls when they came along,"[17] won the match 27 to 20 and, upon returning to St. Louis, were treated as conquering heroes.

Although the history of the Empire Club was reasonably well chronicled, there are no references in the contemporary source material yet found regarding its demise. Tobias, who ends his series on the history of baseball in St. Louis with the 1875 season, did speak to the difficulties the club was having in the face of a new era. He wrote that it "was not until May [1875] that the club was able to definitely complete its nine and enter upon any engagements, it having been a much mooted question among the amateur clubs as to whether or not it was possible to maintain their organizations with two out and out professional teams in the city. Many amateur clubs disorganized but the Empire and a few others determined to hold fast for the season at least.... As the season advanced it was made apparent that the famous old Empire Club was in its declining days and though it struggled hard to keep up with the procession bad luck followed it through the season and with the exception of an occasional spurt recalling its former glory, its record was that of a sick old man with the grip of death in its vitals."[18]

The club did elect officers and field a nine in 1876. In 1877, the Empire Club joined a new St. Louis Amateur Association, which replaced the old Missouri State Association, but by 1881 the club was being referred to in the past tense in the *St. Louis Globe-Democrat*. The inference is, of course, that the club disbanded sometime between the end of the 1877 season and 1881. This would fit with the general pattern of baseball in St. Louis during the period.

After the 1877 season, the Brown Stockings folded due to a combination of financial losses and the repercussions of a gambling scandal. During this interregnum period, when St. Louis did not have a professional baseball club competing in a major league, there was a desperate struggle to keep a professional team alive as interest in baseball in the city was at an ebb. It is likely that the Empire Club decided to end its baseball activities during this low point in the history of baseball in St. Louis.

Club Members

The Empire Club was the largest and most popular amateur club in St. Louis during the decade following the Civil War, and they also had the longest history of any St. Louis club during the pioneer era, being in existence for twenty years. Known club members number in the hundreds; as a result, the following biographical sketches, like those for the Union Club, must focus on players from the first nine and officers of the club, with a few notable exceptions.

Herman Barklage: An original member of the club, Barklage was born in 1833. He served as the treasurer of the club for fourteen years "and a good one he was too."[19] A boot maker, Barklage's shop on Locust Street served as the club's first headquarters. An "enthusiastic if not an A 1 player,"[20] he played first base for the Empire Club.

Barklage died on March 2, 1878, of consumption and his "death caused sincere grief among the fraternity."[21]

John Barrett: Barrett was born in Canada in 1833 and moved to St. Louis when he was twenty years old, where he originally found work as a tinner. A catcher and outfielder, he served as a field captain for the Empire Club in 1863.

In 1862, Barrett began working for the St. Louis Fire Department as a pipeman. Steadily promoted, by 1867 he was the "engineer of the Old Franklin, No. 13, on Eleventh street ... and there he remained almost until the day of his death.... Outside of the department he had one favorite — base-ball. He helped to organize the Empire Club ... and remained with it until disbandment."[22]

Barrett died of pneumonia in St. Louis on February 18, 1883.

James Barron: Born in Ireland in 1834, Barron was a mainstay at shortstop for the Empire Club and was one of the cornerstones of their championship clubs. Playing with the first nine from at least 1867 through 1875, he was a member of seven championship seasons and was a field captain for the 1869 team.

A plasterer by trade, Barron died on January 1, 1890.

William Bay: William V. N. Bay, a politician and jurist, was born in New York in 1818. By 1840, he had moved to Missouri and served in the state legislature from 1844 to 1848. From 1849 to 1851, Bay was a representative in the United States Congress and served as a justice on the Missouri Supreme Court from 1862 to 1865.

He died in Eureka, Missouri, on February 10, 1894.

Frank Billon: Frank Charles Billon was born on July 17, 1844. A bookkeeper with the StLFD, he died in St. Louis on March 7, 1918.

Joe Ellick: Born in Cincinnati on April 3, 1854, Ellick was a professional baseball player who was with the R. E. Lee Club of New Orleans in 1872 when that club made a trip to St. Louis to play the Empire Club. "A year or so afterwards, I received a letter from the Empires asking me to join them."[23]

In 1875, Ellick joined the Red Stockings of St. Louis, who were trying to strengthen their club after deciding to compete in the National Association. After the Reds stopped playing championship matches in July of that year, Ellick jumped to the Eagles of Louisville, where he claimed he was "the first professional player Louisville ever had...."[24] Over the course of his professional career, Ellick played for Milwaukee and Worcester in the National League as well as three different clubs in the Union Association in 1884.

Ellick, who died on April 21, 1923, in Kansas City, also served as an umpire for the National League in 1886. He published an article in *Lippincott's Monthly Magazine* in October of that year detailing the travails and difficulties of the major league umpire.

Thomas Farmer: Born in 1841, Thomas H. Farmer was one of the owners of Farmer & McCoy, a printing firm in St. Louis. There is evidence that he may also have worked at some point for the StLFD.

Farmer died in 1916 in York, Ontario.

James Fitzgerald: Fitzgerald, one of the original members of the Empire Club, was born in Ireland in 1837. Immigrating to the United States in 1850, he was living in St. Louis and working as a painter in 1860. In 1880, Fitzgerald was working for the StLFD and living with fellow club member and fireman Adam Wirth.

Fitzgerald died in St. Louis in October of 1908.

James Fitzgibbons: A prominent St. Louis contractor, Fitzgibbons was born in Ireland on June 28, 1843, and immigrated to the United States with his family around 1848. At the age of nineteen, he moved to Hartford, Connecticut and worked as a machinist at the Phoenix Iron Works. While living in Hartford, Fitzgibbons played with the Charter Oak Club of that city. In April of 1860, he moved to St. Louis where he worked as a foreman for his uncle's construction company. Starting a general contracting company in 1873, he became one of the city's prominent businessmen as well as a leader in the Irish immigrant community.

A pitcher for the club who once threw the last four innings of a game with a gaping bleeding cut on his pitching hand, Fitzgibbons was named field captain in 1870. He died in Sidney, Ohio, on January 25, 1930. (For more details on Fitzgibbons, see the Charter Oaks of Hartford, Connecticut.)

Jeremiah Fruin: Jeremiah Fruin was one of the most influential people in the history of St. Louis baseball.

Born in County Tipperary, Ireland, on July 6, 1831, Fruin grew up in Brooklyn and played with that city's Charter Oak Club and also claimed to have played with the Atlantics and Excelsiors. While living in Brooklyn, Fruin served as an officer in New York State Militia. During the Civil War, he was a member of the Union Army, serving in the quartermaster corps.

In 1861, Fruin was transferred to St. Louis and continued his ball playing. Arriving in the city, he "quickly sought the headquarters of the Empire Club ... joined the club, [and] showed that he was a master hand at the game...."[25] As probably the most experienced baseball player in St. Louis, Fruin quickly became the second baseman for the Empire Club's first nine and its field captain.

It was under Fruin's leadership as field captain that the Empire Club developed into a championship baseball club. His significance lies in the fact that he brought first-hand knowledge of the game as it was played in New York and taught the Empire Club the lessons he had learned on the playing fields of Brooklyn. Fruin himself stated that he gave the club "a few lessons on the improved Eastern method [of play] ... [showing] the boys how to trap the ball, to make a double play and ... [how] to catch the ball by giving to it as it was thrown, with the hands low down or high up as the occasion demanded."[26] With Fruin as their teacher and the war years as an apprenticeship, by 1865 the Empire Club had developed into a force to be reckoned with on the diamond.

While Fruin did bring his considerable knowledge of the game to St. Louis and influenced a generation of ballplayers through his instruction and leadership, Shepard Barclay and others claimed that Fruin was actually the first to introduce the game to St. Louis. The fact that the game was being played in St. Louis prior to Fruin's arrival in the city in 1861 proves this to be false, but that has not stopped Barclay's claim from spreading and being accepted as fact. This claim continues to appear in histories of the game, in articles, and on websites even though Fruin himself stated that "I have heard it said that I was the first to introduce baseball into St. Louis.... But I make no such claim."[27]

Fruin, who was extremely well-respected by the members of the club and the baseball fraternity in St. Louis, went on to successful career in the construction business after the Civil War and died in St. Louis on March 10, 1912.

George Gilson: Gilson, a journalist and St. Louis city official, was born in Ohio on March 3, 1832. "Upon the breaking out of the Mexican war, although a mere youth, he became possessed of a noble and patriotic ambition, and joined the army of invasion as a private soldier.... Young Gilson was attached to a battalion of regulars, and spent several months at Pueblo, and marched with the invaders into the city of Mexico."[28] The young veteran came to St. Louis in 1850 and began working in the newspaper business. During the Civil War, Gilson served in the Union Army as a Major and in 1864 and 1865 was the Inspector-General of the St. Louis Military District.

As a newspaper man, Gilson worked for many years for the *St. Louis Democrat* as both a reporter and editor. "Upon the consolidation of the *Globe* and *Democrat* in 1875, he was chosen by the proprietors as city editor of the paper."[29] In 1879, he left the newspaper business to serve as chief of staff for the recorder of deeds and later worked as a bailiff for the federal courts in St. Louis.

Gilson died on August 13, 1910, in St. Louis.

William Godfrey: William H. Godfrey, who worked as a draughtsman with the St. Louis County Assessor's Office and later owned a saloon in St. Louis, was born in 1821 in Illinois. He died in St. Louis on October 28, 1906.

John Grimsley: Grimsley, a "well known and highly esteemed citizen,"[30] was born in St. Louis in 1823 and ran a successful saddle-making company. It appears that he had a contract with the StLFD to provide saddles and harnesses for the department.

Grimsley died in St. Louis in January of 1881.

Charlie Hautz: Born in St. Louis on February 5, 1852, Hautz was a professional baseball player and a slugging first baseman. Along with Joe Ellick, Hautz was brought over from the Empire Club in 1875 to strengthen the Red Stockings' National Association team. In 1876 and 1877, he played with Indianapolis and in 1878 played for a club in Springfield, Massachusetts. Returning to St. Louis, Hautz was a member of the independent professional Brown Stocking club and in 1882 was playing for the Standards of St. Louis. He appeared in seven games with the Pittsburgh Alleghenys of the American Association in 1884.

Hautz died in St. Louis on January 24, 1929, and it appears that he spent his post-baseball career as a traveling salesman.

John Heep: Heep, an outfielder for the Empire Club in the late 1860s, was born in 1847. A cigar maker, he died on October 10, 1883.

Joseph Hollenback or Hallenbeck: According to Edmund Tobias, Hollenback was the founder of the Empire Club, organizing the first meeting of the club in 1860. A deputy constable in St. Louis, he was born in New York in 1836 and may have played baseball in that city prior to moving to St. Louis. The first secretary of the club, Hollenback served with the 10th Regiment of the Enrolled Missouri Militia during the Civil War and most likely died in 1866. Even the exact spelling of his surname remains in doubt.

Charles Johnson: Born in Lebanon, Illinois, on January 18, 1836, Charles P. Johnson was an attorney and politician who has been described as Missouri's "greatest criminal lawyer."[31] Johnson moved to St. Louis in 1855 to study law, was admitted to the bar in 1857, and was elected City Attorney in 1859. At the outbreak of the Civil War, Johnson declined an appointment to the United States Congress but was elected to the Missouri General assembly where he worked on issues surrounding emancipation and the writing of a new state constitution. He was elected lieutenant governor in 1872.

In 1883, he successfully represented Frank James, who was on trial in Missouri on murder and robbery charges related to his actions as a member of the James Gang. Considered a master orator, Johnson also served as a professor at Washington University's law school.

He died in St. Louis on May 21, 1920.

Harry Little: Born in Pocahontas, Missouri, on November 9, 1850, Little was a professional baseball player. A member of the Grand Avenue Base Ball Club of St. Louis in 1876, Little played with the National League's St. Louis Brown Stockings and Louisville Grays in 1877.

After his baseball career ended, Little worked as a store clerk in St. Louis and died in Illinois in 1927.

John Lockett: Born in England on December 21, 1834, Lockett was living in St. Louis by 1860 and earned a living as a grocer. He died of acute bronchitis on January 18, 1915.

John O'Connell: O'Connell, the head of a successful St. Louis painting business, was born in Shangarry, County Cork, Ireland on October 7, 1843, and immigrated to America with his family in 1848, settling in St. Louis. From 1857 to 1862, he served as an apprentice with the painting firm of H. Farmer & Son. O'Connell, during the Civil War, "responded to the call for aid issued by the Confederacy and for seven months did active military duty with the southern army."[32]

After the war, O'Connell started a painting business with his friend and fellow club member Patrick Tobin. A few years later, he bought Tobin out and renamed the business the J.W. O'Connell Painting Co. The success of this company, according to Jeremiah Fruin, made O'Connell wealthy.

One "of the original members of the Empire Base Ball Club ... [who] played with the first nine for seven years,"[33] O'Connell, in 1872, helped organize the American chapter of the Knights of Father Matthew, a Catholic temperance group.

Tom Oran: The first Native American to play major league baseball, Oran, who was born in California in 1847, was a skilled player whose talents were coveted by the best clubs in St. Louis. Playing at different times with the Union Club, the Empire Club, and the Red Stockings, Oran, between 1868 and 1874, had an impact on several championship series in St. Louis.

Oran first appears in the records as a catcher with the Olympic Club of St. Louis in 1867 and then with the first nine of the defending champion Union Club in 1868. In 1869, as the rivalry between the Unions and Empires was at its peak, Oran jumped to the Empire Club, who had lost their starting catcher to injuries. This move, which may have been made with the promise of a job with the StLFD, strengthened the Empires, weakened the Unions, and certainly affected the competitive balance between the two clubs.

For the next several years, Oran was a fixture in the Empire's first nine, as a catcher and third baseman. In 1874, however, Oran jumped clubs once again. On July 4, 1874, Oran was playing for the Empires in a match against the Liberty Club of Springfield, Illinois. A week later, he was playing for the Red Stockings in a match against the Rowena Club of St. Louis. The Empires had already lost their best pitcher, Dan Collins, to the White Stockings of Chicago in May of 1874 and the loss of Oran severely handicapped the club at the same time as it strengthened their rival. A year later, Oran became the first Native American to play in a major league as a member of the Reds' National Association club.

Little is known about Oran's life after 1875. He died in St. Louis on September 22, 1886, and it was insinuated that his death was a result of alcoholism.

Walter Parr: Walter S. Parr, born in Virginia in December of 1838, was a furniture maker who served as president of the Empire Club in 1868, as vice-president from 1866 to 1867 and again from 1870 to 1871, and as field captain in 1874. He also was one of the founders of the Grand Avenue Base Ball Club of St. Louis in 1876.

Parr died in St. Louis in 1900.

Joe Schimper: Schimper was a St. Louis fireman who pitched for the Empire Club in the 1870s. One "of St. Louis' best ball-players,"[34] Schimper was born in Louisiana in 1848 and, for reasons unknown, was also commonly known as Joe Chambers.

Around eleven P.M. on February 9, 1887, a fire broke out at Jesse Arnot's livery stable in St. Louis and Schimper, on duty that day, was one of the firemen who answered the alarm and worked to put out the blaze. About a half hour after the StLFD appeared on the scene, "the entire Ninth street wall of the stable gave way and fell with a crash."[35] One of those trapped under the wall was Joe Schimper.

After the fire was put out, a search for bodies began, and Schimper was the last to be found. "He was carried to the street limp and lifeless to all appearances. His friends thought they detected a faint hope of life, and carried him away as fast as possible to the Dispensary."[36]

He did not survive the night, dying from injuries received "in the discharge of his duty."[37]

Louis Schrader: Born on October 13, 1850, in St. Louis, Schrader was among "the prominent ball players of amateur days and one of the most experienced."[38] Beginning in 1867, he was involved in the establishment of three baseball clubs: the Sherman Club, the Star Club, and the Turner Club. Besides the Empire Club, Schrader was also a member of the Aetna Base Ball Club. His promiscuous membership in St. Louis baseball clubs is unmatched by any other known person. "He was thoroughly conversant of the rules of the game and ... became the most desirable as well as reliable of umpires which reputation he sustained up to the days of professional ball.... No one keeps better posted about ball matters than Lou Schrader."[39]

Schrader, who died in St. Louis on March 14, 1920, made his living as a cigar maker. He was a member of the Cigar Maker's Union and served on its executive board in 1879, helping to organize a strike among cigar makers in St. Louis.

Henry Clay Sexton: The first chief of the all-paid fire department in St. Louis, Sexton was born in Virginia on March 29, 1828, and moved to St. Louis with his family in 1857. His father and older brothers were carpenters and building contractors and, prior to joining the StLFD, he worked for John Sexton and Sons. With contacts and friends in both the fire department and the St. Louis construction industry, Sexton was a natural candidate for membership in the Empire Club and was described as "one of the most prominent early ball players ... [although he] never took much stock in his playing abilities...."[40]

Sexton's election as president of the club in 1864 came during one of the most trying periods of his life. In 1862, he was removed from his position as chief of the StLFD by General John Schofield and confined to the Gratiot Street Prison under suspicion of having Southern sympathies. One of almost five thousand civilians held at the prison during the war, it is unknown how long Sexton was held or when he was released, although it's a safe assumption that he was released prior to his election as president of the Empire Club. It certainly says something about the club that a formerly imprisoned, suspected Southern sympathizer would be elected as president while the Civil War was still ongoing and the fate of the Union in doubt.

In May of 1869, Sexton was reappointed as chief of the

StLFD and held that position until 1885 "when he resigned to become collector of internal revenue."[41] From 1870 to 1873, he also served again as president of the Empire Club, giving him the longest consecutive tenure as president in the history of the club. In 1881, Sexton was one of the original investors in the Sportsman's Park and Club Association and helped to revitalize professional baseball in St. Louis.

"Always alert, sober, clearheaded, quick in perception, [and] powerful in action,"[42] Sexton was a popular chief of the StLFD and "[no] man ... had so large a following among all classes."[43] He died in St. Louis on December 31, 1893.

John Shockey: Shockey, who was born in Pennsylvania in 1839, was an assistant chief with the StLFD and the nephew of Henry Clay Sexton. An outfielder on the Empire Club's first nine in the late 1860s, he also served as a field captain in 1869.

On September 26, 1881, Shockey was seriously injured attempting to put out a fire at a picture frame factory in St. Louis. While trying to move a line of hose to the rear of the building, a wall in the alley collapsed and Shockey was "buried beneath the ruins."[44] He was found "knocked up against a post near the rear of the factory ... lying under some bricks. His left leg was apparently broken, as it was twisted around the post.... Shockey's heavy regulation hat had been cut through with a brick. As soon as it was taken off it was found that the top of Shockey's head was cut open and his face was badly bruised."[45]

A reporter who visited the injured Shockey at his home wrote that his "face appeared badly scorched, and there was a long gash in the top of his head. His leg had just been set and was strung up slightly above the level of his body in a sort of hammock.... The patient endured all this with fortitude, and said he felt perfectly comfortable."[46] Six days later, on October 2, Shockey "died at his residence ... at 2:30 A.M.... The injuries were considered fatal at the time, but many of his friends hoped that his strong constitution would enable him to successfully combat them.... No man in the department was better liked than Shockey—a brave and competent fireman—whose death is universally regretted."[47]

Augustus Solari: Born in 1835 in Switzerland, Solari was the proprietor of the Grand Avenue Grounds from 1866 to 1880. Having immigrated to United States by 1860, he operated a saloon in St. Louis until his death on May 11, 1898.

With both the Empire and Union Clubs looking for a new ballpark in 1866, Solari secured a five-year lease on a cornfield located near the St. Louis Fairgrounds and the junction of several street car lines. Using the wood from the Union Club's old grounds, Solari was the first person to build a ballpark at the Grand Avenue location that would be home to St. Louis baseball for a century. In 1880, as his latest lease on the land was about to expire and at a low point in the popularity of baseball in St. Louis, Solari tore down the Grand Avenue Grounds. One of the reasons for the formation of the Sportsman's Park and Club Association in 1881 was to assume the lease on the grounds and rebuild the ballpark.

In 1875, Solari organized the Grand Avenue Base Ball Club, a club that suffered only two defeats in its first two seasons, one at the hands of the professional Brown Stockings.

Joseph Solari: The son of Augustus Solari, Joseph Solari was born in St. Louis in 1861. A painter by trade, he was also a catcher with his father's Grand Avenue Club. Solari, who died of pneumonia in July of 1882, "was a young man of promise, and during his father's proprietorship of the ball park he became a deserved favorite, being courteous and kind to all."[48]

James Spalding: A mainstay at third base for the Empires' championship clubs, James Spalding was born on June 1, 1849, in Ireland. One of the club's field captains in 1871, 1872, and 1873, he worked in the legal profession and was a constable after his playing days ended.

Spalding died on January 22, 1918.

Edmund Tobias: The Herodotus of St. Louis baseball history (or, if you'd prefer, the Boswell of the Empire Club), Edmund H. Tobias was born in Steuben, New York, and was living in St. Louis by 1866, where he worked as a clerk in a dry goods store. That year he was elected secretary of the Empire Club and appeared in at least one game with the first nine, playing third base in a tournament in Bloomington, Illinois.

Tobias's significance rests not in his playing abilities or even in his membership in the Empire Club but rather in an epistolary series of articles that were published weekly in *The Sporting News* between October 26, 1895, and February 15, 1896. In these articles, Tobias chronicled the history of baseball in St. Louis from its advent through the 1875 season. In his attempt to "faithfully outline the birth and growth of baseball in St. Louis,"[49] he produced a document which is invaluable to anyone studying the history of 19th century baseball in St. Louis.

E.H. Tobias died on January 12, 1898.

Patrick Tobin: An original member of the Empire Club, Tobin was born in Ireland in 1844. A painter and childhood friend of fellow club member John O'Connell, he was the president of the Tobin Brothers Paint Company. Tobin died on May 23, 1910.

Adam Wirth: Arguably the best St. Louis baseball player of his generation, Wirth was born in Missouri on April 10, 1840. For the entire decade following the end of the Civil War, he was the cornerstone of the Empire Club's championship teams, manning first base and center field and earning a reputation as an outstanding defensive player.

Wirth was described as "a first-class ball-player. His strong points of play are his accuracy in throwing and his certainty in holding a ball, these two physical attributes making his services exceedingly useful in other positions besides the one he has made his specialty—viz., the first base of the nine. To these desirable qualifications he adds calmness and steadiness of play, and presence of mind and evenness of temper in exciting and critical positions of the game.... [He] possesses a manly physique, and considerable power of endurance, and his strength of muscle is shown in his batting skill — his average play at the bat being of the best of his club."[50]

In the 1860s, Wirth worked as a printer with the *Missouri Democrat* before joining the St. Louis Fire Department. On September 21, 1881, Wirth was injured while fighting a massive fire that destroyed four square city blocks. "He had ventured too far amidst blinding and stifling smoke in a small alleyway on Tenth street, and had fallen senseless with his lungs clogged with smoke. He was rescued promptly by his comrades. After treatment at the Dispensary he was taken to the engine house, where he was treated.... In the course of two hours he recovered somewhat and insisted upon returning to the fire. He showed up, but was very properly cleared home by Assistant Chief Judd Bame."[51]

Wirth died on February 9, 1912.

James Yule: James C. Yule was born in Scotland in 1836 and worked with his younger brother Alexander, who was also a member of the Empire Club, as a painter and interior decorator. An outfielder who served as a field captain in the early 1860s, Yule died on September 15, 1891.

Other known members of the Empire Club: J.C. Adams, John Bailey, John W. Bain, A.C. Bernoudy, Joseph Clinton, Peter Clinton, Fred M. Coburn, Martin Collins, P.J. Cooney, Daniel Coyle, Fran Dillon, David J. Duffy, Robert Duncan, William Duncan, J.H. Farrar, Richard Fruin, Lewis P. Fuller, William D. Gorman, A.J. Hazelton, James B. Hazelton, William J. Henley, Bernard J. Higgins, John M. Johnson, Joseph Kinwiddy, John T. Murphy, Jake Murphy, Thomas Murphy, Peter Naylor, Hank Noble, Charles C. Norton, John Quinn, James Reynolds, William Robinson, Jacob Ruppenthal, Frank Ruth, William W. Sanford, Charles Stevens, George Stevens, William H. Swift, William P. Thorn, James Utley, John F. Walton, Thomas Walsh, James S. Wilgus, John W. Williams and John Young.

Notes

1. Spink, *The National Game*.
2. *Ibid*.
3. Tobias, October 26, 1895.
4. *Ibid*.
5. Spink, *The National Game*.
6. *Ibid*.
7. Tobias, October 26, 1895.
8. Tobias, November 2, 1895.
9. Tobias, October 26, 1895.
10. *St. Louis Globe-Democrat*, October 18, 1881.
11. Tobias, January 11, 1896.
12. *Ibid*.
13. *St. Louis Globe-Democrat*, February 19, 1883.
14. Tobias, November 9, 1895.
15. *St. Louis Daily Bulletin*, July 7, 1860.
16. Tobias, November 9, 1895.
17. *Ibid*.
18. Tobias, February 8, 1896.
19. Tobias, October 26, 1895.
20. *Ibid*.
21. *St. Louis Globe-Democrat*, March 3, 1878.
22. *St. Louis Globe-Democrat*, February 19, 1883.
23. *Lippincott's Monthly Magazine*, October 1886.
24. *Ibid*.
25. Tobias, October 26, 1895.
26. Spink, *The National Game*.
27. *Ibid*.
28. Reavis, *St. Louis: The Future Great City of the World*.
29. *Ibid*.
30. *St. Louis Globe-Democrat*, January 27, 1881.
31. Connie Nisinger, entry on Charles Johnson at Find A Grave.
32. David Lossos; *Irish St. Louis* (Charles, SC: Arcadia, 2004).
33. Albert Nelson Marquis, *The Book of St. Louisans* (St. Louis: St. Louis Republic, 1912).
34. *St. Louis Globe-Democrat*, February 10, 1887.
35. *Ibid*.
36. *Ibid*.
37. *Ibid*.
38. Tobias, November 16, 1895.
39. *Ibid*.
40. *St. Louis Daily Republic*, February 9, 1896.
41. Nisinger, entry on Henry Clay Sexton at Find A Grave.
42. J.A. Dacus and James William Buel, *A Tour of St. Louis* (St. Louis: Western Pub. Co., 1878).
43. Spink, *The National Game*, p. 38.
44. *St. Louis Globe-Democrat*, September 27, 1881.
45. *Ibid*.
46. *Ibid*.
47. *St. Louis Globe-Democrat*, October 3, 1881.
48. *St. Louis Globe-Democrat*, July 14, 1882.
49. Tobias, February 15, 1896.
50. *Frank Leslie's Illustrated Newspaper*, August 4, 1866.
51. *St. Louis Globe-Democrat*, September 22, 1881.

Selected Bibliography

Although numerous and varied sources were used to put together this history of early St. Louis baseball clubs, several deserve prominent mention.

From October 1895 to February 1896, Edmund H. Tobias published a history of early St. Louis baseball in *The Sporting News*. Appearing as an epistolary series of articles, this history covered the beginnings of the game in St. Louis through the 1875 season. Tobias was a contemporary as well as a participant in the events he chronicled and his remarkably detailed account is an invaluable resource for those wishing to understand the origins and development of the game in St. Louis.

Al Spink, the founder of *The Sporting News*, published *The National Game* in 1910. This general baseball history included a chapter on the history of 19th century baseball in St. Louis as well as an interview with Jeremiah Fruin and a letter from Merritt Griswold. The Fruin interview and Griswold letter are extraordinarily important documents that, when taken together, give an accurate description of the advent of the New York game in St. Louis. Most of the modern accounts of the beginnings of baseball in St. Louis are exposed as myth and legend by the testimony of Fruin and Griswold that was supplied by Spink. Other books that deserve mention are

James Neal Primm's *Lion of the Valley*, the best general history of St. Louis, and Louis Gerteis's *Civil War St. Louis*, which is an outstanding account of the period of St. Louis history that included the introduction of the New York game.

Although St. Louis had a number of outstanding baseball writers working in the city and several newspapers that covered the game, it is necessary to single out two. The first was the *St. Louis Daily Bulletin*, published by William Swift. Swift, by his own account, was a baseball fan who had played the game throughout his life, and the *Bulletin*, in 1860, gave significant coverage to what was essentially the first baseball season in St. Louis. The second newspaper that must be mentioned is the *St. Louis Globe-Democrat* under sports editor William Spink. No paper in St. Louis had better baseball coverage than the *Globe*, and there was no better baseball writer in St. Louis than Al Spink's older brother.

Newspapers and Periodicals

Alton Weekly Courier
Bangor Daily Whig & Courier
Brooklyn Daily Eagle
Frank Leslie's Illustrated Newspaper
Kennedy's 1860 St. Louis City Directory
Lippincott's Monthly Magazine
Milwaukee Sentinel
Missouri Republican
Missouri Democrat
New York Times
Porter's Spirit of the Times
St. Louis Daily Bulletin
St. Louis Daily Republic
St. Louis Globe-Democrat
St. Louis Post-Dispatch
St. Louis Republic
The Sporting News
Washington Post

Books and Documents

Adler, Jeffrey S. *Yankee Merchants and the Making of the Urban West*. Cambridge: Cambridge University Press, 2001.
Anderson, Galusha. *The Story of a Border City During the Civil War*. Boston: Little, Brown, 1908.
Bay, William Van Ness. *Reminiscences of the Bench and Bar of Missouri*. St. Louis, F.H. Thomas and Co., 1878.
Conrad, Howard Louis. *Encyclopedia of the History of Missouri*. New York: Southern History Co., 1901.
Cox, James. *Notable St. Louisans in 1900*. St. Louis: Benesch Art Publishing Co., 1900.
Dacus, J.A., and James William Buel. *A Tour of St. Louis*. St. Louis: Western Pub. Co., 1878.
Darby, John Fletcher. *Personal Recollections of Many Prominent People Whom I Have Known*. St. Louis: G.I. Jones and Co., 1880.
Duke, Basil. *Reminiscences of General Basil W. Duke*. Garden City, NY: Doubleday, Page, 1911.
Forbes, Bertie Charles. *Men Who Are Making America*. New York: B.C. Forbes, 1917.
Gerteis, Louis. *Civil War St. Louis*. Lawrence: University of Kansas, 2001.
History of the St. Louis Fire Department: with a review of great fires and sidelights upon the methods of fire-fighting from ancient to modern times, from which the lesson of the vast importance of having efficient fireman may be drawn. St. Louis: Central Publ. Co., 1914.
Kelsoe, W.A. *St. Louis Reference Record: A Newspaper Man's Motion-Picture of the City*. St. Louis, 1927.
Lossos, David. *Irish St. Louis*. Charleston, SC: Arcadia, 2004.
Marquis, Albert Nelson. *The Book of St. Louisans*. St. Louis: St. Louis Republic, 1912.
Matthews, Leonard. *A Long Life in Review*. 1927.
Miller, Clarence, and Mayner Wallace. *Shepard Barclay*. St. Louis, 1931.
Munson, John Williams. *Reminiscences of a Mosby Guerilla*. New York: Moffat, Yard and Co., 1906.
Powell, William H. *Officers of the Volunteer Army and Navy Who Served in the Civil War*. Philadelphia: L.R. Hamersly & Co., 1893.
Primm, James Neal. *Lion of the Valley*. Boulder, CO: Pruett Pub. Co., 1981.
Reavis, L.U. *Saint Louis: The Future Great City of the World*. St. Louis: C. R. Barns, 1876.
Ryczek, William J. *When Johnny Came Sliding Home*. Jefferson, NC: McFarland, 1981.
St. Louis City Plan Commission. *Physical Growth of the City of St. Louis*.
Scott, John. *Partisan Life with Col. John S. Mosby*. New York: Harper & Brothers, 1867.
Seymour, Harold. *Baseball: The Early Years*. New York: Oxford University Press, 1960.
Spink Al. *The National Game*. N.p.: National Game, 1910.
Snow, Marshall Solomon. *History of the Development of Missouri: And Particularly of Saint Louis*. St. Louis: National Press Bureau, 1908.
Stevens, Walter Barlow. *Centennial History of Missouri*. Chicago: S. J. Clarke, 1921.
Taylor, Jacob N. *Sketch Book of St. Louis*. N.p.: G. Knapp & Co., Printers, 1858.
The Bench and Bar of St. Louis, Kansas City, Jefferson City, and Other Missouri Cities. Chicago: American Biographical Publishing Company, 1884.
Thomas, August. *A Print of My Remembrance*. New York: C. Scribner's Sons, 1922.
Wright, Marshall D. *The National Association of Base Ball Players, 1857–1870*. Jefferson, NC: McFarland, 2000.

Websites

Baseball-Reference (http://www.baseball-reference.com/)
Catholic Cemeteries of the Archdiocese of St. Louis (http://www.archstl.org/cemeteries/)
Civil War St. Louis (http://www.civilwarstlouis.com/index.html)
Civil War Soldiers & Sailors System (http://www.itd.nps.gov/cwss/)
Descendents of Pierre de Laclede Liguest and Marie Therese Bourgeois Chouteau (http://genealogyinstlouis.accessgenealogy.com/laclede.htm)
Earl Fischer Database (http://stlgs.org/publicationsSurnamesEarlFisher.htm)
Find A Grave (http://www.findagrave.com/)
Genealogy in St. Louis (http://www.pddoc.com/cw-chronicles/)
Life in St. Louis: The Matthews Family Exhibit 1851–1933 (http://www.umsl.edu/~whmc/exhibits/matthews/index.html)
Missouri Digital Heritage (http://www.sos.mo.gov/mdh/)
Neal and Garesché Ancestry (http://www.garesche.com/rick/index.html)
SABR's Baseball Biography Project (http://bioproj.sabr.org/)
This Game of Games (http://thisgameofgames.blogspot.com/)
University of Missouri Digital Library (http://digital.library.umsystem.edu/)
Washington University Libraries (http://library.wustl.edu/units/spec/archives/facts/co-founders.html)
Whitney Research Group (http://wiki.whitneygen.org/wrg/index.php/Main_Page)

Chapter Nine

Louisville and Atlanta

❖ *Introduction* (William J. Ryczek) ❖

If baseball were played on horseback, the South might have taken the lead in the sport's development. During the years when baseball was gaining a foothold in New York, field sports dominated the heritage of the southern states in a way that games did not. Most organized sporting activity involved contestants of the four-legged variety. During the first decades of the nineteenth century, there were a number of horse racing tracks in the South, and Tennessee native Andrew Jackson was both an owner of racehorses and an avid gambler on the results.

Baseball originated and grew in cities, especially large ones, and there were not many of those in the South. In 1850 New York was America's largest city, with a population of 814,000. New Orleans was the only Southern city in the top ten, ranking sixth with 169,000 residents. Charleston had a population of just 41,000, Richmond only 38,000, and Savannah, Nashville, Mobile, and Memphis were small towns with just 10,000 to 20,000 inhabitants.

A second factor inhibiting the spread of baseball from New York was the considerable distance to Southern cities. In the antebellum United States, new ideas were slow to infiltrate other areas, for regions were highly parochial and communication between them was limited and often greatly distorted. Travel was slow and arduous, electronic transmission was decades away, and newspapers often contained highly colored and inaccurate accounts.

The rigid ideological bifurcation that eventually led to the Civil War was fueled by a very rudimentary knowledge of Northerners by Southerners and vice versa. Most Southerners viewed their Northern brethren as uncouth, soft, and consisting of far too many undesirable immigrants. They were in turn seen by Northerners as embodying the social order of a time gone by, with their chivalry, plantations, and slaves. Few Northern customs were readily accepted in the South, and baseball had originated in the city that represented all Southerners despised about the Yankees.

Although the Southern climate was conducive to outdoor sports, there was little organized activity other than horse racing. One can find scattered reports of "ball games" beginning in the late eighteenth century, but they were of the highly informal variety. While the Knickerbockers, Eagles, and Gothams drafted bylaws and constitutions, held meetings, levied fines, and sometimes played baseball, there were no similar organizations in the South.

It was not until the end of the 1850s that the first Southern baseball clubs were formed. The first big cluster appeared in New Orleans, 1,172 miles from New York by land but closer to the latter in spirit than most Southern cities. New England, although contiguous to New York, was slow to adopt baseball, in part due to its predominantly puritan culture that considered sport sinful and indulgent. New Orleans, with its Creole mores and history of gambling, dancing, and prostitution, had no such scruples.

In the summer of 1859, baseball received its first notice in New Orleans newspapers. By late summer the Louisiana Base Ball Club, the Empire Base Ball Club, the Magnolia Base Ball Club, and the Southern Base Ball Club were all playing enthusiastically on local fields. With baseball, cricket, and racket clubs playing regularly, there was an inadequate number of venues, and the various clubs vied for priority.

The New Orleans baseball clubs began in the same manner as the early New York organizations, playing intramural, informal games, sometimes with nine to a side, sometimes with the cricket standard of eleven. On some occasions two captains picked sides, other times the players divided up by marital status or weight. Finally, on September 14, 1859, the Louisiana and Empire clubs met in the first interclub match in New Orleans. The *New Orleans Crescent* noted that each team would have nine players and the duration of the match would be nine innings, an indication that this was not always the case. So many runs were scored by the eighteen players that the game was stopped by darkness before nine innings were completed. When the match was concluded the following week, the final score showed the Empires were victors by a 77–64 score.

The following year, during the last summer of peace, the

New Orleans baseball scene was quite active, as the clubs played against each other more frequently. In the year that baseball fever enveloped New York, it appeared that the sport was finally generating the same degree of enthusiasm in the South.

On April 4, 1861, a group of Texans formed the Houston Club, an aggregation that very shortly boasted 35 members. Eight days later, however, cannonballs landed inside the walls of Fort Sumter, and for the next five years, there was virtually no organized baseball played in the Southern states. With limited experience in the game, few Confederate soldiers took bats and balls to war. A great deal of baseball playing by the Union Army has been documented in journals and newspapers, but there are only scattered references to Confederates playing the game. Most of the baseball played in the South was by Union soldiers, and the most widely reported incident of Southern soldiers participating in baseball took place in a Northern prison. A number of Confederate officers imprisoned at Johnson's Island, Ohio, several of whom came from New Orleans, played a series of games, and some of the players later formed the nucleus of the city's postwar Southern Club.

During the first summer of peace, there was little baseball played in the South, for conditions were anything but favorable for the development of sport. Even in 1869, four years after the end of the war, the countryside still reflected the devastation wrought by the conflict. When the Mutuals traveled to New Orleans for a series of games in late 1869, the players looked out of their coach windows and, all along the tracks, saw mangled locomotives and twisted steel rails. Other factors also inhibited the development of baseball. The cities that had been relatively small in 1860 remained small and many were in chaos immediately following the war. Healthy young men who might have taken up baseball in 1860 were dead or maimed by 1865. Most baseball activity in the "South" took place in Maryland and Washington, D.C., rather than in the Deep South, and the ballyhooed "Championship of the South" was generally contested for between clubs from Washington and Baltimore.

Beginning in 1866, reports of baseball from Southern cities like Richmond and New Orleans filtered into the New York sporting journals. The following summer, young men from Georgia, Kentucky, Arkansas, Alabama, West Virginia, and Tennessee began to form clubs and play the game. In some cases, expatriate New Yorkers and Union soldiers were the instigators. In September 1867, in the first game played in the city of Columbia, South Carolina, the Phil Sheridan Club of the 5th U.S. Artillery inflicted a crushing 82–29 defeat on the local Chicora Club.

By 1867 and 1868 there were a sufficient number of clubs to enable state associations to be formed and for contests to be arranged for local championships. Following the visit of the Nationals of Washington in 1867, the players of Louisville became more active. "The visit of the Nationals," reported *Wilkes' Spirit of the Times*, "has made the people crazy on baseball in the cities they have visited."[1] The spirit of the Confederacy was retained by Southern nines that called themselves the R.E. Lees, the Stonewalls, and the Bonnie Blue Flag. A more disturbing remnant of the Old South was reflected in a major racial disturbance at an 1869 game between picked nines of Savannah and Charleston, instigated, according to a local paper, by "idle, vagabond, lawless negroes."[2]

As it had been in antebellum days, New Orleans remained the leading Southern baseball city. Some of its clubs even fielded second nines. In the late 1860s the Lone Stars and Southerns were generally considered the best teams in the city, and by 1870 the two clubs' financial situation was strong enough to enable them to undertake tours that encompassed a number of Northern cities. The Southerns made the first trek, in 1869, and the Lone Stars followed the next year. The Southerns won six of seven games, losing only to the powerful Red Stockings of Cincinnati, and returned home to a torchlight parade. The Lone Stars were either less successful or less selective in their choice of opponents, winning just six of fourteen contests in 1870. At the 1870 convention of the amateur National Association, the last meeting of the dying association, the Louisiana State Association was represented by Henry Chadwick.

From 1867 to 1870, a number of top Eastern clubs toured portions of the South. The Nationals of Washington stopped in Louisville in 1867, as did the Atlantics and Athletics in 1868. During the winter of 1869-1870 the Mutual Club of New York ventured to New Orleans. The best club of the late 1860s, the Red Stockings of Harry Wright, went to Louisville and New Orleans in the spring of 1870. Every visit of a talented Eastern club stimulated enthusiasm and spurred the locals to greater efforts to bolster the home team.

In 1870, despite the postwar growth in the number of teams, the South lagged well behind the North in terms of both activity and prestige. The big games took place in New York and Philadelphia, and clubs from Cincinnati and Chicago, with their roster of imported New Yorkers, were among the most talented nines in the country. It would be a long time before professional baseball became established in the South, and it was not until 1966, one hundred years after the end of the Civil War, that the Atlanta Braves became the first major league franchise in the Deep South.

NOTES

1. *Wilkes' Spirit of the Times*, August 24, 1867.
2. Reported in *Wilkes' Spirit of the Times*, August 7, 1869.

❖ *Louisville Base Ball Club* (Peter Morris) ❖

CLUB HISTORY

The activities of a club known as the Louisville Base Ball Club were described in the *Louisville Democrat* on July 15, 1858. The write-up provided a box score of an intrasquad game, reported that the club played on Tuesday and Thursday afternoons, and described the players' uniforms as consisting of "blue cottonade pants, white flannel shirts with blue piping, dark blue caps, leather belts." This club also published its bylaws and was at least in nominal existence as late as 1860.[1] But nothing else is known about its doings and it does not appear that it shared more than a name with the post-war Louisville Base Ball Club.

Once the Civil War ended, a new Louisville Base Ball Club emerged — indeed announcements of the club's formation in the second week of April 1865, ran alongside articles about the surrender of Robert E. Lee. The new club's first act was the election of a slate of officers that year: President Alexander G. Booth; vice president Daniel S. Fullerton; secretary Benjamin L. McDougall; and treasurer Archie M. Quarrier. Grounds were established on Park Barracks Road ("near the grounds of the Old Phoenix Club") and a series of intrasquad games were played and reported to the local newspapers.[2]

The Louisville Base Ball Club soon moved to more spacious grounds at 18th and Rowan streets, by the old Portland Railroad station. In July the club got its first local rival when the Olympic Base Ball Club of Louisville was formed. The new club soon issued a challenge, a course that in the view of one reporter "evinced the unconquerable *spirit* of the [Olympics], but was generally looked upon as the extreme of rashness." And indeed the Louisville club won, 55–14, in a contest that was "not such a one as a critic of the art world would eulogize."[3]

Nevertheless, contests between the two clubs continued throughout the summer. Coverage in the Louisville papers did not have much to say about the finer points of the game, but it was commendatory. "The game of base ball," remarked one reporter, "is becoming fashionable as well as popular in this city. Yesterday afternoon we had the pleasure of witnessing a match game played between the Louisville and Olympic clubs, on their beautiful grounds in the lower part of the city. The game was not concluded when we left, but it was very interesting and exciting, each club bent on outplaying the other. Quite a large number of ladies and gentlemen were present, all of whom seemed highly entertained with the game. We are glad to notice the enthusiasm displayed on the part of the young men composing the clubs, and the deep interest displayed on the part of the handsome young ladies who honored the occasion with their presence. The clubs, no doubt, think base ball is a game 'that two can play *at*.'"[4]

In the fall the rivalry took on added excitement when a member of the Louisville Base Ball Club, George B. Blanchard, offered a silver service to the winner of the state championship. There were no signs that there were any other baseball clubs in the state, so on September 7, 1865, the Louisville and Olympic clubs met in a "fly game" contest. The big match took place at the new grounds of the Louisville Club in front of a "very large" crowd that included a "goodly number of ladies." Rain ended the game after eight innings with the Louisville Club the winner by a 36–13 score.

At the match's conclusion, the Louisville Club was presented with the silver service by Louisville newspaper editor George Baber. Baber delivered a lengthy speech in which he praised the play of the winners, pointed out that the Olympic Club would not give up and warned the Louisville Club to be prepared to defend the championship, and then discoursed upon "the origin, popularity, and beauty of the game." When he was finally finished, Louisville captain Alec Booth accepted the trophy with a "brief, Grant-like speech."[5]

By 1866 the Louisville Base Ball Club had taken on a new degree of formality with the incorporation of the Louisville Base Ball and Skating Park Company, in which R.A. Browinski, George B. Blanchard, Barry Coleman, George P. Nash, Archie M. Quarrier, J. Lewis Shallcross, and Thomas C. Timberlake served as directors.[6] A club room was established at the corner of Main and Bullit streets and a uniform was selected that consisted of a gray flannel shirt trimmed with scarlet, black and white check cap, blue jean pants, and black patent leather belt.[7]

But there were already signs that business concerns were interfering with the club's activities, and it was not until July that the "long-talked about match for the championship of the State and the splendid silver service now held by the Louisville Base Ball Club" was finally scheduled.[8] The Olympic Club was once again the challenger in a best-of-three series that opened on July 17.

The first game was played in heat so oppressive that it could hardly be endured, making it fortunate that seats with awnings were available for the ladies who attended. The large crowd included the mayor of Louisville and many city officials, as well as representatives of the Rock City and Cumberland clubs of Nashville, the Olympic Club of Covington, the Shelby Club of Shelbyville, and an unidentified Chattanooga club. The visitors were rewarded by a well-played game that showed that both clubs had made "great improvement" since the end of the 1865 season. The Olympics had "everything their own way" in the early going and held a 13–6 lead after sixth innings, only to have the Louisville Base Ball Club mount a furious rally and eke out a 21–20 win. After the final out, the two clubs each gave three cheers for the umpire and then joined in giving three cheers and a "tiger"—a distinctive cheer used by Princeton students—for umpire John W. Dickins. Not to be outdone, Dickins then called for three cheers for "base ball in general."[9]

The series concluded nine days later with a far less noteworthy game. According to one account, a number of the Olympic Club's starters "had their hands badly hurt so that they were unable to play as well as usual. It appeared to us that they thought they were defeated from the start, and they did not play with that vim which usually characterized them."[10] The result was a lackluster match that the Louisville Club won, 31–6. But at least there was excitement at the end of the match when Dickins, a member of the Cumberland Club of Nashville who had again served as umpire, challenged the Louisville Club to face his club for the championship of Kentucky and Tennessee. Although it is not clear that the two clubs had the right to contest for this honor, no such doubts seem to have troubled anyone in Louisville.

Great anticipation thus surrounded this series, which began in Nashville on July 31. The members of the Louisville Club boarded the night train for the 183-mile trip to Nashville the night before. They were accompanied by several members of the Olympic Club and were seen off from the station by many loyal supporters. "As we moved out of the depot," recorded one of the travelers, "we were followed by the shouts and cheers of the numerous friends of the Club, assembled to see us off.... Once under way the exhalerant [sic] spirits of the boys could not be contained, but were manifested by many a lusty shout and cheer for all that pertained to base ball either generally or specifically. Deeming it prudent, however, in view of the struggle to-morrow, to retire early, after an hour or two spent in laughter, jest and song ... the party sought their berths."

When they awoke in the morning, they were in Nashville, where they were greeted at the station by their hosts, provided with a "substantial breakfast" and then shown the sights. In the afternoon the big showdown took place and it ended with the Louisville Club the winner by a 30–23 score. The two clubs then joined in the usual courtesies and in "an additional three cheers for the ladies who had honored the game with their presence." The day concluded with a hearty dinner, after which "corks began to pop" and were accompanied by "many hospitable and patriotic toasts."[11]

The second game in the series was scheduled to take place in Louisville on August 15 but had to be postponed until the following day when the train carrying the visitors was delayed by an accident. But when the contest did come off it was quite the event.[12]

All afternoon "cars running to the ground were crowded with ladies and gentlemen," and by the 2:30 start time a crowd estimated at between 5,000 and 7,000 was on hand. The ladies in attendance were seated under a "spacious and well-ventilated awning," and there were also many "delegates from clubs in other cities and the different clubs in this city on the grounds, all in full uniform." The spectators were treated to "sweet and soul-stirring music" played by the 2nd United States Infantry's band.

The contest itself was described by the Louisville papers as "exciting" and the "greatest game ever played in the West or South," but these were gross exaggerations. In fact the Louisville Club won by the lopsided score of 72–11. The result led the *Daily Democrat* into still more hyperbole, as its reporter called the win "an epoch in the history of base ball," and described the Louisville Base Ball Club as "entitled to the proud CHAMPIONSHIP OF THE SOUTH" and as "the equal of any in the country."[13]

Under the terms stipulated by George Blanchard when he donated the state championship trophy, its winners would become the permanent owner of the silver service if they retained it for an entire year. Since this date was fast approaching and no other contestant had emerged, the Olympic Club issued another challenge. The first game of a new best-of-three series was played "rather unexpectedly" on August 23 but it proved very lackluster—both sides were missing several of their best players and, "with the wind blowing the ball out of its direction, and somewhat benumbing the players," Louisville won, 51–46. The series was never completed, and the 1866 season closed on that note.[14]

After two seasons of play, the Louisville Base Ball Club had still not lost a match game and now bore the title of champion of Kentucky and Tennessee. The unblemished record had already led the *Daily Democrat* to grossly exaggerate the club's credentials, and even the more temperate *Journal* asked, "Why can't we have a match game with some Eastern club—the Atlantics or Athletics? Let us by all means have a match game next season."[15] But realistically, the Louisville Club had beaten only two opponents, neither of which had a national reputation, and there was no reason to believe it ready for such a test. As it turned out, the club was soon to get that opportunity and did indeed fall short.

In light of the elevated expectations and the large crowds that had turned out the preceding summer, the Louisville Base Ball Club began playing at a more spacious location known as Cedar Hill in 1867. Before the first big match of the year, the *Louisville Journal* raved that the new grounds

> are without dispute surpassed by few in the country for such purposes. Spread out as they are in every direction, a beautiful carpet of living green, with a gentle slope rising for nearly two hundred yards towards the cool, shady and inviting groves which surround almost the entire field, and where, under the refreshing protection of the trees from the sun, the spectators can see the honors of the manly game won and lost. We notice, too, that the natural advantages of the place have been greatly added to in other respects. Directly upon the right and left of the home base or striker's position, commodious seats have been erected by the club for the players and their friends, representatives of other clubs, and those friends to whom the club wish to extend

the courtesy; and last though not least to be thought of, suitable arrangements have been made for the newspaper fraternity."[16]

The *Daily Democrat* added praise for the many conveniently located shade trees and similarly concluded that the grounds "are the best appointed we have ever seen, and will compare favorably with those of any other place."[17]

The new grounds opened just in time for clubs with national reputations to visit Louisville for the first time. The Buckeyes of Cincinnati were the first such visitors, on July 2, 1867, and when the Louisville Club triumphed by a 45–37 score, many locals began to believe that the club was on the verge of national prominence.

Two weeks later, the Nationals of Washington arrived in town on their precedent-setting trans–Allegheny tour. The match was Louisville's number one "topic of conversation in base ball circles" and some locals believed that the home side had a chance to pull off a major upset.[18] The *Journal*'s reporter wrote,

> Our boys are determined to oppose them manfully, and bravely defend their title so nobly won and skillfully maintained as the champions of the South. They have abler work and sterner stuff before them than they have ever confronted before, and, with the exaggerated stories and overrated abilities of the club they propose to play sounding in their ears whenever the game is spoken of, they may well have cause to be apprehensive of their laurels. Still, the deserved fine reputation — exaggeration aside — of the Washington nine was not easily nor idly won, and the contest promises severe work for the Louisville. We are confident, however, that our boys will prove no mean opponents, but foemen worthy of their ambitious challengers, that should they be defeated the Washington club will have cause to congratulate themselves upon accomplishing the hardest part of their task in consummating their proposed tour of victory.[19]

A huge crowd turned out and the playing field was "fringed with a deep living cordon of people, all seemingly deeply interested in the exciting contest." But instead of showing that the ability of the Nationals had been exaggerated, the game was an 82–21 rout for the visitors that showed that it was the Louisville Club that was not worthy of the press coverage it had received. Undaunted, the *Journal*'s reporter congratulated the Louisville players "upon the fact that it was the best game that has been played in the series arranged by the 'Nationals' since they left Washington." He did admit that "our boys ... have considerable to learn" but he predicted that the loss "will do them good" by providing "a better standard to play by in the future."[20]

But the *Daily Democrat*'s reporter took a gloomier view, expressing disappointment that the Louisville players had "not come up to other games we have seen them in." He also offered specific criticisms of the performance of a couple of the home players — second baseman Walter Brooks and shortstop John Dickins, the former captain of the Cumberlands of Nashville, who had recently moved to Louisville.[21] More ominously, the *Democrat* offered scant coverage of baseball for the remainder of the season.

The eternal optimist who covered baseball for the *Journal* soldiered on, penning a forceful defense of Louisville's female baseball supporters when Henry Chadwick referred to them as "haughty beauties."[22] But even he had a hard time finding much to write about during the remainder of the season. The Olympics were quickly losing interest in baseball and played their old rivals only once all season. The Louisville Club seems to have also been struggling to remain intact, playing with eight men for the first three innings of one of the rare match games it played that summer.

The season wrapped up in early September with a visit from the Cincinnati Base Ball Club (the club later to become famous as the "Red Stockings"). The *Journal*'s reporter worked as hard as ever to find encouraging signs, writing that "the lady and gentleman auditors" displayed "an emulative spirit of enthusiasm that gave singular éclat to the whole affair. This enthusiasm was entirely spontaneous — evoked by the brilliant and quickly repeated *coups de grace* of the players on each side." Even the loss was presented with optimism: "Although the Cincinnati Club won by an extraordinary score, 44 to 22, the substantial honors of the game were equally shared by the Louisville Club."[23] But it was becoming increasingly clear that the best days of the Louisville Base Ball Club were in the past.

That reality became undeniable in 1868. The Louisville Club's longtime rival, the Olympics, lost what little interest they still had in the game.[24] A new challenger did emerge in the Eagles, a junior club "composed of young fellows courting their first mustaches, [who] are as full of spirit and life as so many deers."[25] The Eagles played a close and exciting series with the Louisville Club, but the games failed to elicit the enthusiasm from the public that the rivalry with the Olympics had done.

The Louisville Base Ball Club also had the chance to play the mighty Athletics of Philadelphia and the Atlantics of Brooklyn in 1868. But while the possibility of visits of these clubs had once been discussed with excitement, things had changed. When the Athletics paid a visit on June 10, the formerly optimistic *Journal* tried to lower expectations by predicting that the "clever amateur" Louisville club would make a "creditable" showing against the "celebrity" Athletics in the "friendly 'strike, catch, and run'" at the Cedar Hill grounds.[26]

Tickets for the match were sold beforehand at the Louisville Hotel, Willard's Hotel, Warner's Cigar Store, and W. Scott Glore's bookstore, and a crowd of close to 3,000 showed up — a fine turnout but a far cry from the estimates given in 1866 and 1867.[27] Nobody expected that the home side would win or even keep the score close, so it was a pleasant surprise when the first inning ended with a deficit of only 5–3. But the Louisville Club could not manage another run and the contest ended with a final score of 51–3.

As usual, the *Journal* went to great lengths to put a

positive spin on the game, offering this explanation: "It was not thought that our amateur nine could make an exhibition of skill to compare very favorably with a club of such repute, in batting and base playing, but they determined to make an attempt to keep down the score of their opponents as close as possible by good fielding; and they succeeded very creditably, although the Athletic score in comparison with theirs looks very large. The trouble was, however, that the Athletics would never let the ball get out of reaching distance, which accounts for the number of blank scores on the Louisville side."[28] But the *Daily Democrat* was not as sanguine, remarking that the match was "not as close as we expected, our boys appearing discouraged from the commencement."[29] Thereafter the *Daily Democrat* ceased regular coverage of the doings of the Louisville Base Ball Club.[30]

The *Journal* continued to cover the visits of noted clubs and to try to find encouraging signs in the results. Its irrepressible reporter wrote that the baseball season had been "unusually brisk" after the Atlantics of Brooklyn came to town on July 2 and opened up an 18–0 lead after the first inning, then cruised to a 66–11 win.[31] And when the Unions of Morrisania paid a visit in August, the "rather unequal" 59–11 final score was characterized as "expected," while the "large number of our citizens" who turned out were said to have come only "to see the champions and an exhibition of their skills."[32]

Five days later, the Louisville Base Ball Club beat the Eagles in a close contest to retain local bragging rights. But that was the club's swan song and it soon disbanded and passed into memory.

Club Members

George B. Blanchard: Born in Kentucky around 1837, George Blanchard ran a gentleman's furnishing store in Louisville along with his brother Albert. He played for the Louisville Base Ball Club only in 1865 but he made an important contribution by donating the silver service that became the symbol of the state championship. He was also a director of the Louisville Base Ball and Skating Park Company and arranged an 1868 train excursion in which more than 100 Louisville baseball enthusiasts accompanied the Eagle Club to Frankfort for a contest billed as being for the junior championship of Kentucky.[33] He left Louisville in the mid–1870s and died in Campbell, Virginia, on November 17, 1879.

Alexander Galt Booth: Alec Booth was the club's pitcher for almost all of its existence and a member of the board of directors. He was born around 1842 and became a partner in the law firm of Mix & Booth. He died on October 29, 1876.

Walter B. Brooks: Brooks was born in Charleston, Virginia (later West Virginia), on May 1, 1846. He was a member of a wealthy family that moved to Louisville shortly before the Civil War, and his new home was next door to that of fellow Louisville Base Ball Club member A.L. Robinson. After the war he attended college in Louisville and worked at Robinson's tobacco store to learn the tobacco business. He was a fixture in the lineup of the Louisville Base Ball Club, playing a variety of positions. But like many players, he had less time for baseball after the 1866 season, and he played only occasionally in 1867 and 1868. He soon returned to Charleston and became president of the Rosin Coal Lamp Company. Brooks died there on February 4, 1929, after a long and successful life.

Roman Alexander Browinski: Club secretary R.A. Browinski was born around 1843 and graduated from the University of Pennsylvania. He was one of the directors of the Louisville Base Ball and Skating Park Company. He died of tuberculosis on September 20, 1876.

Edward Randall Coleman: E.R. Coleman was one of two younger brothers of Barry Coleman who became involved in the club during its later years, being a regular in the outfield in 1867 and 1868. He was born in Louisville in 1847 and was still there in 1880 but left soon afterward. A family genealogy states that he died in St. Louis in 1886, but no matching death record could be found.

Martin Barry Coleman: Barry Coleman was born on January 31, 1840, into one of Louisville's most prominent families; the house in which he was born was long known in Louisville simply as the Coleman residence. He played on the Louisville Base Ball Club in 1865 and served briefly as its secretary, but did not play in subsequent years. He became a partner in Thomas Meikle & Co., a successful plow manufacturer. Eventually he moved to San Francisco, where he founded the United Carriage Company. He died there on July 29, 1907.[34]

William Pritchard Coleman: Will P. Coleman was another brother of Barry Coleman. He was born in Louisville on December 3, 1844, and graduated from the University of Pennsylvania. He lived in numerous places in the courses of a successful career and eventually retired to Macon, Georgia, where he died on March 28, 1924.

William Cornwall, Jr.: Born in Lexington, Kentucky, on September 19, 1845, William Cornwall, Jr., was a regular on the Louisville Base Ball Club during its first three seasons, mostly playing third base. He joined his father in running a successful soap and candle manufacturing business and twice served as president of the Louisville Board of Trade. He died in Louisville on March 29, 1921.

John Whitby Dickins: John W. Dickins was born in Wigan, Lancashire County, England, on June 24, 1841. He arrived in New York in 1857 and attended Williston Seminary in Massachusetts. He taught school and studied law with the Brooklyn law firm of Hagner & Smith. When the Civil War broke out, he enlisted in the 71st New York State Militia and was captured at the Battle of Bull Run, spending four months in Libby Prison in Richmond and four months in Parish Prison in New Orleans. While imprisoned, he became the associate editor of "The Stars and Stripes in Rebeldom," a collection of writings of prisoners. He spent another three months in the

Confederate Prison in Salisbury, North Carolina, before finally being exchanged. He next enlisted in the 165th New York and was wounded at the battle of Port Hudson, Louisiana, on May 27, 1863. After earning promotion to sergeant-major, he was transferred to the 100th U.S. Colored Troops as a captain. He was breveted major and lieutenant colonel for "uniform gallantry and good conduct, and for especial bravery at the battle of Nashville." After the war, he returned to England briefly to get married. He and his bride settled in Nashville, where Dickins had a position in the Bureau of Freedmen and Abandoned Lands. While in Nashville he became captain of the Cumberland Base Ball Club of Nashville. After umpiring two championship games in Louisville in 1866, he arranged a series between his club and the Louisville Base Ball Club for the "championship of Kentucky and Tennessee." In 1867 he moved to Louisville and became an accountant, also playing shortstop for the Louisville Base Ball Club for the next two years. He remained in Louisville for the rest of his life, raising one set of children and then remarrying around 1898 and starting a second family. In 1902 he accepted a commission in the Internal Revenue Service. He died on October 17, 1916.

Henry Vowles Escott: Escott was born in Louisville on December 21, 1845. He was a regular for the Louisville Base Ball Club in 1865, but he played mostly for the second nine in later years. Perhaps that was because, according to one game account, he was in the habit of "turning his back to a ball whenever it did not come exactly where [he] chose it to come."[35] Escott became a Presbyterian minister and died in Louisville on February 19, 1930.

James Stephens Lyman: James S. Lyman was born in Virginia on June 23, 1844. He was the Louisville Club's regular catcher in 1865 and played a variety of positions in subsequent seasons. He went into the insurance business and died in Louisville on August 12, 1890.

Donald MacPherson: Don MacPherson was born in Scotland around 1833 and worked in insurance after moving to Louisville. He also became the secretary and treasurer of the Louisville Public Schools. Despite being older than most of the other members of the Louisville Base Ball Club, he was a regular during the club's first two seasons. MacPherson died in Louisville on January 2, 1908.

Benjamin L. McDougall: Ben McDougall was the club's first secretary and played in most of its games in 1865, but none thereafter. He was born in Kentucky around 1839 and worked in Louisville as a bank teller until the mid-1870s. By 1880, he was a patient at the Central Kentucky Lunatic Asylum. He died on August 12, 1897.

Charles D. Pope: Pope was a graduate of Miami University in Oxford, Ohio, who practiced law in Louisville until his untimely death on October 4, 1871. He was only 24.

Archie Monroe Quarrier: Archie M. Quarrier, the club's first treasurer and a participant in most of its 1865 contests, was born in Virginia in 1841 and attended West Point. He then moved to Louisville and took a job as a clerk for the Louisville & Nashville Railroad. Slowly but surely he worked up to vice president of the company. In 1891 he was transferred from Louisville to New York City, where he died on June 11, 1900.

Arthur Lee Robinson: A.L. Robinson was born in Louisville on December 24, 1843, and graduated from Washington & Lee University. He was a regular for the Louisville Base Ball Club during its first three seasons, but did not play at all in 1868. He and his brother Goldsborough ran a tobacco manufacturing firm in Louisville. In the early 1880s A.L. Robinson was diagnosed with tuberculosis and he moved to Mesa, Arizona, in hopes that the climate would prolong his life. It seems to have done some good, as he lived for nearly two more decades before the disease claimed his life on February 3, 1899.

Lawrence Carr Robinson: Larry Robinson was born in Virginia on March 15, 1845. His father, the Rev. Stuart Robinson, moved the family to Louisville in 1858 when he became pastor of the Second Presbyterian Church in Louisville. After the outbreak of the Civil War, the Rev. Robinson's defense of slavery led the family to go into exile in Toronto. While there, Lawrence earned a degree from the University of Toronto. The family returned to Louisville in 1866, with Stuart Robinson resuming his church and his son opening a bookstore. Larry Robinson played for the Louisville Base Ball Club in all four years of its existence, even appearing in two games in 1868 when he was beginning to suffer the effects of tuberculosis. The recently married young man traveled to Florida and then to St. Paul, Minnesota, in hopes of recovering his health but he died in St. Paul on October 2, 1869. He was the sixth of his parents' eight children to die, and their last surviving son.

Theodore Freulinghuysen Tracy: Theodore F. Tracy was born on September 21, 1846, in Louisville. He played in only intrasquad games in 1865, but thereafter became the star catcher of the Louisville Base Ball Club. The local papers referred to him in such terms as "Tracy, the only Tracy," "little Tracy, no better catcher in the East or West," and "Tracy, the reliable and invincible."[36] He later ran a wallpaper business and died on April 30, 1921, on the outskirts of Louisville.

Other Members: F.O. Anderson, Bell, D.S. Benedict, Jr., John M. Cannon, L.N. Clark, Craik, Fishback, David (or possibly Daniel) L. Fullerton, George S. Graham, John Green, W.B. Gurley, R.G. Hawkins, William Johnston or Johnson, William W. Powell, E.G. Robbins, Smith, Symmes, Edward Tyler, E. G. Wood, Jake Wood, Thomas J. Wood.

Sources

Dean Alan Sullivan, "The Growth of Sport in a Southern City: A Case Study of the Organizational Evolution of Baseball in Louisville, Kentucky, As An Urban Phenomenon 1860–1900," (M.A. Thesis, George Mason University, 1989); contemporaneous newspaper accounts.

Notes

1. David Block, *Baseball Before We Knew It* (Lincoln: University of Nebraska Press, 2005), 224; Dean Alan Sullivan, "The Growth of Sport in a Southern City: A Case Study of the Organizational Evolution of Baseball in Louisville, Kentucky, As An Urban Phenomenon 1860–1900," M.A. Thesis, George Mason University, 1989, 17.
2. *Louisville Journal*, April 14, 1865, 3; *Louisville Daily Democrat*, April 14, 1865, 2, July 4, 1865, 2, July 13, 1865, 2.
3. *Louisville Journal*, July 27, 1865, 3.
4. *Louisville Daily Democrat*, August 24, 1865, 2.
5. *Louisville Journal*, September 8, 1865, 3.
6. The entire act of incorporation is reprinted in Dean Sullivan, *Early Innings* (Lincoln: University of Nebraska Press, 1995), 55.
7. Charles Peverelly, *The Book of American Pastimes* (New York, 1866), 496.
8. *Louisville Journal*, July 10, 1866, 3.
9. *Louisville Journal*, July 18, 1866, 3; *Louisville Daily Democrat*, July 18, 1866, 2.
10. *Louisville Daily Democrat*, July 27, 1866, 2.
11. *Louisville Journal*, August 2 and 3, 1866, 3.
12. *Louisville Daily Democrat*, August 16, 1866, 2.
13. *Louisville Daily Democrat*, August 17, 1866, 2; *Louisville Journal*, August 17, 1866, 3.
14. *Louisville Daily Democrat*, August 24, 1866, 3; *Louisville Journal*, August 24, 1866, 3.
15. *Louisville Journal*, August 24, 1866, 3.
16. *Louisville Journal*, July 17, 1867, 3.
17. *Louisville Daily Democrat*, July 3, 1867, 1.
18. *Louisville Daily Democrat*, July 18, 1867, 1.
19. *Louisville Journal*, July 17, 1867, 3.
20. *Louisville Journal*, July 18, 1867, 3.
21. *Louisville Daily Democrat*, July 18, 1867, 1.
22. *Louisville Journal*, July 30, 1867, 2.
23. *Louisville Journal*, September 7, 1867, 3.
24. *Louisville Daily Democrat*, August 15, 1868, 1; *Louisville Journal*, July 11, 1868, 4.
25. *Louisville Daily Democrat*, July 21, 1868.
26. *Louisville Journal*, June 9, 1868, 4.
27. *Louisville Journal*, June 9, 1868, 4, and June 10, 1868, 4; *Louisville Daily Democrat*, June 10, 1868, 1.
28. *Louisville Journal*, June 10, 1868, 4.
29. *Louisville Daily Democrat*, June 10, 1868, 1.
30. There was a brief account of one game between the Louisville Club and the cross-town Eagle Club, but I found no mention of the visits of the big Eastern clubs.
31. *Louisville Journal*, July 3, 1868, 4.
32. *Louisville Journal*, August 20, 1868, 4.
33. *Louisville Journal*, August 6, 1868, 4.
34. *Sacramento Bee*, July 30, 1907.
35. *Louisville Journal*, July 30, 1867, 2.
36. *Louisville Journal*, July 3, 1867, 2, August 17, 1866, 3, and July 17, 1867, 3.

❖ Gate City Base Ball Club of Atlanta (Peter Morris) ❖

Club History

As one of the earliest prominent Southern clubs, the Gate City Base Ball Club of Atlanta played an important role in spreading baseball to other parts of Georgia and to other Southern cities. While contemporary accounts of the club's doings are very difficult to come by, later retrospectives leave us with an intriguing glimpse into this pioneer club.

According to Atlanta journalist and early ballplayer Smith Clayton, the city's first ball club was known as the Atlanta Base Ball Club and it began to play in 1866. The city was familiar with the "time-honored pastime of townball or bull pen" but baseball was still a novelty. As a result, fielders often forgot themselves and threw the ball at the base-runners, while there was great excitement "when by accident the catcher would take a foul on the bound."[1]

Nevertheless, baseball fever soon swept Atlanta. The city's baseball pioneers discovered a plot of vacant land near the Oakland Cemetery that was ideally suited for their needs—the field was covered "with a carpet of short, green grass" and "surrounded by a grove of stout young oaks."[2] They began practicing there and in no time "hundreds of people [were] flocking to the grounds three afternoons in the week to see the gentlemen blister their white hands in the effort to stop the ball and wear themselves into absolute exhaustion in running from base to base."[3]

The excitement spawned the birth of a rival known as the Gate City Base Ball Club. The new club practiced for a few weeks and held a "dress rehearsal" to get used to their new uniforms, which consisted of "light blue knee pants with a broad red stripe, orange shirts, and black glazed military caps." Then Robert Dohme, the captain of the Gate City Club, boldly challenged the Atlanta Base Ball Club.

The historic match was scheduled for May 18, 1866, and there was great anticipation as the big day approached. "The public were paralyzed," recalled Clayton, "at the audacity of the Gate Citys in calling the great Atlantas out and were filled with profound pity for the daring youngsters. For many days before the match it was the universal theme of conversation. So great was the interest felt that men neglected their business, and gathered in groups on the street corners to discuss the great event and to utter profuse predictions concerning the disastrous defeat that was sure to befall Captain Dohme and his men."

When game day finally arrived, the weather was perfect and a huge throng turned out. There was no seating at the grounds at all, except for a huge armchair for the umpire and stray chairs for the players to share. But that didn't deter the spectators, and "By ten o'clock the people began pouring out to the ball ground. The wealth, beauty and fashion of Atlanta rolled out in carriages, and the rest of the populace took it afoot, for there were no street cars in those days. It was strictly a free show, and by two o'clock the grounds were encircled by cordons of carriages, several deep, the grove was densely crowded with pedestrians and the trees overhead were alive with human beings." The time finally came for the players to make their appearance and they did so in style—"Presently, music was heard in the distance and pretty soon the two nines marched upon the field headed by a colored brass band."

The game turned out to be as lopsided as everyone expected but it was not the Gate City Club that ended up on the short end. The newly formed club counted 25 runs in the first inning alone, while the Atlantas were puzzled by Gate City pitcher Jimmy Gregg's slow twisters, which "started as if going just where the hitter wanted it, and would then fly up under his chin or curl around his feet or zig-zag out into the sociable crowd." It took the Atlanta Club most of the game to match the first-inning output of the Gate Citys, with the final score a staggering 127–29. In spite of the one-sided score and the four and a half hours it took to play the game, the excitement over the match was so great that the crowd stayed until the very end.

The Atlanta Base Ball Club was demoralized by the trouncing and soon disbanded. By contrast, the exultant Gate Citys had the ceremonial ball presented at the match's conclusion covered "with gilt, on which was written in black letters the date of the memorable match and the name of the club from which it was won, and placed it in Taylor's drug store on exhibition. People would go in there and look at that ball as if it was some great man lying in state."[4]

The spoils of the historic match went to the victors in more ways than one. The Gate City Club also inherited the splendid ball field of their now-defunct rivals and began issuing challenges to the clubs that had sprung up in other Southern cities. While dates and scores are not available, Clayton maintained that the Gate City Club won nine matches before their first defeat.[5] Over the next few years, the club won thirty-six ceremonial balls that were "glazed with gold and bore the date of the match game in which captured, and where played" along with "several trophy bats of exquisite workmanship."[6]

An exact list of opponents is also unavailable, but the accounts we do have suggest that baseball had spread to a significant number of Southern cities. Clayton reported that the vanquished clubs represented such cities as Chattanooga, Augusta, Macon, Savannah, Columbus, and Montgomery.[7] A 1906 article also cited wins over clubs from Mobile, New Orleans, Rome, Columbia, Charleston, and Richmond.[8]

In addition, Clayton believed that the Gate City Club's greatest match was one played in Knoxville on July 4, 1866. The host Holston Club had

> sworn to down the Gate Citys. Several hundred people went up from Atlanta to see the game. The Holstons had everything fixed up for a grand ball, which they proposed to give the night after the game to celebrate their grand victory over Atlanta. The Gate Citys got to Knoxville, and were treated most royally by the Holstons before the game. They were wined and dined world without end. The game was played before nearly 10,000 people. It was the most stoutly contested game ever played in Tennessee. It was not decided until the last inning, when the Gate City got there. The score was 21 to 19, and although professionals may smile, for those times it was a superb fight. The Holstons were so chagrined at their defeat, that none of them spoke to the visiting players after the game. They countermanded the order for the ball that night—and refused to have anything whatever to do with the great Atlanta team ever after.

Fortunately, the young women of Knoxville were more gracious to their guests. A Miss Laura Baxter had baked a cake to present to the winners and she presented it to the Gate City Club as promised.[9]

Another memorable victory came against a club from Chattanooga. The match went on "pretty much all day" and Smith Clayton, who was not yet a member of the club, missed his dinner in order to watch until the end. But he felt amply compensated when the hometown heroes emerged triumphant by the count of 86 to 27.[10]

The success of the Gate City Club was especially sweet because the club "was composed of young men who belonged to the best families in the city, and who played ball for glory." As Gordon Noel Hurtel later put it, "It was no hired team, playing for money, but it was composed of loyal citizens who played ball from pure patriotic motives. At that time nearly every city in the south had a local baseball team, and they played for 'blood,' as was said. No games were thrown away; there was no juggling with the umpire; no money was charged to see the games, and every player was prompted by a loyal desire to see his native city win out."[11]

As a result, baseball interest in Atlanta remained at fever pitch. According to Hurtel, at the home games of the Gate City Club, "Ladies crowded the grounds and wore the team colors as is now done in football."[12] Clayton confirmed, "There was the local fire, the corps d'esprit, in those days, real town against town, and maybe the fans were not something fierce."[13]

The unbroken string of triumphs eventually came to an end. In 1867, a University of Georgia student named J.H. Rucker organized a college nine named the Dixies and boldly challenged the Gate City nine. The first match, played on the day before Christmas in 1867 resulted in a comfortable win for the Atlanta side. But a rematch followed in Athens in August of 1868 and "so great was the interest taken in the game that the commencement exercises, which were to have been held in the chapel that afternoon, were suspended for lack of an audience. To the great amazement of the Gate City club, the Dixie club was victorious in this game by the score of 51 to 14."[14]

It appears that a club from Griffin, Georgia, may have also beaten the Gate Citys, although again the lack of contemporary accounts makes it difficult to be sure of the details.[15] More important, by this time, many of the original club members were moving on with their lives and devoting their time and attention to more pressing matters. According to Smith Clayton, the Gate City "original nine were never defeated.

They would have won the game at Athens but for the fact that they played with several of their second nine." Clayton knew whereof he spoke because he took Bob Dohme's place at shortstop for that game (with Dohme instead umpiring) and "did not stop a ball."[16]

The Gate City Base Ball Club endured long enough to collect thirty-six ceremonial balls, but eventually faded out of existence. In the elegiac words of Hurtel, "Then came the day when paid ball teams took the place of the volunteer clubs, just as paid fire departments caused the passing of the old volunteer fire fighters. Maybe it gave the people more scientific ball, but it surely witnessed the decadence of a sport that had far more to recommend it than that in which aliens and hirelings bear the city's name and battle for her prestige."[17]

Club Members

Hugh Angier: Hugh Angier was not an original member of the Gate City nine, but became the club's left fielder and was included in an 1867 photograph of the nine. Unfortunately, there were two men of the same age named Hugh Angier in Atlanta at the same time. The former member of the Gate City was reported to be alive in 1906, so he was likely an Atlanta civil engineer who eventually moved to Naples, Italy, and was still living there in 1926.

Willis Robert Biggers: Willis Biggers was born on January 17, 1846, the son of a physician. He was the first chief of the Atlanta fire department after the war and was a lieutenant in the Gate City Guard. He was subsequently elected city clerk but contracted tuberculosis and died in Atlanta on June 25, 1882.

George S. Cassin: According to Clayton, George Cassin was "a born catcher. He was quick as lightning and active as a cat, and would often play right up under the bat; and he could throw to second like a shot out of a shovel, often getting the ball to Biggers before the runner measured half the ground from first. But the trouble was that Biggers couldn't always hold 'em, and when they passed him, as they frequently did, they would be sure to give the center fielder a long chase among the carriages on the hill." Cassin was born around 1849 in South Carolina and became a physician. He was also member of volunteer fire department and became very active in local politics, serving on the board of education. Cassin was seriously injured in 1892 when a cable fell on his head and knocked him unconscious. He apparently recovered, but when he died in Atlanta on December 10, 1897, some believed that the 1892 accident was responsible and a lawsuit ensued.

Smith A. Clayton: Smith Clayton was not an original member of the Gate City Club, but most of what we know about the club comes from his reminiscences. He was born in December of 1850, the son of an Atlanta judge. He became a club member in 1868, but blamed his poor play at shortstop for the Gate Citys' first loss at the hands of the club from the University of Georgia. Clayton himself then attended the University of Georgia and became a reporter, working for the *Atlanta Journal* and later for the *Atlanta Constitution*. He mostly wrote feature articles. Clayton never married and around 1913 his failing health forced him to retire. He died in April of 1916 at a Home for Incurables.

John W. Collier: Gate City center field John Collier was born on September 6, 1846, in Decatur, Georgia. The family moved to Atlanta at two, where his father, Judge John Collier, helped craft the city charter. The younger John Collier acted as a courier for General Lucius Gartrell during the Civil War. After the war, he joined the Gate City Club, while his brother Charlie was a member of the Dixie Club that gave the Gate Citys their first defeat. Charlie later became mayor of Atlanta, while John W. Collier became an auditor in the city comptroller's office. He still held that position when he died in Atlanta on April 25, 1910.

Robert Dohme: Bob Dohme was the shortstop and captain of the Gate City nine, and the club was so closely identified with him that it was sometimes referred to as Dohme's Gate City Club. He was born in Germany in May of 1845, but his family moved to Danville, Kentucky, when he was five. He fought in the Union Army but moved to Atlanta after the war, remaining there for the rest of his life with the exception of a few years in Rome, Georgia. For most of that time he was a grocer, being one of the principals of the Dohme and Duffy Gate City Tea and Coffee Company on Whitehall Street and later of a grocery called Dohme & Corrigan. He sold the latter business in 1902 and died in Atlanta on July 2, 1904, of Bright's Disease, having outlived two wives.

Jimmy Gregg: Jimmy Gregg was the pitcher of the Gate City Club and his twist deliveries baffled opposing batters. But there was no man by that name in the census in Atlanta, so his identity remains just as baffling.

Tom Johnson: Tom Johnson was the club's third baseman and best hitter. Clayton described him as "the hitter en grande. He rarely failed to knock the ball over the fielders' heads, and very often he would lift it over the carriages and the umpire would have to call time until the relays of small boys could get it back to the fielders. Tom never swung his bat, but seemed just to tap the ball in a sharp, quick way." He became famed for his home runs and according to Clayton, he hit a ball in a game in Chattanooga that was not found until two weeks later and then was determined to have traveled "a quarter of a mile to the inch." Tom Johnson appears to have been a military man, but his common name has made him difficult to firmly identify.

William N. Judson: Bill Judson was born on August 19, 1843, in Warrenton, Georgia. By 1860, his father, a marble dealer, had moved the family to Atlanta, where their neighbors included fellow Gate City Club member George Cassin. Bill Judson enlisted as a Confederate soldier in the 9th Georgia Battalion Artillery, being captured at the Cumberland Gap and spending eighteen months as a prisoner at Camp Douglas. After the war, he became a physician and set up an Atlanta practice with Drs. John and Willis Westmoreland. He died on August 14, 1893 in Indian Springs, Georgia.

William Clay Sparks: Bill Sparks played right field for the Gate Citys in their first game, but afterward "was promoted to first base, which he played as no man has ever played it since. He could pick up the swiftest ball batted or thrown, with either his right or left hand, right from the ground as easily as most professionals can take a ball with both hands." Born in Kentucky in 1848, Sparks was a butcher by trade. His parents were driven out of Kentucky by the war and they settled in Atlanta around 1866. Like many members of the Gate City Base Ball Club, he was active in civic matters, serving as an early volunteer firefighter and as Captain of the Gate City Guard. He ran an Atlanta meat market for many years and as of 1912 was reportedly the only member of the club who was still alive. He died in Atlanta on December 8, 1913, and an obituary mentioned that "when baseball was yet in its infancy, Billy Sparks was a live factor in its interest and was a member of one of Atlanta's best amateur teams, on whose roster appeared the names of some prominent citizens."[18]

Reuben W. Tidwell: Rube Tidwell was the only son of William de Graffenried Tidwell, who owned a 1,500-acre plantation in Meriwether and Coweta counties before the war. Reuben was born on the plantation on December 30, 1840, and father and son both fought in the Confederate Army and returned home to find the plantation destroyed. William Tidwell did his best to build a new and much smaller plantation, while his son moved to Atlanta and founded a successful wholesale tobacco house. Rube was not an original member of the Gate City nine but was included in an 1867 photograph of the nine. He married the sister of fellow club member Bill Judson on September 20, 1868. He died on March 16, 1915.

Dick Williford: Williford was the center fielder of the original nine, but his identity is a complete mystery.

SOURCES

Smith Clayton, "After 22 Years," *Atlanta Constitution*, May 27, 1888, 5; Smith Clayton, "By Way of As You Like It," *Atlanta Constitution*, September 15, 1911, 8; D.G. Bickers, "History of First Georgia Baseball and Football Teams; Some Famous Stars," *Atlanta Constitution*, May 30, 1915, C14; E.C. Bruffey, "Steve Grady Remembers Macon-Atlanta Battle on Brisbine Diamond," *Atlanta Constitution*, November 30, 1919, A2; untitled articles in the *Atlanta Constitution* on July 22, 1884 and October 21, 1906, C2.

NOTES

1. Smith Clayton, "After 22 Years," *Atlanta Constitution*, May 27, 1888, 5.
2. *Ibid.*; Smith Clayton, "By Way of As You Like It," *Atlanta Constitution*, September 15, 1911, 8.
3. Smith Clayton, "After 22 Years," *Atlanta Constitution*, May 27, 1888, 5.
4. *Ibid.*
5. *Ibid.*
6. Smith Clayton, "By Way of As You Like It," *Atlanta Constitution*, September 15, 1911, 8.
7. Smith Clayton, "After 22 Years," *Atlanta Constitution*, May 27, 1888, 5.
8. Gordon Noel Hurtel, *Atlanta Constitution*, October 21, 1906, C2.
9. Smith Clayton, "After 22 Years," *Atlanta Constitution*, May 27, 1888, 5.
10. Smith Clayton, "By Way of As You Like It," *Atlanta Constitution*, September 15, 1911, 8.
11. Gordon Noel Hurtel, *Atlanta Constitution*, October 21, 1906, C2.
12. *Ibid.*
13. Smith Clayton, "By Way of As You Like It," *Atlanta Constitution*, September 15, 1911, 8.
14. D.G. Bickers, "History of First Georgia Baseball and Football Teams; Some Famous Stars," *Atlanta Constitution*, May 30, 1915, C14.
15. "Steve Grady Remembers Macon-Atlanta Battle on Brisbine Diamond," *Atlanta Constitution*, November 30, 1919, A2.
16. Smith Clayton, "After 22 Years," *Atlanta Constitution*, May 27, 1888, 5.
17. Gordon Noel Hurtel, *Atlanta Constitution*, October 21, 1906, C2.
18. *Atlanta Constitution*, December 9, 1913.

Chapter Ten

San Francisco Bay Area

❖ *Introduction* (Angus Macfarlane) ❖

Baseball was played in San Francisco as early as 1851, but the history of club baseball officially began on February 22, 1860, when the San Francisco Base Ball Club (later the Eagles) met the Red Rovers near where Seals Stadium would be built in 1930.

In 1859, amid frequent reports of cricket matches, the *California Spirit of the Times and Fireman's Journal* (hereafter referred to as *Times*), a weekly publication with a sporting orientation, regularly chastised and editorially harangued the young men of San Francisco to form a baseball club for the purpose of "following up this most exhilarating and delightful form of out-door sports." After several months of prompting, the Sacramento Base Ball Club was formed in November 1859. A month later the *Times* reported that San Francisco finally had its own club — the San Francisco Base Ball Club (S.F.B.B.C.). By the end of January a second club had been organized in each city and on Washington's Birthday 1860 baseball matches were underway in San Francisco and Sacramento.

In the capital city it was the Sacramentos vs. the Union Club, while 90 miles to the south the S.F.B.B.C. faced the Red Rovers. The San Francisco match began at 11 A.M., three hours before the scheduled inauguration of baseball in Sacramento.

In San Francisco the clubs played to a contentious and controversial 33-all tie after 9 innings. The Red Rovers refused to play extra innings against what they argued was illegal pitching. After the umpire ruled the pitching fair, the Red Rovers still refused to play, leading the umpire to declare a forfeit against the Red Rovers and award the game to the San Franciscos.

The first completed game in California saw Sacramento win a controversy-free match 20–14. Two months later the Sacramentos extended their winning streak to two games, defeating the Unions, 15–10, while San Francisco remained idle.

Shortly after, two more clubs were formed in the Stockton area near Sacramento: the Live Oaks and the Stocktons. They faced each other once, the Stocktons winning, but no score was reported.

While the game was being played in other cities, the San Franciscos changed their name to Eagle, and printed challenge letters in the *Times* "to any nines in the state" — but emphasizing that they would not consider any responses from the Red Rovers. Eventually another San Francisco club was formed, the Em Quads (possibly a professional reference or term, as several members were in the printing trade), and these two clubs met on June 20, 1860, with the Eagles earning their first victory, 55–27 in 7 innings.

During the summer the state's two undefeated teams were unable to agree on the conditions of a match, but they finally met at the State Fair in Sacramento in September to compete in a baseball tournament for the title of state champion.

The powerhouse Sacramentos were 4–0 while the Eagles, at 2–0, had added "cricket" to their name, becoming the Eagle Base Ball and Cricket Club. The Eagles won both games of this greatly anticipated confrontation, 31–17 and 36–32, earning them, in addition to the title of State Champion, a silver ball and $100. Additionally, the best players at each position were awarded medals — California's first all-star team. San Francisco had five players honored for their performance while Sacramento had four selected.

A rematch between the two clubs was expected at San Francisco's Bay District Agricultural Fair, to be held two weeks later. However, shortly after the state fair bad feelings between the two clubs erupted. Lengthy letters were exchanged, summaries of which were printed in the *Times* over a period of several weeks. Each club accused the other of dishonorable, ungentlemanly, and unsportsmanlike behavior before, during, and after the Sacramento tournament. In lieu of a baseball match, the sporting public was entertained with charges, denials, accusations, and counter-charges that passed between the presidents of the two clubs.

In on-field baseball competition, the Eagles faced the Em Quads at the San Francisco Fair, winning 33–14. The Eagle cricketers were also active at the fair, playing the Pioneer Cricket Club, losing a close match. In December the Eagles posted a series of baseball challenges in the *Times*, but there were no takers.

As suddenly as the game had appeared, baseball vanished after the San Francisco Fair. No official records were kept for the 1860 baseball season, but based on matches reported in the *Times*, the final *unofficial* standings for the year were:

Club	W-L-T	Runs For	Runs Against
Eagles	4-0-1	188	123
or	5-0		
Sacramentos	4-2	205	109
Stocktons*	1-1	11	48
Red Rovers	0-0-1	33	33
or	0-1		
Unions	0-2	24	35
Em Quads	0-2	41	88
Live Oaks*	0-2	7	73

*Stocktons defeated the Live Oaks but no score was provided.

The first mention of any baseball activity in the next two years was an *Alta* item that a splendid match between the Eagles and nine other crack players would take place on November 27, 1862. Two days later it was reported that a match was played at Mission Dolores, but no names or results were provided.

Another two years went by before the next reference to baseball — a match between the first and second nines of a group called the West End Base Ball Club on May 4, 1865. The second nine was victorious 9–7 after five innings. Two weeks later it was written that the two nines would meet again, but there was no follow up, and nothing was ever heard of the West End Base Ball Club again.

On December 7, 1865, Thanksgiving Day, two unnamed teams met at the Pioneer Race Track. An examination of the 18 names in the box score reveals that 14 players who were or would be associated with the Eagles and the Pacifics were evenly distributed between the two teams.

A month later readers of the *Alta* learned that the Eagles and the Pacifics would contend for the baseball championship of California. Apparently that match was not played, but on February 16, 1866, six years after baseball's first appearance at Center's Bridge, the game made a reappearance as the Pacifics defeated the Eagles 32–18. This event received little notice in the press.

Early in the spring of 1866 the Bay Area's baseball eyes were turned toward the East Bay community of Clinton, a suburb of Oakland, where the Live Oak (not the 1860 club of the same name from Stockton) and San Francisco City College Base Ball Clubs were waging a spirited three-match contest. The Live Oak Club consisted of nine of the eleven men who made up the male student body of the College of California, which would become the University of California in 1868.

These three matches drew large, boisterous, and very partisan crowds. The *Alta*'s coverage reveals a grand rivalry, not just between the two schools, but between San Francisco and Oakland. It was estimated that over one thousand people witnessed the second game.

This was in sharp contrast to the February game between the Eagles and Pacifics, ostensibly for the Championship of California, which received little publicity or fanfare, and subsequent matches, which received absolutely no publicity. These East Bay matches mark the beginning of a seven-year heyday of club baseball in the Bay Area that could be called "The Era of the Bat," the "Bat" being the official symbol of baseball supremacy in the Bay Area during this period.

At various times during Era of the Bat (1866–1872), up to four dozen clubs belonged to the Pacific Base Ball Convention, the governing body of baseball in the Bay Area. Of all of these clubs, only three held the prized Bat at the end of the season, signifying that they were the champion for that year.

Plaza/Portsmouth Square January 1851, site of first recorded baseball games in San Francisco in February and March 1851 (Daguerreotype Collection, Prints and Photographs Division, Library of Congress).

These were the Pacific, Eagle, and Wide Awake clubs. A few other clubs, notably the Cosmopolitans, the Atlantics, and the Libertys were legitimate contenders and did in fact hold the Bat at various times during these seasons. The other clubs, having no expectations of seriously competing for the Bat, much less holding it, played the invigorating and manly game of baseball for the enjoyment of the game and the social camaraderie of their club mates.

Within weeks of these Live Oak–City College matches more than a dozen newly formed clubs were regularly hitting the horsehide. This phenomenal growth of the sport called for some form of oversight and regulation. Accordingly, on July 22, 1866, six clubs (the Eagle, City College, Live Oak, Independent, Cosmopolitan, and Latin School clubs) met to establish order over what was potentially a very chaotic situation. These six clubs were not the only baseball clubs in the Bay Area, but they were the most prestigious, representing the top tier of baseball talent.

On August 17, 1866, the clubs met again, this time with five additional clubs sending representatives: Wide Awakes, Pacific, Occidentals, Eclipse, and Broderick. This was the origin of the Pacific Base Ball Convention, the governing body for baseball in California for the next decade.

If any single element can be credited for sustaining the explosive growth of baseball in San Francisco in 1866, it has to be the availability of a long-forgotten and unnamed baseball grounds. For lack of an official name, it will be referred to here as Pioneer Park.

After the July convention of clubs, games were moved from Clinton to San Francisco's Pioneer Race Track. The facility had been closed to horse racing for several years and was undergoing residential development, but a portion had not been subdivided, and was adaptable to baseball. This particular parcel was bounded by Park (now 24th Street), Temple (now 25th Street), Howard, and Folsom Streets. It had been bought from George Treat, the owner of the Pioneer Race Track, by Frank Livingston, "a capitalist" on April 7, 1866. It's not known if there were any *understandings* between Livingston and the convention of baseball clubs, but it was a very advantageous arrangement for the sport. The grounds were unused, easily accessible, and, most importantly, still had the stands from horse racing days, allowing spectators comfortable seating while watching their favorite clubs compete. In addition, it was in better condition than any field in San Francisco, Oakland, or the East Bay.

Since the majority of the convention clubs were in San Francisco, it made sense to have the "field of choice" situated in the city rather than a suburb. When San Francisco's clubs played out of town, the press gleefully pointed out the wretched condition of the fields and boasted that the best grounds for baseball were in San Francisco.

On August 18, 1866, the Pacific Base Ball Convention met again, this time with eleven clubs sending representatives.

Looking back on the recent explosive growth of baseball, the *Alta* wrote on October 30, 1866: "An impetus unlooked for has of late been given to base ball playing in San Francisco and it is most truly welcome. We are pleased to see such an interest taken in the game.... The present season is the proper one for the game, and it is quite an easy matter to find good flat land, within reach of the cars, where the game may be played."

On November 29, in a game witnessed "by a large concourse of people," the Pacifics defeated the Cosmopolitans 27–20, claiming the championship of California.

That year the press reported forty-eight baseball games in the Bay Area. Unfortunately, very few reports provided box scores. Most accounts were very brief summaries with a final score.

The next year was even more lively, beginning on January 23 with a meeting of the 21 clubs now comprising the Pacific Base Ball Convention to settle a dispute between the Eagles and Pacifics regarding who was the legitimate champion for 1866. The press did not report on the basis of the Eagles' protest, nor was there any explanation why the convention ruled in favor of the Pacifics. This would become a regular tradition for the Eagles: to protest the championship if they didn't win it. The convention ruled that the Pacifics were indeed the legitimate champions, although the substance of the Eagles' protest and the basis for the convention's ruling in favor of the Pacifics is unknown. Undeterred, two days later the Eagles issued a challenge to any nine in the state to play for the championship of California on February 23, 1867.

On February 2, 1867, the twenty-three clubs now belonging to the Pacific Base Ball Convention adopted a constitution, by-laws, and rules of play of the National Association of Base Ball Players. The convention agreed to meet quarterly and as special circumstances warranted.

The convention decided that the champion club would be determined by a challenge format rather than most victories or best won-lost percentage. Under this format, any other club could challenge the champion club. The champion and challenger would then play a best-of-three series. The winner was the champion, and the loser could not issue a challenge for sixty days. The champion club could also challenge another club, but in this "downward" challenge the title was not at stake.

A Championship Bat was designed, which would go to the reigning club. Whichever club held the Bat at the end of the season, November 30, was the champion club for that year and retained that trophy. A new bat was created for each new season, leading the newspapers to call championship matches "Battles for the Bat." The first Bat was made of highly polished Spanish cedar mounted in silver with a scroll for the end-of-season inscription.

Play began on Washington's Birthday 1867 with the Independents and Libertys meeting at Pioneer Park at 9 A.M. followed by a 1 P.M. game between the old rivals Eagles and Pacifics. In anticipation of the games, the *Alta* wrote: "Two very interesting games of base ball will be played on the 22d of this month ... at the corner of Park and Folsom Streets.... This game [Eagles-Pacifics] will probably be the most exciting of any ever played on the Pacific Coast. A large audience will probably witness the game. We understand that ample accommodations will be provided for spectators."

Following the game, won by the Eagles 68–32, the *Alta* reported that the contest "was witnessed by upwards of fifteen hundred spectators who manifested the most intense interest during the whole game."

In almost no time baseball had become a victim of its own success, necessitating this disclaimer in the *Alta* of February 17: "Owing to the large number of games now being played, we are no longer able to publish the full scores names of workers, umpires, best fly catchers, etc., unless the game is of unusual interest."

The 1867 season ended with the Pacifics again defeating the Cosmopolitans for the Bat in what were not only the last games played at Pioneer Park, but (in this writer's opinion) a championship game unlike any ever played before or since in California and perhaps in the nation.

Summing up the 1867 season, the various San Francisco newspapers reported on 108 baseball games, or, according to the *Alta*, "this manly and healthy amusement; the very best of manly sports in favor in America." This was more than double the 48 games reported in 1866.

Predictably, 1868 began with the Eagles charging two Pacific players with fraud in a championship match won by the Pacifics the previous July.

Given the expansion of baseball activity from 1866 to 1867, one would expect that 1868 would have been a glorious season for the sport. However, a researcher who relied on reports printed in the San Francisco papers would have reason to conclude that almost no baseball was played in 1868.

In fact, this drop in activity was both real and apparent. Fewer games were played in 1868, and even fewer of those games were reported.

There was a real drop in the number of games played because of the loss of the finest piece of athletic property in the Bay Area. If the availability of Pioneer Park stimulated the growth of baseball in 1866 and 1867, conversely, its loss after 1867 stunted the game's development. Why it was never used after the 1867 season was never explained. Perhaps Mr. Livingston had plans for his property that were incompatible with baseball.

Also contributing to the appearance that the game had declined was the dominance of the Wide Awakes, an Oakland Club. On June 5 the Wide Awakes took the Championship Bat from the Pacifics and held it to the end of the season, forcing all challengers to come to Clinton.

Instead of playing up the natural East Bay–San Francisco rivalry, as they had in the 1866 Live Oaks–City College matches (and a later Live Oaks–Cosmopolitan series in October), the San Francisco newspapers ignored the Wide Awakes and the games played outside of the city. Thus the provincialism of San Francisco's newspapers created the illusion that there was no baseball in 1868.

Another element was the unannounced and unexplained demise of the very competitive and twice runner-up Cosmopolitan Club.

In April 1868, undoubtedly in response to the loss of Pioneer Park, the Bay City Base Ball Club bought two blocks of land that the ballplayers planned to fence in and make into baseball grounds. They intended to charge a small admission fee (something not done at Pioneer Park) for the upkeep and maintenance of their grounds. Ultimately they planned to sell their investment when real estate prices rose in that part of San Francisco.

After the initial announcement of the Bay City Club's plans, no further reports were given on the progress, if any, on their new grounds. In mid–August, while the Wide Awakes were defending their Bat against the Eagles in Clinton, a notice appeared in the San Francisco papers calling for all cricket, baseball, and other out-door sports enthusiasts to meet to discuss a plan to convert two blocks of land into a public recreation ground.

These were not the same two blocks owned by the Bay City Club. These blocks (also part of the former Pioneer Race Track) were bounded by 25th, 26th, Folsom, and Harrison streets, catty-corner to the former site of Pioneer Park. This would become Recreation Grounds, San Francisco's "first" baseball grounds.

Credit for the vision of Recreation Grounds must go to Richard W. Kohler, an English musician, and William J. Hatton, who had the foresight to lease the property from Eugene Casserly, one of California's United States Senators.

Through the summer of 1868 and into the fall, while the plan for Recreation Grounds was taking shape, the Wide Awakes held onto the Bat against all challengers. Finally, on Thanksgiving Day, November 26, Recreation Grounds opened to the public. For 25 cents, which included admission to the grounds, round-trip car fare, a two-part instrumental concert (given under the direction of Mr. Kohler), a half-mile race, a 300-yard sack race and a ¾ mile hurdle race, between three and four thousand people witnessed the return of baseball to San Francisco as the Wide Awakes and Eagles played for the championship. The Eagles had won the first game of the match, 27–16, at Clinton. By winning the inaugural game at Recreation Grounds, 37–23, the Eagles could justifiably claim their first championship.

Despite its grand opening, Recreation Grounds was not the remedy to halt baseball's decline. In fact, Recreation Grounds became the cause and source for even further slippage in 1869.

Whereas Pioneer Park was exclusively a baseball facility, Recreation Grounds was to be, according to the announcement in the *Daily Morning Call* of August 13, 1868, "a public recreation ground designed for cricket, quoits, Caledonian and other athletic and healthful games and outdoor amusements, military parades and reviews," in addition to being used for baseball.

The profit-driven motive of the grounds' operators contributed to another lackluster baseball season in 1869. In order to entice the public to pay for what they had been seeing for free for two years at Pioneer Park, the proprietors of the Recreation Grounds made a burlesque of the national game. Between such offerings as instrumental concerts, Roman Hippodromes, circuses, chariot racing, horse racing, pedestrian racing and a 100-mile horse race against the clock, baseball nines made up of theater troupes would play against opera companies and non-convention teams such as the Horribles, Unknowns, and Invincibles would compete. While fat men's clubs played against each other to the amusement of the paying customers, time was somehow found to schedule some serious baseball into Recreation Grounds.

The short 1869 season began without the Wide Awakes, which didn't field a nine. The season's first match was played on Washington's Birthday with the Eagles and Pacifics facing each other and ended with the same two clubs facing each other on June 5 as the Eagles won their second consecutive championship.

The transcontinental railroad was completed in May. Sensing a sure-fire promotional opportunity that would draw large paying crowds to the Recreation Grounds, William Hatton invited the "Red Stockings" of Cincinnati to come to San Francisco to play a series of games against the local clubs. On August 30 the Red Stockings accepted Hatton's invitation, and for a month the baseball clubs were frantic with delight as they prepared to welcome baseball's royalty.

San Francisco was now on the national baseball map. The Red Stockings would play five games: two against the Eagles and Pacifics and one against the Atlantics. In addition, a game against a picked nine and a mixed game were scheduled. Nobody expected San Francisco's clubs, some of which hadn't played competitively in over three months, to do much against the professional juggernaut.

On September 25, a blisteringly hot day, the Red Stockings kept the Eagles and two thousand fans who paid $1.00 to witness the first game waiting for over forty minutes past the announced starting time. When the Eagles finally came to bat in the top of the first inning, they faced Asa Brainard, "the most accurate and swiftest pitcher in the country." Brainard ushered in the era of professional baseball in San Francisco by striking out right fielder James Aitken. The Red Stockings won 35–4.

Despite admission being cut in half (still including round-trip car fare), only about 1,000 showed up for the second match on September 27 to witness the 58–4 rout of the Eagles.

Two-game total: Red Stockings 93, Eagles 8.

The Pacifics fared even worse, losing both games by a combined score of 120–9.

Next up were the Atlantics, undoubtedly grateful that they only had to face the Red Stockings once. Just 400 were on hand to witness a five-inning 76–5 drubbing that included a 40-run 4th inning by the Red Stockings. After having seen how the Red Stockings handled the Eagles and Pacifics, it was no wonder that the *Chronicle* said the Atlantics were "afraid of their opponents from the start, and muffed many balls and made some very bad overthrows."

The highlight of the Red Stockings' visit was a game against a "picked nine": the best players in California. William Hatton must have been elated to see the largest crowd of the series on hand for this contest.

The *Chronicle* called this match, won by the Red Stockings 46–14, "one of the most exciting and interesting games which has ever been played in this city. The picked nine determined to redeem their reputation and they have done so, for they played unusually well; and, besides, it is no crime to be defeated by a club which has beaten every crack nine in the United States. Every one of the picked nine exerted themselves."

The final match, a mixed-team affair with one side made up of five Red Stockings and four Eagles and the other made up of five Red Stockings and four Pacifics, entertained 1,500 spectators. The game was delayed after five innings and finally halted after seven by something that would vex baseball players in San Francisco for the next 140 years: wind. The *Alta* described a situation not unfamiliar to players today: "occasionally a ball would be carried out of the way by the force of the wind." The *Chronicle* added: "Shortly before the game was called the wind set in and continued for the rest of the day, blowing dust in everybody's eyes and almost paralyzing the players."

On October 4, 1869, the grandest ten days in the history of San Francisco baseball was celebrated at the farewell banquet where dinner, speeches, songs, and toasts kept the party together till past 1 A.M. Not until the San Francisco Giants played the New York Yankees in the 1962 World Series would there be another ten days to compare with these.

The *Times* bid the Red Stockings adieu with this summation of their visit to California:

> Our clubs, as a matter of course, deserve a great deal of credit for entering the field in competition with an association of such established reputation as the Red Stockings.... The vast disproportion between the [Red Stockings] and our own [clubs] is so palpable that, in our judgment, it will not do for the Cincinnatians to say much about the result in California when making up their record of victories because those obtained here carry no credit with them when the result is studied.... Probably no where else would the Red Stockings have found men with the courage that characterized the Californians, because when they went to the field, they were well assured it was a field of defeat.

Professional baseball had come and gone.

Having, for better or worse, played against the best club in the country, San Francisco's clubs ought to have been inspired to get the ball rolling again. Instead, when the 1870 season began, San Francisco found itself exactly where it had been ten years earlier: with only two clubs. The Eagles and Atlantics were the city's only representatives in the 9-member Pacific Base Ball Convention.

Almost all of the clubs from the 1867 convention, including the two-time champion Pacifics and the perennial challenger Libertys, were gone. There was no explanation for this mass extinction. The only good news for 1870 was the return of the Wide Awakes, which were inspired to re-group by the Red Stockings.

Noting that the previous two baseball seasons had been uninteresting, the *Alta* wrote at the beginning of the 1870 season: "It is hoped that we will now have the pleasure of seeing our National Game once more on the Pacific Slope. And now that the players have taken a new life, it is to be expected that the public will encourage them with their presence on match days."

Ironically, the *Alta*, like other papers, seldom reported on the games that it had urged the public to attend. On the basis of newspaper reports, 1870 seems to have been another dull year for the sport, although a mid-season surprise was the reestablishment of the Liberty Club. The Eagles continued their winning ways, posting 10 victories in 11 games and earning their third consecutive championship by defending the Bat against the Atlantic, Liberty, and Vallejo clubs.

Eight clubs began the 1871 season. Play began in April with the Eagles successfully defending the Bat against the Atlantics, two games to one.

Shortly afterward the Eagles were accused of using illegal players in the Atlantics series. The Eagles at first denied the charge and then admitted the violation. They were suspended by the Pacific Base Ball Convention for six months and had to surrender the 1871 Bat.

The Libertys won the drawing for the Bat and accepted the Wide Awake Club's challenge, and the 1871 season began anew without the Eagles.

Or so it seemed.

Eagle Club delegate John Durkee interrupted the first game of the Liberty–Wide Awake match with a protest that the championship was illegal and, somehow forgetting that the truth of the charges had been admitted and that he had personally surrendered the Bat, claimed that only the Eagles were rightfully entitled to hold the Bat. The Wide Awakes defeated the Libertys in this contest, but lost a subsequent championship re-match.

In October a civic relief fund for the victims of Chicago's Great Fire included a benefit game between the reigning champs Libertys and a picked nine. Seven of the picked nine were Eagle players.

Facing each other for the third time for the Bat, the Wide Awakes concluded the 1871 season by defeating the Libertys and become the first non–San Francisco club to hold the Bat at the end of a season.

Predictably, the first 1872 meeting of the Pacific Base Ball Convention began with the litigious Eagles vainly continuing their protest that they had been wrongfully suspended the previous year. Ignoring the facts of the case, and that he had admitted the charges of wrongdoing, John Durkee argued that the convention's action was invalid due to procedural errors. He also accused the Wide Awakes of orchestrating a grand conspiracy to defraud the Eagles of their rightful prize. What remedy he sought had he been successful in his protest was never revealed.

Including the reinstated Eagles, there were nine convention clubs. In 1872 the Wide Awakes and the Eagles met three times during the year for the championship, each meeting generating increasingly bad feelings between the two clubs. The year ended with the Eagles winning the Bat on a technicality in what the *Call*, an unfailingly unabashed Eagle supporter, called "a miserable close" to the season.

As their first order of 1873 business, the six clubs of the Pacific Base Ball Convention had to find a better way to determine the champion—after, of course, dealing with the vexatiously litigious Eagles and their protest of a game that they had lost to the Wide Awakes in September. The clubs decided on a new method for determining the champion. Unfortunately, this was too little too late, for there were no reports of any baseball games played in 1873, bringing an end to the Era of the Bat.

Play resumed in 1874 with the old clubs gone, replaced by new ones—the Oaklands, Occidentals, Athletics, Grand Centrals, Californias, and Mutuals—although with many familiar names on the rosters. At the end of the season the Eagles, the sole remaining club from the Era of the Bat, made their only appearance on the field, defeating the Californias, 41–31.

❖ *Eagles of San Francisco* (Angus Macfarlane) ❖

CLUB HISTORY

Even the most casual student of early San Francisco baseball history knows of the Eagles. And for good reason: they were the first club; the most enduring; arguably the most dominant; and, for some reason, the club's roster is recorded in Seymour Church's *Baseball: The History, Statistics and Romance of the American National Game*. Thanks to an unattributed source, Church provides membership information on 218 Eagles (although only 86 names actually appear in box scores) who joined the club between November 18, 1859, and October 3, 1871. These are the only records of any San Francisco club that exist in any form.

What is not generally known about the Eagles is that they were also the most contentious club, virtually destroying the game in San Francisco with their rule-bending, tolerance-testing, limit-pushing obsession with winning at all costs.

Made up of a mixture of working men, tradesmen, civil servants and "white collar" types, the Eagles began as the San Francisco Base Ball Club in either November or December of 1859.[1]

Legend has it that they had originally been the San Francisco Cricket Club before adopting baseball. Indisputably, many of the original members were indeed cricketers, but they were *not* members of the San Francisco Cricket Club. On June 20, 1859, the *real* San Francisco Cricket Club played a match against a combined team from the Union and Pioneer Cricket Clubs that were made up of a number of future Eagles.[2]

After the November 19, 1859, announcement that a baseball club had been organized in Sacramento, the formation of the San Francisco Base Ball Club was reported in the *Spirit of the Times* (*Times*) of December 24, 1859, and included the names of the following pioneers: President, J.F. Miller; Vice President, John Hall; Secretary, Thomas D. Carroll; Treasurer, John L. Durkee; Committee of Arrangements and Finance, John M. Fisher, John L. Durkee and James Willock.

On January 28, 1860, the S.F.B.B.C. issued a challenge:

> We the undersigned members of the San Francisco Base Ball Club hereby challenge any nine base ball players to a match game to be played according to the rules of the Base Ball Convention held in New York, March 19, 1859, to be on the 22d of February, weather permitting.
> T.D. Carrol; John L. Durkee; J[ames] Willock; T.G. Vandeveer; J[ohn] M. Fisher; J.R. Nealy; A[bner] F[reeman] Barston; J. Anderson; C. Boyce.

(Obligingly, in order to promote the game, the *Times* had published the *Rules and Regulations of the Game of Base Ball, adopted by the National Association of Base Ball Players, held in New York, March 19th, 1859* in its issue of July 2, 1859.)

Responses were received from the Red Rovers of San Francisco and the Sacramento Club. The reply from the Red Rovers having arrived first, the San Franciscos arranged to play them on Washington's Birthday 1860, at Center's Bridge, a site near where Seals Stadium would be built 70 years later.

After a spell of drizzly weather, the conditions were clear and brisk on game day, with the temperature at game time in the high 50s. On that historic date the *Times* reported, "The day was all could be wished for, there being just breeze enough to be refreshing. [This was the first reference to San Francisco's notorious game-affecting wind.] The ground was very good and in fact everything was as could be desired."

Except for one thing: the game was scheduled to begin at 10 A.M., but by 10:15 the San Franciscos had not arrived. SECTION 35 of the New York rules, under which the match was to be played, clearly stated: "Play shall be called at the exact hour appointed; and should either party fail to produce their players within 15 minutes thereafter, the party so failing shall admit defeat."

The Red Rovers could have claimed a forfeit victory. Instead they graciously waited for their opponents to arrive.

At 10:55 the San Franciscos finally appeared, and after hurried preparations, they were ready to play at 11 A.M. Why were the San Franciscos an hour late? Are we to believe that the San Franciscos were unaware of the start time requirement — that they had to be on the field no later than 10:15 A.M.?

In 1888 A.G. Spalding stopped in San Francisco on his worldwide baseball tour. At a banquet given by Mr. Spalding, John Durkee related how the first ball ever used in San Francisco came to be. It was reported in the *Examiner* of November 19, 1888:

> Two clubs had been organized and all preparations made for a game when it was found that such a thing as a ball could not be had in San Francisco. Mr. Durkee was appointed one of a committee to secure one in some way. While searching for material he came across a German immigrant who was the possessor of a pair of rubber overshoes. These he bought, after much dickering, for $10, and with the yarn unraveled from a woolen stocking and a piece of a rubber overshoe the first ball ever used in this city was made.

Is it conceivable that the San Franciscos were an hour late to their first game because at the last minute, if we are to believe the literal truth of John Durkee's 1888 story, they discovered that they didn't have a ball?

If so, did the first baseball game in San Francisco *really* come off because of John Durkee's last-minute luck and resourcefulness, along with his desperate willingness to part with the exorbitant amount of $10 for a used pair of rubber overshoes? "After much dickering," conveys a sense of urgency on Durkee's part that he had no alternative to dealing with the possessor of the highly desired galoshes.

Are we supposed to believe that the San Franciscos *really* were an hour late because Durkee spent so much time looking for and then dickering over the overshoes on the morning of the first match; or because Durkee took too long to unravel his woolen stocking; or because the assembly of the first ball used in San Francisco ran overtime?

Are we supposed to believe that such bad luck and poor planning really occurred, nearly resulting in San Francisco's first baseball game ending in a forfeit?

Although the *Examiner* report of Durkee's version leads one to believe this, it seems highly improbable. SECTION 1 of the New York rules specified that the ball "must be composed of India rubber and yarn, and covered with leather, and in all

San Francisco

Names	H.L.	Runs
1. Carroll, catcher	3	3
2. Willock, pitcher	3	4
3. Fisher, 2d base	3	3
4. Boyes, short	2	5
5. Henderson, left field	2	5
6. Vandeveer, 3d base	4	2
7. Dixon, 1st base	4	2
8. Durkee, centre field	3	4
9. Baston, right field	3	4
Total		33

Red Rovers

Names	H.L.	Runs
1. Hughes, pitcher	2	6
2. Brokaw, catcher	0	7
3. J. Kerrigan, 1st base	3	4
4. Astley, 2d base	5	2
5. E. Kerrigan, short	3	1
6. Ackerson, right field	3	3
7. Colby, centre field	4	3
8. Simpson, 3d base	5	2
9. Swift, left field	2	5

Runs Made at Each Inning

Innings	1	2	3	4	5	6	7	8	9	
S.F.	3	6	3	3	3	0	3	3	9	—33
R.R.	3	4	4	1	13	1	2	4	1	—33

Scorer for the San Franciscos: J. Hall
Scorer for the Red Rovers: Chas. Allen
Umpire: Mr. McClosky

match games shall be furnished by the challenging Club [San Francisco, in this case] and becomes the property of the winning Club as a trophy of victory."

(The original ball, whatever its origin and construction, was given to the Eagle Club of New York in 1868 by John Durkee, according to a *Times* article published on December 20, 1884.)

Or was there another reason that the San Francisco Base Ball Club was an hour late?

The *Times* only provides teasing hints at what happened before the match that morning without details or answers, although the *Times* did report somewhat enigmatically "[San Francisco batted first] *after settling some objections that were made to some of their players.*" (Italics added.)

Again the question: why were the San Franciscos an hour late?

Was there any connection between their tardiness and *the objections to some of their players* by the Red Rovers?

Could it be that San Francisco was an hour late, not because they couldn't find a *ball*, but because they couldn't find *enough players?*

SECTION 27 of the New York rules stated that players must have been members of the club for 30 days prior to the match.

The San Francisco players whose names appeared in the *Times'* box score that day were Willock, Carroll, Dixon, Fisher, Vandeveer, Boyes, Henderson, Durkee and Baston.

According to the Eagle membership roster in Church, three players — Dixon, Baston (or perhaps *Barston?*) and Vanderwater (*Vandeveer?*) — had joined the club in February. Henderson was not even listed as a member, nor did his name appear among the San Francisco challengers.

Additionally, of these four men, only Dixon ever appeared in a box score again. The others played just the one game, never again to be involved in baseball in San Francisco.

Again the question: could it be that the San Francisco Base Ball Club was late because they didn't have enough players?

Questions regarding the eligibility of San Francisco/Eagle players would be a theme throughout the club's history.

Once the objections to the Eagle players were settled, San Francisco batted, three of them crossing the plate before the Red Rovers came up. Immediately they protested the pitching of James Willock. Umpire Matt McCloskey ruled that since Willock didn't violate the rule by throwing or jerking the ball, there was no basis for their objection, so play resumed.

The game was closely contested for 4 innings: San Francisco 15, Red Rovers 12. In the fifth San Francisco changed pitchers, and the Red Rovers scored 13 runs. After that debacle Willock returned to the box in the 6th, and San Francisco went ahead with 9 runs in the top of the 9th. The Red Rovers scored once to tie the game 33-all after nine innings, but they refused to continue unless Willock was replaced.

Again Umpire McCloskey ruled that there was no substance to their complaints, and since the Red Rovers refused to play extra innings, he declared San Francisco the winner by forfeit.

The Red Rovers appealed, asking for time to consider their options. McCloskey granted them the same amount of time they had waited for their opponents. After one hour of deliberation the Red Rovers again refused to continue, and for the second time McCloskey declared the San Franciscos the winner by forfeit.

At stake was a dinner for 25 to be paid for by the losing club. Feeling that they hadn't exactly lost, the Red Rovers offered to pay for half the dining bill. This offer was refused, and the San Francisco Base Ball Club celebrated their victory on their own tab.

This ended any relations with the Red Rovers, who never played another game.

Three weeks later the San Francisco Base Ball Club changed their name to Eagle Base Ball Club, ostensibly to honor the Eagle Base Ball Club of New York.

One version holds that New York members of the Eagles who had relocated to San Francisco missed their pastime so much that they formed the San Francisco Base Ball Club. There is absolutely no basis for this story.

Another version is that the specific honoree was M.E.

(Marion) Gelston, a well-known Eagle base ballist who played shortstop in the famous New York–Brooklyn Fashion Race Course matches in 1858. The time-line of this explanation raises questions regarding its validity. Gelston became a member of the Eagles on March 30, 1860, more than two weeks *after* the club changed its name.

Another possibility for the name change, presented here for the first time, is that the New York honoree might have been Robert Greglette,[3] who played shortstop and catcher for the New York version of the Eagles in 1859. He became a member of the San Francisco club on February 18, 1860, almost a month *before* the club's name change. He was elected the club's third president on December 28, 1860.

Regardless of the actual origin of the name, the Eagles of San Francisco definitely claimed affinity with their New York namesakes. On a trip to New York in 1868, John Durkee was feted by some 30 or 40 veteran members of the original Eagle Club and he presented them with the ball from the first San Francisco game.

The Eagles played their second game of the season against the Em Quads on June 23, winning 55–27 in seven innings.

During the summer there were a number of unsuccessful attempts to play the Sacramento Club, but disagreements over the conditions and terms of the match forced postponements. When it was announced that there would be a baseball tournament at the Sacramento State Fair in September, both clubs accepted invitations, and a meeting between the state's two undefeated clubs was greatly anticipated.

By Sacramento Fair time the Eagles had added "Cricket" to their name, becoming the Eagle Base Ball and Cricket Club. Marion Gelston was the leader of the Eagle nine, and E.N. Robinson, formerly of the Putnam Club of Brooklyn, led the Sacramentos.[4]

The first game against the Sacramentos was a bifurcated affair. Starting so late that by the third inning the game was called because of darkness, it was continued the next day with the Eagles winning, 36–32. The second game was won by the Eagles, 31–17, earning them $100, a silver ball, and the title of State Base Ball Champion.

A feature of the tournament was the selection of best players at each position, effectively the state's first all-star team. Five Eagles were honored: original Eagles John Fisher at second base, John Durkee in right field, and James Willock at first base, along with the recently recruited Ed Kerrigan from the Red Rovers at pitcher, and the former Em Quad Sam Wade at 3rd base.

A week after the two clubs and their guests profusely toasted one another and the spirit of baseball at the departing banquet, selections of the clubs' nines for the San Francisco Fair were published in the *Times*. Included in the article was a reference to the *Sacramento Democrat*'s "covert attack upon the Eagle Base Ball Club."

Rumors on the streets of Sacramento during the state tournament regarding the eligibility of some Eagle players had found their way onto the pages of Sacramento newspapers after the Eagles had left. The post-tournament toasts, good will, and congratulations apparently masked some very hard feelings between the two clubs.

Although Sacramento had selected its nine, the club did not come to San Francisco for a return match. Instead the Eagles easily put away the Em Quads, 33–14, in five innings.

Rather than leading their clubs in competition on the diamond, the presidents of the Eagles and Sacramentos waged a war of words over a period of several weeks, which the *Times* provided to the public in summaries of the lengthy letters exchanged between the two men.[5] Without naming names, Robinson charged that some of the Eagles who had played in Sacramento had resigned from the club, or that their memberships had lapsed, rendering them ineligible to play according to New York rules, Section 27. He requested information on the membership status of the Eagles who had played, but Gelston was evasive and not forthcoming.

In referring to the Eagles' behavior as "Red Roverish," Robinson wrote: "These facts and sentiments are not alone confined to our own city, but have been mentioned and commented upon by other base ball clubs and organizations in other parts of our state."

In his final letter, a completely frustrated Robinson condemned the Eagles for their "clannish, selfish and round-about way of doing that which were better not done at all"—a characterization that would echo down the years.

Meanwhile, the Eagle *Cricket* Club, in its first match, was immersed in its own controversy. Having lost to the Pioneer Cricket Club at the San Francisco Fair, the Eagles rationalized away their defeat, and passed this resolution: "WHEREAS, the E.B.B. and C.C. lost the recent match with the Pioneer Cricket Club through unavoidable absence of their players, they are not willing to acknowledge defeat as a club."

The Eagles promptly issued a challenge to any cricket club in the state to play in a friendly match "*for the championship of the state*" (italics added). The Pioneers, who had defeated the Eagles in the previous match, accepted the challenge. In a formality-laden process, committees were formed, but the match never came off. On December 15, 1860, the Pioneers explained in the *Times* that they had accepted the Eagles' challenge but refused to play them because the Eagles persisted in having an umpire whom the Pioneers felt was biased and incompetent. Challenges that the Eagles posted in the *Times* in December 1860 went unanswered, and the year ended with, as Robinson described them, the "clannish" and "selfish" Eagles having no one to play with.

With the Red Rovers and the Em Quads gone from the diamond and no cricket matches, there was no activity for the Eagles. Consequently, only three new members were accepted in 1861 and no others until November of 1862 when 15 new men joined the Eagles' aerie.

Almost all histories of baseball in San Francisco say that

in 1863 members of the Eagles split off and formed a new club, which became the Pacifics, and that these two clubs played their first match on February 23, 1863, in back of the old Mission Dolores. However, there is no contemporaneous report of that event, supposedly won by the Eagles, 27–18.

On January 7, 1866, readers of the *Alta* learned that the Eagles and the Pacifics would contend for the baseball championship of California the next day. That match was not played, but on February 16, 1866, six years after baseball's first appearance at Center's Bridge, the game made a reappearance in San Francisco. The Eagle Club lost to the Pacifics 32–18 — its first loss ever — igniting the internecine rivalry that would define the two clubs for the next four years.

When the two clubs met a week later, the *Alta*'s report was terse: "CROWDED OUT: The score of the championship base ball match between the Eagle and Pacific clubs which took place yesterday has been furnished to us, but is laid over till tomorrow for want of room."

The results were never published, although Church records that the Pacifics won 35–15. The Eagles, the first champions of California, had been upended by their little brothers in two straight games. The Eagles split four games with the Pacifics over the course of the year.

Only one other Eagle game was reported in 1866: the Thanksgiving Day game against the Independents, which the Eagles won 44–25.

On the morning that the Pacifics and Cosmopolitans were to play in what had been designated the championship match, the Eagles preemptively posted a noticed in the *Call* stating that regardless of the outcome of the Pacifics-Cosmopolitan match, neither club could claim the title because it belonged to the Eagles.

How many matches the Eagles actually played and the basis for their claim to the 1866 championship is not known. Their claim that they were the 1866 state champions had to be settled by the Pacific Base Ball Convention at its first meeting of 1867. The convention ruled against the Eagles.

On June 1, 1867, the Eagles defeated the reigning champs Cosmopolitans twice to gain possession of the championship Bat. For the first time the Eagles were the undisputed champions of the state. But they held the Bat for just a month before they lost it to the Pacifics in July and would not hold the Bat again in 1867.

In the season-ending championship game between the Pacifics and Cosmopolitans the Eagles had a unique opportunity to frustrate their rivals, but they were unable to keep the Pacifics from repeating as champions. (This game is discussed in the Pacific and Cosmopolitan sections.)

The Eagles began the 1868 season by charging the Pacifics with fraud in one of the championship games played the previous July. No public details were provided, but William Hale and John Kerrigan were the targets of the Eagles' unspecified complaint of fraud.

In August 1868, the Eagles played their first Battle for the Bat of the year against the new champion Wide Awakes of Oakland, losing the series, 2–1. The Eagles met the Wide Awakes again in November, this time sweeping the series, 2–0. The second game was played at the grand opening of Recreation Grounds before 3,000–4,000 spectators, the largest crowd to witness a baseball game in San Francisco up to that time. By winning the final championship series of the year, the Eagles earned the title of baseball champion of California of 1868.

Eighteen sixty-nine was both a high and low year for the Eagles. In a shortened season, they took the coveted Bat, defeating their archrival Pacifics in all three matches. The low point was playing the Red Stockings of Cincinnati in September. In a contest between the champions of the state of California versus the undefeated professional juggernaut from the East there was no doubt as to the outcome, which seems to have led to rumors that the Eagles would back out of the match. These reports were taken seriously by Eagle Club president John Durkee, who posted a notice in the *Alta*: "**BASE BALL NOTICE — RED STOCKINGS v. EAGLES**. Reports having been circulated that the Eagles were not to play the Red Stockings, I hereby give notice that the Eagles and Red Stockings will play at the Recreation Grounds THIS DAY, 25th instant, and MONDAY, 27th inst. Game is called for two o'clock punctually."

Commenting on Durkee's notice, the *Alta* wrote:

> The President of the Eagle Base-Ball Club publishes a card in another column denying the report that the nine of the "Eagles" would fail to play with the "Red Stockings"; they will be promptly at their posts when game is called at two o'clock, and will do their "level best" to win. The nine of the Eagle Club is as good a nine as can be picked in the State, in the estimation of most "base-ball sharps," and they will give ample opportunity to bring out the play of the famous visitors for Cincinnati.

The Eagles were true to their word: they did arrive and were ready to play. However, reminiscent of the Eagles' tardiness at Center's Bridge a decade earlier, the visitors were inexplicably 40 minutes late.

The Eagles batted first and lead-off batter, right fielder James Aitken, struck out. Next up was second baseman John Fisher, the only remaining Eagle from the first game. One can only imagine what thoughts went through his mind as he came to bat. After fouling off two Brainard offerings, he singled to right field. For the day the veteran Fisher would get three of the Eagles' eight hits in his five at-bats. The *Call* wrote: "The Eagles went on the ground thoroughly demoralized, through fear of their adversaries."

As they took the field for the bottom of the first, the *Alta* described the Eagles as "discomfited by their defeat [at bat] and fearful of their renowned opponents, so muffs were the order of the day, and the Cincinnatis made their largest score, mostly off the muffed ball by the fielders and passed balls by the catcher."

Twelve red-stockinged runners crossed the plate in the bottom of the first. The Eagles were held scoreless until the 6th inning when they scored three runs, ultimately losing, 35–4. Nonetheless, against a club that averaged 40 runs a game, holding them to 35 tallies definitely counted as a symbolic victory. For the next game the *Call* helpfully advised the Eagles: "What you should do, gentlemen of the Eagles, is to keep down the score of the Red Stockings, with no expectation of winning.... It will be a feather in the cap of that club that allows the visiting club to get the least number of runs."

After the Eagles were plucked 58–4, the *Chronicle* commented: "The Eagles seemed to have lost every particle of their energy and agility before they came upon the field." There was no silver lining in the slaughter, unless "whitewashing" the Red Stockings in the second inning reflected some faint sparkle. The combined total for two games was 93–8.

Two weeks after the Red Stockings left, arsonists set fire to Recreation Grounds, destroying the grandstands and the adjoining buildings in which the Eagles stored their equipment.

The 1870 baseball season didn't begin until July, with the Eagles and Atlantics as the only San Francisco Clubs in the nine-member Pacific Base Ball Convention contending for the Bat. The Eagles had little difficulty that year, winning ten of eleven games and their third consecutive Bat.

Before the 1871 season got underway, three Eagles, catcher John Curran, pitcher Miller, and left fielder Taylor left for the Liberty Club for unknown reasons. Competition began with the Eagles retaining their Bat against the Atlantics two games to one. They then began a series with the Wide Awakes, winning the first game on April 21, 1871.

The next evening, at a meeting of the Pacific Base Ball Convention, the Eagles were charged with having knowingly used three ineligible players in their recent match against the Atlantics, a violation of convention rules. The Eagles' initial response was to vehemently protest the procedure by which the charges had been brought. Their objections were overruled, and witnesses testified that indeed three of the Eagle players had been members of the Atlantic Club within the past 60 days. After the prosecution rested its case, Eagle delegate John Durkee "very quietly remarked that the Eagle Club pleaded guilty and offered no defence whatever." The convention voted to suspend the Eagles for six months — essentially the remainder of the 1871 season — and they had to surrender the Bat. As he did so, Durkee said: "Mr. President: I hand you the bone of contention, and am sorry to say that you cannot obtain it any other way. Good night gentlemen."

The clubs then drew lots for the Bat, which was won by the Liberty Club. They immediately accepted a challenge from the Wide Awakes, and the 1871 season began anew without the Eagles.

Durkee's admission that the Eagles were guilty of wrongdoing was not the end of the dispute. The words of Sacramento Club President E.N. Robinson echoed down the corridors of time: the Eagles' "*clannish, selfish and round-about way of doing that which were better not done at all*" would bring an end to baseball in San Francisco. Despite being suspended as a club, a number of Eagles continued to play as members of the Vallejo Club.

In October a civic relief fund for the victims of Chicago's Great Fire included a benefit game between the reigning champs Libertys and a picked nine. Seven of the picked nine were Eagle players.

True to form, the first 1872 meeting of the Pacific Base Ball Convention began with the litigious Eagles continuing their protest that they had been wrongfully suspended the previous year. Ignoring the facts of the case, and that he had admitted the charges of wrongdoing, John Durkee persisted in arguing that a flawed process had illegally resulted in his club's suspension. His objections were again overruled.

The Wide Awakes and the Eagles met three times during the year for the Bat, with each meeting producing more ill will and controversy than the previous one, ending with the Eagles winning the Bat in a game that even the *Call* reporter, who normally supported the Eagle Club, called "a miserable close" to the season.

On May 1, 1872, three days before the first Eagle–Wide Awake Battle for the Bat, the sympathetic *Call* printed a letter rehashing the issues of the past year that also asserted that the Wide Awakes could never defeat the Eagles on the field. On May 4, the assertions of the letter writer were put to the test as the two clubs met in the first game of their championship match. The Wide Awakes thrashed the Eagles. The result of the game, according to the *Oakland Daily News* of December 2, 1872, "was not to increase the good feeling between these clubs, and many harsh expressions were used against 'our country cousins.'"

The Wide Awakes won the second game and the Bat, but the Eagles won the next two series and the Bat on the final day of the season in ways that brought discredit to the game of baseball and dishonor to the Eagles. (This is discussed in the Wide Awake section)

As described in the introduction, the Era of the Bat ended in 1873 and the Eagles played no known games that season. Late in 1874, the Eagles made one final appearance on the field, defeating the Californias 41–31. A game account in the *Chronicle* noted that the venerable second baseman John Fisher, "despite his advanced age and corpulancy [sic]," played well, making only one out at bat and scoring six runs.

Notes

1. The *California Spirit of the Times* announced the formation of the San Francisco Base Ball Club in its December 24, 1859, edition. The Eagle membership roster in Church notes that the earliest members were admitted on November 29, 1859.

2. Charles Boyce, Thomas Carroll, Ed Kerrigan, John Kerrigan,

William Dunn and C.C. Dunn were the cricketers who played against the San Francisco Cricket Club who would become Eagles.

3. There are four spelling variations. Church lists *GREGGLETTE* in the Eagle membership roster. His name appears as *GREGLIETER* in the June 23, 1860, *Times* box score of the Eagles–Em Quads game. Marshall D. Wright in *The National Association of Base Ball Players, 1857–1870*, p. 33, has *GREGLIETA* playing shortstop and catching for the New York Eagles in 1859. The *Times* reports his election to president of the Eagles on January 12, 1861, with the spelling *GRIGLIETTI*.

4. On September 29, 1860, the *Times* wrote: "*Gelston is of the Eagle Club of New York, and Robinson is of the Putnam Club of Brooklyn.*" Gelston appears in Wright, but there is no mention of Robinson playing for any club, Brooklyn or New York.

5. The letters were printed in the *Times* between October 13 and November 10, 1860.

❖ *Pacifics of San Francisco* (Angus Macfarland) ❖

CLUB HISTORY

For two years following the 1860 baseball "season," the sport was moribund in San Francisco. Of the three original clubs of 1860, only the Eagles remained and there is no record of any baseball activity during this time. Then in a two-week period between November 12 and November 26, 1862, fifteen new members were added to the Eagle roster.

On November 26, 1862, the *Alta* urged its sporting-minded readers to "[witness] a splendid match on Thanksgiving Day, which is to take place at the Mission Dolores between the Eagle Base Ball Club's nine and nine other crack players. After the sport is over a grand dinner is to be partaken of by the Company and invited guests." Two days later the *Alta* followed with "The Eagle Base Ball Club went out to the Mission to have a bout at their favorite game. The day being so charming, was enjoyed with all the greater zest."

Fred Lange, in his *History of Baseball in California and Pacific Coast Leagues 1847–1938*, wrote "With the assistance of the two Shepard brothers [James and William] and some of the Eagles, the Pacifics were organized on *November 26, 1862*" (italics added).

If Lange's information is correct, then the game at Mission Dolores on Thanksgiving Day 1862 was, in fact, the debut of the Pacifics.

William Shepard recalled in Church:

> In 1861 we crossed the plains to California, and to San Francisco. But one club existed in San Francisco at that time, which we joined soon after our arrival. [Church's records indicate that Shepard and his brother James became Eagles on November 12, 1862.] And as we were direct from the center of the base ball universe, and brought with us the newest ideas upon the game, we were regarded as quite a valuable acquisition to the local organization.
>
> The original club was known as the Eagles. We had been members but a short time, when another club was organized, or rather grew out of the Eagles, the new club being called the Pacifics, and my brother and I cast our lot with the younger club. The entry of the new club into the field gave impetus to the game and created a rivalry and competition that grew to remarkable proportions.

Reports that the two clubs played their first match "back of the old Mission [Dolores] Church on February 23, 1863" may or may not be accurate. Details of the November 27, 1862, and February 23, 1863, matches are absent.

On Thanksgiving Day 1865, the *Alta* reported on a game which clearly didn't recognize any club affiliations. The two sides were unnamed; one was captained by John Fisher, an Eagle, and the other was captained by John Kerrigan, a Pacific. Yet both sides were amalgamations of Eagle and Pacific players. Captain Kerrigan was the pitcher for his team, but his catcher was John Calvert, an Eagle. The Shepard brothers, the stalwart Pacifics, played against each other.

Regardless, this was the only reported baseball activity of any kind involving Eagle and/or Pacific players since the formation of the Pacifics three years earlier, and the first box score since the Eagles faced the Em Quads at the San Francisco Fair in October 1860. Unless there were many unreported matches, Shepard's statement that the entry of the Pacifics gave impetus to the game wasn't immediately evident. However, he was correct when he said that it created a rivalry that "grew to remarkable proportions." Having spun off from the Eagle club, the members of the Pacifics shared the same backgrounds: working men who enjoyed baseball. Their distinguishing characteristic was, of course, that they were *not* Eagles.

Although claiming to trace its heritage back to 1862 or 1863, the first mention of "Pacifics" in the press was a match against the Eagles scheduled to occur on January 8, 1866. That contest, promoted as being *for the Championship of California* (italics added), didn't come off and was rescheduled to February 16. The Pacifics won that match, and the state championship, 32–18, becoming the first club to defeat the mighty Eagles. A week later the Pacifics again defeated the Eagles; the results were never published in the *Alta*, but Church provides the score: Pacifics 35, Eagles 15.

A third match between the nascent rivals was played in Oakland on April 28. The following day the *Alta* printed the box score of the Rincon-Eureka match but not a word about the Pacific-Eagle game. The Eagles' first triumph over the Pacifics, 49–23, is recorded in Church, however. The final match of the year between the two clubs was on July 4, won by the Eagles, yet again unreported in the press but preserved in Church.[1]

When the six clubs convened to form the Pacific Base Ball Convention in July 1866, the Pacifics did not send a delegate, but they were present at subsequent meetings. On Thanksgiving Day 1866, the Pacifics found themselves in a match against the Cosmopolitans, of which the *Alta* wrote:

> At Oakland will be played a game by the Pacifics and Cosmopolitans for the championship of the State. The Pacifics have been reputed *the* Club of the State, but tomorrow they must look well to their laurels, as the Cosmopolitan fellows have been traveling over the course pretty lively of late. They have done well for an organization that has been in existence but twelve months.

In a game "that was not of long duration, lasting only three and a half hours," the Pacifics defeated the Cosmopolitans 27–20, garnering the title of Champion of the State. It was never explained how this particular game was the determining one for the state championship. The Eagles had their own questions regarding the legitimacy of this championship match, posting their objection in the *Call* the morning of the contest, claiming the Championship for themselves.

As its first order of business on January 12, 1867, the Pacific Base Ball Convention recognized the Pacifics as the legitimate baseball champions of California for 1866 and called the Eagles' actions an injustice to the Pacifics.[2] In knee-jerk response the Eagles promptly issued a challenge to any nine to play for the championship of the state on February 22, 1867. Just as promptly the Pacifics accepted the challenge and the season was on. The Pacifics split eight matches with the Eagles, but they won the important matches—the ones for the Championship Bat.

In July the rivals met in a battle royal for the Bat. The first game was on July 4 before 2,000 spectators. Considerable open betting was conducted in the see-saw contest. In the final innings, with the excitement building, a portion of the spectators would yell loudly just as the fielder was about to catch the ball. Consequently balls were "muffed." The Eagles won 46–42.

The second game, played on July 12, was, according to the *Chronicle* and its customary hyperbole, "probably the finest ever played on the coast." There was another large crowd on hand, but the "shenanigans" of the first game were not repeated and there was little "muffing." Betting had abated, probably accounting for the good behavior of the spectators. The Pacifics won 29–22, setting the stage for the grand finale.

The third and deciding game was played on July 19. Another large crowd witnessed what the *Alta*, crediting *those posted in such matters*, and being a touch provincial, described as "the closest ever played in California, and probably in the United States."

During the game Eagle first baseman Willock broke three bones in his right hand, and Pacific shortstop Kerrigan sprained his ankle. Both men gamely stayed in the game.

Leading by 13 runs after three innings, the Pacifics held on for a 35–31 victory to win the Bat. Casting a pall on an exciting series, the *Chronicle* wrote, "The muffed fly balls were too numerous. There are a great many rumors floating about, which, if true may place some of the players in a very unenviable position." The paper went on to report that "one or two" Eagle players reported that they had been offered considerable sums of money to "throw off the match." According to other sources, the umpire had also been "implicated."[3]

These were the last games that the Pacifics and the Eagles would play against each other for almost two years.

Over the course of the 1867 season, the Pacifics successfully defended the Bat against the Actives and the Bay Citys before facing the Cosmopolitans in another season-ending championship game.

On the road to the Championship, however, the Pacifics encountered some unusual circumstances. They defeated the Actives two games to none, but the Actives were only able to field eight players for the first game. A full team of Actives couldn't do any better in the second game.

The Pacifics next faced the Bay City Club, who did the Actives one better—or fewer—by fielding a team of only seven players for the first game. Of course the Pacifics won 44–37 despite a furious finish by the Bay Citys when they scored 10 runs in the bottom of the 9th. The Pacifics won the second game more handily, 51–12, against a full complement of Bay City players.

The Pacifics moved on to the Cosmopolitans. The *Alta* hyped the Championship match with this report on November 9, 1867:

> The most exciting topic of conversation among the admirers of the exciting sport of base-ball, is the final match game that will be played this season for the possession of the champion bat, to come off today at one P.M. on the vacant square at the corner of Folsom and [Park] street. The contesting Clubs, the Pacific and the Cosmopolitan, are noted rivals and each included some of the best players in the state. The Pacifics gloriously won the championship in 1866 and from the excellent practice they display at exercise, they are now more formidable than ever before.

Due to unexplained circumstances, only six Cosmopolitans were available to play in the Championship series. Through conscription, recruitment, or volunteers, their places were taken by players from—amazingly enough—the Eagles, undoubtedly with the knowledge and consent of the Pacifics.

The clubs split the first two games: the Pacifics winning the first, 24–18, and the composite Cosmopolitans taking the second, 33–25. Despite playing against ringers, the Pacifics ran away with the third game, 39–15, to win their second championship Bat.

The repeat champions began 1868 with two of their players, pitcher William Hale and shortstop John Kerrigan, accused of fraud. The charges were brought by the Eagles, stemming from the July 1867, championship series. No specifics were reported in the press, but after a lengthy investigation it was announced at the January 18, 1868, meeting of the Pacific Base Ball Convention that Hale was found guilty and suspended for six months while Kerrigan was acquitted.

The consequences for the Pacifics were all but fatal. Hale had been their iron man, appearing in 14 of their 16 games in 1867. Without Hale, the Pacifics had to rely on three different players at pitcher. (William Hale never played baseball again. John Kerrigan continued to play and, as a member of the Atlantic Club in 1871, would gain a measure of satisfaction against the Eagles.)

Probably for a host of very good reasons, the Pacifics and Eagles did not play each other in 1868. The Pacifics played five reported matches in 1868, all against the Wide Awakes of Oakland for the championship, winning just one game.

The next year the Pacifics played in only three reported games, all losing efforts against the Eagles. There probably would not have been a Pacific Club in 1869 if there hadn't been an infusion of players from the Wide Awakes, which didn't field a team that year. Four members of the 1868 runner-up club played for the Pacifics: George Cobb, at third base; W. W. Carter in center; James Perkins in left; and Everett Pomeroy in right. Also joining the Pacific nine was Frank DeLong, a former Cosmopolitan.

The final regular season game for the club was on June 5, 1869. The Pacifics took the field the next time on September 29, and they were facing the legendary Red Stockings of Cincinnati, which had just defeated the Eagles in two games by a combined score of 93–8.

The Pacifics batted first and scored, leading 1–0 after their top of the first inning. This was not just the highlight of the game, it was the highlight of the entire series for the San Francisco clubs, being the only time that the Red Stockings ever trailed. Whatever euphoria the Pacifics may have been experiencing, it didn't last long. Cincinnati scored 8 in the bottom of first on their way to a six-inning 66–4 drubbing of the Pacifics. The Red Stockings hit five home runs, including a grand slam by Andy Leonard.

The *Chronicle* wrote, "Carter, centerfielder, muffed 11 balls, 5 of which were right in his hands. Wade, on 2b did poorly. When he muffed he muffed terribly. Wachtel, pitching, gave the Red Stockings just the kind of balls they wanted and the result is in the score." The paper then suggested a strategy to the Pacifics for the second game: "It would greatly increase the Pacific's chances of scoring if they would play with more precision and not get excited." The Pacifics lost the second game 54–5 in nine innings. In the second game the Red Stockings hit 11 home runs, 4 of them by George Wright, including a grand slam.

A face-saver in the last game played by the Pacifics was the 5 runs they scored, the most so far against the Red Stockings. They also out-scored the Eagles, 9–8, but the total score for two games, 120–9, was an ignominious ending to a classic club.

And there was a final indignity. In their last box score the *Alta* misnamed them "Eagles."

Sam Wade and the Shepard brothers were the only players who were in the Pacific Club's first box score against the Eagles on February 18, 1866, and the final one against the Red Stockings.

John Kerrigan joined his brother David on the Atlantic club in 1870. Sam Wade took a year off before joining the Atlantics in 1871. David E. Allison, who came to the Pacifics from the disbanded Cosmopolitans in 1868, joined the Eagles in 1870. Three former Wide Awakes would rejoin that club: George Cobb, James Perkins, and Everett Pomeroy. For the other Pacifics this was the end of the ride.

Nonetheless, the Pacifics were not entirely forgotten. On February 22, 1882, the Eagles and Pacifics faced each other for one final time in an old-timers' reunion to commemorate the 22nd anniversary of the Center's Bridge match of 1860. Twenty-two players were divided into two teams competing under the names of Pacifics and Eagles. On the Pacific side were former Pacific members David Allison, Thomas Welch, William and James Shepard, Frank DeLong, Sam Wade, John Kerrigan, and Howard Whitbeck. Three other players from other clubs rounded out their side.

Facing them were ten former Eagles and Harry Hook, a ringer from the Liberty Club. Among the venerable Eagles that day were John Durkee and John Fisher, who were present at the historic Center's Bridge match. The Pacifics defeated their nemesis one last time, 30–29, to claim superiority in their series, 9 games to 8.

Unlike previous Pacific-Eagle matches, this one was filled with the greatest joviality and merriment, and at the postgame banquet pleasant reminiscences were shared.

Notes

1. One source for Church's unpublished information might have been an article in the *Daily Evening Bulletin* of September 24, 1869, summarizing San Francisco's brief baseball history, including the scores of all Eagle matches, on the arrival of the Cincinnati Red Stockings. The source of the *Bulletin's* information was attributed to records kept by John Durkee.

2. Between pages 37 and 38 in Church is a team picture captioned "THE PACIFICS," 1866. It shows nine men in formal pose with two baseball bats. A close examination of the bat to the right, held by W.F. Hale, reveals that it is the 1866 Championship Bat. However, it is not the 1866 Champion Pacifics. It is the 1867 Pacifics displaying the bat won the previous year. Four of the identified Pacifics played on both 1866 and 1867 Championship Clubs: James Shepard, first base; John Kerrigan, shortstop; William Shepard, third base; and John Harrison, catcher. H.T. Whitbeck, center field, was not on the 1866 team. That position was covered by Welch and Cahill. S.L. Wade, second base, was the pitcher in 1866. W.F. Hale, Jr., pitcher, did not play in 1866. T. Campbell, Jr., left field, did not play for the Pacifics in 1866. J.H. Wetmore did not play for the Pacifics in 1866. Additionally, there was no 1866 Championship Bat in 1866. The first bat was made for the 1867 season.

3. Two men had umpired the three-game match: the first by Frank

DeLong of the Cosmopolitans and John Williams of the Atlantics for the final two. There was never any report that either man had not discharged his duties fairly and responsibly. The *Chronicle* even noted that Williams's umpiring of the second game was excellent.

❖ *Cosmopolitans of San Francisco* (Angus Macfarland) ❖

CLUB HISTORY

The Cosmopolitan Club, organized on May 24, 1866, was the most professionally oriented of the amateur clubs during the Era of the Bat. Comprised mainly of young attorneys, law clerks and upwardly mobile retail clerks, and up-and-coming young capitalists, these young men, most in their early- to mid-twenties, were serious contenders for the Bat for two seasons. Unfortunately, these were the only seasons that the club was in existence. Other than facing the Pacifics at the end of the 1866 and 1867 seasons for the Bat, the "Cosmops" or "Cosmos" had no defined rivalry.

The Cosmops had a unique player in their catcher, David Allison. Possessing two perfectly good arms, Allison, nonetheless, chose to bat one-handed. Behind the plate, he received the tosses from Frank DeLong. With brothers (and attorneys) George and William Leviston in the outfield and infield, respectively, and A.L. Farish, John Davis, and Charles LeBreton as utility players appearing in most of their games, the Cosmops had the most consistent line-up of the clubs.

At the end of the 1866 season they were the toast of San Francisco when they defeated the Live Oak Club of Oakland, but the historical legacy of the Cosmops is their involvement, through no fault of their own, in controversial championship games. The 1866 Championship match against the Pacifics (which they lost 27–20) generated a protest from the Eagles, who asserted that neither club had any claim to the title and that they — the Eagles — were the rightful baseball champion of the state.

The Cosmopolitans hold the distinction of being the first club to win the Bat by victory rather than by lottery. In February 1867, the Pacific Base Ball Convention created the Championship Bat, and the 1867 season began with a lottery to determine which club would hold the Bat to start the season. The winner of the drawing was the Atlantic Club. On April 27, 1867, the Cosmopolitans defeated the Atlantics in the third game of the first Battle for the Bat to claim the prize. The Cosmops defended the Bat against the Libertys, sweeping the series and setting the stage for a battle with the Eagles. The Cosmopolitans then were swept by the Eagles and had to surrender the Bat.

Another "situation" arose when the Cosmops met the Pacifics in a season-concluding Battle for the Bat. When the Cosmopolitans took their defensive positions for the top of the first inning, some observant spectators may have noticed an unusual trio in the infield. Instead of the usual Cosmopolitans, they saw John Fisher at shortstop, John Calvert at second base, and Hugh Dean at first. All were current members of the Eagle Club. This was unprecedented in the history of San Francisco baseball, but the Pacifics did not lodge any public protests. Undoubtedly the Pacifics were consulted in this matter and perhaps even challenged to allow it, since in their previous championship matches against the Bay City and Active clubs, they defeated short-handed teams. Under these circumstances, would the Pacifics have felt that they had really earned the championship by either forcing the Cosmopolitans to field only six players, or to win by forfeit? How much "needling" did the Eagles provide?

The Pacifics were honorable opponents and allowed a mixed team to face them. How the Eagle players came to fill the voids in the Cosmopolitan infield will never be known, but it might be fun to speculate. Did the Eagles approach the Cosmopolitans? Or did the Cosmopolitans approach the Eagles? Might the Pacifics and Cosmopolitans have discussed the matter initially and agreed on the Eagle substitutes and then approached the Eagles?

Regardless, on November 9, 1867, nine Pacifics faced six Cosmopolitans and three Eagles in the first match. The game went to the Pacifics, 24–18, without any notice or comment from the press on the unusual composition of the Cosmopolitan line-up.

At the second game on November 23, the press noticed and noted that "three of [the Cosmopolitan] nine were absent, whose places had to be supplied by three of the second [club of the Cosmopolitans]." In a game marred by Pacific second baseman Sam Wade's falling and possibly breaking a collar bone, the hybrid Eaglepolitans won 33–25.

On the morning of the final match the *Call* correctly reported:

> It will no doubt be a very interesting match, as it is to be the deciding game between these two Clubs as to who shall hold the Championship Bat until next season. Owing to the absence of three of the First Nine of the Cosmopolitans, their places have been supplied by three of the Eagles. Both Clubs have some of the best players in the city, and the game will be closely contested, as each Club feels confident of success.

On Thanksgiving Day the Pacifics scored nine runs in the first inning and led 30–4 after three innings, then coasted to a 39–15 victory.

On page 49 of Church, the top photo is titled "THE COSMOPOLITAN BASE BALL CLUB." Beneath the names of the players is the caption: "Team of the Cosmopolitan Base Ball Club against the Pacific Base Ball Club in the final match for the championship in the year 1867." Of course not all the men in the picture were club members, since Hugh Dean, John Fisher and John Calvert of the Eagle Club also played for the Cosmopolitans in that match.

This was the final match for the Cosmopolitans, making them the first of San Francisco's competitive clubs to disband.

Eventually Cosmopolitans Charles LeBreton, George R.B. Hayes, William Leviston, and David Allison became members of the Eagle Club. Before joining the Eagles, however, Allison would play with the Pacifics for two seasons.

❖ *Wide Awakes of Oakland* (Angus Macfarland) ❖

CLUB HISTORY

Tracing the lineage of the Wide Awakes is neither a straightforward nor a difficult task.

Originally there was the Live Oak Club, comprised of young men from the College of California (later the University of California), which brought baseball back from the brink of the grave in 1866 with a 3-game match against the City College Club of San Francisco.[1]

In the spring of 1866 a bunch of brash college youngsters overshadowed the claimants to the state championship — the Eagles and Pacifics — with their well-attended and well-reported matches played in Oakland for nothing more than boyish bragging rights and perhaps the favoring glances of the young ladies sporting the team colors.

Pitching the first game for the Live Oaks was 20-year-old John Glascock, who gave up 46 runs in a 46–25 loss. He never pitched again. For the second game he switched positions with his catcher, Charles A. Garter. Alas, Garter also gave up 46 runs, but the Live Oaks scored 48 to win.

As the third game approached, the *Alta* wrote:

> SAN FRANCISCO AGAINST OAKLAND: To-day, between the hours of ten A.M. and four P.M., at Oakland, will be played the third and final match between the "Live Oak Base Ball Club" of Oakland, John Glascock, Captain, and the "City College Base Ball Club" of this city, A.L. Farish, Captain. It bids fair to be the most interesting day's sport of the season. We learn that a great number of ladies and gentlemen intend to go over on the boat at eleven o'clock A.M. and also some at two o'clock P.M.. The ladies are taking quite an interest in the game. The last match that was played some two weeks ago, was witnessed by over one thousand persons.... We advise all of our readers, who desire to see sport, to go over.

In the final match, the Live Oaks crushed their cross-bay rivals 84–39.

The Live Oaks played four more matches in 1866, one against the Independents and three against the Cosmopolitans. The *Alta* made a monumental deal of these matches, terming one of them

> a decisive contest between the Live Oak Base Ball Club, of Oakland, and the Cosmopolitan Base Ball Club of this city.... The Cosmopolitan is composed of young merchants and lawyers, and the Live Oak, of the representative young men of our lovely little sister city of Oakland. The Live Oaks have always been victorious in their games with our San Francisco boys, and for that reason the contestants must see the necessity of preparing more thoroughly for this contest and endeavor to win the flag, which will be a beautiful affair. Base ball is one of the very best of manly sports in favor in America, and we hope to see it growing more popular every day.

The Live Oaks defeated the Cosmopolitans in the first game in Oakland. On October 20, over 500 people gathered at Pioneer Park to witness the return match. With John Glascock behind the plate, but this time with Samuel Redington in the box, the "Cosmops" evened the series with a 54–42 victory.

The Cosmopolitans were so elated with their win that they gave an impromptu banquet at the exclusive Hotel de France in honor of their vanquished rivals. The *Alta* observed that the party was almost wholly composed of young men, "and it is due them to say that their sentiments and speeches were worthy of men of elder years."

On November 3, the *Alta* followed the clubs to Oakland to report on the third game, won by the Cosmopolitans 45–30. Capitalizing on the civic rivalry between San Francisco and Oakland, the *Alta* noted, "The San Franciscans may well be proud of the victory they have gained, as it is the first time the Live Oaks have ever been beaten by any Club, while they have continually added to their laurels by their frequent victories over our city Clubs." The Live Oaks concluded their season with a match against the Independents, while the Cosmopolitans continued on to the season's championship match against the Pacifics.

The next year the Live Oaks would play and lose four matches: two against the Pacifics and two against the Excelsiors, a new club made up of the combined rosters of the Independent and the City College Clubs. Previously they had handily defeated the individual clubs that became the Excelsiors, but lost to the combined rosters by large margins. After these losses no more was heard of the Live Oaks.

The College of California was located on a four-block "campus" bounded by 12th, 14th, Harrison and Franklin streets in today's downtown Oakland. On 12th and Harrison was a school known as the College School and sometimes called the Brayton School, after its principal, Isaac Brayton. This school, which was affiliated with the College of California, was a preparatory school for young men who wished to matriculate to the College of California. In other words, the Brayton School was the equivalent of today's high school, and the Wide Awakes was comprised of the teen-aged students from the College, or Brayton, School.

Both the Live Oaks and the Wide Awakes were members of the Pacific Base Ball Convention and had distinct rosters until 1868 when former Live Oak John Glascock, by then a graduate of the College of California, appeared behind the plate for the Wide Awakes in the Battle for the Bat against the Eagles.

During the 1868 season, even though they played in virtual anonymity, the Wide Awakes were the dominant club in the Bay Area. On June 3, despite the *Alta*'s encouragement that the Pacifics should not let the Bat go to the cow county, the Wide Awakes defeated the reigning champions 30–17 in the deciding match in the Battle for the Bat. The young prep school students held the Bat against the Eagles, the Atlantics, and Pacifics before facing the Eagles for a second series in November, culminating with the opening of Recreation Grounds and their subsequent loss to the Eagles.

Whether discouraged by their loss to the Eagles, saddened by the death of their principal in April, or absorbed by the demands of higher education, the Wide Awakes did not field a team for 1869. However, a number of players joined other clubs. First baseman George Cobb, catcher Everett Pomeroy, and utility players Carter and James Perkins went to the Pacifics. Outfielder James Aitken played for the Eagles.

Inspired to regroup by the recent visit of the Red Stockings, the Wide Awakes appeared again on the playing field in November 1869, defeating the Occidentals, 47–20. In announcing the rebirth of the University-based club, the *Alta* wrote on November 1, 1869:

> Since the assembling of the University of California the students have reorganized this Club, and now have a first nine that will compare favorably with any Club in the State. As many will recollect, this Club was the champion for the greater part of last year, but being defeated at the end of the season, grew discouraged and disbanded. The Red Stocking instilled fresh vigor into the national game on this coast, and the Wide Awakes have renewed spirits.

The Wide Awakes played in only one reported match in 1870, but by 1871 the club was again ready to compete. Little did the young scholars from the East Bay know what controversies and social upheaval they would be precipitating when they donned their uniform of blue cap, white shirt, light blue knee breeches and white stockings.

The Wide Awakes began their 1871 season on April 21 against the Eagles, the holders of the Bat for the past three seasons. The Eagles had just defeated the Atlantics in the season's first Battle for the Bat. The difference in age between the two clubs may have made it look like a David vs. Goliath clash, that wasn't really the case.

The Wide Awakes were young, but they were not inexperienced. Pitcher James Aitken was only 18, but had already played for both the Wide Awakes and the Eagles. Catching for the young Aitken was veteran John Glascock, 26 years old. George Cobb, who would graduate in June, was at first base. James Perkins, a freshman, was at second. Fourteen-year-old Andy Piercy, who would begin his Preparatory Classes at the University in the fall, was starting his second season in organized baseball at third base.[2] Senior Everett Pomeroy, a returning Wide Awake, was at short. Thomas Temple, also a returning Wide Awake, was in the outfield along with Lafayette Smith and "Willey."

Facing them that day were veteran Eagles David Allison, 30 years old, with four previous seasons as a Pacific and Cosmopolitan; Francis E. Beck, in his fourth season with the Eagles; 23-year-old James Stroud, also in his fourth season as an Eagle, Francis Williams, in his sixth season, and his 31- year-old brother Joseph. Isaac Beard, a blacksmith, who had pitched for the Atlantics the previous season, was the pitcher.

In the top of the first the Eagles scored two unearned runs on a bad throw from pitcher Aitken to first baseman Cobb. The Wide Awakes responded with 5 in their half of the first and held a 10–8 lead after five innings. In the 6th the Eagles tied the score with two runs. With two men out Stroud attempted to steal third. In a controversial call, the umpire ruled him safe, even though Stroud acknowledged that he had been tagged out. The Eagles then scored three more runs to go up 13–10.

The Wide Awakes went ahead with 4 runs to lead 14–13 after 6. In the next inning the Eagles pushed three across, but the young men from Oakland didn't yield and scored two to tie. Unfortunately, the runs scored as a result of the umpire's bad call on Stroud's steal were the margin of victory as the Wide Awakes were held scoreless through the final two innings while the Eagles scored two in the 8th to win, 18–16.

The next day the Eagles were suspended for the remainder of the 1871 season and stripped of the Bat for using ineligible players. The Wide Awakes and Libertys played in the first post–Eagle Battle for the Bat on May 6, 1871. Just before play began, John Durkee gave each club a written protest stating that the game for the championship was illegal and that only the Eagles were rightfully entitled to hold the Bat, "and all further games ... are not legal games for the championship; that honor and position now rightfully belonging to the Eagle Base Ball Club." The game was played despite Durkee's protest and the Wide Awakes won the match two games to one.

After sweeping the Atlantics, the Wide Awakes accepted the challenge of the Vallejos. Because former Eagles had joined that club within the previous 60 days, the Vallejos did not appear, choosing to lose by forfeit than to suffer the fate of the Eagles.

Facing the Libertys a second time, the Wide Awakes lost both games.

In November the Wide Awakes and Libertys played for the third time. The Wide Awakes won the Bat, the first time that a San Francisco Club didn't hold it at the end of the season. Previously the Pacifics had won it in 1866–67 and the Eagles 1868–1870.

Surprising nobody, at the first convention meeting of the year, John Durkee attempted to rescind the suspension of the Eagles the previous April but was again overruled.

On May 1, 1872, three days before the Wide Awakes and Eagles were to compete for the Bat, an opinion piece, laced with venom and vitriol, appeared in the *Call*. The writer rehashed the issues of 1871 from the Eagles' point of view and complained of the injustice of the Eagles' suspension the year before, bringing to mind the written exchanges more than a decade earlier between the Eagle and Sacramento club presidents. E.N. Robinson's blasting of the Eagles and their *clannish, selfish and round-about way of doing that which were better not done at all* was both reminiscent and prophetic.

Boasting that the Wide Awakes could never defeat the Eagles on the playing field, the writer claimed that they contrived to defeat the Eagles in the convention room so they could take the Bat by deceit. Referring to "a packed convention with illegal proxies," the writer assailed the Wide Awakes, yet conveniently and carefully avoided all references to the actual violation to which Eagle representative John Durkee admitted. The article had John Durkee's fingerprints all over it.

On May 4, the Wide Awakes faced the Eagles, and the arena shifted from wishful thinking to reality. But the letter had already set the tone for the upcoming season, which would be a travesty and an embarrassment to the national pastime and a gross insult to the Wide Awakes.

The result of the first game, according to the *Oakland Daily News*, "was not to increase the good feeling between these clubs, and many harsh expressions were used against 'our country cousins.'" Batting around in the top of the first, the Wide Awakes scored 7 runs and led the Eagles 10–2 after two. The Wide Awake pitcher, R. de la Toba, a Preparatory Classman from La Paz, Mexico, held the Eagles to one run or less in five of the nine innings. The *coup de grace* was applied in the 8th when the Wide Awakes scored 10 runs, with the first 7 batters of the inning getting on base before an out was made. The Wide Awakes won convincingly, 34–11.

The *Call*, the mouthpiece of the Eagles, peppered its game report with a litany of handicaps that the Eagles had to overcome, such as an uneven playing field and lousy weather conditions. It concluded with the observation: "A large number witnessed this farce, and many were considerably disgusted with the Eagles, *but it was not their fault that the game was lost*" (italics added). The report did not explain why these factors only affected the Eagles.

The second game, according to the *Oakland Daily Transcript*, was marred by "one of the most disgraceful acts on the part of a club or its members that could be committed in base ball ... [an] outrage [that] will long be remembered by those who witnessed it." An unnamed Eagle player who disagreed with the umpire's decisions charged at him. If Eagle catcher Charles Keating hadn't restrained his teammate, the umpire (who was described as a cripple who couldn't defend himself) would have been seriously injured.

The game itself was a ten-inning, come-from-behind victory for the Wide Awakes, which the *Transcript* described as "the closest and most exciting meeting ever held on the coast."

The next encounter between the young club from the East Bay and the aging one from San Francisco was in September. The Wide Awakes took a 39–20 lead into the 7th inning, only to see it vanish as the Eagles scored 19 to tie. The Wide Awakes then scored 11 over the final two innings while whitewashing the Eagles to accomplish something that no other club had ever done: defeat the Eagles three times in a row.

Unfortunately, due to the school break, most members of the club were unavailable for the subsequent two matches, losing both games and the Bat to the Eagles by forfeit because they couldn't field a full nine. This was the first Eagle "victory" over the Wide Awakes since just before their suspension the year before.

At the start of the new school year, the reassembled Wide Awakes challenged the Eagles after the mandatory sixty-day waiting period had passed. Although the challenge letter was sent on November 19, giving the Eagles ample time to select dates for the Battle for the Bat, the Eagles chose the final day of the season, November 30, and the unusually late hour of 2 P.M. to play for the Bat.

Since the Eagles set the game for the last day of the season, only one official game could be played — an all-or-nothing proposition — contrary to the convention rule that all championship matches were to be three games. At the appointed date, time, and place, eight Wide Awakes were on hand but there were only five Eagles. At 2:40 P.M., rather than admit defeat and lose the Bat by forfeit, the Eagles chose to play with five men.

What followed prompted the umpire to say that never in his life had he umpired a game where there was so barefaced an attempt to win the game by foul means. After four innings the Wide Awakes were ahead, 36–2. However, in order for the game to be legal, five innings had to be completed. By muffs, overthrows, bad stops, and a grim determination to keep the Bat no matter what they had to resort to, the Eagles prolonged the game until the umpire was forced to call it on account of darkness before five innings had been played. Since this was the final day of the season, no further official games could be contested, so the Eagles retained the Bat through a technicality.

The newspapers saw through the Eagles' cynical and disingenuous manipulation of the rules and excoriated them in print. Even the *Call* reporter, who had been a steadfast Eagle apologist, wrote of the season's farcical conclusion:

A most inglorious close it was. The days of chivalry have indeed passed so far as base-ball matters are concerned, when the championship trophy can be held by such tricks as were practiced at the Recreation Grounds on Saturday. Some of our young ball tossers do not seem to know that there is no honor in holding a trophy which has not been won in a fair fight.

The bat, therefore, remains with the Eagles, together with their three "technical victories" [forfeit wins]. The honor remains with the Wide Awakes together with the glory of several victories won face-to-face with their opponents in daylight.

Eighteen seventy-three began with the Eagles, although champions, protesting a game that they had lost to the Wide Awakes in September, contending that three of the Wide Awake players were ineligible to play. After hearing all the evidence, the Convention found that there was no basis for the Eagles' protest.

The *Alta* didn't miss the transparency of the Eagles' charge:

> The charges in this instance were brought by the Eagles in retaliation for those brought against them some two years ago, by which they were suspended for six months. They have never got over feeling sore for that, and they sought here to get even on the Wide Awakes, to whom they felt they were indebted for their suspension, although the charges were brought by another club and they pleaded guilty to them.

The Convention heard the evidence and ruled against the Eagles' charges.

The next order of business was to find a new method of determining the champion. The previous season had demonstrated how the challenge system could be abused, prompting the *Alta* to editorialize,

> We want an entire new deal in base-ball matters on this coast. If things go on as they are going now, base-ball will die out. We want fresh life infused into it. Something should be done by which the emblem of championship should be awarded to the club winning the most games of a season, which will give every club a fair and equal show. These reforms are absolutely necessary for the welfare of base-ball.

Sending an unveiled message of contempt to Durkee and the Eagles, the *Alta* admonished, "Let the clubs prove their superiority as base-ball players and not as lawyers."

In a demonstration of what can only be called hypocrisy, Durkee addressed the Convention: "The Championship Bat business had created so much trouble and contention that it had almost caused the death of baseball in the State and it was time that some measures were taken to restore a better feeling among base-ball players than had heretofore existed."

A new system was arrived at but it made no difference. There were no reports of baseball games being played by any convention clubs in 1873, thus ending the Era of the Bat.

Notes

1. The 1866 City College has absolutely no connection with the current City College of San Francisco, the city's community college established in 1935. All traces of that 19th century institution are gone.

2. According to University records, Andrew Piercy was in the University's Fifth (Preparatory Class) in the 1871-1872 academic year. In 1870 the University took over the Brayton School to meet the needs of a rapidly growing Fifth Class at a time when the University accepted students to the Fourth (Freshman) Class at age 16. According to University regulations: "Fifth (Preparatory) Class candidates for the advanced grade of the Fifth Class must be not less than 14 years of age and must pass a satisfactory examination in English Grammar, Arithmetic, Geography and United States History." Additionally, all applicants to the University were required to provide testimonials of good moral character.

Bibliography

Books

Church, Seymour Roberts. *Base Ball: The History, Statistics and Romance of the American National Game From its Inception to the Present Time.* San Francisco: Seymour R. Church, 1902.

Lange, Fred W. *History of Baseball in California and Pacific Coast Leagues, 1847–1938. Memories and Musings of an Old Time Baseball Player.* Oakland, CA: Self-published, 1938.

Wright, Marshall D. *The National Association of Base Ball Players, 1857–1870.* Jefferson, NC: McFarland, 2000.

Newspapers

Alta
California Spirit of the Times and Fireman's Journal
Oakland Daily News
Oakland Daily Transcript
San Francisco Chronicle
San Francisco Daily Evening Bulletin
San Francisco Daily Morning Call
San Francisco Examiner

San Francisco Bay Area Club Members

Allison, David E.
   Born: 1841, Iowa
   Died: 11/25/1903; age 62
Cosmopolitans   1866, 1867
Pacifics   1868, 1869
Eagles   1871

One-handed batter (he in fact had two good hands and two good arms but chose to swing a bat with one). Became a prominent produce wholesaler.

Beck, Francis E.
   Born: 1852, New York
   Died: 05/03/1910; age 58
Eagles   1868–1871
Vallejos   1871
Eagles   1872

Shifted to Vallejo club following suspension of Eagles in 1871. Became a bank executive.

Birdsall, George
   Born: 1844, New York
   Died: 04/20/1903; age 59
Eagles   1866–1867

Twenty-five year veteran of San Francisco Police Department; became captain.

Dean, Hugh E.
Born: 1841; Ireland
Died: 06/21/1890; age 49
Eagles   1866–1868
One of the 1867 "Eaglepolitans" in Battle for the Bat against the Pacifics. Clerk in dry goods store.

DeLong, Frank C.
Born: 1843, New York
Died: 06/27/1910; age 66
Cosmopolitans   1866, 1867
Pacifics   1869
Only pitcher for the Cosmopolitans during their two-season existence. Salesman.

Dixon, Thomas J.
Born: 1836, England
Died: 02/16/1883; age 47
Eagles   1860
Played first base in first game at Center's Bridge on February 22, 1860. Became a court clerk.

Durkee, John Leonard
Born: 1826, Baltimore, Md.
Died: 01/29/1897; age 70
Eagles   1860
Eagles   1866–1868
Original Eagle. Played center field at Center's Bridge as well as the 22nd anniversary game commemorating that game in 1882. He was awarded a medal as the best right fielder at the Sacramento State Fair tournament in 1860. Came to California in 1849. Joined San Francisco Police Department, serving as patrolman, detective and captain, then joined Sheriff's Department. In 1856 he joined the Vigilance Committee and was involved in the *Julia* incident, the seizing of state-issued weapons from a sloop in San Francisco Bay. He was indicted for piracy by a federal grand jury and spent almost two months in custody awaiting trial with penalty of death if found guilty. After three hours of testimony the jury found him not guilty in less than three minutes. He ran for chief of police that November but lost. He believed that he lost because of a rumor that he had been paid to withdraw from the election. He horsewhipped the person he thought was responsible for the rumor. Durkee was arrested, found guilty, and fined $270. He rejoined the police department in 1858, then became a city fire marshal in 1864; investigated the arson-set fire of Recreation Grounds in 1869.

Farish, Anthony L.
Born: 1843, Tennessee
Died: 11/14/1917; age 74
City College   1866
Cosmopolitans   1866, 1867
Played infield in the Live Oak/City College matches of 1866. Became U.S. deputy marshal for 25 years.

Fisher, John Matthew
Born: 1829, Sydney, New South Wales, Australia
Died: 06/27/1909; age 80
Eagles   1860
Eagles   1866–1872
Original Eagle second baseman at Center's Bridge. Played shortstop in Old-Timers' reunion of 1882. He was "Mr. Keystone" for the Eagles, covering shortstop and second base for the entire Era of the Bat. He won a medal for best second baseman at the Sacramento State Fair base ball tournament in 1860. He was a smelter; a melter of metals.

Garter, Charles A.
Born: 1841, New York
Died: 10/29/1911; age 69
Live Oaks   1866, 1867
Original Live Oak; played in debut series against City College. After graduation from the College of California he earned a law degree from Harvard. Appointed U.S. district attorney for Northern California by Pres. Harrison. Later went into private practice.

Gelston, Marion E.
Born: around 1837, New York
Died: unknown
Eagles   1860
Previously played for Eagle Club of New York City. Played in the Fashion Course New York vs. Brooklyn All Star games of 1858. Marion E. Gelston, sometimes known as Joe Gelston, played for the Eagle Base Ball Club of New York in the late 1850s. The July 4, 1857, issue of *Porter's Spirit of the Times* described him as "'the little man,' and the finest player of his inches that the city can boast." Gelston arrived in California in 1859 as an Eastern baseball star and left California in 1866 as a fugitive. After his early involvement with the Eagles, he moved to Sacramento, where he quickly immersed himself in the political and social whirl, becoming a deputy clerk of the state supreme court, a clerk in the California Adjutant general's office, and then engrossing clerk for the state senate. He also followed in the grand tradition of becoming a member of a fire company: the Confidence Engine Company No. 1 of Sacramento.

Life could not have been better for the young man, but there was a darker side that was exposed when he was arrested for forgery on January 20, 1866. According to the *Sacramento Union*, he had always been an efficient political worker, and had generally been able to command a responsible position in one of the state offices. But, also according to the *Union*, Gelston was "skillful in the legerdemain of politics, but was yet another example of the many young men who, falling into the habits of profligacy and vice, found it necessary to resort to crime to sustain themselves financially in their chosen course."

Shortly after being taken to the station house, Gelston admitted his guilt to Governor Frederick Low, claiming his act was the result of gambling losses.

Some 30 forged documents were found, amounting to about $5,000. He was indicted by the grand jury on 16 counts of forgery and bail was set at $2,000 on each count. On February 24, 1866, he escaped from jail. Needing to use the "facilities" after dinner, he was escorted to the outhouse, which was built into the brick wall surrounding the jail yard and was divided into four separate compartments. Two of the compartments (for use by the inmates) were accessed from the yard and two other compartments were accessible through doors on the other side of the yard wall. The "inner" and "outer" compartments were separated by a one-inch thick redwood wall.

When Gelston didn't come out after several minutes, the deputy checked and found the wall between the inner and outer compartments had been breached. Gelston was gone. The sheriff of Sacramento County posted a $250 reward for the capture of the fugitive Gelston. While false reports of Gelston sightings were spread by his friends, claiming that he had been seen in Panama or had joined the Mexican Army, new forgeries were uncovered, raising the total to over $60,000.

On May 31, official word was received from Nevada that Gelston had been arrested in Austin. However, either through a mix-up or intervention by his friends in high places, Gelston was released and was never seen again.

His mother's 1887 obituary made no mention of Gelston. There was a final reference to him on March 26, 1899, when he was fondly recalled in a *San Francisco Call* retrospective of the genesis of baseball in San Francisco. No mention was made of the fugitive status of the former president of the Eagle Base Ball Club.

Glascock, John R.
   Born: 1845, Mississippi
   Died: 10/10/1913; age 68
Live Oaks   1866, 1867
Wide Awakes   1868, 1870–1872

Original Live Oak; played in debut series against City College. Valedictorian of his 1865 College of California graduation class. The son of an attorney, he studied law in his father's office and then received his law degree in 1871. Elected district attorney of Alameda County (Oakland), U.S. congressman, and mayor of Oakland.

Hale, William
   Born: 1845, Detroit, Michigan
   Died: 07/26/1908; age 63
Pacifics   1867

In his only season he was the full-time pitcher for the Pacifics in their best season. Suspended for undisclosed reasons at the start of the 1868 season and never played again. Became a prominent real estate man in San Francisco.

Land, Howard B.
   Born: 1845, New York
   Died: 11/29/1918; age 73
Cosmopolitans   1866, 1867

Part-time Cosmopolitan utility player. Public accountant.

LeBreton, Charles
   Born: 1843, Mass.
   Died: 08/16/01; age 58
Cosmopolitans   1866, 1867

He was a stalwart infielder for the Cosmopolitans. Became a bookkeeper. Committed suicide over poor health.

Leviston, George
   Born: 1846, Illinois
   Died: 12/29/1907; age 61
City College   1866
Cosmopolitans   1866, 1867

Outfielder with Cosmopolitans. Played with his brother William and shared a law practice with him also.

Leviston, William
   Born: 1845, Illinois
   Died: 05/17/1906; age 60
Cosmopolitans   1866, 1867

Played infield while brother George patrolled the outfield for the Cosmopolitans. Shared a law practice with his brother.

McKee, Robert L.
   Born: 1848, California
   Died: 07/31/1915; age 67
Live Oak   1866
Wide Awakes   1871, 1872

Part-time utility player. Established a law practice in Oakland after his playing days.

Peplow, Edward A.
   Born: 1848, Tennessee
   Died: 08/02/1900; age 52
Eagles   1866–1869

Utility player. Worked as a printer/pressman.

Piercy, Andrew J.
   Born: 1856, San Jose, California
   Died: 12/27/1932; age 76
Wide Awakes   1870–1872

Broke into organized baseball at age 13 with the Wide Awakes at third base, where he was their stalwart player for three seasons. Although enrolled in the University's Preparatory Class, he did not continue his education but pursued a base ball career which included a brief stint with the National League's Chicago White Stockings in 1881. Played on San Francisco/Bay Area teams up to 1887. He was also involved in the management of ball parks in San Francisco and the Bay Area while a player. He was probably the last of the Era of the Bat players to die.

Pomeroy, Everett B. (also spelled Pomroy)
    Born: 11/05/1850, Ritchfield, Ohio
    Died: 12/05/1895; age 45
Wide Awakes   1867, 1868
Pacifics   1869
Wide Awakes   1870–1872

Joined "original" Wide Awakes at age 16 as a prep student at the Brayton School in 1867. He was the starting shortstop in their 1871 Championship season. Graduated from the University of California in 1871, the first graduating class from the "new" Berkeley campus. He became an attorney and in 1875 President Grant appointed him U.S. district attorney for the Arizona Territory. He returned to the Bay Area in 1885 for health reasons. In 1894 he bought the Oakland *Times*, which he edited till his death in 1895.

Redington, Samuel
    Born: 1847, Maine
    Died: 11/18/1886; age 39
Live Oaks   1866, 1867
Pacifics   1867, 1868

Original Live Oak; played outfield against City College in 1866. Became a grain broker. Died from injuries received in a cable car accident.

Rising, Alfred W.
    Born: 1847, New York
    Died: 03/27/1884; age 37
Cosmopolitans   1866, 1867

Part-time utility player. Became an attorney.

Shepard, James
    Born: 1837, England
    Died: 10/12/1919; age 82
Pacifics   1866–1869

Played baseball for the Alpine Club of New Jersey before coming to San Francisco. One of the early Eagles who branched off to form the Pacifics in 1862–63. Along with brother William, perhaps the most well-known brother tandem of pioneer San Francisco baseball. He was the Pacifics' stalwart first baseman. Operated a successful plumbing business with brother William.

Shepard, William
    Born: 1838, England
    Died: 11/11/1914; age 76
Pacifics   1866–1869

Like his brother James, played baseball for the Alpine Club of New Jersey before coming to San Francisco and was one of the early Eagles who branched off to form the Pacifics in 1862–63. He was a utility infielder, making throws to his brother James at first base from second, short and third for the entire life of the Pacifics. Operated a successful plumbing business with brother William.

Slicer, Walter R.
    Born: 1844, Pittsburgh, Pa.
    Died: 08/04/1879; age 35
Cosmopolitans   1867

Center fielder for Cosmopolitans. Became a deputy sheriff. Died in a boating accident.

Wade, Joseph L.
    Born: 1831, Maine
    Died: 09/09/1902; age 71
Em Quads   1860

One-game wonder. Along with brother Simon, Joseph played in Em Quads' first match against Eagles on June 23, 1860. He never played again. Printer/pressman with brother Simon.

Wade, Simon L. (Sam)
    Born: 1834, Maine
    Died: 05/20/1914; age 80
Em Quads   1860
Eagles   1860
Pacifics   1866–1869
Libertys   1871

Played in Em Quads' first game on June 23, 1860, against the Eagles; then jumped to Eagles where he played second and third base. Won medal at Sacramento Fair for best third baseman of the tournament. Broke from Eagles to join Pacifics where he was "second-to-none" as a second baseman during the Era of the Bat. Operated a printing business with brother Joseph.

Welch, Thomas J.
    Born: 1840, Australia
    Died: 10/18/1918; age 77
Pacifics   1866, 1867

Part-time utility player. Became one of San Francisco's best-known architects.

Wiggin, Marcus P.
    Born: 1847, Maine
    Died: 10/18/1900; age 53
Live Oaks   1867
Pacifics   1868

Part-time player for both clubs. Became a lawyer after graduation and elected judge of Mono County. Later became an editorial writer for the San Francisco *Chronicle*.

General Bibliography

Each entry in this work contains a listing or discussion of specific sources used by the author of that entry. The following works, however, are national in scope and are listed here instead of being repeated entry after entry.

Adelman, Melvin L. *A Sporting Time: New York City and the Rise of Modern Athletics, 1820–70.* Urbana: University of Illinois Press, 1986.

Bingham, Dennis, and Thomas R. Heitz. "Rules and Scoring." In John Thorn and Pete Palmer with Michael Gershman, eds., *Total Baseball: The Official Encyclopedia of Major League Baseball,* 4th ed. New York: Viking, 1994.

Block, David. *Baseball Before We Knew It.* Lincoln: University of Nebraska Press, 2005.

Chadwick, Henry. *The American Game of Base Ball* (aka *The Game of Base Ball: How to Learn It, How to Play It, and How to Teach It. With Sketches of Noted Players*). 1868. Columbia, SC: Camden House, 1983.

_____. *Beadle's Dime Base-Ball Player.* 1860. Morgantown, PA: Sullivan Press, 1996.

Charlton, James, ed. *The Baseball Chronology: The Complete History of Significant Events in the Game of Baseball.* New York: Macmillan, 1991.

Church, Seymour R. *Base Ball: The History, Statistics and Romance of the American National Game from Its Inception to the Present Time.* 1902. Princeton, NJ: Pyne Press, 1974.

Deming, Clarence. "Old Days in Baseball." *Outing,* June 1902, 357–360.

Dickson, Paul, ed. *The Dickson Baseball Dictionary: The Revised, Expanded, and Now Definitive Work on the Language of Baseball,* 3d ed. New York: W.W. Norton, 2009.

Fox, Stephen. *Big Leagues: Professional Baseball, Football, and Basketball in National Memory.* New York: Morrow, 1994.

Goldstein, Warren J. *Playing for Keeps: A History of Early Baseball.* Ithaca: Cornell University Press, 1989.

Henderson, Robert W. *Ball, Bat, and Bishop: The Origin of Ball Games.* 1947. Urbana: University of Illinois Press, 2001.

"How Baseball Began—A Member of the Gotham Club of Fifty Years Ago Tells About It." *San Francisco Examiner,* November 27, 1887, 14 (interview with William Wheaton).

Ivor-Campbell, Frederick, Robert L. Tiemann, and Mark Rucker, eds. *Baseball's First Stars.* Cleveland: Society for American Baseball Research, 1996.

Kirsch, George B. *The Creation of American Team Sports: Baseball and Cricket, 1838–72.* Urbana: University of Illinois Press, 1991.

Levine, Peter. *A.G. Spalding and the Rise of Baseball: The Promise of American Sport.* New York: Oxford University Press, 1985.

Lowry, Philip J. *Green Cathedrals: The Ultimate Celebration of All 271 Major League and Negro League Ballparks Past and Present.* Reading, MA: Addison-Wesley, 1992.

Melville, Tom. *Early Baseball and the Rise of the National League.* Jefferson, NC: McFarland, 2001.

Morris, Peter. *A Game of Inches: The Stories behind the Innovations That Shaped Baseball: Volume 1: The Game on the Field.* Chicago: Ivan R. Dee, 2006.

_____. *A Game of Inches: The Stories behind the Innovations That Shaped Baseball: Volume 2: The Game Behind the Scenes.* Chicago: Ivan R. Dee, 2006.

_____. *But Didn't We Have Fun: An Informal History of Baseball's Pioneer Era, 1843–1870.* Chicago: Ivan R. Dee, 2008.

Nemec, David. *The Rules of Baseball.* New York: Lyons & Burford, 1994.

Orem, Preston D. *Baseball (1845–1881) from the Newspaper Accounts.* Altadena, CA: n.p., 1961.

Peverelly, Charles A. *Book of American Pastimes.* New York: n.p., 1866.

Protoball, http://www.retrosheet.org/Protoball/index.htm.

Richter, Francis C. *Richter's History and Records of Base Ball.* 1914. Jefferson, NC: McFarland, 2005.

Ryczek, William J. *Baseball's First Inning: A History of the National Pastime Through the Civil War.* Jefferson, NC: McFarland, 2009.

_____. *Blackguards and Red Stockings: A History of Baseball's National Association, 1871–1875.* Jefferson, NC: McFarland, 1992.

_____. *When Johnny Came Sliding Home: The Post–Civil War Baseball Boom, 1865–1870.* Jefferson, NC: McFarland, 1998.

Seymour, Harold. *Baseball: The Early Years.* New York: Oxford University Press, 1960.

Shieber, Tom. "The Evolution of the Baseball Diamond." Originally printed in the *Baseball Research Journal* 23 (1994), 3–13; reprinted in an expanded version in John Thorn and Pete Palmer with Michael Gershman, eds., *Total Baseball: The Official Encyclopedia of Major League Baseball,* 4th ed. New York: Viking, 1994, 113–124.

Spalding, Albert Goodwill. *America's National Game: Historic Facts Concerning the Beginning, Evolution, Development, and*

Popularity of Base Ball, with Personal Reminiscences of Its Vicissitudes, Its Victories, and Its Votaries. 1910. Lincoln: University of Nebraska Press, 1992.

Spink, Alfred H. *The National Game*. 1911. Carbondale: Southern Illinois University Press, 2000.

Sullivan, Dean A., comp. and ed. *Early Innings: A Documentary History of Baseball, 1825–1908*. Lincoln: University of Nebraska Press, 1995.

Thorn, John, and Pete Palmer. *The Hidden Game of Baseball*. Garden City, NY: Doubleday, 1984.

Tiemann, Robert L., and Mark Rucker, eds. *Nineteenth Century Stars*. Kansas City: Society for American Baseball Research, 1989.

Wood, James Leon, as told to Frank G. Menke. "Baseball in By-Gone Days." Syndicated series, *Indiana* (PA) *Evening Gazette*, August 14, 1916; *Marion* (OH) *Star*, August 15, 1916; *Indiana* (PA) *Evening Gazette*, August 17, 1916.

Wright, Marshall D. *The National Association of Base Ball Players, 1857–1870*. Jefferson, NC: McFarland, 2000.

Zoss, Joel, and John Bowman. *Diamonds in the Rough: The Untold History of Baseball*. New York: Macmillan, 1989.

About the Contributors

David **Arcidiacono** is a member of the Society for American Baseball Research, specializing in 19th century baseball. He has written three books on Connecticut baseball history; his latest is *Major League Baseball in Gilded Age Connecticut*, which was published by McFarland in 2010. He has been a featured speaker at the National Baseball Hall of Fame in Cooperstown, New York.

Priscilla **Astifan** has made numerous contributions to the knowledge of local and national baseball history, including five articles in the quarterly *Rochester History*. She serves as an advisor to the vintage baseball program at the Genesee Country Village and Museum in Mumford, New York, and on the board of directors of the AAA Rochester Red Wings.

David **Ball** was employed at the Classics Library at the University of Cincinnati, where he obtained a degree in ancient history. He published book reviews, biographies and articles on 19th century baseball in various publications, and was book review editor for the journal *Base Ball*. David Ball died in 2011.

Beloit College Archivist since 1986, Fred **Burwell** is a former editor of the *Beloit Fiction Journal* and former publisher and editor of the literary journal *Acorn Whistle*. He is the author of *Fridays with Fred*, a weekly online column on Beloit College history, and has published both fiction and non-fiction.

Scott **Fiesthumel** is a former newspaper columnist, and the author of several books on baseball and history. He has served as the official scorer for the New York State League. He and his wife Kathleen live in Kirkland, New York.

A retired English professor and a member of SABR since 1994, Jan **Finkel** has contributed to *Deadball Stars of the National League*, *Deadball Stars of the American League*, *Spahn, Sain and Teddy Ballgame*, *Sock It to 'em Tigers*, the *Baseball Research Journal*, *NINE*, and the SABR Biography Project. He serves as chief editor of the Biography Project.

Robert E. **Gregory**, a long-time SABR member, became interested in 19th century baseball the first time he opened his new 1969 Big Mac. He currently resides with his wife and daughter in Fort Wayne, Indiana—hence his interest in canals and all things Kekionga.

Richard **Hershberger** is a paralegal in Maryland. He has written numerous articles on early baseball, concentrating on its origins and its organizational history. He is a member of the SABR 19th Century and Origins committees.

Jeffrey **Kittel**, a lifelong resident of the St. Louis area, studied history at the University of Illinois and Southern Illinois University. He is the webmaster of *This Game of Games* (http://thisgameofgames.blogspot.com/), a research blog focused on the history of 19th-century St. Louis baseball.

Len **Levin**, who would be happy to watch a baseball game in any century, is a retired newspaper editor who keeps his brain sharp by working on SABR-sponsored publications. He has been a member of SABR since 1977, and has been a national officer twice. He lives in Providence, Rhode Island.

Angus **Macfarlane**'s first brush with baseball history was attending the San Francisco Seals' final game at Seals Stadium when he was 10 years old. He is a retired probation officer, and when he wasn't rooting for the Giants, he cheered for his son, Clifford, from Little League through high school baseball. He has contributed articles to the San Francisco Historical Society and *Base Ball: A Journal of the Early Game*.

Now retired from work as a picture framer, Richard **Malatzky** has an accounting degree from Queens College. He joined SABR in 1976 and has worked with Bill Haber through SABR's Biographical Committee researching missing players. Living in the Bronx, he enjoys traveling throughout the United States and abroad visiting art museums and seeing the sights.

Peter **Morris** of Haslett, Michigan, is a baseball historian whose books include *A Game of Inches*, *Baseball Fever*, *But Didn't We Have Fun?* and *Catcher: How the Man Behind the Plate Became an American Folk Hero*.

Greg **Perkins** studied American urban history at Northern Kentucky University and the University of Cincinnati. His Pioneer Project contributions arose from entries on baseball, cricket, and townball that he contributed to the *Encyclopedia of Northern Kentucky* (University Press of Kentucky, 2009).

William J. **Ryczek** has written a trilogy (*Baseball's First Inning*, *When Johnny Came Sliding Home* and *Blackguards and Red Stockings*) covering the history of baseball from its beginnings through 1875. He has also written of New York baseball in the 1960s. Bill is a principal in a finance company and lives in Wallingford, Connecticut.

Index

Prepared by Skip McAfee (Bibliography Committee, Society for American Baseball Research).

Abrams, Thomas E. 53, 56–58, 62
Actives of Cheshire (CT) 22
Actives of San Francisco 330, 332
Actives of Washington (DC) 273
Adams, George E. "Teddy" 78, 83, 99
Adams, John C. "Jack" 42, 46–47
Addy, Bob 225–229, 231
admission charges 5–6, 27, 79, 88, 92, 108–109, 127, 142, 147, 176, 178, 211, 215, 256, 272–273, 292, 321–322
Adrian (MI), Anchora Club of 177
African Americans 137, 160–162, 169, 266, 308
Air, William 167
Aitken, James 322, 327, 334
Albany (NY), Beaverwyck Club of 50
Albany (NY), Champions of 50–51, 96
Albany (NY), Empires of 68
Albany (NY), Excelsiors of 67–69
Albany (NY), Knickerbockers of 44, 51, 68, 69–70, 78, 81
Albany (NY), Nationals of 54, 56, 68–69, 80
Alerts of Cleveland 126
Alerts of Elmira (NY) 4, 45–46
Alerts of Newburgh (NY) 46
Alerts of Plainville (OH) 160
Alerts of Rochester (NY) 82, 88, 99, 107, 110–111, 116
Alerts of Washington (DC) 266
Alerts of West Troy (NY) 50
Alexander, C.M. 266
Alexander, Maurice W. 283–284
all-star games/teams 115–116, 177, 194, 318, 322, 326
Allegheny Base Ball Club of Allegheny City (PA) 118, 122–125
Allegheny City (PA), Allegheny Base Ball Club of 118, 122–125
Allegheny City (PA), Enterprise Club of 122–123
Allegheny City (PA) game with Pittsburgh in 1857 121–122
Allen, Augustus C. 116
Allen, Frank Erwin "Ham" 29
Allen, George Roderick 29
Allen, Orlando, Jr. 101, 104
Allison, Arthur Algernon 128, 132
Allison, David E. 331–334, 336
Allison, Doug 147, 150, 267, 278
Allison, Robert 139
Alston, David Gordon 212, 217–218
Altoona (PA), Mountain City Club of 120
Altoona (PA), Mountain Club of 118, 119–121
Alvord, Charles Earle 38
Alvord, Joseph Dana 38, 40n26
Alvord, Williston Isaac 38
American Hotel Fire (Buffalo, 1865) 104, 106, 113

Americans of East Bridgeport (CT) 32–37
Ames, Coman Cheney 89
Anchora Club of Adrian (MI) 177
Ancient Cities of Schenectady (NY) 54
Anderson, Robert Henry 170, 179
Andrews, Ezra R. 98
Andrews, William D. 98
Androscoggins of Lewiston (ME) 10–11, 14
Andrus, Fred 169
Angell, George R. 99
Angier, Hugh 316
Ann Arbor (MI), Monitors of 190
Annan, William Howard 260, 262–263
Anson, Adrian "Cap" 64, 203, 228, 233
Armistead, John I. 258
Armstrong, Robert Livingston 263
Arnold, Willis 29
Arnot, John 4
Askew, Joseph Wilkinson 120
Association of Base Ball Clubs of Baltimore 252, 255–256
Athletic Club of Cheshire (CT) 22
Athletics of Philadelphia 27, 57–58, 80–81, 110, 112, 118–120, 122, 127, 142, 178, 215, 227, 255–256, 258, 311–312
Athletics of Portland (ME) 10–11, 14
Athletics of Rochester (NY) 99
Atkins, Edward 172
Atkins, George E. 170, 172
Atkins, John H. 172
Atlanta, Gate Citys of 314–317
Atlanta Base Ball Club 314–315
Atlantics of Brooklyn (NY) 5, 19–20, 54, 57–58, 69, 79–80, 109–110, 112, 127, 142, 148, 178, 215, 227, 312
Atlantics of Chicago 142, 153, 207, 210, 212–213, 215, 217, 224, 226
Atlantics of San Francisco 320, 322–323, 328, 332, 334
Atwater, Edward Pease 108, 110, 112–113
Auburn (NY) Base Ball Club 109
Augusta (ME), Cushnocs of 10–11
Avery, John M. 193, 195
Avery, Matthew Henry 71, 74
Avery, Sidney S. 91–93
Ayres, Stephen Cooper 204

Baars, J[ohn] Frederick, Jr. 195
Baars, W[illiam] Henry 194–195
Babcock, James L. 68
Babcock, Lewis H. 70
Babcock, Otis Hunt 195
Bach, James Brown 101, 104
Bach, Robert 101, 104
Backus, James 91, 94–96

Badger Club of Beloit College 241
Bailey, Moses M. 70
Bailey, Rufus C. 228–229
Bailey, Thomas 70
Baker, Byron W. 77–78, 81, 83
Baker, Everett L. 92, 102
Baldwin, Lyman Hayden 179
Ball, James Pressley 3, 160–161
Baltimore, Enterprise Club of 256–257, 262
Baltimore, Excelsiors of 253–254
Baltimore, Marylands of 58, 255–257, 261–265, 266
Baltimore, Pastimes of 58, 112, 254–261, 261–262
Baltimore, Peabody Club of 262
Baltimore, Waverlys of 254, 261
Banker, Benson Beriah 218
Barbour, Edwin S. 187
Barbour, William Blakney 229
Barclay, Shepard 293, 302
bare feet, playing in 54–55, 64
Barker, Alfred L. 229, 251
Barker, James H. 113
Barker, Richard 96
Barklage, Herman 297, 300
Barnes, Charles 74, 83–84
Barnes, C[harles] Roscoe "Ross" 225–226, 228–230
Barnes, George 74–75, 84
Barnes, James 74
Barnes, John 98
Barnes, Pearce 164
Barnum, Henry 116
Barnum, Samuel 70
Barrett, John 299–301
Barron, James 301
Barry, David E. 177, 179
Barry, James S. 222
Barstow, Galen W. "Gale" 228, 230
Bartlett, Marion Louville 15
Bartow, John H. 108, 113
The Base Ball Polka 92, 95, 102, 104
Batavia (NY), Stars of 115
bats (trophies) 19, 34–35, 37, 50, 126–127, 163, 176, 190, 210, 212, 220, 265, 315, 319–320, 323, 327–328, 330–332, 334–336
Baxter, William Henry 172, 179, 188
Bay, William V.N. 298, 301
Bay Citys of San Francisco 321, 330, 332
Beach, Waddy 265, 267
Beadle, Harry W. 4
Beam, George F. 253, 255, 258
Beard, Isaac 334
Beardsley, Cyrus 96
Beaverwyck Club of Albany (NY) 50
Beck, Francis E. 336

Index

Beckler, Michael 138–139
Belden, John 19
Belknap, John J. 194
Bell, Algernon Sidney 123
Bell, James Dorland 134–135
Bellán, Estevan B. 58, 61–62
Beloit College, Badger Club of 241
Beloit College, Olympians of 202, 239–247, 247
Beloit College Base Ball Club 244
Belvidere (IL), Mystics of 224
Benteen, Frederick D., Jr. 264
Benteen, Frederick William 3, 264, 284–285
Bentley, Clytus "Cy" 29
Benton Harbor (MI), Wolverines of 169
Bergen [Detroit Base Ball Club] 179
Berning, Henry 293
Bernoudy, Edward A. 285
Berthrong, Henry Washburn "Harry" 267, 273, 276
Bettinger, Stephen 111, 113
Bevier, Andries 195
Bicknell, Charles H., Jr. 240, 244
Biddle, William Shepard 179
Bierman, Charles S. "Charley" 57–58, 62, 263
Bigger, John Comly 237–238
Biggers, Willis Robert 316
Billings, Billie J., Jr. 191
Billon, Frank Charles 301
Bingham, Charles F. 116
Binghamton (NY) Club 45
Bird, George 228, 251
Birdsall, David Solomon 276
Birdsall, George 336–337
Bishop, Albert W. 104
Bishop, C[ampbell] Orrick 293
Bittenbender, John 200
Blackstock, William John 124
Blackwell, Josiah "Si" 20
Blair, James R. 139
Blair, Wash 138
Blakeslee [Excelsiors of Chicago] 218
Blanchard, George B. 309–310, 312
Bleaks, David M. 139
Blodgett, J[ohn] Randolph 92, 102, 104–105, 109
Bloomingtons of Bloomington (IL) 214, 217, 227
Blossom, Frank 4
Blumrich, Dick 194
Blymyer, George Washington 134–135
Boake, John Leonard 138, 143, 166
Boake, William H.K. 138, 143
Bolen, Henry 194
Bond, Jared D. 204
Bonker, Eugene H. 57, 62
Bonta, Frank Manley 84
Bonte, A[lbert] P[earley] C[ross] 148, 150
Booth, Alexander Galt "Alec" 309, 312
Booth, Edward H. 29–30
Booth, Edwin 253
Booth, John Wilkes 253
Bostock, Francis H. 208
Boston Red Stockings 150
Bostwick [Niagaras of Buffalo postwar] 112, 114
Boswell, Eugene S. "Buzzy" 78, 80, 84
Bowdoin College 11–14
Bower Citys of Janesville (WI) 240–241, 247–248
Bowman, George H. 135
Bowser, Lafayette M. 204
Boyd, James T. "Jimmy" 46–47
Brackenridge, Charles Starr 204–205
Brady, William Hartman 205
Brainard, Asa 30, 64, 147, 150–151, 267, 276, 322, 327
Branch, Theodore Francis "Theo" 128, 130
Bredell, Edward, Jr. 282, 284–285
Brewster, H.S. 42
Bricker, David 162

Bridgeport (CT), base ball clubs of 32–41
Bridgeport (CT), Business College Club of 33–34
Bridgeport (CT), Liberty Club of 37
Bridgeport (CT), Pequonnocks of 35–37
Bridgeport (CT), Veni Vidi Vici Club of 35
Bridgeport (CT) Club 34–39; see also Business College Club of Bridgeport (CT)
Bright, John G. 205
Brighton (NY), Unions of 93
Brock, Darryl 152
Brockway [Syracuse Base Ball Club] 76
Brockway, Albert A. 200
Brockway, John R. 58–60, 138–139
Brooklyn (KY), Eagles of 137–138, 162–163, 163–164
Brooklyn (NY), Atlantics of see Atlantics of Brooklyn (NY)
Brooklyn (NY), Eckfords of 6, 43–44, 82, 88, 129, 262
Brooklyn (NY), Enterprise Club of 44–45
Brooklyn (NY), Excelsiors of 5, 42–43, 50–51, 68, 90, 93, 96, 98, 101, 103, 254, 256, 272
Brooklyn (NY), Independents of 43
Brooklyn (NY), Resolutes of 42–44
Brooklyn (NY), Stars of 27, 43–44, 257
Brooks, Thomas Hope 130
Brooks, Walter B. 311–312
Brookshaw, Ben 138, 142–143, 153, 164
Brother Jonathans of Detroit 190
Browinski, Roman Alexander 309, 312
Brown, Charles 128, 130
Brown, Charles Francis "Frank" 44, 46–47
Brown, Edward T. 10
Brown, Harvey Huntington 130
Brown, John A. 178–179
Brown, Thomas 258
Brownell, Oscar L. 84
Brumelkamp, Peter John "P.J." 74
Brush, John T. 62
Bruyn, Jacobus C. 74
Bryan, Alf. 124
Buchanan, Frank 167
Buckeyes of Cincinnati (1861) 138
Buckeyes of Cincinnati (1866–1868) 137–138, 141–145, 146–149, 162–164, 166, 215–216, 227, 311
Buckman, Royal Miller 230
Budd, Stephen B. 218
Buffalo, Cliftons of 109–110, 112, 115–117
Buffalo, Columbias of 111–112, 116
Buffalo, Erie Club of 95, 102
Buffalo, Frontier Club of 102
Buffalo, Niagaras of (postwar) 45, 61, 81–82, 88, 103, 107–115, 115–116, 177, 216
Buffalo, Niagaras of (prewar) 92, 95, 98–99, 101–107, 127
Buffalo, Queen City Club of 103
Buker, Horace E. 226, 228, 231, 234, 236
Bull, Henry 113
Bullymore, John 116
Bump, "Del" 250
Bunce, Frederic L. 20
Bunce, Henry L. 20
Burke, Martin 289
Burnham, Silas H. 11–16
Burnham, Sumner W. "Sum" 11–13, 15–16
Burns, J[ames] Irving 267–268
Burns, John Caldwell 134–135
Burrall, Arthur 240, 244
Burroughs, Henry S. 176–179, 268
Burt, Arthur Edwin 127, 130
Burt, David Wales 103, 105
Bushong, Albert "Doc" 250
Business College Club of Bridgeport (CT) 33–34
Butler, John Germond 74
Butler, Thomas Mifflin 238
Buttery, Frank 29–30

Butts, Samuel A., Jr. 138–139
Byron (IL) Base Ball Club 202, 221–223

Cabanne, Joseph Charless 293–294
Cahill [center fielder for Pacifics of San Francisco] 331
Caldwell, David T. 120
California, College of 319, 333–334
California Club of San Francisco 323, 328
Callender, M.P. 70
Calloway, Frederick C. 218
Calnon, Jeremiah 170, 172
Calumet (MI), German Socks of 199
Calvert, Cecil 151
Calvert, John 329, 332–333
Cameron, Addison M. 124
Campbell, George G.
Campbell, John H. 62
Campbell, T., Jr. 331
Campbell, T.H. 191
Canadian base ball clubs 88, 103, 112
Canandaigua (NY), Pioneers of 96
Canandaigua (NY) Club 94
Canastota (NY) Club 72
Canton (OH), Stark Club of 123
Capital Citys of Madison (WI) 240, 242–243, 248
Carey, Thomas Joseph 263
Carleton, James Leslie 132
Carpenter, Edwin F. 244
Carr, Henry Chills 291, 294
Carr, James M. 122, 124
Carroll, Francis Edward 71, 74, 75, 84
Carroll, Thomas D. 324–325
Carter, W.W. 331, 334
Carton, Thomas 70
Cassedy, Abram S. 43, 47
Cassin, George S. 316
Castle, Tommy 116
catchers, playing close to batter 85, 156, 254, 316
Cate, Stephen M., Jr. 37–38
Cazenovia (NY) Club 73
Central Citys of Syracuse 61, 76–87, 88–90, 109–110, 112
Central Club of Jackson (MI) 191–192
Centralia (IL), Egyptians of 214
Chadwick, Edward Sanborn 240–241, 244–245
Chadwick, Henry 28, 110, 224, 308, 311
Chaffin, James B. 11, 17
Chambers, Beverly R. 216, 218
Chambers, Joe see Schimper, Joe
Champion, Aaron B. 146, 148–151, 154–155
Champions of Albany (NY) 50–51, 96
Champions of the South see Louisville (KY) Base Ball Club
Champions of the West see Empires of St. Louis
Champions of West Troy (NY) 53
Champions of Yorkville (NY) 50
Chandler, George H. 43
Chapin, Edward Payson 105
Chapman, Jack 55
Chapman, Nicholas P. 258
Chapman, William 151
Charter Oaks of Hartford (CT) 18–21, 38
Chase, George B. 70
Cheney, Augustus Byron 74
Cheney, O[wen] Lee 228, 230
Cheshire (CT), Actives of 22
Cheshire (CT), Athletic Club of 22
Chicago, Atlantics of 142, 153, 207, 210, 212–213, 215, 217, 224, 226
Chicago, Columbia Club of 207
Chicago, Enterprise Club of 215–216
Chicago, Eurekas of 215–216
Chicago, Excelsiors of (postwar) 111, 128, 142, 177–178, 202, 210–221, 225–228, 236, 274

Index

Chicago, Excelsiors of (prewar) 206–210
Chicago, Garden City Club of 216–217
Chicago, Ogdens of 210
Chicago, Pacifics of 210
Chicago, Pioneers of 210
Chicago, Unions of 206–207
Chicago Base Ball Club 6, 61, 88, 112, 228
Chicago Fire, Great (1871) 65, 70, 113, 129, 139, 172, 208–209, 218, 228, 267, 323, 328
Chicago White Stockings *see* Chicago Base Ball Club
Chicora Club of Columbia (SC) 308
Chittenden, Erastus L. 205
Chittenden, Ward B. 205
Church, R.B. 51
Cincinnati, Buckeyes of (1861) 138
Cincinnati, Buckeyes of (1866–1868) 137–138, 141–145, 146–149, 162–164, 166, 215–216, 227, 311
Cincinnati, Live Oaks of 96–97, 137, 138–141, 147, 149–150, 162–164
Cincinnati, Mount Auburn Base Ball Club of 137
Cincinnati, Resolutes of 146
Cincinnati, Western Unions of 137, 160–162
Cincinnati Base Ball Club 6, 26, 57–61, 82, 88, 111, 127–128, 130, 134, 137–138, 142–143, 146–160, 164, 166–167, 216, 228, 237, 265–267, 308, 311, 322, 327–328, 331, 334
Cincinnati Red Stockings *see* Cincinnati Base Ball Club
City College Club of San Francisco 319–320, 333
Civil War 5–6, 19, 26, 32, 44, 51, 73–75, 93, 99, 103, 176, 180, 190, 207–208, 210, 254–255, 284, 298, 308
Clapp, John 29–30, 134–135
Clark, John 3, 176–177, 180
Clark, Peter Humphries 160–161
Clarke, James Waite 130
Clayton, Smith A. 314–316
Cleveland, Alerts of 126
Cleveland, Eagles of 126
Cleveland, Forest Cities of 82, 109, 112, 119, 125–133, 134, 142, 177, 216
Cleveland, Occidental Club of 126
Cleveland, Railway Unions of 119, 126–128, 134
Cleveland, Stars of 126
Cleveland, Young America Club of 126
Cleveland Base Ball Association 128
Cliftons of Buffalo 109–111, 112, 115–117
Clugston, George A. 134–135
Cobb, George 331, 334
Cobean, James 134–135
Cochran (sometimes spelled Cochrane), William Avery 240–244, 246
Cohoes (NY), Endeavor Club of 51
Cohoes (NY), Unions of 51
Cohoes (NY), Vanguards of 49–50
Cole, Darius 93
Coleman, Edward Randall 312
Coleman, M[artin] Barry 309, 312
Coleman, William Pritchard "Will" 312
Collier, Charlie 316
Collier, John W. 316
Collier, Jonathan Pierre "Jack" 285
Collins, T. 178
Collins Club of East Liberty (PA) 122
Colton, Charles Erastus 81, 83–84
Columbia (SC), Chicora Club of 308
Columbia Club of Chicago 207
Columbias of Buffalo 111–112, 116
Comet Club of New Haven (CT) 37
Commercials of St. Louis 283, 298
Commerford, Charles C. 35–36, 38
Conant, Theodore Pearson "Theo" 250
Cone, J[oseph] Frederick 227–228, 230
Conely, Thomas Jefferson 191
Conger, Stephen M., Jr. 35, 37

Connecticut Association of Base Ball Players 22, 27, 38
Conner, John Sanborn 138–139
Coon, Charles Edward 272, 274, 276
Cooper, George W. 88–89
Cope, Elias P. 262–263, 268
Copecs of Covington (KY) 137, 164–166
Cordin, A., Jr. 33
Corning (NY), Monitors of 45
Cornwall, William, Jr. 312
Corwine, Quinton 151
Cosmopolitans of San Francisco 320–321, 327, 330, 332–333, 333
Coughlin, Dennis H. 273, 276
Courtney, James A. 258
Covell, Henry 194
Covington (KY), Copecs of 137, 164–166
Covington (KY), Stars of 164
Covington (KY) Base Ball Club 137, 142, 147, 163–166
Cowan, Ad 172
Cowing, Stanley Bagge 108, 112–113
Cowing, William K. 116–117
Craig, James 180
Crane, Thomas 172
Craven, William Darcy 276
Craver, William H. "Bill" 53–54, 56, 58–65
Cream Cities of Milwaukee 226, 242–245, 248–249
Creighton, George 167
Creighton, Jim 5, 97–99, 151, 254, 272
Crescents of Saccarappa (ME) 14
cricket 1, 6, 9, 32, 87, 147, 158–159, 281, 318, 324, 326
Crocker, Albert DeForrest 70
Crocker, Augustus L. "Gus" 14, 16
Cronin, Richard A. 276
Crosman, Alexander 285
Cruttenden, William Henry "Will" 78, 81–84
Cuban players 57–58, 62, 65–66
Culp, Philip *see* Kulp, Philip
Cumberlands of Nashville (TN) 310
Cummings, Arthur "Candy" 87–88, 264
Curran, George Langford 70
Curran, John 328
Curtis, Edward Gansevoort 50, 52
Curtis, Philip H. 98
curveball 16, 20, 43, 71, 77–78, 83, 87–88, 94–96, 127, 151, 155, 258–259, 264, 279, 315
Cushnocs of Augusta (ME) 10–11
Custers of Ionia (MI) 169, 194, 197
Cutter, Charles Long 130
Cyclones of St. Louis 282–288, 288–289, 291

Dagwell, Charles M. 70
Daly (sometimes spelled Dailey) [Live Oaks of Rochester] 96
Dana, George 93
Danby (IL), Rustics of 214
Danforth, James "Jimmie" 15–16
Daniels, Henry C. 95, 99
Davis, Charles D. 74
Davis, Henry Alfred "Allie" 57, 63
Davis, John 332
Davis, John Corwin 138–139
Davis, John J. 70
Davis, Jonathan T. 285
Davis, S[imon] S[tevens] 146, 151
Davis, Townsend 108, 113
Davis, William C. 166–167
Dawson, George Ellis 178, 180
Dawson, George Seward 68
Day, George J. 52
Day, Horace 70
Daybreaks of Jackson (MI) 169, 176, 186, 189–193
Dean, Hugh E. 332–333, 337

Deane, Charles Herman 195–196
Deane, Harry 203
DeBeck, B[odo] O[tto] M[organ] 143–144
DeBeck, Jesse P.J. 144
Decatur (IL), McPhersons of 203
Degnan, James 23
DeGraff, A. 68
DeGraff, William 180
DeLand, Hooker Ashton 191
de la Toba, R. 335
De La Vergne, Benjamin 50–52
DeLong, Frank C. 331–332, 337
Demarest, Frank 102, 105
Deming, Clarence 18, 20
Dempsey, Michael 172
Denison, Henry Willard 268
Dennison, Henry 10
Detroit, Brother Jonathans of 190
Detroit, Early Risers of 169, 171, 176, 185–189, 189
Detroit, Franklins of (1857–1861) 169–176
Detroit, Franklins of (1874) 171
Detroit Base Ball Club 108–111, 123, 126–127, 169, 171, 176–185, 185–186, 189, 211–216, 235, 237
Dexters of Grand Rapids (MI) 195
Dick, William S. "Billy" 268
Dickins, John Whitby 309–313
Dietz, Henry C. 134–135
Dillon, John A. 294
Dixies of University of Georgia 315–316
Dixon, Thomas J. 325, 337
Dobbins, John R. 108, 113
Dockney, Patsy 142–144
Dodge, A. 271
Dodge, Fredric 78, 81–82, 84–85
Dodge, George Henry 88–89
Dohme, Robert "Bob" 314, 316
Doolittle, William J. 70, 247, 250
Doubleday, Abner 3
Douglas, Benjamin, Jr. 24, 26–30
Douglas, Stephen A. 207
Dowagiac (MI) Club 190–191
Doyle, Joe 128
Doyle, Joseph E. 128, 145, 228, 230
Drake, Frederick J. 205
Draper, John 138–139, 149, 151
Dripps, William Augustus 205
Duffy, David J. 299, 305
Duke, Basil Wilson 284–285
Dumon, Justin J. 180
Duncan, William 294
Duncklee, Benjamin French 172–173
Dundas, Ont. 112
Dunkirk (NY), Excelsiors of 107
Dunlap, Robert A. 139
Dunn, Elisha Charles 230
Dunne, Finley Peter 236
Dupont, Charles 180
Duquesne Base Ball Club of Pittsburgh 122
Durkee, John Leonard 323–328, 331, 334–337
Durney, Henry R. 173
Duryea, John Jacob 173
Dyer, Marcellis 138–140

Eagles of Brooklyn (KY) 137–138, 162–163, 163–164
Eagles of Cleveland 126
Eagles of Florence (MA) 22–23
Eagles of Louisville (KY) 311–312
Eagles of New York 102, 325–326
Eagles of San Francisco 318–323, 323–329, 329–332, 334–336
Eagles of Washington (DC) 273
Earle, Lawrence Carmichael 193–194, 196
Earle, William Sylvester 193, 196
Early Risers of Detroit 169, 171, 176, 185–189, 189
East Bridgeport (CT), Americans of 32–37

347

East Bridgeport (CT), Eurekas of 35–36
East Bridgeport (CT), Pembrokes of 34–36
East Bridgeport (CT), Protectors of 35–36
East Bridgeport (CT), Wheeler and Wilson Club of 35–36
East Bridgeport (CT) base ball clubs 32–41
East Liberty (PA), Collins Club of 122
East Tawas (MI), North Stars of 169
Easton, Archibald G. 294
Eaton, Charles W. "Charlie" 194, 196
Eaton, James D. 242–243
Eckfords of Brooklyn (NY) 6, 43–44, 82, 88, 129, 262
Eclipse Club of Kingston (NY) 43
Eddie, Clarence E. 173
Edgar, William Boyce 294
Egyptians of Centralia (IL) 214
Elkhorn (WI) Club 249
Ellard, George Brabazon 146, 149, 151–152
Ellerbeck, George 96
Ellick, Joe 301
Ellicotts of Jamestown (NY) 107–108
Ellis, Sylvanus A. 98
Elmira (NY), Alerts of 4, 45–46
Elmira (NY), Unions of 45
Elton, Robert 122, 124
Em Quads of San Francisco 318–319, 326, 329
Emerson, Thomas E. 108, 111–113
Emminger, A. 134
Empire State Club of New York 44
Empires of Albany (NY) 68
Empires of Freeport (IL) 210, 224, 300
Empires of New Orleans 307
Empires of St. Louis 282–283, 288–289, 291–292, 296–305
Endeavor Club of Cohoes (NY) 51
Enterprise Club of Allegheny City (PA) 122–123
Enterprise Club of Baltimore 256–257, 262
Enterprise Club of Brooklyn (NY) 44–45
Enterprise Club of Chicago 215–216
Eons of Portland (ME) 10–11, 14–15
Erby, Frederick Wise 217–218
Erie Club of Buffalo 95, 102
Ernst, James Clarence 164
Ernst, John Preston 164–165
Erwin, Alexander J. 205
Escott, Henry Vowles 313
Eurekas of Chicago 215–216
Eurekas of East Bridgeport (CT) 35–36
Eurekas of Granville (NY) 51
Evans, Eli H. 43
Evans, Ezra H. 222
Evans, George 51
Evers, Johnny 64
Ewell, George W. "Shorty" 268
Ewer, John 124
Excelsior Juniors of Janesville (WI) 247–248
Excelsiors of Albany (NY) 67–69
Excelsiors of Baltimore 253–254
Excelsiors of Brooklyn (NY) 5, 42–43, 50–51, 68, 90, 93, 96, 98, 101, 103, 254, 256, 272
Excelsiors of Chicago (postwar) 111, 128, 142, 177–178, 202, 210–221, 225–228, 236, 274
Excelsiors of Chicago (prewar) 206–210
Excelsiors of Dunkirk (NY) 107
Excelsiors of Pana (IL) 203
Excelsiors of Rochester (NY) 78, 82, 99, 108–110
Excelsiors of St. Louis 291
Excelsiors of San Francisco 333
Excelsiors of West Troy (NY) 50–51

Faass, F. Louis 70
Fairchild, H.L. 116–117
Falley Seminary of Fulton (NY) 87
Fancher, Leonard 81
Farish, Anthony L. 332–333, 337

Farish, Edward Tilghman 283, 285
Farmer, Thomas H. 301
Farwell [Ontarios of Oswego] 87, 90
Farwell, Henry Byron 238
Farwell, Simeon 208
Fashion Race Course, Queens (NY) 5, 92
Fast Days 34
Faulkner, Stephen 144
Fellers, Morgan S. 180
Ferguson, Charles C. 288, 290
Ferry, Dexter Mason, Sr. 180–181
Field, George Lindsey 187
Field, Henry G. 187
Fields, George 29–30
fines 4, 43, 91, 193, 307
Finley, Billy 90
Finney, Edward Forsyth 291, 294
First Nationals of Hancock (MI) 169, 169–176, 199–201
Fisher, Bob 203
Fisher, James Watson 47
Fisher, John Matthew 324–329, 331–333, 337
Fisher, William B. 204–205
Fisher, William Charles "Cherokee" 58, 63, 142–144, 228
Fitzgerald, James 297–298, 301
Fitzgerald, Thomas 43
Fitzgibbons, James Daniel 20, 301
fixing of games 6, 58, 63, 65, 110–111, 153, 213, 227, 257, 274, 330
Fletcher, George Horace Elliot 276–277
Fletcher, John 23
Florence (MA), Eagles of 22–23
Flour Cities of Rochester (NY) 91–93, 94–95, 97–98, 102
Floyd, John R. 208
Flynn, William "Clipper" 56, 58, 61–63
Foard, Addison K. 258
Fogarty, James, Jr. 138, 140, 162
Foley, Bushrod Walton, Jr. 164–165
Foley, James L. 241–242
Foley, Thomas J. 212, 216–218, 228, 230
Foley, Tom [manager of the White Stockings] 61
Follett, Benjamin Franklin 50, 52
Folsom, Frank 173, 181, 187–188
football 90
Force, Charles Harvey 181
Force, David W. "Davy" 265–268
Ford [Knickerbockers of Albany] 69
Forest Cities of Cleveland 82, 109, 112, 119, 125–133, 134, 142, 177, 216
Forest Cities of Marquette (MI) 199
Forest Cities of Middletown (CT) 22
Forest Cities of Rockford (IL) 112, 142, 178, 203, 211–217, 222, 224–235, 245, 248, 274
Forker, Thomas J. 263, 277
Forlorn Hope Club of Ovid (MI) 236
Fort Dodge (IA) Club 203
Fort Wayne (IN), Kekiongas of 203, 262
Fort Wayne (IN), Summit Cities of 202, 204–206
Foster, Walter H. 169–170, 173
Fowler, Edwin 289
Fowler, James 152
Fox, George H. 268, 273, 277
Francis, George W. 23
Franklin, George 288, 290
Franklin, Henry H. 288–289
Franklin, Joseph 289–290
Franklins of Detroit (1857–1861) 169–176
Franklins of Detroit (1874) 171
Freeman, James P. 291, 296
Freeport (IL), Empires of 210, 224, 300
Freeport (IL), Shaffers of 210, 224
French, Edmund Flagg 271–273, 277
French, Ezra B. 265
French, James G. 70

Frontier Club of Buffalo 102
Frontier Club of Oswego (NY) 72–73
Frost, Theodore Carr 96–97, 138, 140
Fruin, Jeremiah 282–283, 295, 297–302
Fry, Joseph B. 205
Fuller, Eugene F. "Gene" 11, 13, 16
Fuller, L.P. 297
Fullerton, Daniel S. 309
Fullerton, Joseph Scott 285–286
Fulmer, Charles John "Chick" 132, 228
Fyfe, Richard Henry 186–188

Gamble, Joseph 286
gambling 6, 44–45, 50, 58–61, 65, 69, 73, 80, 102–103, 108, 110–111, 153, 213, 215, 243, 252, 267, 330
Garden City Club of Chicago 216–217
Garesché, Ferdinand 283–284, 286
Garter, Charles A. 333, 337
Gate Cities of Atlanta 314–317
Gee, Charles 194
Gee, Walter S. 194
Geer, George H. 61, 79, 83, 85–86
Geer, William Henry Harrison "Harry" 71, 74
Gelston, Marion E. "Joe" 102, 325–326, 337–338
Gemmell, Robert Brown 120
Georgia, University of 315–316
German Socks of Calumet (MI) 199
Gibb, Cornelius Smith "Nealie" 46–47
Gibbons, Robert 173
Gibbs, Charles W. 68
Gibney, Andrew 268, 277
Gifford, Sidney Brooks 74–75
Gill, Clayton Eugene 196
Gillespie, John J. 208, 218
Gillett, Thomas S. 173
Gilmore, Julius Porter 173
Gilson, George 302
Girty, Albert R. 124
Glascock, John R. 333, 338
Glassford, Henry A. 146–147, 152
Glenn, John W. 268, 277
Godfrey, William H. 302
gold ball (trophy) 78, 81–83, 88–89, 108–110, 116, 226, 283, 315
Golden, Simeon 88–89
Goldsmith, Warren "Wally" 263
Goodrich, Alphonso 218–219
Goodwin, Thomas Laing 68
Gorham, John Melancthon "Lank" 130
Gorman, Arthur Pue 255–256, 271–273, 277
Goshorn, Alfred Traber 3, 152
Gothams of New York 44–45
Gould, Charles H. "Charlie" 142, 144, 147, 152–153
Grace, Patrick Ambrose 81–82, 84
Grady, Henry B. 196
Grand Rapids (MI), Dexters of 195
Grand Rapids (MI), Kent Base Ball Club of 169, 193–198
Grand Rapids (MI), Peninsulars of 193–195
Grand Rapids (MI), Pioneer Base Ball and Wicket Club of 193
Grand Rapids (MI), Valley Cities of 194
Grant, Jesse 252
Grant, Moses V. "Mose" 147, 153, 164–165
Grant, Richard 165
Grant, Ulysses S. 252
Grant, William S. 165
Granville (NY), Eurekas of 51
Gratton, George W. 71, 75, 256–257, 261n37
Graves, L.G. 51
Great Chicago Fire (1871) *see* Chicago Fire, Great (1871)
Great Hancock (MI) Fire (1869) 199, 201
Great Portland (ME) Fire (1866) 15

Green, Robert 51–52
Green, Robert F. 261, 263
Green River Club of Greenfield (MA) 23
Greene (sometimes spelled Green), John B. 112–113
Greenfield (MA), Green River Club of 23
Greenleaf, William Eugene 291, 294
Gregg, Jimmy 315–316
Gregg, John Newton 258
Greglette, Robert 326
Gridley, Howard Hampton 191
Grieve, Robert 173
Griffin, Henry 69–70
Griffith, William Ridgely 252–258
Griggs, Edward H. 230
Grimsley, John 302
Griswold, John Augustus 63
Griswold, Merritt W. 282–284, 286, 288–289
Griswolds of Lansingburgh (NY) 51
Gunnison, Deloney 196
Gwinner, Henry Wynkoop 120
Gwynn, Walter 263

Hackley, Luck 169
Hade, Jacob 134–135
Hale, William F. 327, 330–331, 338
Hall, John 324
Hallam, Orrin B. 165
Hallenbeck, Joseph *see* Hollenback, Joseph
Halsey, Lewis B. 44–45, 47
Hamilton, Andrew Holman 205
Hamilton, Milo Dwight 173
Hamilton, W.K. 124
Hamilton College 77
Hamilton (Ont.), Maple Leafs of 88
Hammond, Henry Chester 245
Hancock (MI), First Nationals of 169, 169–176, 199–201
Hancock (MI) Fire, Great (1869) 199, 201
Hank, John William Fletcher 258
Hanna, Leonard Colton "Doc" 130–131
Harding, Frederick J. 70
Harlan, Robert James 160–161
Harmon, Judson 3, 144
Harrington [Daybreaks of Jackson (MI)] 191–192
Harris, George S. 93
Harris, Thomas 42–43
Harrisburg (PA), Keystone Club of 119
Harrison, John 331
Harry, William 200
Hartford (CT), Charter Oaks of 18–21, 38
Hartford (CT), Independents of 18–19
Hartford (CT), Mechanics of 19
Hartman, Henry "Harry" 94, 96
Hartshorne, W. 208
Harvard University 19–20, 59, 81, 85–86, 88, 90, 106, 112, 129, 146, 149, 151–158, 179, 220, 262–263, 337
Harvey, Frank 144
Harwood, J. 36
Harwood, John E. 84–85
Harwood, William A. 23
Hasbrouck, Eli 42
Haskell, Washington H. 205
Hastings, W[infield] Scott 228, 230–231
Hatfield, John 147–148, 150, 153
Haughton (sometimes spelled Houghton), William 208
Hautz, Charlie 302
Havill, Dundas 87–89
Hawley, Edward Selden 108, 110, 112–113
Hayes, George R.B. 333
Haymakers of Troy (NY) 53–55, 58–67, 112; *see also* Unions of Lansingburgh (NY)
Haynie, James Henry 219
Hays (sometimes spelled Hayes), J.A. 208
Hazlitt, Boston 258

Heep, John 302
Hegeman, William Henry 50–52
Heiner, G[eorge] Payson 263
Heintz (or Hines), R. 96
Heller, William G. 250
Henley, William J. 298, 305
Henry, Frederick Porteous 258–259
Henry, John 290
Henry, Robert Lind 288, 290
Henry, William H. 290
Herrick, George D. 196
Hersey, Ellis Tristram 14, 16
Hewett, Walter F. 274
Hewitt, William F. 192
Hickory Club of Howell (MI) 190
Hicks, Nathan Woodhull "Nat" 277
Hicks, Sylvester 97, 138, 140
Higgins, John 105
Highlands of New Windsor (NY) 42–43
Hill, David 3
Hill, John Evans 204–205
Hill, John S. 70
Hills, Theron J. 36, 38
Hinchman, Ford De Camp 181
Hinchman, John Marshall 126, 177, 181
Hine, William H. 36–38, 40n40
Hitchcock, G[eorge] Jerome 231
Hodges, William H. "Billy" 273, 277
Hoey (sometimes spelled Hoyle or Hoy), Patrick 277
Hoge, Holmes 153
Hollenback, Joseph 297, 302
Hollenbeck, William 138, 140
Hollingshead, John Samuel, Jr. "Holly" 268, 277–278
Holloway, Benjamin Allen 117
Holly, Alfred A. 113
Holly (sometimes spelled Holley), Myron "Mina" or "Mynie" 89, 111–114
Holmes, Charles S. 54, 66
Holstons of Knoxville (TN) 315
Holt, William 166–167
Holts of Newport (KY) 137, 163–164, 166–168
Holyrod, Simeon 89
Home Run Polka 275
home runs 127, 166, 180, 203, 223, 227, 240–243, 250, 316, 331
Hook, Harry 331
Hooper, Michael H., Jr. 261, 263
Hopkins, Benjamin E. 140
Horn, John, Jr. 181
Hotchkin, Albert Leet, Sr. 51–52, 63
Houghton (MI) Base Ball Club 199–200
Houston (TX) Club 308
Howe (sometimes spelled How), John Condit "Con" 138, 150, 153
Howell (MI), Hickory Club of 190
Hoyt, James 215–216, 219
Hubbard, William O. 194, 196
Hubbell, Gershom B. 19–21, 34, 38–39
Hudson, John H. 173
Hudson, William Allen 288, 290
Hudson Rivers of Newburgh (NY) 43–49, 56, 108
Hulbert (sometimes spelled Hurlbut or Hurlburt), William L. 131, 293
Hulburt, Dwight K. 193, 196
Hunt, Asbel 36
Hunt, Edward H. 196
Hunt, Joseph H. 222
Hunt, William Carlton 207–208
Huntington, Edwin T. 98
Hurley, William F. "Dick" 143–144, 148, 153, 265, 268
Hyatt, Charles L. 23

Hyatt, Isaiah Smith 231
Hyde, Willard Tenney 240, 245

ice skates, playing on 73, 92, 95–96, 98, 186
Independents of Brooklyn (NY) 43
Independents of Hartford (CT) 18–19
Independents of Mansfield (OH) 118, 134–136
Independents of Newtown (OH) 160–161
Independents of Ripley (MI) 199–200
Independents of San Francisco 320, 327, 333
Ionia (MI), Custers of 169, 194, 197
Ireland, John H. 75
Irvine, Edwin A. 222
Ishpeming (MI) Club 199
Ives, Butler 181

Jacklin, Rufus William 188
Jackson, Samuel 99
Jackson (MI), Central Club of 191–192
Jackson (MI), Daybreaks of 169, 176, 186, 189–193
Jackson (MI), Mutuals of 169, 191–192
Jackson (MI), Unknowns of 123, 191–192
Jamestown (NY), Ellicotts of 107–108
Janesville (WI), Bower Citys of 240–241, 247–248
Janesville (WI), Excelsior Juniors of 247–248
Janesville (WI), Mutuals of 202–203, 245, 248–251
Janesville (WI), Titans of 248
Janesville (WI), Whitewater Club of 241–243, 245, 248
Jefferds, Thomas Lewis 205
Jeffersons of Washington (DC) 252, 262, 271
Jewell, Edward 21
Johns, W. Corwin 203
Johnson, Charles P. 302
Johnson, J. William 138, 146, 150, 153–154
Johnson, James T. "Jim" 61, 78, 82, 85
Johnson, Joseph 200
Johnson, Tom 316
Johnson, William P. 127, 131
Jones, Daniel 35, 40n25
Jones, Frank 213, 272, 278
Jones, John 278
Jones, Milo C. 240, 245
Jones, Nathaniel H. 35, 39
Jones, Seth Benjamin, Jr. 33, 35, 39, 40n25
Jones, William H. 35–36, 38–39, 40n25
Jopson, John 23
Joslin, Fred C. 194, 196
Joyce, George 278
Joyce, John P. 146, 148–150, 154–155
Judson, William N. "Bill" 316–317
junior clubs 5, 33, 35, 40n23, 45, 77, 81, 83, 91–93, 99, 109–110, 113, 128, 138–139, 151, 158, 164, 167, 207, 213, 224, 227, 229–230, 232–233, 235, 247–248, 251, 263, 265, 275–276, 299, 311–312

Kalbfleisch, J.H. 95
Kauffman, George S. 205
Kearny, Charles 286
Keating, Charles 335
Keenan [Excelsiors of Chicago] 214–215, 219
Keerl, George Henry 263
Kehoe, Thomas 87
Keilholtz, Otis 259
Kekiongas of Fort Wayne (IN) 203, 262
Keller, William C. "Will" 120
Kelley, Andy 61
Kelley, John C. 70
Kelley (often spelled Kelly), William H. 42, 44, 46–47
Kellogg, Robert 20
Kemper, Samuel L. "Sammy" 155
Kendall, David S. 200
Kennedy, Alexander D. "Alec" 208–209, 212, 216, 219

Kennedy, Michael 162
Kennedy, William Wallace 207–209
Kent Base Ball Club of Grand Rapids (MI) 169, 193–198
Kernan, John D. 70
Kernan, Joseph 263–264
Kernan, Nicholas 70
Kerrigan, David 331
Kerrigan, Ed 325–326
Kerrigan, John 325, 327, 329–331
Ketchum, George B. 105
Keystone Club of Harrisburg (PA) 119
Keystones of Philadelphia 266
Kidder, John F. 75
Kimball, Eugene Boynton "Gene" 99, 132
Kinder, John M. 23
King, George E. 228, 231
King, Marshall Ney "Mart" or "Marty" 55–58, 61–665
King, Rufus 155–156, 164
King, Stephen [Hudson Rivers of Newburgh] 42, 47
King, Stephen F. [Unions of Lansingburgh] 53, 58, 60–62, 64
Kingsbury, Carl C. 205
Kingsley, Gale B. 89
Kingston (NY), Eclipse Club of 43
Kirkwood, John Henry 131
Kirtland, Charles E. 70
Knickerbocker rules 5, 71, 101–102, 119, 169; *see also* New York rules
Knickerbockers of Albany (NY) 44, 51, 68, 69–70, 78, 81
Knickerbockers of New York 5, 297
Knight, Enoch 12, 14–16
Knoxville (TN), Holstons of 315
Kulp (often misspelled Culp), Philip 268–269
Kunath, Otto Charles 200

Lackland, Rufus James, Jr. 294
Lafayette Base Ball Club of Paw Paw (MI) 187
Lamphier, Le Dran B. 117
Land, Howard B. 338
Lane, Enos 21
Lane, Samuel C. 124, 178, 181–182, 216
Lane, Samuel W. 70
Lane, Y.E. 69
Lansingburgh (NY), Nationals of 50, 53
Lansingburgh (NY), Unions of 44, 46, 53–67, 80, 257; *see also* Haymakers of Troy (NY)
Latimer, Everton Judson 131
Latta, Fergus 21
Laverack, George Edward 114, 117
Lawton, Frank 36
Lawton, Hugh 36
Leach, Henry 35, 37
Leavenworth, Seaman (or Seamon) J. "Sonny" 53, 57, 62
LeBreton, Charles 332–333, 338
Lee, William W. 54, 66
Leech, Edward Owen 265, 269
LeFavour, Heber 182, 188
Leffingwell, Lucius Dexter 126, 131
Leggett, Joe 50, 253–254
Lenehan, Pete 250
Lennon, William H. "Billy" 216, 219, 264
Leonard, Andrew J. 142–144, 148, 156, 267, 331
Leviston, George 332, 338
Leviston, William 332–333, 338
Lewis, Charles 88–89
Lewis, Enoch 120–121
Lewis, Samuel L. 204–205
Lewiston (ME), Androscoggins of 10–11, 14
Lex, Harry 215, 219
Liberty Club of Bridgeport (CT) 37
Liberty Club of Norwalk (CT) 36

Libertys of San Francisco 320, 323, 328, 332, 334–335
Lighthart, Wallace "Fred" 231
Lincoln, Abraham 207
Lincoln Club of New Britain (CT) 26
Lincolns of Pittsburgh 122
Lindley, Alfred F. 46–48
Lishawa, Philip N. 144
Little, Harry 302
Little Falls (NY), Pastimes of 82
The Live Oak Polka 95
Live Oaks of Cincinnati 96–97, 137, 138–141, 147, 149–150, 162–164
Live Oaks of Oakland (CA) 319–321, 332–333
Live Oaks of Rochester (NY) 91–92, 93–97, 97–98, 102, 138, 185
Live Oaks of Stockton (CA) 318–319
Livingston, Frank 320–321
Lockett, John 302
Lockhart, William H. 122, 124
Lockport (NY) Club 94–95
Loder, Ed 94–97
Loder, George 96
Lone Stars of Matteawan (NY) 46
Lone Stars of New Orleans 308
Lone Stars of Rochester (NY) 91–97, 98–100, 103
Lone Stars of St. Louis 283, 291
Loomis, William Nelson 105
Lorillards of Rhinebeck (NY) 44
Lothrop, George Howard 182
Louisiana Base Ball Club of New Orleans 307
Louisville (KY), Eagles of 311–312
Louisville (KY), Olympics of 309–311
Louisville (KY) Base Ball Club 309–314
Love, George Maltby 105
Lowe, William 219
Lowell (MA) Base Ball Club 90
Lucas, Robert 294
Lyman, H[enry] Leslie 115, 117
Lyman, James Stephens 313
Lynch, Ambrose 123–124, 214
Lynch, Michael J. 121–122, 124

MacDonald (sometimes spelled McDonald), John A. 51–52, 64, 114
Mack, Denny 228
MacPherson, Donald 313
Madison (WI), Capital Citys of 240, 242–243, 248
Magnolia Base Ball Club of New Orleans 307
Mahaffey, James 162
Maine State Association of Base Ball Players 10, 14–15
Malcolm (sometimes spelled Malcomb or Malcom), James 207, 209
Maledon, J[oannes] J[acobus] 173
Mallinckrodt, Louis Warner 259
Mallinckrodt, William 259
Malone, Fergus G. 269
Mandelbaum, Max H. 200
Manny, James H. 228, 231
Mansfield (OH), Independents of 118, 134–136
Mansfields of Middletown (CT) 26–32
Mapes, A[lbert] S[idney] 47–48
Mapes, Charles H. 48
Maple Leafs of Hamilton (Ont.) 88
Mariani, Ed 167
Marquette (MI), Forest Citys of 199
Marr, Samuel Stewart 269
Marsh, Francis A. 75, 82, 86
Marshall (MI), Red, White and Blue Club of 189–190
Marston, George White 240, 245, 250
Martin, Isaac M. 42
Martin, Robert J. 234
Martin, William "Billy" 52

Marvin, Dwight 194
Marylands of Baltimore 58, 255–257, 261–265, 266
Mason, Frank 23
Massachusetts game 9
Mathews, Robert T. "Bobby" 262, 264
Matteawan (NY), Lone Stars of 46
Matthews, E[dmund] Orville 284, 286–287
Matthews, Leonard 282–284, 286
Mattoon, John Henry 88–89
Mayo, Levi Snow 75, 86
McArthur, John W. 204–205
McAtee, Michael James "Bub" 53–54, 56–58, 61–62, 64–65
McBride, Dick 255
McCarton, Frank 29–30
McClelland, David 75
McCloskey, Matt 325
McCormick [Unions of Lansingburgh] 65
McCreery, Wayman Crow 294
McCulloch, Charles 205
McDougall, Benjamin L. 309, 313
McDowell, John 43
McGeary, Mike 62, 66
McGee, Melville 191–192
McIntosh, Ichabod Collins 70
McKee, James F. 225
McKee, Robert L. 338
McKelvey, John 99
McKeon, James M. 60, 65
McKeon (sometimes spelled McCune), Peter 53, 62, 65
McKim, Louis 259
McKnight, Woodruff 123
McLaughlin, J.C. 124
McLean, Harry Clay 265, 269, 272, 274–275
McLean, John Roll 156
McMillan, John F. 182
McMillan, Jordan P. 173
McNally, C.J. 211–212, 215–216, 219
McNally, Thomas 123
McNamara, John 75
McPhersons of Decatur (IL) 203
McQuade, John W. 70
McQuide (sometimes spelled McQuade), Andrew 53–54, 56, 62, 65
McQuide, James 53, 54, 65–66
McQuigg, J.C. 203
McReynolds, Benjamin Franklin 196–197
McVey, Cal 148, 156, 203
Meachem, Edward C. 294
Meads, Thomas D. 200–201
Mechanics of Hartford (CT) 19
Mercantiles of Rockford (IL) 224
Meriden (CT), Nationals of 22
Meriden (CT), Quinnipiacks of [West] 22–26
Michigan, University of 177–178, 190
Middletown (CT), Forest Citys of 22
Middletown (CT), Mansfields of 26–32
Miles, Marcus M. 70
Millard, Edward Eames 70–71
Miller, Gerrit Smith 81, 88–90
Miller, J.F. 324, 328
Miller, James W. 42, 48–49
Miller, John 42–43, 48
Miller, Samuel W. 48
Miller, Wells B. 105
Miller, William 269
Miller, William C. 42–43, 48
Miller, William F. 105
Mills, A[braham] G[ilbert] 265, 267, 269–270
Mills, Charles Warren 194, 197
Millspaugh, Henry C. 48
Milwaukee, Cream Citys of 226, 242–245, 248–249
Mincher, Edward M. 264

Minis, Philip 254, 259
Missouri State Association of Base Ball Clubs 291, 300
Mitchell, Thomas J. 254, 259
Mix, William Harry 222
Mohawk Club of Schenectady (NY) 51
Monitors of Ann Arbor (MI) 190
Monitors of Corning (NY) 45
Monitors of Niles (MI) 190
Monitors of Westport (CT) 36–37
Moore, Alfred 75
Moore, DeWitt C. 119
Moore, J.J. 122, 124
Moore, William F. 173
Morey, John 97–99
Morgan, Arthur R. 197
Morgan, George H. 197
Morgan, Thomas H. 54, 66
Morin, James Riley 166–167
Morning Stars of St. Louis 282–283, 288–290, 300
Morrill, Isaac P. 16
Morris, Bennett F. 36
Morrisania (NY), Unions of 19, 37, 44, 56–57, 80, 127, 129, 216, 227
Morrison, Clark 90
Morrissey, John 60–61, 65
Morrow, James 271
Morse, Horatio 87
Moses, Gratz A. 287
Mosher [catcher for Lone Stars of Rochester] 99
Mosher, Franklin D. 76, 86, 99
Mosher, John D. 71
Mount Auburn Base Ball Club of Cincinnati 137
Mountain City Club of Altoona (PA) 120
Mountain Club of Altoona (PA) 118, 119–121
Mowry, John N. 135
muffery 78, 80, 152, 330–331
muffin games/nines 15, 159, 167, 214, 297–299
Murdock, James 71
Murnane, Tim 29–31
Murray, William 254
Mutuals of Jackson (MI) 169, 191–192
Mutuals of Janesville (WI) 202–203, 245, 248–251
Mutuals of New York 6, 44–46, 54–55, 57–58, 64, 66, 69, 129, 147–148, 257, 262, 308
Mutuals of Oshkosh (WI) 249, 251
Mutuals of Pittsburgh 127
Mutuals of Rochester (NY) 77, 99
Mutuals of Washington (DC) 266
Myrick, E.F. 182
Myrick, Raymond S. 90
Mystics of Belvidere (IL) 224
Mystics of New York 44–45

Nash, George P. 309
Nashville (TN), Cumberlands of 31
National Association of Base Ball Players (NABBP) 5–6, 8, 38, 59–60, 91, 93, 101, 109, 122, 128, 138, 142, 144, 149, 162, 169–171, 178, 202, 217, 219, 227, 241, 253, 266, 291, 308, 324
National Association of Professional Base Ball Players (NA) 8, 26, 28, 61, 129, 139, 228, 267
national game/pastime 1, 59, 109, 127, 138, 200, 240, 254, 272, 276, 323
Nationals of Albany (NY) 54, 56, 68–69, 80
Nationals of Lansingburgh (NY) 50, 53
Nationals of Meriden (CT) 22
Nationals of Oswego (NY) 77, 87–88
Nationals of Washington (DC) 6, 20, 57, 118, 129, 142, 147, 152, 203, 212–213, 217, 226–227, 236, 252, 255–257, 262, 265–267, 271–280, 292, 308, 311
Naylor, David H. 288, 290
Nealeans, George 167

Neff, J[ames] M[oore] Wayne 153, 156–157
Nelson, William Rockhill 205
New Britain (CT), Lincoln Club of 26
New Haven (CT), Comet Club of 37
New London (CT), Pequots of 20
New Mills (NY), Uniteds of 45–46
New Orleans, Empires of 307
New Orleans, Lone Stars of 308
New Orleans, Louisiana Base Ball Club of 307
New Orleans, Magnolia Base Ball Club of 307
New Orleans, Southerns of 292, 307–308
New Windsor (NY), Highlands of 42–43
New York, Eagles of 102, 325–326
New York, Empire State Club of 44
New York, Gothams of 44–45
New York, Knickerbockers of 5, 297
New York, Mutuals of 6, 44–46, 54–55, 57–58, 64, 66, 69, 129, 147–148, 257, 262, 308
New York, Mystics of 44–45
New York, Washington Club of 5
New York game 9, 19, 42, 73, 240–241, 252, 281–283, 286
New York rules 5, 9, 138, 162, 170, 191, 206–207, 289, 324–325; see also Knickerbocker rules
Newberry, John Stoughton, Sr. 182, 187–188
Newburgh (NY), Alerts of 46
Newburgh (NY), Hudson Rivers of 43–49, 56, 108
Newburgh (NY) Base Ball Club 42–43
Newport (KY), Holts of 137, 163–164, 166–168
newspapers, role of 5, 7, 22, 72–73, 78, 80, 88, 94–96, 109, 115, 134, 171, 178, 212, 216, 248–249, 283, 311–312, 318, 321, 323, 328, 331, 336
Newtown (OH), Independents of 160–161
Niagaras of Buffalo (postwar) 45, 61, 81–82, 88, 103, 107–115, 115–116, 177, 216
Niagaras of Buffalo (prewar) 92, 95, 98–99, 101–107, 127
Nichol, H. 123–124
Nicholds, Alfonzo Noble 231
Nichols, W.C. 209
Niggeman, Robert 291, 294
Niles, George 182
Niles (MI), Monitors of 190
Noakes, James G. 85
North Stars of East Tawas (MI) 169
Northwestern Association of Base-Ball Players 202, 210
Norton, Frank Prescott 270, 278
Norwalk (CT), Liberty Club of 36
Norway (ME), Pennesseewassees of 10–18
Notunck (MA) Club 23

Oakland (CA), Live Oaks of 319–321, 332–333
Oakland (CA), Wide Awakes of 320–323, 327–328, 331, 333–336
Oberlander, John 219
Oberlin College 126
O'Brien, H.L. 182
O'Brien, Noel C 182
O'Brien, T.J. 182
O'Brien, W.C. 182
Occidental Club of Cleveland 126
Occidentals of San Francisco 320, 334
O'Connell, John 297–299, 302–303
O'Donnell, Malachi J. 173–174
Ogdens of Chicago 210
old-timers games 46, 153, 299, 331
Olds, Henry G. 20
Oliver [Excelsiors of Chicago] 212, 220
Oliver, Richard 101, 106
Olympians of Beloit College 202, 239–247, 247
Olympics of Louisville (KY) 309–311
Olympics of Paterson (NJ) 44
Olympics of Rochester (NY) 91–96, 97–98, 98
Olympics of St. Louis 283, 303
Olympics of Syracuse 72–73

Olympics of Washington (DC) 88, 112, 118, 149–150, 157, 252, 265–271, 275
Ontarios of Oswego (NY) 79, 81, 83, 87–91
Oran, Tom 299, 303
Orem, W[illiam] Morris 259
O'Rourke, James "Orator Jim" 29, 31, 32, 37, 39
O'Rourke, John 36, 40n29
Orr, Edward S. 182
Osborn, Morris P. 222
Osborn, Walter C. 68
Osborn, W[illiam] Ballard 222–223, 231
Osborn [Nationals of Washington (DC)] 278
Oshkosh (WI), Mutuals of 249, 251
Ostrander, Homer A. 83
Ostrander, William W. 75
Oswego (NY), Frontier Club of 72–73
Oswego (NY), Nationals of 77, 87–88
Oswego (NY), Ontarios of 79, 81, 83, 87–91
Ousterhout, N.F. 209
Ovid (MI), Forlorn Hope Club of 236
Owen, Guss R. 219

Pacific Base Ball Convention 319–320, 323, 327–328, 330–332, 334–336
Pacifics of Chicago 210
Pacifics of Rochester (NY) 77–78, 99, 108
Pacifics of San Francisco 319–322, 327, 329–332, 332–334
Page, Charles T. 231–232
Paine, Richard, Jr. 75
Pana (IL), Excelsiors of 203
Parcher, William K. 182
Paris Hill Academy (South Paris, ME), Resolutes of 9–10
Parker, C. 23
Parker, Charles Adelbert "Brick" 88, 90
Parker, Edward 278
Parker, J.D. 52
Parker, Richard Husted 75
Parker, S[tephen] Olin 23
Parr, Walter S. 303
Parris, Percival Josiah 9–10, 12, 15–16
Parsons, Nahum Fisher 222–223
Pastimes of Baltimore 58, 112, 254–261, 261–262
Pastimes of Little Falls (NY) 82
Paterson (NJ), Olympics of 44
Patterson, Jimmy 274, 278
Paw Paw (MI), Lafayette Base Ball Club of 187
Peabody Club of Baltimore 262
Pecatonica (IL) Base Ball Club 202, 213–214, 226, 235–239
Pecatonica Club of Shepardsville (MI) 236
Pecatonica horn 213–214, 236–238
Peirce, David Russell 178, 180, 182–183
Pembrokes of East Bridgeport (CT) 34–36
Pendleton, Charles Gay 34–35, 37, 39
Penfield, Burr 65
Penfield, Carrol F. "Cal" 53, 54, 64–65
Penfield Club of Oberlin College 126
Peninsulars of Grand Rapids (MI) 193–195
Pennesseewassees of Norway (ME) 10–18
Pennington, William Clapham 255, 259
Pennsylvania Base Ball Association 120
Peplow, Edward A. 338
Pequonnocks of Bridgeport (CT) 35–37
Pequots of New London (CT) 20
Perkins, Frederick Barker 197
Perkins, Frederick J. 22–23
Perkins, Gaius William 194, 197
Perkins, James 331, 334
Perry, Carlton L. 21
Perry, Richard 281–282, 288–290
Perry, Valette D. 21
Pettingill, Charles B. 132
Phelps, Frank J. 183, 187
Phil Sheridan Club of the 5th U.S. Artillery 308

Philadelphia, Athletics of *see* Athletics of Philadelphia
Philadelphia, Keystones of 266
Philips, John 174
Pickering, Charles E. 108, 114
Pickering, Cyrenius Chapin "C.C." 117
Pierce, John C. 188
Pierce, Silas Kellogg 193, 197
Piercy, Andrew J. 334, 336, 338
Pierson, Hiram Bacon 192
Pike, Lipman 46
Pinkham, Ed 267
Pioneer Base Ball and Wicket Club of Grand Rapids (MI) 193
Pioneers of Canandaigua (NY) 96
Pioneers of Chicago 210
Pioneers of Rockford (IL) 224–225
Pitcairn, Robert "R.P." 121
Pittman, Edward G. 259
Pittsburgh, Duquesne Base Ball Club of 122
Pittsburgh, Lincolns of 122
Pittsburgh, Mutuals of 127
Pittsburgh game with Allegheny City (PA) in 1857 121–122
Plainview (OH), Alerts of 160
Plantsville (CT), Winooski Club of 22
Plantz, Earl F. 174
Poe, Neilson (often misspelled Nelson), Jr. 254, 259
poems 13, 78, 92, 102, 227
Pomeroy (also spelled Pomroy), Everett B. 331, 334, 339
Pope, Charles D. 313
Popplein, Andrew 259, 261
Popplein, George J. 259, 261
Popplein, Joseph 259–260
Porter, Alonzo Burton "Lon" 194, 197
Porter, George A. 77–79, 81, 85
Porter, George S. 7
Portland (ME), Athletics of 10–11, 14
Portland (ME), Eons of 10–11, 14–15
Portland (ME) Fire, Great (1866) 15
postgame rituals 14, 19, 23, 26, 37, 43, 50, 54, 61, 69–70, 72–73, 77–78, 92–93, 102, 108–109, 123, 190, 194, 207, 241, 243, 254–256, 266–267, 272, 310, 322, 333
Potomacs of Washington (DC) 252–254, 271–272
Potter, A. Stuart 71
Powell, George W. 42, 48
Powers, Charles 93
Powers, Mike 58, 65
Prather, George 167
Prather, John Griffith "Griff" 287
Pratt, Albert G. 123–124, 128, 132, 134
Pratt, W.S. 203
Priam Club of Troy (NY) 50, 53
Price, Henry W. 232
professionalism 5–6, 26–28, 57–58, 79–82, 84, 111, 128, 142–143, 147–151, 158, 178–179, 195, 211–212, 214–215, 217, 225, 227–228, 248–249, 257, 262, 267, 292, 299, 316
Protectors of East Bridgeport (CT) 35–36
Proudfit, George 190, 192
Prouty, M.F. 209
Pudder, Henry 162–163
Pullan, Frederic Brown 250
Putnam, George 96
Putnam, Henry 96
Putnam, Thomas Garret 75
Pythians of Washington (DC) 271, 279

Quarrier, Archie Monroe 309, 313
Queen City Club of Buffalo 103
Quickstep Club of Toledo (OH) 127, 177
Quinnipiacks of [West] Meriden (CT) 22–26

Radcliffe, John 154
Railway Unions of Cleveland 119, 126–128, 134
Ralston, William, Jr. 124
Randall, Charles B. 75
Rankin, John M. 68
Rathbun, Julius 19–20
Rawson, Lemuel O. 131
Reach, Al 255
Reach, Robert "Bob" 270
Red Rovers of San Francisco 318–319, 324–326
Red Stockings, Boston 150
Red Stockings, Cincinnati *see* Cincinnati Base Ball Club
Red Stockings, St. Louis 300–303
Red, White and Blue Club of Marshall (MI) 189–190
Redfield, George Davis 75
Redington, Samuel 333, 339
Reed, Thomas, Jr. 165
Reeve, S.B. 42, 48
Remington, Leonard C. "Leon" 197
Rensselaer County (NY), Unions of 53
Resolutes of Brooklyn (NY) 42–44
Resolutes of Cincinnati 146
Resolutes of Paris Hill Academy (South Paris, ME) 9–10
Reynolds, Jack 21
Reynolds, James 305
Reynolds, John 298
Rhinebeck (NY), Lorillards of 44
Rhinehart, Frank 124
Rice, Clark Wilder 117
Richards, Edwin 101, 106
Richards, George, Jr. 35–36, 39
Richardson, James B. 71
Riggin, John, Jr. 287
Riley (sometimes spelled Reilly), John 132
Ring, Thomas C. 43
Ripley (MI), Independents of 199–200
Rising, Alfred W. 339
Robertson, George W. 117
Robertson, Richard L. 117
Robinson, Alfred Valentine "Val" 265, 270
Robinson, Arthur Lee 313
Robinson, Charles C. 174
Robinson, D.C. 4
Robinson, E.N. 326, 328, 335
Robinson, Eugene 170, 174, 183
Robinson, Henry 43, 48
Robinson, Henry H. 205–206
Robinson, Lawrence Carr "Larry" 313
Robinson, Marshall D. "Marsh" 170, 174
Robinson, Marvin S. 206
Robinson, Theodore Pearson 170, 174
Rochester (NY), Alerts of 82, 88, 99, 107, 110–111, 116
Rochester (NY), Athletics of 99
Rochester (NY), Excelsiors of 78, 82, 99, 108–110
Rochester (NY), Flour Citys of 91–93, 94–95, 97–98, 102
Rochester (NY), Live Oaks of 91–92, 93–97, 97–98, 102, 138, 185
Rochester (NY), Lone Stars of 91–97, 98–100, 103
Rochester (NY), Mutuals of 77, 99
Rochester (NY), Olympics of 91–96, 97–98, 98
Rochester (NY), Pacifics of 77–78, 99, 108
Rochester (NY), Unions of 96–97
Rochester (NY), Washingtons of 99
Rockefeller, John D. 126, 177
Rockford (IL), Forest Citys of 112, 142, 178, 203, 211–217, 222, 224–235, 245, 248, 274
Rockford (IL), Mercantiles of 224
Rockford (IL), Pioneers of 224–225
Rockford (IL), Sinnissippis of 224–225
Rockford (IL), Unions of 224
Rogers, Robert 42

Rogerson, W. 183
Root, James Clinton 166–167
Root, Oliver J. 87
Rose, B[enjamin] F[ranklin] 120–121
Ross, Franklin D. 174
Ross, "Ike" 123
Rough and Readys of South Bend (IN) 216
roundball 9, 170
Rousseau, Charles M. 174
Rowland, Robert H. 134–135
Rúa, Rafael Julián de la 57, 63, 65–66
Rucker, J.H. 315
Rurode, Ernst Christian Heinrich 206
Rust, Stiles Mortimer 75
Rustics of Danbury (IL) 214

Saccarappa (ME), Crescents of 14
Sacramento, Unions of 318–319
Sacramento Base Ball Club 318–319, 324, 326
Sage, John B. 103, 106, 110
Sagendorf, George Henry 52
St. John, James W. 250
St. Louis, Commercials of 283, 298
St. Louis, Cyclones of 282–288, 288–289, 291
St. Louis, Empires of 282–283, 288–289, 291–292, 296–305
St. Louis, Excelsiors of 291
St. Louis, Lone Stars of 283, 291
St. Louis, Morning Stars of 282–283, 288–290, 300
St. Louis, Olympics of 283, 303
St. Louis, Red Stockings of 300–303
St. Louis, Unions of 274, 282–283, 291–296, 297–300, 303, 312
St. Paul (MN), Saxon Base Ball Club of 203
Salmon, Charles B. 245–246
Sands, George Fox 142, 144, 149
Sandy Creek (NY), X.L. Club of 87
Sanford, David 77–78, 80, 82, 85
San Francisco, Active of 330, 332
San Francisco, Atlantics of 320, 322–323, 328, 332, 334
San Francisco, Bay Citys of 321, 330, 332
San Francisco, California Club of 323, 328
San Francisco, City College Club of 319–320, 333
San Francisco, Cosmopolitans of 320–321, 327, 330, 332–333, 333
San Francisco, Eagles of 318–323, 323–329, 329–332, 334–336
San Francisco, Em Quads of 318–319, 326, 329
San Francisco, Excelsiors of 333
San Francisco, Independents of 320, 327, 333
San Francisco, Libertys of 320, 323, 328, 332, 334–335
San Francisco, Occidentals of 320, 334
San Francisco, Pacifics of 319–322, 327, 329–332, 332–334
San Francisco, Red Rovers of 318–319, 324–326
San Francisco, Vallejos of 323, 328, 334
San Francisco, West End Base Ball Club of 319
San Francisco Base Ball Club 318, 324–325
Saugerties (NY), Ulsters of 43
Sawin, Jay Sprague 108, 112, 114
Sawyer, Delancy 22–23
Sawyer, Denton F. "Dent" or "Danny" 227, 232
Sawyer, Sylvester J. 232
Saxon Base Ball Club of St. Paul (MN) 203
Scheidemantle, John B. 144
Schenectady (NY), Ancient Citys of 54
Schenectady (NY), Mohawk Club of 51
Schimper, Joe 299, 303
Schmidt, Fred 266
Schoeffel, Frank 99
Schrader, Louis 303
Schwartz, David 157
scientific playing 71, 73, 126

Index

Scofield (sometimes spelled Schofield), John W. 66
Scott, Archibald J. 201
Scott, David A. 46, 48
Scovell, Henry Mason "Harry" 174
Scribner, Nestell Bonee "Ness" 194, 197
Scudder, Charles 288, 290
Sears, John K. 260
second nines 44–46, 72, 77, 92, 110, 186, 190, 207, 210, 234, 240–241, 254, 292, 299, 308, 316, 319, 332
Seddens, Albert C. 167
Sellman, Arthur W. 264
Sellman, Charles Francis "Frank" 260, 264
Sexton, Henry Clay 298–299, 303–304
Shaffers of Freeport (IL) 210, 224
Shallcross, J. Lewis 309
Sharpsteen, Francis A. 192
Shaw, Joseph P. 95
Sheffield, Charles J. 131
Shelley, Ed 278
Shepard, James 329, 331, 339
Shepard, William 329, 331, 339
Shepardsville (MI), Pecatonica Club of 236
Sherman, R.M. 68
Sherman, W.S. 4
Sherman, William Tecumseh 290, 294
Shermans of Utica (NY) 82
Sherwood, Harvey C. 75
Sherwood, James Edmund 144–145
Shiels, Thomas 101, 106
Shipman, Henry W. 192
Shoaff, Thomas B. 204, 206
Shockey, John 299, 304
shoes 54–55, 64, 110
Shoup (sometimes spelled Shoupe), John H. "Jack" 164–165
Shreves, Pete 278
Shriver, J. Hervey 253, 260
Shumway, Edward Haines 23–25
Shurtz, William D. 260
Sicard, George J. 71
Sicard, Stephen G. 71
Sidway, Franklin 102, 104, 106
Sidway, James Henry 106
silver ball (trophy) 10–15, 27, 44, 54, 56, 69, 126–127, 163, 177, 193–194, 210, 247–248, 252, 255–257, 261, 277, 318, 326
Simmons, Edward C. 294–295
Simmons, Joe 216, 219, 228, 232
Simoneau, Henry 183
Simoneau, Leander 183
Sinclair, A[lexander] Porter 193, 197
Sinclair, Sam B. 197
Sinnissippis of Rockford (IL) 224–225
Skiff, William H. "Will" 138, 145
Skinner, Aaron 240
Skinner, Beecher 174
Slattery, J. 60, 66
Slicer, Walter R. 339
Sligh, Charles Robert, Sr. 197
Smith, A.J. 210
Smith, Asa W. 291–293, 295
Smith, Austin R. "Pikey" 125–127, 131
Smith, Clarence M. "Clare" 11–16
Smith, Eben Griffin "Eb" 128, 132, 278
Smith, Edgar M. 250
Smith, Edward B. 111, 114
Smith, Frank L. 203, 247–251
Smith, G. Charles 206–207, 209, 210, 219
Smith, George W. 138, 145
Smith, Julius H., Jr. 295
Smith, Lafayette 334
Smith, Levi 60
Smith, Simeon B. 188
Smith, T.M. 122
Smith, Thaddeus 295

Smith, Thomas G. 146, 148, 157
Smith, William B. "Policy Bill" 154, 157
Snedaker (also spelled Snediker) [Detroit Base Ball Club] 178, 184
Snyder, E. 134
Snyder, George 134–135
soccer 90
Solari, Augustus 304
Solari, Joseph 304
songs 92, 95, 102, 104, 227, 257, 267, 272, 274–275
South Bend (IN), Rough and Readys of 216
South Paris (ME) Club 10
Southard, Richard P. 260
Southerns of New Orleans 292, 307–308
Spalding, Albert Goodwill 213–215, 221–224, 226–229, 231–233
Spalding, David W. 223
Spalding, Harriet 221–222, 225, 231
Spalding, James 304
Sparks, William Clay "Billy" 317
spectators, behavior of 5, 55–57, 59–60, 69, 81, 83, 108–109, 126, 213–214, 216–217, 225, 288, 330
Spink, Alfred H. 225
Spotten, James H. 60, 66
Sprague, Henry S. 114
Sproul, Thomas A. 124
Stacy, Edwin D. 87, 90
Stafford, William D. 75
Stansbury, Henry 295
Stanton, Thomas 98
Stapleford, Francis A. 206
Stark, Herbert 82, 85
Stark Club of Canton (OH) 123
Starkey, Henry Mitchell 170–171, 174–175
Starr, Chandler 227, 232
Starr, Henry Nevins "Harry" 228, 232
Stars of Batavia (NY) 115
Stars of Brooklyn (NY) 27, 43–44, 257
Stars of Cleveland 126
Stars of Covington (KY) 164
Stars of Syracuse 83
Stearns, George 219–220, 233
Stearns, James 220
Stearns, John Walker, Jr. 220
Stearns, Warren S. 232–233
Stearns, Woodbury Eaton "Woody" 217, 220
Stebbins, John 94–95, 97–99
Steigers, William Colbert 295–296
Stein, Frank 167
Stephens (real name Stevens), Charles Asbury 11, 16–17
Sterling, Hugh S. 35–36, 39
Stevens, A.S. 194
Stevens, Benjamin F. 197
Stevens, Charles C. 238
Stevens, E. Gerry 48
Stevens, Erastus Corning 238
Stevens, Thomas Asaph 238
Stimpson, William 117
Stires, Garret C. "Gat" 222–223, 225, 227–228, 231, 233
Stitsel, Daniel A. 238–239
Stockley, George W. 130–131
Stockton (CA), Live Oaks of 318–319
Stockton (CA) Base Ball Club 318–319
Storer, Bellamy 157
Stratford (CT) Base Ball Club 34
Straw, Lendon S. 42, 48
Strong, Lyman Arlington 134–135
Stroud, James 334
Studley, Seymour "Seem" 278
Sturges, Arthur Dimon 134–135
Sullivan, Patrick 99
Summit Citys of Fort Wayne (IN) 202, 204–206

Sunday baseball 292
Sutherland, James A. 251
Sutherland, Orion S. 249–251
Sutton, Ezra Ballou 99, 132
Sutton, Thomas 57
Swasey, Charles J. 158, 233
swearing 4, 60, 147
Sweasy, Charles "Charley" 142–143, 145, 148, 157–158, 233, 267
Sweet, Planter 23
Swezey, Lester Samuel 245–246
Swift, John W. 162–163
Swift, William H. 299, 305
Syracuse, Central Citys of 61, 76–87, 88–90, 109–110, 112
Syracuse, Olympics of 72–73
Syracuse, Stars of 83
Syracuse Base Ball Club 71–76, 77

Taft, William Howard 3, 137
Taggart, Capt. 241
Tamkin, Charles 74–76
Tanner, William E. 112, 114, 116–117
Tappan, Myron Augustus 278
Tarrant, Richard 93
Tatem, Henry Hammond "Harry" 145
Taylor [Forest Citys of Cleveland] 131
Taylor [left fielder for Eagles of San Francisco] 328
Taylor, Oakley Robinson "Oak" 138, 158
Taylor, William 69, 71
Teed, Herbert G. 177, 220
Telford, William L. "Will" 78, 80, 82, 85
Teller, W.C.B. 183
Temple, Thomas 334
Thomas, Charles Henry 164–165
Thomas, Gaylord "Gail" 134–135
Thompson, Andrew M. 239
Thompson, Byron S. 206
Thompson, Edward J. 239
Thompson, John B. 22–23
Thompson, William J.G. 206
Thomson, LaMott 69, 71
Thomson, Mortimer G. 69, 71
Thorn, William P. 298–299, 305
Throop, George 209
Thurston, George 175
Tidwell, Reuben W. "Rube" 317
"tiger" cheer 12, 72, 77, 102, 310
Timberlake, Thomas C. 309
Tinges, George W. 260
Tipper, Jim 29, 31
Titans of Janesville (WI) 248
Titus, Jonas H., Jr. 175
Tobias, Edmund H. 281–283, 291–293, 295, 297, 299–300, 304
Tobin, Patrick 297–299, 304
Toledo (OH), Quickstep Club of 127, 177
Toledo (OH) Base Ball Club 109
Toms, J.W. 183
Tone, James 98
Torrence, William Irwin 140
Torrey, David 88, 90
Town (sometimes spelled Towne), Robert Miller 240, 246
townball 9, 71, 137–138, 141–142, 146, 162–163, 166–167, 224, 247, 281, 288–289, 314
Townsend, Edward Bennet 117
Tracy, Theodore Freulinghuysen 313
Travis, William H. 160–161
Treacey [sometimes spelled Treacy], Fred 216, 220
Trembath, James Walls 201
Trembath, John T.V. "Victor" 201
triple plays 13, 283–284
trophies see bats; gold ball; Pecatonica horn; silver ball
Trowbridge, Luther Stephen 186–189

Troy (NY), Priam Club of 50, 53
Troy (NY), Victorys of 49–53, 56, 63, 69, 93, 96
Troy (NY) Haymakers *see* Haymakers of Troy (NY)
Trumbull, Frank Edward 233–234
Tucker, Cyrus Shaw 11, 13, 17
Tudor, Octavius 138, 140
Turchin Base Ball Club of 19th Illinois Infantry 210, 212
Turnbull, Nesbitt 260
Turner, Charles Hunt 296
Tuttle, Harmon Bascom 240, 246
Twain, Mark 19

Ulsters of Saugerties (NY) 43
umpires 4–5, 10, 35–37, 43, 47, 58–61, 64, 69–70, 73, 94–96, 102, 119, 122–123, 129–130, 134, 151, 166, 177, 184, 190, 210, 214, 217–219, 257, 274, 301, 303, 309–310, 318, 325, 334–335
uniforms 13, 22, 27, 34, 45, 50, 55–56, 69, 71, 73, 81, 88, 92–93, 97–98, 100n27, 104, 107, 110, 115, 123, 128–129, 138, 146, 160, 167, 176, 194, 200, 207, 210, 212, 214, 226–227, 241, 247, 254, 262, 265, 271–272, 282, 289, 309, 314, 334
Union Springs (NY) Base Ball Club 73
Unions of Beloit College 240
Unions of Brighton (NY) 93
Unions of Chicago 206–207
Unions of Cohoes (NY) 51
Unions of Elmira (NY) 45
Unions of Lansingburgh (NY) 44, 46, 53–67, 80, 257; *see also* Haymakers of Troy (NY)
Unions of Morrisania (NY) 19, 37, 44, 56–57, 80, 127, 129, 216, 227
Unions of Rensselaer County (NY) 53
Unions of Rochester (NY) 96–97
Unions of Rockford (IL) 224
Unions of Sacramento 318–319
Unions of St. Louis 274, 282–283, 291–296, 297–300, 303, 312
Unions of Washington (DC) 252
Unions of Whitehall (NY) 50
Uniteds of New Mills (NY) 45–46
Unknowns of Jackson (MI) 123, 191–192
Upton, Charles 93
Urell, Michael Emmet 270, 279
Utica (NY), Shermans of 82
Utica (NY) Base Ball Club 51, 69–71, 73, 77–78
Utley, James 298, 305

Vail, George 56
Vallejos of San Francisco 323, 328, 334
Valley Citys of Grand Rapids (MI) 194
Vanguards of Cohoes (NY) 49–50
Van Ness, Eugene 254, 260
Van Norman, Arthur 183–184
Van Norman, Jonathan Mack 178, 184
Van Rensselaer, Walter A. 68
Van Velsor, John W. 103, 108, 110–112, 114
Van Voorhis, John 97, 99
Veni Vidi Vici Club of Bridgeport (CT) 35
Vernor, Charles H. 175, 184
Vickery, John 98
Victorys of Troy (NY) 49–53, 56, 63, 69, 93, 96
Vilas, Royal Cooper 130–132
Voorhies, Abraham 207, 209

Wachtel [pitcher for Pacifics of San Francisco] 331
Waddell, John 287
Wade, Joseph L. 339
Wade, Simon L. "Sam" 326, 331–332, 339
Wadleigh, Martin V. "Mart" 88, 90
Waidner, Jacob B. 260
Waldo, Hiram Hungerford "Hi" 222, 224–225, 228, 233–234, 237
Waldron, James G. 68

Waldron, Lewis F. 197
Walker, James Henry 175
Walker, Willis Collins "Willie" 287
Walpole, Horace H. 76
Ward, Charles Harrison "Charley" 178–179, 184
Ward, Frank 194
Ward, James 53, 62, 66
Ward, John "Jack" 128, 132, 134
Ward, John Montgomery 250
Ward, Milton Duane 184
Wardwell, George S. 106
Wardwell, William T. 101, 106
Waring, Charles G. 48
Warner, Henry Spalding 224, 233
Warren, Hylan P. 36
Warren, Joseph 102, 106
Washington (DC), Actives of 273
Washington (DC), Alerts of 266
Washington (DC), Eagles of 273
Washington (DC), Jeffersons of 252, 262, 271
Washington (DC), Mutuals of 266
Washington (DC), Nationals of *see* Nationals of Washington (DC)
Washington (DC), Olympics of 88, 112, 118, 149–150, 157, 252, 265–271, 275
Washington (DC), Potomacs of 252–254, 271–272
Washington (DC), Unions of 252
Washington Club of New York 5
Washingtons of Rochester (NY) 99
Washingtonville (NY) Base Ball Club 45
Waterbury (CT) Club 37
Waterman, Frederick A. 147, 151, 158, 267
Watson [pitcher for Western Unions of Cincinnati] 160
Waverlys of Baltimore 254, 261
Waxham, Ernest L. 233, 251
Webster, George C. 101, 106
Weed, J[onathan] Irving 87, 90
Welch, Seth P. 54, 66
Welch, Thomas 331, 339
Weller, John H. 190, 192
Welling, Stephen Alling 191–192
Welton, Dwight 22–23
Wentworth, Willard Francis 216, 220
West End Base Ball Club of San Francisco 319
West Troy (NY), Alerts of 50
West Troy (NY), Champions of 53
West Troy (NY), Excelsiors of 50–51
Western Reserve College 126–127
Western Unions of Cincinnati 137, 160–162
Westport (CT), Monitors of 36–37
Wetmore, J.H. 331
Wheeler, Algar Monroe 108, 114
Wheeler, Benjamin Ide 10
Wheeler, Martin L. "Mart" 225, 233–234
Wheeler, Park 82, 86
Wheeler and Wilson Club of East Bridgeport (CT) 35–36
Whitbeck, Howard T. 331
White, David P. 71
White, Horatio Stevens 82, 85–86
White, James Laurie "Deacon" 119, 127–129, 132
White, John Baldwin 194, 197
White, Nathan Curtis 71
White, T[homas] Stewart 193, 197–198
White, W[illard] Elmer 129, 132
White Lot, Washington, D.C. 252–253, 271–273
White Stockings, Chicago *see* Chicago Base Ball Club
Whitehall (NY), Unions of 50
Whitewater Club of Janesville (WI) 241–243, 245, 248
Whitney, Robert Sanford 287
Whittlesey, Henry 96
wicket 9, 42, 98
Wickwire, Irvin M. 62

Wide Awakes of Oakland (CA) 320–323, 327–328, 331, 333–336
Wiggin, Marcus P. 339
Wilder, Joseph H. 206
Wilkins, Walter L. 198
Wilkinson, Alfred 73–74, 76, 79, 82
Wilkinson, John 74, 76
Wilkinson, John, Jr. 73
Wilkinson, J[oshua] Forman 76
Willard, Gardner Goodrich 220
Williams, Francis 334
Williams, John 332
Williams, Joseph 334
Williams, William F. "Billy" 275, 279
Williams College 54
Williamson, Calvin H. 71
Williamson, Samuel E. 126, 132
Williford, Dick 317
Willis, Richard 94–95, 97–99
Willock, James 324–326, 330
Wilson, James Evert 46, 48
Wilstach, Charles 142
Winooski Club of Plantsville (CT) 22
Winter, Joseph 189
Wirth, Adam 299, 304–305
Wisconsin Association of Base Ball Players 241, 247
Withey, Lewis H. 193, 198
Wolf, Simon 265, 270
Wolff, Eugene Ulrice 296
Wolverines of Benton Harbor (MI) 169
women 34, 44, 50, 56, 69, 73, 95, 102, 110, 126–127, 151, 160, 190, 199, 204, 207, 272, 274, 288, 309–311, 315, 333
Wood, Charles Beers 192
Wood, Daniel 95
Woods, Alexander P. 260
Woods, Daniel C. 260
Woods, Edward P. "Neddy" 270
Woodstock, Frank 22–23
Woodward (sometimes spelled Woodworth), Charles B. 206
Worthington, J[ohn] Tolly 264
Worthington, William 158
Wright, B.F. 178–179
Wright, Charles S. 189
Wright, C.W. 193
Wright, Darwin E. 132
Wright, George 86, 148, 158, 227, 237, 273, 275, 331
Wright, Harry 28, 58, 60, 95, 143–145, 147–150, 152, 158–159, 166, 203, 216, 223, 229
Wright, Henry T. 240
Wright, Joseph L. 271
Wulsin, Drausin 140, 159

X.L. Club of Sandy Creek (NY) 87

Yale, A.E. "Ed" 78, 81–82, 86
Yale, J[ohn] W[esley] 76, 86
Yale University 37
Yeatman, Samuel B. 270
Yeatman, William Suter 279
Yergason, Henry 21, 159
Yorkville (NY), Champions of 50
Yorston, Matthew McKay 96–97, 138, 140
Young, Albert Barnes 117
Young, Benjamin Rush, Jr. 189
Young, Clinton 17
Young, Nicholas Ephraim "Nick" 266–267, 270
Young America Club of Cleveland 126
Young Canadian Club 103
Yule, James C. 305

Zeller, John H. 214–216, 220